South Africa, Lesotho & Swaziland

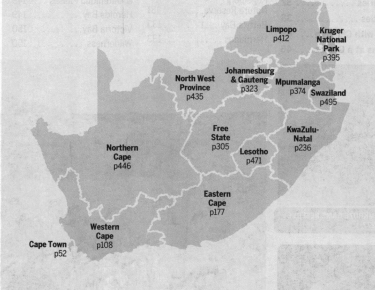

Limpopo
p412

Kruger
National
Park
p395

Johannesburg
& Gauteng
p323

North West
Province
p435

Mpumalanga
p374

Swaziland
p495

Free
State
p305

KwaZulu-
Natal
p236

Northern
Cape
p446

Lesotho
p471

Eastern
Cape
p177

Western
Cape
p108

Cape Town
p52

James Bainbridge,
Robert Balkovich, Jean-Bernard Carillet, Lucy Corne, Shawn Duthie,
Anthony Ham, Ashley Harrell, Simon Richmond

Contents

WOLF AVNI / SHUTTERSTOCK ©

UMKHUZE GAME RESERVE P277

ROGER DE LA HARPE / GETTY IMAGES ©

BATELEUR EAGLE P556

KEREN SU / GETTY IMAGES ©

Contents

KGALAGADI TRANSFRONTIER PARK P459

Contents

ON THE ROAD

MAPUNGUBWE NATIONAL
PARK P424

MAXIMILIANE WAGNER / GETTY IMAGES ©

Contents

Welcome to South Africa, Lesotho & Swaziland

South Africa, Lesotho and Swaziland are a microcosm of the African continent, containing dramatic mountain ranges, golden crescent beaches, wildlife-stalked wildernesses, vibrant cities and centuries of history.

Dramatic Landscapes

The region's landscapes are stunning, from the burning Karoo and Kalahari semideserts to the misty heights of the Drakensberg range and the massive Blyde River Canyon. Even in urban Cape Town, you need only look up to see the beautiful *fynbos* (indigenous flora) climbing the slopes of Table Mountain, while nearby, two of the world's most dramatic coastal roads lead to Cape Point and Hermanus. Add the vineyards carpeting the Cape Winelands, the Garden Route's old-growth forests, mountain ranges from the Cederberg to the Maluti, Indian Ocean beaches and the Swazi highveld, and there's a staggering variety to enjoy.

History

Museums from Jo'burg to Robben Island, many including exhibits on the apartheid era, will help you to understand the fabric of South African society. Continue your history lesson with a township visit to the likes of Soweto (Jo'burg) or Langa (Cape Town), chatting to locals and learning that, despite the heart-wrenching past, there is great pride here and an immense sense of promise for the future. Lesotho and Swaziland's backstories are intertwined with South Africa; learn more at spots such as the mountain lodges occupying Lesotho's historic trading posts.

Outdoor Adventure

The three countries' ever-changing scenery is the perfect canvas on which to paint an activity-packed trip. Try rock climbing in the Cederberg, surfing off the Eastern Cape coast, abseiling from Cape Town's Table Mountain, bungee jumping from the Garden Route's Bloukrans Bridge, swinging into Graskop Gorge, or rafting and mountain biking in Swaziland. If adrenaline sports aren't your thing, opt for a hike: options include multiday treks through wildlife reserves, day walks in the Karoo semidesert, 'slackpacking' trails along the Cape coast, and hikes into the Drakensberg and Maluti ranges.

Wildlife

South Africa and Swaziland comprise one of the continent's best safari destinations, offering the Big Five (lion, leopard, buffalo, elephant and rhino) and more in accessible parks and reserves. You can drive right into renowned parks such as Kruger, Kgalagadi and Swaziland's Hlane Royal, or join khaki-clad rangers on guided drives and walks. But it's not all about big-game sightings – wildlife watching here also teaches you to enjoy the little things: a leopard tortoise ambling alongside the road, a go-away bird chirping its distinctive chant, or a coastal encounter with seals, whales or a great white shark.

Why I Love South Africa, Lesotho & Swaziland

By James Bainbridge, Writer

Before my first trip to South Africa, I was, despite my travel experience, slightly nervous about visiting this country with a reputation for crime. Then I touched down in Jo'burg and headed into the bushveld, finding all the beauty and wildness of Africa accompanied by excellent lodges, restaurants and wildlife reserves. By the time I caught Shosholoza Meyl's train across the Karoo to Cape Town, I was hooked. After experiencing the Mother City's varied lifestyle of gastronomy, culture, mountain walks and beaches, I met my wife here and got to stay.

For more about our writers, see p648

Above: Valley of Desolation (p231)

South Africa, Lesotho & Swaziland

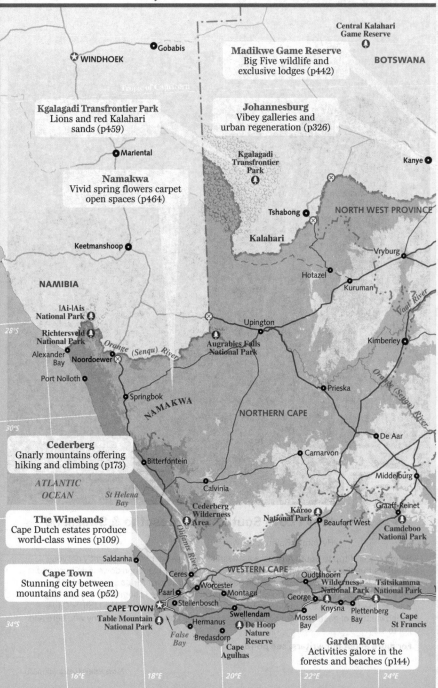

Madikwe Game Reserve
Big Five wildlife and
exclusive lodges (p442)

BOTSWANA

Central Kalahari
Game Reserve

WINDHOEK
Gobabis

Kgalagadi Transfrontier Park
Lions and red Kalahari
sands (p459)

Johannesburg
Vibey galleries and
urban regeneration (p326)

Mariental

Kanye

Namakwa
Vivid spring flowers carpet
open spaces (p464)

Kgalagadi
Transfrontier
Park

Keetmanshoop

Tshabong

NORTH WEST PROVINCE

Kalahari

Vryburg

NAMIBIA

Hotazel

Kuruman

|Ai-|Ais
National Park

Richtersveld
National Park

Alexander
Bay

Noordoewer

Orange (Senqu) River

Upington

Augrabies Falls
National Park

Kimberley

Port Nolloth

Prieska

Orange (Senqu) River

Springbok

NAMAKWA

NORTHERN CAPE

De Aar

Cederberg
Gnarly mountains offering
hiking and climbing (p173)

Bitterfontein

Carnarvon

Middelburg

_ATLANTIC
OCEAN_

_St Helena
Bay_

Calvinia

Cederberg
Wilderness
Area

Karoo
National Park

Graaff-Reinet

The Winelands
Cape Dutch estates produce
world-class wines (p109)

Olifants River

Beaufort West

Camdeboo
National Park

Saldanha

Ceres

WESTERN CAPE

Cape Town
Stunning city between
mountains and sea (p52)

Paarl

Worcester

Montagu

Oudtshoorn

Wilderness
National Park

**Tsitsikamma
National Park**

George

Stellenbosch

Knysna

Plettenberg
Bay

Cape
St Francis

CAPE TOWN

Table Mountain
National Park

Swellendam

Mossel
Bay

Hermanus

De Hoop
Nature
Reserve

_False
Bay_

Bredasdorp

Cape
Agulhas

Garden Route
Activities galore in the
forests and beaches (p144)

28°S

30°S

34°S

16°E

18°E

20°E

22°E

24°E

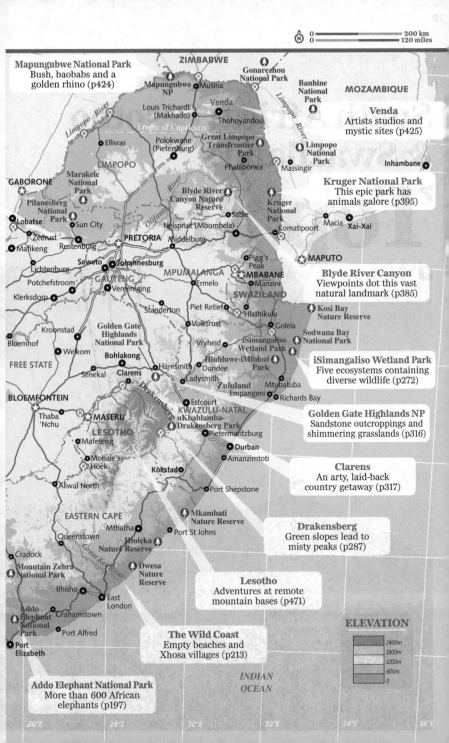

N 0 ————— 200 km
0 ————— 120 miles

ZIMBABWE

Mapungubwe National Park
Bush, baobabs and a
golden rhino (p424)

Gonarezhou National Park

Banhine National Park

MOZAMBIQUE

Mapungubwe NP • Musina

Louis Trichardt (Makhado)

Venda

Thohoyandou

Limpopo River

Venda
Artists studios and
mystic sites (p425)

Tropic of Capricorn

Polokwane (Pietersburg)

Great Limpopo Transfrontier Park

Limpopo National Park

Inhambane •

Ellisras

LIMPOPO

Phalaborwa

Massingir

GABORONE

Marakele National Park

Olifants River

Kruger National Park
This epic park has
animals galore (p395)

Pilanesberg National Park

Sun City

Blyde River Canyon Nature Reserve

Nelspruit (Mbombela)

Sabie

Kruger National Park

Lobatse

Zeerust

Rustenburg

PRETORIA

Middelburg

Komatipoort

Macia Xai-Xai

Mafikeng

Lichtenburg

Soweto **Johannesburg**

GAUTENG

MPUMALANGA

Pigg's Peak

MAPUTO

Potchefstroom

Vereeniging

Ermelo

MBABANE

Blyde River Canyon
Viewpoints dot this vast
natural landmark (p385)

Klerksdorp

Standerton

SWAZILAND

Manzini

Kroonstad

Golden Gate Highlands National Park

Piet Retief

Hlathikulu

Kosi Bay Nature Reserve

Bloemhof

Welkom

Volksrust

Golela

Sodwana Bay National Park

FREE STATE

Bohlakong

Vryheid

iSimangaliso Wetland Park

iSimangaliso Wetland Park
Five ecosystems containing
diverse wildlife (p272)

Senekal

Clarens

Harrismith

Dundee

Hluhluwe-iMfolozi Park

BLOEMFONTEIN

KWAZULU-NATAL

Ladysmith

Zululand

Mtubatuba

Golden Gate Highlands NP
Sandstone outcroppings and
shimmering grasslands (p316)

MASERU

uKhahlamba-Drakensberg Park

Estcourt

Empangeni • • Richards Bay

Thaba 'Nchu

LESOTHO

Pietermaritzburg

Durban

Clarens
An arty, laid-back
country getaway (p317)

Mafeteng

Amanzimtoti

Mohale's Hoek

Kokstad

Aliwal North

Port Shepstone

Drakensberg
Green slopes lead to
misty peaks (p287)

EASTERN CAPE

Mkambati Nature Reserve

Queenstown

Mthatha

Port St Johns

Cradock

Hluleka Nature Reserve

Great Kei River

Mountain Zebra National Park

Dwesa Nature Reserve

Lesotho
Adventures at remote
mountain bases (p471)

Bhisho

East London

Addo Elephant National Park

Grahamstown

Port Alfred

The Wild Coast
Empty beaches and
Xhosa villages (p213)

Port Elizabeth

INDIAN OCEAN

Addo Elephant National Park
More than 600 African
elephants (p197)

ELEVATION

2400m
1800m
1200m
600m
0

26°E   28°E   30°E   32°E   34°E   36°E

South Africa, Lesotho & Swaziland's
Top 25

Cape Town

1 Overlooked by flat-topped Table Mountain, with its cable car, walking trails and abseiling, Cape Town (p52) is one of the world's most beautiful cities. Fill your days here visiting beaches and Constantia wine estates, wandering the V&A Waterfront, catching the ferry to Robben Island and, above all, meeting the easy-going Cape locals. In complement to its considerable natural charms, the city is benefitting from ongoing urban renewal, with world-class restaurants, hip food markets and design-savvy arcades opening in once-industrial neighbourhoods such as Woodstock and the Waterfront's Silo District. Below left: view from the Table Mountain Cableway (p56)

Kruger National Park

2 Kruger (p395) is one of Africa's great wilderness experiences and the mightiest of the country's national parks – a trip here will sear itself in your mind. Its accessibility, quantity and variety of wildlife, and staggering size and range of activities make Kruger unique and compelling. From wilderness trails and bush walks to mountain biking and remote 4WD trails, there are myriad opportunities to enjoy the wild environment and its four-legged inhabitants. Kruger is simply one of the best places to see animals – big and small – in the world. Below: a leopard perched on a branch

Drakensberg Region

3 The mountains and foothills of the World Heritage–listed uKhahlamba-Drakensberg Park (p287) are among the country's most awe-inspiring landscapes. Drakensberg means 'Dragon Mountains' in Afrikaans, while the Zulu named the range Quathlamba ('Battlement of Spears'); both convey the area's back-drop of incredible peaks. With its San rock art, Zulu villages, wilderness areas and wildflowers, the Drak-ensberg region is the perfect place for photographers, hikers and adventurers.
Above: Amphitheatre in Royal Natal National Park (p298)

The Winelands

4 Whitewashed Cape Dutch architecture dots this endlessly photo-genic landscape. The Winelands (p109) is the quintessential Cape, where world-class wines are the icing on the viticultural cake. Stellenbosch, Franschhoek and Paarl, the area's holy trinity of wine-tasting towns, host some of the southern hemisphere's oldest and prettiest wine estates. But this is not the only wine region: head to Tulbagh for sparkling wines; the heights of the Cederberg for crisp sauvignon blancs; and Her-manus' Hemel-en-Aarde (Heaven on Earth) valley for boutique wineries. Above right: Stellenbosch vineyards (p109)

Wild Coast Walks

5 With its rugged cliffs plunging into the sea, remote sandy beaches, rural Xhosa villages and history of shipwrecks and stranded sailors, the aptly named Wild Coast (p213) is ideally explored on foot. From the Great Kei River to Port St Johns, pathways hug the shoreline, cutting through dense vegetation or snaking across denuded hillsides and gorges, and often overlook southern right whales and dolphins in the turquoise seas. Power down in rustic ac-commodation, or overnight with families in traditionally designed rondavels (round huts with conical roofs).

HOUGAARD MALAN PHOTOGRAPHY / GETTY IMAGES ©

Kgalagadi Transfrontier Park

6 Kgalagadi (p459) covers almost 40,000 sq km of raw Kalahari in the Northern Cape and Botswana, an area roamed by some 2000 predators. But such statistics, albeit impressive, barely scrape the surface of this immense land of sizzling sunsets, velvety night skies and rolling red dunes. The park is one of the world's best places to spot big cats, and you might spy black-maned lions napping under thorn trees, or cheetahs and leopards purring along the roadside. Best of all, you don't need a 4WD to access the park. Right: gazelle

JOHAN SWANEPOEL / 500PX ©

ROBERT BERINGER / 500PX ©

GROBLER DU PREEZ / SHUTTERSTOCK ©

iSimangaliso Wetland Park

7 iSimangaliso (p272), meaning 'miracle' or 'wonder' in Zulu, has a fitting name. This Unesco World Heritage site stretches for a glorious 220km, from the Mozambique border to Maphelane, at the southern end of Lake St Lucia. The 3280-sq-km park protects five distinct ecosystems, offering everything from beaches, offshore reefs and coastal forests to lakes, wetlands and woodlands. It's nature's playground, which travellers can enjoy on wildlife drives, kayak safaris, cycling and cruises. The animals here include turtles, whales, dolphins, antelope, zebras and hippos galore. Top: zebras

Clarens

8 The odd international star popping in for a lungful of fresh mountain air gives this well-heeled town (p317) celebrity credentials. But with galleries, antiques, classy restaurants, a microbrewery and adventure activities in the surrounding countryside, there's something to appeal to most visitors. The laid-back town is perfect for an evening stroll after a day exploring the nearby Golden Gate Highlands National Park. And with plenty of pubs to drop into and a bookshop to browse, Clarens is the best place in the Free State's Eastern Highlands to simply wind down.

Blyde River Canyon

9 This canyon (p385), the third largest in the world and possibly the greenest, is one of South Africa's great sights. Even the coachloads of domestic and foreign visitors to the canyon, where the Blyde River snakes down from the Drakensberg Escarpment to the lowveld, cannot spoil the majesty of sights such as Bourke's Luck Potholes. On a clear day, viewpoints including the Three Rondavels and God's Window will leave you breathless. This vast natural landmark scarring northern Mpumalanga can be appreciated on foot or by car.

Mapungubwe National Park

10 A standout among South Africa's national parks, this transfrontier conservation area (p424) in the making has been declared a World Heritage site for its cultural heritage (explained at its interpretative centre). The landscape is riveting, too: arid, ancient terrain that's twisted and knotted, with rocky bluffs offering majestic views, and mighty rivers that intersect. The climate is harsh, but lions, leopards, cheetahs, elephants and rhinos can be found here, as well as smaller species such as caracals. Getting around can be tough but the rewards are sublime. Above: Klipspringers

WESTEND61 / GETTY IMAGES ©

GILL K / SHUTTERSTOCK ©

BILDAGENTUR ZOONAR GMBH / SHUTTERSTOCK ©

Addo Elephant National Park

11 At Addo (p197) more than 600 African elephants roam through low bushes, tall grass and distant hills. The land (reclaimed after being decimated by farmers) and the park represent a conservation success story. Also roaming free are hyenas and lions, introduced in 2003 to bring the kudu, ostrich and warthog populations down. Buffaloes, rare Cape mountain zebras and endemic dung beetles can also be seen, but elephants are the showstoppers – particularly when they burst from the undergrowth, flap their ears and dwarf all that is before them.

Golden Gate Highlands National Park

12 Beneath the open skies of the Free State's Eastern Highlands, this park (p316) enjoys extraordinary sunsets, and hides plenty of antelope, zebras, jackals and birds among its grasslands. It's great walking territory, but you can also drive short, scenic loops. Either way, views of the Drakensberg and Maluti Mountains loom large and there's something almost fairy tale about the wind sweeping patterns through the grass. If you don't have the chance to explore Lesotho, it's worth visiting the Basotho Cultural Village here. Top right: Basotho Cultural Village

Garden Route

13 The enduring popularity of this verdant coastal strip, where woodcutters once dodged elephants in the old-growth forests, lies not only in its undeniable scenic beauty. The Garden Route (p144) is also a magnet for those in search of a little outdoor adventure. Whether you're hiking the Knysna Forests, surfing in Victoria Bay, canoeing on Wilderness Lagoon or getting up close with great whites in a cage in Mossel Bay's waters, the Garden Route guarantees an adventure for every taste and budget.

Lesotho Trading Posts

14 Travel in Lesotho has been arduous since long before the 19th-century, when King Moshoeshoe ruled from atop Thabo-Bosiu. The British established trading posts to maintain commercial (nay, political) links with the Basotho nation and today's traveller benefits greatly from this spirit of endeavour – the former trading posts afford some spectacular adventures. At Malealea (p491), Semonkong (p490), Ramabanta (p481) and Roma (p481), hikers, pony riders, motorbikers and those seeking a village getaway gather at mealtimes to rejoice around the bonfire. Below: Maletsunyane valley

Namakwa Wildflowers

15 Namakwa is one of South Africa's forgotten corners, stretching up the west coast towards Namibia. Crossing the remote region, and reaching Port Nolloth's refreshing Atlantic vistas after hundreds of kilometres on empty roads, is wonderful throughout the year. In spring, there's the added bonus of the wildflower bloom, which turns Namakwa's rocky expanses into a technicolour carpet. You could spend days travelling around multicoloured patches of the rugged area, stopping at spots such as Namaqua National Park (p468) and Goegap Nature Reserve (p465).

Hiking & Stargazing in the Cederberg

16 By day the clear blue skies provide an arresting contrast to the Cederberg's fiery orange peaks; by night the Milky Way shines so brightly you can almost read by its light. But the Cederberg (p173) is the promised land for more than just stargazers – its otherworldly landscape is perfect for hikers, rock climbers and those simply in search of silent nights. Tackle the challenging Wolfberg Arch and Maltese Cross Trails, the shorter Wolfberg Cracks hike, or the Wupperthal Trail, visiting remote and forgotten mission villages.

Hluhluwe-iMfolozi Park

17 Sometimes overshadowed by Kruger National Park, Hluhluwe-iMfolozi (p270) is nonetheless one of the country's most evocative parks. Stunningly beautiful, it features a variety of landscapes, from open savannah to mountains with wildflowers. It teems with wildlife, including the Big Five and other amazing creatures. The park can be visited at any time because there's always plenty to see, from elephants munching marula trees to impala, zebras, wildebeest and giraffe babies. Great wildlife drives, accommodation and hiking trails ensure a memorable experience.

WANSON LUK / 500PX ©

JEREMY WADE SHOCKLEY / GETTY IMAGES ©

Madikwe Game Reserve

18 One of the country's most exclusive reserves on such a large scale, Madikwe (p442) occupies 760 sq km of bushveld, savannah grassland and riverine forest. There's a good chance of spotting iconic African wildlife, and the lodges are experiences in themselves, from an ecolodge to five-star options offering creature comforts in the wilderness. Visits to Madikwe are on an all-inclusive basis, allowing you to relax once you're through the gates.

Sani Top

19 Africa's highest pub is a hell of a place to get to. From the west it's an endurance drive through Lesotho's awesome Central Highlands, past huge dams containing Gauteng's water supply. From KwaZulu-Natal, it's a vertiginous drive up the Sani Pass (2874m), which climbs 1300m through uncountable hairpin bends from the South African border post. At the top, raise a beer in the bar of Sani Mountain Lodge (p487) and celebrate being in the highest country (that is, the nation with the highest low point) in the world. Bottoms up!

Top right: Sani Mountain Lodge

Johannesburg

20 With a grisly reputation, the City of Gold (p326) is a surprisingly vibey and inspiring place thanks to the regeneration uplifting its inner city. The cultural enclaves of Braamfontein, Newtown, 44 Stanley and the Maboneng precinct are dynamic and exciting spots by any city's standards, with galleries, restaurants, bars and boutiques. Take a walking tour to understand the background of this urban transformation and spot Maboneng's public art by international muralists. Try to time your visit to coincide with Braamfontein and Maboneng's weekly markets. Above: Maboneng precinct (p334)

HEIN VON HORSTEN / GETTY IMAGES ©

HEIN VON HORSTEN / GETTY IMAGES ©

BAYAZED / SHUTTERSTOCK ©

Mkhaya Game Reserve

21 You're more likely to meet rhinos here than anywhere else, thanks to Mkhaya's rhino protection program. Named after its *mkhaya* (knobthorn) trees, this private reserve (p513) in eastern Swaziland might also be one of Africa's best-value spots; accommodation rates include wildlife drives, walking safaris, park entry and meals. And as for the accommodation – where else can you sleep in luxurious semi-open stone-and-thatch cottages in a secluded bush zone? All that, plus a loo with a bush view. Above: oxpecker bird perched on a rhinoceros

Venda Region

22 A lush region (p425) steeped in mystique and traditional customs, this is the Africa of mist-clad hills, dusty red tracks and mud huts. Sprinkled with lakes and forests containing enormous spiritual significance, and marking the primeval ties between indigenous culture and the land, the Limpopo province's former homeland is well worth exploring with a local guide. Stay in Elim or Louis Trichardt (Makhado) and begin with the Venda arts and crafts trail; the area is noted for its fine original artwork, with studios hidden throughout the landscape. Top right: mud huts

Pilanesberg National Park

23 Sprawling away from the Sun City casino complex is this underrated park, where the Big Five and day-tripping Jo'burgers roam an extinct volcanic crater. With its tarred roads, Pilanesberg (p440) is sometimes dismissed as tame, yet the rhinos lapping at waterholes seem to disagree. To escape the other cars and score an up-close sighting, hit the gravel roads through the bush and stake out a dam. Guided drives and walks are available, as is a range of accommodation, making this a winner for families and those short on time.

Umhlanga Reed Dance Festival

24 Africa has many colourful festivals that seem bizarre to outside eyes, but none is more curious than Swaziland's reed dance (p502), which takes place in late August/early September. The weeklong event is essentially a debutante ball for young Swazi maidens, who collect *umhlanga* (reeds) to help repair the queen mother's house. The festivities climax with the debs dancing with tall swaying reeds in hand, hoping to catch King Mswati III's eye. Up to 40,000 dancers wear beaded skirts and sashes denoting their tribes. A similar event happens in Zululand.

Cradle of Humankind

25 As you'll discover at this palaeontological zone, it began in Africa – Western Gauteng to be precise. The Cradle of Humankind (p360) nurses hundreds of square kilometres of beautiful green and brown veld, and an increasing migration of tourists, descended from hominids, who sit with the fossils of their ancestors deep underground, before returning to civilisation at fine restaurants and day spas. There's a serene sculpture park at the Nirox Foundation and wilderness to be enjoyed. Only 50km northwest of Jo'burg are free-roaming elands, zebras, giraffes and gazelles.

Need to Know

For more information, see Survival Guide (p585)

Currencies

South African rand (R),
Lesotho loti (plural maloti,
M), Swazi lilangeni
(plural emalangeni, E)

Languages

Zulu, Xhosa, Afrikaans,
English, Northern Sotho,
Tswana, Southern Sotho
(Lesotho), Tsonga, Swati
(Swaziland), Venda,
Ndebele

Visas

Not required for most
Western nationals to
visit South Africa for up
to 90 days, Lesotho for
14 and Swaziland for 30.

Money

ATMs widespread and
cards widely accepted
in South Africa. ATMs
common in Lesotho and
Swaziland, but cards
rarely accepted outside
the capitals.

Mobile Phones

Most foreign phones
can be used on roaming.
Local SIM cards can be
used in most unlocked
foreign phones.

Time

South Africa Standard
Time (GMT/UTC plus
two hours)

When to Go

Warm to hot summers, mild winters
Dry climate
Desert, dry climate

Johannesburg
GO Mar–Apr & Sep–Oct

Mbabane
GO May–Sep

Maseru
GO Apr–May & Sep–Oct

Durban
GO Apr–Nov

Cape Town
GO Nov–Apr

High Season (Nov–Mar)

➡ Peak times are
around Christmas
and Easter.

➡ Coastal and
national-park
accommodation
books up months
ahead.

➡ In popular
spots, accommo-
dation prices can
rise by 50%.

Shoulder (Apr–May & Sep–Oct)

➡ Sunny autumn
(Apr–May) and
spring (Sep–Oct)
weather.

➡ Optimum
wildlife-watching
conditions from
autumn through
winter.

➡ Whale watch-
ing best around
spring.

Low Season (Jun–Aug)

➡ Winter brings
snow to the
mountains.

➡ Rainy season in
Cape Town and the
Western Cape.

➡ A good time
to visit arid areas
such as the Karoo.

Useful Websites

Brand South Africa
(www.brandsouthafrica.com)
News and information.

South African National Parks
(www.sanparks.org) Information, bookings and forums.

Visit Lesotho (www.visitleso tho.travel) Tourist information.

Swaziland Tourism (www. thekingdomofswaziland.com)
News, info, listings and blog.

BBC (www.bbc.com/africa)
News and features.

Lonely Planet (www.lonely planet.com/south-africa)
Destination information, hotel bookings, traveller forum and more.

Important Numbers

South Africa country code	☑27
Lesotho country code	☑266
Swaziland country code	☑268
International access code (all three countries)	☑00
South Africa Police	☑10111

Exchange Rates

Australia	A$1	R9.62
Canada	C$1	R9.63
Euro zone	€1	R14.74
Japan	¥100	R10.93
Lesotho	M1	R1
New Zealand	NZ$1	R8.73
Swaziland	E1	R1
UK	£1	R16.78
USA	US$1	R11.86

For current exchange rates see www.xe.com.

Daily Costs

Budget: Less than R1000

➡ Hostel dorm bed: from R160

➡ Budget main dish (cheaper areas): less than R75

➡ Two-week hop-on, hop-off Baz Bus pass: R4100

➡ Free entry to some museums

Midrange: R1000–2500

➡ Double room: R700–4000

➡ Midrange main dish: R75–200

➡ Jo'burg–Cape Town tourist-class train: R690

➡ Single-room supplements common, usually 30–40%

Top end: More than R2500

➡ Double room (more expensive areas): over R4000

➡ Top-end main dish (more expensive areas): over R200

➡ Pretoria–Cape Town Blue Train: R20,280

➡ Cape Town–Jo'burg flight: from R1000

➡ Wildlife drive: from R350

Opening Hours

Banks 9am–3.30pm Monday to Friday, 9am–11am Saturday

Bars noon–midnight

Businesses & shopping 8.30am–5pm Monday to Friday, 8.30am–1pm Saturday; some supermarkets open weekday evenings, and all day Saturday and Sunday; major shopping centres until 9pm daily

Cafes 8am–5pm

Government offices 8am–3pm Monday to Friday

Post offices 8.30am–4pm Monday to Friday, 8.30am–11am Saturday

Restaurants 11.30am–3pm & 6.30pm–10pm (last orders); many open 3pm–6.30pm

Arriving in South Africa

OR Tambo International Airport (Johannesburg) The Gautrain serves central Jo'burg (R162, 28 minutes) and Pretoria (R174, 34 minutes) every 12 to 30 minutes. Shuttles and taxis take about one hour to Jo'burg (about R500) and Pretoria. There are car-hire companies at the airport.

Cape Town International Airport Shuttle (from R220), taxi (around R250) and MyCiTi bus (R100, every 30 minutes) to central Cape Town take about 30 minutes. There are car-hire companies at the airport.

Getting Around

Car A great option, with affordable rental rates, a good road network and the car-based local lifestyle; the drawback is dangerous drivers.

Baz Bus The backpacker shuttle is a convenient and social option between Cape Town, Durban and Jo'burg/Pretoria. Mzansi Experience offers a similar service.

Train Tourist class is an underused secret (with sleeper coaches and dining car), linking Jo'burg to Cape Town, Durban and the coast.

Air An affordable way to cover long distances.

Bus Lines including Greyhound, Intercape and Translux cover South Africa in comfortable vehicles at reasonable rates.

Shared taxi OK for short journeys but less practical over long distances, as there are safety and security issues.

For much more on **getting around**, see p610

First Time South Africa, Lesotho & Swaziland

For more information, see Survival Guide (p585)

Checklist

➡ Make sure your passport is valid for at least 30 days (six months for Swaziland) after your visit.

➡ Organise vaccinations, and malaria prophylatics if visiting northeast South Africa and Swaziland.

➡ For popular areas, book accommodation well in advance.

➡ Inform your credit-card company you're visiting the region.

➡ Arrange travel insurance.

What to Pack

➡ Yellow-fever certificate if you've recently visited a yellow-fever zone.

➡ Extra documents for children to clear South African immigration.

➡ Visa, if required.

➡ Practical shoes, for safaris and hiking.

➡ Warm evening wear, even in summer.

➡ Credit and/or debit card and backup.

➡ Sunscreen.

Top Tips for Your Trip

➡ Don't try to cover the whole region; focus instead on one or two areas, such as Cape Town and Kruger.

➡ This is a car-driving culture, given the security issues associated with walking and taking shared taxis, so consider renting a vehicle for part of your trip.

➡ South Africa has a network of domestic flights, plus public-transport options including tourist-class trains and backpacker buses.

➡ Don't be paranoid about crime: do as the locals do, take precautions and remain watchful and attuned to your surroundings, and you should have a fantastic time.

➡ Most travellers will be at most risk on the dangerous roads: drive cautiously and don't cover too much ground.

➡ Avoid the peak Christmas and Easter seasons, when accommodation fills up, prices are highest and roads are the most dangerous.

What to Wear

Take a practical wardrobe of shorts and T-shirts, athletic shoes or hiking boots for going on safari, plus warmer layers for the evenings; it can be cold in the bush, and you'll want to hide your arms and legs from mosquitoes. The same mix of clothing will be useful in mountainous Lesotho, along with jeans or other pants you'll be comfortable in while riding a horse. Women may want to avoid wearing shorts in Lesotho, as its culture is fairly conservative. You don't need to worry about fashion in these casual countries, but do pack your favourite outfits for Jo'burg and Cape Town's smart restaurants and nightspots.

Sleeping

You can often book a few days in advance, or not at all, but if you're travelling at Christmas or Easter, plan several months ahead. Always book national-park accommodation in advance.

Lodges Can be uber-luxe or fairly rustic, and boast some of the best locations.

Guesthouses Often owner-run, offering comfortable rooms, hearty breakfasts and local info.

Self-catering cottages Usually spacious and excellent value.

Backpacker hostels Often have a bar, swimming pool and campsites; ideal for budget or solo travellers.

Hotels Everything from boutique hotels to vast and luxurious chains.

Money

ATMs are common throughout the region, and cards are widely accepted across South Africa and in the capitals of Lesotho and Swaziland. Inform your bank of your travel plans to avoid declined credit-card transactions. **For more information, see p595.**

Bargaining

Haggling is common in African craft markets; in most other instances you're expected to pay the stated price.

Tipping

Wages are low here, and tipping is expected.

Restaurants & cafes Tip 10% to 15% of the total in restaurants; 10% in cafes.

Hotels A standard tip of R10 to R20 is welcomed.

Car guards Offer R2, or R5 for longer periods.

Petrol stations Anything from R5 – more if the attendant washes the windscreen and checks the tyres etc.

Taxis Tips not expected but rounding up the fare will be appreciated.

Languages

South Africa has 11 official languages and some of these, such as Afrikaans, Xhosa and Zulu, predominate in parts of the country. However, you will get around easily with English in all three countries – it's the unofficial language of business, especially in the tourist industry, and the sole language of many locals.

Etiquette

Informality South Africa is largely informal; behaviour and expectations familiar from Western countries prevail in tourist venues.

Cultural diversity In this multicultural region, etiquette varies wildly between ethnic and demographic groups, so check with your guide or a local if unsure.

Religion Christianity is taken more seriously and followed more widely than in secular Western countries; jokes about religion may offend.

Grace Saying grace before meals, while possibly holding hands, is common in Afrikaner households.

Greetings Shake hands with men and women when meeting for the first time. Women greet friends and acquaintances with a light hug. In Lesotho and Swaziland, the handshake is a three-part process, best observed before you give it a try.

Hello Be sure to say hello to everyone in Lesotho; if you don't, be prepared for people to be offended.

Conversation It's possible to discuss most subjects, including race, as long as you maintain a positive and tactful tone.

Drink driving This is widespread and locals have a relaxed attitude to it, but definitely don't do it yourself.

Time In rural areas, being punctual is not a thing; people may arrive an hour or two late.

Photos Ask before taking photos of people, particularly if they are in traditional dress or at a cultural event.

Eating

South Africa's culinary diversity reflects its multicultural society, ranging from African staples in the townships to seafood and steaks in globally acclaimed restaurants, and eating is an excellent way to the heart of the Rainbow Nation. The dining scene is more limited in Lesotho and Swaziland, but you'll find good restaurants and cafes in their capital cities and rural lodges.

What's New

Museums

Cape Town's Zeitz MOCAA Museum (p64) occupies a boldly repurposed 1920s grain silo at the V&A Waterfront. Mthatha's Nelson Mandela Museum (p221) is dedicated to the great man's life.

Township tourism

New attractions range from the Emjindini tour under development in Barberton (p393), which will be Mpumalanga's first township tour, to Cape Town's 18 Gangster Museum (p73), Isivivana Centre (p98), restaurants and cafes.

Mackeurtan Avenue

This strip in Durban North (www.durban experience.co.za) is generating a lot of buzz as a bar and restaurant hub, with some calling it the new Florida Road.

Mzsansi Experience

Plying the east coast between Cape Town and Jo'burg, this hop-on, hop-off backpacker bus offers an alternative to the long-running Baz Bus. (p612)

Philippolis

This up-and-coming Free State town has attractions including Tiger Canyons, where wild tigers breed and thrive. (p322)

South African Hall of Fame

Pay homage to South Africa's great and good in this impressive exhibition space at Sun City. Sportspeople dominate, but musicians and other luminaries from the arts also receive their due. (p439)

Hiking and driving routes

The Crayfish slackpacking trail explores an oft-ignored stretch of the West Coast, between the Western Cape fishing villages of Elands Bay and Doring Bay (p173). The Barberton Makhonjwa Geotrail (p394) travels 3.5 billion years into the past on Rte 40.

Urban regenerations

George (p148) has seen a culinary awakening, with some excellent restaurants and a decent coffee scene. Likewise, Polokwane (p413) is slowly transforming from a stolid bastion of Afrikaans tradition, with great coffee, craft beer and a rising tide of good places to eat and stay.

Cultural centres

There's a cultural centre atop Graskop Gorge Lift (p383), the glass elevator descending into the Mpumalanga town's dramatic ravine, and Workshop Ko Kasi (p456) adds appeal to Kuruman. Numerous community tourism projects are afoot in Prince Albert (p167), joining the art deco theatre.

KwaZulu-Natal South Coast

Popular with surfers and divers, the stretch of coast south of Durban is promoting its many boutique hotels, unique natural sights and good restaurants to international travellers. (p256)

Taxis

Uber has taken off in Cape Town, Jo'burg, Pretoria, Durban and Port Elizabeth, and there's an online database of minibus shared-taxi routes, fares and other info. (p617)

Swaziland's new name

The country's king announced in April 2018 that Swaziland would become known as the Kingdom of eSwatini. (p497)

For more recommendations and reviews, see lonelyplanet. com/south-africa

If You Like...

Dramatic Landscapes

From the Cape's mix of coastline and mountains to expanses such as Namakwa, the Kalahari and Karoo, South Africa features some of Africa's most impressive landscapes.

Drakensberg The Dragon Mountains bristle with awesome peaks and formations such as the Amphitheatre. (p287)

Cape Peninsula A spine of mountains runs down the peninsula from Table Mountain to Cape Point. (p69)

Wild Coast Green hills dotted with pastel rondavels (round, conical-roofed huts), rugged cliffs and empty beaches. (p213)

Augrabies Falls National Park The world's sixth-tallest waterfall, created by the Orange River thundering into a ravine. (p463)

Blyde River Canyon Breathtaking viewpoints overlook waterfalls and rock formations where the Drakensberg Escarpment and lowveld meet. (p385)

Wildlife

Diverse, accessible and swarming with animals, these parks and reserves are some of Southern Africa's best destinations to spot wildlife, including the Big Five (lion, leopard, buffalo, elephant and rhino) in most cases.

Kruger National Park South Africa's famous park has more than 13,000 elephants alone, in landscapes from woodland to savannah. (p395)

Kgalagadi Transfrontier Park Deep in the Kalahari, this is an unbeatable place to spot big cats, including black-maned lions. (p459)

Elephant Coast KwaZulu-Natal's ecotourism destination offers sightings in tropical settings; highlights include Hluhluwe-iMfolozi Park. (p269)

Madikwe Game Reserve This exclusive reserve hosts the Big Five in bushveld, savannah grassland and riverine forest. (p442)

Addo Elephant National Park South Africa's third-largest national park offers some of the world's best elephant viewing. (p197)

Cultural Experiences

Escaping the comfortable, Westernised bubble of South Africa's tourist industry, and having hands-on experiences of the region's diverse traditions and beliefs, is hugely rewarding.

Townships From Soweto to Khayelitsha, take an interactive, themed tour or spend the night in a homestay. (p356)

Wild Coast The former Xhosa homeland's community-run lodges such as Bulungula offer accommodation, activities and volunteering opportunities. (p213)

!Xaus Lodge Learn Khomani San tracking skills at one of a few locations offering culture alongside wildlife. (p461)

Venda region Meet the former homeland's artists and explore a sacred forest above Lake Fundudzi. (p425)

Zululand Learn about South Africa's largest ethnic group on visits to villages and ceremonies. (p263)

History

Numerous sights remember South Africa's tumultuous history, and a strong sense of the past lingers in rural areas such as the Winelands and Karoo.

Cape Town Walking tours cover sights from the Castle of Good Hope to the District Six Museum. (p78)

Kimberley A Victorian diamond-mining settlement, historic pubs, ghost tours and Cecil Rhodes' club. (p447)

Liberation trail Spots from Jo'burg's Constitution Hill to Robben Island celebrate the anti-apartheid struggle. (p331)

Apartheid Museum Entered through racial classification gates, Jo'burg's museum evokes the era of segregation. (p335)

Mapungubwe National Park The Unesco World Heritage site was home to a significant Iron Age civilisation. (p424)

Oudtshoorn Mansions built by ostrich-farming 'feather barons', and pioneering engineer Thomas Bain's Swartberg Pass (1886). (p165)

Cape Dutch Gabled museum houses in South Africa's oldest settlements: Cape Town, Stellenbosch, Swellendam and Graaff-Reinet. (p109)

Food & Drink

From Cape Dutch wine estates to braais (barbecues) smoking away on township corners, sampling South Africa's *lekker* (tasty) produce is the best way to this agricultural country's heart.

Cooking safari Make Cape Malay curries in Cape Town's Bo-Kaap, and Xhosa dishes in the townships. (p72)

Food markets Try farm-fresh goodies at Cape Town and Jo'burg's Neighbourgoods Markets and other weekly events. (p102)

Wine tour Toast three centuries of local viticulture on stunning estates in Stellenbosch, Franschhoek and beyond. (p109)

Beer cruise Sample South Africa's burgeoning beer scene in

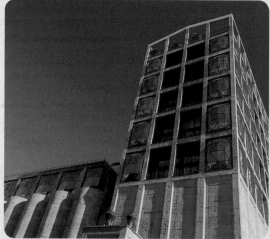

Top: Blyde River Canyon (p385)
Bottom: Zeitz MOCAA Museum (p64), Cape Town

microbreweries and bars such as Long St's Beerhouse. (p94)

Bunny chow Regional specialities include this creation from Durban: a hollow bread loaf filled with curry. (p250)

Wine on the River Quaff by the Breede River, Robertson; one of the Western Cape's many wine festivals. (p129)

Potluck Boskombuis Near Mpumalanga's Blyde River Canyon, this electricity-free riverside 'bush kitchen' is a classic hidden gem. (p386)

Altitudinous eats Africa's highest restaurant, in Lesotho, offers mountain views and novelty value. (p486)

Art

Artworks reflecting South Africa's dramatic landscapes and social issues can be seen in galleries old and new, with vibrant cultural scenes in Jo'burg and Cape Town.

Zeitz MOCAA Museum This contemporary African art gallery is inside a repurposed grain silo at Cape Town's V&A Waterfront. (p64)

Eastern Karoo Refined Graaff-Reinet has well-preserved architecture, and concrete sculptures populate Nieu Bethesda's Owl House. (p227)

Clarens South Africa's foremost art town, this Free State gem has a dozen galleries. (p317)

Ecoshrine This ecological Stonehenge overlooks the

Amathole Mountains in alternative, environmental Hogsback. (p211)

Jo'burg Cultural districts such as the Maboneng precinct have galleries, street art and walking tours. (p326)

Venda region Down red tracks in Limpopo's former homeland, studios produce woodcarvings, pottery, batiks and textiles. (p425)

William Humphreys Art Gallery Artists in Kimberley's gallery range from locals to Dutch and Flemish old masters. (p451)

Eccentric Corners

Isolated from the outside world while under apartheid, South Africa's country towns and villages, by turns quirky and refined, have been preserved in all their idiosyncratic glory.

Matjiesfontein The Karoo railway village has a Victorian hotel and three museums on its single street. (p167)

Hogsback High in the Amathole Mountains, gardens, forests and waterfalls surround this green village. (p211)

Haenertsburg A mountain village in Limpopo's Letaba Valley, with pine plantations and congenial pubs. (p428)

Wild Coast Community-run backpacker hostels mix friendly Xhosa locals with surfers, travellers, sandy beaches and hammocks. (p213)

Barberton Mpumalanga's gold-rush town is rich in history, geology and characterful accommodation. (p392)

Roma In one of Lesotho's most attractive towns, the country's university nestles among sandstone cliffs. (p480)

Open Spaces

Whether you head inland or along the coast, the largely rural countryside offers an invigorating sense of freedom.

Namakwa The rocky hills and plains covering the country's western quarters fill with spring wildflowers. (p464)

Free State Discover golden sunflower and corn fields and, in Golden Gate Highlands Natural Park, simmering grasslands with a mountain backdrop. (p305)

Karoo The semi-arid plateau experiences blazing summers and icy winters, as well as stunning sunsets and starscapes. (p167)

Beaches Quiet beaches are common on South Africa's 2500km-plus coastline, from Cape Point upwards. (p536)

Kalahari Red dunes ripple away to the horizon, with added greenery by the Orange River. (p455)

Southern Lesotho This mountainous area has musk- and orange-coloured valleys, rivers and off-the-beaten-track villages. (p490)

Month by Month

TOP EVENTS

Wildlife watching, July

Kirstenbosch Summer Sunset Concerts, November

Whale watching, September

Oyster Festival, July

Jo'burg festivals, September

January

South Africans descend on tourist areas, including the coast and major parks, during summer school holidays (early December to mid-January). Book accommodation and transport well in advance. High season for accommodation is November to March.

⚶ Cape Town Minstrel Carnival (Kaapse Klopse)

The Mother City's colourful new-year celebration begins with a carnival on 2 January and continues for a month. With satin- and sequin-clad minstrel troupes, ribald song-and-dance routines, floats and general revelry, it's the Cape's Mardi Gras. (p79)

February

Summer continues, with smiles on the beaches, half-price cable cars up Table Mountain for sunset, and dramatic lightning storms in Jo'burg. Elephants munch marula trees, and baby antelope, zebras and giraffes cavort in the parks.

March

Summer rolls towards autumn, although days remain sunny, the lowveld steamy and the landscapes green. Good for walking and beach bumming in the Western Cape. Cultural and music festivals happen in Cape Town and Jo'burg.

🏃 Cape Town Cycle Tour

This 109km spin around the Cape Peninsula is the world's largest timed cycling event. More than 30,000 contestants, from serious racers to costumed Capetonians, tackle Table Mountain and Chapman's Peak Dr. There's a mountain-biking challenge in the Winelands around the same time. (p79)

April

There's a two-week school holiday around Easter, generally regarded as the beginning of autumn. Temperatures drop, and wildlife watching in the bushveld starts to look more attractive than beach bumming. Rutting season runs until May.

⚶ AfrikaBurn

Africa's entry in the global calendar of festivals inspired by the USA's Burning Man is a subcultural blowout and a survivalist challenge. Art installations and themed camps turn a corner of the Tankwa Karoo into a surreal paradise. (p469)

July

Winter brings rain to the Cape and clouds to Table Mountain. Northern areas experience fresh, sunny days and clear night skies. Low season is June to September, apart from the mid-June to mid-July school holidays.

◉ Wildlife Watching

Cooler, drier winter weather is perfect for wildlife watching. Thirsty animals congregate at waterholes and foliage is sparser, making spotting easier. The lower temperatures make toasty northern areas such as the bushveld and Kalahari more enjoyable. (p537)

🏃 Lesotho Ski Season

That's right, skiing in Southern Africa. Lesotho's peaks and passes receive snow in winter – particularly around Oxbow, where the season runs from June to August at the modern and well-equipped Afriski resort. (p485)

🍴 Oyster Festival

Knysna's 10-day oyster orgy is one of a few seafood-oriented events on the South African coastline. Fixtures include oyster-eating and -shucking competitions, wine tastings, a mountain-bike race and the Knysna Marathon. (p155)

☆ National Arts Festival

Feel Africa's creative pulse at the continent's largest arts festival, held over 10 days in early July in studenty Grahamstown. Performers from every conceivable discipline descend on the refined spot, and Fingo Village township holds an associated festival. (p203)

🏃 Open JBay

The winter months bring big waves to the Eastern Cape, and Jeffrey's Bay holds its international Open JBay surf competition. Part of the 10-day Winter Fest in mid-July, the contest on the town's famous Supertubes break attracts thousands of spectators; accommodation fills and prices rise. (p187)

September

Winter starts giving way to spring. Cherry trees bloom in the Free State Eastern Highlands in September and October, which are also the last dry months for wildlife viewing. School holidays run from late September to early October.

⊙ Namakwa Wildflowers

In late August and early September, nature plays a springtime trick and covers this barren area with wildflowers. Namakwa's parched terrain sprouts meadows of flowers in rainbow hues. The spectacle also happens elsewhere in the Northern and Western Capes. (p465)

⊙ Whale Watching

Watch southern right whales calve in Walker Bay throughout the second half of the year; the best time to spot them is the period around Hermanus Whale Festival in September/October. During this time, Hermanus is the world's best land-based whale-watching destination. (p133)

🎆 Jo'burg Festivals

Jozi's two-month festival season starts with Arts Alive, the Soweto Festival Expo, featuring music, poetry, food stalls and a lifestyle expo, and Joy of Jazz. There's more in October, including the monthly First Thursday and First Sunday in the Valley Jozi! (p337)

October

A great month to visit, offering mostly sunny weather without the worst of the summer crowds and prices. There is a 10-day South African school holiday at the beginning of the month.

🎆 South African National Gold Panning Championships

This contest involves hopeful panners from local schoolchildren to semiprofessionals and takes place in a line of watery troughs by the Blyde River. (p382)

🎆 Soweto Festivals

Following Jo'burg's September festival fun, the city's largest township hosts the Soweto Beer Festival, featuring some 40 different types of beers, including local and traditional African brews, and Soweto Fashion Week. (p359)

November

Spring drifts into summer: wildflowers in the Drakensberg, beach potential before the worst humidity hits KwaZulu-Natal, and all of the above in Cape Town and the Western Cape. Rain in the lowveld. High season begins.

☆ Kirstenbosch Summer Sunset Concerts

Summer music festivals take place in stunning settings nationwide. In the Western Cape alone, the choice includes the Kirstenbosch Summer Sunset Concerts in Cape Town's botanical gardens (November to April), the West Coast's indie Endless Daze (www.endlessdazefest.com) and numerous trance parties. (p67)

Itineraries

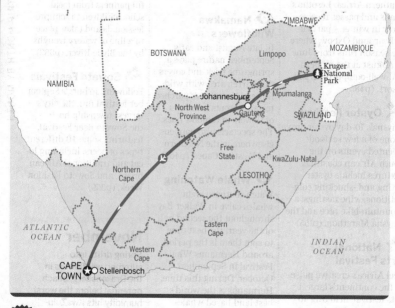

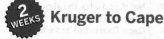

2 WEEKS Kruger to Cape

This trip combines wildlife watching with the Cape's scenery and culture.

Head directly east from Jo'burg's OR Tambo International Airport to **Kruger National Park**, where more than 20,000 growly members of the Big Five (lion, leopard, buffalo, elephant and rhino) roam the bushveld. Staying in a bush camp or luxurious private reserve and going on self-drive safaris, guided drives and walks will keep you and your binoculars busy. From Kruger, head back to the bright lights of **Jo'burg**. Spend a night in the inner-city Maboneng precinct's art hotel or hostels, experiencing Afro-globalisation and meeting local hipsters in the galleries and bars.

Next, pick up a flight to **Cape Town**; alternatively, take a scenic overnight train ride in tourist class on Shosholoza Meyl's trans-Karoo service (or the Blue Train or Rovos Rail from Pretoria). Relax and enjoy one of the world's most beautiful cities, spending your days exploring the likes of Table Mountain and Kirstenbosch National Botanical Garden, and your nights dining in world-class restaurants and drinking in the 'Tavern of the Seven Seas'. The Mother City is surrounded by beaches and vineyards; have lunch in winemaking **Stellenbosch** and wander the refined Cape Dutch student town's lanes.

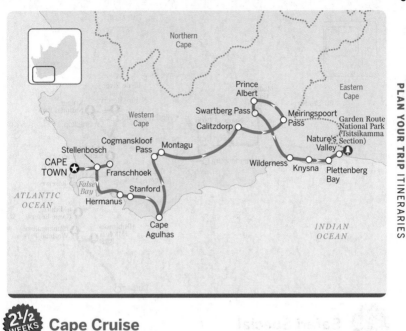

2½ WEEKS Cape Cruise

Beautiful scenery, excellent infrastructure and numerous attractions make this the South Africa of the glossy brochures. The route can be covered on public transport, but is perfect for a road trip in your own car.

After a few days in **Cape Town**, fitting in historical and cultural sights such as the Bo-Kaap neighbourhood, Zeitz MOCAA Museum and Irma Stern Museum alongside the scenic Cape Peninsula, head out to the Winelands. Spend a night or two wine tasting in the vineyard-clad valleys of **Stellenbosch** and **Franschhoek**. From Stellenbosch take Rte 44 for one of the world's most beautiful coastal drives, to **Hermanus**, where you can watch southern right whales (June to December). Overnight or stop for lunch in the 19th-century village of **Stanford**, before making your way to **Cape Agulhas**, Africa's southernmost point.

Next, head along the **Cogmanskloof Pass** in the Langeberg range to countrified **Montagu**. With its whitewashed cottages and rustic accommodation, the quaint town is a great base for rock climbing and the Robertson Wine Valley. Continue along Rte 62 through the Little Karoo, between rolling mountains dotted with farms and charming little towns such as port-making **Calitzdorp**.

Cross the Swartberg range on the **Meiringspoort Pass**, from Oudtshoorn to the Great Karoo and **Prince Albert**. This pretty 18th-century village is green and fertile, with irrigation channels in the streets. The nearby N1 highway leads back to Cape Town; alternatively, backtrack south, possibly via the untarred **Swartberg Pass**, to **Wilderness'** beaches and lagoons. East along the Garden Route, old-growth forests rise into the mountains above **Knysna** and **Plettenberg Bay**, both offering water sports and activities.

Finally, descend a windy road to the beach village of **Nature's Valley**, where happy hikers finishing the five-day Otter Trail hang their boots in a tree outside the pub. Shorter hikes also lead into the surrounding **Garden Route National Park (Tsitsikamma Section)**.

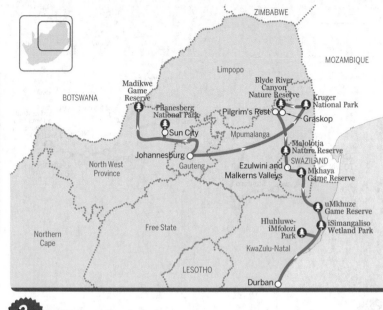

2 WEEKS Safari Special

South Africa is one of the continent's best safari destinations – in a fortnight it's possible to cover several parks and reserves, plus a few extra stops such as the dramatic Blyde River Canyon.

From Jo'burg's OR Tambo International Airport, head east to the country's safari showpiece, **Kruger National Park**. The wildlife here and in the adjoining private wildlife reserves will hold you captivated. **Blyde River Canyon Nature Reserve**, near Kruger's southern and central sections, offers views of the river as it snakes from the Drakensberg Escarpment to the lowveld. Stay overnight in nearby **Graskop**, a good base for outdoor activities and a visit to **Pilgrim's Rest**, a 19th-century gold-rush village.

If time is tight, hit the N4 west for wildlife watching on sealed roads in **Pilanesberg National Park**, within four hours' drive of OR Tambo International Airport. Stay in the Big Five park or the adjoining **Sun City** casino complex. A little further, **Madikwe Game Reserve** is an exclusive destination with accommodation in five-star lodges (and one ecolodge).

If you have a full two weeks, head south from the Kruger area to Swaziland's **Malolotja Nature Reserve**, where hiking trails cross grasslands and forests, and along the **Ezulwini** and **Malkerns valleys** – stop to admire the woodlands and pick up local craftwork. Swaziland's highlight is the wildlife-rich **Mkhaya Game Reserve**, known for its unsurpassed black and white rhino populations. Explore the bushveld thickets and open veld on a guided walking safari.

Leaving Swaziland, hit the N2 to **uMkhuze Game Reserve**, where animals lap at waterholes in pans surrounded by fever trees. Nearby are the waterways and diverse eco-systems of **iSimangaliso Wetland Park**, and **Hluhluwe-iMfolozi Park**, where hiking the wilderness trails is a once-in-a-lifetime experience. From there, continue south along the Indian Ocean to **Durban's** well-connected airport and beaches, restaurants and bars.

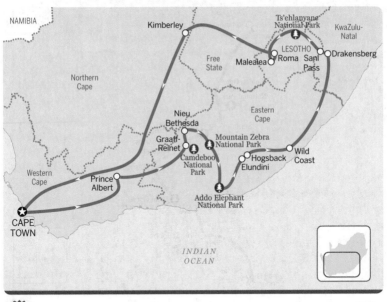

Grand Circuit

4 WEEKS

This epic itinerary covers the bottom half of South Africa, including Wild Coast beaches, the Karoo semidesert and mountainous Lesotho.

From **Cape Town** head along Rte 62 and over the Swartberg Pass to **Prince Albert**. Venture further into the Great Karoo's open spaces to reach the refined oasis of **Graaff-Reinet**, nicknamed the 'jewel of the Karoo' for its 220-plus national monuments and history stretching back to 1786. Also in this corner of the Karoo are **Camdeboo National Park**, with Cape buffaloes and the Valley of Desolation's views over the plains, and arty **Nieu Bethesda**, home of the sculpture-adorned Owl House. Stop at **Mountain Zebra National Park** for cheetah tracking and more Karoo panoramas, or continue straight to **Addo Elephant National Park**, where great white sharks and southern right whales complete the 'Big Seven'.

Moving east, the Amathole Mountains are worth an inland detour for the eco-backpackers in **Hogsback** and **Elundini**. Staying in a rondavel hut by a **Wild Coast** beach is likely to be a trip highlight when mixed with cultural experiences and community-run activities. Heading north to the jagged green sweep of the iconic **Drakensberg**, take South Africa's highest pass, the **Sani Pass** (2876m), to Lesotho, where Africa's highest pub awaits.

Hiking and pony trekking in altitudinous Lesotho, you will meet Basotho people clad in conical hats and patterned woollen blankets. Spend at least a few days crossing the mountain kingdom, stopping at beautiful lodges in the likes of **Ts'ehlanyane National Park** and **Malealea**. Pass your last Lesothan night among sandstone cliffs in **Roma**, a 19th-century mission station and now the country's seat of learning.

Over the international border, zip through the Free State's shimmering golden fields to the Northern Cape and its capital, **Kimberley**. The city that witnessed the world's greatest diamond rush is a great place to get a feel for South African history. From here, Shosholoza Meyl's trans-Karoo Express will whisk you back to Cape Town (or up to Jo'burg).

3 WEEKS Eastern Wander

This eastern jaunt mixes awesome mountain scenery with Xhosa and Zulu culture, and rural calm with urban vibes, giving a good look at the classic South Africa.

After touching down at OR Tambo International Airport, linger a few days in dynamic **Jo'burg**, seeing how urban regeneration is transforming the inner city and creating hip enclaves of restaurants and bars. Go on a city walking tour or head out to South Africa's most famous township, **Soweto**.

Moving on from Jozi, cross the Free State and leave the N3 at Harrismith, to take scenic Rte 712 past Sterkfontein Dam to **Clarens**. The arty town, with its galleries and microbrewery, has surroundings worthy of an impressionist landscape. Next, stay in a chalet in the nearby **Golden Gate Highlands National Park**, with its hiking trails between sandstone outcrops in the foothills of the Maluti Mountains bordering Lesotho.

Just outside the park, the day-long **Sentinel Hiking Trail** climbs the iconic Amphitheatre to the top of the Drakensberg Escarpment. Next, spend a couple of days enjoying the spectacular Drakensberg day walks, such as Tugela Gorge, in **Royal Natal National Park**. Declimatise from the Draks on the twee **Midlands Meander**, with its guesthouses and ceramic studios, before hitting **Durban**, a city of beaches and Indian cuisine that is slowly being revitalised.

Near the Eastern Cape border, **Oribi Gorge Nature Reserve** is an oft-overlooked reserve with cliffs and forests above the Umzilkulwana River. From here, detour off the N2 and along the coast through Pondoland to **Port St Johns** – a laid-back introduction to the Wild Coast's pristine beaches and friendly Xhosa locals. Pastel rondavel huts dot the green hills overlooking the region's gravel roads, which lead to some stunning community-run hostels around **Coffee Bay**.

At the southern end of the Wild Coast, spend a final night by the Indian Ocean in **Chintsa**, and pick up a plane, train or bus from nearby **East London** to Jo'burg or Cape Town.

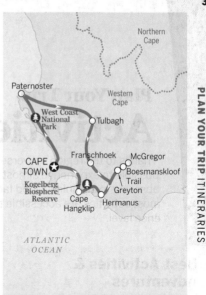

2½ WEEKS The Wild Northwest

Some of South Africa's gnarliest terrain is found in the vast Northern Cape province, which this itinerary tours in conjunction with the Western Cape's wilder corners.

From **Cape Town**, head north to the mountainous **Cederberg Wilderness Area**, with its sandstone formations, lodges and campgrounds. Continue to the Hantam Karoo outpost of **Calvinia**, before hitting the N7 through the Namakwa region, its rocky expanses carpeted with wildflowers in spring. Almost at the end of the region's straight roads is remote **Port Nolloth**. If you have a 4WD, continue to the surreal mountain desert of **|Ai-|Ais/ Richtersveld Transfrontier Park**.

Head east to **Augrabies Falls National Park** for hiking, rafting and canoeing, followed by a sunset cruise in **Upington**. Continue north through the Kalahari to **Kgalagadi Transfrontier Park**, an excellent place to spot big cats, and see more of the thirsty semidesert at **Witsand Nature Reserve**. Return to Cape Town via the Great Karoo, with stops including **Karoo National Park** and historic **Matjiesfontein**.

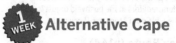

1 WEEK Alternative Cape

With its mountains, culture and wine, the Western Cape is a justly popular holiday destination. This itinerary suggests a few spots to escape the crowds alongside some old favourites.

From **Cape Town**, head north to the **West Coast National Park**, which offers a glimpse of the spring wildflower bloom alongside Langebaan Lagoon. Overnight here or in **Paternoster**, with its white-washed cottages and glorious beaches.

Turning inland, mountain ranges surround the wineries of **Tulbagh**. Further into the Winelands, **Franschhoek** distils the area's refined charm, with its Huguenot heritage, vineyards and restaurants. Cross the Franschhoek Pass to the village of **Greyton**, for thatched cottages, restaurants, mountain views and Genadendal Mission Station. The **Boesmanskloof Trail** leads hikers to the New Age village of **McGregor**.

Return to Cape Town via **Hermanus**, the world's best land-based whale-watching destination (June to December), and along Rte 44, passing **Cape Hangklip** and **Kogelberg Biosphere Reserve**.

Plan Your Trip
Activities

Thanks to the region's diverse terrain and pleasant climate, it's possible to experience almost any outdoor activity here, from abseiling to zip lining. Good facilities and instruction mean that most activities are accessible to all visitors, whatever their experience level.

Best Activities & Adventures

Whether you want to cross vast wildernesses, search for predators in the bushveld or just lounge on the beach, South Africa has it covered.

Garden Route (p144)

The holiday strip offers surfing, canoeing, diving, kloofing (canyoning), horse riding, hiking and more.

Bloukrans Bridge Bungee (p180)

The world's third-highest bungee jump is one of many thrills in the Tsitsikamma forests.

Multiday hikes (p181)

Carry your equipment or take the easy 'slackpacking' option and have your bags transported.

Kalahari (p455)

The semidesert makes use of the Orange River for rafting, canoeing and wine tasting.

Canopy tours (p67)

Stroll Kirstenbosch's 'Boomslang' walkway, and zip line in the Drakensberg, the Mpumalanga lowveld and beyond.

Lion's Head paragliding (p71)

Take a tandem flight from Cape Town's sphinx-like mountain down to the beach.

Abseiling (p57)

Shimmy 112m down Table Mountain.

Birdwatching

With its enormous diversity of habitats, South Africa is a paradise for birdwatchers. There are birdwatching clubs nationwide, and most parks and reserves can provide birding lists, with information available from SANParks (p153). Many parks, reserves and accommodation places also have field guides, but it's still worth bringing your own.

Birding Africa (www.birdingafrica.com) Day trips from Cape Town and tours further afield, covering birds and flowers.

BirdLife South Africa (www.birdlife.org.za) Useful information and links. Promotes avitourism (birding ecotourism) routes.

Bird-Watch Cape (www.birdwatch.co.za) Small, Cape Town–based outfit for twitchers, with tours including a nationwide 17-day package.

Cape Birding Route (www.capebirdingroute.org) Information relating to western South Africa, from Cape Point to the Kalahari.

Indicator Birding (www.birding.co.za) Information, articles and tours. Based in Gauteng.

Limpopo Birding Routes (www.limpopobirding.com) Lists guides and four routes, including one taking in the Soutpansberg mountains and Limpopo River Valley.

Southern African Birding (www.sabirding.co.za) Multimedia guides and information.

Zululand Birding Route (www.zululandbirding route.co.za) Avitourism project in an area of northern KwaZulu-Natal featuring over 600 bird species.

Canoeing, Kayaking & Rafting

South Africa has few major rivers, but those it has flow year-round and offer rewarding rafting and canoeing. Rafting is highly rain dependent, with the best months in most areas from December/January to April.

Felix Unite (☎087 354 0578; www.felixunite.com) Runs trips on the Breede and Orange (Gariep) Rivers.

Induna Adventures (www.indunaadventures. com) White-water rafting and tubing ('geckoing') on the Sabie River.

Intrapid (www.raftsa.co.za) Rafting trips on rivers including the Orange, Doring and Palmiet.

Kaskazi Kayaks (www.kayak.co.za) Sea-kayaking trips in Cape Town.

PaddleYak (www.seakayak.co.za) Sea-kayak online shop, news and tours.

Swazi Trails (p618) Offers trips on Swaziland's Great Usutu River (Lusutfu River) and around the country.

Diving

Take the plunge off the southern end of Africa into the Indian and Atlantic Oceans. Strong currents and often windy conditions mean advanced divers can find challenges all along the coast. Sodwana Bay on KwaZulu-Natal's Elephant Coast is a good choice for beginners, while Aliwal Shoal and Port Elizabeth are also popular.

When to Go Conditions vary widely. The best time to dive the KwaZulu-Natal shoreline is from May to September, when visibility tends to be highest. In the west, along the Atlantic seaboard, the water is cold year-round, but is at its most diveable, with many days of high visibility, between November and January/February.

Costs Prices are generally lower in South Africa than elsewhere in the region. Expect to pay from R5000 for a four-day PADI open-water certification course, and from R350 for a dive.

Equipment Coastal towns where diving is possible have dive outfitters. With the exception of Sodwana Bay during the warmer months (when a 3mm wetsuit will suffice), you'll need at least a 5mm wetsuit for many sites, and a dry suit for some sites to the south and west.

Fishing

Sea fishing is popular, with a wide range of species in the warm and cold currents that flow past the east and west coasts, respectively.

River fishing, especially for introduced trout, is popular in parks and reserves, with some particularly good highland streams in the Drakensberg (for example, in the Rhodes area). Dullstroom is the capital of highveld fly fishing and Lesotho is an insider's tip among trout anglers.

SAFE DIVING

In popular diving areas such as Sodwana Bay, there is a range of diving companies – including some slipshod operations. When choosing an operator, make quality – rather than cost – your priority. Factors to consider include an operator's experience and qualifications, knowledge and seriousness of staff, whether it's a fly-by-night operation or well-established with a good reputation locally, and the type and condition of equipment and frequency of maintenance. Assess whether the overall attitude is professional, and ask about safety considerations – radios, oxygen, emergency evacuation procedures, boat reliability and back-up engines, first-aid kits, safety flares and life jackets. On longer dives, do you get an energising meal, or just tea and biscuits?

Using operators offering courses certified by the Professional Association of Diving Instructors (www.padi.com) gives you the flexibility to go elsewhere in the world and have your certification recognised at other PADI dive centres.

Pony trekking in Lesotho (p480)

Licences are available for a few rand at park offices, and some shops and accommodation rent out equipment.

Bass Fishing South Africa (www.bassfishing.co.za) Forum and details of fishing sites.

Cape Piscatorial Society (www.piscator.co.za) Licences for sites around Cape Town and the Winelands.

Sealine (www.sealine.co.za) Angling and boating community.

Southern African Trout & Flyfishing Directory (www.flyfisher.co.za) Inspiration for a fly-fishing safari.

Wild Trout Association (www.wildtrout.co.za) Rhodes-based repository of fishing lore.

Hiking

South Africa is a wonderful destination for hiking – as are Lesotho and Swaziland – with an excellent system of well-marked trails varied enough to suit every ability.

Accommodation Some trails offer accommodation, from camping and simple huts with electric-ity and running water, to hotels on slackpacking trails in the Eastern Cape and elsewhere. Book well in advance.

Guided walks Various parks, including Kruger, offer hikes ranging from two- to three-hour bush walks to overnight or multiday wilderness trails. Accompanied by armed rangers, you won't cover much distance, but they offer the chance to experience the wild with nothing between you and nature. Numerous tour operators also offer guided hikes in areas such as the Wild Coast and Drakensberg – excellent ways to get off the beaten track and experience African village life.

Off-trail hiking Some designated wilderness areas offer this. Routes are suggested, but it's basically up to you to survive on your own.

Regulations Many trails have limits as to how many hikers can be on them at any one time, so book ahead. Most longer routes and wilderness areas require hikers to be in a group of at least three or four, although solo hikers may be able to join a group.

Safety Not a major issue on most trails, but longer trails have seen muggings and burglaries of accommodation, while robberies and attacks can occur on the contour paths on Table Mountain, neighbouring Lion's Head, Signal Hill and especially Devil's Peak. Check with the local hiking club or park office. On longer and quieter trails, hike in a group and limit the valuables you carry. In Cape Town, do not walk alone, and avoid early mornings, evenings and other quiet times. The Table Mountain plateau is usually safe.

When to go Hiking is possible year-round, although you'll need to be prepared in summer for extremes of heat and wet. The best time in the northern half of the country is March to October. For Cape Town and the Western Cape, spring (September to November) and autumn (March to May) offer cool, dry weather.

Resources

Recommended books:
Best Walks of the Drakensberg by David Bristow.

Easy Walks in the Cape Peninsula by Mike Lundy.

Hiking Trails of South Africa by Willie and Sandra Olivier.

Online resources:
CapeNature (www.capenature.co.za) Administers numerous trails in the Western Cape.

SANParks (www.sanparks.org) SANParks and the various forestry authorities administer most trails. Lots of information on its website.

Ezemvelo KZN Wildlife (www.kznwildlife.com) Controls various trails in the KwaZulu-Natal Drakensberg and Elephant Coast.

Hiking Organisation of Southern Africa (www.hosavosa.co.za) Information and links to hiking clubs.

Horse Riding & Pony Trekking

It's easy to find horse rides ranging from hours to days, and for all experience levels. Riding trips are offered in national parks, including Addo Elephant, Golden Gate and Mountain Zebra. In Swaziland there are stables offering fully kitted-out horse rides in the Ezulwini Valley, Malkerns, Mlilwane Wildlife Sanctuary and Malolotja Nature Reserve. Pony trekking (p480) is one of Lesotho's top drawcards.

Chubeka Trails (www.biggameparks.org/chubeka) At Mlilwane Wildlife Sanctuary.

Fynbos Trails (www.fynbostrails.com) In the Western Cape.

Haven Horse Safaris (www.havenhotel.co.za) One of many operators offering rides on the beaches of the Wild Coast and Eastern Cape.

Horizon Horseback (www.ridinginafrica.com) In the Waterberg, Limpopo.

Khotso Trails (www.khotsotrails.co.za) In the Southern Drakensberg, including Lesotho.

Nyanza Farm (www.nyanza.co.sz) In the Malkerns Valley.

Savannah Horse Trails (www.savannahhorsetrails.co.za) In the Waterberg, Limpopo.

Kloofing (Canyoning)

Kloofing (called canyoning elsewhere) is a mix of climbing, hiking, swimming and some serious jumping. It has a small but rapidly growing following in South Africa, where you can enjoy it in locations from the Western Cape to Mpumalanga.

There's an element of risk in the sport, so when hunting for operators, check their credentials carefully before signing up.

Mountain Biking

There are trails almost everywhere in the region, from the Garden Route to Lesotho. Cape Town is an unofficial hub for the activity.

Bike Hub (www.bikehub.co.za) General cycling site, with articles, classifieds and popular forums.

Linx Africa (www.linx.co.za/trails/lists/bikelist.html) Lists trails by province.

MTB Routes (www.mtbroutes.co.za) Maps the locations of more than 400 bike trails nationwide.

Paragliding & Microlighting

Favourable weather conditions year-round and an abundance of high points to launch yourself from make South Africa a fine destination for aerial pursuits. Taking to the South African skies is fairly inexpensive; a helpful contact for getting started is the **Aero Club of South Africa** (☎011-082 1100; www.aeroclub.org.za).

South Africa is one of the world's top paragliding destinations – especially Lion's Head in Cape Town, with further opportunities throughout the Western Cape and nationwide. The strongest thermals are from November to April; outside these months, Barberton in Mpumalanga is a good winter-flying destination. For experienced pilots, airspace restrictions are minimal and there's great potential for long-distance, cross-country flying. **South African Hang Gliding & Paragliding Association** (SAHPA; ☑074 152 2505; www.sahpa.co.za) can provide information on flying sites, schools and clubs.

For microlighting, a useful resource with forums and a list of airfields for ultralight aviation can be found at http://microlighters.co.za.

Rock Climbing

Top spots for climbing include Table Mountain, the Cederberg, Montagu, the Drakensberg, and Waterval Boven (Emgwenya) in Mpumalanga.

Climb ZA (www.climbing.co.za) News, articles, directory and forum.

Mountain Club of South Africa (www.mcsa.org.za) Information and links to regional clubs.

SA Climbing Info Network (www.saclimb.co.za) Has listings and photos of climbing and bouldering routes.

Surfing

The best time of year for surfing the southern and eastern coasts is autumn and early winter (from about April to July). Boards and gear can be bought in most of the big coastal cities. New boards start around R4500 – check out www.gumtree.co.za.

Good spots for beginners – with lessons and gear hire aplenty – are Muizenberg (Cape Town), Jeffrey's Bay and Durban.

Wavescape (www.wavescape.co.za) Surf forecasting and coastal lifestyle website.

Zig Zag (www.zigzag.co.za) South Africa's main surf magazine.

Wildlife Watching

South Africa and Swaziland's populations of large animals are one of the countries' biggest attractions. In comparison with other countries in the region (Botswana and Zambia, for example), wildlife watching here tends to be very accessible, with good roads and accommodation for all categories of traveller. It is also comparatively inexpensive, although there are plenty of pricier choices for those seeking a luxury experience in the bush.

Whale Watching

South Africa is considered one of the world's best spots to sight whales from land. Whale-watching spots dot the southern and eastern coastlines, from False Bay to iSimangaliso Wetland Park. Hermanus, where southern right whales come to calve, is the unofficial whale-watching capital.

Southern right and humpback whales are regularly seen offshore between June/July and November, with occasional spottings of Bryde's and killer whales.

Whale-watching boat trips are offered on both coasts, everywhere from Cape Town and Hermanus to Port Elizabeth and Durban.

Plan Your Trip

Travel with Children

With its abundance of national parks, beaches, swimming pools and hiking trails suitable for a wide range of competencies, plus a good collection of museums and a handful of amusement parks, South Africa offers plenty for children of all ages in hazard-free settings.

Southern Africa for Kids

Most South Africans are welcoming to children, and you will probably receive many offers of assistance. Get used to passing your child around like a curio; they will excite much interest and attention, particularly in rural and traditional parts of the country.

Lesotho can be a welcoming destination for children, though the rugged terrain and conditions are better suited to older children who would enjoy hiking or pony trekking. Most pony trekking centres arrange treks only for people over 12 years old.

Swaziland is a good family destination, with a child-friendly attitude and a relaxed pace, although malaria is a real risk in lower-lying areas of the country.

Children's Highlights

Beaches

Clifton 4th Beach, Cape Town (p65) Sitting on a Mother City beach such as this Blue Flag beauty, among multicultural Capetonians, will be an interesting experience for all the family.

Arniston, Western Cape (p141) Has a sheltered beach with caves and rock pools near Africa's southernmost point.

Best Regions for Kids

Cape Town

Botanical gardens, an aquarium, the Table Mountain cable car, beaches, Greenmarket Square market, harbour cruises, activities, good facilities and a relaxed atmosphere – the vibrant Mother City is a superb family destination.

Western Cape

Surrounding Cape Town, the Western Cape has good infrastructure as well as stunning scenery. Near the city, the Winelands offers numerous family-friendly wine estates, markets and attractions. Further afield, Garden Route spots such as Mossel Bay and Nature's Valley are particularly well set up for family holidays, with beaches and activities galore.

KwaZulu-Natal

Durban has beaches, one of the world's largest aquariums and hot weather. The sandy fun continues along the surrounding Indian Ocean coastline, with activities from whale watching to kayak safaris in iSimangaliso Wetland Park. Head inland for walking and camping opportunities in the stunning Drakensberg.

Water sports (p38) South Africa offers lots of water sports for older children to get stuck into, including surfing, diving, canoeing, kayaking, tubing and rafting.

Jeffrey's Bay, Eastern Cape (p185) One of the world's best surf spots.

Horse Riding

Noordhoek Beach, Cape Town (p53) Riding along this scenic beach at the foot of Chapman's Peak is a breezy day out.

Horseback safaris and tours (p41) Many operators offer these, in areas from Limpopo's Waterberg range to the Wild Coast.

Wildlife

Kruger National Park (p396) Inhabited by the Big Five, Kruger has easy accessibility and family-friendly rest camps.

Pilanesberg National Park, North West Province (p440) Constructed with weekend-ing families in mind, this malaria-free park near Jo'burg (and Sun City) has sealed roads.

Addo Elephant National Park, Eastern Cape (p197) There is a good chance of spotting elephants in this malaria-free park.

Oudtshoorn, Western Cape (p165) Has ostrich farms and a meerkat conservation project.

Penguin colonies and rehabilitation centres Found at Boulders Beach (Cape Town), Betty's Bay (Western Cape), Cape St Francis (Eastern Cape) and Port Elizabeth (Eastern Cape).

Walking

Table Mountain, Cape Town (p44) Walking up the mountain will give older children a tremendous sense of achievement.

Royal Natal National Park, KwaZulu-Natal (p298) Hiking and camping in Drakensberg parks such as this will be a memorable experience for older children and teenagers.

Hogsback, Eastern Cape (p211) With its fairy meander and easy trails through gardens and forests, it's suitable for nature-loving parents with small children.

Planning

Accommodation

➡ Family-oriented accommodation, such as triple or quadruple hotel rooms and four- to six-person self-catering cottages, is common throughout South Africa.

➡ Camping and self-catering are good options for families seeking affordability and privacy, with quality campgrounds and well-equipped cabins, cottages and chalets found nationwide.

➡ In KwaZulu-Natal, Ezemvelo KZN Wildlife (p287) offers good-value accommodation to groups and families – although animals roam freely in many of its parks.

➡ SAN (South Africa National) Parks accommodation is generally excellent, but pricey; it often works out cheaper to stay outside the park.

➡ Many wildlife lodges have restrictions on children under 12 years, so in parks and reserves the main accommodation options will sometimes be camping and self-catering.

➡ Many hotels and self-catering options can provide cots.

Activities

➡ Safaris are suitable for older children who have the patience to sit for long periods in a vehicle or hide, but less suitable for younger kids.

➡ Guided drives in large vehicles are excellent, with more chance of sightings and an expert to answer questions and take care of safety.

➡ Activities for children are offered in Kruger, Pilanesberg and other parks.

Childcare

➡ Many upscale hotels and resorts in tourist areas can arrange childcare, and short-term day care may also be available.

➡ Especially during the high season, many South African coastal resorts have kids' clubs, offering daily children's activities.

Discounts

➡ Children are usually admitted at discounted rates to national parks, museums and other sights (often free for babies and toddlers, and discounted for teenagers and younger).

➡ Many hotels and transport operators, including bus companies, offer children's discounts.

➡ Restaurants often have children's menus with dishes at good prices, or offer smaller portions of regular dishes at discounted prices.

IMMIGRATION REGULATIONS

Since 2015 all children under 18 years travelling to South Africa have been required to show an unabridged birth certificate (UBC) in addition to their passport. If you do not have one already, UBCs are easy to apply for in most Western countries; unlike abridged birth certificates, they show the parents' details.

If one or neither parent is travelling with a child, the new immigration regulations ask for paperwork over and above the UBC, namely an affidavit giving permission for the child to travel, a court order in some cases and a death certificate if a parent is deceased. Where only one parent's particulars appear on the UBC or equivalent document, no parental consent affidavit is required when that parent travels with the child. The controversial new regulations, which, according to the Department of Home Affairs, are designed to combat child trafficking, have received immense opposition and may possibly be relaxed in the future.

For further information and updates, check www.brandsouthafrica.com, www.home-affairs.gov.za, or with your government's travel advisory or your airline.

Facilities

➡ Baby-changing rooms are not common in South Africa, but clean restrooms abound; in most, you should be able to find a makeshift spot to change a nappy (diaper).

Health

For more on health, see p621.

➡ Breastfeeding in public won't raise an eyebrow among many Africans, but in other circles it's best to be discreet.

➡ Overall there are few health risks, and should your child become ill, good-quality medical care is available in the cities.

➡ Avoid government hospitals where possible and use private hospitals.

➡ Mediclinic (www.mediclinic.co.za) operates private hospitals from Cape Town to Limpopo.

➡ There are reasonable medical facilities in Maseru (Lesotho) and Mbabane (Swaziland), but for anything serious you'll need to go to South Africa.

➡ Seek medical advice about vaccinations months before your trip; not all are suitable for children or pregnant women.

➡ Specifically, seek medical advice on malaria prophylactics for children if you'll be in malarial areas (including Kruger National Park, the lowveld and lower-lying regions of Swaziland).

➡ Think twice before taking young children to malarial areas and try to visit in the winter, when the risk of mosquito bites is lower.

➡ Regardless of malaria, insect bites can be painful, so come prepared with nets, repellent and suitable clothing.

➡ Swimming in streams should generally be avoided, due to the risk of bilharzia (schistosomiasis) infection.

➡ In drought-struck areas such as Cape Town, drink bottled or treated water in preference to tap water.

Supplies

➡ Nappies, powdered milk and baby food are widely available in South Africa, except in very rural areas.

➡ In Lesotho and Swaziland, they are available in Maseru, Mbabane and Manzini, with only a limited selection in smaller towns.

➡ Outside supermarkets in major towns, it's difficult to find processed baby food without added sugar.

➡ Merry Pop Ins (www.merrypopins.co.za) in central Cape Town sells used clothes, furniture and equipment for children from newborns to 12-year-olds.

Transport

➡ Most car-rental agencies can provide safety seats, but you'll need to book them in advance and usually pay extra.

➡ Distances can be vast (the bus from Cape Town to Port Elizabeth takes 12 hours), so try to stagger journeys where possible.

➡ Tourist-class trains with private sleeper compartments, such as the 27-hour trans-Karoo service from Jo'burg to Cape Town, have ample space and dining cars.

Regions at a Glance

Cape Town and the Western Cape are refined, developed spots, where you can sip wine and enjoy activities on beaches and mountains. Head north to the Northern Cape and North West Province for rugged wildernesses and wildlife parks.

Surfers, hikers and lovers of African culture will enjoy the Eastern Cape, bordering the mountain kingdom of Lesotho and the Free State. The latter's golden fields and open spaces lead to the Drakensberg range, which stretches into KwaZulu-Natal, where beaches, wildlife parks and Zululand spread north from Durban.

Turning northwest, Swaziland has excellent reserves; Mpumalanga offers lowveld, the Drakensberg Escarpment and activities; and Gauteng, home of Jo'burg and Pretoria, is South Africa's urban heartbeat. The Big Five's hang-out, mighty Kruger National Park, crowns the country, alongside Limpopo's diverse landscapes and Venda culture.

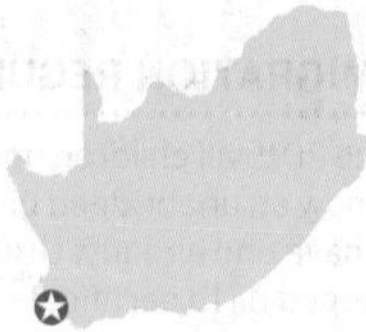

Cape Town

Outdoor Activities
Eating
Shopping

Accessible Adventures

Its mountainous national park, beaches and ocean make Cape Town a scenic hiking location, with a walk up one of the trails on Table Mountain crowning many to-do lists. Even just strolling along Sea Point promenade is a sheer pleasure beneath the Mother City's towering peaks, and kitesurfing, rock climbing and paragliding are also offered.

Diverse Cuisine

Cape Town's multi-ethnic peoples have bequeathed it a range of cuisines. Enjoy meats and fish from the braai (barbecue), world-class restaurants, Cape Malay curries in the Bo-Kaap neighbourhood, and Xhosa dishes in township restaurants.

Contemporary Craftwork

The 2014 World Design Capital is bursting with creativity: intricately beaded dolls, light fixtures made from recycled plastic, stylish buckskin and leather pillows – Cape Town's emporiums and artisan craft markets have it all.

p52

Western Cape

Food & Drink
Outdoor Activities
Adventure Sports

Wine Tasting

The Winelands around Stellenbosch, Franschhoek and Paarl are justifiably famous for their beautiful wine estates. Intrepid tasters should also explore areas such as Wellington, Stanford, Tulbagh and Robertson. Pairing wines with chocolate or cheese adds an extra dimension to tastings.

Hiking

Longer hikes include the five-day Oystercatcher Trail, De Hoop Nature Reserve's five-day Whale Trail and the Greyton–McGregor Boesmanskloof Trail. Hikes ranging in duration from hours to days lead into the bush around towns such as Swellendam and wildernesses including the Cederberg.

Water Sports

Among the many water sports and activities taking advantage of the Garden Route's beaches and lagoons are surfing, canoeing and diving. Gansbaai is the place to brave shark-cage diving.

p108

Eastern Cape

Hiking
Nature & Scenery
Wildlife

Multiday Hikes

In the Garden Route National Park's Tsitsikamma section are the Otter, Dolphin and Tsitsikamma Mountain Trails; overnight routes run the length of the Wild Coast; and the Amathole Trail climbs through waterfall-flecked forests.

Beaches

The Wild Coast is lined with empty beaches, which come with Xhosa culture at backpacker lodges such as Bulungula, Mdumbi and Buccaneers. The Jeffrey's Bay sands are dedicated to surfing, and forests overlook the dunes at Nature's Valley.

Diverse Sightings

Addo Elephant National Park boasts the 'Big Seven', including great white sharks and southern right whales. The nearby private wildlife reserves make the most of the Big Five with diverse programs of activities, while Mountain Zebra National Park offers Karoo panoramas, Cape mountain zebras and cheetah tracking.

p177

KwaZulu-Natal

Wildlife
Culture
Activities

Tropical Sightings

The steamy, tropical Elephant Coast in northern KwaZulu-Natal features three of South Africa's great wildlife parks – iSimangaliso Wetland Park, uMkhuze Game Reserve and Hluhluwe-iMfolozi Park – offering Big Five sightings with backdrops from savannah grasslands to Lake St Lucia.

Zulu Culture

Eshowe and Ulundi are capitals of Zulu culture, while Shakaland offers a Disneyfied look at the ethnic group. Three big events take place in Zululand in September and October, including a 'reed dance' akin to the famous Swazi Umhlanga festival. Durban's Campbell Collections hold documents and artworks relating to early Zulu culture.

Water Sports

On the South Coast, Umkomaas and Shelly Beach are diving centres, with the Aliwal Shoal and Protea Banks sites. Water-based activities in beachfront Durban include surfing, diving, fishing and ocean safaris.

p236

Free State

Landscape
Relaxed Travel
Hiking

Mountains & Foothills

The rugged Eastern Highlands offer views of the Drakensberg and Maluti Mountains. One of South Africa's most scenic drives crosses this region bordering mountainous Lesotho, taking in Clarens and the Golden Gate Highlands National Park.

Rustic Experiences

Mellow to the province's safe and rural pace: small towns such as Clarens promote their streets as some of the safest nationwide, and as you travel dusty roads between golden fields and open skies, you will pass old bakkies (pick-up trucks) and tumbledown Sotho houses.

Mountain Trails

The Rhebok Hiking Trail and others cross the Golden Gate Highlands National Park, with views of the Drakensberg and Maluti Mountains. The nearby Sentinel Hiking Trail, one of South Africa's most impressive day walks, climbs the Drakensberg.

p305

Johannesburg & Gauteng

History
Guided Tours
Culture

Mandela Trail

The Apartheid Museum powerfully evokes the dark era ended by Nelson Mandela et al. Also in Jo'burg, Constitution Hill covers both apartheid and today's democracy. Soweto is a hotbed of social history, and Pretoria's Freedom Park sits opposite the Voortrekker Monument.

Walking Tours

Jo'burg's tours scratch the concrete surface of what can be a grimy Afro-Gotham. Inner-city walking tours showcase the urban regeneration transforming former no-go zones. In Soweto, meet the township locals on foot, bike or tuk-tuk.

Art & Design

Pick up local artwork and cool threads at galleries and shops in Jo'burg's Maboneng precinct, Braamfontein and Newtown. Head to Maboneng's Market on Sunday for design and decor, and to 44 Stanley for local fashion labels. Out of town is the Cradle of Humankind's Nirox Foundation sculpture park.

p323

Mpumalanga

Landscape
Activities
Country Breaks

Natural Wonders

This province between Jo'burg and Mozambique covers both lowveld and the Drakensberg Escarpment. At the dramatic meeting of the two regions is the Blyde River Canyon, the world's third-largest canyon, with viewpoints, rock formations and waterfalls.

Adventure Sports

Graskop has one of the world's highest cable gorge swings. Sabie offers kloofing (canyoning), candlelight caving, tubing, swimming holes and waterfall abseiling. There's more of the latter in climbing centre Waterval Boven (Emgwenya), while Barberton offers 4WD adventures and a geology trail. Head to Hazyview for river rafting, zip lining and more.

Historic Towns

Pilgrim's Rest is a well-preserved gold-rush town. Across the Long Tom Pass (which commemorates Anglo-Boer War history), Lydenburg (Mashishing) has a fascinating museum. Barberton, another gold-rush town, was home to South Africa's first stock exchange.

p374

Kruger National Park

Wildlife
Landscape
Activities

Big Five

With around 148 mammal species, including more than 1600 lions, 13,000 elephants, 37,000 buffaloes, 1000 leopards and endangered rhinos, Kruger is one of Africa's most epic places to see the Big Five acting out the daily drama of life and death.

Wilderness

Kruger is about the size of Belgium or Wales, with landscapes ranging from tropical riverine forest to mopaneveld. If you visit at a quiet time (such as mid-January to March) or go on a bush walk, nature will ring in your ears.

Walks

To access parts of the bush not glimpsed from a vehicle, strike out with gun-toting rangers on a three-hour bush walk, or disappear into the wild on a four-day wilderness trail.

p395

Limpopo

Arts & Crafts
Diverse Environments
African Culture

Studio Visits

The Venda region's artists, from woodcarvers to potters, are famous far and wide; tour their studios and pick up some distinctive work. Further south are Kaross, producing Shangaan embroidery, and the Mapusha Weavers Cooperative, where women make carpets and tapestries in Acornhoek township.

Mountain Escapes

Escape the heat by climbing to Haenertsburg and the Magoebaskloof Pass, where the pine plantations and waterfalls make a refreshing change from the steamy surrounds. In the Modjadji Nature Reserve, summer mists wrap around cycads and the Bolobedu Mountains.

Significant Sites

Mapungubwe National Park, which is World Heritage listed for its cultural significance, contains an important Iron Age site. There's vivid African culture in the Modjadji area, mystic home of rain-summoning queens, and the Venda region.

p412

North West Province

Wildlife
Luxury
Activities

Accessible Animals

Collectively covering more than 1000 sq km of Big Five–inhabited bushveld, Pilanesberg National Park has tarred roads near the Sun City casino complex, and Madikwe Game Reserve's exclusive lodges offer guided drives.

Accommodation

Sun City's hotels, particularly the Palace of the Lost City, are South Africa's last, Vegas-style word in glitz. Madikwe's five-star lodges offer wildlife watching in the lap of luxury.

Family Fun

The kitschy Sun City's endless swimming pools, wave pools, slides and flumes keep children happy on hot bushveld days. The outlandish theme of a lost African civilisation, with simulated volcanic eruptions and life-size fake elephants, entertains everyone, and the more active can explore neighbouring Pilanesberg. The Magaliesberg has an aerial cableway and zip-line canopy tours.

p435

Northern Cape

Wilderness
Wildlife
Activities

Semideserts

This most epic province covers all of South Africa's cracked, arid wildernesses. Like a tumbleweed along a back road, the Karoo sweeps past attractive towns such as Sutherland and Calvinia. Further north, nature is an untrammelled, awe-inspiring force in the sandy Kalahari and rocky Namakwa, respectively home to the vast transfrontier parks of Kgalagadi and |Ai-|Ais/ Richtersveld.

Big Cats

Kgalagadi Transfrontier Park is one of the world's best places to spot big cats, including cheetahs, lions and leopards. You might spy a black-maned lion snoozing under a thorn tree or purring down the road.

Adventure Sports

Raft and canoe down the Orange River, 4WD around Riemvasmaak and the transfrontier parks, go on wildlife drives and walks, and sandboard and mountain bike in Witsand Nature Reserve.

p446

Lesotho

Adventure
Craftwork
Wilderness

Trading Posts

Malealea, Semonkong, Ramabanta and Roma lodges, former trading posts, are mountainside way stations that wow adventurers. Superb hiking and Basotho culture are offered alongside trekking on sturdy Basotho ponies, a classic Lesotho activity that literally takes travellers to another level. At Semonkong, abseilers descend Maletsunyane Falls.

Tapestries

The Basotho people have maintained cultural autonomy for centuries, resulting in distinctive craftwork. You can pick up tapestries in the lowland craft villages Teyateyaneng ('TY'), Leribe, Thaba-Bosiu and Morija.

National Parks

Lesotho's national parks are little-visited gems: Ts'ehlanyane National Park, lush and rugged, is becoming the nation's poster child, with excellent accommodation at Maliba Mountain Lodge. Bokong and Sehlathebethebe are seldom visited but packed with natural beauty.

p471

Swaziland

Craft Shopping
Parks & Reserves
Swazi Culture

Markets

Manzini Market's handicrafts and textiles are sold by a colourful mix of marketers, ranging from rural vendors to Mozambican traders. The neighbouring Ezulwini and Malkerns Valleys have a well-earned reputation for their craft markets, filled with surprises such as animal-shaped candles and zesty contemporary batiks.

Activities

In addition to African bush and wildlife, Swaziland's parks and reserves offer various activities. Options include hiking and canopy tours in Malolotja Nature Reserve; and walks, mountain biking and horse riding in Mlilwane Wildlife Sanctuary.

Festivals

Swaziland's traditional ceremonies are famous African festivals, among them the Umhlanga (reed) dance, essentially a debutante ball for Swazi maidens, and the Buganu (marula) Festival.

p495

On the Road

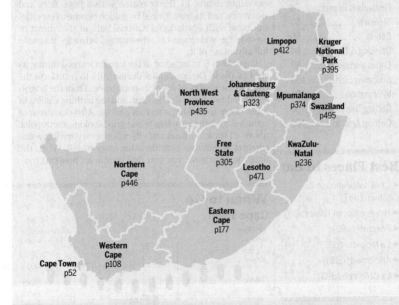

Cape Town

Best Places to Eat

➡ Chef's Warehouse & Canteen (p87)

➡ Reverie Social Table (p89)

➡ Foxcroft (p92)

➡ La Mouette (p92)

➡ 4Roomed (p93)

➡ La Colombe (p92)

Best Places to Stay

➡ Tintswalo Atlantic (p85)

➡ Mannabay (p84)

➡ Backpack (p83)

➡ La Grenadine (p84)

Why Go?

Known as the 'Mother City' for its historical role in the development of modern South Africa, Cape Town is dominated by magnificent Table Mountain, its summit draped with cascading clouds, its flanks coated with unique flora and vineyards, and its base fringed by golden beaches. Few cities can boast such a wonderful national park at their heart or provide the wide range of adventurous activities that take full advantage of it.

Cape Town is using some of the lessons learned during its stint as World Design Capital during 2014 to transform the city and the quality of life of its population. From the brightly painted facades of the Bo-Kaap and the bathing chalets of Muizenberg to striking street art and the Afro-chic decor of countless guesthouses, this is one good-looking metropolis. Above all it's a multicultural city where everyone has a fascinating, sometimes heartbreaking story to tell. When the time comes to leave, you may find your heart breaking too.

When to Go
Cape Town

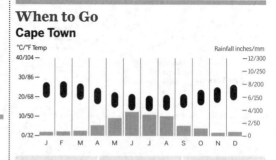

°C/°F Temp   Rainfall inches/mm

Dec–Feb Summer brings warm, dry weather and lively festivals. Peak season.

Mar–Apr Lovely autumn colours and sunshine, plus more festivals. Avoid the busy Easter period.

Oct–Nov Spring sees beautiful flowers bloom and the start of Kirstenbosch sunset concerts.

History

Long before the Dutch East India Company (Vereenigde Oost-Indische Compagnie; VOC) established a base here in 1652, the Cape Town area was settled by the San and Khoekhoen nomadic tribes, collectively known as the Khoe-San. The indigenous peoples shunned the Dutch, so the VOC was forced to import slaves from Madagascar, India, Ceylon, Malaya and Indonesia to deal with the colony's chronic labour shortage. Women were in even shorter supply, so the Europeans exploited the female slaves and the local Khoe-San for both labour and sex. In time the slaves also intermixed with the Khoe-San. The offspring of these unions formed the basis of sections of today's coloured population and also helps explain the unique character of the city's Cape Muslim population.

Under the 150-odd years of Dutch rule, Kaapstad, as the Cape settlement became known, thrived and gained a wider reputation as the 'Tavern of the Seas', a riotous port used by every sailor travelling between Europe and the East. Following the British defeat of the Dutch in 1806 at Bloubergstrand, 25km north of Cape Town, the colony was ceded to the Crown on 13 August 1814. Cape Town continued to prosper after the slave trade was abolished in 1808, and all slaves were emancipated in 1833.

The discovery and exploitation of diamonds and gold in the centre of South Africa from the 1870s led to rapid changes. Cape Town was soon no longer the single dominant metropolis in the country, but as a major port it too was a beneficiary of the mineral wealth that laid the foundations for an industrial society. The same wealth led to imperialist dreams of grandeur on the part of Cecil John Rhodes (premier of the Cape Colony in 1890), who had made his millions at the head of De Beers Consolidated Mines.

An outbreak of bubonic plague in 1901 was blamed on the black African workers (although it actually came on boats from Argentina) and gave the government an excuse to introduce racial segregation: blacks were moved to two locations, one near the docks and the other at Ndabeni on the eastern flank of Table Mountain. This was the start of what would later develop into the townships of the Cape Flats.

The townships grew under apartheid, which affected Cape Town as heavily as the rest of the country, and saw Nelson Mandela spend 18 years on Robben Island. In 1990 Mandela became a free man 75km from the city, hailing the start of a democratic South Africa. For most of the post-apartheid period, Cape Town has forged an independent political path, run by the DA (Democratic Alliance) rather than the ANC (African National Congress). Its reputation as the city of choice for South Africans to live was dented by the recent drought, which necessitated harsh water restrictions in 2017 and 2018.

◎ Sights

From many points on the Peninsula you'll be able to see and climb up to Table Mountain (p70), Cape Town's top sight. However, most visitors ride the cableway that starts in Oranjezicht on the mountain's north side.

In terms of visitor numbers, it's the V&A Waterfront (p63), a dynamic mix of shopping, eating and entertainment based around a working harbour, that is Cape Town's most popular attraction. The new Zeitz MOCAA Museum (p64) makes spending time here a greater pleasure for art lovers, and the Waterfront is also where you'll need to go to board ferries to the World Heritage site of Robben Island (p64).

In and around the City Bowl the key sights are the colourful houses of the Bo-Kaap, the lush Company's Garden (p57), the historic fortifications of the Castle of Good Hope (p56) and the District Six Museum (p56), an important place to gain an understanding of the impact of apartheid on the city.

Moving south around the east side of Table Mountain you'll find the beautifully manicured Kirstenbosch National Botanical Garden (p67) and the heritage vineyards of Constantia. Continuing to the Peninsula's deep south, don't miss the charming fishing village and arty enclave of Kalk Bay (p71), the naval base at Simon's Town and the majestic wild spaces of the Cape of Good Hope (p69).

Heading back up the western side of the peninsula you'll pass the sweeping expanse of **Noordhoek beach** (Beach Rd, Noordhoek) at the foot of the stunning Chapman's Peak Drive. There are several more lovely beaches to discover here too, including those at **Sandy Bay** (Llandudno; 🚇 Llandudno), **Camps Bay** (Map p68; Victoria Rd; 🚇 Camps Bay) and Clifton (p65).

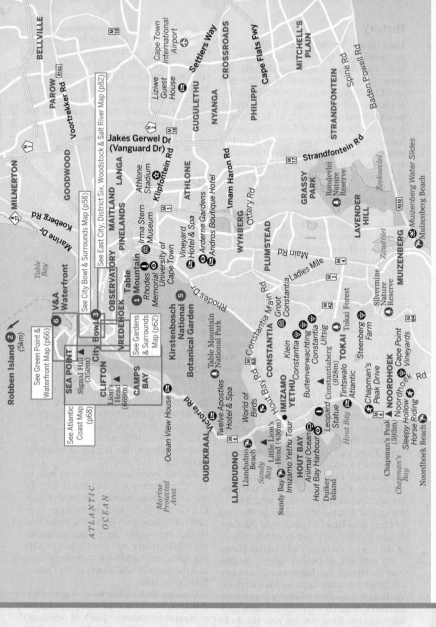

Cape Town Highlights

1 Table Mountain (p70) Taking the cable car to the top of the magnificent mountain and looking down on the city.

2 Robben Island (p64) Sailing out to the infamous prison and pondering the country's past and present.

3 City Bowl (p57) Exploring the area's museums, the Company's Garden and the wonderful art deco and Victorian architecture.

4 Cape of Good Hope (p69) Heading south for wide open spaces, wildlife, empty beaches and the dramatic scenery of the peninsula's rugged tip.

5 Kirstenbosch National Botanical Garden (p67) Wandering through

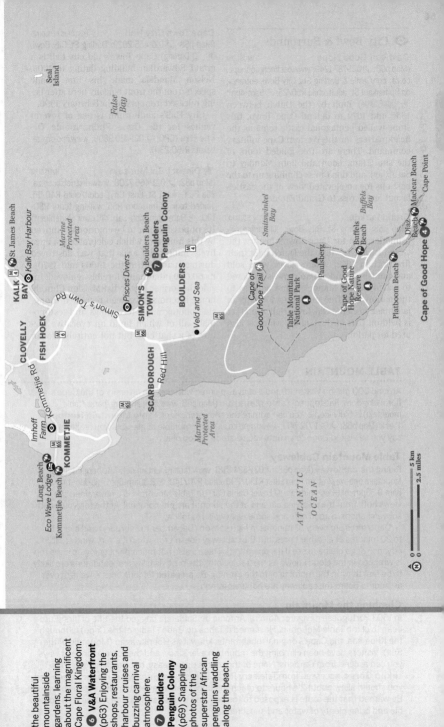

the beautiful mountainside gardens, learning about the magnificent Cape Floral Kingdom.

6 V&A Waterfront (p63) Enjoying the shops, restaurants, harbour cruises and buzzing carnival atmosphere.

7 Boulders Penguin Colony (p69) Snapping photos of the superstar African penguins waddling along the beach.

◉ City Bowl & Surrounds

Castle of Good Hope
MUSEUM

(Map p58; ☑ 021-787 1249; www.castleofgoodhope. co.za; cnr Castle & Darling Sts, City Bowl, entrance on Buitenkant St; adult/child R50/25; ◷ 9am-4pm; 🅿; ▣ Castle) Built by the Dutch between 1666 and 1679 to defend Cape Town, this stone-walled pentagonal castle remains the headquarters for the Western Cape military command. There are free guided tours of the site (11am, noon and 2pm Monday to Saturday), and don't miss climbing up to the bastions for an elevated view of the castle's layout and across to Grand Parade.

Grand Parade
SQUARE

(Map p58; Darling St, City Bowl; ▣ Darling) A prime location for Cape Town's history, the Grand Parade is where the Dutch built their first fort in 1652; where slaves were sold and punished; and where crowds gathered to watch Nelson Mandela's first address to the nation as a free man after 27 years in jail, made from the Old Town Hall. A market is held on part of the square, which is also used for parking.

Cape Town City Hall
HISTORIC BUILDING

(Map p58; ☑ 021-455 2029; Darling St, City Bowl; 🅿; ▣ Darling) Cape Town's old city hall is a grand Edwardian building dating to 1905. Nelson Mandela made his first public speech from the front balcony here after being released from prison in February 1990.

City Hall's auditorium is one of several venues for the **Cape Philharmonic Orchestra** (CPO; ☑ 021-410 9809; www.cpo.org.za; tickets R160-230).

★ District Six Museum
MUSEUM

(Map p82; ☑ 021-466 7200; www.districtsix.co.za; 25a Buitenkant St, East City; adult/child R40/15, guided tour of museum R55, walking tours R80-100; ◷ 9am-4pm Mon-Sat; ▣ Lower Buitenkant) It's impossible not to be emotionally moved by this museum, which celebrates the once lively multiracial area that was destroyed during apartheid in the 1960s and 1970s, its 60,000 inhabitants forcibly removed. Inside the former Methodist Mission Church, home interiors have been recreated, alongside photographs, recordings and testimonials, all of which build an evocative picture of a shattered but not entirely broken

---

TABLE MOUNTAIN

Around 600 million years old, and a canvas painted with the rich diversity of the Cape's floral kingdom, flat-topped **Table Mountain** (Map p68; www.sanparks.org/parks/table_mountain) is truly iconic. You can admire the showstopper of **Table Mountain National Park** (Map p68; ☑ 021-712 7471; www.tmnp.co.za) from multiple angles, but you really can't say you've visited Cape Town until you've stood on top of it.

Table Mountain Cableway

Riding the **cableway** (Map p68; ☑ 021-424 8181; www.tablemountain.net; Tafelberg Rd, Table Mountain; one-way/return from adult R150/290, child R70/140; ◷ 8.30am-6pm mid-Jan–mid-Dec, 8am-9.30pm mid-Dec–mid-Jan; ▣ Lower Cable Car) up Table Mountain is a no-brainer: the views both from the revolving car and at the summit are phenomenal. At the top you'll find souvenir shops, a good cafe and some easy walks to follow.

Departures are every 10 minutes in high season (December to February) and every 15 to 20 minutes at all other times, but the cableway doesn't run when it's very windy (call in advance or go online to see if it's operating). There's also not much point going up if the top is wrapped in the cloud known as the 'tablecloth'; the best visibility and conditions are likely to be first thing in the morning or in the evening. Be prepared for long lines – waits of over an hour to board the cableway are not uncommon.

Climbing the Mountain

In 1503 Portuguese navigator Admiral Antonio de Saldanha bagged the title of 'first European to climb Table Mountain'. He named it Taboa do Cabo (Table of the Cape), although the Khoe-san, the Cape's original inhabitants, knew it as Hoerikwaggo (Mountain of the Sea). Visitors have been climbing the mountain ever since, and there are a range of ways you can ascend from Gardens. None of the routes up are easy, but the 3km-long **Platteklip Gorge**, accessed from Tafelberg Rd, is at least straightforward. It's very steep and you should allow about 2½ hours to reach the upper cableway station at a steady pace. Be warned that the route is exposed to the sun, so climb as early in the morning as possible and bring plenty of water and sunscreen.

community. Many township tours stop here first to explain the history of the pass laws.

★**Company's Garden** GARDENS
(Map p58; City Bowl; ⊙7am-7pm; 🚌Dorp/Leeuwen) These shady green gardens, which started as the vegetable patch for the Dutch East India Company, are a lovely place to relax. They are planted with a fine collection of botanical specimens from South Africa and the rest of the world, including frangipanis, African flame trees, aloes and roses. At the garden's southern end there's a re-creation of the **VOC Vegetable Garden** (Map p58; Queen Victoria St, City Bowl; ⊙7am-7pm; 🚌Upper Loop/Upper Long).

Iziko Slave Lodge MUSEUM
(Map p58; ☑021-467 7229; www.iziko.org.za; 49 Adderley St, City Bowl; adult/child R30/15; ⊙10am-5pm Mon-Sat; 🚌Groote Kerk) Dating back to 1660, the Slave Lodge is one of the oldest buildings in South Africa. Once home to as many as 1000 slaves, the lodge has a fascinating history; it has also been used as a brothel, a jail, a mental asylum, a post office, a library and the Cape Supreme Court in its

time. Today, it's a museum mainly devoted to the history and experience of slaves and their descendants in the Cape.

Houses of Parliament NOTABLE BUILDING
(Map p58; ☑021-403 2266; www.parliament.gov.za; Parliament St, City Bowl; ⊙tours 9am-4pm Mon-Fri; 🚌Roeland) FREE A tour around parliament is fascinating, especially if you're interested in the country's modern history. Opened in 1885, the hallowed halls have seen some pretty momentous events: this is where British Prime Minister Harold Macmillan made his 'Wind of Change' speech in 1960, and where President Hendrik Verwoerd, known as the architect of apartheid, was stabbed to death in 1966. Call ahead and present your passport to gain entry.

Long Street ARCHITECTURE
(Map p58; City Bowl; 🚌Dorp/Leeuwen) A stroll along Long St is an essential element of a Cape Town visit. This busy commercial and nightlife thoroughfare, partly lined with Victorian-era buildings featuring lovely wrought-iron balconies, once formed the border of the Muslim Bo-Kaap. By the 1960s, Long St had fallen into disrepute and

At the Top

Concrete paths lead from the upper cableway station to the restaurant, shop and various terraces. These are easy enough to stroll around without a guide, and from them you may even be able to spot a dassie, a large native rodent which – believe it or not – is related to the elephant. Free volunteer-guided walks across Table Mountain's plateau run at 10am and noon daily from beside the upper cableway station.

To reach the mountain's 1088m summit you'll need to go a bit further along the track to **Maclear's Beacon**, a distance of around 5km, which should take one hour for the round trip. Don't attempt this route if there's low cloud or mist on the mountain, as it's very easy to lose your way.

Top Tips

➡ From mid-December to mid-January, online tickets are available for access to the cable car from 7.30am, before the ticket office opens at 8am. They cost R400 and are valid for two days from purchase.

➡ MyCiTi (p107) buses stop at the Lower Cable Car where you take the Table Mountain Aerial Cableway to the mountain top.

➡ Near the upper cableway station, **Table Mountain Cafe** (Map p68; ☑021-424 0015; www.tablemountain.net; Table Mountain; mains R35-95; ⊙8.30am-30min before last cableway down; 🚌Upper Cable Station) offers tasty deli items and meals, compostable plates and containers, and good coffee. It also sells wine and beer so you can toast the view.

➡ The 112m drop off the top of Table Mountain with **Abseil Africa** (Map p58; ☑021-424 4760; https://abseilafrica.co.za; 297 Long St; abseiling R995; 🚌Upper Long/Upper Loop) is a guaranteed adrenaline rush – don't even think of tackling it unless you've got a head for heights. Take your time, because the views are breathtaking. Tack on a guided hike up Platteklip Gorge (R1745) or just do the hike without the abseil (R800).

City Bowl & Surrounds

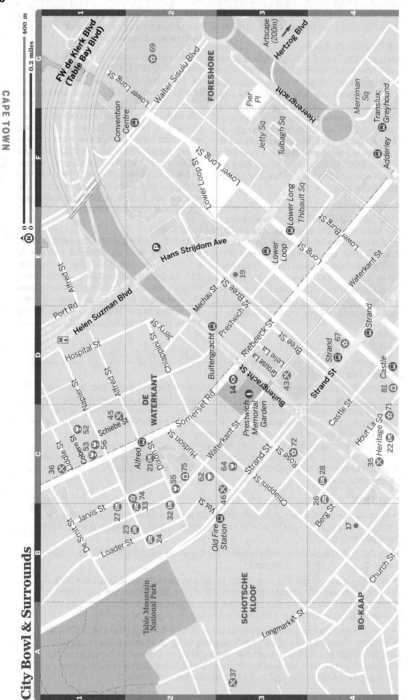

FW de Klerk Blvd
(Table Bay Blvd)

Convention Centre

FORESHORE

Artscape (200m)

Hertzog Blvd

Heerengracht

Pier Pl

Jetty Sq

Tulbagh Sq

Merriman Sq

Translux: Greyhound

Adderley

Walter Sisulu Blvd

Lower Long St

Lower Loop St

Lower Long St

Thibault Sq

Lower Burg St

Strand

Long St

Lower Loop

Waterkant St

Hans Strijdom Ave

Port Rd

Helen Suzman Blvd

Hospital St

Alfred St

Napier St

Liddle St

Cobern St

Schiebe St

De Smit St

Jarvis St

Loader St

Chiappini St

Jerry St

Mechau St

Bree St

Buitengracht

Prestwich St

Riebeeck St

Bree St

Grouse La

Lelie La

Strand

Waterkant St

Castle St

Strand St

Hout La

Heritage Sq

Castle

Buitengracht St

Prestwich Memorial Garden

Somerset Rd

Waterkant St

Hudson St

Dixon St

Rose St

Strand St

Chiappini St

Berg St

Vos St

Old Fire Station

SCHOTSCHE KLOOF

BO-KAAP

Church St

Longmarket St

Table Mountain National Park

DE WATERKANT

Alfred St

0   0.2 miles
0   400 m

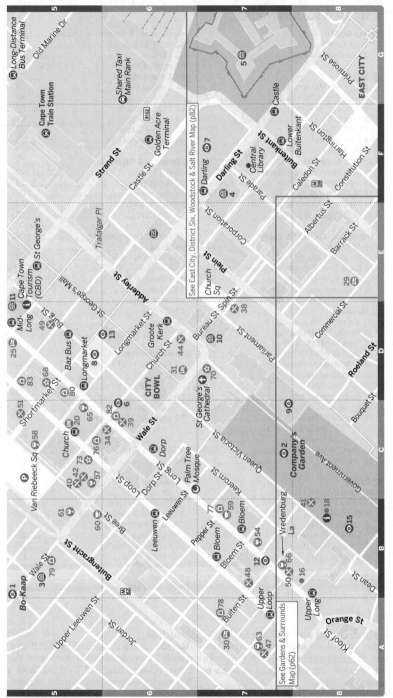

EAST CITY

Long-Distance Bus Terminal
Old Marine Dr
Shared Taxi Main Rank
Cape Town Train Station
Golden Acre Terminal
R102
Strand St
Castle St
Castle
Darling St
Darling
Central Library
Parade
Caledon St
Lower Buitenkant
Buitenkant St
Harrington St
Constitution St
Primrose St

See East City, District Six, Woodstock & Salt River Map (p82)

7

5

Albertus St
Barrack St
29

Trafalgar Pl
Plein St
Corporation St

St George's
Cape Town Tourism (CBD)
11
Mid-Long
25
49
Burg St
St George's Mall
Adderley St
Baz Bus
Longmarket
83
68
Shortmarket St
80
Longmarket St
8
13
Church St
Groote Kerk
Bureau St
Spin St
38
Church Sq
10
Commercial St

CITY BOWL

5i
58
Church
Van Riebeeck Sq
20
65
82
6
39
Wale St
34
76
31
44
St George's Cathedral
70
Roeland St
Bouquet St

40
42
73
57
Dorp St
Dorp
Palm Tree Mosque
Keerom St
Queen Victoria St
9
Company's Garden
2
Government Ave

61
60
Bree St
Leeuwen St
Leeuwen
Vredenburg La
41
18
15

Pepper St
Bloem St
77
59
54
Bloem St
12
48
Buitengracht St

1
Bo-Kaap
3
79
Wale St
Upper Leeuwen St
Jordan St
78
30
63
47
Buiten St
Upper Loop
50
66
16
Upper Long
Dean St
Kloor St
Orange St
Upper Long

See Gardens & Surrounds Map (p62)

City Bowl & Surrounds

it remained that way until the late 1990s, when savvy developers realised its potential. The most attractive section runs from the junction with Buitensingel St north to around Strand St.

Church St STREET

(Map p58; Church St, City Bowl; 🚌 Church/Longmarket) The pedestrianised portion of this street, between Burg and Long Sts, hosts a flea market (8am to 3pm Monday to Saturday) and has several interesting art galleries. At the Burg St end *The Purple Shall Govern* memorial is a piece of graphic art by Conrad Botes commemorating a 1989 anti-apartheid march.

Greenmarket Square   SQUARE
(Map p58; City Bowl; Church/Longmarket) This cobbled square is Cape Town's second-oldest public space after the Grand Parade. It hosts a lively and colourful crafts and souvenir market daily. Apart from the Old Town House, the square is also surrounded by some choice examples of art deco architecture, including Market House, an elaborately decorated building with balconies and stone-carved eagles and flowers on its facade.

Koopmans-de Wet House   MUSEUM
(Map p58; 021-481 3935; www.iziko.org.za; 35 Strand St, City Bowl; adult/child R20/10; 10am-5pm Mon-Fri; Strand) Step back two centuries from 21st-century Cape Town when you enter this classic example of a Cape Dutch town house, furnished with 18th- and early-19th-century antiques. It's an atmospheric place, with ancient vines growing in the courtyard and floorboards that squeak just as they probably did during the time of Marie Koopmans-de Wet, the socialite owner after whom the house is named.

★ Bo-Kaap   AREA
(Map p58; Dorp/Leeuwen) Meaning 'Upper Cape', the Bo-Kaap, with its vividly painted low-roofed houses, many of them historic monuments, strung along narrow cobbled streets, is one of the most photographed sections of the city. Initially a garrison for soldiers in the mid-18th century, this area of town was where freed slaves started to settle after emancipation in the 1830s. The most picturesque streets are Chiappini, Rose and Wale.

Bo-Kaap Museum   MUSEUM
(Map p58; 021-481 3938; www.iziko.org.za/museums/bo-kaap-museum; 71 Wale St, Bo-Kaap; adult/child R20/10; 10am-5pm Mon-Sat; Leeuwen) This small museum provides some insight into the lifestyle of a prosperous 19th-century Cape Muslim family, and a somewhat idealised view of Islamic practice in Cape Town. The most interesting exhibit is the selection of black-and-white photos of local life displayed in the upstairs room, across the courtyard. The house itself, which was built between 1763 and 1768, is the oldest in the area.

Noon Gun   VIEWPOINT
(Military Rd, Bo-Kaap) FREE At noon, Monday to Saturday, a cannon is fired from the lower slopes of 350m-high Signal Hill, which separates Sea Point from the City Bowl; you can hear it all over town. Traditionally, this allowed the burghers in the town below to check their watches. It's a stiff walk up here through the Bo-Kaap – take Longmarket St and keep going until it ends, just beneath the gun emplacement (which is off limits) – the view is phenomenal.

Prestwich Memorial   MEMORIAL
(Map p58; cnr Somerset Rd & Buitengracht St, De Waterkant; 8am-6pm Mon-Fri, to 2pm Sat & Sun; Strand) FREE Construction in 2003 along nearby Prestwich St unearthed many skeletons. These were the unmarked graves of slaves and others executed by the Dutch in the 17th and 18th centuries on what was then known as Gallows Hill. The bones were exhumed and this memorial building, with an attractive facade of Robben Island slate, was created. It includes an ossuary and excellent interpretive displays, including a replica of the remarkable 360-degree panorama of Table Bay painted by Robert Gordon in 1778.

⊙ Gardens & Surrounds

South African Jewish Museum   MUSEUM
(Map p62; 021-465 1546; www.sajewishmuseum.co.za; 88 Hatfield St, Gardens; adult/child R60/free; 10am-5pm Sun-Thu, to 2pm Fri; P; Annandale) You need a photo ID to enter the secure compound that's home to this imaginatively designed museum, which partly occupies the beautifully restored Old Synagogue (1863). The permanent exhibition *Hidden Treasures of Japanese Art* showcases a collection of exquisite *netsuke* (carved pieces of ivory and wood). There are also temporary exhibitions that are usually worth seeing.

South African National Gallery   GALLERY
(Map p62; 021-481 3970; www.iziko.org.za/museums/south-african-national-gallery; Government Ave, Gardens; adult/child R30/15; 10am-5pm; Annandale) The impressive permanent collection of the nation's premier art space harks back to Dutch times and includes some extraordinary pieces. But it's often contemporary works, such as the *Butcher Boys* sculpture by Jane Alexander – looking rather like a trio of Tolkienesque orcs who have stumbled into the gallery – that stand out the most.

Gardens & Surrounds

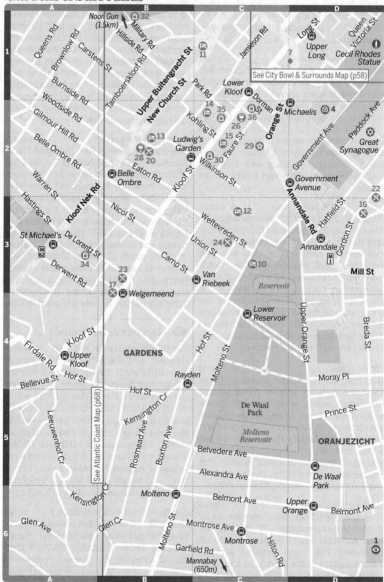

South African Museum MUSEUM
(Map p62; ☏021-481 3800; www.iziko.org.za/
museums/south-african-museum; 25 Queen Victoria St, Gardens; adult/child R30/15; ☺10am-5pm;
🚌Michaelis) South Africa's oldest museum
was undergoing renovations at the time
of research, so some galleries were closed.
The museum contains a wide and often intriguing series of exhibitions, many on the
country's natural history. Look out for an
amazing example of San rock art – there's
an extraordinary delicacy to the paintings,

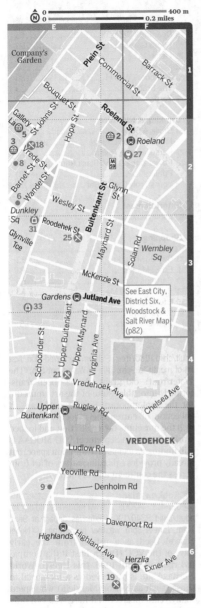

Rust en Vreugd
GALLERY, GARDEN

(Map p62; ☎021-467 7205; www.iziko.org.za; 78 Buitenkant St, Gardens; adult/child R20/10; ⏲10am-5pm Mon-Fri; ☐Roeland) This delightful mansion, dating from 1777–78 and fronted by a period-style garden (recreated in 1986 from the original layout), was once the home of the state prosecutor. It now houses part of the Iziko William Fehr collection of paintings and furniture (the major part is in the Castle of Good Hope); you may see detailed lithographs of Zulus by George Angus and a delicately painted watercolour panorama of Table Mountain (from 1850) by Lady Eyre.

Oranjezicht City Farm
FARM

(OZCF; Map p62; ☎083 508 1066; www.ozcf.co.za; Upper Orange St, Oranjezicht; ⏲8am-4pm Mon-Fri, to 1pm Sat; ☐Upper Orange) **FREE** Local residents and volunteers have created this fantastic nonprofit venture on land where, in 1709, 'Oranje Zigt', the original farm in the Upper Table Valley, was founded. Grounds once occupied by a disused bowling green have been crafted into a beautiful neighbourhood market garden. You are free to wander around, though guided tours can also be arranged: see the website for details.

Signal Hill
VIEWPOINT

(Map p68; ☐Kloof Nek) The early settlement's lookout point is so named because it was from here that flags were hoisted when a ship was spotted, giving the people below time to prepare goods for sale and dust off their tankards. Walk, cycle or drive to the summit, which is part of Table Mountain National Park, by taking the first turn-off to the right off Kloof Nek Rd onto Military Rd.

⊙ Green Point & Waterfront

★V&A Waterfront
AREA

(Map p66; ☎021-408 7500; www.waterfront.co.za; **P**; ☐Nobel Square) This historic working harbour has a spectacular setting and many tourist-oriented attractions, including masses of shops, restaurants, bars, cinemas and cruises. The Alfred and Victoria Basins date from 1860 and are named after Queen Victoria and her son Alfred. Too small for modern container vessels and tankers, the Victoria Basin is still used by tugs, fishing boats and various other vessels. In the Alfred Basin you'll see ships under repair.

Two Oceans Aquarium
AQUARIUM

(Map p66; ☎021-418 3823; www.aquarium.co.za; Dock Rd, V&A Waterfront; adult/student/child R165/120/80; ⏲9.30am-6pm; ❸; ☐Aquarium)

particularly the ones of graceful elands. Another highlight is a 2m-wide nest – a veritable avian apartment block – of the sociable weaver bird, in the Wonders of Nature Gallery.

Gates & Surrounds

Gardens & Surrounds

This excellent aquarium features denizens of the deep from the cold and the warm oceans that border the Cape Peninsula. It's a chance to see penguins, turtles, an astounding kelp forest open to the sky, and pools in which kids can touch sea creatures. Qualified divers can get into the water for a closer look (R870 including dive gear).

Chavonnes Battery Museum MUSEUM
(Map p66; ☑021-416 6230; www.chavonnes battery.co.za; Clock Tower Precinct, V&A Waterfront; R70; ◎9am-4pm; ☐Nobel Square) This museum houses the remains of an early-18th-century cannon battery, one of several fortifications the Dutch built around Table Bay. It was partly demolished and covered over during the construction of the docks in 1860, but an excavation of the site in 1999 revealed the remains. You can walk around the entire site and get a good feel for what it would have originally been like. **Historical walking tours** (Map p66; ☑ bookings 021-408 4600; Chavonnes Battery Museum, V&A Waterfront; adult/child R150/20; ◎11am & 2pm; ☐Nobel Square) of the Waterfront start from here.

★**Zeitz MOCAA Museum** MUSEUM
(Map p66; ☑087 350 4777; www.zeitzmocaa. museum; Silo District, South Arm Rd, V&A Waterfront;

adult/child R180/free; ◎10am-6pm Wed-Mon, first Fri of month to 9pm; ℗; ☐Waterfront Silo) The Waterfront's old grain silo has been transformed into this state-of-the-art museum for the contemporary Southern African art collection of entrepreneur Jochen Zeitz, as well the museum's own collection and loaned works. Opened in September 2017 MOCAA is still finding its feet as an exhibition space, but already provides a dazzling survey of art from across the continent and beyond.

★**Robben Island** HISTORIC SITE
(☑021-413 4200; www.robben-island.org.za; adult/child R340/190; ◎ferries depart at 9am, 11am, 1pm & 3pm, weather permitting; ☐Nobel Square) Used as a prison from the early days of the VOC (Dutch East India Company) right up until 1996, this Unesco World Heritage site is preserved as a memorial to those (such as Nelson Mandela) who spent many years incarcerated here. You can only go here on a tour, which lasts around four hours including ferry rides, departing from the **Nelson Mandela Gateway** (Map p66; Clock Tower Precinct, V&A Waterfront; ◎9am-8.30pm; ☐Nobel Square) **FREE** beside the Clock Tower at the Waterfront. Booking online well in advance is highly recommended as tours can sell out.

⊙ Atlantic Coast

★ **Sea Point Promenade** WATERFRONT
(Map p68; Beach Rd, Sea Point; 🚇; 🚆 Promenade)
Strolling along Sea Point's wide, paved and
grassy promenade is a pleasure shared by
Capetonians from all walks of life. Once a
white-only area, it's now a great place to observe the city's multiculturalism. There are
kids' playgrounds, a well-maintained outdoor gym and several public artworks.

The coast here is rocky and swimming
is dangerous, although you can get in the
water at **Rocklands Beach** (Map p68; Beach
Rd, Sea Point; 🚆 Rocklands). If you're too thin-
skinned for the frigid sea, try the **Sea Point
Pavilion** (Map p68; 🗹 021-434 3341; adult/child
R23/12; ⊙ 7am-7pm Dec-Apr, 9am-5pm May-Nov;
🚆 Sea Point Pool) pool complex, towards the
promenade's southern end.

Clifton 4th Beach BEACH
(Map p68; Victoria Rd, Clifton; 🚆 Clifton 4th) The
only Blue Flag beach among the four sheltered stretches of sand strung along Victoria
Rd at Clifton is popular with families. On
calm summer evenings, especially the night
of Valentine's Day, couples and groups of
young people have candlelit picnics on 4th
from sunset onwards.

Hout Bay Harbour HARBOUR
(Harbour Rd, Hout Bay) Partly given over to
tourism with complexes such as **Mariner's
Wharf** (🗹 021-790 1100; www.marinerswharf.
co.za; mains R70-245; ⊙ 10am-8.30pm; 🚆 North-
shore), Hout Bay's harbour still functions
and the southern side is a fishing port and
processing centre. Cruises and snorkelling/
diving trips to Duiker Island (p72) depart
from here.

DON'T MISS

CONSTANTIA WINE ROUTE

South Africa's wine industry began here back in 1685, when Governor Simon van der
Stel chose the area for its grape-growing potential. After Van der Stel's death in 1712,
his 7.6-sq-km estate, which he had named Constantia, was split up. The area is now the
location for the Constantia Wine Route (www.constantiawineroute.com), comprising 15
upmarket wine estates and restaurants.

Groot Constantia (🗹 021-794 5128; www.grootconstantia.co.za; Groot Constantia Rd, Constantia; tastings R80, museum adult/child R30/free; ⊙ tastings 9am-6pm, museum 10am-5pm;
🅿) Simon van der Stel's manor house, a superb example of Cape Dutch architecture, is
maintained as a museum at Groot Constantia. Set in beautiful grounds, the estate can
become busy with tour groups, but is big enough for you to escape the crowds. The large
tasting room is first on your right as you enter the estate. Further on is the free orientation centre, which provides an overview of Groot Constantia's history, and the beautifully
restored homestead.

Klein Constantia (🗹 021-794 5188; www.kleinconstantia.com; Klein Constantia Rd, Constantia; tastings R50; ⊙ tastings 10am-5pm Mon-Fri, to 4pm Sat & Sun; 🅿) Part of Simon
van der Stel's original Constantia estate, Klein Constantia is famous for its Vin de
Constance, a sweet muscat wine. It was Napoleon's solace on St Helena; and in Jane
Austen's *Sense and Sensibility*, Mrs Jennings advocates 'its healing powers on a disap-
pointed heart'. There's a small bistro and excellent tasting room – be sure to sample the
champagne-style sparkler.

Buitenverwachting (🗹 021-794 5190; www.buitenverwachting.com; Klein Constantia Rd, Constantia; tastings R50; ⊙ tastings 10am-5pm Mon-Sat; 🅿) Buitenverwachting means 'beyond
expectation', which is certainly the feeling one gets on visiting this Cape Dutch estate. It's
a lovely estate to visit with an unusual late-18th-century manor house overlooking verdant
lawns, as well as the Quaffee coffee roastery. **Coffee Bloc** (🗹 021-794 4468; mains R75-135;
⊙ 8am-5pm Mon-Fri, 8.30am-3pm Sat) cafe, a restaurant and gift shop.

Steenberg Farm (🗹 021-713 2222; www.steenbergfarm.com; Steenberg Estate, Steenberg
Rd, Constantia; tastings R60-80; ⊙ tastings 10am-6pm; 🅿) Steenberg's contemporary
tasting bar and lounge, adjoining **Bistro Sixteen82** (🗹 021-713 2211; lunch mains R170;
⊙ 9am-8pm), is a gorgeous setting for sampling its great merlot, sauvignon blanc,
sémillon and Méthode Cap Classique (MCC) sparkler. The estate is the Cape's oldest
farm, dating back to 1682, when it was known as Swaaneweide (Feeding Place of the
Swans).

Green Point & Waterfront

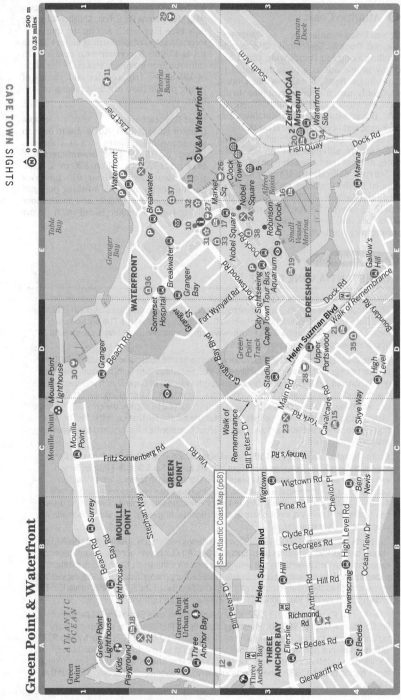

ATLANTIC OCEAN

Green Point

Green Point Lighthouse

Kids Playground

MOUILLE POINT

Mouille Point Lighthouse

Mouille Point

THREE ANCHOR BAY

Three Anchor Bay

GREEN POINT

Green Point Urban Park

See Atlantic Coast Map (p68)

Helen Suzman Blvd

Bill Peters Dr

Wigtown Rd
Pine Rd
Clyde Rd
St Georges Rd
Hill Rd
Antrim Rd
Richmond Rd
St Bedes Rd
Glengariff Rd

Wigtown
Cheviot Pl
Ben Nevis
High Level Rd
Ravenscraig
Ocean View Dr
St Bedes

Table Bay

WATERFRONT

Granger Bay

Breakwater

Somerset Hospital

Granger St

Fort Wynyard Rd

Portswood Rd

Granger Bay Blvd

Green Point Track

Stadium

GREEN POINT

Viel Rd

Fritz Sonnenberg Rd

Surrey
Bay Rd
Beach Rd
Stephan Way

Walk of Remembrance
Bill Peters Dr

Varney's Rd

Main Rd

York Rd

Upper Portswood

Cavalcade Rd

Skye Way

High Level

FORESHORE

Helen Suzman Blvd

Dock Rd

Boundary Rd

Walk of Remembrance

Gallow's Hill

Victoria Basin

Duncan Dock

South Arm

Zeitz MOCAA Museum

Waterfront Silo

Fish Quay

Clock Sq
Nobel Square
Nobel Tower
Robinson Dry Dock
Alfred Basin
Small Vessels Marina
Marina

Aquarium

Market Sq

V&A Waterfront

Green Point & Waterfront

World of Birds BIRD SANCTUARY
(☏021-790 2730; www.worldofbirds.org.za; Valley Rd, Hout Bay; adult/child R95/45; ⊙9am-5pm; Ⓟ⛟; ⓺Valley) Barbets, weavers and flamingos are among the 3000 birds and small mammals – covering some 400 different species – at Africa's largest bird park. A real effort has been expended to make the extensive aviaries as natural-looking as possible, with the use of lots of tropical landscaping. In the monkey jungle (⊙11.30am-1pm & 2-3.30pm) you can interact with cheeky squirrel monkeys.

⊙ Southern Suburbs

★ **Kirstenbosch**
National Botanical Garden GARDENS
(☏021-799 8783; www.sanbi.org/gardens/kirstenbosch; Rhodes Dr, Newlands; adult/child R65/15; ⊙8am-7pm Sep-Mar, to 6pm Apr-Aug; Ⓟ⛟; ⓺Kirstenbosch) 🌿 Location and unique flora combine to make these 5.28-sq-km botanical gardens among the most beautiful in the world. Gate 1, the main entrance at the Newlands end of the gardens, is where you'll find the information centre, an excellent souvenir shop and the conservatory (⊙9am-5pm) 🌿.

Added for the garden's centenary in 2013, the popular Tree Canopy Walkway (informally known as the 'Boomslang', meaning tree snake) is a curvaceous steel and timber bridge that rises through the trees and provides amazing views.

The gardens run free guided walks, or you can hire the MyGuide electronic gizmo (R40) to receive recorded information about the various plants you'll pass on the signposted circular walks.

More than 7000 of Southern Africa's 22,000 plant species are grown here, including the Cape Floral Kingdom's famous fynbos (literally, 'fine bush'; primarily proteas, heaths and ericas). You'll find a fragrance garden that has been elevated so you can more easily sample the scents of the plants; a Braille trail; a kopje (hill) planted with pelargoniums; a sculpture garden; a section devoted to 'useful' medicinal plants; two hiking trails up Table Mountain (Skeleton Gorge and Nursery Ravine); and the significant remains of Van Riebeeck's Hedge, the wild almond hedge planted by Jan van Riebeeck in 1660 to form the boundary of the Dutch outpost.

The outdoor Summer Sunset Concerts (adult/child from R180/135), held here on

Atlantic Coast

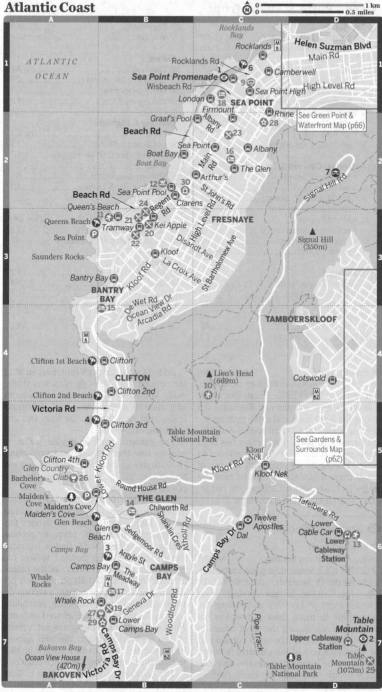

Atlantic Coast

Sundays between November and April, are a Cape Town institution. The gardens are a stop on the City Sightseeing (p78) bus. The quiet Gate 3 (aka Rycroft Gate) is the first you'll come to if you approach the gardens up Rhodes Dr from the south. There are three cafes, including the excellent **Kirstenbosch Tea Room** (☎021-797 4883; www.ktr. co.za; Gate 2; mains R90-160; ☺8.30am-5pm).

★**Irma Stern Museum**   MUSEUM
(☎021-685 5686; www.irmastern.co.za; Cecil Rd, Rosebank; adult/child R10/5; ☺10am-5pm Tue-Fri, to 2pm Sat; ☒Rosebank) The pioneering 20th-century artist Irma Stern (1894–1966), whose works are some of the most sought-after among modern South African painters, occupied this 19th-century house for about 40 years. Her studio has been left virtually intact, as if she'd just stepped out into the verdant garden for a breath of fresh air. The flamboyant painter's ethnographic art-and-craft collection from around the world is as fascinating as her own art, which was influenced by German expressionism and incorporates traditional African elements.

◉ Southern Peninsula

★**Cape of Good Hope**   NATURE RESERVE
(Cape Point; www.tmnp.co.za; adult/child R135/70; ☺6am-6pm Oct-Mar, 7am-5pm Apr-Sep; ℗) This 77.5-sq-km section of Table Mountain National Park includes awesome scenery, fantastic walks, great birdwatching and often-deserted beaches. The reserve is commonly referred to as Cape Point, after its most dramatic (but less famous) promontory. Bookings are required for the two-day **Cape of Good Hope Trail** (R280, excl reserve entry fee), a spectacular 33.8km circular route with one night spent in a basic hut. Contact the **Buffelsfontein Visitor Centre** (☎021-780 9204; Cape of Good Hope; ☺8am-5pm Mon-Fri) for further details.

★**Boulders Penguin Colony**   BIRD SANCTUARY
(www.tmnp.co.za; adult/child R70/35; ℗) This picturesque area, with enormous boulders dividing small, sandy coves, is home to a colony of some 3000 delightful African penguins. A boardwalk runs from the **Boulders Visitor Centre** (☎021-786 2329; Kleintuin Rd, Seaforth, Simon's Town; ☺7am-7.30pm Dec & Jan, 8am-6.30pm Feb, Mar, Oct & Nov, 8am-5pm Apr-Sep; ☒Simon's Town) at the Foxy Beach end of the protected area – part of Table Mountain National Park – to Boulders Beach, where you can get down on the sand and mingle with the waddling penguins. Don't, however, be tempted to pet them: they have sharp beaks that can cause serious injuries.

★**Silvermine**
Nature Reserve   NATURE RESERVE
(☎021-712 7471; www.tmnp.co.za; Ou Kaapse Weg; adult/child R50/25; ☺7am-6pm Sep-Apr, 8am-5pm May-Aug; ℗) The **Silvermine Reservoir**,

CAPE TOWN SIGHTS

CAPE TOWN FOR CHILDREN

Soft sand beaches, the mountain and its myriad activities, wildlife spotting, the carnival atmosphere of the Waterfront and much more: Cape Town takes the prize as a *lekker* (Afrikaans for 'brilliant') location for family vacations.

There's no shortage of beaches, with those on the False Bay side of the peninsula lapped by warmer waters than those on the Atlantic Coast. Good choices include Muizenberg, St James (off Main Rd, St James; St James), or lovely Buffels Bay (Cape of Good Hope, Table Mountain National Park; P) at Cape Point. Boat tours (p72) are abundant: *Tommy the Tugboat* and the *Jolly Roger Pirate Boat* are at the V&A Waterfront, while cruises leave from the harbours at Simon's Town and Hout Bay.

There are two inventively designed playgrounds at Green Point Urban Park (Map p66; www.gprra.co.za/green-point-urban-park.html; Bay Rd, Green Point; tour adult/child R35/11; 7am-7pm; P; Stadium) . Mouille Point has a big play area, toy train (Map p66; 084-314 9200; www.thebluetrainpark.com; Erf 1141/1061 Beach Rd, Green Point; R25; 9.30am-6pm Tue-Sun; Three Anchor Bay) and golf-putting course (Map p66; Beach Rd, Green Point; R25; 9am-9pm; Three Anchor Bay). Sea Point Promenade (p65) also has playgrounds, and swimming at the pavilion. In Vredehoek, there's a good playground beside Deer Park Café (Map p62; 021-462 6311; www.deerparkcafe.co.za; 2 Deer Park Dr West, Vredehoek; mains R55-90; 8am-9pm; ; Herzlia).

Check out the local marine life at the excellent Two Oceans Aquarium (p76); the birds and monkeys at Hout Bay's World of Birds (p67) or the wetland reserve of Intaka Island (021-552 6889; www.intaka.co.za; Park Lane, Intaka Island, Century City; adult/child R20/12, incl ferry ride R60/50; 7.30am-7pm Sep-Apr, to 5.30pm May-Aug; P; Central Park) ; a happy-footed African penguin colony at Boulders (p69); wild ostriches, baboons and dassies at Cape Point (p69); and the birds at Rondevlei Nature Reserve (021-706 2404; rondevleinaturereserve@capetown.gov.za; cnr Perth Rd & Fishermans Walk, Zeekoevlei; 7.30am-5pm; P) FREE. Farm animals live at Oude Molen Eco Village (021-448 9442; www.oudemolenecovillage.co.za; Alexandra Rd, Pinelands; pool adult/youth/child R30/20/10; 9am-5pm Tue-Sun; ; Pinelands) and at Imhoff Farm, where you can even arrange camel rides!

Science and technology is made fun at the Cape Town Science Centre (021-300 3200; www.ctsc.org.za; 370B Main Rd, Observatory; R55; 9am-4.30pm Mon-Sat, from 10am Sun; P; Observatory), where there's usually some special activity scheduled. The South African Museum (p62) offers giant whale skeletons and star shows at the attached planetarium (Map p62; 021-481 3800; www.iziko.org.za/museums/planetarium; 25 Queen Victoria St, Gardens; adult/child R60/30; 2pm Mon-Fri; Michaelis). The Castle of Good Hope (p56), with its battlements, museums and horse and carriage rides, offers an entertaining visual history lesson.

Toy and kids' clothing stores are found at all the major shopping malls. For a fine selection of secondhand items and a play area visit Merry Pop Ins (Map p58; 021-422 4911; www.merrypopins.co.za; 201 Bree St, City Bowl; 9.30am-5pm Mon-Thu, 9am-4pm Fri, 10am-2pm Sat; Upper Loop/Upper Long). The Book Lounge (p101) has a great kids' book section and story readings.

Weekly markets, including Neighbourgoods (p102), Bay Harbour Market (p102) and Blue Bird Garage (082 920 4285; www.bluebirdgarage.co.za; 39 Albertyn Rd, Muizenberg; 4-10pm Fri; False Bay), have play areas and kid-friendly food. For fish and chips, try the Waterfront, Hout Bay and Simon's Town.

a beautiful spot for a picnic or a leisurely walk on the wheelchair-accessible boardwalk, is the focal point of this section of Table Mountain National Park. The placid reservoir waters are tannin-stained and, despite the signs forbidding swimming, you'll often find locals taking a dip here. Some excellent half-day hiking trails lead into the mountains from this area, named after the fruitless attempts by the Dutch to prospect for silver here in the late 17th century.

Muizenberg Beach
BEACH

(Beach Rd, Muizenberg; P; Muizenberg) Popular with families, this surf beach is famous for its row of colourfully painted Victorian bathing chalets. Surfboards can be hired and lessons booked at several shops along Beach Rd. The beach shelves gently and the sea is generally safer here than elsewhere along the peninsula. At the eastern end of the promenade is a fun **water park** (☎021-788 4759; www.muizenberg slides.co.za; off Beach Rd, Muizenberg; 1hr/day passes R45/85; ☻1.30-5.30pm Mon-Fri, from 9.30am Sat & Sun, plus 6-9pm Fri Nov-Feb; 📵; 🚉Muizenberg).

Kalk Bay Harbour HARBOUR

(Essex Rd, Kalk Bay; ☻fish market 9am-5pm; 🅿; 🚉Kalk Bay) This picturesque harbour is best visited in the morning, when the community's fishing boats pitch up with their daily catch and a lively quayside market ensues. This is an excellent place to buy fresh fish for a braai (barbecue), or to spot whales during the whale-watching season.

Nearby, next to Kalk Bay Station and the **Brass Bell** (☎021-788 5455; www.brass bell.co.za; Kalk Bay Station, Main Rd, Kalk Bay; ☻11.30am-10pm; 🚉Kalk Bay) pub, are a couple of tidal swimming pools.

★Cape Point Vineyards WINERY

(☎021-789 0900; www.cpv.co.za; Silvermine Rd, Noordhoek; tastings per wine R10; ☻tastings 11am-6pm Fri-Wed, to 2pm Thu; 🅿📵) This small vineyard known for its fine sauvignon blanc has a spectacular setting overlooking Noordhoek Beach. Enjoy the wines with a picnic (R395 for two, book at least a day ahead; 11am to 5pm Friday to Wednesday) on the grounds, or at the restaurant (noon to 3pm Friday to Wednesday, plus 6pm to 8.30pm Friday and Saturday).

The Thursday evening community market (4.30pm to 8.30pm), selling mainly food, is a weekly highlight for locals and great for kids, who can play on the lawns above the farm dam.

🏃 Activities

Aerial Adventures

Cape Town Tandem Paragliding PARAGLIDING
(☎076 892 2283; www.paraglide.co.za; flight R1150) Feel like James Bond as you paraglide off Lion's Head, land near the Glen Country Club, and then sink a cocktail at Camps Bay. Novices can arrange a tandem paraglide, where you're strapped to an experienced flyer who takes care of the technicalities. Make enquiries on your first day in Cape Town, as the weather conditions have to be right.

Cape Town Helicopters SCENIC FLIGHTS
(Map p66; ☎021-418 9462; www.helicopters capetown.co.za; 220 East Pier, Breakwater Edge, V&A Waterfront; per person from R1650; 🚉Waterfront) Unforgettable views of the Cape Peninsula are guaranteed with these scenic flights. A variety of packages are available, from a 30-minute journey out to Robben Island and back to the hour-long journey down to Cape Point (R4800 per person).

Skydive Cape Town SKYDIVING
(☎082 800 6290; www.skydivecapetown.co.za; Delta 200 Airfield, Brakkefontein Rd, Melkbosstrand; R2850; ☻9am-4pm; 🚉Koeberg Power Station) Based about 40km north of the city centre in the Melkbosstrand area, this experienced outfit offers tandem skydives. Needless to say, the views – once you stop screaming – are spectacular. No Cape Town pickups offered, but the staff can recommend transport operators if you don't have your own vehicle.

Climbing

Mountain Club of South Africa CLIMBING
(Map p62; ☎021-465 3412; www.mcsacape town.co.za; 97 Hatfield St; joining fee R175, annual membership from R460; ☻climbing wall 10am-2pm Mon-Fri plus 6.30-9pm Tue & 7.30-9.30pm Fri; 🚉Government Ave) This club, which can

WORTH A TRIP

PENINSULA HUBS

There's plenty to see and do at the attractive, historic **Imhoff Farm** (☎021-783 4545; www.imhofffarm.co.za; Kommetjie Rd, Kommetjie; ☻9am-5pm; 🅿📵), just outside Kommetjie. Among the attractions are craft shops and art studios; a cafe, sushi bar and the Blue Water Cafe (p93) restaurant; a snake and **reptile park** (adult/child R70/50); the **Higgeldy Piggeldy Farmyard** (R20), stocked with animals; **camel rides** (☻noon-4pm Tue-Sun; adult/child R70/50); and a **farm shop** selling tasty goat's cheeses (made on-site by a French cheesemaker) and other provisions.

Noordhoek Farm Village (☎021-789 2654; www.thefarmvillage.co.za; cnr Main Rd & Village Lane, Noordhoek; ☻9am-5pm; 📵), which has the pastoral charm of a Cape Dutch farmstead, is a pleasant place to buy gifts and souvenirs, from African craft to local fashion. There are restaurants, a children's playground and a weekly **food market** (☻4-8pm) on Wednesday.

TOWNSHIPS TOURS

The best township tours provide a clear understanding of the Mother City's split nature and the challenges faced by the vast majority of Capetonians in their daily lives. They also reveal that these lives are not uniformly miserable and deprived, and that there are many inspiring things to see and do and people to meet.

Typically lasting half a day, township tours usually involve travel in a car or small coach, but there are also walking, cycling and even running tours, if you'd prefer.

Uthando (☑021-683 8523; www.uthandosa.org; tours R912) These township tours cost more because half of the money goes towards the social upliftment projects that the tours visit and are specifically designed to support. Usually three or so projects are visited: they could be anything from an organic farm to an old folks' centre.

Juma's Tours (☑073 400 4064; www.townshiparttours.co.za) Zimbabwean Juma is a talented street artist who lives and works in Khayelitsha where he leads excellent walking tours of the street art brightening up the area around Khayelitsha station. He's also the go-to guide for insights into the rich stock of street art in Woodstock where he used to live and where he still leads walking tours.

Andulela (☑083 305 2599, 021-790 2592; http://andulela.com; cooking tours from R985) Offers a variety of cultural and culinary-themed tours, including an African cooking tour in Langa and a Cape Malay one in Bo-Kaap.

Siwive Tours (☑076 483 5539; www.siviwetours.com; tours from R350) Personable guide Siviwe Mbinda is the founder of this company, offering two-hour walking tours around Langa. Itineraries often include a performance by the Happy Feet gumboot dance troupe that Siviwe established. Another of Siviwe's tour companies is **Vamos** (☑083 452 1112, 072 499 7866; www.vamos.co.za; cycling tours R320), which offers cycling tours of Langa.

Dinner@Mandela's (☑021-790 5817, 083 471 2523; www.dinneratmandelas.co.za; tours R400) A highly recommended alternative or addition to daytime township tours is this evening tour and dinner combination at Imizamo Yethu, which runs Mondays and Thursdays from 7pm (with pick-ups in the city centre). The meal, which includes African traditional dishes and is vegetarian-friendly, is held at Tamfanfa's Tavern and is preceded by lively African dancing and a choir singing.

Imizamo Yethu Tour (☑083 719 4870; www.suedafrika.net/imizamoyethu; tours R75; ⊙tours 10.30am, 1pm & 4pm; ▢Imizamo Yethu) Local guide Afrika Moni offers a two-hour walking tour

recommend guides to serious climbers, also has a climbing wall (R5) and its own hut accommodation on the top of Table Mountain.

Cruises

Simon's Town Boat Company   BOATING
(☑083 257 7760; www.boatcompany.co.za; Town Pier, Simon's Town; ▢Simon's Town) Runs cruises to Cape Point (adult/child R600/500, two hours) and Seal Island (adult/child R450/350, 1½ hours), plus whale-watching trips from June to November that allow you to get up close to these magnificent animals (adult/child R900/600, 2½ hours).

Duiker Island Cruises   BOATING
(⊙cruises 8am-3.30pm; ▢Fishmarket) From Hout Bay Harbour you can catch a boat to Duiker Island, also known as 'Seal Island' for its colony of Cape fur seals (not to be confused with the official Seal Island in False Bay). Circe Launches (☑082 552 2904;

www.circelaunches.co.za; adult/child R75/45), **Drumbeat Charters** (☑021-791 4441; www.drumbeatcharters.co.za; adult/child R90/50) and **Nauticat Charters** (☑021-790 7278; www.nauticatcharters.co.za; adult/child R85/45) run these 40- to 60-minute cruises daily, usually with guaranteed sailings in the mornings.

Waterfront Charters   CRUISE
(Map p66; ☑021-418 3168; www.waterfrontcharters.co.za; Shop 5, Quay 5, V&A Waterfront; ▢Breakwater) One-stop shop for cruises by a variety of operators, including recommended 1½-hour sunset cruises (adult/child R360/180) on the handsome wood-and-brass-fitted schooner *Esperance*. A 30-minute jet-boat ride is R440.

Yacoob Tourism   CRUISE
(Map p66; ☑021-421 0909; www.ytourism.co.za; Shop 8, Quay 5, V&A Waterfront; ▢; ▢Breakwater) Among the several trips that this company runs are those on the *Jolly Roger Pirate*

of Hout Bay's township, meeting local residents at the police station and then visiting the *spaza* (shop), *shebeen* (bar) and *sangoma* (traditional healer).

Transcending History Tours (☑084 883 2514; http://sites.google.com/site/capeslaveroute tours; 2½hr tours from R200) Lucy Campbell is the go-to academic for these tours, which offer a deeper insight into the rich and fascinating indigenous and slave history of the Cape.

18 Gangster Museum (☑021-821 7864, 073 707 3639; www.18gm.co.za; Dullah Omar St, Mandela Park, Khayelitsha; tours R60; ⊙8.30am-6pm Mon-Fri, 10am-3pm Sat & Sun) One-hour walking tours include this tiny museum (housed in a shipping container), which illustrates the treacherous path that too many in these communities follow into crime. They also offer a half-day walking, cycling and taxi tour, incorporating the museum alongside a visit to a reformed gangster's house, Khayelitsha Mall and Lookout Hill, as well as a braai (barbecue) lunch.

Maboneng Township Arts Experience (☑021-824 1773; www.maboneng.com) These walking tours of Langa, normally including Guga S'Thebe, the Langa Pass Museum, street art and a local artist's home gallery, are a fun way to experience the township's creative side. One-hour, half-day and full-day options are offered.

Self-Guided Langa Tour

Cape Town's oldest township is also one of the closest to the city centre, and the proximity of Langa's sights to the N2 highway makes this a straightforward option if you would like to visit a township independently. Catch a taxi or drive to **Guga S'Thebe Arts & Cultural Centre** (☑021-695 3493; cnr King Langalibalele Ave & Church St, Langa; ⊙8am-4.30pm Mon-Fri, to 2pm Sat & Sun; P; Langa) FREE, where there is a car guard, and take a short stroll along thoroughfare King Langalibalele Ave, past the **Langa Mosaic Plinths** (King Langalibalele Ave, Langa; Langa), to the **Langa Pass Museum** (Langa Heritage Museum; ☑084 949 2153, 072 975 5442; cnr King Langalibalele & Lerotholi Aves, Langa; entry by donation; ⊙9am-4pm Mon-Fri, to 1pm Sat; P; Langa).

There are a few eating options in the vicinity, including **Kaffa Hoist** (☑071 120 6345; www.facebook.com/kaffahoist; Guga S'thebe Arts & Cultural Centre, cnr King Langalibalele Ave & Church St, Langa; ⊙7am-7pm) at Guga S'Thebe, where you can get a cup of locally roasted Deluxe Coffeeworks coffee. If you'd like to stay overnight, **Nomase's Guesthouse** (☑083 482 8377, 021-694 3904; cnr King Langalibalele & Sandile Aves, Langa; r incl breakfast R480; P) is also nearby.

Boat (adult/child from R170/85) and *Tommy the Tugboat* (adult/child R50/25), both perfect for families. Adults may prefer their *Adrenalin* speed-boat jaunts or a cruise on the catamarans *Ameera* and *Tigress*.

Cycling & Mountain Biking

Downhill Adventures　　CYCLING
(Map p62; ☑021-422 0388; www.downhill adventures.com; cnr Orange & Kloof Sts, Gardens; ⊙8am-5pm Mon-Fri, to 1pm Sat; Upper Loop/Upper Long) Trips include a thrilling ride down from the lower cable station on Table Mountain (R995), as well as more leisurely pedals in the Tokai Forest or through the Constantia Winelands and the Cape of Good Hope. You can also hire bikes (R550 per day) and arrange surf or sandboarding lessons.

Awol Tours　　CYCLING
(Map p66; ☑021-418 3803; www.awoltours.co.za; Information Centre, Dock Rd, V&A Waterfront; ⊙9am-6pm; Nobel Square) Discover Cape Town's cycle lanes on this superb city bike tour (daily, three hours, R600) from Awol's Waterfront base. Other pedalling itineraries include the Winelands, Cape Point and the township of Masiphumelele – an interesting alternative to traditional township tours either by bus or on foot. Guided hikes on Table Mountain (from R1850) are also available. Bikes can be rented from R200/300 per half/full day.

Day Trippers　　CYCLING, TOUR
(☑021-511 4766; www.daytrippers.co.za) Many of this long-established outfit's tours include the chance to go cycling. Their city cycle tour is R450.

Diving & Snorkelling

There has been much controversy regarding shark-cage diving, with detractors arguing that it is leading to increased shark attacks, while others (including some marine

SERGEY URYADNIKOV / SHUTTERSTOCK ©

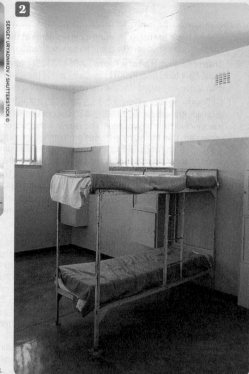

DAVID FORMAN / GETTY IMAGES ©

1. Boulders Penguin Colony (p69)
Visit this picturesque area and watch African penguins waddle along the shores.

2. Nelson Mandela's cell, Robben Island (p64)
Tour this Unesco World Heritage site and gain a deeper understanding of South Africa's history.

3. Kirstenbosch National Botanical Garden (p67)
Stroll through one of the world's finest botanic gardens, home to more than 7000 plant species.

4. Cape Town views
Take in stunning vistas of Table Mountain and Devil's Peak.

QUALITY MASTER / SHUTTERSTOCK ©

WORTH A TRIP

LION'S HEAD

It was the Dutch who coined the term Lion's Head (Leeuwen Kop) for the giant, nipple-like **outcrop** (Map p68; Signal Hill Rd, Tamboerskloof; ⬚ Kloof Nek) that over-looks Sea Point and Camps Bay. It takes about an hour each way to cover the popular 2.2km-hike from Kloof Nek to the 669m summit. There are also hiking routes up from the Sea Point side.

A lot of people do the hike as an early-morning constitutional, and it's a local ritual to hike up and watch the sun go down on a full-moon night. The moonlight helps the walk back down, al-though you should always bring a torch (flashlight) and go with company.

scientists and environmentalists) believe that it is a positive educational tool to en-courage conservation.

★ **Animal Ocean**   SNORKELLING, WILDLIFE, DIVING
(☏ 072 296 9132; www.animalocean.co.za; 8 Al-bert St, Hout Bay; snorkelling/diving per person R800/2150; ⊛; ⬚ Lower Victoria) Although it's weather-dependent (and not for those who suffer seasickness), don't miss the chance to go snorkelling or diving off Duik-er Island. Chances are you'll be visited by some of the thousands of playful, curious Cape fur seals that live on the island and swim in the shark-free waters around it. All necessary gear, including thick neoprene wetsuits, is provided. Trips run from Sep-tember to May.

Apex Shark Expeditions   WILDLIFE
(☏ 021-786 5717; www.apexpredators.com; Quay-side Bldg, Simon's Town; shark-watching tours from R2400; ⬚ Simon's Town) Run by naturalists, this outfit offers small-group marine expe-riences in False Bay, including shark-cage diving between February and September.

Into the Blue   DIVING
(Map p68; ☏ 021-434 3358; www.diveschoolcape-town.co.za; 88 Main Rd, Sea Point; open-water PADI courses R4995-5995, shore/boat dives R400/650, gear hire per day R650; ⬚ Sea Point High) Con-veniently located near Sea Point's accom-modation, this operator runs diving courses and offers regular dives around the Cape, focusing on themes from shipwrecks to cow sharks, including shark-cage dives.

Adrenalised Cape Town   DIVING
(Map p66; ☏ 021-418 2870; www.adrenaliseddiving. co.za; Shop 8, Quay 5, V&A Waterfront; ⊙ 9.30am-6pm Mon-Sat, from 10am Sun; ⬚ Breakwater) Scuba diving is just one of the several water-based activities that this outfit offers, with PADI open-water courses at R5995 and a two-shore dive package at R1540. You can also learn or go freediving with them or sea snorkelling in Ouderkrall where you can hang out with a colony of Cape fur seals.

Two Oceans Aquarium   DIVING
(Map p66; ☏ 021-418 3823; www.aquarium.co.za; Dock Rd, V&A Waterfront; dives R870, Discover Scu-ba course R750; ⬚ Aquarium) A guaranteed way to swim with turtles and rays is to dive in the tanks at the Two Oceans Aquarium. With no sharks around to worry about, this makes for a delightful diving experience. The cost includes gear hire, and you need to be a certi-fied diver, otherwise you also need to pay for the Discover Scuba course.

Pisces Divers   DIVING
(☏ 021-786 3799; www.piscesdivers.co.za; Goods Shed, Main Rd, Simon's Town; guided dives from R1200, courses from R1300; ⬚ Simon's Town) Just metres from the water's edge, this PADI dive centre offers a range of courses and sched-uled dives.

Hiking

Table Mountain offers up scores of routes, from easy strolls to extreme rock climbing. You can choose to conquer the summit or traverses around buttresses, up ravines and through valleys.

As well as the companies listed below, Ab-seil Africa (p70), Awol Tours (p73) and Down-hill Adventures (p73) all offer guided hikes in the park. Hiking clubs that arrange day and weekend hikes include Cape Union Mart Hiking Club (www.cumhike.co.za), Trails Club of South Africa (www.trailsclub.co.za) and Mountain Club of South Africa (p71).

Venture Forth (☏ 021-555 3864, 084 700 2867; www.ventureforth.co.za; per person from R825, minimum 3 people) Excellent guided hikes and rock climbs with enthusiastic, savvy guides.

Walk in Africa (☏ 021-785 2264; www.walk-inafrica.com) Steve Bolnick, an experienced and passionate safari and mountain guide, runs this company. He offers various half- and full-day hiking trips within Table Mountain National Park as well as further afield.

South African Slackpacking (☑ 082 882 4388; www.slackpackersa.co.za; under/over 4hr from R1100/1400) Registered nature guide Frank Dwyer runs this operation, which offers one-day and multiday hikes.

Table Mountain Walks (☑ 021-715 6136; www.tablemountainwalks.co.za; per person from R550) Offers a range of guided day hikes in different parts of the park, from ascents of Table Mountain to rambles through Silvermine.

Christopher Smith (☑ 073 727 0386; http://tablemountain.my-hiking.com; per day from R600) This personable and knowledgeable freelance guide is National Park–trained and has plenty of experience guiding across Table Mountain's terrain.

Karbonkelberg Hikers (www.facebook.com/Karbonkelberg-hikers-791126257689574/) Brent Thomas, Donita Puckpas and Colin Delcarme (all Rastafarians) are a guided-hiking team in Hout Bay. As Hangberg residents they know the area intimately and can guide you safely through this beautiful part of the Table Mountain National Park (do not walk here unguided, as the area is a mugging hotspot).

Horse Riding

Sleepy Hollow Horse Riding HORSE RIDING
(☑ 083 261 0104, 021-789 2341; www.sleepyhollowhorseriding.com; Sleepy Hollow Lane, Noordhoek; beach rides R530, bush trails R350; ☉ beach rides 9am, 1pm & 4pm, bush trails 11.30am & 3.30pm) This reliable operation offers two-hour rides along the wide, sandy beach at Noordhoek, as well as one-hour explorations of the mountainous hinterland. Advance booking is essential. Pony rides and lessons are also available.

Kayaking

★**Kayak Cape Town** KAYAKING
(☑ 082 501 8930; www.kayakcapetown.co.za; Wharf St, Simon's Town; ⊠ Simon's Town) Paddle out to the penguin colony (p69) at Boulders (R300, two hours) with this Simon's Town–based operation.

Kaskazi Kayaks KAYAKING, TOUR
(Map p66; ☑ 074 810 2224, 083 346 1146; www.kayak.co.za; Shell service station, 179 Beach Rd, Three Anchor Bay; per person R400; ⊠ Three Anchor Bay) Get up early to join the two-hour guided kayak trips (weather dependent) run by this professional operator from Three

---

SAFE HIKING

Just because Table Mountain National Park is on the doorstep of the city doesn't make this wilderness area, extending above 1000m, any less dangerous and unpredictable. Accidents on the mountain are common, often due to a climbing expedition gone wrong; more people have died on Table Mountain than on Mt Everest. Mountain fires have also claimed their victims, and muggings on the slopes of Table Mountain and Lion's Head are unfortunately not rare events.

There are staff patrolling the park, but it covers such a large area that they cannot be everywhere, so be well prepared before setting off. Even if taking the cableway to the summit, be aware that the weather up top can change very rapidly. The main emergency numbers are ☑ 086 110 6417 to report fires, poaching, accidents and crime, and ☑ 021-948 9900 for Wilderness Search and Rescue.

Hiking Tips

➡ Hike with long trousers. Much of the fynbos (literally 'fine bush', primarily proteas, heaths and ericas) is tough and scratchy. There's also the seriously nasty blister bush (its leaves look like those of continental parsley).

➡ If your skin does brush against the blister bush, cover the spot immediately – exposure to sunlight activates the plant's toxins, which can leave blisters on your skin that may refuse to heal for years.

➡ Tell someone the route you're planning to climb, and take a map (or better still, a guide).

➡ Stick to well-used paths. Don't be tempted to take shortcuts.

➡ Take plenty of water, some food, weather-proof clothing and a fully charged mobile phone.

➡ Wear proper hiking boots or shoes and a sun hat.

➡ Don't climb alone – park authorities recommend going in groups of four.

➡ Don't leave litter on the mountain or make a fire – they're banned.

DON'T MISS

CHAPMAN'S PEAK DRIVE

Take your time driving, cycling or walking along Chapman's Peak Drive (☑ 021-791 8220; www.chapmanspeak-drive.co.za; Chapman's Peak Dr; cars/motorcycles R45/29; ☒ Hout Bay), a 5km toll road linking Hout Bay with Noordhoek – it's one of the most spectacular stretches of coastal highway in the world. There are picnic spots and viewpoints, and it's certainly worth taking the road at least one way en route to Cape Point.

Anchor Bay to either Granger Bay or Clifton. There are astounding views of the mountains and coastline, as well as possible close encounters with dolphins, seals and penguins. Whale sightings in season are also on the cards.

Surfing, Kitesurfing & Stand-Up Paddleboarding

Gary's Surf School SURFING
(☑ 021-788 9839; www.garysurf.co.za; 34 Balmoral Bldg, Beach Rd, Muizenberg; 2hr lessons R500; ☺ 8am-5pm; ☒ Muizenberg) Genial surfing coach Gary Kleynhans and his team teach wave-riding novices aged four and upwards, using longboards and plenty of happy-go-lucky surf attitude. You can also hire boards and wetsuits (per hour/day R150/600) or join a sandboarding trip to the dunes at Fish Hoek (R350).

Surfstore Africa WATER SPORTS
(☑ 076 202 3703, 021-788 5055; www.surfstore.co.za; 48-50 Beach Rd, Muizenberg; kite-surfing lessons from R1600; ☒ Muizenberg) You can take lessons in kite-surfing and stand-up paddleboarding (SUP), as well as regular surfing, with these folks. Also here is a shop stocking a wide range of surf-related gear, and a cafe.

Best Kiteboarding Africa WATER SPORTS
(☑ 021-556 2765; www.bestkiteboardingafrica.com; Portico Bldg, Athens Rd, Table View; half-/full-day lesson R1185/2350; ☺ 9.30am-5pm Mon-Fri, 10am-3pm Sat & Sun; ☒ Marine Circle) The long, broad, windswept beach at Table View is ideal for the sport of kite-surfing. This outfit, overlooking the beach, can teach you how to do it, or just rent you some gear if you already know how. It also teaches SUP; two-hour lesson R1185.

☞ Tours

City Sightseeing Cape Town BUS
(☑ 086 173 3287; www.citysightseeing.co.za; adult/child 1 day R180/100, 2 days R280/200) These hop-on, hop-off buses, running two main routes, are perfect for a quick orientation, with commentary available in 16 languages. The open-top double-deckers also provide an elevated platform for photos. Buses run at roughly half-hourly intervals between 9am and 4.30pm, with extra services in peak season. They also offer a variety of other add on tours and excursions – see the website for details.

Coffeebeans Routes CULTURAL
(Map p62; ☑ 021-813 9829; https://coffeebeansroutes.com; iKhaya Lodge Hotel, Dunkley Sq, Gardens; tours from US$90; ☒ Roodehek) The Coffeebeans Routes concept – hooking up visitors with interesting local personalities, including musicians, artists, brewers and designers – helps it stand out from the tour-operator pack. Among innovative routes in Cape Town and surrounds are ones focusing on South Africa's recent revolutionary history, creative enterprises, and organic and natural wines.

Cape Town on Foot WALKING
(Map p58; ☑ 021-462 2252; www.wanderlust.co.za; 66 Loop St, City Bowl; tours R250; ☺ 11am Mon, Wed & Fri; ☒ Church/Longmarket) These 2½-hour walking tours, departing from outside Huguenot House – home to the jeweller Prins & Prins (Map p58; ☑ 021-422 0148; www.prinsandprins.com; ☺ 9am-5pm Mon-Fri, to 1pm Sat; ☒ Church/Mid-Long) – cover the central city sights and are led by a knowledgeable guide speaking either English or German.

African Story TOURS
(☑ 073 755 0444; www.africanstorytours.com; R850) Full-day tours include wine, cheese and chocolate tastings at four estates in the Stellenbosch, Franschhoek and Paarl regions.

Run Cape Town RUNNING
(Map p62; ☑ 072 920 7028; www.runcapetown.co.za; tours from R600) Go sightseeing while you get a workout on this innovative company's variety of running routes across the city, both within Table Mountain National Park and further afield in Gugulethu and Darling (R550 with your own transport to Darling).

☆ Festivals & Events

Cape Town loves to party and there's always something happening, particularly in the warmer months (October to March). For a full rundown of festivals and events, check Cape Town Tourism (p106).

January

Cape Town Minstrel Carnival CULTURAL

(www.facebook.com/capetownminstrelca; ⊙ Jan & Feb) *Tweede Nuwe Jaar* (2 January) is when the satin- and sequin-clad minstrel troupes traditionally march through the city for the Kaapse Klopse (Cape Minstrel Festival) from Keizergracht St, along Adderley and Wale Sts to the Bo-Kaap. Throughout January into early February there are Saturday competitions between troupes at **Athlone Stadium** (☑ 021-637 6607; Cross Blvd, Athlone; ⊠ Athlone).

February & March

Design Indaba ART

(www.designindaba.com; ⊙ Feb) This creative convention, bringing together the varied worlds of fashion, architecture, visual arts, crafts and media, is held at the end of February, usually at the Cape Town International Convention Centre.

Infecting the City ART

(☑ 021-418 3336; http://infectingthecity.com; ⊙ Mar) Cape Town's wonderful squares, fountains, museums and theatres are the venues for this innovative performing-arts festival, held every two years, featuring artists from across the continent. The next festival is in 2019.

Cape Town Cycle Tour SPORTS

(www.capetowncycletour.com; ⊙ mid-Mar) Held on a Saturday, this is the world's largest timed cycling event, attracting more than 30,000 contestants. The route circles Table Mountain, heading down the Atlantic Coast and along Chapman's Peak Dr.

Cape Town Carnival CULTURAL

(www.capetowncarnival.com; Walk of Remembrance, Green Point; ⊙ mid-Mar) Held along the Walk of Remembrance (the former Fan Walk), this is a city-sponsored parade and street party that celebrates the many facets of South African identity.

Old Mutual Two Oceans Marathon SPORTS

(☑ 087 740 5260; www.twooceansmarathon.org.za; ⊙ mid-Mar) This 56km marathon follows a route around Table Mountain. It generally attracts about 9000 competitors.

DON'T MISS

REGULAR EVENTS

First Thursdays (www.first-thursdays.co.za; ⊙ 5-9pm, 1st Thu of month Feb-Dec) This massively popular event is centred on the galleries and design shops of the City Bowl – it's a chance to dip into the local art scene, as well as join a roving street party. Food trucks and stalls gather around St Georges Mall, Van Riebeek Sq and Upper Bree St, where you're also likely to encounter events on Orphan Lane.

Tuning the Vine (☑ 083 357 4069; www.tuningthevine.co.za; ticket online/at venue R200/220; ⊙ 5.30-8.30pm, 2nd Wed of month) A successful monthly event enlivening midweek nightlife in the City Bowl. Follow this 'inner-city wine route' around some 13 different venues showcasing local wines and winemakers.

Museum Night V&A Waterfront (www.museum-night.co.za; V&A Waterfront) Held quarterly, usually on a Wednesday evening between 5pm and 10pm, this is when the district's museums and galleries stay open late and have free entry. Other attractions have half-price entry, and various cultural events are usually scheduled.

Promenade Mondays (Map p68; www.facebook.com/promenademondays; off Beach Rd, Sea Point) Every Monday at 6pm, up to 300 skateboarders, rollerbladers and cyclists gather at the parking lot beside Queen's Beach to join this super-social push/roll/skate-a-thon along Sea Point Promenade. It's organised by town planner and longboarder Marco Morgan, who is also a founding member of the National Skate Collective – which has been lobbying the city to improve facilities for skaters.

Art Thursday (www.facebook.com/ARTthursdaysInObz; Observatory) Held on the second Thursday of the month, galleries, shops and local bars and restaurants stay open late to promote various exhibitions and art and music events. Pick up a leaflet showing participants from AHEM! Art Collective (p101). Among the things that you may end up doing is listening to open-mic poets at **Touch of Madness** (☑ 021-447 4650; http://atouchofmadness.webflow.io; 12 Nuttall Rd, Observatory; mains R55-70; ⊙ noon-10pm Tue-Sat, to 6pm Sun; 🅿 🛜; ⊠ Observatory) or watching an art film at Armchair Theatre & Pub.

Cape Town International Jazz Festival
MUSIC

(☑021-671 0506; www.capetownjazzfest.com; ⊙Mar or Apr) Cape Town's biggest jazz event, attracting big names from both South Africa and overseas, is usually held at the Cape Town International Convention Centre at the end of March. It includes a free concert in Greenmarket Sq.

May

Good Food & Wine Show
FOOD & DRINK

(www.goodfoodandwineshow.co.za; ⊙May) Cape Town goes gourmet with this three-day event held at the Cape Town International Convention Centre.

September & October

Open Book Festival
LITERATURE

(http://openbookfestival.co.za; ⊙Sep) The city's main literature festival has a packed schedule with talks, readings and discussions with local and international writers. It's organised by the Fugard Theatre, with events held there, the District Six Homecoming Centre and the Book Lounge.

Cape Town Fringe
ART

(☑086 000 2004; www.capetownfringe.co.za; ⊙mid-Sep–early Oct) A jamboree of the performing arts, organised in conjunction with the respected Grahamstown Festival, that peppers the Mother City with interesting happenings for 11 days at the end of September and into October.

OUTsurance Kfm 94.5 Gun Run
SPORTS

(http://thegunrun.co.za; ⊙early Oct) This popular half-marathon (21km) is the only time that the Noon Gun on Signal Hill gets fired on a Sunday – competitors try to finish the race before the gun goes off. There are also 10km and 5km races.

Mama City Improv Festival
COMEDY

(www.mamacityimprovfest.com; ⊙Oct) Five laughter-packed days of shows at venues in Observatory – including Obviouzly Armchair (☑021-460 0458; http://obviouzlyarmchair.com; 135 Lower Main Rd, Observatory; ⊙5pm-2am Mon-Wed, noon-2am Thu-Sun; ☒Observatory) – for this stand-up comedy and improvisation festival with workshops and performances by local and international talents.

November & December

Adderely Street Christmas Lights
MUSIC

(www.capetown.gov.za; ⊙Dec) Join the tens of thousands who turn out for the concert in front of Cape Town Railway Station that precedes the switching on of festive lights along Adderley St, and a parade. The same street is pedestrianised each night from around 17 to 30 December for a night market, with live music.

🛏 Sleeping

From five-star pamper palaces and designer-chic guesthouses to creatively imagined backpackers, Cape Town's stock of sleeping options caters to all wallets. Choose your base carefully depending on your priorities – not everywhere is close to a beach or major sights. Reserve well in advance, especially if visiting during school holidays (from mid-December to the end of January); most places slash their rates in the quiet winter season from May to October.

🛏 City Bowl & Surrounds

★91 Loop
HOSTEL $

(Map p58; ☑021-286 1469; www.91loop.co.za; 91 Loop St, City Bowl; dm/r incl breakfast from R270/1000; ❋☎; ☒Church/Longmarket) Jo'burg investors are behind this new and buzzing place offering a good range of rooms, including pods – essentially a dorm bed but instead of a bunk you sleep in a concrete, oblong pod with a tad more privacy. Rooms and dorms (all named after major world cities) offer big mattresses, and there are high housekeeping standards throughout.

Scalabrini Guest House
GUESTHOUSE $

(Map p58; ☑021-465 6433; www.scalabrini.org.za; 47 Commercial St, City Bowl; dm/s/d R280/560/780; @☎; ☒Roeland) The Italian monastic-order Scalabrini Fathers have provided welfare services to Cape Town's poor and to refugees since 1994. Housed in a former textile factory, they run several social programs, and a pleasant guesthouse with 11 immaculately clean en-suite rooms – plus a great kitchen for self-catering where you can also watch satellite TV.

St Paul's B&B Guesthouse
B&B $

(Map p58; ☑021-423 4420; www.stpaulsguesthouse.com; 182 Bree St, City Bowl; s/d incl breakfast R600/800, with shared bathroom R500/800; ☐☎; ☒Upper Long/Upper Loop) This spotless, characterful B&B in a very handy location is a fine alternative to the backpacker lodges along Long St. The simply furnished and spacious rooms have high ceilings, and there's a vine-shaded courtyard where you can relax or eat breakfast.

APARTMENT & HOUSE RENTALS

For longer-term stays, a self-catering or serviced apartment or villa can be a good deal. Reliable agencies include the following:

African Elite Properties (Map p58; 021-421 1090; www.africaneliteproperties.com; Shop A21, Cape Quarter, Dixon St, De Waterkant; 1-bed apt from R3000; Alfred) Agency handling rental of luxury apartments atop the Cape Quarter.

Cape Stay (www.capestay.co.za) Accommodation across the Cape.

De Waterkant Cottages (Map p58; 021-421 2300; www.dewaterkantcottages.com; 40 Napier St, De Waterkant; apt/house from R1650/2200; Old Fire Station) Classy villas and apartments in De Waterkant, sleeping from two to eight people.

In Awe Stays (083 658 6975; www.inawestays.co.za; d from R1600) Stylish studios and cottages in Gardens and Fresnaye, with doubles from R1600.

Village & Life (Map p68; 021-437 9700; www.villageandlife.com; 69 Victoria Rd, Camps Bay; Old Fire Station) Focused mainly on properties in De Waterkant and Camps Bay.

★ **Cape Heritage Hotel** BOUTIQUE HOTEL $$
(Map p58; 021-424 4646; www.capeheritage. co.za; Heritage Sq, 90 Bree St, City Bowl; d/ste/ apt incl breakfast from R2850/4420/7000, parking per day R85; P✼@☎; Church/Longmarket) Each of the 19 rooms at this elegant boutique hotel, part of the Heritage Sq redevelopment of 18th-century buildings, has its own character. Some have four-poster beds and all have modern conveniences such as satellite TV and clothes presses. There's a roof terrace and a jacuzzi.

★ **Rouge on Rose** BOUTIQUE HOTEL $$
(Map p58; 021-426 0298; www.rougeonrose. co.za; 25 Rose St, Bo-Kaap; s/d incl breakfast R1600/2300; ✼☎; Old Fire Station) This great Bo-Kaap option offers nine rustic-chic suites with kitchenettes, lounges and lots of workspace. The fun wall paintings are by a resident artist and all rooms have luxurious, open bath spaces with standalone tubs.

Grand Daddy Hotel BOUTIQUE HOTEL $$
(Map p58; 021-424 7247; www.granddaddy.co.za; 38 Long St, City Bowl; r/trailer from R2895/3695; P✼@☎; Mid-Long/Church) The Grand Daddy's star attraction is its rooftop 'trailer park' of penthouse suites, made from seven vintage, artistically renovated Airstream trailers. The hotel's regular rooms are also stylish and incorporate playful references to South African culture.

La Rose B&B B&B $$
(Map p58; 021-422 5883; www.larosecapetown. com; 32 Rose St, Bo-Kaap; s/d incl breakfast from R1000/1200; P✼☎; Old Fire Station) Adheena and Yoann are the very welcoming South African–French couple running this charming B&B, which has been so successful it has expanded into nearby properties. It's beautifully decorated and has a rooftop garden with the best views of the area. Yoann's speciality is making authentic crêpes for the guests.

The Charles GUESTHOUSE $$
(Map p58; 021-409 2500; www.thecharles.co.za; 137 Waterkant St, De Waterkant; s/d incl breakfast from R1300/1550; ✼@☎; Alfred) This appealing guesthouse and cafe has a central position in De Waterkant. The cafe's tables spill out onto a terrace with good views of the area. Rooms vary in size, the cheapest being small. Larger ones are open plan and come with kitchens for self-catering.

★ **Taj Cape Town** LUXURY HOTEL $$$
(Map p58; 021-819 2000; www.tajhotels.com; Wale St, City Bowl; r/ste incl breakfast R3000/5000; P✼@☎⌘; Groote Kerk) India's luxury hotel group has breathed new life into the old Board of Executors building. There's plenty of heritage here, but a new tower also houses the chic contemporary-styled rooms, many offering spectacular views of Table Mountain. Service and facilities, including the excellent restaurant **Bombay Brasserie** (mains R110-200, tasting menus R625; ⊙6-10.30pm), are top grade.

🏠 East City, District Six, Woodstock & Salt River

★ **Wish U Were Here** HOSTEL $
(021-447 0522; www.wishuwereherecapetown. com; 445 Albert Rd, Salt River; dm R280, d R845, s/d with shared bathroom R550/780; ☎; Kent) The designers clearly had a lot of fun with this place, just a short stroll from the Old

East City, District Six, Woodstock & Salt River

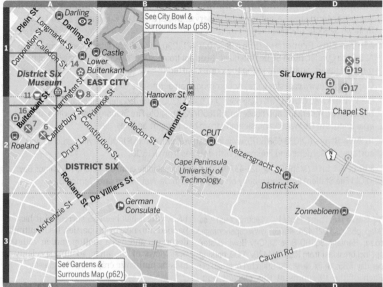

East City, District Six, Woodstock & Salt River

◉ Top Sights
1 District Six Museum A1

◉ Sights
2 Grand Parade A1

⬤ Sleeping
3 DoubleTree by Hilton Hotel
    Cape Town – Upper
    Eastside H3

⊗ Eating
4 Andalousse F2
    Downtown Ramen ....(see 6)
5 Kitchen D1
6 Lefty's A2
    Ocean Jewels ....(see 22)
    Pot Luck Club ....(see 18)
7 Raptor Room A2
    Test Kitchen ....(see 18)

⊙ Drinking & Nightlife
8 Babylon A1
9 Brewers Co-op F1
    Espressolab Microroasters ....(see 18)
10 Hidden Leaf G3
11 Truth A1
12 Woodstock Brewery H1
13 Woodstock Gin Company H1

✪ Entertainment
14 Fugard Theatre A1

⬡ Shopping
15 Art It Is F1
16 Book Lounge A2
17 Goodman Gallery Cape D1
    Neighbourgoods Market ....(see 18)
18 Old Biscuit Mill H1
19 South African Print Gallery D1
20 Stevenson D1
21 Streetwires H1
22 Woodstock Exchange F1

Biscuit Mill. One dorm is Barbie-doll pink; a romantic double has a swinging bed made from a suspended fishing boat; another is styled after an intensive care unit! The building's wraparound balcony overlooks the Salt River roundabout (which is noisy during the day).

Green Elephant   HOSTEL $
(☏021-448 6359; www.greenelephant.co.za; 57 Milton Rd, Observatory; dm R210, s/d R600/750, with shared bathroom R500/650, camping per tent R100; ℗@🛜🏊♿; 🚃Observatory) This long-running backpackers, split between four houses, remains a popular alterna-

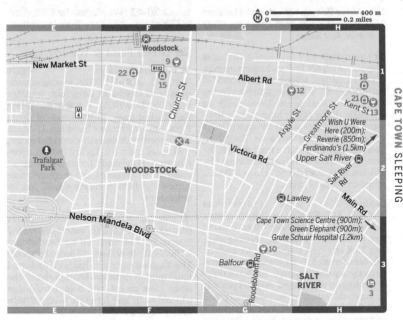

tive to the city-centre hostels. The en-suite rooms in the houses across the road from the main hostel are particularly pleasant, with wooden floors and rustic-chic furnishing. Rates include a basic breakfast.

DoubleTree by Hilton Hotel
Cape Town – Upper Eastside   HOTEL **$$**
(Map p82; ☎021-404 0570; www.doubletree. hilton.com; 31 Brickfield Rd, Woodstock; r/ste from R1395/2595, parking per day R60; ◉❋@☎☒; ❑Upper Salt River) This snazzily designed property is tucked away in the revamped buildings of the old Bonwitt clothing factory. Rooms are large and pleasant, offering either mountain or city views. Most loft suites have kitchenettes. There's an indoor pool and a gym. Rates exclude breakfast.

🛏 Gardens & Surrounds

Once in Cape Town   HOSTEL **$**
(Map p62; ☎021-424 6169; http://onceincapetown. co.za; 73 Kloof St, Gardens; dm/d incl breakfast from R260/1260; ◉@☎; ❑Ludwig's Garden) Once has a great vibe and location, and every room has its own bathroom. While the rooms are pretty compact, they are all pleasantly decorated. There's a courtyard to chill in and a big kitchen for self-catering.

Backpack   HOSTEL **$**
(Map p62; ☎021-423 4530; http://backpackers.co.za; 74 New Church St, Tamboerskloof; dm R390, s/d from R1150/1440, with shared bathroom R910/1150; ◉@☎☒; ❑Upper Long/Upper Loop) This Fair Trade in Tourism–accredited operation offers affordable style, a buzzing vibe and fantastic staff. Its dorms may not be Cape Town's cheapest but they're among its best, while the private rooms and self-catering apartments are charmingly decorated. There's a lovely mosaic-decorated pool and relaxing gardens with Table Mountain views to chill out in. Rates include breakfast.

Ashanti Gardens   HOSTEL **$**
(Map p62; ☎021-423 8721; www.ashanti.co.za; 11 Hof St, Gardens; dm R300, d R1100, s/d with shared bathroom R620/840, camping R180; ◉@☎; ❑Government Ave) This is one of Cape Town's slickest backpackers, with much of the action focused on the lively bar and deck that overlook Table Mountain. The beautiful old house, decorated with a tasteful collection of contemporary art, holds the dorms and rooms with shared bathrooms; there's also a lawn where you can camp. Excellent self-catering en-suite rooms are in two separate heritage-listed houses around the corner. There's also another branch in **Green Point** (Map p66; ☎021-433 1619; 23 Antrim Rd,

Three Anchor Bay; dm/s/d with shared bathroom R320/640/900, d with private bathroom R1100; [P][@][🛜][♨]; [♿] St Bedes).

★ **La Grenadine** GUESTHOUSE $$
(Map p62; ☑ 021-424 1358; www.lagrenadine.co.za; 15 Park Rd, Gardens; r/2-bed cottage incl breakfast from R2590/3980; [❄][@][🛜][♨]; [♿] Ludwig's Garden) Expat couple Maxime and Mélodie ladle on the Gallic charm at this imaginatively renovated former stables, where the ancient stone walls are a feature of the rooms. The garden planted with fruit trees is a magical oasis, the lounge is stacked with books and vinyl LPs, and breakfast is served on actress Mélodie's prized collection of china.

Cloud 9 BOUTIQUE HOTEL $$
(Map p62; ☑ 021-424 1133; www.hotelcloud9.com; 12 Kloof Nek Rd, Tamboerskloof; s/d incl breakfast from R1945/2590; [❄][@][🛜][♨]; [♿] Ludwig's Garden) This arty new boutique hotel and spa has been created from combining several formerly separate properties. Rooms differ depending on what part of the hotel you stay in, but could feature pressed-tin ceilings and tiled fireplace surrounds, kept as part of a contemporary makeover. Major pluses are the spacious rooftop bar and jacuzzi pool with Table Mountain views.

★ **Mannabay** BOUTIQUE HOTEL $$$
(☑ 021-461 1094; www.mannabay.com; 8 Bridle Rd, Oranjezicht; r/ste incl breakfast from R7000/8700; [P][❄][@][🛜][♨]; [♿] Upper Orange) Nothing seems too much bother for the staff at this knockout property, decorated with stunning pieces of contemporary art by local artists. The eight guest rooms are decorated in different themes. Its high hillside location on the edge of the national park provides amazing views. Rates include high tea, which is served in the library lounge.

Belmond Mount Nelson Hotel HOTEL $$$
(Map p62; ☑ 021-483 1000; www.belmond.com; 76 Orange St, Gardens; r/ste incl breakfast from R10,050/12,635; [P][❄][@][🛜][♨]; [♿] Government Ave) A world apart from the rest of the city, sitting in three hectares of gardens, the sugar-pink-painted 'Nellie' is a colonial charmer with its chintz decor and doormen in pith helmets. Rooms sport elegant silver and moss-green decorations. Facilities include a large pool, tennis courts, a luxurious spa and several restaurants.

It's great for families since it pushes the boat out for the little ones, with kid-sized robes and bedtime cookies and milk. Even if you don't stay here, drop by for **afternoon**

tea ([☑] 021-483 1948; afternoon tea R365; ⊙ 1pm or 3.30pm; [🛜]) – it's a Cape Town institution.

🛏 Green Point & Waterfront

★ **B.I.G. Backpackers** HOSTEL $
(Map p66; ☑ 021-434 0688; www.bigbackpackers.co.za; 18 Thornhill Rd, Green Point; dm/s/d/tr R420/1050/1400/1900; [P][❄][@][🛜][♨]; [♿] Skye Way) Tucked away on the slopes of Green Point, this backpackers has a fun, laid-back atmosphere with decently decorated rooms, chill areas and a big kitchen (with an honesty bar). Homemade bread is sometimes available for breakfast and there are three guitars and bicycles handy should you require them.

★ **Villa Zest** BOUTIQUE HOTEL $$
(Map p66; ☑ 021-433 1246; www.villazest.co.za; 2 Braemar Rd, Green Point; s/d incl breakfast from R2070/2990; [P][❄][@][♨]; [♿] Upper Portswood) This Bauhaus–style villa has been converted into a quirkily decorated boutique hotel. The seven guest rooms have bold, retro-design papered walls and furniture accented with furry pillows and shag rugs.

La Splendida HOTEL $$
(Map p66; ☑ 021-439 5119; www.lasplendida.co.za; 121 Beach Rd, Mouille Point; s/d from R1170/1420, parking per day R25; [P][❄][♨]; [♿] Lighthouse) You'll pay slightly extra for rooms with sea views at this hotel located on the Mouille Point Promenade, but the ones looking towards Signal Hill are just as nice and they're all quite spacious. There's a retro pop-art feel to the decor.

★ **Cape Grace** LUXURY HOTEL $$$
(Map p66; ☑ 021-410 7100; www.capegrace.com; West Quay Rd, V&A Waterfront; r/ste incl breakfast from R9700/23,000; [P][❄][@][🛜][♨]; [♿] Nobel Square) One of the Waterfront's most appealing hotels, Cape Grace sports an arty combination of antiques and crafts decoration – including hand-painted bed covers and curtains – providing a unique sense of place and Cape Town's history.

One&Only Cape Town LUXURY HOTEL $$$
(Map p66; ☑ 021-431 5888; www.oneandonlycapetown.com; Dock Rd, V&A Waterfront; r/ste incl breakfast from R12,795/27,565; [P][❄][@][🛜][♨]; [♿] Aquarium) Little expense seems to have been spared creating this luxury resort. Choose between enormous, plush rooms in the main building (with panoramic views of Table Mountain) or the even more exclusive island beside the pool and spa.

Silo Hotel
BOUTIQUE HOTEL **$$$**

(Map p66; ☑021-670 0500; www.theroyalportfolio.com/the-silo; Silo Sq, V&A Waterfront; r/ste from R18,000/25,000; P❄️🛜🏊; 💻Waterfront Silo) In counterpoint to its former industrial surroundings, and the clean lines of Thomas Heatherwick's redesign of the grain silo (p64), Silo Hotel opts for eye-popping maximalism in its interior decor. Be prepared for lush fabrics, floral prints, glitzy chandeliers and plenty of zingy colours everywhere.

Proving so popular you'll need to make a booking is the hotel's **Granary Bar** (afternoon tea from R160, 2pm to 5pm), but the **Willaston Bar** is open to all comers without reservation – both are on the 6th floor. The spectacular rooftop pool and bar area is for guests only.

🛏 Atlantic Coast & Hout Bay

★Ocean View House
GUESTHOUSE **$$**

(☑021-438 1982; www.oceanview-house.com; 33 Victoria Rd, Bakoven; r incl breakfast from R2200; P❄️🛜🏊; 💻Bakoven) It's all about location at this family-run guesthouse, set in a fynbos (literally 'fine bush') garden between the Twelve Apostles range and the rocky shoreline, in Camps Bay's neighbouring suburb of Bakoven. Rooms are crisp, white and minimal, and each has a private balcony or terrace to enjoy the views.

Winchester Mansions Hotel
HOTEL **$$**

(Map p68; ☑021-434 2351; www.winchester.co.za; 221 Beach Rd, Sea Point; s/d incl breakfast from R2785/3135; P❄️🛜🏊; 💻London) Offering a waterfront location (you'll pay extra for seaview rooms), this elegant Sea Point institution dates to the 1920s, but adds contemporary appeal to its historic home with a spa and 50-sq-metre pool. There's a lovely courtyard with a central fountain – a romantic place to dine. **Harvey's** (bar snacks R80, lunch mains R100-200; ⊙7am-10pm Mon-Sat, from 11am Sun) bar is a popular spot for a sundowner, and its legendary jazz brunch.

★Ellerman House
HISTORIC HOTEL **$$$**

(Map p68; ☑021-430 3200; www.ellerman.co.za; 180 Kloof Rd, Bantry Bay; r/ste/villas from R12,000/30,000/95,000; P❄️@🛜🏊🏋️; 💻Bantry Bay) Imagine you've been invited to stay with an immensely rich, art-collecting Capetonian friend – that's what the vibe is like at the Ellerman House, an elegant mansion overlooking the Atlantic. The rooms are studies in tasteful design, with heated floors, studded headboards, ocean-facing bay windows and original artworks. Beautiful gardens and oodles of luxe services and conveniences are all on hand.

Tintswalo Atlantic
LODGE **$$$**

(☑021-201 0025; www.tintswalo.com/atlantic; Chapman's Peak Dr, Hout Bay; s/d incl breakfast from R8085/10,780; P❄️🛜🏊; 💻Hout Bay) The only hotel in Table Mountain National Park has been rebuilt with its secluded seaside charm intact following a disastrous fire in March 2015. Luxurious Tintswalo hugs the edge of Hout Bay beneath Chapman's Peak, with an unbroken view of the Sentinel towering over town, and whales passing in season.

Camps Bay Retreat
RESORT **$$$**

(Map p68; ☑021-437 8300; www.campsbay retreat.com; 7 Chilworth Rd, The Glen; r/ste incl breakfast from R6200/9200; P❄️🛜🏊🏋️; 💻Glen Beach) Based in the grand Earl's Dyke Manor (dating from 1929), this splendid place is set in a secluded nature reserve a short walk from the Camps Bay strip. Rooms range from those with dark wooden furniture, Turkish rugs and free-standing Victorian bath in the manor, to open-plan contemporary spaces with private decks nuzzling the treetops.

🛏 Southern Suburbs

Andros Boutique Hotel
BOUTIQUE HOTEL **$$**

(☑021-797 9777; www.andros.co.za; cnr Phyllis & Newlands Rds, Claremont; s/d incl breakfast from R2050/2550; P❄️🛜🏊; 🚉Kenilworth) Set in expansive gardens, this handsome Cape Dutch Revival homestead dating from 1908 was designed by Sir Herbert Baker. The rooms and suites are spacious and comfortable affairs, and some have private terraces – perfect for people in town to work or socialise. There's a restaurant, bar, pool and spa, with an appealing mix of history and contemporary style throughout.

★Vineyard Hotel & Spa
LUXURY HOTEL **$$$**

(☑021-657 4500; www.vineyard.co.za; Colinton Rd, Newlands; r/ste incl breakfast from R3320/5420; P❄️🛜🏊; 🚉Claremont) This delightful hotel's rooms have a contemporary look and are decorated in soothing natural tones. Built around the 1799 home of Lady Anne Barnard, it's surrounded by lush gardens with Table Mountain views, where you can enjoy a guided walk and afternoon tea. The fabulous Angsana Spa, a great gym and pool, and a gourmet restaurant, Myoga, complete the picture.

🛏 Southern Peninsula

African Soul Surfer
HOSTEL $

(☑ 021-788 1771; www.africansoulsurfer.co.za; 13 York Rd, Muizenberg; dm/s/d R190/580/750; 🖥; 🚇 Muizenberg) Set in a heritage-listed building with splendid sea views, this backpackers is ideal for those who don't want to be more than 30 seconds from the sand. As well as nicely designed rooms with private or shared bathroom, there's a kitchen, comfy lounge, and ping-pong and pool tables.

Eco Wave Lodge
HOSTEL $

(☑ 073 927 5644; www.ecowave.co.za; 11 Gladioli Way, Kommetjie; d R700, dm/s/d with shared bathroom R200/550/600, apt R1200; 🅿🖥) Just 100m from the beach – perfect for surfers – this spacious suburban house has a large dining room (complete with chandelier), lounge with pool table, and sun deck. Rooms range from a four-bed dorm, with exposed brickwork and wooden beams, to minimal doubles and twins with splashes of surf decor, most sharing bathrooms.

⭐ Bella Ev
GUESTHOUSE $$

(☑ 021-788 1293; www.bellaevguesthouse.co.za; 8 Camp Rd, Muizenberg; s/d from R1000/1200; 🅿🖥; 🚇 Muizenberg) This charming guesthouse, with a delightful courtyard garden, could be the setting for an Agatha Christie mystery, one in which the home's owner has a penchant for all things Turkish – hence the Ottoman slippers for guests' use.

Chartfield Guesthouse
GUESTHOUSE $$

(☑ 021-788 3793; www.chartfield.co.za; 30 Gatesville Rd, Kalk Bay; r R900-1200, f R2400; 🅿🖥🖨; 🚇 Kalk Bay) This rambling, wooden-floored 1920s guesthouse is decorated with choice pieces of contemporary local arts and crafts. There's a variety of rooms, each with crisp linens and a bathroom with rain-style shower. You can eat breakfast on the lovely terrace and garden overlooking the harbour.

🛏 Cape Flats

There are a number of family-run homestays and B&Bs on the Cape Flats, usually in or adjoining private homes. Staying with a Xhosa matriarch is an excellent and fun way to experience more of township life than you might on a day tour, including an African meal or two. You can book through Vamos (p72), Ikhaya Le Langa (☑ 076 530 5065; http://ikhayalelanga.co.za), Khayelitsha Travel (☑ 021-361 4505, 082 729 9715; www.facebook.com/Khayelitsha-Travel-618660584966170;

Lookout Hill complex, cnr Mew Way & Spine Rd, Ilitha Park, Khayelitsha; 🚇 Makabeni) and the usual home-sharing services.

⭐ Kopanong
B&B $

(☑ 082 476 1278, 021-361 2084; www.kopanong-township.co.za; 329 Velani Cres, Section C, Khayelitsha; s/d incl breakfast R500/1000; 🅿; 🚇 Nonkqubela) Thope Lekau, also called 'Mama Africa', runs this excellent B&B with her equally ebullient daughter, Mpho. Her substantial brick home offers three stylishly decorated guest rooms, two with private bathroom. Dinner (per person R140, minimum two diners) is delicious and walking tours (one hour per person R150), guided by members of the local community, are available.

Liziwe Guest House
B&B $

(☑ 021-633 7406; www.sa-venues.com/visit/liziwesguesthouse; 111 NY 112, Gugulethu; r R750-900; 🅿; 🚇 Heideveld) Liziwe has made her home into a palace, with seven delightful en-suite rooms all sporting TVs and African-themed decor. She was featured on a BBC cooking show, so you can be sure her food is delicious; all meals are available and nonguests are welcome to book for lunch or dinner.

🍴 Eating

It's a wonder that Capetonians look so svelte on the beach, because this is one damn delicious city to dine in – probably the best in the whole of Africa. There's a wonderful range of cuisines to sample, including local African and Cape Malay concoctions, superb seafood fresh from the boat, and chefs working at the top of their game.

🍴 City Bowl & Surrounds

Royale Eatery
BURGERS $

(Map p58; ☑ 021-422 4536; www.royaleeatery.com; 279 Long St, City Bowl; mains R78-96; ⊙ noon-11.30pm Mon-Sat; 🚇 Upper Loop/Upper Long) They've been grilling gourmet burgers to perfection here for years; downstairs is casual and buzzy while upstairs is a restaurant where you can book a table. For something different, try the Sprinter ostrich burger. For non-red meat lovers, there are chicken, fish and veggie burgers, too.

Plant
VEGAN $

(Map p58; ☑ 021-422 2737; www.plantcafe.co.za; 8 Buiten St, City Bowl; mains R40-70; ⊙ 8am-10pm Mon-Sat; 🖊; 🚇 Upper Loop/Upper Long) As their name suggests, Plant serves only vegan food, and it's so tasty that you may become converted to the cause. Mock cheese and egg substitutes are incorporated in sandwiches and salads, and giant portobello mushrooms or a mix of flaked potato and seaweed do service as alternative burgers. Their vegan cupcakes and brownies are delicious.

Bread, Milk & Honey SANDWICHES $
(Map p58; ☑ 021-461 8872; www.breadmilk honey.co.za; 10 Spin St, City Bowl; mains R45-65; ☉ 6.30am-3.45pm Mon-Fri; 🚇 Groote Kerk) The spirited debate of politicos and bureaucrats from nearby parliament rings through this smart family-run cafe. The menu is delicious: the cakes and desserts are especially yummy and they have a pay-by-weight daily lunch, as well as plenty of stuff to go.

Hokey Poke HAWAIIAN $
(Map p58; ☑ 021-422 4382; www.hokeypoke.co.za; 1 Church St, City Bowl; mains R85-135; ☉ noon-9pm Mon-Sat; ✍) Cape Town's first poke spot is a pleasing hole-in-the-wall with splashes of Asian-inspired kitsch livening up the white tiled walls. There are seven poke bowls to choose from, or you can build your own from scratch. Ingredients are fairly traditional, including raw tuna, salmon and prawns, shredded seaweed and fish roe. It's an upbeat place with friendly service.

Olami MIDDLE EASTERN $
(Map p58; www.facebook.com/Olami-549503688 551991; 231 Bree St, City Bowl; mains R75-100; ☉ 8am-4pm Mon-Fri; 🚇 Upper Loop/Upper Long) All the flavours of the Mediterranean and Middle East are represented at this spotlessly white space serving delicious falafel sandwiches, salads, sweets and drinks. They can rustle up a takeaway box of goodies and sell you a copy of their cookbook as well as the cook's wonderful hand-crafted pottery dishes.

Clarke's Bar & Dining Room AMERICAN $
(Map p58; ☑ 021-424 7648; www.clarkesdining. co.za; 133 Bree St, City Bowl; mains R75-105; ☉ 7am-10.30pm Mon-Fri, 8am-3pm Sat & Sun; 🚇 Dorp/Leeuwen) A focus of the Bree St hipster scene is this convivial spot with counter seating that pays homage to the US diner tradition. All-day breakfast dishes include grilled cheese sandwiches and huevos rancheros. There are Reubens and pork-belly sandwiches from lunchtime, as well as burgers and mac and cheese.

Hidden behind is Hail Pizza (Map p58; www.hailpizza.com; pizza small/large R60/114; ☉ 7am-10.30pm Mon-Fri, from 8am Sat & Sun).

Café Mozart CAFE $
(Map p58; www.themozart.co.za; 37 Church St, City Bowl; mains R70-90; ☉ 9am-4pm Mon-Fri, 8am-

3pm Sat; 🕾; 🚇 Church/Longmarket) Order a coffee and sandwich at this charming cafe with street-side tables amid the daily flea market. Upstairs is a lovely quiet space in which to surf the net and catch up on emails on your laptop.

Bo-Kaap Kombuis CAPE MALAY $
(Map p58; ☑ 021-422 5446; www.bokaapkombuis. co.za; 7 August St, Bo-Kaap; mains R75-95; ☉ noon-4pm & 6-9.30pm Tue-Sat, noon-4pm Sun) You'll receive a hospitable welcome from Yusuf and Nazli and their staff at this spectacularly located restaurant, high up in the Bo-Kaap. The panoramic views of Table Mountain and Devil's Peak alone make it worth visiting. There are all the traditional Cape Malay dishes on the menu, plus vegetarian options such as sugar-bean curry.

Loading Bay BISTRO, CAFE $
(Map p58; ☑ 021-425 6320; www.loadingbay. co.za; 30 Hudson St, De Waterkant; mains R80-100; ☉ 7.30am-5pm Mon-Fri, 8.30am-4pm Sat, 9am-2pm Sun; 🚇 Old Fire Station) Hang with the De Waterkant style set at this spiffy cafe serving coffee with 'microtextured milk' (it's only heated to 70°C) and bistro-style dishes such as crispy bacon and avocado on toast.

★ Chef's Warehouse & Canteen TAPAS $$
(Map p58; ☑ 021-422 0128; www.chefswarehouse. co.za; Heritage Sq, 92 Bree St, City Bowl; tapas for 2 people R700; ☉ noon-2.30pm & 4.30-8pm Mon-Fri, noon-2.30pm Sat; 🚇 Church/Longmarket) Hurry here for a delicious and very generous spread of small plates from chef Liam Tomlin and his talented crew. Flavours zip around the world, from a squid with a tangy Vietnamese salad to comforting coq au vin. If you can't get a seat (there are no bookings), try their takeaway hatch Street Food in the space under the stoop.

★ Hemelhuijs INTERNATIONAL $$
(Map p58; ☑ 021-418 2042; www.hemelhuijs. co.za; 71 Waterkant St, Foreshore; mains R125-175; ☉ 9am-4pm Mon-Fri, to 3pm Sat; 🕾; 🚇 Strand) A quirky yet elegantly decorated space – think deer heads with broken crockery and contemporary art – showcases the art and culinary creations of Jacques Erasmus. The inventive food is delicious and includes local ingredients such as sandveld potato, plus lovely fresh juices and daily bakes.

Addis in Cape ETHIOPIAN $$
(Map p58; ☑ 021-424 5722; www.addisincape.co.za; 41 Church St, City Bowl; mains R110-150; ☉ noon-10.30pm Mon-Sat; 🕾✍; 🚇 Church/Longmarket) Sit at a low basket-weave table and enjoy

tasty Ethiopian cuisine served traditionally on plate-sized *injera* (sourdough pancakes), which you rip up and eat with in place of cutlery. They have a good selection of vegetarian and vegan dishes. Also try their homemade *tej* (honey wine) and authentic Ethiopian coffee.

Company's Garden Restaurant
CAPE MALAY **$$**

(Map p58; ☑021-423 2919; www.thecompanys garden.com; Company's Garden, Queen Victoria St, City Bowl; mains R75-130; ☺7am-6pm; 🐾🖼; 🚊Dorp/Leeuwen) The old Company's Garden cafe has been transformed into a chic contemporary space with charming outdoor features such as a giant chess set and wickerwork nests for kids (and young-at-heart adults) to play in. Menu items run from excellent breakfasts (try the French toast) to several Cape Malay dishes, some with a modern twist such as the spiced-mince spring rolls.

Izakaya Matsuri
JAPANESE **$$**

(Map p58; ☑021-421 4520; www.izakayamatsuri. com; Shop 6, The Rockwell, Schiebe St, De Waterkant; mains R50-125; ☺10.30am-3pm, 5-10pm Mon-Sat; 🚊Alfred) Genial Arata-san serves some of the best sushi and rolls to be found in Cape Town, along with other Japanese *izakaya* pub-grub including noodles and tempura. When the weather's warm, tables shift from the attractive interior hung with giant white and red paper lanterns out to the courtyard area.

Raw and Roxy
VEGAN **$$**

(Map p58; ☑079 599 6277; www.facebook.com/ rawandroxy; 38 Hout St, City Bowl; mains R110-135; ☺10am-6pm Mon-Thu, to 9.30pm Fri, 10am-5pm Sat; 🐾; 🚊Kent) Beatrice Holst seduces meat-loving Capetonians with her delicious raw and vegan repasts and drinks, including super vitamin-charged juices, a raw lasagne that has foodies reaching for superlatives, and a silky-smooth and super-rich avocado chocolate ganache cake.

★Shortmarket Club
INTERNATIONAL **$$$**

(Map p58; ☑021-447 2874; http://theshortmar ketclub.co.za; 88 Shortmarket St, City Bowl; mains R150-290, 7-course tasting menu R790; ☺12.30-2pm & 7-10pm Mon-Sat; 🐾; 🚊Church/Longmarket) Star chef Luke Dale-Roberts' latest venture hides in plain sight on the street it is named after. It's a gorgeous attic space with a wall of paper butterflies and clubby leather chairs and booths. Dishes include sustainable fish, grass-fed beef (displayed on wheeled trolleys), and plenty of locally grown vegetables. White-jacketed waiters provide a sleek European touch.

Africa Café
AFRICAN **$$$**

(Map p58; ☑021-422 0221; www.africacafe.co.za; 108 Shortmarket St, City Bowl; set banquets R360; ☺6-11pm Mon-Sat; 🚊Church/Longmarket) Touristy, yes, but it's still one of the best places to sample African food. Come with a hearty appetite as the set feast comprises some 15 dishes from across the continent, of which you can eat as much as you like. The talented staff go on song-and-dance walkabout around the tables midmeal.

✗ East City, District Six, Woodstock & Observatory

★Kitchen
DELI **$**

(Map p82; ☑021-462 2201; www.lovethekitchen. co.za; 111 Sir Lowry Rd, Woodstock; sandwiches & salads R60-75; ☺8am-3.30pm Mon-Fri; 🐾; 🚊District Six) Of all the swanky restaurants in town, it was this little charmer that Michelle Obama chose for lunch, proving the ex-First Lady has excellent taste. Tuck into plates of divine salads, rustic sandwiches made with love, and sweet treats with tea served from china teapots.

Ocean Jewels
SEAFOOD **$**

(Map p82; ☑083 582 0829; www.oceanjewels. co.za; Woodstock Exchange, 66 Albert Rd, Woodstock; mains R50-95; ☺shop 8.30am-4.30pm, restaurant 11am-3pm Mon-Fri; 🚊Woodstock) 🐟 Fish straight from Kalk Bay Harbour is served at this seafood cafe and fishmonger that supports the South African Sustainable Seafood Initiative (SASSI). It does a mean tuna burger with wedge fries, and despite being in the industrial-chic Woodstock Exchange the vibe is as relaxed as the seaside, with whitewashed wooden tables and food served on rustic enamel plates.

Lefty's
AMERICAN **$**

(Map p82; ☑021-461 0407; 105 Harrington St, East City; mains R60-95; ☺4-10pm; 🚊Roeland) Appealing to students and lovers of grunge and shabby chic, this artfully crafted dive bar amps up its hipster cred with sticky BBQ pork ribs and Kentucky chicken waffles, alongside brick-oven-baked pizza and beetroot and ginger falafel. There's plenty of craft beers to wash it all down, too.

Food orders finish at 10pm but the bar cranks on until midnight. Upstairs is the noodle bar **Downtown Ramen** (noodles R80; ☺4-10pm Mon-Sat).

★**Pot Luck Club** INTERNATIONAL $$

(Map p82; ☑021-447 0804; www.thepotluckclub. co.za; Silo top fl, Old Biscuit Mill, 373-375 Albert Rd, Woodstock; dishes R60-150; ⊘12.30-2.30pm & 6-10.30pm Mon-Sat, 11am-3pm Sun; ⊡Kent) The sister restaurant to Test Kitchen is a more affordable Luke Dale-Roberts option. Sitting at the top of an old silo, it offers panoramic views of the surrounding area, but the star attraction is the food. Dishes are designed to be shared; we defy you not to order a second plate of the beef with truffle-café-au-lait sauce. Sunday brunch (without/ with bottomless bubbly R450/650) is highly recommended. Book ahead.

Andalousse MOROCCAN $$

(Map p82; ☑021-447 1708; http://andalousse-mo roccan-cuisine.business.site; 148 Victoria Rd, Woodstock; mains R90-150; ⊘noon-9.30pm; ⊡Woodstock) Hiding in plain sight along a sketchy stretch of Victoria Rd is this little gem of a place. Started in 2016 by a group of friends from Morocco, this is the real deal, serving flavourful tagines, couscous, filo-pastry pastilla and a very moreish *harira* soup that, served with a crispy, cheese bread, is a meal in itself.

Ferdinando's PIZZA $$

(☑084 771 0485; www.ferdinandospizza.com; 205 Lower Main Rd, Observatory; pizza R80-110; ⊘Wed-Sat 6-11pm; ⊡Observatory) Bookings are required for this charming 'pizza parla' that's found its natural home in Obs. Diego is the pizza maestro and Kikki the bubbly host and creative artist, while their adorable mutt Ferdinando keeps them all in line. Toppings for their fantastic crispy thin-crust pizzas change with the season.

★**Reverie Social Table** INTERNATIONAL $$$

(☑021-447 3219; www.reverie.capetown; 226a Lower Main Rd, Observatory; lunch R60-70, 5-course dinner with wine R700; ⊘noon-2.30pm Tue-Fri plus 7.30pm-late Wed-Sat; ⊡Salt River) With just one long wooden table seating up to 18, and the charming chef and host Julia Hattingh in charge, it's easy to see why this place is called Social. Book ahead for her five-course dinners where the dishes are matched with a particular region's wines, or sometimes with local gins. Daytimes see regular visits from the artists and creatives in the area, who come to lunch on lovely dishes such as rare beef salad with peach achar or a cauliflower and gorgonzola soup.

★**Test Kitchen** INTERNATIONAL $$$

(Map p82; ☑021-447 2622; www.thetestkitchen. co.za; Shop 104a, Old Biscuit Mill, 375 Albert Rd, Woodstock; menu without/with wine R1650/2250;

⊘6.30-9pm Tue-Sat; ℗; ⊡Kent) Luke Dale-Roberts creates inspired dishes with top-quality local ingredients at his flagship restaurant – generally agreed to be the best in Africa. However, the restaurant is so popular now that securing a reservation here is like winning the gourmet lottery – online bookings open three months ahead and you need to be quick off the mark.

✖ Gardens & Surrounds

Tamboers Winkel INTERNATIONAL $

(Map p62; ☑021-424 0521; www.facebook.com/ Tamboerswinkel; 3 De Lorentz St, Tamboerskloof; mains R50-110; ⊘7.45am-5pm Sun-Tue, to 10pm Wed-Sat; ⊡Welgemeend) A serious contender for the award for best breakfast or lunch spot around Kloof St, this rustic, country-kitchen-style cafe-shop is a charmer. The chicken pie, wrapped in flaky filo pastry, is indeed legendary. They also have free wine tastings for different vineyards on Wednesday from 6pm to 8pm.

Yard INTERNATIONAL $

(Map p62; www.facebook.com/YARDCT; 6 Roodehek St, Gardens; mains R85-99; ⊘7am-10.30pm Mon-Fri, 9am-10.30pm Sat & Sun; ⊡Roodehek) The Dog's Bollocks' blockbuster burgers got this hip grunge spot going a few years ago; they've now expanded to all-day dining, with Mucky Mary's for breakfast fry-ups and sandwiches, and the Bitch's Tits for tacos. Deluxe coffee is also served.

★**The Stack** INTERNATIONAL $$

(Map p62; ☑021-286 0187; www.thestack.co.za; Leinster Hall, 7 Weltevreden St, Gardens; mains R125-190; ⊘8am-10pm; ℗⬛; ⊡Van Riebeeck) Given a stylish makeover to become a brasserie and bar downstairs and a private members club upstairs, old Leinster Hall is a delightful place for a meal. The food is beautifully presented and includes dishes such as tuna Niçoise, springbok loin and a sinful smoked-chocolate mousse.

★**Chefs** INTERNATIONAL $$

(Map p62; ☑021-461 0368; www.chefscapetown. co.za; 81 St Johns Rd, Gardens; mains R150-190; ⊘noon-8.30pm Mon-Fri; ⬛; ⊡Annandale) So called because you can see all the chefs at work in the open kitchen, this is a fab new addition to Cape Town's dining scene with an original concept of 'fast fine dining' that really works. The daily choice of three mains (always including a vegetarian option) look exactly as they do on the touchscreen menu and taste wonderful.

Kyoto Garden Sushi JAPANESE $$

(Map p62; ☑ 021-422 2001; https://kyotogarden sushict.com; 11 Lower Kloof Nek Rd, Tamboerskloof; mains R140-220; ⊙ 5.30-11pm Mon-Sat; ☐ Ludwig's Garden) Beechwood furnishings and subtle lighting lend a calm, Zen-like air to this superior Japanese restaurant with an expert chef turning out sushi and sashimi. Splurge on the sea urchin and try their peppy Asian Mary cocktail.

Maria's GREEK $$

(Map p62; ☑ 021-461 3333; www.facebook.com/MariasGreekCafe; 31 Barnet St, Dunkley Sq, Gardens; mains R75-135; ⊙ 8am-10.30pm Tue-Fri, from 9am Sat; ☑ ☑; ☐ Annandale) There are few places more romantic or relaxing for a meal than Maria's on a warm night, when you can tuck into classic Greek mezze and dishes such as moussaka on rustic tables beneath the trees in the square. There are tons of vegetarian and vegan options on the menu, too.

Cafe Paradiso ITALIAN $$

(Map p62; ☑ 021-422 0403; www.cafeparadiso.co.za; 101 Kloof St, Tamboerskloof; mains R90-205; ⊙ 9am-10pm Mon-Sat, 10am-4pm Sun; ☑) Travellers with kids will love this place: it features a kitchen where little ones can make their own pizza, cookies, cupcakes or gingerbread figures (R55) while the adults dine in a pleasant garden setting.

★**Chef's Table** INTERNATIONAL $$$

(Map p62; ☑ 021-483 1864; www.belmond.com/mountnelsonhotel; Belmond Mount Nelson Hotel, 76 Orange St, Gardens; lunch R545, dinner without/with wine R820/1395; ⊙ noon-3pm & 6.30-9pm; ☑ ☑; ☐ Government Ave) There are several dining options at the Mount Nelson Hotel, but for a real treat book one of the four tables with a front-row view onto the drama and culinary magic unfolding inside the kitchen of this restaurant. The food is superb (vegetarians are catered for) and presented by the chefs who will take you on a behind-the-scenes tour.

★**Aubergine** INTERNATIONAL $$$

(Map p62; ☑ 021-465 0000; www.aubergine.co.za; 39 Barnet St, Gardens; 3-course lunch R465, 3-/4-/5-course dinner R620/780/945; ⊙ noon-2pm Wed-Fri plus 5-10pm Mon-Sat; ☑; ☐ Annandale) German-born Harald Bresselschmidt is one of Cape Town's most consistent chefs, producing creative, hearty dishes served with some of the Cape's best wines, several of which are made specially for the restaurant. Vegetarian menus are available, and the service and ambience are impeccable.

✖ Green Point & Waterfront

The Waterfront has a plethora of restaurants and cafes, many with outdoor decks with great ocean and mountain views.

★**Café Neo** CAFE $

(Map p66; ☑ 021-433 0849; 129 Beach Rd, Mouille Point; mains R85-100; ⊙ 7am-7pm; ☑ ☑; ☐ Three Anchor Bay) This popular seaview cafe has a pleasingly contemporary design and atmosphere that sways from buzzy (at meal times) to laid-back – it's great for a late afternoon drink. Check out the big blackboard menu, featuring several Greek dishes, while sitting at the long communal table inside, or grab a seat on the deck overlooking the red-and-white lighthouse.

Giovanni's Deli World DELI $

(Map p66; ☑ 021-434 6893; 103 Main Rd, Green Point; mains R40-70; ⊙ 7.30am-8.30pm; ☐ Stadium) Its menu bursting with flavourful food, Giovanni's can make any sandwich you fancy, which is ideal for a picnic if you're on your way to the beach. The pavement cafe is a popular hangout.

V&A Food Market FOOD HALL $

(Map p66; www.waterfrontfoodmarket.com; Pump House, Dock Rd, V&A Waterfront; mains from R75; ⊙ 10am-8pm Sun-Thu, until 9pm Fri & Sat; ☑ ☑ ☑; ☐ Nobel Square) There's no need to spend big to eat well (and healthily) at the Waterfront, thanks to this colourful, market-style food court in the old Pump House. Grab a coffee or freshly squeezed juice to go with a wrap or muffin, or opt for a larger meal such as Thai, Indian or Cape Malay curry.

Willoughby & Co SEAFOOD $$

(Map p66; ☑ 021-418 6115; www.willoughbyandco.co.za; Shop 6132, Victoria Wharf, Breakwater Blvd, V&A Waterfront; mains R70-180; ⊙ noon-10.30pm; ☑ ☑; ☐ Waterfront) Commonly acknowledged as one of the better places to eat at the Waterfront – and with long queues to prove it. Huge servings of sushi are the standout from a fish-based menu at this casual restaurant inside the mall.

✖ Atlantic Coast

Sea Point is one of the city's most exciting neighbourhoods for food, with its cosmopolitan mix of restaurants, cafes and shops. Main and Regent Rds yield the most interesting culinary discoveries, with numerous options, including the daily Mojo Market (p103), around the meeting of the two thoroughfares. Camps Bay and Clifton have wonderful

---

LEARNING FROM NATURE

Cape Town Fynbos Experience (Map p58; ☑ 021-426 2157; www.gettothepoint.co.za; Visitor Information Centre, Company's Garden, City Bowl; fynbos tasting/apothecary workshop R450/1254; ☐ Upper Long/Upper Loop) The Cape Floral Kingdom is home to over 9000 different species. Over an hour, Giselle Courtney will introduce you to eight of those species – including honeybush, buchu, snow bush, rooibos, cancer bush and rose pelargonium – in a variety of teas, infusions, cordials and boozy digestifs. The presentation is beautiful and the explanations of the plants' health properties fascinating.

Veld and Sea (☑ 060 509 4288; www.veldandsea.com; Good Hope Gardens Nursery, Plateau Rd, Scarborough; adult/child R550/250; ⊙ 9am-4.30pm) Based at the Good Hope Gardens Nursery (www.goodhopegardensnursery.co.za) of indigenous plants, Veld and Sea runs fynbos and coastal foraging courses. Experienced guides will teach you sustainable techniques to harvest Mother Nature's edibles, including seaweed and mussels from nearby rock pools in Scarborough and the Cape of Good Hope (p69) nature reserve. Lunch is made from whatever you find.

---

seafront cafes for an al fresco bite with beach views among Cape Town's beautiful people. Head to Hout Bay for fish and chips and the weekly Bay Harbour Market (p102).

★ **Jarryds Espresso Bar & Eatery**　CAFE $
(Map p68; ☑ 060 748 0145; www.jarryds.com; 90 Regent Rd, Sea Point; mains R95; ⊙ 7am-4pm) When Jarryd and brother Ariel moved home from Sydney, they brought with them the concept of the come-as-you-are daytime eateries beloved of the Aussies. This has consequently become Sea Point's go-to for breakfasts, which range from coconut granola to eggs Benedict, and lunchtime sticky ribs or falafel bowls. Ingredients are sourced locally, including the coffee from Espresso Lab in Woodstock.

★ **Kleinsky's Delicatessen**　DELI $
(Map p68; ☑ 021-433 2871; www.kleinskys.co.za; 95 Regent Rd, Sea Point; sandwiches R50; ⊙ 8am-4pm Mon-Fri, to 3pm Sat & Sun; ☎; ☐ Tramway) A hip homage to classic New York Jewish delis, Kleinsky's is a great casual daytime option, offering dishes such as toasted bagels with smoked salmon or free-range chicken-liver pâté, chicken soup with matzo balls, and latkes (potato pancakes). The deli serves good coffee, too. Its walls act as a gallery for local artists.

Fish on the Rocks　SEAFOOD $
(☑ 021-790 0001; www.fishontherocks.com; Harbour Rd, Hout Bay; mains R50-92; ⊙ 10am-8pm; ☐ Atlantic Skipper) This Hout Bay institution dishes up some of Cape Town's best fish and chips, in a breezy bayside location with outdoor tables. Watch out for the dive-bombing seagulls if you do eat on the rocks, though.

★ **La Boheme Wine Bar & Bistro**　BISTRO $$
(Map p68; ☑ 021-434 8797; www.laboheme bistro.co.za; 341 Main Rd, Sea Point; mains R100, 2-/3-course dinner menus R150/180; ⊙ noon-11pm Mon-Sat; ☎; ☐ Firmount) Although you can fuel up on delicious tapas and espresso here during the day, La Boheme is best visited in the evening, when candles twinkle on the tables and you can take advantage of its superb-value two- or three-course menus. The dishes mix local ingredients with French and Spanish influences, resulting in a Capetonian take on European gastronomy.

★ **Fuego**　MEXICAN $$
(Map p68; ☑ 021-200 4278; www.fuegotacos.co.za; 77 Regent Rd, Sea Point; tacos R60-75; ⊙ 11am-10pm Tue-Sat, 9am-4pm Sun) Established by a New York chef, this taco joint specialises in Mexico's beloved corn snack, and cocktails. Enjoy fillings such as pulled pork and 'drunken' chicken (cooked in tequila), and tipples including the homemade rooibos-infused tequila. Tacos and drinks are both discounted during happy hour (4pm to 6.30pm).

Massimo's　ITALIAN $$
(☑ 021-790 5648; www.pizzaclub.co.za; Oakhurst Farm Park, Main Rd, Hout Bay; mains R70-135; ⊙ noon-9.30pm; ☎☑☀; ☐ Imizamo Yethu) There's pasta and *spuntini* (tapas-style small plates) on offer, but the wood-fired thin-crust pizzas are Massimo's speciality – and very good they are, too. It's all served up with warmth and humour by the Italian Massimo and his Liverpudlian wife Tracy. There are plenty of vegetarian and vegan options, plus one of the best kids' play areas in Cape Town.

★ **La Mouette**   FRENCH $$$
(Map p68; ☑ 021-433 0856; www.lamouette-res
taurant.co.za; 78 Regent Rd, Sea Point; tapas R90,
3-/5-course menus R395/445, with wine pairings
R720/820; ⊙ 6-10.30pm, plus noon-3pm Sun;
☐ Kei Apple) New takes on the classics (such
as herb gnocchi and smoked pork belly)
and fresh inventions (including kudu loin
with fermented cabbage, BBQ carrot puree
and bolognese sauce) make this a standout
culinary experience. Local art hangs in the
maroon-walled interior and there's a lush
outdoor courtyard with a bubbling fountain.
Tapas are served for Sunday lunch.

Codfather   SEAFOOD $$$
(Map p68; ☑ 021-438 0782; www.codfather.co.za;
37 The Drive, Camps Bay; meals R500; ⊙ noon-
11pm; ☐ Whale Rock) Book ahead to get a table
at this Camps Bay institution, where an
enjoyable meal awaits, whether you spend
it at the sushi bar or dining with a view of
Lion's Head. Order your wine and sides,
then let your knowledgeable waiter talk you
through the glistening choices on the counters, from angelfish and butterfish to hake
and kingklip.

✖ Southern Suburbs

★ **Starlings Cafe**   INTERNATIONAL $
(☑ 021-671 6875; www.starlings.co.za; 94 Belve-
dere Rd, Claremont; mains R60-120; ⊙ 7am-5pm
Mon-Fri, 8am-4pm Sat; ☑; ☐ Claremont) One
of the Southern Suburbs' most charming
dining spots. With its relaxed, arty cottage
and shady garden environment, it's great for
a lazy breakfast or lunch. Excellent coffee,
too. For breakfast, choose the likes of French
toast and poached eggs with parmesan and
basil pesto; lunch dishes include aubergine
bake and Asian yellow chicken curry.

★ **Four & Twenty Cafe & Pantry**   DELI $$
(☑ 021-761 1000; www.fourandtwentycafe.co.za;
23 Wolfe St, Wynberg Village; mains R120; ⊙ 8am-
3.30pm Mon-Sat, from 9am Sun; 🛜; ☐ Wynberg) A
favourite among the Little Chelsea (Wynberg
Village) crowd, this rustic but chic spot serves
a small menu of delicious creations, from
gourmet salads and sandwiches to inventive
dishes such as 'man-sized' herbed fish cakes
and sticky-beef-short-rib-filled steamed buns.
The courtyard, draped with bougainvillea, is
a lovely spot even just for tea and cake.

★ **Rare Grill**   STEAK $$
(☑ 076 460 0423; www.facebook.com/raregrillcpt;
166 2nd Ave, Kenilworth; mains R98-190; ⊙ 6-10pm
Mon-Sat; ☐ Kenilworth) In the unlikely setting
of a scruffy car park next to Kenilworth train
station, this small steakhouse is one of the
best in town, serving the finest wet-aged
South African cuts overlooked by photos
of cows. Book well ahead to experience this
meltingly tender fillet and sirloin bursting
with flavour; order the 500g T-bone if it's on
the specials board.

★ **Greenhouse**   INTERNATIONAL $$$
(☑ 021-795 6226; www.greenhouserestaurant.
co.za; The Cellars-Hohenort Hotel, 93 Brommerslvei
Rd, Constantia; tasting menus R1200; ⊙ 6-9.30pm
Tue-Sat, plus noon-2pm Fri & Sat; ☑) Chef Peter
Tempelhoff's culinary imagination runs riot
in this elegant restaurant that's one of the
Cape's top dining destinations. The finest
local produce and recipes, from Cape Malay
curried octopus to Outeniqua springbok,
feature on the 12-course tasting menu. For
serious foodies only; desserts are served on
petrified Madagascan wood, to remind din-
ers of the circle of life and death.

★ **La Colombe**   FUSION $$$
(☑ 021-794 2390; www.lacolombe.co.za; Silvermist
Estate, Constantia Nek; tasting menus R780-1280,
with wine pairings R1530-2180; ⊙ 12.30-2pm &
7-9.30pm) A veteran of Gordon Ramsay's
kitchen, chef Scot Kirton rustles up skilful
dishes combining French and Asian techniques and flavours, such as quail breast
in coconut and miso, and Karoo lamb-loin
bolognese. The coolly elegant setting and
personable service couldn't be better.

Foxcroft   FUSION $$$
(☑ 021-202 3304; www.foxcroft.co.za; High Constan-
tia Centre, Groot Constantia Rd, Constantia; tasting
menus R435; ⊙ noon-2pm & 6-8.30pm) With a
seasonal menu featuring dishes such as slow-
cooked lamb with nettles and whisky mus-
tard, Foxcroft is a delectable addition to the
Southern Suburbs fine-dining scene. Tackle
the four-course tasting menu in the minimal-
ist dining room or on sunny days take tapas
on the patio. It sits at the edge of the car park,
but the mountain views are marvellous.

✖ Southern Peninsula

Kalk Bay is replete with vibey cafes and good
restaurants, with plenty of options also in
Muizenberg and Simon's Town. Noordhoek
Farm Village (p71) and Imhoff Farm (p71)
are rustic, family-friendly complexes with
cafes, delis and restaurants; weekly food
markets take place in the former as well as
at Blue Bird Garage (p70) and Cape Point
Vineyards (p71).

Empire Cafe CAFE $
(☑ 021-788 1250; www.empirecafe.co.za; 11 York Rd, Muizenberg; mains R80; ☺ 7am-4pm Mon-Thu & Sat, to 9pm Fri, 8am-4pm Sun; ☏; ☒ Muizenberg) The local surfers' favourite hang-out is a great place for a hearty breakfast of Mexican huevos rancheros or poached eggs on butternut rosti, accompanied by Tribe coffee, and lunches ranging from burgers to pastas. Local art enlivens the walls and a dramatic chandelier dangles from the ceiling.

Salty Sea Dog FISH & CHIPS $
(☑ 021-786 1918; saltydog@telkomsa.net; 2 Wharf St, Simon's Town; mains R70; ☺ 8.30am-9pm Mon-Sat, to 4.30pm Sun) The Sea Dog is always packed with Cape Point day-trippers feasting on fish and chips (the hake is excellent), with equally palatable milkshakes to follow. It's casual, licensed and has indoor and outdoor seating. Booking ahead recommended.

★**Foodbarn** INTERNATIONAL $$
(☑ 021-789 1390; www.thefoodbarn.co.za; cnr Main Rd & Village Lane; mains R180; ☺ noon-2.30pm daily, plus 7-9.30pm Tue-Sat; ☏) ✔ Expect rustic, delicious bistro dishes with suggested wine pairings at master chef Franck Dangereux's restaurant in the relaxed surrounds of Noordhoek Farm Village (p71). The separate, book-lined deli-bakery-cafe (mains R35 to R145) and tapas bar (6pm to 9pm Tuesday to Saturday; small plates R50) is just as good, and stocks its freshly baked goodies and other locally sourced food and drinks.

The cafe is open 8am to 4.30pm daily; the deli 8am to 9pm Tuesday to Saturday, and until 5pm Sunday and Monday.

★**Blue Water Cafe** INTERNATIONAL $$
(☑ 021-783 4545; www.imhofffarm.co.za; Kommetjie Rd, Kommetjie; mains R100; ☺ 9am-9pm Wed-Sat, to 4pm Tue, to 6pm Sun; ☒) A lovely place to enjoy breakfast, simple-but-good lunch dishes including pizza, pasta, seafood and gourmet salads, or a craft beer with a sweeping view. The stoep (porch) of this historic property at the heart of Imhoff Farm (p71) looks out over Noordhoek Beach and Chapman's Peak. There's good service, a garden, a jungle gym and the Higgeldy Piggeldy Farmyard next door.

★**Olympia Cafe & Deli** BAKERY $$
(☑ 021-788 6396; http://olympiacafe.co.za; 134 Main Rd, Kalk Bay; mains R90-180; ☺ 7am-9pm; ☒ Kalk Bay) Setting a high standard for relaxed rustic cafes by the sea, Olympia bakes its own breads and pastries. It's great for breakfast, and its Mediterranean-influenced lunch dishes are delicious, too – particularly the heaped bowls of mussels. There's live jazz on some Friday and Saturday nights.

Lighthouse Cafe INTERNATIONAL $$
(☑ 021-786 9000; www.thelighthousecafe.co.za; 90 St Georges St, Simon's Town; mains R70-140; ☺ 8.30am-4pm Sun-Tue, to 10pm Wed-Sat; ☒ Simon's Town) Relaxed, beachcomber-chic cafe, with a menu big on seafood – from mussel-and-chorizo pasta to Jamie Oliver's beer-battered fish and chips. The Lighthouse Cafe also does burgers, pizzas and a mezze platter.

Salt TAPAS $$
(☑ 021-788 3992; 136 Main Rd, Kalk Bay; mains R100; ☺ 7am-9.30pm; ☒ Kalk Bay) Offering a gastronomic take on False Bay cool, Salt serves mains such as wild kudu goulash, but your best bet is to focus on the small plates (R45), which range from wasabi-dusted calamari to bratwurst with homemade kimchi. The seafood dishes use what's available from the harbour, normally yellowfish; order the angelfish ceviche when it's going.

Live Bait SEAFOOD $$
(☑ 021-788 5755; www.livebait.co.za; Kalk Bay Harbour, Kalk Bay; mains R75-180; ☺ noon-11pm; ☒ Kalk Bay) This breezy, Aegean-style fish restaurant, set within arm's reach of the crashing waves and the bustle of Kalk Bay Harbour, is one of the best options around for a relaxed seafood meal. Dishes range from sushi to West Coast mussels, and there's another branch in Muizenberg.

✖ Cape Flats

You don't go to the Cape Flats for fine dining, but there are a few small restaurants where you can try traditional Xhosa cuisine or enjoy a braai (barbecue), often known as *shisa nyama* in the townships. It's best to call ahead to check that restaurants will be open, as they often don't stick to their advertised hours of business.

★**4Roomed eKasi Culture** AFRICAN $$
(☑ 076 157 3177; https://4roomedekasiculture.com; A605 Makabeni Rd, Khayelitsha; 3-course meals R165-230; ☺ noon-3.30pm & 6-8.30pm Fri-Sun; ☏) As gourmet as it gets in Khayelitsha with the lovely Abigail Mbalo, a self-taught cook and former contestant on SA's *MasterChef* TV show, in charge. Expect African food with a twist: delicious wedges of pap (maize porridge) mixed with butternut squash and nutmeg, a rich lamb curry and a red velvet cake made with beetroot.

Drinking & Nightlife

Cape Town didn't become known as the 'Tavern of the Seven Seas' for nothing. There are scores of bars and there's bound to be a club to suit.

City Bowl & Surrounds

★ Beerhouse
BAR

(Map p58; ☑ 021-424 3370; www.beerhouse.co.za; 223 Long St, City Bowl; ⊙ 11am-2am; ☑ Upper Loop/Upper Long) With 99 brands of bottled beer, both local and international, and several more brews on tap, this brightly designed and spacious joint in the heart of Long St will have beer lovers thinking they've died and gone to heaven. The balcony is a great spot from which to watch the world go by.

★ Orphanage
COCKTAIL BAR

(Map p58; ☑ 021-424 2004; www.theorphanage. co.za; cnr Orphange & Bree Sts, City Bowl; ⊙ 4pm-2am Mon-Thu & Sat, to 3am Fri; ☑ Upper Loop/Upper Long) Named after the nearby lane, the mixologists here prepare some tempting artisanal libations with curious names including Knicker-Dropper Glory, Dollymop and Daylight Daisy, using ingredients as varied as peanut butter, kumquat compote and 'goldfish'! It's dark, sophisticated and stylish, with outdoor seating beneath the trees on Bree St.

★ Honest Chocolate Cafe
BAR

(Map p58; ☑ 076 765 8306; http://honestchoc olate.co.za; 64a Wale St, City Bowl; ⊙ 9am-6pm Mon-Fri, to 9pm Sat, to 4pm Sun; ☑ Dorp/Leeuwen) Following a successful crowdfunding campaign, Honest Chocolate launched this homage to fine dark chocolate in liquid, solid, ice-cream and cake form. It's a chocoholic's dream come true, with vegan and gluten-free options.

★ Lady Bonin's Tea Bar
TEAHOUSE

(Map p58; ☑ 021-422 0536; http://ladyboninstea. com; 213 Long St, City Bowl; ⊙ 9am-5pm Mon-Fri, 9.30am-2.30pm Sat; ☑ Upper Loop/Upper Long) A charmingly decorated, relaxing place in which to sample organic and sustainable artisanal teas, fruity and herbal brews, and vegan baked treats. At front is the shop selling all their blends, while the tea room is a through the vine-covered courtyard to the rear.

Openwine
WINE BAR

(Map p58; ☑ 021-422 0800; http://openwineza. co.za; 72 Wale St, City Bowl; ⊙ noon-10pm Mon-Fri, from 5pm Sat; ☑ Church/Longmarket) The motto here is 'wine first, food second', so while there is a short menu, it's the range of 200-plus different wines from across the Western Cape that are the focus. Check out what they have by the glass on their 'drinkable blackboard' and then settle down either inside or outside to enjoy a drop or two.

Publik
WINE BAR

(Map p58; https://publik.co.za; 11D Kloof Nek Rd; ⊙ 4-11pm Mon-Fri, noon-6pm Sat; ☑ Ludwig's Garden) This relaxed, unpretentious bar does a brilliant job at digging out hidden gems of the Cape's wine and gin scenes. Taste drops from sustainably farmed vineyards, interesting and unusual varietals, and rare vintages.

The Vue
LOUNGE

(Map p58; ☑ 021-418 3065; www.the-vue.com; 15th fl, 40 Chiappini St, De Waterkant; ⊙ 6.45am-midnight; ☑ Old Fire Station) Knockout views of the city, mountains and harbour envelop this rooftop bar, restaurant and lounge. Exhibitionists should bring their swimming cossies, as they also have a small plunge pool in which to relax and splash about in. Food ranges from breakfast buffets (R195) to tapas (R50 to R90).

Nitro Brew
CAFE

(Map p58; ☑ 078 455 7955; http://nitrobrewbev. co; 130 Bree St, City Bowl; ⊙ 6.30am-4.30pm Mon-Fri, 8.30am-2pm Sat; 🛜; ☑ Dorp/Leeuwen) This small cafe, stylish in its simplicity, serves nitro coffee – iced coffee poured from a draught tap. The nitrogen lends the appearance of a pint of Guinness and adds a smooth, velvety texture. Also on tap are various flavours of kombucha, all brewed on site. There are salads, sandwiches and a couple of heartier meals on the menu.

Gin Bar
COCKTAIL BAR

(Map p58; www.theginbar.co.za; 64a Wale St, City Bowl; ⊙ 5pm-2am Mon-Thu, 3pm-2am Fri & Sat; ☑ Dorp/Leeuwen) Tucked away in the courtyard of what used to be a mortuary (but set to move to the same building's upper floor), this secret little bar is the perfect place to get a taste for Cape Town's burgeoning craft gin scene. Grab one of the four expertly made house cocktails to sip on the interior patio.

Find the bar by heading through Honest Chocolate Cafe.

La Parada
BAR

(Map p58; ☑ 021-426 0330; http://laparada.co.za; 107 Bree St, City Bowl; ⊙ noon-10pm Mon-Sat, to 9pm Sun; ☑ Church/Longmarket) Cerveza-quaffing and tapas-munching crowds spill out from this authentically Spanish-looking bar all days of the week. They also have branches at Camps Bay and Constantia Nek.

Tjing Tjing
BAR

(Map p58; ☑021-422 4920; www.tjingtjing.co.za; 165 Longmarket St, City Bowl; ⏱4pm-2am Tue-Fri, 6.30pm-2am Sat; 🛜; 🚇Church/Longmarket) This slick rooftop bar is a stylish hangout for cocktails and wine. The barnlike interior has exposed beams, a photo mural of Tokyo and a scarlet lacquered bar. Down one floor is the restaurant Tjing Tjing Tori, serving Japanese-influenced tapas with a contemporary twist (not always successful!).

Waiting Room
BAR

(Map p58; ☑021-422 4536; www.facebook.com/ WaitingRoomCT; 273 Long St, City Bowl; cover Fri & Sat R50-70; ⏱7pm-2am Mon-Sat; 🚇Upper Loop/ Upper Long) Climb the narrow stairway beside the Royale Eatery to find this hip bar decorated in retro furniture with DJs spinning funky tunes. Climb even further and you'll eventually reach the roof deck, the perfect spot from which to admire the city's glittering night lights.

Origin
COFFEE

(Map p58; ☑021-421 1000; http://originroasting. co.za/v3; 28 Hudson St, De Waterkant; ⏱7am-5pm Mon-Fri, 8am-3pm Sat, 8am-2pm Sun; 🛜; 🚇Alfred) Apart from great coffee, the traditional bagels are pretty awesome too. They train baristas here and you can book online for their courses – a three-hour home barista class is R600.

East City, District Six, Woodstock & Observatory

★Espressolab Microroasters
COFFEE

(Map p82; ☑021-447 0845; www.espressolab microroasters.com; Old Biscuit Mill, 375 Albert Rd, Woodstock; ⏱8am-4pm Mon-Fri, to 2pm Sat; 🅿; 🚇Kent) Geek out about coffee at this lab staffed with passionate roasters and baristas. Their beans, which come from single farms, estates and co-ops from around the world, are packaged with tasting notes such as those for fine wines.

★Brewers Co-op
CRAFT BEER

(Map p82; ☑061 533 6699; www.facebook.com/ BrewersCoopCPT; 135 Albert Rd, Woodstock; ⏱1-10pm Mon-Fri) Some 16 craft beer brewers get to showcase their efforts at this co-op bar. You could have a very entertaining time working your way through their various IPAs, and golden and summer ales (lager and pilsner fans note there are few of those types of beer on offer). Happy hour is 4.30pm to 6pm.

★Truth
COFFEE

(Map p82; ☑021-200 0440; www.truthcoffee.com; 36 Buitenkant St, East City; ⏱7am-6pm Mon-Thu, 8am-midnight Fri & Sat, 8am-2pm Sun; 🛜; 🚇Lower Buitenkant) This self-described 'steampunk roastery and coffee bar', with pressed-tin ceilings, naked hanging bulbs and mad-inventor-style metalwork, is an awe-inspiring space in which to mingle with city slickers. Apart from coffee, craft beers, quality baked goods (including fresh croissants) and various sandwiches are on the menu.

★Woodstock Gin Company
DISTILLERY

(Map p82; ☑021-821 8208; www.woodstockginco. co.za; 399 Albert Rd, Woodstock; ⏱9am-6pm Mon-Fri, to 4pm Sat; 🚇Kent) Sample the small-batch premium gins of this company here. Buchu (a local type of fynbos), citrus and lavender flavours feature in the 'wine-base' gin; the 'beer-base' one has a more malty profile, and the High Tea gin offers a rooibos and honeybush aftertaste. They also make their own tonic as a mixer.

Woodstock Brewery
BREWERY

(Map p82; ☑021-447 0953; www.woodstockbrew ery.co.za; 252 Albert Rd, Woodstock; ⏱taproom noon-7pm Tue-Thu, to 8pm Fri, 10am-3pm Sat, restaurant 10am-10pm Mon-Sat; 🚇Kent) In the ground-floor taproom you can do a tasting (R30) of the eight seasonal beers produced here. If you'd prefer to pair the beers with food, there's a large restaurant upstairs serving the usual suspects of burgers, steaks and the like. It's all very slick and professional.

Hidden Leaf
BAR

(Map p82; ☑021-447 4868; www.hiddenleaf.co.za; 77 Roodebloem Rd, Woodstock; ⏱11.30am-11pm Tue-Sat; 🚇Balfour) It's hard to beat the views of Table Mountain and Devil's Peak from the wrap-around, plant-potted balcony of this appealing and very Woodstock restaurant and bar. They do some interesting cocktails and have craft beer and wine as well as a tasty, low-alcohol, homemade pineapple beer.

Gardens & Surrounds

★Yours Truly Cafe & Bar
BAR

(Map p62; ☑021-426 2587; http://yourstrulycafe. co.za; 73 Kloof St, Gardens; ⏱6am-11pm; 🚇Ludwig's Garden) This place is hopping from early morning to late at night. Travellers mingle with hipster locals, who come for the excellent coffee, craft beer, gourmet sandwiches, thin-crust pizzas and the occasional DJ event.

Power & the Glory/Black Ram
BAR

(Map p62; ☑021-422 2108; www.facebook.com/The-Power-and-the-Glory-129092450488495; 13b Kloof Nek Rd, Tamboerskloof; ⊙8am-midnight Mon-Sat; ⊠Ludwig's Garden) The coffee and food (pretzel hot dogs, crusty pies and other artisanal munchies) are good, but it's the smoky, cosy bar that packs the trendsters in, particularly on Thursday to Saturday nights.

Perseverance Tavern
PUB

(Map p62; ☑021-461 2440; http://perseverance tavern.co.za; 83 Buitenkant St, Gardens; ⊙noon-10pm; ⊠Roeland) This convivial, heritage-listed pub, which is affectionately known as 'Persies' and has been around since 1808, was once Cecil Rhodes' local. There are beers on tap and the pub grub is decent.

★Chalk & Cork
WINE BAR

(Map p62; ☑021-422 5822; www.chalkandcork.co.za; 51 Kloof St, Gardens; tapas R25-90, pizza R95-110; ⊙11am-10.30pm Mon-Sat, to 6pm Sun; ⊠Lower Kloof) This wine bar and restaurant has a pleasant courtyard fronting Kloof St. The menu runs the gamut from breakfast dishes to tapas and sharing platters, but you're welcome to drop in just for the wines, plenty of which are served by the glass and sourced from some of the region's best estates.

Green Point & Waterfront

★Bascule
BAR

(Map p66; ☑021-410 7082; www.basculebar.com; Cape Grace Hotel, West Quay Rd, V&A Waterfront; ⊙9am-1am; ⊠Nobel Square) Over 480 varieties of whisky are served at the Grace's sophisticated, nautical-themed bar, with a few slugs of the 50-year-old Glenfiddich still available (at just R18,000 a tot). Outdoor tables facing the marina are a superb spot for drinks and tasty tapas.

★Shift
COFFEE

(Map p66; ☑021-433 2450; 47 Main Rd, Green Point; ⊙6.30am-6pm Mon-Sat, 7am-3pm Sun; ☎; ⊠Upper Portswood) Sporting an industrial-chic look with a cosy library corner inside and sheltered, spacious front courtyard outside, this is one of the area's most inviting cafes. Owner Luigi Vigliotti works hard to please customers, and he's come up with a few intriguing signature brews, including Hashtag, which blends espresso with vanilla gelato and Oreo cookies.

★Tobago's Bar & Terrace
COCKTAIL BAR

(Map p66; ☑021-441 3414; www.radissonblu.com/en/hotel-capetown/bars; Radisson Blu Hotel Waterfront, Beach Rd, Granger Bay; ⊙6.30am-10.30pm; ☑; ⊠Granger Bay) Walk through the hotel to the spacious deck bar and restaurant with a prime Table Bay position. It's a great place to enjoy a sunset cocktail; you can take a stroll along the breakwater afterwards.

★Life Grand Cafe
CAFE

(Map p66; ☑021-205 1902; www.life.za.com/home/lifegrandcafe; Old Pierhead, V&A Waterfront; ⊙7.30am-11pm; ☑; ⊠Nobel Square) The food is so-so, but the drinks are fine at this classy all-day cafe serving everything from breakfast coffee and croissants to nightcaps. It's a lovely spot to rest your feet and have some refreshments with a grandstand view onto the buzz of the Waterfront.

Mitchell's Scottish Ale House
PUB

(Map p66; ☑021-418 5074; www.mitchells-alehouse.com; cnr East Pier & Dock Rd, V&A Waterfront; ⊙10am-2am; ☑; ⊠Nobel Square) Check all airs and graces at the door of South Africa's oldest microbrewery (established in 1983 in Knysna), which serves a variety of freshly brewed ales and good-value meals. The 7% proof Old Wobbly packs an alcoholic punch.

Shimmy Beach Club
CLUB

(Map p66; ☑021-200 7778; www.shimmybeach club.com; 12 South Arm Rd, V&A Waterfront; cover charge for events R250; ⊙11am-4am Mon-Sat, until 2am Sun; ⊠Waterfront Silo) Drive past the smelly fish-processing factories to discover this glitzy mega-club and restaurant, arranged around a small, fake beach with a glass-sided pool. There are pool parties with scantily clad dancers shimmying to grooves by top DJs, including the electro-jazz group Goldfish, who has a summer residency here (bookings advised).

Atlantic Coast

Every visitor to Cape Town should experience at least one seafront cocktail or smoothie in chi-chi Camps Bay or Clifton. Bay Harbour Market (p102) is atmospheric on Friday nights and weekends, as is Sea Point's Mojo Market (p103).

★Leopard Bar
COCKTAIL BAR

(☑021-437 9000; www.12apostleshotel.com; Twelve Apostles Hotel & Spa, Victoria Rd, Oudekraal; ⊙7am-2am; ☎; ⊠Oudekraal) With a dress-circle view over the Atlantic, the Twelve Apostles Hotel's bar is an ideal spot to escape the hoi polloi of nearby Camps Bay for a classy cocktail or – better yet – a deliciously decadent afternoon tea (R295; served from 10am to 4pm).

★ **Bungalow** BAR

(Map p68; ☑021-438 2018; www.thebungalow. co.za; Glen Country Club, 3 Victoria Rd, Clifton; ☺noon-2am; 🚗 Maiden's Cove) This Euro-chic restaurant and lounge bar is a great place for a long lunch, languorous-afternoon craft beers or sunset mojitos and martinis, overlooked by the Twelve Apostles range. Crash on a daybed under a billowing white awning, or dangle your feet in the tiny barside splash pool. DJs create a more clubby atmosphere by night. Bookings are advised.

★ **Dunes** BAR

(☑021-790 1876; www.dunesrestaurant.co.za; 1 Beach Rd, Hout Bay; ☺9am-11pm; 🚻; 🚗Hout Bay) You can hardly get closer to the beach than this – in fact, the front courtyard *is* the beach. Up on the terrace or from inside the restaurant-bar, you'll get a great view of Hout Bay, along with some decent sushi, nibbles and pub grub ranging from pizza to seafood. There's also a safe play area for kids.

🍸 Southern Suburbs

★ **Banana Jam** CRAFT BEER

(☑021-674 0186; www.bananajamcafe.co.za; 157 2nd Ave, Harfield Village, Kenilworth; ☺11am-11pm Tue-Sat, to 10pm Sun; 🚗; 🚗Kenilworth) Real beer lovers rejoice – this convivial Caribbean restaurant and bar is like manna from heaven, with over 30 beers on draught (including Banana Jam's own brews) and bottled ales from all the top local microbrewers, including Jack Black, Devil's Peak and CBC.

★ **Forester's Arms** PUB

(☑021-689 5949; www.forries.co.za; 52 Newlands Ave, Newlands; ☺11am-11pm Mon-Sat, 9am-10pm Sun; 🚻; 🚗Newlands) 'Forries' has been around for well over 150 years. The English-style pub offers a convivial atmosphere in which to enjoy a dozen draught beers, good pub meals (including wood-fired pizzas), and a pleasant beer garden with a play area for the kids.

🍸 Southern Peninsula

★ **Tiger's Milk** BAR

(☑021-788 1860; www.tigersmilk.co.za; cnr Beach & Sidmouth Rds, Muizenberg; ☺11am-2am; 🚗; 🚗Muizenberg) There's a panoramic view of Muizenberg Beach through the floor-to-ceiling window of this hangar-like bar and restaurant. It's open all day for food (good pizza and steaks; mains R110), but is more of a sundowner venue and nightspot with its long bar, stools and exposed-brick walls hung with quirky decor, including a motorbike.

Beach Road Bar BAR

(☑021-789 1783; cnr Beach Rd & Pine St, Noordhoek; ☺noon-11pm Tue-Sun, from 4.30pm Mon) If you're down this way – say, after a drive along Chapman's Peak Dr (p78) – the bar above the Red Herring restaurant is a pleasant place for a craft beer and a pizza. The sunset deck has excellent beach views, there's occasional live music and the bar serves beers made on-site by Aegir Project Brewery (www.aegirprojectbrewery.com).

☆ Entertainment

Rappers and comedians performing in a mix of Afrikaans and English; a cappella township choirs and buskers at the Waterfront; theatre on the streets and in old churches; intimate performances in suburban living rooms – the Mother City dazzles with a diverse and creative range of entertainment, with live music a particular highlight.

Find book readings at Book Lounge (p101) and Kalk Bay Books (☑021-788 2266; www. kalkbaybooks.co.za; 124 Main Rd, Kalk Bay; ☺9am-5pm; 🚗Kalk Bay), and poetry slams occasionally at A Touch of Madness (p79).

☆ City Bowl & Surrounds

Artscape THEATRE

(☑021-410 9800; www.artscape.co.za; 1-10 DF Malan St, Foreshore; 🅿; 🚗Civic Centre) Consisting of three different-sized auditoriums, this behemoth is the city's main arts complex. Theatre, classical music, ballet, opera and cabaret shows – Artscape offers it all. The desolate nature of the area means it's not recommended to walk around here at night; there's plenty of secure parking.

Cape Town International Convention Centre CONCERT VENUE

(CTICC; Map p58; ☑021-410 5000; www.cticc. co.za; 1 Lower Long St, Foreshore; 🅿; 🚗Convention Centre) Since opening in 2003, the CTICC has barely paused for breath, packing in a busy annual programme of musical performances, exhibitions, conferences and other events, such as the Cape Town International Jazz Festival and Design Indaba.

★ **Alexander Bar & Café** THEATRE

(Map p58; ☑021-300 1088; www.alexanderbar. co.za; 76 Strand St, City Bowl; ☺bar 11am-1am Mon-Sat; 🚗Strand) Playwright Nicholas Spagnoletti and software engineer Edward van Kuik are the driving duo behind this fun, eccentric space in a gorgeous heritage building. Downstairs is a very popular LGBT-friendly bar, while upstairs is a studio theatre with a

ℹ ENTERTAINMENT

Tickets

Computicket (http://online.computicket.com/web)

Webtickets (www.webtickets.co.za)

Quicket (www.quicket.co.za)

Information

Cape Town Magazine (www.capetownmagazine.co.za)

Inside Guide (https://insideguide.co.za)

IOL (www.iol.co.za/entertainment/whats-on/cape-town)

The Next 48 Hours (http://48hours.co.za)

Cinema

Labia (Map p62; ☑ 021-424 5927; www.thelabia.co.za; 68 Orange St, Gardens; tickets R50; 🚋 Michaelis) Retro-cool cinema in Gardens specialising in art-house titles.

Isivivana Centre (☑ 021-361 0181; https://isivivanacentre.org.za; 8 Mzala St, Khayelitsha; 🚋 Khayelitsha) Free screenings of Africa-themed and family-oriented movies at the centre's Bertha Movie House.

Galileo Open Air Cinema From November to April at the Waterfront, Kirstenbosch and Hillcrest Estate in Durbanville.

Film & Music Festivals

Encounters (www.encounters.co.za) Documentary films in June.

Shnit (http://new.shnit.org) Short film fest in October.

Cape Town Electronic Music Festival (www.ctemf.com) Three-day event in February.

Rocking the Daisies (www.rockingthedaisies.com) Three-day music fest in October.

packed programme of plays, musical performances and other speaking events.

★ Café Roux   LIVE MUSIC
(Map p58; ☑ 061 339 4438; www.caferouxsessions.co.za; 74 Shortmarket St, City Bowl; tickets R100-150; ⏱ 6pm-midnight; 🚋 Church/Longmarket) The City Bowl has been crying out for a quality live-music venue for a while and it's taken Café Roux (which already runs a successful operation in Noordhoek) to provide it. Most nights a different singer or band plays here, and with tiered seating (and all seats bookable online) you're guaranteed to get a good view.

Piano Bar   LIVE MUSIC
(Map p58; ☑ http://thepianobar.co.za; 47 Napier St, De Waterkant; cover Fri & Sat R50; ⏱ 12.30pm-midnight Mon-Sat, to 11pm Sun; 🚋 Alfred) Proving a hit with one and all in the heart of De Waterkant is this slick music revue bar and restaurant with a nightly line-up of different performers who hit the piano keys around 8pm. Expect top-class pianists, jazz singers and players.

Crypt Jazz Restaurant   JAZZ
(Map p58; ☑ 079 683 4658; www.thecryptjazz.com; 1 Wale St, City Bowl; cover R100; ⏱ 7pm-midnight Tue-Sat; 🚋 Groote Kerk) Occupying part of the St George's Cathedral's vaulted stone crypt, this restaurant, which serves a continent-hopping menu of dishes, is best visited for its live jazz. Concerts start at around 8pm and last most of the evening. Some very accomplished performers take to the stage here; for some concerts booking ahead is advisable.

OnPointe Dance Studios   DANCE
(Map p58; ☑ 061 198 6355, 021-422 3368; www.onpointedancestudio.wordpress.com; 5th fl, 112 Loop St, City Bowl; tickets R100, classes from R150; 🚋; 🚋 Dorp/Leeuwen) Theo Ndindwa and Tanya Arshamian use dance to change the lives of kids in the townships. On the first Thursday of the month this studio, where classes are held, hosts Art in the City with iKapa Dance, a wonderful chance to meet up with a host of local dance companies and watch them perform in a very relaxed environment.

Marco's African Place   LIVE MUSIC
(Map p58; ☑021-423 5412; www.marcosafrican place.co.za; 15 Rose Lane, Bo-Kaap; ⏱noon-midnight Tue-Fri, 3pm-midnight Sat-Mon; 🚇Old Fire Station) Marco Radebe's highly popular African restaurant (mains R130 to R170) offers top-class entertainment from a range of singers, dancers and bands each night. Musical styles including the local marimba, Afro-jazz, traditional Xhosa beats and the Congolese kwasa-kwasa. Alongside enjoy game-meat platters, Xhosa dishes including 'smilies' (sheep heads) and home-brewed African beer.

☆ East City, District Six, Woodstock & Salt River

Fugard Theatre   THEATRE
(Map p82; ☑021-461 4554; www.thefugard.com; Caledon St, District Six; 🚇Lower Buitenkant) Named in honour of Athol Fugard, South Africa's best-known living playwright, this very impressive arts centre was created from the former Congregational Church Hall. There are two stages, the largest theatre also doubling up as a 'bioscope' – a fancy word for a digital cinema where top international dance and opera performances are screened.

☆ Green Point & Waterfront

The Waterfront's **Market Square Amphitheatre** (Map p66; www.waterfront.co.za/events/overview; off Dock Rd, V&A Waterfront; 🚇Nobel Square) is the focus for much free entertainment, including buskers and various musical and dance acts. Comedy fans can check out the acts at the long-running **Cape Town Comedy Club** (Map p66; ☑021-418 8880; www.capetowncomedy.com; Pump House, Dock Rd, V&A

Waterfront; tickets from R60; ⏱6-10pm, shows 8.30pm; 🚇Nobel Square).

Mainstream movies are screened at two multiplexes in Victoria Wharf (p103). From November to April, **Galileo Open Air Cinema** (Map p66; www.thegalileo.co.za/waterfront.html; Croquet Lawn, off Portswood Rd, V&A Waterfront; tickets R100, blanket/chair hire R10/20; ⏱Nov-Apr; 🚇Nobel Square) screens classic movies on Thursday nights on the croquet lawn next to the **Dock House** (Map p66; ☑021-421 9334; www.dockhouse.co.za; Portswood Close, Portswood Ridge, V&A Waterfront; d/ste incl breakfast R8000/10,000; 🅿❄@🛜🏊; 🚇Nobel Square).

☆ Atlantic Suburbs

Bay Harbour Market (p102) and **Ta Da!** (☑021-790 8132; its.ta.da.4@gmail.com; 37 Victoria Rd; ⏱8am-5pm; 🚻; 🚇Lower Victoria) in Hout Bay host live music, as do Sea Point's Mojo Market (p103) and **Dizzy's** (Map p68; ☑021-438 2686; www.dizzys.co.za; 41 The Drive; ⏱noon-2am; 🚇Whale Rock) in Camps Bay, while the Harvey's (p85) Sunday jazz brunch is a Sea Point institution.

★**Theatre on the Bay**   THEATRE
(Map p68; ☑021-438 3301; www.theatreonthebay.co.za; 1 Link St, Camps Bay; 🚇Lower Camps Bay) A great venue for an evening of lighthearted theatrical entertainment, offering everything from comic plays to classic musicals.

Studio 7 Sessions   LIVE MUSIC
(Map p68; www.studio7sessions.com; 213 High Level Rd, Sea Point; 🚇Rhine) These bimonthly live gigs, going since 2010, are hosted in unique, unusual venues throughout the city and surrounds. They mix new, up-and-coming artists with inspiring keynote speakers

SPORTS GROUNDS

Newlands Cricket Ground (☑021-657 2003; www.newlandscricket.com; 146 Campground Rd, Newlands; 🚆Newlands) Newlands would be a shoo-in for the title of the world's prettiest cricket ground – if it weren't for a nearby mega-brewery messing up the view towards the back of Table Mountain. With room for 25,000, the ground is used for all international matches. Tickets cost around R60 for local matches and up to R250 for internationals.

Newlands Rugby Stadium (☑021-659 4600; www.wprugby.com; Boundary Rd, Newlands; 🚆Newlands) This hallowed ground of South African rugby is home to the Stormers (www.thestormers.com). Provincial, international and Super Rugby matches are played here.

Cape Town Stadium (Map p66; ☑021-417 0120; www.capetown.gov.za/capetownstadium/home; Granger Bay Blvd, Green Point; tours adult/child R45/17; ⏱tours 10am, noon & 2pm Tue-Sat; 🅿; 🚇Stadium) Shaped like a giant traditional African hat and wrapped with a Teflon-mesh membrane designed to catch and reflect natural light, this R4.5-billion stadium, built for the 2010 World Cup, is Cape Town's most striking piece of contemporary architecture. The hour-long tours will take you behind the scenes into the VIP and press boxes and the teams' dressing rooms.

from various fields to appeal to both mind and soul. Venues include the relaxed and intimate surroundings of founder Patrick Craig's Sea Point living room, as well as libraries, rooftops, gardens and beaches.

☆ Southern Suburbs

★ Baxter Theatre Centre   THEATRE
(☑ 021-685 7880; www.baxter.co.za; Main Rd, Rondebosch; tickets R100-380; ☒ Rosebank) Since the 1970s the Baxter has been the focus of Capetonian theatre. There are three main venues at the centre – a 674-seat theatre, a concert hall and a studio – and between them they cover everything from comedy and kids' shows to classical music and African dance spectaculars.

☆ Southern Peninsula

This being a creative part of the Cape, many bars and restaurants offer live music on summer weekends.

Kalk Bay Theatre   THEATRE
(☑ 021-788 7257; www.kalkbaytheatre.co.za; 52 Main Rd, Kalk Bay; ☒ Kalk Bay) One of the city's intimate dinner-and-a-show venues, this theatre is housed in an atmospheric converted church. You don't need to eat here to see the productions, which are fun showcases of local talent and often reasonably short, and after a performance you can join the cast at the upstairs bar.

🔒 Shopping

Bring an empty suitcase, because chances are you'll be leaving Cape Town laden with booty.

🔒 City Bowl & Surrounds

★ Africa Nova   ARTS & CRAFTS
(Map p58; ☑ 021-425 5123; www.africanova.co.za; Cape Quarter, 72 Waterkant St, De Waterkant; ☒ 10am-5.30pm; ☒ Alfred) One of the most stylish and desirable collections of tribal and contemporary African textiles, arts and crafts. You'll find potato-print fabrics made by women in Hout Bay, Ronel Jordaan's handmade felt rock cushions (which look like giant pebbles) and a wonderful range of high-end ceramics and jewellery.

★ Monkeybiz   ARTS & CRAFTS
(Map p58; ☑ 021-426 0145; www.monkeybiz.co.za; 61 Wale St, Bo-Kaap; ☒ 9am-5pm Mon-Thu, to 4pm Fri, 9.30am-1pm Sat; ☒ Church/Longmarket) Colourful beadwork crafts, made by local township

women, are Monkeybiz's super-successful stock in trade – you'll find their products around the world, but the largest selection – in myriad colour combinations – is here. Profits are reinvested back into community services such as soup kitchens and a burial fund for artists and their families.

★ Stable   DESIGN
(Map p58; ☑ 021-426 5922; www.stable.org.za; 65 Loop St, City Bowl; ☒ 9am-5pm Mon-Fri, 10am-1pm Sat; ☒ Strand) A one-stop shop for a variety of South African designers' products, including very portable items such as clothes hooks, fridge magnets, skinny leather ties and jewellery. If you've a house to decorate, there are bigger pieces of furniture, too, such as chairs and sofas, as well as wall art.

Chandler House   ARTS & CRAFTS
(Map p58; ☑ 021-424 4810; www.chandlerhouse. co.za; 53 Church St, City Bowl; ☒ 10am-5pm Tue-Fri, to 2pm Sat; ☒ Church/Longmarket) Michael Chandler showcases his quirky ceramic homewares and decorative pieces in this well-edited collection of imaginative local arts and crafts, which includes cushions, prints and playful design pieces. He also has an expert eye for art as showcased on the walls and in a small gallery section.

Rialheim   ARTS & CRAFTS
(Map p58; ☑ 021-422 2928; www.rialheim.co.za; 117 Long St, City Bowl; ☒ 9am-5pm Mon-Fri, to 3pm Sat; ☒ Church/Longmarket) Locally sourced clay is used in the Robertson-based factory to make these stylish, mainly monochrome ceramics that range from plates and mugs to decorative items such as dogs and rams' heads. Upstairs check out the Walter Battiss Gallery (https://walterbattiss.co.za) – they have the rights to reproduce images of this important South African artist.

Pan African Market   ARTS & CRAFTS
(Map p58; 76 Long St, City Bowl; ☒ 8.30am-5.30pm Mon-Sat; ☒ Church/Longmarket) A microcosm of the continent, packed into three floors, with a bewildering range of arts and crafts (which you should certainly bargain over). On the top floor you'll find an art gallery and Chimurenga (www.chimurenga.co.za), publishers of the pan-African newspaper *Chronic* and other publications.

Clarke's Bookshop   BOOKS
(Map p58; ☑ 021-423 5739; www.clarkesbooks.co.za; 199 Long St, City Bowl; ☒ 9am-5pm Mon-Fri, 9.30am-1pm Sat; ☒ Dorp/Leeuwen) Take your time leafing through the best range of books on South Africa and the continent, with a great second-

hand section upstairs. If you can't find what you're looking for here, it's unlikely to be in any of the other bookshops around town (although there's no harm in browsing).

East City, District Six, Woodstock & Salt River

If you're looking for a locally created artwork, design piece or interesting fashion then this is the area to zone in on. Pick up a copy of the free *Woodstock Design District Map* or go online to http://woodstock designdistrict.co.za.

★**Old Biscuit Mill**   SHOPPING CENTRE
(Map p82; ☑021-447 8194; www.theoldbiscuitmill. co.za; 373-375 Albert Rd, Woodstock; ⊙10am-4pm Mon-Fri, 9am-2pm Sat; ⬚Kent) This former biscuit factory houses an ace collection of arts, craft, fashion and design shops, as well as places to eat and drink.

★**Book Lounge**   BOOKS
(Map p82; ☑021-462 2425; www.booklounge. co.za; 71 Roeland St, East City; ⊙9.30am-7.30pm Mon-Fri, 8.30am-6pm Sat, 10am-4pm Sun; ⬚Roeland) The hub of Cape Town's literary scene, thanks to its great selection of titles, comfy chairs, simple cafe and busy program of events. There are up to three talks or book launches a week, generally with free drinks and nibbles, and readings for kids on the weekend.

★**Woodstock Exchange**   SHOPPING CENTRE
(Map p82; ☑021-486 5999; www.woodstockex-change.co.za; 66 Albert Rd, Woodstock; ⊙8am-5pm Mon-Fri, to 2pm Sat; ⬚Woodstock) As well

as good places to eat and drink, there's a fair amount of original retail at the Exchange, including the boutique Kingdom, which mixes fashion and accessories with interior design, and Ballo, which makes trendy eyewear from a combo of recycled paper and off-cut timber.

Streetwires   ARTS & CRAFTS
(Map p82; www.streetwires.co.za; Maxton Centre, 354 Albert Rd, Woodstock; ⊙8am-5pm Mon-Fri, 9am-2pm Sat; ⬚Salt River) Their motto is 'anything you can dream up in wire we will build'. And if you visit this social project, designed to create sustainable employment, and see the wire sculptors at work, you'll see what that means! They stock an amazing range, including working radios and chandeliers, life-sized animals and artier products such as the Nguni Cow range.

Gardens & Surrounds

Kloof St is the main shopping strip, offering a good range of boutiques and interior design stores; it's anchored near its base by the **Lifestyles on Kloof** (Map p62; www.life styleonkloof.co.za; 50 Kloof St, Gardens; ⊙9am-7pm Mon-Fri, to 5pm Sat, 10am-3pm Sun; ⬚Lower Kloof) mall. Another handy shopping mall is **Gardens Centre** (Map p62; ☑021-465 1842; www.gardensshoppingcentre.co.za; cnr Mill & Buitenkant Sts, Gardens; ⊙9am-7pm Mon-Fri, to 5pm Sat, to 2pm Sun; ⬚Gardens). There's also a couple of weekly markets, of which **City Bowl Market** (Map p62; ☑083 676 6104; www.citybowlmarket.co.za; 14 Hope St, Gardens; ⊙4.30pm-8.30pm Thu; ⬚Roodehek) is the longest established and liveliest.

WORTH A TRIP

WOODSTOCK & OBSERVATORY GALLERIES

A good reason for heading to Woodstock and Observatory is to check out the many commercial galleries there. All put on interesting shows and there's no pressure to buy. The following are a few of the best:

Goodman Gallery Cape (Map p82; ☑021-462 7573; www.goodman-gallery.com; 3rd fl, Fairweather House, 176 Sir Lowry Rd, Woodstock; ⊙9.30am-5.30pm Tue-Fri, to 4pm Sat; ⬚District Six)

Stevenson (Map p82; ☑021-462 1500; www.stevenson.info; 160 Sir Lowry Rd, Woodstock; ⊙9am-5pm Mon-Fri, 10am-1pm Sat; ⬚District Six)

AHEM! Art Collective (☑071 585 3423; www.ahemartcollective.com; 77 Lower Main Rd, Observatory; ⊙9am-5pm; ⬚Observatory)

Art It Is (Map p82; ☑021-447 9179; http://artitis.co.za; 76 Albert Rd, Woodstock; ⊙10am-5pm Mon-Fri, 10am-3pm Sat; ⬚Woodstock)

South African Print Gallery (Map p82; ☑021-462 6851; http://printgallery.co.za; 109 Sir Lowry Rd, Woodstock; ⊙9.30am-4pm Tue-Fri, 10am-1pm Sat; ⬚District Six)

WEEKEND MARKETS

Neighbourgoods Market (Map p82; www.neighbourgoodsmarket.co.za; Old Biscuit Mill, 373-375 Albert Rd, Woodstock; ⊙9am-3pm Sat; 🚊Kent) This is the artisanal goods markets that kickstarted the craze for similar markets across the Cape – and it's still one of the best. Food and drinks are gathered in the main area where you can pick up groceries and gourmet goodies or just graze, while the separate Designergoods area hosts a must-buy selection of local fashions and accessories. Come early, unless you enjoy jostling with crowds.

Bay Harbour Market (www.bayharbour.co.za; 31 Harbour Rd, Hout Bay; ⊙5-9pm Fri, 9.30am-4pm Sat & Sun; 🚊Atlantic Skipper) This imaginatively designed indoor market at the far end of Hout Bay Harbour is one of Cape Town's best. There's a good range of stalls selling items from clothes to craftwork, as well as very tempting food and drink. Live music gives the former fish factory a relaxed, party-like atmosphere. In the adjoining **Harvest Centre** are the **Urban Brewing Co** (http://urbanbrewery.co.za) craft brewery, **Ethno Bongo** (☑021-791 0757; www.andbanana.com; ⊙10am-5.30pm Mon-Fri, to 4pm Sat & Sun), and metalwork and wooodwork studios and shops.

OZCF Market Day (Map p66; www.ozcf.co.za/market-day; Granger Bay Rd, Granger Bay, V&A Waterfront; ⊙9am-2pm Sat; 🚊Upper Orange) Produce grown on the Oranjezicht City Farm (p63) and other local farms is sold every Saturday here alongside many other edible and souvenir products. It's a great event – one of the best of its kind in Cape Town – with plenty of food and drink stalls for brunching, a DJ and a community-coming-together atmosphere.

Earth Fair Food Market (☑071 121 7367; www.earthfairmarket.co.za; South Palms Shopping Centre, 333 Main Road, Tokai; mains R60-100; ⊙3-8.30pm Wed, 9am-2pm Sat; 🚼; 🚊Steenberg) Popular for dinner and a beer on Wednesday and brunch and a beer on Saturday, this community market sells free-range, organic and ethically farmed food, with live music often adding to the fun. It also takes place on St George's Mall in town, from 11am to 3pm on Thursday.

Milnerton Flea Market (www.milnertonfleamarket.co.za; Marine Dr (R27), Paarden Eiland; ⊙8am-2pm Sat, to 3pm Sun; 🚊Zoarvlei) Hunt for vintage pieces and collectables among the junk and cheap goods at this car-boot sale that fills up a car park on the edge of Table Bay. The views of Table Mountain are matched by the interesting characters you'll encounter here. Established in Milnerton, the market now takes place in neighbouring Paarden Eiland.

Hout Bay Lions Craft Market (Baviaanskloof Rd, Hout Bay; ⊙10am-3pm Sun; 🚊Military) Browsing the stalls at this little village-green market, a fundraiser for the Lions Club of Hout Bay social-upliftment organisation, is a lovely way to while away an hour or so on a Sunday. You'll find crafts made by locals, including impressive beadwork, colourfully printed cloths and cute guinea-fowls crafted from pine cones.

Erf 81 Market (Map p62; www.facebook.com/tyisanabanye; cnr Leeuwenvoet & Military Rd, Tamboerskloof; ⊙10am-2pm Sun; 🚊Lower Kloof) This small market is one of the projects of a worthy, nonprofit urban agriculture scheme that exists without a lease on prime city land. Food security activists Tyisa Nabanye (Xhosa for 'feed the others') moved from the townships into this former military site, cleaned up a shed and planted a market garden with a spectacular view of Table Mountain. Follow the road uphill to find the market and garden.

★ **Ashanti** HOMEWARES
(Map p62; ☑021-461 0367; www.ashantidesign. com; 77 Kloof St, Gardens; ⊙8am-5pm Mon-Fri, 10am-3pm Sat; 🚊District Six) Baskets, mats, lampshades, pillows, bags and cushions are among the many rainbow-coloured products on sale at this great artisan design shop that creates its own fabric from T-shirt offcuts that would otherwise go to landfill. No two pieces are alike and you can also buy their fabrics by the metre.

★ **Handmade by Me** HOMEWARES
(Map p62; www.handmadebyme.co.za; 21 De Lorentz St, Tamboerskloof; ⊙11am-5pm Tue-Fri, 9.30am-1pm Sat; 🚊Welgemeend) Sera Holland is the artist responsible for the colourful, floral and abstract designs on the fabric items – cushion covers, napkins, table runners etc – and other products at this cute shop that also sells plants.

Wine Concepts
WINE

(Map p62; ✆021-426 4401; http://wineconcepts.
co.za; Lifestyles on Kloof, 50 Kloof St, Gardens;
⊗9am-7pm Mon-Fri, to 5pm Sat; 🚇Lower Kloof)
You'll get expert advice on a broad range of
local wines at this small but appealing cellar.
Free wine tastings are held on Friday evening
and Saturday from noon to 5pm.

Mabu Vinyl
BOOKS, MUSIC

(Map p62; ✆021-423 7635; www.mabuvinyl.co.za;
2 Rheede St, Gardens; ⊗9am-8pm Mon-Sat, 11am-
3pm Sun; 🚇Lower Kloof) New and secondhand
LPs, CDs, DVDs, books and comics are
bought, sold and traded at this reputable
shop that features in the award-winning
documentary *Searching For Sugarman*.
Ask here about independently released CDs
by local artists.

🏠 Green Point & Waterfront

★ Watershed
SHOPPING CENTRE

(Map p66; www.waterfront.co.za/shop/watershed;
Dock Rd, V&A Waterfront; ⊗10am-6pm; 🚇Nobel
Square) One of the best places to shop for souvenirs in Cape Town, this inventively designed
retail market gathers together over 150 ten-
ants representing the cream of Capetonian
and South African producers of fashion, arts,
crafts and design – there's something here for
every pocket. On the upper level is an exhibition space, and a wellness centre offering
holistic products and massages.

★ Guild
ARTS & CRAFTS

(Map p66; ✆021-461 2856; www.southernguild.
co.za; Shop 5b, Silo 5, South Arm Rd, V&A Waterfront; ⊗9am-6pm Mon-Fri, 10am-2pm Sat; 🚇Wa-
terfront Silo) Trevyn and Julian McGowan
have made a business out of cherry-picking
the cream of the South African design community and promoting it to the world in annual collections. Opened in 2017, this is their
permanent showcase, so the go-to location
for spotting emerging talent and to buy incredible, distinctive pieces.

★ Out of this World
ARTS & CRAFTS

(Map p66; ✆021-434 3540; www.outofthisworld.
co.za; 1 Braemar Rd, Green Point; ⊗8.30am-4.30pm
Mon-Fri) Buddha statues meet Nigerian tribal crowns at this interior design emporium
piled high with treasures from across Africa
and Asia. Here also, in a courtyard garden, is
the pleasant **Stranger's Club** cafe, which is
good for a quiet coffee and snack.

Victoria Wharf
SHOPPING CENTRE

(Map p66; ✆021-408 7500; www.waterfront.co.za;
Breakwater Blvd, V&A Waterfront; ⊗9am-9pm;
🚇Breakwater) All the big names of South African retail (including Woolworths, CNA, Pick
n Pay, Exclusive Books and Musica), as well as
international luxury brands, are represented
at this mall – one of Cape Town's best.

Everard Read
ART

(Map p66; ✆021-418 4527; www.everard-read-cape
town.co.za; 3 Portswood Rd, V&A Waterfront; ⊗9am-
6pm Mon-Fri, to 4pm Sat; 🚇Nobel Square) Browse
or buy works by some of South Africa's leading contemporary artists at this classy gallery.
Works on display include paintings by John
Meyer and Lionel Smit, mixed media projects
from Velaphi Mzimba, and sculptures by
Brett Murray and Angus Taylor.

🏠 Atlantic Coast

Mojo Market
MARKET

(Map p68; www.mojomarket.co.za; 30 Regent Rd,
Sea Point; ⊗shops 10am-6pm, food stalls 7am-
10pm) Pick up items ranging from contemporary African craftwork to fashion at this
buzzing indoor market, where 45 shops mix
with 25 food stands and a fresh produce section. Between shopping, enjoy goodies such
as masala dosas and poke bowls. The live music (at 7pm during the week, 12.30pm, 4pm
and 7.30pm Saturday and 12.30pm Sunday)
draws the locals for a beer on Friday night
in particular. At other times, such as Sunday
morning, some traders can be disorganised
and you are better off going elsewhere.

🏠 Southern Suburbs

★ Montebello Design Centre
ARTS & CRAFTS

(✆021-685 6445; www.montebello.co.za; 31 Newlands Ave, Newlands; ⊗9am-4pm Mon-Sat, to 3pm
Sun; 🚻; 🚇Newlands) This development project has helped several great craftspeople and
designers along the way. In the leafy compound, artists' studios are scattered around
the central craft shop, where you can buy a
range of gifts, from Irma Stern cushions to
tyre handbags. There's also a plant nursery,
the excellent **Gardener's Cottage cafe**
(✆021-689 3158; mains R80; ⊗8am-4.30pm Tue-
Fri, from 8.30am Sat & Sun) and a farm shop.

Cavendish Square
MALL

(✆021-657 5600; www.cavendish.co.za; Dreyer St,
Claremont; ⊗9am-7pm Mon-Sat, 10am-5pm Sun;
🚇Claremont) The focal point of Claremont's
shopping scene, this top-class mall has outlets of many local and international fashion
designers, as well as supermarkets, department stores, restaurants and a Ster-Kinekor
multiplex cinema (www.sterkinekor.com).

LGBT CAPE TOWN

Africa's pinkest city is a glam-to-the-max destination that any LGBT traveller should have on their bucket list. De Waterkant, the queer precinct, is welcoming to everyone, from Cape Town's finest drag queens to leathered-up Muscle Marys. Throughout the year the city hosts several gay festivals and events.

Cape Town's lesbian community continues to party on with the M.I.S.S (Make It Sexy Sisters; www.facebook.com/MISSmakeitsexysisters) events, and the Unofficial Pink Parties (www.facebook.com/pinkpartyza). These are lesbian-run but welcoming to everyone.

If you fancy going hiking with gays and gay-friendly folk while in the Mother City, check out the Cape Town Gay Hiking Club (www.facebook.com/groups/6068816435).

Rights & Challenges

With democracy, South Africa became the first country in the world to enshrine gay and lesbian rights in its constitution. There's an equal age of consent and LGBT people are legally entitled to marry, too. Sadly, alternative lifestyles are not embraced by all South Africans. Hardly a year goes by without several gay hate crimes being reported in the Western Cape. It is not unheard of for lesbians in black communities to be subjected to 'corrective rape'.

Information

Pink South Africa (www.pinksa.co.za)

GayCapeTown4u.com (www.gaycapetown4u.com)

Mamba (www.mambaonline.com)

Mambagirl (www.mambagirl.com)

SA Leather South Africa (www.sal.qw.co.za)

Don't Miss

Glen Boutique Hotel (Map p68; ☑021-439 0086; www.glenhotel.co.za; 3 The Glen, Sea Point; r incl breakfast from R2980; P❋@🛜🏊; 🚌The Glen) Glam Sea Point digs and Cape Town's best 'straight-friendly' hotel.

Crew Bar (Map p58; ☑021-461 4920; www.facebook.com/CrewBarCapeTown; 30 Napier St, De Waterkant; cover after 10pm Fri & all Sat R50; ⊗7pm-2am Sun-Thu, to 4am Fri & Sat; 🚌Alfred) The most happening of De Waterkant's clubs, with muscular barmen.

Alexander Bar & Café (p97) Classy venue with theatre that puts on a range of shows.

Clifton 3rd Beach (Map p68; Victoria Rd, Clifton; 🚌Clifton 3rd) See and be seen on the cruisiest of Clifton's quartet of beaches.

Pienk Piesang (☑081 249 5604; www.facebook.com/HeSheLangarm; R50) Learn to dance Afrikaans-style at these Northern Suburbs parties.

Sandy Bay (p53) Shed your clothes and inhibitions at this gorgeous nude beach.

Stays

Purple House (Map p58; ☑021-418 2508; www.purplehouse.co.za; 23 Jarvis St, De Waterkant; s/d/apt from R1450/1650/1700; ❋@🛜; 🚌Alfred) Go B&B or self-catering – it's all good.

Colette's (☑083 458 5344, 021-531 4830; www.colettesbb.co.za; 16 The Bend, Pinelands; s/d incl breakfast from R500/650; P🛜; 🚌Pinelands) Women-friendly B&B with pet ducks in Pinelands.

Rondebosch Potters Market CERAMICS (www.ceramics-sa-cape.co.za; Rondebosch Park, Campground Rd, Rondebosch; 🚌Rondebosch) If you're interested in local ceramics, the date to mark in your diary is the twice-yearly Rondebosch Potters Market, held from 8am to 2pm on the second-to-last Saturdays of March and November.

Kirstenbosch Craft Market ARTS & CRAFTS (☑074 333 2170; cnr Kirstenbosch Dr & Rhodes Av, Newlands; ⊗9am-3pm last Sun of month; ♿; 🚌Kirstenbosch) There's lots to choose from at this large craft market spread across the commons outside Kirstenbosch (p67). It's possible to use a credit card to pay for most purchases. Proceeds from the market go to the development fund for the botanical gardens.

The Grey (Map p58; ☑ 021-421 1106; www.thegreyhotel.co.za; 49 Napier St, De Waterkant; s/d from R1320/2750; ✲ @ ☈ ✖; ☐ Alfred) The rooftop bar and pool are its pull factor.

De Waterkant House (Map p58; ☑ 021-409 2500; www.dewaterkant.com; 35 Loader St, De Waterkant; s/d incl breakfast from R1300/1550; @ ☈ ✖; ☐ Old Fire Station) One of several gay-friendly Village & Life properties.

Bars, Clubs & Cabaret

Babylon (Map p82; 44 Constitution St, East City; cover R50; ☺ 8-4pm Fri & Sat; ☐ Lower Buitenkant) Plush velvet upholstered booths, topless twinks and cubs, and views of Table Mountain from its balcony.

Bar Code (Map p58; ☑ 076 469 1825; https://versatbar.wixsite.com/barcode; 18 Cobern St, De Waterkant; cover after 11pm Wed-Sat R70; ☺ 4pm-2am; ☐ Alfred) Depending on the night, clothing may be optional.

Beaulah (Map p58; ☑ 021-418 5244; 28 Somerset Rd, De Waterkant; cover R50; ☺ 9pm-4am Fri & Sat; ☐ Alfred) Fun club for the girls – but welcoming to the boys, too.

Gate69 Cape Town (Map p58; ☑ 021-035 1627; http://gate69.co.za; 87 Bree St, City Bowl; dinner & show from R450; ☐ Strand) Glam it up for the dinner-theatre shows at this camp and glitzy drag venue.

Evita se Perron (p170) Head to Darling for the home theatre of local legend Pieter-Dirk Uys.

Eats

Beefcakes (Map p58; ☑ 021-425 9019; www.beefcakes.co.za; 40 Somerset Rd, De Waterkant; burgers R55-85; ☺ 7pm-midnight; ☐ Gallow's Hill) Burger bar with campy bingo, drag shows and topless muscle-boy waiters.

Lazari (Map p62; ☑ 021-461 9865; www.lazari.co.za; cnr Upper Maynard St & Vredehoek Ave, Vredehoek; mains R60-85; ☺ 7.30am-4pm Mon-Fri, 8am-2.30pm Sat & Sun; ☈; ☐ Upper Buitenkant) Ditch the diet: the cakes and bakes here are divine.

Cafe Manhattan (Map p58; ☑ 021-421 6666; www.manhattan.co.za; 74 Waterkant St, De Waterkant; ☺ 4-11pm Mon-Fri, from noon Sat & Sun; ☐ Alfred) Pioneer of the De Waterkant gay scene.

Raptor Room (Map p82; ☑ 087 625 0630; www.raptorroom.co.za; Shop 2, 79 Roeland St, East City; ☺ 10am-11pm Mon-Fri, to 5pm Sat, to 3pm Sun; ☐ Roeland) Cute pink dinosaurs and sassy staff at this fun diner in the East City.

Festivals & Events

Cape Town Pride (www.capetownpride.org) End of Feburary; in De Waterkant.

Miss Gay Western Cape (www.missgay.co.za; Joseph Stone Auditorium, Klipfontein Rd, Athlone) November; beauty pageant in Cape Town.

MCQP (Mother City Queer Project; ☑ 021-461 4920; https://mcqp.co.za) December; fancy-dress dance party in Cape Town.

Pink Loerie Festival (p595) A flamboyant Mardi Gras at the end of April and beginning of May in Knysna on the Garden Route.

🏠 Southern Peninsula

The peninsula is a popular base for artists, and consequently has a high number of galleries, pottery shops and so on. Muizenberg and Kalk Bay offer the best selection, as well as regular markets including Kalk Bay Market (Kalk Bay Community Centre, Main Rd, Kalk Bay; ☐ Kalk Bay). Noordhoek Farm Village (p71) and Imhoff Farm (p71) are pleasant complexes to shop for crafts and souvenirs.

★ **Kalk Bay Modern** ARTS & CRAFTS
(☑ 021-788 6571; www.kalkbaymodern.co.za; 136 Main Rd, Kalk Bay; ☺ 9.30am-5pm; ☐ Kalk Bay) 🖉 This gallery is stocked with an eclectic

and appealing range of arts and crafts, and there are often exhibitions here by local artists. Check out the Art-I-San collection of printed cloth.

Quagga Rare Books & Art BOOKS
(☑ 021-788 2752; www.quaggabooks.co.za; 86 Main Rd, Kalk Bay; ⊙ 9am-5pm Mon-Sat, from 10am Sun; ☒ Kalk Bay) It's hard to pass by this appealing bookshop if you're looking for old editions and antiquarian books. The shop also has local art, as well prints and maps, for sale.

ⓘ Information

DANGERS & ANNOYANCES

Cape Town is one of the most relaxed cities in Africa, which can instil a false sense of security. Paranoia is not required, but common sense is.

➡ The townships and suburbs on the Cape Flats have an appalling crime rate – these are not places for a casual wander and it's safest to visit with a trustworthy guide.

➡ Public transport and walking are not recommended after dark, so take a taxi or drive (and carry a mobile phone).

➡ Muggings are common in Table Mountain National Park. Check locally for current information and never hike alone (preferably take a local guide).

➡ At beaches, check for warning signs about rips and rocks, and only swim in patrolled areas.

MEDICAL SERVICES

Medical services in Cape Town are of a high standard; make sure you have health insurance and be prepared to pay for services immediately. In an emergency call 107 from a landline (or 112 from a mobile) for directions to the nearest hospital.

Many doctors make house calls; look under 'Medical' in the phone book or ask at your hotel.

Groote Schuur Hospital (☑ 021-404 9111; www.westerncape.gov.za/your_gov/163; Main Rd, Observatory; ☒ Observatory) Has a casualty (emergency) department.

Netcare Christiaan Barnard Memorial Hospital (☑ 021-441 0000; www.netcarehospitals. co.za/Hospital/Netcare_Christiaan_Barnard_Memorial_Hospital; cnr DF Malan St & Rua Bartholemeu Dias, Foreshore; ☒ Church/Longmarket) Excellent private hospital.

Netcare Travel Clinic (☑ 021-419 3172; www. netcare.co.za/Netcare-travel-clinics; 11th fl, Picbal Arcade, 58 Strand St, City Bowl; ⊙ 8am-4pm Mon-Fri; ☒ Adderley) For vaccinations and travel health advice.

TOURIST INFORMATION

Cape Town Tourism (Map p58; ☑ 086 132 2223, 021-487 6800; www.capetown.travel; Pinnacle Bldg, cnr Castle & Burg Sts, City Bowl;

⊙ 7am-6pm Mon-Fri, 8.30am-2pm Sat, 9am-1pm Sun; ☒ Church/Mid-Long) Head office books accommodation, tours and car hire, and provides information on national parks and reserves. There are several other branches around town.

ⓘ Getting There & Away

AIR

Cape Town International Airport (CPT; ☑ 021-937 1200; www.airports.co.za), 22km east of the city centre, has a tourist information office.

BUS

Interstate buses arrive at the bus terminus at Cape Town Railway Station, where you'll find the booking offices for the bus companies, all open from 6am to 6.30pm daily.

Baz Bus (☑ 021-422 5202, SMS bookings 076 427 3003; www.bazbus.com) Offers hop-on, hop-off fares and door-to-door service between Cape Town and Jo'burg/Pretoria via Northern Drakensberg, Durban and the Garden Route.

Greyhound (☑ 021-418 4326, reservations 083 915 9000; www.greyhound.co.za; Cape Town Railway Station; ⊙ 6am-6.30pm)

Intercape (☑ 021-380 4400; www.intercape. co.za)

Translux (☑ 021-449 6209, 086 158 9282; www.translux.co.za; Cape Town Railway Station; ⊙ 6am-6.30pm)

TRAIN

Long distance trains arrive at **Cape Town Railway Station** on Heerengracht in the City Bowl. There are services Wednesday, Friday and Sunday to and from Jo'burg via Kimberley on the **Shosholoza Meyl** (☑ 0860 008 888, 011-774 4555; www. shosholozameyl.co.za); these sleeper trains offer comfortable accommodation and dining cars. Other services include the luxurious **Blue Train** (☑ 012-334 8459; www.bluetrain.co.za) and **Rovos Rail** (☑ 012-315 8242; www.rovos.co.za).

ⓘ Getting Around

TO/FROM THE AIRPORT

Expect to pay around R250 for a nonshared taxi.

MyCiTi buses (☑ 0800 656 463; www.myciti. org.za) Run every 30 minutes between 4.45am and 10.15pm to the city centre and the Waterfront. A single trip is R100; if you use a 'myconnect' card (which costs a non-refundable R35), the fare varies between R90.40 and R98.80 depending on whether you travel in off-peak or peak times.

Backpacker Bus (☑ 082 809 9185; www.backpackerbus.co.za) Book in advance for airport transfers (from R220 per person) and pick-ups from hostels and hotels.

BICYCLE

If you're prepared for the many hills and long distances between sights, the Cape Peninsula is a terrific place to explore by bicycle. Dedicated cycle lanes are a legacy of the World Cup: there's a good one north out of the city towards Table View, and another runs alongside the Walk of Remembrance from Cape Town Train Station to Green Point. Unfortunately, bicycles are banned from suburban trains.

The following offer bicycle hire:

&Bikes (☑ 021-823 8790; www.andbikes.co.za; 32 Loop St, Foreshore; half-/full day from R150/250; ☻7.30am-5pm Mon-Fri, 8am-1pm Sat)

Awol Tours (p73)

Bike & Saddle (☑ 021-813 6433; www.bike-andsaddle.com; half-/full day R950/1380)

Cape Town Cycle Hire (☑ 084 400 1604, 021-434 1270; www.capetowncyclehire.co.za; per day from R300)

Downhill Adventures (p73)

Up Cycles (☑ 076 135 2223; www.upcycles.co.za; 1hr/half-day/full day R70/200/250)

BOAT

The **Mellow Yellow Water Taxi** (☑ 073 473 7684; www.watertaxi.co.za; single/return R100/150) shuttles between Kalk Bay and Simon's Town. We recommend taking the train to Simon's Town and the water taxi back to Kalk Bay, not the other way around.

BUS

The **MyCiTi** (☑ 0800 656 463; www.myciti.org.za) network of commuter buses runs daily between 5am and 10pm, with the most frequent services between 8am and 5pm. Routes cover the city centre up to Gardens and out to the Waterfront; along the Atlantic seaboard to Camps Bay and Hout Bay; up to Tamboerskloof along Kloof Nek Rd, with a shuttle service to the cableway; to Woodstock and Salt River; to Blouberg and Table View; to Khayelitsha; and to the airport.

Fares have to be paid with a stored-value 'myconnect' card (a non-refundable R35), which can be purchased from MyCiTi station kiosks and participating retailers. It's also possible to buy single-trip tickets (R30 or R100 to or from the airport). A bank fee of 2.5% of the loaded value (with a minimum of R1.50) will be charged, eg if you load the card with R200 you will have R195 in credit. The card, issued by ABSA (a national bank), can also be used to pay for low-value transactions at shops and businesses displaying the MasterCard sign.

Fares depend on the time of day (peak-hour fares are charged from 6.45am to 8am and 4.15pm to 5.30pm, Monday to Friday) and whether you have pre-loaded the card with the MyCiTi Mover package (costing between R50 and R1000), which can cut the standard fares by 30%.

For journeys of under 5km (ie from Civic Centre to Gardens or the Waterfront), standard fares are peak/off-peak R13.90/9.10; city centre to Table View is R17.50/11.70; city centre to airport is R98.80/90.40; and city centre to Hout Bay is R17.50/11.70.

CAR & MOTORCYCLE

Cape Town has an excellent road system. Rush hour is from around 7am to 9pm and 4.30pm to 6.30pm. Drive with caution, as Capetonian drivers are inveterate rule breakers. You can hire both cars and motorbikes (p613); major car-hire companies have desks at the airport and offices in the city.

SHARED TAXI

The main shared minibus taxi (p617) rank is on the upper deck of Cape Town Railway Station, accessible from a walkway in the Golden Acre Centre or from stairways on Strand St. It's well organised and finding the right rank is easy. Anywhere else, you just hail shared taxis from the side of the road and ask the driver where they're going.

TAXI

Consider taking a nonshared taxi at night or if you're in a group. Rates are about R10 per kilometre. Uber is very popular and works well.

Excite Taxis (☑ 021-448 4444; www.excitetaxis.co.za)

Marine Taxi (☑ 0861 434 0434, 021-447 0384; www.marinetaxis.co.za)

Rikkis (☑ 021-447 3559, 086 174 5547; www.rikkis.co.za)

Telecab (☑ 021-788 2717, 082 222 0282) For transfers from Simon's Town to Boulders and Cape Point.

TRAIN

Cape Metro Rail (☑ 0800 656 463; http://capetowntrains.freeblog.site) trains are a cheap and – potentially – handy way to get around. However, there are few (or no) trains after 6pm on weekdays and after noon on Saturday. The service is also very unreliable, prone to breakdowns and, on certain services, sometimes unsafe. Over 100 carriages have been lost to arson and vandalism since October 2015, all having an impact on punctuality and reliability.

The difference between MetroPlus (first class) and Metro (economy class) carriages in price and comfort is negligible. The most important line for visitors is the Simon's Town line, which runs through Observatory and around the back of Table Mountain, through upper-income suburbs such as Newlands, and on to Muizenberg and the False Bay coast. These trains run at least every hour from 6am to 9pm and, in theory, as often as every 15 minutes during peak times (6am to 9am and 3pm to 6pm).

Metro trains also run out to Strand on the eastern side of False Bay, and into the Winelands to Stellenbosch and Paarl. They are the cheapest and easiest means of transport to these areas. For all routes security is best at peak times when the carriages are busy – but then they can also be dangerously overcrowded.

Western Cape

Best Places to Eat

➡ La Petite Colombe (p122)

➡ Die Strandloper (p172)

➡ Karoux (p131)

➡ Boschendal at Oude Bank (p115)

Best Places to Stay

➡ Views Boutique Hotel (p151)

➡ Grootbos Private Nature Reserve (p141)

➡ Oudebosch Eco Cabins (p132)

➡ Pat Busch Mountain Reserve (p129)

Why Go?

The splendours of the Western Cape lie not only in its world-class vineyards, stunning beaches and mountains, but also in lesser-known regions, such as the wide-open spaces of the Karoo, the many nature reserves and the wilderness areas. Make sure you get out into these wild, less-visited areas for birdwatching and wildlife adventure, as well as pure relaxation under vast skies.

The Western Cape offers a huge range of activities, from sedate endeavours such as wine tasting and scenic drives to more hair-raising encounters such as skydiving and rock climbing.

The melting pot of cultures in the region also begs to be explored. Khoe-San rock art is at its best in the Cederberg mountains, and there are some fine opportunities to learn about the fascinating culture of the Xhosa people.

When to Go
Knysna

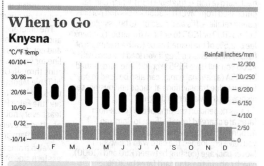

Feb, Mar & Nov	Jun-Aug	Dec & Jan Prices
Temperatures are perfect: not too hot to hike but still beach weather.	Whale-watching season begins; flowers bloom on the West Coast.	rise and visitor numbers increase. Hot days and abundant festivals.

Climate

The Western Cape has dry, sunny summers (December to March) where average temperatures are warm to hot – in some regions it can reach 40°C. It is often windy, and the southeasterly 'Cape Doctor', which buffets the Cape, can reach gale force and cool things down. Winters (June to August) can be cool, with average minimum temperatures around 7°C, and maximums around 19°C, though there are still warm, sunny days dotted around. There is plenty of winter rain, and occasional snow on the higher peaks. As you head north from Cape Town, things become progressively drier and hotter. Along the southern coast the weather is temperate.

Language

The Western Cape is the only province in South Africa where the majority of the population is coloured. Most 'Cape coloureds', who can trace their roots back to the Khoe-San or imported slaves from Indonesia and Madagascar, speak Afrikaans as a first language, though English is spoken everywhere.

WINELANDS

Venturing inland and upwards from Cape Town you'll find the Boland, meaning 'upland'. It's a superb wine-producing area, and indeed the best known in South Africa. The magnificent mountain ranges around Stellenbosch and Franschhoek provide ideal microclimates for the vines.

There's been colonial settlement here since the latter half of the 17th century, when the Dutch first founded Stellenbosch and the French Huguenots settled in Franschhoek. Both towns pride themselves on their innovative young chefs, many based at wine estates, and the region has become the mainspring of South African cuisine.

Along with Paarl, these towns make up the core of the Winelands, but there are many more wine-producing places that are worth exploring. Pretty Tulbagh, with its many historical buildings, is known for MCC (Méthode Cap Classique – which is the local version of Champagne), and Robertson's scattered wineries offer unpretentious, family-friendly places to enjoy tastings.

Stellenbosch

☎ 021 / POP 155,000

If there's one thing that Stellenbosch is renowned for, it is wine. There are hundreds of estates scattered around the outskirts of the town, many of which produce world-class wines. A tour of the wineries with their many tasting options and superlative restaurants will likely form the backbone of your visit, but there is a lot more to see.

An elegant, historical town with stately Cape Dutch, Georgian and Victorian architecture along its oak-lined streets, Stellenbosch is full of interesting museums, quality hotels and a selection of bars, clubs and restaurants. A university town, it is constantly abuzz with locals, students, Capetonians and tourists.

Established by the governor of the Cape (Simon van der Stel) in 1679 on the banks of the Eerste River, Stellenbosch was – and still is – famed for its rich soil, just what was needed to produce vegetables and wine for ships stopping off at the Cape.

◉ Sights & Activities

If you need to walk off all those wine tastings, you could take a **guided walk** (☎021-883 3584; 36 Market St; R140; ⊗11am & 3pm Mon-Fri, 9.30am Sat & Sun) from Stellenbosch Tourism (p118). Bookings are essential for weekend walks.

Village Museum   MUSEUM
(Map p112; ☎021-887 2937; www.stelmus.co.za; 18 Ryneveld St; adult/child R35/15; ⊗9am-5pm Mon-Sat year-round, 10am-1pm Sun Apr-Aug, to 4pm Sun Sep-Mar) A group of exquisitely restored and period-furnished houses dating from 1709 to 1850 make up this museum, which is a must-see. At each house you'll

WESTERN CAPE STELLENBOSCH

WORTH A TRIP

JONKERSHOEK NATURE RESERVE

This small reserve (Map p116; ☎021-866 1560; www.capenature.co.za; Jonkershoek Rd; adult/child R40/20; ⊗7.30am-4pm) is 8km southeast of town and set within a timber plantation. There is a 10km scenic drive, plus hiking trails ranging from 5km to 18km. A hiking map is available at the entrance.

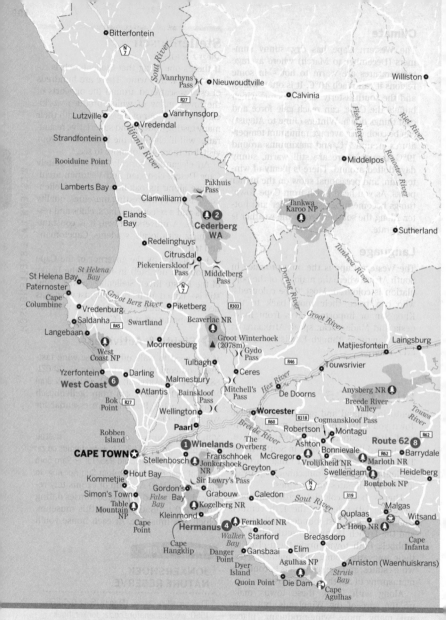

Western Cape Highlights

1 **Winelands** (p109)
Sampling magnificent wines – and food – in the historic wine towns, particularly Stellenbosch and Franschhoek.

2 **Cederberg Wilderness Area** (p173) Exploring Khoe-San culture and hiking past bizarre rock formations.

3 **Wilderness** (p150) Strolling along the windswept

beach and kayaking the lagoons.

4 **Hermanus** (p133) Walking the cliff path or taking to the seas in a kayak to watch for whales.

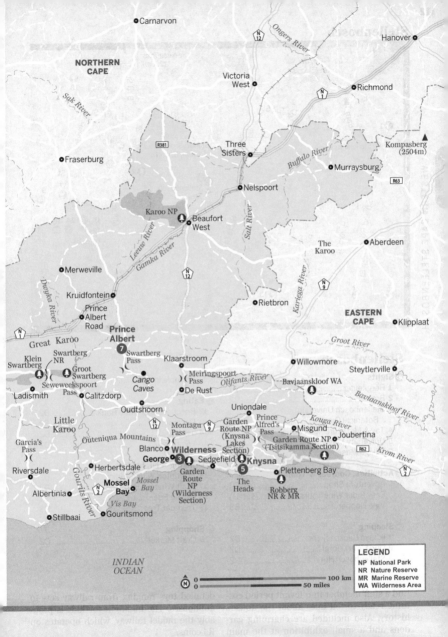

5 **Knysna** (p152) Hiking and biking through the forests or exploring the lagoon by boat.

6 **West Coast** (p170) Learning to kite-surf and rewarding yourself with

a beachside seafood extravaganza.

7 **Prince Albert** (p167) Feasting on fine food and then working it off with a mountain hike.

8 **Route 62** (p162) Driving from Robertson to Oudtshoorn, stopping off to sip wines, climb rock faces and relax in hot springs along the way.

Stellenbosch

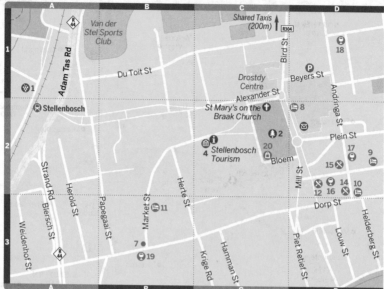

Stellenbosch

find a staff member in relevant period costume ready to tell tales about the house's history. Also included are charming gardens and a small exhibition at the main entrance.

Toy & Miniature Museum   MUSEUM
(Map p112; ☎021-882 8861; Rhenish Parsonage, 42 Market St; adult/child R15/5; ☺9am-4.30pm Mon-Fri, to 2pm Sat; ⓐ) This delightful museum features a remarkable collection of

detailed toys ranging from railway sets to dollhouses. The highlight for kids is probably the model railway, which operates on R5 coins.

Bergkelder   WINERY
(Map p112; ☎021-809 8025; www.fleurducap. co.za/die-bergkelder; George Blake St; tastings R65; ☺9am-5pm Mon-Fri, to 2pm Sat; ⓟ) For wine lovers without wheels, this cellar a short walk from the town centre is ideal.

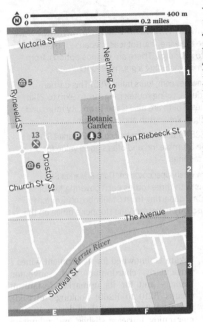

Hour-long tours (R60) are followed by an atmospheric candlelit tasting in the cellar. The tours run at 10am, 11am, 2pm and 3pm Monday to Friday, and at 10am, 11am and noon Saturday. A wine and salt pairing (R110) is also on offer. Bookings are required for all activities.

University Museum
MUSEUM

(Map p112; 52 Ryneveld St; entry by donation; ⊙10am-4.30pm Mon, 9am-4.30pm Tue-Sat) This fabulous Flemish Renaissance–style building houses an interesting and varied collection of local art, an array of African anthropological treasures and exhibits on South African culture and history.

Stellenbosch University Botanical Garden
PARK

(Map p112; ☎021-808 3054; www.sun.ac.za/botanicalgarden; cnr Neethling & Van Riebeeck Sts; R10; ⊙8am-5pm) This glorious inner-city garden is an unsung Stellenbosch sight and well worth a wander. Themed gardens include a bonsai area and tropical glasshouse, and there's a host of indigenous plants. For those not mad about botany, it's a peaceful place to walk and there's a pleasant tea garden for coffee, cake or a light lunch (mains R55 to R130).

Around Stellenbosch

There is an abundance of good wineries in the Stellenbosch area. Get the free booklet *Stellenbosch and Its Wine Routes* from Stellenbosch Tourism (p118) for the complete picture.

Vergenoegd
WINERY

(☎021-843 3248; www.vergenoegd.co.za; Baden Powell Dr; tastings R50; ⊙8am-5pm Mon-Sat, 10am-4pm Sun;) Other than tastings, there's lots of kid-friendly fun, including a chance to meet the workforce of ducks that help keep the vineyards pest- and pesticide-free. There's also plenty for adults including the opportunity to blend your own tea, coffee, wine and olive oil (R250 per experience). Picnics (adult/child R450/125) can be nibbled on the lawns or in the old barn, and there's a popular market on Sundays, featuring food, crafts and an awesome kids' area.

★ Spier
WINERY

(Map p116; ☎021-809 1100; www.spier.co.za; Rte 310; tastings from R40; ⊙9am-5pm Mon-Wed, to 6pm Thu-Sat, 11am-6pm Sun;) Spier has some excellent shiraz, cabernet and red blends, though a visit to this vast winery is less about wine and more about the other activities available. There are superb birds-of-prey displays (adult/child R75/65), Segway tours through the vines, three restaurants, and picnics to enjoy in the grounds. Look out for special events in the summer months, including open-air cinema evenings and live entertainment.

★ Vergelegen
WINERY

(☎021-847 2100; www.vergelegen.co.za; Lourensford Rd, Somerset West; adult/child R10/5, tastings from R30, tours R50; ⊙9am-5pm, garden tour 10am, cellar tour 11am & 3pm;) Simon van der Stel's son Willem first planted vines here in 1700. The buildings and elegant grounds have ravishing mountain views and a 'stately home' feel to them. You can take a tour of the gardens, a cellar tour or just enjoy a tasting of four of the estate's wines. Tasting the flagship Vergelegen Red costs an extra R10. There are also two restaurants.

Waterkloof
WINERY

(☎021-858 1292; www.waterkloofwines.co.za; Sir Lowry's Pass Village Rd, Somerset West; tastings from R40; ⊙10am-5pm Mon-Sat, 11am-5pm Sun;) The stunning contemporary architecture here is a fine contrast to the familiar Cape Dutch buildings at older estates. The

WINE TOURS

Joining a tour is probably the best way to see the wineries, not least because it means you don't have to worry about driving back to your digs. There are various options, from basic hop-on, hop-off transport to bespoke trips including a gourmet lunch.

Bikes 'n Wines (☏ 021-823 8790; www.bikesnwines.com; tours from R795) This carbon-negative company comes highly recommended. Cycling routes range from 9km to 21km and take in three or four Stellenbosch wineries. There are also Cape Town city tours and trips to lesser-visited wine regions such as Elgin, Wellington and Hermanus.

Easy Rider Wine Tours (Map p112; ☏ 021-886 4651; www.winetour.co.za; 12 Market St) This long-established company operates from the Stumble Inn and offers good value for a full-day trip at R650, including lunch and all tastings.

Vine Hopper (Map p112; ☏ 021-882 8112; www.vinehopper.co.za; cnr Dorp & Market Sts; 1-/2-day pass R300/540) A hop-on, hop-off bus with three routes each covering five or six estates. There are seven departures per day, departing from Stellenbosch Tourism (p118), where you can buy tickets. You can also buy tickets at Vine Hopper's office on the corner of Dorp and Market Sts.

estate specialises in biodynamic wines and ecofriendly farming methods – take a two-hour guided walk (10am and 4.30pm, R710 with two-course lunch/dinner) around the estate to learn more. Horse riding (R750 with lunch) is also offered, and if you're feeling particularly flush you could fly in from Cape Town by helicopter (R11,250 per person with six-course meal).

★ **Warwick Estate**   WINERY
(Map p116; ☏ 021-884 4410; www.warwickwine.com; tastings R50, wine safari R80; ☺9am-5pm; P🏄) Warwick's red wines are legendary, particularly its Bordeaux blends. The winery offers an informative Big Five wine safari (referring to grape varieties, not large mammals) through the vineyards, and picnics (R550 for two people) to enjoy on the lawns. Advance bookings are required for picnics, but simple cheeseboards are available if you just rock up.

Villiera   WINERY
(Map p116; ☏ 021-865 2002; www.villiera.com; tastings R30; ☺9am-5pm Mon-Fri, to 3pm Sat; P) Villiera produces several excellent Méthode Cap Classique wines and a highly rated and well-priced shiraz. Excellent two-hour wildlife drives (adult/child R220/110) with knowledgeable guides take in antelope, zebras, giraffes and various bird species on the farm and are followed by a tasting. Bookings are essential for the game drives.

Tokara   WINERY
(Map p116; ☏ 021-808 5900; www.tokara.co.za; Rte 310; tastings R75-100; ☺10am-5.30pm; P)

Tokara is renowned for its excellent wines – particularly chardonnay and sauvignon blanc – and for its upmarket restaurant (mains R210 to R260; bookings advised), fine art collection and sleek design. In summer enjoy intricate dishes and mountain views. In winter, snuggle up by the fire with a taster of the noble late harvest (dessert wine) or pot still brandy (R25). There's a fantastic deli/sculpture gallery for less fancy lunches (mains R110 to R150), and you can taste the estate's olive oil.

Delaire Graff Estate   WINERY
(Map p116; ☏ 021-885 8160; www.delaire.co.za; Helshoogte Pass; tastings from R65; ☺tastings 10am-5pm; P) The views are magnificent from this 'vineyard in the sky', which has a gorgeous hotel and spa and two gourmet restaurants including **Indochine** (mains R225 to R410), which specialises in pan-Asian cuisine. The estate's wines also get top marks from the critics.

🎪 Festivals & Events

Stellenbosch Wine Festival   WINE
(www.stellenboschwinefestival.co.za; ☺Feb) This event in late February offers visitors the chance to sample wines from more than 60 vineyards all in one spot as well as attend talks and tutorials on wine. There's also live music and kids' entertainment.

🛏 Sleeping

Stellenbosch has some decent backpacker options, historical hotels, friendly guesthouses and, in the suburbs, self-catering cottages for rent. Many wine estates offer luxury accommodation. Stellenbosch Tourism (p118) can assist with bookings.

★ Banghoek Place
HOSTEL $

(Map p116; ☑ 021-887 0048; www.banghoek.co.za; 193 Banghoek Rd; dm/r incl breakfast R200/700; P 🛜 ☒) This stylish suburban hostel provides a quiet budget alternative, away from the town centre. The recreation area has satellite TV and a pool table and there's a nice swimming pool in the garden.

Ikhaya Backpackers
HOSTEL $

(Map p112; ☑ 021-883 8550; www.stellenbosch backpackers.co.za; 56 Bird St; dm R165, d with shared bathroom R460; 🛜) The central location means you're within easy stumbling distance of some of the more popular bars. Rooms are in converted apartments, so each dorm comes with its own kitchen and bathroom, shared with the adjoining double rooms.

Stumble Inn
HOSTEL $

(Map p112; ☑ 021-887 4049; www.stumbleinn backpackers.co.za; 12 Market St; camping per site R120, dm R180, d with shared bathroom R500; P 🛜 ☒) Although it's grown up in recent years, this is still Stellenbosch's party hostel. It's split over two old houses – the second building is the quieter option, away from the bar. The wine tours are recommended.

Summerwood Guesthouse
GUESTHOUSE $$

(Map p116; ☑ 021-887 4112; www.summerwood. co.za; 28 Jonkershoek Rd; s/d incl breakfast from R1750/2400; P ✳ 🛜 ☒) In a suburban neighbourhood bordering a small nature reserve east of the town centre is this elegant guest-

house. The immaculate rooms are bright and spacious, with excellent amenities. Rates drop considerably between April and September.

Oude Werf Hotel
HISTORIC HOTEL $$

(Map p112; ☑ 021-887 4608; www.oudewerfhotel. co.za; 30 Church St; r incl breakfast from R2400; ✳ 🛜 ☒) This appealing, old-style hotel dates back to 1802, though it has had a dramatic facelift. Deluxe rooms are furnished with antiques and brass beds, while the superior and luxury rooms are bright and modern.

Stellenbosch Hotel
HISTORIC HOTEL $$

(Map p112; ☑ 021-887 3644; www.stellenbosch hotel.co.za; 162 Dorp St, cnr Andringa St; s/d incl breakfast from R1290/1490; P ✳ 🛜) A comfortable country-style hotel with a variety of rooms, including some with self-catering facilities and others with four-poster beds. A section dating from 1743 houses the Stellenbosch Kitchen (mains R110 to R190), a good spot for a drink and some people-watching.

🍴 Eating

The town centre has a few excellent restaurants and plenty of casual cafes. Many of the best restaurants though are found on wine estates. These often offer a fine-dining experience and should be booked ahead.

★ Boschendal at Oude Bank
BAKERY $

(Map p112; ☑ 021-870 4287; www.decompan je.co.za; cnr Church & Bird Sts; mains R75-120; ◷7am-5pm Mon-Fri, 8am-5pm Sat & Sun; 🛜) A vibrant bakery and bistro priding itself on locally sourced ingredients. The menu features salads, sandwiches and mezze-style

---

DON'T MISS

FOOD MARKETS IN THE WINELANDS

Farmers markets are South Africa's favourite foodie craze, and there is a particularly good selection in the Winelands. Rather than places to do your shopping, these tend to be spots for meals in situ – expect to find anything from freshly baked bread and artisanal cheese to paella, Thai snacks and spicy curries, plus piles of cake, local wine and plenty of craft beer. Here are a few of our favourites:

Blaauwklippen Market (Map p116; www.blaauwklippen.com; Blaauwklippen Vineyards, Rte 44; ◷10am-3pm Sun; ⊞) A family-friendly market with carriage and pony rides on offer.

Franschhoek Market (Map p119; ☑ 082 786 7927; 29 Huguenot Rd; mains R40-70; ◷9am-2pm Sat; ⊞) Based in the grounds of the church, this market has a real country fete vibe.

Root 44 Market (Map p116; ☑ 021-881 3052; www.root44.co.za; Audacia Winery, Rte 44; dishes R40-90; ◷10am-4pm Sat & Sun; P ⊞) A large indoor-outdoor market with plenty of crafts and clothing as well as the usual food and drink offerings.

Around Stellenbosch

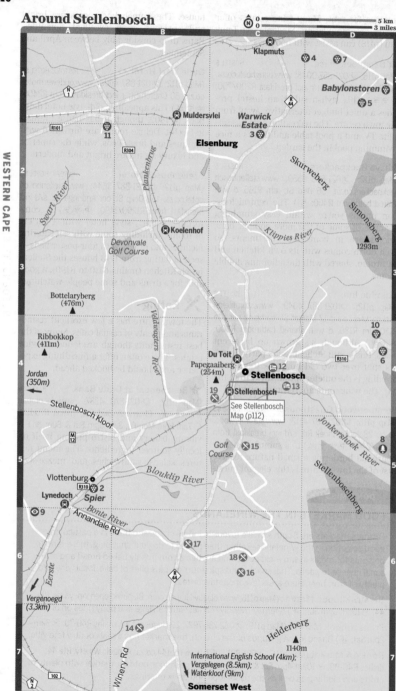

Around Stellenbosch

◉ **Top Sights**
1 Babylonstoren......................................D1
2 Spier A5
3 Warwick Estate C2

◉ **Sights**
4 Anura...D1
5 Backsberg..D1
6 Delaire Graff Estate D4
7 Glen Carlou...D1
8 Jonkershoek Nature Reserve.............D5
9 Lynedoch EcoVillage..........................A6
10 Tokara..D4
11 Villiera...A2

⊜ **Sleeping**
12 Banghoek Place C4
13 Summerwood Guesthouse C4

⊗ **Eating**
14 96 Winery Road..................................B7
15 Blaauwklippen Market C5
Glen Carlou.............................(see 7)
16 Overture Restaurant C6
17 Root 44 Market..................................B6
18 Rust en Vrede....................................C6
19 Slow Market.......................................C4

◉ **Entertainment**
Oude Libertas
Amphitheatre.........................(see 19)

platters, as well as fresh cakes and pastries and local craft beer. There are tables on the pavement, while inside has a market-hall feel, with plenty of seating and some shops to browse.

Slow Market MARKET $
(Map p116; ☑021-886 8514; www.slowmarket. co.za; Oude Libertas Rd, Oude Libertas; ⊙9am-2pm Sat; ℗) Stellenbosch's original farmers market features lots of artisanal produce as well as crafts.

96 Winery Road INTERNATIONAL $$
(Map p116; ☑021-842 2020; www.96wineryroad. co.za; Zandberg Farm, Winery Rd; mains R135-225; ⊙noon-10pm Mon-Sat, to 3.30pm Sun; ℗) Off Rte 44 between Stellenbosch and Somerset West, this is a long-established restaurant, best known for its dry aged beef. There's plenty of other meat on the menu, plus two token vegetarian dishes.

Wijnhuis ITALIAN $$
(Map p112; ☑021-887 5844; www.wijnhuis.co.za; cnr Andringa & Church Sts; mains R120-220; ⊙9am-11pm) There's an interesting menu and an extensive wine list with more than

500 choices. Around 20 wines are available by the glass and tastings are available (R50).

Decameron ITALIAN $$
(Map p112; ☑021-883 3331; 50 Plein St; mains R85-165; ⊙noon-9.30pm Mon-Sat) This Italian-food stalwart of Stellenbosch's dining scene has a shady patio next to the botanical garden.

★**Rust en Vrede** FUSION $$$
(Map p116; ☑021-881 3757; www.rustenvrede. com; Annandale Rd; 4-course menu R720, 6-course menu with/without wines R1450/850; ⊙6.30-11pm Tue-Sat) Expect innovative dishes like rabbit-leg wontons or beetroot chocolate fondant at this stylish winery restaurant. Book ahead.

Jardine FUSION $$$
(Map p112; ☑021-886-5020; www.restaurant jardine.co.za; 1 Andringa St; lunch R160-220, 3-/6-course dinner R380/580; ⊙noon-2pm & 6.30-8pm Wed-Sat) Celebrated chef George Jardine of the long-established Jordan restaurant opened this small and very special spot in 2016. The emphasis is on local produce showcased in simple but extraordinarily good dishes. Book ahead.

Jordan BISTRO, BAKERY $$$
(☑021-881 3612; www.jordanwines.com; Stellenbosch Kloof Rd; bakery R90-135, 3-course menu R425; ⊙bakery 8am-4pm, restaurant noon-2pm & 6.30-10.30pm Thu-Sat, noon-2pm Sun-Wed; ℗) It's a little off the beaten Stellenbosch path, but it's worth the drive to get to this well-respected restaurant in a winery. The delectable menu is filled with high-end, inventive dishes, and, for those looking for something more casual, the bakery serves salads and cheese platters with freshly baked bread.

Overture Restaurant FUSION $$$
(Map p116; ☑021-880 2721; https://bertusbas son.com; Hidden Valley Wine Estate, off Annandale Rd; 3-/6-course menu R510/735; ⊙noon-3pm daily, 7-11pm Thu-Sat) A very modern wine estate and restaurant where celebrated TV chef Bertus Basson focuses on local, seasonal produce prepared to perfection and paired with Hidden Valley wines.

Drinking & Nightlife

Stellenbosch's nightlife scene is geared largely towards the interests of the university students, but there are classier options. It's safe to walk around the centre at night, so a pub crawl could certainly be on the cards – if you're staying at the Stumble Inn (p115), one will probably be organised for you.

★ **Craft Wheat & Hops** CRAFT BEER
(Map p112; ☑ 021-882 8069; www.craftstellen bosch.co.za; Andringa St; ⊙11am-10pm) This place has a dozen local craft beers on tap and plenty more in bottles. There's also a decent wine list and a great selection of spirits. If you can't decide, ask to do the beer tasting (R65) or a gin sampler (R60). Open sandwiches and burgers (R60 to R110) are available to soak it all up.

Brampton Wine Studio WINE BAR
(Map p112; ☑ 021-883 9097; www.brampton.co.za; 11 Church St; ⊙10am-9pm) Scribble on chalkboard tables while sipping shiraz at this trendy pavement cafe that also serves as Brampton winery's tasting room. Sandwiches, wraps and cheeseboards (R60 to R130) are served throughout the day.

Mystic Boer BAR
(Map p112; ☑ 021-886 8870; www.diemysticboer.co.za; 3 Victoria St; ⊙11am-2am Mon-Sat, to midnight Sun) This funky bar is a Stellenbosch institution. There's regular live music and decent bar food.

Trumpet Tree PUB
(Map p112; ☑ 021-883 8379; www.thetrumpet tree.com; Dorp St; ⊙11am-11pm) Popular with both locals and students, Trumpet Tree has a shady beer garden where you can nibble pizzas and sip on craft beer during the lengthy happy hour (2pm to 5pm Monday to Friday).

☆ Entertainment

Oude Libertas Amphitheatre PERFORMING ARTS
(Map p116; www.oudelibertas.co.za; Oude Libertas Rd; ℗) Open-air performances of theatre, music and dance are held here from November to March.

🛍 Shopping

Craft Market MARKET
(Map p112; Braak; ⊙9am-5pm Mon-Sat) This open-air market is a great place to haggle for African carvings, paintings and jewellery.

ℹ Information

Stellenbosch Tourism (Map p112; ☑ 021-883 3584; www.stellenbosch.travel; 36 Market St; ⊙8am-5pm Mon-Fri, 9am-2pm Sat, 9am-1pm Sun; 🖥) The staff are extremely helpful. Pick up the excellent brochure *Historical Stellenbosch on Foot* (R10), with a walking-tour map and information on many of the historic buildings (also available in French and German).

ℹ Getting There & Away

Long-distance bus services charge high prices for the short sector to Cape Town and do not take bookings.

Shared minibus taxis (cnr Bird & Merriman Sts) to Paarl (about R50, 45 minutes) leave from the stand on Bird St.

Metro trains run the 46km between Cape Town and Stellenbosch (1st/economy class R19.50/13, about one hour). For enquiries, call **Cape Metro Rail** (☑ 0800 656 463; http://capetowntrains.freeblog.site). To be safe, travel in the middle of the day. If coming from Jo'burg, change to a metro train at Wellington.

ℹ Getting Around

Stellenbosch is navigable on foot and, being largely flat, is good cycling territory. Bikes can be hired from the **Adventure Shop** (Map p112; ☑ 021-882 8112; www.adventureshop.co.za; cnr Dorp & Market Sts; per hour/day R80/250). **Tuk Tuk Stellies** (☑ 076 011 3016; www.tuktuk stellies.co.za) offers short trips around town on a tuk-tuk (wine tours are also available).

Franschhoek

☑ 021 / POP 17,500

French Huguenots settled in this spectacular valley over 300 years ago, bringing their vines with them. Ever since, this Winelands town has clung to its French roots, and July visitors will find that Bastille Day is celebrated here. Franschhoek bills itself as the country's gastronomic capital, and you'll certainly have a tough time deciding where to eat. Plus, with a clutch of art galleries, wine farms and stylish guesthouses thrown in, it really is one of the loveliest towns in the Cape.

◉ Sights

Huguenot Memorial Museum MUSEUM
(Map p119; ☑ 021-876 2532; www.museum.co.za; Lambrecht St; adult/child R20/5; ⊙9am-5pm Mon-Sat, 2-5pm Sun) This museum celebrates South Africa's Huguenots and houses the genealogical records of their descendants. Behind the main complex is a pleasant cafe, in front is the **Huguenot Monument** (⊙9am-5pm), FREE, opened in 1948, and across the road is the **annexe** (admission included; ⊙9am-5pm Mon-Sat, 2-5pm Sun), which offers displays on the Anglo-Boer War and natural history.

Ceramics Gallery GALLERY
(Map p119; ☑ 021-876 4304; www.davidwalters.co.za; 24 Dirkie Uys St; ⊙10am-5pm) Fran-

Franschhoek

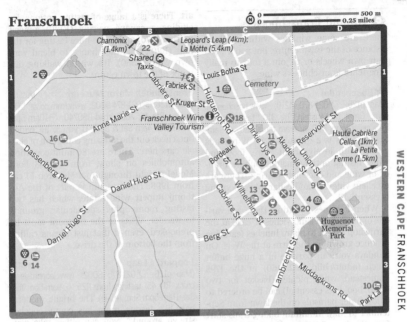

Franschhoek

schhoek boasts many fine galleries, mostly along Huguenot Rd. At the Ceramics Gallery you can watch David Walters, one of South Africa's most distinguished potters, at work in the beautifully restored home of Franschhoek's first teacher. There are also exhibits of work by other artists.

Mont Rochelle   WINERY
(Map p119; ☎021-876 2770; www.montro chelle.co.za; Dassenberg Rd; tastings from R45;

⊙10am-7pm; ℗) Along with the uberplush **hotel** (☎central reservations 011-325 4405; s/d incl breakfast from R4950/6600; ✱🛜🏊) of the same name, this winery was bought by Richard Branson in 2014. You can pair your wines with a trio of canapés (R140), or enjoy lunch (mains R95 to R245) with a view of the town and the mountains beyond.

There are free cellar tours on weekdays at 11am.

⊙ Around Franschhoek

There are some wineries within walking distance of the town centre, but you'll need your own wheels or to join a tour to really experience Franschhoek's wines.

★ Boschendal WINERY

(Map p126; ☑ 021-870 4210; www.boschendal. com; Groot Drakenstein, Rte 310; tastings from R45, cellar tours R50, vineyard tours R80; ☺ 9am-5.30pm) This is a quintessential Winelands estate, with lovely architecture, food and wine. Tasting options include bubbly, brandy or wine and chocolate pairing. There are excellent vineyard and cellar tours; booking is essential.

When it comes to eating, there are various options, from sandwiches or cake at the Farmshop & Deli to bistro lunches featuring produce grown on the farm at the Werf. On Sundays you can partake in a huge buffet lunch (adult/child R325/160) in the 1795 homestead, while picnics (basket for two R480, bookings essential) can be ordered to enjoy under parasols on the lawn from September to May. Mountain-biking trails start from the farm, for those who feel like working up an appetite.

★ La Motte WINERY

(Map p126; ☑ 021-876 8000; www.la-motte.com; Main Rd; tastings R50; ☺ 9am-5pm Mon-Sat) There's enough to keep you occupied for a full day at this vast estate just west of Franschhoek. As well as tastings of the superb shiraz range, wine-pairing lunches and dinners are served at the Pierneef à la Motte (mains R185-240; ☺ 11.30am-3pm Tue-Sun, 7-10pm Thu-Sat) restaurant. The restaurant is named for South African artist Jacob Hendrik Pierneef and a collection of his work is on show at the on-site museum.

This is also the starting point for historical walks (R50) through the estate, taking in four national monuments and a milling demonstration and ending with a bread tasting (Wednesday 10am, bookings essential). If you've overindulged, walk off a few calories on the 5km circular hike that starts at the farm.

Grande Provence WINERY

(Map p119; ☑ 021-876 8600; www.grande provence.co.za; Main Rd; tastings from R40, cellar tours R40; ☺ 10am-7pm, cellar tours 11am & 3pm Mon-Fri) A beautifully revamped, 18th-century manor house that is home to a stylish restaurant and a splendid gallery showcasing contemporary South African art. There is a range of tasting options, including a canapé pairing (R120), nougat pairing (R70) and grape-juice tasting for the kids (R20), plus the chance to blend your own wine (R350). It's within walking distance of the town centre.

Franschhoek Motor Museum MUSEUM

(Map p126; ☑ 021-874 9002; www.fmm.co.za; L'Ormarins, Rte 45; adult/child R80/40; ☺ 10am-5pm Mon-Fri, to 4pm Sat & Sun) If you're all wined out, check out the amazing collection of classic cars here. There are 80 mint-condition automobiles on show, from a 1903 Ford Model A right through to a McLaren F1 car from 1998. The museum is part of the Anthonij Rupert wine estate, which has two tasting rooms plus spectacular grounds to wander. Visits to the museum must be prebooked, even if that just means calling from the bottom of the drive.

Leopard's Leap WINERY

(Map p126; ☑ 021-876 8002; www.leopardsleap. co.za; Rte 45; tastings from R25; ☺ 9am-5pm Tue-Sat, 11am-5pm Sun; ℗) The bright, modern, barn-like tasting room has comfy couches strewn around – you can either take your tasters to enjoy at leisure or sit at the bar for a slightly more formal affair. The large lawns have a jungle gym for kids, while the rotisserie restaurant (11.30am to 3pm Wednesday to Sunday) is very popular with families. You pay by weight, but you can budget for around R150 per person. Cooking classes are available once a month – booking ahead is essential.

Solms-Delta WINERY

(Map p126; ☑ 021-874 3937; www.solms-delta. com; Delta Rd, off Rte 45; tastings from R25, tours R50; ☺ 9am-5pm Sun & Mon, to 6pm Tue-Sat; ℗) In addition to tastings and sales, various heritage tours are available at this excellent winery. The museum here covers Cape history and tells the Solms-Delta story from the perspective of farm workers throughout the years. On the culinary side, there's Fyndraai Restaurant (mains R140-185; ☺ 10am-5pm; ☑), serving original dishes inspired by the Cape's varied cultures and using herbs from the on-site indigenous garden. You can also opt for a picnic (adult/child R235/75), to be enjoyed along an enchanting riverside trail.

⚘ Activities

Franschhoek Wine Tram TOURS

(Map p119; ☑ 021-300 0338; www.winetram.co.za; 32 Huguenot Rd; adult/child R220/90) This is a fun alternative to the usual Winelands tour. The tram line is short and only two wineries have a stop. The rest of the hop-on, hop-off service makes use of an open-sided bus. There are four routes, each visiting up to seven wineries. Bookings are advisable, as is dressing warmly – the bus in particular can get pretty chilly.

Paradise Stables HORSE RIDING
(☑021-876 2160; www.paradisestables.co.za; per hour R300; ⊙rides 7.30am, 8.45am, 1.15pm & 5.45pm Mon-Sat) As well as hour-long rides through Franschhoek's surrounds, there are four-hour trips taking in two vineyards (R950 including tastings).

Franschhoek Cycles CYCLING
(Map p119; ☑021-876 4956; www.franschhoek cycles.co.za; 2 Main Rd; half/full day R250/350) Rent bikes or have staff arrange a guided cycling tour of surrounding wineries – tour prices depend on the itinerary and number of people.

🛏 Sleeping

Otter's Bend Lodge HOSTEL $
(Map p119; ☑021-876 3200; www.ottersbendlodge. co.za; Dassenberg Rd; camping per site R220, dm/d R220/600; P🐾🛜🅿) A delightful budget option in a town not known for affordable accommodation. Basic double rooms lead to a shared deck shaded by poplar trees, and there's space for a couple of tents on the lawn. There are also two four-sleeper cabins (R880) with kitchenette, one of which is wheelchair-friendly. It's a 15-minute walk from town and close to a winery.

★Reeden Lodge CHALET $$
(Map p119; ☑021-876 3174; www.reeden lodge.co.za; Anne Marie St; cottage from R1000; P🛜🅿♿) A good-value, terrific option for families, with well-equipped, self-catering cottages sleeping from two to 10 people, situated on a farm about 10 minutes' walk from town. Parents will love the peace and quiet and their kids will love the sheep, tree house and open space.

La Cabrière Country House GUESTHOUSE $$
(Map p119; ☑021-876 4780; www.lacabri ere.co.za; Park Lane; s/d incl breakfast from R2100/2850; P🐾🛜🅿) The sumptuously decorated rooms at this boutique guesthouse have underfloor heating and sweeping views to the mountains. You can stroll into town.

La Fontaine GUESTHOUSE $$
(Map p119; ☑087 095 2017; www.lafontaine franschhoek.co.za; 21 Dirkie Uys St; s/d from R1375/1950; 🐾🛜🅿) A stylishly appointed,

very comfortable family home featuring 14 spacious rooms with wooden floors and mountain views.

Chamonix Guest Cottages CHALET $$
(☑021-876 8406; www.chamonix.co.za; Uitkyk St; d from R2100) There are various lodges and self-catering cottages at this wine farm-cum-game reserve. You can walk to town (though it's a long slog uphill to get back).

Le Ballon Rouge GUESTHOUSE $$
(Map p119; ☑021-876 2651; www.ballonrouge. co.za; 7 Reservoir East St; s/d incl breakfast from R1000/1200; 🐾🛜🅿) A small, friendly guesthouse with good-quality rooms and stylish suites with stunning bathrooms.

Akademie Street BOUTIQUE HOTEL $$$
(Map p119; ☑082 517 0405; www.aka.co.za; 5 Akademie St; r incl breakfast R5500; P🛜🅿) If there's anywhere in South Africa that you're going to blow the budget, Franschhoek might as well be it. The luxurious rooms at this quiet hotel are a fine place to splurge. Part of the guesthouse dates back to 1860 and rooms honour the building's history with heavy four-poster beds and occasional antiques, though there is a distinctly modern flair.

Le Quartier Français BOUTIQUE HOTEL $$$
(Map p119; ☑021-876 2151; www.lqf.co.za; cnr Wilhelmina & Berg Sts; r incl breakfast from R7500; P🐾🛜🅿) Set around a leafy courtyard and pool, the large rooms at this opulent hotel have fireplaces, huge beds and stylish decor. If you're feeling flush, try one of the suites (from R12,500), which come with private pools.

🍴 Eating & Drinking

Marigold INDIAN $$
(Map p119; ☑021-876 8970; www.marigoldfran schhoek.com; Heritage Sq, 9 Huguenot Rd; mains R80-150; ⊙noon-2.30pm & 6-9pm; 🌿) If you fancy a change from all the French-inspired fine dining, Marigold serves elegant North Indian cuisine in its contemporary dining room.

Reuben's FUSION $$
(Map p119; ☑021-876 3772; www.reubens.co.za; 2 Daniel Hugo St; mains R175-235; ⊙noon-3pm & 6-9pm Wed-Mon) Franschhoek's favourite son, celebrity chef Reuben Riffel, is behind this Asian fusion restaurant in a fabulous, light-filled space off the main road. In summer, grab a poke bowl to enjoy on the large patio. There's a carefully curated wine list plus beers from a nearby microbrewery.

DON'T MISS

BABYLONSTOREN
....

Babylonstoren (Map p116; ☑ 021-863 3852; www.babylonstoren.com; Simondium Rd, Klapmuts; entry R10, tastings R30; ⊙9am-5pm; P), a 2.5-sq-km wine and fruit farm, is on the north slope of the Simonsberg mountain between Klapmuts and Paarl. Its highlight is an 800-sq-metre, formally designed garden; inspired by Cape Town's Company's Garden, it is an incredible undertaking, featuring edible and medicinal plants, lotus ponds and espaliered quince trees, chicken coops and a maze of prickly-pear cacti. Reserve a place on one of the garden tours (10am).

Better yet, check into one of the super-chic guest rooms (single/double from R4200/5700), crafted from the old workers' cottages, so that once the day visitors have left you can enjoy the gardens – not to mention the spa and pool in one of the farm's old reservoir tanks.

There's no need to reserve if you'd like lunch at the **Greenhouse** (mains R75-100), hidden deep in the garden. However, bookings are essential for the **Babel** (mains R100-280), which serves delicious meals made with produce from the garden and quaffable wines that the farm has recently resumed making. The new wine cellar is a model of contemporary design with interesting exhibits related to the wine-making process. There are cellar tours on the hour (R35, including tasting). You can also buy freshly baked bread and charcuterie cured on-site if you feel like picnicking.

Lust Bistro & Bakery
BISTRO $$

(Map p126; ☑021-874 1456; www.lustbistro.com; cnr Simondium Rd & Rte 45; mains R85-160; ⊙7.30am-5pm Mon-Sat, 8am-4pm Sun) Based at Vrede en Lust winery, this is a refreshingly unfussy place to eat in a region known for haute cuisine. You'll find salads, sandwiches and a build-your-own pizza option. Daily blackboard specials include some Asian-inspired eats and on Sunday there's a buffet lunch (adult/child R195/99) where you can eat away the day – bookings essential.

★La Petite Colombe
FUSION $$$

(Map p119; ☑021-202 3395; www.lapetitecolombe.com; Le Quarter Français, Huguenot Rd; 7-course menu with/without wine R750/395) The award-winning Cape Town restaurant has opened a breezy sister branch here. The French-inspired menu comes in seven- or 12-course versions and you can opt to pair each course with a different wine.

Foliage
FUSION $$$

(Map p119; ☑021-876 2328; http://foliage.co.za; 11 Huguenot Rd; mains R175-265; ⊙noon-2pm & 7-9pm Mon-Sat) Chef and owner Chris Erasmus has brought the foraging culture to the Cape at this hugely popular restaurant. Forest-floor ingredients such as river cress, dandelion and mushrooms complement decadent dishes like roasted swordfish and braised kudu shank. The restaurant is decked out with creations from Chris' artist wife, Alisha. Book ahead.

Haute Cabrière Cellar
FUSION $$$

(☑021-876 3688; www.cabriere.co.za; Franschhoek Pass Rd; 3-course menu R370; ⊙noon-2.30pm daily, 6-9pm Mon-Sat) If you want to go all-out on the French-inspired cuisine, try the five-course menu with wine pairings (R595). Tastings (from R55) are available and there are cellar tours at 11am, which include a demonstration of *sabrage* – slicing open a bottle of bubbly with a sword.

Ryan's Kitchen
FUSION $$$

(Map p119; ☑021-876 4598; www.ryanskitchen.co.za; Place Vendome, Huguenot Rd; mains R170-260, 4-course menu with/without wine R740/540; ⊙12.30-2.30pm & 6.30-9.30pm Mon-Sat) Loved by locals and recommended by travellers, this long-running restaurant marries South African ingredients with fine-dining techniques. Watch chefs prepare intricate dishes such as Madagascan sea bass with seaweed-soya broth in the open kitchen. The menu changes every two weeks.

La Petite Ferme
SOUTH AFRICAN $$$

(☑021-876 3016; www.lapetiteferme.co.za; Franschhoek Pass Rd; mains R155-280; ⊙noon-3.30pm daily, 6.30-9pm Fri & Sat; ☎) In a stupendous setting overlooking Franschhoek Valley, this contemporary restaurant makes a big deal of local ingredients. Try the biltong-dusted ostrich steak or harissa-coated Karoo lamb. There are some luxurious rooms if you can't bear to leave.

Tuk Tuk Microbrewery   MICROBREWERY

(Map p119; ☑ 021-492 2207; www.tuktukbrew.com; 14 Huguenot Rd; ☺ 11am-10pm) There are three permanent beers on tap, plus ever-changing experimental brews so be sure to ask what's new. It also serves beers from Cape Brewing Company in Paarl. The menu is a breath of fresh air if you're looking for a light lunch in Franschhoek – tamales, buffalo wings and tacos.

ℹ Information

Franschhoek Wine Valley Tourism (Map p119; ☑ 021-876 2861; www.franschhoek.org.za; 62 Huguenot Rd; ☺ 8am-5pm Mon-Fri, 9am-5pm Sat, 9am-4pm Sun) Staff can provide you with a map of the area's scenic walks (R40) and issue permits (R40) for hikes in the Mont Rochelle Nature Reserve, as well as book accommodation.

ℹ Getting There & Away

Franschhoek is 32km east of Stellenbosch and 32km south of Paarl. The best way to reach Franschhoek is in your own vehicle. Some visitors choose to cycle from Stellenbosch, but roads are winding and can be treacherous. Alternatively, take a **shared taxi** (Map p119; Huguenot Rd) from Stellenbosch (R25) or Paarl station (R28). If you're looking for a private taxi, try **Call a Cab** (☑ 082 256 6784).

Paarl

☑ 021 / POP 112,000

Surrounded by mountains and vineyards, and set on the banks of the Berg River, Paarl is the Winelands' largest town. It's often overlooked by people heading for Stellenbosch and Franschhoek, but it does have its own charm, including interesting Cape Dutch architecture and gracious homesteads, a good range of places to stay and some decent restaurants. The main road is over 11km long, so not exactly walkable, but there are a couple of wineries within an easy stroll of the train station.

◉ Sights & Activities

KWV Emporium   WINERY

(Map p124; ☑ 021-863 3803; www.kwvwineemporium.co.za; Kohler St; tastings R40-65, cellar tours R55; ☺ 9am-4.30pm Mon-Sat, 10am-5pm Sun, cellar tours 10am, 10.30am & 2.15pm; P) Operating since 1918, this wine-making co-operative is particularly well known for its award-winning fortified wines and brandies. Cellar tours are available and there is a range of tasting options, including chocolate and brandy, biltong and wine, bubbly and cheesecake and a tea and chocolate pairing. It's a short walk from the train station.

Paarl Museum   MUSEUM

(Map p124; ☑ 021-872 2651; 303 Main St; R10; ☺ 9am-4pm Mon-Fri, to 1pm Sat) Housed in the Oude Pastorie (Old Parsonage), built in 1714, this museum has an interesting collection of Cape Dutch antiques and relics of Huguenot and early Afrikaner culture, plus information on the history of Paarl.

Afrikaans Language Museum   MUSEUM

(Map p124; ☑ 021-872 3441; www.taalmuseum.co.za; 11 Pastorie Ave; adult/child R20/5; ☺ 9am-4pm Mon-Fri) Paarl is considered the wellspring of the Afrikaans language, a fact covered by this interesting museum. It also shows, thanks to a multimedia exhibition, how three continents contributed to the formation of the language. There's a discount if you buy a combo ticket for the Taal Monument as well.

Taal Monument   MONUMENT

(Map p126; ☑ 021-863 0543; www.taalmuseum.co.za; adult/child R30/10; ☺ 8am-5pm Apr-Nov, to 8pm Dec-Mar) The somewhat phallic Taal Monument is in the **Paarl Mountain Nature Reserve** (Map p126; per vehicle R52, per person R17; ☺ 7am-7pm). The giant, needle-like edifice commemorates the language (*taal* is Afrikaans for 'language'). On a clear day there are stunning views as far as Cape Town. There's also an adjoining restaurant and curio shop. If you're here when it's a full moon, join locals for a night-time picnic.

Wineland Ballooning   BALLOONING

(Map p124; ☑ 021-863 3192; www.kapinfo.com; 64 Main St; per person R3900) You'll need to get up very early in the morning, but a hot-air balloon trip over the Winelands will be unforgettable. Trips run between November and April when the weather conditions are right.

◉ Around Paarl

★ Avondale   WINERY

(Map p126; ☑ 021-863 1976; www.avondalewine.co.za; Lustigan Rd, Klein Drakenstein; tastings R70, ecotour R300; ☺ 10am-4pm; P) This quiet spot in a gracious old homestead serves delectable, organically made wines. The formal tasting takes around an hour, or you can join a two-hour eco-safari through the vineyards on the back of a tractor, which culminates in a tasting. The restaurant, **Faber** (mains R160 to R220), is one of the Winelands'

WESTERN CAPE PAARL

Paarl

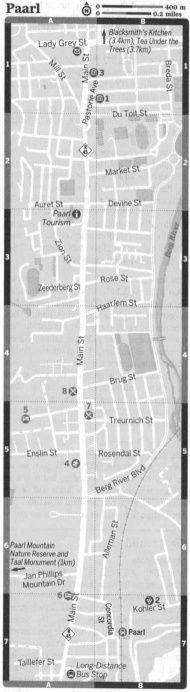

best, with dishes like roasted springbok loin, truffled leeks and sourdough bread-and-butter pudding.

★ Spice Route
WINERY

(Map p126; ☎021-863 5200; www.spiceroute.co.za; Suid-Agter-Paarl Rd; tastings from R40; ⊕9am-5pm; P) Spice Route is known for its complex red wines, particularly the Flagship syrah. Aside from wine there is a lot going on, including glass-blowing demonstrations, wine and charcuterie pairings (R85), a chocolatier (tutored tasting R35), grappa distillery and a superlative microbrewery (tastings R35). As well as the upmarket restaurant headed by celebrity chef Bertus Basson (mains R140 to R215), there is a pizzeria (mains R70 to R150).

Fairview
WINERY

(Map p126; ☎021-863 2450; www.fairview.co.za; Suid-Agter-Paarl Rd; wine & cheese tastings R40; ⊕9am-5pm; P) This hugely popular estate off Rte 101, 6km south of Paarl, is a wonderful winery, but not the place to come for a tranquil tasting. It's great value, since tastings include six wines *and* a wide range of cheeses (you can just do cheese for R20). The well-respected restaurant (mains R90 to R180) is open for breakfast and lunch.

Backsberg
WINERY

(Map p116; ☎021-875 5141; www.backsberg.co.za; tastings from R30; ⊕8.30am-5pm Mon-Fri, 9.30am-4.30pm Sat, 10.30am-4.30pm Sun;) Backsberg is a hugely popular estate thanks to its reliable label and lavish outdoor lunches – book ahead for the Sunday lamb spit braai (barbecue; R295) or a picnic to enjoy in the grounds (R180). Tasting options include wine and chocolate, wine and cheese, and a chance to create your own blend.

Paarl

Glen Carlou
WINERY

(Map p116; 021-875 5528; www.glencarlou. co.za; Simondium Rd, Klapmuts; tastings R25-35; 9am-5pm Mon-Fri, 10am-4pm Sat & Sun; P) Sitting south of the N1, the tasting room has a panoramic view of Tortoise Hill. Enjoy a glass of the sumptuous chardonnay or renowned Bordeaux blend, Grand Classique, over lunch (three-course meal R295). There's an art gallery too, with rotating exhibits.

Drakenstein Correctional Centre
HISTORIC SITE

(Map p126) On 11 February 1990, when Nelson Mandela walked free from incarceration for the first time in over 27 years, the jail he left was not on Robben Island, but here. Then called the Victor Verster, this was where Mandela spent his last two years of captivity in the warders' cottage, negotiating the end of apartheid. It's still a working prison, so there are no tours, but there's a superb statue of Mandela, fist raised in *viva* position.

Anura
WINERY

(Map p116; 021-875 5360; www.anura.co.za; off Simondium Rd, Klapmuts; wine & cheese tastings R60; 9am-5pm; P) Foodies could hang out here for a while, tasting cheese made on the premises, grabbing a platter or picnic featuring cured meats from the deli, or swapping grape for grain and sipping a beer from the microbrewery alongside the pretty pond. Wine-wise, Anura is best known for syrah and malbec.

🛏 Sleeping

Berg River Resort
CAMPGROUND $

(Map p126; 021-007 1852; www.bergriverresort. co.za; Rte 45; camping per site from R330, chalets from R940; P) An attractive campground with simple chalets (sleeping two) beside the Berg River, 5km from Paarl on Rte 45 towards Franschhoek. Facilities include canoes, trampolines and a cafe. It gets very crowded during school holidays and prices rise dramatically.

Oak Tree Lodge
GUESTHOUSE $

(Map p124; 021-863 2631; www.oaktreelodge. co.za; 32 Main St; s/d incl breakfast from R720/980; P) This old house has comfortable, well-appointed rooms, some with balconies. The larger garden rooms are quieter, being off the main road. It's very conveniently located – you can walk to restaurants, wineries and the train station from here.

WORTH A TRIP

BAINSKLOOF PASS

Bainskloof is one of the country's great mountain passes, with a superb caravan park halfway along. It's a magical drive, which, if you have the lungs for it, would be even better experienced on a bicycle. Route 303 runs from Wellington across Bainskloof to meet Rte 43, which runs south to Worcester and north to Ceres.

★ Cascade Country Manor
BOUTIQUE HOTEL $$

(Map p126; 021-868 0227; www.cascademanor. co.za; Waterval Rd; r incl breakfast from R2190; P) Tucked away along a dirt road 10km east of the centre, this place will make you feel like you're far from anywhere, although it's an easy drive back to town. Rooms are just what you'd expect but it's the grounds that wow, with vast lawns, a large pool, olive groves and a short walk to a pretty waterfall. Olive tastings and excellent dinners are on offer.

Under Oaks
GUESTHOUSE $$

(Map p126; 021-869 8535; http://underoaks. co.za; Noord-Agter-Paarl Rd, Northern Paarl; s/d R1150/1440; P) On a peaceful wine farm just 3km north of central Paarl, Under Oaks has spacious rooms decked out in muted shades. There's wine tasting on the premises as well as a rustic pizzeria and some magnificent mountain vistas.

Grande Roche Hotel
LUXURY HOTEL $$$

(Map p124; 021-863 5100; www.granderoche. com; Plantasie St; ste incl breakfast from R3270; P) A superluxurious hotel set in a Cape Dutch manor house, offering wonderful mountain views, a heated swimming pool and the excellent **Bosman's Restaurant** (3 courses R525; noon-2pm & 7-11pm). It's a short walk to Paarl's main road.

🍴 Eating

★ Tea Under the Trees
BISTRO $

(Map p126; 072 871 9103; www.teaundertthe trees.co.za; Main St, Northern Paarl; mains R40-55; 9am-4pm Mon-Fri Oct-Apr; P) The only downside to this fabulous tea garden is that it's only open for half the year. Based on an organic fruit farm, it's a wonderful place to sit under century-old oak trees and enjoy an al fresco cuppa, a light lunch or a large slice of home-baked cake. There's

Around Paarl

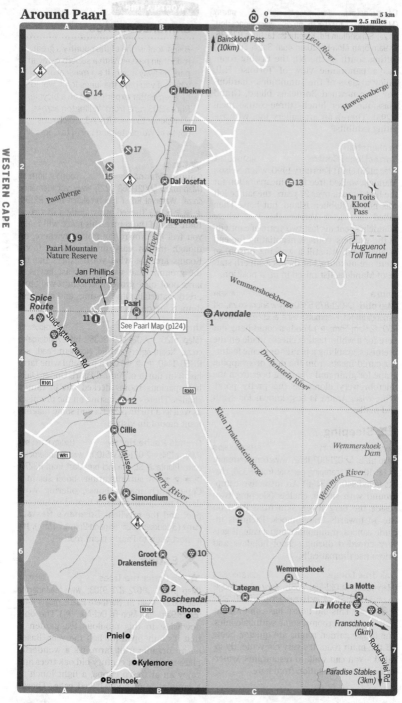

Around Paarl

no indoor seating. Saturdays tend to get booked well in advance. It's 4km north of the town centre.

★ **Glen Carlou** INTERNATIONAL $$
(Map p116; ☑ 021-875 5528; www.glencarlou.co.za; mains R150-190; ⊙ 11am-3pm) The food at this stylish winery is on a par with the views: magnificent. Dishes, such as pan-roasted sea bass, Parmesan mousse and lamb shoulder with sweetbreads, come with a recommended wine pairing. There's also a three-course set menu (R295). Book ahead on weekends.

Terra Mare FUSION $$
(Map p124; ☑ 021-863 4805; 90a Main St; mains R130-200; ⊙ noon-10pm Mon-Sat; ℗) The menu is fairly small but superb, offering a mix of Asian, Italian and South African dishes. Tables inside can be a little noisy due to the proximity to busy Main St, but there's a delightful garden at the back with views of Paarl Mountain Nature Reserve (p123).

Noop FUSION $$
(Map p124; ☑ 021-863 3925; www.noop.co.za; 127 Main St; mains R135-225; ⊙ 11am-11pm Mon-Sat) Recommended by locals all over the Winelands, this restaurant and wine bar has a comprehensive menu of upmarket dishes like slow-roasted lamb neck, roast duck and

wild-mushroom risotto. Check out the South African dessert platter, featuring Malva pudding (a traditional sticky sponge pudding with citrus fruit) and milk-tart millefeuille. Bookings recommended for dinner.

Blacksmith's Kitchen BISTRO $$
(Map p126; ☑ 021-870 1867; www.pearlmountain. co.za; Pearl Mountain Winery, Bo Lang St; mains R65-195; ⊙ 11.30am-9.30pm Tue-Sat, to 4pm Sun; ℗) Grab a table under the trees and enjoy an unfussy lunch of wood-fired pizza or roast pork belly with views of the vineyards, town and mountains beyond.

❶ Information

Paarl Tourism (Map p124; ☑ 021-872 4842; www.paarlonline.com; 216 Main St; ⊙ 8.30am-5pm Mon-Fri, 10am-1pm Sat & Sun) This office has an excellent supply of information on the whole region.

❶ Getting There & Around

All the major long-distance bus companies offer services going through Paarl, making it easy to build the town into your itinerary.

If you don't have your own transport, your only option for getting around Paarl, apart from walking and cycling, is to call a taxi; try **Paarl Taxis** (☑ 021-872 5671; www.paarltaxisandtours. co.za).

Tulbagh

☑ 023 / POP 9000
Beneath the dramatic backdrop of the Witzenberg range, Tulbagh (established in 1699) is a pretty town with historic buildings and delightful places to stay and eat. Church St, lined with trees and flowering shrubs, is a near-perfect example of an 18th- and 19th-century Cape Dutch village street. It was badly damaged in an earthquake in 1969, but the painstaking restoration has paid off.

◉ Sights & Activities

Church Street is one of the Western Cape's most beautiful roads and wandering from house to house is a pleasant way to spend a morning. Many of the buildings are national monuments and have information plaques outside detailing the history of the building. The **community garden** at the northern end of town is also worth a wander. The region is known for its wines, particularly bubbly.

WESTERN CAPE TULBAGH

Oude Kerk Volksmuseum — MUSEUM

(Old Church Folk Museum; 4 Church St; adult/child R15/5; ⊙9am-5pm Mon-Fri, 9am-3pm Sat, 11am-3pm Sun) This museum made up of four buildings is worth a pause. Start at No 4, which has a photographic history of Church St, covering the earthquake and reconstruction; visit the beautiful Oude Kerk itself (1743); move to No 14, featuring Victorian furnishings; and end at No 22, a reconstructed town dwelling from the 18th century.

Saronsberg Cellar — WINERY

(www.saronsberg.com; Waveren Rd; tastings R80; ⊙8.30am-5pm Mon-Fri, 10am-2pm Sat, 10am-1pm Sun) Sip superlative reds while admiring the contemporary art that lines the walls of this smart cellar 6km north of town.

Twee Jonge Gezellen — WINERY

(☎023-230 0680; www.tweejongegezellen.co.za; Waveren Rd; tastings free; ⊙10am-4pm Mon-Sat, cellar tours 11am; P) This long-established winery has had a revamp and is once again a marvellous place to sip bubbly all afternoon. Unpretentious tastings take place in the stylish tasting room, on the deck or in the garden. There are also tours explaining the Méthode Cap Classique–making process.

Detour Bike Shop — CYCLING

(☎084 052 4102; www.detourcycles.co.za; bike hire half/full day R150/250; ⊙8am-5.30pm Mon-Fri, to 1pm Sat) As well as renting out bikes, Detour Bike Shop offers guided cycling tours to nearby wineries (R750 per person).

WORTH A TRIP

KAGGA KAMMA

Far from towns and paved roads, this lodge (☎021-872 4343; www.kagga-kamma.co.za; s/d with full board from R4790/7540, camping R75; P) is the perfect place to recharge. There are wildlife drives exploring the Karoo landscape, hikes to see San rock art and evening 'sky safaris' at the mini-observatory. Rooms are in mock-caves that blend seamlessly with the rugged surrounds. The reserve is 92km northeast of Ceres.

For the ultimate in 'glamping', there are two 'open-air rooms' – entire luxury suites transported into the desert.

🛏 Sleeping & Eating

★ Vindoux Guest Farm — CABIN $$

(☎023-230 0635; www.vindoux.com; Waveren Rd; d incl breakfast R1950; P❀🐾📶🏊) A must for the romantically inclined, these luxury tree houses each have a spa bath and views of a small wildlife area with zebras, wildebeest and springbok. Hire bikes for a self-guided vineyard cycle then revive with a fynbos aromatherapy massage at the day spa (R480). There are also simpler cottages (R850 for two people).

Rijk's Country House — BOUTIQUE HOTEL $$

(☎023-230 1006; www.rijkscountryhouse.co.za; Van der Stel St; r incl breakfast R1550; P❀🐾📶🏊) Rijk's provides pleasant accommodation in thatched cottages on a beautiful wine estate with manicured lawns. There are tours and tastings at the winery and a good restaurant (mains R95 to R170) in the main building. The hotel is 2km north of the town centre.

De Oude Herberg — HISTORIC HOTEL $$

(☎023-230 0260; www.deoudeherberg.co.za; 6 Church St; s/d incl breakfast R865/1130; ❀📶🏊) A guesthouse since 1885, this is a friendly place with traditional country furniture and a lovely patio. There are just four rooms so advance bookings are highly recommended.

Cape Dutch Quarter — GUESTHOUSE $$

(☎079 051 2059; www.cdq.co.za; 33 Van der Stel St; r from R1100; ❀📶🏊) There is a variety of accommodation on offer here, from simple apartments (two people R650) to more luxurious self-catering houses (four people R1600) and smart doubles with four-poster beds. The owner is a mine of information on the area and can arrange hiking and mountain-biking permits and maps. Most of the accommodation is on Church St, but you'll find reception on Van der Stel St.

★ Olive Terrace — INTERNATIONAL $$

(www.tulbaghhotel.co.za; 22 Van der Stel St; mains R75-150; ⊙7am-10pm) Based in the Tulbagh Hotel, this restaurant serves a range of dishes including a few vegetarian options. The shady terrace is a delight in the Tulbagh summer heat.

Readers Restaurant — SOUTH AFRICAN $$

(☎023-230 0087; 12 Church St; mains R105-155; ⊙9am-10pm Wed-Mon) The menu changes regularly, but always features a few traditional South African dishes and plenty of local ingredients. The attached gift shop is aimed at feline lovers, with an array of catty collectables.

ℹ Information

Tulbagh Tourism (📋 023-230 1348; www.
tulbaghtourism.co.za; 4 Church St; ⊙9am-5pm
Mon-Fri, 9am-3pm Sat, 10am-3pm Sun) Helpful
staff provide information and maps about the
area, including the Tulbagh Wine Route.

Robertson

📋 023 / POP 22,000

In a valley located between the Langeberg
and Riviersonderendberge, Robertson is
the prosperous centre of one of the largest
wine-growing areas in the country. It offers
an excellent wine route encompassing the
neighbouring villages of Ashton, Bonnievale
and McGregor, as well as a wider range of
outdoor activities than other towns on Rte
62. There's hiking in the mountains, gentle
rafting on the river and horse riding – the
town is famous for its horse studs.

◉ Sights & Activities

★**Viljoensdrift**   WINERY
(📋 023-615 1017; www.viljoensdrift.co.za; tastings
free; ⊙10am-5pm Mon-Fri, to 4pm Sat; ℗🐕) One
of Robertson's most popular places to sip, especially on weekends. Put together a picnic
from the deli, buy a bottle from the cellar
door and taste on an hour-long boat trip
along the Breede River (adult/child R70/20).
Boats leave on the hour from noon. Bookings essential.

Excelsior   WINERY
(📋 023-615 1980; www.excelsior.co.za; off Rte 317;
tastings free; ⊙10am-4pm Mon-Fri, to 3pm Sat;
℗🐕) Tastings take place on a wooden deck
overlooking a reservoir – it's a delightful
spot. The real draw, though, is the 'blend
your own' experience, where you can mix
three wine varieties to your liking and take
home a bottle of your own creation, complete with your own label (R70). The restaurant serves *roosterbrood* (traditional bread
cooked over coals) sandwiches.

Springfield   WINERY
(📋 023-626 3661; www.springfieldestate.com; Rte
317; tastings free; ⊙8am-5pm Mon-Fri, 9am-3pm
Sat) Some of the wines here are unfiltered –
try the uncrushed Whole Berry for something different. Bring your own picnic to
enjoy in the peaceful grounds, overlooking
a lake. Cellar tours are available on request.

Graham Beck   WINERY
(📋 023-626 1214; www.grahambeckwines.com;
tastings from R75; ⊙9am-5pm Mon-Fri, 10am-4pm

Sat & Sun; ℗) Taste the world-class bubblies
in a striking modern building with huge
plate-glass windows. The winery comes as a
breath of fresh air after all those Cape Dutch
estates.

Nerina Guest Farm   HORSE RIDING
(📋 082 744 2580; www.nerinaguestfarm.com; Go-
ree Rd; hour-long rides R200) This long-running
outfit offers hour-long horse trails along the
Breede River or through the vineyards with
an option to swim with the horses afterwards (R50). Longer rides can be arranged.

✷ Festivals & Events

There are a number of wine-related events,
including the **Hands on Harvest** in February, the **Wacky Wine Weekend** (📋 023-626
3167; www.wackywineweekend.com) in late May/
early June and the **Wine on the River Festival** (📋 023-626 3167; www.wineonriver.com) in
late October. Accommodation in the town
is scarce at these times, so book well in
advance.

🍴 Sleeping & Eating

★**Pat Busch Mountain Reserve**   COTTAGE $
(📋 023-626 2033; www.patbusch.co.za; Bergendal
Rd, Klaasvoogds West; 4-person cottage from R680;
℗📶🐕) These well-equipped cottages are
based on the edge of a nature reserve 15km
northeast of Robertson off Rte 60. Hiking,
mountain biking, fishing and birdwatching
are available. If you fancy some glamping,
there are also luxury tents (doubles R1490)
operated by Africamps. The tents have two
bedrooms, a bathroom, well-equipped kitch-
en and stellar views of the Langeberg.

Robertson Backpackers   HOSTEL $
(📋 023-626 1280; www.robertsonbackpackers.
co.za; 4 Dordrecht Ave; campsites R100, dm/s/d
with shared bathroom R160/350/420, d R520;
℗📶🐕) A suburban backpackers with spacious dorms and pleasant en-suite doubles in
the garden. There's a big grassy backyard and
a shisha lounge, and wine and activity tours
can be arranged, including a gentle half-day
rafting trip on the Breede River (R550).

Ballinderry   GUESTHOUSE $$
(📋 023-626 5365; www.ballinderryguesthouse.com;
8 Le Roux St; s/d incl breakfast from R1100/1500;
℗❄📶🐕) This colourful boutique guest-
house is impeccable, thanks to hosts Luc and
Hilde. A champagne breakfast is served, as
are superb dinners on request, and Dutch,
French and German are spoken. Try to get
one of the rooms that opens onto the garden.

Gubas De Hoek GUESTHOUSE $$
(☑023-626 6218; www.gubas-dehoek.com; 45 Reitz St; s/d from R720/1160; 🛜⛱🌐) 🅿 Highly recommended by readers is this friendly home with well-appointed rooms and family-friendly self-catering units (from R1200). Owner-chef Gunther Huerttlen will cook you dinner (three courses R360) and there's a shared self-catering kitchen for preparing light meals. The owners are working to produce all of their own electricity.

★**Strictly Coffee** CAFE $
(☑023-626 6691; www.strictlycoffee.co.za; 5 Voortrekker St; mains R70-90; ⊗7am-5.30pm Mon-Fri, 9am-2pm Sat; 🛜) As well as excellent coffee roasted on-site, you'll find a selection of cakes, plus tasty salads and sandwiches made with the freshest ingredients. Locals rave about the eggs Benedict for breakfast.

@ **Four Cousins** INTERNATIONAL $$
(☑023-615 1505; www.fourcousins.co.za; 3 Kromhout St; mains R80-160; ⊗8.30am-9.30pm Mon-Sat, to 5pm Sun; 🅿🛜🌐) There's something to keep everyone entertained here – wine tasting, a microbrewery, sweetie pairings for the kids and an excellent jungle gym. The menu runs the gamut from salads and wraps to pizzas, burgers and steaks.

❶ Information

Robertson Tourism Bureau (☑023-626 4437; www.robertsontourism.co.za; 9 Voortrekker St; ⊗8am-5pm Mon-Fri, 9am-2pm Sat, 10am-2pm Sun) A friendly office with information about the wine region, Rte 62 and hiking trails in the mountains.

❶ Getting There & Away

Translux (www.translux.co.za) buses stop opposite the police station on Voortrekker St. Routes include Knysna (R250, five hours), Cape Town (R240, two hours, daily) and Port Elizabeth (R390, nine hours, daily).

Shared taxis (Voortrekker St) to and from Bellville in the northern suburbs of Cape Town (R95, 1½ hours) also stop opposite the police station.

McGregor

☑023 / POP 3100
Dreaming away at the end of a road going nowhere, quiet and sleepy McGregor makes for a delightful retreat with good accommodation, an arts route and plenty of spa treatments on offer. The main thoroughfare,

Voortrekker St, has pretty whitewashed cottages dating from the mid-19th century, and the village is surrounded by farmland. It's a good base for hiking in the nearby Riviersonderendberge and is also one end of the excellent Boesmanskloof Trail. There are half a dozen wineries in the McGregor area, which are encompassed in the Robertson Wine Valley route.

◉ Sights & Activities

Eseltjiesrus Donkey Sanctuary ANIMAL SANCTUARY
(☑023-625 1593; www.donkeysanctuary.co.za; entry by donation; ⊗10am-4pm Thu-Sun; 🅿) This long-running donkey sanctuary is a peaceful spot with a couple of dams offering good birdwatching, a tearoom serving homemade goodies and, of course, the chance to meet the donkeys, many of which were neglected in their former homes. Guided tours are offered or you can wander at will.

Tanagra Private Cellar WINERY
(☑023-625 1780; www.tanagra-wines.co.za; tastings free; ⊗by appointment) Tanagra is a family-run farm offering tastings of its range of reds as well as the grappa distilled on-site. There's self-catering accommodation (two-person cottage from R900) and a range of short hikes on the farm, which can be extended to explore the adjoining Vrolijkheid Nature Reserve.

★**Boesmanskloof Trail** HIKING
(Greyton McGregor Trail; www.capenature.co.za; day permit adult/child R40/20) One of the best reasons for coming to McGregor is to hike the trail to Greyton, roughly 14km through the spectacular fynbos-clad Riviersonderendberge mountains. The hike actually starts at Die Galg, about 15km south of McGregor. The McGregor-to-Greyton direction is easier. During peak times you must book in advance; only 50 people per day are allowed on the trail.

Most hikers stay the night in Greyton and return the following day. Permits are available from the tourism bureau and staff there can also offer advice on transfers to Die Galg.

Oakes Falls HIKING
(day permit adult/child R40/20) If you don't fancy hiking the full Boesmanskloof Trail (p130), it's feasible to do a six-hour round-trip to these lovely waterfalls, roughly 6km from Die Galg, where you can cool off with

a swim in the tannin-stained waters. You'll still need to get a permit from the tourism bureau before you set off.

🛏 Sleeping & Eating

Temenos Retreat   CABIN $
(☏ 023-625 1871; www.temenos.org.za; cnr Bree & Voortrekker Sts; s/d R550/795; ☎☒) These cottages set in spacious gardens aren't just for those on retreat. This is a peaceful place, with a decent lap pool, health treatments and a popular **restaurant** (☏ 023-625 1115; mains R65-160; ⊙9am-3pm & 7-10pm Tue-Sat, 9am to 1pm Sun) serving light lunches and daily dinner specials. Accommodation prices drop considerably during the week. No children under 12 years.

★Lord's Guest Lodge   GUESTHOUSE $$
(☏ 023-625 1881; www.lordsguestlodge.co.za; s/d cottage incl breakfast R1000/1450; ☒☎☒) If McGregor isn't quiet enough for you, head to this luxury lodge north of town. The thatched, stone cottages sit atop a hill and have wow vistas across the region. Look out for the turn-off 10km before McGregor, from where it's a further 3km along a gravel road.

There's also a quaint pub and the Lady Grey Restaurant (mains R90 to R160), which is open to the public (bookings essential).

Green Gables Country Inn   GUESTHOUSE $$
(☏ 023-625 1626; www.greengablescountry-inn.co.za; Mill St; s/d incl breakfast R650/1100; ☒☎☒) Sitting on the southern border of town, this is a family-friendly place with well-kept grounds, affable hosts and a nice pool. There's a restaurant (also open to nonguests), free bikes to borrow and the owners can arrange transfers to Die Galg for the Boesmanskloof hike.

★Karoux   SOUTH AFRICAN $$
(☏ 023-625 1421; www.karoux.co.za; 42 Voortrekker St; mains R90-160; ⊙6-10pm Wed-Sat, noon-3pm Sun) Well known for its gourmet cuisine and attentive service, this is one of the Western Cape's best small-town restaurants. The menu changes regularly but always features dishes that somehow manage to be both upmarket and rustic. Reservations highly recommended.

ⓘ Information

McGregor Tourism Bureau (☏ 023-625 1954; www.tourismmcgregor.co.za; 53 Voortrekker St; ⊙9am-1pm & 2-4.30pm Mon-Fri, to 4pm Sat) Based at the museum, the tourism office arranges hiking permits. There's also a self-guided walking tour brochure for sale (R25) or if you prefer to cycle, grab a map of the local routes and rent a bike (R200 per day). The small museum covers the history of McGregor and is free to enter.

THE OVERBERG

Literally meaning 'over the mountain', Overberg refers to the region east of the Hottentots Holland range, where rolling wheat fields are bordered by the Breede River, the coast and the peaks of three mountain ranges.

There are no unattractive routes leading to the Overberg: the N2 snakes up Sir Lowry's Pass, which has magnificent views from the top, while Rte 44 stays at sea level and winds its way round Cape Hangklip, skirting the Kogelberg Nature Reserve. It's a breathtaking coastal drive, on a par with Chapman's Peak Dr in Cape Town, but without the toll.

Hermanus is a major draw for whales in the calving season (June to December) and for people wanting to watch them from easily accessed points throughout the town. If you're keen to escape the throngs that gather here, head for less crowded whale-watching spots in Gansbaai, Arniston and the magical De Hoop Nature Reserve.

Kogelberg Nature Reserve

Proclaimed in 1988 as South Africa's first Unesco Biosphere Reserve, the Kogelberg biosphere lies 60km east of Cape Town and encompasses 100,000 hectares. The **reserve** (☏ 087 288 0499; www.capenature.co.za; Rte 44; adult/child R40/20; ⊙7.30am-7pm) has incredibly complex biodiversity, including over 1880 plant species. Birdlife is prolific, wild horses live in the wetlands, and whales can be seen offshore. There are day hikes and overnight trails, and the reserve is used by mountain bikers; permits are required for all activities.

The entrance lies about 60km east of Cape Town between Betty's Bay and Kleinmond on Rte 44.

The modern, glass-fronted **Oudebosch Eco Cabins** (☏ central reservations 021-483 0190; www.capenature.co.za; d cabin from R1170; ☒☎; ✎) were designed to meld with the natural surrounds and be as ecofriendly as possible. Delightful and well equipped, they are highly sought after so book ahead.

The Overberg & Route 62

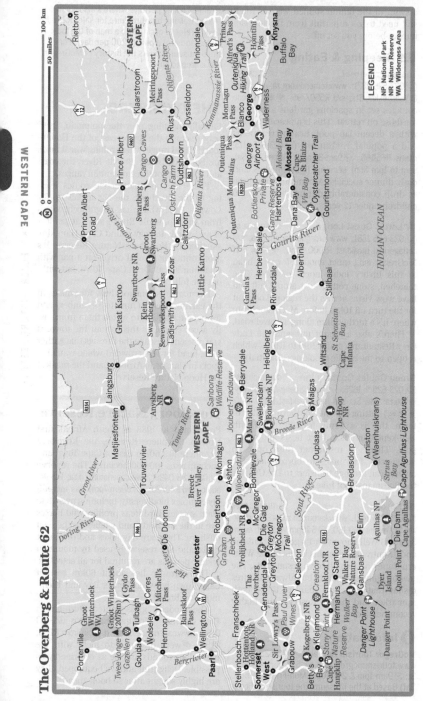

50 miles
100 km

LEGEND
NP National Park
NR Nature Reserve
WA Wilderness Area

Betty's Bay

📞 028 / POP 1400

The small, scattered holiday village of Betty's Bay is sandwiched between mountains and ocean. It's worth a pause for its penguin colony (📞 028-272 9829; www.capenature.co.za; off Wallers Rd; adult/child R20/10; ⊗ 8am-4.30pm; 🅿) and delightful botanical gardens.

There are self-catering cottages and holiday homes for rent throughout the town, plus one or two guesthouses.

The often delightfully empty Harold Porter National Botanical Gardens (📞 028-272 9311; www.sanbi.org; adult/child R25/10; ⊗ 8am-4.30pm Mon-Fri, to 5pm Sat & Sun; 🅿) are well worth a visit. Paths explore the region's indigenous plant life – try the Leopard Kloof Trail, a 3km round-trip walk leading through fern forests and up to a waterfall. You'll need to pay a key deposit (R50) and get your key and permit before 2pm. Picnic spots are plentiful and there's also a tearoom. The gardens sit on the slopes of the Kogelberg at the eastern edge of Betty's Bay.

Hermanus

📞 028 / POP 10,500

Hermanus is generally considered the best land-based whale-watching destination in the world. From June to December, the bay becomes the swimming grounds for a large number of southern right whales. So what might have otherwise just been a small fishing village is today a large, bustling town with an excellent range of accommodation, restaurants and shops.

The town stretches over a long main road but the centre is easily navigable on foot. There's a superb cliff-path walk and plenty of other hikes in the hills around the town, as well as good wine tasting, and the Hermanus Whale Festival (www.whalefestival. co.za) in September. The town gets very crowded at this time and during the December and January school holidays.

Only 122km from Cape Town, Hermanus is also perfect for a day trip.

◉ Sights & Activities

While Hermanus is renowned for its land-based whale watching, boat trips are also available. Approaching whales in the water is highly regulated and the boats must stay a minimum of 50m from the whales.

Fernkloof Nature Reserve   NATURE RESERVE
(📞 028-313 0819; www.fernkloof.com; Fir Ave; ⊗ 7am-7pm) FREE This 15-sq-km reserve is wonderful if you're interested in fynbos (literally 'fine bush' – shrubby plants with thin leaves). There's a 60km network of hiking trails for all fitness levels, and views over the sea are spectacular. A hiking map is available from the tourist information office. Guided tours are available – book ahead.

Old Harbour   HISTORIC SITE
The harbour clings to the cliffs in front of the town centre and is the hub of Hermanus. You'll find three museums here: the Old Harbour Museum (📞 028-312 1475; www. old-harbour-museum.co.za; Marine Dr; adult/child R20/5; ⊗ 9am-4.30pm Mon-Sat, noon-4pm Sun), Whale House Museum (Market Sq; adult/child R20/5; ⊗ 9am-4.30pm Mon-Sat, noon-4pm

---

WINE TASTING AROUND HERMANUS

The area is best known for whales but there are also some superb wineries just outside Hermanus. The Hemel-en-Aarde (Heaven and Earth) valley starts 5km west of the town and follows a winding route north for 15km.

If you don't have a nondrinker in your party, the highly recommended Tuk-Tuk Transporter (📞 084 688 5885; www.hermanustaxi.com) provides transport between three wine farms, a stop for lunch and return to your accommodation for R275 per person.

For an alternative way to see the wineries, join a quad-biking tour (per person R650) with SA Forest Adventures (📞 Cape Town 021-795 0225; www.saforestadventures.co.za; activities from R350).

Creation (📞 028-212 1107; www.creationwines.com; Hemel en Aarde Rd; tastings R50; ⊗ 10am-5pm; 🅿 👶) is best known for its various wine-pairing options, which include a superb brunch pairing (R495) as well as tea pairings (R435) and even a juice pairing for kids (R115). The restaurant menu lists the local butchers, bakers, cheese makers and the like who supply the ingredients. It's 20km from Hermanus on the Hemel-en-Aarde road. Bookings essential for pairing experiences.

Hermanus

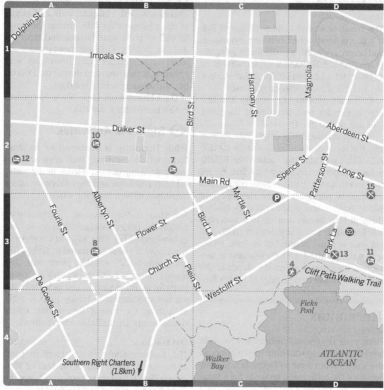

Sun) and **Photographic Museum** (Market Sq; adult/child R20/5; ⊙9am-4.30pm Mon-Sat, noon-4pm Sun). There's a permanent craft market in the square as well.

★Cliff Path Walking Trail   HIKING
FREE This scenic path meanders for 10km from New Harbour, 2km west of town, along the sea to the mouth of the Klein River; you can join it anywhere along the cliffs. It's simply the finest thing to do in Hermanus, whales or not.

Walker Bay Adventures   WATER SPORTS
(✆082 739 0159; www.walkerbayadventures. co.za; Old Harbour; kayaking R400, boat-based whale watching adult/child R800/380) Watching whales from a sea kayak is a gobsmacking, if at times rather nerve-racking, experience. Other activities on offer include sandboarding, horse riding and boat trips.

Southern Right Charters   BOATING
(✆082 353 0550; www.southernrightcharters. co.za; 2hr trip adult/child R800/380) A licensed boat operator that runs whale-watching trips from New Harbour.

🛏 Sleeping

There is a huge amount of accommodation in Hermanus but you might still find yourself searching in vain for a bed in the holiday season, so take care to book ahead.

Hermanus Backpackers   HOSTEL $
(✆028-312 4293; www.hermanusbackpackers. co.za; 26 Flower St; dm R170, d R490, with shared bathroom R440; P🐕🛜🏊) This is a great place with upbeat decor, good facilities and clued-up staff who can help with activities. The simple, help-yourself breakfast is free, and evening meals are available. It's a pretty chilled spot and the annexe around the corner is even quieter.

comfortable rooms are set around a swimming pool. Owner-run, it's a friendly and welcoming spot.

Marine   LUXURY HOTEL **$$$**
(✆ 028-313 1000; www.themarinehotel.co.za; Marine Dr; r incl breakfast from R4700; P✳︎☞⊛) The town's poshest option is right on the sea with immaculate grounds and amenities, including two sea-facing restaurants. The **Pavilion** (breakfast R180; ⊙ 7-10.30am) is only open for breakfast, while **Origins** (mains R135-250; ⊙ noon-2.30pm & 7-9.30pm; P) boasts gourmet fare with a focus on seafood.

Auberge Burgundy   GUESTHOUSE **$$$**
(✆ 028-313 1201; www.auberge.co.za; 16 Harbour Rd; s/d incl breakfast from R1080/1440; P☞⊛) This wonderful place, built in the style of a Provençal villa, is right in the centre of town. Many rooms have ocean views. Rates do not rise during peak season.

Windsor Hotel   HOTEL **$$$**
(✆ 028-312 3727; www.windsorhotel.co.za; 49 Marine Dr; s/d incl breakfast R950/1150, with sea views R1450/1650; P☞) A sea-facing room at this stalwart overlooking the ocean means you'll be able to whale-watch from your bed in

Zoete Inval Travellers Lodge   HOSTEL **$**
(✆ 028-312 1242; www.zoeteinval.co.za; 23 Main Rd; dm from R200, d R650, with shared bathroom R550; P☞) ⬧ A budget option in suburbia, this is a quiet place with good amenities (including a spa bath) and neatly furnished rooms.

★Potting Shed   GUESTHOUSE **$$**
(✆ 028-312 1712; www.thepottingshedaccommodation.co.za; 28 Albertyn St; d incl breakfast from R1100; P☞⊛) This friendly guesthouse offers delightful personal touches, including homemade biscuits on arrival. The neat rooms are comfortable and have bright, imaginative decor. There's a spacious loft studio and the owners also operate self-catering apartments (four people R1450) closer to the sea.

Baleia de Hermanus   GUESTHOUSE **$$**
(✆ 028-312 2513; www.baleia.co.za; 57 Main Rd; s/d incl breakfast R630/1100; P☞⊛) The smart,

LOCAL KNOWLEDGE

THE ELGIN VALLEY

Best known for its apple orchards, this verdant and sparsely populated region is little known to travellers. This makes its wineries (known for sauvignon blanc, chardonnay and pinot noir), hiking trails and other outdoor activities refreshingly uncrowded, except for the very popular Canopy Tour, which must be booked in advance. The main town in the region is Grabouw. It's easy to visit on a day trip from Cape Town.

The valley begins after you reach the top of Sir Lowry's Pass in the Hottentots Holland Mountains east of Somerset West.

Hottentots Holland Nature Reserve (☑ 028-841 4301; www.capenature.co.za; adult/child R40/20; ☺ 7am-5pm) This mountainous and forested reserve stretches from Jonkershoek in the west to Villiersdorp in the east, skirting the Theewaterskloof Dam. There are day walks and overnight hikes, mountain-bike routes and *kloofing* (canyoning) trails, but the main attraction is the Canopy Tour (☑ 021-300 0501; www.canopytour.co.za; per person R895), a zip-lining adventure that sees you soaring above the treetops.

Paul Cluver Wines (☑ 021-844 0605; www.cluver.com; N2, Grabouw; tastings R40; ☺ 9am-5pm Mon-Fri, 10am-2pm Sat & Sun) A worthy stop on the Elgin wine route, offering fine wine, a pleasant country-style restaurant and mountain-bike trails (permits R80).

Green Mountain Trail (☑ 028-284 9827; www.greenmountaintrail.co.za; s/d with full board R13,520/19,350) A four-day, 57km, 'slackpacking' hike through the mountains, where your bags are transported as you hike in relative luxury – think white-table-clothed picnics with fine wines and, at the end of the day, a handsome country manor to stay in.

Hickory Shack (☑ 021-300 1396; www.hickoryshack.co.za; N2; mains R70-165; ☺ 9am-5pm Tue-Fri & Sun, to 9pm Sat; P ♨) This smokehouse has quickly gained a huge following for its slow-cooked and perfectly seasoned meats and Texan-inspired sides like corn salad, baked beans and slaw. There's craft beer on tap and a selection of ciders from around the Elgin Valley.

Peregrine Farm Stall (☑ 021-848 9011; www.peregrinefarmstall.co.za; N2; ☺ 7.30am-6pm; ♨) Locals love to stop here for a freshly baked pie and some just-pressed apple juice before heading off on a road trip. As well as the farm stall, there's a cafe (mains R60 to R120) serving excellent lemon meringue pie and a range of shops and attractions, including the tasting room of Everson's Cider (tastings R42).

season. Rooms have had a bit of a revamp but are still true to the hotel's Victorian roots. There are also large, sea-facing apartments (four people R2100).

✗ Eating

Eatery CAFE $
(☑ 028-313 2970; Long St Arcade, Long St; mains R55-95; ☺ 7am-4pm Mon-Fri, to 1pm Sat; ☎) Tucked away in a side street, this is a local hang-out lauded for its excellent coffee, fresh salads and sandwiches plus a range of tasty cakes baked on-site.

Burgundy Restaurant SEAFOOD $$
(☑ 028-312 2800; www.burgundyrestaurant.co.za; Marine Dr; mains R95-240; ☺ 8am-9pm) This long-standing restaurant is still going strong, popular with both locals and tourists as much for its superb sea view as for

its menu. Seafood is the star, though vegetarians and carnivores are also well served.

Bistro at Just Pure CAFE $$
(☑ 028-313 0060; www.justpurebistro.co.za; cnr Marine Dr & Park Lane; mains R65-115; ☺ 8.30am-4.30pm Mon-Fri, to 3pm Sat & Sun; ☎) ✎ Adjoining a shop selling natural cosmetics, this seafront bistro is all about fresh, local, organic ingredients. Try the 'famous' cheesecake and watch whales from the patio as you eat. Dinners are served from October to February.

★ Pear Tree FUSION $$$
(☑ 028-313 1224; http://peartree-hermanus.co.za; 2 Godfrey Cottages, Village Sq; mains R110-180; ☺ 11am-11pm) One of the town's top restaurants is an intimate venue decorated in bodega style – all bare brick and wine bottles. The small menu features delights like pulled

lamb tagliatelle with truffle oil, braised pork belly and naartjie Malva pudding (a traditional sticky sponge pudding with citrus fruit) with pink peppercorns. Book ahead.

Bientang's Cave   BAR
(☑028-312 3454; www.bientangscave.com; Marine Dr; ⊙11.30am-8pm) This cave, occupied by the last Strandlopers (coastal indigenous people) at the turn of the 19th century, has a truly remarkable setting and is definitely worth a stop for a drink. Consider moving elsewhere for lunch. Access is only via a steep flight of cliff-side stairs.

❶ Information

Although **Hermanus Tourism** (☑028-313 1602; www.hermanustourism.info; Market Sq; ⊙9am-5pm Mon-Fri, to 4pm Sat, 10am-2pm Sun) is not the main tourism office, it's in a much more convenient location. Staff are exceptionally helpful.

The larger **tourism office** (☑028-312 2629; www.hermanustourism.info; Old Station Bldg, Mitchell St; ⊙8am-5pm Mon-Fri, 9am-4pm Sat, 10am-2pm Sun) is just north of the town and can help with accommodation bookings.

❶ Getting There & Away

Bernardus Tours (☑028-316 1093; www.bernardustransfershermanus.co.za) offers shuttles to Gansbaai (R450, 30 minutes) and Cape Town (R1000, 1½ hours). Prices are per vehicle (up to three passengers).

The hostels run a shuttle service (one way from R100, 30 minutes) to the **Baz Bus** (☑Cape Town 021-422 5202, SMS bookings 076 427 3003; www.bazbus.com) drop-off point in Botrivier, 50km west of town. There are shared taxis from Bellville (R90, two hours) in Cape Town's northern suburbs.

Stanford
☑028 / POP 4800

This picture-perfect village on the banks of the Klein River is a popular spot with Capetonians on weekends, and for good reason. The surrounding area boasts a handful of uncrowded wineries, while in Stanford itself you'll find trips on the river, kayaks for hire, a couple of good restaurants and a picturesque **brewery** (☑028-341 0013; www.walkerbayestate.com; Rte 326; tour & tasting R80; ⊙10am-5pm, tours 10am & 3pm Wed-Fri; ℗🐾).

◉ Sights & Activities

★**Stanford Hills**   WINERY
(☑028-341 0841; www.stanfordhills.co.za; off Rte 43; tastings R40; ⊙8.30am-5pm; ℗🐾) Taste

the Jacksons pinotage here – a fine example of South Africa's home-grown grape variety. There's also charming self-catering accommodation available (cottages from R1100), a glamping option (single/double luxury tent R1290/1490) and a family-friendly restaurant (mains R95 to R120) offering a chalkboard menu of rustic fare. The views are marvellous.

Klein River Cheese Farm   FARM
(☑028-341 0693; www.kleinrivercheese.co.za; Rte 326; ⊙9am-4pm Mon-Sat; ℗🐾) The cheese from this farm has become wildly popular – the aged Gruyère is particularly good. Taste and buy a selection of cheese and put together your own picnic to eat in the grounds. Children will love the petting farm and playground.

Robert Stanford Estate   WINERY
(☑028-341 0647; www.robertstanfordestate.co.za; Rte 43; tastings free; ⊙9am-4pm Thu-Mon) The white wines here are good, particularly the sauvignon blanc. There's also a small distillery producing grappa and *mampoer* (moonshine) and a country restaurant open for lunch.

🛏 Sleeping & Eating

Stanford has lots of charming self-catering cottages as well as a couple of guesthouses. The **tourist office** (☑028-341 0340; www.stanfordinfo.co.za; 18 Queen Victoria St; ⊙8.30am-4.30pm Mon-Fri, 9am-4pm Sat, 9am-1pm Sun) can provide a detailed list of the options in and around town.

Marianna's   BISTRO $$
(☑028-341 0272; 12 Du Toit St; mains R120-145; ⊙noon-2pm Sat & Sun; 🐾) This award-winning, eclectic place serves a mixture of traditional and contemporary fare, much of it made with produce from the owner's garden. Advance booking is essential. If all the private tables are taken, you might end up sharing with other guests. No children under 10.

Havercroft's   BISTRO $$$
(☑028-341 0603; Rte 43; mains R140-165; ⊙noon-2.30pm Thu-Sun; ℗) The food from husband-and-wife team Brydon and Innes gets excellent reviews. The small menu is inventive and refined, utilising plenty of local produce. Sunday lunch is highly recommended. Bookings essential and no under 12s allowed. It's based in a farmhouse on Rte 43 as you enter Stanford from Hermanus.

WESTERN CAPE STANFORD

PETER UNGER / GETTY IMAGES ©

1. Franschhoek (p118)
Linger over long lunches in this delightful Winelands town.

2. Knysna (p152)
Admire the beautiful lagoon, sandstone cliffs and ancient forests of this famed town on the Garden Route.

3. Hermanus (p133)
Catch a glimpse of majestic southern right whales in the bay from June to December.

4. Cederberg Wilderness Area (p173)
Spend a night stargazing amid the spectacular landscapes.

3

SAMI SARKIS / GETTY IMAGES ©

Greyton

📞 028 / POP 2800

With a magnificent mountain backdrop, Greyton is a pleasant village, best seen in conjunction with the old Moravian mission of neighbouring Genadendal, with its well-preserved historic buildings that couldn't be more authentic. Greyton itself is rather twee but still a lovely place to wander between galleries and cafes.

Greyton and Genadendal are linked to McGregor via the very popular Boesmanskloof Trail (p130).

🛏 Sleeping

Greyton Ecolodge   HOSTEL $

(📞082 545 1240; www.ecolodgegreyton.co.za; 2 Park St; dm R140, s/d with shared bathroom R270/450; P@) Once the hostel for Greyton's boarding school, this cavernous place has a rather institutional feel. It is part of a larger environmental project and all proceeds from accommodation go towards funding its work. Views of the Riviersonderend mountains are awesome and it's a perfect base for hiking.

★ Post House   HISTORIC HOTEL $$$

(📞028-254 9995; www.theposthouse.co.za; 22 Main Rd; s/d incl breakfast from R1390/1850; P🖥🗲) Based in the town's historic former post house, with rooms set around a pretty garden, this is a peaceful place right in the centre of Greyton's restaurants and shops. Its English-style pub is an atmospheric spot for a drink.

High Hopes   B&B $$$

(📞028-254 9898; www.highhopes.co.za; 89 Main Rd; s/d incl breakfast from R1090/1450; P🖥🗲) This delightful place has tastefully furnished rooms and a small pool in the rambling gardens. It's close to the start of the Boesmanskloof Trail, and if you've overdone it, you can book a treatment – reiki, reflexology and massages are offered. Fully catered retreats are also available, featuring activities such as yoga, art and gardening.

🍴 Eating & Drinking

Peccadillos   FUSION $$

(📞028-254 9066; www.peccadillos.co.za; 23 Main Rd; mains R130-160; ⊙noon-3pm & 6-10pm Thu-Mon) The chalkboard menu changes often, but always features no-nonsense dishes like rump steak, lamb shank and curries, largely created with local, organic produce.

Old Potter's Inn   MICROBREWERY

(📞028-254 9690; www.oldpottersinn.co.za; 16 Main Rd; ⊙8am-10pm) The courtyard is a lovely shady spot to retreat from Greyton's summer heat with a taster tray (R35) of four beers, brewed in-house. The menu features bar food like chicken and waffles, nachos, burgers and noodle bowls. There is accommodation on-site too.

ℹ Information

Tourist Information Office (📞028-254 9414; www.greytontourism.com; 29 Main Rd; ⊙9am-5pm Mon-Fri, 10am-1pm Sat) Staff can provide information on short hikes in the area.

Gansbaai

📞 028 / POP 11,600

Gansbaai's unspoilt coastline is perfect for those wishing to explore more out-of-the-way Overberg nature spots. The town's star has risen in recent years thanks to shark-cage diving, though most people just visit on a day trip from Cape Town.

The nearby village of De Kelders (on the road to Gansbaai from Hermanus) is a great spot for secluded whale watching. Shark boats leave from the harbour at Kleinbaai.

⊙ Sights & Activities

A number of shark-cage diving operators are clustered around Kleinbaai's harbour, including Marine Dynamics (📞079 930 9694; www.sharkwatchsa.com; 5 Geelbek St, Kleinbaai; adult/child R1900/1100) and White Shark Projects (📞076 245 5880; www.whitesharkprojects.co.za; 16 Geelbek St, Kleinbaai; dives R1800), which both have Fairtrade accreditation. Note that there has been much controversy regarding shark-cage diving, with detractors arguing that it leads to increased shark attacks, while others (including some marine scientists and environmentalists) believe that it's a positive educational tool to encourage conservation.

★ Walker Bay Nature Reserve   NATURE RESERVE

(📞028-314 0062; www.capenature.co.za; adult/child R40/20; ⊙7am-7pm) This coastal reserve has excellent hikes and is a prime bird-watching spot. The main attractions though, other than the ocean vistas, are the impressive Klipgat Caves, site of an archaeological discovery of Khoe-San artefacts. There are informative panels within the caves.

The reserve is in two sections, though most people stick to the area just north of De Kelders. You can also access the park from Stanford and from Uilenkraalsmond, south of Gansbaai.

Sleeping & Eating

Gansbaai Backpackers   HOSTEL $
(☑083 626 4150; www.gansbaybackpackers.com; 6 Strand St; dm R180, d R500, d with shared bathroom R450; [P][📶]) This efficient and friendly place close to the harbour offers homely budget accommodation, including small garden studios with TV and basic kitchen facilities (doubles R500). Staff can assist with booking adventure activities in the area.

Aire del Mar   GUESTHOUSE $$
(☑028-384 2848; www.airedelmar.co.za; 77 Van Dyk St, Kleinbaai; s/d incl breakfast R765/1275; [P][📶]) A friendly place offering a good range of prices, including basic self-catering units (for two people R950). Rooms have panoramic sea views out to Dyer Island.

★Grootbos Private Nature Reserve   LODGE $$$
(☑028-384 8008; www.grootbos.com; Rte 43; s/d with full board R9600/12,800; [P][❄][📶][≋]) ✈ This superb luxury choice set on 25 sq km includes horse riding, hiking, local excursions and excellent food in the price. Each of the free-standing cottages has an outdoor shower on the deck. The Grootbos Foundation runs a number of environmental and community projects – ask about the Progressive Tourism Package.

★Coffee on the Rocks   CAFE $$
(☑028-384 2017; http://coffee-on-the-rocks.com; 81 Cliff St, De Kelders; mains R50-110; ⊗10am-5pm Wed-Sun; [📶]) All bread is baked daily on-site and everything else is homemade too. The ocean-facing deck is a great place for a sandwich, a salad or just a coffee while you look out for whales in season.

ℹ Information

Gansbaai Tourism (☑028-384 1439; www.gansbaaiinfo.com; Main Rd, Great White Junction; ⊗9am-5pm Mon-Fri, 9am-4pm Sat, 10am-2pm Sun) Staff can help with activities and accommodation.

ℹ Getting There & Away

Bernardus Tours (p137) runs shuttles to Hermanus (R450, 30 minutes) and Cape Town (R1400, two hours).

Cape Agulhas

☑028 / POP 10,000

Encompassing **Struisbaai** and **L'Agulhas**, Cape Agulhas is the southernmost tip of Africa, where the Atlantic and Indian Oceans collide. It's a rugged, windswept coastline and the graveyard for many a ship. Most people head straight for a photo with the sign marking where the oceans meet.

Cape Agulhas Lighthouse   LIGHTHOUSE
(☑028-435 6078; adult/child R26/13; ⊗9am-5pm) It's a vertiginous climb up increasingly narrow ladders to the top, but is well worth it for the coastal views. Inside you'll find a small museum looking at lighthouses around the world, as well as the **tourism bureau** (☑028-435 7185; www.discovercapeagulhas.co.za; ⊗9am-5pm).

Agulhas National Park   NATIONAL PARK
(☑028-435 6078; www.sanparks.org; adult/child R160/80; ⊗7am-7pm) Africa's southernmost national park has exceptional birdwatching possibilities and hikes ranging from 3km to 10km in length. Recommended is the 5.5km **Rasperpunt Trail**, which takes in the *Meisho Maru* shipwreck. Information booklets for each hike, plus a birding list, are available at the park office for R10. There is also charming self-catering **accommodation** (☑central reservations 012-428 9111; www.sanparks.org; chalet from R1180) by the sea. You don't need to pay the park entrance to visit Africa's southernmost point.

Cape Agulhas Backpackers   HOSTEL $
(☑082 372 3354; www.capeagulhasbackpackers.com; cnr Main & Duiker Sts, Struisbaai; camping per site R120, dm/d R160/420; [P][📶][≋]) A laid-back place in Struisbaai, with a cheery pool and bar area. Breakfast and dinner are available, or you can make use of the shared kitchen. It's in a prime kite-surfing spot, and offers lessons as well as surfboard and kayak rentals.

Arniston

☑028 / POP 1300

Arniston (Waenhuiskrans) is a picturesque village in a dramatic, windswept setting. It has a bit of an identity crisis – it's named after both the vessel wrecked off its treacherous coast in 1815 and the **sea cave** large enough to turn an ox-wagon (Waenhuiskrans means 'wagon house cliff'); not that a wagon could have got inside the cave as the small entrance is, as the name suggests, down a cliff.

Colourful boats, warm blue-green waters and the backdrop of Kassiesbaai, the 200-year-old hamlet of whitewashed cottages that forms the core of the town, make a very pretty picture. South of Kassiesbaai is Roman Beach with white sand and gentle waves. It's a good place to bring the children as there are caves, coves and rock pools filled with sea urchins and colourful anemones at both ends. Be careful not to touch the sea urchins, because they can cause nasty cuts.

🛏 Sleeping & Eating

Arniston Resort
CAMPGROUND, CHALET $

(Waenhuiskrans Oord; ☑ 028-445 9620; arniston@ capeagulhas.com; Main Rd; camping/chalets from R190/500; ℗) This decent budget option has campsites and basic chalets a short walk from the beach. Bring your own bedding and provisions. Prices rise sharply during school holidays.

Arniston Seaside Cottages
CABIN $$

(☑ 028-445 9772; www.arnistonseasidecottages. co.za; Huxham St; s/d self-catering R570/760) There are more than 20 whitewashed, thatched cottages dotted around the town. All are well equipped and comfortable, with some offering ocean views. Reception is at Huxham St.

★ Arniston Spa Hotel
HOTEL $$$

(☑ 028-445 9000; www.arnistonhotel.com; Beach Rd; s/d sea-facing incl breakfast from R1700/2280; ℗ 🛜 ⛱) The Arniston is a light-filled luxury hotel with a nautical theme and its own spa. Sea-facing rooms have floor-to-ceiling windows. The ocean-view restaurant serves sushi, seafood and pizzas (mains R60 to R180) and has an extensive wine list.

★ Willeen's Restaurant
SOUTH AFRICAN $

(☑ 028-445 9995; House C26, Kassiesbaai; mains R40-85; ⊘8am-9pm; ℗) You can sample true local cooking at this restaurant overlooking the ocean in Kassiesbaai. It's a cheap and very cheerful place serving South African specialities like *bobotie* (mild curried mince dish topped with a savoury egg custard), chicken pie, boerewors (farmer's sausage) and fresh fish.

De Hoop Nature Reserve

This magnificent coastal reserve (☑ 028-542 1114; www.capenature.co.za; adult/child R40/20; ⊘7am-6pm) comprises long, un-touched beaches, huge dunes and low-lying vegetation that's home to Cape mountain zebras and bontebok. Southern right whales are often seen along the coast and, for bird enthusiasts, the reserve is home to the Western Cape's only remaining breeding colony of the rare Cape vultures.

The village of Ouplaas, 15km from the reserve entrance, is the nearest place to buy fuel and supplies.

The reserve is about 260km from Cape Town, and the final 57km from either Bredasdorp or Swellendam is unsealed. The only access to the reserve is via Wydgeleë on the Bredasdorp–Malgas road. Note that if you approach via Malgas, you'll have to take the manually operated pont (river ferry) over the Breede River (between dawn and dusk). It costs R50 per vehicle.

There is no public transport to De Hoop.

Whale Trail
HIKING

(☑ 021-483 0190; www.capenature.co.za; per person R2195) Although there are numerous day walks, an overnight mountain-bike trail and good snorkelling along the coast, the De Hoop Nature Reserve's most interesting feature is the five-day Whale Trail. The 55km hike offers excellent opportunities to see whales between June and December. Accommodation is in modern, fully equipped, self-catering cottages.

De Hoop Collection
CAMPGROUND, CABIN $$

(☑ 021-422 4522; www.dehoopcollection.co.za; camping per site R425, rondavel with shared bathroom from R1200, cottage from R1900; ℗ 🛜 ⛱) There's a staggering range of accommodation and something for every budget, from campsites and rondavels with shared ablutions to elegant guesthouse rooms in the old manor (double including breakfast and dinner from R1550). The whole place looks out onto the vlei (marsh) and is a perfectly peaceful escape. If you need further relaxation there is also a spa.

The on-site restaurant is open all day, or most of the accommodation comes with self-catering facilities. Bring your own provisions.

Swellendam

☑ 028 / POP 17,500

Surrounded by the undulating wheat lands of the Overberg and protected by the Langeberge mountain range, Swellendam is perfectly positioned for exploring the Little Karoo and makes a good stopover on the way further east to the Garden Route. One of the

Swellendam

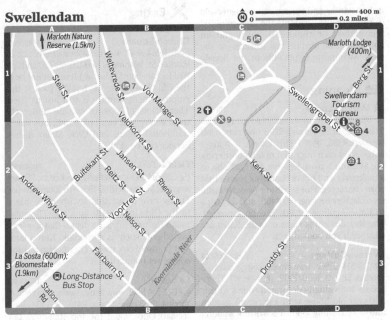

oldest towns in South Africa (it dates back to 1745), it has beautiful Cape Dutch architecture and a worthwhile museum.

Sights & Activities

Drostdy Museum MUSEUM
(028-514 1138; www.drostdymuseum.com; 18 Swellengrebel St; adult/child R25/5; 9am-5pm Mon-Fri, 10am-3pm Sat & Sun) The centrepiece of this excellent museum is the beautiful *drostdy* (residence of an official) itself, which dates from 1747. The museum ticket also covers entrance to the nearby **Old Gaol** (Swellengrebel St; 9am-5pm Mon-Fri, 10am-3pm Sat & Sun), where you'll find part of the original administrative buildings and a watermill; and **Mayville** (Hermanus Steyn St; 9am-5pm Mon-Fri, 10am-3pm Sat & Sun), another residence dating back to 1853, with a formal Victorian garden.

Marloth Nature Reserve NATURE RESERVE
(028-514 1410; www.capenature.co.za; adult/child R40/20) Perched in the Langeberge, 1.5km north of town, this reserve is particularly pretty in October and November when the ericas are in flower. If the day hikes don't hit the spot, try the demanding **Swellendam Hiking Trail**, generally regarded as one of South Africa's top hikes. You can choose to walk any distance

Swellendam

Sights
1 Drostdy Museum	D2
2 Dutch Reformed Church	C1
3 Mayville	D2
4 Old Gaol	D2

Sleeping
5 Braeside B&B	C1
6 Cypress Cottage	C1
7 De Kloof	B1

Eating
8 Field & Fork	D2
9 Old Gaol on Church Square	C1

from two to six days. There are two basic overnight huts, and you'll need to be self-sufficient. Entrance to the reserve is via Andrew Whyte St.

Bontebok National Park NATIONAL PARK
(028-514 2735; www.sanparks.org/parks/bontebok; adult/child R112/56; 7am-7pm Oct-Apr, to 6pm May-Sep) Some 6km south of Swellendam is this national park, proclaimed in 1931 to save the remaining 30 bontebok. The project was successful, and bontebok as well as other antelope and mountain zebras can be found in this smallest of South Africa's national parks. The fynbos that flowers

in late winter and spring, rare renosterveld (scrubby plants including the grey-coloured renosterbos, or rhinoceros bush) and an abundance of birdlife are features of the park. Swimming is possible in the Breede River.

🛏 Sleeping

★ Marloth Lodge
LODGE $

(☑ 082 494 8279; www.marlothhikinglodge.co.za; 5 Lichtenstein St; camping R200, r per person incl breakfast R380; P🐾) This excellent budget lodge is set on a huge plot of land bordering the Marloth Nature Reserve. It's had a bit of a makeover and offers charming rooms that ooze character. Horse riding (www.twofeathers.co.za; 1½hr beginner ride R400) and day trips to Cape Agulhas (R750) can be arranged. The Baz Bus stops right outside. Rates are cheaper if you book direct.

Cypress Cottage
GUESTHOUSE $$

(☑ 028-514 3296; www.cypress-cottage.co.za; 3 Voortrek St; s/d R600/1000; P❄🐾≋) There are six individually decorated rooms in this 200-year-old house with a gorgeous garden and a refreshing pool. It's within walking distance of the church (Voortrek St), museum (p143) and a handful of restaurants.

Braeside B&B
B&B $$

(☑ 028-514 1692; www.braeside.co.za; 13 Van Oudtshoorn Rd; s/d incl breakfast from R800/1200; P❄🐾≋) This quiet, gracious Cape Edwardian home boasts a lovely garden, fantastic views and an excellent breakfast.

★ De Kloof
BOUTIQUE HOTEL $$$

(☑ 028-514 1303; www.dekloof.co.za; 8 Weltevrede St; s/d incl breakfast from R1905/2750; ❄🐾≋) One of Swellendam's swankiest options, this is a supremely stylish guesthouse with a surprisingly personal touch. It's on a large estate dating back to 1801. The luxurious rooms are set around lawns where ducks wander, and a couple of the suites come with spa bath and king-size heated waterbed. There's a spa and delectable restaurant for overnight guests only.

Bloomestate
GUESTHOUSE $$$

(☑ 028-514 2984; www.bloomestate.com; 276 Voortrek St; s/d incl breakfast from R1875/2500; P❄🐾≋) A modern, friendly guesthouse set on a beautiful property, it offers Zen-like privacy to go with the luxurious, colourful rooms. Health and beauty treatments are available and, if relaxing around the pool isn't enough, you can hop in the spa bath that's sitting on a deck under the trees.

🍴 Eating

Old Gaol on Church Square
SOUTH AFRICAN $$

(☑ 028-514 3847; www.oldgaolrestaurant.co.za; 8a Voortrek St; light meals R60-120; ⊙ 7.30am-10pm Wed-Fri, 8am-5pm Sat-Tue; 🌱) It might not be in the Old Gaol any more, but the food at this empowerment venture is still just as good. There's lots of seating outside under the trees where you can enjoy delicious cakes, traditional breads and Cape Malay dishes. Service can be slow.

Field & Fork
FUSION $$$

(☑ 028-514 3430; www.fieldandfork.co.za; 26 Swellengrebel St; mains R160-195; ⊙ 6-10pm Mon-Sat) Locals rave about this stylish place based in the Old Gaol (p143) building. The small menu features intricate dishes that use local ingredients such as springbok, Karoo lamb and Franschhoek trout. There's also a three-course set menu (R365).

La Sosta
ITALIAN $$$

(☑ 028-514 1470; www.lasostaswellendam.com; 45 Voortrek St; 3-course menu R410; ⊙ 6.30-9.30pm Tue-Sat) Once voted the top Italian restaurant in the country, La Sosta is something special. The beautifully presented food includes treats like butternut-and-truffle ravioli, homemade gnocchi and coconut panna cotta. Bookings advisable. The restaurant and adjoining guesthouse usually closes for the winter – often from June to August or September.

ℹ Information

Swellendam Tourism Bureau (☑ 028-514 2770; www.visitswellendam.co.za; 22 Swellengrebel St; ⊙ 9am-5pm Mon-Fri, to 2pm Sat & Sun) A helpful office based in the Old Gaoler's Cottage. It rents out mountain bikes (R150 per day) and staff can advise on biking routes.

ℹ Getting There & Away

All three major bus companies pass through Swellendam on their runs between Cape Town (R300, 3½ hours) and Port Elizabeth (R430, eight hours), stopping opposite the Swellengrebel Hotel on Voortrek St.

GARDEN ROUTE

High on the must-see lists of most visitors to South Africa is the Garden Route, and with good reason: you can't help but be seduced by the glorious natural beauty. The distance from Mossel Bay in the west to Storms River in the east is just over 200km, yet the range of topography, vegetation, wildlife and outdoor activities is remarkable.

The coast is dotted with excellent beaches, while inland you'll find picturesque lagoons and lakes, rolling hills and eventually the mountains of the Outeniqua and Tsitsikamma ranges that divide the verdant Garden Route from the arid Little Karoo.

Mossel Bay

🍴 044 / POP 30,000

With gnarly surf spots, some fine beaches, a menu of outdoor activities that covers everything from coastal hikes to leaping out of a plane, and a solid range of places to stay for every budget, Mossel Bay is an excellent destination for the independent traveller.

At first glance, the town is the ugly sister of the Garden Route. It was a hugely popular destination until the 1980s, when the building of the world's largest gas-to-oil refinery and concomitant industrial sprawl marred it, and it fell into a slump. But if you can see beyond the unimpressive approach road, you'll find a cheery town with plenty of sunny-day pursuits.

Much of the holiday action happens around the Point, a promontory with an old-school seaside vibe. There are ice-cream kiosks, a caravan park and minigolf, and it's also a prime spot to surf.

◉ Sights

★ **Dias Museum Complex**   MUSEUM
(🍴 044-691 1067; www.diasmuseum.co.za; Market St; adult/child R20/5; ⊙ 9am-4.45pm Mon-Fri, to 3.45pm Sat & Sun; 🅿 🐾) This excellent museum offers insight into Mossel Bay's role as an early stomping ground for European sailors. Named for 15th-century Portuguese explorer Bartholomeu Dias, the museum contains the 'post office tree' where sailors left messages for one another, the 1786 Dutch East India Company (Vereenigde Oost-Indische Compagnie; VOC) granary, a small aquarium and a local history museum. The highlight is the replica of the caravel that Dias used on his 1488 voyage of discovery.

Its small size brings home the extraordinary skill and courage of the early explorers. The replica was built in Portugal and sailed to Mossel Bay in 1988 to commemorate the 500th anniversary of Dias' trip. There's an extra fee to board the boat (adult/child R20/5).

Botlierskop Private Game Reserve   WILDLIFE RESERVE
(🍴 044-696 6055; www.botlierskop.co.za; Little Brak River; 🅿) This reserve contains a vast range of wildlife, including lions, elephants, rhinos, buffaloes and giraffes. Day visitors are welcome for a variety of activities including three-hour wildlife drives (adult/child R450/225) and horseback safaris (per hour R310). The reserve is about 20km northeast of Mossel Bay along the N2 (take the Little Brak River turn-off and follow the signs towards Sorgfontein). Bookings essential.

⚡ Activities

It's easy to see where Mossel Bay's tourism slogan comes from. 'Do stuff', the authorities tell you, and the town is chock-full of stuff to do, including surfing, skydiving, hiking and boat trips.

Oystercatcher Trail   HIKING
(🍴 044-699 1204; www.oystercatchertrail.co.za; per person self-catering/full board R6200/7450) Hikers can tackle this fabulous coastal trail over five days. It follows 48km of coastline from Mossel Bay to Gourits River via Cape St Blaize, where you're likely to see the endangered black oystercatcher. You can self-cater or choose the fully catered option. All rates include accommodation and guides.

Point of Human Origins   CULTURAL
(🍴 079 640 0004; www.humanorigin.co.za; tours R450) Led by an archaeology professor, this fascinating four-hour tour includes a hike to the Pinnacle Point Caves, where discoveries have shed light on human life from 162,000 years ago. You can also visit the caves on a 90-minute scramble with a local guide (R350).

Romonza   BOATING
(🍴 082 701 9031; www.romonzaboattrips.co.za; Mossel Bay Harbour; 1hr boat trips R170) Regular boat trips head out to Seal Island to see the seals, birds and dolphins that frequent these waters. From July to October there are also whale-watching trips (adult/child R730/430, 2½ hours).

Skydive Mossel Bay   ADVENTURE SPORTS
(🍴 082 824 8599; www.skydivemosselbay.com; Mossel Bay Airfield, 69 Rooikat St, Aalwyndal; from R2800) Tandem skydives start from 3000m and when the weather and tides cooperate you get to land on Diaz Beach.

Garden Route

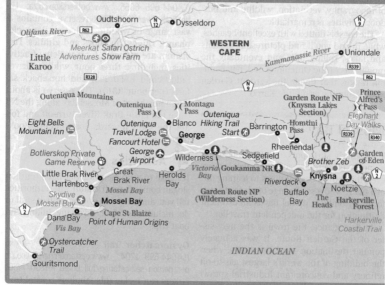

White Shark Africa
DIVING

(☎044-691 3796; www.whitesharkafrica.com; 7 Church St; adult/child R1750/1050) Half-day cage-diving trips to view great white sharks, including breakfast, lunch, drinks and snacks.

Waves School of Surfing
SURFING

(☎078 297 3999; www.wavesschoolofsurfing.com; 47 Marsh St; 1½hr lesson R300) Mossel Bay is one of the Garden Route's top surfing spots; beginners can get started here. Board rental is also available (R150 per day).

🛏 Sleeping

De Bakke Santos
Caravan Park
CAMPGROUND, CHALET $

(☎076 058 7153; www.debakkesantos.co.za; Santos Beach; camping per site from R190, chalet from R550; ℗) As well as more than 300 campsites – many of which have ocean views – there are well-equipped thatched chalets here (the chalets were about to be renovated when we last visited). Rates rise slightly on weekends and during school holidays.

Mossel Bay Backpackers
HOSTEL $

(☎044-691 3182; www.mosselbaybackpackers.co.za; 1 Marsh St; dm R180, d R580, d with shared bathroom R380; ☎⊠) This well-run and long-established backpackers has two sec-

tions – a backpacker wing where rooms share a bathroom and a more upmarket wing with en-suite rooms and dorms. There's even a honeymoon suite, complete with spa bath (R890). Staff can arrange surfing, boat trips and other water sports.

Park House Lodge
& Travel Centre
HOSTEL $

(☎044-691 1937; www.park-house.co.za; 121 High St; camping R110, dm R170, s/d R385/640, with shared bathroom R290/480; ☎) This place, in a gracious old sandstone house next to the park, is friendly, smartly decorated and has beautiful gardens. Breakfast is R55, and staff can organise activities.

★ Point Village Hotel
HOTEL $$

(☎044-690 3156; www.pointvillagehotel.co.za; 5 Point Rd; s/d R600/1100; ℗☎) The quirky, fake lighthouse on this exceptionally well-priced hotel's exterior speaks to what you'll find inside: a range of fun, funky, bright rooms and cheery service. Rooms have a kitchenette and some have balconies. There are also two- and three-bedroom apartments with good sea views (from R1800).

Protea Hotel Mossel Bay
HOTEL $$$

(☎044-691 3738; www.oldposttree.co.za; cnr Market & Church Sts; s/d from R1235/1530;

Sat) Close to the museum (p145), Carola Ann's serves inventive breakfasts, delicious, healthy lunches and not-so-healthy slabs of cake. Grab a packet of the chocolate-chip cookies for the road. Delicious.

★ Kaai 4
BRAAI $$

(☑ 044-691 0056; www.kaai4.co.za; Mossel Bay Harbour; mains R60-100; ⊙ 10am-10pm) Boasting one of Mossel Bay's best locations, this low-key restaurant has picnic tables on the sand overlooking the ocean. Most of the dishes – including stews, burgers, boerewors (farmer's sausage) and some seafood – are cooked on massive fire pits and there's local beer on tap.

Route 57
SOUTH AFRICAN $$

(☑ 044-691 0057; www.route57.co.za; 12 Marsh St; mains R90-190; ⊙ 11am-10pm Tue-Sun) This elegant place in a century-old house is one of Mossel Bay's swankiest dining options. Try the seafood *potjie* (stew) or the fillet steak topped with marrow bone. Dinner bookings recommended.

Big Blu
INTERNATIONAL $$

(☑ 044-691 2010; www.bigblu.co.za; Point Rd; mains R85-185; ⊙ 10am-11pm) This ramshackle place right on the rocks at the Point serves burgers, seafood and steaks. The deck overhanging the ocean is a perfect spot for sundowners.

Kingfisher
SEAFOOD $$

(☑ 044-690 6390; www.thekingfisher.co.za; Point Rd; mains R75-195; ⊙ noon-9.30pm; ⊕) Locals love the seafood dishes and ocean views at this long-standing place. It also serves salads, sushi and meat, and has a children's menu and playground.

🄿❄🛜⛶) Part of the Protea chain, this is a classy hotel set in the old post office building. Its restaurant, **Café Gannet** (www.cafegannet.co.za; mains R115-225; ⊙ 7am-10pm; 🄿), has a large seafood, meat and pizza menu.

Point Hotel
HOTEL $$$

(☑ 044-691 3512; www.pointhotel.co.za; Point Rd; s/d with half board R2200/2500; 🄿🛜) This modern hotel boasts a spectacular location, right above the wave-pounded rocks at the Point. There's a decent restaurant (mains R60 to R120) and the spacious rooms have balconies with ocean views – request a south-facing room for the best vistas. There's no pool, but there are tidal rock pools nearby.

🍴 Eating & Drinking

Mossel Bay Oyster Bar
SEAFOOD $

(☑ 044-333 0202; www.mosselbayoysterbar.co.za; Mossel Bay Harbour; sushi R40-50; ⊙ 9.30am-9pm) On the water's edge, this is one of the best places in town for a sundowner. Sushi and oysters are on the menu alongside a selection of cocktails (R40 to R60).

Carola Ann's
CAFE $

(☑ 044-690 3477; www.carolaann.com; 12 Church St; mains R60-95; ⊙ 8am-5pm Mon-Fri, to 2pm

---

WORTH A TRIP

EIGHT BELLS MOUNTAIN INN

Oozing old-world charm, **Eight Bells Mountain Inn** (☑ 044-631 0000; www.eightbells.co.za; Rte 328; s/d from R1010/1610; 🄿🛜⛶⊕) boasts a lovely mountain setting at the foot of the Robinson Pass. Its large grounds feature tennis and squash courts, horse trails, kids' play areas and hiking routes. You'll find a variety of rooms; the rondavels (round huts with conical roofs) are delightful. Prices rise sharply during school holidays.

Mossel Bay

WESTERN CAPE GEORGE

Mossel Bay

◎ Top Sights
1 Dias Museum Complex...........................A1

◉ Activities, Courses & Tours
2 Oystercatcher Trail................................D2
3 Romonza..A1
4 Waves School of Surfing.......................B1
5 White Shark Africa................................A1

◉ Sleeping
6 Mossel Bay Backpackers.......................C2
7 Park House Lodge & Travel
   Centre..A2
8 Point Hotel...D2

9 Point Village Hotel................................D2
10 Protea Hotel Mossel Bay......................A1

◉ Eating
11 Big Blu..D2
   Café Gannet ....(see 10)
12 Carola Ann's.......................................A1
13 Kaai 4...A1
14 Kingfisher...D2
15 Mossel Bay Oyster Bar........................A1
16 Route 57...C2

◉ Drinking & Nightlife
17 Blue Shed Coffee Roastery..................C1

★ **Blue Shed Coffee Roastery** CAFE
(☑ 044-691 0037; www.blueshedroasters.co.za; 33 Bland St; ⊙ 6.30am-8pm; 🛜) Enjoy great coffee and homemade cakes at this funky cafe with eclectic decor and ocean views from the deck. It's an awesome spot to spend a couple of hours chilling or playing vinyl on the old-school jukebox.

❶ Information

Tourism Bureau (☑ 044-691 2202; www.visitmosselbay.co.za; Market St; ⊙ 8am-6pm Mon-Fri, 9am-4pm Sat & Sun) Staff are very friendly and can help with accommodation bookings. Pick up a brochure detailing a self-guided walking tour of historic Mossel Bay.

❶ Getting There & Away

Mossel Bay is off the highway, so the long-distance buses don't come into town; they drop passengers at the Voorbaai Shell petrol station, 8km away. The hostels can usually collect you

if you give notice, but private taxis (R80) are often waiting for bus passengers who need onward travel. Try **Smith Taxis** (☑ 072 924 5977), or during the day take a shared taxi (R12). The Baz Bus (www.bazbus.com) will drop you in town.

Translux (www.translux.co.za), Greyhound (www.greyhound.co.za) and Intercape (www.intercape.co.za) buses stop here on their Cape Town–Port Elizabeth runs. Intercape fares from Mossel Bay include Knysna (R230, 1½ hours), Plettenberg Bay (R260, 2½ hours), Cape Town (R410, six hours) and Port Elizabeth (R390, 6½ hours).

George

☑ 044 / POP 114,000

George, founded in 1811, is the largest town on the Garden Route yet remains little more than a commercial centre and transport hub. It has some attractive old buildings, including the tiny St Mark's Cathedral and the more imposing Dutch Reformed Mother Church, but it's 8km from the coast and for most visitors its chief draw is the range of championship golf courses.

★ **Outeniqua Power Van** TOURS
(☑082 490 5627; Outeniqua Transport Museum, 2 Mission St; adult/child R150/130; ☺Mon-Sat) A trip on this motorised trolley van is one of the best things to do in George. It takes you from the Outeniqua Transport Museum (☑044-801 8289; www.outeniquachootjoe.co.za/museum.htm; adult/child R20/10; ☺8am-5pm Mon-Fri, to 2pm Sat; ℗) on a 2½-hour trip into the Outeniqua mountains with a brief picnic stop. Departure times vary and all bookings are done via SMS.

🛏 Sleeping & Eating

Outeniqua Travel Lodge HOSTEL $
(☑082 316 7720; www.outeniqualodge.co.za; 19 Montagu St; s/d R430/580; ℗🗗🛜❄) It's about 6km from the centre, but this is a decent budget option with en-suite rooms in a quiet, residential area. Staff can arrange activities.

★ **French Lodge**
International GUESTHOUSE $$
(☑044-874 0345; www.frenchlodge.co.za; 29 York St; s/d incl breakfast from R750/900; ℗✳@❄) Rooms at this town-centre guesthouse are in luxurious thatched-roof rondavels (round huts with a conical roof) set around the pool, with satellite TV and bathrooms with spa baths.

Fancourt Hotel LUXURY HOTEL $$$
(☑044-804 0000; www.fancourt.co.za; Montagu St, Blanco; s/d incl breakfast from R2580/3440; ℗✳🛜❄) This is the area's most luxurious option, with three 18-hole golf courses designed by Gary Player, a health spa and four restaurants. It's about 6km from the town centre.

★ **101 Meade** FUSION $$
(☑044-874 0343; www.101meade.co.za; 101 Meade St; mains R80-210; ☺7am-9.30pm Mon-Sat, 9am-9pm Sun; 🛜) Whether you're after freshly baked bread and good coffee to start the day, inventive tapas plates to share at lunchtime or heavier evening fare like braised springbok shank or Durban lamb curry, the excellent cuisine and minimalist decor at 101 Meade make it George's top eating option.

Old Townhouse STEAK $$
(☑044-874 3663; Market St; mains R75-200; ☺11.30am-5pm & 6-10pm Mon-Fri, 6-10pm Sat) In the one-time town administration build-ing dating back to 1848, this long-standing restaurant is known for its excellent steaks and ever-changing game-meat options. The homemade ice cream is a great way to finish off a meal.

ℹ Information

George Tourism (☑044-801 9299; www.georgetourism.org.za; 124 York St; ☺7.45am-4.30pm Mon-Fri, 9am-1pm Sat) Information for George and the surrounding area.

ℹ Getting There & Away

Kulula (www.kulula.com), Airlink (www.flyairlink.com) and SA Express (www.flyexpress.aero) fly to **George Airport** (☑044-876 9310; www.airports.co.za), which is 9km southwest of town.

Buses stop in George on their route between Cape Town and Port Elizabeth and between Jo'burg and the Garden Route. Greyhound services stop at the Caltex petrol station on York St, while Translux and Intercape stop at the main station at the end of Hibernia St.

Intercape fares include Knysna (R310, 1½ hours, twice daily), Plettenberg Bay (R330, two hours), Port Elizabeth (R420, 5½ hours, twice daily), Cape Town (R440, seven hours, twice daily), Bloemfontein (R680, 10 hours, daily) and Jo'burg (R750, 16 hours, daily).

The Baz Bus (www.bazbus.com)) drops off passengers in town.

Montagu & Outeniqua Passes

Montagu Pass is a quiet dirt road that winds its way through the mountains north of George; it was opened in 1847 and is now a national monument. Head back on the Outeniqua Pass, a tarred road where views are even better. Alternatively, you could opt for the Outeniqua Power Van. You can even take a bike and cycle back down the Montagu Pass.

Herolds Bay

☑044 / POP 700
On a beautiful stretch of beach with decent surf is this tiny village. It's generally quiet, although it can become crowded on summer weekends. The town is 16km southwest of George.

Makarios APARTMENT $$
(☑044-872 9019; www.makariosonsea.co.za; 4 Gericke's Cnr; apt from R1260) Luxury sea-facing apartments a stone's throw from the sand

SURFING ALONG THE GARDEN ROUTE

With the water warming up as you round Cape Agulhas, where the Indian Ocean takes over, you can be happy surfing in just board shorts or a short suit during summer. You'll need a full suit in winter. There are good waves along the coast, but Mossel Bay and Victoria Bay are considered the best spots.

In Mossel Bay, the main surf spot is Outer Pool (left of the tidal pool) – a great reef and point break. There's also a soft wave called Inner Pool to the right of the tidal pool. Elsewhere there's a good right in a big swell called Ding Dangs that's best at a lowish tide, especially in a southwesterly or easterly wind. If might be a bit of a hassle paddling out, but the right is better than the left.

You might find something at Grootbrak and Kleinbrak, but better is Herolds Bay. When it's on, there's a left-hand wedge along the beach, and it's unusual in that it works in a northwesterly wind.

Best of all is Victoria Bay, which has the most consistent breaks along this coast. It's perfect when the swell is about 1m to 2m and you get a great right-hander.

A little further along is Buffalo Bay (Buffel's Bay) where there's another right-hand point. Buffalo Bay is at one end of Brenton Beach; at the northern end, you'll find some good peaks but watch out for sharks.

On to Plettenberg Bay: avoid Robberg Peninsula, which is home to a seal colony. But the swimming area at Robberg Beach (where lifeguards are stationed) can have some good waves if the swell isn't too big. Central Beach has one of the best known waves, the Wedge, which is perfect for goofy-footers. Lookout Beach can have some sandbanks and the Point can be good, but there's a lot of erosion here and the beach is slowly disappearing. Watch out for rip currents, especially when there are no lifeguards on duty.

with self-catering facilities. Prices rise in school holidays and everything gets booked months in advance.

Dutton's Cove　　　　INTERNATIONAL $$
(☑ 044-851 0155; www.duttonscove.co.za; 21 Rooidraai Rd; mains R70-180; ⊙10am-9pm Mon-Sat, to 4pm Sun; P) A popular local lunch spot sitting high above the beach. There's lots of seafood, including a selection of combo platters.

Victoria Bay

Victoria Bay is tiny and picturesque, and sits at the foot of steep cliffs, around 8km south of George. It's considered one of the Western Cape's top surfing spots and also has a tidal pool for children. It gets overrun during school holidays and on long weekends.

Most of the apartments on the promenade are available to rent – check out www.vicbay.com for prices and bookings. There's also an excellent campground (☑ 044-889 0081; www.victoriabaycaravanpark.co.za; camping per site from R330).

Surfari　　　　LODGE $$
(☑ 044-889 0113; www.vicbaysurfari.co.za; dm/s/d R220/350/800; P 🛜) It might not be close enough to smell the ocean, but Surfari is

highly recommended. A family-run boutique backpacker lodge, it has bright, beautifully decorated rooms with breathtaking views of the coastal forest and ocean beyond. The enormous lounge has a bar, large TV and pool table, plus the owners rent out surfboards (R300 per day).

Wilderness
☑ 044 / POP 6200

The name says it all: dense old-growth forests and steep hills run down to a beautiful stretch of coastline of rolling breakers, kilometres of white sand, bird-rich estuaries and sheltered lagoons. All this has made Wilderness very popular, but thankfully it doesn't show – the myriad holiday homes blend into the verdant green hills, and the town centre is compact and unobtrusive. Beach bums beware: the beach here is beautiful, but a strong rip tide means swimming is not advised. The only other drawback is that everything is quite widely scattered, making life difficult if you don't have a vehicle.

Eden Adventures　　　　ADVENTURE SPORTS
(☑ 044-877 0179; www.eden.co.za; Fairy Knowe Hotel, 1 Dumbleton Rd) Offers canoe rental (R250 per day), abseiling (R600), kloofing (canyoning; R600) and tours of the area.

🛏 Sleeping

Fairy Knowe Backpackers   HOSTEL $
(☑044-877 1285; www.wildernessbackpackers.
com; Dumbleton Rd; camping R120, s/d R400/600,
dm/s/d with shared bathroom R160/250/400;
P🗢) Set in leafy grounds overlooking the
Touws River, this long-running hostel is
based in a 19th-century farmhouse. The bar
is in another building some distance away,
so boozers won't keep you awake. There's an
activity centre offering kayaking, abseiling,
horse riding and paragliding. To get here,
drive through town and follow the road for
2km to the Fairy Knowe turn-off.

Wilderness Beach
House Backpackers   HOSTEL $
(☑044-877 0549; www.wildernessbeachhouse.
com; Wilderness Beach; d from R550, dm/d with
shared bathroom R180/450; P🗢) Southwest
of town, this breezy hostel provides awesome ocean views, simple rooms, and a *lapa*
(circular area with a fire pit) bar and cafe
serving breakfast and dinner. If you're after
a dorm bed, request the upstairs dorm with
its ocean-facing balcony.

Interlaken   GUESTHOUSE $$
(☑044-877 1374; www.interlaken.co.za; 713 North
St; s/d incl breakfast from R1100/1200; P🗢🏊) It
gets rave reviews from readers, and we can't
argue: this is a well-run and very friendly guesthouse offering magnificent lagoon
views. Delicious dinners are available on
request.

★ Views Boutique
Hotel   BOUTIQUE HOTEL $$$
(☑044-877 8000; www.viewshotel.co.za; South
St; sea-facing s/d incl breakfast R3715/4800;
P🅿🗢🏊) With bright, modern, glass-fronted rooms looking on to the glorious beach,
this hotel makes the most of its awesome
location. It's worth paying the premium for
an ocean-facing room if you can, though
the mountain-view rooms are also delightful (and are half the price). The hotel has a
rooftop pool, spa and steps leading straight
to the sand.

🍴 Eating & Drinking

Beejuice   CAFE $
(☑044-877 0608; www.beejuicecafe.co.za; Sands
Rd; light meals R50-120; ☺8.30am-9pm Mon-Sat,
to 4pm Sun; P🚗) Although no trains ply the
tracks any more, this cafe filling the old station building is still a nice spot for salads
and sandwiches. In the evenings, traditional
South African fare is served.

★ Serendipity   SOUTH AFRICAN $$$
(☑044-877 0433; www.serendipitywilderness.com;
Freesia Ave; 5-course menu R495; ☺6.30-9.30pm
Mon-Sat; P) Readers and locals all recommend this elegant restaurant with a deck
overlooking the lagoon. The South African–
inspired menu changes monthly but always
features original takes on old classics, such
as cardamom milk tart brûlée. It's the town's
fine-dining option; bookings essential.

Girl's Restaurant   INTERNATIONAL $$$
(☑044-877 1648; www.thegirls.co.za; 1 George Rd;
mains R110-285; ☺7-9.30pm Tue-Sun; P🗢) It
doesn't look much from afar – a restaurant
tucked down the side of a petrol station –
but Girl's gets rave reviews. Try the venison
fillet or the fresh prawns in a range of increasingly spicy sauces.

Blind Pig   CRAFT BEER
(☑083 640 5403; Palms Garden Sq, Owen Grant St;
☺1-8pm Tue-Thu, noon-midnight Fri & Sat, 11am-7pm
Sun; P🚹) This tiny bar serves a wide range
of craft beer from around the country and
there's even an tiny brewery on-site. Grab a
pint and a bar snack to enjoy on the patio.

ℹ Information

Wilderness Tourism Bureau (☑044-877
0045; George Rd; ☺7.45am-4.30pm Mon-Fri,
9am-1pm Sat) Just past the cluster of restaurants on the right as you enter the village.

LOCAL KNOWLEDGE

GARDEN ROUTE PIT STOPS

Timberlake Organic Village (www.
timberlakeorganic.co.za; N2; ☺9am-5pm;
🚹), off the N2 between Wilderness and
Sedgefield, has the pleasant **Zucchini**
(☑044-882 1240; www.zucchini.co.za;
mains R90-195; ☺9am-5pm Sun-Wed, to
9pm Thu-Sat; P🚗🚹) restaurant and
some small shops selling fresh produce,
boutique foodstuffs and crafts. You can
also partake in quad biking and zip-line
tours here.

A Garden Route institution, **Wild
Oats Community Farmers Market**
(☑082 376 5020; www.wildoatsmarket.
co.za; N2, Sedgefield; ☺7.30am-noon Sat;
🚹) has been operating for over a decade. Arrive early to get your pick of the
pies, biltong, cheese, cakes, bread, beer
and fudge – all from small, local producers. The market is just off the N2, 1.5km
east of Sedgefield's town centre.

Garden Route National Park (Wilderness Section)

Formerly the Wilderness National Park, this section has been incorporated into the vast and scattered **Garden Route National Park** (☎ 044-877 1197; www.sanparks.org; adult/child R130/65; ☺ 7am-6pm) along with the Knysna Forests and Tsitsikamma. This section covers a unique system of lakes, rivers, wetlands and estuaries that are vital for the survival of many species.

There are several nature trails for all levels of fitness, taking in the lakes, the beach and the indigenous forest. The Kingfisher Trail is a 5km walk that traverses the region and includes a boardwalk across the intertidal zone of the Touws River. The lakes offer anglers, canoeists, windsurfers and sailors an ideal venue. Canoes can be hired at Eden Adventures in Wilderness.

There is just one camp in this section of the park, the expansive **Ebb & Flow Rest Camp** (camping per site from R200, d rondavel from R480, with shared bathroom R425). Alongside the river, it has campsites and a variety of self-catering cabins, chalets and rondavels (round huts with conical roofs).

ⓘ GARDEN ROUTE NATIONAL PARK (WILDERNESS SECTION)
....

Why Go Mountain-meets-forest-meets-lake vistas; shady hikes; spotting smaller wildlife species; superlative birdwatching; a host of outdoor activities including kayaking and kloofing (canyoning).

When to Go By September the rains have passed, and the park is at its most gorgeous; December and January are the busiest times; June to August are the wetter months.

Practicalities The park is tricky to access by public transport – if you don't have your own car, hiking in or joining a tour are your only options. By car, access is via the N2, 2km east of Wilderness village. Gates are open 7am to 6pm.

Budget Tips You don't have to enter the park proper for some hiking trails, meaning you can just pay hiking permit fees and not the park entrance fee.

Buffalo Bay

☎ 044 / POP 71

Buffalo Bay is a blissful place with an almost deserted surf beach, the **Goukamma Nature Reserve** (☎ 044-383 0042; www.capenature.co.za; adult/child R40/20; ☺ 8am-6pm) and only a tiny enclave of holiday homes. That's about it, and it's all you need. It's 17km west of Knysna; signposts also read Buffel's Bay or Buffelsbaai.

CapeNature (☎ 021-483 0190; www.capenature.co.za) rents out numerous cabins, cottages and chalets throughout Goukamma Nature Reserve. **Buffelsbaai Waterfront** (☎ 044-383 0038; www.buffelsbaai.co.za; Walker Dr; apt from R850) offer apartments and houses. Accommodation in the reserve was badly damaged during wildfires in 2017 but was being rebuilt when we last visited.

There are only a couple of eating options – the **Buffelsbaai Waterfront** (☎ 044-383 0038; Walker Dr; mains R80-130; ☺ 9am-5pm; 🅿) in town and the backpacker resort **Riverdeck** (☎ 078 134 5873; www.riverdeckaccommodation.co.za; Buffalo Bay Rd; camping R80, d R600, with shared bathroom R300; 🅿 ⬛), which serves wood-fired pizzas and traditional meals alongside the river (restaurant open 8am to 7pm).

Knysna

☎ 044 / POP 51,000

Embracing an exquisitely beautiful lagoon and surrounded by ancient forests, Knysna (pronounced ny-znah) is probably the most famous town on the Garden Route. Formerly the centre of the timber industry, supplying yellowwood and stinkwood for railway lines, shipping and house-building, it still has several shops specialising in woodwork and traditional furniture. The lagoon is popular with sailing enthusiasts, and there are plenty of boat trips on offer.

With its serene setting, arty and gay-friendly vibe, excellent places to stay, eat and drink, and wide range of activities, Knysna has plenty going for it. But if you're after something quiet and undeveloped, you might like to look elsewhere – particularly in high season.

In June 2017, a massive wildfire ravaged the area, destroying more than 1000 homes and devastating the landscape. It will take decades for the forests to recover, though the town was welcoming tourists back within a couple of weeks.

◉ Sights

Knysna Lagoon
PARK

(Map p157) FREE The Knysna Lagoon opens between two sandstone cliffs known as the Heads – once proclaimed by the British Royal Navy to be the most dangerous harbour entrance in the world. There are good views from the eastern head, and from the **Featherbed Nature Reserve** (Map p157; www. knysnafeatherbed.com) on the western head.

The best way to appreciate the lagoon is by boat; the Featherbed Company operates various vessels.

Mitchell's Brewery
BREWERY

(Map p154; ☑044-382 4685; www.mitchellsbrewing.com; 10 New St; tastings R75, tour & tastings R150; ⊙11am-5pm Tue & Wed, to 10pm Thu-Sat, tours 12.30pm & 2.30pm Mon-Sat; ℗) South Africa's oldest microbrewery occupies bright, new premises on the edge of the lagoon. You can join a tour or just taste its range of English-style brews in the beer garden. Pub meals (R65 to R110) are also served. Bookings essential for tours.

Belvidere
VILLAGE

(Map p157) Belvidere, 10km from Knysna, is so immaculate it's positively creepy. But it's worth a quick look for the beautiful Norman-style **Belvidere church** (Map p157) that was built in the 1850s by homesick English expats. Further on is the Featherbed Nature Reserve and, on the seaward side, Brenton-on-Sea.

Old Gaol Museum
MUSEUM

(Map p154; ☑044-302 6320; cnr Main & Queen Sts; ⊙9am-4pm Mon-Fri, to noon Sat) FREE Since this region has plenty of wet weather, a rainy-day option is welcome. The main museum is a pleasant complex in a mid-19th century building that was once the jail. There's a gallery showcasing local art, a display on the Knysna elephants and a community art project.

🏃 Activities

The Garden Route is known for its adventure sports and outdoor activities. In and around Knysna you can hike, bike, surf, kloof, kayak, horse ride and more.

Hiking & Mountain Biking

There are excellent short walking trails, some suitable for wheelchairs, and hikes in the Knysna forests north and east of town; book walking trails and collect maps and information at **SANParks** (Map p154; ☑044-302 5600; www.sanparks.org; Long St, Thesen's

Island; ⊙7.30am-4pm Mon-Fri). Exploring the old gold mine at Millwood, elephant-spotting at Diepwalle or simply finding a picnic spot are all a treat in these ancient, atmospheric forests, which fall under the Knysna Lakes section of the Garden Route National Park.

At the easy end of the hiking scale is the **Garden of Eden** (adult/child R40/20; ⊙8am-6pm), where there are lovely forest picnic spots and a wheelchair-friendly path. The **Millwood Gold Mine Walk** is also a gentle hike, while the **Elephant trails** (adult/child R68/34) at Diepwalle offer varying degrees of difficulty.

More challenging is the **Harkerville Coastal Trail** (per person R256), a two-day hike that leads to the popular Outeniqua Trail. The Harkerville Coastal Trail sustained serious damage in the 2017 wildfires and was closed when we last visited, but park authorities were working to rehabilitate the paths.

The **Outeniqua Trail** (☑044-302 5606; adult/child per day R134/67) is 108km long and takes a week to walk, although you can do two- or three-day sections. The daily fee (adult/child R134/67) includes accommodation in basic huts along the trail; bring your own bedding.

There are also plenty of mountain-biking trails – contact **Knysna Cycle Works** (Map p154; ☑044-382 5153; www.knysnacycles. co.za; Waterfront Park, Queen St; per day R250; ⊙8.30am-5pm Mon-Fri, 9am-1pm Sat) for rentals and maps.

On the Lagoon

Featherbed Company
BOATING

(Map p154; ☑044-382 1693; www.knysnafeatherbed.com; Remembrance Ave, off Waterfront Dr; boat trips adult/child from R140/75; ⊙8am-5pm) Operates various boat trips, ranging from a short ferry trip into the Heads to a sunset catamaran cruise (adult/child R730/375). The most popular trip is a 90-minute cruise on the *John Benn,* leaving at 12.30pm and 5pm (adult/child R190/90).

Knysna

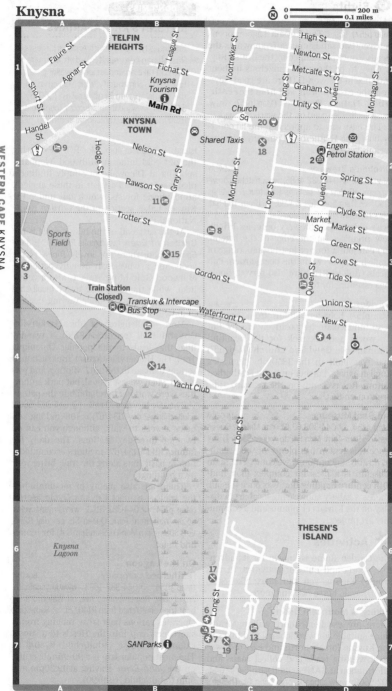

Ocean Odyssey
WATER SPORTS

(Map p154; ✆044-382 0321; www.oceanodyssey.co.za; Thesen's Island; boat trip adult/child R710/510) As well as 1½-hour boat trips on the lagoon, Ocean Odyssey rents out stand-up paddleboards (per hour R180) and offers sunset yachting trips (from R900). From June to November there are whale-watching trips as well (adult/child R900/700).

Oyster Tour
BOATING

(Map p154; ✆082 892 0469; www.knysnacharters.com; jetty at Quay 4, Thesen's Island; adult/child R570/160; ☺3pm) In South Africa, Knysna is synonymous with oysters. Learn about cultivation on this 90-minute lagoon cruise, which includes tasting of wild and farmed oysters and some wine to wash them down with.

Knysna Kayak Hire
KAYAKING

(Map p154; ✆082 892 0469; www.knysnacharters.com; per hour R100) A peaceful way to explore the lagoon – just steer clear of the Heads! Book online and collect the kayaks from Whet Restaurant on Thesen's Island.

Trip Out
WATER SPORTS

(✆083 306 3587; www.tripout.co.za; 2hr surfing class R400) Offers surfing classes for beginners in nearby Buffalo Bay, snorkelling around the Heads (R350) and boat cruises, as well as a half-day kloofing (canyoning) trip (R650).

🕝 Tours

The tourism office has an up-to-date list of the numerous operators offering tours to Knysna's hilltop townships. If you want to stay overnight in the townships, contact Knysna Tourism (p157) and ask for its brochure, *Living Local*.

★ Emzini Tours
CULTURAL

(✆044-382 1087; www.emzinitours.co.za; adult/child R400/150; ☺10am & 2pm Mon-Sat) Led by township resident Ella, this three-hour trip visits some of this tour company's community projects. Tours can be tailored to suit your interests, but generally end at Ella's home for tea, drumming and a group giggle as you try to wrap your tongue around the clicks of the Xhosa language.

🎉 Festivals & Events

Pink Loerie Festival
LGBT

(www.pinkloerie.co.za) Knysna celebrates its gay-friendliness with a flamboyant Mardi Gras around the end of May.

Oyster Festival
FOOD & DRINK

(www.oysterfestival.co.za; ☺late Jun/early Jul) This is an homage to the oyster, with oyster-based specials at restaurants around town, live concerts and sporting events including the Knysna Marathon.

🛏 Sleeping

Island Vibe
HOSTEL $

(Map p154; ✆044-382 1728; www.islandvibe.co.za; 67 Main St; dm R170, d R600, with shared bathroom R550; ☎🖥) A funky backpackers with excellent communal areas, cheery staff and nicely decorated rooms. There's a lively bar and a small pool on the deck.

Jembjo's Knysna Lodge
HOSTEL $

(Map p154; ✆044-382 2658; www.jembjosknysnalodge.co.za; 4 Queen St; dm R170, s/d R550/600, s/d with shared bathroom R450/500; P☎) A small, friendly hostel run by two former overland truck drivers. There's lots of info on activities in the area, mountain bikes to rent (R20 per hour) and a free DIY breakfast.

Inyathi Guest Lodge
CHALET $

(Map p154; ✆044-382 7768; www.inyathiguestlodge.co.za; 38 Trotter St; chalets from R600; ☎) This lodge has changed address and had a

Knysna

👁 Sights
1 Mitchell's Brewery	D4
2 Old Gaol Museum	D2

🎯 Activities, Courses & Tours
3 Featherbed Company	A3
4 Knysna Cycle Works	D4
5 Knysna Kayak Hire	C7
6 Ocean Odyssey	C7
7 Oyster Tour	C7

🛏 Sleeping
8 Inyathi Guest Lodge	C3
9 Island Vibe	A2
10 Jembjo's Knysna Lodge	D3
11 Knysna Log Inn	B2
12 Protea Hotel Knysna Quays	B4
13 Turbine Hotel & Spa	C7

🍴 Eating
14 34 South	B4
15 Chatters Bistro	B3
16 Freshline Fisheries	C4
17 Ile de Pain	C6
18 Olive Tree	C2
19 Sirocco	C7

🍷 Drinking & Nightlife
20 Vinyl	C2

complete overhaul, but the cheery owners and tasteful African decor remain. Accommodation is in self-catering chalets each with its own private garden. It's an excellent budget option for those who don't fancy a backpackers.

Woodbourne Resort
CAMPGROUND $

(Map p157; ☑ 044-384 0316; www.woodbourneknysna.com; George Rex Dr; campsites/chalets R250/650; ☒) Here you'll find spacious, shaded camping and simple chalets with TVs. It's a quiet place a little way out of town; follow the signs to the Heads. Prices more than double from mid-December to mid-January.

Brenton Cottages
CHALET $$

(Map p157; ☑ 044-381 0082; www.brentononsea. net; 242 CR Swart Dr, Brenton-on-Sea; 2-person cabins R990, 6-person chalets R1680; P☒☎☒) On the seaward side of the lagoon, the hills drop to Brenton-on-Sea, overlooking a magnificent 8km beach. The chalets have a full kitchen while cabins have a kitchenette; many have ocean views. There are plenty of braai (barbecue) areas dotted around the manicured lawns. Prices rise steeply in December and January.

★Turbine Hotel & Spa
BOUTIQUE HOTEL $$$

(Map p154; ☑ 044-302 5746; www.turbinehotel. co.za; Sawtooth Lane, Thesen's Island; s/d incl breakfast from R1900/2840; P☒☎☒) The clever design of this power station-turned-boutique hotel makes it one of Knysna's coolest places to stay. Elements of the original building have been cleverly incorporated into the rooms and public areas. It's a great location a short walk from cafes and restaurants, and some rooms have magnificent views of the lagoon.

★Under Milkwood
CHALET $$$

(Map p157; ☑ 044-384 0745; www.milkwood. co.za; George Rex Dr; s/d cabin from R950/1460; P@☎) Perched on the shores of Knysna Lagoon are these highly impressive self-catering log cabins, each with its own deck and braai (barbecue) area. There's no pool but there is a small beach. The water-facing chalets are more expensive and prices skyrocket in December.

Protea Hotel Knysna Quays
HOTEL $$$

(Map p154; ☑ 044-382 5005; www.protea.marriott. com; Waterfront Dr; s/d R1520/1920; ☒☎☒) Rooms are tastefully decorated at this stylish hotel. It has an inviting, heated pool and is moments away from shopping and eating options at the Waterfront. You'll want a lagoon-facing room.

Knysna Log Inn
HOTEL $$$

(Map p154; ☑ 044-382 5835; www.log-inn.co.za; 16 Gray St; s/d incl breakfast R1540/2160; ☒☎☒) This inn is said to be the largest log structure in the southern hemisphere. The rooms are comfortable, many with balconies, and there's a lovely pool in the garden.

Belvidere Manor
HOTEL $$$

(Map p157; ☑ 044-387 1055; www.belvidere.co.za; Duthie Dr; s/d incl breakfast R1330/2220; P☎☒) A tremendously peaceful place to stay, with luxury cottages around an immaculate lawn, some with lagoon views. There is a restaurant (mains R85 to R170) in the historical main house serving regional and international dishes, and an atmospheric pub, open to nonguests.

✖ Eating

★Ile de Pain
CAFE, BAKERY $$

(Map p154; ☑ 044-302 5705; www.iledepain.co.za; Thesen's Island; mains R55-115; ⊙8am-3pm Tue-Sat; ☎☑) Ile de Pain is a wildly popular bakery and cafe that's as much a hit with locals as it is with tourists. There's an excellent breakfast menu, lots of fresh salads, some inventive lunch specials and quite a bit for vegetarians. Expect to queue for a table at weekends or in peak season – reservations are not accepted.

Freshline Fisheries
SEAFOOD $$

(Map p154; ☑ 044-382 3131; www.freshlinefisheries.co.za; Long St, Railway Siding Dockyard; mains R70-170; ⊙11.30am-8pm Mon-Sat; P) It can work out to be quite pricey since sides are ordered separately, but the seafood here really is worth it. It's a simple spot with tables on a sandy terrace. It has so much character you quickly forget you're basically lunching at the side of a car park. Bring your own booze – there's no corkage fee.

Olive Tree
BISTRO $$

(Map p154; ☑ 044-382 5867; 21 Main St; mains R100-170; ⊙6-9pm Mon-Sat) One of Knysna's more upmarket restaurants is a romantic spot with a blackboard menu that changes regularly. Bookings advisable.

East Head Café
INTERNATIONAL $$

(Map p157; ☑ 044-384 0933; www.eastheadcafe. co.za; 25 George Rex Dr, Eastern Head; mains R75-145; ⊙8am-3pm; P☑☒) There's an outdoor deck overlooking the lagoon and ocean, lots of fish and seafood, plus a few vegetarian dishes. It's a very popular spot so expect to wait for a table in high season. Reservations not accepted.

Around Knysna

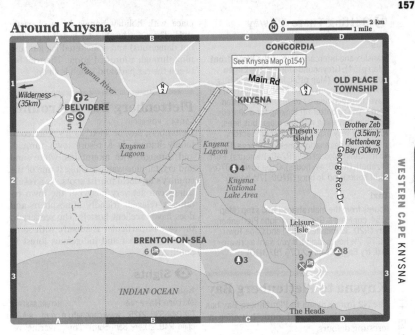

Sirocco
INTERNATIONAL **$$**

(Map p154; ☑044-382 4874; www.sirocco.co.za; Main Rd, Thesen's Island; mains R60-150; ☺11am-10pm) Inside, it's a stylish place to dine on sushi, steak and seafood; outside, it's a laid-back bar with wood-fired pizzas and a range of Mitchell's beers. The cocktail menu is also worth a look.

Chatters Bistro
PIZZA **$$**

(Map p154; ☑044-382 0203; www.chattersbistro.co.za; 9a Gray St; mains R60-130; ☺noon-10pm Tue-Sat) Restaurants seem to come and go in Knysna, but this pizza joint has been around a while. You'll also find burgers, pasta and some salads, plus a pleasant garden to enjoy them in.

34 South
INTERNATIONAL **$$**

(Map p154; ☑044-382 7331; www.34south.biz; Knysna Waterfront; mains R70-170; ☺8.30am-10pm) With outdoor tables overlooking the water, decent sushi, deli produce and lavish seafood platters, this is a nice spot for lunch. The wine selection is one of the best in town.

🍷 Drinking & Nightlife

Head along Main St and check out the local bars, many of which are seasonal. The town's microbrewery, Mitchell's (p153), is South Africa's oldest.

Around Knysna

◎ Sights

Vinyl
CLUB

(Map p154; ☑044-382 0386; Main St; ☺7pm-2am) Knysna's top spot for late-night dancing offers a relaxed vibe and a balcony area for lounging. DJs play when there are no live bands.

ℹ️ Information

Knysna Tourism (Map p154; ☑044-382 5510; www.visitknysna.co.za; 40 Main St; ☺8am-5pm Mon-Fri, 8.30am-1pm Sat year-round, plus 9am-1pm Sun Dec, Jan & Jul) An excellent office, with very knowledgeable staff.

ⓘ Getting There & Away

Bus

Translux and Intercape stop at the **Waterfront** (Map p154); Greyhound stops at the **Engen petrol station** (Map p154; Main St); Baz Bus (www.bazbus.com) drops at all the hostels. For travel between nearby towns on the Garden Route, you're better off looking for a shared taxi than travelling with the major bus lines, which are very expensive for short sectors.

Intercape destinations include George (R240, 45 minutes), Mossel Bay (R240, 1½ hours), Port Elizabeth (R330, 4½ hours), Cape Town (R370, eight hours) and Jo'burg (R700, 17½ hours).

Taxi

Routes from the main **shared taxi stop** (Map p154; cnr Main & Gray Sts) include Plettenberg Bay (R20, 30 minutes, daily) and Cape Town (R270, 7½ hours, daily). If you want a private taxi, try **Eagle Cabs** (☑ 076 797 3110).

Knysna to Plettenberg Bay

The N2 from Knysna to Plettenberg Bay has turn-offs both north and south that offer interesting detours.

The Knysna–Avontuur road, Rte 339, climbs through the Outeniqua range via the beautiful **Prince Alfred's Pass**, regarded by some as even better than the Swartberg Pass. Be warned that the road is a bit on the rough side and it's slow going. The road has few really steep sections but the pass reaches a height of over 1000m, and there are great views to the north before the road winds its way into the Langkloof Valley.

Reached by a turn-off along the N2 10km east of Knysna, **Noetzie** is a quirky little place with holiday homes in mock-castle style. There's a lovely surf beach (spacious but dangerous) and a sheltered lagoon running through a forested gorge. The trail between the car park and beach is steep.

Plettenberg Bay & Around

☑ 044 / POP 6500

Plettenberg Bay, or 'Plett' as it's more commonly known, is a resort town through and through, with mountains, white sand and crystal-blue water making it one of the country's top local tourist spots. As a result, things can get very busy, but the town retains a relaxed, friendly atmosphere and does have excellent hostels. The scenery to the east in particular is superb, with some of the best coast and indigenous forest in South Africa.

◉ Sights

Keurbooms River Nature Reserve
NATURE RESERVE

(☑ 044-533 2125; www.capenature.co.za; adult/child R40/20; ☉8am-6pm) This riverine reserve is a glorious place to swim, angle, picnic or paddle. There are canoes to rent (R135 per day) or you can take a **ferry trip** (☑ 083 254 3551; www.ferry.co.za; N2; adult/child R180/90) down the river.

Bramon
WINERY

(☑ 044-534 8007; www.bramonwines.co.za; N2; tastings per wine R10; ☉11am-5pm) Operating since 2000, this was the first wine estate in the region. It's best known for its bubbly. Tucked away in the vines is the mezze-style restaurant (dishes R35 to R90), where bread

Plettenberg Bay

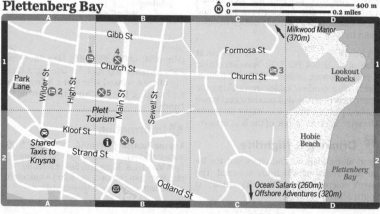

is baked to order and the whole wine range is available by the glass.

Monkeyland · WILDLIFE RESERVE
(☑044-534 8906; www.monkeyland.co.za; The Crags; 1hr tour adult/child R210/105; ☺8am-5pm) This very popular attraction helps rehabilitate wild monkeys that have been in zoos or private homes. The walking safari through a dense forest and across a 128m-long rope bridge is superb. A combo ticket with Birds of Eden (☑044-534 8906; www.birdsofeden. co.za; The Crags; adult/child R210/105; ☺8am-5pm) costs R320/160 per adult/child.

Robberg Nature & Marine Reserve · PARK
(☑044-533 2125; www.capenature.co.za; adult/child R40/20; ☺8am-6pm May-Sep, 7am-8pm Oct-Apr) This reserve, 8km southeast of Plettenberg Bay, protects a 4km-long peninsula with a rugged coastline of cliffs and rocks. There are three circular day walks of increasing difficulty, but it's very rocky and not for the unfit or anyone with knee problems!

Basic accommodation is available at the spectacularly located Fountain Shack (☑044-802 5300; www.capenature.org.za; 4 people R920), which is reachable only by a two-hour hike. To get to the reserve head along Robberg Rd, off Piesang Valley Rd, until you see the signs.

You can also take a boat trip to view the peninsula – and its colony of Cape fur seals – from the water and even take a dip to see if the seals come for a closer look. Contact Offshore Adventures (☑082 829 0809; www.offshoreadventures.co.za; Hopwood St; boat trip R400, swimming with seals R700) to book.

🏃 Activities

Apart from lounging on the beaches or hiking on the Robberg Peninsula there's a lot to do in Plett; check with Albergo for Backpackers (p160), which can organise anything from hiking, horse riding and surfing to bungee jumping, blackwater tubing or skydiving, often at a discount.

Ocean Safaris · BOATING
(☑082 784 5729; www.oceansafaris.co.za; Milkwood Centre, Hopwood St; whale watching adult/child R750/450) Two-hour boat trips to view southern right and humpback whales operate at 9.30am, noon and 2.30pm from July to December. Dolphin-viewing trips (adult/child R500/250) operate throughout the year.

Sky Dive Plettenberg Bay · ADVENTURE SPORTS
(☑082 905 7440; www.skydiveplett.com; Plettenberg Airport; tandem jump from R2600) Although all skydives offer pretty impressive views, you can't beat soaring over the Garden Route coast. This recommended operator has over a decade of skydiving experience.

Learn to Surf Plett · SURFING
(☑082 436 6410; www.learntosurfplett.co.za; 2hr group lesson incl equipment R400) A long-running surfing outfit that also offers stand-up paddleboarding lessons (R100 per hour) and rents out equipment.

Africanyon · ADVENTURE SPORTS
(☑044-534 8055; www.africanyon.com; Forest Hall Rd, The Crags; 2hr tour R550) Travellers rave about this canyoning trip, which sees you swimming through rock pools, whooshing down natural waterslides and abseiling down a waterfall. There is also a four-hour option (R750) if you just can't get enough. If you prefer to stay dry, opt for the abseiling trip (R400), on which you'll descend a 50m rock face.

🛌 Sleeping

The tourism bureau (p161) has a full list of accommodation and can tell you about the many camping options, all in nearby Keurboomstrand. In low season there are bargains to be found.

Nothando Backpackers Hostel · HOSTEL $
(☑044-533 0220; www.nothando.com; 5 Wilder St; dm R180, d R550, with shared bathroom R480; ℗🛜) This excellent budget option is owner-run and it shows. There's a great bar area with satellite TV, yet you can still find peace and quiet in the large grounds. Rooms are worthy of a budget guesthouse.

Abalone Beach House · HOSTEL $
(☑044-535 9602; www.abalonebeachhouse.co.za; 13 Milkwood Glen, Keurboomstrand; d R700, with shared bathroom R600; ℗🛜) This extremely

---

Plettenberg Bay

WORTH A TRIP

NATURE'S VALLEY

Nature's Valley is nestled in yellowwood forest next to a magnificent beach and lagoon in the Tsitsikamma section of the Garden Route National Park. This is where the 46km Otter Trail (p181) ends and the 60km Tsitsikamma Mountain Trail (p181) begins. There are also plenty of shorter hikes in this part of the park.

Mzansi Experience (www.mzansi.travel) stops in the Crags (near Nature's Valley) en route between Cape Town and Hogsback. Baz Bus (www.bazbus.com) also stops in the Crags en route between Cape Town and Port Elizabeth. The other bus companies stop in Plettenberg Bay, from where accommodation in Nature's Valley will pick you up, if given advance notice.

Rocky Road (☏044-534 8148; www.rockyroadbackpackers.com; Loredo South; dm R190, safari tent s/d R240/480, cabin s/d R270/540; P☎) Rocky Road is like an enchanted clearing in the wood. Swing chairs, a donkey-boiler hot tub and offbeat bathrooms are scattered on the fringes of indigenous forest. Accommodation options include two dorms, comfortable safari tents and cabins with adjoining bathrooms. Breakfast and dinner are available on request. It is signposted from Rte 102 about 1km from the N2.

Nature's Valley Rest Camp (☏044-531 6700; www.sanparks.org; camping per site R205, chalet R1120, cabin with shared bathroom R550) The national park campground is a lovely spot at the edge of the river east of town, and it's a 2km walk from the beach. There are clean bathrooms and shared kitchens and laundry. Keep food well stored: there are pesky primates everywhere. In addition to accommodation charges, guests must pay the park's daily conservation fee (adult/child R96/48).

Nature's Valley Guesthouse & Hikers Haven (☏044-531 6805; www.hikershaven.co.za; 411 St Patrick's Ave; s/d incl breakfast R490/960, d with shared bathroom R380; ☺closed Dec; P☎) This thatched brick building has a big lawn, a self-catering kitchen, a lounge, and small, tidy rooms with outdated bathrooms. Transport to the start of the Otter Trail is offered (R480 for up to four people).

Tranquility B&B (☏044-531 6663; www.tranquilitylodge.co.za; 130 St Michael's Ave; s incl breakfast R650-750, d incl breakfast R1300-1500; ☎) Soundtracked by a trickling fountain and the roaring waves, Tranquility has seven clean rooms decked out with beach-house furniture, African art and surf trimmings. Guests get free kayaks for the lagoon and discounts on bungee jumping at Bloukrans Bridge.

Nature's Way Farm Stall (☏044-534 8849; Rte 102; snacks R35-40; ☺9am-5pm; ☎) This charming roadside store on a dairy farm sells light breakfasts and lunches, tapas, cake, coffee and a smorgasbord of local produce, including cheese, jam and fruits. It also rents out a few fully equipped cottages.

Nature's Valley Trading Store (☏044-531 6835; 135 St Michael's Ave; mains R60-125; ☺9am-7.30pm; ☎) A spade's throw from the beach (but without sea views), the only eatery in the village serves burgers, salads, steaks and seafood, and the adjoining shop sells basic groceries. Also offers local information and brochures.

friendly backpackers hostel is two minutes' walk from a magnificent beach; body boards are provided free. To reach the house, follow the Keurboomstrand signs from the N2 (about 6km east of Plett), then turn into Milkwood Glen. You need your own transport to get here.

Albergo for Backpackers HOSTEL $
(☏044-533 4434; www.albergo.co.za; 8 Church St; camping R90, dm R160, d with shared bathroom R450; P☎) Well-run and friendly, Albergo

can organise just about any activity in the area and there are free body boards to use. The upstairs dorm has huge windows and a spacious balcony.

★**Hog Hollow** LODGE $$$
(☏044-534 8879; www.hog-hollow.com; Askop Rd, The Crags; s/d incl breakfast R2700/3975; P☎☎☎☎) Hog Hollow, 18km east of Plett along the N2, provides delightful accommodation in African-art-decorated units overlooking the forest. Each luxurious unit

comes with a private wooden deck and hammock. You can walk to Monkeyland (p159) from here; staff will collect you if you don't fancy the walk back.

Plettenberg
LUXURY HOTEL $$$

(☑044-533 2030; www.theplettenberghotel. com; 40 Church St; r incl breakfast from R4300; P❋☎☀) Built on a rocky headland with breathtaking vistas, this five-star place is pure decadence, with fantastic rooms, a spa and a top-class restaurant (mains R150 to R250).

Milkwood Manor
HOTEL $$$

(☑044-533 0420; www.milkwoodmanor.co.za; Salmack Rd, Lookout Beach; r incl breakfast from R1400; P☎) A remarkable location, right on the beach and overlooking the lagoon. Rooms have a bright, beachy feel. There's an on-site restaurant (mains R110 to R200) and kayaks are free for guests.

Periwinkle Guest Lodge
GUESTHOUSE $$$

(☑044-533 1345; www.periwinkle.co.za; 75 Beachy Head Dr; s/d incl breakfast from R2145/2860; P☎) This bright beachfront guesthouse offers airy rooms, all with great views – you might even be able to spot whales and dolphins.

✖ Eating

Le Fournil de Plett
CAFE $

(☑044-533 1390; Lookout Centre, Church St; mains R60-115; ⊙8am-5pm Mon-Fri, to 4pm Sat, to 1pm Sun; ☎) Enjoy a good cup of coffee and a freshly baked pastry in the courtyard or on the balcony overlooking Plett's main road. There's also a small lunch menu, largely focusing on salads and sandwiches.

Ristorante Enrico
SEAFOOD $$

(☑044-535 9818; www.enricorestaurant.co.za; Main Beach, Keurboomstrand; mains R90-170; ⊙noon-10pm Tue-Sun; P) Highly recommended by readers and right on the beach, this is *the* place for seafood in Plett (well, just outside Plett). Enrico has his own boat that, weather permitting, heads out each morning. If you book ahead you can join the fishing trip and have your catch cooked at the restaurant.

Table
ITALIAN $$

(☑044-533 3024; www.thetable.co.za; 9 Main St; mains R60-115; ⊙noon-11pm Mon-Sat, to 6pm Sun; ☜) A funky, minimalist venue with pizzas, seafood and a very tasty lamb shank. There's an indoor kids' play area and live music on Fridays.

★ Nguni
STEAK $$$

(☑044-533 6710; www.nguni-restaurant.co.za; 6 Crescent St; mains R135-225; ⊙11am-10pm Mon-Fri, from 6pm Sat) Tucked away in a quiet courtyard, this is one of Plett's most upscale eateries. The speciality is dry-aged beef, though you'll also find some South African favourites including ostrich, springbok and the odd traditional dish such as a vegetarian version of *bobotie* (curry topped with beaten egg baked to a crust). Reservations recommended.

❶ Information

Plett Tourism (☑044-533 4065; www.plett-tourism.co.za; Melville's Corner Shopping Centre, Main St; ⊙9am-5pm Mon-Fri, to 1pm Sat) Plenty of useful information on accommodation plus walks in the surrounding hills and reserves.

❶ Getting There & Away

All the major buses stop at the Shell Ultra City on the N2; the Baz Bus comes into town. Intercape destinations from Plett include George (R230, one hour), Port Elizabeth (R250, four hours), Cape Town (R470, eight hours), Jo'burg (R770, 18 hours) and Graaff-Reinet (R480, seven hours).

If you're heading to Knysna you're better off taking a **shared taxi** (Kloof St, near cnr High St, R20, 30 minutes). Long-distance shared taxis stop at the Shell Ultra City on the N2.

ROUTE 62

Route 62 takes you through some spectacular scenery changes, from the rugged mountain passes between Montagu and Calitzdorp to the arid semidesert of the Little Karoo region around Oudtshoorn. It's touted as the longest wine route in the world and is a great alternative to the N2 if you're travelling from Cape Town towards the Garden Route.

Montagu

☑023 / POP 15,000

Pretty Montagu's wide streets are bordered by 24 restored national monuments, including some fine art deco architecture. There's plenty to do here for visitors, including hot springs, a number of walks and superlative **rock climbing** (☑082 696 4067; www.montagu-climbing.com; 45 Mount St; 2hr climbing/abseiling trip R750/400), as well as excellent accommodation and some good restaurants.

If travelling into town along Route 62 from Robertson, the road passes through a narrow arch in the Langeberg Mountains.

◉ Sights & Activities

Joubert House   NOTABLE BUILDING
(☑ 023-614 1774; 25 Long St; adult/child R5/2; ⊙ 9am-1pm &1.30-4.30pm Mon-Fri, 10.30am-12.30pm Sat & Sun) Joubert House is the oldest house in Montagu (built in 1853) and has been restored to its Victorian glory.

★ Protea Farm   ECOTOUR
(☑ 023-614 3012; www.proteafarm.co.za; adult/child R130/55; ⊙ tours 10am Wed & Sat) Wonderful three-hour tractor rides explore Protea Farm, 29km from Montagu. There are sweeping views of the Breede River Valley and the trip includes snacks and drinks. There's an option to extend the day with a traditional lunch of *potjiekos* (pot stew) with homemade bread for R130/55 per adult/child. Farm accommodation is available (two-person cottage from R700).

There's a booking office within the **tourism bureau** (☑ 023-614 2471; www.montagu-ashton.info; 24 Bath St; ⊙ 8.30am-5.30pm Mon-Fri, 9am-5pm Sat, 9.30am-4pm Sun).

🛏 Sleeping

Cottage on Long   COTTAGE $
(☑ 023-614 2398; www.cottageonlong.co.za; 16 Long St; d R600; P 🛜 ☷) Perched on the edge of town but within easy walking distance of many restaurants, this is a cute and well-equipped cottage with great views from the garden. You can use the pool in the owner's home. It's opposite the Kloof farm stall.

Montagu Caravan Park   CAMPGROUND $
(☑ 082 920 7863; www.montagucaravanpark.co.za; 4 Middel St; camping R100, 4-person chalet from R800; P 🐾) This park is in a pleasant location with apricot trees and lots of shade and grass. As well as campsites there are chalets and simple backpacker cabins (for two R550). You'll need your own bedding for the latter.

Mimosa Lodge   HOTEL $$
(☑ 023-614 2351; www.mimosa.co.za; 19 Church St; s/d incl breakfast from R900/1320; P ❄ 🛜 ☷) A delightful, upmarket lodge in a restored Edwardian landmark building with lovely gardens and a pool with a thatched-roof gazebo for shade. The attached restaurant serves four-course dinners (R495) and is open to nonguests. Wines from the owner's vineyard are served.

🚗 Driving Tour
Route 62

START ROBERTSON
END OUDTSHOORN
LENGTH 260KM; THREE TO FOUR DAYS

If you're heading east towards the Garden Route, Route 62 makes for a marvellous drive and a great alternative to taking the N2 both there and back. The route begins in Robertson, a farming town on the Breede River, where you can spend a day or two riding horses, rafting on the river or hopping between unpretentious wineries before heading out to enjoy Route 62.

After about 15km you pass through the untidy town of Ashton with its sizeable wine cellar. There's not much to hold you here, but once you leave Ashton the route quickly takes a turn for the scenic as you near the Langeberg range. The road twists and turns towards Cogmanskloof (Cogmans Gorge). Here you'll see a sign denoting the ❶ **Old English Fort**. Built in 1899 in anticipation of the Anglo-Boer War, the fort sits above the road – keep an eye out for it as you pass through an archway in the mountains.

This archway heralds your arrival in Montagu, an adorable town with good restaurants, superlative ❷ **rock climbing** (p161) and a cheery ❸ **hot springs resort** (p164). Once you leave Montagu, the road straightens out and passes by orchards – the area is known for its fruit, particularly dried fruit.

This is perhaps the least interesting stretch of the trip, but do keep an eye out for ❹ **Joubert-Tradauw** after about 50km. The winery makes for a lovely lunch stop and offers tastings – grab a bottle of its R62 red blend as a memento of your drive. From here it's only 12km to Barrydale. Most people drive straight past, but if you veer off the main road, the town has some interesting galleries and restaurants and a very pretty church.

Some 27km east of Barrydale, you can't miss the tatty whitewashed building on the right, with fluttering flags and untidy lettering proclaiming that you have reached 'Ronnies Sex Shop'. ❺ **Ronnies** has become one of the most famous spots on Route 62. It began life as a simple shop

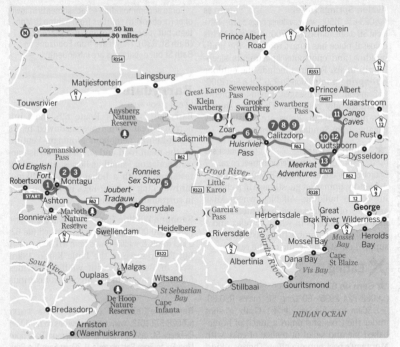

and the owner, struggling to get customers in, painted 'Ronnies Shop' on the facade. Some prankster pals added the word 'sex' and suggested he start a bar rather than sticking with the road stall idea. Today Ronnies is a dingy biker bar and most don't stick around longer than it takes to snap a few photos of the bar, endowed with row upon row of bras and knickers. Nearby there is a spa with warm water pumped from underground springs.

The scenery remains the same – undulating semidesert scrubland typical of the Little Karoo – until you pass Ladismith, a pleasant town with a couple of decent farm stalls, and Zoar, a small farming settlement. Suddenly the mountains begin to rise and you reach the highly scenic ⑥ **Huisrivier Pass**, which counts two river crossings along its 13km of dips and hills. This is the prettiest part of the drive, so take time to stop at one of the lay-bys set up for view-hunters.

On the other side of the pass is Calitzdorp, best known for its port-style wines. The main road isn't the most relaxing place to pause, but turn right onto Van Riebeek St and you'll find a higgledy-piggledy maze of roads lined with handsome old buildings. There are wineries within walking distance of the town, including ⑦ **Boplaas** and ⑧ **De Krans**. Sample the various dessert wines or pop into ⑨ **Porto Deli** for a lunch inspired by Portuguese and Mozambican cuisine.

The road once again flattens out as you leave Calitzdorp and soon enough you start to see the first ostrich farms. Oudtshoorn likes to call itself the 'ostrich capital of the world', with its industry that dates back to Victorian times. The town lies 55km east of Calitzdorp and is home to a number of ⑩ **ostrich farms** (p165) where you can learn about the industry and meet the birds. This is also the home of the impressive ⑪ **Cango Caves**, the interesting ⑫ **CP Nel Museum** (p165) and a much-loved ⑬ **meerkat experience**.

It is also the end of the trip, although Route 62 actually stretches all the way to Port Elizabeth in the Eastern Cape. Celebrate the drive with an ostrich dinner and some local red wine in one of Oudtshoorn's restaurants, then wave goodbye to Route 62 and make for the N12, which connects Oudtshoorn with the Garden Route.

Avalon Springs Hotel
HOTEL $$

(☑023-614 1150; www.avalonsprings.co.za; Uitvlucht St; d/apt from R1300/1700; P🖢❄💻🐾) This colossal place has smart rooms in the main building and enormous apartments sleeping up to six. Features include the outdoor **hot-spring pools** (Mon-Fri R55, Sat & Sun R100; ⊙8am-8pm; 🐾), massages, a gym and plenty of kid-friendly activities. There's a shuttle bus into Montagu. Rates are considerably cheaper from Sunday to Thursday.

★7 Church Street
GUESTHOUSE $$$

(☑023-614 1186; www.7churchstreet.co.za; 7 Church St; d incl breakfast from R1500; P🐾❄❄💻) A friendly, upmarket guesthouse in a charming Karoo building. Affable owners Mike and May offer large, well-appointed rooms, manicured gardens in which to relax and a particularly memorable breakfast. They also supply honest tourist info on the region.

✕ Eating

★Barn on 62
CAFE $

(☑082 824 2995; 60 Long St; mains R50-80; ⊙8.30am-4pm Tue-Sun; P🐾) Grab a spot under the trees and enjoy a lunch of homebaked pie and salad or a slice of cake with Montagu's best cup of coffee. There's a kids' play area in the garden. It's at the start of Long St as you arrive from Barrydale and ideal for a lunch stop if you're just passing through.

Rambling Rose
SOUTH AFRICAN $$

(☑083 401 4503; 36 Long St; mains R75-160; ⊙8am-5pm Wed-Mon; P❄) Great for brunch, lunch or cake, this shop-cum-restaurant serves an array of dishes including Cape Malay curry, seafood, steak and salad. The shop sells all manner of local produce and is a great place to stock up on *padkos* (road snacks) such as biscuits and dried fruit.

Simply Delicious@Four Oaks
FUSION $$

(☑023-614 3483; www.four-oaks.co.za; 46 Long St; mains R115-150; ⊙6.30-9.30pm) Set in a lovely old building, this sleek place has a seasonal menu. The emphasis is on home cooking, with everything from the bread to the ice cream made in-house. The lamb pie is delicious.

❶ Getting There & Away

Buses stop at Ashton, 9km from Montagu. Translux buses stop on the run between Cape Town (R280, 2½ hours) and Port Elizabeth (R450, eight hours).

Some accommodation establishments in town offer (prebooked) shuttles from Ashton to Montagu, but you could also jump in a **shared taxi** (Bath St; R30). They leave from Foodzone on Bath St but departures are infrequent.

Barrydale
☑028 / POP 4200

Barrydale is one of Route 62's most underrated treats, often overshadowed by its better-known neighbour Montagu. Venture off the main road and you'll find stylish accommodation, small galleries and quirky restaurants with a bohemian feel. Hiking, birdwatching and the Big Five are on offer in surrounding nature reserves.

Sanbona Wildlife Reserve
WILDLIFE RESERVE

(☑021-010 0028; www.sanbona.com; off Rte 62; d incl meals & wildlife drives from R11,900; 🐾) A Big Five reserve in the Little Karoo, 18km west of Barrydale, with wildlife activities for those staying in its three ultra-luxurious lodges.

Barrydale Cellar
WINERY

(☑028-572 1012; www.barrydalewines.co.za; 1 Van Riebeeck St; tastings R30; ⊙tasting room 9am-5pm Mon-Fri, to 3pm Sat, pizzeria 11.30am-5pm Tue-Sun; P🐾) Although it looks like a characterless industrial cellar from the roadside, the tasting room and restaurant on the river bank are actually quite charming. The cellar is best known for brandy but you can also taste wine or beer brewed at the on-site microbrewery. There's a kids' play area inside and wood-fired pizzas on the menu (mains R75 to R90).

Calitzdorp
☑044 / POP 4300

This attractive little town, with architecture typical of the Little Karoo, has a stunning setting on rolling farmland overlooked by the Groot Swartberge range to the north and the Rooiberge to the southwest. You have to leave the scruffy main road and explore the backstreets to get a feel for Calitzdorp's charm.

Of the seven wineries in the area, four are within walking distance of the town centre – they all specialise in port-style wines (known as Cape Ruby, Cape Tawny or Cape Vintage) though there are table wines as well.

Port-Wine Guest House
GUESTHOUSE $$

(☑044-213 3131; www.portwine.net; 7 Queen St; d incl breakfast R900; ❄❄💻) A beautifully appointed, thatched Cape cottage with four-poster beds. It's a short walk from three of the wineries.

Tourism Bureau TOURIST INFORMATION
(☑044-213 3775; www.calitzdorp.org.za; 3 Voortrekker St; ☺9am-5pm Mon-Fri, 10am-1pm Sat) Provides details on accommodation and the local wineries. It's in a building at the side of the Shell petrol station.

Oudtshoorn

☑044 / POP 29,000
Oudtshoorn is famous for its ostriches, but it has much more to offer. It makes a great base for exploring the Little Karoo, the Garden Route (it's 55km to George along the N12) and the Great Karoo to the north.

In the late 1860s, no self-respecting society lady in the Western world would be seen dead without an ostrich plume adorning her headgear. The fashion lasted until the slump of 1914 and during this time the 'feather barons' of Oudtshoorn made their fortunes.

You can still see their gracious homes, along with other architectural pointers to Oudtshoorn's former wealth such as the **CP Nel Museum** (☑044-272 7306; www.cpnelmuseum.co.za; 3 Baron van Rheede St; adult/child R25/5; ☺8am-5pm Mon-Fri, 9am-1pm Sat), formerly a school. The town remains the 'ostrich capital of the world' and is now the prosperous tourist centre of the Little Karoo.

◉ Sights & Activities

There are four ostrich farms that offer guided tours, though two still offer riding as an activity. We don't recommend riding the birds as it causes them unnecessary distress. Both **Safari Ostrich Show Farm** (☑044-272 7312; www.safariostrich.co.za; Rte 328; adult/child R130/65; ☺8am-4pm; P) and **Cango Ostrich Farm** (☑044-272 4623; www.cangoostrich.co.za; Cango Caves Rd; adult/child R100/60; ☺8am-4.30pm; P) run interesting tours that do not feature ostrich riding.

Two Passes Route SCENIC DRIVE
A wonderful day's excursion is the round-trip from Oudtshoorn to Prince Albert taking in two magnificent passes. Head up the unsealed **Swartberg Pass** and all the way down to Prince Albert, then return via the **Meiringspoort Pass**. Halfway down the latter is a waterfall and small visitor centre. Both passes are engineering masterpieces.

Ask at your accommodation or the tourism bureau for a route map.

If driving isn't challenging enough, then hop on a mountain bike and ride from the top of Swartberg Pass down into Oudtshoorn. Book with **Backpackers Paradise** (☑044-272 3436; www.backpackersparadise.net; Backpackers Paradise, 148 Baron van Rheede St; tours R450) to be driven up. Be warned: it's not all downhill and it's a long ride.

🎊 Festivals & Events

ABSA Klein Karoo Nationale Kunstefees ART
(Little Karoo National Arts Festival; www.kknk.co.za; ☺Apr) This festival dedicates itself to the 'renaissance of Afrikaans' and showcases local artists, poets, thespians and musicians in a riotous week-long festival of creativity.

🛏 Sleeping

★**Karoo Soul Travel Lodge** HOSTEL $
(☑044-272 0330; www.karoosoul.com; 1 Adderley St; dm R160, d with shared bathroom R480; P🐾🛜🏊) The gracious old house is more about doubles than dorms, though there is one small dorm. Try to get one of the west-facing doubles for a romantic sundowner from your bed, or ask about the garden cottages with en suite (R580).

Backpackers Paradise HOSTEL $
(☑044-272 3436; www.backpackersparadise.net; 148 Baron van Rheede St; camping R100, dm R175, d R560, with shared bathroom R500; P🛜🏊) In a large old house, this lively hostel has a bar, ostrich braais (barbecues) and free ostrich-egg breakfasts (in season, you'll be given an egg – cook it any way you please). It also offers discounts to attractions in the area and can set you up with a host of activities.

Kleinplaas Resort CAMPGROUND $
(☑044-272 5811; www.kleinplaas.co.za; North St, near cnr Baron van Rheede St; camping per site R275, 2-/4-person chalet from R642/775; P🛜🏊) A superb caravan park, with a big pool and decent chalets, some of which have been renovated. The restaurant is only open for breakfast.

★**La Pension** GUESTHOUSE $$
(☑044-279 2445; www.lapension.co.za; 169 Church St; s/d incl breakfast from R800/1200; P❄🛜🏊) An excellent midrange choice with spacious, stylish rooms and superb bathrooms, La Pension also has one self-catering cottage (single/double R700/1200), plus a good-size pool and a large, immaculate garden.

Oudtshoorn

Oudtshoorn

⊙ **Sights**
1 CP Nel Museum A3

⊟ **Sleeping**
2 88 Baron van Rheede..........................B2
3 Oakdene Guesthouse..........................B1
4 Queen's Hotel......................................A3

⊗ **Eating**
5 Bella Cibo..B2
6 Black Swan B1
   Café Brulé ....(see 4)
   Colony Restaurant.......................(see 4)
7 Jemima's...B1
8 Nostalgie...B2

✕ Eating

Café Brulé CAFE **$**
(☑044-279 2412; Queen's Hotel, 5 Baron van
Rheede St; mains R50-75; ⊙7am-5pm; ☎) A popular cafe, recommended for its freshly baked
bread and cakes. Light lunches are on the
menu, or if you're suffering in the morning,
give the hangover breakfast a try.

Nostalgie BISTRO **$$**
(☑044-272 4085; www.nostalgiebnb.co.za; 74
Baron van Rheede St; mains R55-140; ⊙7.30am-
10pm Mon-Sat; ☎) This quaint tea garden,
complete with lace tablecloths, is great for
breakfast, or coffee with a slice of home-
baked cake. There are more than a dozen
ostrich dishes on the lunch and dinner
menu, including carpaccio, burger, kebabs
and pie.

Black Swan INTERNATIONAL **$$**
(☑044-272 0982; http://blackswanoudtshoorn.
co.za; 109 Baron van Rheede St; mains R85-165;
⊙5-10pm; ☎) There are tables outside and
in the atmospheric dining room at this large
restaurant at the northern end of town. The
menu is small but fairly varied, featuring
a few traditional dishes and, of course, the
requisite ostrich steaks.

Bella Cibo ITALIAN **$$**
(☑044-272 3245; www.bellocibo.co.za; 79 St Sav-
iour St; mains R65-120; ⊙5-11pm Mon-Sat) Pop-
ular with locals and widely recommended
around town, this Italian restaurant serves
well-priced pizza, pasta and seafood. Reser-
vations recommended.

★ Jemima's SOUTH AFRICAN **$$$**
(☑044-272 0808; www.jemimas.com; 94 Baron
van Rheede St; mains R75-200; ⊙11am-11pm)

88 Baron van Rheede GUESTHOUSE **$$**
(☑044-272 5288; www.88bvr.com; 88 Baron van
Rheede St; s/d incl breakfast from R650/850;
P❋☎☒) This friendly guesthouse re-
ceives rave reviews for its neat rooms,
hearty breakfast and above all for the
friendly service. Welcoming hosts Zoe and
Huw are full of useful information on what
to see in the area, and offer discount cou-
pons for various local attractions.

Oakdene Guesthouse GUESTHOUSE **$$**
(☑044-272 3018; www.oakdene.co.za; 99 Bar-
on van Rheede St; s/d incl breakfast R745/1390;
P❋☎☒) Fitted out with modern decor
largely made of recycled wine crates, the
rooms here perfectly marry the modern
with the classic – in keeping with the house's
status as one of Oudtshoorn's oldest buildings. There's a lovely garden at the back.

Queen's Hotel HOTEL **$$$**
(☑044-272 2101; www.queenshotel.co.za; 5 Bar-
on van Rheede St; s/d incl breakfast R1070/1760;
❋☎☒) On the main street, close to the
museum, this attractive old-style country
hotel with spacious, understated rooms is
an inviting option and refreshingly cool
in summer. The attached **Colony Res-
taurant** (mains R90-170; ⊙6-11pm) serves a
range of local and international dishes.

With a small menu specialising in traditional South African fare, this long-running restaurant is set in an attractive old house and garden. After your meal try a *swepie,* a mix of brandy and *jerepigo* (a dessert wine).

Shopping

Ostrich goods are naturally in demand, particularly items made from ostrich leather, which, along with feathers, eggs and biltong, is available everywhere. The leather is pricey because of the low yield per bird, so it's worth shopping around, including at show ranches and in hotels.

Information

Oudtshoorn Tourism Bureau (☑ 044-279 2532; www.oudtshoorn.com; cnr Baron van Rheede & Voortrekker Sts; ⊗ 8.30am-5pm Mon-Fri, 9.30am-12.30pm Sat) Behind the CP Nel Museum.

Getting There & Away

Buses stop in the Queen's Mall off Voortrekker St. Intercape has services to Johannesburg (R720, 14½ hours), Cape Town (R550, eight hours) and Mossel Bay (R250, two hours).

The Baz Bus stops at George, from where you can arrange a transfer to Oudtshoorn with **Backpackers Paradise** (R150 one way).

Shared taxis leave from behind the Spar supermarket on Adderley St en route to George (R60, 30 minutes) or Cape Town (R250, five hours). Bookings are required for the latter – contact the tourism bureau.

CENTRAL KAROO

The seemingly endless Karoo has a truly magical feel. It's a vast, semi-arid plateau (its name stems from a Khoe-San word meaning 'land of thirst') that features stunning sunsets and starscapes. Inhabited by humans and their ancestors for over half a million years, the region is rich in archaeological sites, fossils, San paintings, wildlife and some 9000 plant species.

The Karoo covers almost one-third of South Africa's total area and is demarcated in the south and west by the coastal mountain ranges, and to the east and north by the mighty Gariep (Orange) River. It's often split into the Great Karoo (north) and the Little Karoo (south), but the Karoo doesn't respect provincial boundaries and sprawls into three provinces.

Prince Albert

☑ 023 / POP 7050

To many urban-dwelling South African people, Prince Albert – a charming village dating back to 1762 – represents an idyllic life in the Karoo. Victorian, art deco and traditional Karoo buildings rub shoulders in the pretty streets, their residents intent on preserving the town's architecture. Despite being surrounded by harsh country, the town is green and fertile (producing peaches, apricots, grapes and olives), thanks to the run-off from the mountain springs. It's something of a foodie town and there's an Olive Festival each April.

WORTH A TRIP

MATJIESFONTEIN

One of the most curious and fascinating places in the Karoo, Matjiesfontein (pronounced 'mikeys-fontein') is an almost entirely privately owned railway siding around a grand hotel that has remained virtually unchanged for 100 years. It has a slight theme-park feel, but visiting the Victorian buildings, staffed by folks in period costume, is a lot of fun.

Rooms at the purportedly haunted **Lord Milner Hotel** (☑ 023-561 3011; www.matjiesfontein.com; Logan St; s/d from R900/1740; P ⑤ ☒) are decked out in period style. Dinner is available and guests are invited to join tour guide Johnny for a ghost walk around the town at dusk.

There's also an atmospheric **pub** (Logan St; mains R90; ⊗ noon-2.30pm) and a **cafe** (Logan St; mains R50-70; ⊗ 9am-5pm) serving light lunches.

Matjiesfontein is just off the N1, 240km from Cape Town and 230km from Beaufort West. Trains running between Cape Town and Jo'burg stop here and the Blue Train also pauses for an hour, with travellers given a tour of town on the double-decker London bus that stands outside the station.

OFF THE BEATEN TRACK

THE ROAD TO HELL

The main attraction in the Swartberg Nature Reserve (Die Hel; ☑ 044-203 6300; www. capenature.org.za; adult/child R40/20) is Gamkaskloof, a narrow valley better known as Die Hel. One of the most remote settlements in the country, Die Hel is reached by a vertiginous dirt road that is best tackled in a 4WD. On arrival you'll find a tearoom, small museum and self-catering accommodation. Elsewhere in the reserve, there are excellent hiking and mountain biking trails and plenty of birdwatching possibilities.

The dirt road to Die Hel turns off the Swartberg Pass 18km from Prince Albert and extends for another 50km or so before hitting a dead end. Be warned: this short distance takes at least two hours to drive each way. The road is in terrible condition so you might want to leave your car in Prince Albert and opt for a guided tour. Lindsay Steyn from Dennehof Tours (☑ 023-541 1227; www.dennehof.co.za; Dennehof Guesthouse, 20 Christina de Wit St; day tour R1150) is a mine of information on the region and offers superb full-day tours taking in the Swartberg Pass before descending the winding road to Die Hel for lunch.

It's also a great base to explore the mountains, either on foot, by mountain bike or, if it's just too hot for exertion, by driving the spectacular Swartberg and Meiringspoort Passes.

If you have your own transport, you can easily visit Prince Albert on a day trip from Oudtshoorn or even from the coast, but once you're here you're guaranteed to want to stay for a few days.

⊙ Sights & Activities

There is over 100km of hiking trails in the surrounding countryside, all administered by CapeNature (p152) – check with staff there for updates on which trails are open and to book overnight walks. For guides, contact Prince Albert Tourism.

Fransie Pienaar Museum   MUSEUM
(☑ 023-541 1172; 42 Church St; adult/child R20/10; ⊙ 9am-1pm & 2-4.30pm Mon-Fri, 9.30am-12.30pm Sat, 10.30-11.30am Sun) Named for a local resident who started the collection, the museum is a magnificent hotchpotch of everything from old matchboxes, ornate 19th-century bibles and a room full of sewing machines to San artefacts, then-and-now photos of the town and an interesting exhibition on the construction of the Swartberg Pass.

★ Story Weaver   HISTORY
(☑ 023-5411 211; www.storyweaver.co.za; adult/ child R60/30) Joining local character Ailsa Tudhope for a walking tour of Prince Albert is the very best way to kick off your stay. The signature tour is the 90-minute ghost walk, although historical day rambles are also on offer. Bookings are essential for all tours.

Prince Albert Cycles   CYCLING
(☑ 083 395 9038; www.princealbertcycles.co.za; 32 Church St; bike rental per day R250) As well as renting bikes, you can join a three-day culinary cycling tour (R4950 per person) stopping at local eateries and partaking in a cooking course.

🛏 Sleeping & Eating

Known as a foodie destination, the 'culinary capital of the Karoo' offers olive tasting, fruit farms specialising in dried-fruit production, fresh yoghurt, cream, milk and cheese from the local dairy, wine farms to visit and a well-established cooking school, as well as a few superb restaurants. There's also a weekly market (⊙ 8am-noon Sat) showcasing local foodstuffs and crafts next to the museum.

Travellers Rest   B&B $
(☑ 060 765 3955; www.travellersrestpa.com; 107 Adderley St; s/d R495/600) These simple but stylish guest rooms on the edge of town offer excellent value. Friendly hosts Jude and Bryan are passionate and knowledgeable about the region and can help arrange tours and activities. Breakfast is R80. No children under 14.

Karoo Lodge   GUESTHOUSE $$
(☑ 023-541 1467; www.karoolodge.com; 66 Church St; r incl breakfast from R1250; 🅿🕸🛜❄) This owner-run guesthouse has large, uncluttered rooms set around an enormous garden with plenty of shady spots. The restaurant (mains R95 to R150) largely showcases Karoo fare. It's open to nonguests (dinner Wednesday to Sunday) but bookings are essential.

★ **Prince Albert of**
Saxe-Coburg Lodge   GUESTHOUSE **$$$**
(☑ 023-541 1267; www.saxecoburg.co.za; 60 Church St; s/d incl breakfast from R1000/1500; ✱ 🛜 🏊) This place offers quality accommodation in lovely garden rooms. Owners Dick and Regina are a great source of information, particularly on hikes in the area.

★ **Gallery**   FUSION **$$**
(☑ 023-541 1057; www.princealbertgallery.co.za; 57 Church St; mains R95-175; ⊙ 6-9.30pm) Prince Albert's smartest dining option has an ever-changing menu featuring modern takes on local classics such as Karoo lamb and game steaks. There are also a couple of imaginative vegetarian choices.

Karoo Kombuis   SOUTH AFRICAN **$$**
(Karoo Kitchen; ☑ 023-541 1110; 18 Deurdrift St; mains R90-125; ⊙ 7-9pm Mon-Sat) This homely restaurant has been serving the same three traditional dishes since 1998 – *bobotie* (a lightly spiced mince dish), chicken pie and lamb. There's also Malva pudding for dessert – a sticky sponge cake that's a fine way to end a typical South African meal. Bring your own drinks and make sure you book ahead.

☆ **Entertainment**

Showroom   CINEMA
(☑ 023-541 1563; www.showroomtheatre.co.za; 43 Church St) Starting its life as a car showroom in the 1930s, this marvellous art deco building has been reincarnated as a cinema. Movies are shown on Wednesday evenings and there are often live shows on weekends. Even if nothing is happening, it's worth popping in – it's a real homage to the grandeur of bygone cinemas.

🛍 **Shopping**

Prince Albert attracts artists from across the country, and there are galleries throughout town where you can browse and buy. (Even the bins here are arty, each one painted by a local for the town's 250th anniversary in 2012.) There are also a number of community craft projects including **Handmade Karoo Handgemaak** (☑ 083 407 3390; http://karoohandgemaak.com; cnr Market & Chaplin Sts; ⊙ 9am-1pm Mon-Thu) and **Beadkidz** (☑ 082 562 2123; Cape Access Centre, Toegangs Rd, Rondomskrik; ⊙ 2-5pm Mon, Wed & Thu).

ℹ **Information**

Prince Albert Tourism (☑ 023-541 1366; www.princealbert.org.za; 42 Church St; ⊙ 9am-5pm Mon-Fri, 10am-noon Sat) On the main road.

ℹ **Getting There & Away**

Most people visit by driving over one of the area's passes from Oudtshoorn, or from the N1 between Cape Town and Jo'burg. There is no direct bus or train service to Prince Albert; the closest drop-off point is at Prince Albert Rd, 45km northwest of town. The **train** (p618) is cheaper than the bus, and private taxis from the station cost upwards of R200. If you want to book a taxi in advance, try **John Donkey** (☑ 082 575 5133). Some guesthouses also offer pick-ups.

Karoo National Park

Hot, barren and dusty, the 900-sq-km **Karoo National Park** (☑ 023-415 2828; www.sanparks.org; N1; adult/child R192/96; ⊙ 7am-6pm Apr-Sep, 6am-7pm Oct-Mar) features impressive Karoo landscapes and representative flora. You'll likely spot zebras, springboks, kudus and red hartebeests as well as scurrying dassies (agile, rodent-like mammals, also called hyraxes). Lions have been reintroduced and if you're really lucky you might also spot black rhinos.

Wildlife sightings are not as great as in some of the northern parks, but there is plenty to see for the landscape lover. Don't miss the **Klipspringer's Pass**, where you stand a good chance of seeing the small antelope the winding road is named for.

There are two short walks (around 1km each) near the rest camp, which you can do without a guide, and a 400m fossil trail that's accessible by wheelchair. Guided morning walks are also available (R220). The Pointer Trail is a 12km hike that must be undertaken with a guide.

Accommodation is either at pleasant **campsites** (camping per site from R265) or in Cape Dutch–style **cottages** (2 people from R1250; 🅿 🏊). The cottages are fully equipped with kitchens, towels and bedding; two have wheelchair access.

There is one **restaurant** (mains R70-140; ⊙ 7-10am & 6-9pm; 🅿) at the rest camp and a small shop selling the bare essentials. If you're self-catering, be sure to shop in Beaufort West before you arrive.

The road from the entrance gate to the rest camp is tarred, and there is a 12km game-viewing loop that has been tarred. The 45km Potlekkertjie Loop is a rough gravel road, but can be driven in a sedan vehicle.

WEST COAST & SWARTLAND

The windswept coastline and desolate mountains on the western side of Western Cape are a peaceful, largely undeveloped paradise. You'll find whitewashed fishing villages, fascinating country towns, unspoilt beaches, a lagoon and wetlands teeming with birds, plus one of the best hiking regions in the country.

The West Coast National Park is a must for birdwatchers and lovers of seascapes, while inland lies the richly fertile Olifants River Valley, where citrus orchards and vineyards sit at the foot of the Cederberg Mountains – a hiker's heaven. This remote area has spectacular rock formations and a wealth of San rock paintings.

Between the coast and the mountains lies the Swartland, undulating hills of wheat and vineyards. Swartland (black land) received its name from *renosterveld,* a threatened indigenous vegetation that turns dark grey in summer.

Darling

📞 022 / POP 1100

A quiet country town, Darling has long been known as the home of actor and satirist Pieter-Dirk Uys – or more so his alter ego, Evita Bezuidenhout. But in recent years, reasons to visit have multiplied and Darling has become a foodie town of note.

The long-established wineries offer a more relaxed tasting experience than many of their busier counterparts in the Winelands and the region is well known for its olives. In the town centre you'll find boutique outlets specialising in cheese, charcuterie and toffee, among other treats, and on the edge of town is a highly popular brewery that has played an integral part in Darling's culinary awakening.

LOCAL KNOWLEDGE

WILDFLOWER WATCHING

While Swartland may be shades of grey in the summer, it's ablaze with colour in August and September when the veld is carpeted with wildflowers. In season, you can check where the flowers are at their best on a daily basis by calling the **Flower Hotline** (📞 072 938 8186).

Tourist information (📞 022-492 3361; www.darlingtourism.co.za; cnr Hill & Pastorie Sts; ⏱ 9am-1pm & 2-4pm Mon-Thu, to 3.30pm Fri, 10am-3pm Sat & Sun) is in the town museum.

Darling Brewery   BREWERY
(📞 079 182 9001; www.darlingbrew.co.za; 48 Caledon St; tastings from R10; ⏱ 9am-5pm Tue-Thu, 10am-9pm Fri & Sat, 10am-4pm Sun; 🅿 🐾) Darling is one of the country's best-known breweries, pouring a wide range of beers including Africa's first carbon-neutral brew. You can taste any or all of the beers in the cheery tasting room overlooking the brewery itself. The restaurant (mains R60 to R160) serves upscale bar food showcasing produce from Darling's various artisanal producers.

Groote Post   WINERY
(📞 022-492 2825; www.grootepost.com; tastings free, 2hr wildlife drive adult/child R170/75; ⏱ 10am-4pm; 🅿 🐾) Of all the Darling wineries, Groote Post has the most to offer the visitor, with wildlife drives, self-guided nature walks, a superb **restaurant** (mains R110-150; ⏱ noon-2pm Wed-Sun) and, of course, free tastings of its excellent chardonnays and sauvignon blancs. It's 7km along a dirt road, off Rte 307. Book ahead for the restaurant and wildlife drives.

Darling Lodge   GUESTHOUSE $$
(📞 022-492 3062; www.darlinglodge.co.za; 22 Pastorie St; s/d incl breakfast R850/980; 🐾 ❄) An elegant and imaginatively decorated place. Rooms are named after local artists, whose work is displayed on the walls, and there's a lovely garden to relax in.

★ Evita se Perron   CABARET
(📞 022-492 2851; www.evita.co.za; Old Darling Station, 8 Arcadia St; tickets R165, buffet meal R135; ⏱ 2pm & 7pm Sat, 2pm Sun) This uniquely South African cabaret, featuring Pieter-Dirk Uys as his alter ego Evita Bezuidenhout, touches on everything from South African politics to history and ecology. Nothing is off limits – including the country's racially charged past. Although the shows include a smattering of Afrikaans, they're largely in English and always hilarious and thought-provoking. Buffet meals are available for those attending a show.

Even if you're not seeing a show, a visit to the complex is well worth it. There's a politically themed sculpture garden and some fascinating apartheid memorabilia on show. The splendidly kitsch **restaurant** (mains R45-65; ⏱ 10am-4pm Tue-Sun) serves traditional Afrikaner food. Uys also set up the Darling Trust (www.thedarlingtrust.org) to assist Swartland communities to empower themselves through participation in education and health programs. The **A en C Shop** at the complex stocks beading, clothes, wire-art and paintings.

ⓘ Getting There & Away

Darling is 90km north of Cape Town along the scenic Rte 27. **Golden Arrow** (☑ 0800 656 463; www.gabs.co.za) offers a service that leaves Cape Town at 5pm with return buses leaving Darling at 5am.

West Coast National Park

The focal point at this 310-sq-km **park** (☑ 022-772 2144; www.sanparks.org; adult/child R80/40, Aug & Sep R170/85; ⊗ 7am-7pm) is the **Langebaan Lagoon**, whose clear blue waters are perfect for sailing and swimming. The park also attracts birding enthusiasts, its wetlands providing important seabird breeding colonies. Wading birds flock here in summer, with the curlew sandpiper seen in the greatest numbers.

The park's also a popular place to witness spring wildflowers bursting into colour and makes for a much more convenient destination to watch the blooms than Namakwa. It can get crowded in August and September, when the flowers usually bloom, and the entry fee to the park increases at this time.

Apart from the white-sand beaches and turquoise waters of the ocean and lagoon, the park's greatest allure is that it's under-visited. If you visit midweek (and outside school holidays) you might find that you're sharing the roads only with zebras, ostriches and the occasional leopard tortoise ambling across your path.

As well as five park-owned cottages (from R1380 per cottage), the nicest of which is **Jo Anne's Beach Cottage** (www.sanparks. org; cottage from R1380; P), there are various privately run accommodation options in the park, including the **houseboats** (☑ 076 017 4788; www.kraalbaailuxuryhouseboats. com; Kraalbaai; 6-person boat R2530) moored at Kraalbaai.

★ **Duinepos**   CHALET **$$**
(☑ 022-707 9900; www.duinepos.co.za; s/d chalet from R700/1025; P ≋) Bright, modern and well-equipped chalets in the heart of the park. It's an excellent birdwatching spot.

ⓘ WEST COAST NATIONAL PARK

Why Go Easy access from Cape Town; magnificent coastal views; year-round birdwatching; kayaking on the lagoon; largely uncrowded drives to seek out small wildlife species; spectacular spring wildflowers.

When to Go The park is at its finest from August to September when the flowers are in bloom, though this is also the busiest time. The rainy season is between May and August.

Practicalities Drive from Cape Town (120km) or Langebaan (7km). Gates are open 7am to 7pm (to 6pm April to August). Entry fees double in flower season (August and September).

Budget Tips If visiting a number of national parks, consider buying a Wild Card (p592).

Geelbek Visitor's Centre & Restaurant   SOUTH AFRICAN **$$**
(☑ 072 698 6343; mains R95-165; ⊗ 9am-5pm; P) There's a wide menu here, focusing on traditional fare. It's also an information centre for the park and can help with accommodation.

Langebaan

☑ 022 / POP 8300

Its beautiful location overlooking the Langebaan Lagoon has made this seaside resort a favourite holiday destination with South Africans. But, while it is popular, it's fairly spread out so you can still easily find solitude. The town is known for its water sports, particularly kite-surfing and windsurfing on the lagoon. For those seeking something less strenuous there are phenomenal sunset views and a few good beaches, the best of which is **Langebaan Beach** – in town and popular with swimmers. The town is also a good base for exploring the West Coast National Park.

★ **West Coast Fossil Park**   ARCHAEOLOGICAL SITE
(☑ 022-766 1606; www.fossilpark.org.za; guided tour adult/child R80/50, entry only adult/child R35/25; ⊗ 8am-4pm Mon-Fri, 10am-1pm Sat & Sun; P) The first bear discovered south of the Sahara, lion-size sabre-toothed cats, three-toed

WESTERN CAPE WEST COAST NATIONAL PARK

horses and short-necked giraffes are all on display at this excellent fossil park on Rte 45 about 16km outside Langebaan. Fascinating tours depart hourly from 10am to 3pm (until 1pm on weekends) and take you to the excavation sites – among the richest fossil sites in the world. There are also mountain-biking and walking trails, and a coffee shop.

Cape Sports Center   WATER SPORTS

(☑ 022-772 1114; www.capesport.co.za; 98 Main Rd) Langebaan is a water-sports mecca, particularly for windsurfing and kite-surfing. This friendly office offers kite-surfing courses (three-day course from R3950) and windsurfing lessons (two hours R900) and rents out surfboards, SUPs and kayaks (R320/395/395 per day).

🛏 Sleeping

★ Friday Island   B&B $$

(☑ 022-772 2506; www.fridayisland.co.za; Main Rd; s/d R600/880; 🛜) There are bright rooms and cheery staff at this popular beach-front B&B. You're going to want one of the two-level sea-facing rooms (single/double R900/1380), each with its own deck. The popular restaurant (mains R75 to R180) serves seafood, burgers, steak and some budget-friendly breakfast options.

Farmhouse Hotel   HOTEL $$

(☑ 022-772 2062; www.thefarmhousehotel.com; 5 Egret St; r incl breakfast from R1100; 🅿❄🛜🐾) Langebaan's oldest hotel sits on a hill over-looking the bay with lovely sunset views. Rooms are large, with country decor and their own fireplaces. The restaurant is reasonably priced (mains R95 to R190) and has a varied menu. The hotel also has some self-catering cottages (www.kitequarters.co.za) aimed at kite-surfers.

🍴 Eating & Drinking

★ Die Strandloper   SEAFOOD $$$

(☑ 022-772 2490; www.strandloper.com; buffet R310; ⊙ noon-4pm & 6-10pm Dec & Jan, noon-4pm Fri-Sun, 6-10pm Fri Feb-Nov) The West Coast life exemplified – a 10-course fish and seafood braai right on the beach. There's also freshly made bread, bottomless *moerkoffie* (freshly ground coffee) and a local crooner who wanders the tables strumming his guitar. You can BYO (corkage free) or get drinks from the rustic bar, from where the view is sensational. Bookings highly recommended.

Ginja Beanz   COFFEE

(☑ 022-772 2221; www.ginjabeanz.co.za; Water-front Sq, Bree St; ⊙ 8am-4pm Mon-Fri, 9am-3pm Sat) As well as superb coffee from Lange-baan's one and only roastery, Wings, this busy place serves Black Insomnia – the world's strongest cup of joe. Burgers, salads and sandwiches are on the menu.

ℹ Information

Tourist Information Centre (☑ 022-772 1515; www.visitwestcoast.co.za; 120 Oostewal Rd; ⊙ 9am-5pm Mon-Fri, to 2pm Sat & Sun)

ℹ Getting There & Away

Langebaan is about 90 minutes' drive north of Cape Town. **Shared taxis** (Oostewal Rd) run from the OK Mart car park to Cape Town (R110, two hours). **Elwierda** (☑ 021-557 9002; www.elwierda.co.za) operates regular buses to Cape Town (R130, two to three hours); booking a day in advance is essential.

Paternoster

☑ 022 / POP 2000

Paternoster is a lovely town to visit. Not so many years ago, it was the West Coast's last traditional fishing village, little more than a clutch of simple whitewashed homes set against the blue sea. Today it's also a second home to wealthy Capetonians and foreigners who became captivated by its charms: namely calm (if chilly) waters, an expansive and often empty beach and some lovely places to eat and sleep.

!KHWA TTU

!Khwa ttu (☑ 022-492 2998; www.khwattu.org; Rte 27; tours R195; ⊙ 9am-5pm, tours 10am & 2pm; 🅿) is the only San-owned and -operated culture centre in the Western Cape. It's based on an 8.5-sq-km nature reserve within the ancestral lands of the San. Tours involve a nature walk on which you learn about San culture, and a wildlife drive – you'll likely see various antelope, zebras and ostriches. There are hiking and biking trails on the reserve and a quality gift shop stocking work from San artists. A museum was in progress when we last visited.

There is a restaurant open for breakfast and lunch and a range of accommodation including a basic bush camp (R325 per person) and a guesthouse (double R1760). It's off Rte 27, 70km north of Cape Town.

The **tourist information office** (📞 022-752 2323; www.visitwestcoast.co.za; Fish Market, Seeduiker St; ⏰ 9am-5pm Mon-Thu, to 2pm Fri-Sun) is found at the fish market.

Cape Columbine Nature Reserve
NATURE RESERVE

(📞 022-752 2718; adult/child R21/14; ⏰ 7am-7pm) Three kilometres south of Paternoster, along a rutted gravel road, lies this windswept but beautiful reserve. It has campsites with basic facilities at Tieties Bay (R167 per site). The **lighthouse** (📞 021-449 2400; www.transnetnationalportsauthority.net; adult/child R16/8; ⏰ 10am-3pm Mon-Fri; 🅿) tower is worth a climb and you can also stay here in renovated keepers' cottages (double from R650).

Geco Adventures
KAYAKING

(📞 082 584 1907; www.gecoadventures.co.za; per person R200) Hour-long kayaking trips take you out onto the calm but cold waters to see penguins and other seabirds.

🛏 Sleeping & Eating

Paternoster Lodge
GUESTHOUSE $$

(📞 022-752 2023; www.paternosterlodge.co.za; s/d incl breakfast R950/1340; 🅿 🛜) This is a bright, well-priced place offering seven minimalist rooms, all with a sea view, and a breezy restaurant (mains R95 to R190) that's open all day. From the sun deck you can watch the fisherfolk bringing in their catch.

Abalone House
GUESTHOUSE $$$

(📞 022-752 2044; www.abalonehouse.co.za; 3 Kriedoring St; d from R6000; ❄🛜♨) A five-star guesthouse with artsy rooms, a rooftop hot tub and plunge pool and a health spa. The restaurant (mains R145 to R210), also open to nonguests, is part of a small chain of swanky eateries started by local celebrity chef Reuben Riffel.

Voorstrandt Restaurant
SEAFOOD $$

(📞 022-752 2038; www.voorstrandt.com; Strandloperweg; mains R75-185; ⏰ 11am-9pm; 🅿) A better location you couldn't wish for – you can hop from your table right onto the sand. Specialising in seafood, this is also an excellent spot to watch the sunset over a beer.

Elands Bay

📞 022 / POP 1500

Elands Bay is a particularly pretty spot oozing rustic charm and with a supreme setting: mountains run to the sea past a large lagoon frequented by waterbirds – it's a

OFF THE BEATEN TRACK

BIRD ISLAND

Sitting just 100m from the mainland, **Bird Island** (📞 027-432 1672; www.capenature.co.za; Lambert's Bay Harbour; adult/child R40/20; ⏰ 7am-6pm) is an important breeding site for the Cape gannet. You'll likely spot Cape fur seals too. The island is accessible on foot via a breakwater. There's a bird hide and plenty of informative signage.

bird-lover's dream. It's also a good surf spot and is known as a goofy-footer's paradise, with extremely fast left-point waves working at a range of swell sizes. There are a couple of places renting out boards and in peak season (December to January) you might find someone offering lessons.

There are several simple self-catering holiday homes to rent as well as the **Elands Bay Hotel** (📞 022-972 1640; www.elandsbayhotel.co.za; Hunter St; camping per site R250, dm R180, s/d incl breakfast R400/600; 🅿 🛜), which caters to those on a budget.

Eating options are limited to the hotel's restaurant (mains R65 to R130) and **Wit Mossel Pot** (📞 082 496 8931; witmosselpot@gmail.com; Strand St; mains R75-160; ⏰ 9am-4pm Tue-Thu, to 9pm Fri-Sun), both in the northern section of the village. There is a basic supermarket if you're self-catering.

Crayfish Trail
HIKING

(📞 083 553 9107; www.crayfishtrail.co.za; per day from R1650) This 'slackpacking' trail explores an oft-ignored stretch of the West Coast. The five-day trail starts 16km south of Elands Bay and covers 61km of mostly flat terrain, ending in Doring Bay. A two-day version offers a 'best-of' look for those who don't have time for the full trail. Prices include food, accommodation and guides, with your bags transported for you.

Cederberg Wilderness Area

Some of the Western Cape's finest scenery is found in the desolate **Cederberg Wilderness Area** (📞 027-482 2403; www.capenature.co.za; adult/child R60/35). Here, craggy peaks reaching around 2000m harbour weird rock formations, well-preserved San rock art, clear streams and excellent hiking and rock climbing.

The region isn't known for its wildlife, though you might glimpse a baboon or one of the small antelope that hop along the rocks here. Elusive leopards do roam at night, but you'd be extremely lucky to sight one. The region is better known for its plant life – mountain fynbos (shrubby vegetation with fine leaves) abounds, and wildflowers erupt in spring. Vegetation varies with altitude, with the eponymous cedar stands living between 1000m and 1500m. This is also the only place in the world where rooibos (red bush) grows and is processed into tea.

There is a vast network of hiking trails in the mountains. Two of the most popular hikes take in some of the region's more famous rock formations, the **Maltese Cross** and the **Wolfberg Arch**. The former is a relatively easy three-hour hike, the latter an all-day slog with some steep sections. Other hikes take in waterfalls, natural pools and rock art.

The Wolfberg Arch hike was closed in late 2017 to allow the vegetation to recover following a wildfire – it should hopefully be open again by the time you read this.

Permits are required for all hikes. At quiet times you can pick up a permit on the spot at **Algeria** (☑027-482 2403; www.capenature. co.za; camping per site R300, chalets/cottages from R580/800) campground, but during school

---

ℹ CEDERBERG WILDERNESS AREA

Why Go Spectacular scenery; mountain hikes ranging from a few hours to a few days; ancient rock paintings; secluded farmstays; stargazing.

When to Go Spring (September to November) is the best time, when temperatures are ideal and the wildflowers are in bloom. Summer (December to February) days can be scorching, while nights in winter (June to August) often plummet below zero.

Practicalities There are only gravel roads within the park. The main route is a public road and there is no fee to drive through. Entrance fees generally only apply to those undertaking activities.

Budget Tips With campsites and braai (barbecue) areas galore, this is a well-priced region to travel.

---

holidays it's best to book ahead through CapeNature (p152), since hiker numbers are limited. The maximum group size is 12 and, for safety, the minimum is two adults.

Stadsaal Caves   HISTORIC SITE
(adult/child R40/20) Once occupied by the San, these sandstone caves are glorious at sunset. First visit the rock-art site, on the right as you drive through the gate, then explore the network of caves with their marvellous views. Permits are available from Sanddrif (p175) (Dwarsrivier Farm).

ℹ Getting There & Away

The Cederberg range is about 200km from Cape Town, accessible via gravel roads from Citrusdal, Clanwilliam and the N7. You can also drive from Rte 303 via Ceres on the eastern side; this route avoids any vertiginous drops but the road is badly rutted.

It takes about an hour to get to Algeria from Clanwilliam by car. Algeria is not signposted from Clanwilliam, but just follow the gravel road above the dam to the south – it's fairly rough going. Algeria is signposted from the N7 and is about 30 minutes from the main road; it's also a gravel road, but in decent condition.

Unfortunately, public transport into the mountains is nonexistent.

Citrusdal & Around

☑022 / POP 7200

The small town of Citrusdal is a good base for exploring the Cederberg Wilderness Area (p173). August to September is wildflower season, which can be spectacular. This is also one of the best times for hiking. Make sure to explore beyond the town limits – the scenery is stupendous.

🛏 Sleeping & Eating

Ukholo Lodge   HOSTEL $
(☑022-921 3988; www.ukholo-lodge.co.za; camping/dm/d R100/200/700; 🐾) The rooms are stylish, there's plenty of space to pitch a tent and there are bathrooms all over the place. Activities include tubing on the adjacent river or mountain hiking. It's 21km from Citrusdal on the N7 towards Clanwilliam.

Beaverlac   CAMPGROUND $
(☑022-931 2945; www.beaverlac.co.za; Beaverlac Nature Reserve; per car R30, camping per adult/child R65/40, hut from R270) A valley hidden beneath pine trees is the site for this wonderful campground, which also has very basic huts.

There are rock pools for swimming and fascinating terrain to explore. Day visitors are not permitted and all visits must be booked in advance. There are a lot of rules and red tape, but the setting is worth the hassle.

★ **Baths**   RESORT $$
(☑ 022-921 8026; www.thebaths.co.za; camping R100, 2-person chalet from R900; P ☀) In a glorious location thick with trees and right up against craggy peaks is this hot-spring resort with outdoor pools and a range of private baths filled with spring water at 43°C. Booking is essential both for day visits (adult/child R100/50) and overnight stays. Accommodation is cheaper from Sunday to Thursday. It's 18km from Citrusdal and well signposted.

Cederkloof Botanical Retreat   COTTAGE $$
(☑ 022-300 0118; www.cederkloof.co.za; Baths Rd; 2-person cottage R1250; P ⚘ ☀) Set in gloriously landscaped grounds rich in endemic flora, the simple cottages here are well equipped and peaceful, and each comes with its own hot tub filled with water piped from an underground spring. There are short hiking trails on the grounds and the owners were planning to add stargazing decks when we last visited. Rates are considerably cheaper on weekdays.

★ **Hebron**   FUSION $$
(☑ 022-921 2595; www.hebron.co.za; Piekenierskloof Pass, N7; mains R60-130; ☉ 9am-5pm Wed-Sun, 7-10pm Wed, Thu & Sat; P ⚘ ⛟) It doesn't look much from the road, but this farm stall at the top of Piekenierskloof Pass serves some delightful cuisine. The imaginative dishes include green-pea falafel and saffron crème brûlée. It's a stop on the Rooibos Route so you'll find goodies like rooibos scones and rooibos milkshakes on the menu, and there's a shop selling the tea itself.

ℹ Information

Tourism Bureau (☑ 022-921 3210; www.citrusdal.info; Kerk St; ☉ 9am-4pm Mon-Fri, to 1pm Sat)

ℹ Getting There & Away

Intercape buses stop at the Caltex petrol station 6km out of town on the N7. Destinations include Cape Town (R300, three hours) and Springbok (R350, 5½ hours).

There's an excellent scenic road (Rte 303) over Middelberg Pass into the Koue Bokkeveld and a beautiful valley on the other side, which is topped by the Gydo Pass. The back road into the wilderness area is also excellent.

DWARSRIVIER FARM

Deep in the Cederberg, this is an excellent base for hiking – both the Wolfberg Arch and Maltese Cross hikes start nearby. At **Sanddrif** (☑ 027-482 2825; www.sanddrif.com; Dwarsrivier Farm; camping per site R220, 4-person chalets R920) there are shady campsites by the river or chalets with patios gazing out at the mountains. Don't miss the **Cederberg Winery**, also on the premises – the sauvignon blanc in particular is stupendous – and there's a microbrewery on-site too. There's an excellent **Astronomical Observatory** (www.cederbergobs.org.za; entry by donation; ☉ 8pm Sat) nearby.

To get to Dwarsrivier, follow the Algeria turn-off from the N7. From here a gravel road winds into the mountains; it's 46km to Dwarsrivier from the N7.

Clanwilliam & Around

☑ 027 / POP 7700

The adjacent dam and some adventurous dirt roads into the Cederberg Wilderness Area (p173) make the compact town of Clanwilliam a popular weekend resort. The dam is a favourite with water-skiers, though if plans to raise the dam are ever fulfilled, this and the landscape of the region will change somewhat.

Clanwilliam is the centre of the rooibos (red bush) tea industry. The tea is made from the leaves of the *Aspalathus linearis* plant, which only grows in the Cederberg region. Rooibos contains no caffeine and much less tannin than normal tea and is said to have numerous health benefits. The owners of **Rooibos Teahouse** (☑ 027-482 1007; www.rooibosteahouse.co.za; 4 Voortrekker St; ☉ 8am-5.30pm Mon-Fri, to 2pm Sat; P) in town have also set up the Rooibos Route (www.rooibos-route.co.za), which recommends restaurants, tea producers and accommodation highlighting the region's most famous export.

◉ Sights & Activities

Sevilla Rock Art Trail   HISTORIC SITE
(www.travellersrest.co.za; permits R40) There are nine San rock-art sites along a relatively easy 5km hike here. The permit fee includes an informative pamphlet deciphering the

paintings and giving some history on the San. It's based at the Traveller's Rest, 36km from Clanwilliam on the way to Bushmans Kloof.

Cedarberg African Travel TOURS
(☏ 027-482 2444; www.cedarbergtravel.com; per person from R2650) This company works with community guides to run a three-day route through the Cederberg Wilderness Area (p173), staying in mission villages along the way. Opt for the donkey cart trail on day three – a fairly exhilarating way to round off the trip.

🛏 Sleeping & Eating

Lebanon Citrus CAMPGROUND $
(☏ 027-482 2508; www.lebanon.co.za; camping per site R340, 2-person cabins from R480; P) There are campsites and cute wooden cabins at this gorgeous spot on the edge of the dam, with stupendous views of the Cederberg (p173). Hiking trails and horse rides are available. It's 28km from Clanwilliam, mostly along a rutted gravel road.

Daisy Cottage COTTAGE $
(☏ 027-482 1603; 13 Foster St; s/d R450/700; P) In a quiet street close to the town centre, this adorable thatched cottage has a beautiful garden. There are two bedrooms plus a sleeper couch.

⭐ Bushmans Kloof LUXURY HOTEL $$$
(☏ 027-482 8200; www.bushmanskloof.co.za; s/d with full board from R4660/7900; P✳🛜❄) This upmarket private reserve, 46km east of Clanwilliam along the Pakhuis Pass, is known for excellent San rock-art sites and extensive animal- and birdlife. Guests are assigned a guide and can partake in all manner of retreat-type activities or just gorge on excellent food.

Saint du Barrys Country Lodge GUESTHOUSE $$$
(☏ 027-482 1537; www.saintdubarrys.com; 13 Augsburg Rd; s/d incl breakfast R1000/1600; P✳🛜❄) A 150-year-old banyan tree looms over this pleasing guesthouse with five en-suite rooms and a pint-size pool in the pretty garden. The charming hosts offer honest advice on what to see and do in the area.

⭐ Floris INTERNATIONAL $$
(☏ 027-482 2896; www.florisrestaurant.co.za; cnr Augsburg Rd & Main St; mains R85-150; ⊙8am-10pm Mon, Tue & Thu-Sat, from 5pm Wed, from noon Sun; P🍴) Locals are loving this excellent addition to Clanwilliam's otherwise uninspiring culinary scene. There's plenty of choice on the menu, from pizzas to traditional dishes such as *bobotie,* but it's all done with finesse. The rooibos crème brûlée is worth trying. Bookings recommended.

ℹ Information

The **information centre** (☏ 027-482 2024; Main St; ⊙8.30am-4.30pm Mon-Fri, to 12.30pm Sat) is opposite the old jail, which doubles as the town's museum.

ℹ Getting There & Away

Buses that go through Citrusdal also pass Clanwilliam, stopping at the **Shell petrol station** (Augsburg Rd) in town. Shared taxis running between Springbok (R350, five hours) and Cape Town (R190, three hours) go through Clanwilliam. To book a spot in a taxi, try **Van Wyk's** (☏ 027-713 8559).

Eastern Cape

Best Places to Eat

➡ Haricot's Deli & Bistro (p205)

➡ Edge Restaurant (p213)

➡ Victoria Manor (p235)

➡ Remo's (p195)

➡ Decadent (p209)

Best Places to Stay

➡ Drostdy Hotel (p230)

➡ Prana Lodge (p216)

➡ Mdumbi Backpackers (p219)

➡ Die Tuishuise & Victoria Manor (p234)

➡ Edge Mountain Retreat (p212)

Why Go?

From lush tropical forests to uninhabited desert expanses, and from easy-going hammock time to adrenaline-pumping adventures, the Eastern Cape offers a wide range of topography and experiences. Compared with the more developed Western Cape, it can feel like a different country and provides opportunities to learn about Xhosa culture. Some of South Africa's finest hiking (and slackpacking) trails wind along the province's largely undeveloped coastline and through its mountainous, waterfall-filled landscapes.

Private wildlife reserves and national and regional parks abound: see the Big Five (lion, leopard, buffalo, elephant and rhino) or migrating whales and dolphins. You'll find tranquillity and culture in the towns of the semi-arid Karoo; the imposing Drakensberg peaks and little-known valleys in the Highlands; good surfing in the Indian Ocean, coupled with amazing cultural experiences on the Wild Coast; and history throughout, including the legacy of some famous local sons – Nelson Mandela, Oliver Tambo and Steve Biko.

When to Go
Port Elizabeth

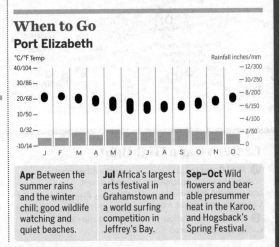

Apr Between the summer rains and the winter chill; good wildlife watching and quiet beaches.

Jul Africa's largest arts festival in Grahamstown and a world surfing competition in Jeffrey's Bay.

Sep–Oct Wild flowers and bearable presummer heat in the Karoo, and Hogsback's Spring Festival.

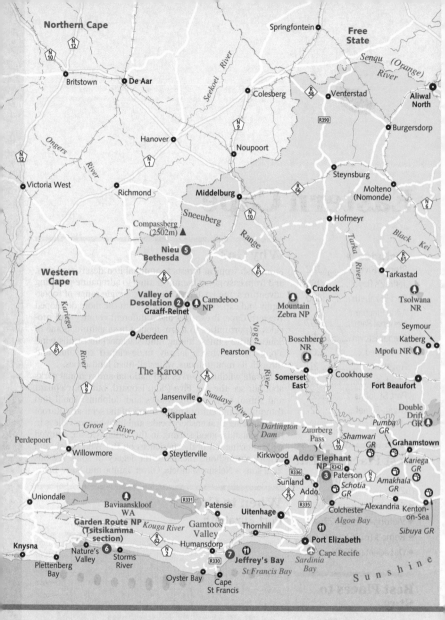

Eastern Cape Highlights

1 **Wild Coast** (p213)
Walking the coastal pathways
and secluded beaches near
Coffee Bay and Port St John's.

2 **Valley of Desolation**
(p231) Taking in a Karoo

sunset with views of
Graaff-Reinet.

3 **Addo Elephant National
Park** (p197) Observing African
elephants up close.

4 **Hogsback** (p211) Hiking
forested trails to waterfalls or
simply chilling out.

5 **Nieu Bethesda** (p231)
Gazing at star-filled skies in
this artistic Karoo outpost.

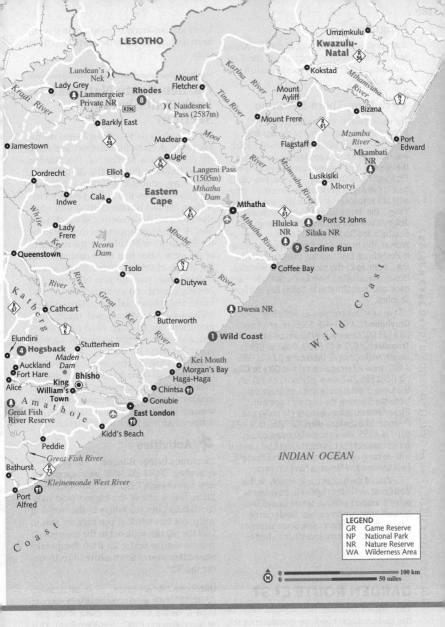

LESOTHO

KwaZulu-Natal

Umzimkulu

Kokstad

Lundean's
Nek
Lady Grey

Lammergeier
Private NR

R396

Rhodes
8

Mount
Fletcher

Naudesnek
Pass (2587m)

Mount
Ayliff

Bizana

N
2

Barkly East

Maclear

Ugie

Langeni Pass
(1505m)

Mount Frere

Flagstaff

Mzamba
River

Port
Edward

Mkambati
NR

Jamestown

R
58

R
56

Dordrecht

Elliot

Eastern
Cape

Mthatha
Dam

Lusikisiki

Mbotyi

Indwe

Cala

R
61

Mthatha

Lady
Frere

White

Kei

Ncora
Dam

Queenstown

Tsolo

Dutywa

N
2

Hluleka
NR

R
61

Port St Johns

Silaka NR

9 Sardine Run

Coffee Bay

Katberg

R
67

River

Great

Cathcart

N
6

Butterworth

Kei

Dwesa NR

1 Wild Coast

Wild Coast

Elundini

4 Hogsback

Stutterheim

Maden
Dam

Auckland
Fort Hare

Bhisho

Alice

King
William's
Town

Amathole

Great Fish
River Reserve

Kei Mouth
Morgan's Bay
Haga-Haga

Chintsa

Gonubie

East London

Kidd's Beach

INDIAN OCEAN

Peddie

Great Fish River

Bathurst

R
72

Kleinemonde West River

Port
Alfred

Coast

LEGEND
GR   Game Reserve
NP   National Park
NR   Nature Reserve
WA   Wilderness Area

0   100 km
0   50 miles

---

6 **Garden Route National
Park (Tsitsikamma Section)**
(p180) Enjoying hiking,
snorkelling and tubing among
churning rivers and ancient
trees.

7 **Jeffrey's Bay** (p185)
Marvelling at (or surfing, if
you dare) some of the world's
top-ranked waves.

8 **Rhodes** (p226) Finding
mountain solitude in this

southern Drakensberg
hamlet.

9 **Sardine Run** (p220)
Experiencing one of the
most spectacular marine
interactions on earth.

Language

Start practising those tongue clicks – Xhosa is the predominant language in the Eastern Cape. Local whites speak English and Afrikaans.

ℹ Getting There & Around

The easiest way to explore the province is by car, but backpacker shuttle the **Baz Bus** (☑ 021-422 5202, SMS bookings 076 427 3003; www.bazbus.com) is a good option for touring the coast. It runs between Cape Town and Port Elizabeth (R2020 one way – hop-on, hop-off; 15 hours) five days a week in both directions, stopping at backpackers in the Crags (near Nature's Valley), Bloukrans Bridge, Storms River and Jeffrey's Bay. Baz Bus also runs between Port Elizabeth and Durban (R1830 one way – hop-on, hop-off; 15¼ hours) four days a week, stopping in Port Alfred, East London, Chintsa and Mthatha. Seven- to 21-day passes are also available. Hostels run shuttles from East London to Hogsback, and from Mthatha to Coffee Bay and Port St Johns.

The major bus companies, including **Greyhound** (☑ 021-418 4326, reservations 083 915 9000; www.greyhound.co.za), **Translux** (☑ 021-449 6209, 086 158 9282; www.translux.co.za), **Intercape** (☑ 021-380 4400; www.intercape.co.za) and **City to City** (☑ 0861 589 282; www.citytocity.co.za), ply the same coastal route and also serve the hinterland, linking the Eastern Cape with Bloemfontein, Johannesburg (Jo'burg) and Pretoria. **Shosholoza Meyl** (☑ 0860 008 888, 011-774 4555; www.shosholozameyl.co.za) trains connect Port Elizabeth and East London with Jo'burg via Bloemfontein. Port Elizabeth, East London and Mthatha have airports.

Further off the beaten track, notably on the Wild Coast and in the Highlands, travellers on public transport will have to take shared taxis to reach more-obscure spots. Roads can be impassable after heavy rains. Some places on the Wild Coast are only accessible on foot or horseback.

GARDEN ROUTE EAST

This region includes the western edge of the Eastern Cape coast, an extension of the well-travelled Garden Route (p144) and, for that reason, is probably the most visited part of the province. The Tsitsikamma section of Garden Route National Park is deservedly well known, but other lesser-known destinations such as Baviaanskloof Wilderness Area (p183) are also worthy of attention. Nature lovers and outdoorsy types will be in seventh heaven with plenty of activities to keep them busy.

Garden Route National Park (Tsitsikamma Section)

Cut through by dark, coffee-coloured churning rivers, deep ravines and dense forests, the Tsitsikamma section of the **Garden Route National Park** (☑ 042-281 1607; www.sanparks.org; adult/child R216/108; ⊗ gate 6am-9pm) encompasses 650 sq km between Plettenberg Bay and Humansdorp, as well a Marine Protected Area covering 80km of coastline. A 77m-long suspension bridge spans the Storms River Mouth near the rest camp of the same name (not to be confused with the village of Storms River), where several walking trails pass thickets of ferns, lilies, orchids, coastal and mountain *fynbos* (fine bush), and yellowwood and milkwood trees. Millennia-old sandstone and quartz rock formations line the gorges and rocky shoreline, and southern right whale and dolphins are visible out in the ocean.

Elusive Cape clawless otters, after which the Otter Trail (a multiday hike) is named, inhabit this park; there are also baboons, monkeys, small antelope and furry little dassies. Birdlife is plentiful, including endangered African black oystercatchers.

🏃 Activities

Bloukrans Bridge Bungee   BUNGEE JUMPING
(Map p146; ☑ 042-281 1458; www.faceadrenalin.com; bungee jumps R990; ⊗ 8.30am-4.45pm) At 216m, this is one of the highest (and most spectacular) bungee jumps in the world. If you're not sure whether you have the guts to take the plunge, walk out to the jumping-off point under the bridge for R150. Jumps take place 21km west of Storms River directly under the N2.

Untouched Adventures   ADVENTURE SPORTS
(☑ 073 130 0689; www.untouchedadventures.com; kayak & lilo trip R450, scuba diving R600, guided snorkelling trip R400; ⊗ 8.30am-6pm) This renowned venture offers a popular three-hour kayak and lilo trip up Storms River, plus scuba diving and guided snorkelling trips in the national park Marine Protected Area (trips are weather dependent). Located near the beach at Storms River Mouth Rest Camp.

❶ GARDEN ROUTE NATIONAL PARK (TSITSIKAMMA SECTION)

Why Go Mountainous landscape covered with indigenous forest, rolling down to rocky coastline. Activities include kayaking, tubing and bungee jumping; walking trails range from short strolls to famous multiday hikes.

When to Go June and July are the driest months, and their relatively mild temperatures continue into August and September.

Practicalities The park's main information centre is at Storms River Mouth Rest Camp.

Budget Tips Accommodation in Storms River and Nature's Valley is cheaper than at the park's rest camp; in Storms River, you can walk from accommodation to companies offering activities in the park. If you don't have a car, stay at accommodation on the Baz Bus or Mzansi Experience route and organise shuttles into the park, rather than taking taxis.

Hiking

If you don't have time for the long, overnight trails, don't worry: shorter walks ranging from 1km to 4km are also available in the park.

Otter Trail
HIKING
(☑ Pretoria 012-426 5111; www.sanparks.org; per person R1200) The 45km Otter Trail is one of South Africa's most acclaimed hikes, hugging the coastline from Storms River Mouth to Nature's Valley. The five-day, four-night walk involves fording a number of rivers and gives access to some superb stretches of coast. A good level of fitness is required, as it goes up- and downhill quite steeply in many places.

Accommodation is in six-bed rest huts with mattresses (without bedding), rainwater tanks, braais (barbecues) and firewood. Camping is not allowed.

Book at least nine months ahead (six months if you are flexible about dates). There are often cancellations, however, so it's always worth trying, especially if you are in a group of only two or three people. Single hikers are permitted; you'll be tagged onto a group so you do not walk by yourself.

Tsitsikamma Mountain Trail
HIKING
(Map p146; ☑ 042-281 1712; www.mtoecotourism.co.za; per night R155) This 62km trail begins at Nature's Valley and ends at Storms River, taking you inland through the forests and mountains. The full trail takes six days, but you can also opt for two, three, four or five days, because each overnight hut has its own access route. Porterage is also available, as are day hikes (R50) and mountain-bike trails.

Dolphin Trail
HIKING
(☑ 042-280 3588; www.dolphintrail.co.za; s/d R7080/11,800) Ideal for well-heeled slackpackers who don't want to hoist a rucksack or sleep in huts, this two-day, 17km hike runs from Storms River Mouth Rest Camp to Misty Mountain (p183), and then onto the Fernery Lodge & Chalets (p183) for the last night. Book through the trail's website at least a year in advance (yes, really!).

🍴 Sleeping & Eating

Storms River Mouth Rest Camp
CAMPGROUND $$
(☑ 042-281 1607; www.sanparks.org; camping per site from R370, hut/cottage/chalet from R600/1100/1200; [P][☎][🐾]) This camp offers accommodation ranging from rustic forest huts to chalets, family cottages and waterfront 'oceanette' cottages with top ocean views. Most have single beds with bedding and, apart from the forest huts, kitchens (including utensils) and bathrooms. The turn-off for the camp is between Bloukrans Bridge and Storms River on the N2; from here, the camp is 10km.

Rates do not include the park's conservation fee (adult/child R216/108).

Cattle Baron
STEAK $$
(☑ 042-281 1190; www.cattlebaron.co.za; mains R70-140; ⏰ 8.30am-9pm; 🐾) At the reception complex for Tsitsikamma National Park, this busy place has a wide selection of seafood and meat dishes at reasonable prices and superb views of the coast. There's also a small shop and an outdoor terrace with a boardwalk over the rocks to the river mouth.

❶ Getting There & Away

There is no public transport to Storms River Mouth. Greyhound, Intercape, Translux and City to City stop in Plettenberg Bay and Storms River Bridge. Baz Bus stops at Bloukrans Bridge en route between Cape Town and Port Elizabeth. **Mzansi Experience** (☑ 021-001 0651;

www.mzansi.travel) stops at the hostels in Storms River en route between Cape Town and Port Elizabeth.

Hiking Trail Transfers (☑ 083 232 7655; www.ottertrailtransfers.co.za) offers transfers to walkers on the Otter and Tsitsikamma Mountain Trails.

Storms River

☑ 042 / POP 1670

Tree-lined Storms River is a charming little hamlet with a well-developed tourist industry, in large part because of its location in the Tsitsikamma section of Garden Route National Park near Bloukrans Bridge. It's a big draw for outdoor enthusiasts, with plenty of adventure options readily available, including hiking, ziplining and rafting. It's also a comfortable base if you're travelling between Cape Town and Port Elizabeth.

If you're driving, don't confuse Storms River with the turn-off 4km to the west for Storms River Mouth (Stormsriviermond in Afrikaans), located in the park.

◉ Sights & Activities

Big Tree   FOREST
(adult/child R16/9; ☉ 8am-5pm May-Aug, to 6pm Sep-Apr; ℗) Just east of Storms River on the other side of the N2 is the Big Tree, a 36m-high yellowwood that's over 800 years old, and a forest with many fine examples of candlewood, stinkwood and assegai. The 4.2km Ratel Trail begins here, with signs describing the trees in this forest; it's one of the best preserved in South Africa.

Mild 2 Wild   OUTDOORS
(☑ 042-281 1842; www.mild2wildadventures.com; Darnell St; horse riding R400, mountain bikes per day R300; ☉ 9am-5pm) Runs horse-riding trips and rents out mountain bikes for the recommended 22km cycle through the national park to the Storms River Mouth.

Tsitsikamma Canopy Tours ADVENTURE SPORTS
(☑ 042-281 1836; www.stormsriver.com; Darnell St; zipline from R650, guided forest drives & hikes from R200; ☉ 8am-6pm) This massive operation is the oldest branch in a nationwide network of canopy tours. Ten ziplines up to 100m long cut through the forest covering high in the trees; it's more relaxing than thrilling. The three-hour guided tour departs every half-hour from 8.30am to 3.30pm. Guided forest drives and hikes are also offered.

Blackwater Tubing   ADVENTURE SPORTS
(☑ 079 636 8008; www.tubenaxe.co.za; Darnell St; half-/full day from R595/950; ☉ by reservation) Tubing trips on the Storms River run out of **Tube 'n Axe backpackers** (☑ 042-281 1757; camping/dm R120/210, d R700-760, safari tent R700; ℗ 🛜 🏊). Because the river is susceptible to flooding, there may be no departures for several days after rains of any significance. It's worth asking how the river is flowing; with lower water levels you'll be doing almost as much walking as floating.

Tsitsikamma Falls Adventure   ADVENTURE SPORTS
(☑ 042-280 3770; www.tsitsikammaadventure.co.za; Witelsbos; R400; ☉ 9am-3.45pm) Explore the Kruis River gorge on eight ziplines up to 211m long. Around 12km east of the Storms River just off the N2.

🛏 Sleeping

🛏 In the Village

Dijembe Backpackers   HOSTEL $
(☑ 042-281 1842; www.dijembebackpackers.com; Formosa St; camping/dm/d R120/160/500, safari tent R450; ℗ 🛜) 🌱 Reflecting the spirit of its nature-loving owner – who might arrive with a rescued horse, hang from the rafters and lead a drum circle, all in the space of a typical evening – much of this offbeat backpackers is made from recycled wood. Accommodation includes two dorms, two en-suite doubles and three safari tents.

Tsitsikamma Backpackers   HOSTEL $
(☑ 042-281 1868; www.tsitsikammabackpackers.co.za; 54 Formosa St; dm R220, d R720, with shared bathroom R620, safari tent R600; ℗ @ 🛜) The faux log-cabin facade aside, a stay here feels like bedding down in a clean suburban home. Spick-and-span rooms are decorated with colourful flourishes in the bedding and artwork, while comfortable twin tents stand on covered platforms. Breakfast (R60) and dinner (R90) are available, and the lounge, attractive garden, well-equipped kitchen, and bar with pool sweeten the deal.

At the Woods   GUESTHOUSE $$
(☑ 042-281 1446; www.atthewoods.co.za; 43 Formosa St; s/d incl breakfast R1050/1400; ℗ ❄ 🛜 🏊) This stylish guesthouse has an arty feel, with ceramics on the walls, colourful cushions on the beds and turquoise gar-

den furniture. Rooms upstairs have wooden balconies; number six is particularly spacious. A safe choice.

Tsitsikamma Village Inn INN $$
(☑042-281 1711; www.tsitsikammahotel.co.za; Darnell St; s/d incl breakfast from R950/1350; P✱🖧🏊🛏) In this handsome mini-village, the majority of rooms are in old-fashioned low-slung cottages with private porches surrounding a manicured lawn. Right in the centre of the village, there's a restaurant, bar and playground on the premises plus a microbrewery next door.

Armagh Country Lodge & Spa LODGE $$
(☑042-281 1512; www.thearmagh.com; 24 Fynbos St; incl breakfast s R900-1390, d R1200-1800; P🛜🏊) Just off the main access road into the village from the N2, Armagh is practically hidden from view by a lush and leafy garden. The nine rooms are snug and warm, and most have individual patios. There's a spa and tiny pool, and the on-site restaurant (p183) is one of the best places to eat in town. Book ahead.

🏠 Outside the Village

★ Fernery Lodge & Chalets RESORT $$$
(Map p146; ☑042-280 3588; www.forestferns.co.za/Fernery; s/d incl breakfast from R1800/2600; P🛜🏊) Hugging the edge of a cliff overlooking the Sandrift River gorge, the Fernery takes full advantage of its dramatic setting.

Luxurious chalets and suites are scattered throughout; a hot tub hovers over the void; and the restaurant is a cosy nook with floor-to-ceiling windows. Activities include walking and biking. Access is via a good gravel road from the N2.

Misty Mountain Reserve RESORT $$$
(Map p146; ☑042-280 3699; www.mistymountainreserve.co.za; s/d/f from R1395/1860/2200; P🛜🏊) This rural resort is a terrific place to kick off your shoes for a few days. It has a string of individual A-frame cottages set back from a bluff over the ocean as well as five rustic cottages and four safari tents overlooking a small lake. Access is via a good gravel road from the N2.

✖ Eating & Drinking

★ Tsitrus Cafe CAFE $
(☑076 873 1509; www.tsitruscafe.co.za; Kamassi St; mains R45-80; ⊙8am-8pm; 🛜) Hallelujah! Storms River finally gets the cafe it so deserves. This atmospheric place offers tasty meals, including delicious pancakes and pizzas, as well as good coffee and craft beers. Everything is fresh and homemade. Also sells local crafts and a great selection of gourmet products.

Rafters SOUTH AFRICAN $$
(☑042-228 11587; www.thearmagh.com; 24 Fynbos St; mains R90-140; ⊙8am-8.45pm; 🛜) The Armagh Country Lodge's restaurant has a

[side margin: EASTERN CAPE STORMS RIVER]

WORTH A TRIP

BAVIAANSKLOOF WILDERNESS AREA & THE GAMTOOS VALLEY

One of South Africa's largest conservation areas, **Baviaanskloof Wilderness Area** (Baviaanskloof Mega Reserve; Map p146; ☑044-272 9908; www.baviaans.co.za; R40; ⊙sunrise-4pm) is a World Heritage site that's home to leopards, antelope, buffaloes and Cape mountain zebras, between the Kouga and Baviaanskloof mountains. Stretching between the towns of Patensie and Willowmore, the region is best explored in your own vehicle (with high clearance) or on a tour with **Guarri Safari** (☑042-283 0739; Patensie; full day incl lunch 1-4 people R2900; ⊙by reservation). With a 2WD vehicle, you can explore the Gamtoos Valley, which lies roughly between Loerie and Patensie along R331. The heart and soul of the valley, **Patensie** is a charming agricultural town surrounded with large citrus farms. It's a great place to relax for a couple of days, without being too far from the coast. It has a wide choice of accommodation options.

Recommended stays include **Tropical Eden Villas** (☑082 933 1400, 042-283 0801; www.patensieselfcatering.co.za; Patensie; villas from R800; P), which has four self-catering villas with great views of the countryside, and **Ripple Hill Hotel** (☑042-283 0625; www.ripplehill.co.za; Patensie; s/d R450/650; P🛜), which offers renovated rooms with all mod cons. On the main road, **Tolbos** (☑042-283 0437; www.tolbos.co.za; Main Rd, Patensie; mains R65-115; ⊙8am-7pm Mon-Sat, to 5m Sun; 🛜) is a great little cafe with an alluring menu. It doubles as an informal tourist office.

cosy dining room with an open fire and patio seating. Cape Malay specialities, including ostrich *bobotie* (delicately flavoured curry with a topping of beaten egg baked to a crust), are offered alongside less-local dishes such as lamb shank, burgers, fish of the day and light lunches. A great find.

ℹ Information

Just off the N2 is **Storms River Information Centre** (☑ 042-281 1098; Kamassi St; ☺ 9am-5.30pm), which has a wall of brochures and can help with accommodation, including self-catering options. There's an ATM inside Tsitsikamma Canopy Tours (p182).

ℹ Getting There & Around

Baz Bus and Mzansi Experience (p181) both stop at the hostels in Storms River en route between Cape Town and Port Elizabeth, and your accommodation can organise shuttles to the Tsitsikamma section of Garden Route National Park as well as local activities. The main bus companies stop at Storms River Bridge, 5km east of town on the N2; arrange a pickup with your accommodation from there.

SUNSHINE COAST

The Sunshine Coast has everything the country is known for – pristine beaches, wildlife, stunning scenery, great outdoor activities and culture. It covers a significant chunk of the Eastern Cape coastline, including Port Elizabeth, the seaside towns of Jeffrey's Bay and Port Alfred, and numerous sandy beaches. In the hinterland are the best wildlife-watching areas within easy reach of the coastline between Cape Town and Durban: Addo Elephant National Park and the nearby private reserves.

The region has an English heritage and flavour, thanks to the influence of the 1820 Settlers. These hardy Brits landed at Algoa Bay and, having tried to farm in the midst of internecine clashes between the Boers and the Xhosa, they ultimately ended up in Grahamstown, Port Elizabeth and beyond.

St Francis Bay

☑ 042 / POP 5275

St Francis Bay is an upmarket resort partially constructed around a network of canals. It has a uniform building code that calls for black thatched roofs and white stucco walls. The beach here is fairly narrow but pleasant

nonetheless, and the surf is good for beginners. Off season, it's pretty much deserted, and its golf course and twee crescents create an air of immaculate sterility. However, it does come to life in the high season, and is a safe and tranquil spot for a night or two throughout the year. Nearby Port St Francis is one of the centres of the calamari fishing industry; catches include Cape Hope squid, known as chokka and often used as bait. A few kilometres further south, Cape St Francis has a wind-whipped beach and the Seal Point surf break. Whales can be seen offshore between July and November; dolphins are seen throughout the year.

⊙ Sights & Activities

Seal Point Lighthouse LIGHTHOUSE
(Seal Point Reserve, Cape St Francis) **FREE** Built in 1878, this lighthouse is the tallest masonry tower on the South African coast, and marks the second-most-southern tip of Africa.

SANCCOB Sea Bird Rehabilitation Centre BIRD SANCTUARY
(☑ 042-298 0160; www.sanccob.co.za; Seal Point Reserve, Cape St Francis; admission free, guided tour adult/child R50/30, penguin adoption R1000; ☺ 9am-4pm; ℗) **FREE** This haven for endangered African penguins is funded entirely by donations. You can adopt a penguin that will be cared for and released when healthy.

Chokka Trail HIKING
(☑ 073 825 0835; www.chokkatrail.co.za; per person R4770; ☺ Apr-Sep) This 56km slackpacking trail meanders around the headland's beaches, *fynbos*, forests and dune fields. The four-day package includes three nights of full-board guesthouse accommodation, a canal cruise and calamari tasting.

Cruises

St Francis Safaris & Adventures CRUISE
(☑ 042-294 0634; www.stfrancissafaris.com; Triton Ave, Port St Francis; from R250; ☺ by reservation) This reputable operator specialises in whale- and dolphin-watching trips as well as ocean, canal and river cruises.

Resort Adventures CRUISE
(☑ 042-298 0054; www.capestfrancis.co.za; St Francis Bay; canal cruise R250, upriver trip R500) Offers canal cruises in St Francis Bay and day-long trips upriver to a farm for kayaking and a braai (barbecue).

BriSan on the Canals CRUISE

(📞042-294 1894; www.brisan.co.za; 7 Spray Ave; 1hr cruise R200; ⊘by reservation) Specialises in canal cruises. It's also a B&B, with six straightforward rooms (singles/doubles incl breakfast from R800/1300).

🛏 Sleeping

St Francis Bay Backpackers HOSTEL $

(📞042-294 1747; www.stfrancisbaybackpackers.com; 167 St Francis Dr, St Francis Bay; dm/d R180/500; P 🛜) Clean, neat and close to shops and restaurants, this hostel is a great choice if you're counting the pennies. The dorms and rooms have been renovated and feature spacious bathrooms and excellent bedding. There's a well-tended communal kitchen.

Cape St Francis Resort RESORT $$

(📞042-298 0054; www.capestfrancis.co.za; Da Gama Way, Cape St Francis; camping R120-160, backpackers s/d from R480/640, apt s/d from R1300/1730, villas & cottages from R3050; P 🛜 🏊 🍴) The various chalets and units at this sprawling oceanfront resort are attractive and well-equipped, with self-catering and B&B options available. In the thatched and whitewashed village are Cape Dutch-style cottages, beachfront luxury villas (with their own small pools), backpacker rooms, apartments and more. There's also a spa, restaurant, small shop and bar on-site. Plenty of activities are offered.

⭐**St Francis Golf Lodge** BOUTIQUE HOTEL $$$

(📞042-294 0028; www.stfrancisgolflodge.co.za; 10 Jack Nicklaus Dr, St Francis Bay; s/d incl breakfast R1625/2190; P ❄ 🛜) The best thing about this efficiently run venture with a boutique feel is its peaceful location inside the golf course. The 10 rooms, eight of which have top views over the golf course, are all sparkling clean and tastefully decorated.

🍴 Eating & Drinking

St Francis Brewing Company GASTROPUB $$

(📞063 274 3743; 167 St Francis Dr, St Francis Bay; mains R70-120; ⊘11am-10.30pm Wed-Mon; 🛜) The trendiest choice in town, this venue is part bar and part restaurant. Eclectic decor, casual service, a tempting menu focusing on seafood, burgers and pasta, as well as a small selection of craft beers (from R30), make this a great place to chill out.

Big Time Taverna GREEK $$

(📞042-294 1309; Mayotte Circle, St Francis Bay; mains R70-175; 🛜) This restaurant is the only one in town that is located on the canals,

with heavenly views from the deck. It specialises in traditional Greek food, such as mezze, moussaka and *youvarni* (lamb with Greek noodles and parmesan).

Christy's Catch SEAFOOD $$

(📞042-294 1644; www.christyscatch.co.za; 165 St Francis Dr, St Francis Bay; mains R90-200; ⊘5-9pm Mon-Wed, 11am-3pm & 5-9pm Thu-Sat, 11am-3pm Sun) Seafood lovers rave about Christy's, which has superb calamari burgers, fish steaks, prawns and oysters. It's also renowned for its grilled meat, including spare ribs and rib-eye. The thatched bar and themed decor (think fishing tackle and a boat) add nautical flavour to the courtyard. There is also an Asian counter offering stir-fries, sushi, curries and spring rolls.

ℹ Getting There & Around

You'll need your own wheels to explore the area as public transport is unreliable.

Jeffrey's Bay

📞042 / POP 27,107

Once just a sleepy seaside town, 'J-Bay' is now one of the world's top surfing destinations. It's certainly South Africa's foremost centre of surfing and surf culture. Boardies from all over the planet flock here to ride waves such as the famous Supertubes, generally rated as one of the world's most perfect waves. June to September are the best months for experienced surfers, but novices can learn at any time of year. If you don't surf, or want something different, there are plenty of other water sports on offer. And if all you want to do is recharge the batteries, a couple of superb expanses of white sand beckon.

🏃 Activities

For nonsurfers, there's windsurfing, kite-surfing, stand-up paddleboarding, sandboarding, horse riding, dolphin- and whale-watching from the beaches, and birdwatching at **Kabeljous Estuary**, which makes a pleasant 6km coastal walk from town (for security reasons, don't go by yourself). Alternatively, wander down the boardwalk to **Supertubes** to watch impressive displays of surf skill.

Wavecrest Surf School SURFING

(📞073 509 0400; www.wavecrestsurfschool.co.za; 6 Drommedaris St; 2hr lesson incl board & wetsuit R320; ⊘by reservation; 🚗) This long-running operation offers daily lessons. Good for children and beginners.

Jeffrey's Bay

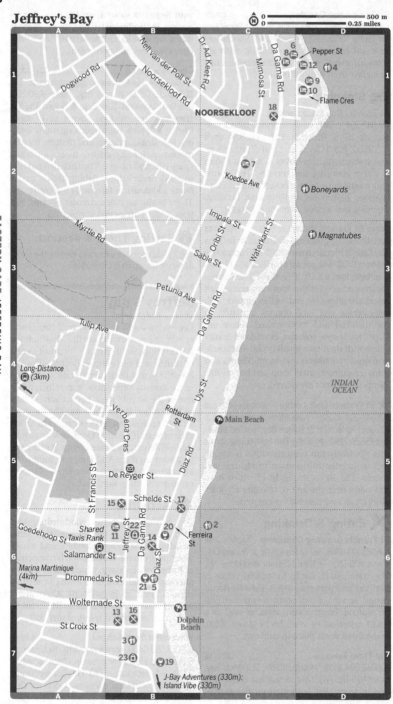

N

0 ——————— 500 m
0 ——————— 0.25 miles

Dogwood Rd

Neil van der Poll St

Dr Ad Keet Rd

Noorsekloof Rd

Mimosa St

Da Gama Rd

Pepper St

6
8
12
4
9
10
Flame Cres

NOORSEKLOOF

18

Koedoe Ave

7

Boneyards

Impala St

Oribi St

Sable St

Waterkant St

Magnatubes

Myrtie Rd

Petunia Ave

Da Gama Rd

Tulip Ave

Long-Distance
(3km)

INDIAN
OCEAN

Uys St

Verbena Cres

Rotterdam St

Diaz Rd

Main Beach

St Francis St

De Reyger St

Schelde St

15

17

Goedehoop St

Shared
Taxis Rank

11

22

Jeffrey St

Da Gama Rd

14

20

2

Ferreira St

Salamander St

Diaz St

Marina Martinique
(4km)

Drommedaris St

21 5

Woltemade St

13   16

St Croix St

1

Dolphin
Beach

3

23

19

J-Bay Adventures (330m);
Island Vibe (330m)

Son Surf School   SURFING

(☑ 076 501 6191; www.surfschools.co.za; 1½hr lesson R340; ◷ by reservation) This reputable outfit is good for intermediate surfers who want a refresher or to improve their technique. Beginner and advanced classes are also on offer, and equipment rental is available.

AfricaSUP   WATER SPORTS

(☑ 042-293 0155; www.africasup.com; 19 Da Gama Road; 1½hr lesson R370, 1½hr equipment hire R250; ◷ by reservation) If you fancy a different way to get wet, try stand-up paddleboarding. As well as beginner lessons, they also rent out equipment.

⭐ Festivals & Events

Winter Fest   SPORTS

(www.jbaywinterfest.com) The biggest surf crowd comes to town every July for the Open of Surfing competition, part of this 10-day festival of sports, live music and entertainment. Demand for accommodation skyrockets during the festivals, and most places charge high-season rates.

🛏 Sleeping

J-Bay has a wide range of accommodation options to suit all budgets, including hostels, B&Bs, self-catering apartments, guesthouses and hotels. It's chock-a-block with holidaymakers between mid-December and mid-January; book way ahead for accommodation at this time.

Island Vibe   HOSTEL $

(☑ 042-293 1625; www.jbay.islandvibe.co.za; 10 Dageraad St; camping R100, dm R180-200, cabin with shared bathroom R600, d R650-750; ᴘ🛈) A cool spot for budget-conscious travellers, this no-frills venture has a prime beachfront location despite being 500m south of the centre. It has a wide assortment of accommodation options, including four- to 14-bed dorms, five wooden cabins with sea views, a beach house with 12 doubles and a flashpackers with five rooms, as well as a restaurant and communal kitchens.

In-house tour company **J-Bay Adventures** (☑ 042-293 4214; www.jeffreysbayadventures.co.za; 10 Dageraad St; 2hr surf lesson R300, sandboarding R250, waterfall trip R250, horse ride R450, township tours R200; ◷ by reservation) offers surf-camp packages (three, five and seven days), daily lessons and board hire, as well as horse riding, sandboarding and township tours.

African Ubuntu   HOSTEL $

(☑ 042-296 0376; www.jaybay.co.za; 8 Cherry St; camping/dm R110/175, d R450, with shared bathroom R400, all incl breakfast; 🛈) A suburban home transformed into an intimate and colourful backpackers by its passionate surfer owner. It has compact six- to 10-bed dorms and seven serviceable doubles as well as kitchen facilities. Overall, it's well kept but some bathrooms could use an upgrade. There are sweeping views of the ocean from the upstairs lounge and balcony. On-street parking only.

Surfboard rental and activities can be organised.

Cristal Cove   GUESTHOUSE $

(☑ 042-293 2101; www.cristalcove.co.za; 49 Flame Cres; dm R160, d R500-700, with shared bathroom

EASTERN CAPE JEFFREY'S BAY

R400; ☏) This two-storey brick home shelters five tidy, light-filled rooms and a neat four-bed dorm as well as excellent kitchen facilities, a bar and pool table. The laid-back atmosphere is hard to beat. Upstairs rooms are larger and offer more privacy. Hint: room 4 comes with great ocean views.

Aloe Again
HOSTEL $

(☑042-293 1401; www.aloeagainbackpackers.co.za; 20 Pepper St; d R500-800; P☏) Aloe Again has clean, fresh rooms and a large open-plan lounge and kitchen. The courtyard and garden area offer plenty of space to chill.

Beach Music
GUESTHOUSE $

(☑042-293 2291; www.beachmusic.co.za; 33 Flame Cres; s R350-600, d R500-950; ☏) This airy house with a garden leading straight to the beach is great value. The 1st-floor lounge has superb ocean views – including a glimpse of Supertubes – and the tastefully decorated rooms have small private patios. Room 1, upstairs, enjoys the best views. All rooms come with kitchen facilities.

Super Tubes Guesthouse
GUESTHOUSE $$

(☑042-293 2957; www.supertubesguesthouse.co.za; 12 Pepper St; s R750-1500, d R1200-2100, incl breakfast; P☀☏) Just steps away from the beach and Supertubes, this upmarket and friendly guesthouse offers an assortment of tidy, light-filled rooms – most of which come with private balconies and glorious ocean views. The garden area is a great place to recharge the batteries. Before hitting the waves, enjoy the lavish breakfast buffet.

Funky Town
GUESTHOUSE $$

(☑042-293 3860; www.accommodationjbay.co.za; 12a Oosterland St; d R900, penthouse apt R1600; P☏☒) The seven rooms here are all brightly decorated with original art hanging on the walls. There's also a penthouse apartment with kitchen and sitting area. For

---

ⓘ STAY IN J-BAY

There have been cases of people making online bookings for accommodation in J-Bay that turn out to be bogus. Confirm before paying that your chosen accommodation does actually exist in the offline world – in doubt, contact the tourist office. Stay in J-Bay (www.stay-injbay.co.za) is a useful and reputable resource for accommodation.

---

everyone else, there's a shared kitchen and TV lounge inside and a barbecue area, hot tub and tiny pool in the garden. Bikes and boards are available to hire.

African Perfection
GUESTHOUSE $$$

(☑042-293 1401; www.africanperfection.co.za; 20 Pepper St; d incl breakfast R1300-1800; P☀☏) Occupying prime real estate in front of Supertubes (with direct beach access), this luxury option is perfect for surfing voyeurs. Most rooms come with a balcony offering stunning sea views.

✖ Eating

★InFood Deli Bakery & Deli Restaurant
INTERNATIONAL $$

(☑042-293 1880; www.infood.co.za; cnr Schelde & Jeffrey Sts; mains R60-100; ☺7am-5pm Mon-Sat; ☏) The sandwiches, burgers and other food at this cafe, bakery and deli are far from ordinary. This is not surprising, considering the owner-chef's impressive CV – including once having cooked for Prince William. The mix of organic, locally sourced ingredients and wide-ranging culinary tastes (nachos, pasta and Thai chicken curry) makes this a worthy foodie destination.

Kitchen Windows
SEAFOOD $$

(☑042-293 4230; www.kitchenwindows.co.za; 80 Ferreira St; mains R70-170; ☺11am-9pm Mon-Sat, to 3pm Sun; ☏) Great sea views and white stucco walls give this airy restaurant a Mediterranean island feel. It has an informal yet upmarket atmosphere and is known for its flavourful cuisine based on fresh, quality ingredients. Unsurprisingly for Jeffrey's Bay, seafood features heavily, but there's also a tempting selection of tapas.

★Nina's
INTERNATIONAL $$

(☑042-296 0281; www.ninas.co.za; 126 Da Gama Rd; mains R65-190; ☺7am-10pm; ☏) Most locals recommend vibey Nina's, with its quirky decor of surfboards and coastal scenes around a paper-disc chandelier. Seafood abounds on the wide-ranging menu, which also features burgers, curries, pizza, pasta, Thai food and the best ice cream in town. Great beers and cocktails, too. What's missing? A cool location – it's on the main drag next to a petrol station.

J-Bay Bru Co
INTERNATIONAL $$

(☑042-940 0165; www.jbaybruco.co.za; 10 Da Gama Rd; mains R80-150; ☺9am-10pm Tue-Sat, 8am-5pm Sun; ☏) Many locals and tourists rave about this funky place in an imagina-

SURFING THE EASTERN CAPE

Surfing on the Eastern Cape coast is legendary. While Supertubes at Jeffrey's Bay is world class, and Bruce's Beauties at St Francis Bay inspired the movie *Endless Summer*, you can generally check out breaks anywhere along the coast, from Jeffrey's Bay to Port Edward.

The water temperature ranges from 16°C to 22°C, so you can get away with a short wetsuit (or even baggies) in summer, but you'll need a full wetsuit in winter.

Starting in the south, Cape St Francis (p184) is home to legendary Seal Point, one of the most consistent right-handed breaks. Nearby St Francis Bay has Bruce's Beauties and Hullets, the perfect longboard wave.

Jeffrey's Bay (p185) is one of the planet's 10 best surf spots, and ranks high on most people's list of 'waves I must surf before I die'. In July it hosts the Open of Surfing competition. Consequently, it can become crowded when the surf's up: remember your manners and say 'howzit' to the locals. Supertubes (p185) is a perfect right-hand point break, and once you've caught this, you'll be spoilt rotten. If you're a beginner, head to the softer Kitchen Windows.

In the rush to J-Bay, many surfers overlook nearby Port Elizabeth (p190). While the predominant southwesterly winds can blow everything away, Pipe in Summerstrand is PE's most popular break, and on a good day the Fence is another favourite.

Further north in Port Alfred (p206) there are excellent right-handers at East Beach (p206), while West Beach (p206) has a more sheltered left and right.

East London (p210), home to some well-known surfing pros such as Greg Emslie and Rosy Hodge, is best known for the consistent Nahoon Reef; Gonubie Point and Gonubie Lefts can also come up with the goods. Nursery 'grommets' will find what they need at Nahoon Beach (Beach Rd) and Corner. There can be some dirty water in the area, which encourages shark activity, so keep an eye out and don't surf at dusk.

Heading north from East London, there are good waves in the coastal spots collectively known as East Coast Resorts and at the beginning of the Wild Coast. Look out for Queensberry Bay (where Hodge learnt her tricks), Glen Eden, Yellow Sands and Chintsa (p214).

Now you're on the Wild Coast – and wild, it is: a spectacular, often dangerous coastline that hasn't really been explored or exploited. Be careful at polluted river mouths: sharks are common, and in general you're a long way from medical attention. There's Whacky Point at Kei Mouth (p217), and Coffee Bay (p218) has a couple of waves. Mdumbi (p219) has a long, right-hand point break with a nice sandy bottom, Whale Rock is just around the corner, and then there are those secret spots that no one's ever going to tell you about...

tively converted space on the main drag, and we share their unbridled enthusiasm. The food here (and the enticing dining room) won't disappoint, with an assortment of flavoursome wood-fired pizzas, delectable burgers and well-presented salads, among others. Something sweet to finish? Try a homemade pastry. Excellent coffee, too.

Bay Pasta Co
ITALIAN $$

(☑042-293 3564; www.baypasta.co.za; 34 Jeffrey St; mains R65-120; 🕾) If satisfying pasta dishes, wood-fired pizzas, satisfying salads or well-prepared *tramezzini* (sandwiches) make your stomach quiver with excitement, slide into this inviting eatery in cool surrounds. The deck is a popular hang-out, with live music on certain days.

Catch of the Day
SEAFOOD $$

(☑042-293 2614; www.catchoftheday.webs.com; Diaz Rd; mains R60-110; 🕙11am-9.30pm) This convivial restaurant right in the centre is famous for one thing and one thing only: fresh fish (served with fries or rice), savoured in a ramshackle, nautically themed interior. The menu also includes calamari, prawns, sandwiches and grilled meat.

🍷 Drinking & Nightlife

Brewery on the Beach
CRAFT BEER

(☑082 334 8528; www.breweryonthebeach.co.za; 55 Diaz St; 🕙11am-7pm Tue-Sun) Set back from the seafront, this atmospheric bar set in an old fish factory is a good place for getting a bit of local vibe. It has a small selection of craft beers, but if you fancy something different be sure to try the craft cider or craft gin. There's outdoor seating with sea views and pub grub is available.

Je'Vista Social Cafe
COCKTAIL BAR

(☑042-293 3516; www.facebook.com/JeVistaSocialCafe; 1st fl, 33 Diaz St; ⊙11am-midnight) This loungey spot with big, sea-facing windows is popular for cocktails. The rose petal mojito, Baileys banana colada and potent California iced tea are all hits. There's live music on certain evenings.

The Mexican
BAR

(☑042-293 2966; www.themexicanjbay.co.za; 19a Da Gama Rd; ⊙noon-10pm) A popular local hang-out, this 1st-floor Latino bar-restaurant has a long balcony overlooking Da Gama Rd. Mexican classics such as enchiladas, fajitas, burritos and tacos (from R45) are on the menu, and the cocktail list includes the mandatory tequilas and margaritas.

🛍 Shopping

Surf Village
SPORTS & OUTDOORS

(Da Gama Rd; 9am-5pm) This cluster of surf shops, factory outlets and fashion shops offers pleasant browsing in modern, thatched buildings. Stores line Da Gama Rd south of St Croix St, with a few also found one block further inland on Jeffrey St. On Da Gama are the local labels Country Feeling (surf and fashion) and In Step (leather products), as well as Billabong, Rip Curl and RVCA.

Quiksilver
SPORTS & OUTDOORS

(☑042-293 2273; 24 Da Gama Rd; ⊙8.30am-5pm Mon-Sat) This shop has a 'museum' upstairs tracing the development of local surf culture, as well as surfboards, bodyboards, wetsuits and so on.

ℹ Information

Jeffreys Bay Tourism (☑042-293 2923; www.jeffreysbaytourism.org; Da Gama Rd; ⊙9am-5pm Mon-Fri, to noon Sat) Friendly and helpful, and can make bookings for accommodation and activities.

ℹ Getting There & Around

Baz Bus and Mzansi Experience (p181) both stop at several J-Bay hostels en route between Cape Town and Port Elizabeth.

Long-distance buses (St Francis St, Mentors Plaza Caltex garage) plying the Cape Town–Port Elizabeth–Durban route stop at the Mentors Plaza Caltex garage, at the junction of St Francis St and the N2.

Shared taxis depart when full, generally on the hour, from the corner of Goedehoop and St Francis Sts; it's R40 to Humansdorp (25 minutes) and R90 to Port Elizabeth (1¼ hours).

Local taxis, including **J-Bay Cabs** (☑083 611 1003), charge about R10 per kilometre.

Port Elizabeth

☑041 / POP 1.15 MILLION

Port Elizabeth (PE for short) fringes Algoa Bay at the western end of the Sunshine Coast, and offers many good bathing beaches, great surf spots and excellent water sports. Marine life in the bay is also sensational, with plenty of dolphins and whales that can be spotted throughout the year. The city centre, once a place to avoid, has started to smarten up thanks to a few urban regeneration projects, and it boasts numerous heritage buildings that are well worth a gander.

PE is also a convenient gateway to destinations in either direction along the coast, as well as to the eastern Karoo.

◉ Sights

Port Elizabeth's major attractions as a holiday destination are its wide sandy beaches and the warm waters of the Indian Ocean. Sardinia Bay, 20km south of the centre past the airport, is easily the nicest in the area, though beware of strong currents. There are broad beaches south of Central; Kings Beach (off Beach Rd) stretches from the harbour to Humewood. Further east you'll find Hobie Beach (Beach Rd), which is the beach of choice for windsurfers, sailors and kite-surfers, but sunbathers will also love it. There are more beaches at Summerstrand, which are all fairly sheltered.

Donkin Reserve
PARK

(Donkin St; lighthouse adult/child R10/5; ⊙lighthouse 8.14am-4pm Mon-Fri, 9.45am-3pm Sat) This pleasant hilltop park is a good place to get your bearings, particularly if you climb to the top of the lighthouse. The pyramid is a memorial to Elizabeth Donkin, wife of Sir Rufane Donkin, governor of the Cape Colony in the 1820s – who named PE after his beloved spouse. A heritage trail leads between the park's monuments and artworks, which narrate important periods of the city's history, and form part of the wider Route 67 trail through the centre.

Nelson Mandela
Metropolitan Art Museum GALLERY

(☑041-506 2000; www.artmuseum.co.za; 1 Park Dr, St George's Park; ⊘9am-5pm Mon & Wed-Fri, from 1pm Tue) FREE The museum housed in two handsome buildings at the entrance to St George's Park has a small gallery of paintings and sculpture by contemporary South African artists, some older British and Eastern Cape works, plus temporary exhibitions.

No. 7 Castle Hill HISTORIC BUILDING

(☑041-582 2515; 7 Castle Hill; adult/child R10/5; ⊘10am-1pm & 2-4pm Mon-Fri) This museum-house, occupying a picturesque cottage dating from 1827, evokes a settler family's life during the mid-Victorian period.

South End Museum MUSEUM

(☑041-582 3325; www.southendmuseum.co.za; cnr Walmer Blvd & Humewood Rd, South End; ⊘9am-4pm Mon-Fri, 10am-3pm Sat & Sun) FREE Multimedia exhibits relate the history of South End, a vibrant multicultural district destroyed by apartheid bulldozers during forced removals between 1965 and 1975 (under the infamous Group Areas Act). The inhabitants were relocated to other parts of the city, designated by race. Book ahead for a one-hour guided walking tour of the area (R100).

🏃 Activities

There are some excellent dive sites around Port Elizabeth, with shipwrecks and reefs all over Algoa Bay. Expect plenty of colourful soft corals and stunning underwater topography, including huge pinnacles and gullies. Fish life is prolific and includes ragged tooth sharks, which are often found swimming through the network of gully formations at various dive sites inside the bay. Most sites are suitable for novices and experienced divers alike.

PE's best surf breaks are found between the harbour wall and Summerstrand, and at Pollok beach.

Pro Dive DIVING

(☑041-581 1144; www.prodive.co.za; 189 Main Rd, Walmer; introductory dives R1700, single dive trips R350-550, sea kayaking from R400, snorkelling trips from R500; ⊘8am-5pm) Pro Dive is a fully-fledged, well-organised dive shop offering a full menu of underwater adventures, including introductory dives, single dive trips, snorkelling trips and certification courses. Guided sea kayaking trips can also be arranged. It also specialises in dive tours along the South African coastline and offers packages for the annual sardine run (p220).

Surf Centre SURFING

(☑041-585 6027, 082 322 1150; www.surf.co.za; Beach Rd, Humewood; 1½hr lesson R250) The Surf Centre sells and hires out surfboards and bodyboards. Its surf school will teach you how to use them.

☞ Tours

Calabash Tours CULTURAL

(☑082 390 6340; www.calabashtours.co.za; Summerstrand Hotel, Marine Dr; safaris R1450, township tours R600-700; ⊘by reservation) Runs local trips, ranging from Addo Elephant National Park safaris to several township tours, including visits to *shebeens* (taverns) and storytelling in residents' homes. The guides are locals who are proud of the Port Elizabeth townships' part in the anti-apartheid struggle, and they highlight places of historical and political interest along the way.

Raggy Charters BOATING

(☑073 152 2277; www.raggycharters.co.za; Algoa Bay Yacht Club; half-day tours R1400, sunset cruises R500; ⊘8am-5pm) This well-respected outfit offers a range of oceanic boat trips, including half-day tours with a qualified marine biologist to St Croix, Jahleel and Benton Islands, variously focused on penguins, whales and dolphins. Shorter sunset cruises to Cape Recife Lighthouse also offer opportunities to spot birds and marine life. Bookings essential.

Stampede Cruises BOATING

(☑081 766 6749; www.stampedecruises.co.za; Algoa Bay Harbour; cruises R250-750; ⊘by reservation) Offers a variety of boat trips around PE, including half-day tours to the nearby islands and shorter cruises up to Cape Recife.

🛏 Sleeping

🛏 Humewood & Summerstrand

Lungile Lodge HOSTEL $

(☑041-582 2042; www.lungilebackpackers.co.za; 12 La Roche Dr, Humewood; camping R100, dm R180-190, d R560, with shared bathroom R440; 🅿🛜🏊) Uphill from Kings Beach in a suburban neighbourhood, this well-run A-frame home's large entertainment area rocks most nights, and the six- and 12-bed dorms and tiny campground easily get full. The private rooms in the rear annexe are more modern,

Port Elizabeth

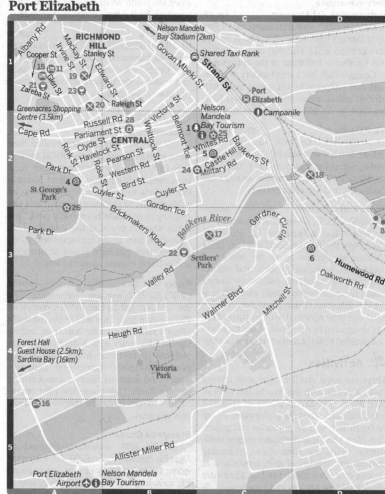

with hefty wooden beds, African masks and shared balconies.

Transfers and activities are offered, including township and Addo tours (more on www.afroventures.co.za).

Kings Beach Backpackers
HOSTEL $

(☑041-585 8113; 41 Windermere Rd, Humewood; camping/dm/d with shared bathroom R120/170/400, f R550; P🖥️) A small, lived-in house on a quiet street a short walk from the beach. There are cabins in the back garden, including an en-suite family room, plus a lounge and outdoor bar. The three dorms

inside the main house feel a bit cramped. The travel desk can organise local activities and transport.

Island Vibe
HOSTEL $$

(☑041-583 1256; www.islandvibe.co.za; 4 Jenvey Rd, Summerstrand; dm/s/d/apt R180/500/700/800; P🖥️🏊) This flashpackers in a nondescript suburban house makes a comfortable base with numerous facilities. The bar, pool table and outdoor hot tub liven up the 'burbs, while the well-equipped kitchen, secure parking and well-maintained dorms and en-suite rooms are welcome. Pollok Beach and the Pipe surf break are within walking distance.

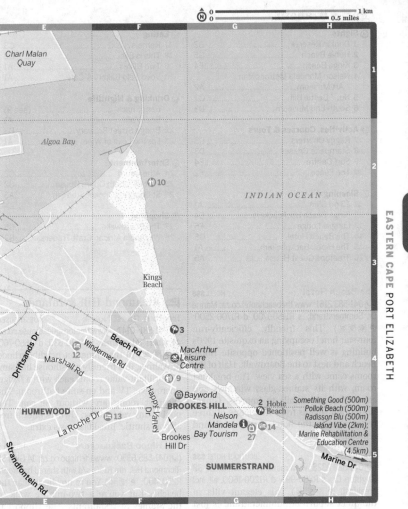

INDIAN OCEAN

Charl Malan Quay

Algoa Bay

INDIAN OCEAN

Kings Beach

Beach Rd

Windermere Rd

Driftsands Dr

Marshall Rd

MacArthur Leisure Centre

Bayworld
BROOKES HILL

HUMEWOOD

La Roche Dr

Happy Valley Dr

Strandfontein Rd

Nelson Mandela Bay Tourism

Brookes Hill Dr

Hobie Beach

Something Good (500m);
Pollok Beach (500m);
Radisson Blu (500m);
Island Vibe (2km);
Marine Rehabilitation &
Education Centre
(4.5km)

Marine Dr

SUMMERSTRAND

★**Ocean Bay**
Guest House　　　　BOUTIQUE HOTEL **$$$**
(☑041-583 1361; www.oceanbay.co.za; 1 Tiran Rd,
Summerstrand; s/d incl breakfast R1100/1650;
P❋🖥️🐾) A short amble from the beach,
this sassy venture with a boutique feel is
the epitome of a refined abode, with seven
elegant, modern and amply sized rooms, all
with private terraces. Although small, the
swimming pool in the landscaped garden is
a little beauty. The beach is just a five-min-
ute stroll down the road.

★**Isango Gate**　　　　BOUTIQUE HOTEL **$$$**
(☑041-811 2225; www.isangogate.co.za; 27
Bournemouth St, Summerstrand; s R1800-2300, d
R2400-3000, all incl breakfast; P❋🖥️🐾) This
venue strikes a perfect balance between
style, functionality and privacy (there are
only 10 rooms), in a residential area close
to the beach. Expect plush, spacious rooms
with carpet floors, squeaky-clean bathrooms and a private balcony. Amenities
include a spa, a small pool, a gym and a
restaurant.

Port Elizabeth

The Beach Hotel
HOTEL $$$

(☑ 041-583 2161; www.thebeachhotel.co.za; Marine Dr, Summerstrand; s R1150-1700, d R1700-2500; P❋🛜🏊) This friendly, efficiently-run four-star hotel occupying an exquisite 1920s building is well positioned opposite Hobie Beach and next to the Boardwalk. Half of the rooms come with a sea view. The breakfast room, with its stained-glass windows and chandelier, never fails to impress. Ginger Restaurant (mains from R125), one of three restaurants in the hotel, serves steak and seafood.

Manor 38
BOUTIQUE HOTEL $$$

(☑ 041-583 2328; www.manorcollection.co.za; 38 Brighton Dr; s R850-995, d R1200-1600, all incl breakfast; P❋🛜🏊) This elegant villa in the quiet suburb of Summerstrand is just the ticket for those seeking a cosy home away from home experience in PE. The eight rooms come in two levels of comfort and the standard ones are fan only. There's a delightful patio complete with a nifty pool.

Radisson Blu
HOTEL $$$

(☑ 041-509 5000; www.radissonblu.com/en/hotel-portelizabeth; Marine Dr, Summerstrand; d from R1700; P❋🛜🏊) You probably won't fall in love with this modern high-rise, but it has the most dramatic beach views you could ever hope for and all the facilities of an international business-class hotel.

🛏 Richmond Hill & Inland

Treetops Guest House
GUESTHOUSE $

(☑ 041-581 0147; www.treetopsguesthouse.co.za; 44 Albert Rd, Walmer; s R510-630, d R650-760; P❋🛜🏊) In the upmarket neighbourhood of Walmer, this friendly guesthouse has simple, brilliant-value rooms each with a fridge, microwave, TV and en-suite bathroom. The cheapest rooms are without air-con. The pool is tiny yet inviting. Owners offer a free airport shuttle. Breakfast costs extra.

The Hippo Backpackers
HOSTEL $

(☑ 041-585 6350; www.thehippo.co.za; 14 Glen St, Richmond Hill; dm R150, s/d with shared bathroom R250/400; P🛜🏊) You're nowhere near the beaches but you're a two-minute walk to the Stanley St restaurants. The Hippo has an inviting backyard pool, a bar and pool table, two attractive lounges, two kitchens, nicely furnished rooms and rather cramped dorms. Overall, it's simple, straightforward and well priced.

23 on Glen
B&B $$

(☑ 041-582 3296, 064 753 4115; www.facebook.com/23onglen; 23 Glen St, Richmond Hill; s R700-800, d R900, all incl breakfast; P🛜) Seeking a relaxing cocoon with homely qualities without the exorbitant price tag? This venture that opened in 2017 has all the key ingredients, with tastefully decorated rooms, a cosy lounge area, prim bathrooms and a copious breakfast. Bonus: the Stanley St bars and restaurants are within walking distance.

Forest Hall Guest House   GUESTHOUSE $$

(☑ 041-581 3356; www.foresthall.co.za; 84 River Rd, Walmer; s R800-900, d R1150-1400, all incl breakfast; P❋☎⊠) An attractive, secure property in a residential area. This efficiently run haven of peace set in park-like gardens is one of PE's most solid options, with 17 well-appointed rooms with individual entrances. The icing on the cake is the two swimming pools and tennis court. Four rooms have air-con.

✖ Eating

The culinary scene in PE is increasingly sophisticated. Stanley St is the centre of the up-and-coming Richmond Hill neighbourhood, with a vibey string of more than a dozen places to eat, serving cuisine ranging from Asian to Mediterranean. Walmer and Baakens Valley also boast excellent restaurants and cafes. Of course, you'll find a great selection of dining options along Beach Rd.

★ Banneton Bakery & Cafe   CAFE $

(☑ 041-450 6737; www.bannetonbakery.co.za; 154 Main Rd, Walmer; mains R20-85; ⊙7.30am-4pm Mon, Tue & Sat, to 9.30pm Wed, 8.30am-3pm Sun; ☎) This snazzy cafe-cum-bakery makes splendid breakfasts, sandwiches, wraps, salads and addictive goodies as well as serving excellent coffee at affordable prices and yummy pastries. There's outdoor seating on warm days.

This is Eat   SEAFOOD $

(☑ 041-582 2161; www.facebook.com/ThisIsEat; Bakens River Harbour, Lower Valley Rd; mains R50-175; ⊙9.30am-5.15pm Mon-Fri, 9.30am-4.30pm Sat & Sun) This crazily popular canteen-style joint has a tempting menu with plenty of simply prepared fish dishes as well as prawns and calamari. The setting (and the area) is less exciting, but the restaurant does takeaway, so you might want to make a picnic of it at the beach of your choice.

★ Remo's   ITALIAN $$

(☑ 082 877 6411; www.remos.co.za; 2 Alabaster St, Baakens Valley; mains R50-115; ⊙7am-10pm Wed-Fri, 7am-4.30pm Sat-Tue) You really need to know this place is here, but luckily now you do. What was once a warehouse in a derelict area is now a snazzy cafe with an industrial-chic decor. Start with fabulous *antipasti* (starters), then delve into the amazing pastas, salads or wood-fired pizzas. Don't miss the homemade pastries for dessert (the chocolate croissant is particularly good).

★ Two Olives   MEDITERRANEAN $$

(☑ 041-585 0371; www.twoolives.co.za; 3 Stanley St, Richmond Hill; tapas R50-70, mains R75-175; ⊙noon-10pm Tue-Sat, 11am-3pm Sun) One of the most attractive restaurants in Richmond Hill, Two Olives serves a range of Spanish-, Portuguese- and Greek-inspired dishes in its busy dining room and on the wrap-around balcony with partial ocean views. The lamb shank is as delicious as it is enormous. For the not so hungry, try the tapas menu.

Something Good   CAFE $$

(☑ 041-583 6986; St Croix Dr, Pollok Beach; mains R60-120; ⊙8am-10pm; ☎) This roadhouse-cum-beach bar is an excellent spot for a sundowner, with a breezy interior and beachfront decks. Dishes include gourmet pizzas, burgers, seafood (try the Cajun calamari) and, for the health conscious, bunless burgers and healthy breakfasts. It also has a takeaway outlet and there's live music on weekends.

Bocadillos on Sixth   INTERNATIONAL $$

(☑ 041-581 1523; www.bocadillos.co.za; 42 Sixth Ave, Walmer; mains R50-120; ⊙7.30am-9pm Mon-Sat, 9am-2pm Sun; ☎) This slick modern place does a brisk business with locals – always a sign that you've found a good bargain. It speedily serves tasty wraps, thin-crust pizzas, crunchy salads, melt-in-the-mouth tarts – make a beeline for the divine salted caramel tart – and grilled meat. Excellent cocktails, too.

Vovo Telo Bakery & Café   CAFE $$

(☑ 011-315 3000; www.vovotelo.co.za; cnr Raleigh & Irvine Sts, Richmond Hill; mains R70-110; ⊙7.15am-3.15pm Mon-Fri, to 2.30pm Sat; ☎) The original branch of a nationwide chain, Vovo Telo kicked off the regeneration of Richmond Hill. In a characterful old house with a wrap-around veranda, locals catch up over thin-crust pizza made with ciabatta dough, gourmet sandwiches, pastries and healthy salads, and numerous breakfast choices.

● Drinking & Nightlife

Nightlife in PE is not especially thriving but there are some great places to sip a cocktail or swill a beer. With outside tables, the Richmond Hill and Walmer restaurants are great for a drink. You'll also find several bars with ocean-facing terraces along

Beach Rd. Baakens Valley has an emerging drinking scene, with a few hip venues serving craft beers.

★ For the Love of Wine WINE BAR

(☑ 072-566 2692; www.ftlow.co.za; 1st fl, 20 Stanley St, Richmond Hill; ⊙ noon-9pm Mon-Sat) At this excellent wine bar and boutique, you can sample the output of Stellenbosch and beyond (tastings and wine by the glass start at R36), with craft beer and cheese platters (R95) also offered. If the wrap-around porch feels too inviting to leave, you can order from a few local restaurants to eat here.

Beer Yard BAR

(☑ 041-582 2444; www.facebook.com/BeerYardPE; 1 Cooper St, Richmond Hill; ⊙ noon-11pm Mon-Sat) With a Bedouin tent and small pool in the backyard, this craft beer and cider bar encapsulates Richmond Hill's urban buzz. Handmade burgers and thin-crust pizzas are on the menu, plus beer from the adjoining microbrewery.

Bridge Street Brewery CRAFT BEER

(☑ 041-581 0361; www.bridgestreet.co.za; Bridge St, Baakens Valley; ⊙ 10am-10.30pm) Craft beer lovers rejoice – this convivial pub and restaurant overlooking the Baakens River is like manna from heaven, with a great selection of beers on tap.

Beer Shack BEER HALL

(☑ 041-582 2354; www.facebook.com/BeerShack-PE; 1 Marine Dr, Humewood; ⊙ 11am-1am; 🛜) Low on aesthetics but high on energy, this beer hall is one of the liveliest bars in PE. It has a good range of craft beers and also serves food.

☆ Entertainment

Nelson Mandela Bay Stadium STADIUM

(☑ 041-408 8900; www.nelsonmandelabaystadium.co.za/; 70 Prince Alfred Rd, North End) Built for the 2010 football (soccer) World Cup, this futuristic stadium in the rundown North End area hosts sports matches and concerts. Call or email to arrange a 30-minute stadium tour (available between 11am and 3pm, Monday, Wednesday and Friday).

Port Elizabeth Opera House OPERA, THEATRE

(☑ 041-586 2256; Whites Rd) The oldest theatre in both Africa and the southern hemisphere, the PE Opera House hosts a wide range of performances, including plays, poetry, concerts and comedy.

Athenæum PERFORMING ARTS

(☑ 041-585 1041; www.theathenaeum.co.za; 7 Belmont Tce, Central) This cultural centre in a renovated Victorian building hosts plays, performances and live music including jazz.

St George's Cricket Stadium STADIUM

(☑ 041-585 1646; www.stgeorgespark.co.za; St George's Park) Home of Eastern Province Cricket, it's famous for its band-playing supporters who turn one-day internationals into tub-thumping affairs.

🛍 Shopping

There are craft shops at the **Boardwalk mall** (☑ 041-507 7777; www.suninternational.com/boardwalk; Marine Dr, Summerstrand; ⊙ 7am-11pm). Head to the Kings Beach flea market on Sunday mornings for curios.

Wezandla African Craft Traders ARTS & CRAFTS

(☑ 041-585 1185; www.wezandla.co.za; 37 Parliament St; ⊙ 8.30am-4.45pm Mon-Fri, 9am-12.45pm Sat) This brightly coloured arts and crafts centre has a huge array of items made by South African and Zimbabwean groups, including basketware, jewellery, woodcarvings, masks, fertility dolls, cushion covers, wall hangings, place mats, handbags, T-shirts and paintings. There's also a small coffee shop.

ℹ Information

Nelson Mandela Bay Tourism (☑ 041-585 8884; www.nmbt.co.za; Donkin Reserve; ⊙ 8am-4.30pm Mon-Fri, 9.30am-3.30pm Sat) has an excellent supply of information and maps, and a cafe with city views. There are also branches at the Boardwalk (☑ 041-583 2030; Marine Dr, Summerstrand; ⊙ 8am-7pm) (a good stop for information about the whole province) and the airport (☑ 041-581 0456; Port Elizabeth Airport; ⊙ 7am-7pm).

Wezandla craft shop also dispenses information.

ℹ Getting There & Away

AIR

Port Elizabeth Airport (☑ 041-507 7319; www.airports.co.za; Allister Miller Rd, Walmer) is about 5km from the city centre.

South African Airways (☑ 0861 606 606; www.flysaa.com) and its subsidiaries **Airlink** (☑ 086 160 6606; www.flyairlink.com), **SA Express** (☑ 086 172 9227; www.flyexpress.aero) and **Mango** (☑ 0861 001 234; www.flymango.com), and **FlySafair** (☑ 0871 351 351; www.flysafair.co.za) and **Kulula** (☑ 086 158 5852; www.kulula.com) all fly daily to/from cities including

Cape Town (from R900, 1¼ hours), Durban (from R1100, 1¼ hours) and Jo'burg (from R800, 1¾ hours). A taxi to the centre costs about R130.

BUS

Greyhound, Translux and City to City depart from the Greenacres Shopping Centre, about 4km inland from the city centre. Intercape departs from its office behind the old post office. They all have buses to/from Cape Town (from R450, 12 hours) via the Garden Route, Jo'burg (from R500, 16 hours) via Bloemfontein (from R480, 9½ hours) and Durban (from R520, 14½ hours) via Grahamstown (from R290, two hours) and East London (from R450, 4½ hours).

Baz Bus stops at the hostels in Port Elizabeth en route between Cape Town and Durban. Mzansi Experience also stops in PE en route between Cape Town and Hogsback (and on to Jo'Burg).

CAR

All the big car-rental operators have offices in Port Elizabeth or at the airport.

TRAIN

Shosholoza Meyl runs to/from Jo'burg (20 hours, Wednesday, Friday and Sunday) via Cradock and Bloemfontein. A sleeper in tourist class costs from R500.

❶ Getting Around

Consider taking a taxi to get around the city. Rates are about R10 per kilometre. Uber (www.uber.com) is very popular and works well.

Addo Elephant National Park

The jewel in Eastern Cape's crown is **Addo Elephant National Park** (☏042-233 8600; www.sanparks.org; adult/child R232/116; ⊙7am-7pm), South Africa's third-largest national park, located 70km north of Port Elizabeth and encompassing both the Zuurberg mountains and the Sundays River Valley. It protects the remnants of the huge elephant herds that once roamed the Eastern Cape. When Addo was proclaimed a national park in 1931, there were only 11 elephants left; today there are more than 600 in the park, and you'd be unlucky not to see some. A day or two at Addo is a highlight of any visit to this part of the Eastern Cape, not only for the elephants but for the lions, zebras, black rhinos, Cape buffaloes, spotted hyenas and myriad birds. The park is also one of few which boasts the 'Big Seven', thanks to sightings of great white sharks and southern right whale (in season) off its coastal sections.

🏃 Activities

Book in advance for wildlife drives, horse riding and other activities, especially during the high season (October to March). Also bear in mind that for most SANParks activities and accommodation, you must pay the park's daily conservation fee on top of SANParks' quoted price.

SANParks Guided Wildlife Drives SAFARI
(☑042-233 8657; www.sanparks.org; Park Headquarters; per person R370-505) The park authorities run two-hour guided wildlife drives in large 4WDs with good viewing angles, departing every few hours between sunrise and evening from the park headquarters. Fee does not cover park entry.

Criss Cross Adventures OUTDOORS
(☑083 330 0480; www.crisscrossadventures.co.za; off R335; half-day guided canoe trip R550, Addo safaris half-/full day R1050/1500; ⊙by

---

❶ ADDO ELEPHANT NATIONAL PARK

Why Go Near-guaranteed pachyderm sightings, plus the chance to spot the rest of the Big Five. Good gravel roads and the absence of malaria sweeten the deal.

When to Go Wildlife watching is good year-round, but autumn (around April) and spring (around September) offer mild weather, avoiding the winter chill and stiflingly hot summer. There should also be a few oranges on the trees; the main citrus season is winter. (Peak rainfall periods are February to March and October to November.)

Practicalities The main gate gives access from R342 to the park reception at Addo Rest Camp, about 10km north of the small town of Addo. There is also a southern gate, Matyholweni, located 40km from Addo Rest Camp near Colchester. It is possible to drive in a 2WD between the two.

Budget Tips Winter is low season; between May and June the park offers discounts on accommodation.

reservation) When in flood, the Sundays River is the fastest flowing river in South Africa, but at other times it's perfect for a guided canoe trip. Tunnels of river grass give way to wider vistas, and kingfishers and spotted eagle owls nest in the riverbanks. Also offers Addo safaris, mountain biking, sandboarding and hiking tours. Prices include park fees.

Adrenalin Addo ADVENTURE SPORTS
(☑ 078 911 1619; www.adrenalinaddo.co.za; off R336, Addo; zipline/giant swing/canoe from R300/150/100; ☺ by reservation) The aptly named outfit claims to offer the highest, longest (500m) and fastest zipline in Africa. Gliding over the Sundays River Valley is a memorable experience. Not enough for you? Try the giant swing. For something less heart-pumping, canoes can be hired for a paddle down the Sundays River.

Self-Drive Safaris

During summer it's best to arrive at the park by mid-morning and stake out one of the waterholes, where the elephants tend to gather during the heat of the day. In winter, early mornings are the best time to see animals.

The elephants of Addo were once addicted to – and even fought violently over – the oranges and grapefruits fed to them by the park's first rangers to encourage them to stay within the park's boundaries. A fruit ban has been in place since the late 1970s; however, as the old adage goes, 'elephants never forget' and the smell alone could provoke an old-timer. And, of course, do not get out of your car except at designated climb-out points.

As at most parks in Southern Africa, it's not compulsory to hire a guide to explore Addo in your own vehicle. You can just turn up, pay the entrance fee and try your luck

PRIVATE EASTERN CAPE WILDLIFE RESERVES

With over a 10,000 sq km of malaria-free wildlife watching, the Eastern Cape's private reserves are a major attraction. Along with Addo Elephant National Park, a wildlife drive on one of these properties, possibly accompanied by a night in the bush, makes an exciting and memorable finale for people travelling along the Garden Route from Cape Town. There's a significant cluster of reserves between Addo and Grahamstown, including Pumba, Kwantu and Lalibela, as well as Schotia, Shamwari and Amakhala, and north of Kenton-on-Sea (Sibuya and Kariega). Most of the reserves are dedicated to restocking large tracts of reclaimed land with animals that were common in the region before the advent of farmers and big-game hunters.

Many reserves offer a range of accommodation, varying in terms of comforts and price, from over-the-top honeymoon-level luxury at the private lodges to more modest tent camps. Rates are generally all inclusive and significant winter discounts are offered between May and September.

A great way to experience a little of the reserves' magic is on a guided day safari. Most have the Big Five, and can be reached by travelling along the N2 between Addo and Grahamstown or the R343 north of Kenton-on-Sea.

Schotia Game Reserve (☑ 042-235 1436; www.schotiasafaris.co.za; safari from R1500, accommodation packages from R2500; ☺ by reservation) is the smallest (and busiest) private reserve in the Addo area, and it's contiguous with Addo (accessed from the N10 south of Paterson). Aiming to evoke the bush before humans arrived, Schotia was the first local reserve to introduce lions that hunt for themselves; their numbers have since been reduced from 18 to three, to give their prey a fighting chance. Its full-day Addo–Schotia tour (R2500 including lunch, dinner and return transfer from Port Elizabeth) is a good way to see the area; the late-afternoon Schotia tour (R1500) includes a bonfire and dinner in the *lapa* (outdoor entertainment area). Tour operators and accommodation around Addo also offer Schotia excursions. The reserve has various lodges and tented camps, and offers packages including accommodation and several wildlife drives (one/two nights from R2500/5000).

Shamwari Game Reserve (☑ Port Elizabeth 041-509 3000; www.shamwari.com; d all-inclusive from R16,000; ☺ by reservation), roughly 40km east of Addo, is one of the most exclusive, luxurious and internationally renowned reserves. Accommodation here ranges from palatial bush tents to an Edwardian manor house. Activities include wildlife drives, spotting elephants between the trees. For novice wildlife watchers, hiring a hop-on SANParks guide (R210 plus park entry fee; available 8am to 5pm) to ride along can be a helpful way of picking up a few tips for spotting animals.

Horse Trails

Morning and afternoon rides are offered by SANParks in the park's Nyathi section (two hours, R540). For mountainous scenery but not wildlife, rides are also offered in the Zuurberg section: there are one- (R240), three- (R330) and five-hour (R350) rides and an overnight trail to Narina Bush Camp. Prices do not include park fees.

🛏 Sleeping

There's a string of convenient sleeping and eating options located just off R335 as it makes its way through the small town of Addo. There are also good options around Kirkwood and Sunland on R336 and in Colchester, less than 5km from Matyholweni gate. Park accommodation can get booked up at busy periods, so, if possible, reserve in advance.

Orange Elephant Backpackers   HOSTEL $
(☑ 042-233 0023; www.addobackpackers.com; off R335; dm R150, d R500, with shared bathroom R450, safari tent R350; P 🛜) Slightly ramshackle but reasonably clean, the Orange Elephant is a good budget base for Addo, offering a shuttle from Port Elizabeth (R250 return) and tours of the park (half-/full day R650/1200). Accommodation ranges from rooms in the main house to the eight-bed dorm in a rondavel, with a rustic yet salubrious ablution block. There's also a safari tent. Breakfast costs R45 and the adjoining Thirsty Herd pub does pizzas and a house ale.

field-guide courses, a rhino awareness centre, and a big-cat sanctuary and wildlife rehabilitation centre with conservation volunteering opportunities.

Amakhala Game Reserve (☑ 041-502 9400; www.amakhala.co.za; half-day safari from R950, s/d all-inclusive from R3900/6000; ☺ by reservation) is roughly 70km from PE and well worth a stay: it's beautiful, tranquil and easily accessible, and it supports a large diversity of fauna, including four lions, six cheetahs, a few rhinos, giraffes, buffaloes, elephants, zebras and plenty of antelope species. The landscape is another highlight, with 75 sq km of rolling hills, bushveld and savannah. There are 11 different accommodation options, ranging from three-star venues to five-star lodges, all in scenic surrounds. Amakhala was created by a group of local landowners, descendants of the 1820 Settlers, who combined their properties. Amakhala also offers conservation activities and volunteering opportunities.

Pumba Private Game Reserve (☑ 041-502 3050; www.pumbagamereserve.co.za; half-day safari R1200, d all-inclusive from R11,000; ☺ by reservation) is a fantastic, luxurious and exclusive reserve, and is home to the Big Five, as well as a pride of white lions (a rarity in Africa, and you're guaranteed to see them), hippos, cheetahs, giraffes, antelopes and about 300 bird species. Accommodation is in two dreamy lodges, one of which overlooks a small lake. Activities include wildlife drives, guided bush walks, fishing, archery and spa treatments.

Kariega Game Reserve (☑ 046-636 7904; www.kariega.co.za; s/d all-inclusive from R6000/7900; ☺ by reservation) is an upmarket (but not luxurious) choice. This 100-sq-km reserve 14km north of Kenton-on-Sea offers a chance to see the Big Five (although leopards are very elusive) as well a large variety of fauna, flora and birdlife. The stunning landscape spans five different ecosystems and incorporates the picturesque Kariega and Bushman's Rivers (hippos!). Guest can enjoy wildlife drives, guided bush walks and river cruises. There are five different lodges scattered around the reserve.

Sibuya Game Reserve (☑ 046-648 1040; www.sibuya.co.za; Kenton-on-Sea; half-/full day R1250/1800, d all-inclusive R9020; ☺ by reservation), a few kilometres north of Kenton-on-Sea, is a wonderfully scenic place to see a variety of wildlife, including a few lions, white rhinos, elephants, buffaloes, giraffes and hippos. And with nearly 400 species of birds, it's a fantastic destination for birders. This reserve is unique in that it's only accessible by a 45-minute boat transfer from the main reception in Kenton-on-Sea. Accommodation consists of three attractive lodges. Day trips include a boat cruise, two wildlife drives and lunch.

JFJACOBSZ / SHUTTERSTOCK ©

WILDESTANIMAL / SHUTTERSTOCK ©

RICHARD DU TOIT / GETTY IMAGES ©

1. Storms River Mouth (p180)
Kayak amid stunning rock formations in the Tsitsikamma section of the Garden Route National Park.

2. Addo Elephant National Park (p197)
A wildlife drive in this park, boasting more than 600 elephants, almost guarantees a sighting.

3. Port St Johns (p222)
Dolphin watching is at its finest in June and July, during the sardine run (p220).

4. Surfing at Jeffrey's Bay (p185)
Catch a wave at 'J-Bay', one of the world's top surfing destinations.

DAVID STEELE / SHUTTERSTOCK ©

Addo Rest Camp
LODGE $$

(☑Pretoria 012-428 9111; www.sanparks.org; camping 1-2 people R330, safari tents R875, cabins/chalets/cottages/houses R1010/1200/1630/4610; P⊠⛨) Addo's main rest camp, at the park headquarters, has myriad cottages, chalets, safari tents and rondavels (round huts with a conical roofs), some overlooking the floodlit waterhole where elephants slake their thirst. Options range from camping, to two-person safari tents with shared bathroom, to luxurious houses with two en-suite bedrooms and air-conditioning.

Chrislin African Lodge
LODGE $$

(☑042-233 0022; www.chrislin.co.za; off R335; s R940-1400, d R1300-1500, all incl breakfast; P✳⛨) Chrislin is set among lawns, trees and aloes on a former citrus farm. The lodge offers thatched huts with stylish African decor and heat-banishing walls of cow dung and mud, and luxurious units with air-con. Activities including open-vehicle Addo safaris are offered, as are delicious three-course dinners (R250). It's a refreshingly cool and rustic spot after a day spotting elephants.

Rosedale Organic Farm B&B
FARMSTAY $$

(☑042-233 0404; www.rosedalebnb.co.za; off R335; s/d incl breakfast R700/1000; P⛨) On an organic citrus farm, Rosedale offers eight simple yet neat cottages with stoeps (porches) overlooking the freshwater swimming pool and tropical trees. Organic breakfasts feature home-baked bread, free-range eggs and of course fresh-from-the-branch orange juice. Owner Keith will show you round the farm. A safe choice.

Addo African Home
GUESTHOUSE $$

(☑042-233 1244; www.addoafricanhome.co.za; off R335; safari tent R600, s R850-1050, d R850-1350, all incl breakfast; P⛨) This handsome guesthouse is set around a manicured lawn down a tree-shaded country lane. Rooms in the main building have solid wood floors and artistic flourishes, and there are en-suite rondavels in the garden. Also available are two attractive safari tents. The on-site restaurant is renowned for its organic meals, with an emphasis on fresh, local produce.

German and French are spoken.

★ Camp Figtree
RESORT $$$

(☑082 611 3603; www.campfigtree.co.za; s/d incl breakfast from R2400/3200; P@⛨) ✿ Offering colonial-chic luxury, this property takes full advantage of breathtaking panoramic views from its perch in the Zuurberg Mountains above Addo. Tastefully appointed cottages with elephantine bathrooms and private porches share the grounds with a pool, library, and restaurant that serves afternoon tea. Figtree is around 11km from the R335 turn-off towards the Zuurberg Pass.

★ Elephant House
LODGE $$$

(☑042-233 2462; www.elephanthouse.co.za; R335; d from R2100, cottage d from R2000, all incl breakfast; P⛨) For panache and design flair, Elephant House is a great place to indulge. The main thatched-roof building shelters six cosy rooms filled with rugs and antique furniture, and there are plenty of chill-out spaces. Across the road, six 'stable cottages' (www.stablecottages.co.za) open onto a manicured lawn. And did we mention the three swimming pools?

There's a set menu for dinner.

✕ Eating

Addo Rest Camp has a shady picnic site overlooking the waterhole, as well as a restaurant and a shop selling basic supplies. There are also a couple of eating options near the town of Addo.

River Front Estate Restaurant
SOUTH AFRICAN $$

(☑042-233 0000; www.facebook.com/rfrestaurant; off R335, Addo; mains R70-120; ⊙9am-9pm Wed-Mon; ⛨) This friendly, offbeat barn of a place overlooking the Sundays River serves up meat dishes such as kudu, impala or ostrich fillet as well as springbok carpaccio. Don't fancy meat? Opt for the wholesome vegeterian plate, with vegetables from the permaculture kitchen garden. It also features five beautifully furnished chalets (doubles R800).

Lenmore
INTERNATIONAL $$

(☑042-233 0505; www.lenmore-addo.com; R335, Addo; mains R95-140; ⊙7am-8.30pm; ⛨) A wide selection of salads, steaks, chicken dishes, seafood and pasta make up the menu here, but the best bet is to opt for a wood-fired pizza. The supermarket and bakery make for a good place to stock up on picnic fodder. It also has five comfortable chalets dotted in the garden (singles/doubles including breakfast R600/1200).

❶ Information

The 'town' of Addo is nothing more than a few shops, a petrol station and a bank with ATMs sharing a dusty car park on Rte 335. Addo Rest Camp also has a shop and petrol station.

ℹ️ Getting There & Around

Private shuttles operate between Port Elizabeth and Addo – ask at PE's tourist information office for recommended operators. Countless companies offer Addo day trips and overnight tours, but the best way to explore is in a hire car.

The park's sealed and gravel roads are mostly passable in a 2WD vehicle, though some may be out of action after heavy rain – if in doubt, call the park headquarters.

Grahamstown

📞 046 / POP 50,217

The historic capital of Settler Country, Grahamstown is also one of South Africa's liveliest university towns, and hosts several annual festivals, including one of the world's largest arts festivals. With its dreaming spires, weathered edifices and pastel shopfronts, the town centre has some fine examples of Georgian, Victorian and early Edwardian architecture.

Yet its genteel conservatism and English prettiness belie a bloody history; the Cape Frontier Wars, fought locally between European settlers and the Xhosa, continued for most of the 19th century. Once rulers of the region, the Xhosa were defeated by British and Boer forces after a fierce struggle.

Socially, while the university students dominate the town, packing out pubs and bars, artists and alternative spirits are settling here and, as the population ages, a more sophisticated side is developing.

👁️ Sights & Activities

A few guides, including **Otto Ntshebe** (📞082 214 4242; ottours@webmail.co.za; half-day tour R450), offer tours of historic Fingo Village, one of South Africa's oldest townships. It was built on land given to the Mfengu people by the British, in exchange for their support in the Cape Frontier Wars.

Church Square HISTORIC SITE
Grand colonial edifices, university buildings, the 19th-century Anglican cathedral and colourful Victorian and Edwardian shopfronts all overlook this square. Good examples of the latter are the **Grocott's Mail** building, the original home of South Africa's oldest independent newspaper, and the neighbouring **Clicks** pharmacy.

Birch's (High St) has a marvellously old-fashioned 'slider' (a pulley system that sends money and change across the ceiling to and from the central till) and a vacuum pipe system used to send notes between floors. Staff will demonstrate the slider if you ask nicely.

Albany History Museum MUSEUM
(📞046-622 2312; www.am.org.za; Somerset St; adult/child R20/10; ⏰9am-4.30pm Mon-Fri) This great museum details the history and art of the peoples of the Eastern Cape, including the Xhosa and 1820 Settlers, with some beautiful beadwork and embroidery on display.

Albany Natural Science Museum MUSEUM
(📞046-622 2312; www.am.org.za; Somerset St; adult/child R20/10; ⏰9am-4.30pm Mon-Fri) Covers a mishmash of subjects, from early human history to astronomy. The collection includes some impressive taxidermy and skeletons.

**International Library
of African Music** MUSEUM
(ILAM; 📞046-603 8557; www.ru.ac.za/ilam; Prince Alfred St, Rhodes University; ⏰8am-12.45pm & 2-5pm Mon-Fri) FREE There are 200 or so instruments to examine here – you can listen to field recordings and try to emulate what you've heard on *nyanga* (pan) pipes from Mozambique, a *kora* (stringed instrument) from Southern Africa or a Ugandan *kalimba* (thumb piano). Call ahead for an appointment.

**1820 Settlers National
Monument** MONUMENT
(www.foundation.org.za; Gunfire Hill; ⏰8am-4.30pm Mon-Thu, to 4pm Fri) FREE This monument to the hardy British settlers and their contributions to South Africa has stupendous views of the surrounding countryside, and contains artworks and a large theatre.

**National English
Literary Museum** MUSEUM
(📞046-622 7042; www.facebook.com/NationalEnglishLiteraryMuseum; 25 Worcester St; ⏰9am-1pm & 2-4.30pm Mon-Fri) FREE Housed in a snazzy building on the outskirts of town, this museum contains South African manuscripts, first editions and works dating back to 1797, with all the famous South African writers represented. It also houses exhibitions on South African literature.

🎉 Festivals & Events

National Arts Festival ART
(📞046-603 1103; www.nationalartsfestival.co.za; ⏰Jul) Africa's largest arts festival runs for 10 days at the beginning of July.

Grahamstown

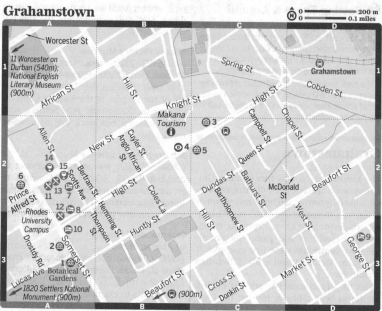

Grahamstown

Sights

Sleeping

Eating

Drinking & Nightlife

Remember two things: book ahead, as accommodation at this time can be booked out a year in advance; and bring something warm, as nights can be freezing. The associated Fringe and Fingo Festivals, the latter showcasing art, music and theatre from the townships, offer hundreds more performances.

Sleeping

Blue Skies Backpackers HOSTEL $
(☏084 278 3193; www.blueskiesbackpackers.co.za; Grahamstown Airfield; dm/d with shared bathroom R150/400; P) Despite its odd location on the edge of the airfield, about 4km north of the centre, this low-key venture run by friendly Sean is a good bet, with a couple of clean dorms and a handful of very simple yet perfectly acceptable cabins. No meals are provided but there's a communal kitchen. No wi-fi.

As it's isolated, you'll definitely need your own wheels if you plan to explore the area.

Kwam eMakana HOMESTAY $
(☏072 448 0520; ribogora@gmail.com; s/d incl breakfast from R400/600) Over 20 homestays are offered by Xhosa women in Grahamstown's townships. Meals are available.

7 Guesthouse
GUESTHOUSE **$$**

(📞083 750 9980; www.7guesthouse.com; 7 Scotts Ave; s/d R650/1100; 🅿🛜🕸) A fine choice in the centre. The three adjoining rooms in a revamped old house are on the small side (try for room 2, which is marginally larger) but well appointed with a modernish feel. No meals are provided, but you're just steps from the town's best restaurants. Just one quibble: there are only two parking spaces.

High Corner
GUESTHOUSE **$$**

(📞046-622 8284; www.highcorner.co.za; 122 High St; s/d incl breakfast R850/1240, s/d cottage R680/1040; 🅿🌸🛜🕸) Appropriately, an account of this gracious house's 200-year history is the first thing you see you see upon entering. Rooms are split between the main building, with its antique furniture and elegant, high-ceilinged lounge and breakfast room, and modern self-catering cottages at the back. It's within easy walking distance from numerous restaurants and bars.

Cock House
GUESTHOUSE **$$**

(📞046-636 1287; www.cockhouse.co.za; 10 Market St; s/d incl breakfast R720/1220; 🅿🌸🛜) Named after William Cock, an enterprising 1820 Settler, and once home to author André Brink, this historic residence with bags of character has nine cosy double rooms in the main house and converted stables. There are also two-bedroom self-catering apartments. Norden's Restaurant, on site, is a great place for a fine meal overlooked by paintings of 19th-century South Africa.

Browns @ 137 High Street Guesthouse
GUESTHOUSE **$$**

(📞046-622 3242; www.grahamstownaccom.co.za; 137 High St; s/d incl breakfast R780/1150; 🅿🛜) This welcoming abode with a central location has seven cramped but comfortable rooms in a 200-year-old house built by Piet Retief, with thick walls and honey-coloured yellow-wood floors. The inhouse restaurant is recommended.

11 Worcester on Durban
B&B **$$$**

(📞072 505 1621; www.11worcesterondurban.co.za; 11 Worcester St; s/d incl breakfast R875/1500, cottage R1800; 🅿🛜) An attractive, secure property in a residential area, this efficiently run haven of peace is a solid option, with four rooms that are well appointed and clean as a whistle. Our favourite is the Mayfield, which opens onto a flourishing garden. The self-catering cottage, which can sleep six people, is great for families.

🍴 Eating & Drinking

Handmade Coffee – The Bakery Grahamstown
CAFE **$**

(📞046-603 1103; www.facebook.com/thebakerykenton; 38 Somerset St; sandwiches R50; ⊗8am-8pm Mon-Fri, 8.30am-1pm Sat; 🛜) Just thinking about the scents wafting from this place makes us swoon. One step into this cafe and you're hooked forever. Don't miss the small bakery in the courtyard at the back – it serves hard-to-resist goodies, including bagels and muffins.

★Haricot's Deli & Bistro
INTERNATIONAL **$$**

(📞046-622 2150; www.facebook.com/HaricotsBistro; 32 New St; mains R80-130; ⊗11am-4pm & 5-9.30pm Mon-Fri, from 10am Sat; 🛜) Eavesdrop on faculty gossip at Grahamstown's best place to eat, which is simultaneously a relaxed courtyard cafe and refined restaurant. The menu drips with panache, with an inventive mix of local ingredients and Mediterranean flair, resulting in gourmet dishes such as a delectable whisky barbecue burger. Its deli heaves with wholesome goodies including quiches, gluten-free muffins and flourless chocolate cake.

Casa de Loco
MEXICAN **$$**

(📞083 549 1837; www.facebook.com/casadelocorestaurant; 36 New St; mains R55-160; ⊗noon-2pm & 5-9.30pm Tue-Sat; 🛜) Delicious tapas, nachos, tacos and fajitas in Grahamstown? Yes, it's possible. Not your average place to eat, Casa de Loco adds a touch of exoticism to the local restaurant scene, with a riotously colourful dining room as well as a tempting menu featuring Mexican-inspired dishes.

Rustic Route
BAR

(📞046-622 8825; www.facebook.com/therusticroute; cnr Scotts & New Sts; ⊗11am-11pm) This hip, convivial bar and restaurant with an open-air terrace is a great spot to swill a craft beer or two. The crowd ranges from students to well-heeled locals. Also serves good South African specialities.

Rat & Parrot
PUB

(📞046-622 5002; 59 New St; ⊗11am-midnight; 🛜) The centre of the student party scene, the Parrot's downstairs bar is wood panelled and cosy, while the upper floor has big windows and a veranda overlooking the street. It offers popular pizzas, pub grub and, like a few pubs in this area, rugby on the TV.

BATHURST

The small, quaint village of Bathurst offers a surprising mix of rural atmosphere and artistic vibes, and attracts a growing number of visitors. You'll find a few curio shops, galleries and restaurants clustered around the village's only intersection.

About 45km from Grahamstown and 17km from Port Alfred, Bathurst is best visited in your own vehicle, although shared taxis do ply R67 daily (R25 to Port Alfred).

Big Pineapple (☎046-625 0515; off Rte 67; adult/child R25/15; ◷8am-3.30pm) Local farmers own the Big Pineapple, a few kilometres from the village en route to Port Alfred. This fiberglass replica of a pineapple stands 16.7m high – you can climb to the top for great vistas of the surrounding countryside, and learn all about the pineapple industry in South Africa. There's a shop that sells various pineapple food items, including jellies and chutneys, as well as souvenirs.

The Historic Pig & Whistle Inn (☎046-625 0673; www.pigandwhistle.co.za; R67; s/d R400/700, with shared bathroom R300/500; ☏) The charmingly old-world hotel, dating from 1832, offers excellent rooms, some with free-standing bath, honey-coloured parquet flooring and period furniture. The cheaper rooms (with shared bathroom) are brilliant value. The on-site restaurant (mains R70 to R130) does homemade burgers, steaks, pies and a Sunday roast, and the adjoining pub is a great place to meet locals. On-street parking only.

❶ Information

The **tourist office** (☎046-622 3241; www.grahamstown.co.za; 63 High St; ◷8am-4.30pm Mon-Fri; ☏) has booklets and information on self-guided walking tours and various themed historical routes.

❶ Getting There & Away

Greyhound, Translux, Intercape and City to City buses depart from the **Frontier Hotel** (cnr High & Bathurst Sts) and the **Conference Centre** (Grey St) on their daily runs to Cape Town (R490, 14 hours), Port Elizabeth (R290, two hours), Durban (R500, 12 hours) and Jo'burg (R490, 13 hours).

Port Alfred

☑046 / POP 9747

Known as 'the Kowie' for the picturesque canal-like river that flows through its centre, Port Alfred is blessed with stunningly beautiful beaches, with some to the north backed by massive sand dunes. Upscale, contemporary holiday homes line the marina and the hills surrounding town. It's generally a quiet place, except for visiting Grahamstown students. Things get busier during the rowing regatta in late September, and from mid-December to January, when the town bustles with South African holidaymakers.

🏃 Activities

Apart from the pristine beaches, there are some truly awesome surf breaks at the river mouth, including **West Beach** and **East Beach**. Drifting up the Kowie River also makes for a relaxing few hours; riverine euphorbia and private wildlife reserves meet the shore, African fish eagles circle overhead, and fishers dig for mud prawns to use as bait.

Oceana Beach & Wildlife Reserve WILDLIFE WATCHING
(☎083 616 0605, 043-555 0305; www.oceanareserve.com; R72, Rietriver; drive R300, incl 3-course lunch R450; ◷by reservation) This five-star reserve, inhabited by antelope, zebras and giraffes, among other animals, offers a two-hour wildlife drive. Book ahead to join the drive, which starts at 10am. Oceana is located 8km from town on the R72 towards East London.

Outdoor Focus OUTDOORS
(☎061 524 6519; www.outdoorfocus.co.za; Beach Rd; 1hr canoe hire R110, river cruise adult/child R100/50, sandboarding R140, horse riding from R200; ◷8am-5pm) A one-stop shop for activities, Outdoor Focus rents out canoes and organises 90-minute river cruises. Other activities include sandboarding and horse riding.

Kowie River Cruises BOATING
(☎083 359 3231, 073 162 1611; www.kowierivercruises.co.za; Ski Boat Club Jetty; adult/child R100/60) This operator offers two-hour cruises in the *Lady Biscay,* an enclosed 13m-long barge, up the Kowie River. Bring a picnic.

Three Sisters Horse Trails   HORSE RIDING

(☑ 082 645 6345; www.threesistershorsetrails.co.za; R72; per hour R400; ⊙ by reservation) Offers rides taking in beach and forest, and overnight trips along a river valley. Beginners and experienced riders are welcome. Located 15km from town on the R72 towards East London.

Kowie Canoe Trail   CANOEING

(☑ 046-624 2230; www.kowiecanoetrail.co.za; 64 Albany Rd; per person R250; ⊙ by reservation) The Kowie Canoe Trail is a fairly easy 21km canoe trip upriver from Port Alfred, with an overnight stay in a hut at Horseshoe Bend in the Watersmeeting Nature Reserve. Mattresses, water and wood are provided, but you'll need your own food and bedding. Your bags can be transported for an extra fee.

🛏 Sleeping

Spinning Reel   CHALET $

(☑ 046-624 4281; www.spinningreel.co.za; Freshwater Rd; cottages/chalets/d from R500/700/750; P🛜🖶) Bargain! A great bet if funds are short, this unpretentious venture about 4km west of the centre has simple self-catering beach cottages and Vermont-style pine chalets surrounded by indigenous dune forest, plus two rooms with sensational sea views in the main house. There's direct beach access. Breakfast is extra.

Wanderlust Adventures   HOSTEL $

(☑ 071 410 3994, 046-624 1659; www.wanderlustadventures.co.za; 11 Stocks Ave; dm/d R200/600, d with shared bathroom R400-480; P🛜) Finally, Port Alfred has produced a great backpackers with plenty of atmosphere. Opened in late 2016, this establishment efficiently run by a friendly couple from Jo'burg features four- to 10-bed dorms and a few inviting private rooms, all with good bedding, as well as a pleasing communal area and kitchen. Meals are available on request.

★ Lookout   GUESTHOUSE $$

(☑ 046-624 4564; www.thelookout.co.za; 24 Park Rd; s R540-600, d R910-1200; P🛜❄) Perched on a hill, this contemporary whitewashed home has five units with kitchenettes and wonderful views. All are in top nick and have individual entrances. Breakfast costs R65. A great find, although you're nowhere near the beach.

Panorama   B&B $$

(☑ 046-624 5853; www.portalfredpanorama.com; 15 Wesley Hill; s/d incl breakfast R500/800; P✳🛜) Dutch–South African couple Rob and Marianne are gracious hosts at this well-priced hilltop guesthouse with winning views. The three rooms are spick and span and open onto a lovely garden with an alluring pool. Rob, a pilot and speedboat owner, is full of suggestions for local activities.

Links Coastal Inn   INN $$

(☑ 046-624 4533; www.thelinks.co.za; 14 Wesley Hill; s/d incl breakfast R675/875, cottages R750/950; P🛜) A decorative African theme pervades this friendly inn's rooms and self-catering garden cottages that have been refurbished and modernised. The bar-restaurant (mains R60 to R150) has a splendid deck for sundowners with a river view, and serves South African specialities such as kudu and ostrich steaks as well as springbok carpaccio.

Medolino Caravan Park   CAMPGROUND $$

(☑ 046-624 1651; www.medolinocaravanpark.co.za; 28 Hards St; camping/chalet R130/950; 🛜❄) This highly recommended tranquil, shaded park has excellent two-bedroom chalets (sleeping four) as well as fully grassed areas for campers and well-maintained ablution blocks.

★ Royal St Andrew   LUXURY HOTEL $$$

(☑ 046-604 5400; www.royalstandrewshotel.co.za; 19 St Andrews Rd; d incl breakfast R1850-2500; P✳🛜❄) Directly across from the golf club and within walking distance of the beach,

EASTERN CAPE PORT ALFRED

WORTH A TRIP

SHIPWRECK HIKING & CANOE TRAIL

As graveyard for many errant ships, the coast between the Great Fish River and East London is deservedly known as the Shipwreck Coast. The 67km, six-day **Shipwreck Hiking & Canoe Trail** (☑ 082 391 0647; www.shipwreckhiking.co.za; per person from R1000) leads from Port Alfred to the Great Fish River Mouth and includes canoeing. You are rewarded with wild, unspoiled sections of surf beach, rich coastal vegetation and beautiful estuaries. Accommodation is in huts.

The slackpacking option, with more comfortable lodgings, costs from R1900. A four-night, five-day trip excluding canoeing, and an overnight canoe trail on the Kleinemonde West River, are other options.

Port Alfred

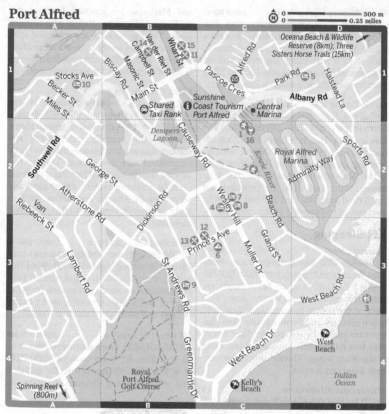

the creatively designed Royal St Andrew is Port Alfred's most prestigious establishment, with 10 individually decorated rooms in the Heritage section and 50 luxury units in the modern wing. Amenities include a high-class restaurant, a gastropub (The Highlander) – both open to nonguests – a pool and a spa.

**Oceana Beach
& Wildlife Reserve**　BOUTIQUE HOTEL **$$$**
(☑083 616 0605, 043-555 0305; www.oceana reserve.com; R72, Rietriver; d incl breakfast from R6000; ⓟ❊☎⛱) No, you're not hallucinating, the view is real. Poised on a greenery-shrouded hillside, the four tastefully appointed Ocean Suites overlook the beach – full frame. The Lodge Suites are a bit less impressive but equally comfortable. The three-bedroom Private House is ideal for a group of friends or families. There's direct beach access. It's 8km from town on R72 towards East London.

Fine dining is available at the on-site restaurant. There's also a lovely wildlife reserve (p206).

Richmond House Cottages　COTTAGE **$$$**
(☑046-624 8543; www.richmondhousecottages. com; 19 Wesley Hill; cottage 2/4 people R1880/ 3600; ⓟ☎) Three luxury self-catering cottages among lawns and coral trees on the site of a historic homestead atop Wesley Hill. Offers seclusion, privacy and tranquillity in the town centre.

🍴 Eating & Drinking

C'est La Vie　DELI **$**
(☑046-624 1225; www.facebook.com/cestlavie portalfred; 18 Prince's Ave; mains R50-80; ⏱8.30am-4pm Mon-Fri, to 2pm Sat; ☎) Fill up at this great little den before (or after) heading to the beach. Come for excellent breakfasts, gourmet burgers, well-presented salads and changing lunch specials. Oh, and it serves delectable cakes and cheese platters.

Port Alfred

★ **Decadent**   CAFE $$
(📞046-624 8282; 20 Prince's Ave; mains R65-90; ⊙9am-4pm Mon-Fri, to 2pm Sat; 🕷) Fresh ingredients, great coffee (and tea!), terrific waffles, savoury pancakes and crêpes, and top-notch smoothies make for a winning combination at this attractive venture in a suburban home.

Café Reset   CAFE $$
(📞072 276 5500; www.facebook.com/cafe resetportalfred; 10 Wharf St; mains R60-150; ⊙8.30am-3.30pm Mon-Sat; 🕷) Occupying one of Port Alfred's historic buildings, Café Reset offers a range of light meals as well as daily specials and great coffee. It's also well known for its quality house wines and cocktails. The courtyard garden is a great place to relax.

Graze by the River   HEALTH FOOD $$
(📞046-624 8095; www.facebook.com/graze bytheriverPA; 38 Van der Riet St; mains R85-160; ⊙9am-3pm Mon, Tue & Thu-Sat, 9.30am-4pm Sun; 🕷) 🌿 This eccentric spot at the back of a curio shop serves slow food, organic veg and ethically produced meat, fish and dairy products. They also roast coffee beans and smoke meat and fish. Daily specials include line-caught cob, fresh Transkei mussels and 30-day matured rump steaks, best enjoyed in the private garden at the back.

The Wharf Street Brew Pub   SOUTH AFRICAN $$
(📞046-624 4947; 18 Wharf St; mains R70-145; ⊙noon-9.30pm Tue-Sat, to 2.30pm Sun; 🕷) Try beers from the neighbouring Little Brewery on the River in this 19th-century building on the old wharf, with a handsome dining room of exposed stone and brick, wood floors and poster-sized photos.

The menu features salads, fresh line fish, steaks, crumbed calamari, prawn curry, schnitzel, prego rolls and delectable pub grub.

Tash's Craft Bar   CRAFT BEER
(📞076 707 0963; www.facebook.com/tashscraft-bar; Ski Club Jetty, Harbour; ⊙8.30am-11.30pm) A lively bar overlooking the harbour. It also serves meals.

ℹ Information

Sunshine Coast Tourism Port Alfred
(📞046-624 1235; www.sunshinecoasttour-ism.co.za; Causeway Rd; ⊙8am-4.30pm Mon-Fri, 8.30am-1pm Sat) Brochures and maps, plus information about accommodation and activities including boat cruises and fishing charters.

ℹ Getting There & Away

Baz Bus passes through four days a week between Port Elizabeth (R295, two hours) and Durban (R1970, 13 hours). **Let's Go Tours** (📞083 644 6060, 046-624 2358; www. facebook.com/LetsGoToursAndShuttleService) runs a daily shuttle between Port Elizabeth and Port Alfred (R150).

From the **shared taxi rank** (Biscay Rd) outside the Heritage Mall, there are daily services to Port Elizabeth (R105), Grahamstown (R50) via Bathurst (R25), and East London (R105).

AMATHOLE

Running inland from East London, the Amathole region (pronounced 'ama-*tawl*-eh', from the Xhosa for 'calves') includes the eponymous mountain range, home to the enchanting, quirky village of Hogsback, and some wild and little-visited nature reserves. A good part of this area was the apartheid-era Xhosa homeland of Ciskei. If meeting the Xhosa people against a mountain backdrop sounds appealing, a few backpacker hostels offer cultural experiences on a par with the Wild Coast.

East London

☑ 043 / POP 267,007

While the centre of East London may not be much to look at – it's mostly industrial and fairly drab – the city's bay-front location, which curves round to huge sand hills, is eminently pleasurable, and the eastern suburbs are well worth a gander, if only for the pristine beaches and neat gardens. With its airport and location at the meeting of the Sunshine and Wild coasts, East London is also a convenient transport hub.

◉ Sights & Activities

East London Museum   MUSEUM
(☑ 043-743 0686; www.facebook.com/eastlondonmuseum; 319 Oxford St; adult/child R20/10; ⊙ 9am-4.30pm Mon-Thu, to 4pm Fri) Given the Eastern Cape's rich past, this museum is worth a visit, with an excellent natural-history collection, a great section dedicated to Xhosa culture and exhibits on subjects from trace-fossil human footprints to maritime history.

Imonti Tours   CULTURAL
(☑ 083 487 8975; www.imontitours.co.za; Mdantsane half-day tour R350, Xhosa village vista R420, Nelson Mandela tour R850, cultural tour R300; ⊙ by reservation) Owner Velile Ndlumbini runs a variety of tours in the area including to Mdantsane, South Africa's largest township after Soweto; a visit to a typical Xhosa village; a cultural tour of East London; and a Nelson Mandela–themed day trip. He also offers airport transfers and shuttles to Chintsa. Prices include hotel pick-up (and drop-off).

🛏 Sleeping

There isn't much reason to overnight in East London when a range of more appealing accommodation is available in nearby Chintsa. If you get stuck here overnight, the best options are the many midrange and top-end B&Bs in the suburbs, only a few kilometres north of Eastern Beach. There is a good selection on and around John Bailie Rd, which runs north from the eastern end of Moore St.

John Bailie Guest Lodge   GUESTHOUSE $$
(☑ 043-735 1058; www.johnbailieguestlodge.co.za; 9 John Bailie Rd, Bunkers Hill; s R600-700, d R700-800, s/d with shared bathroom R400/600; P ⊠) This restful guesthouse near the golf course has unpretentious yet clean carpeted rooms

(two of which have sweeping ocean views), a pool and braai area, all surrounded by a manicured garden. Breakfast and dinner are available on request. For shoestringers, there's a 'backpacker' room with external bathroom.

The Hampton   HOTEL $$
(☑ 043-722 7924; www.thehampton.co.za; 2 Marine Tce; s/d incl breakfast from R990/1200; P ❋ ☎) This renovated 1920s landmark building with a waterfront location and contemporary furnishings is a good choice for the centre. Sea-facing rooms, while slightly more expensive, have panoramic views.

Quarry Lake Inn   HOTEL $$$
(☑ 043-707 5400; www.quarrylakeinn.co.za; Quartzite Dr, off Pearce St; s/d incl breakfast R1420/1985; P ❋ ☎ ⊠) One of East London's best sleeping options, this intimate hotel overlooking a small lake is an oasis of calm and security north of the centre. It offers bright, spotless rooms, a good breakfast, a small pool and friendly staff. Weekend rates are cheaper.

🍴 Eating

The Beach Break   CAFE $
(☑ 083 438 7784; www.facebook.com/nahoonbreak; Beach Rd; mains R60-80; ⊙ 7.30am-4pm; ☎) This little gem just off Nahoon Beach (but without sea views) serves delectable light meals and superb coffee in a wonderfully relaxed environment. Bag a table under the trees and order a pancake, an omelette, a salad, a wrap or a sandwich. Amazing value.

Sanook Cafe   BURGERS $$
(☑ 043-721 3215; www.sanook.co.za; 11 Chamberlain Rd; mains R70-150; ⊙ 9am-10pm Mon-Sat; ☎) It's official – the gourmet-burger and craft-beer craze has reached East London, and Sanook does it particularly well. Burgers are juicy, tasty and come with a range of inventive toppings. Try the trio of sliders with a taster tray of Eastern Cape–brewed beer. Pizza, grills and salads also grace the menu at this vibrant, cheery spot.

Café Neo   MEDITERRANEAN $$
(☑ 043-722 4531; www.facebook.com/CafeNeoEastLondon; 128 Moore St; mains R70-110; ⊙ 8.30am-8pm; ☎) Views from the outdoor balcony of this stylish 1st-floor restaurant and cocktail bar extend from the car park to the ocean. The large menu runs the gamut from wraps and linefish to steaks and decadent desserts.

Grazia Fine Food & Wine   MEDITERRANEAN **$$**
(☑ 043-722 2009; www.graziafinefood.co.za; Upper Esplanade, Aquarium Rd; mains R75-175; ☺ noon-10pm; 🐾) This stylish, centrally located restaurant has large windows with sea views as well as an outdoor deck for dining. The Italian-born owner has helped create a sophisticated menu with a variety of European influences; the menu includes pasta, pizza, salads, meat, seafood and delicious desserts.

ℹ Information

Buffalo City Tourism (☑ 043-736 3019; www.bctourism.co.za; Fleet St; ☺ 9am-5pm Mon-Fri) Has brochures and maps.

ℹ Getting There & Away

AIR
East London Airport (☑ 043-706 0306; www.airports.co.za; R72) is 10km southeast of the centre. SA Express, FlySafair and Kulula fly daily to Jo'burg (from R650, 1½ hours). SA Express and FlySafair also serve Cape Town (from R1200, two hours) and Durban (from R1160, one hour) daily.

BUS
Baz Bus stops in East London en route between Port Elizabeth and Durban.

All the major bus lines serve the central **bus station** (Moore St, Windmill Park), near Eastern Beach.

Greyhound, Translux, Intercape and City to City offer daily services to Mthatha (from R300, three hours), Port Elizabeth (from R450, 4½ hours), Durban (from R420, 9½ hours), Cape Town (from R550, 16 hours) and Jo'burg (from R450, 16 hours).

SHARED TAXI
Shared taxis leave from Oxford St and the surrounding streets. On the corner of Buffalo and College Sts (near East London Zoo) are long-distance **taxis** (Buffalo St) to destinations north of East London, including Mthatha (R135, four hours).

TRAIN
On Wednesdays, Fridays and Sundays, **Shosholoza Meyl** (p618) runs a tourist-class (with sleepers) train both to and from Jo'burg (R490, 20 hours) via Bloemfontein (R310, 13 hours).

Hogsback

☑ 045 / POP 1029

There's something about Hogsback that inspires people. An Edenic little village 1300m up in the beautiful Amathole Mountains above Alice, the village's name is derived from the 'bristles' (known geologically as a 'hogsback') that cover peaks of the surrounding hills.

Artists, poets, alternative therapists and other like-minded folk have helped create an environmentally inclined community here – an easy sensibility to adopt with fabulous views of mountains and forested valleys. The town's climate and history of green-fingered English settlers mean it's blessed with gorgeous (though seasonal) market-garden estates. Expect occasional snowfall and freezing temperatures in winter.

Locals will tell you that JRR Tolkien, who lived in Bloemfontein until he was three, visited Hogsback, sowing the seed of his fantastical novels. That is extremely unlikely, but the area may well have inspired him via his son Christopher, who came here while stationed in South Africa with the British Royal Air Force.

◉ Sights

Ecoshrine   SCULPTURE
(www.ecoshrine.co.za; 22 Summerton Dr; adult/child R30/free; ☺ 9.30am-3.30pm Wed, Fri, Sat & Sun) Well-known mixed-media artist Diana Graham, a passionate environmental advocate, has created a concrete sculpture garden dedicated to the forces of nature. The images, which Graham will explain, cover the origins of the earth, and ecological and scientific themes.

The property has beautiful views (when the haze in the valley has cleared off) and can be reached from the village centre by road or a forest walking trail.

Mirrors Gallery
& Crystal Corner   GALLERY
(Bramble Close; admission by donation; ☺ 10am-5pm) Mirrors has a magical 180-sq-metre garden with a stone circle and labyrinth, a gallery of owner Ken's landscape photography, and a crystal shop.

Prayer Trail   GARDENS
(Main Rd) This meditative path meanders through the garden of St Patrick on the Hill chapel.

Fairy Realm Garden   GARDENS
(☑ 045-962 1098; Main Rd; adult/child R30/15; ☺ 9.30am-4.30pm) A 400m path winds past the garden's ponds, cascading water and over 80 fairy sculptures. It's a great place to relax.

🏃 Activities

There are some great walks, bike rides and drives through the area's indigenous forests and pine plantations. A recommended hike (three to five hours) leaves from behind Away with the Fairies backpackers and passes various waterfalls. Purchase a R10 hiking permit at the backpackers.

Hogsback Adventures ADVENTURE SPORTS
(☑ 045-962 1070; www.hogsbackadventures.co.za; 9 Main Rd; mountain-bike trip R600 per person, bike rental per hour R70, abseiling R320, archery R90; ⊙ 9am-3pm Tue-Sat, 9am-1pm Sun) On the main road, this one-stop activities shop offers an 18km, four-hour guided mountain-bike adventure through the forest, plus bike rental, archery, and abseiling 35m down the Madonna & Child Falls.

Amathole Horse Trails HORSE RIDING
(☑ 082 897 7503; www.terrakhaya.co.za; off Plaatjieskraal Rd; ⊙ by reservation) Shane offers rides at all levels of experience, and practises 'natural horsemanship'. Outings last from 1½ hours (R300) to four days (R3500), with accommodation on the latter in a Xhosa homestay and dairy farm.

✨ Festivals & Events

Spring Festival CULTURAL
(www.hogsbackgardens.blogspot.com; ⊙ late Sep-late Oct) Hogsback's biggest annual event throws open the green-fingered town's lovingly tended gardens and, in early October, prompts a weekend of fire dancing, drum circles, children's events and general merriment.

🛏 Sleeping

Visit www.hogsback.com, www.hogsback.co.za and www.hogsbackinfo.co.za for listings.

Terra-Khaya FARMSTAY $
(☑ 082 8977 503; www.terrakhaya.co.za; off Plaatjieskraal Rd; camping/dm incl breakfast R95/165, d incl breakfast with shared bathroom R385; P ☜) Get way off the grid at this unique and inspiring mountainside farm retreat situated at 1350m. The DIY aesthetic and philosophy of the owner (bareback-riding Shane of Amathole Horse Trails) is suffused throughout: everything is made with wattle, daub and recycled materials; electrical plug points are only found in the lounge; and ablutions consist of donkey-boiler showers and composting toilets.

With its sweeping views, this wonderfully tranquil place is difficult to leave. It's accessed via a steep, rough road, which is normally passable in a 2WD vehicle in dry weather. Wi-fi is available on request.

Away with the Fairies HOSTEL $
(☑ 045-962 1031; www.awaywiththefairies.co.za; Ambleside Close; camping/dm/d/cottage from R110/180/600/1500; P ☜☒) Terrific views abound at this offbeat clifftop backpackers where you can take an al fresco bath in the cliff-side tub. It has four- to eight-bed dorms, a few doubles and 'hobbit' rooms as well as fully-equipped cottages. Activities include Xhosa lessons and hiking. The Wizard's Sleeve Bar, a colourful spot to down a few beers, serves meals including made-to-order pizzas.

★ Edge Mountain Retreat LODGE $$
(☑ 045-962 1159; www.theedge-hogsback.co.za; Perry Bar Lane; s/d incl breakfast R495/900, self-catering cottages R650-1800; P ☜) The tastefully decorated cottages and garden rooms are strung out along a dramatic plateau edge. The cottages, some with sensational valley views, vary in size but all have log fires and a small kitchen. The vibe here is peace and relaxation. It's an unbeatable place for a healthy rest or a romantic weekend. Amazing value.

Laragh-on-Hogsback COTTAGE $$
(☑ 045-962 1187; www.laragh-on-hogsback.co.za; 1 Orchard Lane; d R850-1000; P ☜) Run by affable owners, this place offers three

OFF THE BEATEN TRACK

AMATHOLE TRAIL

The 120km, six-day **Amathole Trail** (per person incl accommodation from R1250) starts at the Maden Dam, 23km north of King William's Town, and ends at the Tyumie River near Hogsback. It ranks as one of South Africa's top mountain walks, but it's pretty tough and in poor condition. Only attempt the walk if you are reasonably experienced and fit, and seek local advice before doing so. About a third of the route crosses dense forest and numerous streams with waterfalls and swimming holes.

Accommodation is in huts and it is possible to walk a shorter section of the trail. Contact **Amatola Trails** (www.amatolatrails.co.za; per person from R1250), who will book the trail on your behalf and can arrange shuttles at either end of the hike.

ELUNDINI BACKPACKERS

About 15km south of Hogsback, located in Elundini village on the gravel road to Seymour, **Elundini Backpackers** (☑ 078 357 3285; www.elundinibackpackers.com; Elundini; camping/ dm R100/165, d/tr/q with shared bathroom R390/550/750; [P] 🛜) offers total immersion in a Xhosa village nestling in the Amathole countryside. Accommodation is in four rondavels with shared rainwater showers and composting toilets, all gazing at the forested hills, and meals are served in the living area.

What really makes this Xhosa-Belgian venture special is the community-run activities, ranging from guided hikes and village tours to bread-making and Xhosa lessons. Pick-ups are offered from Hogsback and Alice (R60); you can also hike here in four hours from Hogsback. You can access Elundini by 2WD car from both Hogsback and Seymour. Wi-fi is available on request.

amply-sized, well-thought-out cottages with separate bedrooms, immaculate en suites and well-equipped kitchens, but what really makes it special are the verdant gardens and sense of privacy.

✖️ Eating & Drinking

★ **Edge Restaurant** INTERNATIONAL $$
(☑ 045-962 1159; www.theedge-hogsback.co.za; Perry Bar Lane; mains R75-175; ☺ 8-10.30am, noon-2.30pm & 6.30-8.30pm; 🛜) The charming garden restaurant at the Edge serves French toast with local berries and Hogsback's best coffee for breakfast, recommended wood-fired pizzas for lunch, and hearty but refined meat dishes for dinner. Throw in homemade bread, fresh, organic local produce, a cosy dining room, and paths leading to the nearby labyrinth and viewpoint. Dinner bookings essential.

The Lighthouse Ranch INTERNATIONAL $$
(☑ 045-962 1101; www.facebook.com/light-houseranch.hogsback; Main Rd; mains R60-140; ☺ 11.30am-9pm Tue-Sun; 🛜) This venerable local haunt, which is set in a large building with outdoor seating, serves up copious pizzas and burgers, crunchy salads and grilled meat dishes in rustic surrounds (think stone floors, beamed ceilings and a fireplace).

The Hog & Hornbill PUB
(☑ 073 600 4644; www.facebook.com/hogand-hornbill; off Main Rd; ☺ 10am-10pm Fri-Wed) This intimate pub off the main street has tap beer aplenty and serves good pub grub.

❶ Information

There's an ATM in the small supermarket, just off the main road, and a petrol station.

The helpful **information centre** (☑ 045-962 1245; www.hogsbackinfo.co.za; Main Rd;

☺ 9am-3pm Mon-Sat, to 1pm Sun) can provide accommodation advice and maps for walks.

❶ Getting There & Away

The way up to Hogsback on R345 (the turnoff is 4km east of Alice) is sealed, but try to arrive in daylight due to mountain bends and occasional itinerant livestock. Coming from Queenstown and the north, take R67 towards Fort Beaufort and turn off in Seymour, following the good gravel road to Elundini and the backpackers there; after 22km, this road meets R345 south of Hogsback. Do not attempt the more direct dirt road to/from Cathcart in a 2WD car.

The easiest way to get to Hogsback without a car is in the shuttle run by Away with the Fairies hostel on Tuesday, Wednesday, Friday and Sunday. It picks up at Buccaneers Lodge in Chintsa (R180, 2½ hours) and East London Airport (R180, two hours). Mzansi Experience also stops in Hogsback en route between Cape Town and Southern Drakensberg.

City to City stops in Alice daily en route between East London (from R150, two hours) and Pretoria via Queenstown, Bloemfontein and Jo'burg.

THE WILD COAST

This shipwreck-strewn coastline rivals any in the country in terms of beauty and wilderness, stretching over 350km from just east of East London to Port Edward. Often referred to as the 'Transkei' (the name of the apartheid-era homeland that once covered most of this area), the Wild Coast region also stretches inland, covering pastoral landscapes where clusters of *rondavels* (round huts with a conical roofs) scatter the rolling hills covered in short grass.

The local Xhosa people have a reputation for friendliness, and you might be invited inside a home. In this land of far-flung river estuaries and backpackers resembling Xhosa settlements, numerous outdoor activities and cultural tours are on offer. In June and July, the Wild Coast is prime territory for the natural phenomenon known as the 'sardine run' (p220), an absolute highlight on the marine calendar which attracts divers and snorkellers from all over the world.

The Wild Coast is the place to forgo transport for a while and make use of the paths that connect the coastal villages. There are a number of trails, some making use of hotels along the way and offering porterage, and some where you can stay with locals. It's likely you'll enjoy yourself more when you're off the road, so pick one of the out-of-the-way backpacker lodges – such as Bulungula, Mdumbi or Wild Lubanzi – and spend several days there.

Tours

Even if guided tours aren't your usual style, a few reputable outfits can help immeasurably with your understanding of the rich and complex culture of the Xhosa and Mpondo peoples who live on the Wild Coast. Contact African Heartland Journeys and the various hostels along the Wild Coast, which can all offer a cultural immersion.

African Heartland Journeys ADVENTURE
(082 269 6421; www.ahj.co.za; Chintsa West; ☺by reservation) A well-regarded tour company. Their intrepid tours venture deep into the Wild Coast's rural corners, encompassing travel by foot, canoe, 4WD and mountain bike, with accommodation options ranging from hotels to villages. They also

have a surf school, and offer two- to 12-week volunteering opportunities through Volunteer Africa 32° South (www.volunteerafrica.co.za). Prices vary – contact the company for a quote.

Wild Coast Holiday Reservations WALKING
(East London 043-743 6181; www.wildcoastholidays.co.za) Organises three multiday hikes along the length of the coast, with accommodation in the area's great resorts and hotels, including the classic six-day, five-night Wild Coast Meander from the Kob Inn resort to Morgan Bay Hotel. Local guides are employed. Accommodation and transfers can also be booked through this outfit.

WESSA Wild Walk WALKING
(Chintsa 043-738 5523; www.wessa.org.za; per person R8500) This seven-day trail, highlighting the rich and fragile coastal environment protected by WESSA (Wildlife and Environment Society of South Africa), runs from Mtentu to Port St Johns twice a year (usually May and October). Minimum six people.

Chintsa

🅙 043 / POP 1803

Fronted by a spectacular white-sand beach with good, swimmable surf, Chintsa comprises two small villages – Chintsa East and Chintsa West, on either side of the Chintsa River Mouth. It's a great place to hang out for a few days (or weeks) on this part of the coast. And despite being less than an hour's drive north of East London, it feels a world away from the big city.

WORTH A TRIP

STRANDLOPER & SUNDOWNER TRAILS

The 60km, four-day **Strandloper Hiking Trail** (043-841 1046, 083 285 4773; www.strandlopertrails.org.za; per person R650) runs from Kei Mouth to Gonubie, just outside East London. It traverses splendid sandy beaches, rocky shores, sea cliffs and coastal grasslands with plenty of birdlife. You're always within sight and sound of the sea. It is fairly easy, but good fitness is required.

Nights are spent in dorms and the Haga-Haga Hotel, and accommodation is included in the trail fee, with a two-night option (R275) also available. Profits are channelled into environmental education for local children.

A slackpacker option for those looking to end their vigorous days of hiking with a little luxury, the five-day, four-night **Sundowner Trail** (083 285 4773, 043-841 1046; www.strandlopertrails.org.za; per person R6500) runs from Trennerys Hotel to Chintsa East. A six-day, five-night option leads from Kob Inn to Morgan Bay. All meals, transfers and accommodation are included.

❶ SAFE TRAVEL ON THE WILD COAST

Access to the coast from the N2 (which connects East London with KwaZulu-Natal via Mthatha) is limited by the rugged terrain, and exploring the area inevitably leads travellers down more than one bone-jarring road. Even tar roads here, such as the road linking Coffee Bay with the N2, should be approached with caution. They can be dangerously potholed, and the potholes may be difficult to see, so it's best to drive slowly unless you want to lose a hubcap – or worse.

Don't drive after dark; remember that many of the roads here don't appear on maps; and expect that signposts will be few and far between. Your GPS might even not be useful as it may indicate shortcuts that are not suitable for a car. It's also important to watch out for animals and people in the middle of the roads.

In general, whether you are travelling by car or public transport, do make advance contact with the accommodation option you are travelling to. Despite their remoteness, the Wild Coast's hotels, lodges, backpackers and resorts do fill up; phoning ahead could save you a long journey back to the N2 in search of alternative accommodation. Even if you have a booking, making advance contact will let your hosts know you are making your way through their section of the Wild Coast.

Many of the gravel roads can often be navigated in a 2WD hire car (preferably with high clearance), provided you are a reasonably confident driver. Tarring and upgrading are also slowly improving the local road network. However, unsealed roads often become impassable after rain. Again, phone ahead or seek local advice about the current state of the roads you plan to tackle.

Allow much longer travel times here than you would in other parts of South Africa, even on the tar roads. This applies to both drivers and travellers taking shared taxis, which only leave when they are full and make multiple stops along the way.

◉ Sights & Activities

Buccaneers Lodge is a one-stop shop for activities, including horse riding (R450) and surf lessons (R265).

Inkwenkwezi
Game Reserve   WILDLIFE RESERVE
(☑043-734 3234; www.inkwenkwezi.com; wildlife drives per person from R800, tented bush camp incl meals & activities per person R2300) The private Inkwenkwezi is well worth a visit (or a stay). It's beautiful, upmarket, well organised and features the Big Five (although the elephants and lions are kept separately) and five biomes. In addition to wildlife drives, the reserve offers guided hiking, canoeing and quad biking – great for outdoor lovers. Bookings essential for all activities. Find it between the Chintsa East and West turnoffs (it's signposted).

⊨ Sleeping

The Chintsa area offers excellent accommodation for all budgets, making it a great alternative to East London.

Areena Riverside Resort   RESORT $
(☑043-734 3055; www.areenaresort.com; Glengariff; camping/r/cottage from R190/510/1250; P � ⇲ ⛱ ⊞) Hugging the tree-shaded shore of the Kwelera River, Areena has self-catering rondavels, thatched cottages, timber chalets, riverside tents and caravan sites – and a 3.5-sq-km wildlife reserve with herbivores. There's a tennis court, a bar-restaurant open Wednesday to Sunday (mains R70 to R120), plus abseiling, ziplining, sea kayaking and river cruises. It's low-key, unpretentious and family-oriented. Located 8.5km south of Chintsa.

Buccaneers Lodge   HOSTEL $$
(☑043-734 3012; www.cintsa.com; Chintsa West; camping/dm/r/suite/cottage from R120/190/470/860/1080; P @ ⇲ ⛱) Offering an accessible taste of the Wild Coast, fabulous 'Buccs' is a sort of all-inclusive holiday resort for backpackers and beach bums. Sleeping options cover the spectrum from comfortable eight- to 12-bed dorms and safari tents to self-catering cottages and gorgeous suites for two with sea-facing decks.

Various activities and tours are offered, while on-site entertainments include free use of canoes and boogie boards, complimentary wine and Sunday breakfast, beach volleyball, yoga and spa treatments. Meals (from R75) are served, family-style, in the charming candlelit dining room and outdoor deck.

The Wild Coast

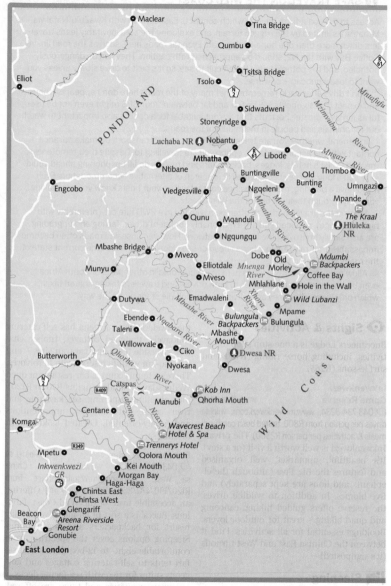

Maclear

Tina Bridge

Qumbu

Elliot

Tsitsa Bridge

Tsolo

Sidwadweni

PONDOLAND

Mntafufu River

Stoneyridge

Luchaba NR · Nobantu

Mthatha

Libode

Mzimvubu River

Ntibane

Buntingville

Old Bunting

Thombo

Mngazi River

Engcobo

Viedgesville

Ngqeleni

Umngazi

Mpande

Qunu

Mqanduli

Mthatha River

The Kraal
Hluleka NR

Ngqungqu

Mbashe Bridge

Mvezo

Dobe

Old Morley

Mdumbi Backpackers

Munyu

Elliotdale

Mnenga River

Coffee Bay

Mveso

Mhlahlane

Hole in the Wall

Dutywa

Emadwaleni

Xhora River

Wild Lubanzi

Mbashe River

Ebende

Nqabara River

Mpame

Taleni

Bulungula Backpackers

Bulungula

Willowvale

Ciko

Mbashe Mouth

Butterworth

Nyokana

Dwesa NR

Qhorha River

Dwesa

Catspas

R409

Wild Coast

Kabonsa

Manubi

Kob Inn
Qhorha Mouth

Centane

Komga

Wavecrest Beach Hotel & Spa

Mpetu

R349

Trennerys Hotel

Qolora Mouth

Inkwenkwezi GR

Kei Mouth

Morgan Bay

Haga-Haga

Chintsa East
Chintsa West

Beacon Bay

Glengariff

Areena Riverside Resort

Gonubie

East London

★ **Prana Lodge**   RESORT $$$

(☏043-704 5100; www.pranalodge.co.za; Cintsa Dr, Chintsa East; s/d incl breakfast from R2400/3500; P✿@🛜🏊) Combining old-world European sumptuousness with the tranquillity of a Southeast Asian resort, this intimate proper-

ty hidden in a dune forest a short walk from the beach is ideal for those seeking top-flight pampering. The eight suites mostly have a private plunge pool and enclosed garden courtyard, and there's an open-air dining area and bar, a library and luxurious spa facilities.

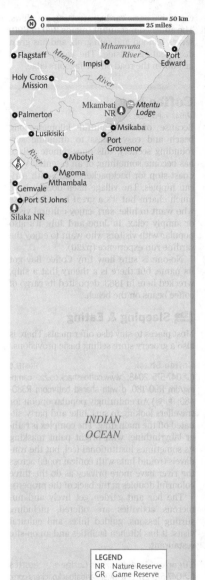

0
0
50 km
25 miles

● Flagstaff
Mthamvuna River
Mtentu River
Impisi ●
Port Edward

Holy Cross ●
Mission

Mkambati
NR ●
Mtentu Lodge

● Palmerton

● Lusikisiki
● Msikaba
Port Grosvenor

● Mbotyi

● Mgoma
Mthambala
Gemvale

● Port St Johns
Silaka NR

INDIAN OCEAN

LEGEND
NR   Nature Reserve
GR   Game Reserve

Cape Dutch and Cape Cod, contains stylishly appointed rooms, a poolside bar-restaurant with glorious beach views, a spa, tennis courts and easy beach access. The more expensive units have great sea views.

Eating

The C Club
SOUTH AFRICAN $$

(☑ 043-738 5226; www.theclub.co.za; Heron Loop, Chintsa East; mains R60-120; ☺ noon-9pm; 🛜) The C Club's well-earned reputation comes from its scrumptious specialities and atmospheric setting, with a large dining room, a charming garden and excellent sea views. Local gourmands rave about the burgers and the flame-grilled steaks. The seafood buffet (R165) served on Sunday is very popular.

Emerald Vale
PUB FOOD $$

(☑ 043-738 5397; www.emeraldvalebrewery.co.za; Chintsa East; tour & tasting R75, mains R70-120; ☺ 11am-6.30pm Wed-Sat, to 4pm Sun, tours by appointment noon-4pm; 🅿🛜👪) Half-hour tours of this brewery in a converted barn on a working farm include tasters of the four ales. The bar-restaurant serves food to complement the beer, including burgers and a few veggie options. There's a playground and milkshake bar for the kids. It's about 10km west of Chintsa West.

❶ Information

Chintsa East has a shop, a liquor store, an ATM and a petrol station.

❶ Getting There & Away

Baz Bus stops at Buccaneers en route between Port Elizabeth and Durban. Mzansi Experience also serves Chintsa between Hogsback and Mthatha. Many accommodation options at this end of the Wild Coast will arrange a transfer from East London with prior notice.

With your own transport, follow the brown signpost to Chintsa from the N2, about 30km north of East London. Chintsa East and West are both about 15km further on.

Morgan Bay & Kei Mouth
POP 612

Morgan Bay is an excellent place for some peace and quiet. It's also a fantastic playground for outdoorsy types, with a startling variety of adventure options available, including surfing, hiking, horse riding, mountain biking and abseiling. A few kilometres

Crawfords Beach Lodge
RESORT $$$

(☑ 043-738 5000; www.crawfordsbeachlodge.co.za; Off Steenbras Dr, Chintsa East; s/d with half board from R1250/2000; 🅿❄🛜🏊) This sprawling complex of attractive thatched white units, wavering somewhere between

north, the sealed road ends in the somewhat ramshackle Kei Mouth, where taking the pontoon ferry (pedestrian/car R1.50/80; ☺7am-5.30pm) across the Great Kei River feels a little like crossing into the Wild Coast proper. Indeed, the river was once the southern border of the Xhosa homeland of Transkei.

Yellowwood Forest Campsite
& Morgan Bay Backpackers HOSTEL $
(☎043-841 1598; www.yellowwoodforest.co.za; Morgan Bay; camping R115, dm R130, d R270-600; P🛜🐾) Yellowwood Forest, about 1km from Morgan Bay beach, is a tranquil riverside camp surrounded by indigenous forest and frequented by louries and hornbills. There a variety of rustic, Hobbit-style lodgings, including a loft room, a cabin, a bush camp, a dorm and a better-equipped (and more expensive) cottage, plus a charming tea garden, craft shop, and wood-fired pizzas on offer.

Morgan Bay Hotel HOTEL $$$
(☎043-841 1062; www.morganbayhotel.com; Beach Rd, Morgan Bay; camping R290, s incl breakfast R950-1390, d incl breakfast R1460-2140; P🛜🏊🐾) This local landmark perched directly over the beachfront provides an excellent level of comfort and service. The sun-filled rooms boast pristine bathrooms, well-sprung mattresses and, in the more

OFF THE BEATEN TRACK

DWESA NATURE RESERVE

One of South Africa's most remote and beautiful reserves, Dwesa Nature Reserve (☎043-705 4400; www.visiteasterncape.co.za; adult/child R30/15; ☺6am-6pm) blends lush forests, winding rivers, open grassland and rugged coastline, with walking trails and wildlife including buffaloes, zebras, antelope, warthogs, and crocodiles in the rivers. Some 290 bird species have been identified, including the rare Narina trogon and mangrove kingfisher. Community-run activities include guided nature walks and boat trips over the Mbashe River.

There is self-catering accommodation (one-/two-bedroom chalets R320/650) and camping (R240) in Dwesa near the beach, accessed via a 47km gravel road from Willowvale. You need a high-clearance vehicle to get here.

expensive ones, cardiac-arresting sea views. The attached restaurant (mains R60 to R90) serves seafood and pub grub, and has great deck seating outside. The campground is just down the road on the lagoon's edge.

Coffee Bay
🌐 047 / POP 258

Because of its beautiful kilometre-long beach and easy access to dramatic surrounding scenery, this once-remote village has become something of an essential Wild Coast stop for backpackers and South African hippies. The village itself doesn't have much charm but it's a great base for those who want to hike, surf, enjoy cultural visits or simply relax. In June and July, it's also popular with visitors who want to enjoy the sardine run experience (p220).

No-one is sure how tiny Coffee Bay got its name, but there is a theory that a ship, wrecked here in 1863, deposited its cargo of coffee beans on the beach.

🛏 Sleeping & Eating

Most places to stay also offer meals. There is also a grocery store selling basic provisions.

Coffee Shack HOSTEL $
(☎047-575 2048; www.coffeeshack.co.za; camping/dm R90/180, d with shared bathroom R380-480; P🛜) An enduringly popular option for travellers looking to surf, hike and party, situated off the main drag. The complex is rather labyrinthine, with bright paint masking its sometimes institutional feel, but the rondavels (round huts with conical roofs) across the river have more privacy as do the three colourful doubles at the back of the property.

The bar and garden get lively and numerous activities are offered, including surfing lessons, guided hikes and cultural visits. It has kitchen facilities and an on-site restaurant.

Sugarloaf Backpackers Lodge HOSTEL $
(☎047-575 2175; www.sugarloafbackpackers.com; dm R160, d R680, with shared bathroom R550, safari tent s/d R280/420; P🛜) On the main drag, Sugarloaf is a relaxed and relatively orderly budget choice, with a full complement of facilities and hang-out areas in leafy grounds atop a river bank. Safari tents stand on decks overlooking the Mnenga River and the beach, which is a short walk away. The on-site restaurant (mains from R50) serves simple meals.

White Clay
CHALET **$$**

(☑083 979 4499; www.whiteclayresort.co.za; camping R150, s/d with half board R850/1700, chalets s/d R350/700; P) Around the headland en route to Hole in the Wall, White Clay boasts an adorable setting on a hillside with stupendous ocean views. It comprises standard rooms and self-catering chalets – all simple but tidy and with sea views. Food here is a definite plus; you'll eat delicious seafood at the on-site restaurant (mains R110 to R180), overlooking a pebble beach.

Ocean View Hotel
HOTEL **$$**

(☑047-575 2005; www.oceanview.co.za; s/d with half board from R900/1500; P🖥🏊) This venerable hotel offers a great mix of old-fashioned charm and modern elements, with generous buffet meals, a lovely thatched beach bar and chalet-style rooms with private patio overlooking the sea or garden. Located at the far end of the main beach from the Coffee Bay melee, it offers activities including guided hikes and drives, kayaking outings and cultural tours.

The hotel is usually full during the sardine run (June and July) – book well ahead. It's off the main drag.

Papazela's
PIZZA **$$**

(☑076 165 9299; pizzas R90-95; ☺4-9pm Tue-Sat) Off the main drag, this popular shack serves wood-fired pizzas with predictably wacky names, eaten with fingers and accompanied by sweeping beach views and cold quarts of beer. Also does takeaway.

❶ Getting There & Away

A sealed road runs to Coffee Bay from the N2 at Viedgesville – beware of children, potholes and stray farm animals. Backpacker shuttles (R90) meet the Baz Bus and the Mzansi Experience bus at the Shell Ultra City garage, 4km south of Mthatha.

Around Coffee Bay

The walks around Coffee Bay are spectacular – one of the best and most popular is to Hole in the Wall, an offshore rock formation featuring a large, photogenic natural arch created by the pounding of the ocean waves. A gravel road also leads there from Coffee Bay (about 9km). The road is passable in a 2WD car as far as Hole in the Wall, after which it disintegrates.

The three-hour walk to Hole in the Wall is doable without a guide (though not alone), but is safer and easier with one, partly because you will get a lift back to Coffee Bay at the end. Coffee Shack charges about R100 per person for the guide and transfer back.

Further south, Wild Lubanzi (p220) can be reached in a day. Overnight guided hikes can also be arranged to Bulungula (two days, one night) and, to the north, Port St Johns (five days, four nights) via Hluleka and Silaka Nature Reserves; prices are typically about R350 per person, per day (including river crossings) plus accommodation and food. Nights on the hikes are generally spent in comfortable community-run hikers' huts and Xhosa rondavels in the villages en route (typically R300 including dinner and breakfast). Book guides through local backpackers or Wild Coast Hikes (p223).

Adventurous sorts can jump into the ocean from the rocks above the Mapuzi Caves, around 7km north of Coffee Bay, and the grass-covered cliffs there are an ideal sundowner spot. Guides will take you there for about R100 per person, including transport back – contact your accommodation. If you go without a guide, find out when high tide is to avoid getting trapped.

🛏 Sleeping

★ Mdumbi Backpackers
HOSTEL **$**

(☑081 407 9273; www.mdumbi.co.za; Mdumbi; camping/dm R90/160, r/safari tent with shared bathroom R360/350; P🖥) 🏆 Marvellous Mdumbi, a 23km drive north of Coffee Bay (the 17km gravel road is normally passable in a 2WD car), is a rural retreat set in rolling hills above a wide white-sand beach. A collection of simply furnished rondavels (round huts with a conical roofs) and safari tents share the grounds with a former chapel and cafe. Excellent meals are provided.

There are lots of activities, including surfing, boat trips, kayaking and hiking, plus numerous opportunities to meet the local Xhosa people in a genuine setting. Volunteers looking to stay longer can also get involved in various community projects undertaken by Mdumbi's affiliated nonprofit organisation, Transcape (www.transcape.org). Book a day ahead for the shuttle here from Coffee Bay (R60).

Bulungula Lodge
HOSTEL **$**

(☑047-577 8900; www.bulungula.com; Bulungula; camping/dm R110/190, d/tent with shared bathroom R500/430; P🖥) 🏆 Bulungula is legendary for its stunning location, community-based activities and ecofriendly ethos. It's 100% owned by the local Xhosa community, which run tours including horse riding, hiking, canoeing, cultural visits and pancakes at sunrise on the beach. Creatively painted, Xhosa-style rondavels serve as no-frills quarters. A few tents are also available.

Beats liven up the shipping container–like reception and lounge, but tranquillity is as close as the bonfire; the overall vibe will make you want to linger indefinitely. Ablution blocks include ecofriendly composting toilets and paraffin-rocket showers. All meals are offered; self-caterers should bring their own supplies because there isn't much available nearby.

Bulungula is around 2½ hours' drive from Coffee Bay, via a gravel road; it's normally doable with a 2WD. If you're driving, visit Bulungula's website, phone or ask in Coffee Bay backpackers for a map. Shuttles run from Mthatha (R120), and should be booked in advance.

Wild Lubanzi HOSTEL $
(📞078 530 8997; www.lubanzi.co.za; Lubanzi; dm/d from R160/450, safari tent R350; 🅿🛜) 🏊
Partly owned by the local community, Wild Lubanzi focuses on sustainable living and sociable evenings at the dinner table in its cosy lounge made of stone and wood. Accommodation includes two safari tents, one 10-bed dorm and four enchanting en-suite rooms fit for a Hobbit. There's an on-site restaurant that serves breakfast, lunch and dinner on request (mains from R70).

The rooftop deck overlooks a wild and woolly stretch of coastline, where surfing, chilling and hiking opportunities abound (Hole in the Wall is 1½ hours away, Bulungula is five hours). If you don't fancy inflicting the bumpy 6km gravel road on your 2WD car, a shuttle is available from the end of the tar road (R20 per person, plus R15 per night for secure parking) or from Mthata (R90).

Mthatha
📞 047 / POP 96,114

Busy, bustling and at times clogged with traffic, Mthatha (formerly Umtata) has some elegant, historic buildings in among the modern blocks, and the not-to-be-missed Nelson Mandela Museum.

The town was founded in 1882, when Europeans settled on the Mthatha River at the request of the Thembu tribe, to act as a buffer against Pondo raiders. During the apartheid era it became the capital of the Transkei, the largest of the black homelands, and it remains a regional centre.

THE SARDINE RUN EXPERIENCE

The sardine run is one of the most spectacular natural phenomena on earth. It usually occurs between mid-June and mid- to late July, when massive schools of sardines migrate from the colder water around the Cape to the warmer waters of KwaZulu-Natal to spawn. They are closely followed by an array of predators, including Cape gannets, huge pods of dolphins, various species of sharks and massive Bryde whales, all eager to feed on these massive shoals, which creates incredible marine action in less than 10m of water. The thrill is unforgettable. Some say it's the marine equivalent of the famous Masai Mara wildebeest migration in East Africa.

A number of reputable operators, including Pro Dive (p191) and Offshore Africa (p222), offer multiday sardine run packages along the Wild Coast. A few popular bases include Chintsa, Morgan Bay and Port St Johns. Divers are taken to the action aboard inflatable boats; the highly skilled crew is in contact with a pilot who flies over the ocean in search of animal activity and gives direction. The boat carefully approaches the area where the action is, and divers are only allowed to slide into the water when its safe – they can then watch the sensational scene from a depth of approximately 5m to 7m. In fact, you don't even need to dive – a mask, snorkel and fins suffice. The activity can last anything from a few minutes to an hour or longer. You are frequently getting on and off the boat, which requires a certain level of fitness, and the water is chilly and the sea usually choppy. The excursion lasts about six to seven hours.

Note that sightings can't be guaranteed. One day might be very quiet while the next day can be extremely busy – it's important to remember that nature is ultimately unpredictable.

Most travellers will pass through or stop here briefly, either en route along the N2 highway or while transferring to a shuttle to Coffee Bay or Port St Johns.

★ **Nelson Mandela Museum** MUSEUM
(☎047-501 9500; www.nelsonmandelamuseum. org.za; Nelson Mandela Dr; ⏱9am-4pm Mon-Fri, to 3pm Sat, to 1pm Sun) `FREE` Set aside at least two hours for this inspiring museum right in the centre. It offers visitors a fascinating journey through the life of Nelson Mandela. There are four rooms that contain a mix of memorabilia, photographs and panels as well as videos and sound documents.

🛏 Sleeping & Eating

Mthatha is not a foodie heaven. You'll find the usual chain restaurants in the various shopping malls dotted around town. For something more authentic, make a beeline for Ebony Lodge, which has an excellent restaurant.

Mthatha Backpackers HOSTEL $
(☎047-531 3654; www.mthathabackpackers.co.za; 12 Aloe St; dm R180, s with shared bathroom R300, d R400; P🅿🛜🅿) This suburban compound is a nice surprise and a bonanza for budgeteers. It shelters three dorms and three standard rooms in wooden cabins. Owner Angus is full of local recommendations and can help with booking bus tickets, catching shared taxis etc. He offers pick-ups from Shell Ultra City, transfers to Coffee Bay, and day trips to spots such as waterfalls.

Ebony Lodge GUESTHOUSE $$
(☎047-531 3933; ebonylodge@telkomsa.net; 22 Park Rd; s/d incl breakfast from R800/975; P🅿🛜🅿) This early 20th-century mansion in a leafy garden has stylish rooms with African decor. The restaurant (mains from R80) is one of Mthatha's best, serving healthy salads, a Thai seafood pot and the usual steaks and wraps to young professionals in cosy surrounds. Sadly, the restaurant is not open on weekends. Great value.

ℹ Getting There & Away

The N2 and R61 (for Port St Johns) cross in the town centre. The intersection can be a gridlocked mess, so try to avoid weekday rush hours.

AIR

Mthatha Airport is 17km north of the centre on R61. **Airlink** (☎086 160 6606; www.flyairlink.

com) has daily flights to/from Jo'burg (from R1200). Most hotels and B&Bs can arrange transfers to/from the airport.

BUS

Baz Bus stops at Shell Ultra City, 4km south of town, en route between Port Elizabeth and Durban. Mzansi Experience also stops at Shell Ultra City, en route between Port Elizabeth and Jo'burg.

Greyhound, Translux, Intercape and City to City stop at Shell Ultra City on their daily runs between Cape Town (from R680, 20 hours) and Durban (from R350, six hours).

All lodgings in Mthatha can organise pick-ups from Shell Ultra City.

CAR

The major car rental companies have desks at the airport.

SHARED TAXI

Shared taxis in Mthatha depart from both Shell Ultra City and the main bus stop and taxi rank near Bridge St. Destinations include Port St Johns (R60), Coffee Bay (R60) and East London (R135).

Mthatha to Port St Johns

The road between Mthatha and Port St Johns provides access to a great section of coast, including the **Hluleka Nature Reserve** (☎043-701 9600; www.visiteasterncape. co.za; adult/child R20/10; ⏱8am-5pm), which conserves a spectacular coastline of rocky seashores, pristine beaches and lagoons, as well as evergreen forests and grassy hilltops. Burchell's zebras, blesboks and blue wildebeest have all been introduced, and bird life is abundant. A 47km gravel road leads to the reserve from near Libode on R61. You need a high-clearance vehicle to get there.

🛏 Sleeping

Kraal HOSTEL $
(☎082 871 4964; www.thekraal.co.za; Mpande; camping/dm R120/170, d with shared bathroom R400-600; P🅿🛜) 🍃 Power down and disconnect at this ecologically minded coastal retreat, which offers accommodation (six doubles and one eight-bed dorm) in traditionally designed rondavels. A rustically cosy lounge and dining area open onto a back porch where the ocean view is framed by a V in the hillside.

Hiking, surfing and dolphin- and whale-watching are possibilities, as are visiting the preschool or lunching with a Xhosa family. There are also three beaches within walking distance. Meals are available in the nearby village restaurant. The turnoff to the Kraal is about 80km from Mthatha and 20km from Port St Johns. It is another 16km on a sealed road; the last stretch (about 4km) is a rough road that requires a high-clearance vehicle after rains.

★ **Umngazi River**
Bungalows & Spa   RESORT $$$
(☑ 047-564 1115; www.umngazi.co.za; Umngazi; s/d with full board from R1800/2500; P 🛜 🏊) Overlooking a large estuary and a deserted beach, this splendid resort at the mouth of the Umngazi River features 69 bungalows that were modernised in 2017. It's popular with honeymooners and families alike. Activities include canoeing, fishing, mountain biking and sunset cruises; there's also a babysitting service and kids' club for when you want to hit the spa.

To get here in your own car from Port St Johns, take R61 towards Mthatha for 14km to the signposted turn-off on your left, from where it is another 11km on a relatively good gravel road.

Port St Johns

☑ 047 / POP 6441

Dramatically located at the mouth of the Mzimvubu (or Umzimvubu) River and framed by towering cliffs covered with tropical vegetation, the laid-back town of Port St Johns is the original Wild Coast journey's end. There's a vibrant, if somewhat run-down, quality to the town, which is the largest between East London and Port Edward. In June and July, Port St Johns attracts divers and snorkellers from all over the world who come to experience the annual sardine run (p220).

Bull Zambezi sharks calve upriver and there have been several fatal attacks in recent years, all at Second Beach. Until shark nets are installed, it's recommended that you do nothing more than wade off the town's beaches, and even then with caution.

👁 Sights & Activities

Walk to the **Gap blowhole**, between First and Second Beach, at high tide (but stay well away from the shore because of dangerous waves). Another great natural site that can be accessed on foot is **Bulolo Waterfall**, which requires a rather strenuous 90-min-

ute walk to get there. For the waterfall, you'll need a guide – contact your accommodation. An easier walk goes from Second Beach to Third Beach along the coastline; you don't really need a guide, but if you're on your own it's safer to take one.

Second Beach   BEACH
Second Beach is Port St Johns's heart and soul. Locals come to this idyllic stretch of sand to while away the hot days and party as the sun goes down. Wandering down to the shallows for a paddle and spotting Nguni cows lounging on the sand are classic Port St Johns experiences. That said, be aware of rip currents and sharks.

Mt Thesiger   VIEWPOINT
Just north of the town centre on the banks of the Mzimvubu River, a sealed road (Concrete Rd) climbs to this favourite sunset spot – a flat-topped hill with a disused airstrip and one of the more spectacular views on the Wild Coast.

Silaka Nature Reserve   NATURE RESERVE
(☑ 047-564 1177; www.visiteasterncape.co.za; adult/child R20/10; ⊙ 6am-6pm) This small reserve, 6km south of Port St Johns, is worth a visit if you want to soak up the stunning scenery. It runs from Second Beach past Third Beach to Sugarloaf Rock, near the estuary where the Gxwaleni River flows into the sea. Clawless otters are often seen on the beach, white-breasted cormorants clamber up onto Bird Island, and you might spot vervet monkeys and birds. You can overnight here; well-equipped self-catering chalets (from R550) overlook Third Beach.

The overgrown 2km pathway (wear long trousers) from Second Beach to **Third Beach**, which is cleaner, quieter and normally untroubled by sharks, leaves from near Lodge on the Beach. Alternatively, follow the hilly road.

★ **Offshore Africa**   WHALE WATCHING
(☑ 084 951 1325; www.offshoreportstjohns.com; 1565 Ferry Point Rd; sardine run packages from R22,000, whale-watching trips R750, boat cruises R120; ⊙ by reservation) Offshore Africa is the most experienced sardine run operator in the country and the only locally based sardine run specialist along the entire Wild Coast. In season (June to July), it offers various packages – book well ahead. During the rest of the year, it organises dolphin- and

Port St Johns

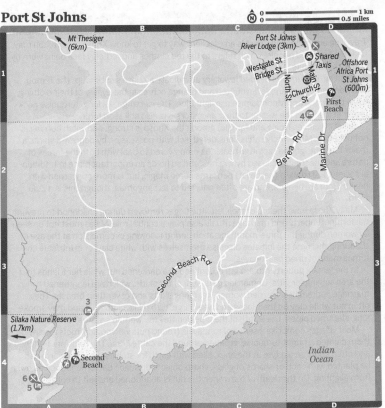

Port St Johns

⊙ Sights

❸ Activities, Courses & Tours

⊜ Sleeping

⊗ Eating

whale-watching trips as well as two-hour
boat cruises up the Mzimvubu River.

Wild Coast Hikes   HIKING
(⬛082 507 2256; www.wildcoasthikes.com;
per person per day from R250) Jimmy leads hikes
from Second Beach in Port St Johns to destinations ranging from Silaka (five hours) to
Coffee Bay (five days), with accommodation
in Xhosa villages on the overnight trails. Accommodation is an extra R300 per person
per night.

⊨ Sleeping

Delicious Monster   GUESTHOUSE $
(⬛083 997 9856; www.deliciousmonsterpsj.
co.za; Second Beach; s R380, d R470-650, cottage
d/q R800/1200; ⓟ) Just steps from the restaurant of the same name you'll find this
airy loft-style cottage with lovely ocean
views from its front porch. It features a
well-equipped kitchen, a cosy lounge embellished with artistic touches and three
tastefully done-out rooms. The mezzanine
room has an outside bathroom. Also available is a self-catering cottage with two
bedrooms.

THE XHOSA

Travelling along the Wild Coast is an excellent way to get to know Xhosa culture. You may hear the term 'red people', which refers to the red clothes and red-clay face paint worn by some Xhosa adults.

Clothing, colours and beaded jewellery all indicate a Xhosa's subgroup. The Tembu and Bomvana, for example, favour red and orange ochres in the dyeing of their clothing, while the Pondo and Mpondomise use light blue. The *isi-danga* – a long, turquoise neck-lace that identifies the wearer to their ancestors – is also still seen today.

Belief in witches (male and female) among the Xhosa is strong, and witch burning is not unknown. Most witchcraft is considered evil, with possession by depraved spirits a major fear. The *igqirha* (spiritual healer) is empowered to deal with both the forces of nature and the trouble caused by witches, and so holds an important place in tradition-al society. The *ixhwele* (herbalist) performs some magic, but is more concerned with health. Both are healers, and are often referred to as *sangomas*, though this is a Zulu word.

Many Xhosa have the top of their left little finger removed during childhood to prevent misfortune. Puberty and marriage rituals also play a central role. Males must not be seen by women during the three-month initiation period following circumcision at the age of 18; during this time the initiates disguise themselves with white clay, or in intricate cos-tumes made of dried palm leaves.

In the female puberty ritual, a girl is confined in a darkened hut while her friends tour the area singing for gifts. Unmarried girls wear short skirts, which are lengthened as marriage approaches. Married women wear long skirts and cover their breasts. They often put white clay on their faces and wear large, turbanlike cloth hats and may smoke long-stemmed pipes. The length of the pipe denotes the woman's status in the clan.

Most villages comprise a series of rondavels (round huts with conical roofs), many of them painted a bright turquoise, grouped around the cattle *kraal*. The roofs are thatched and often sport an old tyre at the apex, filled with earth for stabilisation. The earth can be planted with cacti or shards of glass: sharp objects dissuade bad omens such as owls from alighting. On the death of the owner, the hut is abandoned and left to collapse.

Jungle Monkey
HOSTEL $

(☏047-564 1517; www.junglemonkey.co.za; 3 Berea Rd; camping/dm R100/150, d R550, with shared bathroom R370-450; 🅿🛜❄) Music booms through the trees as you approach this casual hang-out, with its desert-island bar-restaurant overlooking the pool. Rooms are colourful and comfortable (especially the Monkey View) and distant from any party noise, while dorms are more basic. Hiking, activities and day trips are on offer. Lights meals are available. A safe choice, just south of the centre.

Lodge on the Beach
GUESTHOUSE $

(☏083 374 9669; www.lodgeonthebeach.co.za; Second Beach; d R500; 🅿) Perched on a slight rise with unobstructed views of Second Beach, this well-kept thatch-roofed retreat has three rooms, each with its own small deck and an individual bathroom in the hallway. Breakfast can be provided, and there's a communal kitchen. There is no wi-fi.

Amapondo Backpackers
HOSTEL $

(☏083 315 3103; www.amapondo.co.za; Second Beach Rd; camping R110, dm from R170, s/d with shared bathroom from R350/450, cottages R700-800; 🅿🛜) A mellow place where several low-slung buildings line a hillside with ex-cellent views of Second Beach. A rambling network of verandas, leafy walkways and chill spaces leads to the simple (and rather dark) rooms and dorms, while smarter cot-tages stand on the hill above. Various activ-ities are offered, including hiking to Silaka or Bulolo Waterfalls, and sundowners at the airstrip.

The bar-restaurant, where driftwood hangs from the beams, gets lively with a mix of locals and travellers. A hot shower is avail-able in the morning and late afternoon.

Port St Johns River Lodge
LODGE $$

(☏047-564 0005; www.portstjohnsriverlodge. co.za; Mzimvubu Dr; s/d incl breakfast R700/1200, chalets R1100-1500; 🅿❄🛜❄) One of a few riverside lodges north of town, this well-run complex in a verdant property in has comfortable rooms, self-catering chalets and a restaurant (mains from R85) gazing across a lawn at the river cliffs. Rates are cheaper on weekends. In June and July, it's fully booked with divers who want to experience the annual sardine run.

✖ Eating

Delicious Monster　　　　　INTERNATIONAL $
(☑083 997 9856; Second Beach; mains R40-115; ☺8am-3pm & 6-9pm Mon-Sat; ☎) This funky restaurant has a fabulous view of Second Beach and the sea, and an eclectic menu that includes a recommended mezze platter, delicious *shwarma,* line fish, salads and steaks.

The Waterfront　　　　　INTERNATIONAL $$
(☑047-564 1234; www.facebook.com/PSJWaterfront; Main St; mains R70-140; ☺10am-8pm; ☎) Grab a table on the rear deck with views of the river and Mt Sullivan, then choose from a large selection of wood-fired pizzas, salads and seafood, including fresh calamari and line fish. Carnivores, fear not: meat dishes are also available. It also does takeaway.

ℹ Getting There & Away

The R61 from Mthatha to Port St Johns is in excellent condition, but it involves switchbacks and sharp curves – beware of speeding minibus taxis. Amapondo and Jungle Monkey hostels will pick you up from the Shell Ultra City, 4km south of Mthatha (where Baz Bus and Mzansi Experience stop) for around R100, but it's essential to book ahead (and turn up when you've booked).

There are regular **shared taxis** (Main St) to Port St Johns from Mthatha (R60, two hours) and Durban (R190, five hours).

You'll find a couple of petrol stations in town.

Pondoland

Some of the most biologically rich landscape of the whole region is found on the 100km stretch of coast between Port St Johns and the Mthamvuna River. Currently unspoiled, there are velvety hills dotted with brightly painted houses, serene tea plantations and waterfalls galore.

Mbotyi

Well off the beaten path thanks to its splendid isolation, the Mbotyi area is a dream come true for seekers of the offbeat. You'll soon realise that the journey to get there is worth the effort when the road drops down through indigenous subtropical forest to a pristine river mouth and beach.

Mbotyi is roughly two hours' drive from Port St Johns. Just before Lusikisiki, 45km north of Port St Johns on R61, turn right at the Mbotyi River Lodge sign; if you reach the Total garage, you've gone too far. Concrete and gravel roads (normally passable in a 2WD car) lead 19km through the Magwa Tea plantations to Mbotyi.

🛏 Sleeping & Eating

Mbotyi River Lodge has a restaurant with lots of fish and meat dishes; book ahead. The nearest place to stock up on food supplies is Port St Johns.

Mbotyi Campsite　　　　　CAMPGROUND $
(☑039-253 7200; www.mbotyi.co.za; camping R140, d with shared bathroom R450-550; ℙ) Mbotyi Campsite, a joint venture between neighbouring Mbotyi River Lodge and the local community, is the place for total relaxation and long walks on the beach. It has rondavels (round huts with conical roofs) and plenty of grassy, shady areas for campers. You'll need to be self-sufficient with food.

Mbotyi River Lodge　　　　　RESORT $$$
(☑082 674 1064, 039-253 7200; www.mbotyi.co.za; s/d with half board from R1260/1700; ℙ☀☂) Mbotyi River Lodge, a low-key resort at the river mouth, has thatched rooms and a cluster of log cabins overlooking the beach and lagoon. Numerous activities can be arranged, including horse riding, hiking trails, canoeing and visits to the area's many waterfalls. Not all rooms have air-con. No wi-fi.

Mkambati Nature Reserve

Breathtaking Mkambati Nature Reserve (☑079 496 7821; www.visiteasterncape.co.za; adult/child R20/10; ☺6am-6pm) covers 77 sq km with some spectacular waterfalls, the deep Msikaba and Mtentu River gorges, rock pools, swamp forests and several hundred thousand square metres of grassland, where antelope species, including red hartebeests and blue wildebeest, graze. The magnificent coastal scenery is a haven for birds, including trumpeter hornbills and African fish eagles, while dolphins and whales can be seen.

Activities include canoe and walking trails, and self-drive wildlife viewing.

From Flagstaff on R61, a tar road leads 32km east past Holy Cross Mission. From the end of the tar, a gravel road runs 40km to the reserve, requiring a 4WD or bakkie (pick-up truck).

Mtentu Lodge HOSTEL **$**
(☑ 083 805 3356; www.mtentulodge.co.za; dm/cabin R150/700) On the isolated northern bank of the beautiful Mtentu Estuary, just across from Mkambati, is this lodge. Six comfortable wood cabins and a dorm with ocean views are linked by a boardwalk running through the naturally landscaped property. Toilets are communal and showers are gas or solar powered. Three meals a day can be provided for R340 per person.

A range of activities is on tap, including hiking, horse riding, canoeing and cycling – as is good ol' fashioned chilling out on the surrounding beaches. In dry weather, Mtentu can be reached in a 2WD car with high clearance, and there are other options including shuttles, guided shared taxi rides and guided hikes. In all cases, contact the lodge in advance to arrange your visit.

NORTHEASTERN HIGHLANDS

The Northeastern Highlands, climbing up from the lush valleys of the Wild Coast to the south and bordered by the sharply ascending peaks of Lesotho to the north, has some of South Africa's most beautiful mountain scenery. There are tranquil towns little visited by tourists; rushing streams and rivers where trout and other fish abound; day hikes through bucolic landscapes; and even snow-covered mountain passes north of Rhodes in the winter.

It's worth approaching this region as a scenic road trip because, while the towns are appealing stop-offs, you will likely find the journey more satisfying.

❶ Getting There & Away

The major transport hub is Queenstown, which has bus services to major destinations in the country; it also has train services to Cape Town, Jo'Burg and East London. The rest of the region is best explored with your own wheels as public transport is infrequent.

If you have covered the Wild Coast and you have a little time, R56 makes a scenic alternative to the N2 for crossing the province. It runs east from Middelburg in the Karoo to Kokstad in KwaZulu-Natal, and is particularly scenic in the highlands between Elliot and Maclear. A dramatic route linking the area with the Wild Coast is the Langeni Pass (1505m), one of South Africa's newest passes, which climbs 720m from Mthatha to Ugie. Drive cautiously, as weather and road conditions can be harsh.

Lady Grey
☑ 051 / POP 1395
Backed by the imposingly steep and sunbaked cliffs of the Witteberge mountain range, Lady Grey is a peaceful agricultural community at the foot of Joubert's Pass (2236m) – the scenery couldn't be more stunning. It's popular with fishermen, hikers and artists.

The **tourist office** (www.ladygreytourism.co.za; cnr Joubert & Murray Sts; ⊗ 8am-1pm & 2-4pm Mon-Fri, to noon Sat) has an accommodation list as well as brochures and a guide to fly-fishing in the Highlands.

Public transport is scarce in this area. City to City has daily services to Johannesburg (R280, 10 hours).

The delightful guesthouse **Comfrey Cottage** (☑ 051-603 0407; www.comfreycottage.co.za; 51-59 Stephenson St; s/d incl breakfast R800/1360; 🅿🛜) has three upmarket cottages with alpacas grazing the lawns of its beautiful park-like garden. Geological and botanical tours can be arranged, and dinners can be prepared on request.

Rhodes
☑ 045 / POP 696
Deep in the southern Drakensberg, in a spectacular valley setting alongside the Bell River, the little village of Rhodes is a lovely bucolic escape that's well worth the detour. The architecture remains as it was when the town was established in 1891 as a base for agriculture and commerce. In this mountain outpost, all four seasons can be experienced in a single day, and extremes are not uncommon – temperatures have reached -15°C in winter and 35°C in summer.

Wild Trout Association FISHING
(☑ 045-971 9003; www.wildtrout.co.za; 1 Vorster St) Trout fishing is extremely popular throughout the southern Drakensberg, and the Wild Trout Association headquarters, which issues permits, is in the Walkerbouts Inn.

🛌 Sleeping

There is a handful of reliable places to stay in town, including one inn. You'll also find several self-catering cottages in the village and surrounding farms – book online at www.rhodesinfo.co.za and www.linecasters.co.za. You'll need to book early for high season (there are three brief high seasons: 1 December to 15 January, 15 March to 30 April, and 25 May to 31 August) and bring warm clothes and blankets in winter.

Walkerbouts Inn   INN $$
(☑ 045-974 9290; www.walkerbouts.co.za; 1 Vorster St; s/d with half board R905/1550) Oozing character, Walkerbouts has polished wood floors and cosy rooms with all-important panel heaters and electric blankets. The dining room serves wholesome country fare, while the beckoning pub does build-your-own pizzas. The lovely garden has magnificent views, and genial host Dave 'Walkabout' Walker knows just about everything there is to know about Rhodes and fly fishing.

Tenahead Mountain Lodge   LODGE $$$
(☑ 045-971 8901; www.tenaheadmountainlodge.info; Naudesnek Pass; d incl breakfast R4050; 🅿 🛜) This spectacular five-star lodge, perched at 2500m and surrounded by the Drakensberg, Witteberg and Maluti ranges, has seven luxurious rooms with fireplaces. Wooden decks make the most of the view and, for bad-weather days, the library has 2000 books. Although it's on the Naudesnek Pass, it's best to drive via Rhodes from Barkly East. A high-clearance vehicle is recommended.

❶ Getting There & Away

There is no public transport to Rhodes.

Fuel is sometimes available here, but it's not unusual for the supply to run out, so fill up before driving to Rhodes. The unsealed road from Barkly East (60km, 1½ hours) is fine for 2WD cars but can become tricky after rains. Check locally for the latest road and weather conditions. The road on to Maclear (110km, three hours) cuts through the imposing Naudesnek Pass (2587m), the country's highest, and should only be undertaken in a high-clearance vehicle (preferably a 4WD).

EASTERN KAROO

The Karoo is the vast and beautiful semidesert stretching across the great South African plateau inland from the Cape coast; its southeastern section covers a chunk of the Eastern Cape. The dry region, with its variety of grasses, hardy shrubs, *tolbos* (tumbleweed in Afrikaans) and succulents, is a surprisingly rich cultural and historic destination. Graaff-Reinet, the architectural 'jewel of the Karoo', is complemented by artistic Nieu Bethesda and literary Cradock, while Camdeboo and Mountain Zebra National Parks offer stunning scenery and rare Cape mountain zebras. Throughout, the overwhelming sense of space, peace and freedom stand in sharp contrast to the busier coastline – and make the region perfect road-trip territory.

Between December and February temperatures in Karoo towns can reach 45°C, and things barely cool down in March and April. June and July see the thermometer plummet to -5°C, with snow in the mountain passes and frosts. Come prepared!

Graaff-Reinet

☑ 049 / POP 26,585

Cradled in a curve of the Sundays River and encircled by the Camdeboo National Park, Graaff-Reinet is often referred to as the 'jewel of the Karoo'. South Africa's fourth-oldest town, the 'far-off colony of Graaff-Reinet', as the Dutch East India Company called the remote spot when they established it in 1786, has a superb architectural heritage. More than 220 buildings designated as national monuments include gabled Cape Dutch houses, flat-roofed Karoo cottages and ornate Victorian villas. Add in small-town charm, some excellent accommodation and restaurants, plus a handful of museums, and you'll begin to understand why Graaff-Reinet acquired its nickname.

◉ Sights & Activities

You can buy a combined **pass** (www.graaffreinetmuseums.co.za; adult 2/3/4/5 museums R40/60/80/100, child R15/20/30/40) that gives access to any of the town's museums, apart from the Hester Rupert Art Museum.

Hester Rupert Art Museum   MUSEUM
(☑ 049-807 5700; www.rupertartmuseum.co.za; Church St; R10; ⊙ 9am-12.30pm & 2-5pm Mon-Fri, to noon Sat & Sun) Located in one of South Africa's oldest churches, a Dutch Reformed Mission church consecrated in 1821, this museum hosts an art collection of work by more than 100 South African artists from the 1950s and '60s, including Irma Stern and Alexis Preller.

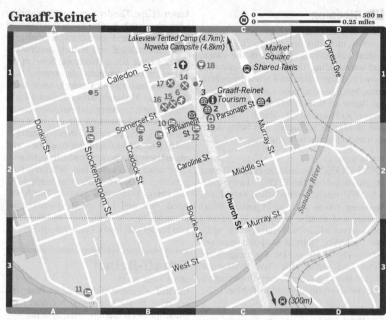

Graaff-Reinet

Lakeview Tented Camp (4.7km);
Nqweba Campsite (4.8km)

Market Square
Shared Taxis

Cypress Gve

Caledon St

Graaff-Reinet Tourism
Parsonage St

Somerset St
Parliament St

Donkin St

Stockenstroom St

Cradock St

Caroline St

Middle St

Church St

Bourke St

Murray St

Sundays River

West St

(300m)

Graaff-Reinet

◎ Sights
1 Dutch Reformed Church	B1
2 Hester Rupert Art Museum	C1
3 Old Library	C1
4 Reinet House	C1

◎ Activities, Courses & Tours
5 Camdeboo Adventure Tours	A1
6 Fly Karoo	B1
7 Karoo Connections	B1

◎ Sleeping
8 Aa 'Qtansisi	B2
9 Buiten Verwagten	B2
10 Camdeboo Cottages	B2
11 Cypress Cottage	A3

12 Drostdy Hotel	C2
Karoopark Guest House	(see 5)
13 Profcon Resort	A2

◎ Eating
14 GRT Brewery	B1
15 Our Yard	B1
16 Polka Cafe	B1
17 The Muller House	B1

◎ Drinking & Nightlife
18 Graaff-Reinet Club	C1

◎ Shopping
19 Annette Oelefse Mohair Products	C1

Dutch Reformed Church CHURCH
(Church St) This landmark 19th-century church, one of South Africa's finest examples of Victorian Gothic architecture, stands in the town's main square. It was built using local sandstone and has beautiful stained-glass windows.

Old Library MUSEUM
(cnr Church & Somerset Sts; adult/child R25/10; ☺8am-1pm & 1.45-4pm Mon-Fri, 9am-1pm Sat & Sun) This former library, built in 1847, houses a wide-ranging collection of historical artefacts. There's fossils from the Karoo, displays on Khoe-San rock paintings and slavery, and an exhibition about local son Robert Sobukwe, founder of the Pan African Congress (PAC).

Reinet House MUSEUM
(Murray St; adult/child R25/10; ☺8am-4pm Mon-Fri, 9am-1pm Sat & Sun) This Dutch Reformed parsonage, built between 1806 and 1812, is a beautiful example of Cape Dutch architecture, with high ceilings and yellow wood floors. The cobblestone rear courtyard has

a grapevine that was planted in 1870 and is one of the largest in the world.

Camdeboo Adventure Tours TOURS
(☏ 049-892 3410; www.karoopark.co.za; 81 Caledon St; township tour R500, wildlife-watching drive R650, historical tour R425) Buks and Chantelle Marais of Camdeboo Cottages (☏ 049-892 3180; www.camdeboocottages.co.za; 16 Parliament St; d from R750, cottage from R950; P ✳ 🛜 ☀) and Karoopark Guest House (p229) organise various trips to the Valley of Desolation and wildlife-viewing drives in Camdeboo National Park, as well as township tours and guided walks around Graaff-Reinet. Two people minimum per tour.

Karoo Connections TOURS
(☏ 049-892 3978, 082 339 8646; www.karooconnections.co.za; 7 Church St; sundowner tour R650, historical tour R425, township guided walk R425, Nieu Bethesda from R750, wildlife-watching drive R600) Based at McNaughton's Bookshop, David McNaughton organises a range of tours, including a sundowner tour of the Valley of Desolation by open Land Rover, a historical tour of Graaff-Reinet, a guided walk around the township, a half-day trip to Nieu Bethesda (a full day including Bushman rock art and fossils is also available) and wildlife-watching drives to Camdeboo.

🛏 Sleeping

Profcon Resort RESORT $
(☏ 049-892 2887; www.profconresort.co.za; 88 Somerset St; camping R250, d R550-700, cottages from R850; P ✳ 🛜 ☀ 🐾) This well-run complex with a laid-back vibe features excellent facilities and amenities, including a restaurant and a superb children's playground. With its varied accommodation options – including an excellent campground with a grassy area and a kitchen, modern, well-equipped rooms and comfy garden cottages – it's appropriate for backpackers, couples and families alike. One downside: the pool is miniscule.

Cypress Cottage B&B $$
(☏ 083 456 1795; www.cypresscottage.co.za; 76 Donkin St; s/d incl breakfast R1000/1500, d R1400; P ✳ 🛜 ☀) Is this Graaff-Reinet's best-kept secret? There are six upmarket rooms and three self-catering units in these beautifully renovated Karoo cottages on a quiet street southwest of the centre. Relax in the dreamy lush oasis at the back or take a dip into the quaint reservoir that has been converted in swimming pool.

Aa 'Qtansisi B&B $$
(☏ 049-891 0243; www.aaqtansisi.co.za/graaff-reinet/contact.html; 69 Somerset St; s/d incl breakfast R850/1400; P ✳ 🛜 ☀) Translating as 'We welcome you' in Khoe-San (to pronounce the name, drop the 'Q'), Aa 'Qtansisi's seven lavish rooms are inspired by the owner's travels, with themes including the Karoo, a French chateau and Morocco. The trellis-covered backyard is a tempting oasis with a plunge pool, and the gourmet breakfast includes a fruit platter and shot glass of muesli.

Karoopark Guest House GUESTHOUSE $$
(☏ 049-892 2557; www.karoopark.co.za; 81 Caledon St; s/d from R600/950; P ✳ 🛜 ☀) This family-owned and -run complex with a retro feel is a good base, with a restaurant serving South African specialities, a bar and a tour company, all in a garden environment. Various accommodation options, including biggish rooms and self-catering units, occupy the historic main house and blocks in the leafy grounds.

Buiten Verwagten B&B $$
(☏ 049-892 4504; www.buitenverwagten.co.za; 58 Bourke St; s/d incl breakfast from R800/1100; P ✳ 🛜 ☀) Every aspect of this Victorian-era home is tastefully curated by its friendly and professional owners. Inside are high ceilings, cedar and pine floors, and elegant antiques; outside are a trellis-covered veranda, a perfectly manicured lawn and a courtyard pool. There are two self-catering rooms at the back and three rooms in the main house.

> ## GRAAFF-REINET FROM ABOVE
> **Karoo Ballooning** (☏ 082 562 8876; www.facebook.com/karooballooning; R2500) Drifting across the Karoo's surreal geological formations in a hot-air balloon is a seductive way to take in the captivating countryside. Balloon flights last between 45 minutes and one hour. They are subject to weather forecasts.
>
> **Fly Karoo** (☏ 064 751 6609; www.flykaroo.co.za; Somerset St; R500-3200) Seen from a helicopter (four seats), the Karoo's majesty can bring tears to the eyes. Fly Karoo has a whole range of scenic flights, including a popular 10-minute loop that takes you over Spandau Kop and the Valley of Desolation. Unforgettable.

SOUTH AFRICAN MOHAIR

South Africa is the largest mohair (a fabric made from the hair of an Angora goat) producer in the world, and the majority of South African mohair is produced in the Karoo. At Graaff-Reinet's Annette Oelefse Mohair Products (☑082 466 6174; www. mohairblanket.co.za; Church St) you're guaranteed to find high-quality mohair items, including socks, blankets, scarves, jerseys, beanies and gloves, among others.

★ Drostdy Hotel   HISTORIC HOTEL $$$
(☑049-892 2161; www.newmarkhotels.com; Parliament St; s/d from R1400/1700; P✷⊜✷) The Karoo's flagship hotel offers a fine mix of historic charm and modern luxury. Accommodation is in mid-19th-century cottages, originally built for freed slaves. A long list of facilities make it a world-class hotel, including a spa, an art gallery, several lounge areas, three pools in a manicured garden, a bar and a top-notch restaurant with a unique country-chic interior.

✖ Eating

GRT Brewery   CAFE $$
(☑061 4084 351; 20 Church St; mains R50-120; ⊙9am-9pm Mon-Sat; ⊜) This multipurpose venue – beer garden, deli and cafe – has an inviting courtyard where you can sip a coffee, sample a craft beer, have breakfast or enjoy a light meal. Pick from vegetarian wraps, toasted sandwiches, savoury burgers or cheese and charcuterie platters, all made with locally sourced products.

The Muller House   INTERNATIONAL $$
(☑072 420 5473; www.facebook.com/themullerhouserestaurantbar; 1 Muller St; mains R70-170; ⊙noon-10pm Mon & Wed-Sat, to 3pm Sun) This hip resto-bar near the Dutch Reformed Church is as adept at serving up tapas (from R40) as it is heartier meals. The menu is concise yet inventive, and the breezy courtyard is atmospheric. A chill-out place by day, it gets more romantic at night (think candlelit dinners).

Polka Cafe   CAFE $$
(☑087 550 1363; www.polkacafe.co.za; 52 Somerset St; mains R65-155; ⊙7.30am-9pm Mon-Sat; ⊜) Polka's food will linger long on the palate. Karoo lamb, matured steaks and bobotie (curry topped with beaten egg baked to a crust) are on the dinner menu; lighter lunches include savoury pancakes, salads and pizzas. The candlelit veranda and rear courtyard turn romantic at night, while the nouveau-rustic dining room has a bakery selling homemade pastries and ice creams.

Our Yard   CAFE $$
(☑071 870 5081; 50 Somerset St; mains R50-155; ⊙7.30am-9pm Mon-Sat; ⊜) This trendy 'roastery and culture stop' serves excellent coffees, breakfasts, light meals, fruit juices, scones and cakes in a shady courtyard. The evening menu feature meaty mains, including lamb rib and venison. Also here are a gallery, a T-shirt shop and a deli selling wine, craft beers and local goodies. A cool spot.

Graaff-Reinet Club   CLUB
(English Club; Church St; ⊙1-9pm Mon-Thu, until late Fri & Sat, 11am-2pm Sun) This atmospheric, one-time 'men only' club, one of South Africa's oldest, has walls and halls adorned with hunting trophies and a bar pocked with bullet holes. Visitors are welcome to have a drink with locals. Friday evening is particularly lively, when farmers are in town.

ⓘ Information

Graaff-Reinet Tourism (☑049-892 4248; www.graaffreinet.co.za; 17 Church St; ⊙8am-5pm Mon-Fri, 9am-noon Sat) This helpful office has accommodation information and an abundance of maps.

ⓘ Getting There & Away

Intercape and Translux serve Cape Town (from R380, 12 hours) and Jo'burg (from R360, 11 hours) daily; the latter also runs to East London (from R280, six hours) and Port Elizabeth (R250, four hours). Tickets and information are available at the tourist office.

Shared taxis leave from Market Sq for Port Elizabeth (R210).

Camdeboo National Park

Covering an area of 194 sq km, Camdeboo National Park (☑049-892 3453; www.sanparks. org; adult/child R114/57; ⊙Lakeview Gate 6am-7pm Oct-Mar, 7am-6pm Apr-Sep; P) has plenty of animals, but the real attractions are the spectacular geological formations, and great views of Graaff-Reinet and the sun-baked Karoo plains. The park's name comes from the Khoekhoen for 'green valleys' – probably a reference to the spekboom growing here, which remain verdant throughout the winter.

◉ Sights

★ Valley of Desolation   NATURAL FEATURE
(off Rte 63; adult/child R114/57; ⊙ 6am-7.30pm Oct-Mar, 7am-6pm Apr-Sep) The park's most popular sight, the Valley of Desolation is a hauntingly beautiful valley with outstanding views – the rugged, piled dolerite columns are set against the backdrop of the endless Karoo plains. From the nearby Toposcope viewpoint, Graaff-Reinet is also visible, nestled in a bend of the Sundays River. The valley viewpoint, 14km from town, can be reached by car on a sealed road. The Crag Lizard Trail, a 1.5km circuit walk along the cliff, starts from the parking area.

The best times to visit are sunrise and sunset.

Giant Flag   LANDMARK
(www.giantflag.co.za) A 6600-sq-metre flag is being created from millions of coloured desert plants in the Valley of Desolation. When completed (possibly in 2020), it will be the world's largest flag – visible from space.

🏃 Activities

In the wildlife-watching area, accessed through Lakeview Gate, there are buffaloes, elands, kudus, red hartebeests, black wildebeest and springboks – to name a few of the park's 40-plus mammal species. Rare Cape mountain zebras may be spotted, but they prefer mountainous terrain. Good gravel roads lead 19km around the wildlife-watching area; visitors must stay in their vehicles except at the picnic sites.

There are also animals in the Valley of Desolation section of the park, while 200-plus bird species in the skies above include black eagles, African fish eagles and falcons.

Eerstefontein Day Trail   HIKING
FREE The Eerstefontein Day Trail runs through the park's western section past the Valley of Desolation; there are three route options with distances of 5km, 11km and 14km. The park reception has a map.

🛏 Sleeping

Lakeview Tented Camp   TENTED CAMP $
(☑ 049-892 3453; www.sanparks.org; tent for 2 people R700; 🅿) Near Nqweba Dam, this fenced campground has four pre-erected safari tents furnished with twin beds and a table and chairs on the deck. There's a shared kitchen and ablutions.

Nqweba Campsite   CAMPGROUND $
(☑ 049-892 3453; www.sanparks.org; camping R250; 🅿) This fenced campground near the dam of the same name has 15 gravel sites beneath thorn trees, each with a barbecue, a power point and a self-catering kitchen.

Nieu Bethesda
POP 1540

Hidden in the deep Karoo, the tiny village of Nieu Bethesda has gained some attention for its extraordinary Owl House – the fantastically and unnervingly decorated home of 'outsider' artist, Helen Martins. These days, the village is a minor artistic colony, with creative cred added by *The Road to Mecca*, Athol Fugard's play about Martins.

With its dirt roads, water furrows, pretty cottages and endless stars, Nieu Bethesda is a great place to experience life in a Karoo

EASTERN CAPE NIEU BETHESDA

ℹ CAMDEBOO NATIONAL PARK

Why Go Dramatic landscapes, rock formations and an unlikely ecological feat in the Valley of Desolation; animals including Cape mountain zebras; and day hikes.

When to Go The park is quiet in April, when the Karoo produces autumn colours and you can enjoy amazing sunsets in crisp weather. The vegetation is also thin, making wildlife easier to spot.

Practicalities Camdeboo is divided into three main sections: the wildlife-watching area north of the Nqweba Dam; the western section with the Valley of Desolation; and the eastern section with various 4WD trails. The park reception and accommodation are at Lakeview Gate, which is located on the N9 4km north of Graaff-Reinet. You'll need your own vehicle to visit the wildlife-watching area; otherwise, book a tour in Graaff-Reinet.

Budget Tips Camp and prepare your own food in the self-catering kitchen and barbecue.

village, unwind for a few days and reconnect with nature. Most visitors drive from Graaff-Reinet, about 55km to the south – the route is very scenic, with the Sneeuberg range dominating the region.

⊙ Sights & Activities

Owl House
HISTORIC BUILDING

(☏049-841 1733; www.theowlhouse.co.za; Martin St; R60; ⊙9am-4.45pm) The idiosyncratic vision that inspired artist Helen Martins (1897–1976) to turn her home and studio into a singular work of outsider art is the bedrock of Bethesda's bohemian identity. Martins and her assistant Koos Malgas worked for years designing and constructing the menagerie of concrete owls and other figures in the backyard. Nearly every inch of the shadowy interior is covered with colourful painted glass shards, textiles and knick-knacks, recalling the troubled figure who eventually took her own life.

Kitching Fossil
Exploration Centre
MUSEUM

(☏011-717 6685; Hudson St; R30; ⊙9am-5pm) The models and fossil casts here depict prehistoric animals (gorgonopsians, dicynodonts and the like) around 253 million years old – 50 million years before the age of dinosaurs. Staff will take you to see the real thing, untouched and embedded in rocks in the nearby dry riverbed.

Ganora Guest Farm
CULTURAL

(☏049-841 1302; www.ganora.co.za; per person from R110; ⊙by reservation) Ganora Guest Farm, 7km east of Nieu Bethesda, offers numerous activities, including a guided walk around the on-site museum of fossils and Bushman artefacts. Another tour focuses on medicinal plants. Groups can even enjoy a sheep-shearing demonstration. Ganora rehabilitates meerkats so you might see one or two scurrying around. They also host periodic courses in stargazing, art and cookery.

⌇ Sleeping

Owl House Backpackers
HOSTEL $

(☏049-841 1642; www.owlhouse.info; Martin St; camping per person R100, dm R180, s/d incl breakfast R480/790, with shared bathroom & incl breakfast R370/580) The whitewashed Karoo facade conceals a home with old-fashioned character, funky nooks and crannies, and a sizeable back garden. For more privacy, try the loft-like backyard water tower with circular bedroom, composting toilet and kitch-

enette, or the self-catering garden cottage. En-suite rooms are across the street in Outsiders B&B. The owners can organise tours, including visits to Bushman painting sites.

Bethesda Tower
GUESTHOUSE $

(☏073 028 8887; www.bethesdatower.co.za; Miller St; s/d with shared bathroom R280/400; P) Climbing this three-storey castellated tower is like stepping into a fairy tale. The top room has a round double bed, covered with a quilt made at the adjoining Bethesda Arts Centre, while downstairs is an equally quirky twin room. Two rooms are also available in the neighbouring Priory, decorated with quilts and artwork. The shared bathrooms are clean.

And The Cow Jumped
Over The Moon
GUESTHOUSE $

(☏083 460 3716; casper1@pixie.co.za; Immelman St; s/d R450/600; P) Just north of the 'centre' you'll find this cosy venture in a proudly maintained property; the three rooms are spotless, with simple decor.

★ Ganora Guest Farm
FARMSTAY $$

(☏049-841 1302; www.ganora.co.za; incl breakfast s R750-860, d R1000-1300; P☎✿) If you'd rather be out of town under the soaring skies of the Karoo, this 18th-century farmstead 7km east of Nieu Bethesda is an excellent option. The original stone wall now forms part of the luxurious boutique-style rooms, with further options in whitewashed former workshops and sheds. Meals are served in a rustic pioneer-style dining room.

Activities include hiking and mountain biking.

✗ Eating

Karoo Lamb Restaurant
SOUTH AFRICAN $

(☏049-841 642; www.facebook.com/KarooLamb Restaurant; River St; mains R80-110; ⊙7am-9pm; ☎) When all the elements of breakfast (from R35) at this large eatery-cum-deli-cum-gift shop are laid out, half a picnic table is occupied. For lunch or dinner, hearty dishes such as lamb chops and *potjiekos* (stew cooked in a cast-iron pot) satisfy after a long drive through the Karoo. Tapas are also available.

★ The Brewery & Two Goats Deli
DELI $$

(☏049-841 1602; www.facebook.com/TheBreweryNieuBethesda; Pienaar St; platter R80; ⊙8am-5pm Mon-Sat, to 3pm Sun) Across a bridge from the main part of the village is this charmingly rustic farmhouse on a working dairy farm, where you can sit under the trees sampling a delicious platter of cheeses, salami, pickles and olives. It also sells farm produce and has excellent craft beers. A great find, with plenty of atmosphere.

Die Waenhuis SOUTH AFRICAN **$$**
(☑084 862 8280; Martin St; mains R70-135; ☺9am-5pm Thu-Sat, to 3pm Sun) Occupying a beautifully renovated trading post in the heart of Nieu Bethesda, this atmospheric venue specialises in well-executed South African dishes, including lamb chops, burgers, chicken schnitzel and *bobotie*. There's a small but perfectly formed wine list, and the homemade ice creams and scones are a treat.

ℹ Information

The **tourist office** (☑079 070 8988; www. nieubethesda.info; Martin St; ☺9am-5pm) has a few brochures. Karoo Lamb Restaurant is also a great source of information. Note that there are no petrol stations or ATMs here, and credit cards are generally not accepted by accommodation. The nearest town is Graaff-Reinet.

ℹ Getting There & Away

There is no public transport to Nieu Bethesda. Owl House Backpackers can pick up guests from Graaff-Reinet (R200 per person), but it must be arranged in advance.

Mountain Zebra National Park

Don't miss this largely underrated national park (☑048-801 5700; www.sanparks.org; off R61; adult/child R192/96; ☺7am-7pm Oct-Mar, to 6pm Apr-Sep), 20km west of Cradock on the northern slopes of the Bankberg range (2000m), which encompasses 280 sq km with some superb Karoo vistas. The park was established to protect one of the world's rarest mammals: the Cape mountain zebra. There are now almost 800 in the park; they're distinguished from other zebra species by their small stature, reddish-brown nose, darker stripes and dewlap (a loose fold of skin hanging beneath the throat). It also offers the opportunity to approach cheetahs. The scenery is another draw. Among the silence and wide-open spaces, thick patches of sweet thorn and wild olive are interspersed with rolling grasslands and succulents.

🏃 Activities

In addition to Cape mountain zebras, the park supports many antelope species, buffaloes and black rhinos; a couple of lions, eight cheetahs and several species of small cat; genets, aardwolves, bat-eared foxes and black-backed jackals; and over 200 bird species. The park offers two-hour **wildlife drives** (adult/child from R250/125) and a unique **cheetah-tracking tour** (R410 per person), which takes you as close as 15m from the big cats. Evening drives combine the best of sunset and nocturnal game viewing.

With your own vehicle, it's possible to get a taste of the park in a few hours. Roads are mostly gravel but of good standard and suitable for all vehicles. The road that loops from the main gate across to the rest camp and back can take under two hours, depending on how often you stop.

Hiking

Hiking trails range from free 1km and 2.5km self-guided saunters around the rest camp, to longer guided walks including the

EASTERN CAPE MOUNTAIN ZEBRA NATIONAL PARK

ℹ MOUNTAIN ZEBRA NATIONAL PARK

Why Go Cape mountain zebras, lions, buffaloes and many other mammals; Karoo landscapes on the slopes of the Bankberg range; and numerous activities, including cheetah tracking.

When to Go Anytime outside summer (November to February), to avoid extreme heat in the Karoo's semidesert environment.

Practicalities The roads are mostly good gravel and tar, suitable for 2WD cars, plus three 4WD trails. There's no public transport to the park so bring your own vehicle or come on a tour.

Budget Tips If you don't want to camp, stay in cheaper accommodation in nearby Cradock and visit the park on a day trip. If you do stay in the park, your conservation (entrance) fee will be calculated on a nightly, rather than daily, basis; if you stay one night, you will only pay for one day despite being in the park for two.

Salpeterkop Hike (per person R390; ☺ by reservation), a challenging five- to six-hour walk up a hill with panoramic views.

🛏 Sleeping

Mountain Zebra
National Park Rest Camp   CAMPGROUND $

(🕿 012-428 9111, 086 111 4845; www.sanparks.org; camping 1-2 people R330, cottages from R1300; P ⁂) The park rest camp offers campsites (with power points and a communal kitchen) and comfortable and well-equipped cottages. The rest camp is 10km from the gate, and has the park reception, a shop selling basic items and a bar-restaurant (mains R60 to R160). And yes, there's a swimming pool.

Doornhoek   COTTAGE $$$

(🕿 012-428 9111, 086 111 4845; www.sanparks.org; 1-4 people R3500-3800; P) This restored historic farmhouse, built in 1837 and hidden in a secluded valley near a dam, can sleep six people in two doubles and two singles. It has plenty of charm and character and is ideal if you want to get away from it all.

Cradock

🕿 048 / POP 36,671

The archetypal Karoo town, Cradock has bags of atmosphere and an assortment of historic buildings. Originally established as a military outpost in 1813 to stop the Xhosa from crossing the Great Fish River, Cradock became a bustling agricultural and commercial settlement in later decades. Market St was home to the artisans who served the ox-wagons passing through. Take a closer look at the beautiful old buildings and tree-lined avenues and stroll down lovely Dundas and Bree Sts, the latter the oldest in Cradock, past fine well-preserved 19th-century gabled homes.

◉ Sights & Activities

Schreiner House Museum   MUSEUM

(🕿 048-881 5251; 9 Cross St; ☺8am-12.45pm & 2-4.30pm Mon-Fri) **FREE** Olive Schreiner is best known for her classic Karoo novel, *Story of an African Farm*. Published in 1883 under the pseudonym Ralph Iron, this provocative *plaasroman* (farm novel) and *bildungsroman* (coming-of-age story) advocated views considered radical well into the 20th century. She lived in this typical Karoo house for only three years; however, several

of its small rooms are now dedicated to a chronicle of her life, career and local history seen through writers' eyes.

The bookshop has an excellent collection of South African novels and a booklet detailing a literary walking tour of Cradock.

Karoo River Rafting   RAFTING

(🕿 084 429 9944; www.karoo-river-rafting.co.za; from R500; ☺ by reservation) Offers rafting and canoeing trips down the Great Fish River and its tributaries.

Township Tours   CULTURAL TOUR

(🕿 048-881 1650; tours by donation) Amos, who works at the Victoria Manor hotel, offers tours of the local township.

🛏 Sleeping & Eating

Butler House Guesthouse   GUESTHOUSE $

(🕿 082 629 5648; riana@lightmail.co.za; 53 Bree St; s R450, d R500-800; P ⁂ ⁑) If you look at the overall package – lovely, leafy and bird-filled grounds, a pleasant pool, several cosy lounge areas, quiet location and a renovated historic house dating from 1815 – it's not hard to see why this venue is a respected option. The 11 units, including two chalets and two garden cottages, have bags of character. No air-con, though.

★**Die Tuishuise**
& Victoria Manor   HISTORIC HOTEL $$

(🕿 048-881 1650, 048-881 1322; www.tuishuise. co.za; Market St; cottages s/d R720/1200, hotel s/d R720/1000, all incl breakfast; P ⁑ ⁂) The 'homely home' consists of 31 beautifully restored and handsomely furnished Karoo houses, their *stoeps* (porches) opening onto one of Cradock's oldest streets, and garden cottages. The neighbouring Victoria Manor is an atmospheric small-town inn with a splash pool, a wood-panelled bar-restaurant, and antiques in the charming rooms. Air-con is available on request in some rooms only. The picture-perfect self-catering houses, which each accommodate up to eight, are split between light and modern interpretations of Karoo rusticity and more historic decor, redolent of the Brits and Boers who once trod their floorboards. Lovely.

Albert House B&B   B&B $$

(🕿 048-881 4624; www.alberthouse.co.za; 40 Dundas St; s/d incl breakfast R700/900; P ⁂ ⁑) Relaxed, simple and beautiful seem to be the rule here. All rooms have a pleasing rustic touch. But it's the garden that steals the laurels, with its verdant lawns, blossoming flowers and elegant trees. What's missing? A swimming pool.

★**Victoria Manor**   SOUTH AFRICAN **$$**
(☑048-881 1650; Market St; mains R70-170, dinner buffet R200; ☺noon-2pm & 7-9pm Mon-Fri, 7-9pm Sat & Sun; ☎) This atmospheric hotel dining room has dark-wood panelling and richly upholstered furnishings in 19th-century English style. Service is attentive, and the Karoo cuisine hearty and delicious. Karoo lamb chops, burgers and vegetarian platters are on the menu.

True Living   SOUTH AFRICAN **$$**
(☑048-881 3288; www.truelivingshop.com; 44 JA Calata St; mains R60-105; ☺7.30am-5pm Mon-Thu, to 10pm Fri, to 1pm Sat; ☎) Cafes cluster around the corner of JA Calata and Albert Sts, mostly combined with nurseries or decor shops. In the latter category, this courtyard cafe sells plates and platters of farm-kitchen food, including *bobotie* (curry topped with

beaten egg baked to a crust), Cradock lamb chops, salads, quiches, pies, steaks and burgers. Oh, and divine muffins, too.

ℹ Information

Cradock Tourism (☑048-801 5000; www.cradockmiddelburg.co.za; JA Calata St; ☺9am-4pm Mon-Fri) In the municipal building opposite the Spar Centre.

ℹ Getting There & Away

Translux, Intercape and City to City run daily to Cape Town (from R390, 10 to 15 hours) via Graaff-Reinet (from R150, 1½ hours) or Port Elizabeth (from R180, four hours), and to East London (from R260, 4½ hours) and Jo'burg (from R510, 11 hours). Tickets can be bought at **Shoprite** (Beeren St; ☺8am-8pm), in the centre.

Shosholoza Meyl operates three trains weekly via Cradock between Jo'burg (R380, 15½ hours) and Port Elizabeth (R170, 4½ hours).

EASTERN CAPE CRADOCK

KwaZulu-Natal

Why Go?

Rough and ready, smart and sophisticated, rural and rustic: there's no doubt that KwaZulu-Natal (KZN) is eclectic. It's a region where glassy malls touch shabby suburbs, and action-packed adventurers ooze adrenaline while laid-back beach bods drip with suntan lotion. Mountainscapes contrast with flat, dry savannahs, while the towns' central streets, teeming with African life, markets and noise, are in stark contrast to the sedate tribal settlements in rural areas. Here, too, is traditional Zululand, whose people are fiercely proud of their culture.

Throw in the wildlife – the Big Five (lion, leopard, buffalo, elephant and rhino) and rare marine species – the historic intrigue of the Battlefields, fabulous hiking opportunities, and the sand, sea and surf of coastal resort towns, and you get a tantalising taste of local heritage and authentic African highlights that should be on every 'must-do' list.

Best Places to Eat

➜ Cafe 1999 (p252)
➜ Mali's Indian Restaurant (p251)
➜ Guinea Fowl (p301)
➜ Rosehurst (p285)
➜ Pucketty Farm (p292)

Best Places to Stay

➜ Napier House (p249)
➜ Hilltop Camp (p271)
➜ George Hotel (p265)
➜ Kosi Forest Lodge (p282)
➜ Hlalanathi (p299)

When to Go
Durban

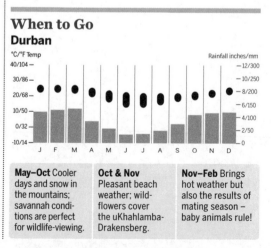

May–Oct Cooler days and snow in the mountains; savannah conditions are perfect for wildlife-viewing.

Oct & Nov Pleasant beach weather; wildflowers cover the uKhahlamba-Drakensberg.

Nov–Feb Brings hot weather but also the results of mating season – baby animals rule!

History

Battled over by Boers, Brits and Zulus, Natal was named by Portuguese explorer Vasco da Gama, who sighted the coastline on Christmas Day 1497, and christened it for the natal day of Jesus. It took the British Empire more than 300 years to set its sights on the region, proclaiming it a colony in 1843. Briefly linked to the Cape Colony in 1845, Natal again became a separate colony in 1856, when its European population numbered less than 5000.

The introduction of Indian indentured labour in the 1860s – sections of the province still retain a subcontinental feel – and the subsequent development of commercial agriculture (mainly sugar) boosted growth. The colony thrived from 1895, when train lines linked Durban's port (dredged to accommodate big ships) with the booming Witwatersrand.

The recorded history of the province up until the Union of South Africa is full of conflict: the *mfeqane* (the forced migration of South African tribes; Zulu for 'the crushing'), the Boer-Zulu and Anglo-Zulu Wars, which saw the Zulu kingdom subjugated, and the two wars between the British and the Boers.

Just after the 1994 elections, Natal Province was renamed KwaZulu-Natal, acknowledging that the Zulu homeland of KwaZulu comprises a large part of the province. From that time, Ulundi (the former KwaZulu capital) and Pietermaritzburg (the former Natal homeland capital) enjoyed joint status as capital of KwaZulu-Natal until 2005, when Pietermaritzburg was named the province's official capital.

Climate

The weather (and the water, thanks to the Agulhas current) stays warm year-round along much of the coast, with Durbanites claiming to lap up a heady 230 sunny days a year. In summer the heat and humidity, combined with the crowds that flood to the coast to enjoy it, can be exhausting, with temperatures regularly in the mid-30s (degrees Celsius). Most of the interior enjoys similarly balmy conditions, but sudden and explosive electrical storms, especially in the Drakensberg mountains and northern KwaZulu-Natal, often roll in during the afternoon. Winter brings a dusting of snow to the higher peaks, and even to some of the higher-elevation towns.

Language

Eleven official languages are spoken in South Africa, but English, Zulu, Xhosa and Afrikaans are most widely used in KwaZulu-Natal.

ℹ Getting There & Around

With flights, buses and trains to destinations across the country, Durban is KwaZulu-Natal's undisputed transport hub, and the city is well connected. King Shaka International Airport, built for the 2010 World Cup, has been steadily increasing in traffic, with more and more international flights that make it easier to head straight to KZN without having to first touch down in Johannesburg or Cape Town.

However, getting around the province itself is a different story. While long-distance buses run to Port Shepstone, Margate and Kokstad in the south, Richards Bay and Vryheid in the north and a string of towns including Estcourt, Ladysmith and Newcastle in the west, many of the more remote locations are a headache to get to by public transport. Shared taxis provide a useful back-up, but relying on minibuses as your sole means of getting about will mean many long hours in the back of a cramped van.

Baz Bus (☑ 021-422 5202, SMS bookings 076 427 3003; www.bazbus.com) links many of the province's hostels.

DURBAN

☑ 031 / POP 3.1 MILLION

Cosmopolitan Durban, South Africa's third-largest city (known as eThekweni in Zulu), is sometimes passed over for her 'cooler' Capetonian cousin. But there's a lot more to fun-loving Durbs (as it's affectionately known) than meets the eye.

The city had a major makeover leading up to the 2010 World Cup, with a sleek new stadium and a revamped waterfront. The renewal of the promenade and the sweeping away of the old sleaze has given municipal authorities new confidence and ambition, which you can see in the development projects all over the city.

Home to the largest concentration of people of Indian descent outside of India, Durban also boasts an unmistakably Asian feel, with the marketplaces and streets of the Indian area replete with the sights, sounds and scents of the subcontinent.

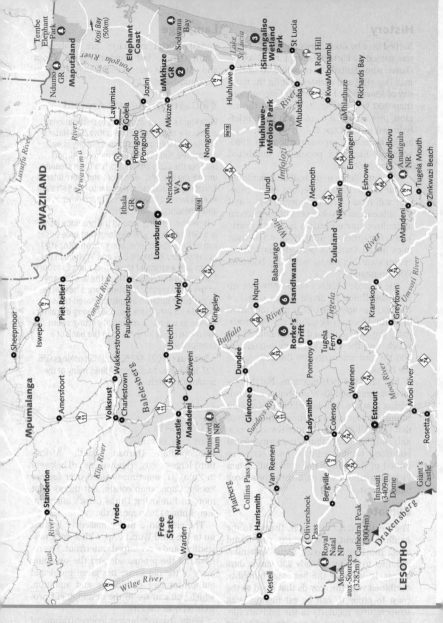

KwaZulu-Natal Highlights

1 Hluhluwe-iMfolozi Park (p270)
Wildlife spotting through the Big Five stomping ground.

2 uMkhuze Game Reserve (p277)
Birdwatching at a pan as the sun rises.

3 iSimangaliso Wetland Park (p272)
Hippo spotting and miles of isolated 4WD trails.

4 uKhahlamba-Drakensberg Park (p287) Walking or horseback riding in the mountainous wonderland.

5 Sani Pass (p293) Driving through the clouds on the way to Lesotho.

6 Isandlwana & Rorke's Drift (p303) Reliving the clashes of the Anglo-Zulu War

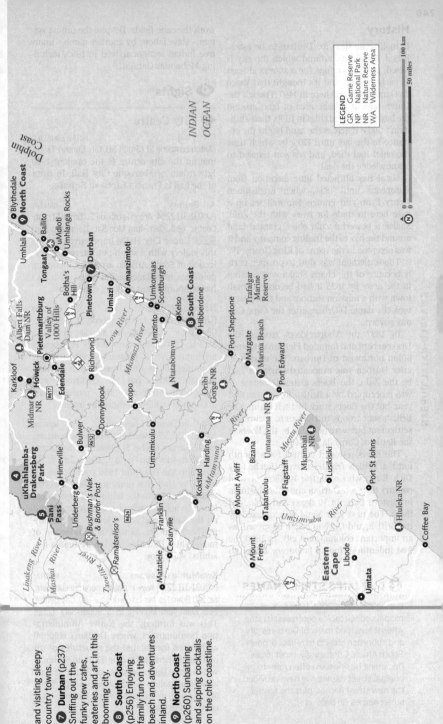

LEGEND
GR Game Reserve
NP National Park
NR Nature Reserve
WA Wilderness Area

100 km
50 miles

INDIAN
OCEAN

Dolphin Coast

North Coast

Blythedale
Ballito
uMdloti
Umhlanga Rocks
Umhlali
Tongaat
Durban
Botha's Hill
Pinetown
Umlazi
Amanzimtoti
Umkomaas
Scottburgh
Kelso
Hibberdene
South Coast
Umhlali

Karkloof
Albert Falls
Dam NR
Howick
Pietermaritzburg
Valley of
1000 Hills
Edendale
Richmond
Umzinto
Midmar
NR
Donnybrook
Ixopo
Umzimkulu

uKhahlamba-
Drakensberg
Park
Sani
Pass
Himeville
Underberg
Bulwer
Bushman's Nek
& Border Post
Ramatseliso's
Franklin
Cedarville
Matatiele
Kokstad
Harding

Port Shepstone
Trafalgar
Marine
Reserve
Margate
Marina Beach
Port Edward
Umtamvuna NR

Oribi
Gorge NR
Natabomvu

Mkambati
NR
Bizana
Flagstaff
Lusikisiki
Mkambati
Port St Johns
Hluleka NR
Coffee Bay

Mount Ayliff
Tabankulu
Mount
Frere
Umzimvubu River
Mount
Frere
Libode
Umtata
Eastern
Cape

Linakeng River
Mashai River
Tsoelike River

Lovu River
Mkomazi River
Mtamvuna River
Mtentu River
Mzimvubu River

and visiting sleepy
country towns.

⑦ Durban (p237)
Sniffing out the
funky new cafes,
eateries and art in this
booming city.

⑧ South Coast
(p256) Enjoying
family fun on the
beach and adventures
inland.

⑨ North Coast
(p260) Sunbathing
and sipping cocktails
on the chic coastline.

History

It took some time for Durban to be established. Natal Bay, around which the city is based, provided refuge for seafarers at least as early as 1685, and it's thought that Vasco da Gama anchored here in 1497. Though the Dutch bought a large area of land around the bay from a local chief in 1690, their ships didn't make it across the sand bar at the entrance to the bay until 1705, by which time the chief had died, and his son refused to acknowledge the deal.

Natal Bay attracted little attention from Europeans until 1824, when Englishmen Henry Fynn and Francis Farewell set up a base here to trade for ivory with the Zulu. Shaka, a powerful Zulu chief, granted land around the bay to the trading company and it was accepted in the name of King George IV.

The settlement was slow to prosper, partly because of the chaos Shaka was causing in the area. By 1835 it had become a small town with a mission station, and that year it took the name D'Urban, after the Cape Colony governor.

In 1837 the Voortrekkers crossed the Drakensberg and founded Pietermaritzburg, 80km northwest of Durban. The next year, after Durban was evacuated during a raid by the Zulu, the Boers claimed control. It was reoccupied by a British force later that year, but the Boers stuck by their claim. The British sent troops to Durban to secure the settlement but were defeated by the Boers at the Battle of Congella in 1842.

The Boers retained control for a month until a British frigate arrived (fetched by Dick King, who rode the 1000km of wild country between Durban and Grahamstown in Eastern Cape in 10 days) and dislodged them. The next year Natal was annexed by the British, and Durban began its growth as an important colonial port city. In 1860 the first indentured Indian labourers arrived to work the cane fields. Despite the unjust system – slave labour by another name – many free Indian settlers arrived in 1893, including Mohandas Gandhi.

◉ Sights

◉ City Centre

City Hall NOTABLE BUILDING
(Anton Lembede St (Smith St), City Centre) Dominating the city centre is the opulent 1910 Edwardian neo-baroque City Hall. In front of the hall is Francis Farewell Square.

Art Gallery GALLERY
(☑ 031-311 2264; Anton Lembede St (Smith St), City Centre; ⊗ 8.30am-4pm Mon-Sat, 11am-4pm Sun) FREE Under City Hall's impressive dome is this gallery with a small but interesting collection of South African artworks, including paintings, mixed media and ceramics. It also has temporary and rotating exhibitions.

Natural Science Museum MUSEUM
(☑ 031-311 2256; Anton Lembede St (Smith St), City Centre; ⊗ 8.30am-4pm Mon-Sat, from 11am Sun) FREE This museum at City Hall boasts an impressive, if pleasantly retro, display of stuffed birds and insects, plus African animals. Check out the cockroach and dung-beetle displays, the reconstructed dodo and the life-size dinosaur model.

Old Courthouse Museum MUSEUM
(☑ 031-311 2229; www.durbanhistorymuseums.org.za; 77 Samora Machel St (Aliwal St), City Centre; ⊗ 8.30am-4pm Mon-Fri, to 12.30pm Sat) FREE Found in the beautiful 1866 courthouse behind City Hall, this museum offers a worthwhile insight into the highs and lows of colonial living. There's also a moving exhibit on the sadly brief life of journalist Nathaniel (Nat) Wakasa, as well as a collection of model ships that kids (and more than a few adults) will enjoy.

KwaMuhle Museum MUSEUM
(☑ 031-311 2237; www.durbanhistorymuseums.org.za; 130 Bram Fischer Rd (Ordnance Rd), City Centre; ⊗ 8.30am-4pm Mon-Fri, to 12.30pm Sat) FREE This was formerly the Native Administration headquarters, where Durban's colonial authorities formulated the structures of urban racial segregation (the 'Durban System'), which were the blueprints of South Africa's apartheid policy. Exhibitions on apartheid are housed in various rooms leading off a central courtyard.

ⓘ DURBAN'S STREET NAMES

During 2007 and 2008 Durban's municipal council took a controversial step when it renamed many of Durban's city and suburban streets to reflect a 'new South Africa'. Confusingly, most locals (including businesses) often refer to the original street names. We have provided the new street names, plus the former street names (in brackets).

Berea & Around

★ **Campbell Collections**   GALLERY
(☑ 031-260 1720; http://campbell.ukzn.ac.za/;
220 Gladys Mazibuko Rd (Marriott Rd); R20; ⊙ by
appointment only) These collections are well
worth seeing. Muckleneuk, a superb house
designed by Sir Herbert Baker, holds the
documents and artefacts collected by Dr
Killie Campbell and her father Sir Marshall
Campbell (KwaMashu township is named
after him), and these are extremely important records of early Natal and Zulu culture.

Killie Campbell began collecting works
by black artists 60 years before the Durban
Gallery did so, and she was the first patron
of Barbara Tyrrell, who recorded the traditional costumes of the indigenous peoples.
Tyrrell's paintings beautifully convey clothing and decoration, and the grace of the people wearing them.

★ **Phansi Museum**   MUSEUM
(☑ 031-206 2889; https://phansi.com; 500 Esther Roberts Rd (Frere Rd), Glenwood; adult/child
R50/20; ⊙ 8am-4pm Mon-Fri, 10am-2pm Sat)
Found southwest of the city centre, this
museum features a private collection of
Southern African tribal artefacts, displayed
in Roberts House, a Victorian monument.
Owner-collector Paul Mikula has amassed
outstanding examples of contemporary
sculptures, beadwork of KwaZulu-Natal,
carved statues, and artefacts from pipes to
fertility dolls. Bookings required.

Kwazulu Natal Society of Arts   GALLERY
(☑ 031-277 1705; www.kznsagallery.co.za; 166
Bulwer Rd; ⊙ 9am-5pm Tue-Fri, to 4pm Sat, 10am-
3pm Sun) FREE This not-for-profit gallery
has temporary exhibitions of modern South
African art. Once you've perused the gallery,
its outdoor cafe, set under shady trees, is a
lovely place to visit. A gift shop is also within
the complex.

★ **Durban Botanic Gardens**   GARDENS
(☑ 031-309 9240; www.durbanbotanicgardens.org.
za; John Zikhali Rd (Sydenham Rd); ⊙ 7.30am-5.15pm
Sep-Apr, to 5.30pm May-Aug) FREE A 2000-sq-me-
tre garden featuring one of the rarest cycads
(*Encephalartos woodii*), as well as many
species of bromeliad, this is a lovely place to
wander. On weekends bridal parties galore
pose with their petals for photographers. The
gardens play host to an annual concert series
featuring the KwaZulu-Natal Philharmonic
Orchestra and other performances.

WORTH A TRIP

GANDHI SETTLEMENT

An often forgotten gem of Durban's
historic past lies just outside the city in
the Phoenix township. At the Gandhi
Settlement (☑ 073-055 5860; Phoenix;
⊙ 8am-4.30pm Mon-Fri, 9am-2.30pm Sat, by
appointment Sun) you can visit the house
where Mahatma Gandhi lived and resisted the oppressive apartheid regime.
There are several exhibits dedicated to
him, his wife Kasturba, and other leaders
of the anti-apartheid movement.

There is secure parking at the museum if you drive yourself. Several tour
compies offer day tours that include the
Gandhi Settlement.

★ **Moses Mabhida Stadium**   STADIUM
(☑ 031-582 8242; www.mmstadium.com; 44 Isaiah
Ntshangase Rd (Walter Gilbert Rd), Stamford Hill;
SkyCar adult/child R60/30, Adventure Walk per person R90, Big Swing per person R695; ⊙ SkyCar 9am-
5pm, Adventure Walk 10am, 1pm & 3pm Sat & Sun, Big
Swing 9.30am-6pm Mon-Fri, 8am-6pm Sat & Sun)
Durbanites are proud of their state-of-the-art
stadium, constructed for the 2010 World Cup.
Resembling a giant basket, it seats 56,000
people, and its arch was inspired by the 'Y'
in the country's flag. Visitors can head up to
the arch in a SkyCar, puff up on foot (550
steps) on an Adventure Walk or plunge off
the 106m arch on the giant Big Swing. All
options offer great views of Durban.

Cafes line a section of the stadium base;
from here you can explore on a Segway, hire
a bike or walk to the beachfront on the pedestrian promenade.

North & West Durban

Umgeni River Bird Park   WILDLIFE RESERVE
(☑ 031-579 4601; www.umgeniriverbirdpark.co.za;
490 Riverside Rd, Durban North; adult/child R55/36;
⊙ 9am-5pm) Found on the Umgeni River,
north of the centre, this bird park makes for
a relaxing escape from the throng. You can
see many African bird species in lush vegetation and aviaries. Don't miss the free-flight
bird show at 11am and 2pm Tuesday to Sunday, featuring birds from around the world.

Temple of Understanding   TEMPLE
(☑ 031-403 3328; www.iskcondurban.net; 50 Bhak-
tivedanta Swami Circle; ⊙ 10am-1pm & 4-9pm) Situated in Durban's west, this is the biggest

Durban

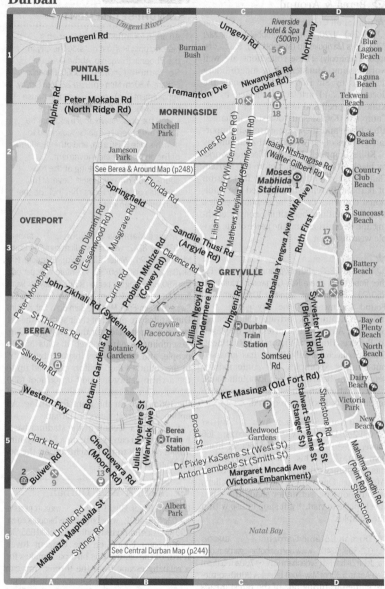

Hare Krishna temple in the southern hemisphere. The unusual building is designed in the shape of a lotus flower and is a treat for those interested in architecture or world religion. There is also a well-respected vegetarian restaurant (open 10.30am to 7pm, to 5pm Sundays) on the temple grounds.

Follow the N3 towards Pietermaritzburg and then branch off to the N2 south. Take the Chatsworth turn-off and turn right towards the centre of Chatsworth.

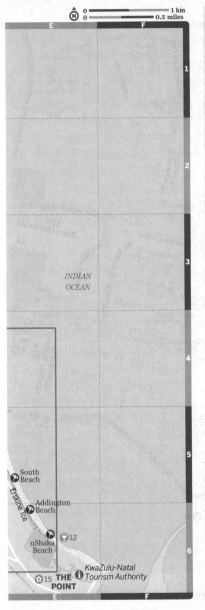

Durban

◎ Top Sights
1 Moses Mabhida Stadium....................D2

◎ Sights
2 Kwazulu Natal Society of Arts............A5
3 Suncoast Beach................................D3

● Activities, Courses & Tours
4 Durban Country Club D1
   STS Sport ....(see 1)
5 Windsor Park Municipal Golf
   Course..C1

▭ Sleeping
6 Blue Waters D3

✕ Eating
7 Cafe 1999..A4
8 Cafe Jiran..D3
9 Habesha Cafe..A5
10 Mali's Indian Restaurant......................C1
11 Neo Cafe D3

● Drinking & Nightlife
12 Moyo uShaka Pier Bar..........................E6
13 Origin..B5
14 S43...C1
   Unity Brasserie & Bar..................(see 7)

● Entertainment
15 Chairman E6
16 Kings Park Stadium..............................D2
17 Sun Coast Casino D3

● Shopping
18 African Art Centre................................C2
19 Musgrave Centre A4

Mon-Thu, 8.30am, 10am & 11.30am Fri) Maydon Wharf, which runs along the southwestern side of the harbour and south of Margaret Mncadi Ave, is home to the Sugar Terminal, which offers an insight into the sugar trade. The trade was the backbone of Durban's early economy.

Wilson's Wharf　　　　　　　WATERFRONT
This once-hip waterside development is now a little tired, but it's the best place to get a view of Durban's harbour and its activities. The harbour is the busiest in Southern Africa (and the ninth busiest in the world). The wharf has a clutch of eateries, boat-charter outfits, shops and a theatre. By car, enter opposite Hermitage St.

Port Natal Maritime Museum　　　MUSEUM
(☏ 031-322 9598; www.durbanhistorymuseums.org.za; Maritime Dr; adult/child R5/3; ◷ 8.30am-4pm

◎ Margaret Mncadi Avenue (Victoria Embankment)

Sugar Terminal　　　　　NOTABLE BUILDING
(☏ 031-365 8100; 25 Leuchars Rd; adult/child R20/10; ◷ tours 8.30am, 10am, 11.30am & 2pm

Central Durban

KWAZULU-NATAL DURBAN

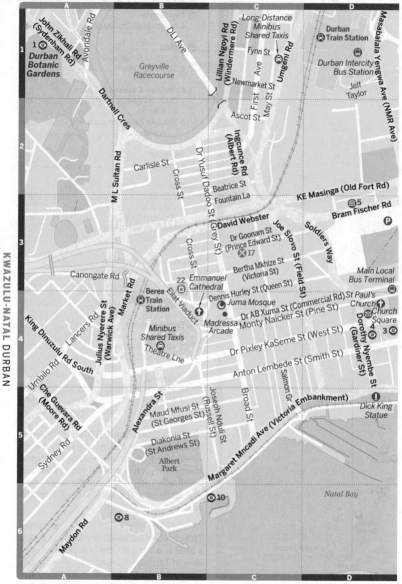

Mon-Sat, 11am-4pm Sun) In the midst of Durban's busy southern seafront you can explore two former steam tugs and see the huge wicker basket once used for hoisting passengers onto ocean liners.

⊙ Beachfront

Durban's beachfront has experienced a resurgence thanks to the massive revamp that was completed prior to the World Cup. The promenade is the town square of Durban.

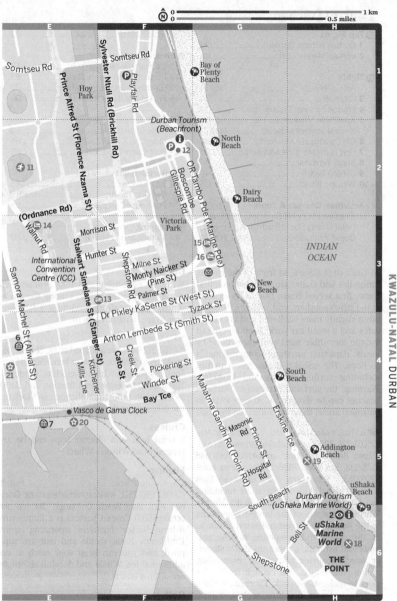

It runs behind the beaches but offers little shade. Both the beaches and promenade extend from the Blue Lagoon (at the mouth of the Umgeni River) to uShaka Marine World on the Point, an area known as the 'Golden Mile', although it's much longer. The road behind this is OR Tambo Pde (Marine Pde), and it's lined with high-rise hotels and a sprinkling of cafes.

Excellent signage at the beaches provides maps and names of the different beaches, as well as what activities are permitted there.

Central Durban

At **Suncoast Beach**, in front of the casino, umbrellas and chairs are available on a first come, first served basis. Due to its location at the strip's southern end, **uShaka Beach** is often slightly more sheltered and is close to cafes and a small car park. Keep an eye out for the incredible sand sculptures done by locals, depicting anything from mermaids to lions. The uShaka Beach has activities including surfing lessons and kayaking. Warning: the surf and currents at Durban's beaches can be dangerous. Always swim in patrolled areas; these are indicated by flags.

★**uShaka Marine World**   AMUSEMENT PARK
(☑031-328 8000; www.ushakamarineworld.co.za; uShaka Beach, the Point; adult/child Wet'n'Wild R178/138, Sea World R186/138, combined ticket R209/168; ⊙9am-5pm, Wet'n'Wild open from 10am Wed-Fri) Divided into areas including Sea World and Wet'n'Wild, uShaka Marine World boasts one of the largest aquariums in the world, the biggest collection of sharks in the southern hemisphere, marine animals and exhibits, a mock-up 1940s steamer wreck featuring two classy restaurants, a shopping centre, and enough freshwater rides to make you seasick. There are various options to 'meet' dolphins, seals and rays, but animal welfare groups suggest such interactions create stress for these creatures.

🏃 Activities

With a temperate climate and excellent facilities to enjoy, Durbanites are passionate about their nature, outdoor and adrenaline-inducing activities.

Cycling

With the pedestrian and bike promenades along the beachfront and linking the stadium to the beachfront, cycling is a fabulous way to see parts of Durban.

STS Sport   CYCLING
(☑031-312 9479; www.stssport.co.za; Shop 6, Moses Mabhida Stadium; per hour from R50; ⊙8am-6pm) Bicycles for hire, including tandems. You'll need to leave identification and R100 as a deposit; unfortunately, you can't lock up the bikes along the way.

Cruises

Several boat and charter trips can be arranged from Wilson's Wharf.

Fishing

Casea Charters   FISHING
(☑083 690 2511; www.caseacharters.co.za; Grannies Pool, Main Beach, Umhlanga; 3hr trip per person R600) Casea Charters is a family-run fishing-charter business operating from Umhlanga. Rods, tackle and bait are supplied, and you can keep your catch at no additional fee. Whale and dolphin sightings are often a bonus.

Golf

Durban has an array of decent golf courses. **Windsor Park Municipal Golf Course** (fax 031-312 2245; Masabalala Yengwa Ave (NMR Ave); green fee R58) is a popular option. On another level is **Durban Country Club** (☑031-313 1777; www.dcclub.co.za; Isaiah Ntshangase Rd; green fee R385), considered by some to be the best golf course in South Africa.

Indoor Extreme Activities

Besides the Big Swing (R695) inside Moses Mabhida Stadium (p241), you can try your surfing prowess at the artificial wave house (R130 per hour) at giant Gateway Mall (☑031-514 0500; www.gatewayworld.co.za; 1 Palm Blvd, Umhlanga Ridge; ☺9am-7pm Mon-Thu, to 9pm Fri & Sat, to 6pm Sun) – the water shots will have you performing tricks left, right and centre (your feet are secured into the board, so nonsurfers can have a go).

Skydiving

Skydive KZN   ADVENTURE SPORTS
(☑072 214 6040; www.skydivekzn.co.za; tandem jumps from R2000) Skydive KZN offers a seagull's view of Durban and surrounds. Jumps depart outside of the city.

Surfing & Kitesurfing

Durban has a multitude of good surfing beaches.

Ocean Ventures   SURFING, KAYAKING
(☑086 100 1138; www.oceanventures.co.za; uShaka Marine World; lessons R200, board hire per hour from R120; ☺8am-4pm) Learn to surf on uShaka Beach, or rent a board and go it alone. Ocean Ventures also hires out kayaks (per person R100, tours/lessons R220/250) and offers tours and tuition in stand-up paddleboarding.

Kitesports   WATER SPORTS
(☑082 572 4163; www.kitesports.co.za; Umdloti Centre) Kite-surfing is very popular around Durban; lessons are available through Kitesports at Umdloti, just north of Umhlanga.

☞ Tours

A good way to experience Durban is in the company of a professional tour guide. Many hostels also arrange backpacker-oriented tours and activities in the Durban area and around KwaZulu-Natal.

Natal Sharks Board Boat Tour   BOATING
(☑082 403 9206; www.shark.co.za; Wilson's Wharf; 2hr boat trip R350; ☺departs 6.30am Mon-Fri) A fascinating trip is to accompany Natal Sharks Board personnel in their boat when they tag and release trapped sharks and other fish from the shark nets that protect Durban's beachfront. Boats depart from Wilson's Wharf, which is not to be confused with the head office, which is located in Umhlanga Rocks.

Ricksha Bus   BUS
(☑031-322 4209; www.durbanexperience.co.za; adult/child R100/50) Durban's open-top bus tour is a good way to see the city. It covers some city highlights and heads to suburbs including the popular Florida Rd in

KWAZULU-NATAL DURBAN

DON'T MISS

KZN'S PARKS & RESERVES

For those planning to spend time in the province's excellent parks and reserves, Ezemvelo KZN Wildlife (p287) is an essential first stop. Accommodation within the parks ranges from shabby to chic, from humble campsites to comfortable safari tents and luxurious lodges; the free *Fees & Charges* booklet lists accommodation options and prices, as well as entrance charges, for all Ezemvelo KZN Wildlife reserves. Maps of the parks are also available here.

All accommodation must be booked in advance by phone, online, or in person through the Pietermaritzburg office. Last-minute bookings (those within 48 hours) must be made directly with the camps.

Officially, the gate entry times of all parks are 5am to 7pm (1 October to 31 March) and 6am to 6pm (1 April to 30 September).

While many of the parks are a must-see for animal-lovers and outdoorsy types, their camps – many of which have high-quality bungalows or safari tents – are also excellent for families and those touring South Africa on a budget.

Tip: If you only have time to visit one or two reserves, highlights include Royal Natal National Park (p298) for some uKhahlamba-Drakensberg vistas; Hluhluwe-iMfolozi Park (p270) for the wildlife and wilderness accommodation options; Ithala Game Reserve (p268) and uMkhuze Game Reserve (p277) for its wonderful bird hides and waterholes; and iSimangaliso Wetland Park (p272) for its diverse scenery and ecological environments.

Berea & Around

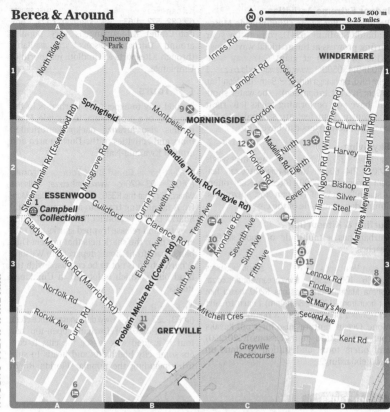

0 ———————— 500 m
0 ———————— 0.25 miles

Morningside. Buses depart daily at 9am and 1pm from the beach branch of Durban Tourism (☎031-322 4205; www.durbanexperience.co.za; Old Pavilion Site, OR Tambo Pde (Marine Pde); ⏱8am-5pm).

🎊 Festivals & Events

Awesome Africa Music Festival   MUSIC
(⏱late Sep/early Oct) Highlighting music and theatre from across the continent.

**Durban International
Film Festival**   FILM
(www.durbanfilmfest.co.za; ⏱Jul) A cinematic showcase of 200-plus films, held in July. One of the oldest and largest film festivals in Southern Africa.

Diwali   RELIGIOUS
The three-day Diwali (towards the end of the year; dates change) is also known as the Festival of Lights.

🛏 Sleeping

Despite what you may think when you see the hotel-lined beachfront promenade, much of Durban's best accommodation is in the suburbs. Unless you are set on sleeping by the sea, accommodation in the suburbs is better value than the beachfront options. You'll also deal with less noise, especially in the summer months.

🛏 City Centre

Note that the city centre shuts down (and is less safe) at night.

Curiocity Backpackers   HOSTEL $$
(☎031-286 0025; http://curiocitybackpackers.com; 55 Monty Naicker Rd, South Beach; dm/s with shared bathroom from R220/320, d from R990; ⏽) After opening a hit backpackers in Johannesburg, Curiocity turned its sights on Durban. Accommodation here is in a perfectly charming colonial building down-

Berea & Around

town. The minimalist room design and large atrium-style lounge give the place a clean, modern feel, without coming off as too sterile. Due to the location some guests do complain about the noise and the safety of the neighbourhood at night.

In addition to hanging out in the lounge, there are also more activities than you can shake a stick at, including city tours, rooftop braais (barbecues) and pub crawls.

Durban Hilton International   BUSINESS HOTEL $$$
(☑ 031-336 8100; www.hilton.com; 12 Walnut Rd; r from R1800; 🅿 ✳ @ 🛜 ☒) Glitzy and chic, this modern behemoth offers a predictable hotel experience and attracts mainly business travellers. Ask about the specials.

🏳 Berea & Around

★ **Concierge**   BOUTIQUE HOTEL $$
(☑ 031-309 4453; www.the-concierge.co.za; 36-42 St Mary's Ave, Greyville; r from R1190; 🅿 ✳ 🛜) One of Durbs' most cutting-edge sleeping options, this cleverly conceived spot – 12 cosy rooms in four pods – is more about the design (urban, funky, shape-oriented) than the spaces (smallish but adequate). The bathrooms are open, so best for singles or close couples. For breakfast, roll out of bed and head to Freedom Cafe, also on the premises.

Napier House   B&B $$
(☑ 031-207 6779; www.napierhouse.co.za; 31 Napier Rd, Berea; s/d incl breakfast R850/1300; 🅿 ✳ 🛜 ☒) On a poky little street near the Botanic Gardens, this is an excellent, homey B&B that is terrific value. The former colonial residence has five en-suite rooms that are spacious, light and tastefully organised and have large bathrooms. Breakfast is a highlight, as are the friendly hosts.

Madeline Grove   B&B $$
(www.madeline.co.za; 116 Madeline Rd, Morningside; s/d incl breakfast from R750/1050; 🅿 🛜 ☒) Close to Florida Rd's bars and restaurants, this largish guesthouse has a range of rooms, including some with balconies and a couple of smaller budget-friendly options (single/double R450/790). There are plenty of places on the grounds to relax with a cup of tea or a sundowner.

Gibela Backpackers Lodge   HOSTEL $$
(☑ 031-303 6291; www.gibelabackpackers.co.za; 119 Ninth Ave, Morningside; dm/s/d R280/545/750; 🅿 @ 🛜 ☒) This hostel (a tastefully converted 1950s Tuscan-style home) gets lots of good reports from travellers, including those travelling by themselves. Continental breakfasts are enjoyed in an attractive indoor-outdoor dining area. The quiet atmosphere is perfect for those looking for a bargain, but aren't interested in the hostel party scene. Friendly owner Elmar knows everything there is to know about life in Durban.

Benjamin   BOUTIQUE HOTEL $$$
(☑ 031-303 4233; www.benjamin.co.za; 141 Florida Rd, Morningside; s/d incl breakfast R1290/1655; 🅿 ✳ 🛜 ☒) This upmarket boutique hotel is filled with 'clipped accents and smart rooms of the 'heavy drapes and floral furnishings' variety, around a pretty paved and green courtyard area. It's in a terrific location at the bottom of Florida Rd and with eating and drinking places galore a short walk away.

Quarters   BOUTIQUE HOTEL $$$
(☑ 031-303 5246; www.quarters.co.za; 101 Florida Rd, Morningside; s/d from R1450/1900; 🅿 ✳ 🛜) Right in the throbbing heart of Durban's busiest eating and drinking quarter, this attractive boutique hotel – at two neighbouring locations – balances colonial glamour with small-scale home comforts. There's an on-site restaurant at both. Some rooms do suffer from the noise on busy Florida Rd.

KWAZULU-NATAL DURBAN

📛 North Durban

The area north of Umgeni River comprises many suburbs, including Durban North and Umgeni Heights. Leafy, quiet and sedate, Durban North is one of Durban's wealthier areas and is still easily accessible to the city and the North Coast. Mackeurtan Ave has recently blossomed as the new hot stretch of restaurants and bars in the city.

★ Smith's Cottage   HOSTEL $
(📞 031-564 6313; http://smithscottage.co.za; 5 Mount Argus Rd, Umgeni Heights; dm/d R230/600, self-catering cottages R1500; P 🛜 ❄) An excellent budget option within chirping distance of the Umgeni River Bird Park. It's set around a suburban garden and has a couple of free-standing (smallish) cabins, a large 12-bed dorm with attached kitchen, a smaller four-bed dorm inside the house and even a caravan for the ultra-budget conscious. The whole place has a great feel; the hosts couldn't be friendlier.

Next door is the sister property **De Charmoy** (www.riverside.decharmoy.co.za; 7 Mount Argus Rd, Umgeni Heights; s/d incl breakfast from R650/850; ❄🛜❄), an upmarket alternative with a similarly friendly demeanour.

Riverside Hotel & Spa   HOTEL $$$
(📞 031-563 0600; www.riversidehotel.co.za; 10 Kenneth Kaunda Rd (Northway), Durban North; r from R1475; P 🛜❄) It's hard to miss this white behemoth just over the Umgeni River on the right-hand side. The pool area has a sprawling LA vibe and the rooms offer all the comforts of an upmarket place. It's close to the city, as well as lots of notable restaurants in Durban North. The restaurant doesn't get great reviews. Some guests complain of noise in rooms on the 1st floor.

📛 Beachfront

Protea Hotel
Edward Durban   BUSINESS HOTEL $$
(📞 031-337 3681; www.proteahotels.com/edwarddurban; 149 OR Tambo Pde (Marine Pde); r from R1235; P ❄@❄) King of the seafront hotels, this is classic and comfortable, with fresh-polish smells and full-on decor.

Blue Waters   HOTEL $$$
(📞 031-327 7000; www.bluewatershotel.co.za; 175 Snell Pde; s/d incl breakfast from R2197/2294; P ❄🛜) At the northern end of the beachfront, away from the promenade crowd, Blue Waters is a classic hotel that has recently undergone an extensive renovation. Rooms have brilliant ocean views, soft bedding and stylish furnishings. There are also rare amenities for the beachfront, such as a sauna and an indoor pool. Rates are significantly cheaper in the off-season, especially during the week.

Garden Court Marine Parade   HOTEL $$$
(📞 031-337 3341; www.tsogosun.com; 167 OR Tambo Pde (Marine Pde); r from R1405; P ❄🛜❄) A superb beachfront option, Garden Court was given a snazzy overhaul in 2014 and now boasts sleek, modern rooms, all with ocean views.

📛 Glenwood & Around

Southwest of the city centre, Glenwood is one of Durban's oldest suburbs and is the most bohemian area. While we're not exactly talking rasta beanies or New York cutting edge, it has nevertheless a genuine sense of creative community, with some great cafes and sleeping options.

Mackaya Bella Guest House   GUESTHOUSE $$
(📞 031-205 8790; www.mackayabella.co.za; 137 Penzance Rd; s/d incl breakfast R950/1350, budget r R475; P ❄🛜❄) 🍴 Located near the university, this pretty spot has a lovely indigenous garden (featuring the Mackaya Bella plant) and stylish rooms in a relaxed home-style environment. The owners, Nicki and Mike, are delightful and whip up a delicious breakfast each morning in the sun-drenched common area. Special amenities, such as an airport shuttle service, make this place extra special.

The budget single rooms have a minimum three-night stay, but are very well appointed and a great choice for travellers on a budget who want to avoid the backpackers scene. There is also a self-catering family suite. Reserve ahead as it's popular with university-associated guests.

Roseland House   GUESTHOUSE $$
(📞 031-201 3256; www.roseland.co.za; 291 Helen Joseph Rd (Davenport Rd); s/d incl breakfast R1000/1400; P 🛜❄) A well-established guesthouse with friendly hosts, an excellent breakfast, two swimming pools and a dozen rooms fitted with wooden furniture. There are restaurants and shops within walking distance.

✕ Eating

Indian and Asian flavours abound in Durban, as do healthy meat and salad dishes (although these can become a little repetitive).

BUNNY CHOW

You can't leave Durban without sampling bunny chow. It's the ultimate takeaway food, where the container (a loaf of bread) is part of the meal and the only utensils are your hands and a chunk of bread. The hollowed-out loaf is filled with curry – usually beans, chicken or lamb – which you scoop out with pieces of the loaf. You can order a quarter or half loaf – a quarter is usually plenty for one person. Bunny chow is available in restaurants and backstreet dives throughout Durban. Here are a few choice spots.

Hollywood Bets (☑031-309 4920; cnr Linze & De Mazenod Rds, Greyville; bunnies R50-105; ☺7am-8pm) This cafe tacked onto a betting shop is an unlikely lunch spot, but the bunnies here are legendary and, indeed, award-winning.

House of Curries (☑031-303 6076; 275 Florida Rd, Morningside; mains R50-120; ☺9am-10.30pm) On Florida Rd, this is a more salubrious spot than many to sample bunny chow.

Little Gujarat (43 Dr Goonam St (Prince Edward St); mains R30-70; ☺7am-7.30pm Mon-Sat; 🍴) A long-running city-centre takeout, specialising in vegetarian dishes.

✖ Beachfront

Hip eateries are starting to pop up on the beachfront alongside the usual spread of burgers, pizza and candy floss. At opposite ends of the promenade, uShaka Marina and the casino both have some excellent choices.

Surf Riders Food Shack   BURGERS **$$**
(☑062 747 7037; 17 Erskine Tce, Addington Beach; mains R65-140; ☺7am-5pm Mon-Thu, to 8pm Fri, to 6pm Sat & Sun; 🍴) Marking a resurgence of beachfront dining, Surf Riders has tables alongside the promenade where surfers, travellers and hip locals meet to chomp on gourmet burgers, wood-fired pizzas, tacos and a few seafood dishes. There's craft beer on tap, or for something healthier try a protein shake with your morning oats.

Neo Cafe   PORTUGUESE **$$**
(☑031-332 2299; Summer Sq, 37 Sol Harris Cres, North Beach; mains R80-175; ☺noon-8.45pm Mon-Sat) Portuguese food isn't a rarity in KwaZulu-Natal, but when it's done as well as it is at Neo Cafe it's worth getting excited about. The menu is simple: chicken and seafood dishes smothered in perfectly spicy peri-peri sauce. Instead of choosing surf or turf go ahead and just get a half chicken and calamari combo.

Cafe Jiran   CAFE **$$**
(☑031-332 4485; 151 Snell Pde; mains R70-140; ☺7am-10pm Mon-Fri, from 8am Sat & Sun) Temporarily located in the garden of the Bel-Aire Suites Hotel, this funky space is the spot for a post-dip coffee, fruit crush or breakfast, or just to mingle with Durban's hip elite. Dining options range from artisanal wraps

and burgers to grilled fish and classic Durban curries. The cafe's regular location, next door to the Bel-Aire, was under renovation at the time of research.

Moyo   INTERNATIONAL **$$**
(☑031-332 0606; 1 Bell St, uShaka Marina, the Point; mains R95-195; ☺restaurant 11am-10pm) Housed in the uShaka complex, Moyo is more novelty than quality cuisine, and makes for a fun (if noisy) night out. The concept is great – the decor features sculptures and decorations from recycled materials, and there's face painting, fabulous table-side serenades and bands of a high quality. Food includes ostrich salad and Knysna oysters.

✖ Berea & Around

Florida Rd is chock-a-block with lively eateries, cafes and bars, and nearby Lilian Ngoyi Rd (Windermere Rd) has some good options, too. There is a wonderful cafe hub opposite Mitchell Park on Innes Rd.

Habesha Cafe   ETHIOPIAN **$**
(☑076 046 2516; 124 Helen Joseph Rd; dishes R50-75; ☺8am-10pm Mon-Thu, to 11pm Fri & Sat; 🍴) Durbanites rave about this casual Ethiopian spot that serves up traditional platters of food with plenty of injera. Everything on the menu is incredible, so it's best to go with a friend or two so you can sample all of the dishes. There are also plenty of veggie options, of course.

★ Mali's Indian Restaurant   INDIAN **$$**
(☑031-312 8535; 77 Smiso Nkwanyana Rd (Goble Rd), Morningside; mains R90-120; ☺12.30-3pm & 6-10pm Tue-Sat, to 9pm Sun) In a city that

boasts a huge Indian population, this place is about as good as Indian food gets in Durban's restaurant scene. The outside looks like it could be a doctor's office, but inside you'll find North and South Indian dishes with a friendly, family-run atmosphere.

Cafe 1999
INTERNATIONAL $$
(☑ 031-202 3406; www.cafe1999.co.za; Silverton Rd, Silvervause Centre, Berea; tapas R80, mains R125-175; ⊘ 12.30-2.30pm & 6.30-10.30pm Mon-Thu, to 11pm Fri, 6.30-11pm Sat; ☏) This classy restaurant looks unassuming inside, but assume that you will get seriously good modern Mediterranean fusion food here. Tapas including stuffed and deep-fried olives, kudu carpaccio and chilli prawns all hit the spot. There are always lots of daily specials, and friendly waitstaff to run you through them.

Market
INTERNATIONAL $$
(☑ 031-309 8581; www.marketrestaurant.co.za; 40 Gladys Mazibuko Rd (Marriott Rd), Greyville; mains R80-175; ⊘ 11am-9.30pm Tue, from 8am Wed-Sat, 8.30am-4pm Sun; ☏) ✐ Breakfast, lunch and dinner are all a hit at this hip Durban restaurant. Imaginative dishes include the likes of calamari, quinoa, feta, red pesto and macadamia salad; produce is locally sourced, free range and organic, where possible. The cafe's tree-lined courtyard and fountain are the perfect antidote to the hot weather and the craft beer is reasonably priced.

Spiga D'oro
ITALIAN $$
(☑ 031-303 9511; www.spiga.co.za; 200 Florida Rd; mains R65-115; ⊘ 7am-11pm Sun-Wed, to midnight Thu, to 1.45am Fri & Sat) It looks like a typical cafe along this very popular strip, but Spiga serves up hearty helpings of Italian food, including delicious pasta dishes. It also makes a great place to grab a cocktail or glass of wine. On the weekends, this place is packed with locals enjoying some people-watching along Florida Rd. A dining section in the rear requires reservations.

Joop's Place
STEAK $$
(☑ 031-312 9135; Ninth Ave, Avonmore Centre, Morningside; mains R95-195; ⊘ 6.30pm-9.30pm Mon-Sat, plus noon-2pm Fri) In a most unlikely location at the rear of a shopping centre, unpretentious Joop's Place has Durbanites flocking in for high-quality steaks – each cooked by Joop himself. Order yours plain or smothered in a delicious sauce of your choice. A local favourite.

9th Avenue Bistro
INTERNATIONAL $$$
(☑ 031-312 9134; www.9thavenuebistro.co.za; Ninth Ave, Avonmore Centre, Morningside; mains R175-199; ⊘ noon-2.30pm Tue-Fri, 6-10pm Mon-Sat) The setting, in the car park of the Avonmore Centre, isn't anything to rave about, but the fine-dining experience is. This smart, modern spot serves up fabulously reliable upmarket fare. The tasting menu changes (often with venison, and the likes of smoked ostrich fillet), while the bistro standards include braised beef short rib and line-caught fish of the day.

🍷 Drinking & Nightlife

Many drinking and dancing dens are found in the suburbs along Florida Rd; the casino also has some good spots. Nightclubs seem to set up and close down to their own very fast beat. Many of the best places to go are in developing neighbourhoods that are otherwise deserted, so it's always best to take a cab when going out.

★ S43
BREWERY
(☑ 031-303 2747; 43 Station Dr, Berea; ⊘ 4pm-midnight Tue-Thu, from noon Fri & Sat) This warehouse-like space alongside the train tracks is in a complex of arty enterprises that is set to gentrify this formerly downtrodden district. Beers from That Brewing Company are brewed and served here – the APA and Weiss are particularly good. The menu is inspired by global street food and features burgers, pulled-pork tacos and, of course, bunny chow.

Unity Brasserie & Bar
BREWERY
(☑ 031-201 3470; www.unitybar.co.za; 117 Silverton Rd, Silvervause Centre; ⊘ noon-10.30pm Mon-Thu, to midnight Fri & Sat) This cosy bar has quality craft beer on tap from a range of breweries from Durban, Johannesburg and the Cape. It's a very friendly place, with families welcome during the day and early evening.

Connor's Public House
PUB
(☑ 031-563 4462; Shop 11 & 13 Mackeurtan Ave; ⊘ 9am-midnight; ☏) Young and old, black and white, hip and square: Connor's Pub on popular Mackeurtan Ave attracts Durbanites from all strata of society. There's nothing particularly special about the drinks or the food, but the friendly atmosphere can't be topped. Come on a weekday afternoon for midday happy hours for a few cheap beers and people-watching.

Origin
CLUB
(☑ 031-201 9959; www.theorigin.co.za; 9 Clark Rd, Lower Glenwood; ⊘ 8.30pm-late Sat) Covering a range of music from deep house to electro, soul and funk (and much more), this stylish

spot remains at the forefront of Durban's club scene. Sometimes open Friday night – check the events page on its website before going.

Moyo uShaka Pier Bar
BAR

(☑031-332 0606; www.moyo.co.za; 1 Bell St, uShaka Marine World, the Point; ☺11am-9pm Mon-Fri, from 10am Sat & Sun) Perched out on the edge of a pier in front of uShaka Marine World, this is a top spot to go for a South African sundowner with fabulous views of the harbour on one side, the Indian Ocean on the other, and the stadium and cityscape beyond. It's laid-back, exotic Durban at its chic best.

☆ Entertainment

Durban is a lively city with a vibrant cultural scene. Hundreds of events, from Natal Sharks rugby games and cricket matches to film festivals and theatre performances, can be booked through Computicket (www.computicket.com). There are outlets at the Playhouse Company, and at Shoprite and Checkers supermarkets throughout the city.

Live Music

Chairman
LIVE MUSIC

(☑after hours 079 753 6313, until 4.30pm 031-368 2133; www.thechairmanlive.com; 146 Mahatma Gandhi Rd (Point Rd); entrance fee R150; ☺7pm-2am Thu-Sat) This classy lounge-bar is in an up-and-coming part of Durban, but for now it's best to grab a cab to get here. This sprawling bar and lounge has a maximalist design with antiques, game trophies and strange paintings covering the walls. There are jazz performances, but it's well worth going just to taste one of the excellent cocktails.

KwaZulu-Natal Philharmonic Orchestra
CLASSICAL MUSIC

(☑031-369 9438; http://kznphil.org.za) The orchestra has an interesting spring concert program with regular performances in City Hall (p240). Check the calendar and events listings on the website.

BAT Centre
LIVE MUSIC

(☑031-332 0451; www.batcentre.co.za; 45 Maritime Pl, Victoria Embankment) One of Durban's more interesting, if unreliable, arty haunts, this venue features semiregular jazz performances – check what's on before heading down. Note that the area is isolated, so it can be dodgy at night. It's off Margaret Mncadi Ave (Victoria Embankment).

Rainbow Restaurant & Jazz Club
JAZZ

(☑031-702 9161; www.therainbow.co.za; 23 Stanfield Lane, Pinetown) In Pinetown, 15km west of the centre, this was the first place in Natal to cater to blacks in a so-called 'white area' in the 1980s. With a reputation as the centre of the jazz scene and still the preferred local haunt, it features gigs on the first or last Sunday of the month. See the website for info.

Zack's
LIVE MUSIC

(☑031-312 0755; www.zacks.co.za; Lilian Ngoyi Rd (Windermere Rd), Windermere Centre; ☺8am-late) Weekends see this unassuming restaurant liven up with performances from local rock, jazz and blues bands. There's another venue at Wilson's Wharf.

Theatre

Playhouse Company
THEATRE

(☑031-369 9555; www.playhousecompany.com; 29 Anton Lembede St (Smith St)) Opposite City Hall, Durban's central theatre is a stunning venue. The Zulu mosaics and beadwork in the foyer are alone worth seeing, as are the dance, drama and music performances.

Catalina Theatre
THEATRE

(☑031-837 5999; 18 Boatman's Rd, Wilson's Wharf) This is a not-for-profit venture that brings new artistic works to the stage. Boatman's Rd runs parallel to Margaret Mncadi Ave (Victoria Embankment).

Sport

Cricket, football and rugby are played in KwaZulu-Natal. Professional teams such as AmaZulu play in town, and international teams also visit.

Moses Mabhida Stadium (p241) was built to host the 2010 World Cup. With 60,000 seats, Kings Park Stadium (☑031-308 8400; Jacko Jackson Dr) is currently home to the Natal Sharks (www.sharksrugby.co.za) rugby team. Cricket fever is cured at Kingsmead Cricket Stadium (Sahara Stadium; ☑031-335 4200; 2 Kingsmead Cl), where the international knockabouts are hosted.

🔒 Shopping

Durban is known for its factory outlets, which stock everything from surfing items to footwear at reasonable prices. For necessities, major shopping centres include the Musgrave Centre (☑031-277 8420; www.musgravecentre.co.za; Musgrave Rd; ☺9am-6pm Mon-Fri, from 8.30am Sat, 9am-5pm Sun) and Pavilion (☑031-275 9818;

STATION DRIVE PRECINCT

Following trends set in Cape Town and Johannesburg, Station Drive Precinct is an artsy complex that's helping to regenerate a run-down part of town. Shops within include designer-clothing boutiques, a photography studio, a distillery and a brewpub. There is a market here on Sunday mornings and a host of events on the first Thursday of each month.

⊙9am-7pm); the latter is in Westville, a 10km drive from the centre on the N3 towards Pietermaritzburg.

Victoria Street Market
MARKET
(☑031-306 4021; www.thevsm.co.za; 151-155 Bertha Mkhize St (Victoria St), City Centre; ⊙8am-5pm Mon-Fri, to 3pm Sat & Sun) This busy market, located at the western end of Bertha Mkhize St, is the hub of the Indian community. It offers a typically rip-roaring subcontinental shopping experience, with more than 160 stalls selling wares from across Asia. It's generally safe, but watch your wallet and don't take valuables. Note: most shops run by Muslims close between noon and 2pm on Friday.

African Art Centre
ARTS & CRAFTS
(☑031-312 3084; www.afriart.org.za; 15A Station Dr; ⊙8.30am-5pm Mon-Fri, 9am-3pm Sat) This not-for-profit gallery has an excellent selection of high-quality work by rural craftspeople and artists. It's a great place to pick up unique, ethically sourced souvenirs. In 2017 it relocated to the trendy Station Dr Precinct.

Ike's Books & Collectables
BOOKS
(☑031-303 9214; http://ikesbooks.com; 48A Florida Rd; ⊙10am-5pm Mon-Fri, 9am-2pm Sat) More like a museum than a bookshop, this antique-filled delight is chock-a-block with first editions and is everything an antiquarian bookshop should be. There is an emphasis on Africana in its selection.

Khaya Records
MUSIC
(☑031-303 2936; 85 4th Ave; ⊙10am-4pm Mon-Fri, 9am-3pm Sat, to 1pm Sun) Durban's hip elite hang out at this delightfully cluttered record shop. There is a coffee shop and expansive veranda where music is always pumping.

ⓘ Information

DANGERS & ANNOYANCES
As with elsewhere in South Africa, crime against tourists and locals can and does occur in Durban. Be aware and careful, but not paranoid.

➡ Muggings and pickpocketing have declined around the beach area since its upgrade, but be careful here at night, and around the Umgeni Rd side of the train station and the Warwick Triangle markets.

➡ Always catch a cab to and from nightspots, as well as uShaka Marine World.

➡ Parking is generally OK outside suburban restaurants, but use off-street parking overnight (most accommodation options offer this).

➡ Never leave valuables exposed on your car seats, even while driving.

EMERGENCY
Ambulance 10177
General emergency 031-361 0000

MEDICAL SERVICES
Entabeni Hospital (☑031-204 1300, 24hr trauma centre 031-204 1377; 148 Mazisi Kunene Rd (South Ridge Rd), Berea) The trauma centre charges around R700 per consultation, the balance of which is refunded if the full amount is not utilised.

St Augustines (☑031-268 5000; 107 JB Marks Rd, Berea) KwaZulu-Natal's largest private hospital has a good emergency department.

Travel Doctor (☑031-360 1122; www.durban-traveldoctor.co.za; 45 Bram Fischer Rd (Ordnance Rd), International Convention Centre; ⊙8.30am-4pm Mon-Fri, to 11am Sat) For travel-related advice.

Umhlanga Hospital (☑031-560 5500; 323 Umhlanga Rocks Dr, Umhlanga) Handy for the North Coast and north Durban.

TOURIST INFORMATION
Durban Tourism (☑031-322 4164; www.durbanexperience.co.za; 90 Florida Road, Morningside; ⊙8am-4.30pm Mon-Fri) A useful information service on Durban and surrounds. It can help with general accommodation and arrange tours of Durban and beyond. There are also branches at the beachfront (p248) and at uShaka Marine World (☑031-322 2858; 1 Bell St, uShaka Marine World; ⊙8am-4.30pm Mon-Fri).

King Shaka Airport Tourist Information Office (☑032-436 6585; international arrivals hall; ⊙8am-9pm Mon-Sat, from 9am Sun) Durban Tourism, KwaZulu-Natal Tourism Authority and Ezemvelo KZN Wildlife all share a desk (the latter is open 8am to 4.30pm Monday to Friday only) at the airport.

KwaZulu-Natal Tourism Authority (KZN Tourism; ☑031-366 7500; www.zulu.org.za; 29

Canal Quay Rd, Ithala Trade Centre, the Point; ⊙8am-4.30pm Mon-Fri) Has lots of glossy brochures, but the assistance stops there.

Tourism KwaZulu-Natal (☑031-816 6600; Shop 1A, uShaka Marine World; ⊙9am-6pm Sun-Thu, to 7pm Fri & Sat) The main tourist information centre for the region, and Durban, is in the uShaka Marine World shopping centre.

ⓘ Getting There & Away

AIR

King Shaka International Airport (DUR; ☑032-436 6585; http://kingshakainternational.co.za) opened in 2010, and is at La Mercy, 40km north of the city.

Several airlines link Durban with South Africa's other main centres. Internet fares vary greatly depending on the day of the week, the month and even the time of day.

Kulula (☑086 158 5852; www.kulula.com) A budget airline linking Durban with Jo'burg, Cape Town and Port Elizabeth.

Mango (☑0861 001 234; www.flymango.com) A no-frills airline that is a subsidiary of SAA, with flights to Jo'burg and Cape Town.

South African Airlink (SAAirlink; ☑011-451 7300; https://flyairlink.com/) Flies daily to Nelspruit, Bloemfontein and George.

South African Airways (SAA; ☑011-978 1111; www.flysaa.com) Flies at least once daily to most major regional airports in South Africa.

There has also been an uptick in international flights direct to Durban in recent years, with a direct flight from Dubai linking King Shaka to the rest of the world for tourism.

BUS

Long-distance buses leave from the **bus station** near the Durban train station. Enter the station from Masabalala Yengwa Ave (NMR Ave), not Umgeni Rd. Long-distance bus companies have their offices here.

Note: tickets for all long-distance buses can be bought from Shoprite/Checkers shops and online at www.computicketravel.com.

Baz Bus (☑021-422 5202; SMS bookings 076 427 3003; www.bazbus.com) Hop-on, hop-off backpacker shuttle service to/from Cape Town and Jo'burg. See the website for routes and ticket options.

Eldo Coaches (☑031-307 3363; www.eldo coaches.co.za) Inexpensive bus liner that runs to many locations around KwaZulu-Natal, as well as the rest of South Africa. Tickets to Johannesburg are around R200, but it's not as nice as other options.

Greyhound (☑087 352 0352; www.greyhound.co.za) Has daily buses to Jo'burg (R350, eight hours), Cape Town (R750, 22 to 27 hours), Port Elizabeth (R600, 15 hours) and Port Shepstone (R350, 1¾ hours). Within KZN, Greyhound buses run daily to Pietermaritzburg (R250, one hour) and Ladysmith (R360, four hours), among other destinations.

Intercape (☑021-380 4400; www.intercape.co.za) Has several daily buses to Jo'burg (R340, eight hours). For connections to Mozambique, buses head to Maputo (via Jo'burg; R810, 22 hours).

Intercity (☑031-305 9090; www.intercity.co.za) Cheap bus option for destinations all over South Africa from Durban's bus depot. Trips to Johannesburg run around R200. The service gets lower reviews from travellers than other options.

Margate Mini Coach (☑039-312 1406; www.margatecoach.co.za) Head to Durban station or King Shaka International Airport to hop on this bus, which links Durban and Margate three times a day (R220, 2½ hours), and also Port Edward (R240, three hours).

Translux (☑086 158 9282; www.translux.co.za) Runs daily buses to nationwide destinations, including Jo'burg (R300, eight hours) and Cape Town (R720, 27 hours).

SHARED TAXI

Some long-distance minibus taxis leave from stops in the streets opposite the Umgeni Rd entrance to the Durban train station. Others running mainly to the South Coast and the Wild Coast region of Eastern Cape leave from around the Berea train station. Check with your cab driver; they usually know the departure points. Be alert in and around the minibus taxi ranks.

TRAIN

Durban train station (Masabalala Yengwa Ave/NMR Ave) is huge. The local inner-city or suburban trains are not recommended for travellers; these are not commonly used and even hardy travellers report feeling unsafe.

However, mainline passenger long-distance services are another matter – they are efficient

KWAZULU-NATAL DURBAN

ⓘ FREEDOM TO EXPLORE

To discover the region's true highlights (the uKhahlamba-Drakensberg region, the national parks and wildlife reserves, and the Battlefields), you're better off hiring a car. Durban has a reasonable choice of operators. Most roads are good, but a few locations, such as Sani Pass (to which you can easily take a tour from Underberg), Tembe Elephant Park and many parts of iSimangaliso Wetland Park, require a 4WD.

ℹ RIDE A 'RICKSHA'

Rickshaws – known locally as 'rickshas' – ply their trade along OR Tambo Pde (Marine Pde), many sporting exotic Zulu regalia. In 1904 there were about 2000 registered rickshaw-pullers, and it was an important means of transport. A 15-minute ride costs about R60 (plus R10 for a happy snap).

and arranged into separate male and female sleeper compartments. These are run by **Shosholoza Meyl** (☑ 0860 008 888, 011-774 4555; www.shosholozameyl.co.za) and include the *Trans Natal*, which leaves Durban on Wednesday, Friday and Sunday evenings for Jo'burg (sleeper R360, 14 hours) via Pietermaritzburg and Ladysmith.

Premier Classe (☑ 086-000 8888; http:// southafricanrailways.co.za) The fully serviced, luxury Premier Classe has trains between Jo'burg and Durban on Wednesday, Friday and Sunday. Tickets should be booked in advance (R1230, about 14 hours).

Rovos Rail (☑ 012-315 8242; www.rovosrail. co.za) The *Rovos* is a luxury steam train on which, from a mere R18,950, you can enjoy old-world luxury on a three-day choof from Durban to Pretoria via the Battlefields and nature reserves.

ℹ Getting Around

TO/FROM THE AIRPORT

Some hostels run their own taxi shuttle services for clients at competitive prices. By taxi, the same trip costs around R400.

The **King Shaka Airport Shuttle Bus** (☑ 031-465 5573; www.shuttle.airportbustransport. co.za; R80; ⊙ to airport 4.30am-8pm, from airport 7.30am-10.30pm) runs hourly from the airport to hotels and key locations in Durban and the beachfront via Umhlanga Rocks.

BUS

The useful **Durban People Mover** (☑ 031-309 2731; www.durban.gov.za/City_Services/ethekwini_transport_authority/Pages/People_Mover. aspx; single/day pass R5.50/16; ⊙ 5am-10pm) shuttle bus operates along several routes. Tickets (R16) can be purchased on board and allow you to get on and off as many times as you like within a day. Single-leg tickets cost R5.50. The service runs daily between 5am and 10pm. The bus links the beachfront to the city centre and runs the length of the beachfront from uShaka Marine World to Suncoast Casino, with designated stops (including the Victoria Street Market and City Hall) along the way.

Durban Transport (☑ 031-309 3250) runs the bus services Mynah and Aqualine. Mynah covers most of the city and local residential areas. Trips cost around R5 and you get a slight discount if you pre-purchase 10 tickets. Stops include North Beach, South Beach, Musgrave Rd/Mitchell Park Circle, Peter Mokaba Ridge/ Vause, Botanic Gardens and Kensington Rd. The larger Aqualine buses run through the greater metropolitan area.

The **Main Local Bus Terminal** is located on Dr AB Xuma St (Commercial Rd).

TAXI

Always use metered cabs. A taxi between the beach and Florida Rd, Morningside, usually costs about R50. Companies running a reliable 24-hour service include **Mozzie Cabs** (☑ 031-303 5787; www.mozziecabs.mobi), **Zippy Cabs** (☑ 031-202 7067; www.zippycabs.co.za) and **Eagle** (☑ 0800 330 336; www.eagletaxicabs. co.za). Uber also operates in Durban and is usually cheaper than metered cabs.

SOUTH COAST

This 160km-long string of coast south of Durban is a surfers' and divers' delight (the latter because of Aliwal Shoal). Lined with similar-looking seaside resorts and suburbs running from Amanzimtoti to Port Edward, near the Eastern Cape border, it has a bit of a *Groundhog Day* feel about it. Most of the developments are spread out along two routes – the N2 and the R102. However, the coastal region's sandy beaches are interspersed with some pretty gardens and grassy areas, especially in the southern section.

Inland, the sugar cane, bananas and palms provide a pleasant, lush, green contrast to the beach culture. The attractive Oribi Gorge Nature Reserve, near Port Shepstone, provides beautiful forest walks.

Warner Beach

Warner Beach, with small-village charm and convenient amenities, offers lots of good surf spots and makes an excellent place to base yourself if you're looking to undertake diving trips to the Aliwal Shoal.

Information is available from Tourism Umdoni (☑ 039-976 1364; www.tourismsouthcoast.co.za; Scott St, Scottburgh; ⊙ 8am-5pm), next to the Scottburgh Memorial Library.

Major bus lines stop at nearby Amanzimtotti, while the Margate Mini Coach (p260) makes a stop at Scottburgh.

Blue Sky Mining
Backpackers & Lodge   HOSTEL $
(📱 031-916 5394; www.blueskymining.co.za; 5 Nelson Palmer Rd, Warner Beach; dm R220, r from R460, with shared bathroom from R400; 🅿 @ 🛜 🏊) Just uphill from the coastal shopping strip, and overlooking the water with magnificent views, Blue Sky can organise a lot of beach- and water-based activities. Spin out at the funky psychedelics, and chill by the pool. Seriously revitalising. From Kingsway (Rte 102), look for Strelitzia Rd, go up the hill, turn left into Meintjies Rd and onto Nelson Palmer from there.

Umzumbe & Umtentweni

Surf's up in these quirky villages that lie between Durban and Port Shepstone. In contrast to the effete pleasantries of Ramsgate and Southbroom, Umzumbe and Umtentweni cater more to those looking to catch waves, take a yoga class on the beach and otherwise chill. Greyhound (📱 083 915 9000; www.greyhound.co.za) has daily services between Port Shepstone and Durban (R390, 1¾ hours). If you are staying at one of the backpackers, ask the driver to drop you in Umzumbe or Umtentweni. The Baz Bus also runs here.

🛏 Sleeping

★ Mantis & Moon
Backpacker Lodge   HOSTEL $
(📱 039-684 6256; www.mantisandmoon.net; 7/178 Station Rd, Umzumbe; dm R165, d R610, with shared bathroom R510; 🛜 🏊) This place has more accommodation options than subtropical tree varieties in its compact jungle garden: a giant teepee, small rustic cabins, and tree houses, some with glass walls. There's a hot tub, a rock pool, a bar and an incredible glass and wood yoga studio. In recent years it has made a shift away from a rowdy party atmosphere and begun catering to those who enjoy a healthy, laid-back lifestyle.

There is no shortage of activities that can be booked from the backpackers, including yoga classes (R100), surf lessons (R350) and day tours to nearby attractions.

Spot Backpackers   HOSTEL $
(📱 039-695 1318; www.spotbackpackers.com; 23 Ambleside Rd, Umtentweni; dm/d with shared bathroom R180/450, cabin d R600; 🛜 🏊) Close to Port Shepstone, this is spot-on for position (a right-on-the-beach deal for sand, sun and surf) and is a justifiably popular, albeit slightly jaded, place. Offers use of

---

SOUTH COAST DIVING

Aliwal Shoal is touted as one of the best dive sites in the world. The shoal was created from dune rock around 30,000 years ago. A mere 6500 years ago the sea level rose, creating a reef. This reef was named after a ship, the *Aliwal*, which ran aground here in 1849. Other ships have since met a similar fate. Today, the shoal's ledges, caves and pinnacles are home to everything from wrecks to rays, turtles, 'raggies' (ragged-tooth sharks), tropical fish and soft corals.

Further down the coast, near Shelly Beach, the extraordinary Protea Banks dive site is restricted to advanced divers and is the place to see sharks.

Numerous operators along the South Coast offer dive charters, PADI courses and accommodation packages. Packages vary enormously in terms of accommodation and equipment. (In some cases, equipment hire may cost extra.) To give you an idea, at the time of writing, a three-night, five-dive package cost around R4900.

Always speak to other travellers about their experiences because safety briefings vary among the operators – incidents can, and do, occur.

The following are based in Umkomaas:

Calypso Dive & Adventure Centre (📱 082 800 4668; www.calypsoushaka.co.za; 1 Maclean St, Umkomaas; ⊙ 6.30am-5pm Mon-Sat) PADI-qualified operator Calypso Diving offers Open Water courses (from R5495), and advanced courses and dives in nearby wrecks and elsewhere.

Aliwal Dive Centre (📱 039-973 2233; www.aliwalshoal.co.za; 2 Moodie St, Umkomaas) A comprehensive dive centre that also has pleasant rooms available (single/double R598/920).

Shoal (📱 039-973 1777; www.theshoal.co.za; 21 Harvey St, Umkomaas)

Oceanworx (📱 039-973 2578; www.oceanworx.co.za; 1 Reynolds St, Umkomaas)

South Coast

kayaks and a host of other activities. It's a great choice for those looking for the classic young, backpackers vibe.

Umdlalo Lodge   LODGE **$$**
(☏ 039-695 0224; www.umdlalolodge.co.za; 5 Rethman Dr, Umtentweni; s/d incl breakfast from R895/1150; ❄☎) With eight luxurious rooms, and even a honeymoon suite, this place is a fabulously upmarket coastal spot. Each bedroom suite leads onto a charming central courtyard. Zizi's Restaurant, on site, with its meat-driven menu, is a great place for a relaxed meal.

Oribi Gorge

The spectacular Oribi Gorge on the Umzim-kulwana River is one of the highlights of the South Coast, with its nature reserve full of beautiful scenery, animals and birds, plus walking trails and pretty picnic spots. The gorge also cuts into the Lake Eland Game Reserve, which has some lovely scenery and plenty of wildlife to view, as well as fishing, canoeing and zip-line tours.

Oribi Gorge Nature Reserve   NATURE RESERVE
(☏ 072 042 9390; www.kznwildlife.com; adult/child R60/30; ⏲ 5am-7pm Oct-Mar, 6am-6pm Apr-Sep) This awe-inspiring gorge is known for its dizzying scenery and family-friendly activities. There are plenty of walking trails, birdwatching opportunities and thrills to be had. Or if you are just looking for a lovely lunchtime backdrop there is a plethora of picnic areas overlooking the gorge as well.

Accommodation is in several two-bed rest huts (R500) and one six-bedroom chalet (R1200) with private bathrooms, a shared kitchen and a marvellous location atop the gorge. Camping (R110) is also available.

Inland from Port Shepstone, the reception office is accessed via the N2 on the southern side of the gorge. There is ample signage to help you find the way.

Lake Eland Game Reserve   WILDLIFE RESERVE
(☏ 039-687 0395; www.lakeeland.co.za; day visitors adult/child R60/40, camping R500, 2-person cabins from R750; ⏲ 7am-5pm) The reserve has over 40 species of animal and 200 bird species. You can head off on a self-drive (R60 per person) or a wildlife drive (R250 per person, minimum four people). There is a 4.7km series of zip lines, as well as the alternative Zip eXtreme, which reaches speeds of 160km/h (R450 to R550, including gate en-

try). A short gorge walk crosses a 130m-high suspension bridge, and fishing and canoeing are possible on the lake if you have the necessary kit (none available for hire). You'll find the reserve 40km from Port Shepstone; drive 26km along Oribi Flats Rd off the N2.

There are well-maintained log cabins overlooking a small lake; fishers cottages; camping; and dorm beds in a massive pipe! A restaurant is open from 7.30am to 4pm.

Wild 5 Adventures   ADVENTURE SPORTS
(☑082 566 7424; www.wild5adventures.co.za; Oribi Gorge Hotel; adult/child R20/15; ☺8am-5pm Dec-Feb, 8.30am-4.30pm Mar-Nov) Organises activities within the Oribi Gorge Nature Reserve, including a 100m Wild Swing (free-fall jump and swing) off Lehr's Falls (R600), abseiling (R450) and white-water rafting (R600). It's located 11km off the N2 along the Oribi Flats Rd.

Leopard Rock Lookout Chalets   CHALET $$$
(☑074-124 0902; www.leopardrockc.co.za; Main Oribi Gorge Rd; chalet incl breakfast from R1700) Accommodation here is in four pleasant chalets, although it's the vista that's the winner. The dining deck boasts a superb view of the uMzumkulu Gorge. Thoughtful touches include a welcome pack of South African goodies like braai (barbecue) spice, rusks and rooibos tea. The coffee shop's open 9am to 4pm Wednesday to Sunday.

Margate, Ramsgate & Southbroom

This string of beach towns (with plenty of smaller villages in between) is a good gateway for those looking to explore the South Coast. Margate is the busiest of the three, where you'll find plenty of loud and lively bars. Ramsgate, and especially Southbroom, offer a more sedate oceanfront experience. Southbroom is nestled in the trees and is a bushbuck conservancy.

◎ Sights & Activities

Umtamvuna Nature Reserve   NATURE RESERVE
(☑039-311 2383; www.kznwildlife.com; adult/concession R25/15; ☺7am-5pm Oct-Mar, 6am-6pm Apr-Sep) This reserve is on a gorge on the Umtamvuna River (which forms part of the border with Eastern Cape). This beautiful dense forest has great nature walks, with wildflowers in spring, plus mammals and many species of bird. To get there from Port

Edward, follow the signs off R61 to Izingolweni and continue for 8km. Pick up a brochure at the reserve's entrance.

Beaver Creek   FARM
(☑039-311 2347; www.beavercreek.co.za; Izingolweni Rd, Port Edward; ☺cafe 8am-4pm, tours at noon) If you stay on the South Coast for long enough you'll most likely drink a few cups of Beaver Creek coffee, so why not visit the source? This coffee farm offers tours and barista courses and has a cafe on-site where you can enjoy expertly made drinks. Wholesale coffee is available for sale.

🛏 Sleeping

Wailana Beach Lodge   B&B $
(☑039-314 4606; www.wailana.co.za; 436 Ashmead Dr, Ramsgate; r incl breakfast from R610; ◉🄿🛜🏊) Comfortable, well-designed rooms with modern amenities net this place glowing reviews from travellers, but it's the ocean views from the deck and pool area that make it truly special.

Vuna Valley Lodge   LODGE $$
(☑071 451 6060; www.vunavalleylodge.com; 9 Mitchell Rd, Banners Rest; dm R165, d R750, with shared bathroom R650; ❄🛜🏊) Right next to the entrance to the Umtamvuna Nature Reserve, Vuna Valley Lodge is an old standby in the area. It came under new ownership in 2017 and has been given a much-needed facelift. The rooms are clean and feature plenty of bright colours and African flair, and the comfortable dorms make for a great budget option.

Days at Sea   BOUTIQUE HOTEL $$$
(☑087 551 7003; 39 Effingham Pde, Trafalgar; r from R3600; ❄🛜🏊) If you make it all the way to paradise why not splurge a bit? Days at Sea was designed by German photographer Guido Schoeldgen and the European influences are very evident in this glass and white-stone structure built into a hill. The rooms are unique, with tasteful, '60s-inspired furniture and large windows throughout. An on-site spa rounds out the luxury experience.

Coral Tree Colony   B&B $$$
(☑039-316 6676; www.thecoraltree.com; 593 Mandy Rd, Southbroom; r incl breakfast R1650; ❄🛜🏊) Rates here are a bit higher than your typical B&B, but it's located in a purpose-built recent construction that offers a comfort level more akin to a swish hotel. Some may find the lack of historic charm disappointing,

but everything, from the linens to the large soaking tubs, is first rate.

✕ Eating & Drinking

Waffle House   WAFFLES $
(☑ 039-314 9424; www.wafflehouse.co.za; Marine Dr, Ramsgate; mains R40-90; ◷ 8am-5pm; 🖋) Tourists flock to this pleasant spot on the edge of a lagoon for fresh Belgian-style waffles with every sweet and savoury topping under the sun. Some locals turn their nose up at it, but the long lines during the holiday season don't lie.

Chef's on Marine   BURGERS $$
(☑ 039-314 4154; 2450 Lifestyle Village, Ramsgate; mains R85-160; ◷ 9am-4pm Mon-Fri, to 3pm Sat & Sun) The best burgers in the South Coast are served in this large, airy restaurant in Ramsgate. If you come for breakfast make sure to treat yourself to one of its house-made pastries.

Trattoria La Terrazza   ITALIAN $$
(☑ 039-316 6162; www.trattoria.co.za; Outlook Rd, Southbroom; mains R95-150; ◷ 6.30-10pm Tue-Sat, plus 12.30-2.30pm Thu-Sat) Ask for a restaurant recommendation in the area and the answer is overwhelmingly this Italian option. It has a popular meaty and pasta-heavy menu, including the likes of tender, grain-fed beef fillet and seafood such as Norwegian salmon. The setting, on an estuary, is gorgeous. Reservations recommended.

Burlesque Cafe   INTERNATIONAL $$
(957 Marine Dr, Ramsgate; mains R60-110; ◷ noon-3pm Tue-Sun, plus 6-9pm Wed-Sat) A quirky little retro treat with a chic vintage interior and cheeky menu items featuring organic produce. Good veggie options.

Pistols Saloon   BAR
(☑ 039-316 8463; www.pistolssaloon.co.za; Old Main Rd, Ramsgate; ◷ 10am-late) Don't be fooled: the kitschy Wild West theme at this bar and restaurant is no joke. The most famous regular at this bar is a donkey that roams around the joint getting cosy with patrons. Gimmicks aside, it's a fun place to grab a drink with the locals (the food is just OK).

ℹ Information

South Coast Tourism (☑ 039-312 2322; www.tourismsouthcoast.co.za; Panorama Pde, Main Beach, Margate; ◷ 8am-5pm Mon-Fri, to 1pm Sat, 9am-1pm Sun) Information is available from here.

ℹ Getting There & Around

Margate Mini Coach (☑ 039-312 1406; www.margatecoach.co.za; Marine Dr) links Durban and Margate three times daily (one way R240).

Intercity Express (☑ 031-305 9090; www.intercity.co.za; Marine Dr) runs regular buses between Margate and Jo'burg (R400, 10 hours).

P.A.C.E. You Drink We Drive (☑ 071 231 3294; pace25@live.com) is a reliable taxi service that can get you all around the South Coast, and even to and from Durban if you need.

NORTH COAST

To the north of Durban you'll find miles of picturesque coastline that calls to those looking to unwind in the sun. Just north of the city are the upmarket beach communities of Umhlanga (high-rise condos, expensive restaurants by the water) and uMdloti (stately beach houses, quiet streets), while further up you'll enter the Dolphin Coast, which gets its name from the bottlenose dolphins that favour the area.

The area is home to a fascinating mix of peoples: descendants of former colonialists, Indians, French-Mauritian sugar-cane growers and indentured labourers from the Indian subcontinent, plus, of course, the Zulu people.

King Shaka is said to have established a military camp on the coast; royal handmaidens gathered salt from tidal pools, a practice since immortalised in the name Salt Rock. A memorial to King Shaka can be found at KwaDukuza (Stanger), slightly inland.

Metropolitan buses run between Durban and Umhlanga Rocks, and buses and minibus shared taxis also run between Durban and KwaDukuza (Stanger) and other inland towns.

Umhlanga Rocks & uMdloti Beach

Gleaming towers and well-maintained beaches draw wealthy Durbanites just north of the city to Umhlanga, 'Place of Reeds'. In this chi-chi suburb you'll find incredible shopping and restaurants, as well as some of the nicest hotels the Durban area has to offer. Further north, uMdloti is a bit quieter and more beachy, although no less moneyed. Both locations are convenient to the airport.

Metro buses 716 and 706 run between Umhlanga and Durban. You can also take cabs and Ubers to and from Durban for about R400 one way.

⊙ Sights & Activities

Natal Sharks Board MUSEUM
(☏031-566 0400; www.shark.co.za; 1A Herrwood
Dr, Umhlanga Rocks; ⊗8am-4pm Mon-Fri, presentations & dissections 9am & 2pm Tue-Thu) FREE
This research institute is dedicated to studying sharks, specifically in relation to their
danger to humans. There are audiovisual
presentations and shark dissections (adult/
child R50/30). The museum has replicas of
sharks and a wealth of information on the
animals and their tumultuous relationship
with mankind. The Natal Sharks Board is
signposted; it's about 2km out of town, up
steep Umhlanga Rocks Dr (the M12 leading
to the N3).

The public can also accompany Sharks
Board personnel on their boat trips (p247)
from Durban.

**Umhlanga Lagoon
Nature Reserve** NATURE RESERVE
(⊗6am-6pm) FREE Found on a river mouth
just north of town, the reserve is home to
many bird species (despite its small size:
2600 sq metres). Trails lead through stunning dune forest, across the lagoon and onto
the beach. Ask at the reception of the Break-
er's Hotel about the walking tours, which
leave at 9am, 11am and 3pm.

🛏 Sleeping & Eating

Umhlanga is crowded with holiday apartments and B&Bs, as well as some legendary
beachfront hotels. In uMdloti you'll find
plenty of upmarket B&Bs and guesthouses.
Prices are seasonal and vary enormously.

On the Beach Backpackers HOSTEL $$
(☏031-562 1591; www.durbanbackpackers.com;
17 The Promenade, Glenashley; dm/s/d from
R270/700/1000; P🐾🛜🏊) While it might be
a little pricier than your average backpack-
ers, there are million-rand views from the
double rooms here that overlook the water.
Or you can slum it in a dorm for a much
more reasonable price. This light and airy
house-turned-backpackers is a great spot for
lazing on the coast. It's on the Baz Bus route.

Oyster Box HOTEL $$$
(☏031-514 5000; www.oysterboxhotel.com; 2
Lighthouse Rd, Umhlanga; r incl breakfast R5645;
❄🛜🏊) For chic, ocean-facing luxury you
can't do much better than this renowned
hotel next to the lighthouse. Rooms have
special amenities such as on-demand movies and heated towels. If you've forgotten

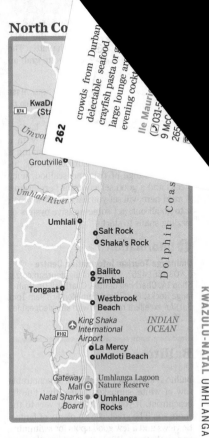

North Co[...]

anything you can grab a bag packed with
umbrella, bats, balls and sunscreen before
heading to the beach. The daily curry buffet
is legendary.

★Mundo Vida INTERNATIONAL $$
(☏031-568 2286; www.mundovida.co.za; 1 South
Beach Rd, uMdloti Centre; mains R120-170; ⊗noon-
3pm & 6-10pm Mon-Sat, noon-5pm Sun) Enjoy
seafood and bistro fare in unpretentious
surroundings at this excellent coastal res-
taurant, where traditional recipes have a
modern twist. For a taste of everything fishy
try the seafood medley or, if your pockets are
deep, tuck into the deluxe version. Excellent
wine list.

Bel Punto INTERNATIONAL $$
(☏031-568 2407; www.belpunto.co.za; 1 South
Beach Rd, uMdloti Centre; mains R80-150; ⊗6-
10pm Tue, noon-10pm Wed-Sun, open Mon Dec-
Feb) With a large terrace overlooking uMdloti Beach, Bel Punto attracts the weekend

. There's a focus on
[...]dining – try the baby
[...]rilled shellfish platter. The
[...]a is a good place to grab an
[...]ail.

[...]e   FRENCH $$$
[...]61 7609; www.ilemauricerestaurant.co.za;
[...]ausland Cres, Umhlanga Rocks; mains R185-
[...], ☺noon-2.30pm & 6.30-9.30pm Tue-Sun;
⚿🅰) For a special seaside splurge with a
Gallic touch, try this chic eatery serving a
variety of French and Mauritian dishes, in-
cluding a range of fish and seafood, juicy
steaks and a good selection for vegetarians.
A meal here will set you back, but it's worth
it to go all out; get some massive oysters or
sizzling snails to start.

ℹ Information

Umhlanga Tourism Information Centre
(☎031-561 4257; www.umhlangatourism.co.za;
Shop 1A, Chartwell Centre, Chartwell Dr, Umh-
langa Rocks; ☺8.30am-5pm Mon-Fri, 9am-1pm
Sat) An excellent resource with knowledgeable
staff.

Ballito
☎032

Ballito is known for the almost impenetrable
row of white, sunbaked hotels that line its
beachfront. If you can find your way to the
shore you'll be greeted with plenty of fantas-
tic views and a few good spots for swimming
and sunbathing. While the town can be a bit
sterile, and it certainly lacks any Zulu fla-
vour, proximity to the airport (about 22km)
makes it worth a visit for beach bunnies.

🛏 Sleeping & Eating

Monkey Bay Backpackers   HOSTEL $
(☎071 348 1278; www.monkeybaybackpackers.
co.za; 9 Jack Powell Rd; dm/d R170/550; 🛜)
Calling all surf-rats. This casual place –
made from recycled materials, and painted
in funky colours inside – has a pleasantly
hippie vibe and a friendly owner. All of the
rooms, everything from classic dorms to sa-
fari tents, are built into the hill, giving the
place an awesome treehouse-style vibe. The
common areas foster a friendly, but not too
rowdy, vibe.

Guesthouse   GUESTHOUSE $$
(☎032-525 5683; www.theguesthouse.co.za; Ip-
ahla Lane, Shaka's Rock; s/d incl breakfast from
R550/950; 🅿🛜🅰🍽) Five rooms (as well as

a self-catering cottage) in a pleasant, neat-
as-a-pin, slightly dated house nestled in the
hills above Ballito. Richard, the owner, is a
delight. Best is the garden-facing room with
private entrance.

Boathouse   GUESTHOUSE $$$
(☎032-946 0300; www.boathouse.co.za; 33
Compensation Beach Rd; s/d R1690/2780;
❄@🛜🏊) Taken over by new management
in 2014, this upmarket choice has a bit
more character than the rest of the behe-
moths that crowd the Ballito coastline. The
bar and restaurant area is big and airy and
some of the rooms have decks with incred-
ible sea views.

Hops   SEAFOOD $$
(☎032-946 2896; 14 Edward Pl; mains R70-160;
☺9am-11.30pm Tue-Thu & Sun, from 11am Mon,
9am-2am Fri & Sat) If a fun seaside vibe and
tasty food is what you're after, Hops has you
covered on both fronts. There is frequently
live music and the large, open dining area is
the ideal place to have a beer or wine while
enjoying the breeze off the ocean.

ℹ Information

Sangweni Tourism Centre (☎032-437 5021;
cnr Ballito & Link Drs; ☺8.30am-5pm Mon-Fri,
9am-1pm Sat) Houses the Dolphin Coast Publicity Association, which lists accommodation
and activities in the area. There's also a small
craft store representing local artisans on-site.
It's located near the BP station, where you
leave the N2 to enter Ballito.

ℹ Getting There & Away

Ballito is conveniently located right off the N2
north of Durban. Several bus lines service Ballito, as do minibus taxis, of course. They drop off
near the Ballito Junction shopping centre, so if
you're travelling without a car you'll have a long
walk down to the beachfront.

KwaDukuza
☎032 / POP 13,500

KwaDukuza, also known as Stanger, is an important stop for those undertaking a Shaka
pilgrimage or those interested in Zulu culture. In July 1825, Shaka established it as his
capital and royal residence. It was here that
he was killed in 1828 by his half-brothers
Mhlangane and Dingaan; Dingaan then took
power. Each year Zulus don their traditional
gear and gather in the Recreational Grounds
for the King Shaka Day Celebration.

The city serves as the central business district for the surrounding rural communities. Other than the museums in town, tourists won't find much to see here. It can be done as a day trip.

KwaDukuza is easily accessible from the N2. Most of the major bus lines stop here, and if you're trying to save money you can catch a minibus taxi into town (from Durban about one hour, R40).

King Shaka Visitor Centre   CULTURAL CENTRE
(☑032-552 7210; 5 King Shaka Rd; adult/child R10/5; ☺8am-4pm Mon-Fri, 9am-4pm Sat & Sun) **FREE** The King Shaka Visitor Centre is worth visiting for limited but clear historical and chronological information about Shaka and his kingdom. Inside you'll find a short informational video and several display cases of historic artefacts. Outside is a reconstructed Zulu house and the famous Shaka's monument and rock where, according to legend, he was assassinated.

Dukuza Museum   MUSEUM
(☑032-437 5075; King Shaka Rd; admission by donation; ☺8.30am-4pm Mon-Fri) Opposite the King Shaka Visitor Centre, the museum has a small collection of related historical exhibits and other displays (there are some nicely preserved gramophones).

Luthuli Museum   MUSEUM
(☑032-559 6822; www.luthulimuseum.org.za; 3233 Nokukhanya Luthuli St, Groutville; ☺8.30am-4pm Mon-Sat, 11am-3pm Sun) **FREE** A tribute to Chief Albert John Mvumbi Luthuli – president of the ANC from 1952 and Africa's first recipient of the Nobel Prize for Peace (1960) for his efforts to end apartheid – the museum is located in Luthuli's house, where he lived and fought against injustice all his life. The house is surrounded by gardens and hosts changing exhibitions.

ZULULAND

Evoking images of wild landscapes and tribal rhythms, this beautiful swath of KwaZulu-Natal offers a different face of South Africa, where fine coastline, mist-clad hills and traditional settlements are in contrast to the ordered suburban developments around Durban. Dominated by the Zulu tribal group, the region offers fascinating historical and contemporary insights into one of the country's most enigmatic cultures. However, while the

name Zulu (which means Heaven) aptly describes the rolling expanses that dominate the landscape here, it doesn't tell the whole story. Intense poverty and all the social problems that come with that are still commonplace, and much of the population struggles in a hand-to-mouth existence. If you head off the main roads this becomes glaringly obvious.

The region is most visited for the spectacular Hluhluwe-iMfolozi Park and its many traditional Zulu villages. Here you can learn about Zulu history and the legendary King Shaka.

Zululand extends roughly from the mouth of the Tugela River up to St Lucia and inland west of the N2 to Vryheid.

Mtunzini

☑035 / POP 2200

A little thatch of neatly tended lawns surrounded by the wild, rolling hills of Zululand, Mtunzini is an outpost of Europe in the heart of Africa. But there's more to this pretty village than herbaceous borders. Sitting above a lush sweep of rare raffia palms, and bordering the Umlalazi Nature Reserve, Mtunzini makes an excellent base for exploring this beautiful slice of Zululand.

The town had a colourful beginning. John Dunn, the first European to settle in the area, was granted land by King Cetshwayo. Dunn became something of a chief himself, taking 49 wives and siring 117 children. He held court here under a tree, hence the town's name (*mtunzini* is Zulu for 'a place in the shade'). After the British defeated Cetshwayo and divided the kingdom, Dunn was one of the chiefs granted power.

The town was declared a conservancy in 1995. Visitors can enjoy its network of nature trails, as well as sight some antelope and bird species.

◉ Sights

Raffia Palm Monument   PARK
FREE *Raphia Australis* palms were first planted here in 1916 from seeds. The idea was to use the palm fibres to make brooms for the prison service, but, as the fibres were too short, the commercial enterprise soon ended. However, the palms (whose leaves are among the largest in the plant kingdom) flourished and by 1942 had been declared a national monument. The palms are home to the palm-nut vulture (*Gypohierax angolensis*), South Africa's rarest breeding bird of prey.

KWAZULU-NATAL MTUNZINI

ZULU FESTIVALS

Throughout the year major festivals celebrate the rich culture of the Zulu people. These peaceful and joyous occasions involve colourful displays of traditional singing and dancing. See www.kzn.org.za for a sneak preview.

King Shaka Day Celebration On 24 September, as a part of the larger nationwide Heritage Day celebration, thousands of Zulus converge on KwaDukuza (Stanger) for the King Shaka Day Celebration. The annual event, attended by the current Zulu king, pays homage to the Zulu hero.

Reed Dance Every year thousands of bare-breasted Zulu 'maidens' gather before their king, honouring the ancient tradition of the Reed Dance. In days long past, the king would select a new bride from among the beautiful throng. The dance takes place at King Enyokeni's Palace (between Nongoma and Ulundi) around the second weekend of September, before the King Shaka Day Celebration.

Shembe Festival During October more than 30,000 Zulus gather at Judea, 15km east of Eshowe, to celebrate the Shembe, the Church of the Holy Nazareth Baptists – an unofficial religion that manages to combine Zulu traditions with Christianity. Presiding is the church's saviour, Prophet Mbusi Vimbeni Shembe. There's much dancing and singing and blowing of the horns of Jericho.

Zululand Eco-Adventures (www.zululandeco-adventures.com; 36 Main St) Zululand Eco-Adventures in Eshowe offers a large range of genuine Zulu adventure activities, from weddings and coming-of-age ceremonies to visits to witch doctors.

Umlalazi Nature Reserve　　　NATURE RESERVE
(☑035-340 1836; www.kznwildlife.com; adult/child R60/30; ☉5am-10pm) This reserve has walking trails through the pretty dune and forest ecosystems and is great for birders. Visit the Indaba Tree, where John Dunn held his court gatherings, and the remains of John Dunn's Pool, which he built so his wives could swim safely, well away from hippos and crocs. The entrance is 1.5km east of town, on the coast.

🛏 Sleeping & Eating

Umlalazi Nature Reserve
Chalets & Campground　　　CAMPGROUND $$
(☑035-340 1836; www.kznwildlife.com; camping R360, 4-bed log cabin R1380) Two well-organised camping areas (Inkwazi and Indaba) are set in gorgeous forest, close to the beach. The log cabins are spacious, have great decks and are well organised inside. Prices drop significantly in the off season.

Mtunzini B&B　　　B&B $$
(☑035-340 1600; 5 Barker St; s/d incl breakfast R550/850; ❊ 🛜 ❄) A no-nonsense, friendly place with beautiful spaces, set around a beautiful garden. There's a range of rooms, from doubles inside the main house to separate cabin, attic and self-catering options. Only some have private bathrooms.

One-on-Hely　　　BOUTIQUE HOTEL $$$
(☑035-340 2499; www.oneonhely.co.za; 1 Hely Hutchinson St; d from R1700; ❊ 🛜 ❄) The village's flashest place, with enormous decks, forest views over Umlalazi Nature Reserve and the ocean, and luxury trimmings. In 2017 the owners added a luxury suite, as well as a newly landscaped lush garden. It's popular, so book ahead.

Clay Oven　　　INTERNATIONAL $$
(☑035-340 1262; www.theclayoven.co.za; 32 Hely Hutchinson Rd; mains R80-180; ☉11am-9pm Mon-Fri, from 9am Sat & Sun) A patio with peaceful sea views makes this restaurant worth the visit alone. The menu is basic bistro fare, but locals rave about the pizzas.

Fat Cat Coffee Shop　　　CAFE $$
(☑035-340 2897; 2 Station Rd; mains R65-110; ☉7.30am-8pm Mon-Sat, to 2pm Sun) Casual, friendly Fat Cat is a nice, open spot tucked away off the main drag. Breakfast is recommended, especially the Mediterranean Surprise.

Eshowe

🗐 035 / POP 14,800

Situated in the hills amid a beautiful indigenous forest and surrounded by green rolling hills, Eshowe has its own particular character. The centre has a rural, rough-and-tumble atmosphere, but the suburbs are leafy and quiet except for the birds. It is well placed for exploring the wider region and there are decent attractions and accommodation options.

Eshowe has been home to four Zulu Kings (Shaka, Mpande, Cetshwayo and Dinuzulu). It was Cetshwayo's stronghold before he moved to Ondini and, like Ondini, it was destroyed during the Anglo-Zulu War. The British occupied the site and built Fort Nongqayi in 1883, establishing Eshowe as the administrative centre of their newly captured territory.

◎ Sights

Fort Nongqayi Museum Village MUSEUM
(www.eshowemuseums.org.za; 7 Nongqayi Rd; adult/child R35/10; ⊗7.30am-4pm Mon-Fri, 10am-4pm Sat & Sun) Based around three-turreted Fort Nongqayi, the museum village also includes the **Zululand Historical Museum**, with artefacts and Victoriana; the excellent **Vukani Museum** with its Zulu basketry collection; and a **missionary chapel**. Well worth a look is the small but delightful **butterfly house**: a walk-in greenhouse where visitors can enjoy indigenous vegetation and hundreds of (mostly local) African butterfly species.

You can walk from here to Mpushini Falls (40 minutes return), but note that bilharzia (snail fever) has been reported here.

Dlinza Forest Reserve FOREST
(www.kznwildlife.com/dlinza-forest) When war approached, King Shaka is said to have hidden his wives in the thick swath of forest that now makes up this 2-sq-km reserve. There is prolific birdlife – look out for crowned eagles (*Stephanoaetus coronatus*) – as well as a few walking trails, some of which are believed to have been made by British soldiers stationed here after the Anglo-Zulu War. The 125m-long **Dlinza Forest Aerial Boardwalk** (www.kznwildlife.com/dlinza-broadwalk; adult/child R40/10; ⊗6am-5pm Sep-Apr, 8am-5pm May-Aug) offers some great views.

🛏 Sleeping & Eating

There aren't many options, but the restaurant at the George Hotel (p265) and **Adam's Outpost** (☏035-474 1787; 5 Nongqayi St, Fort Nongqayi Museum; mains R50-80; ⊗8.30am-4pm Sun-Fri) are both very fine choices.

Dlinza Forest Accommodation CABIN $
(☏035-474 2377; www.dlinzaforestaccommodation.co.za; 2 Oftebro St; s/d R550/700; 🖥) These

four self-catering log cabins are neat, modern, clean and spacious. Follow the signs to the Dlinza Forest Reserve; the guesthouse is just beyond the entrance.

Eshowe Guesthouse B&B $$
(☏035-474 2362; www.eshoweguide.co.za/accommodation/eshowe_guesthouse; 3 Oftebro St; s/d R680/850; 🅿🌐🖥) This place has a top setting, backing onto the bird-filled Dlinza Forest. The owner is delightful and rooms are spotless, modern, airy and spacious. A fabulous pool and garden area doesn't hurt, either. Follow the signs to the Dlinza Forest Reserve; the guesthouse is just beyond the entrance. It gets busy; reserve ahead.

George Hotel HOTEL $$
(☏035-474 4919; www.thegeorge.co.za; 36 Main St; s/d incl breakfast from 780/1045; 🅿🖥) Dripping with character, this grand old hotel (1902) is a good midrange option. Rooms are a bit old and rickety (and water pressure can be hit-and-miss), but the huge beds are very comfy. The budget wing is a bit dingy but offers good value (single/double R450/600). The restaurant menu is limited, but the food is well prepared. Two of the hotel's best features are its veranda, perfect for a sunset drink, and its lounge, with ancient reading material and a cosy vibe. There is a bar–music venue and a cafe is also on-site.

ⓘ Getting There & Away

Minibus shared taxis leave from the bus and taxi rank (downhill from KFC near the Osborne and Main Sts roundabout – go across the bridge and to the right) to Empangeni (R60, one hour), which is the best place from which to catch taxis deeper into Zululand, and to Durban (R110, 1½ hours).

SHAKALAND

Created as a set for the telemovie *Shaka Zulu*, the slightly Disney-fied **Shakaland** (☏035-460 0912; www.shakaland.com; Nandi Experience R560; ⊗display 11am & 12.30pm) beats up a touristy blend of perma-grin performance and informative authenticity. The Nandi Experience (Nandi was Shaka's mother) is a display of Zulu culture and customs (including lunch); the Zulu dance performance is said to be the best in the country. You can also stay overnight in luxury beehives at the four-star **hotel** (s/d with full board R2165/3060).

Zululand & Elephant Coast

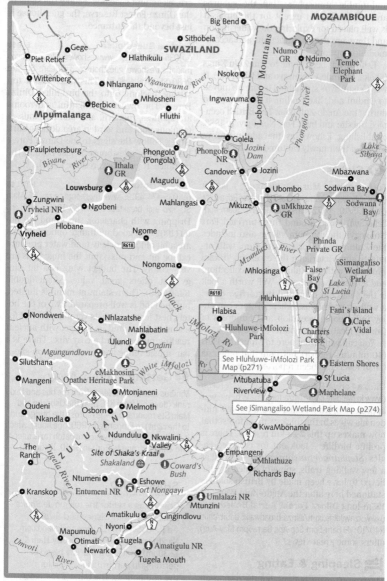

Ulundi

035 / POP 20,000

Once the hub of the Zulu empire and until 2004 a joint capital of KZN (with Pietermaritzburg, which gained pre-eminence), today Ulundi is best known to tourists for its historic Zulu sites, including the interesting Ondini, and its alternative access to Hluhluwe-iMfolozi Park. The town itself is not very attractive, with broad thoroughfares and buildings that are merely serviceable, but once you get outside of the centre there are things to see.

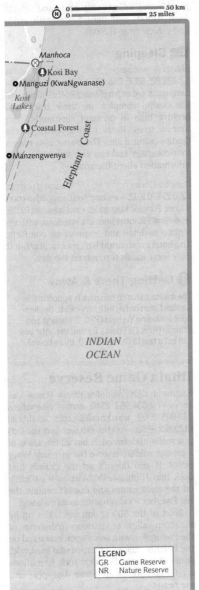

Manhoca

Kosi Bay

Manguzi (KwaNgwanase)

Kosi Lakes

Coastal Forest

Manzengwenya

Elephant Coast

INDIAN OCEAN

LEGEND
GR Game Reserve
NR Nature Reserve

KWAZULU-NATAL ULUNDI

disastrous loss at Blood River. He seized power with assistance from the Boers, but Zululand declined during his reign. The king's grave is here, but there's little else to see.

Ondini
HISTORIC SITE

(High Place; ☎035-870 2050; www.heritagekzn. co.za; adult/child R40/15; ⊗8am-4pm Mon-Fri, 9am-4pm Sat & Sun) Established as Cetshwayo's capital in 1873, Ondini was razed by British troops after the Battle of Ulundi (July 1879), the final engagement of the Anglo-Zulu War. The royal kraal section of the site has been rebuilt and you can see where archaeological digs have uncovered the floors of identifiable buildings. The floors, made of mud and cow dung, were preserved by the heat of the fires, which destroyed the huts above. The area is enclosed in a defensive perimeter of gnarled branches.

It took the British nearly six months to defeat the Zulu army, but the Battle of Ulundi went the same way as most of the campaign, with 10 to 15 times more Zulus than British killed. Part of the reason for the British victory at Ulundi was the adoption of the Boer *laager* tactic (creating a circle with their ox wagons to use for protection), with troops forming a hollow square to protect the cavalry, which attacked only after the Zulu army had exhausted itself trying to penetrate the walls.

To get to Ondini, take the 'Cultural Museum' turn-off from the highway just south of Ulundi centre and keep going for about 5km. Minibus shared taxis occasionally pass Ondini. This road continues on to Hluhluwe-iMfolozi Park (tarred for 30km). En route here from Ulundi you'll pass the Ulundi Battlefield Memorial, a stone structure commemorating the Battle of Ulundi and the final defeat of the Zulus.

◎ Emakhosini Ophathe Heritage Park

Ulundi lies within the Valley of the Kings, the name of which is officially promoted as Emakhosini Ophathe Heritage Park. The area is of great significance to the Zulu. The great makhosi (chiefs) Nkhosinkulu, Senzangakhona (father of Shaka, Dingaan and Mpande) and Dinizulu are buried here. The park itself can be confusing (some sites are advertised but aren't fully functioning). A local guide can help you make sense of all of the sites.

◎ Sights & Activities

KwaNodwengu
HISTORIC SITE

Opposite the large former Legislative Assembly building is the site of King Mpande's iKhanda (palace), KwaNodwengu. Mpande won control from Dingaan after the Zulus'

Mgungundlovu
HISTORIC SITE

(www.heritagekzn.co.za) The military settlement of Mgungundlovu (Ungungundhlovu), Dingaan's capital from 1829 to 1838, is southwest of Ulundi on Rte 34 (the road linking Vryheid and Melmoth). It was here that Pieter Retief and the other Voortrekkers were killed by their host in 1838, the event that precipitated the Boer-Zulu War. Signs point to the Piet Retief memorial marking the spot. In 1990 excavations revealed the site of Dingaan's *indlu* (great hut) nearby. A multimedia information centre (☑035-450 0916; adult/child R35/15; ☉9am-4pm) has high-tech displays and information.

From Ulundi head southwest along Rte 66 to Rte 34, turn right and continue on Rte 34 for several kilometres. Mgungundlovu is signed off Rte 34 to the west; it's another 5km to the site.

Spirit of Emakhosini Monument
MONUMENT

(☉8am-4pm Mon-Fri, 9am-4pm Sat & Sun) This monument comprises a massive bronze Zulu beer pot, surrounded by 18 bronze reliefs depicting Zulu life, and seven large horns symbolising the seven kings buried in the valley. Guides will explain the site's significance. It's on Rte 34 and 2km north of Mgungundlovu perched on a hill.

Tinta Safaris
HISTORY

(☑035-870 2500; www.tintasafaris.co.za) A family-run enterprise offering guided tours of the Emakhosini Valley (with guide and vehicle from R1200) and Battlefields (with guide and vehicle from R2400).

🛏 Sleeping

uMuzi Bushcamp
HUT $$

(☑082 825 6896, 035-870 2500; www.umuzibushcamp.co.za; s/d with half-board R645/940) Inside the Ondini complex are these traditional beehive huts in pleasant surrounds, near marula trees. Rates include entry to the Ondini cultural site. The owner also runs a tour company and can give you some great information about the area.

Garden Court
BUSINESS HOTEL $$

(☑035-870 1012; www.tsogosun.com/garden-court-ulundi; Princess Magogo St; r incl breakfast R1315; 🅿❄🛜🏊) Rooms here are spacious, with attention to detail and no-nonsense comforts. The hotel's restaurant isn't spectacular but it does serve meals throughout the day.

ℹ Getting There & Away

The minibus shared taxi park is opposite the Garden Court hotel, with services to destinations including Vryheid (R80, 1½ hours) and Eshowe (R75, 1½ hours). Behind the hotel you can get a taxi to Durban (R170, three hours).

Ithala Game Reserve

Ezemvelo KZN Wildlife's Ithala Game Reserve (☑034-983 2540, central reservations 033-845 1000; www.kznwildlife.com; adult/child R120/60; ☉5am-7pm Nov-Feb, 6am-6pm Mar-Oct) is severely underrated. It has all the assets of a private wildlife reserve but at much lower prices. It also doesn't get the crowds that flock into Hluhluwe-iMfolozi, as it's slightly off the main routes and doesn't contain the Big Five, but it's captivating in its own way.

Most of the 300 sq km are taken up by the steep valleys of six rivers (tributaries of the Phongolo), with some open grassland on the heights, rugged outcrops and bushveld. Some of the world's oldest rock formations are found here, as are Stone Age spear and axe heads.

Animals include black and white rhinos, elephants, tsessebis, buffaloes and giraffes (the park's emblem, as they are believed to be indigenous to Ithala Game Reserve) and rare bird species.

Guided walks (R250 per person) and wildlife and night drives (R500 per person) are available.

ℹ ITHALA GAME RESERVE

Why Go Panoramic views from the mountainous thornveld, the oldest rock formations in the world and a plethora of wildlife make Ithala unique. It is one of KwaZulu-Natal's most spectacular wildlife reserves.

When to Go Ithala is a year-round destination, although it can get chilly in the evenings between May and August, with frosts not uncommon.

Practicalities Gates are open from 5am to 7pm November to February, and 6am to 6pm March to October. The nearest town with supplies is Louwsburg, 15km away.

Budget Tips Bring your own food, and a tent – campsites start at R180 per person. Take a self-guided walk.

🛏 Sleeping

Doornkraal
CAMPGROUND $

(📞 033-845 1000; www.kznwildlife.com; camping per person R180) This is one of a range of fabulous bush camps; the others have heftier minimum charges. Note, this is your 'real Africa' camping experience – it's cold-water showers only.

Ntshondwe
CABIN $$

(📞 033-845 1000; www.kznwildlife.com; 2-bed chalets per person R1230; 🏊) This is the park's main resort, located at the foot of Ngotshe Mountain, with superb views of the reserve below. It's warthog heaven, and home to the red Pride of De Kaap flower and redbilled oxpeckers. Facilities include a restaurant, a shop and a swimming pool. There's a full-board option for the units, on request.

ℹ Information

Ithala is reached from Louwsburg, about 55km northeast of Vryheid on R69, and about the same distance southwest of Phongolo via R66 and R69.

THE ELEPHANT COAST

Up there on the podium with the world's great ecotourism destinations, and near the top of the scribbled list marked 'Places I Must See in South Africa', the Elephant Coast (formerly 'Maputaland') is a phenomenal stretch of natural beauty, with a fabulously diverse mix of environments and wildlife.

This large stretch of coastline includes some of the country's true highlights, including the perennially photogenic iSimangaliso Wetland Park that runs from Lake St Lucia in the south to Kosi Bay in the north. Uncompromisingly untamed, this region, away from the scattered resort towns, offers a glimpse of precolonial Africa. Slightly further inland, the incredible Hluhluwe-iMfolozi Park is KZN's answer to Kruger National Park.

The climate becomes steadily hotter as you go north and, thanks to the warm Indian Ocean, summers are steamy and tropical. The humid coastal air causes dense mists on the inland hills, reducing visibility to a few metres.

There is a good network of roads connecting the regions. Minibus shared taxis cover the coast. Self-drivers have a world open to them; while a 2WD will get you many places,

ℹ HLUHLUWE SIGNS

Signs to Hluhluwe and surrounds often confuse travellers. Useful to know when exiting the N2 is that Hluhluwe, the village, is on the eastern side of the N2, while Hluhluwe-iMfolozi Park is 12km west of the N2 (14km west of the town).

a 4WD is required for the spectacular sandy road along the coast from Kosi Bay to Sodwana Bay. If driving, be careful of pedestrians and animals that may suddenly appear around a corner.

Hluhluwe

📞 035 / POP 1100

Hluhluwe village (roughly pronounced shloo-*shloo*-wee) is the main gateway to the beautiful Hluhluwe-iMfolozi Park, which sits just to the southwest. There's not much to the village itself – it spans a wide main road that joins the N2.

Emdoneni
Cheetah Project
ANIMAL SANCTUARY

(www.emdonenilodge.com; adult/child R260/130; ⊙ tours at 10.30am & 4pm May-Aug, 4.30pm Sep-Apr) The Emdoneni Cheetah Project is home to rescued and rehabilitated African felines of all varieties. Tours are offered daily that give educational information with a focus on conservation, as well as a chance to get a closer look at the majestic animals. The guides take great care to make sure the cats are comfortable at all times.

🛏 Sleeping & Eating

Hluhluwe County Cottages
BUNGALOW $

(📞 082 494 1047; www.hluhluwecottages.co.za; 1 Ngweni Rd; 1-/2-/3-bedroom cottages R700/1200/1800; 🏊) These self-catering cottages, in a wildlife sanctuary that is part of a larger farm, are a comfy set-up. The cottages are fairly old-fashioned and they definitely have a lived-in feel, but its a good spot just out of town, especially for families. The farm offers wildlife walks, and the famous Ilala Weavers (p270) and Fig Tree Cafe are nearby.

Hluhluwe Backpackers
HOSTEL $

(📞 076 375 3831; www.hlubackpack.co.za; s/d with shared bathroom R370/520; 🅿) Just outside Hluhluwe-iMfolozi Memorial gate, this converted house has a great location. It's a bit dark and dingy inside, but friendly dogs, clean rooms and a very informal approach make it fine for a night or two. The owner is known for fostering a friendly atmosphere. And it's a heck of a lot cheaper than staying in the park.

Isinkwe Backpackers Bushcamp
HOSTEL $$

(☑083 338 3494; www.isinkwe.co.za; Bushlands; self-catering camping R140, dm R200, s/d R450/600, with shared bathroom R300/450; @ 🛜 🌊) Located in a sweep of virgin bush 14km south of Hluhluwe, this budget place has a variety of accommodation options, from huts to rooms with bathrooms, a plethora of bush-focused (and other) activities, and a poolside bar where you can exchange tall-as-a-giraffe stories. The owners take safaris into Hluhluwe-iMfolozi and have half-board and accommodation-activity packages (see the website). Ring for directions.

★ Hluhluwe River Lodge
LODGE $$$

(☑035-562 0246; www.hluhluwe.co.za; s/d with half-board R2030/2900) If you're looking for seclusion you'll find it at this luxurious lodge set deep in the bush overlooking Lake St Lucia. Each chalet is stylish, airy, spacious and private. The communal area features a stunning indoor-outdoor living room with terrace, and the lodge's chef serves up top-notch fare. It's about 11km from Hluhluwe, on the D540.

Bushwillow
GUESTHOUSE $$$

(☑083 502 5556; www.bushwillow.com; Kuleni Game Park; s/d incl breakfast from R1625/2290) Within the privately owned Kuleni Game Park and surrounded by superb forest – flat crown, albizia and, of course, bush willows – is this romantic, relaxing hideaway. Soft wildlife (the likes of zebra, giraffe and duikers) surround the property and there are walking trails. It's 20km from Hluhluwe village on the Sodwana Bay road; look for the Kuleni sign. Half-board available.

Zululand Tree Lodge
LODGE $$$

(☑035-562 1020; http://ubizane.co.za; s/d incl breakfast R1335/1920; ❋ 🌊) Like to wake up to the sound of birdsong? Seven kilometres outside Hluhluwe, and set in the Ubizane wildlife reserve amid fever trees, this romantic spot offers thatched tree houses set on stilts. Each room has its own viewing deck. There are excellent specials that include half-board and safari drives (per person R535); prices are flexible, depending on the package.

🛍 Shopping

About 20km south of Hluhluwe on the N2 is the great-value Zamimpilo market, a women's cooperative that sells a variety of local crafts. Ilala Weavers is also close by.

Ilala Weavers
ARTS & CRAFTS

(☑081 400 0947; www.ilala.co.za; 1 Ngweni Rd; ⊙8am-4.30pm Mon-Fri, 9am-4pm Sat & Sat) Sells a large range of Zulu handicrafts, plus there's a museum and a local, slightly contrived 'village'. It's a good place to pick up souvenirs and worth the coach crowds you may encounter.

Hluhluwe-iMfolozi Park

Rivalling Kruger National Park in its beauty and variety of landscapes, Hluhluwe-iMfolozi Park (☑035-550 8476, central reservations 033-845 1000; www.kznwildlife.com; adult/child R210/105; ⊙5am-7pm Nov-Feb, 6am-6pm Mar-Oct) is one of South Africa's best-known, most evocative parks. Indeed, some say it's better than Kruger for its accessibility – it covers 960 sq km (around a 20th of the size of Kruger) and there's plenty of wildlife including lions, elephants, rhinos (black and white), leopards, giraffes, buffaloes and African wild dogs.

Stunning Hluhluwe-iMfolozi has a mountainous landscape providing jaw-dropping views in all directions. The lack of thick vegetation in parts of the park, such as the drive from Memorial gate to Hilltop Camp, makes for excellent wildlife spotting. You are almost certain to see white rhinos here.

◉ Sights & Activities

Centenary Centre
MUSEUM

(⊙8am-4pm) FREE The Centenary Centre, a wildlife-holding centre with an attached museum, information centre and excellent craft market, is in the eastern section of iMfolozi. It incorporates rhino enclosures and antelope pens, and was established to allow visitors to view animals in transit to their new homes. To see the animals, ask at the Centenary Centre kiosk; you must be accompanied by a guide (around R20 per person).

Wildlife Drives

Wildlife drives here are popular. Hilltop Camp offers morning and evening drives, while Mpila Camp does evening drives only. The camp-run drives are open to resort residents only and cost R330 per person (minimum two people). Most visitors to the area self-drive.

Hluhluwe-iMfolozi Park

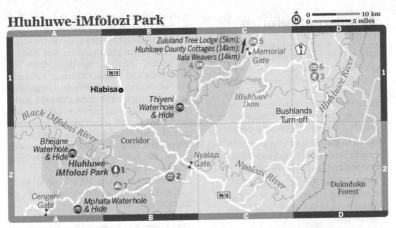

Hiking

One of iMfolozi's main attractions is its extraordinary trail system, in a special 240-sq-km wilderness area (note: these trails are seasonal and there's a four-person minimum) where there are no roads, only walking tracks. The trail walks are guided and last from two to five days. They are run by KZN Wildlife (p287) and all food, water, cooking equipment etc is provided. Accommodation is in tented camps and you can certainly expect to see wildlife. These walks are truly once-in-a-lifetime experiences and thus extremely popular, so book ahead.

The **Base Camp Trail** (3 nights R4185) is, as the name suggests, at a base camp. Trailists carry day packs on the daily outings. The **Short Wilderness Trail** (2 nights R2520) is at satellite camps with no amenities (bucket shower) but are fully catered. Similar is the **Extended Wilderness Trail** (3 nights R3700), but guests must carry their gear for 7km into camp. On the **Primitive Trail** (www.kznwildlife.com; 3/4 nights R2575/3110) you carry equipment, help prepare the food (provided) and sleep under the stars. Some consider this trail to be more fun than the others because you are able to participate more (for example, hikers must sit up in 1½-hour watches during the night).

🛏 Sleeping & Eating

As well as Hilltop Camp and Mpila Camp, there's a range of fabulous lodges within the park, but minimum charges apply; they cater for six to eight guests. You must book accommodation in advance through Ezemvelo KZN Wildlife (p287) in Pietermaritzburg.

Hluhluwe-iMfolozi Park

Last-minute bookings – those made up to 48 hours ahead – should be made directly with the camps. If you're self-catering, remember to bring your own food.

★ Hilltop Camp   CABIN $$
(☎035-562 0848; rondavels R660, 2-person chalets R1305; ❄) The signature resort on the Hluhluwe side; a cold drink followed by dinner on the patio with mountains silhouetted into the distance is a memorable experience. There is a wide range of accommodation, from simple cabins to luxury chalets.

If you want peace and quiet, try one of the private and sedate accommodation options. Although described as 'bush lodges', they are out of this world: fully equipped and reasonably upmarket. Some come with their own chef – although you supply the food.

ℹ️ HLUHLUWE-IMFOLOZI PARK

Why Go This is an incredibly scenic park, very mountainous, and the viewing opportunities allow for excellent wildlife spotting. This is one park in KwaZulu-Natal that should not be missed. Crawling along open mountain ridges spotting wildlife is a wonderful African experience.

When to Go Any time of year is good. May to September is best for wildlife spotting on the open savannah.

Practicalities Petrol is available at Mpila Camp in iMfolozi and at Hilltop Camp in Hluhluwe, where you can also get diesel.

Budget Tips Stay outside the park! Try Hluhluwe Backpackers (p269) or Isinkwe (p270). If you want to try a wilderness trail, stick with the Primitive Trail for good value.

★ **Mpila Camp** TENTED CAMP, CHALET **$$**
(safari tent or chalet for 2 R1000) The main accommodation centre on the iMfolozi side, peaceful Mpila Camp is perched on top of a hill in the centre of the reserve. The safari tents are the most fun, but self-contained chalets are available, too. The accommodation isn't as nice as Hilltop, but it offers a much more peaceful vibe. Note: there's an electric fence, but wildlife (lions, hyenas, wild dogs) can still wander through.

There's a curio shop that sells some canned food, braai (barbecue) supplies, ice cream, beer, wine and souvenirs.

ℹ️ Getting There & Away

You can access the park via three gates. The main entrance, Memorial gate, is about 15km west of the N2, about 50km north of Mtubatuba. The second entrance, Nyalazi gate, is accessed by turning left off the N2 onto R618 just after Mtubatuba on the way to Nongoma. The third, Cengeni gate, on iMfolozi's western side, is accessible by road (tarred for 30km) from Ulundi.

iSimangaliso Wetland Park

The iSimangaliso Wetland Park (http://isimangaliso.com), a Unesco World Heritage site, stretches for 220 glorious kilometres from the Mozambique border to Maphelane,

at the southern end of Lake St Lucia. With the Indian Ocean on one side and a series of lakes (including Lake St Lucia) on the other, the 3280-sq-km park protects five distinct ecosystems, offering everything from offshore reefs and beaches to lakes, wetlands, woodlands and coastal forests. Loggerhead and leatherback turtles nest along the park's shores; whales and dolphins appear offshore and the park is occupied by numerous animals, including antelopes, hippos and zebras. The ocean beaches pull big crowds during the holiday season for everything from diving to fishing.

iSimangaliso means 'Miracle' or 'Wonder' and, given its extraordinary beauty, it's an appropriate title.

Lake St Lucia is Africa's largest estuary. After dipping to its lowest level for around 55 years due to a former environmental-management policy that kept the Lake St Lucia Estuary separate from the iMfolozi River, the two water bodies were naturally linked in 2012. This, along with more consistent rainfall, saw the water return to its former level in 2014 and the reappearance of fish and prawns. A new management strategy is also in place to ensure water levels remain stable and the ecosystem healthy.

There's a wonderful range of accommodation, from camping to private lodges to excellent options managed by Ezemvelo KZN Wildlife (p287). It's a good idea to book at least 48 hours ahead.

St Lucia is the main settlement and a good accommodation and supply base; the Eastern and Western Shores take you into the heart of the wetlands; Sodwana Bay is a separate access point to the park and is popular with divers; Lake Sibaya in the park's northern reaches is both remote and beautiful, while Kosi Bay is within convenient distance of the small but well-equipped town of Manguzi; and uMkhuze Game Reserve is further inland.

🏃 Activities

As part of the iSimangaliso Wetland Park Authority's responsible-tourism practices, every few years an ecotour operator must officially reapply for a permit – known as a concession – to operate activity tours. Go to www.isimangaliso.com for a list of current companies and organisations.

Birdwatching

Birdwatching is a delight in St Lucia and beyond. Check out www.zululandbirdingroute.co.za for heaps of info plus guide services.

Themba's Birding & Eco Tours
BIRDWATCHING

([☑]071 413 3243; https://zulubirding.jimdo.com; St Lucia; per person from R350, minimum 2 people) Themba is a recommended guide who gets great reports from travellers for his birding and local-area knowledge.

Boat Tours & Whale Watching

Whatever you do, keep aside some money in the kitty for a whale-watching experience. In season, there's a high chance of spotting whales here, as well as dolphins and other sea creatures. Trips cost around R1100 per person. You can also head upriver on boat tours to view hippos and crocodiles. Most trips operate from St Lucia, though Sodwana Bay Lodge (p280) offers whale watching out of Sodwana Bay.

Advantage Tours
CRUISE

(St Lucia Tours; [☑]035-590 1259; www.advantage-tours.co.za; 1 McKenzie St, Dolphin Centre) Runs daily whale-watching boat tours (R990 per person) between June and September, weather permitting. You can also head upriver on boat tours to view hippos and crocodiles (R220 per person).

Shoreline Boat & Walking Safaris
CRUISE

([☑]035-590 1555; Shop 1 Reef & Dune complex, McKenzie St) Runs a two-hour hippo and croc cruise up the St Lucia Estuary. Also offers the opportunity to disembark from the boat and continue with a walking tour into the bush and the opportunity to see zebras and antelopes.

Diving & Deep-Sea Fishing

Sodwana Bay (p280) is a hotbed for scuba diving and deep-sea fishing.

Horse Riding

Hluhluwe Horse Safaris
HORSE RIDING

([☑]035-562 1039; www.hluhluwehorsesafaris.co.za; 1½hr ride R495, 2½hr ride R795) Horse riding is a wonderful way to see wildlife; these rides are in the False Bay region. You may spot antelope species, as well as other animals. A second option heads to Falaza Game reserve, where you can see rhinos, buffaloes and giraffes. It operates out of Wildebeest Ecolodge.

Turtle Watching

Fascinating night turtle tours operate from Cape Vidal. Sodwana Bay Lodge (p280) runs trips at Sodwana Bay, as does Kosi Bay Lodge (p282) at Kosi Bay.

Five species of turtle live off the South African coast, but only two actually nest on the coast: the leatherback turtle *(Dermochelys coriacea)* and the loggerhead turtle *(Caretta caretta)*. The nesting areas of both species extend from the St Lucia mouth, north into Mozambique, and both nest at night in summer. About 70 days later, the hatchlings scramble out of the nest at night and make a dash for the sea.

St Lucia Turtle Tours
WALKING

([☑]082 2575 612; www.extremenaturetours.co.za; [☺]per person R750) Run by Extreme Nature Tours, this environmentally focused outfit runs very good turtle-watching tours as part of a local community development project. For example, they walk – they do not drive vehicles – along the beach, to ensure nesting turtles are not disturbed.

EuroZulu Safaris
ECOTOUR

([☑]035-590 1635; www.eurozulu.com; per person incl dinner & drinks R1095) Fascinating night turtle-watching tours operate (from November to March) from Cape Vidal and

---

ℹ ISIMANGALISO WETLAND PARK

Why Go This park is unique in South Africa and indeed on the continent. It contains most of South Africa's remaining swamp forests and is Africa's largest estuarine system.

When to Go Year-round.

Practicalities The park is a huge area spreading over 220km, much of it sand dunes and forest. There are three main regions: the south (easily accessed via St Lucia, from where you can enter the Eastern and Western Shores); the centre (Sodwana Bay, accessed from Rte 22); and the least accessible and appropriately stunning north (Kosi Bay, located at the end of Rte 22). A road west off Rte 22 allows for fairly easy access to uMkuze Game Reserve.

Budget Tips There are a couple of good hostels in St Lucia that can advise on cheap tour options. Self-drive safaris split between three or four people are the cheapest way to see the park. Accommodation outside the park tends to be less expensive.

iSimangaliso Wetland Park

0 ————————— 20 km
0 ————————— 10 miles

Sodwana Bay
(40km)

uMkhuze
Game Reserve

Phinda
Resource
Reserve

Lake
St Lucia

Hluhluwe

iSimangaliso
Wetland Park

Memorial
Gate

Hluhluwe
Dam

Cape
Vidal

Dukuduku
Forest

St Lucia

Mtubatuba

Riverview

White iMfolozi River

Kosi Bay. Other tours include the usual selection of wildlife-watching drives and boat trips.

Wildlife Watching

uMkhuze Game Reserve has some of the best wildlife viewing in the country, and there are a number of operators offering excellent day and night trips on the Eastern and Western Shores. Operators are listed on www.isimangaliso.com. Self-guided drives are also rewarding ways to seek out wildlife.

Shakabarker Tours   TOUR
(☏035-590 1162; www.shakabarker.co.za; 43 Hornbill St) Shakabarker Tours operates out of St Lucia and conducts a range of excellent wildlife trips, including tours of local wildlife parks and a guided bike ride (around R250 per person) around St Lucia with a Zulu guide.

St Lucia
☏035 / POP 1104

Although not officially within the iSimangaliso Wetland Park, the pleasant village of St Lucia is a useful base from which to explore the park's southern sections. In high season St Lucia is a hotbed of activity as the population swells with visitor numbers. The main drag, McKenzie St (a former hippo pathway), is packed with restaurants, lively hostels and bars, but the quieter avenues behind it offer a touch more hush and a good selection of B&Bs. Hippos sometimes amble down the town's quieter streets (beware: these are not cute, just dangerous).

The main banks (Standard Chartered Bank, Nedbank and FNB) have an ATM in the main street.

🛏 Sleeping

There's rarely a shortage of places to stay, but it's worth booking ahead during the summer months.

Monzi Safaris
GUESTHOUSE $

(035-590 1697; www.monzisafaris.com; 81 McKenzie St; dm/tent/r R220/480/570; ⟨icons⟩) St Lucia's best budget option is part upmarket guesthouse, part well-maintained backpacker hostel. The backpacker section has clean, simple rooms with shared bathroom, or pre-erected tents with fans and plug points on a covered balcony. There's an excellent entertainment area with pool table, bar and sparkling pool. The luxury wing offers large tents with en-suite bathroom (R750).

St Lucia Wilds
APARTMENT $

(035-590 1033; www.stluciawilds.co.za; 174 McKenzie St; flatlet/cottage from R660/1650) An excellent budget/midrange alternative with three cottages and one flatlet for those allergic to backpackers; no meals provided.

Sugarloaf Campsite
CAMPGROUND $

(033-845 1000; www.kznwildlife.com; Pelican St; camping R390) This pretty campground on the estuary is within snorting distance of hippos, monkeys and crocodiles.

Santa Lucia Guesthouse
GUESTHOUSE $$

(035-590 1151; www.santalucia.co.za; 30 Pelikaan St; s/d incl breakfast R787/1330; ⟨icons⟩) Off the main drag and opposite a lovely park, this guesthouse has affable hosts who ensure a very comfortable stay. Each room here has a fun, unique theme and there is a small library if you'd like to sit by the pool and read, or relax over a hearty breakfast and enjoy the tropical garden from a lower or upper deck.

Sunset Lodge
CABIN $$

(035-590 1197; www.sunsetstlucia.co.za; 154 McKenzie St; chalets R895-1995; ⟨icons⟩) Seven well-maintained, self-catering log cabins, lined in dark wood and with a safari theme.

Affords a stunning view overlooking the estuary from your private patio should you choose one of the pricier chalets – you can watch the hippos, mongooses and monkeys wander onto the lawn. The owners have recently added a pool that enjoys the estuary views.

Hornbill House
B&B $$

(035-590 1162; www.shakabarker.co.za/hornbillhouse; 43 Hornbill St; r from R1145; ⟨icons⟩) A very pleasant place to nest, with lovely rooms, some with private balconies overlooking the tropical vegetation in the garden, friendly dogs and a small pool for a dip. That is, if you're not flitting about on one of the many eco-friendly trips or activities offered by the knowledgeable owner, Kian, who runs a tour company.

Lodge Afrique
LODGE $$$

(035-590 1696; www.lodgeafrique.com; 71 Hornbill St; s/d incl breakfast R1050/1700; ⟨icons⟩) Smart 'African chic'-style chalets with all the modern trimmings are on offer at Lodge Afrique. The spot is right in the middle of St Lucia, but the garden makes it feel like you're in the bush. Also serves an excellent breakfast.

Serene Estate Guesthouse
GUESTHOUSE $$$

(072 365 2450; www.serene-estate.co.za; 119 Hornbill St; r incl breakfast from R2160; ⟨icons⟩) A world away from St Lucia, minimalist Dutch meets lush African forest and creates a stylish experience in Serene Estate's seven rooms and beyond. The breakfasts, served with one of Olga's daily surprises, are memorable.

Forest Lodge
HOTEL $$$

(035-590 1698; www.forestkzn.co.za; 15 Pelikaan St; s/d from R875/1530) This newish addition to the St Lucia hotel circuit is a good choice for those who want no muss, no fuss

---

HEALTH WARNING

In 2004, the World Health Organization declared KZN – as far northeast as St Lucia – malaria free. Note: a low-risk area extends from Sodwana Bay (iSimangaliso Wetland Park) northwards. The risk may be higher north and northeast near the borders of Swaziland and Mozambique. At the time of writing the recommended precautions were insect spray and long sleeves, but you should consult your doctor about the need for anti-malarial medications if you plan to visit.

There is the risk of bilharzia in some waterways and dams, especially those less than 1200m above sea level. Also beware of crocs and hippos: both can be deadly. Be careful at night (including in the town of St Lucia), as this is when hippos roam. In more remote areas hippos might be encountered on shore during the day – maintain your distance and retreat quietly. Do not enter any inland water (St Lucia Estuary) – there are crocodiles, sharks, hippos and bilharzia. Swimming is possible (in good conditions and at low tide) at Cape Vidal beach.

accommodation. All of the rooms have crisp, white linens and modern furnishings. In the centre of the lodge is a fabulously overgrown courtyard and pool that truly feels like being in the forest, but without as many critters.

Umlilo Lodge LODGE $$$
(☏035-590 1717; www.umlilolodge.co.za; 9 Dolphin Ave; s/d incl breakfast from R1050/1600; ✴🖧🏊) Centrally located with a lovely lush garden. There are 13 separate rooms and a lovely indoor-outdoor lounge in which to kick back after a day's activities. Delightful owner.

🍴 Eating & Drinking

The best place for a sundowner is the **Ski Boat Club** (☏035-590 1376; Sugar Loaf Rd, St Lucia Estuary; mains R50-160; ☺noon-10pm; 🍴) – the only restaurant in town overlooking the estuary.

Rich's Cafe CAFE $
(☏083 453 1621; McKenzie St; mains R45-55; ☺7.30am-6pm Mon-Fri, 8am-2pm Sun) Serves up wraps, sandwiches, real coffee and all-day breakfasts in a nice little courtyard garden.

Barraca INTERNATIONAL $$
(☏035-590 1729; McKenzie St; mains R80-140; ☺8am-9pm) A large, open veranda onto the main street makes this place easy to spot. It's friendly, the food's tasty and it's great for people-watching and grabbing a bite at any time of the day. For lunch there are open sandwiches, while for dinner seafood options include prawn curry or seafood paella.

Braza PORTUGUESE $$
(☏035-590 1242; 73 McKenzie St; mains R80-180; ☺11am-10pm) Cuisine with a touch of Portugal, Brazil, Mozambique and Angola – at least that's what this lively place promotes. It translates as good meaty dishes and grills, although a decent vegetarian platter is also on offer (but not on the menu). Anything featuring the chorizo is superb.

❶ Getting There & Away

Minibus shared taxis connect Durban and Mtubatuba (R120); the latter is 25km from St Lucia, and it's from where you must catch a connecting minibus taxi to St Lucia. Alternatively, buses run between St Lucia, Richards Bay and Mtubatuba; you must change at each point. If you're not doing tours out of St Lucia Estuary, the only way of getting around is to have your own wheels.

For car hire, **Avis** (☏035-590 1634; www.avis. co.za; 110 McKenzie St; ☺8am-5pm Mon-Fri, to noon Sat) has a branch in the main street.

Eastern Shores

The **Eastern Shores** (☏035-590 1633; www. isimangaliso.com; adult/child/vehicle R48/36/58; ☺5am-7pm Nov-Mar, 6am-6pm Apr-Oct), in the southern part of iSimangaliso Wetland Park, is among the most accessible from St Lucia Estuary. It affords opportunities for self-guided drives through the wonderful network of wildlife-viewing roads (there's everything from hippos to antelope, and prolific birdlife). Part of a rehabilitation scheme with Western Shores, this area is where hundreds of thousands of square metres of plantation land has been returned to its former state (yes, that's why there are all those tree stumps).

The Eastern Shores' gate lies 2km north of the town of St Lucia, adjacent to the St Lucia Crocodile Centre.

Mission Rocks WATERFRONT
Mission Rocks is a rugged and rock-covered shoreline known for the rock pools that have a fabulous array of sea life on view during low tide. It's important to note that there's no swimming here. They are located about 14km north of the entrance of the Eastern Shores.

Bats Cave CAVE
At low tide you can walk the 5km from Mission Rocks to this bat-filled cave.

Mt Tabor Lookout VIEWPOINT
Hikers should head to the Mt Tabor lookout, where three trail loops lead to spectacular views of Lake St Lucia and the Indian Ocean. It's about 4km before Mission Rocks.

Cape Vidal BEACH
(http://isimangaliso.com; adult/child/vehicle R48/36/58; ☺5am-7pm Nov-Mar, 6am-6pm Apr-Oct) If you ask anyone in the know what to see in the iSimangaliso Wetland Park they'll most likely suggest Cape Vidal. Some of the forested sand dunes here rise 150m high and the beaches are excellent for swimming. There's also decent wildlife viewing en route to the beach and you'll likely have the sightings of hippos, antelopes, buffaloes and crocs to yourself. It's 20km north of Mission Rocks (30km from St Lucia Estuary), taking in the land between Lake Bhangazi and the ocean.

Cape Vidal Camp CAMPGROUND, CABIN $$
(☏033-845 1000; www.kznwildlife.com; camping per site 1-4 people R540, 5-bed log cabins from

R1575) This Eastern Shores' campground is blessed to be located in the stunning Cape Vidal near the shores of Lake Bhangazi. The campsites are a bit expensive and the cabins a bit run-down (keep a lookout for bats and their leavings), but if you don't mind roughing it the scenery alone is worth the visit.

Western Shores

The region northwest of St Lucia Estuary is called the **Western Shores** (☑035-590 1633; www.isimangaliso.com; adult/child/vehicle R48/36/58; ☺5am-7pm Nov-Mar, 6am-6pm Apr-Oct), and comprises two stunning lakeside spots, known as **Fani's Island** (closed to visitors at the time of research due to drought conditions) and **Charters Creek** (entrance is off the N2, 18km north of Mtubatuba and 32km south of Hluhluwe), an area of dense coastal forest and grasslands.

A new road provides direct access between St Lucia and Charter's Creek (a nice lakeside spot for views, but there's not much to do here), and offers excellent leisurely wildlife-drive opportunities up the western side of Lake St Lucia. The drive up the western shore reveals antelope (waterbuck and kukdu in particular), plus the possibility of hippo sightings.

uMkhuze Game Reserve & Around

The **uMkhuze Game Reserve** (☑035-573 9004, 031-845 1000; www.kznwildlife.com; adult/child/vehicle R48/36/58; ☺5am-7pm Nov-Mar, 6am-6pm Apr-Oct) is, in a phrase, a trip highlight. Established in 1912 to protect the nyala antelope, this reserve of dense scrub and open acacia plains covers some spectacular 360 sq km. It successfully re-introduced lions in 2014, and just about every other sought-after animal is represented, as well as more than 400 bird species, including the rare Pel's fishing owl (*Scotopelia peli*). The reserve has fabulous hides, some at waterholes; the pans, surrounded by fever trees, offer some of the best wildlife viewing in the country. It's 15km from Mkuze town (18km from Bayla if heading north).

🏃 Activities

By day you can self-drive in the park. Night drives (per person R250) are available from Mantuma.

ℹ️ UMKHUZE GAME RESERVE

Why Go uMkhuze has all the Big Five and is a remarkably beautiful park. Nyala and other antelope are often seen around the rest camp. Guides are knowledgeable and a wildlife drive is a highlight.

When to Go The best time for viewing is October and November, when the undergrowth is less dense.

Practicalities The nearest town is Mkhuze.

Budget Tips Rest huts are a bargain; self-cater, as there are plenty of braais (barbecues).

Fig Forest Walk   WALKING
(www.kznwildlife.com; per person R250) Don't miss the wonderful Fig Forest Walk, an escorted walk across multilevel walkways. It's offered by Mantuma.

🛏️ Sleeping

Mantuma   CHALET, TENTED CAMP **$$**
(☑033-845 1000; www.kznwildlife.com; rest hut per person R290, d chalets R1100) Mantuma is in a lovely setting and is unfenced, so there's often wandering wildlife, especially nyala. It's an old camp – the accommodation has seen better days – but it's clean, well positioned and good value. You're better off self-catering than relying on the restaurant, although you can get a tasty sandwich there in a pinch.

Ghost Mountain Inn   INN **$$$**
(☑035-573 1025; www.ghostmountaininn.co.za; Fish Eagle Rd, Mkuze; s/d incl breakfast from R1315/1750; ❄️🅿️📶🏊) Outside of the park, Ghost Mountain Inn is an old-school colonial place with a modern (and luxurious) touch, indoor-outdoor lounge areas and blooming gardens. It's an excellent base for exploring the reserves. There are fascinating cultural tours in the scenic surrounds; recommended tours include trips to uMkhuze Game Reserve and Dingaan's Grave.

Nhlonhlela Bush Lodge   LODGE **$$$**
(☑033-845 1000; www.kznwildlife.com; 8-bed lodges R4080) Nhlonhlela bush lodge features a communal area overlooking a pan, and four comfortable units linked by boardwalks. You have your own ranger and chef (you bring your own food).

KWAZULU-NATAL ISIMANGALISO WETLAND PARK

1. Sani Pass (p293)
Awe-inspiring vistas abound on the highest pass in South Africa.

2. iSimangaliso Wetland Park (p272)
This glorious park offers everything from offshore reefs and beaches to lakes, wetlands, woodlands and coastal forests.

3. Hluhluwe-iMfolozi Park (p270)
Jaw-dropping views and a variety of wildlife, such as buffalo herds, make this one of South Africa's best-known, most evocative parks.

❶ Getting There & Away

Access from the north is via Mkhuze town (from the south, you turn off the N2 around 35km north of Hluhluwe village, but it's on a dirt road). On the eastern side there's access about 40km south of Sodwana Bay, off Rte 22. It's a mix of dirt roads and badly potholed bitumen that's OK for 2WDs, but drive carefully as it can get treacherous. There's also a road from Sodwana Bay.

Sodwana Bay

Sodwana Bay (☎035-571 0051; http://isimangaliso.com; adult/child/vehicle R42/36/58; ☉24hr) is bordered by lush forest on one side and glittering sands on another. The area is best known for its scuba diving – the diversity of underwater seascapes and marine flora and fauna makes it one of South Africa's diving capitals. Serious deep-sea fishing occurs here, too; you can be inundated with huntin', shootin', fishin' types who head out in their water machines. But except during summer holidays, it's a beautifully peaceful place. Most people come here for the diving or fishing; outside of that, there's not much to do here but walk along the beach and admire the gorgeous surrounds.

The main reason people visit Sodwana is for the superlative scuba diving, though oceanic pursuits in general are on offer, including sailing, surfing, snorkelling, fishing or just paddling in the warm waters. There are also some choice birdwatching opportunities, including the four-hour **Ngoboseleni Trail** and driving the shores of Lake Sibaya.

🛏 Sleeping & Eating

Natural Moments
Bush Camp & Diving   HOSTEL $
(☎083-236 1756; www.divesodwana.com; 1A Sodwana Bay Main Rd; huts per person R240, r from R255) This very basic backpackers is of the laid-back, hippie variety has small huts crammed into a lush garden setting. It also runs a campground and Zulu-hut accommodation nearby.

Ezemvelo KZN Wildlife   CAMPGROUND $$
(☎central reservations 033-845 1000; www.kznwildlife.com; camping per site 1-4 people from R640, 4-bed cabins R1800; ❀) Has hundreds of well-organised campsites plus cabins with recently renovated bathrooms and modern appliances set within the park's coastal forest. Minimum charges apply. There's a general store (p280) with two ATMs selling basic supplies, curios and petrol here.

Coral Divers   LODGE $$
(☎035-571 0290; www.coraldivers.co.za; Sodwana Bay; d tent R495, d chalet with/without breakfast & dinner R1030/760; @❀) Inside the park proper, this factory-style operation continues to 'net the shoals' with its diving packages and other activities. There's a large dining area–bar, and a tadpole-size pool. There's something for all budgets, from tents and small dollhouse-style cabins to nicer, upmarket cabins with their own patch of lawn and bathrooms.

It can look a bit overused depending on whether or not maintenance has been done after the hordes have gone.

Sodwana Bay Lodge   LODGE $$$
(☎035-571 9101; www.sodwanabaylodge.co.za; s/d with half-board R1040/1910) This resort has neat boardwalks, banana palms and pine-filled, slightly dated rooms. The chalets here are very comfortable, with huge decks. It caters to divers and offers various dive and accommodation packages, which can be great value. It's on the main road on the approach to the park.

Sodwana Bay Lodge Scuba Centre (☎035-571 0117; www.sodwanadiving.co.za; PADI open-water course R3850; ☉7am-4.30pm) is on the premises. There's also a lively restaurant and bar, as well as an ATM.

Leatherbacks   SEAFOOD $$
(☎035-571 6000; Sodwana Bay Lodge; mains R75-145; ☉7-10.30am, noon-5pm & 6.30-10pm) This lovely eating area is open to the breeze, has a range of simple dishes and is a quiet respite from the main road. Other than the breaks between meals it is open from morning to late night, making it ideal for a bite of pizza, pasta or well-prepared seafood just about any time.

❶ Information

Services, including accommodation options, dive operators, a couple of cafes and tour operators, sprawl along the road leading to the park entrance.

There are two ATMs in the **general store** (☉8am-4.45pm Mon-Fri, to 3pm Sat, to 12.45pm Sun) at the park's entrance, one inside and one outside. The Sodwana Bay Lodge also has one on site. Otherwise you'll need to head to Mbazwana, 14km west.

❶ Getting There & Away

Turn off the N2 at Hluhluwe village heading to Mbazwana, and continue about 20km to the park. Minibus shared taxis ply this route.

Lake Sibaya & Coastal Forest

Remote grassland plains, lush forests and pristine beaches are the main features of the magical Coastal Forest. Its beauty can, in part, be explained by its location – this area is one of the most remote sections of iSimangaliso. Highlights include Black Rock (a rugged rocky peninsula easily reached by climbing over sand dunes) and Lala Nek, a beautiful and seemingly never-ending stretch of sand.

Further south sits Lake Sibaya, the largest freshwater lake in South Africa. It covers between 60 and 70 sq km, depending on the water level. Hippos, crocs and a large range of birdlife (more than 280 species) occupy the lake. Canoeing trips can be arranged through Thonga Beach Lodge.

Entrance to this area of iSimangaliso is free.

All the lodges offer excellent snorkelling, diving and other activities.

🛏 Sleeping

Beauty doesn't always come cheap. Accommodation in this region is made up mainly (but not entirely) of luxury lodges – there is also one spectacularly located campground. The lodges transfer guests from the main road; you leave your car in a secure parking area.

Mabibi Camp   CAMPGROUND **$**
(☏ 035-474 1504; www.mabibicampsite.co.za; camping/chalets R134/728) If you can get here, you'll have heaven to yourself – almost. This rustic community-owned camp is right next to upmarket Thonga Beach Lodge, but this is luxury of a different kind – nestled in a swath of forest and only a hop, skip and 137 steps (via a stairway) from the beach. Bring your own tent, food and gear.

Thonga Beach Lodge   LODGE **$$$**
(☏ 035-474 1473; www.thongabeachlodge.co.za; r with full board from R4780; ❄🛜🛏) Popular with European visitors, this isolated and luxurious beach resort offers spacious huts scattered through coastal forest. Spectacular ocean views – whales sometimes pass by – and activities provide the entertainment, while the wide, white beach and spa treatments (at extra cost) are a welcome relief after the rigours of a safari. The cuisine is excellent, especially the buffet lunches.

Rocktail Beach Camp   LODGE **$$$**
(☏ Johannesburg 011-807 1800; www.wilderness-safaris.com; r per person with full board from R3135; 🛜🛏) Snorkellers, scuba divers, birders and those looking to get away from it all will find lots to love at Rocktail Beach Camp. Twelve safari tents (with pine floors and tasteful wood-sided bathrooms), three family units and a honeymoon suite are nestled in dune forest in a tropical environment, with a choice of forest-canopy or sea views.

Rates include breakfast, lunch and dinner that exceed the normal full-board fare. There is a dive centre on-site and the Maputaland Coastal Forest is just a short walk away.

❶ Getting There & Away

This area is accessed either along the coastal sandy track between Kosi Bay and Sodwana Bay or from Manguzi, in both instances by 4WD. There is no public transport to Lake Sibaya. Gates are open 6am to 6pm.

Kosi Bay

The jewel of iSimangaliso Wetland Park, Kosi Bay (http://isimangaliso.com; adult/child/vehicle R53/26/53; ⏱6am-6pm) features a string of four lakes, starting from an estuary lined with some of the most beautiful and quiet beaches in South Africa. Fig, mangrove and raffia-palm forests provide the greenery (it's the only place in South Africa with five mangrove species in one place). Within the estuary mouth is excellent snorkelling.

Hippos, Zambezi sharks and some crocs live within the lake system. More than 250 bird species have been identified here, including rare palmnut vultures.

Kosi Mouth   OUTDOORS
(adult/child/vehicle R56/23/56) Golden sand, arresting blue water and the sound of birds greet you at the end of the trek to Kosi Mouth, where traditional Thonga fishing kraals still provide an income to local families. The sandy mouth offers great swimming and snorkelling, though stonefish are present so be sure to wear shoes. To get there you'll need a 4WD vehicle and a permit, which you must arrange at the Kosi Bay Camping (☏ central reservations 033-845 1000; www.kznwildlife.com; camping from R560, 2-/6-bed cabins R940/1870) reception the day before. Some lodges can arrange permits for their guests.

🛏 Sleeping & Eating

Utshwayelo Lodge   CAMPGROUND, CHALET $$
(☑ 082 909 3113; www.kosimouth.co.za; camping R200, sahara tents R660, chalets R960; 🛜 ⬛)
This lovely community-run camp offers accommodation that ranges from roomy campsites to bamboo-lined chalets with comfortable outdoor showers, all surrounding a communal kitchen, bar and pool area. It's right by the entrance to the park at the Kosi Mouth access road. Issues car-entry permits to Kosi Mouth and also offers a shuttle service there.

Kosi Bay Lodge   LODGE $$
(☑ 083 262 4865; www.kosibaylodge.co.za; r/safari tent per person from R360/230; 🛜 ⬛) The rooms are a little worn but good value and the resort has decent facilities including a pool, a restaurant and a bar. The comprehensive activities menu includes turtle watching (R680 per person) and shuttle rides down to the Kosi Bay Mouth (R400). Prices increase greatly for school holidays and long weekends.

Maputaland Lodge   CHALET $$
(☑ 082-323 4271; www.maputalandlodge.co.za; Manguzi; s/d incl breakfast R690/1040; ⬛ ⬛) These 23 simple yet pleasant self-catering chalets in Manguzi have all mod cons including DSTV, a restaurant and a bar. Its location makes it a great choice for those looking to explore Kosi Bay or nearby Tembe Elephant Park and Ndumo Game Reserve. Head to the bar at night to meet the friendly owners who love to give insider recommendations for the area.

★ Kosi Forest Lodge   LODGE $$$
(☑ 035-474 1473; www.isibindi.co.za; s/d from R1800/2200; 🛜 ⬛) The only private lodge in iSimangaliso's Kosi Bay region, and surrounded by the sand forest's Umdoni trees, this intimate 16-bed lodge offers a dreamy, luxurious – given the remote circumstances and limited electricity and wi-fi – experience. Accommodation is in romantic safari tents. They're a blend of *Out of Africa* (wooden decor and muted furnishings) and natural (the ultimate in ingenious outdoor bathrooms).

There are activities (some included in the nightly rate) on tap, and guest transfers are available from nearby Manguzi. If you want to get here yourself you'll need a 4WD vehicle to navigate the sand roads.

ⓘ Getting There & Away

A 4WD and permit are required to access Kosi Bay, but don't let this deter you. There are two entrances to the park: at Kosi Bay Camp (7km north of Manguzi) and Kosi Mouth (19km north of Manguzi). Only 4WDs can enter the access roads, and numbers are limited; permits are required to enter Kosi Mouth. These must be arranged a day in advance by visiting the reception at the Kosi Bay Camp, or through some lodgings.

Kosi Forest Lodge organises pick-ups from Manguzi, and some lodges in other areas organise trips to Kosi Bay. You can get to Manguzi via minibus taxi from Durban (R220, about five hours) or some of the nearby villages.

If you are driving – approaching from any direction – the best access is via N2; at Hluhluwe turn onto R22. If heading from Sodwana Bay, continue north up the R22. For those with a 4WD, the sandy coastal route is not to be missed.

Tembe Elephant Park

South Africa's last free-ranging big tusker elephants are protected in the sandveld (dry, sandy coastal belt) forests of **Tembe Elephant Park** (☑ 031-267 0144; www.tembe.co.za; adult/child/vehicle R50/25/110; ⊘ 6am-6pm). This transfrontier park on the Mozambique border is owned by the Tembe tribe and managed by Ezemvelo KZN Wildlife. Around 230 elephants live in its 300 sq km; these are the only indigenous elephants in KZN, and the largest elephants in the world, weighing up to 7000kg. The park boasts the Big Five (lion, leopard, buffalo, elephant and rhino), plus more than 300 bird species.

Tembe Lodge   LODGE $$$
(☑ 082 651 2868; www.tembe.co.za; s/d with full board & activities from R2425/4070; ⬛) Tembe Lodge offers accommodation in lovely, secluded, upmarket safari tents built on wooden platforms (the tents have bathrooms, some with outdoor showers). The room rates include all meals as well as two game drives per day.

Ndumo Game Reserve

On some 100 sq km of postcard-like scenery lies the **Ndumo Game Reserve** (☑ 035-591 0004; www.kznwildlife.com; adult/child/vehicle R60/30/50; ⊘ 5am-7pm Oct-Mar, 6am-6pm Apr-Sep). Here you'll find black and white rhinos, giraffes, hippos, crocodiles and antelope species, but it's the birdlife on the Phongolo

❶ TEMBE ELEPHANT PARK

Why Go Not only does this park contain the legendary big tuskers – the largest elephants in the world – it also has the Big Five. Staying in a safari tent is a delightful way to experience the park, and this accommodation, which includes meals and activities, is very good value.

When to Go The drier months (May to September) offer the best wildlife viewing. Using the hide at the waterhole normally produces excellent results at this time. Day visitors are advised to arrive early, as the park only allows 10 vehicles in per day.

Practicalities There's a sealed road all the way to the park entrance, but only 4WD vehicles are allowed to drive through the park itself; secure parking is available and visitors are collected in open safari vehicles.

Budget Tips While the rates at the lodge in the park seem steep, keep in mind they include all meals, as well as two game drives a day. A cheaper option is to stay outside the park and make sure you make it to the gate early.

and Usutu Rivers, and their flood plains and pans, that attracts visitors. The reserve is known locally as a 'mini Okavango'.

Wildlife-viewing and birdwatching guided walks (R150) and vehicle tours (R250) are available. This is the southernmost limit of the range of many bird species and the reserve is a favourite with birdwatchers, with more than 400 species recorded.

Fuel and limited supplies are usually available 2km outside the park gate. Camping and rest huts are offered by Ezemvelo KZN Wildlife (☑central reservations 033-845 1000; camping R160, 2-bed huts R960); minimum charges apply.

The reserve is just west of Tembe Elephant Park beside the Mozambique border and close to the Swaziland border, about 100km north of uMkhuze.

The road to Ndumo is paved all the way. You need your own vehicle to reach the park.

THE MIDLANDS

The Midlands run northwest from Pietermaritzburg (KwaZulu-Natal's capital) to Estcourt, skirting the Battlefields to the northeast. West of Pietermaritzburg is picturesque, hilly country, with horse studs and plenty of European trees. It was originally settled by English farmers.

Today, the region appeals more to art and craft lovers; it promotes itself heavily as the Midlands Meander, a slightly contrived concoction of craft shops, artistic endeavours, tea shops and B&Bs, winding along and around the R103 west of the N3, northwest of Pietermaritzburg.

Pietermaritzburg

☑ 033 / POP 223,500

Pietermaritzburg comprises a very contemporary mix: the city is home to students attending the numerous private schools in the area, a large Zulu community and a sizeable Indian population. Pietermaritzburg is a reasonable base from which to tackle the Midlands Meander and is also within spitting distance of the Drakensberg.

Billed as a heritage city, and KZN's administrative and legislative capital, Pietermaritzburg and its grand historic buildings around City Hall hark back to an age of pith helmets and midday martinis. While many buildings have been converted into museums, much of the CBD has, sadly, lost its gloss. This is partly due to the dire state of the local-government coffers. Elsewhere, the inner suburbs – plus Hilton, a suburb 9km northwest of the city centre – are green, leafy and pretty.

History

After defeating the Zulu at the decisive Battle of Blood River, the Voortrekkers began to establish their republic of Natal. Pietermaritzburg (usually known as PMB) was named in honour of leader Pieter Mauritz Retief, and was founded in 1838 as the capital (later the 'u' was dropped and, in 1938, it was decreed that Voortrekker leader Gert Maritz be remembered in the title). In 1841 the Boers built their Church of the Vow here to honour the Blood River promise. The British annexed Natal in 1843, but they retained Pietermaritzburg – well positioned

KWAZULU-NATAL PIETERMARITZBURG

and less humid than Durban, and already a neat little town – as the capital. In 2004 it became the provincial capital, and in 2005 street names were altered to reflect the region's broader history.

Alan Paton, author of *Cry, the Beloved Country,* was born in Pietermaritzburg in 1903.

◉ Sights

★**KwaZulu-Natal Museum**　　　MUSEUM
(☑ 033-345 1404; www.nmsa.org.za; 237 Jabu Ndlovu St; adult/child R10/2.50; ⊙ 8.15am-4.30pm Mon-Fri, 9am-4pm Sat, 10am-3pm Sun) This impressive museum has a range of well-curated displays reflecting a diversity of cultures, including settler history, war records, stuffed birds and marine life. The hall of African mammals is particularly stunning, with a huge number of stuffed animals in a relatively small space.

★**Tatham Art Gallery**　　　GALLERY
(☑ 033-392 2801; www.tatham.org.za; Chief Albert Luthuli St (Commercial Rd); ⊙ 10am-5pm Tue-Sun) **FREE** In keeping with Pietermaritzburg's self-styled role as a heritage city, one of its finest sights, the art gallery, was started in 1903 by Mrs Ada Tatham. Housed in the beautiful Old Supreme Court, it contains a fine collection of French and English 19th- and early-20th-century works.

KwaZulu-Natal
National Botanical Garden　　GARDENS
(☑ 033-344 3585; www.sanbi.org; 2 Swartkops Rd, Prestbury; adult/child under 6yr R25/free; ⊙ 8am-6pm Oct-Apr, to 5.30pm May-Sep) Spread over 4200 sq metres, these gardens have exotic species and indigenous mist-belt flora. Guided tours are offered on weekdays and there's a weekly farmers market here on Saturday mornings from 6am. It's located 2km west of the train station on the continuation of Hoosen Haffejee St.

Msunduzi Museum　　　MUSEUM
(☑ 033-394 6834; www.voortrekkermuseum.co.za; 351 Langalibalele St (Longmarket St); adult/child R10/3; ⊙ 9am-4pm Mon-Fri, to 1pm Sat; ℗) Formerly known as Voortrekker Museum, Msunduzi Museum comprises a complex that incorporates the Church of the Vow, the home of Andries Pretorius, a Voortrekker house and a former school now housing exhibits on the history of the region and its varied inhabitants.

Statue of Gandhi　　　MONUMENT
(Church St Mall) A statue of Gandhi, who was famously ejected from a 1st-class carriage at Pietermaritzburg station, stands defiant opposite some old colonial buildings on Church St.

🛏 Sleeping

Most B&Bs cater to the business crowds who stay in town tending to council and other matters of commerce. Pietermaritzburg Tourism can help with bookings, or try the **Pietermaritzburg B&B Network** (☑ 073 154 4444; www.pmbnetwork.co.za; d R600-1500).

Tancredi B&B　　　B&B $$
(☑ 082 818 1555; www.tancredi.co.za; 41 Woodhouse Rd, Scottsville; s/d incl breakfast R690/980; ℗ 🛜) Just south of the city centre in a quiet suburb, Tancredi has seven rooms in a beautifully restored Victorian house. The top-notch breakfast and personal service from owner Ann make this a popular spot. She even sells her own knitted creations at the reception desk.

Smithgrove B&B　　　B&B $$
(☑ 033-345 3963; smithgrove@telkomsa.net; 37 Howick Rd; s/d incl breakfast from R610/865; ❄🛜) This beautiful renovated Victorian home offers English-style B&B comforts with spacious, individually styled rooms, each in a different colour. There are freestanding bathtubs, and the pick of the rooms is No 5 on the 2nd floor, facing away from the main road with two good-sized windows to enjoy the views.

Heritage Guest House　　GUESTHOUSE $$
(☑ 033-394 4364; www.heritageguesthousepmb.co.za; 45 Miller St; s/d incl breakfast R600/800; ℗🛜🏊) It's a good sign when you see the owner in chef's garb cooking a full English breakfast. Here six small units of varying shapes and sizes surround a small, pretty garden and pool. It's handy to the city centre and opposite the cemetery, and with comfortable beds, you'll sleep like the dead. It can get booked out by long-term business travellers.

Redlands Hotel & Lodge　　HOTEL $$$
(☑ 033-394 3333; www.redlandshotel.co.za; cnr Howick Rd & George MacFarlane Lane; s/d from R1320/1630; ℗❄🛜🏊) Swish and stately, this elegant place offers contrived but tasteful colonial-style surrounds. It's a favourite among government dignitaries. The spacious grounds add to the escape-from-

Pietermaritzburg

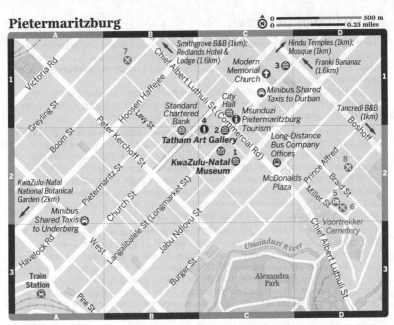

Smithgrove B&B (1km);
Redlands Hotel &
Lodge (1.6km)

Hindu Temples (1km);
Mosque (1km)

Franki Bananaz
(1.6km)

Modern
Memorial
Church

Minibus Shared
Taxis to Durban

City
Hall

Standard
Chartered
Bank

Msunduzi
Pietermaritzburg
Tourism

Tancredi B&B
(1km)

Tatham Art Gallery

Long-Distance
Bus Company
Offices

**KwaZulu-Natal
Museum**

McDonalds
Plaza

KwaZulu-Natal
National Botanical
Garden (2km)

Minibus
Shared Taxis
to Underberg

Voortrekker
Cemetery

Umsinduzi River

**Train
Station**

Alexandra
Park

it-all ambience. It's north of the centre off Howick Rd, past the Royal Agricultural Showgrounds.

Eating & Drinking

Tandoor INDIAN **$**
(033-345 1379; 319 Bulwer St; mains R40-105; 10am-3pm & 5-10pm) Durban enjoys most of the glory when it comes to Indian food, but Tandoor helps Pietermaritzburg give it a run for its money. Takeaway is best as the dining area is nothing special, but the food is absolutely flavourful. Locals swear by the butter chicken.

Tatham Art Gallery Cafe CAFE **$**
(033-342 8327; www.tatham.org.za; Chief Albert Luthuli St (Commercial Rd); mains R60-90; 9am-4pm Tue-Sat) Dip into quiche, beef curry or lasagne at the upstairs cafe at Tatham Gallery, or grab a table on the outside balcony. Also on offer are sweet treats such as muffins and brownies.

Mo-G's Restaurant INTERNATIONAL **$$**
(083 637 8861; 43 Miller St; mains R140-185; noon-3pm & 5.30-9.30pm Tue-Thu & Sat, from 2pm Fri) A new addition to the Pietermaritzburg dining scene, Mo-G's Restaurant has already developed a reputation as one of the best fine-dining establishments in

Pietermaritzburg

the city. Here classics such as lamb shanks and duck confit are prepared with a slight modern twist courtesy of homegrown chef Muhammed Moosa.

Rosehurst INTERNATIONAL **$$**
(033-394 3833; 239 Boom St; mains R60-80; 8.30am-4.30pm Mon-Fri, to 2pm Sat) This delightful oasis, in a lovely Victorian house behind a rather chintzy gift shop, is a quintessential English garden in the middle of 'Maritzburg – complete with topiary trees

THE MIDLANDS MEANDER

For the uninitiated, the Midlands region can be a bit overwhelming. It's full of twee venue names such as 'Piggly Wiggly' and 'Ugly Duckling', with little explanation as to whether they're tasteful galleries or kitsch gift shops. There's also a couple of microbreweries and the Nelson Mandela Capture Site.

The Meander – stretched out over a valley and its offshoots – is relaxing and enjoyable and well worth a detour off the N3. The *Midlands Meander* brochure is available from tourist offices and contains a detailed colour-coded map of the area.

Nelson Mandela Capture Site (☑ 071 834 4349; www.thecapturesite.co.za; Rte 103, Lions River; adult/child R25/15; ☺ 9am-4pm; ■) On 5 August 1962, Nelson Rolihlahla Mandela was captured by apartheid police on the R103 outside of Howick. This would mark the start of his 27 years of incarceration. In 2012 a monument was installed here in the form of 50 steel columns which, when viewed from the correct angle, come together to produce a marvellous portrait of the great man. At the time of writing, exhibits were housed in a temporary shed while a permanent museum was constructed. There's a cafe serving excellent coffee, a craft shop and a kids' playground on-site.

Ardmore Ceramic Studio (☑ 033-940 0034; www.ardmoreceramics.co.za; Caversham Rd, Lidgetton; ☺ 8am-4.30pm) This extraordinary gallery was started by artist Fée Halset-Berning in 1985. She trained Bonnie Ntshalintshahli, the daughter of a farm employee. Sadly, Bonnie has since passed away, but the studio flourished, firstly in the Drakensberg with a group of highly gifted artists. In 2009 the studio moved to its current site, set among greenery and stunning trees. The studio's artists create the most extraordinary pieces of ceramic art, some functional, others ornamental. So renowned are the pieces that Christie's holds an annual auction of selected items. You can see the artists at work in the studio and visit the gallery; works are for sale, too.

Dargle Valley Pottery (☑ 082 420 7729; D66; ☺ 9am-5pm) Started by famous South African potter Ian Glenny, this old-school, '70s-style pottery place is at the earthy and rural end of Ardmore's range of arts centres but no less captivating for that. You can wander through the barnlike gallery and watch the current local potter as he turns the pots. The pieces are noted for their stunning glazing; the tagines are popular.

Sycamore Avenue Tree Houses (☑ 033-263 5009; www.treehouse-acc.co.za; 11 Hidcote Rd, Mooi River; s/d incl half board from R695/1390) These extraordinary tree houses are functional art at its best: recycled materials, unique carvings, wooden hinges and ingenious artistic touches have been incorporated into comfortable surroundings. One house even has a 'Jacuzzi in the sky', connected by a walkway. Near Hidcote, Sycamore is located 50km from Giant's Castle, Drakensberg; see the website for directions.

Granny Mouse Country House (☑ 033-234 4071; www.grannymouse.co.za; Old Main Rd, Balgowan; d incl breakfast from R2595) This deceptively named place near the village of Balgowan, south of Mooi River, is not one abode but more a resort-style range of neat, thatched, luxurious cottages, complete with a chapel and spa. Specials are often available.

Cafe Bloom (☑ 033-266 6118; Nottingham Rd, Country Courtyard; mains R50-85; ☺ 7.30am-4.30pm, closed Tue) One of the nicest cafes in the area. Located in a small complex with a garden, this homely, funky place is decked out in a melange of retro decor. You'll find great coffee, snacks and all-day breakfasts, and all products are made on the premises, from bread and cakes to the daily seasonal special (the likes of veggie curries and quiches).

and quaint chairs and tables. Relax under blossoms and pink bougainvillea while enjoying fresh and very tasty salads, sandwiches and pastries. There are excellent breakfasts, too.

Franki Bananaz BAR
(☑ 033-345 7373; 9 Armitage Rd, Bird Sanctuary; ☺ noon-2am) This upmarket cocktail bar is a great spot to mix with a cross-section of locals. It's particularly popular with stu-

dents and young professionals, especially on Friday night. It also does tasty burgers and other quality pre-prepared offerings, but service isn't too speedy. Local bands play here monthly. Note: only ever take a taxi to and fro.

❶ Information

DANGERS & ANNOYANCES

Keep an eye out for pickpockets, especially in the more crowded sections of the CBD such as the Church St Mall.

MEDICAL SERVICES

Medi-Clinic (☏ 033-845 3700; www.medi-clinic.co.za; 90 Payn St; ⊙24hr emergency) Well-equipped hospital with emergency department on the banks of the Umsinduzi River.

TOURIST INFORMATION

Ezemvelo KZN Wildlife Headquarters (☏ 033-845 1000; www.kznwildlife.com; Peter Brown Dr, Queen Elizabeth Park; ⊙8am-4.30pm Mon-Fri to 1pm Sat) Provides information and accommodation bookings for all Ezemvelo KZN Wildlife parks and reserves. To get to the office, head out to Howick Rd (an extension of Chief Albert Luthuli St) and after several kilometres you'll come to a roundabout. Veer right and head over the N3. This road has a very small sign directing you to 'Country Club', which is 2km further.

It's hard to get to without your own transport, although some minibus shared taxis pass the roundabout on their way to Hilton. Note that at least 48 hours' notice is required for bookings.

Msunduzi Pietermaritzburg Tourism (☏ 033-345 1348; www.pmbtourism.co.za; Publicity House, 177 Chief Albert Luthuli St/Commercial Rd; ⊙8am-5pm Mon-Fri, to 1pm Sat) is located in the stately Publicity House building in the middle of the CBD (although there have been long-delayed plans to move the office to a nearby building). It houses friendly staff and a healthy cache of brochures and maps.

❶ Getting There & Away

AIR

The **airport** (☏ 033-386 9577) is 7km south of the city. A taxi costs around R90. **SAAirlink** (☏ 033-386 9286; www.flyairlink.com) operates flights to Johannesburg (R800, one hour).

BUS

The offices of most bus companies, including Greyhound and Intercape, are in Berger St, or directly opposite in McDonalds Plaza (267 Burger St). Translux and its no-frills affiliate, City to City, are based at the train station.

Destinations offered from Pietermaritzburg include Jo'burg (R330, seven hours), Pretoria (R330, seven hours) and Durban (R220, 1½ hours). Offices are generally open 7am or 8am until 11pm. Tickets for all major services can be purchased at Checkers/Shoprite or online at www.computickettravel.com.

NUD Express (☏ 079 696 7108; www.underbergexpress.co.za) offers a daily service to Durban's King Shaka International Airport (R300) and Durban Central (R300). You must book these services; note that the buses are not known for their reliability in sticking to times.

Baz Bus travels between Durban and Pietermaritzburg three times a week.

SHARED TAXI

Minibus taxis to Durban leave from behind City Hall (R55, 1½ hours), while those to Underberg depart from the corner of West and Pietermaritz Sts. Destinations from this stop also include Ladysmith (R90, 2½ hours) and Jo'burg (R200, eight hours).

TRAIN

Shosholoza Meyl offers a service to Johannesburg (R320, 12 hours) on Wednesday, Friday and Sunday.

❶ Getting Around

To order a taxi, phone **Metro Taxis** (☏ 033-397 1910; www.metrotaxis.co.za).

DRAKENSBERG & UKHAHLAMBA-DRAKENSBERG PARK

If any landscape lives up to its airbrushed, publicity-shot alter ego, it is the jagged, green sweep of the Drakensberg's tabletop peaks. This forms the boundary between South Africa and the mountain kingdom of Lesotho, and offers some of the country's most awe-inspiring landscapes.

Within the area is a vast 2430-sq-km sweep of basalt summits and buttresses; this section was formally granted World Heritage status in 2000, and was renamed uKhahlamba-Drakensberg Park. Today, some of the vistas are recognisably South African, particularly the unforgettable curve of the Amphitheatre in Royal Natal National Park.

Drakensberg means 'Mountain of the Dragons'; the Zulu named it Quathlamba, meaning 'Battlement of Spears'. The Zulu word is a more accurate description of the

ⓘ UKHAHLAMBA-DRAKENSBERG PARK

Why Go This is one of South Africa's greatest sights. The sheer majesty of the mountains is worth travelling here to see; add to this brilliant hiking opportunities and San rock art. Be aware, though, that this is not a traditional South African wildlife park where you can drive around and see the animals. The parks inside uKhahlamba-Drakensberg have few or no roads – instead they are specifically set up for walking and hiking.

When to Go Autumn (March to May) and spring (September to November) offer good hiking weather. Winter nights can be bitterly cold, while summer rains can make trails treacherous.

Practicalities There is no single road linking all the main areas of interest – you have to enter and exit and re-enter each region of the park from the N3, R103 and R74 or, if road conditions permit, from secondary roads.

Budget Tips Stick to camping and the few budget accommodation places in the area. If you're travelling in a group it's worth hiring a car and splitting the costs.

sheer escarpment, but the Afrikaans name captures something of the Drakensberg's otherworldly atmosphere.

People have lived here for thousands of years – this is evidenced by the many San rock-art sites (visit Didima, Cathedral Peak, Kamberg and Injisuthi). The San, already under pressure from the tribes that had moved into the Drakensberg foothills, were finally destroyed with the coming of white settlers. Some moved to Lesotho, where they were absorbed into the Basotho population, but many were killed or simply starved when their hunting grounds were occupied by others. Khoe-San cattle raids annoyed the white settlers to the extent that the settlers forced several black tribes to relocate into the Drakensberg foothills to act as a buffer between the whites and the Khoe-San. These early 'Bantu locations' meant there was little development in the area, which later allowed the creation of a chain of parks and reserves.

Climate

The frosts come in winter, but the rain falls in summer, and snow has been recorded on the summit every month of the year. The summer weather forecasts, posted in each of the Ezemvelo KZN Wildlife park offices, can often make bleak reading for those hoping for blue skies and sunshine. Whenever you visit, always carry wet-weather gear, and be prepared for icy conditions and snowfalls.

Hiking

The Drakensberg range is one of the best hiking destinations in Africa. Valleys, waterfalls, rivers, caves and the escarpment, which rises to an impressive 3000m, provide spectacular wilderness experiences for walkers of all levels. Climbing is popular throughout the Drakensberg; only experienced climbers should attempt peaks in this region.

Broadly speaking, there are three main degrees of difficulty: gentle day walks, moderate half-day hikes and strenuous 10- to 12-hour hikes. Overnight treks and multiday hikes are for more serious and experienced hikers.

The trails are accessed through any of the park's entrances – Royal Natal National Park (renowned for its excellent day walks), Cathedral Peak, Monk's Cowl, Injisuthi and Giant's Castle, and the remote wilderness areas in the Southern Drakensberg.

To plan any walk, hike or trek, make sure you obtain the relevant 1:50,000-scale maps that show trails and have essential information for hikers. You should always seek advice on the current status of any trail – consult with experienced hikers, accommodation owners and Ezemvelo KZN Wildlife officers. You must always fill in a register, and permits are needed on all hikes within the park – organise them with Ezemvelo KZN Wildlife offices at the various trailheads. The only trail accommodation is at Giant's Castle; in some areas hikers can use caves, but always carry a tent.

If you prefer to hike with a guide, most accommodation options can arrange an experienced one, or enquire at park offices. Guides for overnight hikes can be booked through Ezemvelo KZN Wildlife – rates per guide vary and there is also a R60 permit fee (per person per night). Hikers are not allowed to light fires, so you'll need to bring a stove.

April to July are good months for hiking. Summer hiking can be made frustrating, and even dangerous, by rain and flooding rivers; in winter, frost is the main hazard, and snow occurs occasionally. Snakes inhabit the area.

Wildlife

With plentiful water, a range of up to 3000m in altitude and distinct areas such as plateaus, cliffs and valleys, it isn't surprising that the uKhahlamba-Drakensberg has extremely varied flora. The park is mainly grassland, wooded gorges and high basalt cliffs with small forests in the valleys. There's also some protea savannah and, during spring, swaths of wildflowers. At higher altitudes grass yields to heath and scrub. At lower levels, but confined to valleys (especially around Royal Natal National Park), are small yellowwood forests.

The park is home to numerous and varied animals and hundreds of bird species. Altogether there are thought to be about 60 mammal species. There are several species of antelope, with relatively large numbers of elands (more in the Southern Berg). The rarest antelope is the klipspringer, which is sometimes spotted on the higher slopes. There are otters, African wildcats, porcupines and even the odd leopard. Baboons forage for food on some of the steepest mountains. The rarest species is a small, short-tailed rodent called the ice rat, which lives in the boulders near the mountain summits. The bearded vulture (a rare bird of prey), black eagles and other vultures are found around the cliffs, capitalising on the peaks' thermals. Various hides throughout the park allow for closer viewing.

Accommodation

The perfect way to see the park is to stay at one of Ezemvelo KZN Wildlife's excellent accommodation options – campgrounds, safari tents, equipped cabins and chalets. A minimum charge may apply. Other more-upmarket options include private resorts, which dot the foothills. For hikers, caves and camping are the only options, with a few huts on the mountains – mainly in the Southern Berg, which also has a couple of superb hostels.

ℹ️ Information

Ezemvelo KZN Wildlife Headquarters (p287) In Pietermaritzburg; it can provide information on the various parks and accommodation options. In general, you must book all Ezemvelo KZN Wildlife accommodation in advance.

Central Drakensberg Information Centre (☎ 036-488 1207; www.cdic.co.za; R600, Info Centre Building; ⊙9am-5pm) This private enterprise based in the Thokozisa complex, 13km outside Winterton on R600, stocks tons of promotional literature.

Southern Berg Tourism (p292) Friendly, helpful office. Has the useful *Southern Drakensberg Pocket Guide*.

ℹ️ Getting There & Around

There is little public transport to and within the Drakensberg, although there is a lot of tourist traffic and the occasional minibus shared taxi ferrying resort staff. The main jumping-off points are on or near the N3. The Baz Bus drops off and picks up at a couple of hostels in the area. Through hostels in Durban you can arrange a shuttle to the hostels near Sani Pass and Himeville.

Sani Pass is the best-known Drakensberg route into Lesotho, but note that you can only go in a 4WD. Further south there are other passes over the escarpment, but most don't connect with anything larger than a walking track (if that) in Lesotho.

Many back roads in the Drakensberg area are unsealed, and after rain some are impassable – stick to the main routes.

It's important to note that GPS can be very finicky and sometimes downright misleading when trying to navigate to various spots in the mountains. It's best to rely on confirmed directions from those in the know and the ample signage on the roads in the area.

Southern Berg

The Southern Berg boasts one of the region's highlights: the journey up to Lesotho over Sani Pass. It is also renowned as a serious hiking area. As well as some great walks (including the fabulous Giant's Cup Trail), the region also offers a smorgasbord of wilderness areas.

Southern Drakensberg Wilderness Areas

This area is good for hiking, and encompasses Highmoor, Kamberg, Lotheni and Cobham. All south of Giant's Castle, they are administered by Ezemvelo KZN Wildlife. These areas are more isolated, although they're accessible for those with time. Rates for overnight-hiking permits are dependent on which hikes you're embarking on.

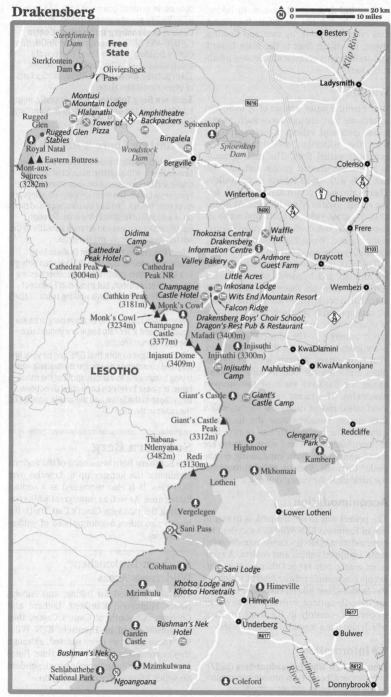

KWAZULU-NATAL SOUTHERN BERG

0 ___ 20 km
0 ___ 10 miles

Sterkfontein Dam

Free State

Sterkfontein Dam

Besters

Klip River

Oliviershoek Pass

Montusi Mountain Lodge

Hlalanathi

Rugged Glen

Tower of Pizza

Amphitheatre Backpackers

Rugged Glen Stables

Royal Natal

Eastern Buttress

Mont-aux-Sources (3282m)

Woodstock Dam

Spioenkop

Bingalela

Bergville

Spioenkop Dam

R616

Ladysmith

Colenso

Winterton

R600

N3

R74

Chieveley

Frere

R103

Draycott

Didima Camp

Cathedral Peak Hotel

Cathedral Peak (3004m)

Cathedral Peak NR

Thokozisa Central Drakensberg Information Centre

Valley Bakery

Waffle Hut

Ardmore Guest Farm

Little Acres

Inkosana Lodge

Wits End Mountain Resort

Falcon Ridge

Wembezi

Cathkin Peak (3181m)

Champagne Castle Hotel

Monk's Cowl

Monk's Cowl (3234m)

Champagne Castle (3377m)

Drakensberg Boys' Choir School; Dragon's Rest Pub & Restaurant

Mafadi (3400m)

R29

Injasuti Dome (3409m)

Injisuthi

Injisuthi (3300m)

Injisuthi Camp

KwaDlamini

Mahlutshini

KwaMankonjane

LESOTHO

Giant's Castle

Giant's Castle Camp

Giant's Castle Peak (3312m)

Glengarry Park

Redcliffe

Thabana-Ntlenyana (3482m)

Redi (3130m)

Highmoor

Kamberg

Lotheni

Mkhomazi

Vergelegen

Lower Lotheni

Sani Pass

Cobham

Sani Lodge

Mzimkulu

Khotso Lodge and Khotso Horsetrails

Himeville

Himeville

R617

Garden Castle

Bushman's Nek Hotel

Underberg

R617

Bulwer

Bushman's Nek

Sehlabathebe National Park

Mzimkulwana

Ngoangoana

Coleford

Umzinkulu River

Donnybrook

R612

⊙ Sights

Highmoor Nature Reserve NATURE RESERVE
(🖵 central reservations 033-845 1000; www.kzn-wildlife.com; adult/child R80/40; ⊙ 5am-7pm Oct-Mar, 6am-6pm Apr-Sep) Although more exposed and less dramatic than some of the Drakensberg region, the undulating hills of this reserve make for pleasant walks. It's also one of the few places where you're driving 'on top of' the foothills. There are two caves – Aasvoel Cave and Caracal Cave – both 2.5km from the main office, and Fultons Rock, which has rock art (a 4km easy walk), plus caves for overnight hikers. Access is via the towns of Nottingham Road or Rosetta (it's well signed).

Trout fishing is also popular. There are no chalets here, but campsites (R190) are available.

Kamberg Nature Reserve NATURE RESERVE
(🖵 033-267 7251; www.kznwildlife.com; adult/child R80/40; ⊙ 5am-7pm Oct-Mar, 6am-6pm Apr-Sep) Southeast of Giant's Castle, Kamberg Nature Reserve has a number of antelope species and a mustn't-miss rock-art experience. It begins with a multimedia presentation, then you join a three-hour guided walk to the famous Game Pass Shelter, known as the 'Rosetta Stone' of Southern African rock art, for it was here that archaeologists first interpreted the symbolism of the San paintings. You can get to Kamberg from Nottingham Road or Rosetta, off the N3 south of Mooi River.

🛌 Sleeping & Eating

Kamberg Chalets CHALET $
(🖵 033-267 7251; www.kznwildlife.com; 2-/6-bed chalets R940/1080) Ezemvelo KZN Wildlife has well-equipped two- and six-bed chalets in the Kamberg section, tastefully decorated with small kitchens and floor-to-ceiling glass overlooking lawns and mountains. Accommodation in the Highmoor section is limited to camping. Bring your own supplies if you're staying in either reserve.

Glengarry Park LODGE $$
(🖵 033-267 7225; www.glengarry.co.za; camping R150, self-catering chalets per person R440; 🎿) Perfect for families, Glengarry Park has pleasant, unpretentious chalets with a lovely green outlook, facing a small lake. Although in need of a renovation, the chalets are sturdy and homely and have fireplaces. Amenities include a bowling green, a small golf course, a tennis court and great walks,

and the owner is happy to lead the way on a mountain-bike trail.

Cleopatra Mountain Farmhouse RESORT $$$
(🖵 033-267 7243, 071 687 7266; www.cleomountain.com; Balgowan; r per person from R2495) If God were to top off the beauty of the Drakensberg with a gourmet treat, Cleopatra Mountain Farmhouse would be it. Guests enjoy a nightly, innovative seven-course menu of quality produce, and accompanied by rich, creamy sauces. Rooms are decked out in modern amenities and fireplaces, and each has a theme and features quirky touches, such as a picket-fence bedhead and Boer memorabilia.

Underberg, Himeville & Around

POP 4400

Clustered in the foothills of the southern Drakensberg, the small farming town of Underberg fills up in summer, when Durbanites head to the peaks for a breath of the fresh stuff. It has good infrastructure, and is the place to go to organise trips in the region. Only a few kilometres from Underberg, Himeville is a pretty, if sedate, jumping-off point for the southern Drakensberg.

Himeville Museum MUSEUM
(🖵 033-702 1184; Arbuckle St; admission by donation; ⊙ 9am-3pm Tue-Sat, to 12.30pm Sun) One of the best rural museums in the country. Housed in a retired fort dating back to 1899, the museum now contains an incredible array of bric-a-brac, from antiques from daily life in 20th-century South Africa to the Union Jack flown at the siege of Ladysmith to a map of El Alamein signed by Bernard Montgomery.

⟳ Tours

Several companies offer day tours up Sani Pass (excluding lunch from around R800), as well as tailored special-interest packages.

Drakensberg Adventures TOURS
(🖵 033-702 0330; www.drakensbergadventures.co.za; Sani Lodge, Sani Pass) 🪁 Started by the owners of Sani Lodge. Practises responsible tourism through involvement with local communities. Tours of Sani Pass, Lesotho and hiking throughout the Drakensberg are available.

Sani Pass Tours TOURS
(🖵 033-701 1064; www.sanipasstours.com; Shop 22, Trout Walk Centre, Underberg) Highly regarded

tours up the Sani Pass (from per person R850) as well as multiday tours into Lesotho.

Major Adventures
TOURS

(☎033-701 1628; www.majoradventures.com; Main Rd, Underberg) Major Adventures offers Sani Pass day tours that focus on the history of the pass, local plants and animals, and the Basotho people. There are also overnight tours through Lesotho for those looking to dig further into the culture.

Thaba Tours
TOURS

(☎033-701 2333; www.thabatours.co.za; 54 Sani Rd) Runs a wide variety of tours, including mountain biking, hiking, San rock art and trips up Sani Pass and into Lesotho.

🛏 Sleeping

Khotso Lodge
HOSTEL $

(☎033-701 1502; www.khotso.co.za; Treetower Farm, Underberg; camping R120, dm R160, d from R600, rondavels from R800; 🛜) After having a less-than-stellar reputation as a backpackers, this local institution rebranded as Khotso Lodge. Gone is the rowdy vibe (though a fun community atmosphere is still fostered in the quaint common areas), and the facilities have been refurbished with upmarket fixtures that add a much-needed sense of modernity while retaining the overall rustic charm.

What remains are the incredible **horse-riding trips** (☎033-701 1502; www.khotso.co.za/; horse rides per hour/day R200/680) to Lesotho, hikes and tubing at the nearby dam. It's worth it to stay in one of its recently added rondavels, which have unbeatable views and modern amenities.

Yellowwood Cottage B&B
B&B $

(☎033-702 1065; 8 Mackenzie St, Himeville; self-catering/B&B/dinner B&B per person R350/450/595; 🅿🛜) An enjoyable, homey experience: four cosy, frilly rooms in a pretty house overlook a spectacular English garden with views of Hodgson's Peaks. Host Elsa is delightful and attentive.

Tumble In
B&B $

(☎033-701 1556; www.tumbleinunderberg.co.za; 60 Sani Rd, Underberg; r incl breakfast per person R335, self-catering per person R170) This unpretentious place offers spacious, old-style rooms. The rooms overlook a lovely garden of pear and apple blossoms, with birds galore. It's 2.5km from Underberg on Himeville Rd. No credit cards. Great budget option.

Himeville Arms
HISTORIC HOTEL $$

(☎033-702 1305; www.himevillehotel.co.za; Arbuckle St, Himeville; standard r/B&B R790/890; 🐾) Now operated by the Premier Hotels group, this old-fashioned inn dates back to the start of the 20th century. Rooms blend antique furniture with modern decor and there's an atmospheric old bar, as well as an impressive pool area and garden. B&B options are available.

Albizia House B&B
B&B $$

(☎061-462 5741; www.albiziahouse-tours.co.za; 62 Arbuckle St, Himeville; s/d incl breakfast R650/990; 🅿🛜) Neat, clean and carpeted, with trimmed-lawn views, this place is perfect for those looking for a more traditional South African countryside experience. A family room is available with cot and high chair. The friendly owners ensure an enjoyable stay.

🍴 Eating

Pucketty Farm
DELI $

(☎033-701 1035; www.puckettyfarm.co.za; Main Rd, Underberg; mains R30-70; ⏲9am-4.30pm) Beatrix Potter meets Jamie Oliver: there's more to this extraordinarily cute place than meets the eye. There's a huge selection of great-value gourmet products, plus an art gallery and a small tea garden. Perfect for self-caterers. The farm is 1.5km southeast of the Himeville turn-off.

Lemon Tree Bistro
INTERNATIONAL $$

(☎033-701 1589; www.lemontreeb.co.za; Clocktower Centre, Main Rd, Underberg; mains R60-130; ⏲8am-5pm, dinner Tue-Sat) This friendly place serves up zesty pastas, burgers, wraps and pancakes at lunchtime. In the evenings dine out on trout, kudu fillet and springbok carpaccio.

Grind Cafe
CAFE $$

(Trout Walk Centre, Underberg; mains R60-95; ⏲8am-9pm Mon-Sat, to 5pm Sun; 🛜) One of the most popular eateries in Underberg, this big barn of a place in the Village Mall has great coffee, good cakes and a wide selection of pasta, burgers and pizzas. There's also wi-fi.

ℹ Information

Southern Berg Escape (☎033-701 1471; www.drakensberg.org; Old Main Rd, Clocktower Centre, Underberg; ⏲7.45am-4.15pm Mon-Fri, 9am-1pm Sat & Sun) Friendly and helpful office. Has the useful *Southern Drakensberg Pocket Guide*.

ℹ Getting There & Away

One daily minibus shared taxi runs between central Kokstad and Underberg, departing Underberg (Spar car park) at 9am and Kokstad at 2pm. Baz Bus and bus arrivals in Kokstad are at Mount Currie Inn, 2.5km from the centre; you will have to ask the minibus to take you there, for an extra cost.

Minibus taxis run between Himeville and Underberg (R12, 10 minutes) and from Underberg to Pietermaritzburg (R90, 1½ hours).

BUS

NUD Express (☏079 696 7108; www.under bergexpress.co.za) operates shuttle-bus services between Underberg (and Sani Lodge) and central Durban (R550), Durban's King Shaka International Airport (R650) and Pietermaritzburg (R350). You must book these services; note that they are not known for their reliability in sticking to times.

TAXI

Easy Move Junior Cabs (☏076 199 5823, 076 719 2451; easymovejuniorcabs@gmail.com) Can take up to four passengers to the South Coast (R1200), and Kokstad (R600).

Sani Pass

At 2865m, this is the highest pass in the country and the vistas (on a clear day) are magical, offering stunning views out across the Umkhomazana River to the north and looming cliffs to the south. There are hikes in almost every direction, and inexpensive horse rides are available. Amazingly, this is also the only road link between Lesotho and KwaZulu-Natal.

The drive up here is a trip to the roof of South Africa: a spectacular ride around hairpin bends up into the clouds to the kingdom of Lesotho. At the top of the pass, just beyond the Lesotho border crossing, is Sani Top Chalet – various operators run 4WD trips up to the chalet.

Daily minibus shared taxis bring people from Mokhotlong (Lesotho) to South Africa for shopping; if there's a spare seat going back, this is the cheapest way to head over the pass to Lesotho, and you are taken to a town, not just the isolated lodge at the top of the pass. Ask at the tourist office. You need a passport to cross into Lesotho. The border is open from 6am to 6pm daily, but check beforehand; times alter. Make sure you allow sufficient time to arrive at either end. Also be aware that coming back into South Africa will require another visa.

Although there has been talk of sealing the pass for years, it remains a gravel road and a 4WD is required.

Sani Lodge Backpackers   HOSTEL **$**
(☏033-702 0330; www.sanilodge.co.za; camping per person R90, dm/d with shared bathroom R165/460, rondavel R590) At the bottom of the pass and on a sealed road, Sani Lodge tops the pops in the local-knowledge stakes, offering a range of fabulous tours, activities and insider tips about the region through its company, Drakensberg Adventures. Some rooms do have the sparse quality often found in hostels (the rondavels are nicer), but it's worth it for the communal, ski-lodge-style atmosphere. A kitchen is available for

---

GIANT'S CUP TRAIL

If you are planning to stretch your legs anywhere in South Africa, this is the place to do it. Without doubt, the Giant's Cup Trail (60km, five days and five nights), running from Sani Pass to Bushman's Nek, is one of the nation's great walks. Any reasonably fit person can walk it, so it's very popular. Early booking, through Ezemvelo KZN Wildlife (p287), is advisable in local holiday seasons. Weather-wise, the usual precautions for the Drakensberg apply – expect severe cold snaps at any time of the year. Fees are based on the composition of the hiking party.

The stages are: day one, 14km; day two, 9km; day three, 12km; day four, 13km; and day five, 12km (note that it's not a circuit walk). An unofficial sixth day can take you from Bushman's Nek up into Lesotho to Sehlabathebe National Park (passports required). Highlights include the Bathplug Cave, with San rock art, and the breathtaking mountain scenery on day four. You can make the trail more challenging by doing two days in one, and you can do side trips from the huts if the weather is fine. Maps are sold at Sani Lodge for R45.

Camping is not permitted on this trail, so accommodation is in limited shared huts (R120), hence the need to book ahead. No firewood is available, so you'll need a stove and fuel. Sani Lodge is almost at the head of the trail; arrange for the lodge to pick you up from Himeville or Underberg.

general use, or pre-arranged dinners cost R130. It's about 10km from Himeville on the Sani Pass road.

Bushman's Nek

This is a South Africa–Lesotho border post (although with no vehicles). From here there are hiking trails up into the escarpment, including to Lesotho's Sehlabathebe National Park. You can trot through the border and into Lesotho on horseback with Khotso Horsetrails (p292).

Bushman's Nek Hotel RESORT $$
(☏033-701 1460; www.bushmansnek.co.za; r/cabins from R1050/1160; ❋ ☋ ☲) Bushman's Nek Hotel is a full-on resort with log cabins, apartments and standard hotel rooms in an idyllic mountain setting. Activities include horse riding, fishing, archery, trail walks and spa treatments. It's about 2km east of the Lesotho border post and 24km from Underberg. The road is bumpy, but can be tackled cautiously in a 2WD car.

Silverstreams Caravan Park CAMPGROUND $$
(☏082 331 6670; www.silverstreams.co.za; camping/cottages R520/950; ☲) At the foot of the Drakensberg in a beautiful natural setting, the Silverstreams Caravan Park has campsites and cottages next to the Lesotho border. Rates are at their cheapest during the week. An on-site store sells groceries, curios and braai gear and also has information about activities to do in the area. Pets welcome with an extra fee.

Central Berg

Crowned by some of the Drakensberg's most formidable peaks, including Giant's Castle peak (3312m), Monk's Cowl (3234m) and Champagne Castle (3377m), the Central Berg is a big hit with hikers and climbers. But with dramatic scenery aplenty, this beautiful region is just as popular with those who prefer to admire their mountains from a safe distance.

The sedate little town of Winterton is the gateway to the Central Drakensberg. The tiny, parochial **Winterton Museum** (☏036-488 1885; Kerk St; admission by donation; ⊗8am-4pm Mon-Fri, 9am-noon Sat) offers an insight into San rock art (there are some excellent photos with notes) and the history of local peoples, and there are photos relating to the Spioenkop battle.

Bridge Lodge (☏036-488 1554; www.bridgelodge.co.za; 18 Springfield Rd, Winterton; s/d from R395/730) offers spartan, but comfortable, accommodation at great rates for the area. The cheap pub grub is a favourite among the locals.

You can hail minibus shared taxis around the Central Berg that head to Cathedral Peak (approximately 30 minutes), Bergville (approximately 15 minutes) and Estcourt (approximately 45 minutes).

Cathedral Peak Nature Reserve

In the shadow of the ramparts of Cathedral Peak, **Cathedral Peak Nature Reserve** (☏036-488 8000; www.kznwildlife.com; adult/child R80/40; ⊗5am-7pm Oct-Mar, 6am-6pm Apr-Sep) backs up against a colossal escarpment of peaks between Royal Natal National Park and Giant's Castle, west of Winterton. With the Bell (2930m), the Horns (3005m) and Cleft Peak (3281m) on the horizon, this is a beautifully photogenic park.

Cathedral Peak is 45km southwest of Winterton on a sealed road. The park office offers information on hikes in the area. Sadly, many of the exhibits in the **Didima San Rock Art Centre** (☏036-488 1332; adult/child R20/5; ⊗8am-4pm), at Didima Camp, were out of action when we last visited.

Didima Camp CAMPGROUND, CHALET $$
(☏central reservations 033-845 1000; www.kznwildlife.com; camping R100, chalets from R1120; ℗@☲) One of Ezemvelo KZN Wildlife's swankiest offerings, this upmarket thatched lodge, constructed to resemble San rock shelters, boasts huge views, a restaurant, tennis courts and two- and four-bed self-catering chalets. The campsites have braai facilities, shared ablutions and kitchen, and lovely views. You may still encounter typical lodge problems (broken appliances, jammed doors), but the overall feel is spectacular.

Minimum charges apply. Full-board options are also available, on request.

Cathedral Peak Hotel HOTEL $$$
(☏036-488 1888; www.cathedralpeak.co.za; r from R3560) Upmarket rooms at this private hotel have stupendous views and all the mod cons you would expect from a swish hotel. The exterior doesn't quite match its incredible mountain surroundings, and the restaurant service and food doesn't match the prices, but if you have money to spend on one of its luxury suites you'll see why it retains its reputation.

Monk's Cowl & Champagne Valley

Within uKhahlamba-Drakensberg Park, **Monk's Cowl** (☑036-468 1103; www.kznwildlife. com; adult/child R80/40; ⊙6am-6pm), another stunning slice of the Drakensberg range, offers superb hiking and rock climbing. Within the reserve are the three peaks Monk's Cowl, Champagne Castle and Cathkin Peak.

The area en route to the park is known as Champagne Valley. This is full of cafes, pleasant accommodation options, bakeries and enough (nonhiking) tourist activities to keep you busy for days.

The Thokozisa complex, 13km out of Winterton on R600 and at the crossroads to Cathedral Peak, Monk's Cowl and Giant's Castle (via Estcourt), is a useful spot to orient yourself. It has a clutch of craft shops.

◎ Sights & Activities

Overnight hiking (per person R70) is possible, but the shelter caves must be booked in advance through Ezemvelo KZN Wildlife (p287).

Falcon Ridge   WILDLIFE RESERVE
(☑082-774 6398; adult/child R90/45; ⊙displays 10.30am Sat-Thu) Falcon Ridge, with awesome raptor-flying demonstrations and talks, is 7km from the Drakensberg Sun turn-off.

**Drakensberg
Canopy Tour**   ADVENTURE SPORTS
(☑036-468 1981; www.drakensbergcanopytour. co.za; per person R650; ⊙8am-1pm) Drakensberg Canopy Tour boasts superlatives – 12 slides, of which seven are over 100m; the highest point is 65m and the longest is 179m. You 'fly' above a beautiful canopy of an ancient indigenous forest, with a stream and waterfalls. It's an extreme sport – don't attempt it if you have vertigo. Book ahead.

Ushaka Horse Trails   HORSE RIDING
(☑072 664 2993; www.monkscowl.com; 4 Bell Park Dam Rd; 2hr/day R250/950) One-hour to full-day horse trails are available through Ushaka Horse Trails. Ring for directions.

🛏 Sleeping

Inkosana Lodge   HOSTEL $
(☑036-468 1202; www.inkosana.co.za; R600; camping/dm R125/250, d R900, with shared bathroom R700; ℗🅿🛜❄🐾) Travellers rave about this lodge. Its indigenous garden, rustic swimming dam, clean rooms and lovely rondavels (round huts with conical roofs) make

ℹ TAKING CARE IN THE MOUNTAINS

Ezemvelo KZN Wildlife warns that walkers should not go alone – even on day walks. Usually, guides are available for hire. For any walk, including short walks, you must always sign the rescue register. Be sure to obtain instructions and times regarding the hikes. For overnight treks, Ezemvelo KZN Wildlife recommends a minimum of four people. Note: attempting peaks in a day – as opposed to the more leisurely 'day walks' – is only for the very fit and experienced.

it one of the best spots around. Although promoted as a 'backpacker lodge', its range of rooms (from backpackers to en-suite private rooms) would suit any discerning traveller. Centrally located for activities in and around the area.

Wits End Mountain Resort   CHALET $$
(☑036-468 1133; www.witsend.co.za; R600; chalets per person from R450; 🛜❄) The excellent four-, six-, and eight-sleeper chalets here have braai (barbecue) areas, large kitchens, fireplaces and wonderful views of the mountains and the nearby dam, where there are plenty of aquatic activities on offer. Cheaper rates on weekdays.

Ardmore Guest Farm   LODGE $$
(☑087 997 1194; www.ardmore.co.za; r from R705; ℗🅿🛜❄) A refreshing change from the area's resorts, this pleasant place, situated on a working farm, has a range of comfortable options. There are cottages and thatched rondavels – some with log fires – and meals are served in the original farmhouse. Many of the accommodations have comfortable modern amenities, such as plush recliners.

Little Acres   B&B $$
(☑082 305 3387; www.littleacres.co.za; R600; s/d incl breakfast from R1010/1070, self-catering from R890; 🛜) Modern luxuries such as flat-screen TVs and underfloor heating in the bathroom meet rustic charm at this B&B. There is a variety of room types, including bungalows with kitchenettes, and the hosts are friendly and very knowledgeable about activities in the area. Guests rave about the black Labradors, James and Bentley, who live on the property.

Champagne Castle Hotel
RESORT $$$

(☑036-468 1063; www.champagnecastle.co.za; R600; s/d with full board from R2025/2700; ☎☒) The ever-reliable and predictably 'nice' Champagne Castle is one of the area's best-known resorts, conveniently in the mountains at the end of R600 to Monk's Cowl. It's a proper resort with a pool, a tennis court, a games room and a spa on-site.

✖ Eating

★ Valley Bakery
BAKERY, CAFE $

(☑036-468 1257; R600; mains R35-60; ⏱8am-5pm Mon-Fri, to 2pm Sat; ☎♨) Baguettes, croissants and a range of sticky treats are baked on the premises (the owners even grow and grind their wheat). A quaint wrought-iron veranda is the place for a wonderful selection of breakfasts, including eggs Benedict or muesli with fresh fruit. Wraps, sandwiches and homemade pies feature later in the day.

Waffle Hut
CAFE $

(R600; mains R40-70; ⏱8am-4.30pm) After you've stuffed yourself with savoury and sweet waffles, get your fill of handmade rugs (some locally made, others imported) at this cafe located at KwaZulu Weavers. It's on the R600 south of Winterton.

Dragon's Rest
Pub & Restaurant
PUB FOOD $$

(☑036-468 1218; mains R80-110; ⏱10.30am-2.30pm & 6-8.30pm) Sit outside at this delightful place and drink in the dam-side and mountain views while enjoying some fine Berg cooking and a cold drink. Inside is a log fire and a cosy bar. Service is painfully slow but the food is tasty and the setting sublime. It's near the auditorium of the boys' choir.

☆ Entertainment

Drakensberg Boys'
Choir School
LIVE PERFORMANCE

(☑036-468 1012; www.dbchoir.com; R600; from R120) Just off Dragon Peaks Rd are South Africa's singing ambassadors, the Drakensberg Boys' Choir School. There are public performances at 3.30pm on Wednesday during school terms, which come highly recommended by locals and visitors alike.

❶ Information

The **park office** (☑036-468 1103; ⏱8am-12.30pm & 2-4.30pm) is 3km beyond Champagne Castle Hotel, which is at the end of the R600 running southwest from Winterton. The

Central Drakensberg Information Centre (p289), based in the Thokozisa complex, 13km outside Winterton, is also helpful, especially with directions if your GPS fails you.

Injisuthi

Injisuthi (☑central reservations 033-845 1000; www.kznwildlife.com; adult/child R80/40; ⏱5am-7pm Oct-Mar, 6am-6pm Apr-Sep), on the northern side of Giant's Castle, is another 'wow' spot of the Drakensberg. It's a secluded and extraordinarily beautiful place with a terrific view of the Monk's Cowl peak. This reserve, originally a private farm, was purchased by KZN Wildlife in the late 1970s. Injisuthi features the Drakensberg's highest points, Mafadi (3400m) and Injisuthi (3300m). Note: these peaks cannot be done in a day.

Injisuthi is the departure point for the guided hike to the extraordinary Battle Cave, a massive rock overhang featuring remarkable San paintings. The extraordinary scenes – depicting figures and animals – were believed to represent a battle, but this has been disproven, with experts now proposing that they represent hallucinatory dreams or a spiritual trance.

The hike to Battle Cave (around R140 per person) is a six-hour round-trip, both exposed and shady. You must reserve in advance directly with Injisuthi Camp and there needs to be a minimum three people – rates will vary depending on numbers.

There are many day walks, include to Marble Baths (four to five hours), where you can swim.

Injisuthi Camp
CAMPGROUND, CHALET $

(☑central reservations 033-845 1000, hike reservations 036-431 9000; www.kznwildlife.com; camping R115; safari camps for 2 people R430, chalets R790) There are self-contained chalets that sleep up to four people as well as campsites here. The area has caves for overnight hikers (however, check on their state before setting out).

Giant's Castle

Established in 1904, mainly to protect the eland, Giant's Castle is a rugged, remote and popular destination, with varying dramatic landscapes. The Giant's Castle ridge itself is one of the most prominent features of the Berg. (If coming from the south on the N3, use the off-ramp exit 175, which was not marked on all maps.)

The office at Giant's Castle Camp (p297) gives out a basic map of the trails (distances not stated).

Lammergeier Hide VIEWPOINT

(☑036-353 3718; www.kznwildlife.com; group of 3 per person R840, additional person R280) The rare lammergeier, also known as the bearded vulture *(Gypaetus barbatus)*, which is found only in the Drakensberg, nests in the reserve. Reserve staff sometimes give guests bones to put out to encourage the birds to feed here. The Lammergeier Hide is the best place to see these raptors. The hide is extremely popular, so it's essential to book in advance. You need a 4WD or a sturdy pair of hiking boots to reach the hide and there are no facilities whatsoever.

Main Cave HISTORIC SITE

(per person R45; ⊙9am-3pm) The Giant's Castle area is rich in San rock art. It's thought that the last San lived here at the beginning of the 20th century. To see some of these paintings, you can visit Main Cave, 2.3km south of Giant's Camp. Thandeka, the resident guide, waits at the cave's entrance where, every hour, she conducts an explanatory tour.

The walk from Giant's Camp to the cave takes 45 minutes; there's a shorter return of 1.5km.

🛏 Sleeping

There are several excellent accommodation options inside the reserve, as well as caves and trail huts for hikers.

Giant's Castle Camp CHALET $$

(☑036-353 3718, central reservations 033-845 1000; www.kznwildlife.com; trail huts per person R85, chalets from R1065) The main camp here is an impressive and remote set-up 8km from the main gate. Two-, four- and six-bed chalets have fireplace, kitchenette, floor-to-ceiling windows, TV and thatched veranda. The restaurant has a lovely deck with superb mountain views (but when the summer mists descend visibility gets down to a few metres). Hiker accommodation is available in caves and in an eight-bed hut.

❶ Getting There & Away

If coming from the north or south along the N3, take Rte 29 to Giant's Castle (it links with Estcourt, to the east). From Winterton or Champagne Valley you can get here on Rte 10 and then south via Draycott (from Draycott there's 25km of good gravel road meandering through pine plantation, which joins the tar at White Mountain Lodge – from here it's 23km on tarred roads to Giant's Castle, hooking up with Rte 29).

Infrequent minibus shared taxis do the run from Estcourt to villages near the main entrance (KwaDlamini, Mahlutshini and KwaMankonjane), but these are still several kilometres downhill from Giant's Camp.

Northern Berg

The Northern Berg is crowned with the beautiful Royal Natal National Park, with some excellent day walks and wonderfully empty spaces. The area is an ideal stopover if you're making the journey between Durban and Jo'burg.

Bergville

☑036 / POP 1200

Bergville, a small and rough-around-the-edges town, is a useful stocking-up and jumping-off point for the Northern Drakensberg.

Bingalela CHALET $$

(☑036-448 1336, 082 390 3133; bingelela@mweb. co.za; r per person from R450; 🐾) Bingalela is a bit far from the Drakensberg action, but if you don't mind a trek to your accommodation it offers affordable and comfortable rooms. Attractive double and family-size rondavels are set in dusty, slightly car-park-like surrounds, under lovely eucalypts. Note that it holds its own beerfest in October, so the action might not be for everyone.

There's a lively restaurant and bar that attracts the locals.

❶ Information

Okhahlamba Drakensberg Tourism (☑036-448 1296; www.drakensberg.org.za; ⊙8am-5.30pm Mon-Fri, 9am-12.30pm Sat) The privately owned Okhahlamba Drakensberg Tourism has plenty of brochures, but the help stops there.

❶ Getting There & Away

The minibus-taxi park is behind the tourist office. None of the long-distance bus lines run very close to Bergville. You'll have to get to Ladysmith and take a minibus shared taxi from there (45 minutes). A daily Greyhound bus stops at Estcourt and Ladysmith. Taxis run into the Royal Natal National Park area for about R20, but few run all the way to the park entrance.

KWAZULU-NATAL NORTHERN BERG

ℹ PUBLIC TRANSPORT

Bus services travel to Ladysmith and Harrismith in the Free State, which are both close to the Northern Berg. Additionally, the Baz Bus stops at Amphitheatre Backpackers. Minibus taxis can take you to Bergville, which is a great launching point for the rest of the area. Some accommodations may be able to provide shuttle services from these nearby towns.

Royal Natal National Park

Fanning out from some of the range's loftiest summits, the 80-sq-km Royal Natal National Park (☑036-438 6310; www.kznwildlife.com; adult/child R80/40; ⊙5am-7pm Oct-Mar, 6am-6pm Apr-Sep) has a presence that far outstrips its relatively meagre size. With some of the Drakensberg's most dramatic and accessible scenery, the park is crowned by the sublime Amphitheatre, an 8km wall of cliff and canyon that's spectacular from below and even more so from up on high. Here, the Tugela Falls drop 850m in five stages (the top one often freezes in winter). Looming behind is Mont-aux-Sources (3282m), so called because the Tugela, Elands and Western Khubedu Rivers rise here; the last eventually becomes the Senqu (Orange) River and flows all the way to the Atlantic. The park is renowned for its excellent day walks and hiking opportunities.

Other notable peaks in the area are the Devil's Tooth, the Eastern Buttress and the Sentinel. Rugged Glen Nature Reserve adjoins the park on the northeastern side.

The park's visitors centre (☑036-438 6310; ⊙8am-4.30pm) is 3km in from the main gate. It doubles as a shop selling basic provisions. Day walks are explained in a simple map provided by the centre.

◉ Sights & Activities

San Rock Art
HISTORIC SITE

(R50; ⊙9am-4pm) Of several San rock-art sites within the park, this is the only one open to tourists. Siyaphambili Elijah tours, whose representatives you can usually find near the visitor centre, offers guided walks to the rock art. The return trip takes about an hour, including time to rest and chat.

Rugged Glen Stables
HORSE RIDING

(☑036-438 6422; 2hr rides R260) Just outside the Royal Natal National Park gates, Rugged Glen Stables organises a wide range of horse-riding activities, including two-day trails.

Elijah Mbonane
HIKING

(☑073 137 4690; elijahmbonane@yahoo.com) Offers guided hikes ranging from hour-long strolls to overnight treks. Prices vary greatly depending on number of hikers and length of the walk – minimum charge is R800.

🛏 Sleeping & Eating

INSIDE THE PARK

Mahai
CAMPGROUND $

(☑033-845 1000; campsites with/without outlets R420/390) You can camp at the beautiful Mahai inside the Royal Natal National Park.

Rugged Glen Campsite
CAMPGROUND $

(☑central reservations 033-845 1000; www.kznwildlife.com; camp sites with/without plugs R260/280) A basic campground with an impressive setting inside Royal Natal National Park.

Thendele
CHALET $$

(☑central reservations 033-845 1000; www.kznwildlife.com; 2-/4-bed chalet from R980/1920) The park's fabulous main camp has two- and four-bed chalets as well as cottages and a lodge for larger groups. The chalets are set around lawns and driveways; all have in-your-face views of the peaks opposite. Those at the top are slightly more expensive because of their wondrous views, but all are good. It's a great base for walkers.

OUTSIDE THE PARK

Amphitheatre Backpackers
HOSTEL $

(☑082 855 9767; www.amphibackpackers.co.za; R74, 21km north of Bergville; camping/dm R95/200, r from R210; P🐾) Amenities at this five-star backpackers are superb, including a bar, a hot tub, a sauna and a restaurant serving top-notch food. Facing out over the Amphitheatre, it has a selection of sleeping options from dorms to comfortable four-person en-suite rooms and a great campground. Things get rowdy at night, so request a room far from the common areas if you're a light sleeper.

Staff at the front desk here get mixed reviews – some report feeling pressured to do the organised trips (when there are other options around); others enjoy the rolled-out convenience. On the other hand, the bartenders here are legendary for their good service and friendly demeanour.

⭐**Hlalanathi**   RESORT $$
(☎036-438 6308; www.hlalanathi.co.za; camping R220, 2-/4-bed chalets R1300/2200; ❄) With a location lifted straight from an African chocolate-box lid and next to the local golf course, this pretty, unpretentious resort offers camping and excellent accommodation in thatched chalets on a finger of land overlooking the Tugela River. Go for a site facing the river and mountains. Prices are substantially cheaper outside high season.

Montusi Mountain Lodge   LODGE $$$
(☎036-438 6243; www.montusi.co.za; s/d with half-board from R2600/4150; ❄❄) With oodles of bush-lodge exclusivity, this opulent place blends a thatch-and-fireplace homeliness with plenty of luxury comforts in very swish chalets. There's guided hiking, including a daily morning walk on the property, and horse riding can be arranged. Wi-fi and DVD players keep the rooms modern despite the mountain setting. The turn-off is just after the Tower of Pizza; follow the signs.

Tower of Pizza   ITALIAN $
(☎036-438 6480; www.towerofpizza.co.za; pizzas R75-100; ⊙noon-8.30pm Tue-Thu, to 9pm Fri & Sat, 10am-9pm Sun, open Mon in high season) Yep, there really is a tower, where very good wood-fired pizza is prepared. Grab a table on the outside decking and enjoy the clean air and mountain views at this excellent place near the Drakensberg mountains. Be warned: it doesn't accept cash – credit cards only!

If you like the food so much you want to stay the night, it also offers quaint rondavels and cottages (single/double R770/1100).

❶ Getting There & Away

The road into Royal Natal runs off R74, about 30km northwest of Bergville and about 5km from Oliviershoek Pass.

BATTLEFIELDS

Big wildlife, big mountains and big waves may top the agenda for many visitors to the province, but the history of KwaZulu-Natal is intrinsically linked to its battlefields, the stage on which many of South Africa's bloodiest chapters were played out. The province's northwestern region is where fewer than 600 Voortrekkers avenged the murder of their leader, Piet Retief, by defeating a force of 12,000 Zulu at Blood River, and where the British Empire was crushed by a Zulu army at Isandlwana. It's where the British subsequently staged the inconceivable defence of Rorke's Drift, and where the Boers and the Brits slogged it out at Ladysmith and Spioenkop. These days, the region offers some luxurious accommodation options, and for history buffs it can be most rewarding.

See www.battlefields.kzn.org.za or pick up KZN Tourism's *Battlefields Route* brochure, which can be found at most hotels and museums, as well as at Tourism Dundee (p303) and the Siege Museum (p301) in Ladysmith.

Spioenkop Nature Reserve

The 60-sq-km **Spioenkop Nature Reserve** (☎036-488 1578; www.kznwildlife.com; adult/child R50/30; ⊙5am-7pm Oct-Mar, 6am-6pm Apr-Sep) is based on the Spioenkop Dam, on the Tugela River. The reserve is handy for most of the area's battlefield sites and not too far from the Drakensberg for day trips into the range. Animals include zebras, white rhinos, giraffes, various antelope species and over 290 bird species.

There are two driving tracks, both quite short – the dam is huge but you only access a small part of the shoreline as a visitor. You can even head out among the wildlife at a vulture hide, or on horse-riding trips and guided walks. There's a lovely stroll through aloe plants and woodlands.

Ezemvelo KZN Wildlife   CAMPGROUND $
(☎036-488 1578; www.kznwildlife.com; camping R216) Inside the reserve in a valley are campsites in very pretty surrounds, overlooking a reservoir. It's peaceful and offers plentiful bird life, plus the odd specimen of hoofed wildlife. Book accommodation directly through the reserve.

Three Tree Hill Lodge   LODGE $$$
(☎036-448 1171; http://threetreehill.co.za; s/d with full board R3510/5400; ❄❄) ✿ This upmarket eco-friendly house with plush contemporary-meets-colonial creature comforts is a treat for those who want to explore the Spioenkop area. Beautiful setting and views, a delightful open-plan living area, luxury ammenities and an eco focus make for a fabulous stay. Horse riding and battlefield tours are made to order.

Battlefields

0 — 40 km
0 — 20 miles

Battlefields

◉ Sights

The lodge is conveniently located near Spioenkop, between Ladysmith and Bergville off the R616, a great location to launch day trips into the battlefields and Drakensberg mountains.

ℹ Getting There & Around

The Spioenkop Nature Reserve is northeast of Bergville, but the entrance is on the eastern side, 13km from Winterton off the R600. If you're coming from the south on the N3, take exit 194 for the R74 towards Winterton. The Spioenkop battlefield is accessed from the R616 (not the R600; follow the signs). You will need a car to access both places.

The roads inside the reserve are just OK for 2WDs. You'll want to make sure you have good traction and high clearance – drive slowly, and keep your eyes open for eroded parts of the track.

Ladysmith

📞 036 / POP 65,000

Ladysmith is a bustling base to tour the area's battlefields. It was named after the wife of Cape governor Sir Harry Smith and achieved fame during the 1899–1902 Anglo-Boer War, when it was besieged by Boer forces for 118 days. Musical group Ladysmith Black Mambazo has its roots here. The town's pretty colonial vestiges are faded, to be sure, but history enthusiasts will still find lots to enjoy.

👁 Sights

Siege Museum
MUSEUM

(📞036-637 2992; Murchison St; adult/child R11/5.50; ⊙9am-4pm Mon-Fri, to 1pm Sat) This museum, next to the town hall in the old Market House (built 1884), which was used to store rations during the Anglo-Boer War siege, may be small but it's full to bursting with lovingly curated exhibits. It has winding hallways full of displays about the town and surrounds, stocks information about the town and surrounds, and can provide a list of battlefield tour guides.

Castor & Pollux
MONUMENT

Outside the town hall are two guns, Castor and Pollux, used by the British in defence of Ladysmith.

Long Tom
MONUMENT

A replica of Long Tom, a Boer gun capable of heaving a shell 10km, is near the town hall. Long Tom was put out of action by a British raiding party during the Anglo-Boer War siege, but not before it had caused a great deal of damage.

Fort
NOTABLE BUILDING

(King St) Opposite Settlers Dr is a wall with loopholes from the original fort, built as a refuge from Zulu attack and now part of the police station.

🛏 Sleeping & Eating

There are plenty of B&Bs out of town off Short St. They are often booked out by business travellers – it's best to reserve ahead.

Buller's Rest Lodge
B&B $$

(📞036-637 6154; www.bullersrestlodge.co.za; 59 Cove Cres; s/d incl breakfast from R790/1100; 🌐🖥) This smart thatched abode has a snug 'Boer War' pub, scrumptious home cooking (three courses R170, book in advance) and views from the attractive sundeck–bar area. In 2017

the owners added two luxury rooms (single/double R1050/1300), complete with deep soaking tubs and panoramic views of Ladysmith and the surrounding areas. Budget options (from R620) are also available.

Turn right at Francis Rd off Harrismith (Poort) Rd, and follow the signs.

Budleigh Guesthouse
B&B $$

(📞036-635 7700; 12 Berea Rd; s/d incl breakfast R600/850; 🌐🖥) Just like something out of a BBC TV production with its verandas, trimmed lawns and stunning garden, this mansion has a range of neat, sophisticated rooms with wooden bedsteads, modern appliances and faux antiques. It's in the heart of Ladysmith, within walking distance of the main drag of historic buildings, as well as the town's scant few restaurants.

Penelope's
CAFE $

(📞036-637 2176; 140 Murchison St; mains from R40; ⊙9am-5pm) Look past the declarations, which are a bit cutesie, and you'll be treated to a nice little cafe that serves tasty lunches and incredible home-baked pastries and cakes. It's located right in the central business district, which makes it a good place to stop after touring some of the museums.

Guinea Fowl
INTERNATIONAL $$

(📞036-637 8163; San Marco Centre, cnr Harrismith & Francis Rds; mains R105-160; ⊙11.30am-9.30pm, bar open late) One of the only reasonable restaurants in Ladysmith, this eatery does curries along with steak, chicken and seafood dishes at an unassuming location in a shopping centre. The food is surprisingly good and there's an impressive list of South African wines available by the glass or bottle.

ⓘ Getting There & Away

BUS

Bus tickets can be purchased from Shoprite/Checkers in the Oval Shopping Centre. Greyhound buses depart from the Guinea Fowl petrol station (not to be confused with the restaurant) on Murchison Rd, and they connect Ladysmith with Durban (around R370, four hours), Jo'Burg/Pretoria (R395, seven hours) and Cape Town (R670, 19 hours).

SHARED TAXI

The main minibus taxi rank is east of the town centre near the corner of Queen and Lyell Sts. Taxis bound for Jo'burg are nearby on Alexandra St. Destinations include Pietermaritzburg (1½ hours), Durban (2½ hours) and Jo'burg (five hours).

KWAZULU-NATAL LADYSMITH

A GUIDE TO THE BATTLE SITES

With a knowledgeable guide at hand, and with a bit of swotting up before you go, the so-called Battlefields Route can be extremely rewarding. Without a guide the battlefields can be a challenge to find, let alone understand. Guides generally charge between R800 and R1500 for a one-day tour of sites including Rorke's Drift and Isandlwana. Note: some guides quote these rates per person, others per group; rates are cheaper in your own vehicle.

BushBaby Safaris (☏034-212 3216; www.bushbaby.co.za; 110 Victoria St, Dundee) is a more formal addition to the battlefield guide scene. It offers a day tour to Isandlwana and Rorke's Drift for R1800 per person (minimum two people; rates exclude lunches and admission charge). It also offers a shuttle to the Battlefields for R390 per person, picking up in Dundee at 8am, for the more budget minded.

The following guides are also recommended:

Bethuel Manyathi (☏083 531 0061; Nquthu)

Elisabeth Durham (☏072 779 5949; www.cheznousbb.com; 39 Tatham St, Dundee; day tour per person R1800)

Ken Gillings (☏031-702 4828; ken.gillings@mweb.co.za; Durban)

Thulani Khuzwayo (☏072 872 9782; thulani.khuzwayo@gmail.com; Rorke's Drift)

Liz Spiret (☏072 262 9669; lizs@telkomsa.net; Ladysmith)

Paul Garner (☏082 472 3912; garner@jenny.co.za; Dundee)

Evan Jones (☏034-212 4040; www.battlefieldsroute.co.za)

Anthony Coleman (☏034-212 3401; tonytish@worldonline.co.za)

Lists of further battlefield guides are available from Talana Heritage Park & Battlefield, plus tourism offices in Dundee and Ladysmith. Be sure to pick up a Battlefields brochure or to consult www.battlefields.kzn.org.au.

Main Battles

Battle of Blood River Voortrekker–Zulu conflict (1838).

Battle of Isandlwana, Battle of Rorke's Drift Anglo-Zulu War (1879).

Battles of Laing's Nek, Schuinshoogte and Majuba First Anglo-Boer War (Transvaal War of Independence; 1880–81).

Battle of Talana, Battle of Elandlaagte Second Anglo-Boer War (1899–1902), which led to the Siege of Ladysmith.

Battle of Spioenkop Occurred on 23 and 24 January 1900, when the British fought to relieve the besieged town of Ladysmith from the surrounding Boer forces.

Battle of Colenso One of the largest battles (15 December 1899) in the southern hemisphere, between Boers and Brits.

Dundee

☏034 / POP 35,000

Dundee is a quiet town with tree-lined streets, classic Dutch reform churches and a busy, but generally safe, central business district. The reason to come here is to explore the Battlefields and regional history sites.

Talana Heritage
Park & Battlefield   HISTORIC SITE
(☏034-212 2654; www.talana.co.za; adult/child R35/5; ☺8am-4.30pm Mon-Fri, 9am-4.30pm Sat & Sun) Talana means 'the shelf where precious items are stored' – strangely appropriate for this excellent battlefield site turned heritage park. There are memorials, cairns and 27 historic buildings relating to the 1899 Anglo-Boer Battle of Talana (the first Anglo-Boer battle was fought on the site). Spread around these buildings are comprehensive displays on the Anglo-Zulu and Anglo-Boer Wars.

It's located on the Vryheid road, 1.5km out of town.

🛏 Sleeping

Penny Farthing
Country House   GUESTHOUSE $
(☑ 034-642 1925; www.pennyf.co.za; r from R500; ❋ @ ☒) This quaint guesthouse, located 30km south of Dundee on the R33 towards Greytown, is well placed for visits to Rorke's Drift and Isandlwana. Owner Foy Vermaak is a renowned tour guide. Half-board option and tours to the Battlefields available.

★ Lennox Guest House   GUESTHOUSE $$
(☑ 034-218 2201; www.lennox.co.za; r incl breakfast from R920; ☎) Set on a picturesque farm about 8km outside of Dundee, Lennox Guest House offers guests much more than the typical B&B experience. Hosts Dirk (a former rugby star) and Salome truly open their home to their guests, cooking incredible meals (dinner R175) and offering wildlife drives on their property. The rooms are a rustic delight, with animal pelts and antique furnishings.

Chez Nous   B&B $$
(☑ 034-212 1014; www.cheznousbb.com; 39 Tatham St; s/d incl breakfast from R650/900, self-catering units from R2250; ❋ @ ☎) This centrally located, comfortable place, run by Elisabeth Durham, efficient French *madame* and tour guide (with a special interest in Prince Imperial Louis Napoleon, who died near Dundee in 1879), is a great choice for those in Dundee to immerse themselves in the battlefield tours. The rooms are comfortable and clean and the breakfasts offer more than just the usual full English.

Royal Country Inn   HOTEL $$
(☑ 034-212 2147; www.royalcountryinn.com; 61 Victoria St; dm/d/s per person R385/490/690; ☎) This old dame exudes a slightly faded, late-19th-century charm, and its English-style flavour is perfect for a spot of post–Rorke's Drift R&R. The rooms are tidy, but the furnishings and other amenities are quite dated, although they are generally comfortable. What you come for, though, is the eclectic lounge and restaurant area that's dripping with colonial airs.

The restaurant (dinner R225) and bar are worth checking out whether or not you're checked in to the hotel. Wi-fi is available in the common areas.

Ingudlane Lodge   LODGE $$$
(☑ 034-218 5094; www.ingudlane.co.za; s/d self-catering chalet R1100/2200; ☎ ☒) Dundee is not known for its wildlife viewing, but Ingundlane is an excellent private reserve that features a superb lodge with upmarket accommodation. Its self-catering chalets come with modern furnishings and a pool or hot tub on-site. In the afternoons you can relax in the expansive restaurant and bar area that looks out over the reserve, which is also the perfect place for a sundowner.

The on-site restaurant (open 10am to 9pm Monday through Saturday, until 4pm Sunday) is one of the few places to get a good meal in Dundee (mains R75 to R195).

ℹ Information

Tourism Dundee (☑ 034-212 2121; www.tourdundee.co.za; Victoria St; ⊙ 8.30am-4.30pm Mon-Fri, to noon Sat) can put you in touch with Battlefields guides and accommodation options. It's by the gardens in the centre.

ℹ Getting There & Away

There is very little transport to Dundee; this is a location where your own vehicle is ideal. Minibus shared taxis head to and from nearby towns such as Ladysmith, as well as some further locations, such as Durban.

Isandlwana & Rorke's Drift

If you've seen *Zulu* (1964), the film that made Michael Caine a star, you will doubtless have heard of Rorke's Drift, a victory of the misty-eyed variety, where on 22 and 23 January 1879, 139 British soldiers successfully defended a small mission station from around 4000 Zulu warriors. Queen Victoria lavished 11 Victoria Crosses on the survivors and the battle was assured its dramatic place in British military history.

However, for the full picture you must travel 15km across the plain to Isandlwana, the precursor to Rorke's Drift. It's here that, only hours earlier, the Zulu dealt the Empire one of its great Battlefields disasters by annihilating the main body of the British force in devastating style. Tellingly, *Zulu Dawn* (1979), the film made about Isandlwana, never became the cult classic *Zulu* is now. Victory sells better than defeat.

⊙ Sights

Isandlwana Battlefield   HISTORIC SITE
(☑ 034-271 0634; adult/child R35/20; ⊙ 8am-4pm Mon-Fri, from 9am Sat & Sun) The Isandlwana Visitors Centre has a small museum;

the entrance fee includes the battlefield. The battlefield itself is extremely evocative. White cairns and memorials mark the spots where the bodies of British soldiers were gathered en masse for burial and there are several memorials throughout. It's best seen with a local guide.

Rorke's Drift Battlefield · · · · · · · · · · HISTORIC SITE
(☑ 034-642 1687; adult/child R35/20; ☺ 8am-4pm Mon-Fri, from 9am Sat & Sun) Rorke's Drift Orientation Centre, on the site of the original mission station, is an impressive museum, especially for fans of the film *Zulu*. The Zulu know this site as Shiyane, their name for the hill at the back of the village.

Zulu was actually filmed in the Drakensberg, so the scenery around Rorke's Drift may come as a bit of a disappointment to those familiar with the film. The landscape is still beautifully rugged, however. The *Rorke's Drift–Shiyane Self-Guided Trail* brochure (R5) is a helpful reference. For the full experience it's best to go with a guide who can give context to the exhibits and buildings on-site.

Evangelical Lutheran Church Art & Craft Centre · · · · · · · · ARTS & CRAFTS
(☑ 034-642 1627; www.centre-rorkesdrift.com; ☺ 8am-4pm Mon-Fri, from 9am Sat & Sun) Behind the Rorke's Drift Orientation Centre, this operation was one of the few places to offer artistic training to black artists during apartheid. As well as the beautiful craft shop, several workshops – for weaving, printmaking and pottery – are in separate buildings in the vicinity; you are welcome to visit these, with the artists' permission.

🛏 Sleeping

Several lodges and hotels – of varying degrees of luxury – are in the surrounding area; all organise tours of the Battlefields.

Isandlwana Lodge · · · · · · · · · · · · · · · LODGE $$$
(☑ 034-271 8301; www.isandlwana.co.za; s/d with full board R4320/7200; P 🛜 🛱) Top marks for location: the lodge is perched in the hills above a village and the stunning rooms have expansive views over Mt Isandlwana, the Anglo-Zulu battle site. Although it is a modern construction, it has the feel of an idyllic wildlife lodge of yore and perfectly blends

with its surroundings. Tours, hikes and other actives can be booked through the staff.

Rorke's Drift Hotel · · · · · · · · · · · · · · LODGE $$$
(☑ 034-642 1760; www.rorkesdrifthotel.com; s/d with half-board R1780/2270; @) For the best view in the Battlefields area check out the common areas and restaurant of this hotel. A large rotunda with walls of windows, massive sofas and an enormous central fireplace make this place worth the price. It's also the nearest place to Rorke's Drift and the restaurant is a popular snack spot for day-trippers.

❶ Getting There & Away
The battle sites are southeast of Dundee. Isandlwana is about 70km from Dundee, off R68; Rorke's Drift is 42km from Dundee, accessible from R68 or R33 (the R33 turn-off is 13km south of Dundee). The roads to both battlefields can be dusty and rough. A dirt road connects Isandlwana and Rorke's Drift.

Blood River

On 16 December 1838 a small force of Voortrekkers avenged the massacre of Piet Retief by crushing an army of 12,000 Zulu. More than 3000 Zulu died – the river ran red with their blood – while the Voortrekkers sustained a few casualties. The battle became a seminal event in Afrikaner history, seen as proof that the Boers had a divine mandate to 'civilise' Southern Africa, and that they were, in fact, a chosen people.

It has been argued that the importance of Blood River was deliberately heightened and manipulated for political ends. The standard interpretation of the victory meshed with the former apartheid regime's world view: untrustworthy black savages beaten by Boers on an Old Testament–style mission from God.

The story of this historic battle is told at two rewarding sites, the **Blood River Heritage Site** (☑ 034-632 1695; www.bloedrivier.org.za; adult/child R40/25, car R15; ☺ 8am-4.30pm) and **Ncome Museum** (☑ 034-271 8121; www.ncomemuseum.co.za; admission by donation; ☺ 8am-4.30pm), which speak from the perspective of the Voortrekkers and Zulus respectively.

Free State

Best Places to Eat

➡ Seven on Kellner (p311)

➡ New York (p311)

➡ O's Restaurant (p314)

➡ Hoi Polloi Bistro (p314)

➡ Clementines Restaurant (p319)

Best Places to Stay

➡ Kalm Guest Suites (p319)

➡ Cranberry Cottage (p322)

➡ Karma Backpackers (p320)

➡ Fisant Bokmakierie & Hoephoep Guest House (p320)

➡ Otters' Haunt (p314)

Why Go?

A place of big skies and open pastureland, the Free State is ideal for a road trip. Broad horizons are interrupted only briefly by a smattering of towns and villages and, apart from Bloemfontein, the urban centres are small and manageable.

The Eastern Highlands, around the Drakensberg and the Lesotho border, is a vast area of rocky mountains, steep valleys and summer electrical storms. It's spectacular country, well known for its fruit farms, especially cherries. There are some excellent accommodation options in this part of the country, along with the stunning and walkable Golden Gate Highlands National Park.

The Free State tends to be a place travellers pass through rather than a destination in its own right. However, it's well worth exploring for its natural beauty, adventure sports and history – especially Bloemfontein, which, although historically an Afrikaner city, is also the birthplace of the African National Congress (ANC).

When to Go
Bloemfontein

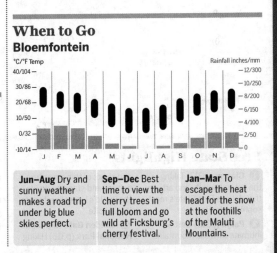

Jun–Aug Dry and sunny weather makes a road trip under big blue skies perfect.

Sep–Dec Best time to view the cherry trees in full bloom and go wild at Ficksburg's cherry festival.

Jan–Mar To escape the heat head for the snow at the foothills of the Maluti Mountains.

Free State Highlights

1 **Clarens** (p317) Taking in the natural beauty and artistry that defines Free State's most sophisticated town.

2 **Parys** (p313) Getting intimate with the mountains and rivers of this adventure capital, and standing inside the world's largest meteorite impact site.

3 **Golden Gate Highlands National Park** (p316) Hiking among grasslands, spectacular sandstone formations and thriving wildlife.

4 **Sentinel Hiking Trail** (p320) Scaling the dizzying

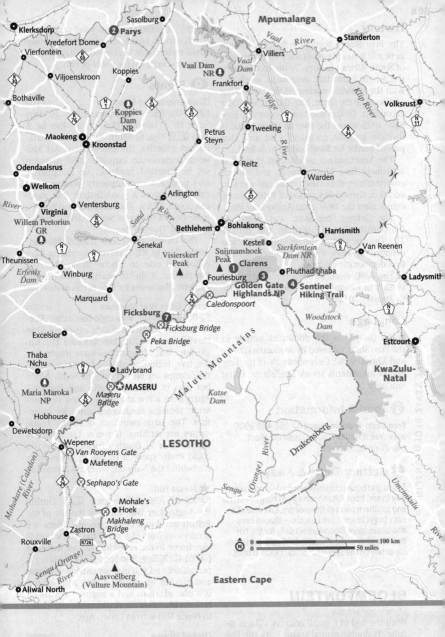

Map Labels

Mpumalanga

Klerksdorp
Sasolburg
2 Parys
Standerton
Vredefort Dome
Vierfontein
R59
Villiers
Vaal River
R30
Viljoenskroon
Koppies
Vaal Dam NR
Vaal Dam
Frankfort
Volksrust
Bothaville
N1
Koppies Dam NR
R34
R26
Wilge River
N3
N11
Klip River
Maokeng
Kroonstad
R76
R57
Petrus Steyn
Tweeling
Odendaalsrus
Reitz
Welkom
Arlington
Warden
Virginia
Ventersburg
River
R57
Harrismith
Willem Pretorius GR
Sand River
Bethlehem
Bohlakong
N5
Van Reenen
Theunissen
N1
R25
Senekal
Kestell
Snijmanshoek
Sterkfontein Dam NR
Ladysmith
Erfenis Dam
Winburg
N5
Visierskerf Peak
Snijmanshoek Peak
1
Clarens
Phuthaditjhaba
Marquard
Fouriesburg
3
Golden Gate Highlands NP
4
Sentinel Hiking Trail
Excelsior
Ficksburg
7
R26
Caledonspoort
Woodstock Dam
N3
Thaba 'Nchu
Ficksburg Bridge
Peka Bridge
Maluti Mountains
Estcourt
Maria Maroka NP
N8
Ladybrand
MASERU
Katse Dam
KwaZulu-Natal
Hobhouse
R25
Maseru Bridge
Dewetsdorp
LESOTHO
Orange River
Drakensberg
Wepener
Van Rooyens Gate
Mafeteng
Senqu (Orange) River
Umzinkulu River
Mohakare (Caledon) River
R25
Sephapo's Gate
Mohale's Hoek
Makhaleng Bridge
Zastron
R726
Rouxville
Senqu (Orange) River
Aasvoëlberg (Vulture Mountain)
Eastern Cape
Aliwal North

0 100 km
0 50 miles

Callouts

heights of the Drakensberg plateau.
5 **Bloemfontein** (p308) Checking out history museums and the province's most lively culinary scene.

6 **Philippolis** (p322) Time-traveling to the 1800s in the Free State's oldest town, and sipping craft beer at a historic bar filled with locals.

7 **Ficksburg** (p321) Dropping in on the cherry festival, when this friendly town brims with visitors, fruit and merriment.

History

The Free State's borders reflect the prominent role it has played in the power struggles of South Africa's history. To the east is Lesotho, where forbidding mountains, combined with the strategic warfare of the Sotho king Moshoeshoe the Great, halted the tide of Boer expansion. To the southeast, however, Free State spills across the river as the mountains dwindle into flat grassland – an area that proved harder for Moshoeshoe to defend.

The Voortrekkers established their first settlement near Bloemfontein, and various embryonic republics then came and went. In addition, there was a period of British sovereignty after the 1899–1902 Anglo-Boer War.

The 'Orange Free State' was created in 1854, with Bloemfontein as the capital. The 'Orange' part of the province's title was dropped in 1994, following South Africa's first democratic elections.

The ANC celebrated its centenary anniversary in Bloemfontein, where it was born, in January 2012.

Language

Sotho (64.4%) is the dominant tongue in the Free State, followed by Afrikaans (11.9%) and Xhosa (9.1%). Only about 2% of the Free State's inhabitants speak English as a first language.

❶ Tourist Information

Free State Tourism Board (☏ 051-409 9900; www.freestatetourism.org) is an excellent trip-planning resource.

❶ Getting There & Away

Trains and buses stop in Bloemfontein on their way to and from Johannesburg (Jo'burg), Pretoria and southern parts of the country. Likewise, it's easy to get to and from Lesotho – shared taxis and buses leave Bloemfontein daily for the border. Elsewhere, you'll need to take your own vehicle or rely on the sporadic minibus shared taxis.

BLOEMFONTEIN

☏ 051 / POP 369,568

With the feel of a small country village, despite its double-capital status – it's the Free State's capital and the judicial capital of the country – Bloemfontein is one of South Africa's most relaxed and welcoming cities. Although it doesn't possess the type of big-name attractions that make it worth a visit in its own right, you'll likely pass through 'Bloem' at some point on your way across South Africa's heartland, and there are some small-scale sights and good restaurants to keep you occupied for a day or two.

◉ Sights

Oliewenhuis Art Museum　　　GALLERY
(☏ 051-011 0525; www.nasmus.co.za; 16 Harry Smith St; ⊙ 7am-5pm Mon-Fri, 9am-4pm Sat & Sun) FREE One of South Africa's most striking art galleries, the Oliewenhuis Art Museum occupies an exquisite 1935 mansion set in beautiful gardens. An imaginative and poignant contemporary photographic exhibition gives a good insight into modern South Africa. The museum also holds a collection of works by South African artists, including Thomas Baines.

The on-site **tea room** (closed Monday; mains R40 to R195) serves everything from coffee and cake to T-bone steak. There's a functioning, if slightly scary, carousel in the gardens, plus lawns for kids to run around on.

Anglo-Boer War Museum　　　MUSEUM
(☏ 051-447 3447; www.anglo-boer.co.za; Monument Rd; adult/child R10/5; ⊙ 8am-4.30pm Mon-Fri, 10am-5pm Sat, 11am-5pm Sun) The Anglo-Boer War Museum has some interesting displays, including photos from concentration camps set up not only in South Africa but also in Bermuda, India and Portugal. Apart from a few modern touches, this museum remains unchanged since its inception. The large paintings depicting battle scenes are striking. If you're interested in this chapter of South African history you could easily spend a couple of hours here. It's behind the National Women's Memorial.

★**Naval Hill**　　　PARK
(☏ 051-412 7016; ⊙ 8am-6pm) FREE During the Anglo-Boer War, this was the site of the British naval-gun emplacements. There are good views from the top of the hill, which is also home to the **Franklin Nature Reserve** (☏ 051-412 7016; ⊙ 8am-5pm) FREE. Walking is permitted, and you may see ostriches, zebras and giraffes wandering about. Also on top is a **planetarium** and a gigantic **statue of Nelson Mandela** overlooking the city. Entry to Naval Hill is from Union Ave.

Orchid House　　　GARDENS
(☏ 051-405 8481; Union Ave; ⊙ 10am-4pm Mon-Fri, to 5pm Sat & Sun) FREE This glasshouse has a beautiful, if small, collection of flowers and some dazzling orchids. The surrounding **Hamilton Park** is an ideal place to take the kids for a picnic.

JRR TOLKIEN: LORD OF BLOEMFONTEIN

JRR Tolkien, author of *The Lord of the Rings*, was born in Bloemfontein in 1892. Although he moved to England when he was five, his recollection of the Bloemfontein district as 'hot, dry and barren' is considered a sign by Bloem's residents that his years here inspired him to create the legendary kingdom of Mordor. Or perhaps, as some graffiti in a Cape Town pub once said, 'Tolkien was just another Bloemfontein boy on acid'...

Regardless, if you're interested in learning more about the local Tolkien scene, head over to the Hobbit Boutique Hotel, formerly the home of the Tolkien literary society (before it disbanded). Staff there can direct you to the house where Tolkien was born, the cathedral in which he was baptised and the grave where his father is buried. If you're in the area, and fascinated with all things Tolkien, it's definitely worth strolling over to the Hobbit for a cosy fireside chat.

National Museum   MUSEUM
(📞051-447 9609; www.nasmus.co.za; 36 Aliwal St; adult/child R5/3; ⊘8am-5pm Mon-Fri, 10am-5pm Sat, noon-5pm Sun) A great recreation of a 19th-century street, complete with sound effects, is the most interesting display at this museum. It also has a shop and a cafe.

☞ Tours

Mangaung Township   CULTURAL
(📞051-430 7974) The African National Congress (ANC) was born in the township of Mangaung, 5km outside Bloemfontein, in 1912. Today, you can experience township life and learn some important history on a guided tour. Tours are informal and cost about R500. The operators change, so it's best to ask at the tourist office (p312) for an up-to-date list of guides.

🛌 Sleeping

Odessa Guesthouse   GUESTHOUSE $
(📞084 966 0200; info@odessa.la; 4 Gannie Viljoen St; s/d from R440/600; @🅿) For Ukrainian hospitality in the Free State, check out Odessa. The multilingual (Russian, Ukrainian and Afrikaans are spoken along with English) guesthouse has a good rep for its home-away-from-home vibe and friendly hosts. Set in a quiet suburb just off the N1 (take the Nelson Mandela turnoff, towards the city), its rooms are simple but spotless.

Reyneke Caravan Park   CARAVAN PARK $
(📞051-523 3888; www.reynekepark.co.za; Brendar Rd; camping per site up to 4 people R320, s/d/chalets R480/620/1020; ❄🅿) Two kilometres out of town (take the N8 towards Kimberley), this well-organised park has a swimming pool, trampoline and kids' play area. It's a good place for families. Basic rooms and modern brick chalets sleep up to four. Some

travellers report that it can be noisy due to its proximity to a busy road.

★ De Akker Guest House   GUESTHOUSE $$
(📞051-444 2010; www.de-akker.co.za; 25 Parfitt Ave; r R560-730; ❄🅿) This stylish offering in a central location has 15 rooms, including some with sink-in-and-smile king beds, and both baths and showers in attached en suites. It's very friendly and is popular with visiting cricket teams, so book ahead in summer. Breakfast is R70.

Matanja   GUESTHOUSE $$
(📞082 333 6731; www.matanja.co.za; 74 Albrecht St, Dan Pienaar; s/d incl breakfast from R625/830; ❄🅿) Small luxuries, such as pure goosedown duvets and a stylish, rustic ambience, set this little B&B apart. There are honesty fridges in the bedrooms, and with only seven rooms there's attention to detail. Your comfort seems a priority to the owners, who will even arrange breakfast in bed. Reservations recommended.

Hobbit Boutique Hotel   BOUTIQUE HOTEL $$
(📞051-447 0663; www.hobbit.co.za; 19 President Steyn Ave, Westdene; r incl breakfast from R980; ❄@🅿) This charming Victorian guesthouse, comprising two 1921 houses, is popular with visiting dignitaries and perfect for literati and romantic types. The cottage-style bedrooms have painted bathtubs, plus a couple of teddy bears apiece. The reading room has a chess table, and a local Tolkien society used to meet here to discuss all things JRR.

Check out the pub and lovely outdoor patio. On winter nights, there's a turn-down service with sherry and chocolate.

Protea Hotel Willow Lake   HOTEL $$$
(📞051-412 5400; www.marriott.com/hotels/travel/bfnwi-protea-hotel-bloemfontein-willow-lake; 101 Henry St; r from R1279; ❄@🅿) Part of

Bloemfontein

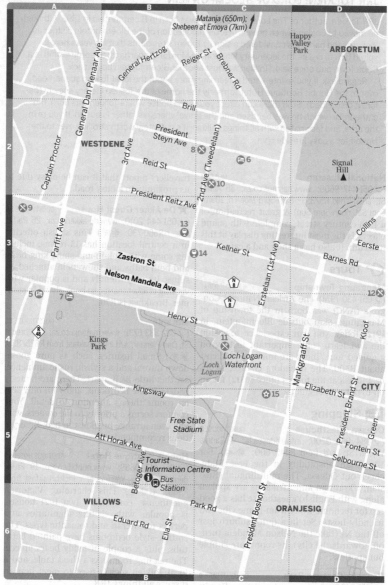

Matanja (650m);
Shebeen at Emoya (7km)

a popular national chain, the Protea offers very stylish rooms. Plump bedding and a shower cubicle that looks like it belongs at NASA complete the experience. It's a genuine touch of luxury. Close to the Waterfront, and overlooking the zoo.

✗ Eating

Modelled after Cape Town's waterfront, the **Loch Logan waterfront** isn't as impressive, but it's a good, safe spot for dinner, drinks or a movie. The main eating street is 2nd Ave, which is loaded with delicious choices.

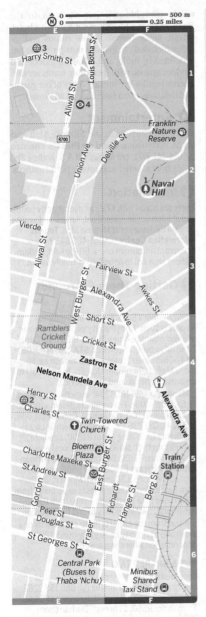

Bloemfontein

and sandwiches. Enjoy the fresh bread, quality ingredients and homemade touches such as tomato chutney (recommended on rye with ham and camembert).

★ Seven on Kellner INTERNATIONAL **$$**
(☑051-447 7928; www.sevenonkellner.co.za; 7 Kellner St, Westdene; mains R80-165; ☺noon-2pm Mon-Fri, from 6.30pm-midnight Mon-Sat) Set in an old house with inside and outside dining options, Seven on Kellner offers an informal, intimate atmosphere. Poultry, meat and seafood dishes are delicately prepared with expert hands along a Middle Eastern and Indian-inspired theme. Excellent wine list.

New York STEAK **$$**
(☑051-447 7279; www.newyorkrestaurant.co.za; cnr 2nd Ave & Reid St; mains R80-180; ☺11.30am-3pm & 6-10pm Mon-Fri, 5-10pm Sat, 11.30am-3pm Sun) Locals love this upmarket steakhouse, with its decor invoking 1920s New York, for special occasions. The menu features seafood, chicken and burgers, but it's the saucy steaks that steal the show. There are a couple of vegetarian options alongside all the meat.

Picnic CAFE **$**
(☑051-430 4590; Loch Logan Waterfront; mains R60-90; ☺8am-5pm Mon-Fri, to 4pm Sat, to 2pm Sun) A cool place with a great outlook over the water, perfect for a long, lazy chill-out. The food is excellent – especially the salads

Euro Caffe CAFE **$$**
(☑051-444 6222; www.eurocaffe.co.za; 131 Kellner St, Mimosa Mall; mains from R85-140; ☺8am-11.30pm) Inexplicably tucked into the Mimosa Mall, this delicious restaurant offers an

ℹ SAFETY IN BLOEM

Note that some areas of downtown are not considered safe, especially at night, so seek local advice before going for a wander around the central business district.

enormous (and ambitious) menu and some of the friendliest service in Bloemfontein. Choose from healthy, fresh salads, piping-hot pizza and an array of meaty mains, including a fall-off-the-bone-tender lamb shank, slow cooked in a wood-fired oven and served in a bacon brandy sauce.

Bella Casa Trattoria ITALIAN $$
(☑051-448 9573, 051-448 9571; 31 President Steyn Ave; mains R85-130; ⊙noon-10pm Mon-Sat; ☞) This efficient Italian trattoria serves lots of pasta choices along with pizzas and salads. It's a cheerful, family-friendly place with a cosy indoors and ample courtyard seating at tables covered with blue chequered cloths. The thin-crust Naples-style pizzas are recommended. Extensive wine list, with most varieties available by the glass.

🍺 Drinking & Nightlife

As a university town, Bloem has a good range of places to drink, party and listen to live music. The corners of 2nd Ave and Kellner St and off Zastron St and Nelson Mandela Ave bustle with revellers in the evening. A slightly older crowd hangs out at the Waterfront.

Patpong BAR
(☑064 139 5603; 16A Second Av; ⊙3pm-midnight Sun-Thu, noon-2am Fri & Sat) Opened in 2016, this self-proclaimed 'Thai fusion bar' is a pleasing amalgam of '80s music, Thai food and yummy cocktails. We recommend pairing the spring rolls with a martini, which the super nice bartenders will expertly prepare.

Mystic Boer PUB
(☑051-430 2206; www.diemysticboer.co.za; 84 Kellner St; ⊙3pm-4am; ☎) Bloem's most popular long-standing pub and live-music venue provides an eccentric twist on Afrikaner culture – check out the psychedelic pictures of long-bearded Boers on the walls. There are regular gigs by DJs and unsigned rock and hip-hop groups, along with beer pong tournaments. Pizza and burgers provide the fuel.

Shebeen Bar at Emoya BAR
(www.emoya.co.za; 7 Frans Kleynhans Rd, Emoya; ⊙4pm-late Mon-Thu, from noon Fri & Sat) This

rowdy township-style bar sits with in the Emoya Estate, a lifestyle complex with a hotel, private game reserve (white rhinos and giraffes included), a spa and putt-putt. The bar is defined by funky and colourful indoor and outdoor spaces, with incredibly warm service. There's regular live music, plenty of bar games and delicious pizza (available at all hours).

☆ Entertainment

There are cinemas in the Mimosa Mall and at the Waterfront. **Sand du Plessis Theatre** (☑051-447 7771; cnr Markgraaff & St Andrew Sts) holds opera, ballet and music performances.

ℹ Information

There are banks with ATMs all over the city centre and at Loch Logan Waterfront. American Express Foreign Exchange is at Mimosa Mall. **Tourist Information Centre** (☑051-405 8489; www.bloemfonteintourism.co.za; 60 Park Rd; ⊙8am-4.15pm Mon-Fri, to noon Sat) is mildly useful.

ℹ Getting There & Around

AIR

Bloemfontein's Bram Fischer International Airport is 10km from the city centre. A number of international airlines fly into Bloem via Cape Town or Jo'burg; check with **STA Travel** (☑051-444 6062; bloemfontein@statravel.co.za; Mimosa Mall; ⊙9am-6pm Mon-Fri, to 3pm Sat) to organise flights around South Africa.

Mango (☑086 100 1234; www.flymango.com; ⊙6am-6pm Mon-Fri) connects Bloem with Cape Town (from R1200, two hours). **CemAir** (☑086 123 6247, 081 736 8473; www.flycemair.co.za) has flights to Jo'burg (from R1200, one hour), Port Elizabeth (from R1600, 1½ hours) and George (from R1700,1½ hours). **South African Express Airways** (☑086 160 6606; www.flyexpress.aero; ⊙5.30am-7pm Mon-Fri, 8.30am-4pm Sat, to 7pm Sun) connects to Jo'burg (from R1041, one hour) and Cape Town (from R1652, two hours). SA Airline flies to and from Durban.

A taxi from the airport (there's often only one available) to the city centre is around R200, depending on where you are going.

BUS & SHARED TAXI

Long-distance buses leave from the tourist centre on Park Rd. **Translux** (☑086 158 9282; www.translux.co.za) runs daily buses to Cape Town (from R550, 13 hours), Durban (from R450, nine hours), East London (R400, nine hours), Jo'burg/Pretoria (R330, five hours) and Port Elizabeth (from R460, nine hours).

Greyhound (☑051-447 1558, 083 915 9000; www.greyhound.co.za; Park Rd) and **Intercape** (☑051-447 1435, 021-380 4400; www.intercape.co.za; Park Rd) have similar services.

Most **minibus shared taxis** (cnr Power & Fort Sts) leave from near the train station and head to Maseru, Lesotho (R100, three hours), Kimberley (R120, four hours) and Jo'burg (R190, six hours). There's usually at least one bus daily, but times vary. Buses to Thaba 'Nchu leave from St George's St (R30, one hour).

TRAIN

Shosholoza Meyl (☏ 0860 008 888, 011-774 4555; www.shosholozameyl.co.za) operates services three times weekly via Bloemfontein between Jo'burg (R230, seven hours) and Port Elizabeth (R330, 15 hours). There's also a service that passes by Bloem on the run between Jo'burg and East London (R230, 13 hours).

NORTHERN FREE STATE

With a pretty countryside of rolling hills, the northern Free State offers a growing number of hiking, mountain-biking and fishing opportunities. Near Parys in the far north, at Vredefort Dome, is the world's largest and oldest visible meteorite crater, now one of South Africa's eight Unesco World Heritage sites. (The crater is too wide to get a good photo of from the ground; to get a real impression of it, you'll need to take a flight.)

Further south is a golden region of maize farms and sunflowers. The small towns around here are rural enclaves where people live and work, and they see few tourists.

Parys & Vredefort Dome Area

☏ 056 / POP 48,169

Parys is a growing, vibrant town that sits beside the Vaal River just 120km south of Jo'burg. It is home to a few impressive buildings, including the 1915 Anglican Church, built from blue-granite blocks. The immediate area is quite beautiful, with its valleys, ravines and cliffs, a covering of lush flora, and many resident plants, animals and birds. But it's the adventure-sport options and the art-and-craft outlets lining the main street that draw most of the town's visitors – particularly Jo'burgers on the weekend.

Parys is also handy for visiting Vredefort Dome, an enigmatic area of hills created by the impact of a gigantic meteorite two billion years ago.

◉ Sights

Vredefort is the oldest and largest meteorite-impact site on earth, measuring about 200km in diameter. In 2005, the dome, which actually refers to the bowl (or upside-down dome) shape that characterises the central part of the crater, was named a Unesco World Heritage site, South Africa's sixth. It's well worth taking a drive across the site – or better yet, a hike – to experience this unique landscape.

Venterskroon
Information Centre   NATURE CENTRE
(☏ 076 485 9212; ◷ 8am-4pm Mon-Fri, 9am-5pm Sat & Sun) At Venterskroon is an information centre where you can watch a brief video on the dome (ask for the English version, unless you understand Afrikaans) and organise guided walks (per person from R80) around the nearby crater.

🏃 Activities

Parys has numerous activities on offer, including abseiling, sky diving, mountain biking, quad biking, rafting, hiking and birding. Otters' Haunt (p314) is the base of the most professionally run adventure operation, and its co-owner Graeme Addison actually pioneered white-water rafting in South Africa in the '80s. He and his wife also lead mountain biking excursions and hiking trips around the Vredefort Dome.

Stone Adventures   OUTDOORS
(☏ 056-811 4664; www.stoneadventures.co.za; Kopjeskraal Rd) Stone Adventures, based at the Stonehenge in Africa lodge, can organise tandem skydives (from R2600), an 8km rafting trip to Rocky Ridge (R280), abseiling with 13m (R220) and 44m drops (R260), and other activities, including a geological tour of Vredefort Dome.

Mountain Biking

Otters' Haunt (p314) can guide visitors to a dozen mountain-bike trails, catering to all skill levels, that snake out from its property 2km outside town. The trails are open to visitors (R90), though not all of them are well marked and it's easy to get lost. Bike rental costs an extra R250 per day.

Tweezer Rocks (about 18km, two hours) is one of the most popular options, and can be done alone or on a guided trip – locals call it the 'breakfast run' because it's a fast wake-up ride.

White-Water Rafting

Riverman (☏ 082 475 8767, 084 245 2490; http://riverman.co.za; Kopjeskraal Rd, Otters' Haunt; rafting half-/full day per person R335/565), based at Otters' Haunt, runs white-water rafting excursions down the Vaal River

FREE STATE PARYS & VREDEFORT DOME AREA

WILLEM PRETORIUS GAME RESERVE

Off the N1, about 70km south of Kroonstad, is the Willem Pretorius Game Reserve (☏ 057-651 4003; per vehicle R70; ◷ 7am-7pm), one of Free State's biggest recreation areas. Divided by the Sand River and Allemanskraal Dam, the reserve encompasses two ecosystems: grassy plains with large herds of elands, blesboks, springboks, black wildebeests and zebras, and, further north, a bushy mountain region with baboons, mountain reedbucks and duikers.

White rhinos and buffaloes are equally at home on either side of the reserve, but elephants and predators such as lions are not found here. If you enter via the West Gate, head up to the nearby lookout for great views of the area. Do not attempt to enter through the east gate; it is permanently closed. There are also chalets here (single/double from R250/850).

below Parys. The Class I to III rapids are not wild by world standards, but they can be quite exciting, especially in high water. The Gatsien Rapid (which translates to 'see your arse') is the best paddle on the 6km stretch – it can be walked up to and ridden down numerous times, and the bold may even opt to tube it. Other companies that run less expensive but also less personal white-water trips include Real Adventures (☏ 072 749 8169; www.parysriverrafting.co.za; 72 Bree St; half-/full day rafting trips per person from R250/400) and Ingwenya Tours (☏ 082 773 8656; www.ingwenyatours.co.za; 25 Van Wouw St, Sasolburg; rafting per person from R250).

🛌 Sleeping

★ **Otters' Haunt** GUESTHOUSE **$**
(☏ 056-818 1814, 084 245 2490; www.otters.co.za; Kopjeskraal Rd; s/d from R450/700; @ 🛜 🏊) The accommodation at this cheerfully overgrown place is decidedly rustic, but the secluded location right on the Vaal River is unbeatable. Options include bungalows, thatched-roof cabins set around a swimming pool, and a three-bedroom cottage with its own pool. Turn left after you cross the bridge out of town and continue for 2km along the river.

Klipdas Boskamp CAMPGROUND **$**
(☏ 072 877 6153; www.facebook.com/klipdas-boskamp; campsite for up to 6 people R400, trailer for up to 3 people R550) Those who would like to feel truly away from it all will flip for this campground, which offers drinking water, a large stove and plenty of unadulterated nature right on the bank of the Vaal River. The property has also got hiking trails through grasslands and over rocky outcroppings, from which much of the Vredefort Dome can be taken in.

Suikerbos CAMPING, CHALET **$$**
(☏ 082 484 8150; www.suikerbos.co.za; camping per person R100, hikers' huts R400, chalets R875-975; 🏊) Herds of impala graze between the buildings at this very popular, self-catering farm-reserve. The chalets are airy and modern, with giant bathtubs and loads of light. A caravan and basic hikers' huts sleeping four are also onsite. The far-flung property is ideal for stargazing, and is also near a former goldmine and a historical site from the Anglo-Boer war.

From Parys head to Potch, take the gravel road to Venterskroon and after 20km it's a left turn to Suikerbos.

🍴 Eating & Drinking

This town closes early, even on weekends. But Pickled Pig (www.pickledpig.co.za; 71 Bree St) is a fantastic spot for an early evening drink, and there are a couple of other good pubs in and out of town, including craft brewery The Dog and Fig (☏ 076 180 6521, 082 451 8634; www.dogandfigbrewery.com; craft beer tasting R95, mains R80-145; ◷ 10am-6pm Mon-Fri, to 10pm Sat, 9am-6pm Sun; 🅿).

★ **O's Restaurant** INTERNATIONAL **$$**
(☏ 056-811 3683; www.osrestaurant.co.za; 1 de Villiers St; mains R95-200; ◷ 11am-10pm Wed-Sat, to 3pm Sun) In this stylish, thoroughly satisfying restaurant down by the river, have some deep-fried calamari strips followed by peri peri steak, or fillet flambé prepared at your table. The pizza menu is also worth a browse, and there are some kids' meals, too. Dine in the elegant interior, out on the deck or amid the foliage in the gorgeous garden.

Hoi Polloi Bistro
& Boutique Caffe BISTRO **$$**
(☏ 056-811 3333; 73 Bree St; bistro mains R75-160, cafe mains R60-160; ◷ bistro 10am-9pm Fri, 9am-

9pm Sat, 9am-4pm Sun, 10am-4pm Wed & Thu, cafe 8am-4pm Thu-Tue) A split-level restaurant adorned from top to bottom in oddities, antiques and memorabilia – but with two distinct menus. The creaky but elegant upstairs is the bistro, serving dishes like warthog carpaccio, gemsbok sausage and karoo ostrich, either indoors or on sunny verandas.

ℹ Information

Parys Info Centre (☑ 056-811 4000; www.parys.info; 30 Water St; ☺ 8am-5pm Mon-Fri, 9am-1pm Sat) Can provide a map of the town and detailed information on accommodation options and activity providers.

ℹ Getting There & Away

The R59 leads into Parys, which is just west of the N1 heading north from Jo'burg.

Translux (☑ 086 158 9282; www.translux.co.za) buses connect Parys with Bloemfontein (R280, 3½ hours) and Jo'burg (R230, 1½ hours). The stop is in front of the Sasol garage.

EASTERN HIGHLANDS & SOUTHERN FREE STATE

With the Kingdom of Lesotho tucked into its crook, the mighty Eastern Highlands are the Free State's star attraction. The wild, rugged border winds its way past snow-shrouded mountains in winter and amber foliage in autumn – the views are spectacular, particularly in the northwest around Clarens.

Encompassing an area roughly from Rte 26 and Rte 49 east of Bethlehem to Harrismith, the region boasts sandstone monoliths towering above undulating golden fields, the fantastic Golden Gate Highlands National Park and trendy Clarens, South Africa's loveliest art destination.

Harrismith

☑ 058 / POP 27,869

Harrismith is a ramshackle, typical country town, with wide streets, picturesque old buildings around a grassy square, and distant Drakensberg views. South Africans refer to it affectionately as 'the half-way house' due to its central location between Durban and Bloemfontein, as well as Jo'burg and Durban, right where the N3 and the N5 intersect.

Harrismith is also a place to get supplies before exploring the Drakensberg range just inside the border of KwaZulu-Natal.

🛏 Sleeping & Eating

The Bergview complex is your best bet for eating, where you'll find the usual chains (Debonairs, Nando's and Ocean Basket) along with a couple of classier cafes.

Platberg Harrismith Backpackers HOSTEL $ (☑ 058-622 3737; www.platbergbackpackers.co.za; 55 Biddulph St; dm R185, s/d from R380/420; @ ⑦) This well-run place with safe parking has three dorm rooms, a double and two family units, all in good shape. You can use the braai (barbecue) outside, and there are great views of Platberg Mountain. If you want to explore your spectacular surrounds you can grab a hiking map, and there's shuttle service to nearby hikes.

La La Nathi Country Guest House CHALET $$ (☑ 058-623 0282; www.lalanathi.co.za; s/d from R650/850; P ⑦ ☒) Just off the N3, 3km from Harrismith (towards Durban), and offering convenience, great value and traditional rondavels (round huts with conical roofs), this is a sure bet – especially if you intend to hit the highway in the morning.

ℹ Information

N3 Help Centre (☑ 080 063 4357; www.n3tc.co.za/contact-us; Warden St; ☺ 8am-4.30pm Mon-Fri) This helpful centre is in the Bergview complex (a cluster of restaurants and retail near the entrance to the N3). It's overflowing with brochures and printed material on the wider region. Staff are knowledgeable and eager to assist with queries.

ℹ Getting There & Away

Intercape runs daily bus services to Durban (R234, four hours) and Jo'burg (from R198, four hours). The bus station is on McKechnie St. There's a Greyhound stop on Warden St near the Quest Garage.

Sterkfontein Dam Nature Reserve

The small **Sterkfontein Dam Nature Reserve** (☑ 083 942 1418, 058-622 3520; car/van R70/250; ☺ 6am-10pm) is in a beautiful area of the Drakensberg foothills, 23km south of Harrismith on the Oliviershoek Pass road into KwaZulu-Natal. Looking out over this expansive dam with its backdrop of rugged peaks feels like gazing across an inland sea. There are many viewpoints, and windsurfing and fishing are popular. Camping (up to five people R200) and rustic four-bed chalets (R550 to R850) are available.

Golden Gate Highlands National Park

Right before the darkness erases the remaining flecks of colour from the sky, something magical happens in Golden Gate Highlands National Park (📞082 233 9111, 058-255 1000; www.sanparks.org/parks/golden_gate; adult/child R192/96). The jagged sandstone outcrops fronting the foothills of the wild, maroon-hued Maluti Mountains glow golden in the dying light; lemon-yellow rays silhouette a lone kudu standing still in a sea of mint-green grasses before the sky explodes in a fiery collision of purple and red. The park might not boast any of the Big Five, but it does feature fantastic nightly sunsets.

There are quite a few animals in the park, though, including grey rheboks, blesboks, elands, oribi antelope, Burchell's zebras, jackals, baboons and numerous bird species, including the rare bearded and Cape vultures as well as the endangered bald ibis. The park is popular with hikers on long treks, but there are also shorter walking trails. There are two easy drives close to park headquarters.

Rhebok Hiking Trail   HIKING
This well-maintained, circular 33km trail is a two-day trek and offers a great way to see the park. On the second day the track climbs up to a viewpoint on the side of Generaalskop (2732m), the highest point in the park, from where Mont-aux-Sources and the Maluti Mountains can be seen. The return trail to Glen Reenen passes Langtoon Dam.

The trail starts at the Glen Reenen Rest Camp, which doubles as park reception. It has some steep sections, so hikers need to be reasonably fit. The trail is limited to 18 people and must be booked through the park board in advance – check the park's website.

Eastern Highlands

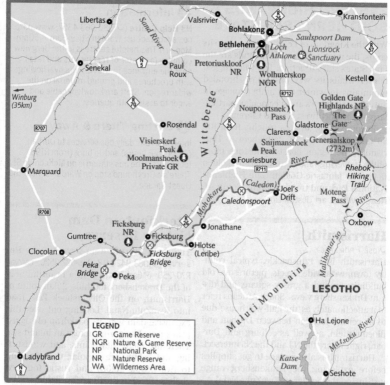

LEGEND
GR   Game Reserve
NGR   Nature & Game Reserve
NP   National Park
NR   Nature Reserve
WA   Wilderness Area

ℹ️ GOLDEN GATE HIGHLANDS PARK

Why Go The opportunity to hike in national parks in South Africa is rare. Not only can you walk without a guide here, but also the landscape is mesmerising and you have a great chance of seeing wildlife including various antelope.

When to Go The park can get very cold in winter, when temperatures can plummet to -15°C (June to August) and snow is common. September to April is the best time for travel to the park, although in summer afternoon thunderstorms do occur.

Practicalities Carry sufficient water if you're hiking and remember that the weather can change unpredictably up here. With your own vehicle you can approach from Harrismith on Rte 74 and then Rte 712.

Budget Tips Bring your own food. Minibus shared taxis run between Bethlehem and Harrismith, via Clarens and Phuthaditjhaba, and go right through the park.

Glen Reenen Rest Camp   CAMPGROUND $

(☎️058-255 0962; www.sanparks.org; Golden Gate Highlands National Park; camping R255, 2-person rondavel from R1010) This place is conveniently located on the main road, buried among the craggy limestone, and has well-maintained chalets and campsites by the river. A shop sells basic supplies and liquor.

ℹ️ Information

Glen Reenen Rest Camp is where tourists pay conservation fees to the park (adult/child R192/96), and obtain information on drives, hikes and horse riding.

ℹ️ Getting There & Away

The R712 cuts through Golden Gates Highlands National Park. You don't have to pay the entrance fee in order to drive through, but be careful to adhere to strict speed limits.

Minibus shared taxis between Bethlehem and Harrismith pass through the park. The trip is about an hour from either destination and costs around R20. You can also hop in a shared taxi from Clarens (R10, 30 minutes) or Phuthaditjhaba (R15, 45 minutes).

Clarens

☎️ 058 / POP 6379

The jewel of the Free State, and at 1850m, its highest town, Clarens is one of those places you stumble upon and find yourself talking about long after you depart. With a backdrop of craggy limestone rocks, verdant green hills, fields of spun gold and the magnificent Maluti Mountains, Clarens is a picture-perfect village of whitewashed buildings and quiet, shady streets. Its mild climate coupled with excellent opportunities for horse riding and trout fishing make it a bucolic country retreat.

It's also an art destination, with many galleries focusing on quality works by well-known South African artists. Charming guesthouses (ranging from very simple to extraordinarily posh), gourmet restaurants, eclectic cafes and myriad adventure activities round out the appeal.

FREE STATE CLARENS

Clarens

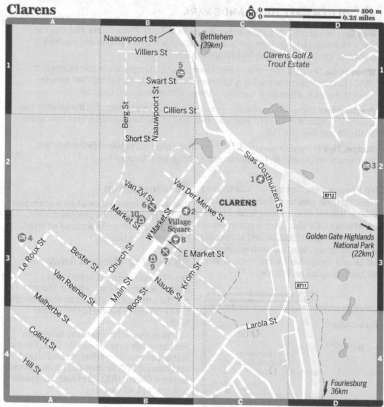

Clarens

🏃 Activities

The top two adventure tour operators are **Clarens Xtreme** (☎058-256 1260; www.clarensxtreme.co.za; 531 Sias Oosthuizen St; ⊗9am-5pm) and **Outrageous Adventures** (☎083 485 9654; www.outrageousadventures.co.za; Main St; rafting half-/full day R580/860, abseiling per person R360). They offer a wide range of trips including white-water rafting on the thrilling Ash River (rapids can flow up to class IV), quad biking, ziplining and even hot air balloon rides (which Outrageous Adventures can arrange through a Jo'burg-based company).

🎉 Festivals & Events

Clarens Craft Beer Festival   BEER
(www.clarenscraftbeerfest.com; ⊗Feb) The town fills up with beer enthusiasts on the last weekend in February for the annual Clarens Craft Beer Festival – one of the country's larg-

est. Tickets sell out and accommodation gets booked months in advance, so plan ahead.

🛏 Sleeping

There are plenty of guesthouses in Clarens, and some wonderful, scenically located lodges in the surrounding area. Things can get busy on weekends and during school holidays so it's wise to book ahead. Rates are often cheaper during the week. A useful site for bookings is www.clarens.co.za.

Clarens Inn & Backpackers   HOSTEL $
(☑076 369 9283; www.clarensinn.com; 93 Van Reenen St; dm R180, s/d from R180/360, self-catering cottages from R400; 🖥) The town's best budget option offers single-sex dorms and basic doubles, built around an artsy central courtyard with a big open fire pit and outdoor bar. The locale is rustic and tranquil, pushed up against the mountain at the bottom of Van Reenen St (look for it after the Le Roux turn-off).

★ Kalm Guest Suites   GUESTHOUSE $$
(☑058-256 1232; www.kalm.co.za; 484 Sias Oosthuizen St; s/d R1200/1640; 🅿🖥) With an ornate style she calls 'maximalism', interior designer extraordinaire Karen Hickman has gone to town on two guest suites, 'Yours' and 'Whose', festooning them in every colour, material, animal print and knick-knack around. The result is genius, and in 2017 Karen also added wood-burning fireplaces and braais to the cosy units, which are surrounded by *Alice in Wonderland*–style gardens.

Karen lives next door with her husband in a home that's received an equal overdose of her artistry – she might let you see it if you ask nicely. And you really should see this.

★ Clarens Country House   GUESTHOUSE $$
(☑082 449 2082; www.theclarenscountryhouse. com; r incl breakfast per person R750; 🖥) Within the Clarens Golf Estate, this collection of spacious, comfortable apartments is set in century-old sandstone architecture, with an attached gallery displaying works by renowned local artist (and co-owner) Peter Badcock-Walters, and views through floor-to-ceiling windows of the Maluti Mountains. The service is exceptional and detail-oriented: think decanters of sherry, electric blankets and home-cooked breakfasts in your private dining room.

Otherwise the cottages are self-catering, with a braai available on the manicured lawn, just beyond the rose garden.

🍴 Eating & Drinking

There are a few atmospheric pubs set around the village square. The brewery (☑058-256 1193; www.clarensbrewery.co.za; 326 Main St; ⊙10am-7pm Mon-Sat, to 6pm Sun; 🖥) and attached distillery are always busy.

Highlander Restaurant & Scotch Bar   SOUTH AFRICAN $
(☑058-256 1912; pizza from R40, mains R85-135; ⊙8am-late) A solid choice in town with longer hours than most other establishments, this high-spirited pub serves delicious wood-fired pizzas, burgers and sandwiches, but also less common and surprisingly delightful items, such as a seafood salad. There's indoor dining and an outdoor beer garden, and though it may seem a contradiction, they've also got a kids' menu *and* a scotch bar.

★ Clementines Restaurant   INTERNATIONAL $$
(☑058-256 1616; www.clementines.co.za; cnr Van Zyl & Church Sts; mains R80-160; ⊙11.30am-3pm & 6-9pm Sun-Thu, to 10pm Fri & Sat; 🖉) The food at this souped-up country kitchen tastes just as good as it looks on the gourmet international menu, featuring everything from rainbow trout with almond butter to tender ostrich fillets. Professional service, intimate ambience, a lengthy wine list and veggie options are more perks. Make sure to check out the daily specials on the wall.

🛍 Shopping

With tidy, tree-lined streets and myriad boutiques and galleries to peruse, Clarens is made for aimless wandering. In the galleries, keep an eye out for pieces by Pieter van der Westhuizen or Hannetjie de Clercq, two well-respected South African artists.

Art & Wine Gallery   ART
(☑082 341 8161, 058-256 1298; www.artandwine.co.za; 279 Main St; ⊙9am-5pm) Offers a fantastic selection of regional wines and paintings.

Bibliophile   BOOKS
(☑058-256 1692; 312 Church St; ⊙9am-4.30pm) A quaint bookshop with a huge range of titles and jazz and world music CDs.

ℹ Getting There & Away

Clarens is 40km (45 minutes' drive) from Bethlehem, and is best reached by private transport.

SENTINEL HIKING TRAIL

The most famous of the hiking trails in the area is the 10km **Sentinel Hiking Trail** (☎058-713 6361; car park R30, hiking R60), which commences in Free State and ends in KwaZulu-Natal. The trail starts at the Sentinel car park, at an altitude of 2540m, and runs for 4km to the top of the Drakensberg plateau, where the average height is 3000m.

It's about a two-hour ascent for those of medium fitness. At one point you have to use a chain ladder that runs up over a set of sheer rocks. Those who find the ladder frightening can take the route up the Gully, which emerges at Beacon Buttress (although some hikers argue that this route is even more hair-raising!). The reward for the steep ascent is majestic mountain scenery and the opportunity to climb Mont-aux-Sources (3282m).

Nearby accommodation includes the following:

Witsieshoek Mountain Lodge (☎073 228 7391, 058-713 6361; www.witsieshoek.co.za; r per person incl breakfast from R595; P) Perched at the foot of Sentinel Peak, this lodge consists of 76 well-appointed rooms and chalets, as well as an elegant dining room with giant windows overlooking the Drakensberg range. It's ideal for those aiming to pass their days with hikes to awe-inspiring rock formations and tumbling waterfalls.

Karma Backpackers (☎058-653 1433; www.karmalodge.co.za; 2 Piet Retief St; camping/ dm/d R100/200/500; @) In Kestell, a small maize-farming village on Rte 57 about 26km north of Phuthaditjhaba, Karma Backpackers is a peaceful, cosy place. The friendly hosts have lots of first-hand knowledge on regional hikes and good regional maps, and there are views of Sentinel Peak and the Maluti Mountains from the gorgeous garden.

Bethlehem

☎058 / POP 16,236

The main commercial centre of the eastern Free State, Bethlehem perches among rippling fields of grain and is famous for wheat and wool production. The town has a nice, wide-open feel, and its historic sandstone buildings date back to the 1840s, when the town was founded by Voortrekkers.

Although it remains of little interest to travellers, the buzzing township makes a good spot to lay your head.

◎ Sights

Lionsrock WILDLIFE RESERVE
(☎058-304 1691; www.lionsrock.org; wildlife safaris from R190) Eighteen kilometres from Bethlehem, Lionsrock is a 12.5-sq-km sanctuary and wildlife park for big cats rescued from all over the world and includes lions, cheetahs and leopards. There are also many species of antelope and wild dog, and guided game drives are offered. Accommodation is also available (per person including breakfast R750, four-person cabins R2310).

★Fisant Bokmakierie & Hoephoep Guest House GUESTHOUSE $$
(☎058-303 7144, 082 776 0322; www.fisant.co.za; 8-10 Thoi Oosthuyse St; s/d incl breakfast from R650/850; @🖥) Amid magnificent bird-at-tracting gardens are rooms and some luxurious self-catering chalets in three combined guesthouses. The rooms are beautifully appointed and very spacious, some with small kitchens and patios in an annex a couple of minutes' drive away. Rooms combine modern facilities such as power showers with classic polished-wood furniture and sumptuous bedding.

① Getting There & Away

Translux buses run to Durban (R300, five hours) and Cape Town (R600, 16 hours) twice a day and stop in Church St. Taxis are available on the streets as well.

Fouriesburg

☎058 / POP 700

Surrounded by wild, craggy mountains and wide open plains, Fouriesburg occupies a magnificent, riverside spot just 12km north of the Caledonspoort border post to Lesotho.

Two nearby peaks, **Snijmanshoek** and **Visierskerf**, are the highest in Free State; you'll also find the largest sandstone overhang in the southern hemisphere, **Salpeterkrans**, around here – look for the signs off Rte 26 just northwest of town. An eerie example of wind erosion and a hikers paradise, the area is also considered sacred and is used by local tribes for ancestral worship.

Camelroc Guest Farm   CAMPGROUND, CHALET $

(☑058-223 0368; www.camelroc.co.za; camping R200, r R700, chalets R800-1800) About 11km outside Fouriesburg, and just 800m from the Lesotho border, Camelroc sits in a spectacular location against a camel-shaped sandstone outcrop, with fine views over the Maluti Mountains. It's a great rustic retreat, offering en-suite rooms in the farmhouse hut and fully equipped chalets that range in size and style. Good hiking, mountain-biking and 4WD trails are nearby.

Di Plaasstoep   PUB FOOD $

(☑083 331 0714; 54 De La Harpe St; buffet breakfast R110; ⊙8am-9pm Mon-Sat, to 3pm Sun) An excellent local Afrikaner pub serving hearty meat dishes, craft beer and a standout buffet Boer breakfast, complete with mince, boiled eggs and oversized sausages. There's also a cosy beer garden where guests are kept warm by a central fire pit.

ⓘ Getting There & Away

Having your own wheels is ideal here. Taxis to the Lesotho border from Fouriesburg cost around R10.

Ficksburg

☑051 / POP 41,248

Ficksburg is a lovely little mountain village on the banks of the Mohokare (Caledon) River that's home to some fine sandstone buildings; keep an eye out for the town hall and the post office. Nestled into the purple-hued Maluti range, Ficksburg is particularly fetching in winter, when dollops of snow cover the craggy peaks.

Mild summers and cold winters make this area perfect for growing asparagus, apples and stone fruits, and Ficksburg is the centre of the Free State's cherry industry. There's a Cherry Festival (☑051-933 6486; www.cherryfestival.co.za) in November, but September and October are the best times to see the trees in full bloom.

Imperani Guest House & Coffee Shop   GUESTHOUSE $$

(☑051-933 3606; www.imperaniguesthouse.co.za; 53 McCabe Rd; s/d incl breakfast from R600/890; P✳☎❄) In a quiet spot, the Imperani has an African-flavoured, country-cottage vibe. The 36 spotless, modern rooms have wooden floors and big windows and are in thatched-roof buildings. The on-site restaurant features two sundecks and is a good lunch stop if you're passing through Ficksburg, with strong coffee, excellent wraps and a kids menu. There's also a great cocktail bar.

★Cafe Chocolate   CAFE $$

(☑082 920 5551, 051-933 3531; 9 Fontein St; mains R65-140; ⊙10am-8pm Mon-Sat) Part restaurant, part chocolate factory and part theatre, this is Ficksburg's top eatery and de facto cultural centre. Popular items include homemade pastas, pizzas and Maluti trout, and there's a good selection of deli items and fresh, homegrown salads. In the chocolate shop, the owners whip up Belgian truffles with all-organic ingredients, and have created the brand McKinley Chocolates.

ⓘ Getting There & Away

You'll need your own wheels to get to and from Ficksburg, unless you hire a private taxi. Intercape buses run to/from Cape Town (from R500, 13 hours) and Durban (from R486, six hours).

FREE STATE FICKSBURG

WORTH A TRIP

MOOLMANSHOEK PRIVATE GAME RESERVE

The breathtaking, family-owned Moolmanshoek Private Game Reserve (☑051-933 2220; www.moolmanshoek.co.za; P❄) protects a 3000-hectare stretch of grasslands, stone rock formations and valleys of the Wittenberg mountains. Springbok, black wildebeest, blesbok, oryx, zebra and ostrich are all accounted for, but what makes the experience unique is the horse operation. Guests are permitted to ride in the reserve, trotting and cantering if they please, alongside wild game.

The horses are top-notch and well cared for, and the comfortable saddles are designed for long-distance trips, which Moolmanshoek arranges to Lesotho and back. The on-site lodge offers rooms (per person including breakfast from R882) that are sumptuous and tastefully adorned, and the property also features a children's playground, a pool, a library and an exquisite restaurant where an elaborate breakfast is served each morning.

The reserve is located on the R70, 20km from the town of Rosendal between Senekal and Ficksburg.

Ladybrand

📞 051 / POP 25,816

In a valley surrounded by jagged peaks, 16km from Lesotho's capital, Ladybrand is an attractive small town loaded with sandstone buildings, dramatic scenery and ancient history – it is home to more than 300 Bushman rock art sites, along with fossilised dinosaur footprints, though these have not yet become tourist sites. Ladybrand is mainly a handy place to overnight on your way to and from Southern Africa's mountain kingdom.

⭐ **Cranberry Cottage** GUESTHOUSE $$
(📞 051-923 1500, 082 660 1168; www.cranberry.co.za; 37 Beeton St; s/d incl breakfast from R640/790; ❄️@🛜🏊) The best place to sleep in Ladybrand (and one of the best in Free State) is this rambling stone guesthouse. Spacious rooms have a touch of luxury and the feel of nature. A foliage-decked garden, a grapevine-covered patio and lovely swimming pool, a cosy dining room with crackling log fire and an old-time polished-wood bar all await. Cranberry also offers cheaper self-catering options down the road.

ℹ️ Getting There & Away

Ladybrand is 4km off the N8 on Rte 26 – the road to Ficksburg – and about 130km south of Bloemfontein. Minibus shared taxis can be found near the church on Piet Retief St and run to Ficksburg (R70, one hour). For a wider choice of destinations, take a minibus taxi to Maseru Bridge (R15), at the Lesotho border, and find a long-distance taxi in the big minibus-taxi rank there.

Gariep Dam Nature Reserve

The Free State's largest **nature reserve** (📞 051-754 0026; per vehicle R70; ⏰ 7am-6pm) is a combination of the 365-sq-km Gariep Dam (which holds back a vast 6 billion cubic litres of water) on the Senqu (Orange) River and an 112-sq-km wildlife sanctuary on its northern shore.

Gariep Boat Cruises BOATING
(📞 079 522 2566, 051-754 0190; www.gariepboatcruises.com) Morning and sunset cruises (from R120) to the Gariep Dam wall.

Forever Resorts Gariep RESORT $$
(📞 051-754 0045; www.forevergariep.co.za; camping/chalets from R180/1035; 🅿️❄️🛜🏊) Families will live it up at this pleasant, activity-oriented resort, where amenities include a swimming pool, minigolf course, volleyball court and trampolines. The layout of the well-appointed, 30-plus chalets allows for excellent views of the water, and the manicured grounds offer comfortable camping. There's a decent on-site restaurant as well.

Philippolis

📞 051 / POP 3648

Founded in 1823 as a mission station, Philippolis, on Rte 717, is a town frozen in time, and the oldest settlement in the Free State. Seventy-five of its buildings have been declared national monuments, including the library, and many places are built in Karoo style, with thick walls to keep the semi-desert heat at bay.

Writers, artists and other luminaries have long congregated in this dusty outpost, which offers a wonderful bookstore, a history museum, several art galleries and proximity to the world's best opportunity to view and photograph wild tigers. Weekends are lively, with seemingly the entire town crammed into the historic Hotel Oranjehof bar.

⭐ **Tiger Canyons** WILDLIFE WATCHING
(📞 051-773 0063; www.jvbigcats.co.za; wildlife drive R2000) 🌿 A wildlife reserve 25km from Philippolis where a South African filmmaker has created a place where wild tigers can breed and thrive. There are 17 Bengal tigers living in the reserve, a few of which are cubs, and two of which are white. Cheetahs live there as well, as do antelopes that the cats hunt. Wildlife drives are offered in the morning and afternoon, and each includes a meal in the **Tigress Julie Lodge** (📞 082 892 4680; per person all-inclusive R7500; 🅿️❄️🛜🏊) 🌿.

Starry Nights Karoo Cottages COTTAGE $$
(📞 051-773 0063, 082 892 4680; www.starrynights.co.za; 16 Tobie Muller St; s/d R750/1000) Four lovely, restored historic homes for self-caterers, sleeping anywhere from one to six people. Interiors feature wooden floors and Victorian tubs; backyards offer lush gardens.

Waterkloof Craft Brewery MICROBREWERY
(📞 082 770 0101; R717; craft beer R35; ⏰ 24hr) Just a few kilometres outside of Philippolis, fronting a tiny ghost town called Waterkloof, this microbrewery proudly serves its signature Karoobossie and Kapokbossie ales, which are named after shrubs found on nearby farms.

Tourism Office & Gift Shop TOURIST INFORMATION
(📞 018-525 8371; R717; ⏰ 9am-5pm) This helpful office has loads of information and maps regarding Philippolis, and is the place to book history tours (R75).

Johannesburg & Gauteng

Best Places to Eat

➡ Fermier (p370)
➡ Breezeblock (p348)
➡ Yeoville Supper Club (p348)
➡ Marble (p347)
➡ La Boqueria (p347)

Best Places to Stay

➡ Satyagraha House (p340)
➡ Gastehys JanHarmsgat (p366)
➡ Alpine Attitude (p367)
➡ Curiocity Johannesburg (p338)
➡ Cradle Boutique Hotel (p360)

Why Go?

Gauteng (pronounced *how*-teng) may be a small province but it also is the economic heart of the nation. Its epicentre is Johannesburg, the country's largest city. And what a city! Jo'burg's old downtown area is undergoing an astonishing rebirth. Once considered a place to avoid, Jo'burg is now one of the most inspiring and happening metropolises in the world.

For a change of scene, head to Pretoria. The country's administrative capital may not be quite as dynamic as Jo'burg, but it still offers stately buildings, good museums and beautiful jacaranda-lined streets. It's also a short drive from here to the attractive village of Cullinan, famous for its diamond mine.

Gauteng also has a unique geological history that's evident at the World Heritage–listed Cradle of Humankind. This vast valley full of caves and fossils is one of the African continent's most important archaeological sites.

When to Go
Johannesburg

°C/°F Temp · Rainfall inches/mm

Mar School's back, so Jo'burg's Melville, Maboneng and Braamfontein hop. High fashion is out in Sandton.

Aug Festival season led by Joy of Jazz, the Dance Umbrella and a hectic calendar of theatre.

Oct–Feb Wonderful displays of jacaranda blossoms in spring. Spectacular near-daily lightning strikes.

Johannesburg & Gauteng Highlights

1 Constitution Hill (p331) Learning about the horrors of apartheid and viewing splendid contemporary art at this significant Jo'burg site.

2 Maboneng (p334) Cruising around this regenerated inner Jo'burg 'burb with its street art, galleries and fab Sunday market.

3 Apartheid Museum (p335) Tracing South Africa's tumultuous modern history at this outstanding museum.

4 Orlando Towers (p358) Bungee-jumping off these former power station towers in Soweto.

5 Sterkfontein Caves (p360) Going deep underground to see one of the world's most significant archaeological sites.

6 Freedom Park (p362) Learning about African history from a whole different perspective.

7 Cullinan (p366) Taking a tour of the diamond mine and exploring the charming village.

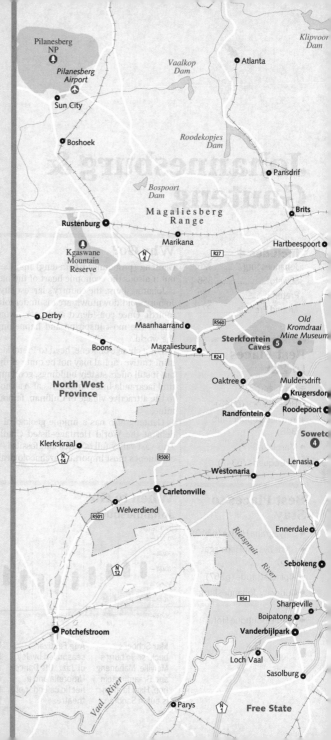

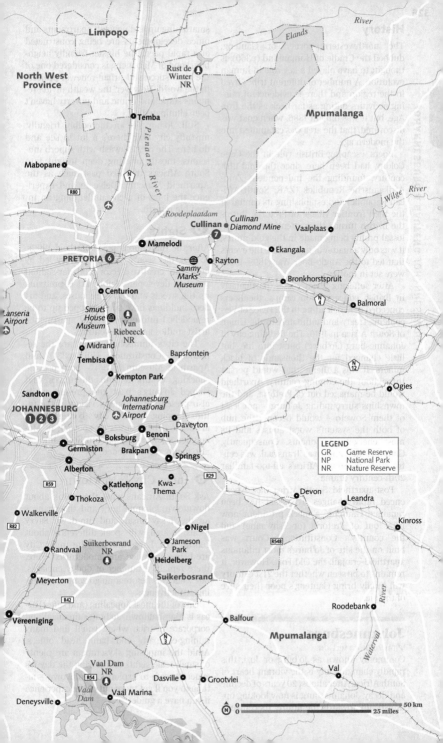

History

The northwestern corner of Gauteng, dubbed the Cradle of Humankind (p360), is thought to have played a key role in human evolution. A number of different tribes lived in the region and there is evidence of mining activities dating as far back as the Iron Age, but it was only in 1886, when gold was discovered, that the area was catapulted into the modern age.

Boers, escaping British rule in the Cape Colony, had been here since the mid-19th century, founding the independent Zuid-Afrikaansche Republiek (ZAR; South African Republic) and establishing its capital in the then frontier village of Pretoria. But as the British turned their attention to the colossal profits being made in the gold mines, it was only a matter of time before the events that led to the Anglo-Boer War (1899–1902) were set in motion.

After suffering severe losses, particularly in British concentration camps, the Boers conceded defeat, leading to the Peace of Vereeniging treaty and ultimately to the Union of South Africa in 1910. The fledgling city of Johannesburg (Jo'burg) burst into life, but little changed for the thousands of black miners. It was a theme that would persist throughout the coming century. Apartheid would be managed out of Pretoria, and the townships surrounding Jo'burg – not least of them Soweto – would become the hub of both the system's worst abuses and its most energetic opponents. Consequently, Gauteng, then known as Transvaal, was centre stage in South Africa's all-too-familiar 20th-century drama.

Post-apartheid South Africa has experienced rapid changes. Transvaal has been renamed Gauteng, a black president now rules out of Pretoria (or Tshwaane) and the country's Constitutional Court was built on the site of Jo'burg's most infamous apartheid-era jail, the Old Fort. However, it remains to be seen whether the 21st century will finally bring Gauteng's poor their slice of the pie.

Johannesburg

♩ 011 / POP 4.4 MILLION

Commonly known as Jo'burg or Jozi, this rapidly changing city is the vibrant heart of South Africa. After almost 20 years of decline and decay, Johannesburg is now looking optimistically towards the future. Its centre is smartening up and new loft apartments and office developments are being constructed at a rapid pace. The hipster-friendly neighbourhood of Maboneng is considered one of the most successful urban-renewal projects in the world. However, the wealth divide remains stark, and crime and poverty haven't been eliminated.

Still, Jo'burg is an incredibly friendly, unstuffy city and there's a lot to see and do here. The city is awash with superb museums, mostly offering deep insight into South Africa's troubled past such as the Apartheid Museum. Delve in and experience the buzz of a city undergoing an incredible rebirth.

◉ Sights

After the tumultuous post-apartheid 1990s, Jo'burg has seen a steady recovery led by both the creative sector and far-sighted property developers. Public art is prettying up the streets and old warehouses, and art deco buildings have been snapped up to be remodelled into offices, rental apartments, artist studios and retail ventures.

The city's unmissbale sights are the remarkable Constitution Hill (p331) and Apartheid Museum (p335) – both provide shocking testimony into the forces that shaped Jo'burg's past and present while also presenting a hopeful vision of the future. Tapping into the city's contemporary art scene – be it street-art-spotting in Maboneng or gallery-hopping in Rosebank – is also highly recommended.

◉ Inner City & Newtown

Ask South Africans what they think about downtown Johannesburg and the chances are they'll say 'unsafe' and 'run-down'. Savvy locals, though, will speak differently about central Jozi. Large areas of the Inner City are being upgraded and modernised. Sure, there remain a number of dodgy enclaves, but what was before a no-go zone is regaining its attractiveness.

One of the most appealing (and safest) areas is Marshalltown, Jo'burg's financial and corporate district, where you'll find many mining-company and bank head offices. Amid the imposing skyscrapers are plenty of small-scale sights and during the day it's generally safe to explore on your own – although you'll get more out of the experience if you have a guide.

The revival of Newtown itself has slowed in recent years as other areas have risen in the hip stakes, but it's still home to some decent museums, the Market Theatre complex and the new Newtown Junction mall.

During the day you can walk pretty safely around the area west of the Carlton Centre and south of Rahima Moosa St, but it pays to keep your wits about you, especially around Park Station. Don't flash around valuables such as cameras and watches, and avoid carrying bags.

Chancellor House NOTABLE BUILDING
(Map p332; 25 Fox St, Ferreiras Dorp) It was in this three-storey building that, in the 1950s, Nelson Mandela and Oliver Tambo set up South Africa's first black-owned law firm. After a 2012 renovation, it features a public 'outside museum' that can be visited any time of the day or night. Photos and panels displayed in the windows give a vivid insight into Mandela's and Tambo's lives.

Opposite is the 5m-tall painted steel sculpture **Shadow Boxing** by Marco Cianfanelli, based on Bob Gasini's famous photo of Mandela sparring in 1952.

Johannesburg Art Gallery GALLERY
(JAG; Map p332; ☑011-725 3130; Joubert Park, Hillbrow; ⊙10am-5pm Tue-Sun) FREE Fenced off from the southern end of sketchy Joubert Park is this elegant Lutyens-designed gallery dating from 1915. The JAG has one of the largest art collections in Africa; however, only a tiny fraction of it is ever on display and usually the gallery rooms that are open host temporary exhibitions. The entrance is just off Klein St.

Top of Africa VIEWPOINT
(Map p332; ☑011-308 1331; 50th fl, Carlton Centre, 150 Commissioner St; adult/child R15/10; ⊙9am-6pm) The Carlton Centre (223m) has been Africa's tallest building since 1973. The basement shelters a buzzing shopping mall. For awesome city vistas, head to the **observation deck** at the top (entrance is via a special lift one floor below street level).

Mary Fitzgerald Square SQUARE
(Map p332; Rahima Moosa St, Newtown) Named after South Africa's first female trade unionist, this square is partly decorated with an array of heads, carved from old railway sleepers by Newtown artists. It's also the start for a **Jazz Walk of Fame**, a walkway

COFFEEBEANS ROUTES

The Jo'burg wing of Cape Town–based tour company **Coffeebeans Routes** (https://coffeebeansroutes.com) offers a great program of highly original cultural tours and connections. Itineraries include contemporary Soweto (US\$120), a farm-to-fork culinary tour (US\$160, minimum eight people) and chances to meet local music makers and artists as well as attend a private symphonic concert.

that pays tribute to South Africa's most influential jazz musicians.

Museum Africa MUSEUM
(Map p332; ☑011-833 5624; Old Market Bldg, 121 Lilian Ngoyi St, Newtown; ⊙9am-5pm Tue-Sun) FREE This museum, housed in the old Bree St fruit market, offers a wide range of exhibitions on historical themes, including the Treason Trials of 1956–61, the development of South African music and housing in the city. The satirical 'Cartoons in Context' are worth a look, as is the Sophiatown display, which contains a mock-up of a *shebeen* (unlicensed bar).

SAB World of Beer MUSEUM
(Map p332; ☑011-836 4900; www.worldofbeer. co.za; 15 Helen Joseph St, Newtown; adult/child R115/45, tour & tasting R195; ⊙10am-5pm) Take a 1½-hour tour through the history of beer at this jovial museum. Taste traditional sorghum beer in a mock African village, sample a cheeky half-pint at a re-created Victorian pub, then nail two free pints in the bar afterwards. You even get a World of Beer glass keepsake.

Sci-Bono Discovery Centre MUSEUM
(Map p332; ☑011-639 8400; www.sci-bono.co.za; cnr Miriam Makeba & Helen Joseph Sts, Newtown; adult/child R130/70; ⊙9am-5pm Mon-Fri, 9am-4.30pm Sat & Sun) Testament to the remarkable reawakening of downtown Jo'burg, this well-organised science museum, full of interactive exhibitions, occupies a former power station. Sci-Bono often hosts internationally acclaimed temporary exhibitions – such as 'Body Worlds' and 'Wonders of Rock Art' featuring the ancient Lascaux cave paintings – and these exhibitions are the best time to visit. Great for kids and adults alike.

Johannesburg

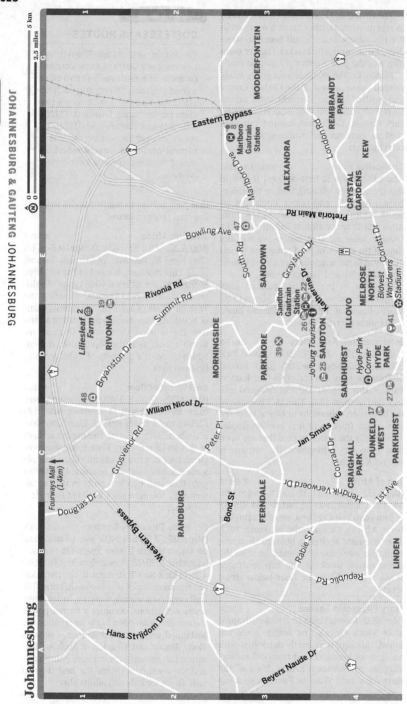

5 km

2.5 miles

MODDERFONTEIN

REMBRANDT PARK

KEW

Eastern Bypass

Marlboro Gautrain Station 8

London Rd

CRYSTAL GARDENS

ALEXANDRA

Marlboro Dr

Pretoria Main Rd

Bowling Ave 47

Corlett Dr

South Rd

Grayston Dr

SANDOWN

MELROSE NORTH

Bidvest Wanderers Stadium

Rivonia Rd

Summit Rd

Sandton Gautrain Station

Katherine Dr

22

ILLOVO

19

Lilliesleaf Farm

Bryanston Dr

RIVONIA

MORNINGSIDE

PARKMORE

26

Jo'burg Tourism

25

39

SANDTON

SANDHURST

Hyde Park Corner

HYDE PARK

41

48

Grosvenor Rd

William Nicol Dr

Peter Pl

Jan Smuts Ave

Conrad Dr

CRAIGHALL PARK

DUNKELD WEST 17

27

PARKHURST

Fourways Mall (1.4km)

Douglas Dr

RANDBURG

Bond St

FERNDALE

Hendrik Verwoerd Dr

1st Ave

Western Bypass

Rabie St

Republic Rd

LINDEN

Hans Strijdom Dr

Beyers Naude Dr

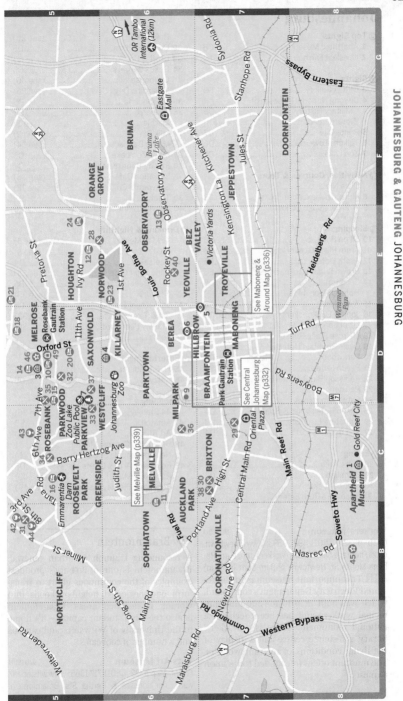

Johannesburg

Workers' Museum   MUSEUM
(Map p332; ☑011-492 0593; www.newtown.
co.za/heritage/view/index/workers_museum; Rahima Moosa St, Newtown; ⊙9am-5pm Tue-Sun)
FREE This important museum is in the restored Electricity Department's compound,
which was built in 1910 for 300-plus municipal workers and has been declared a
national monument. There is a workers'
library, a resource centre and a display of
the living conditions of migrant workers.
The museum offers free guided tours upon
request.

◉ Braamfontein

A resounding triumph of urban renewal,
Braamfontein is one of Jo'burg's proudest
examples of the continuous effort to transform once-neglected neighbourhoods into
vibrant, modernised areas. Braamfontein
is also the city's student capital – it's home
to the University of Witwatersrand campus
and a number of cool cafes.

Wits Art Museum   MUSEUM
(WAM; Map p332; ☑011-717 1365; www.wits.ac.za/
wam; cnr Jorissen & Bertha Sts, Braamfontein;

⊙10am-4pm Wed-Sun) **FREE** Completed in May 2012, this is one of the leading museums of African art on the continent. Although it has an extraordinary collection of 10,000 works – which it shares with the Johannesburg Art Gallery (p327) – you'll only see a tiny fraction here, as there is a dynamic program of events and exhibitions including ones of international artists.

Origins Centre   MUSEUM
(Map p332; ☑011-717 4700; www.origins.org.za; Wits University, cnr Yale Rd & Enoch Sontonga Ave, Braamfontein; adult/child incl audio guide R80/40; ⊙10am-5pm Mon-Sat; P) This stunning museum explores the African origins of humankind through interactive exhibits. The centre is brilliant for school-age children and holds the most formidable collection of rock art in the world, led by the work of the Khoisan people, the original South Africans.

⊙ Hillbrow, Berea & Yeoville

Dominated by two iconic buildings – the 269m **Telkom Tower** (Map p328; Goldreich St) and the cylindrical Ponte City – Hillbrow and neighbouring Berea and Yeoville were once the liveliest and most interesting suburbs in the city where South Africans of all races lived side by side. However, from the late 1980s, when whites began to flee the inner city, they became marked as 'grey zones' devoid of basic utilities and policing.

These densely populated neighbourhoods still have a reputation for crime but are also very lively and colourful, with a mixed pan-African population and vibrant street markets during the day. If you venture here, it's best to do so with a savvy guide, such as those from Dlala Nje.

★**Constitution Hill**   MUSEUM
(Map p332; ☑011-381 3100; www.constitutionhill.org.za; 11 Kotze Rd, Braamfontein; tours adult/child R65/30; ⊙9am-5pm, tours on the hour) Do not leave Jo'burg without visiting Constitution Hill. One of South Africa's most important historical sites, the deeply moving and inspirational exhibitions here are split across four locations: the **Old Fort**, which dates from 1892 and was once a notorious prison for white males; the horrific **Number Four Jail**, reserved for nonwhite males; the **Women's Jail**; and the Awaiting Trial Block – now mostly demolished and replaced by the **Constitutional Court** (Map p332; ☑011-359 7400; www.constitutionalcourt.org.za; 1 Hospital St, Constitution Hill, Braamfontein; tours R22; ⊙8.30am-5pm Mon-Fri, 10am-3pm Sat). Tours depart on the hour and provide essential context.

What you will hear and see will be shocking – the brutal facts of prisoners' incarceration here speak volumes. You will come away with an integral understanding of the legal and historical ramifications of the struggle. Many of the country's high-profile political activists, including Nelson and Winnie

---

PONTE CITY

Nothing encapsulates the changing fortunes of downtown Jo'burg better than **Ponte City** (Map p328; 1 Lily Ave, Berea), which can be visited on tours with **Dlala Nje** (Map p328; ☑011-402 2373; www.dlalanje.org; Shop 1, Ponte City; tours R150-200). This 54-storey cylindrical skyscraper with 484 apartments was conceived in the 1970s as the pinnacle of high-rise living in the city. However, by the late 1980s, as white South Africans abandoned the inner city, the building was hijacked by squatters. As this part of Jo'burg became a 'grey area', Ponte City was declared a vertical urban slum: some 10,000 people lived here with no running water or electricity.

Flash forward a couple of decades and Ponte City's fortunes are swinging back to its original conception. The building's owner, Kempston, has taken back control and refurbished the structure, which is now generally safe and home to an ethnically mixed community of working- and middle-class South Africans. For a great insight into their lives and wonderful photography, search out the book *Ponte City* by Mikhael Subotzky and Patrick Waterhouse.

Dlala Nje's work with the local community, particularly the young, has been a huge success. In December 2017 the social enterprise opened the bar **5101** (Map p328; ☑011-402 2373; www.dlalanje.org) on the 51st floor and there are plans for a climbing wall up the side of 173m building. Dlala Nje also manages a couple of Airbnb rental apartments should you wish to stay overnight here.

Central Johannesburg

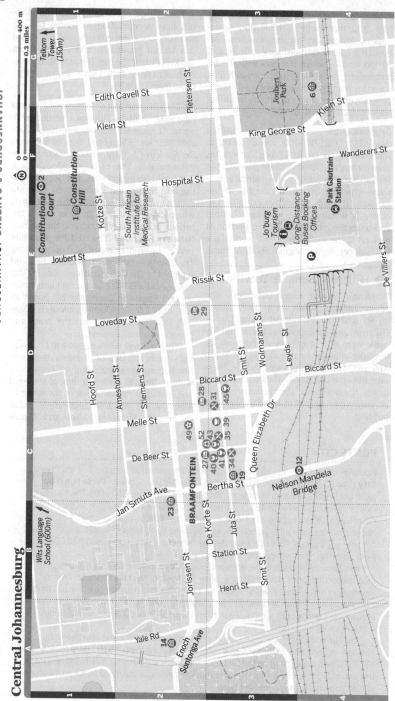

0 400 m
0 0.2 miles

Telkom Tower (150m)

Edith Cavell St

Pietersen St

Klein St

Joubert Park

6

King George St

Klein St

Constitution Hill

Constitutional Court 2

1 Constitution Hill

Kotze St

South African Institute for Medical Research

Hospital St

Wanderers St

Jo'burg Tourism

Long-Distance Buses Booking Offices

Park Gautrain Station

Joubert St

Rissik St

De Villiers St

Loveday St

29

Smit St

Wolmarans St

Leyds St

Biccard St

Hoofd St

Ameshoff St

Stiemens St

Biccard St

28

31

45

Smit St

Melle St

49

52

27

40

41

35

39

34

19

Queen Elizabeth Dr

De Beer St

BRAAMFONTEIN

Bertha St

12

Nelson Mandela Bridge

Jan Smuts Ave

23

Wits Language School (600m)

De Korte St

Juta St

Jorissen St

Station St

Smit St

Henri St

Yale Rd

14

Enoch Sontonga Ave

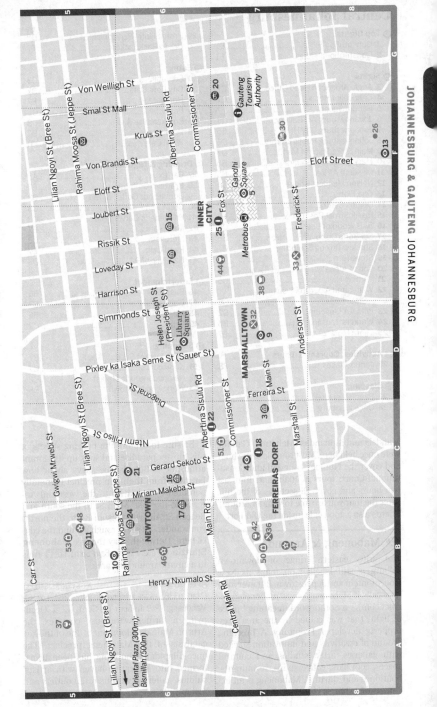

Von Weilligh St

Smal St Mall

Kruis St

Commissioner St

Lilian Ngoyi St (Bree St)

Rahima Moosa St (Jeppe St)

Albertina Sisulu Rd

Gauteng Tourism Authority

20

Von Brandis St

Eloff Street

Eloff St

30

26

13

Joubert St

Gandhi Square

Fox St

5

Frederick St

INNER CITY

15

Rissik St

7

25

Metrobus

Loveday St

44

33

Harrison St

38

Simmonds St

MARSHALLTOWN

32

Helen Joseph St (President St)

Library Square

9

8

Pixley ka Isaka Seme St (Sauer St)

Diagonal St

Main St

Ferreira St

Albertina Sisulu Rd

Commissioner St

Anderson St

Ntemi Piliso St

22

3

51

18

Gwigwi Mrwebi St

Lilian Ngoyi St (Bree St)

Gerard Sekoto St

4

FERREIRAS DORP

Marshall St

21

16

Miriam Makeba St

Rahima Moosa St (Jeppe St)

24

17

NEWTOWN

Main Rd

48

11

53

46

42

36

50

47

10

Carr St

Henry Nxumalo Rd

Central Main Rd

37

Oriental Plaza (300m);
Bismillah (500m)

Lilian Ngoyi St (Bree St)

Central Johannesburg

Mandela and Mohandas (Mahatma) Gandhi, were once held here. Most tours last one hour and cover the Number Four Jail and Constitutional Court; tours at 10am and 1pm last two hours and cover all sections of the hill. After the tour you are free to wander around. There's also a good cafe inside the Old Fort.

◎ Maboneng & Around

The gritty eastern fringe of downtown Jo'burg is still labelled on maps as New Doornfontein and Jeppestown. But everyone now calls it Maboneng (www.mabonengprecinct.com) – a Sotho word, meaning ' place of light', that was coined by the area's key property developer Propituity. A breeding ground of creativity and innovation stacked with galleries, artist studios and cultural spaces, cool bars, coffee shops, restaurants, boutiques and startups, Maboneng is an exemplar of Jo'burg's vision for the future.

Be sure to explore the buzzing streets of this hipster paradise and soak up its vibrant atmosphere. But also be savvy about how far away from the main precinct (generally bordered by Berea Rd to the west and Aurer St to the east, Main St to the south and Beacon St/Albertina Sisulu Rd to the north) you wander – it's still rough around the edges here. During the day the free **Maboneng Shuttle** (◎ every 15min 6am-6pm) **FREE** runs in a circuit around the area.

Arts on Main ARTS CENTRE, GALLERY
(Map p336; www.artsonmain.info; 264 Fox St, Maboneng; ◎ 9am-5pm Tue-Sun) **FREE** Occupying a former warehouse complex, the Arts on Main development is one of the key catalysts of the Maboneng precinct. The once-dilapidated building has been transformed into a creative haven with artists' studios, galleries, various retail outlets and restaurants.

The Cosmopolitan   HISTORIC BUILDING
(Map p336; www.thecosmopolitan.joburg; 24 Albrecht St, Maboneng) Standing out against the more modern warehouse conversions in Maboneng is this former pub dating from 1902. The handsome whitewashed building now hosts a number of businesses, while to the rear is a lovely sculpture garden overlooked by an impressive giant mural of Jan van Riebeeck by Gaia and Freddy Sam.

Here you'll find the art gallery **Hazard** (✆082 831 4217; www.hzrd.co.za; ⏰10am-5pm Tue-Sun), teahouse **Yswara** (✆011-005 5111; www.yswara.com; ⏰9am-4.30pm Mon-Fri) and fine-dining restaurant **Sphere Monk** (✆082 422 8158; www.spheremonk.co.za; mains R150-250, 3-course lunch R350, 5-course dinner R420; ⏰11am-10pm Wed-Sun).

👁 Northern Suburbs

Ditsong National
Museum of Military History   MUSEUM
(Map p328; ✆010-001 3515; www.ditsong.org.za; 22 Erlswold Way, Saxonwold; adult/child R40/30; ⏰9am-4.30pm) If you're fascinated by guns, tanks and aircraft, you can see artefacts and implements of destruction from the 1899–1902 Anglo-Boer War through to WWII at this well-curated musem near the zoo.

Zoo Lake   PARK
(Map p328; www.jhbcityparks.com; Lower Park Dr, Parkview; ⏰24hr) **FREE** This busy park is a firm favourite with Jo'burgers from all walks of life. Lace up your trainers and join locals for a run on the paved paths or games on the basketball and five-a-side football courts. Families and groups of teenagers fill the lush grounds on weekends for picnics.

You can also rent a rowboat (R15) and paddle to the fountain at the centre of the lake. Also here is the Zoo Lake Public Pool and the African restaurant **Moyo** (✆011-646 0058; www.moyo.co.za; mains R60-160; ⏰8.30am-10pm Sun-Thu, to 11pm Fri & Sat).

👁 Southern Suburbs

★ Apartheid Museum   MUSEUM
(Map p328; ✆011-309 4700; www.apartheidmuseum.org; cnr Gold Reef Rd & Northern Parkway, Ormonde; adult/child R85/70; ⏰9am-5pm; 🅿) The Apartheid Museum illustrates the rise and fall of South Africa's era of segregation and oppression, and is an absolute must-see. It uses a broad variety of media to provide a chilling insight into the architecture and implementation of the apartheid system, as well as inspiring stories of the struggle towards democracy. It's invaluable in understanding the inequalities and tensions that still exist today. Located 8km south of the city centre, just off the M1 freeway.

👉 Tours

Despite the positive changes that are underway, Jo'burg may still feel a bit intimidating for a number of travellers. The best (and safest) way to get your bearings and gain confidence is in the company of a knowledgeable tour guide. Whether it's a focus on history, architecture, urban regeneration, cultural life or street art that you're after, you'll find an experienced guide to lead the way.

★ Mainstreetwalks   WALKING
(Map p336; ✆011-614 0163; www.mainstreetwalks.co.za; tours R350) Run out of Curiocity backpackers (p338), Mainstreetwalks specialises in tours of Maboneng, where it is based, but it also offers excellent tours of the Inner City, Troyeville and the utterly fascinating Little Addis Ethiopian district. And if you want to get a taste of Jo'burg nightlife, the Underground Pub Crawl (every Friday or on request) is a must.

JoburgPlaces   WALKING
(Map p332; ✆082 894 5216; www.joburgplaces.com; tours R250-300) Gerald Garner's inner-city tours are sure to change your perceptions of downtown Jo'burg. Along with other

---

WORTH A TRIP

LILIESLEAF FARM

A highlight of Jo'burg's northern suburbs is **Liliesleaf Farm** (Map p328; ✆011-803 7882; www.liliesleaf.co.za; 7 George Ave, Rivonia; adult/child R110/50; ⏰8.30am-5pm Mon-Fri, 9am-4pm Sat & Sun). This was the secret headquarters of the ANC (African National Congress) from 1961 until a dramatic raid in 1963 that saw the capture of several of the organisation's leaders including Nelson Mandela. Free tours provide all the background, but you can also explore at your own pace, learning the story of South Africa's liberation struggle through a series of high-tech, interactive exhibits. There's a cafe at the museum.

Maboneng & Around

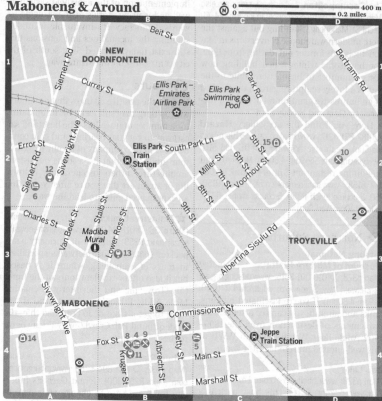

guides Gerald runs five regular itineraries covering the city centre, the mining industry district of Marshalltown, the fashion district and Little Addis, Maboneng, and some of the Inner City's pubs, bars and rooftops.

Past Experiences WALKING
(☏083 701 3046; http://pastexperiences.co.za) Run by Jo Buitendach and her team of hip guides, Past Experiences offers something different, with a range of fascinating tours that have a special focus on graffiti, street art and shopping. Participants have the opportunity to learn about artists' histories and the local graffiti culture. Tours take in Braamfontein, Newtown and the Fashion District.

Mulaudzi Alexandra Tours CYCLING
(Map p328; ☏061 365 7695, 071 279 3654; www.alexandratours.co.za; ⊙2/4hr tour R450/550) Explore Alexandra, one of South Africa's oldest townships, in the company of friendly Jeff Mulaudzi. Born and raised in Alexandra,

this young entrepreneur offers a two- to four-hour bicycle tour where you'll venture into the heart of this lesser-known township. It's a truly enlightening experience. Jeff meets visitors at the Marlboro Gautrain station, where secure parking is available.

🎆 Festivals & Events

Chinese New Year NEW YEAR
(⊙Jan/Feb) Fireworks, street stalls and traditional entertainment mark the start of a new year for Jo'burg's Chinese community at various locations including the First Chinatown on Commissioner St, and Derrick Ave, Cyrildene, the city's biggest Chinatown.

Dance Umbrella DANCE
(www.danceforumsouthafrica.co.za; ⊙Mar) The premier showcase of South African dance performance takes place in March at a variety of venues including Wits Theatre at Wits University.

Maboneng & Around

Rand Easter Show   FAIR
(www.randshow.co.za; ⊘ Apr) All kinds of fun can be had at this entertaining consumer exhibition generally held the first week of April at Jo'burg's Expo Centre.

Joy of Jazz Festival   MUSIC
(www.joyofjazz.co.za; ⊘ Sep) Staged at Sandton Convention Centre, this long-running jazz fest attracts top local and international acts.

Arts Alive Festival   PERFORMING ARTS
(www.arts-alive.co.za; ⊘ Sep) This month-long festival provides a particularly good opportunity to hear excellent music, on or off the official program. Most events are in Newtown.

Johannesburg Carnival   CARNIVAL
(⊘ 31 Dec) This New Year's Eve event sees a parade of choirs, troupes, floats and bands from Hillbrow to Newtown, finishing with a party in Mary Fitzgerald Sq.

🛏 Sleeping

Most accommodation options are scattered across the northern suburbs, and you'll usually need a car or to take a taxi to reach the closest entertainment or shopping options. If you want to be close to the Inner City, your best bet is to stay in Braamfontein or Maboneng. Be mindful, though, that it's not particularly safe to walk around certain inner-city areas alone at night.

Melville, Norwood and Rosebank are the best suburbs to be based if you like to walk to bars and restaurants.

🛏 Inner City & Newtown

Once in Joburg   HOSTEL $
(Map p332; ☑ 087 625 0639; www.onceinjoburg. co.za; 90 De Korte St, Braamfontein; dm/d/tr incl breakfast R372/885/1317) If you like the vibe of a backpackers but the luxury of a hotel, Once in Joburg is the answer. With luxurious white dorms and artfully decorated private rooms, all with en suite, there is something for all travellers. Situated in the heart of Braamfontein, and surrounded by bars, cafes and boutiques, this hostel is a destination in itself.

The facilities such as kitchen and common areas are excellent and the staff clued up and friendly. For a quieter stay, ask for a room on the upper floors.

Urban Backpackers   HOSTEL $
(Map p332; ☑ 081 457 2447; 100 Anderson St, Marshalltown; dm/r with shared bathroom R150/399; 🛜) It's a sign of the improving security of downtown Jo'burg that a fairly cool backpackers has opened here. Basic rooms have some nice decorative touches, such as old movie cameras or LPs. The bathrooms have seen better days, but the rooftop kitchen and the chill-out area are pluses, as is the ground-floor Kafe Noir where you can grab breakfast.

🛏 Braamfontein

Bannister Hotel   HOTEL $
(Map p332; ☑ 011-403 6888; http://bannisterhotel. co.za; 9 De Beer St, Braamfontein; tw & d from R675; 🅿❄🛜) If you're after stumbling access to Braamfontein's bars and restaurants then the Bannister is a no-brainer. Its rooms are modern, cleanly decorated, functional and comfortable, with quality mattresses and prim bathrooms. Another draw is the on-site restaurant and bar. However, expect some traffic noise in most rooms.

Protea Hotel Parktonian
HOTEL $$

(Map p332; ☑ 011-403 5741; https://parktonian. co.za; 120 De Korte St, Braamfontein; s/d from R1100/1300; P❄@❄⊠) The rooms are big but rather plainly decorated at the Parktonian. However, it offers great facilities, rates are good and it's handily set if you want to be close to Park Station (complimentary shuttle to/from the hotel) or Braamfontein's bars and restaurants. There's a fabulous rooftop terrace (with small pool) on which to have an evening drink.

🛏 Maboneng & Around

★Curiocity Johannesburg
HOSTEL $

(Map p336; ☑ 011-614 0163; www.curiocitybackpackers.com; 302 Fox St, Maboneng; dm R180-235, s/d with shared bathroom R330/500; P❄) This is a superlative place to stay thanks to the dedication of young proprietor Bheki Dube. Occupying a converted printing house in the desirable Maboneng precinct, this quirky, offbeat backpackers features clean dorms, unadorned yet neat rooms and a rooftop suite. It also offers good kitchen facilities, a small restaurant and the buzzing Hideout Bar. The congenial atmosphere is hard to beat.

12 Decades Art Hotel
BOUTIQUE HOTEL $$

(Map p336; ☑ 010-410 5460; http://12decadeshotel.co.za; 7th fl, Main Street Life Bldg, 286 Fox St, Maboneng; s/d R950/1260; P❄❄) There are 12 loft-style rooms, each one designed by a different artist and inspired by a particular era in the city's history, at this art-themed hotel in the heart of Maboneng. All have kitchens and, in some, the decor has seen better days. Still, it's a cool concept and all the corridors are plastered in art, too.

Hallmark House
BOUTIQUE HOTEL $$

(Map p336; ☑ 011-402 0220; www.hallmarkhouse. co.za; 54 Siemert Rd, New Doornfontein; r incl breakfast from R990; P❄❄⊠) One of the latest projects of Propertuity, the developers of Maboneng, is this hip hotel with rooms on floors four and five of a renovated 1970s building. The lofty ceiling rooms are spacious, with polished concrete floors, balconies and African print headboards on the beds. There's also a rooftop pool, bar and restaurant with amazing views of central Jo'burg.

A free shuttle bus provides regular transport during the day to the main Maboneng district; walking around here after dark is not advised.

🛏 Melville & Around

★Motel Mi Pi Chi
BOUTIQUE HOTEL $

(Map p339; ☑ 011-726 8844; www.motelmipichi. co.za; 35 4th Ave, Melville; s/d incl breakfast from R645/895; P❄) Book ahead for this gem of a place. The design duo behind Motel Mipichi have transformed several semidetached 1930s abodes along the street into a genuine alternative to the traditional Melville guesthouse experience. It's a minimalist delight, offering a total of 15 calming rooms speckled with pastel splotches and showers that open onto private courtyards.

Sleepy Gecko
GUESTHOUSE $

(Map p339; ☑ 011-482 5224, 082 745 0434; www. sleepygecko.co.za; 84 3rd Ave, Melville; s/d incl breakfast from R550/700; P❄❄⊠) The laidback Gecko is an attractive and very popular guesthouse right at the heart of the 7th St mischief. The rooms outside the house, in a semidetached annexe, are preferable, with less noise and more natural light – our favourites are Fossil and Amarula. The communal areas include a spacious, homey dining area and a tiny front-yard plunge pool.

Arum Place Guest House
GUESTHOUSE $

(Map p328; ☑ 011-482 5247; www.arumplace. co.za; cnr 1st & Motor Sts, Melville; s/d incl breakfast from R780/990; P❄⊠) This 1935 villa on the outskirts of Melville is just the ticket for those seeking a stylish 'home away from home' experience. The eight rooms are different in design and are comfortably spread out on two floors; our choice is 'Touch of Grey', with its own terrace and entrance. In the garden you'll find a highly enticing pool area.

84 on 4th Guesthouse
GUESTHOUSE $

(Map p339; ☑ 011-482 2725; www.84onfourth. co.za; 84 4th Ave, Melville; s/d incl breakfast from R650/800; P❄) A coin's toss from the 7th St hoo-ha, this rambling home is a reliable choice if you want to be in the thick of things. Rooms vary widely – some are small and unpretentious, while others are grand and stylish – and are arranged around a garden.

Hotel QSL on 44
BOUTIQUE HOTEL $$

(Map p328; ☑ 076 222 7700; www.qslon44.com; 12 Quince St, Milpark; s/d incl breakfast from R1200/1320; P❄❄) Adjacent to the 44 Stanley retail development, Hotel QSL takes up the area's industrial makeover theme, of-

Melville

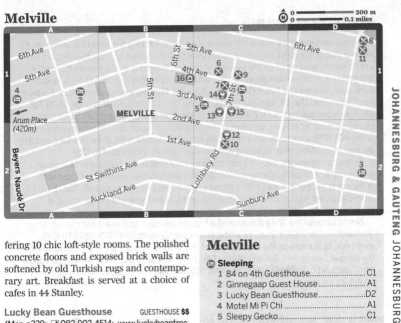

fering 10 chic loft-style rooms. The polished concrete floors and exposed brick walls are softened by old Turkish rugs and contemporary art. Breakfast is served at a choice of cafes in 44 Stanley.

Lucky Bean Guesthouse GUESTHOUSE $$
(Map p339; ☑ 082 902 4514; www.luckybeantree. co.za; 129 1st Ave, Melville; s/d incl breakfast from R820/1130; ⊞ ⚕ ⚟) Owner Conway has turned this villa into a peaceful, welcoming B&B with stylish, large and well-equipped rooms (with private entrances) and great amenities, such as flat-screen TVs, quality bedding, a swimming pool and insider tips on the best Melville has to offer. It's an easy walk to 7th St, Melville's most vibrant strip. Book early, as it fills fast.

Ginnegaap Guest House GUESTHOUSE $$
(Map p339; ☑ 011-482 3507; www.ginnegaap. co.za; 54 4th Ave, Melville; s/d incl breakfast from R770/1000; ⊞ ⚕) Ginnegaap is a contemporary inner-city townhouse attached to an old-world Melville beauty. You can lounge in the established garden that runs right up to the front gate, or slump blissfully on the wrap-around veranda. Service is prompt yet discreet, while the rooms are excellent value for the quality of bedding, the warmth of design and the overall size.

🛏 Northern Suburbs

Brown Sugar Backpackers HOSTEL $
(Map p328; ☑ 011-648 7397; www.brownsugarbackpackers.com; 75 Observatory Ave, Observatory; incl breakfast s/d R475/640, dm/s/d without bathroom R210/425/530; ⊞ @ ⚕ ⚟) This quirky hostel

Melville

🛌 Sleeping
1 84 on 4th Guesthouse	C1
2 Ginnegaap Guest House	A1
3 Lucky Bean Guesthouse	D2
4 Motel Mi Pi Chi	A1
5 Sleepy Gecko	C1

✴ Eating
6 Bambanani	C1
7 Bread & Roses	C1
8 Great Eastern Food Bar	D1
9 Lucky Bean	C1
10 Pablo Eggs Go Bar	C2
11 Service Station	D1

🍸 Drinking & Nightlife
12 Hell's Kitchen	C2
13 Jo'Anna Melt Bar	C1
14 Ratz Bar	C1
15 Six Cocktail Bar & Restaurant	C1

🛍 Shopping
16 27 Boxes	B1

is set in a rambling mansion that looks like a miniature castle and was once the home of a 1970s drugs baron. The wide assortment of options includes en-suite dorms, log cabins and a few quirkily decorated private rooms, as well as TV lounge, pool, and kitchen and laundry facilities.

Joburg Backpackers HOSTEL $
(Map p328; ☑ 011-888 4742; www.joburgbackpackers.com; 14 Umgwezi Rd, Emmarentia; s/d R410/530, dm/s/d with shared bathroom R180/340/440; ⊞ ⚕ ⚟) In the leafy streets of Emmarentia, this pleasant, plainly decorated

MONTHLY ARTS EVENTS

Jo'burg's contemporary visual arts scene is well worth taking the time to discover, and helping that process is First Thursday (www.first-thursdays.co.za/johannesburg). This event, which takes place on the evening of the first Thursday of the month, focuses on the galleries in three main areas: around what is dubbed the Keyes Art Mile in Rosebank such as Everard Read (Map p328; ☑ 011-788 4805; www.everard-read.co.za; 6 Jellicoe Ave; ⊙9am-6pm Mon-Fri, 9am-1pm Sat) FREE and CIRCA Gallery (Map p328; ☑ 011-788 4805; www.everard-read.co.za; 2 Jellicoe Ave; ⊙9am-6pm Mon-Fri, to 1pm Sat) FREE; those clustered close to Wits Art Museum in Braamfontein, such as Stevenson (Map p332; ☑ 011-403 1055; www.stevenson.info; 62 Juta St; ⊙9am-5pm Mon-Fri, 10am-1pm Sat); and the art spaces of Maboneng, including Arts on Main (p334) and Hazard (p335).

Exhibition openings, pop-ups and other special events are scheduled to happen on the night, with participants encouraged to walk between each venue. Rosebank is the most happening area with a street-party atmosphere around Milk Bar (p347), where gourmet food and bar trucks set up and DJs and singers provide musical entertainment.

Not to be outdone, the galleries and art spaces around Troyeville hold the First Sunday in the Valley Jozi! (www.facebook.com/events/1447179428734999/) event during the day on the first Sunday of the month. This is a great time to drop by the unique Spaza Art Gallery (Map p336; ☑ 082 494 3275, 011-614 9354; www.facebook.com/Spaza.Art/; 19 Wilhelmina St, Troyeville; ⊙10am-5pm) as it usually hosts a lunch in its sculpture garden.

---

hostel is clean, safe and well run. The ensuite rooms are terrific value and open onto big grassy lawns; the eight- and 10-bed dorms are spacious and spotless.

Signature Lux Hotel BUSINESS HOTEL $
(Map p328; ☑ 011-085 9500; www.signatureluxhotels.com; 135 West St, Sandton; r R850; P🅿️❄️🛜) We're not sold on the metallic animal print upholstered chairs in the lobby, but otherwise it's a big thumbs up for this new, efficiently run business hotel just steps from Sandton Gautrain station and Nelson Mandela Sq. Wi-fi is high-speed and uncapped, parking free, and rooms small but cleanly decorated.

Rates are R100 cheaper Friday to Sunday, making this a bargain for the area. Plus there's also a day rate (R495, 8am to 4pm) if you just need a place to freshen up before or after a flight or meeting.

★ **Satyagraha House** GUESTHOUSE $$
(Map p328; ☑ 011-485 5928; www.satyagraha-house.com; 15 Pine Rd, Orchards; s/d incl breakfast from R1810/2520; P🅿️🛜) ✈ A wonderful urban sanctuary, Satyagraha is built around the Kraal, a 1907 traditional African-style thatched house where Mohandas (Mahatma) Gandhi lived between 1907 and 1908 with the owner and his friend Herman Kallenbach. This innovative guesthouse offers seven chic

minimalist rooms; two in the original house and the others in contemporary buildings surrounded by a serene garden.

Satyagraha also operates as a museum (admission R70, open 10am to 4pm) detailing the history of Gandhi's time in South Africa and his philosophies on life. A visit can be combined with a vegetarian meal in the Kraal (breakfast/lunch/dinner R170/250/335).

Oasis Boutique Hotel HOTEL $$
(Map p328; ☑ 011-807 4351; www.oasis.sa.com; 29 Homestead Rd, Rivonia; s/d incl breakfast from R1100/1450; P🅿️❄️🛜🖥️) This is a delightful suburban hideaway, presided over by an astute couple who cater for businesspeople and holidaymakers with equal aplomb. The lush garden surrounds feature a kidney-shaped pool and a spacious *lapa* (South African thatched gazebo). The 14 rooms vary in size and price, but all are stylish and tastefully furnished.

Peech Hotel BOUTIQUE HOTEL $$
(Map p328; ☑ 011-537 9797; http://thepeech.co.za; 61 North St, Melrose; r incl breakfast R3050; P🅿️❄️🛜🖥️) ✈ Made up of four converted duplex apartment blocks scattered amid a beautifully landscaped garden, the Peech is indeed a peach. The 16 rooms are amply sized and feature subtle, trendy design details, but it's the setting that's the pull here.

Parkwood BOUTIQUE HOTEL $$
(Map p328; ☑011-880 1748; www.theparkwood.com; 72 Worcester Rd, Parkwood; s/d incl breakfast from R2000/2200; P❋@☎☙) Comfort, charm and atmosphere: this superb venture has it all. It offers the chance to unplug in a series of separate, narrow, self-contained buildings that ensure discretion during your stay. The rooms are all class, thanks to the interior-designer owner, with contemporary art facing stone walls, day beds facing fountains, two lap pools, a library and a gym. Dinners on request.

Liz at Lancaster B&B $$
(Map p328; ☑011-442 8083; www.lizatlancaster.co.za; 79 Lancaster Ave, Craighall Park; s/d incl breakfast from R895/1090; P@☎☙) It's pure pleasure to walk into this modern oasis after a day's sightseeing. The bathrooms are beautifully kept, the rooms are well appointed and comfortable, the breakfasts are generous and the welcome from Liz is more than friendly. All units – two rooms, three flatlets and two family-friendly cottages – have their own entrances and courtyards. A safe choice.

Melrose Place Guest Lodge HOTEL $$
(Map p328; ☑083 457 4021, 011-442 5231; www.melroseplace.co.za; 12A North St, Melrose; s/d incl breakfast R1375/1700; P☎☙) Life feels less hurried in this oasis of calm, between Rosebank and Sandton. This secluded country-style home harbours 33 rooms and is perfect for those who crave space – the expansive garden is a good place to mooch around and soak up the tranquil charm, or you can relax in the large swimming pool. Evening meals are available on request.

Radisson Blu Gautrain Hotel HOTEL $$
(Map p328; ☑011-245 8000; www.radissonblu.com; cnr West St & Rivonia Rd, Sandton; d R1350-5980; P❋☎☙) Rates can vary widely at this slick business hotel that's a brisk jaywalk from Sandton's Gautrain station exit, but are cheapest on the weekends. The rooms sport sophisticated design, good views and large bathrooms. The restaurant is excellent and there's a splash pool on the balcony next to the 3rd floor lobby.

Ascot Hotel HOTEL $$
(Map p328; ☑011-483 3371; www.ascothotel.co.za; 59 Grant Ave, Norwood; r incl breakfast from R1220; P@☎) This is a stylish small hotel with a red-roped lobby entrance, adjacent day spa and friendly management.

The sense of affordable prestige suits the suburb's easy-going attitude. Rooms are smallish but well presented and comfortable. The prime selling point here is the location, within hollering distance of some of the neighbourhoods's best bars and restaurants.

Clico Hotel BOUTIQUE HOTEL $$
(Map p328; ☑086 636 8770; www.clicohotel.com; 27 Sturdee Ave, Rosebank; s/d incl breakfast from R2245/2685; P❋☎☙) There are nine very pleasantly decorated and comfortable rooms at this heritage property that has a Cape Dutch design. Pluses are its highly regarded restaurant (open to nonguests from 6.30pm to 9.30pm) and proximity to the galleries of the Keyes Art Mile and shops of Rosebank.

Ilali House BOUTIQUE HOTEL $$
(Map p328; ☑082 567 5142; http://ilali.co.za; 19 Chester Rd, Parkwood; s/d incl breakfast from R800/1000; P☎) There's no sign for this characterful guesthouse, which offers six generally spacious rooms all differently decorated, most featuring quirky prints of maps, the works of Vladimir Tretchikoff or other South African artists. There's a lovely shaded courtyard to relax in and you're not far from Rosebank and the Keyes Art Mile.

★**Residence** BOUTIQUE HOTEL $$$
(Map p328; ☑011-853 2480; https://theresidence-portfolio.co.za; 17 4th Ave, Houghton; d incl breakfast from R3495; P❋☎☙) If you could smell charm, this super-smooth boutique hotel set in a former embassy would reek of it to high heaven. This quiet little paradise is the epitome of a refined cocoon, with 17 opulent, individually designed suites and swish communal areas. After a day of turf pounding, take a dip in the stress-melting pool or relax in the spa.

Saxon Hotel, Villas & Spa HOTEL $$$
(Map p328; ☑011-292 6000; www.saxon.co.za; 36 Saxon Rd, Sandhurst; ste incl breakfast from R7655; P❋@☎☙) The pride of Sandhurst is a palatial suite hotel, where Mandela completed his famed memoir. If you're not bowled over by features such as private elevators, personal attendants and the country's finest day spa, you certainly will be by the nifty pool, the exclusively designed suites and the top-notch restaurant presided over by famed Cape Town chef Luke Dale-Roberts.

RICH T PHOTO / SHUTTERSTOCK ©

1. Freedom Park (p362), Pretoria

Visit this must-see memorial and museum that honours fallen South Africans in all major conflicts.

2. Apartheid Museum (p335), Johannesburg

This compelling museum examines the rise and fall of South Africa's era of segregation and oppression.

3. Orlando Towers (p358), Soweto

Bungee jump from, or simply admire from a distance, these vibrantly painted towers.

4. Maboneng (p334), Johannesburg

Spend time wandering this buzzing area, filled with galleries, cool bars, restaurants and hip boutiques.

54 on Bath
BOUTIQUE HOTEL **$$$**

(Map p328; ☎011-344 8500; www.tsogosun.com/54-on-bath; 54 Bath Ave, Rosebank; r incl breakfast from R3500; P❄🖥🏊) Best described as 'urban chic', this sexy number is a short amble from Rosebank's shopping malls. The 75 rooms are spacious and elegantly restrained, and the uber-cool 4th-floor garden terrace and pool deck is a great place to decompress. Extra in-house perks include a top-notch restaurant, two bars and free access to a fitness centre in the nearby mall.

Ten Bompas
BOUTIQUE HOTEL **$$$**

(Map p328; ☎011-341 0282; www.tenbompas.com; 10 Bompas Rd, Dunkeld West; ste incl breakfast R4000; P❄🖥🏊) In the upmarket neighbourhood of Dunkeld West and within walking distance of several nice places to eat and shop is this sleek hotel with 10 very spacious, elegant rooms. Dark wood and savannah hues colour an exquisite private collection of African art. Its restaurant is also a destination in its own right.

✖ Eating

Jo'burg is a fabulous city for foodies, with restaurants to suit all tastes and budgets. Areas to zone in on that offer clusters of places to dine and the ability to stroll between venues include Melville, Greenside, Braamfontein, Parkhurst, Norword, Rosebank and Maboneng.

✖ Inner City & Newtown

During weekdays there are plenty of cafes, if you need a break while strolling around, but many places shut at night.

★ Urbanologi
FUSION **$**

(Map p332; ☎011-492 1399; www.urbanologi.co.za; 1 Fox St, Ferreiras Dorp; mains R60-80; ⊙noon-10pm Mon-Sat, to 3.45pm Sun; 🍴) Even if Mad Giant's very quaffable beers are not your thing, do not pass over on the microbrewery's fabulous restaurant. Serving an inventive range of delicious Asian-inspired tapas dishes, you really can't go wrong with taste sensations such as the yakitori chicken with spicy chimichurri sauce or teriyaki poached heirloom baby carrots with kumquat marmalade.

City Perk Café
CAFE **$$**

(Map p332; ☎011-838 9755; www.cityperkcafe.co.za; 70 Fox St, Marshalltown; mains R60-150; ⊙6.30am-3.30pm Mon-Fri; 🛜) Good luck with securing a seat at this deservedly popular cafe, which makes splendid breakfasts, sandwiches, wraps, grills and salads, as well as serving decent coffee at affordable prices. Lunch for under R80? Count us in! There's outdoor seating on warm days.

Homestead
SOUTH AFRICAN **$$**

(Map p332; ☎011-689 1000; http://homestead.co.za; 58 Anderson St, Marshalltown; mains R45-110, lunch/dinner buffet R185/215; ⊙6am-10pm) On the ground floor of the Reef Hotel, this large restaurant has a relaxed vibe and pleasingly kooky industrial interior. The visibly busy kitchen generates traditional meals without fanfare: stir-fried beef, pork ribs, burgers and sandwiches.

✖ Braamfontein

Post
CAFE **$**

(Map p332; ☎072 248 2078; 70 Juta St, Braamfontein; mains R45-75; ⊙6.30am-4pm Mon-Fri, 8.30am-2pm Sat; 🛜) Fill up at this great little cafe before (or after) delving into Braamfontein. Come for delicious breakfasts, gourmet sandwiches, fresh salads and changing lunch specials. The chalkboard menu adds to the casual atmosphere. Oh, and it serves delectable coffee.

WAM Cafe
CAFE **$**

(Map p332; ☎011-717 7123; cnr Jorissen St & Jan Smuts Ave, Braamfontein; mains R20-60; ⊙7am-4pm Mon-Fri, 10am-2pm Sat; 🛜) Attached to the Wits Art Museum (p330), this is one of the most popular cafes in Braamfontein – a slick, modern, design-led eatery with large picture windows looking onto the street. Actually, the real reason most are here is for the lunch buffet – you pay by the weight of what you choose to eat.

86 Public
PIZZA **$**

(Map p332; ☎011-403 3055; www.86public.co.za; cnr Melle & Juta Sts, Braamfontein; mains R65-105; ⊙11.30am-10pm, to midnight Sat) Right in the heart of Braamfontein, 86 Public does brisk business with students and office workers – always a sign that you've found a good bargain. The pie ain't gourmet and doesn't claim to be, but if you're craving a decent slice to go, this is your baby. There's a huge variety of toppings.

Smokehouse & Grill
STEAK **$$**

(Map p332; ☎011-403 1395; http://thesmokehouseandgrill.co.za/; cnr Juta & De Beer Sts, Braamfontein; mains R75-215; ⊙noon-10pm Mon-

Sat) Students, hipsters, moms and pops: everyone dives into this busy steakhouse for a rockin' feed. Get messy with slow-pit-smoked ribs, slabs of juicy steak and succulent burgers, or watch the waist with the lightly seasoned grilled-chicken options or classic salads. Good wines and beers, too.

✗ Maboneng

Little Addis Café
ETHIOPIAN $

(Map p336; ✆082 683 8675; 280 Fox St, Maboneng; mains R50-90; ⊙12.30-9pm Tue-Sun) A great experience for gastronauts, this eatery is all about spicy *doro wot* (chicken stew), *kitfo* (mince meat) and *tibs* (fried meat and vegetables), served traditionally on plate-sized *injera* (sourdough pancakes), which you rip up and use to eat with instead of cutlery.

Eat Your Heart Out
DELI $

(Map p336; ✆072 586 0600; www.eatyourheartout. co.za; cnr Kruger & Fox Sts, Maboneng; mains R50-88; ⊙7.30am-4pm Tue-Sun) The best spot in Maboneng to start the day. The Israeli breakfast – omelette, toasted pita, diced salad, pickled cabbage and cottage cheese – is the highlight, while the bagels and cheesecakes will leave your taste buds reeling. Healthy fruit juices, great coffee and sweet treats are also on offer, and there's outdoor seating.

Che
ARGENTINE $$

(Map p336; ✆011-614 0264; http://cheargentine-grill.co.za; 303 Fox St, Maboneng; ⊙noon-11pm Tue-Sun) This seductive restaurant occupies a dimly lit former warehouse space. On the menu are real-deal Argentine dishes such as *mollejas* (veal sweetbreads cooked in lemon) and *empanadas* (savoury pastries), but its the grilled meats that most customers opt for and we can't blame them.

On the first Tuesday of the month it has a live tango performance. Attached is the secretive cocktail bar Al Lado (✆011-614 0140; ⊙1-11pm Wed, to 2am Thu-Sat, to midnight Sun).

Pata Pata
INTERNATIONAL $$

(Map p336; ✆073 036 9031; 286 Fox St, Maboneng; mains R75-170; ⊙7am-10.30pm) The hip crowd may have moved on, but this Maboneng classic still delivers a winning formula of rustic-chic decor, beautifully presented cuisine and attitude-loaded staff. The eclectic menu runs the gamut from pizzas and burgers to grilled meats and seafood. In the warmer months tables spill out onto the pavement. There's live music most evenings.

✗ Melville

Melville is one of Jo'burg's hippest eating districts, with a wide selection of restaurants and cafes along 7th St and 4th Ave, most with outdoor seating.

Service Station
BISTRO $

(Map p339; ✆011-726 1701; www.servicestation-cafe.co.za; Bamboo Centre, cnr 9th St & Rustenburg Rd, Melville; mains R60-80; ⊙7.30am-5pm Mon-Fri, 8am-5pm Sat, 8.30am-3pm Sun) In a far corner of Melville, Service Station is that easy-to-miss 'secret spot' that locals like to recommend. Come here for bountiful breakfasts featuring flapjacks and brioches, as well as a kaleidoscope of freshly prepared goodies – think grilled vegetables with cheese, gourmet burgers and grilled beef with caramelised onions. It also has irresistible ice creams and superb coffee.

Pablo Eggs Go Bar
BREAKFAST $

(Map p339; ✆063 335 9348; 2 7th St, Melville; dishes R40-100; ⊙6.30am-4pm) You have to love this place for the name alone, but the Middle Eastern–inspired all-day breakfast menu also keeps the hipsters and foodies coming back. Try the upmarket Egg 'n' Soldiers, where fingers of toast are replaced by asparagus wrapped in bacon.

Lucky Bean
SOUTH AFRICAN $$

(Map p339; ✆011-482 5572; www.luckybeantree. co.za; 16 7th St, Melville; mains R110-165; ⊙11am-9.30pm Tue-Thu, to 11pm Fri & Sat; 🐾) Low lighting, slick tunes, a decked-out cocktail bar and waiters who happily skip down a flight of stairs to serve – Lucky Bean is one of most atmospheric places to dine in Melville. The food is spot on, too – light any-time meals, a few vegetarian options, gamey stews, creative starters and scrumptious steaks (teriyaki ostrich fillet, anyone?).

Bread & Roses
CAFE $$

(Map p339; ✆011-482 1858; www.facebook. com/BreadandRosesCafeandBistro; 80 4th Ave, Melville; mains R80-150; ⊙7.30am-6pm Tue-Fri, 8am-5pm Sat, 8am-4pm Sun; 🐾) Colourful and quirky, Bread & Roses is a typical Melville cafe, and the mismatched furniture and African prints are part of the charm. When it comes to the food, however, there are no compromises. The salmon potato rosti is brunch perfection. With free wi-fi it's a popular hangout for local e-entrepreneurs and students.

Great Eastern Food Bar
ASIAN $$

(Map p339; ☑ 011-482 2910; Bamboo Centre, cnr 9th St & Rustenburg Rd, Melville; mains R60-165; ⊙noon-11pm Tue-Fri, 1-11pm Sat, 1-8pm Sun) If you think Jozi is a dud at creative Asian food, prepare to eat your words – and everything in sight – at this well-priced, obscenely delicious eatery located on the roof of the trendy Bamboo Centre. Musts include kimchi dumplings, sashimi tacos and smoked trout.

Bambanani
INTERNATIONAL $$

(Map p339; ☑ 011-482 2900; www.bambanani. biz; 85 4th Ave, Melville; mains R90-180; ⊙8am-8pm, to 9pm Sat & Sun; 🛜🦽) Not your average eatery, Bambanani is a concept restaurant that caters for families. Picture this: at the back is a huge deck and garden area with a massive, multilevelled children's play den. Foodwise, it cooks up a wide array of dishes, including pizzas, pastas, salads and various nibbles that will put a smile on everybody's face.

✖ Milpark

Leopard
INTERNATIONAL $

(Map p328; ☑ 011-482 9356; www.leopardfood-company.com; 44 Stanley Ave, Milpark; mains R60-90; ⊙8am-8pm) Chef Andrea Burgener is known for her excellent take-out deli food, which includes a changing rainbow of eclectic dishes such as taro-leaf masala, and quail stuffed with cashews and coriander, all prepared with the best ingredients available. Its new location inside the 44 Stanley (p352) precinct has a few perch-at-a-counter seats with the promise of more to come.

Salvation Cafe
CAFE $

(Map p328; ☑ 011-482 7795; www.salvationcafe. co.za; 44 Stanley Ave, Milpark; mains R60-100; ⊙8am-3pm Tue-Thu, Sat & Sun, to 8pm Fri) Organic deliciousness awaits at this casual cafe (bonus points for the covered veranda and inviting courtyard). All bases are covered, from baked treats and vibrant salads to made-from-scratch burgers, delicious wraps and scrumptious breakfasts (served until 11.45am). Local gourmands rave about the eggs Benedict and carrot cake.

Il Giardino Degli Ulivi
ITALIAN $$

(Map p328; ☑ 011-482 4978; www.ilgiardino. co.za; 44 Stanley Ave, Milpark; mains R69-210; ⊙11.30am-10pm Tue-Sat, to 4pm Sun) Inside the hip 44 Stanley (p352) precinct, Il Giardino feels like a charming old-world trattoria, its leafy courtyard the backdrop to nourishing dishes at reasonable prices. Top selections: gorgonzola gnocchi, beef carpaccio with Parmesan cheese and bubbling thin-crust pizzas. There's a small but respectable wine list, with equally fair prices.

✖ Greenside & Linden

Not far from Melville, the suburb of Greenside also has a couple of excellent restaurants and trendy bars, mainly clustered along Gleneagles Rd and Greenway Rd.

Heading slightly further northwest is Linden, where the restaurant strip is focused around 4th Ave and 7th St.

Momo Baohaus
ASIAN $

(Map p328; ☑ 010-900 4889; http://momobaohaus.com; 139 Greenway, Greenside; mains R52-90; ⊙11am-3pm & 5-9pm Tue-Sat, 11am-4pm Sun) Minimalist decor greets visitors to Momo Baohaus, where fusion Asian tapas is the order of the day. Dine on crispy pork potstickers, sushi rolls and the fluffiest baos followed by veggie bowls that are as colourful as they are flavourful.

Dukes Burgers
BURGERS $$

(Map p328; ☑ 011-486 0824; www.dukesburgers. co.za; 14 Gleneagles Rd, Greenside; mains R54-130; ⊙11.30am-9pm Sun-Thu, to 10pm Fri & Sat; 🅿) Elevating the humble burger to high art, this inviting and warmly lit eatery on a restaurant-lined stretch of Gleneagles Rd serves up a wide variety of burgers. The vegetarian options are tops, especially when paired with sweet-potato wedges. There's a sheltered courtyard out back.

Brian Lara Rum Eatery
CARIBBEAN $$$

(Map p328; ☑ 076-320 9739; www.facebook.com/ thebrianlara; 54 4th Ave, Linden; mains R150-300; ⊙11am-11pm Tue-Sun) *Now* you're on holiday – you've entered tropical paradise. When you're sipping a pina colada out of a real pineapple and enjoying old fashioneds made the old fashioned way, you'll forget that you're not actually in the Caribbean. The delightful rum-soaked food is likely to contribute to that effect.

✖ Norwood

Grant Ave is lined with cafes and restaurants, most of which are open every day, and provide a cross-section of street life.

Schwarma Co
MIDDLE EASTERN **$$**

(Map p328; ☑ 011-483 1776; www.schwarmacompany.co.za; 71 Grant Ave, Norwood; mains R80-190; ⊘11am-10pm; ⊅) This Jo'burg institution is renowned for delicious platters of shwarma (meat sliced off a spit, served in pitas with chopped tomatoes), yummy kebabs and copious salads; for dessert, try the belt-bustingly good baklava. Grab an upstairs table on the breezy terrace and observe Grant Ave's gentle mayhem down below as you dig in.

Baha Taco
MEXICAN **$$**

(Map p328; ☑ 076 694 7400; www.bahataco.co.za; 39 Grant Ave, Norwood; mains R50-150; ⊘noon-9pm Tue-Sun) Using the freshest ingredients and traditional cooking methods, Baha actually started as a food market stall. But it has grown into the Grant Ave institution that it is today because of the popularity of its consistently excellent food. Handmade tortillas and specials such as goat empanadas ensure an authentic Mexican experience. Wash it down with small-batch craft tequila.

✕ Parkview, Parkhurst, Parktown North & Rosebank

Tyrone Ave in Parkview is a lovely neighbourhood spot to search out an appealing restaurant. Not far away both 4th Ave in Parkhurst and 3rd Ave in Parkton North offer similar tasty pickings. If none of them suffice, there's a good cluster of places in Rosebank along what is becoming known as the Keyes Art Mile, along and around Keyes Ave.

Croft & Co
CAFE **$**

(Map p328; ☑ 011-646 3634; www.facebook.com/CroftAndCo; 66 Tyrone Ave, Parkview; mains R40-110; ⊘6.30am-5pm Mon-Wed, to 8pm Thu & Fri, 7am-2pm Sat, 7am-noon Sun) This popular suburban cafe is the perfect spot for a leisurely brunch or quick coffee. The menu is simple and uses locally sourced ingredients. Bacon and sausage lovers will be hard pressed to find a better serving elsewhere, and the homemade Portuguese bread is a great accompaniment.

La Boqueria
BISTRO **$$**

(Map p328; www.laboqueria.co.za; 17 3rd Ave, Parktown North; mains R80-180; ⊘7am-10pm Mon-Thu, to 11pm Fri & Sat, to 5pm Sun) Taking inspiration from global street food, La Boqueria serves up gourmet snacks and meals in a dramatic double-storey space with walls covered with plants and giant murals. Try tapas with one of the craft gin cocktails, or for something more filling feast on Mexican cola chicken skewers or Hawaiian poke bowls – everything is done well and portions are generous.

Coalition Pizza
PIZZA **$$**

(Map p328; ☑ 010-900 4987; www.coalitionpizza.co.za; 2 Bolton Rd, Rosebank; pizzas R75-125; ⊘noon-10pm Mon-Sat, to 8pm Sun) The white-washed walls and simple decor of this little hole-in-the-wall eatery belie the excellence of the food on offer. Specialising in Neapolitan pizzas, the menu is concise with only a handful of options, but the crispy pies are freshly made in a wood-fired oven with traditional ingredients and will leave you saying 'mama mia!'

Milk Bar
CAFE **$$**

(Map p328; ☑ 083 649 3339; www.facebook.com/milkbarSA; 21 Keyes Ave, Rosebank; mains R80-150; ⊘6am-5pm Mon-Wed, to 11pm Thu & Fri, to 4pm Sat & Sun) Bright colours and traditional African fabrics make this cute little cafe a feast for the eyes. The interesting takes on traditional meals, such as mini bunny chows, are a feast for the taste buds. With tables spilling onto the street it's a popular hangout for locals.

★ Marble
SOUTH AFRICAN **$$$**

(Map p328; ☑ 010-594 5550; www.marble.restaurant; 3rd fl, Trumpet Bldg, 19 Keyes Ave, Rosebank; mains R165-265; ⊘noon-3.30pm & 6-9.30pm; ☏) Currently one of Jo'burg's hottest restaurants, this is braai (barbecue) given a luxe makeover. Chef David Higgs and his cloth-capped team in the open kitchen allow the quality of meat and fish (and occasional vegetable – take a bow, cauliflower) to shine as it hits the flames. Portions are generous and service effusive.

Grillhouse
STEAK **$$$**

(Map p328; ☑ 011-880 3945; www.thegrillhouse.co.za; The Firs, cnr Oxford Rd & Bierman Ave, Rosebank; mains R75-300; ⊘noon-2.30pm & 6.30-9.30pm Sun-Fri, 6.30-9.30pm Sat) Get an honest-to-goodness Jozi steakhouse experience at this New York-style steakhouse institution. Rub elbows with other red-meat lovers and choose your cut: prime sirloin, T-bone, spare ribs or fillet. Thick chops of veal, ostrich medallions and various seafood options are also on tap, as are heaping portions of character thanks to the skilled waiters and cosy decor.

✕ Sandton

The many eating options in this affluent suburb are centred on the huge shopping malls of Nelson Mandela Sq and Sandton City Mall.

Thief   BISTRO $$
(Map p328; ☑011-783 1570; www.thiefrestaurant. co.za; 110 Victoria Ave, Parkmore, Sandton; mains R65-200; ☺7am-11pm Tue-Fri, 8am-11pm Sat, noon-11pm Sun; ☎) Just off 11th St, this easy-to-miss restaurant and wine bar is a convivial place in an otherwise unpromising area. It's a stylish place with exposed beams and industrial touches, serving superb bistro food such pan fried hake and beef fillet. The menu has just a few starters, three or four mains and a handful of desserts – and all are very flavourful.

Bukhara   INDIAN $$
(Map p328; ☑011-883 5555; www.bukhara.com; Nelson Mandela Sq, cnr West & Maude Sts, Sandton; mains R130-210; ☺noon-3pm & 6-11pm Mon-Sat, to 10pm Sun) One of the best Indian restaurants in town, Bukhara manages to be atmospheric despite its mall location. It serves authentic, richly flavoured tikka masala, korma, curry and tandoori dishes. It's a classy place complete with marble floor, teak furniture and ochre walls. Needless to say, service is excellent.

✕ Fordsburg & Brixton

★Breezeblock   CAFE $
(Map p328; ☑076 705 3992; http://breezeblock. co.za; 29 Chiswick St, Brixton; mains R26-65; ☺7am-5pm Tue-Fri, to 4pm Sat & Sun; ☎✐) The designers have a done a grand job transforming this old Chinese restaurant into a pastel-shaded haven of mid-century cool amid the gritty 'burb of Brixton. Many come here for its delicious breakfast dishes, which include tempting options such as huevos rancheros and baked pancakes, but find themselves lingering over coffee, seduced by the appealing atmosphere.

Roving Bantu Kitchen   SOUTH AFRICAN $
(Map p328; ☑072 223 2648; www.facebook.com/ rovingbantu; Caroline St, Brixton; mains R85, music cover charge Sun R100; ☺6pm-midnight Fri, noon-midnight Sat & Sun) Sifiso Ntuli is the genial patron of this great little spot keeping it real in Brixton. Bookings are essential and there's no written menu – instead the cook comes out to introduce the dishes of the day,

which could include crispy light samosas, spicy chicken wings, a chicken curry or a beef stew.

Bismillah   INDIAN $$
(Map p328; ☑011-838 8050; www.bismillahrestaurant.co.za; 78 Mint Rd, Fordsburg; mains R50-140; ☺8am-10.30pm) Over in Fordsburg you'll find the best Indian food in Jo'burg. While it's far from fancy, Bismillah is, we reckon, the pick of the lot. The menu is classic North Indian – tandooris, tikkas, biryanis and masalas are all here, plus a few surprises – while the service is refreshingly earnest. Best of all, it's super cheap.

✕ Eastern Suburbs

Jo'burg's main Chinatown is Derrick Ave, Cyrildene, off Observatory Rd. Here you'll find a number of cheap, good Chinese restaurants.

Troyeville Hotel   PORTUGUESE $$
(Map p336; ☑011-402 7709; www.troyevillehotel. co.za; 1403 Albert Sisulu St, Troyeville; mains R60-280; ☺11am-9pm Sun-Thu, to 10pm Fri & Sat; ☎) This character-filled hotel is a memorable place for a long meal. It has been frequented by the Portuguese community since well before the paint began to peel. The Iberian influence is found in the delicious Mozambican prawns, the tasty *feijoada* (bean stew) and the chilled red wine.

★Yeoville Dinner Club   AFRICAN $$$
(Map p328; ☑083 447 4235; www.facebook.com/ pg/yeovilledinnerclub/community/; 24 Rockey St, Bellevue; dinner R425; ☑) Jo'burg's most memorable meal out is in this artily decorated cramped room with a balcony overlooking Rockey St, heart of the much-bad-mouthed, inner-city area of Yeoville. Sanza Sandile is your host and chef, and what an impression he makes both with his wonderful stories about the city and delicious mainly pan-African vegetarian (there is fish) dishes.

🍷 Drinking & Nightlife

Jo'burg has an ever-revolving bar scene and you'll find everything from crusty bohemian haunts to chic cocktail lounges and conservative wine bars here. Maboneng and Braamfontein have some great lively places (several with rooftop views), but much of the nightlife is in the northern suburbs, particularly around Melville, Greenside and Rosebank.

Inner City & Newtown

★ Mad Giant   BREWERY
(Map p332; ☑ 011-492 0901; www.madgiant.co.za; 1 Fox St, Newtown; ☺ noon-10pm Mon-Sat, to 6pm Sun) A superlative addition to Jozi's inner city, Mad Giant offers excellent craft beers (brewed on-site) paired with delectable Asian-inspired tapas dishes at its classy restaurant Urbanologi (p344). The spectacular steampunk-style space has an award-winning design that seems partly fashioned from a giant Meccano set.

Rand Club   BAR
(Map p332; ☑ 011-870 4276; http://randclub.co.za; 33 Loveday St, Marshalltown; ☺ noon-8pm Tue-Fri, 10am-6pm Sat) Founded in 1887, this version of the illustrious (and once whites- and men-only) club dates from 1904. It's now open to all, and so long as you're not dressed too shabbily you can enter and order a drink at the ground-floor bar, which has a fine antique wooden bar (at 31m, reputed to be the longest in Africa!).

Cramers Coffee   CAFE
(Map p332; http://cramerscoffee.com; 17 Harrison St, Marshalltown; ☺ 6am-6.30pm Mon-Fri, 7am-5pm Sat; ☎) Some say the coffee served at this always-bustling, no-lingering joint west of Gandhi Sq is among the best in town. There's also an array of sweet temptations, including croissants and muffins.

Carfax   CLUB
(Map p332; ☑ 011-834 9187; https://carfax.co.za; 39 Gwigwi Mrwebi St, Newtown) Check online for details of events such as progressive/deep house and hip-hop parties, and the more interesting international acts, at this giant industrial space in Newtown.

Braamfontein

★ Great Dane   BAR
(Map p332; ☑ 081 594 6032; www.facebook.com/greatdanebar; 5 De Beer St, Braamfontein; ☺ noon-2am Thu-Sat) Fun and friendly Great Dane is one of the mainstays of the ever-changing Braamfontein bar strip. The music is very danceable and staff make you feel like friends. Early on it's a good place for warm-up drinks, especially in the appealing courtyard hung with old lampshades; come midnight the tables are cleared and the dancing commences.

Doubleshot Coffee & Tea   COFFEE
(Map p332; ☑ 083 380 4127; www.doubleshot.co.za; cnr Juta & Melle Sts, Braamfontein; ☺ 8am-4.30pm Mon-Sat) Artisanal coffee, tea and a few baked treats is all you'll get at this roaster but, man, are they good. The espresso is dark and intense, brewed by competent baristas and swilled by a bevy of cool kids and clued-in corporate people.

Republic of 94   BAR
(Map p332; ☑ 083 342 3991; www.facebook.com/RepublicOf94; 94 Juta St, Braamfontein; ☺ noon-2am Wed-Sun) The sheer length of the bar makes this high-end Braamfontein haunt worth a visit, and the length of the drinks menu is reason enough to stay. There's also a roomy back courtyard where DJs get the crowds dancing later on.

Metanoia   BAR
(Map p332; ☑ 011-339 1551; www.metanoia.joburg; Shop 1, 73 Juta St, Braamfontein; ☺ 10am-10pm Mon-Thu, to 2am Fri & Sat) Metanoia offers a great terrace overlooking De Beer St (where the entrance is) for people-watching, an enticingly chic interior and a medley of alcoholic libations including cocktails served in fishbowl-like glasses, and a Mediterranean-inspired menu of tapas, flatbreads and the like.

Kitchener's Carvery Bar   PUB
(Map p332; ☑ 011-403 0166; http://kitcheners.co.za; cnr Juta & De Beer Sts, Braamfontein; ☺ 11am-midnight, to 4am Fri & Sat) What used to be a grand colonial hotel is now hipster central and epitomises the contemporary swagger of Braamfontein. By day it's a popular pub, known for its knockout burgers, fish 'n' chips and vast choice of drinks served in vintage surrounds; by night DJs spin soul, funk and electro.

Maboneng & Around

★ Living Room   BAR
(Map p336; ☑ 084 529 9006; www.livingroomjozi.co.za; 5th fl, Main Change Bldg, 20 Kruger St, Maboneng; ☺ 11am-10pm Wed-Sat, 11am-7pm Sun) This plant-packed oasis offers great city views of Jo'burg. Enjoy cold beers, cocktails and bar snacks as you watch the city go by at this rooftop jungle decorated with fairy lights.

Uncle Merv's   CAFE
(Map p336; ☑ 083 659 4233; cnr Fox & Kruger Sts, Maboneng; ☺ 7am-4.30pm) This hole-in-the-wall is famous for its perfectly brewed

coffee, decadent banana bread, yummy croissants and killer shakes. Our favourite is the Macci Porter, a rich blend of tahini, banana, soy milk, cashews and dates. Stackable chairs and nearby pavement benches provide places to sit. Very Maboneng.

Nine Barrels
WINE BAR

(Map p336; ☑079 458 5350; http://ninebarrels. com; 12 Lower Ross St, Maboneng; ☺11am-2am Wed-Sun) Combine your wine sipping in Maboneng with some contemporary art at this bar, which shares a building with the gallery Agog (www.agog.co.za). As well as the ground-floor bar, where monthly events showcasing the products of different South African wine farms are held, there's a rooftop space with superb views of the street-art-decorated district.

Marabi
COCKTAIL BAR

(Map p336; ☑010-591 2872; http://themarabi-club.com; 47 Sivewright Ave, New Doornfontein; ☺6.30am-midnight Wed-Sat, noon-5pm Sun) Mellow live jazz music is the background sound to this slick and sophisticated bar and restaurant hidden behind the Hallmark Hotel. Reservations are advised, as is one of the very tasty cocktails such as the Thai green curry martini or pomegranate mojito.

🍸 Melville

Hell's Kitchen
BAR

(Map p339; ☑079 980 9591; www.hellskitchen. co.za; 4 7th St, Melville; ☺12.30pm-1.30am Mon-Sat, noon-10pm Sun) Forget which year it is as you enter this speakeasy-themed bar that has rooms hidden behind bookshelves and a tattoos and bikers vibe. An extensive cocktail menu, cold craft beer and food prepared on an open flame will snap you back to the present. There's also live music on the weekends.

Jo'Anna Melt Bar
BAR

(Map p339; ☑072 733 5966; www.facebook. com/JoAnnaMeltBar; 7 7th St, Melville; ☺noon-2am Mon-Sat) The massive, rectangular bar takes centre stage in this lively place awash with people getting jolly on the abundant cocktails and craft beers. The decor – exposed brickwork and a pressed tin ceiling – exudes a slightly more sophisticated air than other Melville bars.

Six Cocktail Bar & Restaurant
COCKTAIL BAR

(Map p339; ☑011-482 8306; 7th St, Melville; ☺noon-2am) Six has single-handedly shifted

the 7th St dress code, thanks to its so-far-above-average cocktails and so-better-looking-than-you clientele. This is a wonderful place for a drink. Fabulous artwork, soft orange and red colour scheme, iconic reggae, and soul and house music at a level conducive to hearing key questions: want another one?

🍺 Milpark

Stanley Beer Yard
CRAFT BEER

(Map p328; ☑011-482 5791; www.44stanley. co.za; 44 Stanley Ave, Milpark; ☺noon-11pm Tue-Sun) The cognoscenti of Jo'burg's beer world pack this attractive haven inside the 44 Stanley (p352) precinct. It serves brews from around the country as well as delectable pub grub and hosts live bands on Saturday (from 2pm). Inside is an eye-catching interior complete with armchairs and a huge log fire; outside are long wooden tables under olive trees.

🍺 Linden

Craft Beer Library
CRAFT BEER

(Map p328; ☑071 177 9531; www.craftbeerlibrary. co.za; 3rd Ave, Linden; ☺11am-midnight Tue-Sat) Beer-lovers will think they have died and gone to heaven at this 'library' where the shelves are lined with an impressive range of local bottled brews, from ales and largers to porters and stouts. It has a good selection on tap, too, and offers decent pub grub.

Tonic
COCKTAIL BAR

(Map p328; www.tonic.joburg; Shop 509, Menal Place, 32 7th St, Linden; ☺5-11pm Tue-Thu, 3-11pm Fri, noon-11pm Sat, noon-4pm Sun) A mural of Queen Elizabeth II with a Ziggy Stardust makeover greets you at this cute bar specialising in gin. It has around 50 different and mostly South African craft brands, out of which it makes some seriously good cocktails. You won't regret ordering a bowl of warm gin and citrus olives to snack on alongside.

🍸 Parkview, Parkhurst, Parktown North & Rosebank

Blind Tiger Cafe
COCKTAIL BAR

(Map p328; ☑076 030 4200; http://blindtigerca-fe.co.za; 62 Tyrone Ave, Parkview; ☺3-9pm Mon, to midnight Tue-Sat) There's a cool 1920s prohibition feel to this welcoming space with a

GAY & LESBIAN GAUTENG

Johannesburg Pride (www.johannesburgpride.co.za) is held at the end of October with a jolly anyone-can-join-in march around Melrose Arch.

GALA (Gay and Lesbian Memory in Action; ☑ 011-717 4239; www.gala.co.za; tours per person R200-350) organises both walking and bus tours that offer a fascinating insight into the role of homosexuality in the city's history, taking you deep into Hillbrow and Soweto.

There are few dedicated LGBT bars or entertainment spaces in Jo'burg – most places are welcoming to all comers. Ones that do lean more towards the rainbow crowd are **Ratz Bar** (Map p339; ☑ 011-482-2414; www.ratzbar.co.za; 9 7th St, Melville; ⊘ 4pm-2am Tue-Sun) and the drag-show/burger bar **Beefcakes** (Map p328; ☑ 011-447 5266; http://beefcakes.co.za/illovo; 198 Oxford Rd, Ilovo Park; ⊘ 7pm-midnight Wed-Sat).

At the beginning of October Pretoria hosts its **Pride party** (www.facebook.com/PretoriaPride).

long wooden bar and outdoor tables right on the Tryone Ave shopping strip. It's hard to resist their inventive cocktails – or as their menu would have it, 'giggle water'. From their food menu the hot chorizo and bean dip is recommended.

★ **4PM at Mesh**   COCKTAIL BAR
(Map p328; ☑ 010-594 5545; www.meshclub.co.za; Trumpet Bldg, 21 Keyes Ave, Rosebank; ⊘ 4-11pm) This slickly designed members' club and co-working space in Rosebank's most trendy location throws open its doors each day at 4pm to anyone who would like to enjoy a delicious cocktail and something to eat in its seriously cool bar. Sit in cute pink basket seats and soak up the sunset views over the northern suburbs.

Foundry   CRAFT BEER
(Map p328; ☑ 011-447 5828; www.foundrycafe.co.za; Shop 7, Parktown Quarter, cnr 3rd & 7th Aves, Parktown North; ⊘ 11.30am-10.30pm Mon-Sat, to 5pm Sun) This place stands out for its impressive selection of craft beer from around the country. The bistro-style fare (try the maple-bacon and blue-cheese pizza) is also good. It's a large place but popular, so it's always worth calling ahead to book a table, especially in the evening.

Jolly Roger Pub   PUB
(Map p328; ☑ 011-442 3954; www.jollyroger.co.za; cnr 4th Ave & 6th St, Parkhurst; ⊘ 10am-2am Mon-Sat, to midnight Sun) This long-running two-storey English-style pub on the edge of burgeoning 4th Ave holds its own against trendier upstarts. Upstairs it serves good pub grub and offers fabulous views of the busy street below. Downstairs is a more traditional sports pub with tap beer aplenty.

Sin & Taxes   COCKTAIL BAR
(Map p328; ☑ 010-900 4987; 4 Bolton Rd, Parkwood; ⊘ 6pm-1am Tue-Sat) It's best to make a reservation for this unsigned speakeasy-style cocktail bar as it's a pretty intimate place. Pull up a seat at the bar and the friendly mixologists – all hipster beards and tattoos – will enthuse about their latest seasonal concoctions. Or you could just stick with the classics.

☆ Entertainment

The quarterly print booklet and website **Johannesburg and Surrounds In Your Pocket** (www.inyourpocket.com) has a fairly comprehensive What's On listing – sign up online for weekly updates.

For entertainment bookings by credit card, contact **Computicket** (www.computicket.com). For news on parties, gettogethers and other local events, check out www.jhblive.co.za.

☆ Live Music

Jo'burg is an excellent place to see live music, especially across the jazz-tipped and electronic spectrum.

Many bars in Braamfontein, Melville, Greenside and Sandton host live bands.

Katzy's   JAZZ
(Map p328; ☑ 011-880 3945; www.katzys.co.za; The Firs, cnr Oxford Rd & Bierman Ave, Rosebank; Mon-Wed free, Thu-Sat R150; ⊘ 10am-11pm Mon-Wed, to 1am Thu-Sat) This swanky den recalls the atmosphere of an old NYC jazz club. You'll find mellow, live jazz Tuesday to Saturday evenings from around 8.30pm. It also boasts an exceptional menu of whiskies, cognacs and bourbons.

Bassline
LIVE MUSIC

(Map p332; ☑ 011-838 9145; www.bassline.co.za; 10 Henry Nxumalo St, Newtown) Jo'burg's most respected live-music venue gained prominence as a Melville jazz haunt in the late '90s before getting the world-music tip and relocating to Newtown in 2004. Today it covers the full range of international musicianship and more-popular reggae, rock and hip-hop styles.

Good Luck Bar
LIVE MUSIC

(Map p332; ☑ 084 683 4413; www.thegoodluckbar. com; 1 Fox St) With exposed bricks and iron beams, visible piping and a long bar, the Good Luck Bar has obvious remnants of its previous life as a warehouse for buses and trams. Its latest incarnation is as a grungy live-music venue and bar only open for specific events – so check its website.

Orbit
JAZZ

(Map p332; ☑ 011-339 6645; www.theorbit.co.za; 81 De Korte St, Braamfontein; ⊙11.30am-2am Tue-Sun) This is by far the most famous of the city's jazz clubs. Plenty of freedom is given to young producers and artists, and its convivial atmosphere attracts a mix of jazz fans, students and in-the-know tourists. An upmarket bistro greets you downstairs, while you'll find the highly impressive concert venue upstairs. Its complete monthly agenda is available online.

Johannesburg Philharmonic Orchestra
CLASSICAL MUSIC

(☑011-484 0446; www.jpo.co.za) The city's orchestra stages a regular circuit of concerts at venues such as Wits University and City Hall. Call or check its website for the latest program.

☆ Theatre

Market Theatre
THEATRE

(Map p332; ☑ 011-832 1641; http://markettheatre. co.za; 56 Margaret Mcingana St, Newtown; tickets R90-150) The city's most important venue for live theatre has three performance spaces (John Kani, Mannie Manim and Barney Simon Theatres) as well as galleries and a cafe. There is always some interesting theatre on, from sharply critical contemporary plays to musicals and stand-up comedy – check the program online.

POPArt
THEATRE

(Map p336; ☑ 083 245 1040; https://popartcentre. co.za; 286 Fox St, Maboneng; tickets from R50)

Showcasing up-and-coming performers, fringe productions and other quirky ensembles, POPArt is the kind of place where you see tomorrow's theatre superstars today. The tiny amphitheatre-style set-up ensures intimate interaction between the performers and the audience. Shows include drama, poetry, live music and a regular Sunday night stand-up comedy gig.

🛍 Shopping

Jo'burg has countless bland malls dotted around the suburbs catering to all your chain-store needs. For something bespoke, try the boutiques and small galleries in Maboneng or one of the city's excellent markets, many of which mix up opportunities to graze on or take away artisan food as well as indulge in some fashion, accessory or souvenir consumption.

★ 27 Boxes
SHOPPING CENTRE

(Map p339; ☑ 011-482-1090; http://27boxes.co.za; 75 4th Ave, Melville; ⊙10am-5pm Tues-Sun; 🛜🚻) This shipping-crate complex of boutiques, galleries and eateries is well on its way to establishing its Melville street cred. A newly planted park, indigenous nursery, and fun kids' playground add to the allure. 27 Boxes highlights include fantastic bread from the Baker Brothers, African-inspired clothes and souvenirs from Krag Drag, and delectable Portuguese cuisine from Reserved Cafe.

★ 44 Stanley
MALL

(Map p328; www.44stanley.co.za; 44 Stanley Ave, Milpark) The antithesis of consumer tack, 44 Stanley is a blueprint for future mall development. It's a warren of lanes around shady courtyards and features an eclectic collection of local designers and speciality boutiques as well as pleasant bars, cafes and restaurants.

★ Art Africa
ARTS & CRAFTS

(Map p328; ☑ 011-486 2052; 62 Tyrone Ave, Parkview; ⊙9am-6pm Mon-Fri, to 4pm Sat) Arts and crafts from across South Africa as well as Mali, Ghana and the Ivory Coast are attractively displayed here – you'll be spoiled for souvenir choice whether you're in the market for a carved wooden mask, beaded jewellery or even the incredible ceramics of Ardmore (www.ardmoreceramics.co.za).

Workshop Newtown
FASHION & ACCESSORIES

(Map p332; www.workshopnewtown.com; cnr Miriam Makeba & Gwingwi Mrwebi Sts, Newtown;

10am-6pm Mon-Fri, to 7pm Sat, to 3pm Sun) Occupying part of the 1911 Potato Sheds building that is now part of the Newton Junction mall development, this small arcade offers up emerging fashion labels including the luxe and very Missoni-like knitwear Maxhosa by Laduma. There are also some arts and crafts courtesy of African Image and others.

**Rosebank Arts
& Crafts Market** ARTS & CRAFTS
(Map p328; 011-568 0850; www.artsandcraftsmarket.co.za; Rosebank Mall, Cradock Ave, Rosebank; 9am-6pm Mon-Thu, to 7pm Fri, to 5pm Sat & Sun) If you're not around for the Rosebank Sunday Market (Map p328; www.rosebanksundaymarket.co.za; Cradock Ave, Rosebank; 9am-4pm Sun) then this basement arcade is packed to the ceiling with stalls selling very similar if not identical African arts and crafts. Worth a browse.

Amatuli HOMEWARES
(Map p328; 011-440 5065; www.amatuli.co.za; 6 Desmond St, Kramerville, Sandton; shop 8.30am-5.30pm Mon-Fri, 9am-3pm Sat & Sun,

cafe 7.30am-6.30pm) A treasure trove of pan-African arts, crafts and interior design pieces, Amatuli is the place to head if you're looking for anything from a Zulu headdress to kinti cloth from Nigeria or carved masks from Madagascar – on multiple floors there's a real Aladdin's Cave atmosphere as you explore.

Piece ARTS & CRAFTS
(Map p336; 083 400 5126; www.piece.co.za; 5th fl, Ellis House, 23 Voorhout St, New Doornfontein; 9am-4pm Mon-Sat) Eugénie Drakes scours Southern Africa for her spacious boutique, stocking a colourful and creative range of local arts and crafts, including pottery, wirework baskets, fashion and accessories. Workshops, exhibitions and talks also happen in the space.

Collectors Treasury BOOKS
(Map p336; 011-334 6556; CTP House, 244 Commissioner St, Maboneng; 9am-5pm Mon-Fri, 10am-2pm Sat) The southern hemisphere's largest bookshop is a curious affair. Some two million volumes and around half a million LP records and other collectables are

JO'BURG'S BEST MARKETS

Between Wednesday and Sunday somewhere in Jo'burg there's a market being held where food vendors dish out savoury and sweet treats. You'll usually find a smattering of arts, crafts and fashion vendors at these weekly markets, too, which act more as a reason to hang out with friends while grazing rather than a serious shopping expedition.

Market on Main (Map p336; 082 868 1335; www.marketonmain.co.za; Arts on Main, 264 Fox St, Maboneng; 10am-3pm Sun) Spilling out of Arts on Main onto Fox St is this buzzy weekly market. You'll find the usual selection of takeaway food stalls downstairs (look out for the one serving delicious cups of Ethiopian coffee or spiced teas, served with free popcorn), while upstairs and on the street are colourful arts, crafts, new and pre-loved fashions and accessories.

Bryanston Organic Market (Map p328; 011-706 3671; www.bryanstonorganicmarket.co.za; 40 Culross Rd, Bryanston; 9am-3pm Thu & Sat) Arts and crafts are on offer here, but the main attraction is the splendid organic produce. There are five cafes as well and often live music. On Tuesday evenings (5pm to 9pm) in November and December it also holds a night market.

Neighbourgoods Market (Map p332; 081 416 2605; www.neighbourgoodsmarket.co.za; 73 Juta St, Braamfontein; 9am-3pm Sat) It's mainly about grazing and hanging out at this two-storey brick warehouse, which fills with artisan purveyors and their foodie fans every Saturday. Upstairs you can grab a bench, groove along to the DJ, watch the sun shine off city buildings and also do some souvenir shopping at a small range of fashion and gift stalls.

1 Fox Market Shed (Map p332; www.1fox.co.za; 1 Fox St, Ferreirasdorp; noon-5pm Fri, 10am-4pm Sat & Sun) Occupying part of a former industrial warehouse on the western edge of downtown Jo'burg, this thriving marketplace offers mainly gourmet outlets, food stands and bars, as well as smattering of craft stalls.

piled high and scattered over nearly every crevice and corner of this multifloor depository. However, ask the owners, the Klass brothers, about a particular book and they'll know exactly where to find it.

Kohinoor MUSIC
(Map p332; ☎ 072-486 7662; 33 Ntemi Piliso St, Newtown; ⊗ 9am-5pm Mon-Fri, to 2pm Sat) In a new smaller location on the corner of Ntemi Piliso and Commissioner Sts, Kohinoor is one of the best sources of African music, and sells everything from *kwaito* to jazz.

ℹ️ Information

DANGERS & ANNOYANCES

Johannesburg has a larger-than-life reputation when it comes to crime, but most visits are trouble-free.
➡ The city centre, once a no-go area, is fine during the day. However, large parts of it are best avoided at night – take a taxi if you go there after dark.
➡ The surrounding neighbourhoods of Braamfontein, Ferreirasdorp, Newtown and Maboneng are generally busy at night and safe to visit – just be vigilant when walking back to your car.
➡ It is advisable to explore Hillbrow and Yeoville with a guide – even during the day.

Driving in Jo'burg

Jo'burg is a big city and driving around it can be quite an experience – and not always one for the best. To stay safe, keep in the mind the following:
➡ Be alert to possible robbery when stopped at traffic lights after dark – don't wind down windows to give change to beggars.
➡ Watch out for the erratic behaviour of other drivers –you'll soon realise why there are so many car crashes on Jo'burg's roads.
➡ Avoid driving along bus lanes as this can incur a fine.

➡ There are many one-way streets and street signs are not always clear – check your route carefully before setting off.

EMERGENCY

Ambulance ☎ 011-37 55 911
Fire & Police ☎ 10111

MEDICAL SERVICES

Jo'burg's medical services are good, but they can be pricey, so make sure you get insurance before you leave home.
Netcare Rosebank Hospital (☎ 011-328 0500; www.netcare.co.za; 14 Sturdee Ave, Rosebank; ⊗ 24hr) A private hospital in the northern suburbs, with casualty (emergency), GP and specialist services.

TOURIST INFORMATION

Guesthouses or hostels as well as tour guides are your best sources of tourist information.

Jo'burg Tourism has branches in **Sandton** (Map p328; ☎ 011-883 3525; www.joburgtourism.com; Nelson Mandela Sq, Sandton; ⊗ 8am-5pm Mon-Fri) and at **Park Station** (Map p332; ☎ 011-338 5054; www.joburgtourism.com; Park Station; ⊗ 8am-5pm Mon-Fri).

You can also try **Gauteng Tourism Authority** (Map p332; ☎ 011-085 2500; www.gauteng.net; 124 Main Street, Marshalltown; ⊗ 8am-5pm Mon-Fri).

ℹ️ Getting There & Away

AIR

South Africa's major international and domestic airport is **OR Tambo International Airport** (Ortia; ☎ 011-921 6262; www.airports.co.za; Kempton Park). It's about 25km east of central Johannesburg.

If you're in a hurry to get around South Africa, some domestic flights are definitely worth considering. Smaller budget airlines **Kulula** (☎ 086 158 5852; www.kulula.com), **FlySafair** (☎ 0871 351 351; www.flysafair.co.za) and **Mango** (☎ 0861 001 234; www.flymango.com) link Jo'burg with major destinations.

For regular flights to national and regional destinations try **South African Airways** (☎ 0861 606 606; www.flysaa.com), **Airlink** (☎ 086 160 6606; www.flyairlink.com) and **SA Express** (☎ 086 172 9227; www.flyexpress.aero). All flights can be booked through SAA, which also has offices in the domestic and international terminals of OR Tambo.

BUS

A number of international bus services leave Jo'burg from the **Park Station** (Map p332) complex and head for Mozambique, Lesotho, Botswana, Namibia, Swaziland and Zimbabwe.

The main long-distance bus lines (national and international) also depart from and arrive at the Park Station transit centre, in the northwestern corner of the site, where you'll also find their booking offices.

Baz Bus (☑ 021-422 5202, SMS bookings 076 427 3003; www.bazbus.com) Connects Jo'burg with the most popular parts of the region (including Durban, the Garden Route and Cape Town) and picks up at hostels in Jo'burg and Pretoria, saving you the hassle of going into the city to arrange transport.

City to City (☑ 0861 589 282; www.citytocity. co.za) National and international bus services.

Greyhound (☑ reservations 087 352 0352, 011-611 8000; www.greyhound.co.za) Highly recommended national and international bus services.

Intercape (☑ 021-380 4400; www.intercape. co.za) National and international bus services.

Mzansi Experience (☑ 021-001 0651; www. mzansi.travel) Similar to Baz Bus.

Translux (☑ 086 158 9282; www.translux. co.za) National and international bus services.

CAR

All the major car-rental operators have counters at OR Tambo and at various locations around the city, including Park Station. Cars can also be delivered and picked up from wherever you plan to stay in Jo'burg.

TRAIN

Long-distance train services link Jo'burg with a number of destinations including Pretoria, Cape Town, Bloemfontein, Kimberley, Port Elizabeth, Durban, Komatipoort and Nelspruit. A number of these services have sleeper compartments. Tickets can be booked through **Shosholoza Meyl** (☑ 0860 008 888, 011-774 4555; www. shosholozameyl.co.za) or at Jo'burg's Park Station.

ℹ️ Getting Around

TO/FROM THE AIRPORT

The rapid-transit Gautrain (p356) offers a direct service between the airport and Jo'burg. There are Gautrain stations at Sandton, Rosebank and Park Station. A one-way ticket to Park Station costs R162 (it's R151 to Sandton), on top of which you will have to pay R16 (non-refundable) for the Gautrain card.

Airport transfers to locations in Jo'burg and Pretoria (as well as places further afield) can be arranged through any of the following:

Airport Shuttle (☑ 0861 397 488; www. airportshuttle.co.za)

Citybug (☑ 0861 334 433; www.citybug.co.za)

Get You There Transfers (☑ 082 762 7104; www.getyoutheretransfers.co.za)

Lowveld Link (☑ 083 918 8075; www.lowveld-link.com)

Magic Transfers (☑ 011-548 0800; www. magictransfers.co.za)

By car, the airport is easily accessible (via the R24 and the N12), but if you need to get there during the weekday rush hour (5pm to 7pm) allow up to an extra hour's travelling time.

Some accommodation options offer transfers. If taking a taxi (around R500), ensure that you choose an authorised firm while still inside the terminal building – don't go with taxi touts outside as rip-offs are common.

BUS

Rea Vaya (☑ 0860 562 874; www.reavaya.org. za) These buses provide safe, reliable public transport across Jo'burg and between Soweto (and other townships) and the city's downtown areas. An inner-city circular route costs R7 (green line), while a full trip from the feeder routes to the inner city (blue line) costs R13.50. The fleet is colourful and comfortable, and timetables are more strictly adhered to than metro lines.

Citysightseeing Johannesburg (☑ 0861 733 287; www.citysightseeing.co.za; 1-/2-day ticket R200/300) These hop-on, hop-off buses stop at major tourist sites around Jo'burg. The red city tour route, which includes the Mining District and Carlton Centre and runs out to the Apartheid Museum and Gold Reef City before looping back to Newtown and Braamfontein, connects with the more northern green route at Constitution Hill. Buses run from roughly 9am to 6pm. There's a discount for online bookings and you can also add on tours to Soweto.

Metrobus (Map p332; ☑ 0860 562 874; www. mbus.co.za; Gandhi Sq) A reasonable network of buses across the city.

ℹ️ LANSERIA AIRPORT

Jo'burg's second airport, Lanseria (☑ 011-367 0300; www.lanseria.co.za; Airport Rd, Lanseria), is about 42km northwest of the city. It's often cheaper to fly in and out of Lanseria as it's a smaller airport.

It's a joy to rent a car here and drive onto near-empty roads. There is no public transport from the airport.

Lanseria is 61km southwest of Pretoria. Many of the same shuttle bus companies that serve OR Tambo International Airport also offer transfers to the city from here.

SHARED TAXI

The standard fare in the inner suburbs and the city centre is R8, while longer journeys are R12. There's a complex system of hand/finger signals to tell a passing taxi where you want to go, so it's best to look as though you know where you're going and raise a confident index finger (drivers will stop if they're going the same way).

If you take a minibus shared taxi into central Jo'burg, be sure to get off before it reaches the end of the route, and avoid the taxi rank – it's a mugging zone. Getting a minibus taxi home from the city is a more difficult proposition.

TAXI

There are taxis in Jo'burg, but they are relatively expensive. They all operate meters, but it's wise to ask a local the likely price and agree on a fare from the outset.

Rose Taxis (☑ 011-403 0000) and **Maxi Taxi Cabs** (☑ 011-648 1212) are reputable firms. These days, most Jo'burgers prefer to use Uber (www.uber.com/cities/johannesburg), though Taxify (www.taxify.eu/cities/johannesburg) and Zebra Cabs (www.zebracabs.co.za) are also good options. There are also a number of cab services that will only transport women, such as Cabs For Women (www.facebook.com/cabsforwomen).

TRAIN

Jo'burg's public transport pride and joy, the rapid-transit **Gautrain** (☑ 0800 428 87246; www.gautrain.co.za) offers a direct service between the airport, Sandton, Rosebank, Park Station, Pretoria and Hatfield. Trains depart every 12 minutes at peak times (5.30am to 8.30am and 3pm to 6pm Monday to Friday), and every 20 to 30 minutes outside peak times. A one-way ticket between Pretoria and Park Station costs R76.

If you're travelling in peak periods, or staying near a station, it's a fast, state-of-the-art and cost-effective way to enter/exit the city. You must purchase a Gold Card (R16) first, then load it with credit for your desired journey. The Gautrain is also complemented by a bus service connecting stations to nearby areas. The Gautrain buses are safe, reliable and affordable if you are a rail-user.

Soweto

☑ 011 / POP 1.3 MILLION

The townships are the heart of the nation and none beats louder than Soweto. Standing for 'South West Townships', this area has evolved from one of forced habitation to an address of pride and social prestige as well as a destination in its own right. Come here to experience welcoming township life and to visit places of tremendous historical significance, such as the former home of Nelson Mandela and the Hector Pieterson Museum.

For many years now it has been safe to visit the main sights independently. A stroll down buzzing Vilakazi St offers an insight into modern African sensibilities, while the addition of the Orlando Towers bungee jump, or taking in a show at the marvellous Soweto Theatre, provides quality, fun experiences in what can be a place of great political abstraction.

History

As ANC stalwart and long-time Soweto resident Walter Sisulu once said, the history of South Africa cannot be understood outside the history of Soweto.

Using the outbreak of bubonic plague as an excuse, in 1904 the Jo'burg City Council (JCC) moved 1358 Indians and 600 Africans from a Jo'burg slum to Klipspruit, 18km by road from the city centre. It wasn't until the late 1930s, after the suburb of Orlando had been built and cynically marketed by the JCC as 'somewhat of a paradise', that the population began its astonishing growth.

By the end of WWII, Jo'burg's black population had risen by more than 400,000, and by 1958 more than 20 new suburbs had appeared around Orlando, each filled with row upon row of identical houses.

During the 1950s organisations such as the ANC took a bigger role in opposing apartheid, and before long Soweto (as it was officially named in 1961) would be recognised as the centre of resistance. Confirmation of this came in 1955, when 3000 delegates from around the country gathered in Kliptown Sq (known today as Freedom Sq) at the Congress of the People. The result was the Freedom Charter, which is the pillar of ANC philosophy and integral to the new constitution.

The movement was forced underground in 1960 after the Sharpeville Massacre (p526). While the struggle continued at a slower pace, it was not the only change taking place here. The demographics of the townships were changing, and as second-generation Sowetans matured, so did Soweto style. New forms of music emerged and the youth led development of a unique urban culture. Football also offered an escape, and massive support for teams such as the Moroka Swallows, Orlando Pirates and (after they split from the Pirates) Kaizer

Chiefs reflected the development of an urban black identity.

The development of this new identity only served to strengthen the desire to be treated as equals. Resistance eventually spilled over on 16 June 1976, when a student protest became the precursor to the Soweto uprising. Within days of the fighting, world opinion had turned irreversibly against the apartheid regime and Soweto became the most potent symbol of resistance to a racist South Africa.

Scenes of burning cars, 'necklaced' people and mass funerals flowed out of Soweto throughout the 1980s, while the death throes of apartheid could be felt. Mandela was released in 1990 and returned to live in his tiny home in Vilakazi St, just 200m from Archbishop Desmond Tutu.

However, Mandela's release was no panacea. Encouraged by the government, supporters of rival political parties murdered each other by the hundreds in the run-up to the 1994 free elections.

More recently life has been stable, and since 1994 Sowetans have had ownership rights over their properties. The relative calm has been further promoted by a number of redevelopment projects. The 2010 World Cup brought great positive press for the township, not to mention a much needed upgrade in infrastructure including street lighting, parks and paved roads.

Mirroring much of South Africa, the rising middle class lives here alongside shack dwellers and the mass unemployed, yet all are equally buoyed by the history of Soweto as an icon of the struggle. Many who break the cycle decide to stay and reinvest, and most laud their Sowetan upbringing. Indeed, today many parts of Soweto are safer and more laid-back than Johannesburg's wealthy, high-security northern suburbs.

⊙ Sights & Activities

★ **Hector Pieterson Museum**　　MUSEUM

(☑ 011-536 0611; cnr Pela & Kumalo Sts, Orlando West; adult/child R30/10; ⊙ 10am-5pm Mon-Sat, to 4pm Sun) This powerful museum, named after the 12-year-old boy shot dead during the student protests in Soweto on 16 June 1976, illuminates the role of Sowetan life in the history of the independence struggle. It's a major stop on all tours of Soweto and thus is almost always busy.

★ **June 16 Memorial Acre**　　MEMORIAL

(cnr Pula & Mputhi Sts, Jabavu; ⊙ 9am-5.30pm) **FREE** Opposite one of the schools from which students marched on 16 June 1976 is this stunning open-air memorial to the bloody events that presaged the Soweto Uprising. The key artwork here is the memorial wall that documents the fateful day, hour by hour, in a panorama of gut-wrenching images.

Mandela House Museum　　MUSEUM

(☑ 011-936 7754; www.mandelahouse.com; 8115 Vilakazi St, Orlando West; adult/child R60/20; ⊙ 9am-5pm) Nelson Mandela lived with his first wife, Evelyn, and later with his second

---

BEST SOWETO TOURS

Dozens of companies offer tours of Soweto; opt for one whose guides hail from Soweto and consider a walking or cycling tour to get a better feel for the place.

Lebo's Soweto Bicycle Tours (☑ 011-936 3444; www.sowetobicycletours.com; 2hr/day tour R470/580) Soweto's clay paths and grassy nooks make for fabulous cycling terrain. Walking tours are also offered, and there are tuk-tuk (auto rickshaw) tours for the less energetic (R430 per person). The tours are organised by Lebo's Soweto Backpackers (p360), with discounts available for guests.

Africa My Beginning Tours (☑ 011-075 2201, 082 634 4841; www.sowetovisits.co.za) Runs various tours of Soweto, including minibus-taxi tours (R400, five hours) and bicycle tours (R500, four hours).

Taste of Africa (www.tasteofafrica.co.za) As well as a day tour of Soweto, this operation offers an excellent 24-hour tour (per person R890, or R650 if you self-drive) where you can explore Soweto with locals, far off the beaten track.

Vhupo Tours (☑ 076 601 3204, 011-936 0411; www.vhupo-tours.com; tours R520) Run by Soweto resident Bruce Luthanga, this place offers a range of tours around Soweto, including an evening out at a *shebeen* (unlicensed bar).

Central Soweto

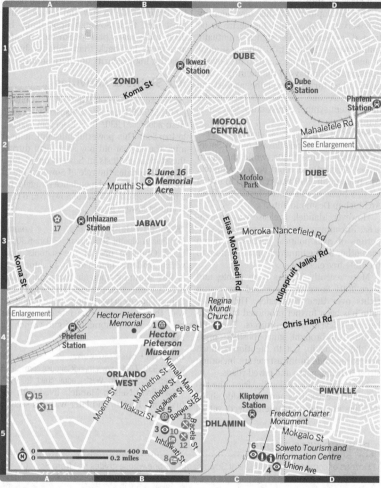

wife, Winnie, in this four-room house, just off Vilakazi St. The museum includes interactive exhibits on the history of the house and some interesting family photos.

Nearby is the home of **Archbishop Desmond Tutu** (Vilakazi St) (not open to visitors); Winnie Mandela has a property a short walk away, too.

Kliptown
AREA

Established in 1891 and found southwest of Orlando West, Kliptown is Soweto's oldest settlement. Informal settlements (shacks) for black families started to appear here in

1903 and it is also where the Freedom Charter was adopted on 26 June 1955. The site of the adoption, once a football field, has become the **Walter Sisulu Square of Dedication** (www.waltersisulusquare.co.za; cnr Union Ave & Main Rd, Kliptown).

★ Orlando Towers
ADVENTURE SPORTS

(☑071 674 4343; www.orlandotowers.co.za; Chris Hani Rd, Klipspruit; viewing platform/bungee jumping R80/550; ⊙noon-5pm Thu, 10am-6pm Fri-Sun) Built originally for Orlando's Power Station, the towers host one of the world's more incongruous bungee jumps. Once painted a

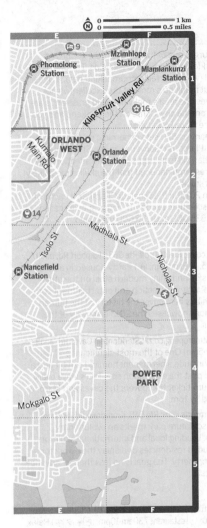

Central Soweto

◎ Top Sights
1	Hector Pieterson Museum	B4
2	June 16 Memorial Acre	B2

◎ Sights
3	Home of Archbishop Desmond Tutu	B5
4	Kliptown	C5
5	Mandela House Museum	B5
6	Walter Sisulu Square of Dedication	C5

☻ Activities, Courses & Tours
	Lebo's Soweto Bicycle Tours	(see 9)
7	Orlando Towers	F3

▣ Sleeping
8	Dakalo B&B	B5
9	Lebo's Soweto Backpackers	E1
10	Nthateng's B&B	B5

✗ Eating
	Chaf Pozi	(see 7)
11	Restaurant Vilakazi	A5
12	Sakhumzi Restaurant	B5
13	Vuyo's	B5

◔ Drinking & Nightlife
14	Ubuntu Kraal Beer Garden	E2
15	Wine Bar	A5

✦ Entertainment
16	Orlando Stadium	F1
17	Soweto Theatre	A3

drab white, one tower is now decorated with a colourful mural depicting, among others, Nelson Mandela, singer Yvonne Chaka Chaka and a football stadium. The other tower displays the Vodacom logo and more colourful designs.

☆ Festivals & Events

Soweto Wine Festival　　　WINE
(www.sowetowinefestival.co.za; ☉ Mar) Meet South Africa's best winemakers at this festival, which takes place at the Soweto Theatre.

Soweto Festival Expo　　　FAIR
(www.sowetofestivalexpo.co.za; ☉ Sep) Enjoy music, poetry, food stalls and a lifestyle expo on the last weekend of September at the Johannesburg Expo Centre.

Soweto Beer Festival　　　BEER
(www.sowetobeerfestival.co.za; SHAP Stadium, Mzilikazi St; ☉ Oct) This festival, held in the last weekend of October at SHAP stadium, opposite Mofolo Park, features some 40 different types of beers including local and traditional African brews.

Soweto Fashion Week　　　CULTURAL
(https://sowetofashionweek.com/; ☉ Oct) Soweto's fashionistas descend on the Soweto Theatre in early October to catch the latest designer styles on the catwalk.

Old Mutual Soweto Marathon　　　SPORTS
(www.sowetomarathon.com; ☉ Nov) Takes place in early November, starting and finishing at the FNB Stadium.

CRADLE OF HUMANKIND

Around 45 minutes' drive northwest of Jo'burg is one of the world's most important palaeontological zones, focused on the Sterkfontein hominid fossil fields. The area is part of the 470-sq-km Cradle of Humankind (www.thecradleofhumankind.net), a Unesco World Heritage site. As well as learning about mankind's roots at the excellent visitor centre, Maropeng, and the Sterkfontein Caves, the area's rocky highveld grasslands are beautiful to look at and a welcome respite from the city. Come on the weekend and you can also tour the serene sculpture park at the Nirox Foundation.

Sites across the region have yielded as many as 850 sets of hominid remains – in 1947 Dr Robert Broom made one of the most famous discoveries, in the Sterkfontein Caves, when he uncovered the 2.5-million-year-old fossilised skull of the affectionately named Mrs Ples. Later, more sophisticated research deduced that the skull is most likely that of an adolescent boy, but the name has stuck.

New fossils are continually being found. In 2013, in the Dinaledi Chamber, a cache of some 1550 fossils was uncovered, enabling scientists to confirm a new species called *Homo naledi* who lived in this area between 335,000 and 236,000 years ago.

Sights

Maropeng (☎014-577 9000; www.maropeng.co.za; Rte 400, off Rte 563, Hekpoort Rd; adult/child R120/65, with Sterkfontein Caves R190/125; ☉9am-5pm; ✋) Partly housed in a building that looks like a giant grassy mound on one side and shiny modern steel on the other, Maropeng is an all-in-one information centre, visitor attraction and entertainment complex. The fascinating series of interactive exhibits here cover the history of the human race since its very beginnings. A new exhibition showcases the 2013 discovery of the *Homo naledi* species in the Rising Star caves.

Sterkfontein Caves (☎014-577 9000; www.maropeng.co.za; Sterkfontein Caves Rd; adult/child R165/97, with Maropeng R190/125; ☉9am-5pm) One of the most significant archaeological sites in the world, Sterkfontein Caves include a permanent hominid exhibit and a walkway down into the impressive caves and past the excavation site. Tours leave every 30 minutes (the last tour is at 4pm). A discount ticket that covers the caves and Maropeng, which is 8km away, must be purchased by 1pm.

Nirox Foundation (☎082 875 2865; www.niroxarts.com; Rte 540, Kromdraai Rd; ☉10am-5pm Sat, Sun & public holidays) This gorgeous sculpture park marks an evolutionary advancement for South African creative arts. Leading local and international sculptors, painters and conceptual artists take up secluded residencies or display their work for public perusal in the 1500-sq-metre private property. The goal is no less than to 'advance Africa's place in the global contemporary arts'.

Sleeping & Eating

Cradle Boutique Hotel (☎087-353 9599; https://cradlehotel.co.za; Rte T9, off Rte 540/Kromdraai Rd, Kromdraai; r incl breakfast from R2500; ☉restaurant 7.30am-10pm; ⓟ❄☎⛱) Relax and revive in one of the 17 very stylish and spacious timber and thatch lodge-style rooms on this property. All have verandas with sweeping views of the Cradle Nature Reserve, as does the hotel's decent and affordable restaurant, which is open to outside guests.

Maropeng Hotel (☎014-577 9000; www.maropeng.co.za; Rte 400, off Rte 563, Hekpoort Rd; s/d incl breakfast R1000/1470; ⓟ❄☎⛱) Inside the Maropeng complex, this low-slung pad offers 24 rooms that are pleasantly decorated with African crafts and earthy colours, and blessed with breathtaking views of the Witwatersberg and Magaliesberg ranges.

🛏 Sleeping

There are many B&Bs in Soweto, several of which are in the immediate vicinity of Vilakazi St.

★**Lebo's Soweto Backpackers** HOSTEL $
(☎011-936 3444; www.sowetobackpackers.com; 10823A Pooe St, Orlando West; camping/dm from R100/185, s/d with shared bathroom from R290/450; ⓟ☎) For a real township

experience, this well-established hostel set by lovely parklands is your answer. It's a healthy walk from the Vilakazi St action, but guests love the shaded beer garden, restaurant (meals from R60) and pool table. Dorms are neat and clean; the double rooms are excellent value. Friendly staff encourage interactivity, and all kinds of tours are available.

Nthateng's B&B GUESTHOUSE $
(☑082 335 7956, 011-051 9362; nthatengmd@gmail.com; 6991 Inhlwathi St, Orlando West; s/d incl breakfast R500/695; P🕾) Dark woods, tan linens, sandy-coloured walls and a few kitschy touches give this spacious guesthouse an air of early-'80s post-disco chill. However, Nthateng is an animated host who insists on top-shelf personal tours, delicious breakfasts and a *mi casa es su casa* state of mind. It's in an ideal location near the museum and restaurants.

Dakalo B&B GUESTHOUSE $$
(☑082 723 0585, 011-936 9328; 6963 Inhlwathi St, Orlando West; s/d incl breakfast R450/800; P🕾) Spitting distance from Vilakazi St (but on a quiet lane), this friendly family home is full of funky decor, from the psychedelic blue-spotted tiles in the bathroom to animal-print curtains and rococo collectibles. There are four rooms; try for the one that opens onto the flower-filled garden at the back.

✗ Eating & Drinking

Vilakazi St is lined with tourist-friendly and atmospheric eateries.

Places to go out for a drink in Soweto range from informal *shebeens* to more upmarket bars, cafes and restaurants. Vilakazi St has some choice spots, including the **Wine Bar** (☑071-154 7459; www.thewinebar.co.za; 7165 Vilakazi St, Orlando West; ⊙noon-10pm Sun-Thu, to 11pm Fri & Sat). The Soweto Gold Brewery (www.sowetogold.co.za) at **Ubuntu Kraal Beer Garden** (☑011-051 5780; www.ubuntukraal.com; 11846 Senokonyana St, Orlando West; ⊙9am-5pm Mon-Fri) is also not far away.

Chaf Pozi BARBECUE $$
(☑081 797 5756; www.chafpozi.co.za; Chris Hani Rd, Klipspruit; set menus R110-275; ⊙noon-6pm Mon-Thu, to 2am Fri & Sat, 11am-10pm Sun) At the base of the Orlando Towers, this large *shisa nyama* (barbecue) restaurant is popular with locals and those needing a beer after leaping from the towers (attached to

a bungee rope, that is). There's a choice of well-seasoned meats, which are served in a range of set menus that also include mealie pap (maize porridge), vegetables and sauces.

Vuyo's AFRICAN $$
(☑011-536 1838; www.vuyos.co.za; 8038 Vilakazi St, Orlando West; mains R110-150; ⊙10am-11pm Mon-Thu, to 2am Fri-Sun; 🕾) A surprisingly hip restaurant with a sleek, design-led interior, this cool culinary outpost demonstrates Soweto's changing sensibilities. Serving up inventive dishes showcasing South African ingredients like *mogodo* (tripe), boerewors (farmer's sausage) and *morogo* (wild spinach), it's frequented more by locals than tourists. A good place to hang out and soak up the atmosphere while nursing a beer on the upstairs terrace.

Restaurant Vilakazi SOUTH AFRICAN $$
(☑011-936 7423; http://restaurantvilakazi.co.za; 6876 Vilakazi St, Orlando West; mains R70-150; ⊙10am-10pm) A seductive setting complete with a breezy terrace is the draw at this well-regarded joint up the top of Vilakazi St. The chef prepares a colourful assortment of palate pleasers, such as salads, fish dishes, burgers and pastas, as well as local-style carnivorous options, including oxtail, boerewors and *mogodu*.

Sakhumzi Restaurant SOUTH AFRICAN $$
(☑011-536 1379; http://sakhumzi.co.za; 6980 Vilakazi St, Orlando West; lunch buffet R185, mains R70-190; ⊙11am-10pm) Brimming with good cheer, Sakhumzi is firmly on the tourist trail and bus parties regularly pass through for the excellent-value daily lunch buffets. Patrons spill onto the street tables and mingle joyfully with passers-by. Expect African staples such as mutton stew, *umleqwa* (traditional-style steamed chicken) and mealie pap, as well as more conventional burgers and steaks.

☆ Entertainment

Check online to see what's playing at the **Soweto Theatre** (☑011-930 7461; www.sowetotheatre.com; cnr Bolani Rd & Bolani Link, Jabulani; ⊙tours 8am-5pm). Soccer is hugely popular, with loyalties split between the Orlando Pirates, who are based at **Orlando Stadium** (☑011-024 5518; Klipspruit Valley Rd, Orlando East), and the Kaizer Chiefs, who call the **FNB Stadium** (Map p328; www.stadiummanagement.co.za/stadiums/fnb; Baragwanath Rd,

Diepkloof) home. Tickets for games are around R40 and can be bought via Computicket (http://online.computicket.com/web).

🛒 Shopping

Vilakazi St is lined with stalls selling local craft souvenirs; you'll also find a good selection outside the Hector Pieterson Museum, at Regina Mundi Church and at the craft market held at Soweto Theatre on the last Saturday of the month. For contemporary fashions check out the Box Shop complex at the top of Vilakazi St.

❶ Information

There are banks with ATMs in Walter Sisulu Sq of Dedication.

Soweto Tourism and Information Centre
(☑ 011-342 4316; www.joburgtourism.com; Walter Sisulu Sq of Dedication, Kliptown; ⊙ 8am-5pm Mon-Fri) Has a few brochures and can help with tours.

❶ Getting There & Away

Many tourists take a half- or full-day guided tour of Soweto, but you can choose to travel independently using the safe Rea Vaya (p355) bus system.

It's also pretty straightforward (and safe) to drive to Soweto with your own wheels.

Pretoria

☑ 012 / POP 741,651

South Africa's administrative centre is a handsome city with some gracious old architecture, significant historical sites for South Africans of all races, prosperous leafy suburbs, and wide streets lined with jacarandas that burst into a beautiful purple haze in October and November.

It's always been more of an Afrikaner city than Jo'burg, and hence more conservative and less cosmopolitan – this was once the beating heart of the apartheid regime, after all, and its very name a symbol of oppression. Today it's home to a multitude of black civil servants and foreign embassy workers, who are infusing the city with a new sense of multiculturalism. The once blighted inner city is also undergoing something of a renaissance.

Officially, the greater Pretoria region, which also includes Centurion and a number of smaller towns, such as Cullinan, and townships such as Mamelodi, is called Tshwane.

History

The fertile Apies River, on which the city of Pretoria sits today, was the support system for a large population of Nguni-speaking cattle farmers for hundreds of years. However, the Zulu wars caused massive destruction and dislocation. Much of the black population was slaughtered and most of the remaining people fled north into present-day Zimbabwe.

In 1841 the first Boers trekked into a temporary power vacuum. With few people around, they laid claim to the land that would become their capital. By the time the British granted independence to the Zuid-Afrikaansche Republiek (ZAR) in the early 1850s, there were estimated to be 15,000 whites and 100,000 blacks living between the Vaal and Limpopo Rivers. The whites were widely scattered, and in 1853 two farms on the Apies River were bought as the site for the republic's capital.

Pretoria, which was named after Boer leader Andries Pretorius, was nothing more than a tiny frontier village with a grandiose title, but the servants of the British Empire were watching it with growing misgivings. They acted in 1877, annexing the republic; the Boers went to war (Pretoria came under siege at the beginning of 1881) and won back their independence.

The discovery of gold on the Witwatersrand in the late 1880s changed everything – within 20 years the Boers would again be at war with the British.

With the British making efforts towards reconciliation, self-government was again granted to the Transvaal in 1906, and through an unwieldy compromise Pretoria was made the administrative capital. The Union of South Africa came into being in 1910, but Pretoria was not to regain its status until 1961, when the Republic of South Africa came into existence under the leadership of Hendrik Verwoerd.

◉ Sights

⭐ **Freedom Park**   MEMORIAL
(Map p372; ☑ 012-336 4000; www.freedompark. co.za; cnr Koch St & 7th Ave, Salvokop; entry incl guided tour R120; ⊙ 8am-4.30pm, tours 9am, noon & 3pm) This stunning park and museum honours fallen South Africans in all major conflicts and adopts an integrated approach to African history. It is a place of architectural imagination and collective healing. Start at //hapo, the museum covering Southern

African history at the bottom of the hill; then proceed up the hill to the main park, which provides wonderful views of the city.

★ **Voortrekker Monument** MONUMENT, VIEWPOINT
(Map p372; ☑ 012-326 6770; www.vtm.org.za; Eeufees Rd, Groenkloof; adult/child R70/35; ⊙ 8am-6pm Sep-Apr, to 5pm May-Aug) The imposing, art-deco-style Voortrekker Monument was constructed between 1938 and 1949 to honour the journey of the Voortrekkers, who journeyed north over the coastal mountains of the Cape into the heart of the African veld. Surrounded by a 3.4-sq-km nature reserve, it's 3km south of the city and clearly signposted from the N1 freeway.

Church Square SQUARE
(Map p364) A **statue of Old Lion** (Paul Kruger) takes pride of place in the centre of Church Square, which is surrounded by some impressive public buildings. The square was given a facelift in 2017 and is now a more pleasant spot to linger and admire the architecture and busy comings and goings from the municipal buildings.

012central NOTABLE BUILDING
(Map p364; ☑ 012-357 1613; www.facebook.com/012central; 381 Helen Joseph St) The rebirth of downtown Pretoria has been given a kickstart by the redevelopment of this set of buildings into an events, arts and social hub. Check out the Facebook page for details of various activities held out of this imaginative, street-art-decorated precinct, such as free guided walks of the city centre and the monthly **Market @ the Sheds** (Map p364; www.marketatthesheds.co.za; ⊙ 11am-6pm last Sat of month) ⊘.

Melrose House HISTORIC BUILDING
(Map p364; ☑ 012-322 2805; 275 Jeff Masemola St; adult/child R22/5; ⊙ 10am-5pm Tue-Sun) On 31 May 1902, the Treaty of Vereeniging, which ended the Anglo-Boer War (1899–1902), was signed in the dining room of this stately mansion. Highlights of the house, which was built in 1886, include a grand billiards room with a vibrant stained-glass smoking nook, and a conservatory containing a collection of political cartoons from the Anglo-Boer War.

Pretoria National Zoological Gardens ZOO
(Map p364; ☑ 012-328 3265; www.nzg.ac.za; cnr Paul Kruger & Boom Sts; adult/child R110/70; cable

---

LOCAL KNOWLEDGE

MONTHLY EVENTS IN PRETORIA

Held in the nature reserve beneath the Voortrekker Monument, either on the last or first Sunday of the month, the **Park Accoustics** (www.parkacoustics.co.za; online/at the gate R120/150) pop concerts have been a huge hit with locals, who bring their picnic baskets and rugs to enjoy the evening's outdoor entertainment.

Also with live music (blues, folk, rock, jazz, reggae and Afro-soul) and worth marking your diary for is Market @ the Sheds. One of the projects of a nonprofit company aiming to rejuvenate central Pretoria, this lively market (usually held on the last Saturday of the month) showcases local creativity in terms of food, drink, fashion, accessories and local arts and crafts.

---

car return R35/25; ⊙ 8.30am-4.30pm) There's a reptile park and an aquarium here, as well as a vast collection of exotic trees and plenty of picnic spots. The highlight, though, is the **cable car**, which runs up to the top of a hill that overlooks the city.

Union Buildings NOTABLE BUILDING
(Map p372; Fairview Ave) **FREE** Designed by Sir Herbert Baker, these sweeping sandstone buildings are the headquarters of government and home to the presidential offices. They're not open to the public, but are worth visiting to view from the front gardens, where you'll find statues of a few former heads of state, including a giant one of an open-armed, grinning Mandela – it's a top selfie spot.

National Cultural History Museum MUSEUM
(Map p364; ☑ 012-324 6082; www.ditsong.org.za; 432 Visagie St; adult/child R35/20; ⊙ 8am-4pm) Concentrating on the cultural history of South Africa, this museum features exhibitions on San rock art, Iron Age figurines from Limpopo and a small gallery of contemporary South African works, among others.

Pretoria Art Museum GALLERY
(Map p372; ☑ 021-358 6750; www.pretoriaartmuseum.co.za; cnr Francis Baard & Wessels Sts, Arcadia Park; adult/child R25/5; ⊙ 10am-5pm Tue-Sun) Specialising in South African art from most

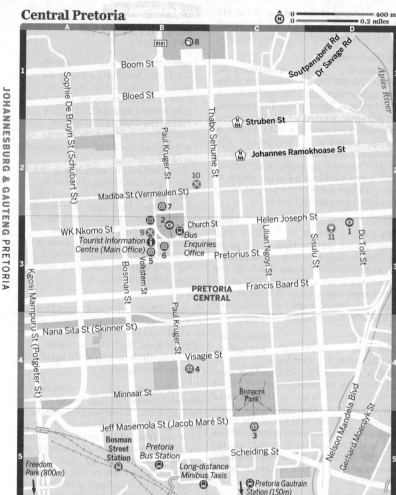

of the country's history, this good gallery contains works by all the big local hitters, from Jacob Hendrik Pierneef and Irma Stern to William Kentridge and Conrad Botes. It also features regularly changing exhibitions.

✹ Festivals & Events

Jacaranda Agricultural Show FAIR
(Pretoria Show; Tshwane Events Centre, 205 Soutter St, Pretoria West; ⊙ end Aug/early Sep) This immensely popular agricultural show and flea market is held at the end of August and early September.

Cool Capital ART
(www.coolcapital.co.za; ⊙ Sep/Oct) An uncurated, DIY, guerrilla arts biennale held every two years, usually between September and October.

🛏 Sleeping

🛏 Arcadia & Hatfield

1322 Backpackers International HOSTEL $
(Map p368; ☎ 012-362 3905; www.1322back-packers.com; 1322 Arcadia St, Hatfield; s/d R400/500, dm/s/d with shared bathroom from

Central Pretoria

R170/300/400; (P@♠☎) This hostel is a welcoming retreat, where travellers congregate around a backyard pool and a buzzing little bar. You can stay in neat three- to eight-bed dorms, or smallish, converted wood-and-brick sheds at the bottom of the garden (chilly in winter, a bit stifling in summer). Shared bathrooms are clean and all guests have kitchen access. Continental breakfast is included.

Pumbas Backpackers   HOSTEL $
(Map p368; ☑012-362 5343; www.pumbas.co.za; 1232 Arcadia St, Hatfield; camping/dm R100/180, s/d with shared bathroom R300/400; P♠☎) Although this budget-friendly hostel won't knock your socks off, it features an assortment of tidy and serviceable private rooms and dorms and is optimally placed in Hatfield, a short stroll from the Gauteng station. There's a kitchen for guest use and a pocket-sized pool.

**Bed & Breakfast
in Hatfield**   GUESTHOUSE $$
(Map p368; ☑083 447 2066, 012-362 5392; www.bandbhatfield.co.za; 1265 Arcadia St, Hatfield; s/d incl breakfast R650/900; P❄♠☎) A short amble from the Hatfield Gauteng station, this B&B is the epitome of a refined cocoon, revelling quietly in minimalist lines, soothing colour accents and well-thought-out decorative touches – it helps that the owner is a retired architect. The pool at the back is a bonus.

East View Guest House   GUESTHOUSE $$
(Map p368; ☑082 451 6516; www.eastviewguesthouse.com; 175 East Ave, Arcadia; s/d incl breakfast R750/800; P♠☎) This calm haven occupies an imposing villa close to the Union Buildings. Owner Lynette Blignaut offers the perfect small B&B experience, with six fresh rooms done out in taupe and grey shades, and modern bathrooms. Breakfasts are copious – mmm, the homemade muffins! – and evening meals can be arranged.

Village in Hatfield   GUESTHOUSE $$
(Map p368; ☑012-362 3737; www.thevillageinhatfield.co.za; 1252 Arcadia St, Hatfield; s/d incl breakfast R660/880; P@☎) This delightful property offers well-presented and spacious self-catering rooms and helpful, friendly service. There's a swimming pool and a shaded courtyard. Excellent value.

Courtyard Arcadia Hotel   HOTEL $$$
(Map p368; ☑012-342 4940; www.clhg.com; cnr Park & Hill Sts, Arcadia; d R1900; P❄♠☎) At the upper end of the City Lodge chain spectrum is this Cape Dutch manor house in the heart of the embassy district. The 69 rooms, which occupy several residences, are a little pedestrian for the grandeur of the setting, but service is assured. Booking online gets you the best deal.

🛏 Brooklyn & Groenkloof

★**Bwelani**   GUESTHOUSE $$
(Map p368; ☑083 200 5939, 012-362 1148; www.bwelani.co.za; 210 Roper St, Brooklyn; s/d incl breakfast from R630/790, apt s/d R1090/1700; P❄♠☎) Concealed behind high walls down near the university, this bright, contemporary B&B has lots of personality. The nine rooms, including two self-catering apartments, are imaginatively designed and embellished with various African art pieces collected by the owner. Our fave is the loft room Jozi, with its funky decor and super-size bedroom. Dinner available on request.

Brooks Cottage   GUESTHOUSE $$
(Map p368; ☑082 448 3902, 012-362 3150; www.brookscottage.co.za; 283 Brooks St, Brooklyn; s/d incl breakfast R800/1100; P♠☎) This attractive address is in high demand, meaning you need to book well in advance to snag one of its cosy, excellent-value rooms with sparkling bathrooms. With its pressed ceilings, wooden floors and soberly elegant living room, this lovingly restored house has charm in spades.

Richtershuyz GUESTHOUSE $$
(Map p368; ☑012-346 2025; www.richtershuyz. co.za; 375 Mackenzie St, Brooklyn; s/d incl breakfast from R930/1150; P❄🛜🏊) In a residential neighbourhood, this low-slung building feels like a warm, soft nest. It conceals seven rooms that offer attractive tiled bathrooms, crisp linen, excellent bedding and complimentary snacks. The swimming pool in the garden is a little beauty and art works celebrating Elvis add a humorous touch.

131 Herbert Baker BOUTIQUE HOTEL $$$
(Map p368; ☑012-751 2070; www.131.co.za; 131 Herbert Baker St, Groenkloof; d/ste incl breakfast from R1750/5000; P❄🛜🏊) A hotel with style, this venture strikes a perfect balance between sophistication, seclusion and privacy (there are only eight rooms), on a hillside

---

WORTH A TRIP

CULLINAN

This pretty, over-100-year-old village offers quaint architecture, including a church designed by Herbert Baker. The reason that the village exists is that it is home to one of the biggest and most productive diamond-bearing kimberlite pipes in the world: three of the largest diamonds ever found came out of the ground here and the mine is still in full operation.

Cullinan is little more than a handful of picturesque streets clustering around the mine, but the last few years have seen a proliferation of accommodation options, restaurants, bistros, antiques shops and art galleries. The relaxed atmosphere, charming architecture and good infrastructures draw crowds, particularly at weekends.

Several tour companies, including **Premier Diamond Tours** (☑083 261 3550, 012-734 0081; www.diamondtourscullinan.co.za; 99 Oak Ave; 90min/4hr tours R130/550; ⊙10.30am & 2pm Mon-Fri, 10.30am & noon Sat) and **Fundani Tours** (☑081 403 1279; www.fundanitours. co.za; 99 Oak Ave; tours R120-450), offer 90-minute tours of the fascinating **Cullinan Diamond Mine** (www.petradiamonds.com/our-operations/our-mines/cullinan).

All tours start with a video about the mine's history and take in the massive hole (1km by 500m and far larger than the Big Hole at Kimberley) and the headgear of the skips that transport the ore from 700m underground. You see a mock-up of an underground tunnel and a display room with replicas of the famous diamonds discovered here, including the largest rough gem diamond ever discovered (in 1905). Named the Cullinan Diamond, this whopping 3106-carat rock was cut to form two major gems that are now part of the British Crown Jewels. Four-hour **underground tours** will get you into the workings of the mine – a fascinating experience (these must be booked a day in advance).

Fundani also offers **cycling tours** (from R350 including lunch, minimum two people) of Cullinan, or the nearby township of Refilwe, which is home to 90% of the miners who work in the diamond mine.

Gastehys JanHarmsgat (☑074 322 5225; www.gastehys.co.za; 8 Hospital Rd; s/d R660/830; P) An attraction in its own right, this four-room B&B in a renovated farmhouse is like something from an interior-design magazine crossed with a conceptual art project. It's all recycled knick-knacks, from old hospital tables and gilt frame mirrors to enamel ware and ironwork. The lush garden and generous breakfast (R80) are other assets, but note there's no wi-fi.

As Greek As it Gets (☑012-734 0707, 083 632 5364; www.asgreekasitgets.co.za; 86 Oak Ave; mains R135-210; ⊙11.45am-3.30pm & 5.45-8pm Thu-Sat, 1.45am-3.30pm Sun; ☑) Stavros Vladislavic, the larger-than-life patron of this place, sits by the door welcoming guests and keeping the staff on their toes as they dish out tasty mezze and other classic Greek dishes to the punters. The whitewash and turquoise decor plus the bright sunshine on the outdoor terrace will lull you into a relaxed mood.

Cockpit Brewhouse (☑012-734 0656; www.facebook.com/cockpitbrewhouse; 80 Oak Ave; mains R60-95; ⊙noon-6pm Wed-Sat, to 5pm Sun; 🛜) The aviation-themed Cockpit Brewhouse serves at least six of its own delicious microbrew draught ales and decent bar food, including a tasty lamb and beef burger. If you eat here a taster set of six of the beers is free, otherwise it's R50.

south of the centre – the location is one of the best in Pretoria. Ask for rooms 1, 2, 3 or 4, which come with city views.

🛌 Lynnwood, Menlo Park & Around

Foreigners Friend Guesthouse
GUESTHOUSE $$

(Map p368; ☑ 082 458 4951; www.foreignersfriend. co.za; 409A Om die Berg St, Lynnwood; s/d incl breakfast from R900/1200; P ❋ 🛜 ≋) Character and charm – this enchanting thatched-roof abode is an oasis of tranquillity in a wonderfully quiet neighbourhood. It has 10 spacious, well-organised rooms; a well-furnished ground-floor living area; a lush garden and a small swimming pool. A beautifully presented breakfast is served on a breezy terrace.

Ambiance Guesthouse
GUESTHOUSE $$

(Map p368; ☑ 083 280 0981; www.ambianceguesthouse.com; 28 3rd St, Menlo Park; s/d R850/1190; P 🛜 ≋) This elegant guesthouse in the leafy suburb of Menlo Park is just the ticket for those seeking a stylish home-away-from-home experience. The four self-catering rooms are different in design and colour scheme and open onto a delightful garden complete with a nifty pool; our choice is 'Petit Paris', replete with claw-footed bath. Breakfast costs R80.

★ Menlyn Boutique Hotel
BOUTIQUE HOTEL $$$

(Map p368; ☑ 086 100 7887; www.menlynhotel. com; 209 Tugela Rd, Ashlea Gardens; s/d from R1500/1700; P ❋ @ 🛜 ≋) Friendly and relaxed service combined with chic, sandstone-colour-scheme rooms make the Menlyn a hit. Even though it's near a busy highway, calm prevails within the grounds scattered liberally with with art and sculptures, including ones by father and son Anton and Lionel Smit. The pool area is so nice you may end up spending all your time here.

Another plus: the fine-dining restaurant Black Bamboo (☑ 084 508 9752; www.theblackbamboo.co.za; mains R165-200; ⊙ 6.30-10am, noon-10pm; 🛜) is also on-site.

★ Alpine Attitude
BOUTIQUE HOTEL $$$

(Map p368; ☑ 012-348 6504; www.alpineattitude. co.za; 522 Atterbury Rd, Menlo Park; s/d incl breakfast from R1500/1900; P ❋ 🛜 ≋) Looking for a night somewhere extra special? Make a beeline for this unique boutique hotel. The

seven rooms have been creatively designed – each one has its own theme and decor. The Transparent room, where pretty much everything (except the bedding and walls) is see-through, has to be seen to be believed. Amenities include a restaurant, a bar and a pool.

It also features five self-catering apartments. It's on a busy thoroughfare, but most units overlook a quiet garden at the back.

🍴 Eating

You'll find a good range of options in Hatfield (zone in on Hatfield Sq on Burnett St) and Brooklyn (around Fehrsen St and the Brooklyn Mall) as well as around Greenlyn Village Centre in Menlo Park and The Club in Hazelwood.

🍴 City Centre

Café Riche
BISTRO $

(Map p364; ☑ 012-328 3173; 2 WF Nkomo St; mains R45-90; ⊙ 6am-6pm; 🛜) This historic, early-20th-century European bistro overlooking Church Sq is the ideal place to sip beer and watch the South African capital roll through its day. The street tables are quickly nabbed by local office workers and politicians, while inside the atmospheric bar, unhurried staff serve sandwiches, pastries, salads and simple bistro meals.

TriBeCa CBD
CAFE $

(Map p364; ☑ 012-321 8876; www.tribeca.co.za; 220 Madiba St; mains R50-80; ⊙ 7am-5pm Mon-Fri) This popular downtown business-lunch place is safe and welcoming. Spitting distance from Church Sq, this chain restaurant is popular with public servants and lawyers in the nearby High Court Chambers. Salads and sandwiches are respectable, and best enjoyed in the outside seating area.

🍴 Arcadia, Hatfield & Villiera

★ Grounded At Echo
CAFE $

(Map p372; ☑ 012-329 0159; http://groundedat. co.za; Shop 1, 353 24th Ave, Villieria; ⊙ 6am-5pm Mon-Fri, 8am-3pm Sat, 8am-1pm Sun; 🛜) It's easy to love this design-savvy cafe run by the nonprofit Echo Youth Development. It's a great spot for breakfast, with a variety of granolas alongside some tempting egg dishes. The coffee and tea are top class and you can buy the beans and leaves (and the adorable mini-gingerbread men served gratis with each cup) to take away.

Brooklyn, Hatfield & Menlo Park

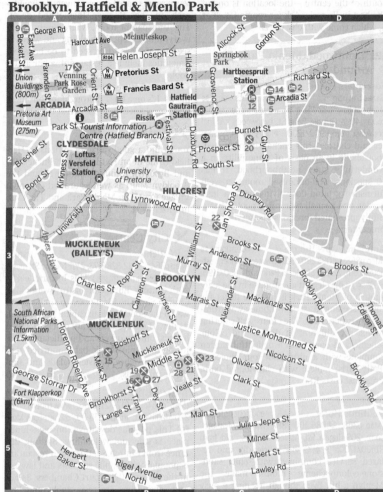

Papa's Restaurant
SOUTH AFRICAN **$$**

(Map p368; ☑012-362 2224; www.papasrestaurant.co.za; cnr Jan Shoba & Prospect Sts, Duncan Yard, Hatfield; mains R70-150; ⊙8am-9.30pm Mon-Sat, 10am-3pm Sun) Papa's serves various South African faves, including steaming *potjies* (meat and vegetables cooked in a cast-iron pot over an open fire) as well as delicious grilled meats, pizzas and pastas. The lovely courtyard gives you a good excuse to take your time, and the surrounding boutique arts, crafts, fashion and antiques shops provide welcome post-meal distractions.

Deli on Duncan
CAFE, DELI **$**

(Map p368; ☑012-362 4054; www.duncanyard.co.za/deli-on-duncan; cnr Jan Shoba & Prospect Sts, Duncan Yard, Hatfield; mains R15-50; ⊙8am-5pm Mon-Fri, to 3pm Sat, to 2pm Sun) This groovy place provides an unceasingly cool terrace for summer chillin'. An array of pastries, cakes, tarts and quiches will tempt the devil in you, or you could opt for the soup of the day. It also serves excellent coffees and fragrant teas.

Café 41
MEDITERRANEAN **$**

(Map p368; ☑012-342 8914; www.cafe41.co.za; Eastwood Village Centre, cnr Eastwood & Pretorius Sts, Arcadia; mains R50-105; ⊙7am-11.30pm Mon-

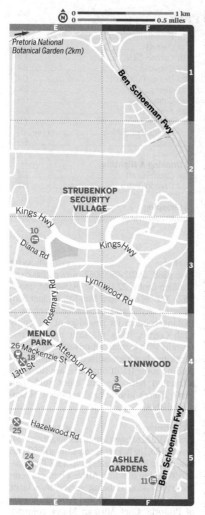

Pretoria National
Botanical Garden (2km)

Ben Schoeman Fwy

STRUBENKOP
SECURITY
VILLAGE

Kings Hwy

10

Diana Rd

Kings Hwy

Lynnwood Rd

Rosemary Rd

MENLO
PARK

26 Mackenzie St

18

13th St

Atterbury Rd

LYNNWOOD

3

25 Hazelwood Rd

24

ASHLEA
GARDENS

11

Ben Schoeman Fwy

0 — 1 km
0 — 0.5 miles

---

peaceful stretch of Bronkhorst St, this neighborhood charmer makes a great setting for a meet-up with a friend or a fine spot to linger over a light meal (sandwiches, pizzas, salads) when you're solo. It also sells baked goods (including highly popular croissants and muffins) and has good coffee.

★ Blue Crane
SOUTH AFRICAN $$

(Map p368; ☎ 012-460 7615; www.bluecranerestaurant.co.za; 156 Melk St, New Muckleneuk; mains R60-170; ⊗ 7.30am-3pm Mon, to 10pm Tue-Fri, 9am-10pm Sat, 9am-3pm Sun; 🔊📶) As part of the Austin Roberts Bird Sanctuary, Blue Crane is famous to ornithologists worldwide (and anyone else who enjoys a cold Castle lager at sunset), with a menu that begins with breakfast and moves on to steaks, salads, burgers and sandwiches. There are various dining rooms, including an atmospheric *boma* and a splendid deck overlooking a pond.

Geet
INDIAN $$

(Map p368; ☎ 012-460 3199; www.geetindianrestaurant.com; 541 Fehrsen St, Brooklyn; mains R90-175; ⊗ 11am-3pm & 5-10pm Mon-Sat, 11am-4pm Sun; 📶) Around the back of Brooklyn Mall, Chef Gita Jivan concocts first-class Indian dishes, fusing Indian flavours with European presentation. The huge menu emphasises North Indian delights, and vegetarians can feast well. The whisky lounge, where you can dine sitting on cushions, is a treat.

Crawdaddy's
BRASSERIE $$

(Map p368; ☎ 012-460 0889; www.crawdaddys.co.za; cnr Middle & Dey Sts, Brooklyn; mains R90-180; ⊗ 11am-10pm Mon-Sat, to 9pm Sun) An old favourite with hungry locals, this brasserie never fails to satisfy the requirements of its loyal punters. The key to its success is an eclectic menu that ranges from curries and stir-fries to grilled meats and seafood. It has several dining rooms and an open-air terrace that overlooks a busy intersection.

Carlton Café
CAFE $$

(Map p368; ☎ 012-460 7996; www.carltoncafe.co.za; Menlo Park Centre, 13th St, Menlo Park; mains R75-110; ⊗ 7.30am-4pm Mon, to 5pm Tue-Fri, to 2pm Sat) Since 2002, stylish Carlton Café and its associated deli Delicious (you'll find it next door) have been keeping Pretorians happy with gourmet treats. It's a great place for a leisurely breakfast offering unusual items such as Indian-style scrambled eggs or savoury French toast. Or just come to enjoy a coffee and one of its cakes.

Sat, 9am-10.30pm Sun; 🔊) A huge menu and a plethora of seating options – go for the outdoor deck – make this one of Pretoria's more enjoyable lunch spots. The pasta dishes and sandwiches won't blow your socks off but are good deals, as are the mezze platters.

✖ Brooklyn, New Muckleneuk & Around

Broodhuijs
BAKERY, CAFE $

(Map p368; ☎ 012-346 5753; www.broodhuijs.com; cnr Bronkhorst & Dey Sts, Brooklyn; mains R20-40; ⊗ 7am-4pm Mon-Fri, 8am-2pm Sat; 🔊) On a

Brooklyn, Hatfield & Menlo Park

Salt
MEDITERRANEAN $$

(Map p368; ☎079 540 3483; www.salteatery. co.za; 11 Hazelwood Rd, Hazelwood; mains R70-185; ⊙7am-9pm Tue-Sat, 8am-4pm Sun) Salt specialises in artisanal cheeses, cured meats and bread, which they bake themselves. You can assemble your own tasting plate from the very tempting range, which includes housecured and smoked pastrami, mild saucisson sausage and Huguenot cheddar, plus some luscious condiments. There's a nice terrace for dining and you're in the heart of the Hazelwood gourmet scene.

Ginger & Fig
CAFE $$

(Map p368; ☎012-362 5926; www.gingerandfig. co.za; Shop 5, Brooklyn Centre, 751 Jan Shoba St, Brooklyn; mains R60-105; ⊙6am-5.30pm Mon-Fri, 7am-3pm Sat) This highly reliable cafe has on-trend industrial-chic decor and a tempting range of breakfast and lunch dishes, all homemade, free range and organic where possible. Try the smocked chuck (beef) open sandwich with coffee barbecue sauce if it's available.

Kream
INTERNATIONAL $$$

(Map p368; ☎012-346 4642; www.kream.co.za; 570 Fehrsen St, Brooklyn Bridge, Brooklyn; mains R120-220; ⊙noon-10pm Mon-Sat, to 2.30pm Sun) Subtle is not a word in Kream's vocabulary. From its dramatic interior design (giant works of art, two water features!) to its sometimes over-the-top dishes (check out its Candy Crush sugar bomb dessert), this restaurant does nothing by halves. The eclectic menu features exotic starters, such as crocodile carpaccio, and the usual grilled suspects for main course.

Pacha's
SOUTH AFRICAN $$$

(Map p368; ☎012-460 5063; www.pachas.co.za; The Club Centre, 22 Dely Rd, Hazelwood; mains R160-200; ⊙noon-9pm Mon-Sat, to 3pm Sun) Offering style and substance, Pacha's is looking good in its new digs at the spiffy Club Centre. It's a pleasant modern restaurant with a small aquarium and quality furniture, but high-calibre meat dishes, including some traditional fare, are the main attraction here. Feeling more surf than turf? There's also a good selection of seafood dishes.

★ Fermier
INTERNATIONAL $$$

(☎076 072 5261; www.fermierrestaurant.com; 141 Lynwood Rd, The Willows; 9-course meal R550, plus wine pairing R900; ⊙seatings 7pm & 7.30pm Tue-Sat) ✎ Some of South Africa's best contemporary cooking is being served in a large mud-walled and tin-roofed shed in the east of Pretoria. Chef Adriaan Maree conjures up a fabulous nine-course, three-hour-long culinary journey with an underpinning ethos of minimum food waste, sustainability and a celebration of fine local produce. The series of small, creative dishes is magnificent.

🍷 Drinking & Nightlife

Hatfield has a decent range of bars, restaurants and clubs, with Hatfield Sq a university-student stronghold after dark. There are also some hip places in Menlo Park and Brooklyn.

★ **Capital Craft**   CRAFT BEER

(Map p368; ☎012-424 8601; www.capitalcraft.co.za; Greenlyn Village Centre, cnr Thomas Edison St & 12th St East, Menlo Park; ☺noon-midnight Tue, 10.30am-midnight Wed-Sat, 10.30am-8pm Sun) Pretoria's premier beer hangout is a huge place whose long tables, both inside the barn-like bar and out in the garden, are perpetually packed. The focus here is craft beer from around the country. The selection is impressive – try a few tasters before ordering a pint. Want something to soak up all that ale? The pulled-pork sandwich is superb.

★ **Carbon Bistro**   BAR

(Map p368; ☎012-340 0029; www.carbonbistro.co.za; 279 Dey St, Brooklyn; mains R99-180; ☺11am-11pm Mon-Sat, to 3pm Sun; 🅿) This places oozes hipster chic, with its minimalist decor, craft-beer taps, and cuts of steak you've maybe never heard of. However, it's the gin menu – featuring over 150 different makes, including many South African ones – that really grabs the attention. Tastings (from R105) of five different types are available.

African Beer Emporium   CRAFT BEER

(ABE; Map p364; ☎064 205 5069; www.africanbeeremporium.com; 012central backyard, 381 Helen Joseph St; ☺9am-6pm Mon-Fri, to 8pm Sat) Capital Craft are the brains behind this new, very welcome and large bar in the hip 012central (p363) precinct. The focus, as the name implies, is on local ales and there's a menu of African dishes to complement them. Seating is at Octoberfest-style long wooden tables.

❶ Information

EMERGENCY

Emergency ☎012-310 6300
Fire & Police ☎10111

MEDICAL SERVICES

Hatmed Medical Centre (☎012-362 7180; www.hatmed.co.za; 454 Hilda St, Hatfield; ☺8am-7pm Mon-Thu, to 6pm Fri, to 1pm Sat, to noon Sun) A well-known suburban clinic.

Tshwane District Hospital (☎012-354 7000; cnr Dr Savage & Steve Biko Rds) For medical emergencies.

TOURIST INFORMATION

South African National Parks (☎012-428 9111; www.sanparks.org) Your best bet for all wildlife-reserve bookings and enquiries.

Tourist Information Centre (Map p364; ☎012-358 1430; www.tshwanetourism.com; Old Nederlandsche Bank Bldg, Church Sq; ☺7.30am-4pm Mon-Fri) There's another branch in Hatfield (Map p368; ☎012-358 1675; Kingston House, 311 Eastwood St, Hatfield; ☺7.30am-4pm Mon-Fri).

❶ Getting There & Away

AIR

Jo'burg's OR Tambo International Airport (p354), 48km south of Pretoria, is South Africa's international hub, accepting flights from across the globe.

BUS

The **Pretoria Bus Station** (Map p364; 4 Scheiding St, Pretoria West) is next to Pretoria's train station. You will also find the major companies' booking and information offices here, as well as a cafe and an ATM.

Most **Translux** (www.translux.co.za), **City to City** (www.citytocity.co.za), **Intercape** (www.intercape.co.za) and **Greyhound** (www.greyhound.co.za) services running from Jo'burg to Durban, the South Coast and Cape Town originate in Pretoria. Services running north up the N1 also stop here. (Translux, Greyhound and Intercape fares from Pretoria are identical to those from Jo'burg, regardless of the one-hour difference in time.) If you only want to go between the two cities, it will cost about R200.

Baz Bus (www.bazbus.com) will pick up and drop off at Pretoria hostels.

Long-distance minibus taxis (Map p364) leave from the rank close to the train station.

WORTH A TRIP

NAN HUA TEMPLE

Rising out of the savannah, 56km east of Pretoria along the N4, is **Nan Hua Temple** (☎013-931 0009; www.nanhua.co.za; 27 Nan Hua Rd, Cultura Park, Bronkhorstspruit; ☺9am-5pm Tue-Sun) FREE, the largest Buddhist temple complex in the southern hemisphere. Opened by the Buddhist order Fo Guang Shan in 2005, the complex is a sight to behold with its brightly painted gates, carved stone lions and yellow-tiled temple roofs glistening in the blazing sunshine. The main shrine houses three beautifully carved wooden Buddhas.

Across the road from the main complex is the guesthouse where it's possible to stay and take part in meditation courses. There's also a dining hall here open to outside guests on Sunday from noon to 12.30pm for a vegetarian buffet (R30).

Around Pretoria

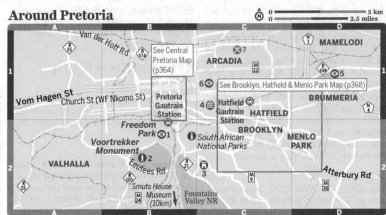

CAR

Many larger local and international car-hire companies are represented in Pretoria.

TRAIN

The historic Pretoria train station is an attractive location to commence or complete a journey.

The **Gautrain** (p356) service offers regular high-speed connections with Hatfield, Johannesburg (Park Station, Rosebank and Sandton) and onwards to the airport. The fare from Pretoria to Sandton is R57.

For long distances, **Shosholoza Meyl** (www.shosholozameyl.co.za) trains running through Pretoria are the *Trans Karoo* (daily from Pretoria to Cape Town) and the *Komati* (daily from Jo'burg to Komatipoort via Nelspruit). The luxury **Blue Train** (www.bluetrain.co.za), which links Pretoria, Jo'burg and Cape Town, originates here.

Because of a high incidence of crime, we don't recommend travelling between Pretoria and Jo'burg by Metro.

❶ Getting Around

TO/FROM THE AIRPORT

If you call ahead, most hostels, and many hotels, offer free pick-up.

Get You There Transfers (p355) operates shuttle buses between OR Tambo and Pretoria. They can pick you up from the airport and deposit you in Pretoria for about R700. Airport Shuttle (p355) offers the same service.

The Gautrain (p356) is a reliable and fairly fast way to get to the airport (you'll need to change at Marlboro). A one-way ticket is R174.

Around Pretoria

◎ Top Sights
1 Freedom Park.................................B2
2 Voortrekker Monument...................B2

◎ Sights
3 Fort Klapperkop............................C2
4 Pretoria Art Museum......................C1
5 Pretoria National Botanical
   Garden....................................D1
6 Union Buildings............................C1

✴ Eating
7 Grounded At Echo.........................C1

BUS

There's an extensive network of local buses – for more details check with the **bus enquiries office** (Map p364; ☎ 012-358 0839; www.tshwane.gov.za/sites/residents/TshwaneBusSerivces/Pages/Bus-Routes-Timetables.aspx; Church Sq; ☉ 4.30am-7pm Mon-Fri, 5am-2pm Sat). Fares range from R8 to R16, depending on the distance. Handy services include buses 5 and 8, which run between Church Sq and Brooklyn via Burnett St in Hatfield.

TAXI

You can get a metered taxi from **Rixi Taxis** (☎ 086 100 7494; www.rixitaxi.co.za; per km around R10). Locals tend to opt for Uber.

Around Pretoria

There are a few sights to the south and east of Pretoria that make interesting day trips from the city.

Fort Klapperkop

There are panoramic views from the 1889 fort that was one of four built to defend Pretoria, although in the end it was never used for that purpose. Located 6km south of the city, it's one of the best-preserved forts in South Africa, and its museum (Map p372; ☑012-346 7703; Johann Rissik Dr, Groenkloof; adult/child R25/5; ⊗10am-5pm Tue-Sun) tells the story of the country's military history from 1852 to the end of the 1899–1902 Anglo-Boer War.

Rietvlei Nature Reserve

This 38-sq-km reserve (☑012-358 1810; http://rietvlei-reserve.co.za; 14 Game Reserve Ave, Rietvallei; adult/child R50/30; ⊗6am-4pm Apr-Aug, 5.30am-5pm Sep-Mar) 🍃, 27km south of Pretoria, off Rte 21, is popular with locals who come for fishing in the dam, but is also great for wildlife viewing. Sightings of rhinos are common, often from the grounds of the small tearoom. You'll also spot zebras, various antelopes and perhaps buffaloes.

Activities on offer include guided hikes, night drives and horse riding.

Pretoria National Botanical Garden

Located around 9km east of central Pretoria, these gardens (Map p372; ☑012-843 5071; www.sanbi.org; 2 Cussonia Ave, Brummeria; adult/child R33/15; ⊗8am-6pm) cover 7700 sq metres and are planted with indigenous flora from around the country. There are 20,000-odd plant species, labelled and grouped according to their region of origin – a visit is a must for keen botanists.

Sammy Marks' Museum

This handsome mansion, 20km east of central Pretoria, was built in 1884 for the industrial, mining and agricultural magnate Sammy Marks. Now it's a fascinating museum (☑012-755 9542; www.ditsong.org.za; R104, Old Bronkhorstspruit Rd, Donkerhoek; adult/child R65/30; ⊗9am-4.30pm, tours Tue-Sun) that you can only enter on a tour (around five a day, each lasting an hour).

It's worth visiting also for the lovely grounds with a shady tea garden overlooking the house. This is as close as you'll get to a South African *Downton Abbey*.

Mpumalanga

Best Places to Eat

➡ Potluck Boskombuis (p386)

➡ Wild Fig Tree (p381)

➡ Kuka Café (p387)

➡ Cicada (p390)

➡ Greek Kouzina (p390)

Best Places to Stay

➡ River House Guest Lodge (p391)

➡ Idle & Wild (p387)

➡ Fountain Baths Guest Cottages (p394)

➡ Acra Retreat Mountain View Lodge (p379)

➡ Critchley Hackle (p378)

Why Go?

Mpumalanga is one of South Africa's smallest provinces and one of its most exciting. Visually, it's as beautiful as it is diverse, with mountain vistas, lush green valleys, arid bush, subtropical plantations and cool-climate towns. Its natural assets make it a prime target for outdoor enthusiasts, who come to abseil down waterfalls, throw themselves off cliffs, raft or tube down rivers, explore subterranean caves, gallop through grasslands, and hike or bike forest trails.

The province's major draw, though, is the massive Blyde River Canyon, which carves its way spectacularly through the Drakensberg Escarpment. The world's third-largest canyon, it's one of South Africa's iconic sights and on a clear day the many vantage points can leave you breathless.

The Eastern Lowveld also provides access to the southern half of Kruger National Park (p395), with an excellent selection of lodges and wilderness activities right on the mighty park's doorstep.

When to Go
Nelspruit

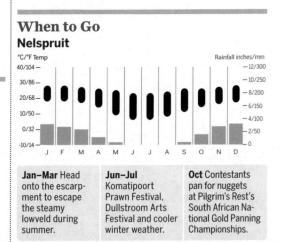

Jan–Mar Head onto the escarpment to escape the steamy lowveld during summer.

Jun–Jul Komatipoort Prawn Festival, Dullstroom Arts Festival and cooler winter weather.

Oct Contestants pan for nuggets at Pilgrim's Rest's South African National Gold Panning Championships.

Mpumalanga Highlights

1 Blyde River Canyon
(p385) Gazing in awe at the
Three Rondavels and other
rock formations in the world's
third-largest canyon.

2 Barberton (p392)
Discovering gold-rush history
and geological prehistory in
the province's most enjoyable
country town.

3 Dullstroom (p376)
Throwing a line in the water for
trout and tasting whisky in this
sophisticated highveld town.

4 Graskop (p383) Picking up
African arts and crafts before
hurling yourself into a gorge on
the Big Swing outside town.

5 Sabie (p379) Taking in the
misty mountain views on hikes

to waterfalls, and sampling
craft beer.

6 Pilgrim's Rest (p382)
Wandering down the main
street of this museum-packed,
19th-century gold-mining town.

7 Waterval Boven (p378)
Enjoying rock climbing,
mountain biking, waterfall
abseiling and hiking.

History

During the *difaqane* (forced migration) of the early 19th century, groups of Shangaan, Swazi and Ndebele entered the area, escaping turbulent times in Zululand. Voortrekkers first arrived on the scene in the late 1830s and had established the Transvaal (including the Eastern Transvaal, now Mpumalanga) as a republic within 10 years.

The Transvaal was the scene of the lesser-known First Anglo-Boer War (1880–81); the Boers were victorious, claiming back their territory and making Paul Kruger their first president. This independence lasted until the end of the Second Anglo-Boer War (1899–1902), when the Transvaal, also known as the South African Republic, was returned to British hands, along with the Orange Free State (today's Free State province). It then became the Transvaal Colony until the Union of South Africa (1910), followed by the Transvaal Province until 1994, when it was divided into Mpumalanga and the neighbouring provinces to the north and west: Limpopo, Gauteng and North West Province.

Language

Swati, Zulu and Ndebele are the main languages spoken in Mpumalanga, but it's easy to get by with English. In and around Nelspruit, you'll also hear a lot of Afrikaans.

ⓘ Information

Mpumalanga Tourism and Parks Agency (www.mpumalanga.com) The website has information on the province's tourist routes, nature reserves and more.

Safcol (www.safcol.co.za) Oversees forest areas, promotes ecotourism and manages hiking trails around Mpumalanga.

DRAKENSBERG ESCARPMENT

Home to some of South Africa's most striking landscapes, the Drakensberg Escarpment was, until a couple of centuries ago, untamed rainforest roamed by elephants, buffaloes and even lions. Today, it's holidaying South Africans and, increasingly, international visitors who wander the highlands, enjoying the beautiful landscape in their droves. The escarpment marks the point where the highveld plateau plunges down 1000m to the lowveld, forming a dramatic knot of soaring cliffs, canyons, sweeping hillsides and cool valleys thick with pine trees and waterfalls – an apt backdrop for the myriad adventure activities that are on offer here.

Dullstroom

📞 013 / POP 600 / ELEV 2053M

This little oasis is all about good food, old-fashioned English pubs, fresh country air and fishing in the surrounding cool waters. When you arrive you would be forgiven for thinking you had taken a wrong turn and ended up in Canada. Replete with pine trees and lined with pretty clapboard buildings, Dullstroom is one of the coldest towns in the country, and a popular place for international athletes to train at altitude.

The area is famous for one thing – trout – but there's lots more to do here, including hiking, playing golf and horse riding. A refined stop-off between Johannesburg and Kruger National Park, Dullstroom has plenty of pleasant spots to toast your first or last night in South Africa.

◉ Sights & Activities

Dullstroom is one of the best places in South Africa for trout fishing. Local flyfishing specialists include the **Mavungana Flyfishing Centre** (📞013-254 0270; www.flyfishing.co.za; Naledi Dr) and the **Village Angler** (📞013-254 0045; theangler@dullstroom.net; Naledi Dr).

ⓘ POLICE FINES

There have been cases of tourists being unlawfully fined by corrupt police, who have pocketed the money. If you are stopped, remember that it is illegal to pay cash to a traffic officer or any other official at the roadside. Fines should be paid at a police station or magistrates court, where a receipt must be issued. Road tolls must be paid at official toll plazas only.

If you have any problems or doubts, call the 24-hour police hotline (📞082 451 7044, 082 462 2557) or contact Kruger Lowveld Ehlanzeni (📞013-755 1988; www.krugerlowveld.com; Crossing Mall, cnr Madiba & Samora Machel Drs; ⊙7am-6pm Mon-Fri, 8am-1.30pm Sat).

Drakensberg Escarpment & Eastern Lowveld

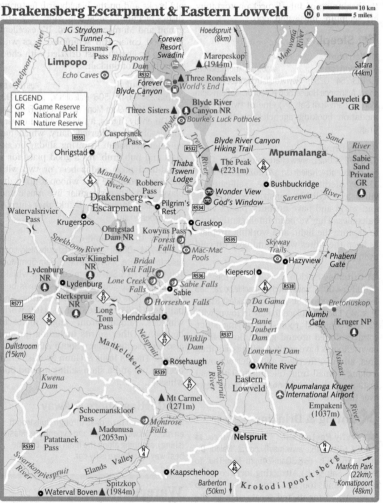

Dullstroom Bird of Prey & Rehabilitation Centre   BIRD SANCTUARY

(☏ 082 899 4108; www.birdsofprey.co.za; adult/child R70/40; ☺ 9am-4pm Wed-Mon, flying displays 10.30am & 2.30pm; P) This centre, south of town off Rte 540, teaches visitors about raptor species and the dangers facing them – you can even spend a morning learning the art of falconry (R400).

There are regular flying displays involving peregrine falcons, kestrels, buzzards and black eagles, among others.

Dullstroom Riding Centre   HORSE RIDING

(☏ 082 442 9766; www.dullstroomhorseriding.co.za; 1/2hr horse ride R200/350, 15min pony ride R60; ☻) This place offers horseback riding among hills, forests, streams and dams on a country estate north of town. It's about 10km from Dullstroom on Rte 540 to Lydenburg (Mashishing).

🎊 Festivals & Events

Dullstroom Arts Festival   CULTURAL

(☺ Jun/Jul) Try catching this platform for showcasing local talent at the end of June or the beginning of July. Expect photography, art, sculpture, music and food.

🛏 Sleeping

Dullstroom

Reservations   ACCOMMODATION SERVICES
(☑013-254 0254; www.dullstroomreservations. co.za; Auldstone House, 506 Naledi Dr; ⊙8am-5pm Mon-Fri, 9am-4pm Sat; P) One of two accommodation booking agencies on the main drag.

Cherry Grove   APARTMENT $$
(☑013-254 0421; www.cherry-grove.co.za; Cherry Grove Centre, Naledi Dr; s/d R675/1190; P🖥) These Mediterranean-style self-catering villas are stylishly constructed in stone and wood and have upstairs 'piazza view' balconies. They've been intelligently built to capture the light, and working fireplaces keep the suites warm and cosy on cold evenings.

★Critchley Hackle   LODGE $$$
(☑013-254 0055; www.critchley-hackle.co.za; 585 Teding van Berkhout St; ⊙r incl breakfast R1850; P🖥🏊) The best place to stay in town, with 12 well-equipped rooms occupying stone cottages dotted around grassy, flower-filled lawns. Rooms have vaulted ceilings, a sitting area, an open fireplace and a terrace overlooking a small trout-filled dam. The great restaurant is glass-fronted and has views over the gardens.

🍴 Eating & Drinking

★Mayfly Restaurant   INTERNATIONAL $$
(☑084 619 4946; www.mayfly.co.za; Naledi Dr; mains R62-183; ⊙8.30am-7.45pm Mon-Thu, to 9pm Fri & Sat; 🖥🍴) Attracting local couples, families and tourists, this classy set-up is renowned for its red meat, such as the recommended Mayfly rump topped with red wine, mushroom sauce and more, but it's also good for a cooked breakfast or light lunch. The cavernous interior with wood-burning heater, exposed beams and simple, stylish furniture creates an intimate dining atmosphere.

Mad Hatter Café   INTERNATIONAL $$
(☑013-254 0086; www.facebook.com/madhatter-dullstroom; Cherry Grove Centre, Naledi Dr; mains R90; ⊙7am-4.30pm Thu-Tue) Overlooking the cobbled piazza in the Italianate Cherry Grove, this creative little cafe in black, white and red has puntastic menus stuck into

old books and on the blackboard, featuring dishes including chicken in wine, beef stroganoff and Moroccan chicken. It's excellent for good coffee and scrambled eggs with chorizo or French toast drizzled with chocolate, honey or dukkah.

Duck & Trout   PUB FOOD $$
(☑013-254 0047; 506 Naledi Dr; mains R90; ⊙kitchen 10am-9pm Mon-Thu, to 10pm Fri & Sat; 🍴) On chilly nights, a fire crackles in every corner of this converted dairy, which has an extensive menu featuring all-day breakfasts and pub grub. It's a good place for a wood-fired pizza and a beer or two with the locals while the kids whoop it up in the playground. There's regular live music and an annual Oktoberfest, **Ducktober** (http:// ducktober.co.za).

★Wild About Whisky   BAR
(☑013-254 0066; www.wildaboutwhisky.com; Auldstone House, 506 Naledi Dr; ⊙9am-5pm Mon-Thu, to 7pm Fri & Sat, to 4pm Sun) This whisky bar, one of the southern hemisphere's best stocked, offers over 30 themed tastings and pairings (R165 to R865) of its 1400 world whiskies, ranging from single malts to bourbons. Other spirits including gin are also represented, as are South African producers. There's Innis & Gunn Scottish craft beer on tap and a shop selling around 300 whiskies.

ℹ Getting There & Away

Minibus shared taxis pass through Dullstroom en route between Belfast and Lydenburg (Mashishing), stopping along the main road, but the best way to get here is by car.

Waterval Boven (Emgwenya)

☑013 / POP 6200

Rock climbers, mountain bikers, waterfall abseilers, hikers and other outdoor enthusiasts flock to this minute town, just off the N4, for serious adventure-sport action. Nestled into the Drakensberg Mountains, it has a spectacular natural setting.

The town is a handy stop-off about 2½ hours' drive from both OR Tambo International Airport (245km) and Kruger National Park's Malelane gate (165km). It was officially renamed Emgwenya, and you will see the name on newer signposts, but most locals continue to use the old title.

🏃 Activities

Roc 'n Rope Adventures
CLIMBING

(📞 013-257 0363; www.rocrope.com; 53 3rd Ave) The cliffs around Waterval Boven are one of South Africa's premier rock-climbing destinations, with almost 1000 climbs. Gustav, who quite literally wrote the guide to climbing here (download it free from www.climbing.co.za/wiki/waterval_boven), offers a range of excursions and courses (including a two-day introduction) as well as equipment rental and a climbers' lodge.

BBK Trails
HORSE RIDING

(📞 082 853 3993; www.bbktrails.co.za; N4) Trots through the mountains, lasting from 30 minutes (R150) to four hours (R750). For a cracking start to the day, try the Champagne Brunch ride to a secluded valley for breakfast with bubbly and orange juice (R400); or finish the day climbing to a viewpoint for sundowners (R400).

🛌 Sleeping & Eating

⭐ Acra Retreat
Mountain View Lodge
LODGE $$

(📞 083 485 7665, 013-257 7088; www.acra-retreat.com; 5th St; s incl breakfast s R560-920, d R850-1120; P✱🅰️💺) A relaxing mountaintop retreat, welcoming Acra has great decks to enjoy the vertiginous valley views, a cosy bar and spacious rooms decked out in African decor. German–South African owner Holger is having fun with this '70s pad; in places it's like Scaramanga's island hideaway, with features such as a hidden room entered through a bathroom. Dinner is R259.

There is a self-catering cottage (breakfast not included) accommodating up to six (R1300).

Shamrock Arms
INN $$

(📞 013-257 0888; www.shamrockarms.co.za; 68 3rd Ave; s/d incl breakfast R835/1250; P✱🅰️) The Shamrock has seven beautifully furnished rooms with modern conveniences, including TV and minibar. In the cosy old pub-restaurant at the front, friendly hosts Terry, Cheryl, Jako and Sue offer guests large portions of local trout, rump steak and other British country food (three-course dinner R260).

Aloes Country Inn
PUB FOOD $$

(Hillbilly Bar; 📞 013-257 7037; www.aloescountry-inn.co.za; N4; mains R50-100; ⊙9am-9pm; 🍴) This slightly ramshackle pub is OK for a light lunch, with outside seating and a jungle gym. Dishes range from toasted sandwiches, burgers and pizzas to steaks, pasta and chicken schnitzel. It's around 7km east of the Waterval Boven turnoff.

ℹ️ Getting There & Away

Minibus shared taxis (3rd Ave) to Nelspruit (Mbombela), about two hours away, cost R65. You can pick one up at the petrol station at the western end of main drag 3rd Ave.

Shuttles (p391) and buses (p390) travelling along the N4 between Nelspruit and Pretoria, Jo'burg and OR Tambo International Airport stop here.

Sabie
📞 013 / POP 9200 / ELEV 1100M

Sabie is a quiet little town, with more of an authentic feel than the likes of Graskop and Dullstroom. There are some excellent eating options and a range of accommodation, and the lush, mountainous countryside makes a delightful backdrop. Out of town, you'll quickly discover hidden waterfalls, streams and walking trails. Sabie is a favourite with outdoorsy types, who enjoy the heart-pumping activities – including rafting, canyoning (known as kloofing around these parts) and abseiling – that abound in the surrounding forests.

◉ Sights

Komatiland Forestry Museum
MUSEUM

(📞 013-754 2700; www.safcol.co.za; cnr Ford St & Tenth Ave; adult/child R10/5; ⊙8am-1pm & 2-4.30pm Mon-Fri, to noon Sat) This museum has displays on local forests and the history

---

SABIE'S WATERFALLS

The area around Sabie positively gushes with waterfalls, including **Sabie Falls**, just north of town off Rte 532 to Graskop; the 70m **Bridal Veil Falls**, northwest of Sabie, off Old Lydenburg Rd; the 68m **Lone Creek Falls**, also off Old Lydenburg Rd, and with wheelchair access; and **Horseshoe Falls**, about 5km southwest of Lone Creek Falls. The popular **Mac-Mac Falls**, about 12km north of Sabie, off Rte 532 to Graskop, take their name from the many Scots on the local mining register. About 3km southeast of the falls are the **Mac-Mac Pools**, where you can swim. Admission to most of the waterfalls is R10 per car.

Sabie

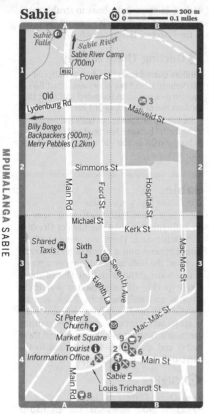

Sabie

◎ Sights
1 Komatiland Forestry Museum............A3

✪ Activities, Courses & Tours
2 Kestell Adventures...............................B4

🛏 Sleeping
3 Sabie Townhouse................................. B1

✪ Eating
4 African Elephant...................................A4
5 Wild Fig Tree...B4
6 Woodsman...B4

◎ Drinking & Nightlife
7 Coffee Etc..B4
8 Sabie Brewing Company.....................A4

✪ Shopping
Bookman's Corner........................(see 6)
9 Mphozeni Crafts...................................B4

of the South African timber industry. There's a historical examination of the use of timber and the introduction of plantations to protect indigenous forests that were disappearing fast. The museum has wheelchair access and information on day and overnight forest hiking trails.

🏃 Activities

Pick up permits and maps from Komatiland Forestry Museum for 4km, 6.5km and 10.2km **day hikes** (R20) in the surrounding pine and eucalyptus plantation forest and indigenous woodland, taking in waterfalls, viewpoints, picnic sites, birdlife and gold-mining history. There's also an **overnight trail** (R105) with accommodation in a basic mountaintop hut with a toilet, shower and bunk beds.

Kestell Adventures   ADVENTURE SPORTS
(🕿 072 351 5553; www.kestelladventures.com; cnr Louis Trichardt & Main Sts) If you're into adventure activities, this outfit can organise kloofing (canyoning), candlelight caving, tubing, abseiling down Sabie Falls and more.

🛏 Sleeping

Sabie River Camp   CAMPGROUND $
(🕿 013-764 3282; www.sabierivercamp.co.za; 30 Plaaswaterval Ave; camping R130) Every level of camping is offered here, from sites where you pitch your own, to ready-pitched tents with beds and bedding (singles/doubles R310/420) and en-suite safari tents with their own kitchenette (singles/doubles R390/550). It's in a lovely location on the banks of the Sabie River just out of town, off the road to Graskop.

Billy Bongo Backpackers   HOSTEL $
(🕿 072 370 7219; www.facebook.com/billybongobackpackers; 173 Old Lydenburg Rd; dm R200; r from R500, with shared bathroom from R400; 🅿🛜) 🌱 This rustic spot has a definite party atmosphere with nights full of drinking, bongo drumming and bonfires. It's clean and well equipped, featuring a lounge with a pool table, a TV room and a kitchen, and the small property packs in accommodation from rooms to garden huts. It's mostly solar powered.

★ Sabie Townhouse   B&B $$
(🕿 013-764 2292; www.sabietownhouse.co.za; 25 Maliveld St; s/d incl breakfast from R795/1100; 🅿🛜🏊) This pretty river-stone house has a fabulous pool terrace with a safari-tent bar

and braai (barbecue), all overlooking the Sabie River valley. Inside are a lounge, pool table and games room. The eight rooms with private entrances include budget, luxury and family options, and travellers appreciate the warm hospitality from Greg and family.

Merry Pebbles CARAVAN PARK $$
(☑013-764 2266; www.merrypebbles.co.za; off Old Lydenburg Rd; camping R180, r R1200-2500; P🛜🏊👶) This leafy and well-run caravan park has riverside campsites, a poolside bar-restaurant, a shop, a liquor store and an ATM. There's a range of cabanas, chalets and cottages with one to three bedrooms.

✖ Eating & Drinking

★**Wild Fig Tree** SOUTH AFRICAN $$
(☑013-764 2239; www.facebook.com/wildfig-treesabie; cnr Main & Louis Trichardt Sts; light meals R50, mains R70-170; ⊙8.30am-8.30pm Mon-Sat) There's a meat-driven menu and a warm atmosphere here, amid candles, wildlife photos and artworks. It's a great place to sample traditional South African dishes, especially game meat – from ostrich kebabs and crocodile curry to *bobotie* and *potjie* stew. The ploughman's or trout platter makes a terrific lunch, while pizzas, tramezzinis and toasted sandwiches are also on offer.

African Elephant INTERNATIONAL $$
(☑013-764 1909; www.facebook.com/theafricanel-ephant; Louis Trichardt St; lunch mains R50-90, dinner mains R100-170; ⊙8.30am-9pm) Locals rate this all-rounder with an expansive menu featuring hearty dinner mains such as surf and turf, ribs and wings, and flame-grilled steaks. There's lighter fare for lunch, including burgers, pancakes and chicken schnitzel, and a wood-burner for cold and misty days. The cavernous interior, adorned with baseball caps, wood-carved antelope heads and pictures of the eponymous pachyderm, is appealing.

Woodsman GREEK $$
(☑013-764 2015; www.thewoodsman.co.za; 94 Main St; mains R80-160; ⊙7am-9pm, bar to midnight; 👶) Half pub, half restaurant, the Woodsman offers great food with a Greek twist. Moussaka, stifado stew, grilled calamari, *mezedhes* (starter plates) and other offerings are mixed with local dishes: panfried trout, and ostrich in red wine and oregano feature. Most folk will find their spot, be it raucous beer drinking at the bar or candlelit fine dining on the balcony.

★**Sabie Brewing Company** CRAFT BEER
(☑013-764 1005; www.sabiebrewery.com; 45 Main Rd; ⊙10am-6pm, kitchen to 5pm) Occupying a 1921 trading post, this microbrewery has a bar-restaurant in its pleasant modern interior. Grab a taster platter of the full range of seven beers (R60) to enjoy on the wooden deck overlooking Main St. It's a nice spot for a sundowner. Pub grub on offer includes burgers, cheese platters, lamb curry and pies (mains R45 to R170).

Coffee Etc CAFE
(☑013-764 2074; Mac-Mac St; ⊙8.30am-5pm Mon-Fri, to 4pm Sat & Sun) Owner Helen bakes everything herself and has even invented two cakes: the Middle Eastern Delight (featuring almonds, Turkish apricots, nutmeg and cloves, with honey and cream-cheese icing) and a pineapple coconut cream concoction. Coffees, milkshakes, smoothies and frappés are on the drinks menu and you sit among tomes from the adjoining bookshop (mainly the gardening and Afrikaans sections).

🛍 Shopping

Mphozeni Crafts ARTS & CRAFTS
(☑013-764 2074; 94 Main St; ⊙8.30am-5pm Mon-Fri, to 4pm Sat & Sun) A lovely selection of African arts and crafts and textiles, including jewellery, statuary, woodcarvings, pottery, basketry and children's T-shirts.

Bookman's Corner BOOKS
(☑013-764 2074; cnr Main & Mac-Mac Sts; ⊙8.30am-5pm Mon-Fri, to 4pm Sat & Sun) Pick up the latest Deon Meyer thriller at this secondhand bookshop, which is one of South Africa's largest, with lots of paperback novels, a South African section and maps. The chat from owner Tiger comes for free.

ℹ Information

Sabie 5 (☑082 736 8253; barbarapetley@gmail.com; cnr Louis Trichardt & Main Sts; ⊙9am-3.30pm Mon-Fri, to noon Sat) This helpful private operation offers information and bookings, covering everything from local activities to Kruger National Park.

Sabie Source of Surprises (www.sabie.co.za) Online directory.

Tourist Information Office (☑013-590 5452; www.sabie-info.com; Market Sq; ⊙9am-4pm Mon-Fri, to 2pm Sat & Sun) Staffed by a personable Afrikaans poet from Cape Town, this helpful office offers accommodation recommendations, brochures, activity bookings and plenty of local information.

ℹ Getting There & Away

There are daily buses from Jo'burg to Nelspruit (Mbombela), from where you can get minibus shared taxis to Sabie (R35, one hour). Minibus shared taxis also run frequently to and from Hazyview (R30, one hour).

Driving north from here, for example to Hoedspruit or Kruger National Park's Orpen gate, the route via the Blyde River Canyon (Rte 532) and the JG Strydom Tunnel (Rte 36) is the most scenic. It can also be quicker, as Bushbuckridge gets busy with traffic, for example on Friday afternoons when the locals descend for banking and shopping.

Pilgrim's Rest

☑ 013 / POP 1730

Tiny Pilgrim's Rest appears frozen in time – a well-preserved 19th-century gold-rush town with wooden and corrugated-iron houses lining a pretty main street. The town is looking slightly scruffy these days and tourism has suffered, leaving many locals without an income, despite the souvenir shops and curio stalls lining the main drag between the museums. Mpumalanga locals roll their eyes at the mention of Pilgrim's Rest and bemoan its municipal mismanagement and subsequent decline, but don't be put off as it remains a historic and atmospheric spot.

◉ Sights

Most points of interest are in the Uptown area; the Downtown (or Onderdorp) area is 300m north. There are seven small museums covering various aspects of Pilgrim's Rest's history – enough to fill a leisurely day of exploring.

Diggings Museum MUSEUM
(www.pilgrims-rest.co.za; off Rte 533; adult/child R20/10; ☺ tours 10am, 11am, noon, 2pm & 3pm) Just southeast of town along the Graskop road is the open-air Diggings Museum, where you can see how gold was panned.

ℹ **PILGRIM'S PARKING**

Beware the competitive ferociousness of the informal car-park attendants waving cars into parks on the side of the road. Tell them firmly that you do not want your car washed, or they may do so without asking and present you with a sign specifying an extortionate fee, such as R80, for the service.

You need to visit on a tour, which you can arrange through the information centre.

Victoria House Museum MUSEUM
(www.pilgrims-rest.co.za; Main St; adult/child R20/10; ☺ 9am-4pm) This restored Victorian home is full of B&W photos, old dolls and furniture, including a wooden carved commode in the main bedroom. Admission includes entry to four other museums.

Alanglade MUSEUM
(☑ 013-768 1060; www.pilgrims-rest.co.za; off Rte 533; adult/child R20/10; ☺ tours 11am & 2pm) A former mine-manager's residence at the northern edge of town, beautifully decked out in 1920s style with original artefacts. Tours need to be booked 30 minutes in advance.

✷✷ Festivals & Events

**South African National
Gold Panning Championships** SPORTS
(off Rte 533) Contestants from local school children to semi-professionals pan for nuggets at this atmospheric annual event, which takes place by the Blyde River at the beginning of October.

⊨ Sleeping & Eating

There is an excellent pancake house Uptown and a good cafe and restaurant Downtown. The Royal Hotel offers half-board accommodation, but consider forgoing their dinner, which is often a buffet affair, to dine at the Vine Restaurant.

Royal Hotel HISTORIC HOTEL $$
(☑ 013-768 1100; www.royalhotelpilgrims.co.za; Main St; s/d incl breakfast R735/1270, s/d with half board R805/1460; ☎) Staying in this elegant 19th-century building in the centre of Uptown is a worthwhile experience; book ahead. The 50 rooms have Victorian baths, brass beds and other period features. Most aren't in the main building but in various houses on the main street, many with porches and great views. The adjoining **Church Bar** is a good spot for a drink.

Pancakes at The Stables CRÊPES $
(Main St; mains R20-75; ☺ 9am-5pm Tue-Sun) Occupying a stable dating from 1895, this cute little place has a corrugated-tin roof and wooden tables and benches outside. They serve a dozen excellent pancakes, with classic South African fillings such as mild springbok coconut curry and milk tart, and good coffee.

Vine Restaurant

SOUTH AFRICAN $$

(☑ 013-768 1080; thevine.pilgrims@gmail.com; Main St; mains R70-100; ⏱ 10am-7pm Mon-Fri, from 8am Sat, 8am-3pm Sun) This nicely restored general dealer's shop, decorated with local animal art, serves traditional dishes such as *bobotie* and ostrich-neck *potjie* stew. Burgers, prego rolls, chicken schnitzels, salads and toasted sandwiches also feature on the menu, and they make their own sauces. Cosy Johnny's Pub at the rear is crammed with old signposts, beer mirrors, sports T-shirts and so on.

❶ Information

For ATMs, go to Graskop, 15km southeast.

Visitor Information Centre (☑ 013-768 1060; www.pilgrims-rest.co.za; Main St; ⏱ 8.30am-4.30pm Mon-Fri, 9am-4pm Sat & Sun) This helpful centre is where you buy a combination ticket (adult/child R20/10) for five of the town's seven museums. It also has an accommodation list.

❶ Getting There & Away

Sporadic minibus shared taxis run between Pilgrim's Rest and Graskop (R15, 30 minutes), but most traffic along this treacherous road is in private vehicles. Go to Graskop for petrol stations.

Graskop

☑ 013 / POP 4000 / ELEV 1450M

This compact town is one of the most appealing in the area, with a sunny disposition, sleepy backstreets and gently sloping hills in every direction. While it's a popular stop with the tour buses, most unload on the main street, leaving plenty of room around town for everyone else. There are numerous guesthouses, restaurants and craft shops for a pleasant stopover. On summer afternoons (October to March), the restaurant terraces are full and there's a friendly buzz.

Graskop is a useful base for exploring the Blyde River Canyon, and the nearby views over the edge of the Drakensberg Escarpment are magnificent. Adding considerable excitement and adrenaline to the vistas are the Big Swing and Graskop Gorge Lift, which face each other across a forested ravine.

◎ Sights & Activities

There's good hiking and mountain biking in the area. The information offices (p385) can point you in the right direction, and you can hire bikes (per half-day R150) from Valley View Backpackers (p384).

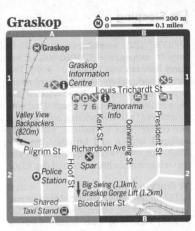

MPUMALANGA GRASKOP

Graskop

◉ **Sleeping**
- 1 Autumn Breeze B1
- 2 Graskop Hotel A1
- 3 Le Gallerie B1

◉ **Eating**
- 4 Canimambo A1
- 5 Finches B1
- 6 Harrie's Pancakes A1

◉ **Shopping**
- 7 Delagoa A1

Graskop Gorge Lift

VIEWPOINT

(☑ 066 305 1572; www.graskopgorgeliftcompany.co.za; Rte 533; adult/child R175/120; ⏱ 8.30am-5.30pm; 🅿) This glass viewing elevator travels 51m down the sheer cliffs of Graskop Gorge, with views of the Big Swing opposite, to an elevated forest boardwalk, which leads 500m to a 70m-high waterfall via suspension bridges and exhibits. At the top of the shaft, a lifestyle centre with a restaurant, craft market and shops perches on the precipice. Tickets are valid for multiple rides during the day of purchase.

Big Swing

ADVENTURE SPORTS

(☑ 079 779 8713; www.bigswing.co.za; Rte 533; single/tandem jump R350/600, zip line only R100; ⏱ 8.30am-4.45pm Tue-Sun) One of the highest cable gorge swings in the world, Big Swing has a free-fall of 68m (that's like falling 19 storeys in less than three seconds) into Graskop Gorge. You then swing like a pendulum across the width of the gorge – which gives you an outstanding view. There's also a 135m-long, high-wire 'foefie slide' (zip line).

🛏 Sleeping

Valley View Backpackers　　　HOSTEL $

(☑ 013-767 1112; www.valley-view.co.za; 47 De Lange St; camping/dm/r R110/160/400, s/d with shared bathroom from R300/340; P🛜) This friendly backpackers has a variety of rooms in good condition, plus basic wooden cabins, a self-catering rondavel (round hut with conical roof) and self-catering cottage. It's a nice country spot to chill out, with a fully equipped kitchen and breakfast available (R25). The owners can organise tours and rent out mountain bikes (per half-day R150).

⭐ **Graskop Hotel**　　　HOTEL $$

(☑ 013-767 1244; www.graskophotel.co.za; cnr Hoof & Louis Trichardt Sts; s/d incl breakfast R850/1320; P🛜🏊) This classy hotel is one of our favourites in the province. The 19 small rooms in the main building are slick, stylish and individual; several feature art and design by contemporary South African artists – room nine is rustic meets pop art – as do the lounge, bar and dining room. Sadly, it's often swamped by coach parties, so book ahead.

The 15 garden bungalow rooms out the back – little wheelchair-friendly country cottages with doll's house-like furniture – are equally comfortable, with glass doors opening onto the lush garden.

If you'd like an early breakfast to beat the crowds heading to the Blyde River Canyon, Graskop Hotel offers a buffet (from R45) from 7am to 9.30am. Nonguests are welcome to join if there's space.

Le Gallerie　　　GUESTHOUSE $$

(☑ 013-767 1093; www.legallerie.co.za; cnr Louis Trichardt & Oorwinning Sts; s/d incl breakfast R780/1300; P@🛜) A luxury guesthouse and art gallery with paintings and photography by owner Maria for sale in the three rooms, which have sumptuous furnishings and private access. Breakfast (R90) and picnic packs (R100) are available.

Autumn Breeze　　　B&B $$

(☑ 076 089 8542, 013-767 1016; www.autumnbreezemanor.co.za; cnr Louis Trichardt & President Sts; incl breakfast s R550-650, d R900-1200; P❄🛜🏊) Autumn Breeze has 15 rooms in the main lodge and the 'manor', two modern buildings facing each other. Ask to see a few rooms if available, as there is a range of facilities and layouts. In the lodge, room 10 is pleasant, with a spa bath and open shower, but note that room nine, a family room, has an open-plan bathroom.

🍴 Eating

Finches　　　PIZZA $$

(☑ 060 642 4713; President St; mains R35-95; ⊘2-8pm, bar to 11.30pm) Named after the finches chirping in the trees by its courtyard, this cosy bar-restaurant serves wood-fired pizzas with toppings such as biltong, blue cheese, garlic and sweet piquanté peppers, as well as burgers, lamb chops, toasted sandwiches and bunny chow (curry in a hollowed bread loaf, a Durban speciality), beneath corrugated iron and exposed beams.

Canimambo　　　PORTUGUESE $$

(☑ 013-767 1868; www.canimambo.za.net; cnr Hoof & Louis Trichardt Sts; dishes R60-230; ⊘11am-9pm; 🛜🍴) A Portuguese and Mozambican joint with a fire pit out front, serving spicy stews and grills as well as seafood dishes such as sardines, lemon and garlic prawns and one- or two-person platters. Try the chicken Chacuti stew or prego roll. Lighter dishes include burgers, salads and, until 5pm, toasted sandwiches.

Harrie's Pancakes　　　CRÊPES $$

(☑ 013-767 1273; www.harriespancakes.com; cnr Louis Trichardt & Kerk Sts; pancakes R90; ⊘8am-5pm Mon-Sat, from 9am Sun) The chic white minimalist interior of Graskop's original pancake house, full of modern art and quirky touches, often fills with coach parties. You won't find breakfast-style pancakes here but mostly savoury and exotic fillings, from Dutch bacon to biltong with mozzarella, as well as sweet offerings such as lemon meringue pie.

Kruger's Gold　　　INTERNATIONAL $$

(☑ 071 590 1510; www.hoyohoyoleisure.co.za; Eagle's View Eco Estate, Rte 533; mains R120; ⊘8am-5pm Sun-Thu, to 6pm Fri & Sat; 🛜) Fine dining comes to Graskop on a country estate, 4km south of town. The restaurant does wonderful things with beef, chicken, lamb and seafood; dishes range from lamb chops and T-bone steak to Dullstroom trout and chicken curry. There are also wood-fired pizzas.

🛍 Shopping

Delagoa　　　ARTS & CRAFTS

(☑ 013-767 1081; www.delagoa.co.za; Louis Trichardt St; ⊘8am-6pm) This busy shop has contemporary crafts from beadwork and woven baskets to engraved ostrich eggs and make-up bags decorated with African proverbs. It's solidly South African in the main, but there are pieces from further afield such as masks from Cameroon and the Côte d'Ivoire. Its line in kids' clothing isn't cheap, but it's high quality and quite distinctive.

❶ Information

Graskop Information Centre (☏013-767 1833; Pilgrim St; ⊙7.30am-4.45pm Mon-Fri, 8.30am-1pm Sat) Private office offering accommodation bookings, maps, second-hand books and memory cards.

Panorama Info (☏013-767 1377; www.panoramainfo.co.za; cnr Louis Trichardt & Kerk Sts; ⊙9am-4.30pm Mon-Fri) This gift shop and tourist office sells maps and helps with accommodation bookings.

❶ Getting There & Away

The **shared taxi stand** (Hoof St) is diagonally opposite the Total garage at the southern end of town. There are daily minibus taxis to Pilgrim's

Rest (R15, 30 minutes), Sabie (R22, 40 minutes) and Hazyview (R28, one hour).

Blyde River Canyon

Blyde River Canyon is both one of the world's largest canyons and one of South Africa's most outstanding natural sights – little wonder that it is increasingly popular with international visitors. The canyon's scale and beauty make a trip here a memorable experience, especially if you're lucky enough to visit on a fine day. Epic rock formations tower above the forested slopes and eagle-eye views abound at the dramatic meeting of the Drakensberg Escarpment and the lowveld.

Appreciating the area's scenery is easy on Rte 532, which largely follows the edge of the canyon as it winds north from Graskop.

TOURING AROUND BLYDE RIVER CANYON

Heading north from Graskop, look first for the **Pinnacle** (Rte 534; adult/child R10/5; ⊙7am-5pm; Ⓟ), a striking skyscraper-like rock formation. Just to the north along Rte 534 (a loop off Rte 532) are **God's Window** (Rte 534; adult/child R10/5; ⊙7am-5pm; Ⓟ) and **Wonder View** (Rte 534; ⊙7am-5pm; Ⓟ) **FREE**, both offering amazing vistas. At God's Window, take the trail up to the **rainforest** (300 steps), where you might spot rare birds, including the elusive loerie, on the boardwalk to the viewpoint.

When you return to Rte 532, take a short detour 2km south to the impressive **Lisbon Falls** (off Rte 532; per car R10; ⊙8am-5pm; Ⓟ) – or if you are coming back to Graskop, catch it on the way back. Continuing north, you'll pass the turnoff for the **Berlin Falls** (off Rte 532; per car R10; ⊙8am-5pm; Ⓟ), the less impressive of the two waterfalls.

The Blyde River Canyon starts north of here, near **Bourke's Luck Potholes** (off Rte 532; adult/child R50/25; ⊙potholes 7am-5pm, office from 8am, cafe from 8.30am; Ⓟ). These bizarre cylindrical holes were carved into the rock by whirlpools at the confluence of the Blyde and Treuer Rivers. Bridges span the rivers, providing impressive views. There's a small museum providing information on the canyon's geology, flora and fauna, a busy cafe and an 80m-long lichen trail.

Continuing north into the heart of the nature reserve, you'll reach the **Lowveld View-point** (off Rte 532; ⊙7am-5pm; Ⓟ) **FREE**. This offers stunning views up the canyon, to the glistening **Blydepoort Dam** at the far end surrounded by forested slopes. The rocky cones of the **Three Rondavels** formations are just visible, and you can see over the ridge to the hazy plains on the far side.

Next, the **Three Rondavels Viewpoint** (off Rte 532; adult/child R20/10; ⊙8am-5pm; Ⓟ) is the area's highlight, with its staggering view of these enormous rounds of rock, their pointed, grassy tops resembling giant huts carved into the side of the canyon. There are short walks in the surrounding area to points where you can look down to the Blydepoort Dam at the reserve's far north.

West of here, outside the reserve and just over the provincial line in Limpopo, are the **Echo Caves** (☏013-238 0015; www.echocaves.co.za; off Rte 36; admission & guided tour adult/child R60/30; ⊙8.30am-4pm; Ⓟ). Stone Age relics have been found in these caves, which were discovered in 1923 and named after dripstone formations that echo when tapped. The one-hour guided tour leads you deep into the caverns on walkways and staircases (sensible shoes required) to a cool underground world of limestone stalactites and stalagmites, some named after figures such as the Madonna. The formations of the **Crystal Palace** chamber are a highlight.

En route, there are numerous scenic stops to make, taking in waterfalls and lookout points. Lying within the 260-sq-km **Blyde River Canyon Nature Reserve** (013-753 3115; www.mtpa.co.za; P), most stops have a nominal entry fee, and their car parks are generally mobbed with craft stalls and tour buses.

Take some coins and small notes to pay entrance fees, and always make sure you are given a ticket. Although the viewpoints have set opening hours, some may open longer or be accessible when unstaffed.

✵ Activities

Hiking here is a magical experience. There are four trails at the Blyde Canyon Forever Resort, which nonguests pay R50 to walk. The short **Kadishi-Tufa Trail** (one hour) runs along the Kadishi River, a tributary of the Blyde, to a tufa waterfall; the **Guinea-Fowl Trail** (three hours) offers beautiful views before descending to the Kadishi; the **Lourie Trail** (three hours) explores indigenous riparian forest and criss-crosses the river; and the **Leopard Trail** (four hours) offers spectacular Blyde River Canyon views.

Thaba Tsweni Lodge also offers guided half- and full-day hikes.

Belvedere Day Walk   HIKING
(082 879 3945; R50) This reasonably strenuous 10km, five-hour walk takes you in a circular route to the Belvedere hydroelectric power station. You'll get awesome canyon views as you descend 400m to the power station, which was built in 1911 and was the largest of its kind in the southern hemisphere. Permits are available between 8am and noon at Bourke's Luck Potholes (p385) trailhead.

🛏 Sleeping & Eating

There are a few restaurants along Rte 532 and a supermarket, liquor store and bar-restaurant at both the Blyde Canyon Forever Resort and **Forever Resort Swadini** (015-795 5141; www.foreverswadini.co.za; off Rte 531; camping per site R170 plus per person R105, safari tent R830, chalet R1725-1785; P ✲ ☀).

★**Thaba Tsweni Lodge**   LODGE $$
(013-767 1380; www.blyderivercanyonaccommodation.com; off Rte 532; d from R850; P ☎) Beautifully located just a short walk from Berlin Falls (p385), these six self-catering chalets have stone walls, African-print bedspreads,

kitchens, garden areas with braai (barbecue) facilities, wood-burning fireplaces and beautiful views. Prebook for breakfast (R120), dinner (R250) and activities including canyon tours and guided half- and full-day hikes.

Blyde Canyon Forever Resort   RESORT $$
(086 122 6966; www.foreverblydecanyon.co.za; Rte 532; camping per site 1/2 people R315/405, 2-/4-/6-person chalet from R1070/1515/2630; P ✲ ☎ ☀) This rambling resort has a wide choice of accommodation. The solid brick chalets on the canyon's edge are well set up, with TV, kitchenette, shower and bath; the pricier ones are worth it for the views and extra space. For jaw-dropping views of the Three Rondavels rock formations, ask for Nos 73 to 98.

★**Potluck Boskombuis**   SOUTH AFRICAN $$
(071 539 6773; www.facebook.com/little-boskombuis; off Rte 532; mains R80-160; ☉10am-4pm; P) Look out for the South African flag and follow the red-dirt track to this 'bush kitchen', a makeshift shelter beneath gnarly boulders and trees decorated with animal skulls, its terrace nudging the rocks in the Treur River. Enjoy a cold craft beer and dishes from steaks and spare ribs to *bobotie* and beef *potjie* stew, cooked without electricity.

Kadisi Restaurant   CAFETERIA $$
(086 122 6966; Blyde Canyon Forever Resort, off Rte 532; mains R50-135; ☉7am-9pm; ✲) The Forever Resort's bar-restaurant should be a pleasant lunch stop with its cavernous, air-conditioned interior and Three Rondavels terrace views. Unfortunately, it's often brimming with coach parties. If you order à la carte, you'll face a long wait; opt instead for the lunch buffet (adult/child R160/80, served from noon to 3pm) featuring a cornucopia of hot and cold choices.

EASTERN LOWVELD

The hot and dry eastern lowveld is mostly used as a staging post on the way into and out of Kruger National Park. You can learn about the history of the gold rush in the feel-good town of Barberton or get your big-city fix in Nelspruit (Mbombela) and there are plenty of bush lodges to whet your appetite for the mighty Kruger.

Hazyview

📞 013 / POP 4300

Spread out along Rte 40 and with no real centre, this farming town surrounded by banana plantations has far outgrown its original size thanks to its proximity to Kruger National Park. There are good facilities, restaurants and accommodation, and even some adventure activities to keep you busy if you stay for a day or two.

Hazyview is close to Kruger's Phabeni (12km), Numbi (15km) and Paul Kruger (47km) gates.

Skyway Trails
ADVENTURE SPORTS

(📞 013-737 6747; www.skywaytrails.com; Perry's Bridge Centre, Rte 40; Aerial Cable Trail R495, Tree Top Challenge adult/child R180/160; 🚹) On 'Mpumalanga's longest aerial cable trail', glide through a forested river valley while safely clipped to a wire. It takes about 2½ hours to complete the 10 platforms and eight 70m- to 230m-long zip-line sections (1.2km in total). There's also the one-hour Tree Top Challenge, a family-friendly obstacle course incorporating balancing beams, rope bridges, spider webs and a 50m zipline.

African Safari Adventures
SAFARI

(📞 013-737 7794; www.tourist.co.za) Experienced outfit running a plethora of day and overnight tours to Kruger and Blyde River Canyon, as well as specialist activity safaris such as birdwatching and river rafting. Also runs tours to Swaziland and Mozambique.

🛌 Sleeping

⭐ Idle & Wild
LODGE $$

(📞 013-737 8173; www.idleandwild.co.za; Rte 536; incl breakfast s R770-850, d R1140-1300; P🅿❄🛜🏊) In a wonderful tropical garden that will make your heart sing (no, really!) are eight excellent rondavels (round huts with conical roofs), with outside tables and chairs to enjoy the beautiful garden outlooks. Standard options are roomy and include kitchenette; the honeymoon rondavel has slightly nicer linen and a large spa bath. It's 5km west of Hazyview, towards Sabie.

Gecko Lodge & Backpackers
LODGE $$

(📞 013-590 1020, 082 721 5830; www.geckolodge.co.za; off Rte 536; camping R90, dm R130-195, s/d R330/470, lodge s/d incl breakfast R765/1190; P🛜🏊) This sprawling, well-equipped lodge's 23 en-suite rooms have vaulted bamboo ceilings, comfy beds and animal-themed decor. The recently renovated hostel, a separate property next door, offers a variety of room configurations and is good value. Gecko is 3km west of Hazyview, just off the Sabie road. There's a bar and a set dinner menu is offered (R185).

Perry's Bridge Hollow
HOTEL $$$

(📞 013-737 7752; www.perrysbridgehollow.co.za; Perry's Bridge Centre, Rte 40; s/d incl breakfast R2285/3070; P🅿❄🛜🏊) Worth it for the sheer convenience of being in a retail centre, and pretty stylish to boot, Perry's Bridge Hollow offers 34 large rooms decorated in dark wood and muted tones. All rooms have patios overlooking the gardens or the pretty pool area.

🍴 Eating

Hazyview has some excellent restaurants and cafes, most of them at the Perry's Bridge Centre on Rte 40. There are supermarkets at the malls in the town centre, including a Woolworths in the Lowveld Mall on Rte 536.

⭐ Kuka Café
INTERNATIONAL $$

(📞 013-737 6957; www.kukasoup.co.za; Perry's Bridge Centre, Rte 40; mains R85-170; ⏰7am-10pm) Its blue-grey walls hung with artwork and cage lampshades, Kuka's glass doors open onto a terrace decorated with fairy lights. It's a contemporary setting for cocktails, tapas, pizzas, seafood, sushi and grills; house specials include slow-braised springbok shank and kudu fillet.

Summerfields Kitchen
GASTRONOMY $$$

(📞 013-737 6500; www.summerfields.co.za; Rte 536; mains R180; ⏰6.30-9pm Tue-Sat) Locals and weekenders in the know head 5km west of town to dine beneath metalwork chandeliers in this barn-like contemporary space, its terrace overlooking the organic kitchen garden. Waiters in black serve dishes such as venison tartare, duck à l'orange, Karoo ostrich fillet and pulled-lamb risotto, accompanied by the finest Cape wines. Bookings essential. On the same premises are the more casual River Café and a spa.

ℹ Information

Tours & Tickets (📞 013-737 7415; www.tours-tickets.co.za; Perry's Bridge Centre, Rte 40; ⏰8am-5pm Mon-Sat, 9am-3pm Sun) Useful for booking local accommodation, activities and transfers, plus Kruger tours.

ℹ️ Getting There & Away

Minibus shared taxis go daily to Nelspruit (R52, one hour) and Sabie (R40, one hour), leaving from near the Shoprite supermarket at the back of the Lowveld Mall on Rte 536. The police often set up speed traps on the southern approaches to town, so stick to the speed limits.

Nelspruit (Mbombela)

📞 013 / POP 58,700

Nelspruit (now officially called Mbombela, though locals rarely use the new moniker) is Mpumalanga's dilapidated but functional provincial capital, where bakkies (pick-up trucks) dodge potholes en route to shiny malls. It's more a place to get things done than a worthwhile destination for tourists, but it's not unpleasant and has the facilities to make it a practical stopover on the way elsewhere. Well connected to Jo'burg, it's a good place to organise a trip to Kruger National Park, the Blyde River Canyon, Swaziland or Mozambique.

◉ Sights & Activities

There are some good (and strenuous) hikes in the area. For information and bookings, contact Komatiland Forests Eco-Tourism (p379) in Sabie.

Chimp Eden   ANIMAL SANCTUARY
(📞079 777 1514; www.chimpeden.com; Umhloti Nature Reserve, Rte 40; adult/child R200/90; ☺tours 10am, noon, 2pm) This is a sanctuary for rescued chimpanzees, which have survived everything from the bush-meat trade to being traumatised for entertainment in circuses, beach resorts and nightclubs. You can see the primates in a semi-wild environment and learn about their behaviour and plight. Entry is on a one-hour guided tour.

Lowveld National
Botanical Garden   GARDENS
(📞013-752 5531; www.sanbi.org.za; off Madiba Dr; adult/child R32/15; ☺8am-5pm) North of the city centre, this 2-sq-km botanical garden (established 1969) is home to tropical African rainforest and is a nice place for a stroll among the flowers and trees. Over 240 bird species have been recorded here.

Discover Kruger   SAFARI
(📞013-744 1310; www.discoverkruger.com; Funky Monkey Backpackers, 102 Van Wijk St) Offers one- to four-day Kruger safaris, as well as day trips to Blyde River Canyon.

🛏️ Sleeping

Old Vic Travellers Inn   HOSTEL $
(📞013-744 0993; www.oldvicinn.co.za; 12 Impala St; dm R160, s/d from R480/560, with shared bathroom R420/460, 6-person self-catering unit from R900; 🅿❄️🛜🏊👪) A solid budget choice, with self-catering facilities, food available and Kruger Flexi Tours (www.krugerandmore.co.za) offering activities from safaris to horse riding. Rooms are basic but spacious and good value with clean linen. Shared bathrooms are in good order, too. There's a big, rambling garden that leads down to the river. About 3km south of the centre, it's a Baz Bus (www.bazbus.com) stop.

Nelspruit Backpackers   HOSTEL $
(📞013-741 2237; www.nelback.co.za; Andries Pretorius St; camping/dm R110/160, s/d with shared bathroom from R280/480; 🅿🛜👪) With a large pool and deck overlooking the adjoining nature reserve, this spick-and-span suburban family home is a refreshingly homely and relaxing hostel. There are rooms in the main house, which has a communal lounge and kitchen, and another in the garden.

Owner Paul leads tours to Blyde River Canyon, Kruger National Park and Swaziland, and can organise car hire.

Vineyard on the Hill   GUESTHOUSE $$
(📞082 925 1182; www.vineyardonthehill.co.za; 18 Sheppard Dr; incl breakfast s R750-1090, d R850-1350; 🅿❄️🛜🏊👪) Nudging the hilltop boulders, this modern guesthouse has seven small but comfy rooms, two of them self-catering, featuring minibar, rustic trimmings and furniture with a natural finish. In the hillside garden are a pool, braai area and jungle gym.

Auberge Guest Lodge   B&B $$
(📞013-741 2866; www.aubergeguestlodge.com; 3 De Villiers St; s R635-690, d R810-870; 🅿❄️🛜🏊) A quiet, well-maintained and sunny guesthouse with a plant-filled courtyard and a pool. The 11 motel-like rooms are comfortable and straightforward, and some have ceiling fans. It's in a good location behind the Sonpark Centre, with cafes and restaurants within walking distance.

★Utopia in Africa   GUESTHOUSE $$$
(📞013-745 7714; www.utopiainafrica.co.za; 6 Daleen St; s/d incl breakfast R1025/1520; 🅿❄️🛜🏊) Simplicity, elegance and a masterly design that keeps the premises cool using the afternoon breeze mark this exceptional accom-

Nelspruit (Mbombela)

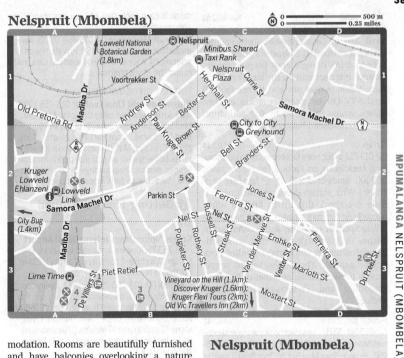

modation. Rooms are beautifully furnished and have balconies overlooking a nature reserve. A contemporary safari aesthetic prevails from the high-ceilinged rooms to the pool, making this a place to unwind and leave urban Nelspruit far behind.

Francolin Lodge GUESTHOUSE $$$
(☑013-744 1251; www.francolinlodge.co.za; 4 Du Preez St; s/d/tr/q incl breakfast R1350/2100/2450/2800; ᴘ❋🛜❄) This is a top Nelspruit guesthouse. Rooms have double-height ceilings, private patios and corner bathrooms with views. There's also a small spa and the excellent Orange Restaurant (p390) on-site. On the same hilltop property is Francolin's marginally cheaper and equally lovely 'Lorie's Call' annexe. Nine plush rooms are set apart from the main house, along decked walkways, each with their own entrance.

✗ Eating & Drinking

Head to bar-restaurants such as Cicada (p390) and the spit-and-sawdust **Jock Pub & Grill** (☑013-755 4969; www.jockpubandgrill.co.za; 23 Ferreira St; mains R55-130; ⊙kitchen 8am-9.30pm Mon-Sat, 10am-4pm Sun; 🛜🅟) for a beer. By day, Food Fundi and Crisp (p390) are good options. The action tends to be spread around the city's many malls, with a

Nelspruit (Mbombela)

multiscreen cinema, ice rink and games arcade adding to the fun at the I'langa Mall on Samora Machel Dr.

Food Fundi SANDWICHES $
(☑013-007 0786; www.thefoodfundi.co.za; Pick n Pay Centre, Madiba Dr; sandwiches R50-100; ⊙7am-5pm Mon-Fri, 8am-4pm Sat, 9am-2pm Sun; 🛜) Using fresh lowveld ingredients, this bustling cafe is an excellent choice for breakfast or lunch among its glass, wood, steel, exposed brick and blackboards. Wraps, sandwiches (try the rooibos-smoked chicken), salads and burgers decorate the menu, alongside more substantial choices such as pie of the day.

★ **Cicada** PUB FOOD $$

(☎013-741 1751; www.facebook.com/cicadanel-spruit; Sonpark Centre, Faurie St; mains R80-165; ⊙11am-9pm Mon-Sat) Nelspruit's youth come here to drink draught craft beers in the industrial interiors and on the large open terrace. Music pumps out and there's football on the TV. On the menu are steaks, chicken dishes, wraps, salads, sushi, fish and chips, and recommended burgers.

Crisp CAFE $$

(☎013-752 3453; www.facebook.com/crisprestau-rant; Absa Square, cnr Parkin & Ferreira Sts; mains R60-100, sandwiches R40-70; ⊙7am-5pm Mon-Fri; 🛜) With stylish decor and seating in a little courtyard, this urban kitchen offers something for most tastes, from eggs Benedict, Spanish omelette and toasted sandwiches to Asian-style pork ribs, an American cheeseburger and barbecue pulled-pork open sandwich. There's also salads, wraps, freshly pressed juices, gourmet milkshakes, smoothies and Pretoria-roasted Tribeca Coffee.

Greek Kouzina GREEK $$

(☎013-741 5371; www.facebook.com/greekkouzi-nanelspruit; Sonpark Centre, Faurie St; mains R65-150; ⊙noon-9pm Mon-Sat, to 3pm Sun) Despite the cars rushing past on Rte 40, the Aegean-blue decor and taverna tunes create a suitable atmosphere for Greek classics such as stuffed peppers, moussaka, seafood, *kleftiko* (roasted lamb shank) and flavoursome lamb *biftekia* (burgers).

Orange Restaurant FUSION $$$

(☎013-744 9507; www.eatatorange.co.za; 4 Du Preez St; mains R100-200; ⊙noon-3pm & 6-10pm Mon-Sat, 6-9pm Sun; 🛜) Put on your finest and treat yourself to some beautifully prepared cuisine – from herb-crusted yellowtail, spinach and ricotta ravioli and Niçoise salad to duck breast, eland loin and kudu fillet – at the Francolin Lodge's classy restaurant. The terrace has terrific views of the city and surrounding bush. Bookings essential for nonguests.

ⓘ Information

EMERGENCY

Police Station (☎013-759 1008; 15 Bester St) Opposite Nelspruit Plaza shopping centre.

MEDICAL SERVICES

Nelmed Medicross (☎013-755 5000; www.nelmed.co.za; cnr Nel & Rothery Sts; ⊙7am-8pm Mon-Fri, from 8am Sat & Sun) Private

medical care, including 24-hour assistance for emergencies.

Nelspruit Mediclinic (☎013-759 0500; www.mediclinic.co.za; 1 Louise St) Private hospital offering 24-hour emergency medical care and a round-the-clock pharmacy.

TOURIST INFORMATION

Kruger Lowveld Ehlanzeni (☎013-755 1988; www.krugerlowveld.com; Crossing Mall, cnr Madiba & Samora Machel Drs; ⊙7am-6pm Mon-Fri, 8am-1.30pm Sat) This helpful office at the Crossing Mall (behind Standard Bank) takes bookings for all national parks, including Kruger, and can help arrange accommodation and tours. It also sells maps and books.

ⓘ Getting There & Around

AIR

Kruger Mpumalanga International Airport (013-753 7500; www.kmiairport.co.za) is Nelspruit's closest commercial airport, 28km northeast of town.

Airlink (☎013-750 2531; www.flyairlink.com; Kruger Mpumalanga International Airport, Rte 538) has daily flights to/from Jo'burg (R1600 to R2200, one hour), Cape Town, Durban, Livingstone (Zambia) and Vianculos (Mozambique). Its Lodge Link flights serve airstrips in Kruger National Park.

BUS

The major bus companies stop in Nelspruit daily, as they travel between Jo'burg/Pretoria (five hours) and Maputo (Mozambique; five hours). Tickets are sold at their offices and at **Computicket** (☎013-757 0009; www.computicket.com; Riverside Mall, Madiba Dr).

City to City (☎013-755 1755; www.citytocity.co.za; Promenade Mall, Samora Machel Dr; ⊙8am-4pm) Budget services to/from Jo'burg (R220) and Maputo (R190).

Greyhound (☎013-753 2100, 083 915 9000; www.greyhound.co.za; Promenade Mall, Samora Machel Dr; ⊙7am-5pm Mon-Fri, 7.30am-2.30pm Sat & Sun) Jo'burg, Midrand, Pretoria (R300) and Maputo (R370).

Translux (☎0861 589 282; www.translux.co.za) Jo'burg, Pretoria (R240) and Maputo (R220). Shares an office with City to City.

CAR RENTAL

Avis (☎013-750 1015; www.avis.co.za), **Europcar** (☎013-750 2871; www.europcar.co.za) and **First** (☎013-750 2538; www.firstcarrental.co.za) all have offices at the airport. There is also a branch of **Avis** (☎013-757 8760; Meander Cr, Riverside Park) north of the city centre, just off Madiba Dr, and a **First** (☎013-753 3313; www.firstcarrental.co.za; Hotel Promenade, Samora Machel Dr) office downtown.

ON THE CROCODILE RIVER

Malelane is essentially a stopover point and service centre for Kruger National Park, which lies over the hippo-inhabited Crocodile River. There is more going on in Nelspruit (Mbombela) and Komatipoort, but the wildness of this outpost in the bush may appeal. Brown tourism signposts alongside the N4 highway identify this part of the province, bordering Kruger, Swaziland and Mozambique, as the Wild Frontier.

Perched right on the park boundary, the cracking, gay-friendly **River House Guest Lodge** (☑013-790 1333; www.riverhouselodge.co.za; 27 Visarend St; r/f incl half board R2600/4355; ▣☞▣) is a great place to relax pre or post Kruger, perhaps with views of wallowing hippos from the thatched riverside terrace. The 12 cool rooms have their own balconies, from which you can see all the way into the park.

Friendly owner Johan 'Daff' Daffue built and decorated the idiosyncratic, antique-packed lodge, with its bikes hanging from the dining-room ceiling and a cosy bar and lounge.

Consider booking through **Around About Cars** (☑021-422 4022, 0860 422 4022; www.aroundaboutcars.com) for good deals.

SHARED TAXI

The local bus and **minibus shared taxi rank** (cnr Henshall & Andrew Sts) is behind the Nelspruit Plaza shopping centre. Taxi destinations include White River (R15, 20 minutes), Barberton (R30, 40 minutes), Hazyview (R52, one hour), Graskop (R50, 1½ hours) and Jo'burg (R200, five hours).

SHUTTLE

Kruger Lowveld Ehlanzeni can arrange private transfers to Kruger Mpumalanga International Airport, starting at R300 per person, and OR Tambo International Airport (Jo'burg; from R2500 per person). **Dana Agency** (☑013-753 3571; www.danaagency.co.za; Crossings Mall, cnr Madiba & Samora Machel Drs; ⊙8am-4.30pm Mon-Fri, 9am-noon Sat) sells tickets for the following shuttles:

City Bug (☑086 133 4433; www.citybug.co.za; 61 Graniet St) Operates a twice-weekly shuttle to Durban (one way R660, 9¼ hours), four daily to OR Tambo (R440, 3¾ hours), three per day to Pretoria (R440, 3½ hours) and Bloemfontein (R660, 8½ to 10½ hours), and one to Lanseria International Airport (R440, 4½ hours). All services depart from Graniet St, off Samora Machel Dr near the I'langa Mall.

JSL Transport (☑083 785 4779, 013-793 7124; www.jsltransport.co.za; Komati Sq) Between Komatipoort and Pretoria, via Malelane, Nelspruit, Waterval Boven (Emgwenya) and OR Tambo. Daily except Tuesday and Thursday.

Lime Time (☑086 999 0978; www.limetime-shuttle.co.za; Sonpark Centre, cnr Madiba Dr & Piet Retief St; ⊙7am-5pm Mon-Fri, 8-11am Sat) Daily to/from Pretoria, OR Tambo, Rustenburg, Lanseria and more destinations.

Lowveld Link (☑013-750 1174; www.lowveld-link.com; Crossing Mall, cnr Madiba & Samora Machel Drs) Operates a convenient daily shuttle to/from Pretoria, OR Tambo (one way R420, 4½ hours) and Sandton (Jo'burg), and in the other direction to/from White River. It leaves from Kruger Lowveld Ehlanzeni, where you can buy tickets.

Mr Chubby (☑074 329 9114; www.mrchubby-shuttles.com) To/from Maputo (Mozambique; R300) daily. It also serves Kruger Mpumalanga International Airport, White River and OR Tambo.

TRAIN

Shosholoza Meyl (☑0860 008 888, 011-774 4555; www.shosholozameyl.co.za) operates a twice-weekly service between Jo'burg (R200, 10 hours) and Komatipoort (R50, 2½ hours) via Nelspruit.

Komatipoort

☑013 / POP 4700

Cradled by the Lebombo Mountains, Komatipoort sits near the confluence of the Komati and Crocodile Rivers, only 10km from Kruger National Park's Crocodile Bridge gate. If you're travelling to/from Mozambique or Swaziland, it makes for a good stopover. One of South Africa's hottest towns, it has a tropical languor and an African feel with Mozambicans selling cigarettes and speaking Portuguese on the streets.

Komatipoort Prawn Festival FOOD & DRINK

(☑082 318 2020; www.komatipoortfestival.co.za; Komatipoort Show Grounds) This festival in late June celebrates the modest crayfish in all its glory. The weekend of entertainment includes live music, food stalls, a craft market and a beer tent.

🛏 Sleeping & Eating

Kruger View Backpackers
HOSTEL $

(☑013-793 7373; kvbackpackers@gmail.com; 61 Bosbok St; dm/s/d/tr R220/450/600/750; P❋🛇🌊) This quiet backpackers, 10km from Kruger's Crocodile Bridge gate, has a spacious lounge, terrace and watchtower gazing at the park across the river, where elephants are often spotted. The shipshape en-suite rooms and dorm have colourful bedspreads, and there are two- to four-bed cabins.

★ Trees Too
GUESTHOUSE $$

(☑013-793 8262; www.treestoo.co.za; 9-11 Furley St; s/d/tr/q/f R770/1040/1250/1470/1600; P❋🛇🌊) This place is a standout, with great thatch and brick rooms featuring quality furniture, honesty bars, wildlife artworks and vintage African tourism posters. There's a poolside bar, a badminton court and breakfast (R130), dinner (mains R100 to R170) and wildlife drives available. The friendly staff have heaps of info on Kruger.

Stoep Cafe
GUESTHOUSE $$

(☑083 457 3909; www.stoepcafeguesthouse.co.za; 74 Rissik St; s/d/tr R500/800/1150; P❋🛇🌊) Stoep is a pretty colonial-style house with a small garden, pool, *lapa* (circular area with a fire pit) and braai (barbecue) in the heart of town. There are six quiet and spacious self-catering rooms and a three-bedroom house.

The coffee shop (mains R60 to R130, open 7am to 9pm Monday to Saturday) serves jaffles, burgers, salads, steaks, chicken dishes, pancakes and Komatipoort's best coffee on its large, shady veranda.

❶ Getting There & Away

Shosholoza Meyl's twice-weekly train to/from Jo'burg (R250, 12½ hours), the Komati, travels via Malelane and Nelspruit (Mbombela). More reliable are the City to City, Greyhound and Translux buses between Jo'burg and Maputo (Mozambique) via Komatipoort; you can buy tickets at the Shoprite and Spar supermarkets on Rissik St.

Even more convenient, Mr Chubby runs a daily shuttle between Nelspruit and the Mozambican capital via Komatipoort. JSL Transport operates a shuttle to/from Pretoria (R450, 6½ hours, daily except Tuesday and Thursday) via Malelane, Nelspruit, Waterval Boven (Emgwenya) and OR Tambo International Airport.

Minibus shared taxis leave regularly from just off Rissik St (Rte 571), outside the Wimpy restaurant by the Spar supermarket, and run 4km east to the Mozambique border post, typically charging R10. On the far side of the border, you can pick up onward transport to Maputo.

If you're driving, there are several tolls along the N4 to/from Jo'burg. There is a petrol station in Komatipoort.

Barberton
☑013 / POP 12,000

Barberton is a friendly, walkable little town with quiet, leafy streets set against a striking backdrop of green and purple mountains. It has a wonderful feel, thanks to its well-preserved historical buildings, the laid-back nonchalance of its inhabitants and its compact centre. The rustic town makes an excellent stop-off en route to Swaziland, Kruger or Mozambique.

Dating back to the gold-rush days, Barberton boomed in the late 19th century and was home to South Africa's first stock exchange. On top of such claims to fame, the fascinating spot's geological significance, rich flora, and sights and activities mixing history, culture and adventure could keep you here for a couple of days.

◎ Sights

Barberton boasts several restored houses dating back to the late 19th and early 20th centuries. All are open for touring and give a glimpse into the town's early history.

Pick up a free *Heritage Walk* leaflet and map from Barberton Tourism (p394). The self-guided tour takes in two-dozen historic sights including the town's restored houses.

Barberton Museum
MUSEUM

(☑013-712 4208; 36 Pilgrim St; ⊙9am-4.15pm; P) FREE The town museum has interesting exhibits on local history, culture and geology, including a great black-and-white photo display of Barberton through the years, covering everything from the gold rush to the local literary canine hero Jock of the Bushveld.

Barberton History and Mining Museum
MUSEUM

(☑072 668 4063; Greenstone Trading Post Bldg, 73 De Villiers St; ⊙8.30am-5pm Mon-Fri, to 1pm Sat, by appointment Sun) FREE In the old Transvaal Hotel (1882), this treasure trove of local history exhibits a hotchpotch of items from weaponry and greenstone samples to some fool's gold and an old R1 note bearing Jan van Riebeeck's face.

Barberton

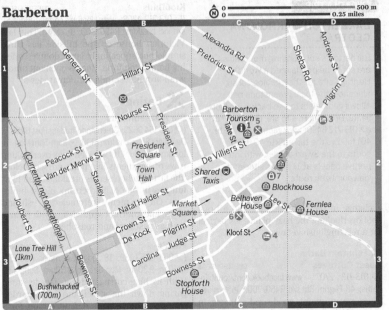

Painted Stone Garden MONUMENT
(www.nukainmabuza.co.za; cnr Rte 40 & Sheba Rd) These rocks at the entrance to town are painted in the style of 'outsider' artist Nukain Mabuza, who turned his humble labourer's accommodation on a nearby farm into a fantastic rock garden by colourfully decorating huts and hillside boulders. The enigmatic figure, who committed suicide in 1981, inspired Athol Fugard's play *The Painted Rocks at Revolver Creek*.

Pilgrim & Crown Gallery (☑ 013-712 5807; www.umjindijewellery.co.za; Pilgrim St; ⏱ 8.30am-5pm Mon-Fri, to 2pm Sat & Sun) ✐ sells books on Mabuza.

🏃 Activities

Ask in Barberton Tourism (p394) about the Emjindini township tour under development. It will focus on Emjindini's role in the struggle against apartheid and be the province's only township tour.

Dusty Tracks ADVENTURE
(☑ 076 825 5794; www.dustytracks.co.za; Greenstone Trading Post Bldg, 73 De Villiers St) Pieter and Wynand offer a fantastic range of historical adventures, including tours of the Barberton Makhonjwa Geotrail (p394), gold-panning experiences, and visits to the 19th-century

Barberton

◎ Sights
1 Barberton History and Mining Museum C2
2 Barberton Museum C2

◈ Activities, Courses & Tours
Dusty Tracks .... (see 1)

⊜ Sleeping
3 Fountain Baths Guest Cottages D2
4 Kloofhuis C3

⊗ Eating
5 Die Plaaskombuis C2
6 Papa's C3

⊜ Shopping
7 Pilgrim & Crown Gallery C2

gold-prospecting ghost town of Eureka City and the subterranean Golden Quarry – camp overnight at Eureka if you dare.

🛏 Sleeping

Bushwhacked FARMSTAY $
(☑ 073 691 5646; Kruger St; r from R550; ⓟ 🛜) ✐ This rustic hillside eyrie has rooms in the main cottage and two chalets. With a fully equipped kitchen, a wood-burner and book

WORTH A TRIP

BARBERTON MAKHONJWA GEOTRAIL

Barberton's surrounding mountains are set to be proclaimed a World Heritage site for their geological significance; the local greenstone belt allows geologists to see back 3.5 billion years. Bringing this to life, the **Geotrail** (☑ 013-712 6490; www.geotrail.co.za; Rte 40) follows the tarred Rte 40 37km south to the Swazi border, with interpretive panels at 11 picnic sites and viewpoints en route.

exchange in the comfy lounge and a braai spot overlooking the hazy plains, it's perfect for a relaxing bush getaway.

★ Fountain Baths Guest Cottages
GUESTHOUSE **$$**

(☑ 013-712 2707; www.facebook.com/fountainbaths; 48 Pilgrim St; s/d R450/700; ⓟⓡ🛜🖥🕹) These seven quaint, good-sized cottages, in a beautiful and historical location on the northeastern edge of town, are well kitted out and full of character. A walking trail leads up the creek from the lovely quiet garden, where the pool was once a bathhouse for 19th-century prospectors. Wake up to the sound of birdsong.

The family-run property has a cute bar and options ranging from self-catering cottages to corrugated-iron affairs, most with their own stoep (porch). Breakfast (R60) is often served in the garden.

★ Jathira Gastehuis
LODGE **$$**

(☑ 082 388 1404; jathira@wol.co.za; Rte 40; r R800; ⓟ❄🛜🖥🕹) Enjoy *platteland* (farmland) hospitality at this very Afrikaans and very friendly lodge 6km northwest of the town centre. Accommodation is in spacious, well-equipped bungalows with braais and there's a poolside bar. Request a braai dinner before 2pm to experience a T-bone the size of Table Mountain.

Kloofhuis
GUESTHOUSE **$$**

(☑ 013-712 4268; www.kloofhuis.co.za; 1 Kloof St; s/d incl breakfast R450/800; ⓟ@🛜) This late Victorian house on the hillside has three simple but appealingly large doubles offering homey comforts. Rooms open out onto a wrap-around veranda with great views.

✖ Eating

Die Plaaskombuis
CAFE **$**

(☑ 076 154 9629; Greenstone Trading Post Bldg, 73 De Villiers St; mains from R30; ⊙ 8am-5pm Mon-Fri, to 2pm Sat & Sun) Its wooden deck overlooking rows of succulents in a plant nursery below, 'the farm kitchen' serves breakfasts and light lunches in one of Barberton's oldest buildings. On the menu are omelettes, fish and chips, and gourmet sandwiches with fillings such as pastrami and roast beef.

Papa's
MEDITERRANEAN **$$**

(☑ 063 626 6189; 18 Judge St; mains R50-150; ⊙ 10am-9.30pm Mon-Sat, to 8.30pm Sun; 🖥) With its blue corrugated-iron facade, stoep gazing down the street and large garden courtyard, Barberton's default option for a bite attracts everyone from bikers to families. The pseudo-Mediterranean establishment serves breakfast, pizzas, pastas, the odd burger, good filter coffee and less impressive shawarmas.

❶ Information

Barberton Tourism (☑ 013-712 2880, 082 959 6670; www.barberton.co.za; Greenstone Trading Post Bldg, 73 De Villiers St; ⊙ 8am-4.30pm Mon-Fri, to 1pm Sat; 🛜) This helpful office in the town centre can assist with accommodation, tours of historic sites, day hikes in the area and private transfers.

❶ Getting There & Away

A few **minibus shared taxis** (cnr Natal Halder & Adcock Sts) stop in town near Shoprite supermarket, but the easiest option is to ask Barberton Tourism to call for a taxi to pick you up there. The fare to Nelspruit (Mbombela) is R30 (40 minutes). Most departures are in the early morning.

Barberton Tourism can also organise private transfers.

Kruger National Park

Best Places to Eat

→ Tshokwane (p407)

→ Lower Sabie Rest Camp
(p403)

→ Olifants Rest Camp (p405)

→ Letaba Rest Camp (p407)

Best Places to Stay

→ MalaMala Main Camp
(p410)

→ Sabi Sabi Earth Lodge
(p411)

→ Singita Boulders (p411)

→ Rhino Post Safari Lodge
(p403)

→ Letaba Rest Camp (p407)

→ Olifants Rest Camp (p405)

Why Go?

Kruger is one of the world's greatest wildlife-watching destinations. All of Africa's iconic safari species – elephant, lion, leopard, cheetah, rhino, buffalo, giraffe, hippo and zebra – share the bushveld with a supporting cast of 137 other mammals and over 500 varieties of bird.

Beautiful granite kopjes (hills) pepper the south, the Lebombo Mountains rise from the savannah in the east, and tropical forests cover the north of the 19,485-sq-km park.

Yes, Kruger can sometimes become crowded. And yes, you may have to wait in line to see those lions. But that's because the vast network of roads makes Kruger one of Africa's most accessible parks (explore on your own or join one of the many guided wildlife activities) and accommodation is both plentiful and great value.

If you think the crowds may overwhelm, consider the private reserves that surround the national park. Among these is Sabi Sand, one of Africa's finest.

When to Go
Skukuza

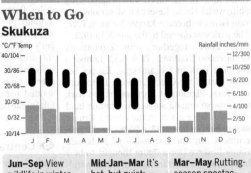

| Jun–Sep View wildlife in winter when the park is driest and animals congregate at water holes. | Mid-Jan–Mar It's hot, but quiet; school holidays are over, accommodation is easy to find. | Mar–May Rutting-season spectaculars see impala, wildebeest and other species go head to head. |

ℹ️ **KRUGER NATIONAL PARK**

Why Go Astounding wildlife, ease of self-drive access and incredible-value safaris. Perhaps Africa's best-run national park.

When to Go Year-round; avoid South African school holidays.

Practicalities Entry costs R328 per adult, R164 per child. Gate times (p409) for the park and camps are strictly adhered to. Speed limits (50km/h on sealed routes, 40km/h on dirt roads) are also stringently enforced. Don't lose your exit receipt (given to you on entry). The detailed park maps (R80) are worth their weight in gold.

Budget Tips Save 5% on SANParks camping and accommodation by booking online. Book tours at backpackers in Hazyview, Nelspruit or Graskop, or group together to share accommodation and car hire. Buy a Wild Card (p592).

History

The area that is now Kruger National Park first came under government protection in 1898, when Paul Kruger (president of the Transvaal Republic) established the Sabie Game Reserve, between the Sabie and Crocodile Rivers, as a controlled hunting area. In 1902, following the second Anglo-Boer War, James Stevenson Hamilton became the reserve's first warden. Hamilton was also the first to see the tourism potential of wildlife watching and conservation. In 1926, Sabie Game Reserve was joined with neighbouring Shingwedzi Game Reserve and various private farms to become Kruger National Park. The park was opened to the public in 1927.

In 2002, together with Zimbabwe's Gonarezhou National Park and Limpopo National Park in Mozambique, Kruger became part of the Great Limpopo Transfrontier Park. Significant portions of the park continue to remain subject to pending land claims. A large claim in the greater Kruger was upheld in late 2013, which saw the government buy the ownership of MalaMala Game Reserve (for a figure thought to be 1 billion rand) and transfer it to the N'wandlamharhi Community Property Association (CPA). Three years later the South African government settled six land claims and compensated community groups – three in Limpopo and three in Mpumalanga – for

land taken from them to make up part of Kruger National Park during the apartheid years. Further land claims remained under negotiation at the time of writing.

⊙ Sights

Kruger (Map p398; ☎ 012-428 9111; www.sanparks.org/parks/kruger) encompasses a variety of landscapes and ecosystems, with each favouring particular species. That said, elephants, impalas, buffaloes, Burchell's zebras, wildebeest, kudus, waterbucks, baboons, vervet monkeys, leopards and smaller predators are widespread, and birdlife is incredible, especially along waterways. Rivers are hubs of activity; the major ones flow from west to east, including the Limpopo, Luvuvhu, Shingwedzi, Letaba, Olifants, Timbavati, Sand and Sabie. All of them are lined with riverine forest (often with enormous fig trees), which supports a wealth of wildlife.

While your drives along the extensive road network will throw up the majority of your animal sightings, there are numerous lookouts that offer great opportunities to see wildlife, or simply enjoy a stunning view.

⊙ Southern Kruger

Southern Kruger is perhaps the most physically beautiful section of the park, with numerous granite kopjes climbing above the undulating grasslands and the thick stands of acacias, bushwillows, sycamore figs and flowering species such as the red-and-orange coral tree. The changes in elevation in the west offer staggering views over the wilderness that at times can look like a never-ending sea of green.

Its flora is fed by the park's highest amount of rainfall, some 50% more than in the north. This has in turn led to Kruger's highest proportion of wildlife calling the area home. The terrain is particularly favoured by white rhinos, buffaloes and zebras. Lions, hyenas and leopards are still spotted regularly, and wild dogs and cheetahs make occasional appearances.

This is the most visited section of Kruger.

⊙ Central Kruger

With the exception of the Lebombo Mountains that flank the Mozambique border to the east, the landscape between the Sabie and Olifants Rivers is less varied than in the south, with large swaths of open savannah, particularly west and southeast of

Satara. The buffalo grass and red grass in these areas is interspersed with knobthorn, leadwood and marula trees, and hosts large populations of impalas, zebras, wildebeest, kudus, giraffes and elephants. Joining them are predators, especially lions. Leopards are commonly sighted, and the road between Satara and Orpen is one of the most likely places in Kruger to spot cheetahs.

☉ Northern Kruger

North of the Olifants River the rolling landscape becomes more and more dominated by the elephant's favourite dish: the mopane tree. So it's no surprise that huge herds roam this region. Towards the Lebombo Mountains in the east the trees are so stunted by the clay soils on the basalt plains that the elephants' backs rise above the canopy. The mopaneveld (woodland) also attracts large herds of buffaloes and numerous tsessebes, elands, roans and sables. Leopards, lions and rhinos are less numerous but nonetheless present.

Kruger's far north, around Punda Maria and Pafuri, lies completely in the tropics and supports a wider variety of plants (baobabs are particularly noticeable), high wildlife concentrations and an exceptional array of birds not found further south. Between the Luvuvhu and Limpopo Rivers is a gorgeous tropical riverine forest with figs, fever trees and jackalberries. The far north is a winter grazing ground for elephants, and lions and leopards are also regularly encountered.

★**Elephant Hall Museum** MUSEUM (Map p398; Letaba Rest Camp; ☉8am-8pm Mon-Sat, to 6pm Sun) FREE Even if you're not staying at Letaba Rest Camp, it's worth swinging by to check out this excellent museum. It has life-size skeletons and dozens of fascinating displays and information panels on everything from Kruger's big tuskers to the place of elephants in world and Kruger history.

🏃 Activities

Despite its mammoth size, Kruger is exceptionally well organised and there are numerous opportunities to enrich your wildlife watching throughout.

Wildlife Drives

Self-driving is fantastic for so many reasons, but do strongly consider joining some guided drives – they are a great way to maximise your safari experience. For starters, all the SANParks options roam the park when you

KRUGER NATIONAL PARK ACTIVITIES

Kruger National Park Highlights

1 **Sabi Sand Game Reserve** (p410) Tracking leopards through one of Africa's premier wildlife destinations.

2 **Kruger Side Roads** (p410) Driving a crowdless, late-afternoon, riverside track, such as the S39.

3 **Lonely Bull Back-Pack Trail** (p401) Waking to the sweet sounds of nature's alarm clock when camping wild.

4 **Wildlife Drives** (p397) Getting stuck behind unforgettable traffic – elephants, rhinos, giraffes – in Kruger's south.

5 **Sweni Hide** (p401) Discovering that birdwatching can be a wonderful way to deepen your enjoyment of Kruger.

6 **Makuleke** (p408) Journeying into the tropics and exploring the fever tree forests and gorges of northern Kruger.

7 **Olifants Rest Camp** (p405) Savouring some of the best views in Kruger, nursing a sundowner.

8 **Satara Rest Camp** (p405) Taking a night drive through big-cat heaven to see Kruger in a whole new light.

Kruger National Park

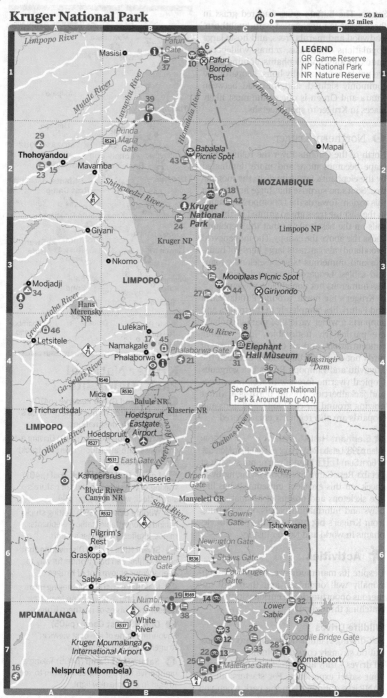

LEGEND
GR Game Reserve
NP National Park
NR Nature Reserve

0 ———————— 50 km
0 ———————— 25 miles

Limpopo River

Masisi

Pafuri Gate
37
10
6

Pafuri Border Post

MOZAMBIQUE

Mutale River

Luvuvhu River

39

29

Thohoyandou
23 15

Mavamba

Punda Maria Gate

R524

Shingwedzi River

Hlambala River

43

Babalala Picnic Spot

Mapai

Limpopo River

Limpopo NP

2 Kruger National Park
24

11
18
42

Giyani

Kruger NP

LIMPOPO

Nkomo

Modjadji
34
9

Hans Merensky NR

Groot Letaba River

35 Mooiplaas Picnic Spot
27 44 Giriyondo

Lulekani

46 Letsitele

Namakgale
17 45
Phalaborwa

41 Letaba River

Phalaborwa Gate
21
4

8
1 Elephant Hall Museum
31
36

Massingir Dam

Go-Selati River

R540

R530

Mica

See Central Kruger National Park & Around Map (p404)

Balule NR

LIMPOPO

Trichardtsdal

Hoedspruit Eastgate Airport

Klaserie NR

Chalons River

Olifants River

Hoedspruit
R527

R531 East Gate

Kampersrus

Klaserie

Orpen Gate

Sweni River

7

Blyde River Canyon NR

Manyeleti GR

Sand River

R532

R40

Gowrie Gate

Pilgrim's Rest

Newington Gate

Tshokwane

Graskop

Phabeni Gate

R536 Shaws Gate

Paul Kruger Gate

Sabie

Hazyview

MPUMALANGA

Numbi Gate
R40

19 R569
38

14

Lower Sabie
32
20

White River
R537

3
12

26

Crocodile Bridge Gate

Kruger Mpumalanga International Airport

25 22
40

13
33

28

Malelane Gate

Komatipoort

16

Nelspruit (Mbombela)

5

can't (ie before camps open and after they've closed), and guides will often shed light on species and behaviours that you weren't aware of. Guides at lodges in private concessions can also take you closer to the wildlife, as off-road driving is permitted in most.

SANParks operates three-hour **sunrise drives** and **sunset drives** at almost all rest camps, bushveld camps and many park gates. Costs vary between R325/160 per adult/child (all camps except Crocodile Bridge) and R425/210 (Crocodile Bridge). Two-hour **night drives** (R255 to R345 for adults depending on the camp, R125 to R170 for children) are great for nocturnal animals such as bushbabies; hippos and big cats are common, too. Book in advance or upon arrival. Children under the age of six are not permitted.

Wildlife Walks

The bush becomes so much more alive and you become so much more *aware* when you step out on foot and leave the security blanket of your vehicle behind. And it's often not the large wildlife that captures your imagi-

nation – the smallest of creatures, whether insects, reptiles or birds, or tracks in the dust – take on a new light of importance and you truly start to understand how the environment works.

Most SANParks rest camps offer three-hour **morning bush walks** (R565; R650 at Crocodile Bridge) with knowledgeable armed guides, as do all of the lodges in the private concessions. Letaba and Skukuza also offer **afternoon walks** (R450), and Olifants offers **river walks** (R325), too. SANParks options can be booked in advance or arranged at the relevant camp upon arrival.

If you truly want to embrace the wilderness, book one of the park's **wilderness trails** or **backpack trails** well in advance of your trip. Lasting four days (departing Wednesday and Sunday), these guided walks provide some of the park's most memorable experiences.

The catered wilderness trails are based out of a remote camp with basic huts or safari tents and are not overly strenuous, covering around 20km per day. They operate out of Berg-en-dal, Satara, Pretoriuskop, Punda

---

Kruger National Park

◉ Top Sights
1 Elephant Hall Museum	C4
2 Kruger National Park	B2

◉ Sights
3 Afsaal Picnic Spot	C7
4 Amarula Lapa	B4
5 Chimp Eden	B7
6 Crooks Corner	C1
7 Echo Caves	A5
8 Engelhard Dam	C4
9 Modjadji Nature Reserve	A3
10 Pafuri Picnic Area	B1
11 Red Rocks	C2
12 Renosterpan	C7
13 Steilberg Loop	C7
Sunset Dam	(see 32)
14 Transport Dam	C6

◉ Activities, Courses & Tours
15 Avhashoni Mainganye	A2
16 BBK Trails	A7
Lebombo Motorised Eco Trail	(see 28)
17 Leka Gape	B4
Lonely Bull Back-Pack Trail	(see 35)
18 Mphongolo Back-Pack Trail	C2
19 Napi Wilderness Trail	B6
20 Nthandanyathi Hide	D7
Olifants River Back-Pack Trail	(see 36)
Pioneer Hide	(see 35)
21 Sable Overnight Hide	B4
Shipandani Overnight Hide	(see 35)
22 Wolhuter Wilderness Trail	C7

◉ Sleeping
23 Avkhom Hotel	A2
24 Bateleur Bushveld Camp	B3
25 Berg-en-dal Rest Camp	C7
26 Biyamiti Bushveld Camp	C7
27 Boulders Bush Lodge	C3
28 Crocodile Bridge Rest Camp	C7
29 Fundudzi African Ivory Route Camp	A2
30 Jock Safari Lodge	C7
31 Letaba Rest Camp	C4
32 Lower Sabie Rest Camp	D6
33 Lukimbi Safari Lodge	C7
34 Modjadji African Ivory Route Camp	A3
35 Mopani Rest Camp	C3
36 Olifants Rest Camp	C4
37 Outpost	B1
38 Pretoriuskop Rest Camp	B7
39 Punda Maria Rest Camp	B1
40 River House Guest Lodge	C7
41 Shimuwini Bushveld Camp	B4
42 Shingwedzi Rest Camp	C2
43 Sirheni Bushveld Camp	B2
44 Tsendze Rustic Camping Site	C3

◉ Eating
Kaross Cafe	(see 46)

◉ Shopping
45 Afrikania	B4
46 Kaross	A4

WILDLIFE WATCHING

Some call it a game of chance, but wildlife watching is actually a skill in its own right. There is never a guaranteed outcome, of course, but play your cards right and you'll increase your chances of unforgettable encounters. And no matter when you visit Kruger, you do have the odds stacked in your favour.

➡ Purchase a detailed map (R80) from a rest-camp shop that denotes pans (water holes), dams, rivers and other key lookouts.

➡ View sighting boards at camps each evening; these map the notable sightings from the day.

➡ If lions were sighted somewhere mid- to late morning, it's almost guaranteed that they'll still be there, or nearby, mid- to late afternoon.

➡ Leopards often start walking along river roads and trails in the last hour before sunset, especially when the daytime temperature has been high. In winter they may start a little earlier.

➡ Wake early and get out of camp when the gates open; many species are most active at this time, particularly big cats (look around water holes). Activity will usually pick up again before sunset.

➡ Drive slowly; going any faster than 25km/h will reduce your chance of noticing game stoppers like leopards and cheetahs.

➡ Be patient, stop frequently and turn the engine off; you'll be amazed how many more species you'll spot coming out of the woodwork while you're at rest.

➡ If you see a herd of herbivores all staring in the same direction, follow their gaze.

➡ Watch for big cats enjoying the breezes from rocky knolls; leopards will often rest high off the ground in tree branches.

➡ Join a guided drive and learn some animal-behaviour patterns.

➡ Main roads yield some fabulous Kruger sightings, but quieter trails can produce some magical moments all to yourself. Buy a copy of *Kruger Self-Drive: Routes, Roads & Ratings* (2015) by Ingrid van den Berg – it describes the pros and cons of every route in the park.

➡ Even if you're not normally a birdwatcher, adding avian sightings to your list can be both rewarding for its own sake and also as a way of sharpening your attention to the world around you.

Maria and Letaba, and advance bookings are essential. Backpack trails are more rugged, with the group camping wild each evening (minimum of four people required). All walking groups limit numbers to eight participants, and no children under 12 are permitted.

Wolhuter Wilderness Trail WILDLIFE
(Map p398; ☎ 012-428 9111; www.sanparks.org; 4 days incl meals R5000; ☺ departs 3.30pm Wed & Sun) Wolhuter is the original wilderness trail and is based in southern Kruger in an area inhabited by lions and white rhinos. The trail has great history, as does the ground it covers – Stone and Iron Age relics abound. Take it all in from high atop a granite kopje. Meet prior at Berg-en-dal Rest Camp (p403).

Napi Wilderness Trail WILDLIFE
(Map p398; ☎ 012-428 9111; www.sanparks.org; 4 days incl meals from R5000; ☺ departs 3.30pm Wed & Sun) Following the Mbyamithi and Napi Rivers between Pretoriuskop and Skukuza, four-day-three-night Napi is known for its black and white rhino sightings at seasonal pans (water holes). Camp consists of four safari tents. Trips commence at Pretoriuskop Rest Camp (p403) and run to Skukuza Rest Camp (p403).

Sweni Wilderness Trail WILDLIFE
(Map p404; ☎ 012-428 9111; www.sanparks.org; 4 days incl meals R5000; ☺ departs 3.30pm Wed & Sun) This rewarding trail is known for herds of wildebeest, zebras and buffaloes (and the lions that stalk them). It's an evocative environment with vast grassy plains. Sweni starts and finishes at Satara Rest Camp (p405).

Olifants River Back-Pack Trail WILDLIFE
(Map p398; ☎ 012-428 9111; www.sanparks.org; 4 days R3100) The 42km trail's superb river-

ine setting offers the chance to get close to elephants, hippos, crocs and more. It's also known for birds, including the African fish eagle and the rare Pel's fishing owl. You must provide your own camping and gas stoves, as well as food and drink. Water can be collected en route. Walks commence from Olifants Rest Camp (p405).

Lonely Bull Back-Pack Trail HIKING
(Map p398; ☑012-428 9111; www.sanparks.org; 4 days R3100; ⊙departure 2pm Wed & Sun Feb-Nov) Following along the Letaba River and crossing various dry riverbeds, this four-day guided trail walk throws up some great sightings of buffaloes, elephants and even leopards. You must be self-sufficient, with your own tent, cooking equipment and food. Water is available. Based from Mopani Rest Camp (Map p398; ☑013-735 6536, reservations 012-428 9111; www.sanparks.org/parks/kruger/camps/mopani; q bungalows with kitchen from R1100, 6-person cottages from R2015; ❄ ❄).

Mphongolo Back-Pack Trail HIKING
(Map p398; ☑012-428 9111; www.sanparks.org; 4 days R3100; ⊙departures 12pm Wed & Sun Feb-Nov) This trail option begins at Shingwedzi Rest Camp (p408) in Kruger's north, and it is especially good for birding. You'll need to be self-sufficient with food, water, tent and cooking equipment. The trail largely follows the Shingwedzi River, so keep an eye out for leopards.

Birdwatching
Kruger offers excellent birdwatching everywhere, but the very far north is arguably one of the best birding regions on the continent. There are many great hides found in prime viewing areas.

For a good overview of the birds you might see in the rest camps, visit www.sanparks.org/groups/birders/krugerbirds.php.

Shipandani Overnight Hide BIRDWATCHING
(Map p398; ☑013-735 3547; overnight 2 people R760) Overlooks a narrow, gullied section of the Tsendze River. Green-backed herons, Burchell's coucals, Diederick cuckoos and African openbills are regular visitors (and so are elephants and hippos, as we found out).

There are six beds that can be hired exclusively for the night (R760 for the first two people, plus R350 for each extra person). You'll need to bring wood/fuel, cooking gear, food and water. There is a braai (barbecue) area and a toilet. Book at Mopani Rest Camp.

Sable Overnight Hide BIRDWATCHING
(Map p398; ☑013-735 3547; overnight 2 people R760) On the edge of the large Sable Dam, this hide provides a good chance to spy on the iconic African fish eagle, as well as black-winged stilts and African cuckoos.

Sable can be hired exclusively for the night (R760 for the first two people, plus R350 for each extra person). There are nine fold-down beds, a toilet and a braai area; you'll need to bring the rest. Book at Phalaborwa Gate (Map p398; ☑013-735 3547; ⊙5.30am-6.30pm Nov-Feb, 5.30am-6pm Mar & Oct, 6am-6pm Apr, Aug & Sep, to 5.30pm May-Jul). Listen for lions and hyenas.

Sweni Hide BIRDWATCHING
(Map p404) One of the most stunning hide locations, this L-shaped hide overlooks a bend in the Sweni River. The blue-cheeked bee-eater, cinnamon-breasted bunting and black-chested snake eagle are species of note. We also enjoyed watching elephants frolicking in the water here.

4WD Trails
If you're travelling by 4WD, trails are an incredible way to experience the remote bush and its wildlife.

Lebombo Motorised Eco Trail DRIVING
(Map p398; ☑012-426 5117, 012-428 9111; www.sanparks.org; per vehicle, max 4 people, R9975; ⊙departs Sun Apr-Oct) Covering a rugged 500km over five days (Sunday to Thursday), the Lebombo Motorised Eco Trail is Kruger's premier 4WD trail. Departing from Crocodile Bridge, the route skirts the park's entire eastern boundary before finishing at Pafuri picnic spot (Map p398) near Crooks Corner. Besides providing your own 4WD and camping gear, you must bring all your food, drink and cooking equipment.

Mountain Biking
SANParks runs guided mountain-bike trails (R805/1085 with your own/SANParks bike, three to four hours) at Phalaborwa Gate. Must be booked in advance.

☞ Tours

At the budget level, the best places to contact for tours into Kruger are the backpacker lodges in Hazyview (p387), Nelspruit (p388) and Graskop (p383), most of which organise tours from about R1850 per day, including entry fees and meals. There are also some hotels in Hoedspruit (p433) and Phalaborwa (p432) that offer central and/or northern Kruger tours.

At the upper end of the price spectrum, or if you're on a tight schedule and want to connect directly from Johannesburg (Jo'burg) or Cape Town, you have plenty of good options, including the following:

Signature Tours (📞 in Cape Town 021-975 1060; www.signaturetours.co.za; 4-day tour incl full board, drinks & activities from R9850) has tailored self-drive and guided packages with a focus on wildlife.

Wildlife Safaris (📞 011-791 4238; www.wild lifesafaris.com; 4-day tour incl accommodation & activities from R11,870) offers four-day panorama tours of Blyde River and Kruger.

🛏 Sleeping & Eating

If you've travelled in other African national parks, you'll know just what a treat Kruger is. Accommodation here ranges from SAN-Parks' rest camps, bushveld camps and satellite camps to five-star luxury lodges within the park's private concessions. The latter include exclusive access to some of Kruger's richest wildlife areas.

All accommodation should be booked far in advance during the high season (October to mid-January) and over school holidays.

The majority of visitors stay in Kruger's 12 large rest camps, most of which offer serviced caravan and camping sites, plus a range of comfortable accommodations. Furnished safari tents and huts are usually the most basic, though they still typically have fans and fridges. Like the campgrounds, they share ablutions (hot showers) and have access to communal cooking facilities consisting of sinks, hotplates and braais (barbecues).

The roomier bungalows and cottages are almost always en suite and often come complete with fans/air-con, kitchen, cutlery, pans

---

NORTH VERSUS SOUTH: A QUICK GUIDE

Kruger is such a massive park that a visit here requires careful planning. If you're unable to visit everywhere, for which you'd need a number of weeks if you were to do it properly, where you go should depend on what sort of experience you'd like to have.

Central Kruger is generally considered a transition zone between north and south – visiting here is easy from either end of the park and contains the best and worst of both worlds.

Northern Kruger

Pros

➡ great birding

➡ quieter trails

➡ quieter rest camps

➡ distinctively Kruger mopane (woodland) vegetation

➡ you may have wildlife sightings to yourself

Cons

➡ generally lower density mammal populations

➡ denser vegetation means wildlife more difficult to see

➡ further distance from major South African cities and towns

Southern Kruger

Pros

➡ fantastic wildlife concentrations (including more rhinos)

➡ open bushveld means great visibility for wildlife

➡ higher number of vehicles means more eyes looking for wildlife – if you see a car stopped, you may be onto something

Cons

➡ busy trails and roads

➡ busy rest camps

➡ higher number of vehicles means you may have to wait in line at a sighting

and plates. Bedding and towels are provided for all noncamping options (including safari tents). All rest camps are fenced and have petrol stations, laundry facilities and reasonably well-stocked shops, and 10 of them have restaurants. As a general rule, they're outstanding value.

Bushveld camps are a recommended option if you want more of a wilderness experience than is possible at the rest camps. The cottages are equipped for self-catering, but only ice and firewood are available on site.

Satellite camps are similar to bushveld camps, but most only have communal kitchens and ablutions blocks. They are usually set within 3km of a rest camp, however.

🛏 Southern Kruger

★ Lower Sabie
Rest Camp   BUNGALOW, CAMPGROUND $$
(Map p398; 📞013-735 6056, reservations 012-428 9111; www.sanparks.org/parks/kruger/camps/lower_sabie; camping per site R330-355, huts with shared bathroom R640, d safari tents/bungalows with kitchen from R1340/1400; ❄🐾) Kruger's most popular rest camp is set on a gorgeous bend of the Sabie River that attracts elephants, hippos, buffaloes and other animals. LST2U-class safari tents and BD2U/BD3U bungalows have river views. The riverside dining area of the **Mugg & Bean** (www.themugg.com; ⊙7am-9pm; mains R64-160) is one of Kruger's most scenic, though the pool area is less so.

Skukuza Rest Camp BUNGALOW, CAMPGROUND $$
(Map p404; 📞013-735 4152, reservations 012-428 9111; www.sanparks.org/parks/kruger/camps/skukuza; camping per site R285-355, d safari tents with shared bathroom from R640, d bungalows R1135-1490; ❄🐾🐾) Although more town than camp, Kruger's largest camp is unobtrusive and has a great location on the Sabie River. There's an extensive range of accommodation, including four-/six-person cottages (from R2320). The attractive pool areas will lead you to linger. Additional services include bank, ATM, post office, doctor, library, museum and information centre.

The riverside **Cattle Baron** (www.cattlebaron.co.za; mains R60-190) has free wi-fi, great food (the fillet steak is divine) and a lovely setting. The takeaway stand is less appetising.

Berg-en-dal
Rest Camp   BUNGALOW, CAMPGROUND $$
(Map p398; 📞013-735 6106, reservations 012-428 9111; www.sanparks.org; camping per site R285-355, d bungalows with kitchen R1150-1555; ❄🐾)

This modern brick-built camp, 12km from Malelane Gate, lacks the old-school bush feel but its location in the Malelane Mountains' shadow makes up for it, with views over Berg-en-dal Dam and its associated wildlife. Options include six-person family cottages (from R2100). There's a visitors' centre, evening nature movies (except Sunday) and the short Rhino Walking Trail on the camp edge.

The Tindlovu restaurant (mains R40 to R155) and cafe serve average food. A couple of birding prizes to watch out for in and around the camp: scarlet-chested sunbird and Heuglin's robin.

Biyamiti Bushveld Camp   COTTAGE $$
(Map p398; 📞013-735 6171, reservations 012-428 9111; www.sanparks.org/parks/kruger/camps/biyamiti; 2-/4-person cottages from R1475/2710) This small self-catering camp's 15 cottages are set along the bank of the ephemeral Biyamiti River (Nos 1 to 9 have the best views). There is a great bird hide – the orange-breasted bush shrike is a local speciality. The shop sells firewood and ice, but no food. The drive to get here is stunning.

Pretoriuskop
Rest Camp   BUNGALOW, CAMPGROUND $$
(Map p398; 📞013-735 5128, reservations 012-428 9111; www.sanparks.org/parks/kruger/camps/pretoriuskop; camping per site R285-355, d bungalows without bathroom R555-685, d bungalows R1055-1490; 🐾🐾) Kruger's oldest and highest (thus coolest) camp is next to Numbi Gate. Located within an attractive region dotted with granite outcrops and frequented by rhinos, it's pretty too, with bougainvillea, flowering trees and a natural rock swimming pool. A wide choice of accommodation, a limited choice of food.

★ Rhino Post Safari Lodge   LODGE $$$
(Map p404; 📞035-474 1473; www.isibindi.co.za; per person all-inclusive R4700-5650; ❄🐾🐾) The most authentic private bush lodge in southern Kruger, Rhino Post has eight suites constructed from wood, canvas, glass and gabion baskets. Each oozes safari appeal, and you feel part of the tree canopy. Sit on the deck and watch wildlife come and go from the Mutlumuvi riverbed.

The lodge is within the only private concession that is a declared wilderness area, so there are no off-road drives. However, SANParks has allowed the lodge access to 130km of park roads after closing. Inquire about the Rhino Walking Safaris.

Central Kruger National Park & Around

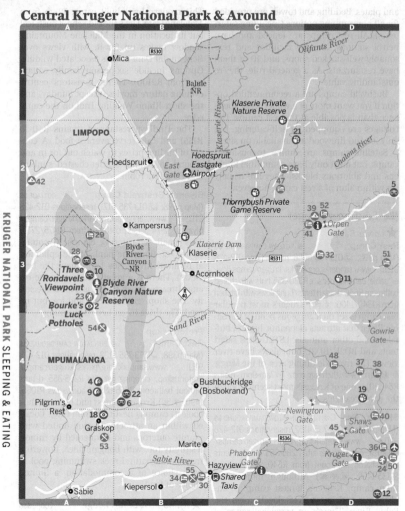

★ **Lion Sands Narina Lodge** LODGE $$$
(Map p404; ☎ 011-880 9992; www.lionsands.com; s/d all-inclusive from R20,130/26,840; ✳ ✿ ≋) Hovering over the bank of the Sabie River in a private concession, Narina's nine bright suites live beneath stepped thatched roofs. They are full of natural woods and modern furnishings, much like the open-plan common areas. Views are everywhere. Bathrooms have warm stone floors and massive eggshell-shaped tubs that radiate light. All decks include plunge pools and private showers.

Exclusive activities take place not only in the concession but also in the renowned Sabi Sand Game Reserve.

Lion Sands Tinga Lodge LODGE $$$
(Map p404; ☎ 011-880 9992; www.lionsands.com; s/d all-inclusive from R20,130/26,840; ✳ ✿ ≋) Tinga's nine luxury suites enjoy beautiful views of the Sabie River. The colonial-feeling rooms feature polished dark-wood floors and furniture, formal leather loungers, huge windows, outdoor showers and private plunge pools. The massive open-plan common areas are more contemporary

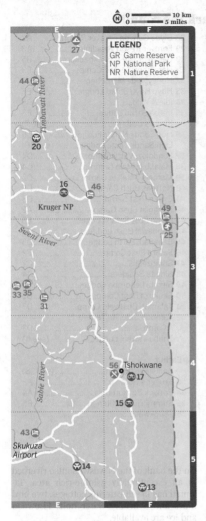

LEGEND
GR Game Reserve
NP National Park
NR Nature Reserve

Kruger NP

Tshokwane

Skukuza Airport

and drop down onto a huge riverside deck surrounding a majestic jackalberry tree.

Activities are within both the concession and the Sabi Sand Game Reserve.

Jock Safari Lodge
LODGE **$$$**

(Map p398; ☑ 041-509 3000; www.jocksafarilodge.com; per person all-inclusive from R7722; ❀ 🤖 🏊) The first private lodge in the park, Jock rests at the confluence of the Biyamiti and Mitomeni Rivers within an exclusive 60-sq-km conservancy. The 12 rooms (some adjoining for families) all have plunge pools and river views. It's something of a Kruger classic, and the rooms remain outstanding.

🛏 Central Kruger

Balule Satellite Camp
HUT, CAMPGROUND **$**

(Map p404; ☑ reservations 012-428 9111, 013-735 6606; www.sanparks.org/parks/kruger/camps/balule; camping per site R285-345, hut tr without bathroom from R415-495) Just south of Olifants, this atmospheric camp has just six huts and 15 campsites. There's no electricity, but lanterns are provided for huts (a torch is still wise). A communal freezer and stove are available. Sunset and night drives are possible on request. Check in at Olifants, Satara, Orpen or Letaba.

Maroela Satellite Camp
CAMPGROUND **$**

(Map p404; ☑ reservations 012-428 9111; www.sanparks.org/parks/kruger/camps/maroela; camping per site R285-355) A few kilometres from Orpen Rest Camp (where check-in is), this campsite is fairly open, without much bush or privacy. There are braai racks, and hotplates and freezers in the communal kitchen. Watch for bushbabies among the rather lovely jackalberry trees.

★ Olifants Rest Camp
BUNGALOW, COTTAGE **$$**

(Map p398; ☑ 013-735 6606, reservations 012-428 9111; www.sanparks.org/parks/kruger/camps/olifants; d bungalows R1120-1765; ❄) High atop a bluff, this camp offers fantastic views down to the Olifants River, where elephants, hippos and numerous other animals roam. Bungalows 10 to 14 have the best views, as do the eight-person Nshawu and Lebombo self-catering guesthouses (from R4050). There's also a camp pool.

Rustic Kitchen (mains R42 to R155) has a small variety of meals and extraordinary sunset views – bring binoculars. At sunset look for the bat colony departing.

★ Satara Rest Camp
BUNGALOW, CAMPGROUND **$$**

(Map p404; ☑ 013-735 6306, reservations 012-428 9111; www.sanparks.org/parks/kruger/camps/satara; camping per site R240-355, d bungalows R1135-1660; ❀ ❄) Satara – the second-largest option after Skukuza (p403) – may lack the riverside views of other camps, but it's optimally situated in the heart of 'big cat' territory, with open plains making viewing easier. When it's busy, it feels like the antithesis of wilderness, but it's still a good base.

Rustic Kitchen (mains R42 to R155) has taken over the restaurant here – the food's fine, and there's a well-stocked shop for those self-catering. Both baboons and honey badgers are considered problem animals

Central Kruger National Park & Around

in the camp – don't leave any food lying around. We also saw an African wild cat within the rest camp's fence.

Tamboti Satellite Tented Camp
BUNGALOW $$

(Map p404; ☑ reservations 012-428 9111; www.sanparks.org/parks/kruger/camps/tamboti; safari tent d without bathroom R580, d with kitchen from R1200) Tamboti has 40 safari tents spread along a curve in the Timbavati River, including 10 very comfy options with kitchens and en-suite bathrooms. All have fridges, fans and views, and dense bush makes most rather private affairs. It has plenty of wildlife and a hide, and residents can use Orpen's nearby pool.

Talamati Bushveld Camp
COTTAGE $$

(Map p404; ☑ 013-735 6343, reservations 012-428 9111; www.sanparks.org/parks/kruger/camps/talamati; 4-/6-person cottages from R1200/2350)

On the bank of the N'waswitsontso riverbed in an exceptionally wildlife-rich area, Talamati has 15 self-catering cottages, two bird hides and a nearby water hole. Firewood and ice are available.

Roodewal Bush Lodge
LODGE $$

(Map p404; ☑ reservations 012-428 9111; www.sanparks.org/parks/kruger/camps/roodewal; up to 8 people R6700-7500, up to 10 people R7855-8655) This 18-person bush lodge on the Timbavati River must be booked in advance and on an exclusive basis. There are no facilities other than equipped kitchens, braai areas and bedding. Solar provides power for just lights and fans. You're in the heart of big-cat country, and watch, too, for nyala, a rather extravagantly patterned large antelope, in the area.

★Singita Lebombo Lodge   LODGE $$$
(Map p404; ☑021-683 3424; www.singita.com; per person all-inclusive R25,750; ❄🅿🌐) This 15-room flagship ultraluxury lodge on Singita's private concession in Kruger's Lebombo Mountains is themed around a bird's nest, with each open-plan suite built among trees high atop a bluff and clad in oversized twigs. All have views down to the Sweni River (Nos 4 and 5 are the best), and you can choose to bed down on your private deck.

★Imbali Safari Lodge   LODGE $$$
(Map p404; ☑013-735 8917; www.imbali.com; d all-inclusive R9770-14,100; ❄🅿🌐) The largest lodge in the Mluwati concession, Imbali is fenced and welcomes children three years and over. There are 12 large suites (each with private plunge pool or hot tub) nestled in riverine forest, nine of which overlook the N'waswitsontso riverbed and its associated wildlife.

Hoyo Hoyo Safari Lodge   LODGE $$$
(Map p404; ☑011-516 4367; www.hoyohoyo.com; s/d all-inclusive R6840/9340; ❄🌐) Partly owned by a local community, the small six-suite lodge in the Mluwati concession embraces Tsonga culture, and you'll be welcomed with the Shangaan greeting of 'Hoyo Hoyo'. The orange-coloured beehive rooms resemble traditional dwellings in style but are full of luxury. It's the most affordable option in Kruger's exclusive private concessions. Big cats are something of a speciality in the surrounding bushveld.

Hamiltons Tented Camp   LODGE $$$
(Map p404; ☑011-516 4367; www.hamiltonstentedcamp.co.za; s/d all-inclusive R9440/12,820; ❄🌐) The highest-end option within the private 100-sq-km Mluwati concession, Hamiltons has six sumptuous safari tents that are built on stilts next to the dry riverbed of the N'waswitsontso. It's arguably the pick of the options within the park.

🛏 Northern Kruger

In addition to the many standard SANParks accommodation options available in this area, Shipandani (p401) and Sable (p401) overnight hides can be hired on an exclusive basis for the night.

Tsendze Rustic
Camping Site   CAMPGROUND $
(Map p398; ☑reservations 012-428 9111; www.sanparks.org/parks/kruger/camps/tsendze; camping R265-305) A basic but well-maintained campground 8km south of Mopani. There are communal gas cookers and fridges, but no electricity. Alexander, one of Kruger's big tuskers, likes the area, while birders will want to watch for the ground hornbills and brown snake eagles that are sometimes seen around here.

★Letaba
Rest Camp   BUNGALOW, CAMPGROUND $$
(Map p398; ☑013-735 6636, reservations 012-428 9111; www.sanparks.org/parks/kruger/camps/letaba; camping per site R285-355, d safari tents/huts with shared bathroom from R580/680, bungalows R1040-1500; ❄🌐) One of Kruger's best rest camps, this leafy Letaba River haven has shady lawns, resident bushbucks, SANParks' most attractive pools and a wide variety of accommodation, with great views from various bungalows (Nos 32, 33 or 59 to 64) and six-person cottages (ask for newly refurbished No 101, class FQ6). There's a Rustic Kitchen garden restaurant and a well-stocked shop, too. Although elephants are a common sight in the river here, be sure to visit the Elephant Hall Museum (p397). Each evening (except Sunday) wildlife films are shown.

★Shimuwini Bushveld Camp   COTTAGE $$
(Map p398; ☑013-735 6683, reservations 012-428 9111; www.sanparks.org; 2-/4-/6-person cottages

KRUGER NATIONAL PARK SLEEPING & EATING

ℹ **PICNIC SPOTS**

There are almost a dozen picnic spots at which you can take a break during your wildlife drives. Besides giving you the chance to alight from your vehicle, they have toilets, and several serve food and drinks. Skukuza's and Letaba's day-visitor sites even include pools. Look out for the following:

Tshokwane (Map p404; mains R30-70; ⊙7.30am-4.30pm) About halfway between the rest camps at Satara and Skukuza, or between Lower Sabie and Satara, Tshokwane has been transformed from an attractive picnic spot into a genuine stopover as you move between central and southern Kruger. The restaurant serves light meals, such as wors roll or kudu wors, jaffles and homemade pies, as well as other sausages off the braai and salads.

Timbavati Picnic Area (Map p404) This designated picnic spot is northwest of Satara. Have a late lunch here as a prelude to a loop along the S127 and S39.

THE MAKULEKE CONTRACT

The heart of Kruger's far north is Makuleke Contract Park – a beautiful and geologically unique area consisting of a 240-sq-km wedge of land rimmed by the Limpopo and Luvuvhu Rivers. In 1969, South Africa's apartheid government forcibly removed the Makuleke people from the area in order to incorporate their traditional lands into Kruger National Park.

In the late 1990s the land was returned to the Makuleke, who in turn agreed not to resettle it but to use it for ecotourism purposes. A 'contract park' was created in which the land is administered and managed environmentally as part of Kruger, with tourism developments owned by the Makuleke, who have since granted concessions to a select few companies.

Elephants favour the area during the winter months, while buffaloes, hippos, lions, leopards and nyalas are plentiful year-round. Birdlife is prolific.

Sleep inside or out, with the press of a button. Set high above the Luvuvhu River at the northern extreme of Kruger, the outward-facing walls of the 12 super-contemporary 'living spaces' at **Outpost** (Map p398; ☎011-327 3920; www.seasonsinafrica.com; s/d all-inclusive from R10,530/16,200; ✳) can be raised by remote, allowing you to wake to a breathtaking panorama. Walks through local gorges and the fever-tree forest are highly recommended, as are wildlife drives.

from R1200/2080/2835) This beautiful small camp and bird hide has a picturesque riverine setting, with 15 self-catering cottages staggered on lawns overlooking a wide stretch of the Letaba River. Ask for No 8 (GC5 class), as it was rebuilt after flooding and is the most comfortable and modern.

Sirheni Bushveld Camp
COTTAGE $$
(Map p398; ☎013-735 6860, reservations 012-428 9111; www.sanparks.org; 2-/6-person cottages from R1150/1930) At this pretty camp in a lightly wooded area in the park's north, all but one of the 15 self-catering cottages overlook the Sirheni Dam (avoid No 13, of CO4 class). It's an excellent spot for birding, with a good hide. There is a deep freeze, and ice and firewood are available.

Bateleur Bushveld Camp
COTTAGE $$
(Map p398; ☎013-735 6843, reservations 012-428 9111; www.sanparks.org/parks/kruger/camps/bateleur; 4-person cottages from R1930; ✳) The oldest and smallest of the bushveld camps, Bateleur has loads of wilderness ambience. The seven thatched-roof self-catering cottages with their 1930s steel-frame windows have a rustic feel, set along the Mashokwe (ask for Nos 1 or 7, of GA6 class). The hide has a light for night viewing. Firewood and ice are available. Night and/or sunset drives cost R325.

Shingwedzi
Rest Camp
BUNGALOW, CAMPGROUND $$
(Map p398; ☎013-735 6806, reservations 012-428 9111; www.sanparks.org/parks/kruger/camps/shingwedzi; camping per site R285-400, d huts without

bathroom from R520, d bungalows R880-1300; ✳✳) Way up in Kruger's north, tall mopane trees and palms shade this relaxed camp, with a mix of old-style bungalows in circle A and some large, new modern options in circle B (Nos 32 to 35 and 69 to 79 of BD2 class, and Nos 38 to 41 of the BG2 class). Although it's on the Shingwedzi River, only the Tindlovu restaurant (mains R55 to R150) offers views.

Punda Maria
Rest Camp
BUNGALOW, CAMPGROUND $$
(Map p398; ☎013-735 6873, reservations 012-428 9111; www.sanparks.org/parks/kruger/camps/punda; camping per site from R240, d bungalows R880-1350, safari tents with kitchen R1045-1275; ✳✳) Quaintly residing up a forested slope in far northern Kruger, this petite camp has plenty of old-world charm, with picturesque thatched-roof bungalows dating back to the 1930s. While those options are a little cramped, seven new 'luxury' safari tents provide more comfort and space (Nos 2 and 3 of ST2 class are the most private).

Boulders Bush Lodge
LODGE $$$
(Map p398; ☎reservations 012-428 9111, 013-735 6535; www.sanparks.org/parks/kruger/camps/boulders; up to 4 people R3730, per additional person R720) Set high among large granite boulders 23km south of Mopani, this five-bungalow self-catering lodge has views over the plains. The lodge must be booked in advance by one party on an exclusive basis. Solar provides power for fans and lights only. Given the terrain, leopards are a possibility, and watch for birds of prey and the giant eagle owl.

ℹ Information

BOOKINGS

Bookings for **South African National Parks** (☏ 012-428 9111; www.sanparks.org) accommodation and most activities can be done up to a year in advance (but only one month prior for accessible facilities) online, by phone or in person. Except for school holidays and weekends, bookings are not essential, although we strongly recommend that you book ahead. Between October and mid-January, book as far in advance as possible. The online booking system is efficient and very easy to navigate once you've registered.

EMERGENCY

Kruger National Park 24hr Emergency Call Centre (☏ 013-735 4325, 076 801 9679)
Kruger National Park Headquarters (☏ 013-735 4000)

ENTRY

Park entry for international visitors costs R328/164 per adult/child per day or for an overnight stay – SANParks' Wild Card (p592) applies. During school holidays park stays are limited to 10 days, and five days at any one rest camp (10 days if you're camping).

Throughout the year authorities restrict the total number of visitors, so in the high season arrive early if you don't have a booking. Bicycles and motorcycles are not permitted.

INTERNET ACCESS

Free wi-fi is limited to a handful of the restaurants at the rest camps, although the situation was in a state of flux at the time of writing – limited wi-fi was available only at Skukuza and there was an internet cafe at Berg-en-Dal at the time of writing. At some other camps, you may be able to purchase air-time, but this remains very much the exception rather than the rule.

MONEY

Payment by credit card is possible just about everywhere, including camp shops and restaurants. Only Skukuza and Letaba have ATMs that take international cards. There are 'mini-ATMs' at rest-camp stores, but they only accept local cards and withdrawals are limited to R800 (or less, depending on cash availability in the store till).

TELEPHONE

You can buy mobile air-time at all park shops. Most camps also have 3G mobile or cell-phone coverage, and the range extends out onto some of the surrounding areas and main roads.

TRAVEL WITH CHILDREN

Kruger is very family friendly, and it is ideally set up for taking children with you on safari. The rest camps are all fenced, almost all have swimming pools and restaurants (with most offering special children's meals), and several have play areas. Berg-en-dal, Letaba, Skukuza, Satara and Shingwedzi also have regular evening wildlife movies (usually Monday to Saturday evenings at 7pm) that are good for all ages, and Letaba has an interesting elephant museum. Camp shops, however, generally don't stock nappies (diapers), processed baby food or formula, so bring these items with you.

Children under the age of 12 are not allowed on SANParks wildlife walks, and those under six are prohibited from the park's wildlife drives. Age of acceptance varies for both activities and accommodation at private lodges.

TRAVELLERS WITH DISABILITIES

Facilities for travellers with disabilities are now available at all rest camps except Orpen. Tamboti Satellite Camp, near Orpen, has two accessible safari tents. The SANParks website (www.sanparks.org) has an excellent overview of facilities at each camp, and is worth investigating. Note that all accessible options have 'Z' in the room-class code, and bookings can only be made one month in advance.

ℹ Getting There & Around

There are nine South African entry gates with unified hours of operation, which vary slightly by season (opening times range from 5.30am

KRUGER NATIONAL PARK INFORMATION

KRUGER ENTRY TIMES

MONTH	GATES/CAMPS OPEN (AM)	GATES & CAMPS CLOSE (PM)
Jan	5.30/4.30	6.30
Feb	5.30/5.30	6.30
Mar	5.30/5.30	6
Apr	6/6	6
May-Jul	6/6	5.30
Aug & Sep	6/6	6
Oct	5.30/5.30	6
Nov & Dec	5.30/4.30	6.30

to 6am; closing times from 5.30pm to 6.30pm). Camp gate times are almost in complete unison with the park gates, and fines are issued for late arrival.

There are also border crossings into Kruger from Mozambique at Giriyondo and Pafuri (p606).

AIR

SAAirlink (www.flyairlink.com) and South African Airways (www.flysaa.com) now team up to provide a direct daily flight to **Skukuza Airport** (Map p404; ☎ 013-735 5074; www.skukuzaairport. com) in Kruger from both Cape Town (three hours) and Johannesburg (50 minutes). The airlines provide more abundant options to **Kruger Mpumalanga International Airport** (Map p398; ☎ 013-753 7500; www.kmiairport.co.za), near Nelspruit, from Jo'burg (one hour), Durban (one hour) and Cape Town (2½ hours). They also make the one-hour flights from Jo'burg to Hoedspruit's **Eastgate Airport** (☎ 015-793 3681; www.east-gateairport.co.za; Rte 40), for Orpen gate, and to **Kruger Park Gateway Airport** (☎ 015-781 5823), near Phalaborwa Gate.

CAR

Kruger's southern gates are all within 475km (five hours' drive) of Jo'burg; Orpen and Phalaborwa gates are around 525km (six hours) away, and Punda Maria and Pafuri gates are over 600km (seven hours) away.

Once in the park most visitors drive themselves as it's very straightforward. Kruger's road system is excellent, with a network of great sealed routes and many well-maintained gravel side roads. However, keep an eye out for other vehicles stopping suddenly, distracted drivers and darting animals. You won't need a 4WD for most secondary gravel roads, though check with rangers if it has been raining heavily. There are petrol stations at all the rest camps.

Avis (☎ 013-735 5651; www.avis.co.za; Skukuza Rest Camp) has a rental branch at Skukuza Rest Camp, and there are numerous agencies at Kruger Mpumalanga International Airport. Eastgate Airport and Kruger Park Gateway Airport have further options.

PRIVATE WILDLIFE RESERVES

Spreading over a vast area just west of Kruger is a string of private reserves that offer some of Africa's most compelling safari viewing – they offer the best of Kruger without the crowds. The Big Five-plus populations roaming these protected areas are no different from those in the park – in fact, there is no fence or physical boundary separating the main reserves – Sabi Sand, Manyeleti and Timbavati – from Kruger itself.

What makes the biggest difference to the wildlife-viewing experience here is the level of guiding, the ability of safari vehicles to go off road, and the exclusivity of walking and driving activities. This all comes at a price, of course, as you must stay in one of the exclusive lodges to gain access. But if your budget permits, consider a night or two at the end of your stay in Kruger.

Most visitors fly into Kruger's Skukuza Airport, Eastgate Airport or directly into Sabi Sand with Federal Airlines (www.fedair. com), which serves Londolozi, Mala Mala, Sabi Sabi and Singita airstrips from Jo'burg and MKIA.

Sabi Sand Game Reserve

Bound by the Sabie River and containing much of the Sand River, this large reserve (Map p404; ☎ 013-735 5102; www.sabisand.co.za; vehicle fee R250, per passenger R110; ⊙ 5am-10pm) straddles what might be the richest wedge of wilderness on the continent. Particularly famous for leopards, it is routinely the choice of wealthy safari cognoscenti. Sabi Sand is actually a conglomeration of smaller private reserves, with each one traditionally hosting only its own vehicles within its unfenced boundaries (some now share traversing rights). Wherever you stay, expect top-notch guiding and an outstanding wildlife experience.

🛏 Sleeping & Eating

★**MalaMala Main Camp**   LODGE $$$
(Map p404; ☎ 011-442 2267; www.malamala.com; s/d all-inclusive from US$1110/1480; ❄ 🛜 🏊) While very comfortable, Main Camp doesn't offer plunge pools, throw pillows or chic interiors. And it doesn't care – everything here is about providing ultimate wildlife experiences. Key is the relationship its guides have fostered with the animals over decades (MalaMala was the first photographic safari reserve in the country). At 135-sq-km, it also dwarfs many other reserves.

Guests are encouraged to dine with their safari guides at each meal, which promotes even more understanding of the environment, wildlife and South Africa – it also makes activities feel much more personal. Apart from anything else, it's considered one of the best places in Africa to see leopards, with other sightings, Big Five and otherwise, all likely as well.

★**Sabi Sabi Earth Lodge**   LODGE $$$

(Map p404; ☑013-735 5261; www.sabisabi.com; s/d all-inclusive R28,500/38,000; ✳☎✉) Subterranean bliss, Earth Lodge is unlike any other lodge in Africa – where else can you look up though a skylight to an elephant looking down at you? Using sloping topography brilliantly, its ultramodern rooms, open communal areas and private plunge pools are flooded with light. The super-thick walls and polished-cement floors are dotted with artwork and natural materials.

★**Singita Boulders**   LODGE $$$

(Map p404; ☑021-683 3424; www.singita.com/lodge/singita-boulders-lodge; per person all-inclusive from R21,634; ✳@✉) Singita has a reputation for having some of the best lodges in Africa. Its Boulders lodge on the bank of the Sand River is our favourite. The dining areas, lounge, library, wine cellar and cavernous suites are all framed by Great Zimbabwe–esque stacks of large dark stones that contrast beautifully with contemporary furnishings and African artwork.

Londolozi Varty Camp   LODGE $$$

(Map p404; ☑011-280 6655; www.londolozi.com; s/d all-inclusive from R17,925/23,900; ✳☎✉) Built on the site of the Varty family's original 1920s Sparta Hunting Camp, Varty Camp was Londolozi's first photographic safari lodge and has metamorphosed into a contemporary safari marvel. The original 1920s huts are still on show behind the modern grand lounge, which stares out over the Sand River and frames a gorgeous jackalberry tree (the very tree that inspired the site of Sparta).

Nottens Bush Camp   LODGE $$$

(Map p404; ☑013-735 5105; www.nottens.com; s/d all-inclusive R7793/10,390; ✉) This comfortable, family-run, six-room camp offers a fine safari experience. The open dining area and two rooms (Nos 3 and 4) overlook the water hole, though the beautiful pool does not. Lighting is limited to candles and paraffin lamps, which is romantic (but not everyone's cup of tea). There is power for fans/plugs in the rooms, but not the common areas.

Manyeleti Game Reserve

During the apartheid era the 230-sq-km Manyeleti (Map p404; www.manyeleti.com; per person/vehicle R110/55; ⊙6am-8pm) was the only wildlife reserve that blacks were permitted to visit. Due to its unfenced boundary with Kruger there is no shortage of animals here (including the Big Five), but you

may have to look a little harder than in Sabi Sand or Timbavati as there's less water. As compensation, prices are much lower here, and the birdwatching, with 300 recorded species, is excellent.

🛏 Sleeping & Eating

★**Honeyguide Mantobeni**   LODGE $$$

(Map p404; ☑021-424 3122, 011-341 0282; www.manyeleti.com; all-inclusive s R4600-5425, d R8200-9850; ☎✉) Aimed at couples, this small camp has 12 East African–style safari tents dotted among trees (No 4 overlooks a water hole; No 1 is the most private). Elevated on platforms, the petite tents are very comfortable and have bathrooms that are partly open to the bush. The lounge and pool area also embraces nature but is very modern in look and feel.

Timbavati Private Nature Reserve

It was the discovery of white lions in the mid-1970s that put this reserve (Map p404; ☑015-793 2436; www.timbavati.co.za; vehicle fee R140, conservation bed levy per person R70-328) on the map. Since then, as white lion populations have come and gone, it's the other wildlife (for which Timbavati is probably second only to Sabi Sand in the area) and the good mix of accommodation that keeps travellers coming back.

🛏 Sleeping & Eating

★**&Beyond Ngala Safari Lodge**   LODGE $$$

(Map p404; ☑reservations 011-809 4300; www.andbeyond.com; Timbavati Private Game Reserve; per person all-inclusive R8485; P✳☎@✉) As we've come to expect over the years with high-end &Beyond, super-stylish rooms in a lovely setting and with plenty of wildlife nearby make for a fabulous stay. The rooms are a beguiling mix of wood, stone and thatch with beautiful khaki hues throughout. Service is impeccable, guides are outstanding and the food is some of the best in the area.

Shindzela   LODGE $$$

(Map p404; ☑087 806 2068; www.shindzela.co.za; s/d all-inclusive R2500/3900) A great entry-level option at reasonable prices, Shindzela has eight safari tents, each with attached loos under thatched roofs. Most tents overlook the busy riverbed and water hole (Nos 7 and 8 are more private and view the riverbed). It offers excellent animal viewing, good food and a lovely setting, so much so that we wonder why you'd pay more.

Limpopo

Best Places to Eat

➜ Saskia Restaurant (p417)

➜ Purple Olive (p423)

➜ Red Plate (p429)

➜ Buffalo Pub & Grill (p433)

➜ Sleepers Railway Station Restaurant (p434)

Best Places to Stay

➜ 57 Waterberg (p422)

➜ Fusion Boutique Hotel (p416)

➜ Marataba Safari Lodge (p422)

➜ Tlopi Tent Camp (p421)

➜ Leokwe Camp (p425)

Why Go?

Limpopo, which occupies South Africa's northern reaches, is a huge and diverse province characterised by traditional cultures, an interesting historical story, vast open spaces and terrific wildlife watching. In Mapungubwe National Park visitors can walk through the country's most significant Iron Age site, gaze from a rocky bluff over the riverine landscape where South Africa, Botswana and Zimbabwe meet, and observe birds, big cats and rhinos. Culture and traditional art shine in the enigmatic region of Venda, an area dotted with landforms of great spiritual significance. Nature takes centre stage in the Waterberg, where the eponymous Unesco biosphere reserve has endless skies, a landscape of distinctly South African beauty and great safari opportunities, particularly in Marakele National Park. Best of all, few travellers make it up here to the north, making it one of the country's most rewarding destinations.

When to Go
Polokwane (Pietersburg)

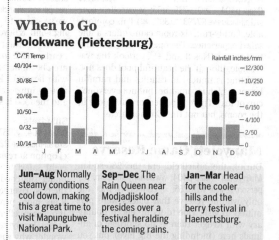

Jun–Aug Normally steamy conditions cool down, making this a great time to visit Mapungubwe National Park.

Sep–Dec The Rain Queen near Modjadjiskloof presides over a festival heralding the coming rains.

Jan–Mar Head for the cooler hills and the berry festival in Haenertsburg.

History

Makapan's Caves, near Mokopane, have offered up an archaeological record stretching back to protohuman times (including tools from over a million years ago), while the area that is now Mapungubwe National Park was once the heart of one of Africa's most technologically advanced civilisations, holding sway over an area of 30,000 sq km and enjoying its heyday in the 8th and 9th centuries.

The Voortrekkers made this region home in the mid-19th century, establishing their base in Pietersburg (now Polokwane) in 1886. Conflict with the local Ndebele people marked a period of resistance against the settlers.

Language

English is widely spoken but Afrikaans remains the language of choice in most areas. The other main languages include Northern Sotho (Sepedi), Tsonga and Venda.

ⓘ Getting There & Around

Other than relatively busy Polokwane Airport, the only air services to/from Limpopo connect Johannesburg with Hoedspruit and Phalaborwa.

Limpopo is bisected by the excellent N1 highway (a toll road), which connects Johannesburg and Pretoria to the Zimbabwe border at Beitbridge. Many of the province's large towns are on this artery and most are connected to Jo'burg and Pretoria by Translux (www.translux.co.za) buses and the company's cheaper City to City (www.citytocity.co.za) services. Greyhound (www.greyhound.co.za) buses make a few stops en route to Harare and Bulawayo, but you can't get off before the border.

Translux also runs along Rte 71 to locations including Tzaneen and Phalaborwa (for Kruger's Phalaborwa Gate). Some destinations are hard to access without a car, but minibus shared taxis trundle to most parts of the province.

Hiring a vehicle is by far the best way to see Limpopo (most roads are good, although many are still undergoing extensive repair work); if you want to save time, you can fly from Jo'burg to Polokwane, Phalaborwa or Hoedspruit (northwest of Kruger's Orpen Gate) and hire a car there.

POLOKWANE

ⓙ 015 / POP 130,000

Limpopo's largest city and provincial capital, Polokwane (formerly Pietersburg) is urban South Africa in all its complications, from the gritty downtown area to a range of worth-

---

ⓘ WARNING

Malaria (p623) and bilharzia (p624) are both prevalent in Limpopo, mainly in the northeast near Kruger National Park and the Zimbabwe border. Malaria is a particular concern after the rains.

---

while attractions. It was once called 'the bastion of the north' by Paul Kruger and has long been a centre of Afrikaans culture, but it's now a little rough around the edges, and although not unpleasant, it's a mishmash of lively, semi-organised African chaos (roughly between Civic Sq and the Indian Centre) and security fences sheltering vast gardens and clipped lawns (in the prim and proper eastern suburbs). Spend any time in the north and you're likely to pass through here.

◉ Sights & Activities

Polokwane Game Reserve   WILDLIFE RESERVE
(ⓙ 015-290 2331; adult/child/vehicle R30/22/45; ⊘ 7am-5.30pm, last entry 3.30pm May-Sep, 7am-6.30pm, last entry 4.30pm Oct-Apr) Go on safari at this 32.5-sq-km reserve less than 5km south of Polokwane. It's one of the country's largest municipal nature reserves, with 21 wildlife species, including zebras, giraffes and white rhinos, plus a good network of roads and hiking trails. It's like a trial run for those going out on safari – if you've already been out in Kruger or elsewhere, it will all feel a little tame, although seeing a rhino is never underwhelming.

Polokwane Art Museum   MUSEUM
(ⓙ 015-290 2177; cnr Grobler & Hans van Rensburgh Sts, Library Gardens; ⊘ 9am-4pm Mon-Fri, 10am-noon Sat) FREE This museum is worth ducking into for its modern take on colonialism, many depictions of Nelson Mandela and interesting displays on women and art in South Africa. It features artists from Limpopo and across the country and is one of South Africa's best regional art galleries.

Bakone Malapa
Open-Air Museum   MUSEUM
(ⓙ 073 216 9912; adult/child R12/7; ⊘ 8am-4pm Mon-Fri) Located 9km south of Polokwane on Rte 37 to Chuniespoort, this museum evokes the customs of the Northern Sotho people who lived here 300 years ago. The tour of the re-created village views pot manufacture and tool demonstrations, such as the antelope-horn trumpet and marula-palm-root matches.

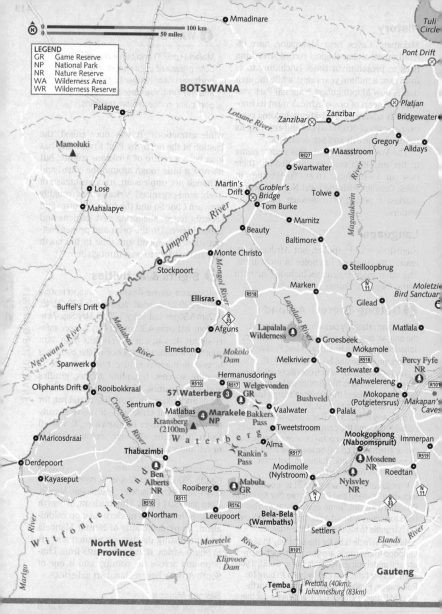

Limpopo Highlights

1 Mapungubwe National Park (p424) Exploring ancient civilisation, stunning landscapes and fab wildlife.

2 Venda (p425) Drawing near to traditional culture

by searching out crafts and colourful weavings.

3 57 Waterberg (p422) Losing yourself in the valleys of the Waterberg watching wildlife from this splendid perch.

4 Marakele National Park (p421) Watching the sun slide behind red cliffs as you search for the Big Five and Cape vultures.

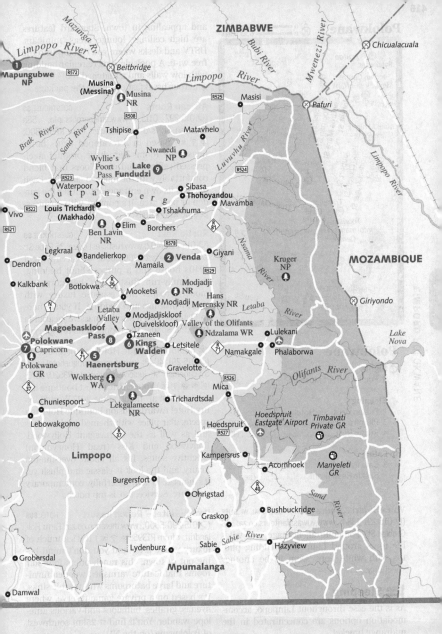

ZIMBABWE

Chicualacuala

Limpopo River Rd

① **Mapungubwe NP**

Beitbridge

Limpopo River

Musina (Messina)
R572
Musina NR

Pafuri

Masisi

R525

Tshipise

R508

Matavhelo

Lavuvhu River

Mwenezi River

Bubi River

Brak River

Sand River

Nwanedi NP

Wyllie's Poort Pass

Lake Fundudzi ⑨

Waterpoor

R523

Soutpansberg

Sibasa

Thohoyandou

Tshakhuma

Mavamba

R522
Louis Trichardt (Makhado)

Vivo

R521

Elim

Ben Lavin NR

Borchers

Nsama River

R524

R81

MOZAMBIQUE

Kruger NP

Legkraal

Bandelierkop

Mamaila

② **Venda**

Giyani

R578

R529

Dendron

Kalkbank

Botlokwa

Mooketsi

R36

Modjadji NR

Modjadji

Hans Merensky NR

Letaba River

Giriyondo

Lake Nova

Letaba Valley

Magoebaskloof Pass

⑦ **Polokwane**

Capricorn

R71

Modjadjiskloof (Duivelskloof)

⑧

Tzaneen

⑥ **Kings Walden**

Letsitele

Valley of the Olifants

Ndzalama WR

Lulekani

Namakgale

Phalaborwa

Polokwane GR

R37

⑤ **Haenertsburg**

Wolkberg WA

Gravelotte

R526

Chuniespoort

Lekgalameetse NR

Trichardtsdal

Mica

R37

Olifants River

Lebowakgomo

Limpopo

Hoedspruit Eastgate Airport

Timbavati Private GR

Hoedspruit

R527

Burgersfort

Kampersrus

Acornhoek

Manyeleti GR

Sand River

Ohrigstad

R40

Bushbuckridge

Graskop

Grobersdal

Sabie

Lydenburg

Sabie River

Hazyview

Damwal

Mpumalanga

Polokwane

Polokwane

◉ **Sights**

🛏 **Sleeping**

🍴 **Eating**

Vuwa Safari & Tours   CULTURAL, WILDLIFE
(☏015-291 1384; www.vuwasafaritours.co.za; 88 Grobler St) For cultural, heritage and wildlife tours around Limpopo. Wedding photos with white lions seem to be another speciality.

🛏 Sleeping

As is the case throughout Limpopo, accommodation options are concentrated in the midrange bracket.

★Plumtree Lodge   GUESTHOUSE $$
(☏015-295 6153; www.plumtree.co.za; 138 Marshall St; s/d incl breakfast R825/1195; 🅿🛜🏊) The bungalow rooms at this German-run guesthouse are some of the most spacious and appealing in town. Standard features are high ceilings, lounge areas, minibars, DSTV and desks where you can tap into the free wi-fi. A poolside *lapa* (circular building with low walls and a thatched roof) bar and generous breakfast complete the package.

African Roots   GUESTHOUSE $$
(☏015-297 0113; www.africanroots.info; 58a Devenish St; s/d incl breakfast from R650/800; 🅿🛜🏊) Based in a revamped 1920s farmhouse, the rooms here have original steel-pressed ceilings and pine floors that blend comfortably with the modern facilities. Each one has its own entrance into either the garden or pool area. It's popular with businesspeople and tourists.

Rustic Rest   GUESTHOUSE $$
(☏015-295 7402; www.rusticrest.co.za; 36 Rabe St; s/d incl breakfast R700/1000; 🅿) Occupying a 1940s house and a purpose-built building, the family-run Rustic Rest has gorgeous, modern rooms that espouse luxury with soft furnishings and bedding. If you're here in October, you'll see the massive jacaranda tree that shades the rooms in its full glory.

★Fusion Boutique Hotel   BOUTIQUE HOTEL $$$
(☏015-291 4042; www.fusionboutiquehotel.co.za; 5 Schoeman St; junior/executive ste R3520/5870; 🅿🛜@🏊) Voted Africa's best boutique hotel (and best art hotel) at the 2017 World Luxury Hotel Awards, Fusion Boutique Hotel is a spectacular place with themed junior suites and as well as the extravagant Hollywood, Bollywood and Kiss (read Honeymoon) executive suites. It's all about over-the-top luxury, and the look is classic and plush yet it's housed in a wonderfully contemporary structure. Service, too, is top notch.

Protea Hotel – Ranch Resort   HOTEL $$$
(☏015-290 5000; www.theranch.co.za; Farm Hollandrift; r from R1395; 🛜🏊) If it's a touch of luxury you're after and you don't mind being out of town, this ranch offers four-star rooms that feature varnished wooden furniture and large bathrooms with marble sinks. It's based on a private game reserve, where hyenas, giraffes, buffaloes and various antelope wander. You'll find it 25km southwest of Polokwane (on the N1).

🍴 Eating & Drinking

You can find the usual takeaways in and around Library Gardens, but the Savannah Centre (Rte 71) offers the widest selection of sit-down meals.

Cafe Pavilion
CAFE $$

(☎015-291 5359; Church St, Sterkloop Garden Pavilion; mains R55-125; ⊙8am-5pm Mon-Sat, to 2pm Sun) Overlooking a garden centre, and boasting its own water feature in the covered outdoor area, the Pavilion is a great spot for breakfast or lunch. The food has the usual focus on meat feasts (think biltong and avocado T-bone) prepared in a variety of styles, with a couple of salads thrown in for good measure.

★ Saskia Restaurant
INTERNATIONAL $$$

(☎015-291 4042; www.fusionboutiquehotel.co.za/ saskia-fine-dining-restaurant; 5 Schoeman St; mains R155-260; ⊙noon-10pm) Decorated with Rembrandt replicas and stories from the master painter at every turn, you might expect this place at Fusion Boutique Hotel to be a bit stuffy. Not so. The cooking is fresh and assured, with Indonesian fish, Norwegian salmon and all manner of steak, lamb, chicken and (a few) vegetarian options to choose from. Start with the sublime garlic mussels.

★ Grind
CAFE

(☎083 633 6479; www.facebook.com/thegrin-drepresent; ⊙7-11am & 3-7pm Mon-Fri) This mobile coffee tuk-tuk is the brainchild of master barista and all-round-coffee-guru Ben Schempers. Keep an eye on Facebook on weekdays then track it down for Polokwane's (Limpopo's?) best coffee. It's a real hipster hangout in the best sense, with gourmet sandwiches complementing the fabulous artisan coffee.

Grounded Container Bar &Cafe
BAR

(☎066 302 9682; www.facebook.com/Grounded-containerbar; Landdros Mare St; ⊙9am-9pm Wed, Thu & Sat, to 10pm Fri, to midnight Sun) We're ready to ignore the rather odd, close-to-the-airport location, and we really wish it'd open later, but this fantastic outdoor venue serves up Polokwane's best mix of craft beer and cocktails. It opened in late 2017 and is already Polokwane's best place for a drink.

ⓘ Information

Limpopo Tourism Agency (☎ office 015-293 3600, visitor info 015-290 2010; www.golimpopo.com; Southern Gateway, ext 4, N1; ⊙8am-4.30pm Mon-Fri) Covers the whole province and offers the useful *Limpopo Explorer* map and the *Know Limpopo* guide. On the N1 south of town.
Medi-Clinic (☎015-290 3600, 24hr emergency 015-290 3747; www.mediclinic.co.za; 53 Plein St) Private hospital with 24-hour emergency centre.

Police Station (☎015-290 6000; cnr Bodenstein & Schoeman Sts)
Tourism Information Centre (☎015-290 2010; cnr Thabo Mbeki & Church Sts, Civic Sq; ⊙8am-5pm Mon-Fri) The best source for Polokwane information; it has brochures and a list of accommodation.

ⓘ Getting There & Away

AIR
Polokwane Airport (☎015-288 1622) is 5km north of town.
Airlink (☎015-781 5823; www.flyairlink.com) Subsidiary of South African Airways with offices at the airport; flies daily to/from Jo'burg.

BUS
Translux (☎0861 589 282; www.translux.co.za; cnr Thabo Mbeki & Joubert Sts) Translux runs services to/from Jo'burg (R260, four hours) via Pretoria (R20, 3½ hours) at least three times daily.

CAR
Major car-rental agencies are located at the airport.

SHARED TAXI
Minibus shared taxis run to destinations including Louis Trichardt (R70, 1½ hours) and Thohoyandou (R80, 2½ hours) from the rank at the Indian Centre, on the corner of Church and Excelsior Sts.

BUSHVELD

Southwest of Polokwane lies the Waterberg, a Unesco biosphere reserve the size of the Okavango Delta. The source of four of Limpopo's perennial rivers, its biodiversity is reflected in the San rock paintings of large mammals on the area's sandstone cliffs. For something more recent, Marakele National Park is one of South Africa's most underrated protected areas. Elsewhere, the Bushveld region is typical African savannah. If you want to break up your journey along the N1, there is a string of roadside towns with some pit-stop potential.

Mokopane

☎015 / POP 30,151

Mokopane is a sizeable Bushveld town that makes a good place to break up a trip along the N1. The main attraction for visitors is Makapan's Caves. Inside the town itself, there's little to detain you.

⊙ Sights

Makapan's Caves
CAVE
(Makapansgat; ☏014-736 4328, 079 515 6491; adult/student R25/15) While not visually arresting, this National Heritage Site carries great palaeontological significance – artefacts from throughout the Stone and Iron Ages have been unearthed here. In the **Historic Cave**, chief Makapan and 1000-plus followers were besieged for a month in 1854 by Paul Kruger and the Voortrekkers. You must prebook visits to the site, 23km northeast of town; the guide also speaks French. The fossilised remains of long-extinct animals – such as the sivatherium, an offshoot of the giraffe clan – have been discovered in the caves, which are still littered with fossils and bones.

Game Breeding Centre
WILDLIFE RESERVE
(☏015-491 4314; Thabo Mbeki Dr; adult/child R20/10, feeding tours R40; ⊙8am-4.30pm Mon-Fri, to 6pm Sat & Sun) This 13-sq-km reserve on Rte 101 is a breeding centre for the National Zoo in Pretoria and has a wide variety of native and exotic animals, including gibbons, wild dogs, giraffes and lions. You can drive through the reserve; go early morning or late afternoon to see the animals at their most active.

🛏 Sleeping & Eating

Game Breeding Centre
GUESTHOUSE $
(☏015-491 4314; Thabo Mbeki Dr; camping/s/d R50/250/320; ✺) Certainly the most novel choice in Mokopane. The rooms are all a bit different – some with interior or exterior kitchens and bathrooms. But all are a good size with a lovely outlook onto the reserve. Room 1 is our fave – you can see the gibbons at play from your window.

Thabaphaswa
HUT $
(☏082 389 6631, 015-491 4882; www.thabaphaswa.co.za; camping R155, hut per person R180-420; ✺) If you don't mind roughing it a little, this unique property offers accommodation in

climbers' huts beneath rocky escarpments. The glass-walled huts have bunk beds and patios with braai (barbecue) pits and open-air showers, but there are a couple of more comfortable options as well. There are biking and walking trails on the property.

★Platinum
GUESTHOUSE $$
(☏015-491 3510; theplatinum@connectit.co.za; 4 Totius St; s/d incl breakfast R600/950; ✺@🖧) The appearance of this suburban house belies the luxury accommodation on offer. Rooms are beautifully presented with touches of elegance and comfort everywhere. The friendly owner is happy to show her rooms, so have a look at a few because layout and size differ – all are first class. It's signposted off the R101 as you enter town from Modimolle.

Park Hotel
HOTEL $$
(☏015-491 3101; www.thepark.co.za; cnr Thabo Mbeki Dr & Beitel St; r from R920; 🅿✺🖧✺) On the town's northern fringe, this three-star hotel has 129 modern rooms and an excellent poolside restaurant. It lacks the personal charm of other places, but the rooms are stylish and service is professional.

La Bamba Restaurant & Sports Bar
PUB FOOD $
(☏083 368 6846; Hooge St; mains R45-90; ⊙11am-late Mon-Sat) This plain, tiled-floor pub – with rugby or cricket usually on the box – is a good place to fuel up on burgers, schnitzels and steaks. It also has a salad bar.

❶ Information

Mokopane Tourism Association (☏015-491 8458; www.mogalakwena.gov.za; 97 Thabo Mbeki Dr; ⊙8am-4.30pm Mon-Fri, 9am-noon Sat) Has plenty of local information.

❶ Getting There & Away

Translux (www.translux.co.za) and City to City (www.citytocity.co.za) have daily buses to Jo'burg (R250, 3¾ hours) via Pretoria; to

WHAT'S IN A NAME?

The changing of apartheid-era town names has always been bound up with wounded sensibilities, but nowhere more so than Mokopane. Under apartheid, Mokopane was originally called Vredenburg, but was later changed to Pieter Potgietersrust (later shortened to Potgietersrus). The name honoured a Boer hero, Piet Potgieter, who was shot during the siege of the Makapansgat, or Makapan's Caves, in 1854. The siege occurred when hundreds of local people, led by Chief Makapan (Mokopane), took refuge inside the cave when surrounded by Voortrekker forces seeking to avenge the killing of some of their members. Hundreds of those hiding in the caves died of thirst and starvation. After South Africa's transition to democracy, the town's name was changed to Mokopane to honour the local chief, considered the direct enemy of Potgieter.

NATURE A STONE'S THROW FROM THE N1

Nylsvley Nature Reserve (☑ 014-743 6925; www.nylsvley.co.za; adult/child/vehicle R25/20/30; ☺ 6.30am-5.30pm May-Aug, 6am-6pm Sep-Apr) This 40-sq-km reserve, on the Nyl River floodplain, is one of the country's best places to see birds: 380 species are listed. The mammal list runs to 79, with brown hyena, leopard, roan antelope, honey badger and aardwolf all present, if elusive. The reserve, 20km south of Mookgophong, is signposted from Rte 101 to Modimolle.

Bundox Bush Camp (☑ 072 523 2796; www.bundox.co.za; per person R275-880; P ☢ ☒) Three kilometres south of Mookgophong off Rte 101, this camp has gorgeous open-plan chalets and East African tents in a reserve that hosts a conservation centre with cheetahs, 129 bird species and a thatched library.

Nylsvley Wildlife Resort (☑ 014-743 6925; www.wildliferesorts.org/limpopo-resorts/waterberg/nylsvley-birding-lodge.html; campsites per person R35, chalets per person from R530) Simple but tidy and well-maintained chalets make this a perfect spot for birders to base themselves while exploring the reserve.

Phalaborwa (R250, 3¾ hours) via Tzaneen; and to Sibasa (R250, four hours) via Polokwane and Louis Trichardt.

Minibus shared taxis leave from outside Shoprite on Nelson Mandela Dr; from Mokopane to Polokwane it's about R50.

Bela-Bela

☑ 014 / POP 66,500

Bela-Bela is a hot, chaotic and seemingly perpetually busy place. And as so often in South Africa, there's an arresting juxtaposition between the township and town. But Bela-Bela works as a spot to break a journey, especially if you like to indulge in 'warm baths'. Bela-Bela (aka Warmbaths) takes its name from the town's hot springs, which bubble out of the earth at a rate of 22,000L per hour and were discovered by the Tswana in the early 19th century. Bathing in the soporific pools is a popular treatment for rheumatic ailments. There are also a couple of interesting attractions just north of town.

◉ Sights & Activities

Bambelela　　　　　　　WILDLIFE RESERVE
(☑ 014-736 4090; www.bambelela.org.za; adult/child R100/50; ☺ by appointment) This private rehabilitation centre, the work of Silke von Eynern and established in 2003, is a testament to persistence. After her husband's death in 1997, she set up this facility, which, after many false starts, now thrives and focuses on vervet monkeys, with more than 300 being cared for here. Join a 1½-hour tour to learn more about the monkeys, from newborns through to those about to be released into the wild. Advance booking is essential. It's 20km north of town.

Hydro　　　　　　　　　　　　SPA
(☑ 014-736 8530; www.foreverwarmbaths.co.za; Chris Hani Dr; per person from R130; ☺ 7am-4pm & 5-10pm) At Warmbaths (a Forever Resort), the Hydro spa has a series of interlinked indoor and outdoor pools. Children head to the cold pools with twisty slides, while those who prefer a relaxing experience can wallow in warm baths (at 38°C to 42°C) or peruse the many other enhancers and therapies involving the cleansing waters.

🛏 Sleeping & Eating

With plenty of chain restaurants across the city centre – for example, steakhouses and Ocean Basket – you won't go hungry.

Flamboyant Guesthouse　　　　　B&B $
(☑ 076 259 7111; www.flamboyantguesthouse.com; 5 Flamboyant St; s/d incl breakfast R380/560; ☢) Among the jacaranda trees on the northern edge of town, the Flamboyant has flowery patios aplenty, decor that may take you back a few years and a personable owner. It's a no-frills place, but excellent value.

Elephant Springs Hotel　　　　　HOTEL $$
(☑ 087 820 5999, 014-736 2101; www.southofafrica.co.za/properties/elephant-springs-hotel-bela-bela; 31 Sutter Rd; s/d R600/1200; ☢ ☢ ☒) Primarily (but not exclusively) used for conferences, this old-fashioned little beauty provides spacious lodging. Although underneath its smiling veneer there are some rough edges, it's very friendly, the beds are comfy and it makes a good change from staying at guesthouses.

Toeka se Dae　　　　　　　INTERNATIONAL $
(☑ 082 570 7923; www.toekasedae.co.za; Rte 516, Roodekuil Padstal; mains R45-90; ☺ 9am-6pm)

LIMPOPO BELA-BELA

Pull up a chair fashioned from old tyres, number plates or tin baths and admire the inimitably quirky decor at this farm stall 15km out of town. Lunches are nothing spectacular – a familiar menu of burgers, toasted sandwiches and a few South African specialities – but it's a fun pit stop. You'll find it on the R516, southeast of Bela-Bela.

ⓘ Information

Bela-Bela Community Tourism Association
(☑ 014-736 3694; www.belabelatourism.co.za; Old Pretoria Rd, Waterfront; ⊙ 8am-5pm Mon-Fri, 9am-1pm Sat) In the Waterfront development, over the bridge from the town centre.

ⓘ Getting There & Away

Minibus shared taxis run from Ritchie St, between the Forever Resort and Elephant Springs Hotel, to destinations including Polokwane (R90, 2½ hours) and Jo'burg (R105, two hours).

The Waterberg

Paul Kruger used to damn troublesome politicos with the phrase 'Give him a farm in the Waterberg'. These days, that fate may not strike you as such a hardship. The 150km-long range, which stretches northeast from Thabazimbi past Vaalwater, is protected by the 15,000-sq-km Waterberg Biosphere Reserve, one of Africa's two savannah biospheres. Rising to 2100m, it has a mild climate and some wild terrain for spotting the Big Five (lion, leopard, buffalo, elephant and rhino), with rivers and distinctive mountains scything through bushveld and sourveld (a type of grassland). Marakele National Park is the undoubted highlight.

The Waterberg Meander, a 350km signposted tourist route around the Waterberg, links 13 community projects, and sites of interest such as those significant in the Anglo-Boer War, along with viewpoints of some stunning landscapes, and arts-and-crafts outlets. Look out for the excellent *Waterberg Meander* booklet in tourist offices. You're most likely to find information in Vaalwater.

Vaalwater & Around

☑ 014 / POP 4000

Vaalwater ('faalvater') makes a top base for exploring the many attractions of the Waterberg, and is by far the most pleasant town between Polokwane and Limpopo's southwestern border – basing yourself here can feel like a world away from gritty, urban South Africa. Otherwise, the town is little more than jumble of tourist and local facilities strung out along the highway.

◉ Sights & Activities

St John's Church   CHURCH
FREE About 10km from Vaalwater on the Melkrivier road, turn right onto the Vierentwintigriviere road, and after 8.7km turn left towards Naauwpoort – St John's will be on your left. The church dates from 1914 and is said to have been designed by Sir Herbert Baker, but is often overlooked in studies of the great colonial architect.

Horizon Horseback
Adventures   HORSE RIDING
(☑ 083 419 1929; www.ridinginafrica.com) Inspiring fervent loyalty in returning riders, this operation near Waterberg Cottages offers adventurous options including cattle mustering and an eight-day horse safari that includes wildlife watching in Botswana.

Waterberg Welfare Society   INFORMATION
(☑ 014-755 3594; www.facebook.com/Waterberg-WelfareSociety; Timothy House, 208-209 Waterberg St; ⊙ 8.30am-5pm) Founded to assist individuals and their families affected by HIV/AIDS, the Waterberg Welfare Society operates a visitor centre, Timothy House, giving the public an opportunity to interact with the orphans and to learn about its programs and work with HIV/AIDS sufferers. Call before visiting.

🛏 Sleeping & Eating

Vaalwater has a handful of OK places to stay at the budget end – for top-end accommodation, you'll need to head out of town into a private game reserve.

Waterberg Cottages   CABIN $
(☑ 014-755 4425; www.waterbergcottages.co.za; per person R420-550; ▣) These cottages, 33km north of Vaalwater off the Melkrivier road, range from the dual-level 'Bushwillow', with its free-standing bath and modern kitchen, to simpler offerings; it's all lent some charm by furniture belonging to the family's ancestors. Activities include astrology with the resident star buff, wildlife watching and farm tours.

La Fleur   ITALIAN $$
(☑ 014-755 3975; 361 Voortrekker St; mains R50-110; ⊙ 8am-10pm Mon-Sat) With a classy setup inside and an outdoor terrace where you can keep an eye on the comings and goings in town, this is Vaalwater's only restaurant

of note. It dabbles in pizza, pasta, salads, pancakes and steaks, and the chatty kitchen staff do everything well.

🛍 Shopping

Beadle ARTS & CRAFTS
(☑ 014-755 4002; www.beadle.co.za; Sterkstroom Rd; ⊙ 7.30am-5pm Mon-Fri, to 1pm Sat & Sun) Next to an essential oils factory and close to Horizon Horseback Adventures (p420), Beadle is a community project that sells attractive leather and beaded crafts, handmade in the workshop by local villagers.

❶ Getting There & Away

A newly laid road along the R33 between Modimolle and Vaalwater has made the journey out to Vaalwater quick and easy. Private transport is your best bet – public transport is rare and unpredictable.

Marakele National Park

One of South Africa's least-known and yet most underrated reserves, this mountainous **national park** (☑ 014-777 6929; www.sanparks.org/parks/marakele; adult/child R192/96; ⊙ 7am-5.30pm May-Aug, to 6pm Sep-Apr) at the southwest end of the Waterberg Biosphere Reserve combines fabulous wildlife with dramatic landscapes. The Big Five are all here, the birdwatching can be excellent and the park is home to one of the world's largest colonies of the endangered Cape vulture (800-plus breeding pairs). But it's the landscape – the dramatic red cliffs and outcrops of the Waterberg massif, forests cauterised by a 2017 fire, and a handful of lakes – that has the power to beguile.

◉ Sights & Activities

The park is divided into two sections, with the second, eastern section (you press a buzzer to open the gate) wilder and richer in wildlife.

In the first, **western section** of the park, rhinos are present, but not the other members of the Big Five. The tracks here are accessible in a 2WD and lead through pretty light woodland that is good for birdwatching – take Kudu Dr and then Kgokong Dr to the **Bollonoto Bird Hide**. The hide overlooks the **Bollonoto Dam**, which can be good for kingfishers and waders.

In the **eastern section**, after passing through the gates, the views are more expansive and the Big Five are all present – lions, elephants and rhinos in particular are

❶ MARAKELE NATIONAL PARK

Why Go The park contains all the larger African species, including the big cats and the Big Five, and has the largest colony of endangered Cape vultures in the world. The Waterberg massif affords spectacular views of the area as well as stunning backdrops at every turn.

When to Go Year-round – but note that heavy rains can occur in February and March.

Practicalities The Marakele 4x4 Eco Trail is sometimes closed due to rain damage. The park entrance booking office is on the Thabazimbi–Alma road, 3km northeast of the intersection with the Matlabas–Rooiberg road.

Budget Tip Stay in Thabazimbi, a few kilometres away – it's much cheaper than the park unless you're camping.

commonly seen. Many of the tracks in this section of park are fine in a 2WD (except after heavy rain) and the best views are along the loop that takes in the Lekganyane Dr and Mbidi Rd.

The eastern sector is also home to the **Lenong Viewing Point** (Vulture-Viewing Point). A narrow, serpentine but paved road climbs to this splendid vantage point with sweeping views; arguably the best views are on the way up. Once at the summit (take the right branch of the roads at the top), ignore the rather ugly communication towers, park your car and then walk for a couple of hundred metres. It may take some looking and false starts, but the breeding colonies of the endangered Cape vulture (800-plus breeding pairs) are worth the effort.

Self-driving is an excellent and easy way to explore the park in your own vehicle, but **wildlife-watching drives** (adult/child R260/120) can be arranged at the park gate for both sunrise and sunset. Adult-only **guided walks** (R350) are also possible.

🛏 Sleeping

⭐**Tlopi Tent Camp** CAMPGROUND $$
(☑ Pretoria 012-428 9111; www.sanparks.org/parks/marakele/tourism/accommodation.php; tents R1365-1670) This two-bed tented accommodation is 15km from reception and is a wonderful spot. The furnished tents, overlooking a dam where antelope and wildebeest come

LIMPOPO THE WATERBERG

to drink, have a bathroom, separate kitchen with refrigerator and braai (barbecue), and an appealing terrace that overlooks the dam. Note: you'll have to bring your own food, as there is no shop in the park.

★ **57 Waterberg** LODGE $$$
(☑ 012-346 5425; www.57waterberg.com; Welgevonden GR; s incl meals & activities R4500-4900, d R7800-8600; ⓟ ⓢ ⓧ) We're yet to hear a bad word about this place in the Welgevonden Game Reserve, northeast of Marakele National Park but part of the same prolific ecosystem when it comes to wildlife. The five suites in earth tones and with plenty of thatch and glass are elegant and spacious and come with private plunge pools. Excellent guides round out a fabulous package.

★ **Marataba Safari Lodge** LODGE $$$
(☑ reservations 011-880 9992; www.marataba.co.za; s all-inclusive R10,343-13,748, d all-inclusive per person R6895-9165; ⓟ ⓢ ⓧ) In a wonderfully remote corner of the Waterberg, Marataba is a magnificent place. The stone-and-canvas accommodation is surrounded by splendid Waterberg views, and there's a real sense of style and sophistication at play in everything it does. We'd be happy to sit on one of the private terraces and not move for a week.

❶ Getting There & Away

The easiest route to the park is on Rte 510 from Thabazimbi. An alternative is the hard-dirt Bakkerspas Rd, which runs alongside the moun-

---

CAPE VULTURE

One of southern Africa's most iconic birds, the Cape vulture is found primarily in South Africa, Botswana and Lesotho, with smaller populations in Namibia, Mozambique, Zimbabwe and Swaziland. Like most African vulture species, the Cape vulture has seen precipitous falls in numbers to the extent that it was classified as Endangered by the IUCN in 2015. They nest on cliffs, lay only one egg per season and are known to range far and wide in search of carrion – one radio-collared Cape vulture had a home range of 22,500 sq km. Poisoning of carcasses, loss of habitat and electrocution from electricity pylons have taken their toll since the 1980s, and numbers may have fallen to as few as 4700 nesting pairs – all of which makes the 800 pairs that nest in Marakele National Park critical to the future of the species.

---

tains, with spectacular views. Turn left 6km west of Vaalwater and, after 60km, right at the T-junction; the park entrance is 45km further, a few kilometres after the tar begins.

SOUTPANSBERG

The Soutpansberg region incorporates the northernmost part of South Africa, scraping southern Zimbabwe and bordered by eastern Botswana. The forested slopes of the Soutpansberg mountains are strikingly lush compared with the lowveld to the north, where baobab trees rise from the dry plains. The highlights here are the mountains, the Venda region and Mapungubwe National Park, which is well worth the 260km drive from Polokwane. Relatively few visitors make it this far north, but the rewards are significant for those who do.

Louis Trichardt

☑ 015 / POP 25,550

Leafy Louis Trichardt (also sometimes known as Makhado) makes a great base when visiting northern Limpopo – its outlying streets reveal verdant parkland, wide roads and shady jacarandas, giving the place a very pleasant feel. The centre is very busy, with streets of booming retail-chain outlets and hordes of shoppers.

Nearby, the spectacular Soutpansberg mountains boast an extraordinary diversity of flora and fauna, with one of the continent's highest concentrations of African leopard and more tree species than there are in the whole of Canada.

🏃 Activities

There are a couple of great hikes in the Soutpansberg mountains, both of which start from the Soutpansberg Hut on the outskirts of town. One is a 2½-hour walk; the other is the two-day, 20.5km **Hanglip Trail**, which climbs through indigenous forest to a 1719m peak with views across the bushveld. Take precautions against malaria (p623), bilharzia (p624) and ticks. Overnight accommodation is in huts (per person R120) with bunk beds, showers and braais (barbecues).

🛏️ Sleeping & Eating

★ **Madi a Thavha** LODGE $$
(☑ 015-516 0220; www.madiathavha.com; camping R100, s/d incl breakfast R855/1520; ⓢ ⓧ) A cleansing Soutpansberg hideaway, this farm lodge is very involved with the local com-

munity. Accommodation is in colourful little cottages, with Venda bedspreads and cushions, tea-light candles aplenty and kitchenettes. The Dutch owners organise tours of local craft studios, and hiking, birding and village tours are also available. It's some 10km west of Louis Trichardt, off Rte 522.

★**139 on Munnik** GUESTHOUSE $$
(📱083 407 0124; www.139onmunnik.co.za; 139 Munnik St; s/d incl breakfast from R750/1150; 🅿🛜💐) Without a doubt Louis Trichardt's most luxurious accommodation. Modern fittings, stylish touches, great beds and facilities such as a bar and coffee shop make this place a standout. According to the owner, it even has the best wi-fi in town. Book ahead: it's popular.

Ultimate Guest House GUESTHOUSE $$
(📱015-517 7005; www.ultimategh.co.za; Bluegumsport Rd; s/d incl breakfast R600/820; 🛜💐) After a long day on the N1, this quirky, colourful, mist-shrouded guesthouse's name seems apt. It has a bar-restaurant (mains R90) with a veranda (ideal for an evening gin and tonic) overlooking a lush valley. It's 10km north of town; turn left off the N1 100m after Mountain Inn, head 1.6km along the dirt track and it'll be on your right.

Purple Olive INTERNATIONAL $
(📱015-516 5946; 129 Krogh St; mains R48-95; ⊗8am-5pm Mon-Sat) Presenting seafood dishes, grills, loads of burger variations, salads and pastas, this place is a great stop any time of day. A formal atmosphere pervades, but it gets more casual at the outside seating area, which opens onto a garden.

ⓘ Information

Soutpansberg Tourist Office (📱015-516 3415; Songozwi Rd; ⊗8am-4.30pm Mon-Sat) Helpful office. Ask about tours around the Venda region.

ⓘ Getting There & Away

Greyhound (📱083 915 9000; www.greyhound.co.za) offers services to Jo'burg (R290, six hours) and Harare, Zimbabwe (R465, 11 hours). Buses stop by the Caltex petrol station on the corner of the N1 and Baobab St. The **Louis Trichardt Travel Agency** (📱015-516 5042; ⊗8am-1pm & 2-4.30pm Mon-Fri, 9-11am Sat), down an alley off Krogh St (opposite Louis Trichardt Stationers), is the local agent for Greyhound and Translux buses.

The minibus shared taxi rank is in the Shoprite supermarket car park off Burger St. Destinations from Louis Trichardt include Musina (R60, 1½ hours) and Polokwane (R60, 1½ hours).

OFF THE BEATEN TRACK

LESHIBA WILDERNESS

Perched in the clouds of the Soutpansberg mountains, this Fair Trade–accredited **resort** (📱015-593 0076; www.leshiba.co.za; chalet per person from R620, s/d incl full board & activity R2800/4600; @💐) is based on a Venda village, created with the help of acclaimed Venda artist Noria Mabasa. Rooms have a lovely traditional feel wedded to high levels of comfort, with adobe walls, thatched roofs and manicured grounds. It's signposted 36km west of Louis Trichardt on Rte 522.

Surrounded by wildlife, including rare brown hyenas and leopards, and with greenery supplied by 350-plus tree species, the hideaway offers self-catering and full-board accommodation in rondavels (round huts with conical roofs), with features such as private plunge pools and views of Botswana.

Musina

📱015 / POP 68,400

Some 18km south of the Beitbridge border crossing into Zimbabwe, Musina (aka Messina) hums with typical border-town tension. It's busy, there are traffic snarls, and you should keep your wits about you when walking the streets.

You will probably pass through the town en route to the spectacular Mapungubwe National Park; the drive passes through a starkly beautiful landscape on empty, baobab-lined roads.

⊙ Sights

Giant baobab trees (*Adansonia digitata*), which look like they have been planted upside down with their roots in the air, characterise this region. You don't have to drive far from Musina to spot some impressive examples. Whoppers such as the largest in the country, known as 'the Big Tree' (located near Sagole in northeast Limpopo), are more than 3000 years old.

Musina Nature Reserve NATURE RESERVE
(📱015-534 3235; ⊗9am-6pm) FREE With South Africa's highest concentration of baobabs, the reserve is 5km south of the town off the N1, and has animals such as zebras, giraffes and the rare sable antelope.

🛌 Sleeping

Hotel restaurants are the only recommended eating choices in Musina.

Ilala Country Lodge LODGE $$
(☑076 138 0699; www.ilalacountrylodge.co.za; Rte 572; s/d incl breakfast R600/800; ☒) The sweeping views of the Limpopo River Valley into Zimbabwe at this old country lodge are something special. And there are few better places in Limpopo for a cold drink in the evening. The accommodation is superb value, with rooms sleeping four in the main homestead, and huge chalets with lounge area, braai (barbecue) facilities and separate kitchen.

It's 8km northwest of town, on the way to Mapungubwe.

Old Mine Guest House GUESTHOUSE $$
(☑082 568 3215; 1 Woodburn Ave; s/d R700/800; ❊🛜☒) In a residence built in 1919 by the first manager of Musina's copper mine, this guesthouse reeks of class and old-world charm (which is seemingly out of place in Musina!). A veranda overlooks the leafy grounds, and there are stylish rooms and self-catering units with private outdoor patio areas.

ℹ Information

ABSA (6 National Rd; ⊙9am-3.30pm Mon-Fri, to 11am Sat) Has change facilities and an ATM. Located on the N1 as it passes through the centre of town.

Musina Tourism (☑015-534 3500; www.golimpopo.com; National Rd; ⊙8am-4pm Mon-Fri) In a thatched hut on the way into town on the N1 from Polokwane. Very helpful office.

PostNet (National Rd; per hr R30; ⊙9am-4.30pm Mon-Fri, 8-11am Sat) Internet access, on the N1.

ℹ Getting There & Away

The Zimbabwe border at Beitbridge, 15km north of Musina, is open 24 hours. There is a large taxi rank on the South African side of the border; taxis between the border and Musina cost R50 (20 minutes). If you want to take a minibus shared taxi further south than Musina, catch one here – there are many more than in Musina.

Greyhound buses between Johannesburg (R455, seven hours) and Harare (R455, nine hours) stop in Musina and across the border in Beitbridge at the Ultra City.

Car rental is available at **Avis** (☑015-534 0124; www.avis.co.za; 3 National Rd, Musina Hotel; ⊙8am-5pm Mon-Fri, to noon Sat) for about R325 a day.

Mapungubwe National Park

Stunningly stark, arid, rocky landscapes reverberate with cultural intrigue and wandering wildlife at **Mapungubwe National Park** (☑015-534 7923; www.sanparks.org/parks/mapungubwe; adult/child R192/96; ⊙6am-6.30pm Sep-Mar, 6.30am-6pm Apr-Aug). A Unesco World Heritage site, Mapungubwe contains South Africa's most significant Iron Age site, plus animals ranging from black and white rhinos to the rare Pel's fishing owl and meerkats. The wildlife here is excellent, with lion, leopards and elephants, as is the birdwatching. But the park is as much about history as wildlife – archaeological finds from the 1930s are on display at the excellent Interpretation Centre, and the site itself can be visited on a tour.

◎ Sights & Activities

The park is divided into eastern and western sections (with private land in between). The main gate is on the eastern side along with the interpretation centre, Mapungubwe Hill, a **Treetop Walk**, Leokwe (the main camp), and the magnificent **viewpoints** that overlook the confluence of South Africa, Botswana and Zimbabwe.

Mapungubwe has excellent organised activities, all of which must be booked in advance at the main park gate. The Heritage Tours are the only way to access the archaeological site, which is otherwise off limits. All activities begin at the main park gate unless otherwise arranged:

Wildlife drives at sunrise (from 5.30am; three hours) and sunset (from 4pm; three hours); both cost R303 per person

Night drives (from 7.30pm; two hours; R303 per person)

Guided walks (from 6am; three hours; R444 per person)

Heritage site tour (from 4pm; two hours; R247 per person)

Heritage tour & museum (from 7am and 10am; two hours; R283 per person)

Interpretation Centre MUSEUM
(www.sanparks.org/parks/mapungubwe/tourism/interpretation_centre.php; guided tour R50; ⊙8am-4pm) The impressive centre, one of the country's finest modern buildings (it won the 2009 World Architecture Award),

---

ℹ️ MAPUNGUBWE NATIONAL PARK

Why Go One of South Africa's best national parks, but it's rarely busy, as it's quite remote. Wonderful combination of history, culture and wildlife. Stunningly beautiful landscapes.

When to Go Year-round, given the diversity of attractions, but June to October is high season and the best weather for a visit. Summer days are stiflingly hot.

Practicalities The only way to get here is to drive, done most commonly from Musina, the border town to the east. The roads heading south through the Waterberg are in a horrendous state, more potholes than tar – plan extra time if heading this way. You'll need to be self-sufficient with your food, although there is a restaurant near the park entrance.

Budget Tips Bring your own food – do your shopping at a supermarket on your way through Musina or elsewhere.

---

was designed in sympathetic resemblance to the landscape. Inside it is contemporary and air-conditioned, and has tastefully curated exhibits. There's plenty of information on the Mapungubwe cultural landscape, including finds from archaeological digs. Keep an eye out for the exquisite beadwork and the **replica of the famous gold rhino**. Guided tours may amount to someone following you around to make sure you don't take pictures.

🛏️ Sleeping & Eating

⭐ **Leokwe Camp** CHALET $$
(☑ Pretoria 012-428 9111; www.sanparks.org/parks/mapungubwe/tourism/accommodation.php; chalets R1175-1520, family chalets from R1865; 🅿️ ❄️ 🏊) These chalets are among the best we've seen in any South African national park. They include a large living space, fully equipped kitchen, outside braai (barbecue) area and a traditional rondavel-thatch-roof design. There are also outdoor showers. The camp has a number of family chalets, and the setting, surrounded by low rocky bluffs with baobabs in the vicinity, is rather lovely.

Limpopo Forest Camp CAMPGROUND $$
(☑ Pretoria 012-428 9111; www.sanparks.org; luxury tents R1100-1315) This lovely forest location, close to the Limpopo River, has well-equipped safari tents, with a kitchen area containing fridge/freezer and a separate bedroom area with twin beds and a fan. It's especially good for birding, with the **Maloutswa Bird Hide** nearby.

Golden Rhino Restaurant INTERNATIONAL $$
(mains R20-155; ⏰ 8.30am-4pm) This simple restaurant at the Interpretation Centre does chicken burgers, steaks and local dishes based around *pap* (a traditional African food made from ground maize) with sauce. It's a good lunch alternative to all that self-catering.

ℹ️ Getting There & Away

The park is a 60km drive from Musina along Rte 572 towards Pont Drift. A 2WD will get you around, but the tracks are pretty rough and you'll see more with a 4WD. The western side of the park is rougher again, and you'll need a 4WD to really see it.

Note that the nearest petrol is in Musina, around 90km away.

Venda

With perhaps the most enigmatic ambience of the Soutpansberg region, this is the traditional homeland of the Venda people, who moved to the area in the early 18th century. Even a short diversion from the freeway takes you through an Africa of mist-clad hilltops, dusty streets and mud huts. A land where myth and legend continue to play a major role in everyday life, Venda is peppered with lakes and forests that are of great spiritual significance, and its distinctive artwork is famous nationwide. It's a somewhat forgotten corner of the country and utterly unlike anywhere else in the region. More than that, if your South African journey is lacking a slice of traditional Africa with an emphasis on culture rather than wildlife, this could be your place.

Thohoyandou

📞 015 / POP 70,000

Created as the capital of the apartheid-era Venda homeland, Thohoyandou (Elephant Head) is a scrappy and chaotic town set amid beautiful Venda scenery – like so many modern African urban creations, it lacks both beauty and any sense of historical resonance. That said, it's useful as a base for exploring the Venda region or to overnight on the way to/from Kruger's Punda Maria Gate,

Venda

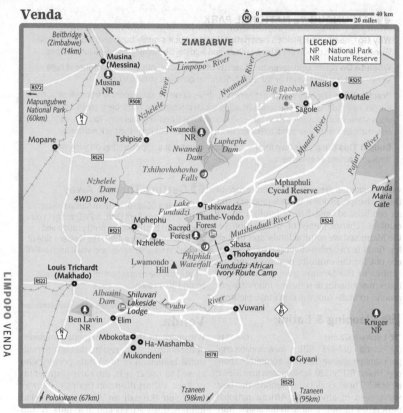

LEGEND
NP   National Park
NR   Nature Reserve

a 60km drive. The adjacent town of Sibasa is 5km north of Thohoyandou.

Dozens of **art and craft studios** dotted around the lush countryside are open to the public. The region is best known for its raw woodcarvings (exemplified by the Venda doyenne Noria Mabasa, whose work adorns Pretoria's Union Buildings); its pottery (often painted silver and maroon using graphite and ochre); and bright, stripy batiks and textiles. Hiring a guide makes finding the studios easy (some can be hidden down dusty backroads) and provides great insight into local culture – a full-day trip costs approximately R1200. Thohoyandou- and Sibasa-based guides include **Avhashoni Mainganye** (Map p398; ☏084 725 9613; a.mainganye@yahoo.com), who has a great knowledge of different media and the artists in the area.

The **Ribolla Route** is a self-drive itinerary that allows you to discover the artistic traditions of the Venda and its people in your own time. Check out www.openafrica. org/experiences/route/96-ribolla-open-africa-route and look for 'open Africa' brochures and maps in tourist offices.

Thohoyandou Arts & Culture Centre
CULTURAL CENTRE

(Punda Maria Rd; ◷8am-4pm) One starting point for cultural explorations is this centre, which displays craftwork including carved wood animals, prints, local pottery and traditional drums. A lot of it is for sale. If you get chatting to the artists, you'll be in for a real treat.

Avkhom Hotel
HOTEL **$$**

(Map p398; ☏015-962 1928; www.avkhomhotel. co.za; Mphephu St; s/d R500/750; ☏) In a central Thohoyandou location and with bucketloads of accommodation, this place has decent rooms.

ℹ Getting There & Away

Translux (www.translux.co.za; from R300, eight hours) and City to City (www.citytocity.co.za; from R250) services to Jo'burg are available, all leaving from the Shell petrol station in Thohoyandou.

The minibus shared taxi rank next to the Venda Plaza in Thohoyandou serves destinations, including Louis Trichardt (R50, 1½ hours).

Lake Fundudzi

Lake Fundudzi is a sacred site that emerges spectacularly from forested hills, a turquoise gem on a bed of green velvet. The python god, who holds an important place in the rites of the Venda's matriarchal culture, is believed to live in the lake and stop it from evaporating in the heat. The water is thought to have healing qualities and ancestor worship takes place on its shores. On the drive to the lake there are panoramic viewpoints and the Thathe-Vondo Forest. A sacred section of the forest is home to primeval tangles of creepers and strangler fig

trees. You should approach the lake with proper respect; the traditional salute is to turn your back to it, bend over, and view it from between your legs.

To visit the lake, 35km northwest of Thohoyandou, you must have permission from its custodians, the Netshiavha tribe. The easiest way to achieve this is to hire a guide in Thohoyandou, Elim or Louis Trichardt.

You need 4WD transport to reach the lake, but a car can manage the dirt tracks in the surrounding hills.

Fundudzi African
Ivory Route Camp   HUT $$
(Map p398; ☑ 072 778 3252; www.africanivory-route.co.za; s self-catering/full board R806/1859, d R1240/2860) Located 25km northwest of Thohoyandou, and gazing across two tea plantations from its 1400m-high perch, is a branch of this community-run network, which offers basic accommodation in rondavels. You'll need a 4WD vehicle or a car with good clearance to get there. Manager Nelson offers local tours. You can either self-cater or arrange for a full-board package.

THE VENDA & NDEBELE PEOPLES

Limpopo's main ethnic group, the Venda people, have obscure origins, although it's believed that they migrated across the Limpopo River in the early 18th century and settled in the Soutpansberg area. When they arrived they called their new home 'Venda' or 'Pleasant Land'.

The Boers came into contact with the Venda at the end of the 18th century and noted their extensive use of stone to build walls. The Venda were skilled in leather and beadwork, and made distinctive grain vessels that doubled as artwork hung from their huts.

Traditional Venda society shows respect for the very young and the very old – the young having recently been with their ancestors and the old about to join them. The Venda *kgosi* (king) is considered a living ancestor and must be approached on hands and knees.

Women enjoy high status within Venda society and can inherit property from their father if there is no male heir. Rituals cannot be performed unless the oldest daughter of a family is present. One of the most important Venda ceremonies is the *domba* (snake) dance, which serves as a coming-of-age ritual for young women.

A subgroup, the Lemba, regard themselves as the nobility of the Venda. The Lemba have long perplexed scholars as they seem to have had contact with Islam. They themselves claim to be one of the lost tribes of Israel, and DNA testing has shown they have a genetic quality similar to Jewish people elsewhere. Traditionally, they keep kosher, wear head coverings and observe the Sabbath.

The Ndebele entered the region from KwaZulu-Natal in around the 17th century. The structure of their authority was similar to the Zulu, with several tiers of governance. An *ikozi* (headman) oversaw each community. Ndebele, who today number around 700,000, and have a strong presence in southern Zimbabwe, are renowned for their beadwork, which goes into making rich tapestries, toys, wall decorations, baskets, bags and clothing. Traditionally, women wear copper and brass rings around their arms and necks, symbolising faithfulness to their husbands. During apartheid, the Venda and Ndebele peoples were forced onto 'homelands' that were given nominal self-rule.

NETWORKED NAPS

The nine community-run camps of **African Ivory Route** (015-781 0690; www.africanivoryroute.co.za; Phalaborwa) offer accommodation in rondavels or safari tents. Meals, tribal dances and activities are on offer; when reserving, call the camp as well as the head office.

Elim

015 / POP 17,000

The backwater town of Elim, some 25km southeast of Louis Trichardt, can be used as a base for touring the Venda and Tsonga-Shangaan art-and-craft studios, where you might come across a zebra-dung notebook or a ceremony taking place at a studio. There are also some worthwhile cooperatives.

Shiluvari Lakeside Lodge LODGE $$$
(015-556 3406; www.shiluvari.com; Albasini Dam; incl breakfast s R861-1113, d R1230-1590;) Set amid the greenery on the shores of Albasini Dam, this lodge is immersed in the local culture and countryside. Thatched chalets, standard rooms and a family suite, reached on walkways lined with sculptures, are adorned with local craftwork (which can be purchased in the on-site shop). There's also a country restaurant and a pub.

Information

Ribolla Tourism Association (015-556 4262; Old Khoja Bldg) Produces a useful brochure on the area's art route.

Getting There & Away

Translux (www.translux.co.za) buses serve Jo'burg (from R230, five to seven hours).

VALLEY OF THE OLIFANTS

These days the Valley of the Olifants may be largely devoid of pachyderms, but the subtropical area feels exotic in places, enough so for the name still to carry a whiff of African magic. The region is also culturally rich, being the traditional home of the Tsonga-Shangaan and Lobedu peoples.

Phalaborwa, a popular entry point to the Kruger National Park, is the start of the 'Kruger to Beach' trail to the Mozambique coast. The main town of Tzaneen and the pretty village of Haenertsburg make pleasant bases for trips to the scenic Modjadji and Magoebaskloof areas.

Letaba Valley

The Letaba Valley, east of Polokwane, is subtropical and lush, with tea plantations and fruit farms overlooked by forested hills. At Haenertsburg, known locally as 'The Mountain', Rte 71 climbs northeast over the steep Magoebaskloof Pass. There are plenty of places where you can stop for short hikes that are signposted from the road.

Haenertsburg

015 / POP 282

A small mountain hideaway with a great pub and a couple of upmarket restaurants, Haenertsburg is well worth a stop to breathe in the fresh, crisp mountain air. When the mist rolls in over the surrounding pine plantations, it's easy to imagine yourself far away from Africa – in the Pacific Northwest or the Scottish Highlands, perhaps. It makes an excellent alternative base to Tzaneen. In short, it's one of the loveliest small towns in Limpopo.

Sights & Activities

There are several good hiking trails near Haenertsburg, including the 11km **Louis Changuion Trail**, which has spectacular views. With 10-plus dams and four rivers teeming with trout, Haenertsburg is a good place for a spot of fly-fishing. Ask around town – try Pennefather or get in touch with **Mountain Flyfishing** (083 255 7817; www.mountainflyfishing.co.za; Veekraal K).

Magoebaskloof Adventures ADVENTURE SPORTS
(083 866 1546; www.magoebaskloofadventures.co.za; R528) On R528, this outfit runs adventure trips in the area, including kloofing (canyoning), tubing, fly-fishing, mountain biking, horse riding and canopy tours.

Sleeping & Eating

Two pubs, a cafe and a good restaurant – Haenertsburg punches well above its weight when it comes to getting a good meal.

Black Forest Mountain Lodge LODGE $
(082 572 9781; www.blackforestlodge.co.za; Black Forest; camping/cabins R110/550) You want privacy? You can have privacy. Set

among a gorgeous forested landscape, this lodge is 4km from town along a dirt road of varying quality, and is well signposted.

Pennefather
CABIN **$$**

([☎]015-276 4885; www.thepennefather.co.za; Rissik St; s/d R500/700) Part of a complex containing antiques, junk, a museum and secondhand books, this old-world place run by charming older women is hot property, especially at weekends. One of its major assets is that it's a short walk from the town's pubs. The red-roofed cottages have comfortable interiors featuring fireplaces and kitchenettes.

Red Plate
INTERNATIONAL **$**

([☎]083 305 2851; www.redplate.co.za; 161 Rissik St; mains R50-89; [⊙]9am-9pm Wed-Sat, to 4pm Sun-Tue; [🖉]) A classy set-up in the middle of the village, the Red Plate offers dishes using fresh ingredients, including crisp salads, a selection of wraps, homemade burgers and deboned whole trout. Vegetarians are also catered for, and it does cooking classes as well.

Pot 'n Plow
PUB FOOD **$**

([☎]082 691 5790; pizza R55-90; [⊙]11am-late) A mountain pub well worth ducking into, this place attracts every expat and eccentric in the mountains. The Pot 'n Plow is an essential stop for pizza, pool and plenty of chat. It also has a beer garden and a legendary Sunday roast. It's about 10km northeast of Haenertsburg on Rte 71.

🛈 Getting There & Away

A car is definitely your best option for accessing the town and for getting around – the attractions and accommodation are quite spread out.

Magoebaskloof Pass

Magoebaskloof is the escarpment on the edge of the highveld, and the road from here careers down to Tzaneen and the lowveld, winding through plantations and tracts of thick indigenous forest.

There are a number of waterfalls in the area, including the glorious **Debengeni Falls** (www.magoebaskloof.co.za/debengeni-waterfall; off Magoebaskloof Rd/Rte 71, De Hoek State Forest; adult/child R20/10; [⊙]8am-5pm).

Of the 10 walking trails in the area, lasting between two and five days, a recommended option is the three-night, 60km **Dokolewa Waterfall Trail**. There are six huts, including some above Debengeni Falls – to book them, contact Komatiland Ecotourism (p379) in Sabie (Mpumalanga).

Tzaneen

[☎]015 / POP 14,600

An affluent town with a chaotic street layout, Tzaneen makes a pleasant place to base yourself for a few days on your way to Kruger, the Blyde River Canyon, or deeper into Limpopo's arts-and-crafts territory further north. The Letaba Valley's largest town has personality, although the town centre is looking worse for wear of late, with especially terrible litter. That said, there are a few attractions and the cool mountainous retreat of Haenertsburg is well worth a visit or even an overnight stop. It's often hot around here, but sudden downpours cool things off.

◉ Sights

Tzaneen Museum
MUSEUM

(Agatha St; entry by donation; [⊙]9am-5pm Mon-Fri, to 1pm Sat) The town museum has an impressive collection of artefacts, ranging from a 'house guard' totem used by the Rain Queens to some pretty spine-chilling Congolese masks. It's particularly interesting if you're visiting Modjadji or the Venda region.

Kings Walden
GARDENS

([☎]015-307 3262; www.kingswalden.co.za; Agatha Rd, Agatha) [FREE] If steamy Tzaneen is making you droop, climb to this spectacular 300-sq-metre English garden at 1050m in the African bush. The views of the Drakensberg Mountains from the sweeping lawn are interrupted only by a lightning-struck tree, and leafy walkways wind away from

LIMPOPO TZANEEN

OFF THE BEATEN TRACK

TRADITIONAL EMBROIDERY

Next to the busy workshop, **Kaross** ([☎]086 276 2964; www.kaross.co.za; [⊙]8am-4pm Mon-Fri, closes at noon last Fri of month) sells vivid wall hangings, cushion covers, tunics and table mats, designed here and embroidered by 1200 local Shangaan women. The quality is very good and the designs are skilful and colourful. There's an excellent courtyard **cafe** (Map p398; [☎]086 276 2964; www.kaross.co.za; mains from R55; [⊙]8am-4pm Mon-Fri) with decadent desserts.

Some 30km east of Tzaneen, turn left onto Rte 529 to Giyani and, after 9km, the Kaross embroidery cooperative is on your right.

Tzaneen

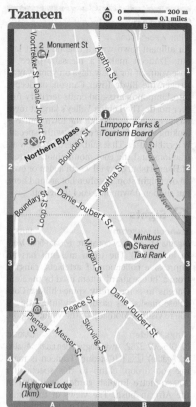

0 — 200 m
0 — 0.1 miles

Tzaneen

the refreshing swimming pool. From town, take Joubert St south then turn right onto Claude Wheatley St. There's no charge for the gardens, but it's good form to get a drink or some cake from the restaurant.

🛌 Sleeping & Eating

Satvik Backpackers
HOSTEL **$**

(☏084 556 2414; www.satvik.co.za; George's Valley Rd/Rte 528; camping per person R85, dm/d/cottage R140/350/710) These cottages, on a

slope above a dam, have a kitchen and a braai (barbecue), along with views of wooded hills. Activities such as fishing are offered, but watch out for the crocs and hippos. Rooms are simple but the overall package is good. It's about 4km southwest of town.

Highgrove Lodge
HOTEL **$$**

(☏082 427 6888; www.highgrovelodge.com; Agatha St; s/d incl breakfast R790/990; P🅿❄🛜🏊) Classy and stylish rooms with tiled floors, muted colour schemes and plenty of space make this a good option. It's in town, but doesn't feel like it is, giving you the best of both worlds.

Silver Palms Lodge
HOTEL **$$**

(☏015-307 9032; www.facebook.com/silverpalmslodge; Monument St; s/d incl breakfast from R820/1200; ❄🏊) This good-value hotel has some pleasant touches such as marula-based shower gel in the smart rooms. Cheaper on the weekends (but with no breakfast included), the luxury rooms are rather lovely. The big plus to staying here is the gorgeous, sunken swimming pool, which backs onto a bar. There's an excellent golf course as well.

★ Kings Walden
HOTEL **$$$**

(☏015-307 3262; www.kingswalden.co.za; Agatha Rd, Agatha; s/d incl breakfast R1265/2266; 🛜🏊) The sizeable rooms here are as dreamy as the gardens and mountains they overlook, with fireplaces, antiquated prints everywhere, and bathrooms you could get lost in. Picnic hampers can be provided; four-course dinners are R350 per person.

Market Cafe
CAFE **$**

(Tzaneen Lifestyle Centre; mains R35-65; ◷8am-6pm) The new 'lifestyle' centre may be lacking in atmosphere (yes, you overlook a car park), but the Market Cafe – a small operation that's part of a larger food market here – delivers quality breakfasts, light lunches (salads and wraps) and more substantial meals such as steaks and pizza. Try the brie, bacon and cranberry-sauce croissant. Excellent coffee.

Highgrove Restaurant
INTERNATIONAL **$$**

(☏015-307 7242; www.highgrovelodge.com/tzaneen-restaurant.php; Agatha St; mains R60-120; ◷7am-8.30pm) Based at Highgrove Lodge, this is one of Tzaneen's most reliable restaurants. Dishes include steaks, pasta, burgers, pizzas from the wood-fired oven and hearty breakfasts. With a pretty poolside setting, it's a lovely spot for dinner.

ⓘ Information

ABSA (Danie Joubert St; ⊙9am-3.30pm Mon-Fri, to 11am Sat) Has an ATM and exchange facilities.

Limpopo Parks & Tourism Board (⌨015-307 3582; Old Gravelotte Rd; ⊙8am-4.30pm Mon-Fri) On Rte 71 towards Phalaborwa.

ⓘ Getting There & Away

There is a daily Translux (www.translux.co.za) bus to Phalaborwa (R220, one hour), and to Jo'burg (R280, seven hours) and Polokwane (R220, two hours). **Checkers** (Agatha St) sells tickets.

Most minibus shared taxis depart from the rank behind the Tzaneen Mall; destinations include Polokwane (R80, two hours).

Modjadjiskloof

⌨015 / POP 1815

Modjadjiskloof, named Duiwelskloof (Devil's Gorge) by European settlers after the devilish time they had getting their caravans up and down the surrounding hills, is a gateway to some worthwhile stops – depending on where you're coming from, you're well placed to go from here to Kruger National Park, the Venda region and the charms of the Letaba Valley. Closer to home, there's a lovely forested reserve and the remains of a majestic old baobab tree.

Modjadji Nature Reserve   NATURE RESERVE
(Map p398; adult/vehicle R10/20; ⊙7am-4.30pm) Covering 30,000 sq metres (or 530 hectares), this reserve protects forests of the ancient Modjadji cycad. In the summer mists, the reserve and surrounding Bolobedu Mountains take on an ethereal atmosphere. Take the Modjadji turn-off from Rte 36 about 10km north of Modjadjiskloof (Duivelskloof); after 10km, turn left at the signpost to the reserve, then right at the signpost 12km further along, and continue for 5km.

Sunland Big Baobab   GARDENS
(⌨082 413 2228; www.bigbaobab.co.za; Sunland Nursery; adult/child R20/free; ⊙9am-4pm) On the road to Modjadji Nature Reserve, look out for signs to the remains of this 22m-high boabab, with a 47m circumference. According to carbon dating it was over 1700 years old, and a bar occupied the two cavities inside the tree. Sadly, this grand old tree fell in April 2017 and the bar has since moved outside.

Modjadji African Ivory Route Camp   CAMPGROUND $$
(Map p398; ⌨015-781 0690; www.africanivory-route.co.za; s/d rondavel self-catering R868/1240, incl full board & activities R2002/2860) This camp is 5km into the Modjadji Nature Reserve and is accessible by car if it hasn't rained recently. Part of a community-run

LIMPOPO MODJADJISKLOOF

MODJADJI, THE RAIN QUEEN

In Africa it is unusual for a woman to be sovereign of a tribe, but the Rain Queen is an exception. The queen resides in the town of GaModjadji in the Bolobedu district near Modjadjiskloof. Every year, around November, she traditionally presides over a festival held to celebrate the coming of the rains. The *indunas* (tribal headmen) select people to dance, to call for rain, and to perform traditional rituals, including male and female initiation ceremonies. After the ceremony, the rain falls. The absence of rain is usually attributed to some event such as the destruction of a sacred place – a situation resolved only with further ritual.

Henry Rider Haggard's novel *She* (1886) is based on the story of the original Modjadji, a 16th-century refugee princess. Successive queens have lived a secluded lifestyle, confined to the royal *kraal*, and following the custom of never marrying but bearing children by members of the royal family. However, the currrent millennium has been a time of crisis for the matrilineal line.

In June 2001 Rain Queen Modjadji V died in Polokwane. In an unfortunate turn of events, her immediate heir, Princess Makheala, had died three days earlier, and it wasn't until April 2003 that the 25-year-old Princess Mmakobo Modjadji was crowned Modjadji VI. It was raining on the day of the ceremony, which was taken to be a good omen. Sadly, Modjadji VI passed away two years later, leaving a baby daughter, Princess Masalanabo. The princess may accede when she reaches the age of 16, but traditionalists point out that her father is not a member of the royal family, and the clan has lost a lot of respect.

network, the camp offers basic rondavels and hiking trails among the 800-year-old cycads.

Phalaborwa

📍 015 / POP 13,100

Phalaborwa eases between suburban tidiness and the bush, with a green belt in the centre and the occasional warthog grazing on a lawn. The town makes a necessary waystation if you're intending to explore central and northern Kruger, and there's the Amarula Lapa distillery to visit, as well as a recommended township tour. Unless you arrive after the park gates have closed for the night, there's little advantage to staying overnight rather than pushing on into Kruger – Letaba Rest Camp is only an hour from gate.

The town is also a gateway to Mozambique – it's possible to drive across Kruger and into Mozambique via the Giriyondo Gate in a vehicle with good clearance.

🏃 Activities

Hans Merensky Estate　　　　　GOLF
(📞015-781 3931; www.hansmerensky.com; 3 Copper Rd; 9-/18-hole round R300/525) Just south of Phalaborwa is an 18-hole championship golf course (designed by renowned golfing architect Bob Grimsdell) with a difference: here you might have to hold your shot while wildlife (elephants included) cross the fairways. Be careful – the wildlife is indeed 'wild'.

Leka Gape　　　　　CULTURAL TOUR
(Map p398; 📞076 986 9281; R680) A half-day township tour with an NGO in Lulekani,

13km northwest of Phalaborwa, includes a visit to a handicrafts workshop. Call Danielle to book – if she is not running a tour on the day you want to go, she may be able to pass you onto other local operators.

Africa Unlimited　　　　　WILDLIFE WATCHING
(📞015-781 7466; www.africaunltd.co.za) Offers activities including culture tours, river cruises, bush walks, visits to animal-rehabilitation centres and trips through Kruger to Mozambique.

Turnkey Tours　　　　　SAFARI
(📞015-781 7760; www.turnkeytours.co.za; 73 Sealene Rd; ⊙9am-4.30pm Mon-Fri) A good locally based company with a range of custom-made tours to Kruger and beyond. It's also the local agent for Translux and City to City buses, with an office at the airport.

🛏 Sleeping

Daan & Zena's　　　　　GUESTHOUSE $
(📞015-559 8732; www.daanzena.co.za; 15 Birkenhead St; r without/with kitchen R400/500, apt from R800; 🅿🛜📶) Though looking a bit worn around the edges these days, Daan & Zena's is brought to life by lashings of colour and a friendly atmosphere, and it still presents great value. The two-room flats across the road from the main establishment are spacious and well equipped; No 1 has a door leading onto a lovely grassed area.

Elephant Walk　　　　　HOSTEL $
(📞082 495 0575, 015-781 5860; elephant.walk@nix.co.za; 30 Anna Scheepers Ave; camping R110, dm/s/tw without bathroom R155/220/440, B&B s/d R350/435; 🅿🛜) Close enough to Kruger

---

THE MIGHTY MARULA

The silhouette of a marula tree at dusk is one of the more evocative images of the African bush, but the real value of this mighty tree is what comes out of it.

In summer, the female marula sags under the weight of its pale yellow fruit. Chacna baboons love the stuff and you can see them by the road chomping on the golden delicacy, which has four times as much vitamin C as an orange. Elephants, also big marula fans, spend their days ramming into tree trunks to knock the fruit to the ground. Their somewhat obsessive behaviour has led to the marula being dubbed the 'elephant tree'.

Local people have long valued the marula fruit's medicinal qualities, particularly its aphrodisiac nature, and it is now used in a popular cream liqueur. Limpopo's answer to Baileys, Amarula debuted in 1989 and is now available in more than 70 countries.

The best way to enjoy a glass of creamy Amarula is to visit the **Amarula Lapa** (Map p398; 📞015-781 7766; www.amarula.com; off Rte 40; ⊙9am-6pm Mon-Fri, to 4pm Sat) FREE, located next to the production plant, 10km west of Phalaborwa. Groups of at least five can visit the plant during harvest season; at other times, exhibits and a seven-minute DVD explain all.

to hear the lions roar, this is a great spot to plan your foray into the park. The owners have quite a few rules that they ask guests to stick to, such as no noise after 10pm. It also has an excellent range of reasonably priced tours and activities. The rooms with en suite are more like a guesthouse.

★ **Kaia Tani**   GUESTHOUSE $$
(☑ 015-781 1358; www.kaiatani.com; 29 Boekenhout St; r per person incl breakfast R690; ❀ 🛜 ☒) This 'exclusive guesthouse' delivers a lot of style for your money. The six rooms with traditional African furniture have flourishes such as rope-lined wooden walls, and a thatch restaurant-bar overlooks the rock swimming pool. It's off Essenhout St.

Hans Merensky Estate   HOTEL $$
(☑ 015-781 3931; www.hansmerensky.com; s/d incl breakfast from R950/1200) Even if you're not the sort to stay at a golfing estate, this place is worth considering. Rooms are an appealing mix of classic safari furnishings (heavy wood frames and chests) and modern colour (rugs, paintings), and the look is at once classy and soothing. The bush setting and the chance of wildlife sightings are also pluses, as is the on-site spa.

★ **Sefapane**   LODGE $$$
(☑ 015-780 6700; www.new.sefapane.co.za; Copper Rd; per person from R1750; ❀ 🛜 ☒) With a whiff of exclusivity, this 1000-sq-metre resort has a restaurant and sunken bar, a long list of safaris for guests and mushroom-shaped rondavels. There are spacious self-catering 'safari houses' overlooking a dam, and donations are made to projects for local children. Lots of packages are available, from two to seven nights.

✕ Eating

Eden Sq, on Nelson Mandela St, has the usual food chains. The small Italian restaurant at Kaia Tani is recommended (book ahead).

★ **Buffalo Pub & Grill**   PUB FOOD $$
(☑ 015-781 0829; 1 Raasblaar St; mains R80-155; ⊙ 11am-10pm; ❀) If you've emerged from Kruger feeling like a hungry lion, stop here for some pub grub. It's a very meat-driven menu – for a lean steak alternative try the ostrich or impala fillet. Excellent service, and there's a terrace for al fresco dining.

Villa Luso   PORTUGUESE $$
(☑ 015-781 5670; 7 Molengraaf St; mains R65-115; ⊙ 8am-late; 🛜) The influence of the Portuguese owner can be seen on the Villa's menu, and it's a nice little taster if you're on your way to Mozambique: seafood, buffalo wings, surf and turf and Portuguese steaks are a few of the dishes on offer. With a garden bar (and long cocktail list), it's a pleasant place to dine. Also has a kids' playground.

🛍 Shopping

Afrikania   CERAMICS
(Map p398; ☑ 015-781 1139; www.afrikania.co.za; ⊙ 10am-5pm Mon-Sat) For a coffee stop and a browse through some wonderful locally made pottery at a little, landscaped, grassroots initiative, venture north of Phalaborwa to Afrikania, hosted by (and signposted as) Bed in the Bush. The pottery reflects traditional patterns found among the Tsonga and Pedi people. Ring ahead to check they're open.

ℹ Information

Bollanoto Tourism Centre (☑ 087 151 1164; www.phalaborwa.co.za; Hendrik van Eck St; ⊙ 8am-6pm Mon-Fri) Helpful information office.

ℹ Getting There & Away

AIR

The **airport** (☑ 076 907 0089) is 2km north of town. **Airlink** (☑ 015-781 5823; www.flyairlink.com) Has an office at the airport, and flies daily to Jo'burg.

BUS

Translux (www.translux.co.za) connects Phalaborwa with Jo'burg (R300, eight hours) via Tzaneen (R190, one hour), Polokwane (R240, 3½ hours) and Pretoria (R300, seven hours); City to City (www.citytocity.co.za) buses travel to Jo'burg (R250, 9½ hours) via Middelburg.

CAR

Hiring a car is often the cheapest way of seeing Kruger National Park, starting at about R300 per day. Major car-rental companies have offices at the airport; they're generally open 8am to 5pm Monday to Friday, and also to meet flights or by appointment at weekends.

Hoedspruit

☑ 015 / POP 3500

Hoedspruit makes a convenient launch pad for exploring Kruger National Park's central and southern sections – it's located just 70km northwest of the park's Orpen Gate – as well as the private game reserves.

The town itself has little to offer, but the Endangered Species Centre is an option on your way here or onwards.

Hoedspruit

Endangered Species Centre ZOO

(Map p404; ☑083 654 2299, 015-793 1633; www.hesc.co.za; R40; tour adult/senior/child from R165/132/83; ☺tours daily 9am, 11am, 1pm & 3pm, during holidays 8am, 10am, noon, 2pm & 4pm) A few clicks south of Hoedspruit along the R40 and attached to the Kapama Private Game Reserve, the Hoedspruit Endangered Species Centre was set up to take a holistic approach to South Africa's endangered species through research and breeding programs, as well as a big focus on education. Daily two-hour tours in open safari vehicles show you the animals and explain the work of the centre, which complements a Kruger safari. Advance bookings are essential for all tours.

Originally the centre's focus was on cheetahs, but it has now broadened to include the rehabilitation of rhino victims of poaching and anti-poaching activities. It also includes elephants, leopards, wild dogs and lions among the many species now at home at the centre.

🛌 Sleeping & Eating

Maruleng Lodge HOTEL $

(☑015-793 0910; www.marulenglodge.co.za; 67 Springbok St; s/d incl breakfast R525/680; P❋🗶) This lodge has enormous rooms. So big in fact that they're kinda spartan – if you like your space you'll love this place. A spruce up in the not-too-distant past, together with the lodge's convenient location – right next to all the services and eating options at the Kamagelo Centre – make it a good bet.

Loerie Guesthouse GUESTHOUSE $$

(☑015-793 3990; www.loerieguesthouse.com; 85 Jakkals St; s/d/f R540/780/820; @🗶🗶) This guesthouse specialises in warm welcomes. The best rooms are upstairs in the separate accommodation wing out the back. All rooms are a decent size and well set up. Breakfast is available (R65).

Pangolin Bush Camp CAMPGROUND $$$

(Map p404; ☑073 049 7494; www.shikwari.co.za; Lydenburg Rd/Rte 36; s/d R1550/2400; 🗶) This utterly charming self-catering option has delightful rondavels set around a pool in a beautiful bush setting. Facilities are communal, including kitchen, bathroom and outdoor shower. There is also a *boma* (traditional enclosure or gathering place) with a fire pit and braai (barbecue) facilities. It's a great set-up and would suit families in particular. Pangolin is on the property of luxury Shikwari Bush Lodge, about 35km from Hoedspruit.

Khula's Cottage COTTAGE $$$

(Map p404; www.hesc.co.za/tourists-visitors/accommodation/khulas-cottage; off R40, Hoedspruit Endangered Species Centre; 4-person cottage R3960) Inside the Hoedspruit Endangered Species Centre (p434), Khula's Cottage has two twin rooms, a double room and a fine terrace overlooking the semi-wild surrounds. It's comfortably rustic rather than luxurious and a terrific option for groups, especially birdwatchers. Meals can be arranged with advance notice for those who don't wish to self-cater.

Sleepers Railway
Station Restaurant INTERNATIONAL $$

(☑015-793 1014; www.sleepersrailwaystationrestaurant1.treetopscafe.com; Rte 40, train station, Hoedspruit Crossings; mains R55-110; ☺8am-10pm Mon-Sat, to 2.30pm Sun Mon-Sat) This old station house is a fantastic venue for devouring quality dishes and has a very extensive menu with local game a speciality (try the organic ostrich medallions). Dine on the outside deck under the branches of two enormous trees.

❶ Getting There & Away

SA Express (p605) flies daily to Jo'burg out of Hoedspruit Eastgate Airport (p410), 7km south of town.

City to City (www.citytocity.co.za) runs a daily bus to Jo'burg (R260, 8½ hours).

North West Province

Best Places to Eat

➡ Cape Town Fish Market (p438)

➡ Brauhaus am Damm (p437)

➡ Mosetlha Bush Camp & Eco Lodge (p443)

Best Places to Stay

➡ Palace of the Lost City (p439)

➡ Mosetlha Bush Camp & Eco Lodge (p443)

➡ Buffalo Ridge Safari Lodge (p443)

➡ Royal Madikwe (p443)

➡ Afri-Chic Guesthouse (p437)

Why Go?

This stretch of bushveld between Pretoria and the Kalahari is famous for Sun City, the southern hemisphere's answer to Las Vegas. Though its slot machines and kitsch edifices are grotesquely fascinating, it's the nearby parks and reserves that we really love – Madikwe Game Reserve is a real gem, while Pilanesberg has terrific wildlife and is *very* accessible. And for that once-in-a-lifetime, romantic *Out of Africa–*style experience, a night in the bush at Madikwe's exclusive lodges can't be beaten.

Conveniently, these opportunities to encounter both big cats and one-armed bandits are all within four hours' drive of Jo'burg. En route, the Magaliesberg area offers detours from the N4, ranging from zip lining to rural accommodation near Rustenburg.

When to Go
Rustenburg

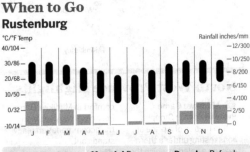

Apr Autumn temperatures drop; wildlife-watching conditions are optimum through to the winter.

May–Jul Dry, sunny winter days, and (bar mid-June to early July) school terms mean thinner crowds.

Dec–Jan Refreshing storms; South Africans head to the coast, leaving more room here for foreign travellers.

History

The North West Province takes in much of the area once covered by the fragmented apartheid homeland of Bophuthatswana ('Bop'), a dumping ground for thousands of 'relocated' Tswana people. The nominally independent homeland became famous for the excesses of the white South African men who visited its casinos and pleasure resorts for interracial encounters with prostitutes – an illegal practice elsewhere in South Africa.

The area was the site of a complex and sophisticated Iron Age civilisation, centred on the 'lost city' of Kaditshwene, about 30km north of modern-day Zeerust. The people who lived here had an economy so developed they traded copper and iron jewellery

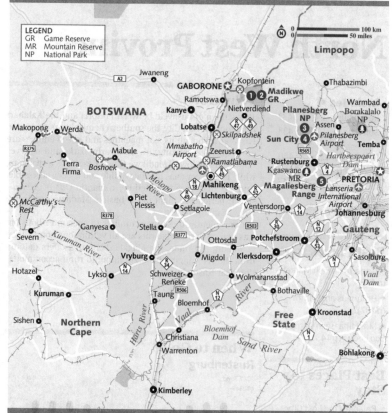

North West Province Highlights

1 Madikwe Game Reserve (p442) Stopping within metres of a pride of lions resting under a thorn tree, on a safari in which the Big Five are never far away.

2 Mosetlha Bush Camp & Eco Lodge (p443) Getting down to basics without sacrificing on comfort in Madikwe Game Reserve, a reserve where the accommodation really stands out.

3 Pilanesberg National Park (p440) Driving the back roads in search of big wildlife you can keep all to yourself while the crowds head elsewhere.

4 Sun City (p438) Bodysurfing the Valley of the Waves and soaking up the deliciously gaudy ambience.

5 Magaliesberg Range (p445) Riding the scenic aerial cableway to the top of this popular mountain range.

with China. By 1820, when European missionaries first visited the city, they found it to be bigger than Cape Town. In the end, Kaditshwene's peace-loving inhabitants proved no match for the Sotho, displaced by Zulu incursions into the Free State. The city was sacked by a horde of 40,000 people in the 1830s and fell into ruins.

ℹ️ Getting There & Around

Convenient for Rustenburg and the Magaliesberg, **Lanseria International Airport** (☑ 011-367 0300; www.lanseria.co.za) is 30km south of Hartbeespoort Dam en route to Jo'burg. Kulula. com has daily flights from Lanseria to Cape Town and Durban; Mango (www.flymango.com) flies daily to Cape Town. Car-hire companies operate from the airport.

Hiring a car is the easiest way to travel around the province. Secure parking is readily available at accommodation, restaurants and sights.

Rustenburg

☑ 014 / POP 105,000

Sitting on the edge of the Magaliesberg range, Rustenburg is a big country town with an urban grittiness to its crowded central business district. Pedestrians weave between honking cars on Nelson Mandela Dr (the main drag through the long downtown area), and sidewalks heave with vendors selling mobile-phone cases and the like in front of takeaway chicken shops and undertakers. There's always a lot happening, although, in truth, it's rarely anything of interest.

It's Rustenburg's location, however, just 40km southeast of Sun City and Pilanesberg National Park, that is its main selling point – it's an option for travellers wishing to visit these major attractions without paying high accommodation rates.

🛏️ Sleeping

Hodge Podge
Backpacker Lodge   HOSTEL $
(☑ 084 698 0417, 074 294 6315; www.hodgepodge backpackers.co.za; Plot 66, Kommiesdrift; camping/dm R80/200, s/d from R380/600; 🛜🏊) Set below some impressive cliffs, Hodge Podge gives a taste of slow-paced country life up a rocky red track. The outdoor pool is refreshing in the heat and the veranda bar is ideal for sundowners. Colourful bedspreads and bushveld scenes brighten the dinky ensuite cabins; airport shuttles and activities

including Sun City and Pilanesberg tours are offered. It's signposted about 10km south of the Waterfall Mall.

⭐ Afri-Chic Guesthouse   GUESTHOUSE $$
(☑ 014-592 2763; www.afri-chic.co.za; 35 Boven St; s/d incl breakfast R965/1150; 🅿❄🛜🏊) Stylish rooms on a quiet street and at a reasonable price – this could just be the pick of Rustenburg's places to stay if you want to be in the town. Animal-skin rugs and some lovely knick-knacks that range from vintage to contemporary add to the sense of sophistication. Professional, friendly service, too.

⭐ Boubou   B&B $$
(☑ 083 457 9954; www.boubou.co.za; Doornlaagte, Kommissiesdrift; s/d incl breakfast from R750/1160; 🅿🛜🏊) This tranquil option in a small nature reserve will likely have you extending your stay in Rustenburg. There's excellent birdwatching and you might spot a range of antelope from your pool lounger. Rooms come with great big comfy beds and French doors opening out onto the garden. Guests can use the kitchen; traditional meals are available if you book ahead.

It's 28km out of town, off the R52 to Koster.

Masibambane   GUESTHOUSE $$
(☑ 083 310 0583; www.masibambaneguesthouse. co.za; Plot 45, Waterglen AH; s/d incl breakfast R540/820; 🅿🛜🏊) This thatched property is a peaceful, relaxing place, its flowerbeds, mature trees and water features attracting a variety of birdlife, from hoopoes to sunbirds. A three-course dinner (R135) can be organised on weeknights. It's signposted 5km south of Waterfall Mall; the guesthouse is on the right at the end of the paved side road, just beyond the 'Private Road' sign.

🍴 Eating

Most restaurants in Rustenburg are found in the **Waterfall Mall** (Augrabies Ave; ⏰ 9am-6pm Mon-Sat, to 1pm Sun), which is sterile but safe and reliable. Options range from standalone restaurants to chains – including Woolworths for self-catering.

Brauhaus am Damm   GERMAN $$
(☑ 014-004 0382; www.brauhaus.co.za; Rte 24, Olifants Nek Dam; mains R62-145; ⏰ 11am-10pm Tue-Sat, to 4pm Sun) On a sunny afternoon join Rustenburg locals and Gauteng weekenders at this cavernous restaurant with a large deck overlooking the Olifants Nek

Dam. German food like sausage platters and *eisbein* (pork knuckle) come accompanied by award-winning beers from the on-site microbrewery, one of the few in the country with a female brewer at the helm. The *weissbier* (wheat beer) is excellent. It's 20km south of Rustenburg on the R24.

Cape Town Fish Market
SEAFOOD $$

(☑083 400 2005; www.ctfm.co.za; Waterfall Mall; mains R92-164; ⊙11am-11pm) The dark interior and blue neon lighting of the Waterfall Mall's most stylish restaurant are probably meant to hint at oceanic depths, but what they conjure up is more like a nightclub feel. Still, it's a spacious place, the service is efficient, and there's lots of seafood to sample, from salmon and crayfish to kingklip and dorado. Sushi and burgers, too.

ⓘ Information

Tourist Information Centre (☑014-597 0904; www.tourismnorthwest.co.za; cnr Nelson Mandela St & Kloof Rd; ⊙8am-4.30pm Mon-Fri, to noon Sat) Rustenburg's helpful, well-stocked tourist information centre is located in the municipal offices that sprawl between Nelson Mandela Dr and Fatima Bhayat St just west of the Rte 24 turn-off. It provides sundry brochures and a local map.

ⓘ Getting There & Away

Rustenburg is just off the N4, about 120km northwest of Jo'burg and 110km west of Pretoria. Intercape has buses from Johannesburg (R180, 1½ hours), but if you want to explore the surrounding region, you'll need your own wheels.

Sun City
☑014

At **Sun City** (☑014-557 1580; www.suninternational.com/sun-city; day visitors adult/child R75/65, hotel guests free; ⊙24hr; 🛪), the legendary creation of entrepreneur Sol Kerzer, Disneyland collides with ancient Egypt in Africa's version of Vegas. Filled with gilded statues of lions and monkeys, acres of artificial beaches, over 1200 hotel rooms and line upon line of clinking slot machines, it serves no other purpose than to entertain. Yet while this gambling-centric resort is almost grotesquely gaudy, a visit can be pretty damn fun.

The complex is dominated by the Lost City, an extraordinary piece of kitsch claiming to symbolise African heritage. In fact, it has even less to do with African culture than Disneyland Paris has to do with French culture, but it's still entertaining.

We'll be honest: this is not our sort of place. But it does have to be seen to be believed, and one thing Sun City does have in its favour is that it has received awards for practising sustainable, environmentally friendly tourism.

If you're travelling with children or on a budget, Sun City is a pretty good bargain. The admission fee covers the main attractions, and there are countless activities on offer for an extra outlay. The complex also boasts one of the world's most luxurious hotels, a shrine to all things glittery and golden.

Sun City opened in 1979 as an apartheid-era exclusive haven for wealthy whites. At the time, gambling was illegal in South

---

DON'T MISS

LOST CITY

Sun City's kitsch heart is the Lost City, a sort of mega amusement park in high-glitz style, teeming with attractions that range from botanic gardens to simulated volcanic eruptions. It's reached from the Entertainment Centre via the Bridge of Time, which is flanked by life-size fake elephants.

Most of the fun takes place in the **Valley of the Waves** (www.suninternational.com/sun-city/activities/valley-of-waves; adult/child R120/70, hotel guests free; ⊙9am-6pm Sep-Apr, 10am-5pm May-Aug) water park, overlooked by the towers of the Palace of the Lost City hotel. The water park is gaudy and outlandish even by Sun City's standards – and children love it. Its centrepiece is the **Roaring Lagoon**, a 6500-sq-metre wave pool with a palm-fringed beach. Slides, flumes and chutes such as the 70m-long **Temple of Courage** get the adrenaline flowing; tubing on the **Lazy River** and swimming in the **Royal Bath** pool are two of the slower activities. Another Lost City attraction is its **Maze** (www.suninternational.com/sun-city/activities/maze; adult/child R120/60; ⊙9am-9pm), an enormous labyrinth in the form of an archaeological site.

Africa, but not in the homelands, so Sun City was built in what was then Bophuthatswana. These days, one of its most prominent features is the mix of black, white and Asian people who flock here on weekends.

⊙ Sights & Activities

Visit the Welcome Centre for the low-down on the mind-boggling range of activities available. These include golfing (on two different courses), a walk-through aviary, jet skiing, parasailing, a crocodile park and zip lining, plus wildlife drives at the neighbouring Pilanesberg National Park.

South African Hall of Fame   MUSEUM
(☑014-557 1978; www.halloffame.co.za; day visitors adult/child R100/50, hotel guests free; ⊙8am-5pm) Opened in 2016, this celebratory exhibition pays homage in words and photos to South Africa's high achievers. Most come from the world of sports, but there are also some musicians and actors among the stars. Think golfer Gary Player, the 1995 World Cup–winning South African rugby team and musicians Ladysmith Black Mambazo.

Entertainment Centre   CASINO
(⊙24hr; ⓹) As well as housing smoking and nonsmoking casinos, this two-storey centre has food courts, shops, cinemas and the Superbowl performance venue. Its style might best be described as 'nouveau Flintstone', embellished by a jungle theme.

Mankwe Gametrackers   SAFARI, OUTDOORS
(☑014-552 5020; www.mankwegametrackers.co.za; Welcome Centre; ⊙5am-7pm) From Sun City, this tour and outdoor activity company runs two three-hour wildlife drives (adult/child R550/275) to Pilanesberg National Park each day, usually departing at 5.30am and 5pm (times vary depending on the time of year). It also runs four-hour, early-morning wildlife walks (per person R650) in the park (ages 16 and over only).

The company also offers hot-air balloon flights (per person R4750), and has an outdoor adventure centre where you can try quad biking, clay-pigeon shooting, archery, paintballing and *djembe* drumming.

Segway Guided Tours   TOURS
(☑014-557 4052; www.segwayguidedtours.co.za/suncity; R240-360; ⊙8am-5pm) Tours of Sun City that allow you to get up a little speed on the golf courses and give an overview of the whole complex. The booking office is in the Welcome Centre.

REGAL LUXURY

The **Palace of the Lost City** (☑bookings 011-780 7855; www.suninternational.com/palace; r incl breakfast from R4731; ❄🛜🏊🍴), its turquoise domes overlooking the Valley of the Waves, is a hallucinatory dazzle of glamour in the bushveld. Frequently rated one of the world's top hotels by travel media, it does a good job of exceeding guests' fantasies of luxury.

The 330-plus rooms and suites have flourishes such as butler service and marble bathrooms, but it's the awesome public spaces that hog the limelight. Confronted by the frescoes, mosaics and painted ceilings in the grand atriums and halls, restaurants and bars, you almost begin to believe this is the kingly residence of an ancient ruler. In the surrounding pleasure garden, fountains, pools and waterfalls sparkle among the thick foliage.

🛏 Sleeping & Eating

Cascades   RESORT $$$
(☑bookings 011-780 7855; www.suninternational.com/sun-city/cascades/accommodation; s/d incl breakfast from R3211/3411; ❄🛜🏊) In this azure, Mediterranean-inspired environment, waterfalls cascade into a lake and cocktails go down nicely in the beach bar. There are multiple pools, al fresco island dining at Santorini restaurant, and luxuries such as dressing rooms in the more expensive palatial bedrooms.

Soho   CASINO HOTEL $$$
(☑bookings 011-780 7855; www.suninternational.com/sun-city/soho/accommodation; r incl breakfast from R3117; ❄🛜🏊) Sun City's liveliest hotel (and its first) packs in casinos, slot machines and an entertainment centre, as well as multiple restaurants and bars. With foliage hanging in the jungle-themed foyer and oversize roulette chips stacked outside the Raj Indian restaurant, it's a good choice for anyone looking for a little hedonism with their gambling. There are nine different room types.

Cabanas   RESORT $$$
(☑bookings 011-780 7855; www.suninternational.com/sun-city/cabanas/accommodation; r incl breakfast from R1911; ❄🛜🏊🍴) Sun City's most informal option is the best one for families, with facilities and activities for children. The modern rooms have retro styling and

upmarket conveniences, and the atmosphere is laid-back, from the balconied foyer and onwards. Family rooms with a fold-out sofa and up to eight beds are available.

ℹ Information

Welcome Centre (☑ 014-557 1543; ⊙ 8am-7pm Mon-Fri, to 10pm Sat & Sun) is at the entrance to the Entertainment Centre. It has maps and just about any information you could possibly need. Also here are lockers and a branch of Hertz car rental.

ℹ Getting There & Away

Sun City is less than three hours' drive northwest of Jo'burg, signposted from the N4. Coming from Gauteng on the N4, the most straightforward route is to stay on the freeway past Rustenburg and take Rte 565 via Phokeng and Boshoek.

The car park for nonguests is at the entrance, about 2km from the Entertainment Centre. Buses and an elevated monorail Sky Train (the latter offering good views of the complex and Pilanesberg) shuttle people from the car park to the Entertainment Centre and Cascades, passing Sun City Cabanas and Sun City Hotel.

Tours from Gauteng combine Sun City and Pilanesberg.

Ingelosi Shuttles (☑ 014-552 3260; www.ingelositours.co.za; Welcome Centre; per 2/4 people R1400/1950) offers a shuttle service from set pick-up points in Johannesburg.

Pilanesberg National Park

Occupying an eroded alkaline crater north of Sun City, in a transition zone between the Kalahari and wet lowveld vegetation,

> ## ℹ PILANESBERG NATIONAL PARK
> ....
> **Why Go** The (malaria-free) park is South Africa's most accessible Big Five reserve; it's less than a three-hour drive from Jo'burg. Wild dogs can also be sighted, as can rarer antelope such as roan and sable.
>
> **When to Go** Dry season is best (June to September), when the grass is short and the animals congregate around water holes. From January to April the bush is very dense, making wildlife spotting more difficult.
>
> **Practicalities** The two southern gates are within about 10km of Sun City.
>
> **Budget Tips** Bring a tent and food.

the 550-sq-km **Pilanesberg National Park** (☑ 014-555 1600; www.pilanesbergnationalpark.org; adult/child R110/30, vehicle R20, map R40; ⊙ 5.30am-7pm Nov-Feb, 6am-6.30pm Mar, Apr, Sep & Oct, 6.30am-6pm May-Aug) is a wonderfully scenic place to see a stunning variety of South African wildlife.

Conceived in the late 1970s as a back-to-nature weekend escape for nearby city dwellers, Pilanesberg remains a haven where lions, buffaloes and day-trippers still roam. In 1979, Operation Genesis reclaimed this area of land from agriculture and released 6000 animals into the new park. Today, all the Big Five are here, as are cheetahs, caracals, African wild dogs, jackals, hyenas, giraffes, hippos, zebras, a wide variety of antelope (including sables, elands and kudus) and 300-plus bird species.

But although the park may appear developed, and even overrun in comparison with some South African wildernesses, leave behind main thoroughfares through the park and you'll likely have any sightings to yourself.

🏃 Activities

Most lodges in the park offer sunrise and sunset wildlife drives, but with nearly 200km of excellent gravel roads, Pilanesberg was designed with self-drive safaris in mind. Although you have a better chance of spotting cats on one of the ranger-led wildlife drives, steering yourself is cheaper, and more rewarding when you do see an animal. Apart from anything else, the organised drives stick to the main roads, stop at every impala sighting and can feel like a circus. Traffic jams along the main byways are also common in late afternoon. Then again, whichever way you visit, you'll never forget the first time you brake to let a lumbering elephant cross your path – or the size of these animals and how tough, dirty and wrinkly a pachyderm's rump looks up close.

Devote at least a few hours to sitting with a cooler full of beverages and a pair of binoculars in one of the many public hides and wait for the action to come to you. Basically big, raised, covered decks with chairs that have been camouflaged so the wildlife doesn't notice you, these hides have been purposefully constructed next to water sources that attract thirsty animals.

The following activities can be booked at any of the park entrance gates. Private operator **Mankwe Gametrackers** (☑ 014-556

Pilanesberg National Park

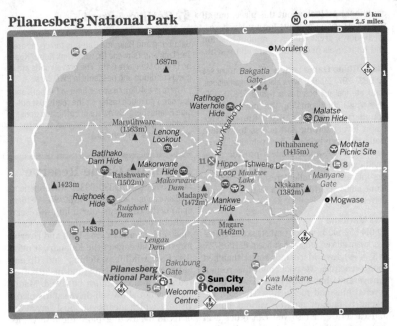

2710; www.mankwegametrackers.co.za; Bakgatla; ⊙5am-7pm) can also make the bookings at no extra cost (and are sometimes cheaper):

Sunrise/sunset game drives (adult/child R610/305; 2½ hours)

Hot-air balloon rides (per person R4750; one to five hours)

Guided hikes (per four people R2600; four hours)

🛏 Sleeping

There are eight lodges in the park. They also have activities and facilities for children, such as pools, playgrounds and minigolf, and offer discounts to families. There are more-exclusive lodges to the west of Kudu/Kgabo Dr.

Tshukudu Lodge　　　　　LODGE $$$
(☑014-552 6255; www.legacyhotels.co.za/en/hotels/tshukudu; s/d incl full board & activities R10,250/14,510) Luxury suites and chalets in an exclusive corner of Pilanesberg will have you wondering what all the fuss is about in terms of visitor numbers to the park. The views from the bathtubs out over the bushveld are worth it on their own, and the combination of African colours and local stone in the decor make for a pleasing aesthetic. Service is excellent.

Pilanesberg National Park

Shepherds Tree Game Lodge　　LODGE $$$
(☑014-551 3910; www.shepherdstreegamelodge.info; ste incl full board & activities from R9794; P🛜☒) Out in Pilanesberg's wild west and far from the madding crowds, Shepherds Tree is an elegant choice. Unlike so many South African lodges, there's a daring,

contemporary look about this place, but all the necessary ingredients for a safari base – great views, great guides, a remote location and high levels of comfort – are all present.

Black Rhino Game Lodge
LODGE $$$

(☏083 297 5020; www.blackrhinogamelodge. com; ste incl full board & activities R5870-7160; ▣✷✿❄) Just outside the northwestern boundary of the park, Black Rhino Lodge has a lovely setting and access to wildlife trails that rarely see safari vehicles. Large and elegant A-frame chalets provide a refined experience and the modern public areas include an excellent restaurant. As the name suggests, rhinos are a feature of game drives.

Kwa Maritane
LODGE $$$

(☏014-552 5100; www.legacyhotels.co.za/en/hotels/kwamaritane; s/d incl half board R5115/6725; ✷✿❄➊) Kwa Maritane's smart thatched rooms encircle its pool, and the restaurant veranda has a bird's-eye view of bush-covered hills and rocky cliffs. The Kwa Lefakeng restaurant puts on various buffets and carveries, or else you can order à la carte out on the terrace. It's a good choice, and slightly less busy than its sister property **Bakubung** (☏014-552 6314; www.legacyhotels. co.za/en/hotels/bakubung; s/d incl half board R4160/5170, chalets from R2100; ✷✿❄➊).

✗ Eating

Of the lodges, Manyane, Bakgatla, Bakubung and Kwa Maritane serve lunch to day-trippers and offer bush braais (barbecues) and full/half-board packages. The **Pilanesberg Centre** (Kgabo Dr; ⊙6.30am-5.30pm Apr-Oct, to 6pm Nov-Mar) has basic supplies for a picnic.

Zebra Crossing
CAFE $

(Kgabo Dr; mains R52-155; ⊙7.30am-4pm Mon-Fri, to 4.30pm Sat & Sun) A cafe with a large terrace that provides good views of a waterhole popular with wildebeest and giraffes. It serves pizza, burgers, wraps and salads, plus some kids' meals.

❶ Getting There & Away

Tours from Gauteng combine Pilanesberg and Sun City. Bakubung and Kwa Maritane gates are convenient if you're driving from Sun City. If you're driving down from Limpopo on the Rte 510 (between Rustenburg and Thabazimbi), Manyane and Bakgatla gates are your closest entry points.

❶ Getting Around

Kubu/Kgabo Dr, crossing the park between Bakubung and Bakgatla Gates, is tarred, as are Tau Link and Tshwene Dr, which link Kubu/Kgabo Dr and Manyane Gate. The gravel roads are in good condition and passable in 2WD cars.

There is a 40km/h speed limit in the park and you can't go much faster on the roads just outside Pilanesberg. Be aware of cattle and donkeys wandering onto the road; locals may wave to warn you of a herd ahead.

Madikwe Game Reserve

Madikwe (☏018-350 9938; www.experience madikwe.com; adult/child R180/90; ⊙6am-6pm) is the country's fourth-largest reserve and one of its best, covering 760 sq km of bushveld, savannah grassland and riverine forest on the edge of the Kalahari. It offers Big Five wildlife watching and dreamy lodging among striking (and malaria-free) red sand and clay-thorn bushveld. Madikwe does not allow self-drive safaris or day visitors, which means you must stay at one of its 16 lodges to explore the reserve. Experiencing Madikwe isn't cheap, but you get what you pay for at these exclusive bush hideaways.

Most lodges include two wildlife drives per day (or one drive and a guided walk) in its full-board rates. Rangers communicate via radio with the other drivers in the reserve, so if a family of lions napping in the shade of a thorn tree is spotted nearby, your driver will hear about it. Restrictions on driving off road are minimal and the jeeps are tough enough to tackle most terrain, getting you close to the animals.

The rules in Madikwe dictate that only three vehicles may be present at any one sighting, and this is strictly observed. While this may be frustrating while you wait in line and out of sight, it ensures that animals are not pursued or harassed by a convoy of vehicles, and retains Madikwe's credentials as a wonderful place to get up close with the animals.

Madikwe was formed in 1991 with a dual mandate to protect endangered wildlife and to use sustainable tourism initiatives to create jobs for the poor, remotely located local people. A massive translocation operation reintroduced more than 10,000 once-indigenous animals, whose numbers had been depleted by hunting and farming. The operation took more than seven years to complete, with animals (including entire herds of elephants) being flown or driven in from other Southern African reserves. Madikwe, run as a joint venture between the North West Parks & Tourism Board, the private sector and local communities, has ultimately provided the promised jobs, as well as a home for healthy wildlife numbers.

🛏 Sleeping & Eating

Madikwe has a full suite of outstanding places to stay. Most of them are exclusive and supremely comfortable. Advance booking is mandatory: you will not be allowed through the gates without a reservation (the guard will telephone your lodge to check you have a booking). For extensive information on all of the lodges, visit www.madikwegamere serve.net.

All Madikwe lodges and tented camps offer three meals a day as part of their accommodation packages.

★**Mosetlha Bush
Camp & Eco Lodge** LODGE $$$
(☎011-444 9345; www.thebushcamp.com; Abjaterskop Gate; s/d per person incl full board R2995/4990) 🐾 Madikwe's second-oldest lodge is also the reserve's only non-five-star option, but Mosetlha's relatively low rates are not its only attraction. With nine open-fronted cabins around the campfire, Mosetlha is truly off the grid – it has no electricity or running water. But staying here is romantic rather than rough.

The ecolodge features in Hitesh Mehta's authoritative book on the subject, *Authentic Ecolodges*. It made it into Mehta's 'innovative technology' category for its donkey boilers, bucket shower and VIP (ventilation-improved pit) toilet. Paraffin lamps stand in for bedside lamps, conversation for TV, and the meals are as delicious as the bushveld air. It's a wonderful choice, with outstanding guides and a prevailing sense of authenticity.

Buffalo Ridge Safari Lodge LODGE $$$
(☎011-234 6500; www.buffaloridgesafari.com; Wonderboom Gate; chalet incl full board & activities s R4745-6825, d R7300-10,500; ❄🏊) This swish lodge exemplifies the sustainable, community-based tourism envisioned by Madikwe's founders – owned by the Balete people from the local village of Lekgophung, it was the first of its kind in South Africa. Designed by a well-known local architect, Buffalo Ridge has eight ultraprivate

thatched chalet suites that blend seamlessly into the bushveld, with a wonderful blend of stone, wood and linen.

★**Royal Madikwe** LODGE $$$
(☎082 568 8867, reservations 082 787 1314; www.royalmadikwe.com; s/d incl full board & activities R11,400/15,200; ❄🏊) You know what to expect at these prices – private plunge pools, large, luxurious and secluded rooms, expansive terraces looking out upon the African wilds – and the Royal Madikwe has these aplenty. But it also has iPod docking stations, velour bathrobes and a private fireplace. Service is faultless.

Tau Game Lodge LODGE $$$
(☎011-466 8715; www.taugamelodge.com; Tau Gate; chalet per person incl full board R3250-4795; ❄🏊👶) When it comes to value for money, Tau is one of the park's best bets. The 30 cosy thatched chalets have giant bathtubs, massive outdoor bush showers, huge beds, and private decks for watching the waterhole action – improved a few years ago by the introduction of a croc family of five. Also on-site are a spa and curio shop.

The Tau Foundation seeks to benefit the local people, and guests can visit schools and community schemes.

Jaci's Lodges
LODGE $$$

(📞 083 700 2071; www.madikwe.com; r per person incl full board from R7895-10,500; ❄️ 🏊 🐾) For panache and design flair, Jaci's contiguous lodges – Safari Lodge and Tree Lodge – are excellent places to indulge. Safari Lodge's eight rooms are constructed to feel like tents, with canvas siding and outdoor showers made from natural stone. Handmade ceramic fireplaces and private decks with waterhole views complete the elegantly natural picture. There are discounts for children under 12, plus child minders and wildlife drives geared towards families.

Even more exclusive, Tree Lodge brushes the canopy, with elevated rooms built around trees and connected by walkways. Constructed from rosewood and thatch, the eight abodes are luxurious but also built to let nature flow in.

Thakadu River Camp
TENTED CAMP $$$

(📞 018-365 9912, 087 740 9292; www.aha.co.za/thakadu; s/d incl full board & activities R5625/7500; ❄️ 🏊) Luxury, air-conditioned safari tents with wooden decks make Thakadu an excellent choice out in Madikwe's east. Of the 12 tents, four can be used for families, and the game viewing is typically excellent. It probably sits in the middle of Madikwe's options in terms of price, the quality is unimpeachable, and the whole atmosphere is nicely unpretentious.

❶ Getting There & Away

AIR

There is one charter flight per day between OR Tambo International Airport in Jo'burg and the landing strip in Madikwe (from where your lodge can arrange a transfer). Tickets are arranged through your lodge at the time of booking.

BUS

Take a Gaborone (Botswana) bus and arrange for your lodge to pick you up from the Kopfontein border crossing, where the bus will stop.

CAR

Madikwe is next to the Kopfontein Gate/Tlokweng Gate border crossing with Botswana, about 400km northwest of Johannesburg and Pretoria via the N4 and Rte 47/49 (the road is referred to by both numbers).

Madikwe's main gates are Abjaterskop and Wonderboom, adjoining Rte 47/49 on the reserve's western side; Tau and Deerdepoort on the northern side; and Molatedi on the eastern side. All the lodges can be reached from Rte 47/49; when you make a reservation, your lodge will give you directions.

If driving yourself between Madikwe and Sun City and Pilanesberg, ask your lodge for directions and take the back roads. This route is quicker and bypasses the Swartruggens toll gate on the N4.

Without your own transport, the best option is to organise a transfer through your lodge.

Magaliesberg Range

An hour's drive from Pretoria and less than two from Jo'burg, but worlds apart in looks and attitude, the 120km-long Magaliesberg range is a favourite weekend escape for Gautengers. These mountains form a half-moon arc from Hartbeespoort Dam in the east to Rustenburg in the west. Forsake overly commercial Hartbeespoort Dam and hit the winding back roads leading off Rtes 104 and 24 to fully appreciate this region of scrub-covered rolling hills, streams, forests and lots of fresh, clean air. An added attraction is the recently resurrected cableway that hoists visitors to the roof of the Magaliesberg.

◉ Sights & Activities

East of the four-way stop in Damdoryn, the road leads through an Arc de Triomphe-style gate, across **Hartbeespoort Dam** and through a tunnel. Art galleries and upscale eateries then line the road as it passes through Schoemansville on the dam's northeastern shore, on its way to a meeting with the N4 to Pretoria.

Welwitschia Country Market
MARKET

(📞 083 302 8085; www.countrymarket.co.za; Damdoryn; ⏰ 9am-5pm Tue-Sun) **FREE** Stock up on 'Boks tops and biltong, leather goods and wirework. Located just west of the four-way stop in Damdoryn, near the northwest corner of Hartbeespoort Dam, this market is more authentic than the nearby Chameleon Village tourist complex, with around 40 stalls housed in wooden cabins. It has a small playground and aviary to keep children occupied, plus three restaurants, and craftwork and classic South African gifts for sale.

Magaliesberg Canopy Tour
OUTDOORS

(📞 014-535 0150; www.magaliescanopytour.co.za; Sparkling Waters Hotel & Spa, Rietfontein Farm; tours incl light meal R595; ⏰ 6.30am-4.30pm Sep-Apr, 7.30am-3pm May-Aug) Skim treetops and whizz between cliffs on steel zip lines up to 140m long, suspended 30m above a stream.

This brilliant eco-adventure takes you on an exhilarating 2½-hour descent through Ysterhout Kloof. Along the way you stop at 11 platforms, built into the cliff's face, for the views and the scoop on local ecology from a guide.

A minimum of two participants is required and advance booking is recommended; Sparkling Waters guests receive a 20% discount.

Aerial Cableway   CABLE CAR

(☑ 072 241 2654; www.hartiescableway.co.za; off Rte 104; adult/child R195/115; ☺ ticket office 9am-4.30pm) Just east of Schoemansville is this cable-car ride that thrived for two decades before closing in 2005, only to re-open after an extensive refitting in 2010. It deposits you atop the Magaliesberg, where you can take in magnificent views of the surrounding region. There's a restaurant at the base station; at the top is another eatery plus a pizza shack-cum-bar and a kids' playground.

🛏 Sleeping & Eating

There is a handful of sleeping options in the area, but you'll need to book ahead on weekends. Pubs and roadside cafes line the roads around Hartbeespoort Dam, but options are decidedly slim out on the country roads further into the mountains.

Sparkling Waters Hotel & Spa   HOTEL $$$

(☑ 014-535 0000; www.sparklingwaters.co.za; Reitfontein Farm; s/d incl breakfast from R1050/1900; ❋ 🛜 🌊) The large grounds of this low-key, Tudor-style hotel contain pools, minigolf, tennis courts, a health spa, a games room and a playground – plenty to keep families occupied – while the Magaliesberg bush lies beyond the sweeping lawns. The rooms, arrayed around the landscaped grounds, sport oddly rendered exteriors and plain furnishings, but they're well maintained, and some standard rooms are huge.

The hotel is 32km southeast of Rustenburg, accessible from Rte 104 near Buffelspoort or Rte 24 via the Oorsaak turn-off in Rex.

Upper Deck   PUB FOOD $$

(☑ 012-253 2586; Welwitschia Country Market, Damdoryn; mains from R76; ☺ 8.30am-5pm Mon, to 10pm Tue-Sat, to 8pm Sun) The large beer garden of this pub-style restaurant is a good place in which to take a break from Welwitschia curio browsing. Grilled meats and burgers dominate the menu, which also offers some salads and a couple of kids' meals. There's live music from Friday to Sunday nights.

❶ Getting There & Away

On weekdays, roads in the area are quiet, although there's no public transport. On weekends, it's something of a procession along the major arteries leading into the mountains.

Northern Cape

Best Places to Eat

➡ Tauren Steak Ranch (p466)

➡ Cluster d'Hote (p470)

➡ Cafe Zest (p459)

➡ Transkaroo Country Lodge (p454)

Best Places to Stay

➡ Gorge Cottage (p464)

➡ Kalahari Tented Camp (p461)

➡ 75 on Milner (p452)

➡ !Xaus Lodge (p461)

➡ Kameeldoorn Tree House (p454)

Why Go?

With only a million people inhabiting its 373,000 sq km, the Northern Cape is South Africa's last great frontier. Its scattered towns are hundreds of kilometres apart, connected by empty roads across the sublime, surreal wilderness expanses of Namakwa, the Kalahari and Upper Karoo. Under the remorseless sun, vehicles share park roads with lions, dune boards swish down roaring sands, and Kimberley's pubs serve cold beer as they have since the 19th-century diamond rush.

It's a raw, elemental land, where gnarly camel thorn, quiver and Halfmens trees break the boundless horizons. Yet some of nature's greatest tricks here are instances of rejuvenating beauty. The Gariep (Orange) River waters the dry region, creating the Green Kalahari with its vineyards and epic Augrabies Falls. Following the rains, red Kalahari sands shimmer with grasses, and Namakwa's spring blooming carpets rocky hills and plains with wildflowers.

When to Go
Kimberley

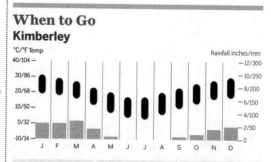

Jan–Mar Augrabies Falls are impressive; weather is scorching but Kgalagadi wildlife watching is excellent.

May–Jul Cooler weather, night skies are brighter and dry conditions bring animals to water holes.

Aug–Sep Namakwa's barren expanses explode with colour during the spring wildflower bloom.

Language & People

English is widely spoken in the Northern Cape but Afrikaans is the dominant language, with about 54% of the province speaking it. Tswana (33%) and Xhosa (6%) are the other main languages. The population includes Afrikaners, Tswana and descendants of the region's earliest inhabitants, the Khoe-San, who can still be seen around the Kalahari.

KIMBERLEY

☑ 053 / POP 97,000

Kimberley, the provincial capital, is the centre of the region known as the Diamond Fields. The city that gave birth to De Beers and 'A Diamond is Forever' remains a captivating place, with a Wild West vibe.

The last earth was shovelled at the landmark Big Hole back in 1914, but the Northern Cape's capital remains synonymous with diamonds. Step inside an atmospheric old pub, with dark interiors, scarred wooden tables and last century's liquor ads, and you'll feel you've been transported back to Kimberley's rough-and-ready mining heyday. Wander the period-perfect Victorian mining settlement at the Big Hole Complex, and you soon find yourself imagining Cecil Rhodes is alive and well and pointing his horse towards Rhodesia.

The Northern Cape's only real city is also home to fantastic museums, some wonderful accommodation and Galeshewe, a township with plenty of its own history.

⊙ Sights

★ Big Hole   MUSEUM

(☑ 053-839 4600; www.thebighole.co.za; West Circular Rd; adult/child R100/60; ⊙ 8am-5pm; 🅿) Although the R50 million that turned the Big Hole into a world-class tourist destination came from De Beers, touring the world's largest hand-dug hole gives an honest impression of the mining industry's chequered past in Kimberley. Visits start with an entertaining 20-minute film about mining conditions and characters in late-19th-century Kimberley, and a walk along the Big Hole viewing platform. The open-air steel contraption, jutting out over the 1.6km-round, 215m-deep chasm, enhances the vertigo-inducing view of the 40m-deep turquoise water.

ARCHITECTURE

Thanks to its fascinating history, Kimberley holds a lot for the architecture enthusiast. Check out **Rudd House** (☑ 053-839 2700; 5 Loch Rd; adult/child R40/20; ⊙ by appointment Mon-Fri), a fine example of the residences constructed for rich Kimberlites in the 19th century, and **Dunluce** (☑ 053-839 2700; 10 Lodge Rd; adult/child R40/20; ⊙ by appointment 9am-4pm Mon-Fri), an elaborate Victorian residence.

For something more modern, head to the striking **Northern Cape Legislature Building** (☑ 053-839 8024; www.ncpleg.gov.za; off Green St, Galeshewe; ⊙ 8am-4pm Mon-Thu, to noon Fri) **FREE**, designed to reflect the culture, nature and history of Kimberley and the Northern Cape. The building is signposted from the city centre, but it is best visited on a guided Galeshewe tour.

A lift takes you down a shaft for the simulated mine experience, where audio and visual effects give an idea of how bad life was for the early diamond miners. Sounds of tumbling rubble and explosions add to the claustrophobia.

After exiting the mine, spend some time in the exhibition centre, which covers South African history and diamonds in general, as well as Kimberley's story. Also here is the guarded **diamond vault**, holding more than 3500 diamonds and replicas of the Eureka and 616 (the world's largest uncut eight-sided diamond, weighing 616 carats), which were unearthed here.

Outside, and entered for free, is a partial reconstruction of Kimberley's 1880s mining settlement, constructed using original relocated buildings, including a corrugated iron church, funeral parlour, sweet shop and bank, as well as a functioning pub-restaurant and guesthouse. Try your luck panning for diamonds and hitting skittles in the bowling alley. There is also a restored **Victorian tram** that takes visitors on a short ride (R10) to the other side of the Big Hole. There are plans to extend the line to City Hall.

If you just want to see the hole itself, a reduced rate is offered (though not generally advertised).

Northern Cape Highlights

① **Kgalagadi Transfrontier Park** (p459) Watching a black-maned lion nap under a thorn tree in this wild crimson Kalahari wonderland.

② **Kimberley** (p447) Stepping back in time to Kimberley's diamond-dealing past at the Big Hole and exploring the city's well-preserved Victorian buildings.

③ **Augrabies Falls National Park** (p463) Gasping at the water surging between vertiginous cliffs then indulging in some low-key wildlife watching.

④ **Namakwa** (p464) Taking a spring hike through a sea of brilliant yellow, purple and golden wildflowers.

⑤ **|Ai-|Ais/Richtersveld Transfrontier Park** (p467) Embarking on an adventure across surreal mountainous desert in this ultra-remote park.

⑥ **Stargazing** (p470) Taking in the astonishingly starry night skies across the province, particularly in Sutherland.

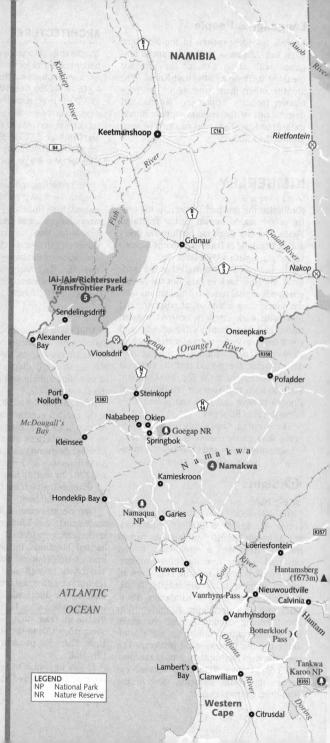

LEGEND
NP   National Park
NR   Nature Reserve

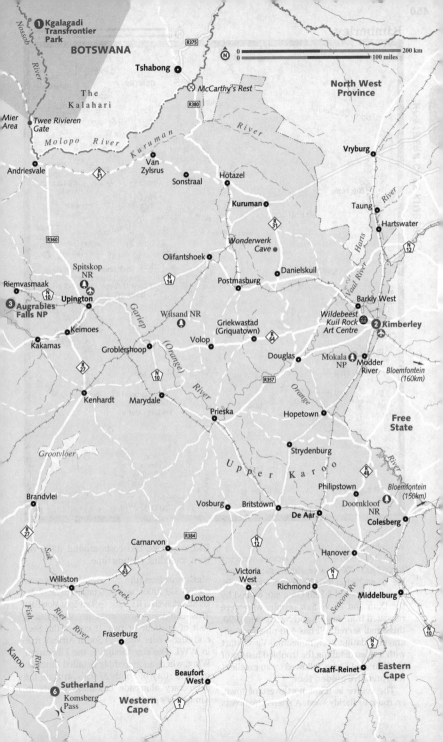

Kimberley

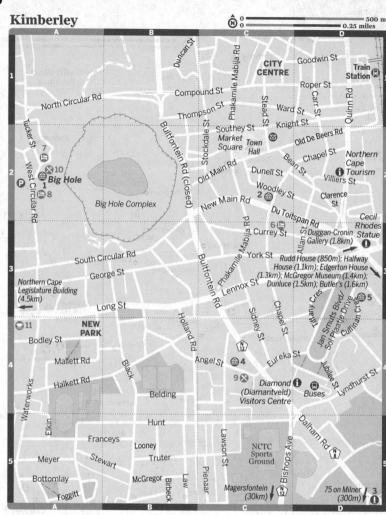

Wildebeest Kuil
Rock Art Centre ARCHAEOLOGICAL SITE
(☎053-833 7069; www.wildebeestkuil.itgo.com;
Rte 31; adult/child R35/20; ☺9am-4pm Mon-Fri,
by appointment Sat & Sun) On a site owned by
the !Xun and Khwe San people, who were
relocated from Angola and Namibia in 1990,
this small sacred hill has 400-plus rock en-
gravings dating back millennia. Visits start
with a video detailing the troubled history of
the !Xun and Khwe, followed by an excellent
interpretative guided tour.

The centre is 16km northwest of town,
en route to Barkly West. A shared taxi costs
R45; a private taxi costs around R390 return, including waiting time.

McGregor Museum MUSEUM
(☎053-839 2700; www.museumsnc.co.za; 7 Atlas St; adult/child R30/20; ☺9am-5pm Mon-Sat)
This comprehensive museum warrants a
visit of an hour or two. It covers the Second Anglo-Boer War and South Africa's role
in WWI. The star though is the Liberation
Wing, where an incredibly detailed timeline
tells the story of South Africa's struggle for
democracy alongside landmark events in
Kimberley's past.

Kimberley

Duggan-Cronin Gallery GALLERY
(4 Egerton Rd; entry by donation; ⊘9am-4pm Mon-Fri; ℗) This ethnographic gallery holds a wonderful collection of photographs of Southern African tribes taken in the 1920s and 1930s, before many aspects of traditional life were lost. Photographer Alfred Duggan-Cronin lived in this 19th-century house before his death in 1954.

William Humphreys Art Gallery GALLERY
(☑053-831 1724; www.whag.co.za; 1 Cullinan Cres, Civic Centre; adult/child R5/2; ⊘8am-4.45pm Mon-Fri, 10am-4.45pm Sat, 9am-noon Sun) One of the country's best public galleries, with changing exhibitions of contemporary South African work, as well as a surprisingly good collection of European masters. The cafe (mains R30 to R80) sits in a lovely garden and is a perfect spot for tea and cake.

Alexander McGregor Memorial Museum MUSEUM
(☑053-839 2700; Chapel St; adult/child R25/15; ⊘by appointment Mon-Fri) Based in a grand old building in the city centre, this museum focuses on Kimberley's history. There's information on the early settlers and forced removals, but best is the collection of photographs showing the Kimberley of yesteryear – it's fun to compare the shots with the city today, because many of the buildings are still standing.

Honoured Dead Memorial MONUMENT
(Memorial Rd, cnr Dalham Rd) This sandstone memorial remembers the soldiers who died defending the British-held city in the 124-day Siege of Kimberley, which took place during the Second Anglo-Boer War (1899–1902). The large gun is Long Cecil, built to repel the Boers' Long Toms.

Sol Plaatje Museum & Library MUSEUM
(☑053-833 2526; 32 Angel St; entry by donation; ⊘8am-4pm Mon-Fri) This museum, dedicated to activist and writer Sol Plaatje, occupies the house where he lived until his death in 1932. Panels tell the story of his life – he was known for being the first black South African to write a novel in English and for translating Shakespeare into Tswana. There are also displays on apartheid-era resistance press and information on forced removals.

⚲ Tours

Several battles from the Second Anglo-Boer War were fought in the area, including Magersfontein, Modder River and Graspan, all southwest of Kimberley off the N12. The most important was at **Magersfontein** (☑053-833 7115; adult/child R25/15; ⊘8am-4pm), where entrenched Boers decimated the famous Highland Brigade. Check with staff at the Diamond Visitors Centre for an updated list of guides offering insightful tours of the battlefields.

Steve Lunderstedt Tours WALKING, HISTORY
(☑083 732 3189; lunderstedt@kimberley.co.za; tours per person from R200; ⊘6.30pm) Given its history of diamond-digging and Anglo-Boer conflict, Kimberley is fertile ground for ghosts. Local historian and raconteur Steve Lunderstedt has been exploring the city for 20 years. As much historical tour as paranormal hunt, his four-hour jaunt has six stops, starting at the Honoured Dead Memorial. Bookings are essential; 10 people are required for a tour to go ahead.

Steve also offers a three-hour Big Hole ghost walk, as well as an evening tour at Magersfontein battlefield.

★**Native Minds** CULTURAL
(☑053-871 3690; www.facebook.com/native-minds.co.za; half-day tours R340) Joy Phirisi leads recommended walking or cycling tours of Galeshewe, a friendly township that was an integral player in the anti-apartheid struggle. Stops include the Mayibuye Uprising Memorial, where anti-apartheid protests

took place in 1952; Robert Sobukwe's house, where the Pan African Congress (PAC) founder was sent on his release from prison; and the Northern Cape Legislature Building.

To visit a home or artist's studio, ask in advance.

Jaco Powell Tours   HISTORY
(☑082 572 0065; per person R200) Jaco offers three-hour walking tours (book in advance; minimum 10 people) departing from the Honoured Dead Memorial at 6pm – just in time for the skies to darken and your guide to inform you that the vault is supposedly haunted with the souls of 27 British soldiers who perished during the siege of Kimberley.

🛏 Sleeping

Heerengracht Guest House   GUESTHOUSE $
(☑053-831 1531; www.heerengracht.co.za; 42 Heerengracht Ave, Royldene; s/d incl breakfast R650/750; P❋🛜➿) Situated on a leafy suburban street, there are simply decorated rooms here as well as spacious self-catering units (R850). It's within walking distance of two malls with fast-food eateries.

Gum Tree Lodge   HOSTEL $
(☑053-832 8577; www.gumtreelodge.com; Hull St; dm R180, r R500, with shared bathroom R250; P❋🛜➿) As close as Kimberley gets to a backpackers, this former convict station occupies leafy grounds off Rte 64, 5km northeast of the centre. Rooms are uninspiring and the furnishings are well-worn but it's a pleasant enough environment, with greenery overhanging the corrugated roofs. There's a restaurant, a pool and a kids' play area.

★ 75 on Milner   GUESTHOUSE $$
(☑082 686 5994; www.milnerlodge.co.za; 75 Milner St; s/d incl breakfast from R750/940; P❋🛜➿🏠) Highly recommended by travellers, this very friendly guesthouse has spacious, well-equipped rooms set around a small patio. Little touches set it apart, including good coffee at breakfast, snacks in the rooms and plug points in the garden so you can catch up on social media while dipping your toes in the pool.

Batsumi Luxury Guesthouse   GUESTHOUSE $$
(☑053-871 1339; www.facebook.com/BatsumiLuxuryGuesthouse; 15 Phakedi St, Galeshewe; r from R800; P❋🛜➿) This opulent new guesthouse in Galeshewe has large, high-ceilinged rooms with huge, modern bathrooms. There's a leafy internal patio with

comfy couches scattered around the edge of the pool. Meals are served in a light-filled dining room and a small pub was in the making when we visited.

Halfway House Hotel   HOTEL $$
(☑053-831 6324; www.halfwayhousehotel.com; 229 Du Toitspan Rd; s/d R800/1000; P❋🛜) Rooms are a little worn, but this hotel attached to a historic pub has a great location, within walking distance of Belgravia's museums and architectural delights. Breakfast is R98. Also under the same ownership is **Edgerton House** (5 Egerton Rd; r from R800; P❋➿), which once hosted Nelson Mandela.

New Rush Guest House   GUESTHOUSE $$
(☑053-839 4455; www.newrushguesthouse.co.za; Tucker St; r incl breakfast R850; P❋🛜) There are 14 simple guest rooms here, scattered across several buildings in the mock-up historical town at the Big Hole. Breakfast is served at the Protea Hotel. A bonus is being able to wander around the largely deserted mining village at night, imagining diamond dealers of yore drinking in the taverns after a long day's digging.

★Kimberley Club   BOUTIQUE HOTEL $$$
(☑053-832 4224; www.kimberleyclub.co.za; 35 Currey St; s/d from R1200/1445; ❋🛜) Founded by Cecil Rhodes and his diamond cronies as a private club in 1881, and rebuilt following a fire in 1896, this reputedly haunted building became a hotel in 2004. The 21 bedrooms are period-elegant, and offer the chance to pad in the slipper-steps of illustrious visitors such as Queen Elizabeth II. Breakfast is R150.

Protea Hotel Kimberley   HOTEL $$$
(☑053-802 8200; www.proteahotels.com/kimberley; West Circular Rd; s/d from R1350/1450; P❋🛜➿) The plush, four-star Protea is the only hotel with Big Hole views – enjoyed from the viewing deck outside the lobby with its magnificent crystal chandeliers and historical photos of the mine. The 120 compact rooms are scattered with faux antiques, but the Victorian-style elegance really shines in the lobby and bar-restaurant (open to nonguests). Weekend specials are normally offered.

🍽 Eating & Drinking

Lemon Tree   CAFE $
(☑053-831 7730; www.nclemontree.co.za; Angel St; mains R55-130; ⊘8am-5pm Mon-Fri, to 1pm Sat; P🛜) A long-established cafe offering

light – and some not-so-light – lunches. There's a build-your-own breakfast option and a range of cakes.

★ **Fusion Gardens** SOUTH AFRICAN **$$**
(☑079 520 9462; www.fusions.co.za; 465 Jenkins Mothibedi St, Galeshewe; mains R80-160; ⊙noon-9pm) ✐ Specialising in traditional cuisine like oxtail, snoek (a type of mackerel), tripe and trotters and chicken's feet, Fusion offers a welcome break from Kimberley's usual menus. Based in a tree-filled garden in Galeshewe, there is a focus on urban gardening, with the herbs and some of the veggies grown on-site. The menu changes daily. Bookings essential.

Fusion can be tricky to find, but can be visited as part of a tour to Galeshewe.

Halfway House PUB FOOD **$$**
(☑053-831 6324; www.halfwayhousehotel.co.za; 229 Du Toitspan Rd, cnr Egerton Rd; mains R70-180; ⊙7am-11pm Mon-Sat; P(꠶)) After a revamp, 'The Half' has sadly lost a little of its soul. Dating back to 1872, this was once one of Cecil Rhodes' watering holes and today it might be the world's only 'drive-in' bar, stemming from Rhodes' insistence on being served beer without dismounting his horse. There's beer on tap and upscale pub grub is served.

Occidental Grill Bar PUB FOOD **$$**
(☑053-830 4418; West Circular Rd, Big Hole Complex; mains R65-165; ⊙10am-10pm Mon-Thu, to midnight Fri & Sat, to 3pm Sun; (꠶)) With a long bar and B&W photos of old-time prospectors, this Victorian-era saloon is a fun place to pause on a Big Hole tour. Dishes include fish and chips, curry and burgers. 'The Ox' also has Kimberley's best beer selection, with craft beers from across the country. You don't have to pay the Big Hole admission to access the Occidental.

Rhodes Grill INTERNATIONAL **$$**
(☑053-832 4224; www.kimberleyclub.co.za; 72 Du Toitspan Rd, Kimberley Club; mains R70-165; ⊙6.30am-9.30pm Mon-Sat, to 8pm Sun; P) Wear closed shoes and smart-casual dress to eat among Rhodes memorabilia in the one-time gentlemen's club he founded, now a boutique hotel. South African specialities like oxtail, kudu loin and Cape Malay curry star on the menu. There's also Café Vitello, an Italian restaurant serving light lunches on the terrace.

Angel Heart CAFE
(☑053-831 5577; 53 Long St; ⊙7am-5pm Mon-Fri, 8am-2pm Sun; P(꠶)) There are a few breakfast items, salads and toasted sandwiches on the menu here but what keeps this convivial cafe busy is its excellent coffee – undoubtedly the best in town.

ⓘ Information

Diamond (Diamantveld) Visitors Centre
(☑053-830 6779; www.kimberley.co.za; 121 Bultfontein Rd; ⊙8am-5pm Mon-Fri) Pick up the *Kimberley Meander* brochure, with suggested self-guided walking and driving tours.

Northern Cape Tourism (☑053 832 2657; www.experiencenortherncape.com; 15 Villiers St)

ⓘ Getting There & Around

AIR

Taxis connect the city centre with the airport, 6km south.

SA Express (☑086 172 9227; www.flyexpress. aero) Flies to/from Jo'burg (from R900, one hour) and Cape Town (from R1000, 1½ hours).

Hamba Nathi (☑053-831 3982; www.hambanathi.co.za; 121 Bultfontein Rd, Diamond Visitors Centre) Sells airline tickets.

BUS

Tickets 4 Africa (☑053-832 6040; tickets4africa@hotmail.com; 121 Bultfontein Rd, Diamond Visitors Centre) sells tickets for **Greyhound** (reservations ☑087 352 0352, customer care 24hr ☑011-611 8000; www.greyhound.co.za), **Intercape** (☑021-380 4400; www.intercape. co.za) and **City to City** (☑0861 589 282; www.citytocity.co.za). There are direct services to Cape Town (R595, 12 hours), Jo'burg (R365, seven hours) and Bloemfontein (R250, 2½ hours). Intercape runs services to Upington (R380, seven hours) on Friday and Sunday.

Translux (☑086 158 9282; www.translux. co.za) buses also serve Kimberley, though there is no booking office in the city.

CAR

Avis, Budget, Europcar, First, Hertz, Sixt and Tempest have desks at Kimberley airport. Hire rates start at around R300 per day.

TAXI

Rikki's Taxis (☑053-842 1764; www.rikkistaxis.co.za) is a reliable option.

TRAIN

Shosholoza Meyl (☑0860 008 888, 011-774 4555; www.shosholozameyl.co.za) Trans-Karoo trains stop in Kimberley en route between Jo'burg (economy/sleeper R160/240, eight hours) and Cape Town (R300/470, 17½ hours).

Blue Train (☑012-334 8459; www.bluetrain. co.za) Stops for a tour of the Big Hole Complex en route from Pretoria to Cape Town.

THE UPPER KAROO

Part of the Great Karoo, which extends into the Eastern and Western Capes, this is a desolate land of big skies and empty spaces. Its inhabitants are predominantly sheep farmers, who live as they have for generations on giant tracts of barren land. Towns are few and far between, and are mostly of interest as stopovers offering spectacular stargazing and a taste of Karoo lamb.

Mokala National Park

Named after the Tswana for 'camel thorn', the dominant tree found here, Mokala (☎053-204 8000; www.sanparks.org/parks/mokala/; adult/child R160/80; ⏰7am-6pm mid-Mar–Apr, Aug & Sep, 7am-5.30pm May-Jul, 7am-7pm Oct–mid-Mar) is South Africa's newest national park. It encompasses grassy plains studded with rocky hills and these trademark trees. Indigenous to Southern Africa, camel thorns can range from small, spiny shrubs standing barely 2m to 16m-tall trees with wide, spreading crowns. The species is an important resource for both the people and wildlife living in this harsh region – the local tribes use the gum and bark to treat coughs, colds and nosebleeds. (Some people even roast the seeds as a coffee substitute.) Mammals in the 200-sq-km park include black and white rhinos, roan antelopes, Cape buffaloes, giraffes and zebras.

Organised activities include sunset wildlife drives, fly-fishing and bush braais (barbecues). Activities should be booked ahead.

TRANSKAROO STOPOFF

The charming restaurant at Transkaroo Country Lodge (☎053-672 0027; www.transkaroocountrylodge.co.za; Market St; mains R60-160; ⏰7am-9pm; P) really sets Britstown apart from other Karoo dorps (villages). Chequered tablecloths in the leafy courtyard give a provincial French feel, yet the food is Northern Cape through and through – try the superlative dinner buffet (R195), with Karoo lamb cooked every possible way.

The quaintly furnished rooms (room with shared bathroom per person R270, single/double from R750/850) are fine for a stopover and there's a pleasant pool in the gardens.

It's a good idea to start your Mokala visit at the small Interpretation Centre (Mofele Lodge; ⏰9am-4pm Mon-Fri, from 10am Sat; P), which gives information on the history and geology of the park. There's a touch station where you can feel the skins of various animals that you'll hopefully see livelier versions of later.

🛏 Sleeping & Eating

There is one restaurant in the park, based at Mosu Lodge. Reservations are required.

Motswedi Campsite CAMPGROUND $
(camping per site R455) A superb campground with just six sites, all overlooking a water hole. Each site has its own ablutions and kitchen.

Stofdam Bird Hide HUT $
(☎053-204 8000; per night R555) A much sought after and very rustic option that sleeps up to four people. It cannot be booked online and only one-night stays are possible. Bring all your own bedding and cooking utensils. Book directly through the park.

★Kameeldoorn Tree House CABIN $$
(☎053-204 8000; www.sanparks.org/parks/mokala/; d R1380) A simply delightful self-catering cabin accommodating one or two people, nestled in a tree in the centre of the park. Bookings should be made directly through the park, rather than central reservations. Book well in advance.

Mosu Lodge LODGE $$
(bungalows from R880; ❄❄) Mokala's most upmarket accommodation, with amenities such as electric blankets, fireplaces and DSTV in the self-catering luxury executive suites. The smart poolside bar-restaurant (mains R70 to R130) is open all day, serving dishes from vegetable stir-fry to venison pie.

Lilydale Rest Camp CHALET $$
(chalets R890; ❄❄) Lilydale is on the banks of the Riet River, which has good fly-fishing. Its self-catering units, especially the thatched chalets, are perfect for getting back to nature.

Haak-en-Steek CHALET $$
(chalets R1440) This rustic cottage tucked away in the west of the park sleeps four. There is a well-equipped kitchen and a braai area, but no restaurant, bar or pool.

ℹ Getting There & Away

To enter the park, head about 60km southwest of Kimberley on the N12, then turn right at the 'Mokala Mosu' sign and follow the rutted dirt road for 21km. It's possible to cross the park and exit by the Lilydale Gate, then follow a dirt road for 16km and meet the N12 about 40km southwest of Kimberley.

In the rainy season, the roads might not be passable with a 2WD – always call in advance to check.

There is no fuel in the park so be sure to fill up before you set out.

Victoria West

🕿 053 / POP 8300

Located roughly halfway between Jo'burg and Cape Town, Victoria West is a gracefully fading old railway town. If you need an overnight stop on the way across the Karoo, and want to get a feel for small-town life, Victoria West has a certain stuck-in-time allure. In fact, it has a distinct Wild West feel, tumbleweeds and all.

Architecture enthusiasts will enjoy wandering along Church St, with its mixture of building styles. The Apollo Theatre was sadly closed when we visited, but its art-deco facade is still worth a photo. The late-19th-century hotel – now a guesthouse – dominates the street, and you can easily imagine a couple of cowboys stepping out into the deserted main road for a high-noon scuffle.

Victoria West has ATMs and a petrol station.

🛏 Sleeping & Eating

Always call ahead if you're planning to eat in Victoria West, just to make sure something will be open, as there aren't many options.

★**Kingwill's B&B**　　GUESTHOUSE $
(🕿053-621 0453; Willow St; r R725; 🅿❄) There are lovely rooms in the main building as well as spacious garden units with flat-screen TV, modern decor, microwave and fridge. Meals are served at the adjoining **Karoo Deli** (mains R45-95; ⊙7am-5pm Mon-Fri, 7am-1pm Sat).

ℹ Getting There & Away

The town is at the junction of the N12 and Rte 63, which leads west to Calvinia via the towns of Loxton, Carnarvon and Williston. Buses stop here on their way from Cape Town (R460, eight hours) to Johannesburg (R475, 10½ hours).

THE KALAHARI

A voyage to the Kalahari is akin to being catapulted into a parallel universe. It's a surreal *Alice in Wonderland* experience, where everything looms larger than life in the scorching desert heat. A collage of fiery sunsets and shifting crimson sands, lush green fields and gushing waterfalls, magnificent parks and tidy vineyards, this region will continue to enchant long after you have departed. Get a feel for it before you leave home in the works of Laurens Van der Post, who brought the Kalahari alive in books including *The Lost World of the Kalahari* and *A Far-Off Place*.

The Kalahari also covers much of Botswana and extends as far as Namibia and Angola.

In South Africa, the Kalahari is divided into two distinct areas: the arid semidesert and desert regions; and the 'Green Kalahari', an irrigated, fertile belt along the banks of the Gariep (Orange) River. In this agricultural area, dunes give way to fruit and wine farms producing goodies such as delicious sultana grapes and vast amounts of table wine. Nonetheless, the Green Kalahari retains a frontier feel, with dazzling night skies and plenty of wide open spaces.

Kuruman

🕿 053 / POP 13,000

A mining town set deep in wild country, rough little Kuruman is not a place to linger, but its remote location makes this a natural stopping point on trans-Kalahari trips.

◉ Sights

Moffat Mission　　HISTORIC SITE
(off Thompson St; adult/child R15/5; ⊙8am-5pm; 🅿) Established by the London Missionary Society in 1816, the mission was named after long-serving Scottish missionaries Robert and Mary Moffat. They converted the local Batlhaping people to Christianity, started a school and translated the Bible into Tswana. The mission became a famous staging point for explorers and missionaries heading further into Africa. The Moffats' daughter married David Livingstone in the mission church, a stone-and-thatch building with 800 seats.

It's a quiet and atmospheric spot shaded by large trees that provide a perfect escape from the desert heat. It is 5km north of

WORKSHOP KO KASI

Serving both as a community centre and a much-needed tourist draw, Ko Kasi (☑081 289 2662; www.facebook. com/workshopkokasi; Tlhabane Rd, Mothibistad; ⊙7am-6pm; 🅿) 🍴 is a must-stop if you're passing through Kuruman. Started by two local entrepreneurs in 2016, the award-wining start-up includes a craft shop, a traditional African spa and a cafe serving pizzas, traditional meals and homemade ginger beer. They can arrange donkey cart trips (R50) around Mothibistad and host pop-up markets and storytelling sessions. The whole place is constructed from recycled materials, including the spa built from old tyres.

There's a small garden that provides fresh greens to the cafe and they also sell starter gardens to local residents.

Kuruman on Rte 31 to Hotazel, signposted from town. If there's no one around, drop your entrance fee into the donations box.

Eye of Kuruman   PARK
(Fontein St; adult/child R14/7; ⊙7.30am-5.30pm Mon-Fri, to 4.30pm Sat & Sun; 🅿) The town's famed natural spring is in the park between the tourist office and Palmgate Centre. Discovered in 1801, the prolific spring produces about 20 million litres of water a day – without fail. Trees ring the clear pond, where sizeable fish dart beneath the lily pads. It's a pleasant enough spot for a picnic, although litter can be a problem.

🛏 Sleeping & Eating

The local mining staff fill accommodation between Monday and Thursday, so book ahead.

Kuru-Kuru Guesthouse   GUESTHOUSE $$
(☑076 781 6669; www.kurukuru.co.za; 1 Albutt St, cnr Buckle St; s/d incl breakfast from R550/700) A friendly guesthouse with simple rooms, some with self-catering facilities and all with a small terrace. There's no swimming pool but there is a bar, a library and a pool table. It's in the suburbs 2km north of town, just off Rte 31.

Palm Gate Centre   SHOPPING CENTRE $
(22 Main Rd) There's a supermarket in this shopping centre, as well as a bar-restaurant serving pizza, pasta, burgers and steaks.

❶ Getting There & Away

Intercape stops daily en route between Jo'burg (R750, eight hours) and Upington (R390, 3½ hours).

Shared taxis leave from a vast and somewhat intimidating rank north of the town centre.

Witsand Nature Reserve

As if a reserve based on a 9km-by-5km and 60m-high white-sand dune system, standing in stark contrast to the surrounding red Kalahari sands, wasn't enough, Witsand also comes with a soundtrack. When conditions are hot and dry, the sand sings. The 'roaring sands' effect is created by air escaping from the tightly packed grains; the bass, organ-like sound is sometimes audible in the reserve office, 5km away.

Activities include hiking, sandboarding (boards per day R150) and mountain biking (bicycles per day R120). Although it's not a major wildlife-watching spot, you can expect to see various antelopes and a host of birdlife. There are no organised activities but you can roam at your will.

🛏 Sleeping & Eating

There is an excellent campsite, simple but well-priced huts with shared ablutions and some fairly plush chalets all within the reserve.

A shop sells the very basics, but you'd do well to come with provisions. The bar-restaurant will do in a pinch but call ahead to check the opening times.

❶ Getting There & Away

From the N14, the turn-off to the reserve is about 5km southwest of Olifantshoek, 105km from Kuruman. From there, the gravel road leads 75km southwest to the reserve. From Rte 62, the turn-off is about 60km east of Groblershoop and 5km east of Volop; the reserve is then 45km north on the gravel road. You shouldn't need a 4WD, but always phone the reserve first to check the condition of the roads. Witsand does not have a petrol station and the shop sells only the very basics, so fill up before you set off, and come equipped with food and water.

Upington

☑054 / POP 57,200

Home to lush gardens and hundreds of date palm trees, Upington is a prosperous, orderly town on the banks of the Gariep (Orange) River. The central hub for the Green Kalahari, it's a good place to recoup after a long desert slog – although it gets blazing hot in summer. Wide boulevards, slightly cluttered with supermarkets and chain stores, fill the town centre. Step onto a side street near the river, however, and you'll enter a peaceful world where refreshing, watery views and rows of palms hold quiet court.

If you yearn to see the Northern Cape's most remote parts but don't have the means to do so on your own, this is also a good place to organise a guided tour.

◎ Sights & Activities

Orange River Cellars　　　　　　WINERY
(☑054-495 0040; www.orangeriverwines.com; 158 Schröder St; tastings from R25; ◷10am-6pm Mon-Fri, to 3pm Sat; ℗) At this smart new tasting centre there's a vast range of well-priced wines to taste, including dessert and sparkling wines. The colombard and muscadel are the best of the bunch. Platters are available if you fancy pairing your wine with cheese, olives or biltong.

Kalahari-Orange Museum　　　　MUSEUM
(☑054-332 5333; 4 Schröder St; adult/child R10/2; ◷9am-12.30pm & 2-5pm Mon-Fri) The highlight of this museum, which occupies the mission station established by Reverend Schröder in 1875, is the story of the Upington 26, who were wrongly jailed under apartheid. Other than that, there are a few printing presses, farming implements and some old photos of the town.

★Sakkie se Arkie　　　　　　CRUISE
(☑082 564 5447; www.arkie.co.za; Park St; adult/child R120/80; ◷5.30pm Fri-Sun, daily during holidays) Soak up the last rays of the Kalahari sun over the Gariep (Orange) River on the top deck of Sakkie's barge. Dire Straits, Afrikaans pop and other classics keep everyone entertained on the two-hour sunset cruise as the water turns silvery and the bartender lines up cold beers.

☞ Tours

Upington is the best place to organise a Kalahari adventure.

Kalahari Safaris　　　　　　ADVENTURE
(☑054-332 5653; www.kalaharisafaris.co.za) Runs small-group (two to five people) trips to locations including the Kgalagadi and Augrabies Falls parks, Witsand Nature Reserve and Namakwa. Tours last from one to seven days and cater to all budgets.

Kalahari Tours & Travel　　　ADVENTURE
(☑054-338 0375; www.kalahari-tours.co.za; 12 Mazurka Curve) Offers itineraries around the province, including three- to nine-day Kgalagadi 4WD adventures.

⌂ Sleeping

Guesthouses on Budler St and Murray Ave overlook the river, their lawns leading to the water.

Oasis　　　　　　　　HOTEL $$
(☑054-337 8500; www.theoasishotel.co.za; 26 Schröder St; s/d from R980/1130; ℗❋⬚) The Oasis offers some of Upington's most stylish accommodation. Afro-chic is the theme and the small but sleek rooms are decorated with paintings from a local Khomani San artist. Guests can use the swimming pool and restaurant at the Protea Upington, across the road. Breakfast is R160.

Island View House　　　　　B&B $$
(☑054-331 1328; www.islandviewhouse.co.za; 10 Murray Ave; s/d incl breakfast R880/1060; ❋⬚⬚) The Mocké family offers a warm welcome and modern rooms with showers, microwaves, fridges and satellite TV. There's a shared lounge, kitchen and balcony and canoeing on the river is offered.

Aqua Viva　　　　　GUESTHOUSE $$
(☑054-331 2524; www.aquaviva.co.za; 26A Schröder St; s/d incl breakfast R690/880; ❋) Tucked behind the Oasis Hotel, this is a peaceful place with spacious if sparsely decorated rooms. They come with large

---

OFF THE BEATEN TRACK

WONDERWERK CAVE

There have been important archaeological finds in this dolomite cave (☑087 310 4356; adult/child R25/15; ◷8am-1.30pm & 2-5pm Mon-Fri), including evidence of hominids using fire. It has a longer record of human occupation than any other known cave. Archaeological digs are still in progress and there's a small information centre with some details on the cave's former inhabitants, including early Stone Age people.

It's a good idea to visit the McGregor Museum (p450) in Kimberley first to get some background on the cave's lengthy history. The cave is 45km south of Kuruman on Rte 31.

Upington

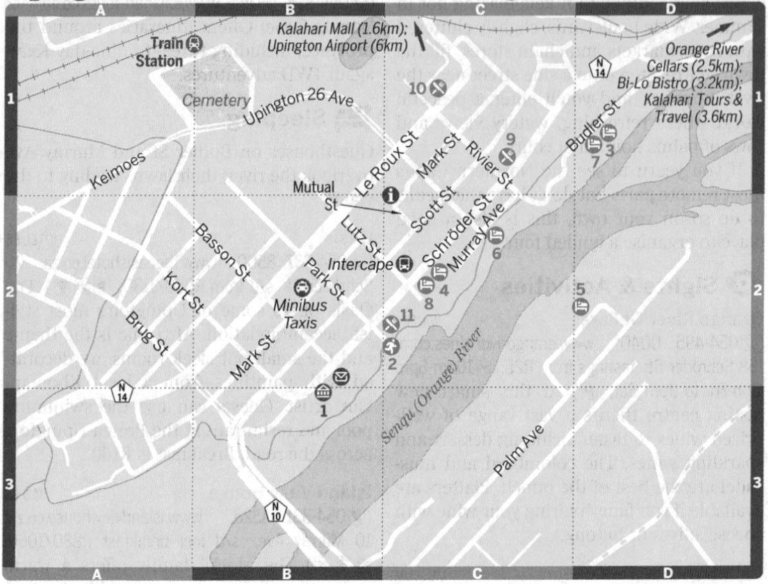

Upington

Sights
1 Kalahari-Orange Museum B3

Activities, Courses & Tours
2 Sakkie se Arkie C2

Sleeping
3 A Riviera Garden B&B D1
4 Aqua Viva C2
5 Die Eiland Holiday Resort D2
6 Island View House C2
7 Le Must River Residence D1
8 Oasis C2

Eating
9 Cafe Zest C1
10 Dros C1
11 Irish Pub & Grill C2

bathrooms, comically small TVs and a shared veranda leading on to a lawn overlooking the river. There are plans to add self-catering cottages and a tea garden on the river bank.

A Riviera Garden B&B B&B $$
(054-332 6554; ariviera@upington.co.za; 16 Budler St; s/d R750/920; P) The gardens at this friendly, family-run guesthouse with two cosy rooms are a fairy-tale creation, and run all the way down to the river.

Die Eiland Holiday Resort CHALET $$
(054-334 0287; resort@kharahais.gov.za; camping from R145, huts with shared bathroom from R330, chalets from R860; P) A palm-lined avenue leads to 'the Island', in a wonderful natural setting on the river's southeastern bank. The somewhat shabby self-catering chalets have kitchenettes with stove and microwave, and tiny bathrooms with shower. Some travellers have reported that it gets quite noisy, particularly on weekends.

★ **Le Must River Residence** GUESTHOUSE $$$
(054-332 3971; www.lemustupington.com; 14 Budler St; s/d incl breakfast from R1190/1700; P) This elegant riverside getaway has 11 African-themed rooms with antique furnishings and crisp linen. Sitting rooms and terraces open onto the artful garden with its Italianate pool.

Eating

There are restaurants of varying levels of quality dotted along the length of Schröder St and you'll find a range of fast-food eateries and chain restaurants at the Kalahari Mall, east of the town centre.

Bi-Lo Bistro INTERNATIONAL, SUSHI $$
(054-338 0616; 9 Green Point Rd; mains R75-190; 8am-10pm; P) Birds hop between

palm trees and kids play on the swings at this popular spot in the suburbs. The vast menu features everything from steak to sushi – the latter is surprisingly decent. There's also a small supermarket and a liquor store on the premises, if you prefer to self-cater.

Irish Pub & Grill PUB FOOD $$
(☑054-331 2005; 20 Schröder St; mains R90-190; ☺9am-11pm) For sundowners or an early evening meal, you can't beat this Irish bar's patio overlooking the river. The menu features pizza, a few salads and plenty of meat.

Dros INTERNATIONAL $$
(☑054-331 3331; www.dros.co.za; Le Roux St, Pick 'n Pay Centre; mains R70-165; ☺9am-11pm; P) A chain bar-restaurant focusing on meat, with a few salads, seafood dishes and pizzas. It's a pleasantly cool spot after a hot drive.

★ **Cafe Zest** INTERNATIONAL $$$
(☑054-332 1413; Schröder St, Ori Bldg; mains R95-220; ☺9am-10pm Mon-Sat) Locals swear that Zest serves the best coffee in town. It also has one of the most appealing menus, featuring salads, seafood, a decadent chicken dish with cafe au lait sauce and, of course, lots of red meat. On summer evenings you'll want a table out in the courtyard. There's local beer on tap and an excellent selection of gin.

❶ Information

Upington Tourist Office (☑054-338 7152; tourism@dkm.gov.za; cnr Mutual & Mark Sts; ☺7.30am-4.30pm Mon-Fri) A helpful office with passionate staff.

❶ Getting There & Away

AIR
South African Airways (☑054-332 2161; www.flysaa.com; Upington Airport) flies to/from Jo'burg (R2800, 1½ hours) and Cape Town (R2900, 1½ hours). The airport is 6km north of town, off the N10.

BUS
Intercape (☑central reservations 021-380 4400; www.intercape.co.za; Lutz St) buses go to Cape Town (R680, 13½ hours, daily), Jo'burg (R950, 11½ hours, daily) and Windhoek, Namibia (R660, 13 hours, Tuesday, Thursday, Friday and Sunday). Buses leave from the Intercape office on Lutz St.

CAR
Rental agencies, including **Avis** (☑054-332 4746; www.avis.co.za; ☺8am-5.30pm Mon-Fri, 10am-1pm Sat, 10am-5pm Sun) and **Europcar** (☑054-332 2383; www.europcar.com; ☺7.30am-6pm Mon-Fri), have offices at Upington airport.

SHARED TAXI
Destinations of **shared taxis** (Mark St) include Springbok (R300, four hours) and Windhoek, Namibia (R680, 13 hours).

Kgalagadi Transfrontier Park

A long, hot road leads between crimson dunes from Upington to Africa's first **transfrontier park** (☑054-561 2000; www.sanparks.org/parks/kgalagadi/; adult/child R328/164), one of the world's last great, unspoilt ecosystems. Once you enter the magical park, tucked away alongside Namibia in the Northern Cape and southwest Botswana, you'll soon see why the journey was well worth the effort.

The Kgalagadi is a wild land of harsh extremes and frequent droughts, where shifting red and white sands meet thorn trees and dry riverbeds. Yet despite the desolate landscape, it's teeming with wildlife. From prides of black-maned lions to packs of howling spotted hyenas, there are some 1775 predators here. It's one of the best places in the world to spot big cats, especially cheetahs. Add in giant, orange-ball sunsets and black-velvet night skies studded with twinkling stars, and you'll feel like you've entered the Africa of storybooks.

We found the section between Urikaruus and Mata-Mata to be particularly good for predator sightings, while the east–west routes linking the two rivers are great for photographing the red dunes this region is known for. The semi-arid countryside also supports large populations of reptiles, rodents, small mammals and antelopes. Most of the animals are remarkably tolerant of vehicles.

KHOMANI SAN COMMUNITY TOURISM

The Khomani San people have inhabited this region for thousands of years, and learning more about their hunter-gatherer culture is a crucial part of visiting the Kalahari. There are a number of community tourism enterprises set up in the region around the Kgalagadi Transfrontier Park, fully owned by the Khomani San community, including accommodation, a living museum, a traditional restaurant and a range of tours that incorporate tracking skills, donkey cart rides and storytelling. For more information, check out www.khomanisan.com.

🏃 Activities

We recommend trying at least one guided activity as you'll have a better chance of spotting predators. The park operates sunrise, sunset, night and full-morning wildlife drives (adult/child from R303/151), departing from Twee Rivieren, Nossob, Mata-Mata and Kalahari Tented Camp. At least two people are needed for safaris to depart.

For an extra fee, there are 4WD trails to tackle (per vehicle R3333).

🛏 Sleeping & Eating

Accommodation should be booked in advance on the South African National Parks website (www.sanparks.org/parks/kgalagadi).

The rest camps have shops selling basic groceries, soft drinks and alcohol, and are open from 7.30am until 15 minutes after the gates close (Nossob and Mata-Mata's also close between 12.30pm and 1.30pm).

Kgalagadi Transfrontier Park

Twee Rivieren Rest Camp has the park's only restaurant.

🛏 Park Rest Camps

The rest camps have a range of campsites, chalets and cottages, with bedding, towels, fully equipped kitchens, braais and bathrooms. Twee Rivieren has 24-hour electricity; at the others, power is cut overnight.

Twee Rivieren   CHALET $$
(camping from R285, cottages/chalets from R1280/1630; P ❄ ☒) The largest camp in the park is also the most convenient, located next to the park entrance and with the most facilities, including a **restaurant** (mains R85-135; ⊙7.30-10am & 6-9pm). The cottages have between two and four single beds; the chalet has six. The cheaper campsites don't have power.

Mata-Mata Rest Camp   CHALET $$
(camping from R330, 2-/4-person chalets from R1015/1745; P ❄ ☒) Surrounded by thorny Kalahari dune bushveld, over three hours from Twee Rivieren Gate, Mata-Mata is a good place to spot giraffes. The riverfront chalets (from R1845) are worth the extra – you stand a good chance of spotting wildlife in the dry riverbed from your patio.

Nossob   CHALET $$
(camping from R330, chalets from R1065; ☒) Situated within the dry Nossob riverbed and surrounded by tree savannah, this camp is a good place to spot predators. The chalets vary in size but all have similar amenities and a somewhat spartan, institutional feel. The premium campsites (from R600) come

❶ KGALAGADI TRANSFRONTIER PARK

Why Go Superlative big cat sightings; beautiful 4WD routes; endlessly photogenic skies; a wilder feel than many South African parks.

When to Go May to August, when the weather is coolest (below freezing at night) and the animals are drawn to the bores along the dry riverbeds. The extreme heat from December to February entices animal to water holes, making wildlife spotting easier.

Practicalities Gates open between 5.30am and 7.30am and shut between 6pm and 7.30pm. Times vary from month to month, but generally follow the rising and setting sun. Petrol and diesel are available at rest camps. Carry drinking water at all times. Kgalagadi tours can be organised in Upington. Visitors must remain in their cars, except at the six designated picnic sites and accommodation.

Budget Tips If you arrive late in the afternoon, consider spending the night outside the park to avoid paying that day's fees.

with their own private ablutions and kitchen. It's over four hours from Twee Rivieren Gate.

🛏 Park Wilderness Camps

These remote camps offer the opportunity to immerse yourself in nature and are highly recommended. The camps are unfenced, which means animals can wander in; a ranger is on duty at all times. Stock up on petrol/diesel, drinking water and wood/charcoal before visiting, and book ahead. Children under 12 are allowed only at Kalahari Tented Camp.

Urikaruus   CABIN $$
(cabins from R1745) Perched on the banks of the Auob River, these four stilted cabins are connected by raised walkways between the camel thorn trees. Urikaruus is the second-closest wilderness camp to Twee Rivieren (over two hours from Twee Rivieren Gate).

Kielekranke
Wilderness Camp   CABIN $$
(cabins from R1745; P) Sunk into a sand dune and with decks gazing over the vast desert, these gorgeous tented cabins feel like they're in the middle of nowhere, though it's only 90 minutes from Twee Rivieren.

Bitterpan Wilderness Camp   CABIN $$
(cabins from R1745) These stilted cabins perch in a very remote section of the park, with excellent sunset vistas across a pan. Access is via a rough, one-way, 4WD-only route over three hours from Nossob. Cabins have private bathrooms but share a kitchen.

Gharagab Wilderness Camp   CABIN $$
(cabins from R1745) Among camel thorn trees and grass savannah, Gharagab's elevated log cabins survey the red dunes. Perks at the remote spot, accessed on a one-way, 4WD-only trail from Union's End, include decks overlooking a water hole popular with brown hyenas. Over three hours from Nossob.

Grootkolk Wilderness Camp   CABIN $$
(cabins from R1745) Nestled amid red sand dunes at a remote spot in the far north of the park, Grootkolk's desert cabins are made from sandbags and canvas. As if the stars and silence weren't enough, predators are often spotted at the water hole.

★ Kalahari Tented Camp   TENTED CAMP $$$
(d safari tents from R1650; P⛱) Kgalagadi's most luxurious wilderness camp has 14 stilted desert tents with rustic furnishings and views of a water hole in the Auob riverbed – a popular hangout for herds of wildebeest. It has a remote, rustic feel while being only 3km from the conveniences of Mata-Mata (and over three hours from Twee Rivieren Gate).

!Xaus Lodge   LODGE $$$
(☑in Cape Town 021-701 7860; www.xauslodge. co.za; s/d incl full board & activities R6045/9300; P⛱) ✔ Kgalagadi's most upmarket option is owned and operated by the local San community. The lodge is a dreamy fantasy in ochre, overlooking a circular pan so perfect it almost looks artificially constructed. Cultural activities and excellent wildlife drives round out a wonderful package.

LOCAL KNOWLEDGE

KOKERBOOM FOOD & WINE ROUTE

With grapes galore (this area is now producing about 10% of the country's wines) and rustic farm stalls selling biltong, dried fruit and other local goodies dotting the lonely highways, the area between Upington and Kakamas offers some offbeat culinary experiences. The Kokerboom Food and Wine Route aims to bring small, local producers together. It's in its infancy but there are already a few stops worth a visit.

Die Mas Van Kakamas (☑054-431 0245; www.diemas.co.za; wine tasting R40, brandy & chocolate pairing R50; ☺8am-5pm Mon-Fri, 9am-2pm Sat; P) The winemaker here experiments with a range of grape varieties, though the hanepoot wines that the region is known for are still the best. Brandy and gin are also on offer. Enjoy a tasting on the deck overlooking the vineyards, and if you have one too many there are campsites and chalets on-site. It's well sign-posted from the N14.

Bezalel (☑054-491 1325; www.bezalel.co.za; N14; tastings R60; ☺8am-5.30pm Mon-Fri, to 3pm Sat; P) Possibly the most varied tasting of any estate in the country, with samples of wine, port, brandy, liqueurs and the challenge of swigging *mampoer* (moonshine) without grimacing. There's a **restaurant** (mains R70 to R125) and a leafy courtyard where you can enjoy your chosen tipple, plus accommodation overlooking the reservoir. It's 25km southwest of Upington on the N14.

Kalahari Gateway Hotel Bar-Restaurant (☑054-431 0838; www.kalaharigateway.co.za; Kakamas; mains R75-190, sushi R30-135; ☺7am-10pm) Although the conveyor belt rarely gets switched on, this Kalahari sushi bar continues to draw curious gourmands. As well as the familiar fishy options (fresh fish is flown in from Cape Town every two days), you'll find local quirks such as a springbok roll stuffed with biltong and avocado. There's also a typically meat-orientated menu if you don't fancy sushi.

Outside the Park

There are dozens of places to stay on Rte 360 from Upington to Twee Rivieren Gate.

Molopo Kalahari Lodge   LODGE $$
(☑054-511 0008; www.ncfamouslodges.co.za; Rte 360; camping per site R300, s/d incl breakfast from R550/800; ❄☏✉) Molopo is a traditional safari lodge offering excellent value. Accommodation includes rondavels (round huts), simple chalets and more luxurious versions, all decorated with Khomani San artwork. There are braai pits dotted around the pretty, landscaped gardens and the restaurant (mains from R110) serves traditional South African fare and light meals. It's 58km south of Twee Rivieren.

Sister properties include Vischgat Game Lodge and Elandspoor Bush Camp, some 60km further south.

ⓘ Getting There & Around

Twee Rivieren Gate is 250km northwest of Upington on the tarred Rte 360.

A 4WD vehicle is useful but not essential – the park's four main routes are gravel/sand roads but they're in decent condition and can be driven in a 2WD if you take care. Beware of patches of deep sand and loose gravel on the park's roads, which can make corners treacherous. The speed limit is 50km/h. Allow plenty of time to get to the camps as no driving is permitted after dark.

TO NAMIBIA & BOTSWANA

You'll find SANParks reception, South African immigration (open 7.30am to 4pm) and border police at Twee Rivieren Gate.

The Botswana side of the park is only accessible by 4WD and there must be at least two vehicles travelling together. Accommodation is in unfenced camps and campsites. Book in advance through **Botswana Wildlife** (☑+267 318 0774; dwnp@gov.bw; Gaborone), which has an office at Twee Rivieren. If you want to exit the park into the rest of Botswana, you must carry out border-crossing formalities at Twee Rivieren and spend at least two nights in the park.

If you want to enter Namibia through Kgalagadi's Mata-Mata Gate, there's also a two-night minimum stay. Present your passport to South African immigration at Twee Rivieren, and to Namibian immigration at Mata-Mata. There's a levy of R242 per vehicle at Namibian immigration.

Augrabies Falls National Park

The Khoe-San people called it 'Aukoerbis', meaning 'place of great noise', and when the waterfall for which this park (☑054-452 9200; www.sanparks.org/parks/augrabies/; adult/child R192/96; ☺7am-6.30pm) is named is fat with rainy-season run-off, its thunderous roar is nothing short of spectacular.

The impressive falls are formed where the Gariep (Orange) River crashes into an 18km-long ravine with 200m-high cliffs. The main falls drop 56m, while the adjoining Bridal Veil Falls plunge 75m. It's a short walk from the visitor centre to the viewing platforms. The park has a harsh climate, with an average rainfall of just 124mm and summer temperatures that can reach 46°C.

The falls are of course the main draw, but the 500-sq-km park also offers little-known wildlife-watching opportunities. The park's 49 mammal species include giraffes, various antelope, African clawless otters and endangered Hartmann's mountain zebras. You're less likely to spot predators, but caracals, black-backed jackals and African wild cats all roam here.

Activities

The road to the rest camp and the main lookout over the falls is tarred and you can easily reach the viewpoints at Ararat and Oranjekom in a 2WD. If you take it slowly, you can explore further without a 4WD, though you'll need one to complete the 94km-long Wilderness Road. Call in advance to check the state of the roads as heavy rains can cause havoc.

Two-hour guided night drives are available – book ahead directly with the park.

Kalahari Outventures RAFTING, CANOEING (☑082 476 8213; www.kalahari-adventures.co.za; Augrabies; half-day rafting trip R450) The flagship rafting trip, Augrabies Rush, is a half-day tour taking in Grade II and Grade III rapids on a 9km section of the Gariep (Orange) River, finishing 300m above the main falls. Overnight and multiday river expeditions are also offered, as are hot-air balloon rides and wildlife-watching trips.

Hiking

The 36km Klipspringer Trail (☑central reservations 012-428 9111; reservations@sanparks.org; per person R590; ☺Apr–mid-Oct) is very popular and must be booked in advance. If you'd like a shorter walk there's the Gorge Trail (2km), the Ebony Trail (2.8km) and the Dassie Trail (5km).

🍽 Sleeping & Eating

There is a restaurant (open 7am to 8pm) at the main camp, offering a decent selection of dishes. There's also a shop here, which will do if you forgot to buy supplies en route to the park.

Augrabies Rest Camp CHALET, CAMPGROUND $$ (☑054-452 9200; www.sanparks.org/parks/augrabies/; camping R260, chalets/cottages from R975/1890; P❋☀) Within the park and close enough to the falls to hear them after rains, the rest camp has self-catering chalets, two-bedroom cottages and a campsite with shared ablutions. Best of all you can visit the falls after dark when they're beautifully floodlit.

Augrabies Falls Lodge & Camp HOTEL $$ (☑054-451 7203; www.augrabieslodge.co.za; Rte 359; camping per site R285, s/d R535/790; P❋) One of a number of sleeping options on the road to the park (8.5km from the park gate), this 1950s building has a modernised interior that is adorned with African art. The spacious rooms have pleasant furnishings and balconies with views across the

---

❶ AUGRABIES FALLS NATIONAL PARK

Why Go Thundering waterfalls; hikes into rugged, otherworldly scenery; uncrowded wildlife drives; gentle river rafting outside the park.

When to Go Spring (March to May) is perfect: the falls are at their most impressive from January but high temperatures make hiking uncomfortable until March. Winter (June to August) nights can be freezing.

Practicalities Your own transport is best; alternatively, get a tour from Upington or Kakamas. Gates are open from 7am to 6.30pm, but late check-ins can be arranged. A well-stocked shop sells basic groceries, alcoholic drinks and firewood.

Budget Tips Park highlights can be seen in a day, so consider staying outside to save on a second day's entrance fees.

countryside. There's a **restaurant** (mains R90 to R190), a bar and a four-person self-catering room (R895).

★ **Gorge Cottage** APARTMENT **$$$**
(d R1715) More a modern studio apartment than a cottage, this is the park's newest and most sought after accommodation. It sits beneath a lookout point over the Oranjekom Gorge, 10km from the main camp. Once the park gates close, you have the magnificent vista – and the soundtrack of birdsong and rushing water – all to yourself.

❶ Getting There & Away

The park is 39km northwest of Kakamas; head west on the N14 for 8km, then northwest on Rte 359.

Shared taxis do pass by the approach road – but you'll then have to walk the remaining 3km to the gate. The park can also be explored by mountain bike.

Riemvasmaak

📞 054 / POP 700

If you're looking for real off-the-beaten-track adventure, this remote village – located in 74 sq km of harsh lunar landscape – will deliver. There are three challenging 4WD trails (41km, 49km and 79km), and activities including hiking, mountain biking (bring your own bike) and birdwatching, plus there's Riemvasmaak's crowning glory, its **hot springs** (adult/child R25/15; ⏱ 8am-5pm). Just beyond the village is the rough and rocky Molopo River gorge.

In 1973 the apartheid government removed the local Xhosa and Nama communities, relocating them to the Eastern Cape and Namibia, respectively, in order to turn this land into a military training camp. Following South Africa's transition to democracy in 1994, the government began a massive effort to return the local population to Riemvasmaak. In 2002 the formerly displaced residents were given plots of land.

Relying on self-sustainable farming, Riemvasmaak remains a poor village, and donkey carts are still a crucial mode of transport across the cracked expanse of frosted orange rock and sand. Unemployment rates are astronomical and community tourism projects offer an important, if sporadic, means of income.

Contact Clarissa Damara at the **Riemvasmaak Community Centre** (📞 083 873 7715) to book activities, accommodation and guides. Don't just rock up in Riemvasmaak on a whim – everything must be booked in advance.

Perched on a hillside overlooking the gorge, there are **chalets** (4 people R525) equipped with bedding, towels and kitchen equipment. Water for the showers comes straight from the spring but you need to bring your own drinking water. There are also campsites (per site R135) along the hiking trails. Book through the community centre.

❶ Getting There & Away

There are two routes to Riemvasmaak from the south. Although the western route, which follows the Augrabies road, is largely tarred, past the national park the road condition becomes terrible and a 4WD is required. If you're in a 2WD, opt for the turn-off 2km east of Kakamas. The first 3km is tarred and while the next 40km is gravel, it's a good road that's doable in a 2WD in all but the wettest of weather. The last 6km to the village is tarred, providing a sort of red carpet as you approach this movie-set-like place.

NAMAKWA & THE HANTAM KAROO

A land of immense skies and stark countryside, rugged Namakwa and the Hantam Karoo are truly South Africa's Wild West. The roads seemingly stretch forever through vast, empty spaces, and scorching days lead to dramatically quiet and still nights, when the stars appear bigger and brighter than anywhere else. From exploring the misty shipwrecked diamond coastline on the country's far western edge to four-wheel driving through the Mars-like landscape of remote |Ai-|Ais/Richtersveld Transfrontier Park, the pleasures here are simple yet flabbergasting.

Namakwa and the Hantam Karoo are proficient magicians, who perform their favourite trick each spring, shaking off winter's bite with an explosion of colour and covering the sunbaked desert in a spectacular, multihued wildflower blanket. The name Hantam actually means 'mountain where the red edible flowers bloom' in Khoi-Khoi. The Namakwa region takes its name from the Nama (also known as Namkwa or Namaqua, which means 'Nama people'), a Khoekhoen tribe.

WILDFLOWERS OF NAMAKWA

For most of the year Namakwa appears an inhospitable desert, where nothing but the hardiest shrubs can survive. But winter rains transform the dry landscape into a kaleidoscope of colours, as daisies, herbs, aloes, lilies and numerous other indigenous flower species blanket the ground. About 4000 species of plant grow in the region, drawing visitors from around the world to this often-forgotten corner of South Africa each spring.

The quality of the bloom and the optimum time to visit are dependent on the rains and vary from year to year. Generally, you have the best chance of catching the flowers at their peak between mid-August and mid-September (sometimes the season can begin early in August and extend to mid-October). The best flower areas also change from year to year, so be sure to get local advice on where to go – the local authorities man a Flower Hotline (079 294 7260) in season.

Most varieties of wildflower are protected by law, and you can incur heavy fines if you pick them.

Springbok

027 / POP 12,800

Springbok sits in a valley surrounded by harsh rocky hills that turn into a rainbow tapestry during the spring wildflower season. When the flowers aren't blooming, the town's remoteness, desolate landscape and 300-plus days of sunshine still make it a pleasant enough place to stop for resupplying or for resting up before continuing your journey.

Its convenience lies in the fact that this once edgy frontier town has grown into a busy service centre for Namakwa's copper and diamond mines, as well as for farmers from remote outlying areas. It's located 120km south of the Vioolsdrif crossing to Namibia, from where it is about 800km to Windhoek.

Sights & Activities

The route to Nababeep, 16km northwest of Springbok via the N7, passes through prime flower-viewing territory in season. If you want to stretch your legs, the Nababeep Mining Museum (Nababeep; R10; 9am-1pm Mon-Fri) is worth a quick look. For info on heading further into the wilds, pick up a leaflet covering the multiday Namakwa 4WD Trail from Springbok tourist office (p466). Permits are required and camping is possible. Richtersveld Challenge, based at Cat Nap Accommodation, hires out 4WD vehicles.

Goegap Nature Reserve NATURE RESERVE
(027-718 9906; R30; 7.30am-4pm; P) This 150-sq-km semidesert reserve, 8km east of Springbok past the airstrip, supports some 600 indigenous plant species, 45 mammal

species and 94 types of bird. It is one of the best places in the region to take a walk during flower season, with circular 4km and 7km hiking trails. There is a 13km circuit for cars and trails for 4WD vehicles, and accommodation is available in basic four-bed huts (R160) and campsites (R90).

Sleeping

During the flower season, accommodation in Springbok fills up and rates rise.

Cat Nap Accommodation HOSTEL $
(027-718 1905; catnap@mweb.co.za; 99 Voortrekker St; dm/s/d R200/400/650;) The walls of this spacious old house are adorned with nature photos, and rooms are cosy, African-themed affairs. There's a self-catering kitchen and dorm beds in the barn, although they're incredibly close together and it gets hot in summer.

Five-day trips into the Richtersveld can be arranged (from R7000 per person), and it also rents out 4WD vehicles (from R1200 per day).

Kliprand Guesthouse GUESTHOUSE $$
(027-712 2604; 2 King St; s/d incl breakfast from R700/1100; P) A friendly place in a quiet side street close to Springbok's top restaurant. Rooms are bright and cosy and there's a large swimming pool in the garden.

Annie's Cottage GUESTHOUSE $$
(027-712 1451; www.anniescottage.co.za; 4 King St; s/d incl breakfast R1050/1350; P) The ornate bedrooms are cutesy in places, but the Afro-themed rooms are fun; you can also request the honeymoon suite at no extra cost. Afternoon tea and cake are served and there is a self-catering room in the garden.

Mountain View GUESTHOUSE $$

(☎027-712 1438; www.mountview.co.za; 2 Overberg Ave; s/d incl breakfast R880/990; ☀☎�) Perched in a tranquil location up against the hills, this guesthouse has pleasant, cool rooms. Some open onto a garden leading to the pool, which has wonderful views.

Naries Namakwa Retreat LODGE $$$

(☎027-712 2462; www.naries.co.za; Rte 355; s/d with half board R1830/2430, s/d ste with full board R2875/3840; ℗) This graceful lodge is the most upmarket place to stay in the area, with large rooms in the manor house, spacious self-catering cottages (from R1850) and elegant mountaintop suites modelled on traditional Nama huts. The accommodation is spread out across the hilltops some 27km west of Springbok.

✗ Eating

★ Tauren Steak Ranch STEAK $$

(☎027-712 2717; 2 Hospital St; mains R70-180; ⏰noon-late Mon-Sat) Meat-lovers rejoice: Tauren serves steaks weighing up to a kilogram, with a host of delectable sauces. The menu also features burgers, a few vegetarian choices and pizzas with toppings including biltong and boerewors (farmer's sausage). The ambience is country-relaxed, with *boeremusiek* on the stereo and the happy hum of content diners in the air.

Herb Garden CAFE $$

(☎027-712 1247; www.herb-garden.co.za; cnr Kruis & Voortrekker Rds; mains R60-110; ⏰8am-10pm Mon-Sat, to 3pm Sun; ☎☐) For breakfast, brunch or lunch, your best bet is this cafe tucked away behind a plant nursery. There are salads, sandwiches and burgers on offer, plus more substantial meals in the evening. The coffee is decent and the service cheery.

Pot & Barrell PUB FOOD $$

(☎027-718 1475; 39 Voortrekker St; mains R70-145; ⏰8am-late Mon-Sat, 11am-10pm Sun) Serves basic pub grub such as burgers and snack baskets and has a decent beer selection.

ℹ Information

Tourist Office (☎027-712 8035; www.namakwa-dm.gov.za; Voortrekker St; ⏰8am-4.15pm Mon-Thu, to 3pm Fri) Has some maps and info on southern Namibia as well as Namakwa.

ℹ Getting There & Away

Overnight buses, including **Intercape** (☎021-380 4400; www.intercape.co.za), serve Cape Town (R500, nine hours) and Windhoek, Namibia (R1150, 13 hours). Buses leave from the Engen garage on Voortrekker St.

Shared taxis serve Upington (R300, four hours), Port Nolloth (R130, two hours) and Cape Town (R450, nine hours). Contact the **Namakwaland Taxi Association** (Van der Stel St) for bookings.

Port Nolloth

☎027 / POP 6100

Way off the beaten path near South Africa's northwest corner, the exposed and sandy little nowhere town of Port Nolloth exudes raw, final-frontier vitality. The bracing air smells of fish and salt, and the town is home to a motley, multicultural group of runaways, holidaymakers and fortune-seekers. The drive alone justifies a visit to this remote seaside town – one minute you're engulfed in nothingness, covered in a layer of red Kalahari sand; the next, you're cresting a hill, watching the icy blue vastness of the Atlantic appear on the horizon.

Established as the shipping point for the region's copper, Port Nolloth is now dependent on the diamond dredgers and crayfish trawlers that gather at its small commercial pier. The dredgers are fitted with pumps, which vacuum diamond-bearing gravel from the ocean floor.

Despite the De Beers complex standing guard, glittery catches do sometimes go astray. However, buying a diamond on the black market is not recommended – pitfalls include slenters (fake diamonds cut from lead crystal) and undercover police officers.

There are ATMs on Beach Rd.

◎ Sights

When we visited, a new section of the Richtersveld National Park was in progress some 20km from Port Nolloth.

Port Nolloth Museum MUSEUM

(Beach Rd; R20; ⏰10am-3pm) A ramshackle and well-loved little museum covering the region's diamond industry. The hotchpotch of exhibits is interesting enough but it's a chat with curator George Moyses that really makes this place shine. A diamond diver for decades, George has plenty of local tales to tell and is a useful source for tourist information since the town lacks an office.

🛏 Sleeping & Eating

⭐ **Scotia Inn Hotel & Restaurant** HOTEL **$$**
(☑ 027-851 8353; www.scotiainnhotel.co.za; Beach Rd; s/d from R450/700; 🛜🐕) There are standard rooms on the ground floor and bright, modern deluxe rooms (single/double R550/850) upstairs, some with huge sea-facing balconies. Request an ocean view – there's no extra fee. Also has a bar-restaurant (mains R65 to R170) serving breakfast, lunch and dinner.

Bedrock Lodge GUESTHOUSE **$$**
(☑ 027-851 8865; www.bedrocklodge.co.za; Beach Rd; s/d incl breakfast from R660/970, s/d cottage R590/840; 🛜🐕) Based in one of Port Nolloth's oldest buildings, Bedrock is a quirky place crammed with all sorts of eccentric knick-knacks and antique collectables. It's right on the seafront, with ocean views through the windows in its corrugated iron facade. There are six nautical-chic self-catering cottages nearby, though most don't boast quite such a marvellous view.

Buttercup Coffee Shop & Bakery CAFE **$**
(☑ 084 706 6959; www.thebuttercup.co.za; Main Rd; mains R25-65; ⊗9am-6pm Mon-Sat) There's decent coffee at this cavernous place a short walk from the ocean. You'll also find home-baked cakes, waffles with sweet and savoury toppings and sandwiches – try the *bobotie*-filled jaffle (a kind of toasted sandwich filled with delicately curried mince).

Vespetti ITALIAN **$$**
(☑ 027-851 7843; 2099 Beach Rd; mains R85-150; ⊗10am-9pm Mon-Sat, to 3pm Sun) This Italian restaurant, its awning twined with fishing rope, serves seafood as well as pizza and pasta. It's a marvellous place to watch the sun dip into the Atlantic with a frosty one in hand, but you'll need to pop to the local liquor store first as the restaurant is un-licensed. There's a small corkage fee.

🛈 Getting There & Away

Namakwaland Taxi Association (☑ 027-718 2840) runs shared taxis to/from Springbok (R130, two hours, Monday to Saturday).

|Ai-|Ais/Richtersveld Transfrontier Park

Sculpted by millions of years of harsh elemental exposure, South Africa's most remote **national park** (☑ 027-831 1506; www.sanparks.org/parks/richtersveld/; adult/child R230/115;

⊗7am-7pm Oct-Apr, to 6pm May-Sep) is a seemingly barren wilderness of lava rocks, human-like trees and sandy moonscapes studded with semiprecious stones. The 6000 sq km of surreal mountain desert joins South Africa's Richtersveld National Park with Namibia's |Ai-|Ais Hot Springs Game Park.

Accessible only by 4WD, the Richtersveld is South Africa's final wild frontier. The South African section of the park covers 1850 sq km, and is most beautiful during the spring wildflower season, when, like elsewhere in Namakwa, it turns into a technicolour wonderland. Hiking here is demanding but spectacular – trails traverse jagged peaks, grotesque rock formations, deep ravines and gorges. This is a place for those who seek to wander way off the beaten track and even those who crave a little survivalist action. There are almost no facilities so you need to be completely self-sufficient.

🏃 Activities

There are three hiking trails on the South African side, open from April to September. **Ventersval** (four days, three nights) encompasses the southwestern wilderness; **Lelieshoek-Oemsberg** (three days, two nights) takes in a huge amphitheatre and waterfall; and **Kodaspiek** (two days, one night) allows the average walker to view mountain desert scenery. It's recommended to hike with a guide.

🚗 Tours

The easiest way to visit the park is on a tour. Accommodation is normally camping, with equipment provided. Tours can be organised in Port Nolloth, Springbok and Upington. Try Richtersveld Challenge, based at Cat Nap Accommodation (p465) in Springbok, or Richtersveld Tours in Port Nolloth.

Richtersveld Tours TOURS
(☑ 082 335 1399; www.richtersveldtours.com; per day from R1950) Johan De Waal runs tailored tours to the Richtersveld region, lasting a minimum of three days. His passion for the region is utterly infectious as he explains the history, botany and geology of the Richtersveld. As well as exploring the national park, tours visit a number of community tourism enterprises.

🛏 Sleeping

There are four rustic campsites (per site from R240) in the park. All have toilets, some have showers and none have hot water.

ⓘ |AI-|AIS/RICHTERSVELD TRANSFRONTIER PARK

Why Go Challenging 4WD terrain; remote, offbeat adventure; wilderness hiking; craggy desert landscapes; far-flung birdwatching; endless photography opportunities.

When to Go August to October, when temperatures are cooler and the flowers are in bloom. November to February is excruciatingly hot.

Practicalities Drive in from Alexander Bay. Basic facilities include a petrol station (open 7.30am to 4pm), small general store and public phone at Sendelingsdrift. Bring all food and drinking water and ideally drive in convoy. Book all tours and accommodation in advance.

Budget Tips Due to its remoteness, the park isn't ideal for budget travellers. Renting a 4WD and camping is the cheapest option.

★ **Tatasberg Wilderness Camp**   CABIN $$
(d cabins from R855) The delightful cabins at this camp each have a covered deck with magnificent views over the Gariep (Orange) River. Made from corrugated tin, reed and canvas, they have a striking, rustic feel that blends perfectly with the park's scenery. Each has two single beds, a fridge, a gas stove and a shower.

Gannakouriep   CABIN $$
(d cabins from R855) Staying in these stone-and-canvas cabins is like upmarket camping. Great efforts have been made to showcase the camp's magnificent setting in a rocky valley. Each cabin comes with two beds, a gas stove and a solar-powered fridge. You need to bring your own drinking water.

Sendelingsdrift   CAMPGROUND, CHALET $$
(camping R240, d chalets from R855; ❋ ⌨) The two- to four-bed self-catering chalets at the park entrance are surprisingly comfortable, with porches overlooking the river. And you'll be glad of the air-con if you dare to visit in summer.

ⓘ Getting There & Around

A tar road leads 82km from Port Nolloth to Alexander Bay, from where a 90km gravel road leads to Sendelingsdrift Gate. This section is just about passable in a car but there's no point driving here in a 2WD as you need a 4WD vehicle in the park – sedans are not permitted. You can hire a 4WD and buy a decent map in Springbok – ask at the tourist office.

You can cross the Gariep (Orange) River into Namibia on a pontoon at Sendelingsdrift; it operates from 8am to 4.15pm, weather permitting.

It's highly recommended that you travel in convoy as the harsh terrain is challenging even for experienced 4WD drivers. Day visits are impractical considering the park's remoteness – you need at least three days, and preferably closer to a week.

Namaqua National Park

Flower-seekers flock to this small, remote park (☏ 027-672 1948; www.sanparks.org/parks/namaqua/; adult/child R80/40; ⊘ 8am-5pm) each spring, when the shrub land and old wheat fields are transformed by the spectacle that is the wildflower bloom. There are short nature trails and drives with viewpoints – the park is one of the best places in Namakwa to photograph the flowers.

For the rest of the year, the 1030 sq km is largely forgotten, although that does make it a peaceful place for a hike. It's also a decent birdwatching destination.

Accommodation in the park is limited and in great demand during August and September, so you need to book as soon as reservations open – usually 11 months ahead. There are basic coastal campsites, chalets and, during flower season, an incredibly popular **tented camp** (s/d tent incl breakfast, high tea & dinner R3375/4500).

Search as well in the nearby towns of Kamieskroon and Garies, desolate places sitting amid the tumbleweed and scrub brush that characterises the Namakwa region.

The park is 20km west of Kamieskroon along a gravel road. The road is in good condition and can easily be driven in a 2WD. Once inside the park, there is a 5km circular drive suited to sedan vehicles, but for everything else you will need a 4WD. If you're staying at one of the coastal campsites, it's better to take the 67km gravel road from Garies. The road is perfectly passable in a sedan vehicle, but you'll need a 4WD – or a sturdy set of hiking boots – to travel much further than the gate.

Intercape (p466) buses stop in Kamieskroon en route to/from Springbok, 67km north on the N7.

Calvinia

⏲ 027 / POP 9700

At the base of the dolerite-covered Hantam Mountains, hundreds of miles from anywhere, is this remote outback town with laid-back charm. Home to blazing bright light during the day, clear skies at night, quaint white-stone buildings and tree-lined streets, Calvinia is the principal town in this sheep-farming region. It's quiet for most of the year but when the rocky countryside blooms in spring, nearly all of the year's tourists arrive in one frenetic burst.

◉ Sights & Activities

There are some fantastic 4WD routes around the surrounding countryside. One of the prettiest is the unpaved Rte 364, which leads southwest to Clanwilliam and the Cederberg via several stunning passes, including the Pakhuis Pass. Ask at the tourist office for access to the Hantam Flower 4WD Route, which traverses an escarpment north of town.

Republic of Rustica GALLERY
(⏲ 027-341 1423; 37 Stigling St; ⊘9am-4pm) Stop at this 'rustic art' emporium to marvel at owner Dirk's collection of found objects, vintage gear and general junk. Road signs, sheep skulls, tin cups, watering cans, bed pans, old shoes, bicycles and farm implements decorate the exterior, and there's an old-school cinema inside. There are five quirkily decorated guest rooms (double from R500 per person) and meals are available for overnight guests.

Calvinia Museum MUSEUM
(⏲ 027-341 1043; 44 Kerk St; entry by donation; ⊘8am-1pm & 2-5pm Mon-Fri) Housed in a former synagogue, this museum is surprisingly large and interesting for a small town. It concentrates on the white settlement of the region, with a section devoted to sheep farming, and has exhibits ranging from Victorian garb to the local telephone exchange switchboard, used until 1991.

Akkerendam Nature Reserve NATURE RESERVE
(⏲ 027-341 8500; Hospitaal St; ⊘8am-7pm; 🅿) FREE North of town, this 275-sq-km reserve has one- and two-day hiking trails. The best time to visit is spring, when the wildflower bloom carpets the mountainous terrain. Head to the **municipal office** (20 Hoof St; ⊘8.30am-3.30pm Mon-Fri) for hiking permits.

✦ Festivals & Events

AfrikaBurn CULTURAL
(www.afrikaburn.com; ⊘Apr) The subcultural survivalist blowout happens about 100km south of Calvinia, off Rte 355 (untarred) to Ceres, near Tweefontein and the Tankwa Karoo National Park. It's a weeklong event, usually taking place in late April.

🛏 Sleeping & Eating

Book well ahead if you plan to visit during the wildflower season as the town's guesthouses fill up quickly.

Die Blou Nartjie GUESTHOUSE $
(⏲ 027-341 1263; www.nartjie.co.za; 35 Water St; s/d incl breakfast R495/710; 🅿❄🌊🐾) At the end of a long, hot day of Northern Cape driving, the garden rooms here are a nice, cool place to relax. There are braai facilities or the restaurant (mains R75 to R135; open 6.30pm to 9.30pm Monday to Saturday) serves traditional tucker such as *bobotie* and Karoo lamb chops.

Hantam Huis GUESTHOUSE $$
(⏲ 027-341 1606; www.calvinia.co.za; 42 Hoop St; s/d incl breakfast from R495/790; ❄🛜) Occupying a series of beautifully restored townhouses, Hantam is the perfect place to soak up Calvinia's country quiet and old-world charm. Die Dorphuis, a Victorian national monument, has luxury rooms packed with antiques. At the rear of the townhouse are cosy standard options in former servants' quarters and rooms once used by visiting church congregation members; Knegtekamer is particularly cute.

Three-course dinners are offered in the 19th-century Hantam Huis itself – Calvinia's oldest house. The restaurant is also open to nonguests from 7am to 4.30pm.

African Dawn B&B $$
(⏲ 084 919 3194; www.calviniaretreat.co.za; 17 Strauss Ave; r incl breakfast from R750; 🅿❄🛜) Set in a pretty garden, this is a peaceful place on the edge of town with just three rooms. Each is decked out in neutral shades with paintings and photos of local flora on the walls. Breakfast is served in a *lapa* (an 'African gazebo'), and the **coffee shop** (mains R55-95; ⊘9am-5pm Mon-Fri & 9am-2pm Sat) serves toasted sandwiches, burgers and light meals.

❶ Getting There & Away

The fastest and easiest route from Cape Town is via the N7 and Rte 27, which climbs the scenic Vanrhyns Pass to Calvinia, then runs northeast to Keimos and Upington. Rte 63 leads east from Calvinia to Victoria West via the pretty Karoo towns of Williston, Carnarvon and Loxton. There is no public transport to Calvinia.

Sutherland

023 / POP 2800

Surrounded by the Roggeveld Mountains, Sutherland is an attractive Karoo *dorp* (village) with sandstone houses, a 19th-century church and gravel side streets. Perched at about 1500m above sea level, it's the coldest place in South Africa and snow carpets the ground every year. The clear skies combined with the minimal light pollution found in Sutherland's remote position make the area perfect for stargazing. The boffins agree: SALT (Southern African Large Telescope), the southern hemisphere's largest single optical telescope, is 14km east of town.

Other than stargazing, there's a 145km self-drive botanical tour, covering both the Roggeveld and lower Tankwa Karoo. The area enjoys an annual wildflower bloom similar to the one that carpets nearby Namakwa.

Sights & Activities

South African
Astronomical Observatory   OBSERVATORY
(023-571 2436; www.saao.ac.za; Rte 356; night tour adult/child R80/40, day tour per person R60; night tour Mon, Wed, Fri & Sat, day tour 10.30am & 2.30pm Mon-Sat;) During the day you can take a guided tour of the huge research telescopes, including the Southern African Large Telescope, but it's the two-hour night tours that are the real draw. After a short video, you head outside to take a sky safari, thanks to two 16in telescopes. Times vary depending on the time of year and bookings are essential. Dress *very* warmly, even in summer.

Tankwa Karoo National Park   PARK
(027-341 1927; www.sanparks.org/parks/tankwa; adult/child R160/80) With a car with good clearance, you can access this 1430-sq-km

park, where Tankwa desert moonscapes meet sheer Roggeveld cliffs. There's great birdwatching, and accommodation is available in the form of campsites, cottages or a wilderness camp with private plunge pools. It's about 120km west of Sutherland.

Sterland Stargazing   OUTDOORS
(023-571 1481; www.sutherlandinfo.co.za; Rte 354, Sterland Caravan Park; stargazing R100) Jurg Wagener's nightly stargazing evenings, on which he reveals the secrets of the Milky Way and beyond with the help of a laser pointer and five powerful telescopes, are highly recommended.

Sleeping & Eating

Sterland
Guesthouses   GUESTHOUSE, CAMPING $$
(023-571 1481; www.sutherlandinfo.co.za; camping R100, d cottage from R790) Jurg and Rita run several cottages around town as well as a caravan park where nightly stargazing evenings take place. The cute 'honeymoon suite' in a cottage on the edge of town is recommended.

Cluster d'Hote   SOUTH AFRICAN $$
(023-571 1436; www.clusterdhote.co.za; Piet Retief St; mains R100-150; 6-10pm) Based in one of the town's oldest houses, Sutherland's best restaurant is cosy, tiny and very popular, so bookings are essential. The menu – like others hereabouts – has a meaty focus, particularly Karoo lamb.

Getting There & Away

There is no public transport to Sutherland and the only tarred road is Rte 354 from Matjiesfontein, 110km south. There are gravel roads from Calvinia and Loxton (via Fraserburg). Contact your accommodation for an update on the state of the gravel roads, which deteriorate in the rain. The town's petrol station keeps short hours – fill up before you set out for Sutherland.

Lesotho

Best Places to Eat

➜ Maliba Lodge (p485)

➜ No.7 Restaurant (p478)

➜ Sky Restaurant (Oxbow; p486)

➜ Semonkong Lodge (p490)

➜ Sky Restaurant (Maseru; p478)

Best Places to Stay

➜ Malealea Lodge (p491)

➜ Maliba Lodge (p484)

➜ Semonkong Lodge (p490)

➜ Sani Mountain Lodge (p487)

➜ Mpilo Boutique Hotel (p478)

Why Go?

Beautiful, culturally rich, affordable and easily accessible from Durban and Johannesburg, mountainous Lesotho (le-*soo*-too) is a vastly underrated travel destination. The contrast with South Africa could not be more striking, with the Basotho people's distinct personality and the altitudinous terrain's topographical extremes. Even a few days in Lesotho's hospitable mountain lodges and trading posts will give you a fresh perspective on Southern Africa.

This is essentially an alpine country, where villagers on horseback in multicoloured balaclavas and blankets greet you round precipitous bends. The hiking and trekking – often on a famed Basotho pony – is world class, offering undulating expanses of pastoral charm, traditional rondavels (round huts with a conical roof) and innumerable grazing sheep.

The 1000m-high 'lowlands' offer craft shopping and sights, but don't miss a trip to the southern, central or northeastern highlands, where streams traverse an ancient dinosaur playground. This is genuine adventure travel.

When to Go
Maseru

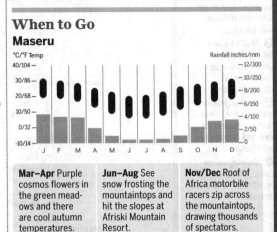

Mar–Apr Purple cosmos flowers in the green meadows and there are cool autumn temperatures.

Jun–Aug See snow frosting the mountaintops and hit the slopes at Afriski Mountain Resort.

Nov/Dec Roof of Africa motorbike racers zip across the mountaintops, drawing thousands of spectators.

Lesotho Highlights

1 **Ts'ehlanyane National Park** (p484)
Horse riding or hiking through breathtaking indigenous forest, and resting well at Maliba Lodge.

2 **Maletsunyane Falls** (p490)
Conquering the world's highest commercial abseil, bragging about it on a donkey pub crawl and sleeping in a rondavel at Semonkong Lodge.

3 **Malealea** (p491)
Staying in the former trading post Malealea Lodge for mountain views, pony treks and authentic village life.

4 **Sani Top** (p487)
Raising a glass of brandy at Southern Africa's highest pub, Sani Mountain Lodge, perched atop the infamous Sani Pass.

5 **Katse Dam** (p489)
Admiring feats of aquatic engineering.

6 **Sehlabathebe National Park** (p493)
Finding rugged isolation and centuries-old San cave paintings.

7 **Mafika-Lisiu** (p488)
Seeing forever from atop a 3000m-plus mountain pass.

8 **Leribe (Hlotse)** (p483)
Discovering dinosaur footprints here and in Quthing and Morija.

9 **Teyateyaneng** (p482)
Shopping for tapestries in this craft capital.

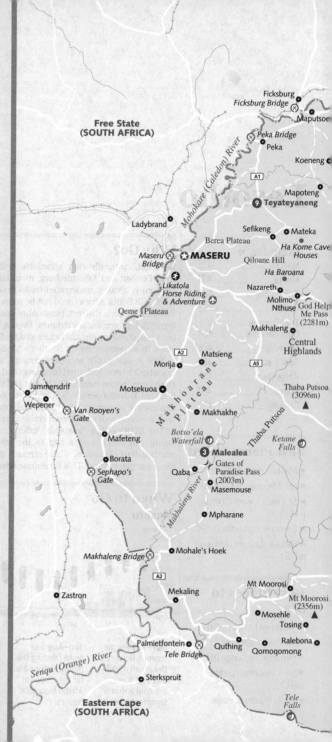

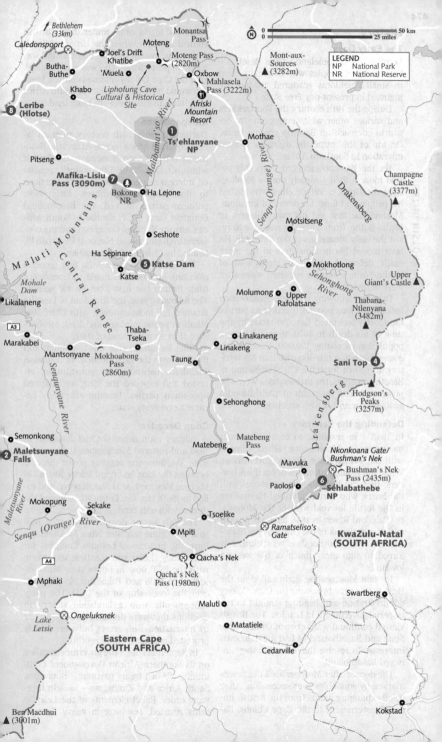

Bethlehem
(33km)

Caledonspoort

Butha-
Buthe

Khabo

**Leribe
(Hlotse)** 8

Pitseng

**Mafika-Lisiu
Pass (3090m)** 7

Bokong
NR

Ha Lejone

Seshote

Ha Sepinare

Katse Dam 5

Katse

*Mohale
Dam*

Likalaneng

Marakabei

Mantsonyane

Mokhoabong
Pass
(2860m)

Thaba-
Tseka

Senqunyane River

Semonkong

**Maletsunyane
Falls** 2

Mokopung

Sekake

Mpiti

Mphaki

Maletsunyane River

Senqu (Orange) River

*Lake
Letsie*

Ongeluksnek

**Eastern Cape
(SOUTH AFRICA)**

Ben Macdhui
(3001m)

Joel's Drift
Khatibe

'Muela

*Liphofung Cave
Cultural & Historical
Site*

Malibamat'so River

Moteng

Monantsa
Pass

Moteng Pass
(2820m)

Oxbow

Mahlasela
Pass (3222m)

*Afriski
Mountain
Resort*

**Ts'ehlanyane
NP** 1

Mothae

Mont-aux-
Sources
(3282m) ▲

Sengu (Orange) River

Motsitseng

Mokhotlong

*Sehonghong
River*

Molumong

Upper
Rafolatsane

Linakaneng

Linakeng

Taung

Sehonghong

Matebeng

Matebeng
Pass

Mavuka

Paolosi

Tsoelike

Qacha's Nek

Qacha's Nek
Pass (1980m)

Maluti

Matatiele

Cedarville

Champagne
Castle
(3377m) ▲

Drakensberg

Upper
Giant's Castle ▲

Thabana-
Ntlenyana
(3482m) ▲

Sani Top 4

Hodgson's
Peaks
(3257m)

*Nkonkoana Gate/
Bushman's Nek*

Bushman's Nek
Pass (2435m)

**Sehlabathebe
NP** 6

**KwaZulu-Natal
(SOUTH AFRICA)**

Ramatseliso's
Gate

Swartberg

Kokstad

LEGEND
NP   National Park
NR   National Reserve

0   50 km
0   25 miles

N

Maluti Mountains

Central Range

A3

A4

History

The Early Days

Lesotho is the homeland of the Basotho – Sotho-Tswana peoples who originally lived in small chiefdoms scattered around the highveld in present-day Free State.

During the 19th century, the Voortrekkers and various other white entrepreneurs began to encroach on Basotho grazing lands. On top of this came the *difaqane* (forced migration in Southern Africa).

Yet the Basotho emerged from this period more united – largely due to Moshoeshoe the Great, a village chief who rallied his people and forged a powerful kingdom. Moshoeshoe first led his own villagers to Butha-Buthe, from where he was able to resist the early incursions of the *difaqane*. He later moved his headquarters to the more easily defended mountain stronghold of Thaba-Bosiu, where he repulsed wave after wave of invaders.

Over the following decades, Moshoeshoe brought various peoples together as part of the loosely federated Basotho state; by the time of his death in 1870, it would have a population exceeding 150,000. He also welcomed Christian missionaries into his territory. In return for some Christianisation of Basotho customs, the missionaries were disposed to defend the rights of 'their' Basotho against Boer and British expansion.

Defending the Territory

In 1843 – in response to continuing Boer incursions – Moshoeshoe allied himself with the British Cape Colony government. While the resulting treaties defined his borders, they did little to stop squabbles with the Boers, who had established themselves in the fertile lowveld west of the Mohokare (Caledon) River. In 1858 tensions peaked with the outbreak of the Orange Free State–Basotho War. Moshoeshoe was ultimately forced to sign away much of his western lowlands.

In 1868 Moshoeshoe again called on the British, this time bypassing the Cape Colony administration and heading straight to the imperial government in London. The British viewed continual war between Orange Free State and Basotholand as bad for their own interests. To resolve the situation, they annexed Basotholand.

The decade after Moshoeshoe's death was marked by squabbles over succession. After briefly changing hands from the British imperial government to the Cape Colony, Ba-sotholand again came under direct British control in 1884. When the Union of South Africa was created in 1910, Basotholand was a British protectorate and was not included. Had the Cape Colony retained control, Lesotho would have become part of South Africa and, later, an apartheid-era homeland.

Independence

During the early 20th century, migrant labour to South Africa increased and the Basotho gained greater autonomy under British administration. In 1955 the council requested internal self-government, with elections to determine its members. Meanwhile, political parties formed: the Basotholand Congress Party (BCP; similar to South Africa's African National Congress) and the conservative Basotholand National Party (BNP), headed by Chief Leabua Jonathan.

The BNP won Lesotho's first general elections in 1965 and made independence from Britain the first item on its agenda. The following year, the Kingdom of Lesotho attained full independence, with Chief Jonathan as prime minister and King Moshoeshoe II as nominal head of state.

Chief Jonathan's rule was unpopular and the BCP won the 1970 election. In response, Jonathan suspended the constitution, arrested and expelled the king, and banned opposition parties. Lesotho effectively became a one-party state.

Coup Decades

A military coup deposed Chief Jonathan in 1986 and restored Moshoeshoe II as head of state. Yet, following ongoing power disputes between the king and coup leader Justin Lekhanya, Moshoeshoe II was deposed and exiled in 1990. His son, Letsie III, assumed the throne, with only ceremonial powers, in 1992.

The '90s were a decade of unrest. A BCP split led prime minister Ntsu Mokhehle to form the breakaway Lesotho Congress for Democracy (LCD) and continue to govern, with the BCP now in opposition. Mokhehle died in 1998 and Pakalitha Mosisili took over the leadership of the LCD. The party subsequently won a landslide victory in elections that were declared reasonably fair by international observers but were widely protested against within Lesotho.

In September 1998 the government called on its Southern African Development Community (SADC) treaty partners – Botswana, South Africa and Zimbabwe – to help it restore order. Rebel elements of the Lesotho army resisted, resulting in heavy fighting and widespread looting in Maseru. The LCD won again in the 2002 elections, but opposition parties gained a significant number of seats.

In 2006, 17 LCD members led by Thomas Thabane, formed the breakaway All Basotho Convention (ABC) party. In the controversial 2007 elections, the LCD retained its majority and national strikes against the government ensued. A two-week curfew was imposed, there was an assassination attempt on Thabane and many people were detained and tortured. In 2009 there was an assassination attempt on Mosisili.

In the hotly contested 2012 elections, Thabane became prime minister after the ABC formed a coalition with other parties including the LCD. Lesotho teetered on the verge of another coup in 2014, when Thabane fled to South Africa, accusing the military of trying to overthrow him. Following SADC mediation, general elections took place in February 2015. Thabane's ABC lost narrowly and a coalition government of seven parties was headed by Mosisili's new party, the Democratic Congress. Mosisili is once again prime minister, with Mothetjoa Metsing of the LCD remaining deputy prime minister.

Climate

Clear, cold winters, with frosts and snow in the highlands, await you in Lesotho, so pack warm clothing. In summer (late November to early March), dramatic thunderstorms are common, as are all-enveloping clouds of thick mist. Summer temperatures can exceed 30°C in the valleys, though it's usually much cooler in the mountains, even dropping below freezing. Nearly all Lesotho's rain falls between October and April. Throughout the year, the weather is notoriously changeable. In 2017 it snowed in the middle of the summer.

Visits are possible at any time; autumn (especially March to April) and spring (especially September) are optimal.

Language

The official languages are Southern Sotho (SeSotho) and English. For more on Sotho language and culture, visit www.sesotho.web.za.

❶ Getting There & Around

Airlink (☑2235 0418; www.flyairlink.com; Moshoeshoe 1 International Airport; ☺6am-5pm Mon-Fri, 9am-5pm Sat & Sun) has daily flights between Johannesburg and Moshoeshoe I International Airport, 21km south of Maseru (from R1100, one hour).

However, it's cheaper to hire a car and drive in and out from South Africa. There are 13 border crossings with South Africa, and getting into Lesotho is generally a pleasant business. Queues at the main crossing **Maseru Bridge** (☺24hr), east of Bloemfontein, are sometimes very long exiting and, on some weekend evenings, entering Lesotho.

You can now access much of Lesotho in a 2WD car, but it is still not possible to do a complete circuit without a 4WD, due to rough gravel roads in the east between Mokhotlong and Qacha's Nek. Bus and shared-taxi networks cover the country; taxis do not normally operate to a schedule but leave only when full.

MASERU

POP 253,000 / ELEV 1600M

Maseru is one of the world's more low-key capital cities. It sprawls across Lesotho's lower-lying western edge, rimmed by the Berea and Qeme Plateaus. Founded by the British in 1869 as an administrative post, over the past few decades Maseru has rapidly expanded and its centre is now congested with traffic. A major city-rebuilding program has hidden many of the once-visible scars of the 1998 political unrest.

The city boasts a temperate climate, well-stocked shops and a decent selection of restaurants and accommodation. While it has few sights, Maseru is where you can get your bearings, sort out logistics and stock up on supplies before heading into the highlands and beyond.

🏃 Activities

Kick4Life FOOTBALL
(☑2832 0707; www.kick4life.org; Lesotho Football for Hope Centre, Nightingale Rd) Watch a game of five-a-side football (soccer) at this sport-focused NGO, which runs the world's first football club exclusively dedicated to social change. If you call ahead, you might be able to join the players for a kick about.

Likatola Horse Riding & Adventure HORSE RIDING
(☑5867 9013; adult/child per hour M80/40; ☺10am-8pm Sun & Tue-Thu, to 10pm Fri & Sat) The closest horse riding to the capital is just a 20-minute drive to the southwest, where rides of varying length take visitors past old sandstone homes and along the banks of the

Maseru

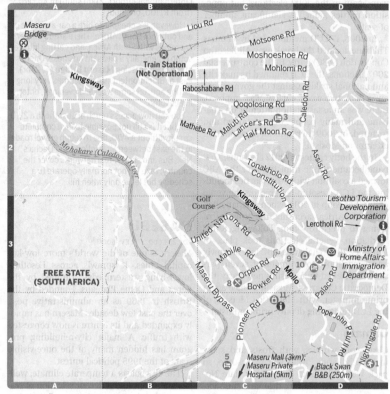

Phuthiatsana River, with a majestic mountain backdrop. Tours of historic villages and inside caves adorned in San paintings can also be arranged.

🛏 Sleeping

Shoeshoe Gardens B&B $
(📞 2232 4190; s/d incl breakfast M590/650; 🅿 🛜) With a savvy young owner and a prime spot near the Maseru Mall, this four-room B&B is on the rise (with plans to expand to include additional units in 2018). It's popular with the NGO set, offering plush rooms and sleek, modern bathrooms.

Foothills Guesthouse GUESTHOUSE $
(📞 5870 6566; www.foothills.co.ls; 121 Maluti Rd; s/d M500/600; 🅿 🛜) This comfortable and friendly suburban guesthouse is good value by Maseru standards. The eight garden rooms are plain and their bathrooms old, but two have a kitchenette. There's also

a self-catering kitchen and thatched *lapa* (a circular area with a fire pit) with braai. Breakfast costs M40.

Maseru Backpackers & Conference Centre HOSTEL $
(📞 2232 5166, 2700 5453; www.lesothodurhamlink.org; Airport Rd; camping/dm M100/180, Durham house dm/r M250/550; 🅿 🛜) Linked to a British Anglican NGO and run by locals, this hostel has sparse, clean four- to eight-bed dorms and four-bed dorms and private rooms in a six-bedroom house. A beautifully adorned, Basotho-style rondavel (M700), with a double, twin and lounge, is perfect for self-catering families, and right on Maqalika Reservoir.

The main reason to stay here is for the outdoor activities, including canoeing and kayaking on the reservoir, rock climbing, abseiling and archery. Meals are available with notice. It's 3km from the city centre; look for the 'Lesotho Durham Link' sign.

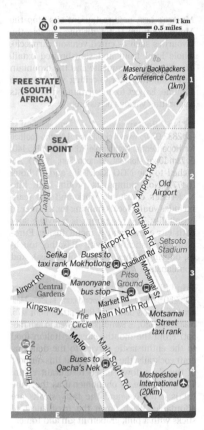

Maseru

⊙ Activities, Courses & Tours
1 Kick4Life...D4

⊜ Sleeping
2 Avani Lesotho Hotel & Casino............E4
3 Foothills Guesthouse C2
  Kick4Life Hotel & Conference
  Centre..(see 1)
4 Lancer's Inn..D3
5 Mohokare Guest House C4
6 Mpilo Boutique Hotel...........................C2

⊗ Eating
  No.7 Restaurant...............................(see 1)
7 Ouh La La D3
8 Piri Piri C3
  Renaissance Café ....(see 11)
  Rendezvous.....................................(see 4)
  Sky Restaurant...............................(see 6)

⊘ Drinking & Nightlife
  Lancer's Inn ....(see 4)

⊟ Shopping
9 Basotho Hat..C3
10 LNDC Centre.......................................D3
11 Pioneer Mall.......................................C4

hotel has renovated rooms with satellite TV and open bathroom, while garden paths meander to pleasant stone rondavels and self-catering chalets. The **Rendezvous** (mains M60-100; ⊙ 6.30am-11.30pm; 🛜) restaurant, bar and nearby travel agency make this a good package.

Mohokare Guest House   GUESTHOUSE **$$**
(📱 2231 4442; www.mohokare.co.ls; 260 Pioneer Rd; s/d incl breakfast from M515/685, luxury s/d/tw M685/800/1000; 🅿❄🛜) By a busy road near Pioneer Mall, Mohokare has a good reputation locally and a cute little bar. The self-catering chalets (M855, including breakfast) have plenty of space; luxury rooms have kitchenette and free-standing bath, although they are not vastly better than the standard options. Shuttles and activities can be organised.

Black Swan B&B   GUESTHOUSE **$$**
(📱 2231 7700; www.blackswan.co.ls; 28 Manong Rd, New Europa; s/d incl breakfast M550/1000; 🅿❄🛜🏊) With its gazebo, braai (barbecue), resident rooster and bird pond, the Black Swan is a calm suburban refuge. The spartan but spacious rooms have satellite TV and all amenities. For a little extra you can have a room or rondavel

★ **Kick4Life Hotel & Conference Centre**   HOTEL **$$**
(📱 2832 0707; www.kick4life.org; Lesotho Football for Hope Centre, Nightingale Rd; s/d incl breakfast from M700/750; 🅿❄🛜) Attached to the sport-focused NGO Kick4Life (p475), this smart hotel with a football (soccer) theme funds the charity's work and its staff includes Kick4Life protégées. In the reception area is a picture of two lucky Basotho lads meeting the English squad, while football strips decorate the 12 attractive rooms, most of which are named after famous footballers.

The terrace offers an excellent city view and also overlooks the 11-a-side pitch. Transfers to/from Ladybrand in South Africa are available (per person M180).

Lancer's Inn   HOTEL **$$**
(📱 2231 2114; www.lancersinn.co.ls; Pioneer Rd; s/d M925/1025; 🅿❄🛜🏊) Owned by the Dutch ambassador, this popular central business

with kitchenette (singles/doubles including breakfast from M800/1600). Rates are lower at weekends.

Mpilo Boutique Hotel BOUTIQUE HOTEL $$$
(📞5220 3000; www.mpilohotel.co.ls; cnr Kingsway & Maluti Rd; r from M2440; 🅿❄🛜) Opened in 2015, Maseru's first true boutique hotel quickly became the gathering spot of choice for the city's upper crust. The hotel features 28 sumptuous rooms, elegant common spaces and the delicious Sky Restaurant, which offers panoramic views of the neighbouring mountains and golf course. It's all adorned in blown-up photographs of the most awe-inspiring landscapes of Lesotho.

Avani Lesotho Hotel & Casino HOTEL $$$
(📞2224 3000; www.minorhotels.com; Hilton Rd; s/d incl breakfast from M2300/2470; 🅿❄@🛜🏊) Surveying Maseru from its hilltop perch since 1979, the capital's landmark hotel has a range of rooms and facilities including two restaurants, two bars, a casino, a travel agent and shops.

🍴 Eating & Drinking

Pioneer Mall (www.pioneer.co.ls; Pioneer Rd; 🕐7am-7pm Mon-Fri, to 6pm Sat, to 2pm Sun) has chain restaurants such as Spur, a Pick n Pay supermarket and the **Renaissance Café** (mains M70; 🕐7am-9pm Mon-Sat, to 6pm Sun). The **LNDC Centre** (cnr Kingsway & Pioneer Rd) has a Shoprite supermarket and cafes.

Kingsway is a good place to head if you want a post-dinner drink, particularly the area around the **Lancer's Inn** (www.lancersinn.co.ls; Pioneer Rd; 🕐9am-midnight). But the best spot for a great cocktail is the Primi Piatti restaurant at the Maseru Mall. A few doors down, **Ba.One** (📞2231 3493; VIP room R300 per person; 🕐4.30pm-6am Wed-Sun) is the hottest club in town (there's even VIP bottle service in a separate lounge).

Ouh La La CAFE $
(📞6335 6570; cnr Kingsway & Pioneer Rd; mains M45-80; 🕐7.30am-9pm Mon-Fri, 8am-7pm Sat, 9.30am-4pm Sun; 🛜) Locals and expats mix easily in this streetside garden cafe, which takes its Gallic theme from the adjoining Alliance Française cultural centre. The light menu is mostly sandwiches, crêpes, pastries and salads, but the coffee is decent and wine is available by the glass.

★Sky Restaurant INTERNATIONAL $$
(📞5220 3000; www.mpilohotel.co.ls/dining; Maluti Rd; mains M120-220; 🕐noon-3pm & 6-11pm)

Maseru's best new restaurant sits atop the Mpilo Boutique Hotel, dishing out Basotho favourites such as cured venison carpaccio, whole local trout and slow-braised oxtail. The wine list is exquisite and the mountain views out the floor-to-ceiling windows are sublime. Expect to be surrounded by guests celebrating various occasions.

★No.7 Restaurant INTERNATIONAL $$
(📞2832 0707; www.kick4life.org; Lesotho Football for Hope Centre, Nightingale Rd; mains M65-140; 🕐7am-10pm Mon-Sat, to noon Sun; 🛜🍴) Attached to the NGO Kick4Life and its hotel (p477), No.7 pumps its profits back into Kick4Life's charitable work and the team includes young locals training for a career in hospitality. The restaurant is a stylish spot with city views and a menu fusing European sophistication with Basotho touches, offering dishes such as fillet steak and bouillabaisse.

Primi Piatti ITALIAN $$
(📞5250 5205; www.primi-world.com; Maseru Mall, cnr Kofi Anan & John Paul Rds; pizzas from M75, mains M60-180; 🕐9am-11pm Sun-Wed, to 1am Thu-Sat) From the mouth-watering Italian food to the enthusiastic service to the delicious craft cocktails, the stars align at this outpost of the Cape Town–based restaurant chain. The pizzas are as phenomenal as the wine list is extensive, and the tasty steaks are affordable. Wash down the fried zucchini sticks with a pink grapefruit gin and tonic.

Piri Piri INTERNATIONAL $$
(Orpen Rd; mains M85-130; 🕐11am-10pm Mon-Sat, to 4pm Sun) This restaurant does Portuguese, Mozambican and South African dishes, including steaks, seafood, *feijoada* (a traditional Portuguese stew) and piri-piri chicken. Choose between romantic, low-lit rooms and a gazebo in the garden.

🛍 Shopping

Maseru Mall MALL
(📞2231 8221; Pioneer Rd; 🕐9am-6pm) Built in 2012, this glitzy mall contains upscale restaurants, several banks and ATMs, a Shoprite, a Woolworths, a nightclub and even a small children's amusement park. It is essentially the social hub of Maseru.

Basotho Hat ARTS & CRAFTS
(📞2232 2523; Kingsway; 🕐8am-5pm Mon-Fri, to 4.30pm Sat) More expensive than elsewhere in Lesotho, but convenient and well stocked with two floors of quality crafts

from across the country. Credit cards are accepted and it's a low-pressure shopping environment.

❶ Information

Maseru Mall offers banks, a pharmacy and many local retailers, while Pioneer Mall has banks, an internet cafe, a currency-exchange bureau, a good souvenir shop and a pharmacy.

EMERGENCY

Fire (☏ 112)
Police (☏ 112)

MEDICAL SERVICES

In an emergency, try contacting your embassy, as most keep lists of recommended practitioners. For anything serious, you'll need to go to South Africa.

Maseru Private Hospital (☏ 2231 3260; off Pioneer Rd, Ha Thetsane) is about 7km south of central Maseru.

MONEY

There are several banks with ATMs on Kingsway. The top-end hotels will do foreign-exchange transactions (at poor rates).
Nedbank (Kingsway; ⊙ 8.30am-4.30pm Mon-Fri, to noon Sat) Does foreign-exchange transactions Monday to Friday.

TOURIST INFORMATION

The **tourist information office** (☏ 2231 2427, 2231 2238; www.visitlesotho.travel; Pioneer Mall, Pioneer Rd; ⊙ 9am-6pm Mon-Fri, to 3pm Sat, to 1pm Sun) has lists of tour guides, information on public transport and, when in stock, free Maseru city maps.

Tourist offices can also be found at **Maseru Bridge Border Post** (☏ 2231 2427; ⊙ 8am-5pm Mon-Fri, 9am-1pm Sat & Sun), **Moshoeshoe I International Airport** (☏ 2835 0479; ⊙ 9am-4.30pm Mon-Fri, 10am-4pm Sat & Sun) and the headquarters of the **Lesotho Tourism Development Corporation** (LTDC; ☏ 2231 2238; cnr Linare Rd & Parliament St; ⊙ 8am-5pm Mon-Fri).

TRAVEL AGENCIES

There are travel agencies at Pioneer Mall, the LNDC Centre and Lancer's Inn (p477) hotel.
Leloli Travel Agency (☏ 5885 1513; maju@leo.co.ls; Pioneer Mall, Pioneer Rd; ⊙ 8am-5pm Mon-Fri, 9am-noon Sat) Books flights and cruises.

Maseru Travel (☏ 2231 4536; palesa.maseru travel@galileosa.co.za; Maseru Book Centre, Kingsway; ⊙ 8.30am-5pm Mon-Fri, 9-11am Sat) Represents Budget hire cars, Intercape buses and airlines including South African Airways.

Shoprite Money Market (Kiosk, LNDC Centre, cnr Kingsway & Pioneer Rd) The easiest place to buy Greyhound, Intercape, Cityliner, Translux and SA Roadlink bus tickets.

❶ Getting There & Away

BUS & SHARED TAXI

There are three main transport stands to the northeast of the main roundabout:
Sefika taxi rank (Airport Rd) A major stand located behind Sefika Mall with services to nationwide destinations, including Roma, Motsekuoa (for Malealea) and points south.
Motsamai Street taxi rank (cnr Motsamai St & Market Rd) Services to local destinations (including Motsekuoa) and points north such as Maputsoe and Leribe (Hlotse). The rank is behind KFC located on Main North Rd, between Pitso Ground and Setsoto Stadium.
Manonyane bus stop (Market Rd) Shared taxis to Thaba-Bosiu and Semonkong, Leribe and points north. Also Lesotho Freight Service buses to destinations including Leribe and Thaba-Tseka. The stop is located near Pitso Ground.

Buses to Mokhotlong depart from Stadium Rd behind Pitso Ground, while those to **Qacha's Nek** (Main South Rd) depart from next to St James Primary and High Schools.

CAR & MOTORCYCLE

Avis (☏ 6270 0088, 5870 0088; www.avis.co.za; Moshoeshoe I International Airport)
Europcar (☏ 5878 5487; Moshoeshoe 1 International Airport; ⊙ 7.30am-5pm Mon-Fri, 10am-3.30pm Sat, 10am-3pm Sun)
Basotho Car Rental (☏ 5885 7225, 2232 4123; www.basothocarrental.com; Camara de Lobos Bldg, Maseru Bridge border post) Competitive rates and airport transfers.

❶ Getting Around

TO/FROM THE AIRPORT

Moshoeshoe I International Airport (MSU; ☏ 2235 0380) is 21km southeast of Maseru, off Main South Rd en route to Morija. Shared taxis to the airport (M24) depart from Sefika taxi rank. Maseru accommodation, tourist offices and travel agencies can organise shuttles (M100) and private transfers (M150).

TAXI

The standard fare for a seat in a shared 'four-plus-one' travelling around town is M6.50. For a private taxi, try **Top Telephone Taxis** (☏ 5063 7822; ⊙ 24hr), **Moon Lite** (⊙ 2231 2695) or **Superb Taxis** (☏ 2831 9647) – the standard fee for a trip around town is M30 to M40. **Luxury** (☏ 2232 6211) taxis is another option.

AROUND MASERU

Maseru's surrounding areas hold several attractions, which make easy day or overnight excursions from the capital.

Thaba-Bosiu

Thaba-Bosiu is regarded as the birthplace of the Basotho nation and, although an unassuming spot, is Lesotho's most important historical site. This famed and flat-topped 'Mountain at Night', about 25km east of Maseru, is where King Moshoeshoe the Great established his mountain stronghold in 1824.

The origins of Thaba-Bosiu's name are unclear and numerous versions exist. The most interesting is that, to intimidate enemies, magic herbs were placed on a rope, which was wrapped around the mountain. When intruders crossed the rope at night, they were overcome with the drugged sensation that Thaba-Bosiu was 'growing' and it was thus an unconquerable mountain.

In the **visitor information centre** (🖉 2835 7207; ⊙ 8am-5pm Mon-Fri, from 9am Sat, 9am-1pm Sun) at the mountain's base, you can organise horse riding, an excursion to rock-art sites or a guide to walk with you to the top. There are good views up there to Qiloane Hill, which allegedly provided the inspiration for the Basotho hat.

PONY TREKKING

Pony trekking is one of Lesotho's top drawcards. It's done on sure-footed Basotho ponies, the result of cross-breeding between short Javanese horses and European full mounts. Good places to organise treks include Malealea Lodge (p491), Semonkong Lodge (p490), Ts'ehlanyane National Park (p484) and Likatola Horse Riding & Adventure (p475).

Advance booking is recommended and no prior riding experience is necessary. Whatever your experience level, expect to be sore after a day in the saddle. For overnight treks, you'll normally need to bring food (stock up in Maseru), a sleeping bag, a torch (flashlight), water-purification tablets and warm, waterproof clothing. Check Malealea's website for more on the provisions and preparation required.

★ **Cultural Village**   MUSEUM

(🖉 5884 0018, 5022 1962; www.thevillage.co.ls; Masekeng St; M20; ⊙ 7am-11pm, tours 8am-5pm; ℗) Revamped in 2016, the well-maintained cultural village is a highly worthwhile stop. Excellent guided tours of the complex explain traditional Basotho culture and history, and end with a visit to a statue of the much-revered Moshoeshoe I. There's a restaurant with a wraparound veranda – a great place for an afternoon drink.

🛏 Sleeping & Eating

Mmelesi Lodge   LODGE $

(🖉 5250 0006; www.mmelesilodge.co.ls; s/d incl breakfast M520/700; ℗ 🛜) Mmelesi Lodge has sandstone, thatched-roof *mokhoro* (traditional Basotho huts), reached along flower-lined paths. The bar often fills with government workers, while the restaurant serves surprisingly good food (mains M50 to M75).

Khotsong Lodge   LODGE $$

(🖉 5250 0113; Thaba Khupa; s/d chalets M645/795; ℗ 🛜 🍴) Lesotho's premier (read: only) wildlife lodge is just a 10-minute drive from Thaba-Bosiu, and though it may look a tad run-down, it offers a rare opportunity to bask in the presence of ostrich, blesbok, wildebeest, zebra, duiker and springbok. A range of accommodation is offered, from standard rooms to basic chalets, and a dining hall serves passable African cuisine.

Cultural Village   RESORT $$

(🖉 5022 1962; www.thevillage.co.ls; Masekeng St; r incl breakfast M1200; ℗ ❄ 🛜) The Cultural Village tourist complex has comfortable chalets and an appealing restaurant (mains M60 to M160).

❶ Getting There & Away

Shared taxis to Thaba-Bosiu (M18, 30 minutes) depart from the Manonyane transport stand in Maseru. If you're driving, take the Mafeteng Rd for about 13km and turn left at the Roma turn-off; after about 6km, take the signposted road left. Thaba-Bosiu is 10km further along.

Roma

POP 11,612

Nestled amid sandstone cliffs about 35km southeast of Maseru, Roma was established as a mission town in the 1860s. Today it's Lesotho's centre of learning, with the country's only university as well as several seminaries and secondary schools. The beautiful National University of Lesotho campus is worth a wander and boots hanging from phone lines confirm Roma's student credentials. The southern entry/exit to town takes you through a striking gorge landscape and is best travelled during the morning or late afternoon when the lower sun lights the cliffs to full advantage.

Shared taxis run throughout the day to/ from Maseru (M20, 45 minutes).

🛏 Sleeping & Eating

★ **Roma Trading Post**   GUESTHOUSE **$**
(☑ 5024 5001; www.tradingpostlodge.com; Ha Basiane; camping M125, s/d per person M400/700, with shared bathroom per person M200; 🅿 🛜 🏊) Roma Trading Post is a charming trading post operated since 1903. The attached guesthouse includes garden rooms, rondavels and the original sandstone homestead, with shared kitchen, set in a lush garden. The accommodating and personable staff can organise adventures including pony trekking, mountain biking, hiking, visits to nearby *minwane* (dinosaur footprints) and local attractions.

It is clearly signposted on the north (Maseru) side of town. Breakfast and dinner are available, costing M90 and M150 respectively.

Kaycees   FAST FOOD **$**
(mains M20-65; ⊙ 8am-midnight) Kaycees, off Roma's main drag, is a popular hangout serving fast food (namely chicken, sausage and fries) and cans of Maluti lager to happy students.

Morija

Tiny Morija is the site of the first European mission in Lesotho. It's an important and attractive town with a rich cultural heritage that makes a pleasant stopover or day trip from Maseru. The Morija Museum is the unofficial national museum.

👁 Sights & Activities

Pony trekking (one person per hour/half-day/day M220/600/880), guided hikes to dinosaur footprints (per person M50) and village sleepovers (per hiker/rider from M440/1060 including full board) can be organised through Morija Guest Houses. Reserve a day in advance. An optional packhorse for luggage is M480 extra.

WORTH A TRIP

RAMABANTA TRADING POST

Set in neat grounds with mountain views, **Ramabanta Trading Post** (☑ 5844 2309; tradingpostram@leo.co.ls; s/d M375/750; 🅿) is located about 40km southeast of Roma, off the tar road to Semonkong and the south. The smart and spacious rondavels (round huts with a conical roof) have a lounge and dining room; three have a kitchenette and the main building features a lounge, bar and restaurant (breakfast M95).

Activities on offer include pony trekking, hiking and village visits. Staying here provides the chance to link up to Semonkong and other places in the area on overnight hikes and pony treks.

Shared taxis serve Ramabanta from Maseru (M50, two hours), continuing to Semonkong.

Morija Museum & Archives   MUSEUM
(☑ 2236 0308; www.morija.co.ls; Church St; M30; ⊙ 8am-5pm Mon-Sat, noon-5pm Sun; 🅿) This small, considered museum contains ethnographical exhibits, archives from the early mission and scientific artefacts. There's an excellent collection of books for sale, including those by curator Stephen Gill. Staff will guide you to **dinosaur footprints** (M50 per person) in the nearby Makhoarane Mountains, a 5km return walk.

Maeder House Gallery   ARTS CENTRE
(☑ 5886 3500, 5991 1853; ⊙ 8am-5pm Mon-Fri, 7am-1pm Sat & Sun; 🅿) This art centre and gallery is near the Morija Museum & Archives in a missionary house dating back to 1843. Various local artists work and exhibit their art here.

🛏 Sleeping & Eating

★ **Morija Guest Houses**   GUESTHOUSE **$**
(☑ 6306 5093; www.morijaguesthouses.com; camping M110, r per person with shared bathroom M260-340; 🅿 🛜) 🍃 At this sterling stone-and-thatch house perched high above the village, guests can choose between cosy rooms in the main building and cottages below. Mountain biking, village tours and pony treks are offered, making this a top spot to experience the area. Backpackers who arrive by public transport pay

MATSIENG

Morija's unremarkable neighbouring village, Matsieng, is the unlikely site of a royal compound. A new palace was built in Maseru in the '60s, but the royals still weekend here. The adjoining **Royal Archives & Museum** (🗹2700 6984; info.royal.archives@gmail.com; M15; ⊙8am-4.30pm Mon-Fri, to 1pm Sat; 🅿) display items from the royal collection and information and documents about the monarchy.

Staff can give you a tour (M40) of the village and point out notable elements of the compound.

R200 per person, regardless of the room. Meals are served (breakfast/lunch/dinner M70/130/150).

Lindy's B&B GUESTHOUSE $
(🗹2236 0732; www.lindysbnb.wordpress.com; s/d from M380/700; 🅿🛜) Lindy offers a large, modern stone duplex with two en-suite rooms and a century-old cottage with two more rooms, both ringed by the Makhoarane Mountains. Meals are available on request (breakfast/lunch/dinner M120/145/165), and wi-fi costs extra.

Cafe Jardin CAFE $
(🗹5910 4153; mains M40-70; ⊙8am-5pm Tue-Sat, noon-5pm Sun) The small courtyard tearoom at the Morija Museum & Archives serves dishes such as pizza, and chicken and chips. It's busy on weekends.

❶ Getting There & Away

Shared taxis run throughout the day to/from Maseru (M25, 45 minutes) and Matsieng (M7, 10 minutes).

NORTHWESTERN LESOTHO

The lowlands of northwestern Lesotho comprise a number of busy little commercial towns. Only the craftwork-selling towns of Teyateyaneng and Leribe (Hlotse) draw travellers, along with the stunning Ts'ehlanyane National Park, but the area gives way to the majestic northeastern highlands and features a few major border crossings.

Teyateyaneng

POP 61,578

Teyateyaneng (Place of Quick Sands; usually known simply as 'TY') is the craft centre of Lesotho and is worth a stop to buy tapestries or watch them being made.

🛏 Sleeping & Eating

Ka-Pitseng Guest House GUESTHOUSE $
(🗹2250 1638; s/d incl breakfast M550/680; 🅿❄🛜) Ka-Pitseng is set in scrubby gardens by the main road on the south (Maseru) side of town. The cool and comfy rooms have satellite TV, plastic flowers, lilac pillars and conference charisma. There is also a bar-restaurant that serves tasty food including a deliciously spicy whole roasted chicken.

Blue Mountain Inn HOTEL $$
(🗹2250 0362; www.bmilesotho.com; Police Station Rd; s/d incl breakfast from M850/900; 🅿❄🛜🏊) Its plain motel-style rooms are enlivened by scattered paintings, but Blue Mountain really shines out the back where the **bar-restaurant** (mains M70-120; ⊙7am-10pm) overlooks a garden and small pool.

🔒 Shopping

Setsoto Design ARTS & CRAFTS
(🗹5808 6312; www.setsotodesign.com; ⊙8am-5pm) Next to a primary school near the Blue Mountain Inn, you can see the painstaking tapestry-making process at Setsoto Design. The project employs more than 60 local women who spin, dye and weave a beautiful selection of tapestries (M250 to M6500) and other crafts. You can even submit your own design to be turned into a tapestry. Credit cards accepted.

Lesotho Mountain Crafts ARTS & CRAFTS
(🗹5855 9960; lesothomountaincrafts@gmail. com; ⊙8am-5pm Mon-Fri, 9.30am-4pm Sat & Sun) You can buy the work of 12 local cooperatives at this showroom and workshop, by the main road about 2km before Teyateyaneng (coming from Maseru). Items include jewellery, shawls, slippers, tapestries, bags and *seshoeshoe* (Basotho dress made of traditional cotton print), incorporating materials such as cow horn, felt, rose leather, sheepskin and wool.

Elelloang Basali Weavers ARTS & CRAFTS
(🗹5355 3737, 5851 0992; www.elelloangbasali@ gmail.com; ⊙8am-5pm Mon-Fri, to 2pm Sat) Elelloang Basali (Be Aware Women) makes

hand-spun mohair rugs with geometric patterns, as well as tapestries and other items. Find it in a building made of recycled cans by the main road on the northern (Maputsoe) side of town.

ⓘ Getting There & Away

Shared taxis run throughout the day to/from Maseru (M25, one hour) and Maputsoe (for Leribe; M25, one hour). Chartering a taxi from Maseru costs about M230 one way (rates can change depending on fuel prices).

Leribe

POP 18,840

Leribe (also known as Hlotse) is a busy regional market hub. It served as an administrative centre under the British, as attested to by a few old buildings slowly decaying in the leafy streets. Nearby dinosaur footprints and its arts and crafts scene are the main attractions.

◉ Sights

Major Bell's Tower   LANDMARK

Leribe's main sight is this crumbling gun tower near the market. It was built for the Gun War in the late 1800s, but spent most of its career as a storehouse for government records. The tower is not open to visitors.

**Subeng River
Dinosaur Footprints**   HISTORIC SITE

(M50; ⏱ 7am-6pm) FREE Dinosaur footprints abound near Leribe. About 7km north of town (en route to Butha-Buthe) are the Subeng River footprints. At the signpost, just before the road crosses the river, walk down about 500m to a concrete causeway. The worn footprints of at least three species of dinosaur are about 15m downstream on the right bank.

**Tsikoane Village
Dinosaur Footprints**   HISTORIC SITE

(⏱ 24hr) FREE This set of footprints is a few kilometres south of Leribe at Tsikoane village. Immediately after the Tsikoane Primary School, take the small dirt road to the right towards some rocky outcrops. Follow it up to the church. Children will vie to lead you the 1km slog up the mountainside to the footprints, in a series of caves, and a guide can be helpful here. The prints are clearly visible on the rock ceiling.

🍴 Sleeping & Eating

There's a Shoprite supermarket for self-caterers stocking up for the highlands.

Monokots'oaing Guest House GUESTHOUSE $

(☎ 5920 3624, 2640 1769; s/d incl breakfast from M400/500; P❄🛜) Perched between farms on a rural hillside, this lovely yellow-brick guesthouse overlooks all of Leribe. The accommodations are set in two buildings, one of which is castle-like, and are charming and tidy, with en suite bathrooms. The restaurant serves up delicious mutton stew and free-range chicken (mains M100), and the owners buy ingredients from local, small-scale farms.

Mountain View Hotel   HOTEL $$

(☎ 2240 0559; www.mvhlesotho.com; Main St; s/d incl breakfast M700/750; P❄🛜🏊) This reliable hotel is adjacent to both the highway and Leribe's main drag. Rooms are bland but spacious and functional, and they outdo most places in town; those upstairs have a shower, while downstairs you get a bath with hand-held shower. The restaurant serves pizzas, burgers, grills and sandwiches.

🛍 Shopping

Leribe Craft Centre   CRAFTS, CLOTHING

(☎ 5877 0251; ⏱ 8am-4.30pm Mon-Fri, to 1pm Sat) Sells a range of high-quality mohair goods from ponchos to stoles, plus craftwork and books on Lesotho, at good prices. Find it on the main road, downhill from the Mountain View Hotel and opposite the hospital.

ⓘ Getting There & Away

Shared taxis run throughout the day between Leribe and Maseru (M46, two hours), usually with a change of vehicles at Maputsoe. There are also several vehicles daily to/from Katse (M120, three hours) and Butha-Buthe (M20, 40 minutes).

Butha-Buthe

POP 30,115

Butha-Buthe (Place of Lying Down) was so named by King Moshoeshoe the Great because it was here that his people first retreated during the chaos of the *difaqane* (forced migration in Southern Africa). Its frontier-town scrappiness is redeemed by an attractive setting alongside the Hlotse River, with the beautiful Maluti Mountains as a backdrop.

THE BASOTHO BLANKET

The Basotho blanket is an important part of public, social and private life, not only as a practical article of clothing but also as a symbol of wealth. In 1860, when European traders presented King Moshoeshoe I with a blanket, the Basotho people were so taken with it that blankets superseded animal hides. By the 1880s, traders were overwhelmed with demand for blankets, which were manufactured from high-quality woven cloth in England.

Today's woollen blanket provides insulation in the heat and the cold, is fireproof and acts as a status symbol (each costs a hefty M500). Look out for a maize cob (a symbol of fertility), a crown or military markings (a legacy of British imperialism) and a cabbage leaf (meaning prosperity). Young married women wear a blanket around their hips until their first child is conceived; and young boys are presented with a blanket upon circumcision, symbolising their emergence into manhood.

The solid lines on a blanket's edges are worn vertically; the Basotho believe that worn horizontally the blanket can stunt growth, wealth and development.

Less common, but still used in rural areas, is the Basotho hat (*mokorotlo* or *molianyeo*), with its distinctive conical shape and curious top adornment. The hat is supposedly modelled on the shape of Qiloane Hill, near Thaba-Bosiu.

There are a couple of chain restaurants and one decent local place, **Karabo** (meals M30; ⊙ 8am-7pm), as well as ATMs in the centre of town.

Many shared taxis travel to/from Maseru via Maputsoe (M25, 20 minutes), where you'll usually need to change vehicles. Shared taxis (M110, three hours) and buses also serve Mokhotlong. Butha-Buthe is the last reliable place to buy petrol if you're heading to Mokhotlong.

Ts'ehlanyane National Park

Lesotho's loveliest and most accessible **national park** (✔ in Leribe 2246 0723; M40, vehicle M10; ⊙ gate 8am-4.30pm; ℗) is a 56-sq-km patch of rugged wilderness, including one of Lesotho's only stands of indigenous forest, at a high altitude of 2000m to 3000m. Dramatic rock formations, caves, cliffs and rich mineral deposits abound, as do crystal-clear rivers and natural pools.

This 'che-che' forest, as the Basotho people call it, offers a canopy of medicinal and ornamental plants, blossoming with wildflowers in the spring and attracting rare migratory butterfly species. This is one of the few areas where eland still roam in Lesotho, and lucky visitors might also spot rhebok, baboon, ice rat or the elusive African wild cat.

The hiking trails and horse riding are top-notch. In addition to short day walks, there's a 39km day hike or pony trek to/from Bokong Nature Reserve (p488), covering some of Lesotho's most dramatic terrain.

Heading north from Bokong to Ts'ehlanyane is easier as Bokong is higher; the challenging route is also better tackled by pony or horse. Hiking guides can be arranged at Ts'ehlanyane gate (M50 within the park, M450 to Bokong) or Maliba Lodge.

Community-run pony trekking and horse riding can be arranged through Maliba Lodge or the park gate (prices vary). Book at least 24 hours ahead.

Maliba Lodge offers community tours (90 minutes, M300 per person) of the villages bordering Ts'ehlanyane National Park.

🛏 Sleeping & Eating

⭐**Maliba Lodge** LODGE $$$
(✔ 6361 6152, in South Africa +27 31-702 8791; www.maliba-lodge.com; s/d from M1080/1440; ℗ 🛜 🏊) Maliba ('Madiba') offers a range of accommodation, from riverside huts to comfy lodge rooms to lavish chalets, in Ts'ehlanyane National Park, along with a fine-dining restaurant, a casual bistro and two bars. The chalets are Lesotho's plushest accommodation, each featuring a four-poster bed, antique furniture, a hot tub facing the mountain range, heated towel racks and welcome sherry.

Walking trails lead to waterfalls and there's a spa and kids' club. Activities include horse riding, birdwatching, archery and village visits.

Accommodation also includes well-equipped self-catering cottages (M1632), with terraces overlooking the river and gazing up a mountain valley, as well as quaint stone-and-thatch riverside huts (singles/doubles M695/800) near swimming holes and hiking trails (hut 3 offers privacy for romantic couples). Rates rise in December and over Easter weekend.

Maliba Lodge INTERNATIONAL $$
(breakfast M190, lunch 2-/3-course set menu M165/245, dinner 2-/3-course set menu M265/390; ☺8-10am, 1-2.30pm & 7-9.30pm) Maliba Lodge's excellent restaurant serves dishes such as braised oxtail, oven-baked trout and Madagascan peppered beef fillet. Advance booking is advised if you're not staying over at the lodge.

❶ Getting There & Away

If you're driving, take the signposted turn-off from the main road about 6km southwest of Butha-Buthe, from where the park gate is 30km along on a tar road. Maliba is 2km further on.

Shared taxis from Butha-Buthe marked 'Ts'ehlanyane' serve the villages en route to the park. If you ask before departure, they can take you to the gate or Maliba for about M40. Take the driver's number to organise transport back.

NORTHEASTERN HIGHLANDS

In the northeastern highlands, the road weaves up dramatically through spectacular mountains – part of the Drakensberg range – with rocky cliffs and rolling hills. South Africa does a good job of marketing its portion of the Drakensberg Escarpment, but the raw beauty of the Lesotho side is hard to beat, with stunning highland panoramas, low population density and plenty of winter snow.

The region is therefore excellent for winter skiing, and offers one of Africa's few ski resorts. Motorbiking and mountain biking are popular in the summertime, as is trekking, but overnighters should be fully equipped with a four-season sleeping bag, waterproof gear, topographical maps and a compass. Trout fishing is reputed to be top-notch.

This area has many of the country's worst stretches of main road, which is the only way in or out. In places the asphalt has actually made the road more pot-holey, making for a wild and slow ride in a regular vehicle. Lesotho's mass, Chinese-run roadwork program is another complication, as the work can further slow traffic.

Shared taxis run through the area regularly and are very affordable, yet crowded.

Liphofung Cave Cultural & Historical Site

This small but historically significant sandstone overhang is adorned in San rock art and served as a temporary hideaway home for King Moshoeshoe the Great back in the early 1800s, before he became the nation's founder. The government-run site (☑2246 0723; adult/child M50/20; ☺8am-4.30pm; ℗) offers guided walks through the cave, along with a cultural centre and shop selling local crafts.

To get here by public transport, take a shared taxi heading from Butha-Buthe towards Moteng and get out at the turn-off to Mamohase or Liphofung (M20, 25 minutes). Liphofung is then an easy 1.5km walk down from the main road along a tarmac access ramp. Daily (except Sunday) buses to Mokhotlong and Maseru pass the turn-offs in the morning (ask around for times); shared taxis to Butha-Buthe pass in the morning and those to Mokhotlong pass all day.

Oxbow

POP 10,000

An ideal place to get away from the bustle while still enjoying amenities, Oxbow consists of a few huts and a couple of lodges nestled amid some wonderful mountain scenery. The area regularly receives snow in winter and boasts one of Africa's few ski resorts. It's also popular with South African trout anglers and birdwatchers.

🏃 Activities

Afriski Mountain Resort SKIING, HIKING
(☑in South Africa 086 123 747 54; www.afriski. net; half-/full-day pass M350/450, half-/full-day equipment rental M295/395; ☺slopes 9am-4pm Jun-Aug) Skiers and snowboarders should make tracks to Afriski Mountain Resort, about 10km from Oxbow via the Mahlasela Pass (3222m), one of Southern Africa's highest road passes. The world-class resort has 3km of slopes, with lessons (half-day/full day M455/655) and packages available.

Try to get here at the very start or very end of the season when the slopes are blissfully empty (winter lasts from June to August). Once school holidays begin, it gets extremely busy.

From September to May, activities including hiking, fly-fishing, quad tours, mountain biking and abseiling are offered.

🛏 Sleeping & Eating

Afriski Mountain Resort
RESORT $$

(☑ in South Africa 086 123 747 54; www.afriski.net; dm M310, r per person from M520, self-catering chalets per person from M1030; 🅿) The ski resort offers myriad accommodation options, all comfortable and modern. Book ahead in June and July, especially over the weekend. Prices peak in July and drop outside the June-to-August ski season.

New Oxbow Lodge
LODGE $$

(☑ in South Africa 051 933 2247; www.oxbow.co.za; s/d incl breakfast M480/880; 🅿) On the banks of the Malibamat'so River, this incongruous alpine chalet would look more at home in the Alps. It fills during winter with South African skiers and snow oglers; at other times, its eerie isolation and intermittent electricity, compounded by golfball-size hailstones clattering on the deserted games room and bar, bring to mind *The Shining*.

The dated rooms and rondavels have showers or baths, tea and coffee, gas fire and bedside candles for the black mountain nights. You can dine in the restaurant or bar (mains M40 to M120); room-only accommodation and à la carte meals will likely work out cheaper than half board. A small shop here supplies the basics. June to August (peak season), full board is compulsory (singles/doubles M990/1630).

★ Sky Restaurant
PIZZA, INTERNATIONAL $$

(mains M80-130; ⊙ 6.30am-10pm Jun-Aug, 7am-9pm Sep-May) Africa's highest restaurant (3010m) overlooks the slopes at Afriski Mountain Resort and reflects the resort's international sheen with its stylish wood finish and big red pizza oven. Lunch choices include pizzas, burgers and steaks, with pasta dishes and Lesotho trout on the dinner menu.

❶ Getting There & Away

The daily (except Sunday) bus between Maseru and Mokhotlong will drop you at Oxbow (M120, 4½ hours), passing in both directions in the morning. Shared taxi is a better option for Mokhotlong, as the bus is packed by the time it reaches Oxbow. Taxis run in the morning to Butha-Buthe from Oxbow (M60, one hour) and Afriski Mountain Resort (M80, 1½ hours), with services to Mokhotlong throughout the day. The road follows a series of hairpin turns up the Moteng and Mahlasela Passes, and can be treacherous in snow and ice.

Mokhotlong
POP 8,784

A remote outpost with a Wild West feel, eastern Lesotho's main town lies below superb high-altitude scenery. There's not much to do other than watch life go by, with locals sporting Basotho blankets passing by on their horses. However, the Senqu (Orange) River – Lesotho's main waterway – has its source near Mokhotlong and the town makes a good base for walks.

🛏 Sleeping & Eating

Shops sell the basics, but it's best to come somewhat equipped.

🛏 In Town

Mokhotlong Hotel
HOTEL $

(☑ 6300 2013, 2292 0212; s/d incl breakfast M520/660; 🅿 🛜) The classiest option in town, Mokhotlong Hotel is fairly basic but adequate for those passing through the region. Staff members are friendly and helpful, the restaurant serves OK buffet meals and the bar is something of a local gathering spot.

Boikhethelo Guesthouse
GUESTHOUSE $

(☑ 6201 8065, 2292 0346; boikhetheloguesthouse@gmail.com; s/d incl breakfast M400/600) A simple, well-run guesthouse with friendly staff and hearty meals (book ahead). Rooms are in cute thatched cottages with marvellous views.

🛏 Outside Town

Molumong Eco Lodge & Pony Trekking Centre
HOSTEL $

(☑ 6203 2253; www.molumongecolodge.wordpress.com; camping/dm/r M100/180/450; 🅿) 🐾 About 15km southwest of Mokhotlong, off the road to Thaba-Tseka, is this former colonial trading post, offering basic (electricity-free) self-catering rooms and rondavels with shared kitchen and bathrooms. The place is charming, but the kilometre-long driveway is treacherous even for a 4WD. Pony treks lasting a few hours or overnight are offered. Breakfast can be ordered in advance for M70, but bring all other food you'll need from Mokhotlong.

Chalets in the Sky
LODGE $$

(Maloraneng Lodge; ☑ 082 686 5847, in South Africa 076 723 6156; www.chaletsinthesky.com; adult/child per person M350/150; 🅿) 🐾 Signposted from

BASOTHO CULTURE

Traditional Basotho culture is flourishing, and colourful celebrations marking milestones, such as birth, puberty, marriage and death, are a central part of village life. While hiking you may see the *lekolulo*, a flutelike instrument played by herd boys; the *thomo*, a stringed instrument played by women; and the *setolo-tolo*, a stringed mouth instrument played by men. Cattle hold an important position in daily life, both as sacrificial animals and as symbols of wealth.

The Basotho believe in a Supreme Being and place a great deal of emphasis on *balimo* (ancestors), who act as intermediaries between people and the capricious forces of nature and the spirit world. Evil is a constant danger, caused by *boloi* (witchcraft; witches can be either male or female) and *thkolosi* (small, mischievous beings, similar to the Xhosa's *tokoloshe*). If these forces are bothering you, visit the nearest *ngaka* (a learned man, part sorcerer and part doctor) who can combat them. Basotho are traditionally buried in a sitting position, facing the rising sun and ready to leap up when called.

the main road near the Letseng Diamond Mine, roughly halfway between Mokhotlong and Oxbow, is this wilderness getaway in the pristine Khubelu Valley. The six riverside self-catering rondavels nestle in a verdant landscape, running on a generator from 6am to 10pm. Only accessible by 4WD or (in decent weather) a high-clearance 2WD.

Activities on offer include pony trekking, fly-fishing and a hot springs trip (via horseback).

❶ Getting There & Away

Mokhotlong's shared-taxi rank is above the main road near the Shoprite grocery store. There are a few shared taxis daily to/from Butha-Buthe (M110, three hours), with occasional direct services to Maseru (M140, six hours). A bus runs Monday to Saturday to/from Maseru (M130), departing from Mokhotlong by about 8am (and from Maseru at around 6am).

Shared taxis to Linakaneng (M40) will drop you by Molumong Eco Lodge & Pony Trekking Centre; change in Linakaneng for Thaba-Tseka, although there are infrequent services on this rough and little-travelled route. There is a daily shared taxi to Sani Top (M100, one hour), departing Mokhotlong around 7am.

Petrol and diesel are normally available in Mokhotlong. You need a 4WD vehicle to tackle the road to Thaba-Tseka but you can travel on to Sani Top in a regular car.

Sani Top

Sani Top offers stupendous views and unlimited hiking possibilities – it sits atop the steep Sani Pass, the famous road into Lesotho through the Drakensberg range in KwaZulu-Natal.

🏃 Activities

Besides local hikes, a rugged three- to four-day trek south to Sehlabathebe National Park (p493) is possible. The route follows a remote Drakensberg escarpment edge and should only be attempted if you're well prepared, experienced and in a group of at least four people.

Thabana-Ntlenyana · HIKING

Africa's highest peak south of Mt Kilimanjaro, Thabana-Ntlenyana (3482m) is a popular but long and arduous hike (12km, nine hours). There's a path, but a guide (from M500) would be handy; arrange the night before through Sani Mountain Lodge. It's also possible to do the ascent on horseback (M1175 per person).

Hodgson's Peaks · HIKING

Hodgson's Peaks (3257m) is a 6km, five-hour hike up a valley. There are views of KwaZulu-Natal from the summit.

🛌 Sleeping & Eating

Sani Stone Lodge · LODGE $
(📞 5631 0331; www.sanistonelodge.co.za; camping M90, dm/d M190/600; 🅿) About 8km from Sani Top, this Basotho-run lodge offers simple rooms, an en-suite dorm and three cosy rondavels (double M1100) with all-important fireplaces. Guided hikes, village visits and pony treks are available, and the bar-restaurant is a welcome sight after a trek in the highlands.

⭐ **Sani Mountain Lodge** · LODGE $$$
(📞 Lesotho 5309 8674, South Africa 078 634 7496; www.sanimountain.co.za; camping/dm from M115/300, s/d with half board M2050/2970; 🅿)

At 2874m, this lodge atop the Sani Pass stakes a claim to 'Africa's highest pub'. Bar trivia aside, cosy rondavels and excellent meals (mains from M55) reward those who make the steep ascent from KwaZulu-Natal. Backpackers doss down the road in modern rooms that hold between two and six people.

In winter, the snow is sometimes deep enough for skiing (you must bring your own equipment, though); pony trekking and village visits can be arranged with notice. A 4WD shuttle (M350) to/from the South African border post is offered to guests staying more than one night.

ⓘ Getting There & Away

The road to Sani Top is tarred all the way from Butha-Buthe. There is a daily shared taxi from Mokhotlong (M100, one hour), departing early in the morning.

Tour operators run day trips and expeditions up the pass from KwaZulu-Natal. Driving, you'll need a 4WD to get up the pass, but confident drivers (with good brakes) can descend it in a car.

CENTRAL HIGHLANDS

Lesotho's rugged interior boasts the country's two trademark sights: the breathtaking Maletsunyane Falls (204m), which are almost twice the height of the Victoria Falls and offer the world's longest commercially operated, single-drop abseil; and the human-made spectacle of Katse Dam, an engineering feat holding a shimmering lake surrounded by rippling mountain slopes.

The area offers an incredible mix of scenery, activities and engineering marvels, accessed from the lowlands up tortuous but stunning passes such as the excellently named God Help Me Pass (2281m) and the Mafika-Lisiu Pass (3090m), one of Lesotho's most beautiful roads.

The central highlands are easily accessible from other regions of Lesotho with the exception of the northeastern highlands, from which a 4WD is needed to tackle the rough gravel road between Mokhotlong and Thaba-Tseka. Shared taxis are unreliable on this remote stretch of road. To travel between Mokhotlong and Thaba-Tseka, you must therefore take the long way around via Leribe (Hlotse).

Bokong Nature Reserve

Bokong (☑5950 2291; adult/child M50/20; ⊙8am-4pm) has perhaps the more dramatic setting of the two northern parks, with stunning vistas over the Lepaqoa Valley from the roadside visitors centre, various short walks and a good, rugged eight-hour hike to Ts'ehlanyane National Park. Bearded vultures, rock shelters, waterfalls and valleyhead fens (wetland areas) are features here.

Hiking guides (M50 within the park, M450 to Ts'ehlanyane) are available and pony trekking (per hour M100) can be booked ahead through the visitors centre. The Lepaqoa Waterfall is a popular destination – in summer it thunders into the gorge; in winter it becomes a highly photogenic pillar of ice

🛏 Sleeping & Eating

The only sleeping option within the reserve is the basic chalets (M500; ℗). Better choices can be found in nearby Leribe or Pitseng.

★ Aloes Guest House   GUESTHOUSE $
(☑2700 5626, 5806 5622; off Mandela Rd; camping M90, dm M195, s/d incl breakfast M450/690; ℗ ❋ ☜) The reception area is situated within an old sandstone trading post, and these charming, old-fashioned bungalows vary in size and decor, with some family-sized units offering full kitchens for self-catering. The grounds are like an English cottage garden with mountain views, and it's a pleasant spot to catch up on writing postcards. Activities include horse riding, quad bikes and guided hikes.

The restaurant (mains M65 to M120) serves light dishes such as burgers and sandwiches, as well as heavier fare including beef stew, mutton chops and chicken curry. Aloes is signposted from the main road in Pitseng village, about 30km from Bokong towards Leribe.

ⓘ Getting There & Away

Bokong lies roughly midway between Leribe (Hlotse) and Katse. Shared taxis from Leribe (M50, two hours) and Katse (M80, 1½ hours) will drop you at the visitors centre, about 2km south of the viewpoint atop the stunning Mafika-Lisiu Pass. When leaving, you may have to wait a while before a taxi with space passes.

There is a bus that travels between Leribe and Katse and costs M35 per trip. The schedule can vary.

Katse Dam

This engineering marvel stores 1950 million cu metres of water bound for thirsty Gauteng, South Africa's most populated province. The high-altitude, 35.8-sq-km body of blue also generates hydroelectric power for Lesotho. Ringed by steep, green hillsides, the dam is a serene if surreal spot; even if you're not impressed by engineering feats, the area makes for a relaxing pause.

◉ Sights

Katse Botanical Garden GARDENS
(www.lhda.org.ls; Katse village; M30; ⊘ 8am-5pm Mon-Fri, 9am-2pm Sat & Sun; P) Katse Botanical Garden was originally established to protect the spiral aloes displaced from the Katse Dam's construction. It has flourished to include gravel, hillside trails passing via a rock garden, indigenous flowers, a medicinal section and a dam viewpoint. A plant-propagation project takes place in the greenhouse.

**Katse Dam
Visitors Centre** VIEWPOINT, MUSEUM
(☏ 2291 0377; www.lhda.org.ls; ⊘ 8am-5pm Fri, 9am-2pm Sat & Sun; P) On the main road in Katse village is the dam's visitors centre, with information, displays and a dam-viewing deck. Look for the bright blue roof a few kilometres east of Katse village. Guided tours of the dam wall (M30, one hour) depart at 9am and 2pm (weekdays) and 9am, 11am and 2pm (weekends and holidays).

⛏ Sleeping & Eating

Katse Lodge HOTEL $$
(☏ 2291 0202; Katse village; s/d incl breakfast M600/880, with shared bathroom M440; P🐾) In a suburban estate-like gated village, this property initially looks rather bland, but it improves when you see the terrace's stunning dam view. Accommodation is comfortable, including the so-called 'dormitory' rooms (private rooms with shared bathroom), and there's also camping (M100) allowed on the lawn and well-equipped self-catering houses (M1100 to M1499) sleeping up to six people.

The restaurant serves light lunches (mains M40 to M90) and dinner mains (M75 to M125) including curries, steaks, poached trout and delicious trout *almandine* (trout garnished with almonds). Activities includ-

ing dam cruises, village tours, guided hikes and pony rides are offered.

❶ Getting There & Away

The 122km road between Leribe (Hlotse) and Katse is excellent but steep and winding, and slick in the rain. Allow at least two hours for driving, longer if going by public transport.

Shared taxis run all day to Leribe (M95, three hours) and Thaba-Tseka (M47, two hours). The quickest and easiest way to travel to Maseru is by taxi via Leribe and Maputsoe (total M150, seven hours).

Daily buses also run to/from Maseru (M120, nine hours) via Thaba-Tseka (M35, 2½ hours), leaving Katse at 5am and Maseru at 9am. In Katse, public transport stops near the Katse village junction.

Thaba-Tseka

POP 5358

Thaba-Tseka is a remote town on the eastern edge of the Central Range, over Mokhoabong Pass (2860m) from Mohale Dam and the west. The town was established in 1980 as a centre for the mountainous district, and is a scrappy place serving mostly as a convenient transport junction for travel north to Katse or west to Maseru.

⛏ Sleeping & Eating

Motherland Guest House GUESTHOUSE $$
(☏ 2890 0404; motherlandguesthouse@gmail.com; s/d incl breakfast from M500/700; P🐾) Motherland Guest House is a decent option in the heart of the town that peeks at the mountains and bubbles with village life, though the staff can be a bit icy. The modern rooms are decorated with photos of Katse Dam and flowery bedspreads, and the bar-restaurant serves curries, steaks and lighter dishes (mains M50 to M70). There are plenty of signs to guide you.

❶ Getting There & Away

The daily bus to/from Maseru (M90, six hours) leaves Thaba-Tseka at 8.30am and Maseru at 9am; shared taxis (M90 to M110, 4½ hours) leave from around 6am. Several daily taxis also serve Katse (M46, two hours); Mokhotlong is trickier, as you must change at Linakaneng and services are infrequent on this rough and little-travelled route.

The road is tarred from Maseru, and the gravel road from Katse is in good condition and suitable for 2WD cars.

Mohale Dam

Built across the Senqunyane River, this impressive 145m-high, rock-filled dam is the second phase of the Lesotho Highlands Water Project, following Katse Dam. There are commanding views of the lake and mountains beyond. Water can flow for 32km along the Mohale Tunnel between here and Katse.

The **visitors centre** (☑2293 6217; ⊙8am-4pm Mon-Fri, 10am-3pm Sat & Sun; P) is 15km from the main road, signposted west of Mohale village. It offers dam views, a guided tour (M10) and boat cruises (per person from M250; book ahead). Tours go at 9am and 2pm on weekdays, and at 11am on weekends.

🛏 Sleeping & Eating

Mohale Lodge HOTEL $$
(☑2293 6134; Mohale village; s/d incl breakfast M830/1100; P✳🛜) The pleasant interiors at Mohale Lodge make up for its distant dam view. The comfortable rooms are replete with modern furnishings and trimmed with Afro-decor, and the restaurant (mains M75 to M180) is a pleasant spot to break up a journey.

ℹ Getting There & Away

Shared taxis from Maseru cost M60 one-way and M120 for a return trip. A bus from Maseru (M40) headed for Thaba-Tseka leaves at 9am and passes the Mohale Lodge at around 11am. Passengers can depart at the bus stop on the main road, but must walk a couple of kilometres to reach the lodge.

Semonkong

POP 17,615

Semonkong (Place of Smoke), a one-pony town in the rugged Thaba Putsoa range, gets its name from the nearby Maletsunyane Falls (204m), which are usually at their loudest in summer but sometimes can be bone dry. The town is the starting point for

---

ROOF OF AFRICA

This annual **motorbike race** (www. roofofafrica.info; ⊙late Nov or early Dec) is one of the world's toughest off-road endurance events, challenging contestants to ride hundreds of kilometres through the Lesotho Highlands.

---

many fine hiking and pony-trekking trails, including the two-day ride via the peaks of the Thaba Putsoa to Ketane Falls (122m).

🛏 Sleeping & Eating

★**Semonkong Lodge** LODGE $$
(☑5888 1021, 6202 1021, 2700 6037; www.semonkonglodge.com; camping M150, dm M250, s/d incl breakfast from M800/1300; P🛗) 🌿 Near the Maletsunyane River, this lodge is a model of community tourism and a great place for everyone from families to adventure seekers. If the inviting accommodation, including cosy rondavels with fireplaces, doesn't make you extend your stay in the mountains, fireside feasts in the lodge's recently expanded Duck & Donkey Tavern (mains M75 to M120) surely will.

There's also a kitchen for those who want to self-cater. Staff can arrange all kinds of tours and hikes, employing locals to navigate the villages and steep trails, including extreme catch-and-release fly-fishing expeditions, overnight pony trekking and even pub crawls by donkey. Then there's the world's longest commercially operated, single-drop abseil 204m down the **Maletsunyane Falls** (☑2700 6037; M1085, includes training, transport, certificate & photos).

The lodge is signposted from the town centre, 2km down a gravel road.

ℹ Getting There & Away

Semonkong is about 110km southeast of Maseru on the tar road to Qacha's Nek; both are a three-hour drive. Shared taxis run all day to/from Maseru (M70) and leave throughout the morning to/from Qacha's Nek (M120). A private taxi to/from Qacha's Nek costs around M250.

If you're heading in from South Africa, it's possible to get a shared taxi from Kokstad in the Eastern Cape, changing at Matatiele.

SOUTHERN LESOTHO

The mountain ranges eat up the sky in southern Lesotho, where a velvety orange-pink light pours over rocky peaks and yawning valleys – it's a place that lingers in the memory banks of all who pass through. If you like hiking and pony trekking in rugged isolation, this little-developed region is for you.

An awe-inspiring permaculture project, a little-explored lake and some far-flung rondavels round out the offerings of the south.

The road from Quthing to Qacha's Nek is one of Lesotho's most impressive drives, taking you along the winding Senqu (Orange) River gorge and through some striking canyon scenery before climbing up onto the escarpment. Another stunner is the road through the interior from Semonkong down to Qacha's Nek. Despite what some maps show, both are tarred all the way to Qacha's Nek. The roads leading to Sehlabathebe National Park are another matter entirely. Do not attempt without a 4WD and a firm backbone.

Shared taxis between destinations in the region are limited, cheap and crowded.

Malealea

This remote village has three travel trump cards: its breathtaking mountain scenery, its trading-post lodge and its successful community-based tourism. Many visitors to Lesotho head straight here to sample traditional Basotho life or, as the sign outside town says, to just 'pause and look upon a gateway of paradise'. The area has been inhabited for centuries, as shown by the many San rock-art sites in the vicinity.

✯ Festivals & Events

Malealea Monster Weekend SPORTS
(www.malealea.com; ⊙ late May) The 'weekend of adventure' hosted by Malealea Lodge features 8km to 80km mountain-bike races, 7km and 15km trail runs and a 2km night run. All take advantage of the mountainous terrain and gorges around Malealea.

Lesotho Sky SPORTS
(www.lesothosky.com; ⊙ late Sep) This six-day, 350km, team mountain-bike race begins in Roma and climbs through the highlands to Malealea and on to Semonkong.

🏃 Activities

Pony Trekking

Options for pony trekking range from easy **two-hour pony rides** (one/two/three people M430/600/750) to San rock art or a gorge viewpoint, to **overnight expeditions** (M900/1140/1575 per day) with accommodation in **Basotho village huts** (M130 per hut for one to three people). Multiday routes include Ribaneng Waterfall (two days, one night); Ribaneng and Ketane Waterfalls (four days, three nights); and Ribaneng, Ketane and Semonkong (six days, five nights).

Hiking

You can hike to spots including **Pitseng Gorge** (8km or 16km), with its gnarly cliffs and swimming holes, and **Botsoela Waterfall** (10km; 13km including San rock art). Guided overnight hikes are also possible (with/without packhorse M600/200 per day), with accommodation in huts.

Village Visits

Village visits provide a stimulating insight into the local people and their customs. Down the slope from Malealea Lodge is a teaching farm where the lodge gets its vegetables, along with a tiny museum and craft shop, housed in traditional Basotho huts, from where you can wander through the village – solo or with a guide. You can pay for **guided visits** (M15 per person per hour) to the *sangoma* (traditional medicine practitioner; only for the genuinely interested), the village school and the late Mr Musi's reclaimed *donga* (eroded ravine used for small-scale agriculture).

Mountain Biking & Scenic Drives

Year-round you can hire bikes (half/full day with guide M250/400 per person). Malealea Lodge can also recommend scenic drives for 4WD and high-clearance 2WD vehicles.

🛏 Sleeping & Eating

★**Malealea Lodge** LODGE $
(✆5840 7816, South Africa 082 552 4215; www.malealea.com; camping M130, s/d from M500/670, with shared bathroom from M300/400; [P]🛜) 🏊 Offering 'Lesotho in a nutshell', Malealea is a deserving poster child for the mountain kingdom. Every sunset, village choirs and bands perform at the mountaintop lodge. Many of the activities are run in partnership with the community, and a proportion of tourist revenue and donations goes directly to supporting local projects. The views, meanwhile, are stupendous.

Accommodation ranges from campsites and twin 'forest' (backpacker) huts in a pretty wooded setting away from the lodge to simple, cosy en-suite rooms and rondavels. A sense of history pervades the site, which began life in 1905 as a trading post, established by teacher, diamond miner and soldier Mervyn Smith. From 1986 the Jones family ran the store before transforming it into accommodation and integrating it with the surrounding community.

Malealea also offers a bar, hearty meals (breakfast/lunch/dinner M95/120/175), self-catering facilities and a shop with basic goods. There are now intermittent wi-fi and mobile-phone signals at the lodge, and the whole place runs on solar power. Bring your own water containers, as the lodge is moving away from plastic bottle usage.

September to December are the busy months.

ⓘ Getting There & Away

Early morning shared taxis connect Maseru and Malealea (M100, 2½ hours). Later in the day, catch a shared taxi to the junction town of Motsekuoa (M50, 1½ hours), from where there are connections to Malealea (M40, one hour). Services from Mafeteng and the south also stop in Motsekuoa. The lodge provides airport transfers for M950 each way.

If driving, beware that Google Maps will lead you astray. Head south from Maseru on the Mafeteng road (Main Rd South) for 60km to Motsekuoa. Opposite the shared-taxi corner, turn left (east) at the sign for Matelile, Qaba and Malealea Lodge. Ten kilometres further on, take the right fork and continue another 15km. When you reach the signposted turn-off to Malealea, travel about 7km along an unsealed road over the Gates of Paradise Pass (2003m) to the village and lodge. It's also possible to approach Malealea from the south, via Mpharane and Masemouse, but this gravel road is rough and not suitable for a 2WD car.

Mohale's Hoek

POP 25,308

Like other towns hereabouts, shabby Mohale's Hoek has little to offer other than a place to overnight, although it does at least boast a decent accommodation option.

Shared taxis, sprinters and buses running between Maseru and Quthing stop here (near Makhaleng Bridge border crossing).

Hotel Mount Maluti (☏ 2278 5224; www. hmmlesotho.com; s/d incl breakfast M700/750; Ⓟ 🛜 ♨) offers dated rooms in cool blocks opening onto pleasant gardens. Its restaurant is a decent lunch stop (mains M70 to M110), serving sandwiches, burgers, pizza and pasta, and the whole shebang is signposted off the main road.

Quthing

POP 20,000

Home to some distinguished sets of dinosaur footprints and close to Lesotho's most innovative and ambitious permaculture project, Quthing is the southernmost major town in Lesotho, and is also known as Moyeni (Place of the Wind).

It was established in 1877, abandoned during the Gun War of 1880 and then rebuilt at the present site. Activity centres on the new part of town, Lower Quthing, with its bustling main road.

◉ Sights

Dinosaur Footprints   ARCHAEOLOGICAL SITE (M15; ⊘ 8am-5pm; Ⓟ) One of Quthing's main claims to fame is the proliferation of dinosaur footprints in the surrounding area. The most easily accessible are signposted on the left as you leave town heading northeast towards Qacha's Nek. In this building are 230-million-year-old footprints and a craft shop. Children will offer to guide you to more footprints for a small tip.

WORTH A TRIP

BETHEL

For travellers (and particularly families) looking to relax in the Lesothan countryside and immerse in permaculture, it's more than worthwhile to venture out to **Bethel Business and Community Development Centre** (BBCDC; ☏ 5901 1384; Bethel; per person M350; Ⓟ ♿), a technical school and learning centre started by a visionary expat in 1993. The school offers a few charming chalets and a good restaurant, along with mountains of expertise in environmental science.

The place runs exclusively on solar power and with its biodigestor cleans thousands of litres of wastewater a day. There are welding and woodworking workshops, and courses in cooking, hospitality and electrical engineering, all of which serve to educate the nation's young people. It's a wonder to see it all in action, and to witness the sheer diversity of plants and trees that thrive on the campus, which was built on soil once thought to be barren.

Although previously the centre was difficult to access, a bridge constructed in 2016 just north of Mt Moorosi, across the Senqu (Orange) River, has made visiting far more convenient. Another lesser-known stay in the vicinity is **Moorosi Chalets** (☏ 6812 1336; huts/chalets per person from M100/M200), a few rondavels on the other side of the bridge, tucked into their own private valley.

Masitise Cave House Museum   MUSEUM
(📱5756 7721; adult/child M10/3; ⊙8.30am-5pm Mon-Fri, to 2pm Sat & Sun; 🅿) Five kilometres west of Quthing is this intriguing section of an old mission, built directly into a San rock shelter in 1866 by Reverend David-Frédéric Ellenberger, a Swiss missionary who was among the first to arrive in Lesotho. There's a cast of a dinosaur footprint in the ceiling, a museum with displays on local culture and history, and fading San rock art nearby.

To get here, take the signposted turn-off near the Masitise Primary School and follow the road about 1km back past the small red church. At the neighbouring house you can ask for the key from the caretaker, the church pastor. From here, the museum is three minutes further on foot.

🛏 Sleeping

Fuleng Guest House   GUESTHOUSE $
(📱2275 0260; info.fulengguesthouse@gmail.com; s/d from M450/600; 🅿🛜) This hillside guesthouse offers rondavels with a view, a restaurant (breakfast/meals M65/90), cheeky garden gnomes, a rock feature and a friendly local experience. Find it by the main road on the way up to Upper Quthing. Rates are higher if you pay by card.

Hillsview Guest House   LODGE $$
(Quthing Lodge; 📱5911 1029; http://hillsviewguesthousequthing.co.ls; s/d incl breakfast M650/750; 🅿🛜) A hillside retreat with 20 lovely chalets and a quaint restaurant (meals M130) serving mostly meat dishes. The owners and management are very tapped into area tourism and can hook you up with a local guide to visit lesser-known attractions such as Lake Letsie (R80).

❶ Getting There & Away

The transport stand is in Lower Quthing. Shared taxis serve Maseru (M70, 2½ hours) and Qacha's Nek (M90, 2½ hours), as do faster, more expensive sprinters and slower, cheaper buses. Services to/from Maseru are more frequent. Shared taxis run to/from Tele Bridge border post (M15, 45 minutes), which is linked by shared taxi to Sterkspruit (South Africa) for onward transport. The gravel road connecting Tele Bridge and the main Quthing–Mohale's Hoek road is passable in a 2WD car.

Qacha's Nek

POP 9417

Originally a mission station, Qacha's Nek was founded in 1888 near the pass (1980m) of the same name. The sleepy border town has an attractive church, a quirky snake park and a variety of colonial-era sandstone buildings, plus nearby stands of California redwood trees, some over 25m high.

Next to the New Central Hotel, the tourist office (📱2295 0331; ⊙8am-1pm & 2pm-4.30 Mon-Fri) assists travellers in making arrangements for Sehlabathebe National Park.

◉ Sights

★**Qacha's Nek Snake Park**   PARK
(📱5330 1880; R30, with carwash R35; ⊙6am-midnight) This site is unique in Lesotho, not only because it is the country's only snake park, but because you can also get your car washed while you visit the anacondas, endemic puff adders and spitting cobras. Oh, and the eccentric, local herpetologist who owns the place also keeps bees. *And* the first chief of Qacha's Nek used to live in a cave above where the snakes are kept. For the full effect, do the tour late at night (don't worry, the place is lit up).

🛏 Sleeping

Letloepe Guesthouse   GUESTHOUSE $
(📱2295 0383; s/d M300/500; 🅿) On the edge of town near the Snake Park, Letloepe offers rustic self-catering rondavels and bungalows with lovely mountain views. Cheaper rooms with shared bathroom (from M200) are also available. Breakfast costs M60.

New Central Hotel   BUSINESS HOTEL $$
(📱2295 0488; s/d incl breakfast from M650/850; 🅿✳🛜) Rooms have mountains of pillows and facilities in this smart hotel at the northern entrance to town. Lunch and dinner (two courses M140) should be ordered in advance.

❶ Getting There & Away

Shared taxis (M160, three hours) begin departing for Maseru at around 7am (this can vary), with a more comfortable sprinter (M160, four hours) departing around 7am. Most services go via Semonkong, but some take the Quthing route.

Small shared taxis link the main transport stand with the border (M6.50), from where shared bakkies (pick-up trucks) and vans run to Matatiele, South Africa (M50), where you can pick up onward transport.

Sehlabathebe National Park

Lesotho's most under-visited **national park** (📱5853 7565, 6253 7565; M30; ⊙headquarters 8am-4.30pm) is remote, rugged and beautiful.

The rolling grasslands, wildflowers and silence provide complete isolation, with only the prolific bird life (including the bearded vulture) and the odd rhebok for company. Hiking (and horse riding from Sani Top or the Drakensberg) is the main way to explore the waterfalls and surrounds, and angling is possible in the park's dams and rivers during the rainy season.

Come well prepared for the changing elements: this is a summer-rainfall area, and thick mist, potentially hazardous to hikers, is common. The winters are clear but it gets cold at night, with occasional light snowfalls.

Camping is permitted in the park, and at the entrance there is a cluster of self-catering **rondavels** (☑ 6253 7565; per person R250). There's also a **lodge** (camping R80) inside the park, though at the time of research it had no operator and its generator was broken.

ℹ Information

Headquarters (☑ 6253 7565, 5853 7565, 6872 5860; ⊙ 8am-4.30pm) Constructed in 2016 at the entrance to Sehlabathebe National Park with a reception area, parking lot and information desk where you can pay park fees and obtain info.

ℹ Getting There & Away

Shared taxis connect Mavuka village, near the park gate, and Qacha's Nek (M70, five hours), leaving Mavuka around 5am and returning at 2pm.

The gravel road from Qacha's Nek is not recommended in a 2WD car, but check locally for updates on its condition. The road from the north is extremely rough and challenging even by 4WD; the 150km road from Thaba-Tseka takes several hours. Both roads can be affected by storms and landslides, so consult locals before setting out. You can arrange to leave your vehicle at the police station in Paolosi village, about 3km south of Mavuka, while you're in the park. The nearest petrol stations are in Qacha's Nek and Thaba-Tseka, but a few shops near the park sell bottles of gas.

On foot, the simplest way into Sehlabathebe is to hike 10km up the escarpment from KwaZulu-Natal. Packhorses can be arranged through the park headquarters. From Bushman's Nek border crossing up the pass to Nkonkoana Gate takes about six hours. To trot up the pass on horseback, **Khotso Trails** (☑ in South Africa 033 701 1502; www.khotsotrails.co.za) offers a two- or three-day expedition from Underberg (Southern Drakensberg).

Swaziland

Why Go?

In short: big things come in small packages. The intriguing kingdom of Swaziland is diminutive but boasts a huge checklist for any visitor. Rewarding wildlife watching? Tick. Adrenaline-boosting activities such as rafting and mountain biking? Tick. Lively and colourful local culture, with celebrations and ceremonies still common practice? Tick. Plus there are superb walking trails, stunning mountain and flatland scenery, varied accommodation options and excellent, handicrafts.

Unlike South Africa, Swaziland has managed to hold on to that slow-down-this-is-Africa feeling and that's why it's gaining in popularity. Everything remains small and personable and the atmosphere is remarkably relaxed. Instead of making a flying visit here on your way to Kruger National Park, KwaZulu-Natal or Mozambique, consider staying at least a week to do the country justice. If you plan a visit during the winter months, try to make it coincide with the Umhlanga (reed) festival, one of Africa's biggest cultural events.

When to Go
Mbabane

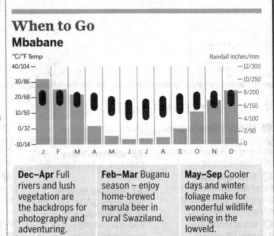

| Dec–Apr Full rivers and lush vegetation are the backdrops for photography and adventuring. | Feb–Mar Buganu season – enjoy home-brewed marula beer in rural Swaziland. | May–Sep Cooler days and winter foliage make for wonderful wildlife viewing in the lowveld. |

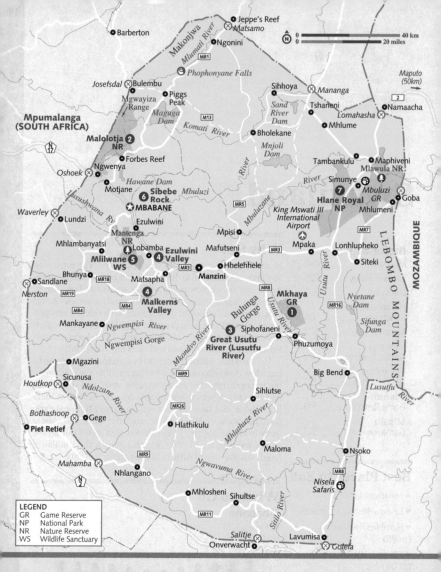

Swaziland Highlights

1 Mkhaya Game Reserve (p513) Watching wildlife, including rare black rhinos, at this excellent reserve.

2 Malolotja Nature Reserve (p509) Walking or hiking in this enchanting wilderness area.

3 Great Usutu River (Lusutfu River) (p514) Shooting over whitewater rapids on a day-long adventure.

4 Malkerns Valley (p505) Checking out the numerous craft shops.

5 Mlilwane Wildlife Sanctuary (p504) Exploring on foot, horseback or by bike and relaxing in the comfortable lodges.

6 Sibebe Rock (p498) Climbing this massive granite dome just outside the capital and soaking up the lovely views.

7 Hlane Royal National Park (p511) Coming face to face with a pride of lions or watching white rhinos congregate at the accessible watering hole.

History

Beginnings of a Nation

The area that is now Swaziland has been inhabited for millennia, and human-like remains possibly dating back as far as 100,000 years have been discovered around the Lebombo Mountains in eastern Swaziland. However, today's Swazis trace their ancestors to much more recent arrivals. By around AD 500, various Nguni groups had made their way to the region as part of the great Bantu migrations. One of these groups settled in the area around present-day Maputo (Mozambique), eventually founding the Dlamini dynasty. In the mid-18th century, in response to increasing pressure from other clans in the area, the Dlamini king, Ngwane III, led his people southwest to the Pongola River, in present-day southern Swaziland and northern KwaZulu-Natal. This became the first Swazi heartland.

Ngwane's successor, Sobhuza I, established a base in the Ezulwini Valley, which still remains the centre of Swazi royalty and ritual. Next came King Mswazi (or Mswati), after whom the Swazi take their name. Despite pressure from the neighbouring Zulu, Mswazi succeeded in unifying the whole kingdom.

From the mid-19th century, Swaziland attracted increasing numbers of European farmers in search of land for cattle, as well as hunters, traders and missionaries.

Over the next decades, the Swazis saw their territory whittled away as the British and Boers jostled for power in the area. In 1902, following the Second Anglo-Boer War, the Boers withdrew and the British took control of Swaziland as a protectorate.

Struggle for Independence

Swazi history in the early 20th century centred on the ongoing struggle for independence. Under the leadership of King Sobhuza II (guided by the capable hands of his mother, Lomawa Ndwandwewho, who acted as regent while Sobhuza was a child), the Swazis succeeded in regaining much of their original territory. This was done in part by direct purchase and in part by British government decree. This was a major development, as Swazi kings are considered to hold the kingdom in trust for their subjects, and land ownership is thus more than just a political and economic issue.

Independence was finally achieved – the culmination of a long and remarkably nonviolent path – on 6 September 1968, 66

> ### SWAZILAND NO MORE?
>
> In April 2018 King Mswati III surprised the world by announcing that his country was now to be called the Kingdom of eSwatini. The new name, which means 'land of the Swazis', has been bandied about before by the king, most notably when he was addressing the UN General Assembly in 2017. The monarch feels that eSwatini reclaims the country's pre-colonial moniker, as well as removes any confusion abroad between his homeland and Switzerland. How quickly eSwatini will be taken up by the public at large is anyone's guess.

years after the establishment of the British protectorate.

The first Swazi constitution was largely a British creation, and in 1973 the king suspended it on the grounds that it did not accord with Swazi culture. Four years later parliament reconvened under a new constitution vesting all power in the king.

Sobhuza II died in 1982, at that time the world's longest-reigning monarch. In 1986 the young Mswati III ascended the throne, where he continues today to represent and maintain the traditional Swazi way of life and to assert his pre-eminence as absolute monarch. Despite an undercurrent of political dissent, political parties are still unable to participate in elections.

Current Events

King Mswati III regularly comes under attack, especially in the foreign press, for his autocratic status, lax spending habits and polygamous practices. Critics say this hinders economic progress and the fight against HIV/AIDS, by which over 27% of the population is believed to be affected. But even his harshest Swazi critics don't seem to want to do away with him altogether, calling for a constitutional, not absolute, monarchy.

The king is hoping to use tourism to bolster Swaziland's struggling economy, which shrunk 0.6% in 2016. However, the construction of a $280 million airport and a state-of-the-art conference venue seem to be more a white elephant rather than an economic boost. A persistent drought hasn't helped the agricultural sector, nor did the fact that Swaziland was removed from the USA's AGOA (African Growth and

Opportunity Act) free-trade agreement in 2014 because it didn't meet some essential criteria – namely respect for workers' rights and freedom of association. While most of the benefits from AGOA would have been limited to low-paying jobs in the textile sector, the loss of any job in a country where the unemployment rate hovers around 28% is problematic.

Climate

Most of Swaziland enjoys a climate similar to that of South Africa's eastern lowveld, with rainy, steamy summers and agreeably cooler winters. Between December and February, temperatures occasionally exceed 40°C and torrential thunderstorms are common. May to August are the coolest months. In the higher-lying areas of the west, winters bring cool, crisp nights and sometimes even frost.

Language

Swaziland's official languages are Swati and English, and English is the official written language.

① Getting There & Around

There are several daily flights with South African Airways Airlink subsidiary **Swaziland Airlink** (☑ in South Africa 0861 606 606, in Swaziland 2335 0100; www.flyswaziland.com) into Swaziland's **King Mswati III International Airport** (SHO; ☑ 2518 4390; www.swacaa.co.sz) from Johannesburg.

Most travellers enter Swaziland overland. Car rental is available from **Avis** (☑ 2518 6226; www.avis.co.za; King Mswati III International Airport; ⊙ 7am-6pm) and **Europcar** (☑ 2518 4393; www.europcar.com; Matshapa Airport; ⊙ 8am-5pm Mon-Fri), or at **Affordable Car Hire** (☑ 7602 0394, 2404 9136; www.affordablecarhire.co.za; Swazi Plaza; daily rates from E215) in Mbabane, but it's usually cheaper to rent a car in South Africa. There is a good network of minibus shared taxis covering Swaziland.

MBABANE

POP 76,000 / ELEV 1243M

Mbabane's main draw? Its lovely setting in the craggy Dlangeni Hills. Swaziland's capital and second-largest city, Mbabane is a relaxed and functional place perched in the cool highveld. Its climate is actually why the British moved their base here from the heat of Manzini in 1902.

Sibebe Rock LANDMARK

(☑ 2404 6070; Pine Valley; E30; ⊙ 8am-5pm Mon-Sat) About 8km northeast of Mbabane is Sibebe Rock, a massive granite dome hulking over the surrounding countryside. It's the world's second-largest monolith, after Australia's Uluru, but is considerably less visited. Much of the rock is completely sheer, and dangerous if you should fall, but climbing it is a good adrenaline charge if you're reasonably fit and relish looking down steep rock faces. Community guides operate guided hikes (E100 per person, three hours) – ask at the visitor centre.

Alternatively, Swazi Trails (p500) in Ezulwini Valley runs half-day nontechnical climbs up the rock (E750 per person, including transport).

🛏 Sleeping

★ **Brackenhill Lodge** GUESTHOUSE **$$**
(www.brackenhillswazi.com; Mountain Dr; s/d incl breakfast E790/1050; [P][🐕][🛜][🏊]) With its wonderfully relaxing atmosphere and bucolic setting, this little cracker located 4.5km northeast of Mbabane is sure to win your heart. It offers eight comfortable, well-equipped and airy rooms, and its 162 hectares have several walking trails, great birdlife and splendid panoramas. Facilities include gym, sauna, swimming pool and even tennis courts. Lovely owners; evening meals on request.

The Place GUESTHOUSE **$$**
(☑ 7638 1880, 7828 5090; www.theplaceswaziland.com; Mantsholo St; s/d incl breakfast E990/1490; [P][❄][🛜][🏊]) Opposite the golf course, this modern guesthouse has impeccable, well-equipped rooms with sparkling bathrooms and a small kitchenette. The free-standing units open onto a manicured garden and a pool, and is in the same complex as **Ramblas Restaurant** (☑ 2404 4147; www.ramblasswaziland.webs.com; mains E80-160; ⊙ 8am-9pm Mon-Sat; [🛜][♿]). A great find.

Foresters Arms LODGE **$$**
(☑ 2467 4177; www.forestersarms.co.za; MR19, Mhlambanyatsi; s/d incl breakfast E670/1140; [P][🛜][🏊]) Hidden 27km southwest of Mbabane in picturesque hills, Foresters Arms has a haunting but beautiful remoteness. The air is clean, the views suggestive, the peace tangible. It's a superb staging post between KwaZulu-Natal and Kruger National Park, with cosy rooms, attractive gardens and a smorgasbord of activities (horse

riding, mountain biking and hiking). Another highlight is the on-site restaurant.

Follow the MR19 from Mbabane in the direction of Mhlambanyatsi.

✕ Eating

There are supermarkets, chain restaurants, fast-food outlets and **Riverside Café** (☑ 2404 9547; mains E30-100; ⊙ 8am-5pm Mon-Fri, to 2.30pm Sat) at **Swazi Plaza** (☑ 2404 3869; www.swaziplazaprop.sz; Dr Sishayi Rd; ⊙ 8am-5pm), which is the main shopping mall in Mbabane's city centre.

eDish   CAFE $

(☑ 2404 5504, 7664 3890; Computronics House, Somhlolo St/Gilfillan St; mains E50-80; ⊙ 8am-5pm Mon-Sat; 🅿 🛜) With gourmet sandwiches, comfy couches, good coffee, cold beer and a deck offering fine Mbabane views, eDish is a worthy place to spend an hour. Best of all, there is free wi-fi at decent speeds.

★ eDladleni   SWAZI $$

(☑ 2404 5743; http://edladleni.100webspace.net; Manzini/Mbabane Hwy, Mvubu Falls; mains E55-80; ⊙ noon-3pm & 6-10pm Tue-Sun; ☑) Delicious food, a serene setting and cracking views – if you're after an authentic Swazi experience, eDladleni is hard to beat. Here you can tuck into traditional specialities that are hard to find elsewhere, and it's got excellent vegetarian options. It's about 6km from Mbabane, off the main highway (follow the sign 'Mvubu Falls'); check the website for directions.

The charismatic owner, Dolores Godefroy, is committed to reviving traditional recipes based on local produce. Service can be rather slow and opening hours are unreliable – it's wise to call ahead.

Albert Millin   CAFE $$

(☑ 2404 9942; Gwamile St; mains E60-120; ⊙ 10am-10pm Tue & Wed, to midnight Thu-Sat; 🅿 🛜) This eatery-pub on the grounds of the Mbabane Club is very popular with expats and has a modern feel. From pizzas and salads to burgers and satisfying grilled meats, the menu covers enough territory to please most palates. It's also a good place to just enjoy the cool atmosphere with a cold beer in hand.

ⓘ Information

EMERGENCY

Police (☑ 2404 2502, emergencies 999; Mhlambanyatsi Rd)

Mbabane

MEDICAL SERVICES

Mbabane Clinic (☑ 2404 2423; www.theclinicgroup.com; Mkhonubovu St; ⊙ 24hr) For emergencies try this well-equipped clinic in the southwestern corner of Mbabane, just off the bypass road.

MONEY

There are banks with ATMs in Corporate Place, next to Swazi Plaza.

TOURIST INFORMATION

Tourism Information Office (☑ 2404 2531; www.thekingdomofswaziland.com; The Mall, Dr Sishayi Rd; ⊙ 8am-5pm Mon-Fri, 9am-1pm Sat)

ⓘ Getting There & Around

Mbabane's main **bus and shared-taxi rank** (Dr Sishayi Rd) is just behind Swazi Plaza. Shared taxis leave for Johannesburg (E220, four hours) throughout the day.

There are several shared taxis daily to Ngwenya and the Oshoek border post (E30, 50 minutes), and Malkerns Valley (E30, 45 minutes). All vehicles heading towards Manzini (E40, 35 minutes) and points east pass through the Ezulwini Valley, although most take the highways, bypassing the valley itself.

Nonshared taxis (Dr Sishayi Rd) congregate just across the street from Swazi Plaza, in the mall parking lot. Nonshared taxis to the Ezulwini Valley cost from E200, more to the far end of the valley (from E250). Expect to pay from E500 to get to King Mswati III International Airport.

TransMagnific ([📞] 2404 9977; www.goswaziland.co.sz; Cooper Centre, Sozisa Rd, Shop 11 behind Cooper Centre) and **Sky World** ([📞] 7664 0001, 2404 9921; www.skyworld.co.sz; Checkers Business Park, Sozisa Rd) offer a daily luxury shuttle service between Johannesburg (stopping at OR Tambo International Airport and Sandton) and Mbabane for E600. Other destinations include Durban (E780) and, on weekends, Nelspruit (from E400).

If you're driving, you can get petrol at **Engen** (Sozisa Rd; ⊗24hr) or **Total** (cnr Sozisa & Mhlambanyatsi Rds; ⊗24hr).

CENTRAL SWAZILAND

The country's tourist hub, central Swaziland is a heady mix of culture, nature and epicurean indulgences, and has plenty to keep you occupied for a few days. There are wildlife reserves to explore, museums to visit, great restaurants to sample and quality handicrafts to bring home.

Ezulwini Valley

What a difference a few kilometres can make! Swaziland's tourism centre, the Ezulwini Valley, begins just outside Mbabane but feels a world away from the hullabaloo of the capital. It makes a wonderful (and convenient) base for many visitors.

◎ Sights & Activities

Mantenga Cultural Village & Nature Reserve   NATURE RESERVE
([📞] 2416 1178, 2416 1101; www.sntc.org.sz/reserves/mantenga.asp; E100; ⊗8am-6pm) The entrance fee to this tranquil, thickly forested reserve covers a guided tour of the Swazi Cultural Village, a 'living' cultural village with authentic beehive huts and cultural displays, plus a *sibhaca* dance (performed daily at 11.15am and 3.15pm) and a visit to the impressive Mantenga Falls. The reserve is also

great for hiking; day hikers pay only E50. Although it's not a big wildlife park, it offers a chance to see vervet monkeys, baboons, warthogs, nyalas and duikers.

There is a free map available of the reserve, with hiking trails, available at reception. Birdlife abounds, including the endangered southern bald ibis. It's located 1km from Mantenga Lodge and is well signposted from the MR103.

Swazi Trails   ADVENTURE SPORTS
([📞] 2416 2180, 7602 0261; www.swazitrails.co.sz; Mantenga Craft Centre; ⊗8am-5pm) Based in the Mantenga Craft Centre, this is one of the country's major activity companies and the place to go to for caving, rafting, hikes and general cultural and highlights tours. Also houses the Ezulwini Tourist Office (p503).

⟟ Tours

All Out Africa   ADVENTURE
([📞] 2416 2260; www.alloutafrica.com; MR103; ⊗8am-5pm) All Out Africa's head office deals with volunteering and experiential tours around Swaziland, South Africa and Mozambique. To book a tour, visit their office located at Malandela's (p505).

Ekhaya Cultural Tours   CULTURAL
([📞] 7644 3257; half/full day R1200/1450, minimum 2 people; ⊗daily by reservation) For a taste of rural Swazi life – including a visit to Lobamba – a good contact is local Mandla Masuku of Ekhaya Cultural Tours. The tours include a traditional lunch and pick-up from your lodging. The full day rate includes a tour of a cultural village. Tours are offered in English and French.

⨳ Sleeping

Legends Backpackers Lodge   HOSTEL $
([📞] 2416 1870, 7602 0261; www.legends.co.sz; Mantenga Falls Rd; camping E90, dm E175, d with shared bathroom E585; [P][🛜][❄️][🏊]) It's far from flash, but this mellow place is the most obvious choice if funds are short, with an assortment of 10- to 12-bed dorms, a self-catering kitchen, a chill-out lounge with TV and a small pool in the garden. Those needing privacy can opt for the plain but restful private rooms in a separate building. Breakfast costs E55.

Swazi Trails, the lodge's sister company and local adventure-activity operator, is just across the road. The nearest supermarket is a 10-minute stroll away.

Ezulwini & Malkerns Valleys

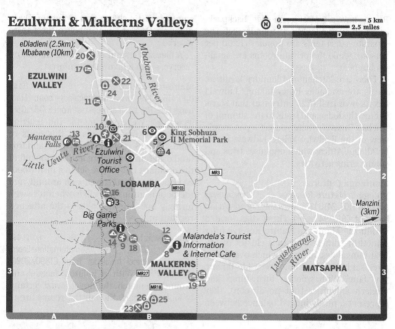

Ezulwini & Malkerns Valleys

★**Lidwala Backpacker Lodge** HOSTEL $$
(☏7690 5865; www.lidwala.co.sz; MR103; camping/dm/d E130/220/715; ❿⊛⊠) What a magical setting! This comfortable, well-run spot is nestled in a splendid garden with a pool, among big boulders and a chuckling stream.

Rooms have a typical dorm-style, backpacker set-up, with a laid-back, friendly feel. The separate safari tents are popular (E200 per person), while the private rooms are smallish but neat.

There are kitchen and laundry facilities; meals are available. Fancy hiking? Lidwala has its own trail (E25 entry fee) that starts behind the lodge and leads to the summit of 'Sheba's Breasts' where you get a panoramic view of the Ezulwini Valley. Lidwala is run by All Out Africa, which organises trips and volunteering activities.

Mantenga Cultural Village & Nature Reserve   BUNGALOW $$

(☑2416 1101, 2416 1178; www.sntc.org.sz; s/d incl breakfast E610/940; P) These digs located within the Mantenga Nature Reserve offer something different, with a cluster of offbeat bungalows, many of which overlook a river, set in lush bushland. Very 'Me Tarzan, you Jane'. With wooden furnishings and modern amenities (but no air-con), they represent a nicely judged balance between comfort, rustic charm and seclusion. Overnight guests don't pay entry to the nature reserve.

A pleasant restaurant is within the nature reserve, set in a luxuriant rainforest.

Mantenga Lodge   HOTEL $$

(☑2416 1049; www.mantengalodge.com; Mantenga Falls Rd; s/d incl breakfast from E745/1050; P ✳ ⊛ ⊠) We're suckers for the relaxing atmosphere that prevails in this oasis of calm. The 38 rooms of varying standards (and different prices) are nothing too out of the ordinary, but they're set in a lush wooded area where you can mooch around, and the pool is an instant elixir when it's swelteringly hot. Another plus is the attached restaurant.

Royal Swazi Spa   HOTEL $$$

(☑2416 5000; www.suninternational.com; MR103; s/d incl breakfast from E1890/2090; P ✳ @ ⊛ ⊠) With a palatial facade and grounds to match, the Royal Swazi certainly looks the part, though the rooms are in

SWAZI CEREMONIES & FESTIVALS

Incwala

Incwala (also known as Ncwala) is the most sacred ceremony of the Swazi people. It is a 'first fruits' ceremony, where the king gives permission for his people to eat the first crops of the new year. It takes place in late December/early January and lasts one week: dates are announced shortly before the event. It's a fiercely traditional celebration and visitors should take note of strict rules, including restrictions on dress and photography.

Umhlanga Reed Dance Festival

The Umhlanga (reed) dance is Swaziland's best-known cultural event. Though not as sacred as the Incwala, it serves a similar function in drawing the nation together and reminding the people of their relationship to the king. It is something like a weeklong debutante ball for marriageable young Swazi women, who journey from all over the kingdom to help repair the queen mother's home at Lobamba. It takes place in late August or early September. Note that visitors are only allowed to take photographs with prior permission from the Ministry of Information.

Buganu Festival

Another 'first fruits' festival, this takes place in February and celebrates the marula fruit. The women gather the fruit and ferment a brew (known as buganu; it packs a punch). Locals – mainly males – gather to drink and celebrate. The festival, which is held in various locations across the country, is becoming one of the country's most popular traditional ceremonies, and is attended by King Mswati III and other royalty.

MTN Bushfire Festival

Held annually for three days over the last weekend of May, this increasingly popular festival features music, poetry and theatre among other performances. It takes place at House on Fire (p506) in Malkerns. Check the website (www.bush-fire.com) for more information about the program.

need of a revamp. Still, they have the requisite comforts and the hotel features a host of facilities and amenities, including two restaurants, three bars, a large pool, a spa, a casino and a golf course.

✗ Eating

Gables Shopping Centre　　SUPERMARKET $
(www.thegables.co.sz; MR 103; ☺ 8am-10pm) This mall has a decent supermarket and a handful of chain restaurants – Ocean Basket is the best bet.

Mantenga Restaurant　　INTERNATIONAL $$
(🖉 2416 1049; Mantenga Lodge & Restaurant, Mantenga Falls Rd; mains E70-185; ☺ 6.30am-9.30pm) Inside Mantenga Lodge, but open to nonguests, this restaurant with a raised wooden deck has a fabulous outlook over the trees. The grilled meats are quite good, as are the pastas.

★ Lihawu Restaurant　　FUSION $$$
(🖉 2416 7035; www.lihawu.co.sz; Royal Villas; mains E95-230; ☺ noon-2pm & 6-10.30pm; 🖉) Within the swish Royal Villas resort nestles Swaziland's most elegant restaurant, with a tastefully decorated dining room and an outdoor eating area that overlooks a swimming pool. The menu is Afro-fusion, with meaty signature dishes such as oxtail stew and pork belly, but there are a couple of vegetarian options. Needless to say the accompanying wine list is top class.

The cigar and whisky bar, attached to the restaurant, is another drawcard.

Calabash　　GERMAN, FRENCH $$$
(🖉 2416 1187; Nyonyane Rd; mains E120-290; ☺ noon-2.30pm & 6-10pm) Grilled *eisbein* (pig knuckle) and *escargots bourguignons* (Burgundy snails) in Swaziland? Yes, it's possible. German and French cuisine are the incongruous highlights at this long-standing and dated, but smart, place located at the upper end of the Ezulwini Valley. It also has an impressive wine cellar.

🔒 Shopping

The Ezulwini Valley, together with the nearby Malkerns Valley, offers some of the best craft shopping in the region, with a wide selection, high quality and reasonable prices.

Ezulwini Craft Market　　ARTS & CRAFTS
(MR103; ☺ 8am-5pm) Don't miss this well-stocked market that's opposite the Zeemans Filling Station on the corner of MR103 and Mpumalanga Loop Rd. Look for the blue tin roofs. The stalls sell a vast array of local carvings, weavings and handicrafts.

Mantenga Craft Centre　　ARTS & CRAFTS
(🖉 2416 1136; Mantenga Falls Rd; ☺ 8am-5pm) This colourful, compact craft centre has several shops featuring everything from weaving and tapestries to candles, woodcarvings and T-shirts.

ⓘ Information

There are ATMs at the Gables Shopping Centre.
Ezulwini Tourist Office (🖉 7602 0261, 2416 2180; www.swazitrails.co.sz; Mantenga Craft Centre; ☺ 8am-5pm) Inside **Swazi Trails** (p500) you'll find this tourist office with information. They can help with bookings services for reserves, community tourism facilities, tour operators, activities and general accommodation.

ⓘ Getting There & Away

Nonshared taxis from Mbabane to the Ezulwini Valley cost E120 to E200, depending on how far down the valley you go. Be ready to haggle for the price.

During the day you could get a shared taxi bound for Manzini, but make sure the driver knows that you want to alight in the valley, as many aren't keen on stopping.

Lobamba

POP 11,000

Welcome to Swaziland's spiritual, cultural and political heart. Within the Ezulwini Valley lies Lobamba, an area that has played host to Swaziland's monarchy for over two centuries. It's home to some of the most notable buildings in the country. Despite its importance, Lobamba feels surprisingly quiet – except during the spectacular Incwala and Umhlanga ceremonies, when the nation gathers on the surrounding plains for several days of intense revelry.

Shared taxis running between Ezulwini and Malkerns Valleys stop in Lobamba several times a day. Fares to both destinations are about E10.

⊙ Sights & Activities

National Museum　　MUSEUM
(🖉 2416 1179; adult/child E80/30; ☺ 8am-4.30pm Mon-Fri, 10am-4pm Sat & Sun) This museum has some interesting displays of Swazi culture, as well as a traditional beehive village

and cattle enclosure, and several of King Sobhuza II's 1940s cars. There's a discounted combo ticket if you visit both the museum and the King Sobhuza II Memorial Park (adult/child E120/40).

King Sobhuza II Memorial Park MEMORIAL
(☑2416 2131; adult/child E80/30; ☺8am-4.30pm Mon-Fri, 10am-4pm Sat & Sun) Across the road from parliament, this memorial was established as a tribute to King Sobhuza II, who led Swaziland to independence from British rule in 1968. Its main highlight is a 3m-tall bronze statue of the late, revered king. There's a small museum with various pictures and documents about his life. The king's mausoleum is also within the park.

Parliament NOTABLE BUILDING
(☑2416 2411, 2416 2407) Opened in 1969 as a post-independence gift from the departing British, this hexagonal building topped with a brass dome is a major landmark in Lobamba. It is sometimes open to visitors; if you want to visit, wear neat clothes and ask at reception for a tour.

Mlilwane Wildlife Sanctuary

Beautiful, tranquil and easily accessible, Mlilwane Wildlife Sanctuary near Lobamba is well worth a visit. The landscape is anoth-

---

ⓘ MLILWANE WILDLIFE SANCTUARY

Why Go Easy access from Mbabane and Ezulwini Valley; rewarding year-round wildlife watching and birding; zebras, warthogs, wildebeest, numerous species of antelope (including the rare blue duiker), crocodiles, hippos and rare bird species; wide range of activities available; no dangerous animals; excellent accommodation options.

When to Go Year-round.

Practicalities From Mbabane or Ezulwini Valley, take the MR103 to the south. Drive past Lobamba; the turn-off to the reserve is well signposted on the right.

Budget Tips For sleeping, the reserve's beehive huts are cheap and pleasant, and there's also a top-notch backpackers.

---

er highlight; its terrain is dominated by the Nyonyane Mountain, whose exposed granite peak is known as Execution Rock (1110m). Small wonder that the reserve is an outdoor-lover's paradise, with a wide range of activities available.

The reserve supports a large diversity of fauna (mostly large herbivores and birds) and flora, and has no dangerous wildlife to worry about (except crocs and hippos). The best wildlife and birdwatching areas are the water hole at the main camp and the main dam to the north. The enclosed area near Reilly's Rock shelters some rare species of antelope and is accessible only on a guided drive.

🏃 Activities

All activities can be booked through reception at Mlilwane Wildlife Sanctuary Main Camp – we recommend exploring the sanctuary on foot, by bike or on horseback.

Horse Riding

Wildlife viewing on horseback (E315 per hour) gives you a fantastic opportunity to explore areas that are otherwise inaccessible to the public, and get up close and personal with a number of species that can be shy around vehicles.

Chubeka Trails HORSE RIDING
(☑2528 3943; www.biggameparks.org/chubeka; per hour E275; ☺daily by reservation) This well-run outfit offers various horse-riding programs for all abilities. The one-hour jaunt is a lovely ramble amid the plains that surround the main camp. The ultimate is the 'Rock of Execution Challenge', which will take you to Nyonyane's peak (about four hours; E900).

Mountain Biking

With its excellent network of roads and trails, the sanctuary is a top two-wheel destination. Bikes are available for hire at the main camp (E130 per hour). You can also hire a guide (E180 per hour per person), but it is more than possible to explore the park without a guide.

Walking

The sanctuary offers a rare opportunity to wander unguided in pristine African bushveld and to explore for yourself the many trails and roads that lead around the reserve. Hiking up the Nyonyane Mountain is a firm favourite. A map is available at reception. Fear not: there are no predators. Guides are available at E150 per hour.

Guided birding walks (two hours, E225) can also be arranged at the main camp.

Wildlife Drives

The sanctuary's guided wildlife drives come recommended. They last 1½ hours and cost E265 (with a minimum of two people). Sunrise and sunset drives are also available (two hours, E345).

🏃 Tours

Want a break from the wildlife? Consider taking a cultural tour (two hours; per person E130), during which you'll visit the homestead of a local chief (a female at the time of research) and get a taste of rural Swazi culture. Bookings (minimum four people) are made at the main camp.

🛏 Sleeping & Eating

All accommodation in the sanctuary can be booked in advance via telephone or email to **Big Game Parks** (📞2528 3943/4; www. biggameparks.org; ⊙8am-5pm Mon-Fri, 8.30am-12.30pm Sat).

★**Sondzela Backpackers**   HOSTEL $
(📞2528 3943; www.biggameparks.org/sondzela; camping E110, dm E125, s/d with shared bathroom E210/325, rondavel s/d with shared bathroom E325/460; 🅿🏊) Sondzela is a top choice for budgeteers, located in the southern part of the Mlilwane Wildlife Sanctuary. It boasts fine, breezy dorms, clean private doubles and a clutch of lovely rondavels (round huts with conical roofs) with wraparound views. And it doesn't end there. The delightful gardens, kitchen, swimming pool and a hilltop perch provide one of the best backpackers' settings in Southern Africa.

Breakfast (E45) and hearty traditional dinners (E75; cooked on the outside braai) are available for a song. If you're driving, you'll need to use the main Mlilwane Wildlife Sanctuary entrance, pay the entry fee and drive through the park to reach Sondzela. Alternatively, Sondzela's own shuttle bus departs the lodge at 8am and 5pm, and from Malandela's B&B in Malkerns Valley 30 minutes later.

Mlilwane Wildlife
Sanctuary Main Camp   CAMPGROUND $$
(📞2528 3943/4; www.biggameparks.org/mlilwane; camping E125, s/d hut E690/1060, rondavel E790/1200; 🅿📶🏊) This homey camp is set

in a scenic wooded location about 3.5km from the entry gate, complete with well-appointed rondavels and simple huts – including traditional beehive huts (singles/doubles E745/1140) – and the occasional snuffling warthog. The Hippo Haunt Restaurant serves excellent grilled meat and overlooks a water hole. There are often dance performances in the evening, and the pool is another drawcard.

Reilly's Rock Hilltop Lodge   LODGE $$$
(📞2528 3943/4; www.biggameparks.org/reilly; s/d with half board from E1870/2580; 🅿) Promoted as 'quaintly colonial', this is an oh-so-delightfully tranquil, old-world, nonfussy luxury experience at its best. The main house is in an incredible setting – a Royal Botanic Garden with aloes, cycads and an enormous jacaranda – and shelters four rooms with striking views of the valley and Mdzimba Mountains. Entry to the reserve is included.

Generous dinners are served communally by the fire and full breakfasts are enjoyed on the veranda, in sight of beautiful birds and even small antelope. If you are looking for something more private, book the Down Gran's Cottage, which stands alone 200m from the main house (E2970 per person). Note that no children under 15 are allowed.

ℹ Getting There & Away

Heading to the sanctuary from Mbabane or Ezulwini Valley, take the MR103 to the south. Drive past Lobamba; the turn-off to the reserve is well signposted on the right. Shared taxis drive this route often – ask at Mbabane or Manzini for a shared taxi heading to Ezulwini (20 minutes, E10) and it can drop you off close to the gate.

Malkerns Valley

Situated in a valley of sugarcane and pineapple fields, Malkerns Valley offers scenic drives, craft shops and a large selection of accommodation options. While less well-known than the neighbouring Ezulwini Valley, the Malkerns Valley is actually home to Swaziland's best craft shop (Swazi Candles) and event venue (House on Fire).

🏃 Tours

All Out Africa   TOURS
(📞2528 3423; www.alloutafrica.com; MR27, Mandalela's complex; ⊙8am-5pm) Located inside

Malandela's tourist information office (☑ 2528 3423; MR27, Mandalela's complex; ⊙ 8am-5pm), you can book adventure and hiking tours throughout Swaziland, plus to Kruger National Park and around South Africa. Highly recommended is the half-day cultural tour through Lobamba (per person E395; minimum two people).

For the ultimate trip, try the 11-day Swazi to Cape adventure tour (R16,430) or the 7-day beach and whale shark experience in Mozambique (R7620)

🛏 Sleeping & Eating

Malandela's B&B   B&B $$
(☑ 2528 3448, 2528 3339; www.malandelas.com; MR27; s/d incl breakfast E670/920; ℗@ 🛜 ☰) This is a wonderfully relaxing option with six tastefully designed rooms, a pool and a terrific sculpture garden. Each room has a different theme and decoration; our fave is the super-sized Purple.

There's an excellent restaurant if you're feeling too lazy to travel elsewhere. Malandela's is located along the MR27, about 1km from the junction with the MR103. Book ahead.

Umdoni   B&B $$
(☑ 2528 3009, 7602 0791; www.umdoni.com; s/d incl breakfast E740/1160; ℗ ✳ 🛜 ☰) An upmarket experience in the heart of the Malkerns Valley. The manicured garden – there's not a leaf out of place – gives a good indication of this abode: chic and stylish rooms in two colonial-style cottages. There are crisp white sheets, DSTV and breakfast on the patio overlooking flower beds. Wonderful staff is a bonus. It's off the MR18.

OFF THE BEATEN TRACK

NGWEMPISI HIKING TRAIL

This 33km trail takes in the forests and hills of the Ngwempisi Gorge. There's excellent birdwatching as well as overnight accommodation operated by the local community. There is no visitors centre, so if you want to stay overnight it is best to arrange it through All Out Africa (p505), which runs river tubing adventures in the area. Even if you are not staying the night, this exceptional region is still worth a visit and a short hike.

Rainbird Chalets   CHALET $$
(☑ 7603 7273; www.rainbirdchalets.com; s/d incl breakfast E750/1300; ℗ ✳ 🛜 ☰) It's the bucolic setting that's the pull here. Eight chalets – three log and five brick A-frames – are set in a manicured private garden near the owners' house and are close to a small dam. All are fully equipped and feature smart bathrooms. Breakfast is served on a veranda blessed with soul-stirring views of the surrounding hills. Located just over 1km off the MR18.

★**Sambane Coffee Shoppe**   CAFE $
(☑ 7677 9902, 2528 3466; Swazi Candles craft centre; mains E60-120; ⊙ 8.15am-5pm; 🖼) If you need to re-energise after a bout of shopping in the adjoining handicrafts outlets, there's no better place than this delightful cafe. It has a fine selection of homemade cakes, sandwiches, burgers and salads. There is also a shaded play area for children. Tip: arrive early, as it's usually packed to the rafters with hungry tourists at lunchtime.

Malandela's Restaurant   INTERNATIONAL $$
(☑ 2528 3115; www.malandelas.com; MR27, Malandela's complex; mains E80-150; ⊙ 9am-10pm; 🛜) This restaurant in the Malandela's complex is a reliable option, with an eclectic menu featuring grilled meats, seafood dishes, frondy salads and scrumptious house desserts – don't miss out on the chocolate cake. There's pleasant outdoor seating; indoors there's a fire for when it's chilly, and it's candlelit at night.

⭐ Entertainment

★**House on Fire**   LIVE MUSIC
(☑ 2528 2110; www.house-on-fire.com; MR27, Malandela's complex) People visit this place especially for the ever-mutating cultural site/living gallery and experimental-performance space. Part of the Malandela's complex, the well-known venue hosts everything from African theatre, music and films to raves and other forms of entertainment.

Since 2007, it has hosted the annual MTN Bushfire Festival (p502).

🛍 Shopping

There's some excellent shopping on the Malkerns Valley loop, particularly for those looking for crafts made in Swaziland.

★**Swazi Candles**   ARTS & CRAFTS
(☑ 2528 3219; www.swazicandles.com; Swazi Candles craft centre; ⊙ 8am-5pm) A manda-

tory stop for the souvenir hunter, Swazi Candles is one of the most famous handicrafts outlets in Southern Africa. Here you can wax lyrical about these creative pigment-coloured candles – in every African-animal shape and hue (E95 to E250); it's fun to watch the workers hand-mould the designs. It's 7km south of the MR103 turn-off for Malkerns.

Yebo Art & Design ARTS & CRAFTS
(☑2416 2984; www.yeboswaziland.com; Swazi Candles craft centre; ☺8am-5pm) Having moved to the Swazi Candles complex, this modern art gallery/shop hosts regular exhibitions and showcases the work of both established and up-and-coming artists, artisans and designers from around Swaziland.

Gone Rural ARTS & CRAFTS
(☑2550 4936; www.goneruralswazi.com; M27, Malandela's complex; ☺8am-5pm Mon-Sat, 9am-5pm Sun) The place to go for good-quality woven goodies – baskets, mats and bowls – made by groups of local women. The shop is found within the Malandela's complex, and on weekdays you can also visit the workshop next door and meet the creators behind the artworks.

Baobab Batik ARTS & CRAFTS
(☑2528 3242; www.baobab-batik.com; Swazi Candles craft centre; ☺8am-5pm) This fairtrade enterprise employs more than 30 local artisans who produce beautiful printed wall hangings, clothing and cushion covers. It's based at the Swazi Candles craft centre.

❶ Getting There & Away

Located about 7km south of Lobamba/Ezulwini Valley on the MR103. Shared taxis run between here and the Ezulwini Valley for around E12. As the craft shops and sleeping places are spread out, you'll really need a car to get around. Private taxis are available from Manzini and will charge around E400 for the day.

Manzini

POP 110,537

Swaziland's largest town, Manzini is a key transport hub so you're likely to pass through if you're getting around on public transport. It's a chaotic commercial and industrial place whose small centre is domi-

OVERNIGHT CULTURAL EXPERIENCE

Headed by proud local Myxo Mdluli, **Woza Nawe Tours** (☑7604 4102, 7642 6780; www.swazivillage.com; day tour/overnight stay E1350/1795) runs highly recommended village visits and overnight stays to Kaphunga, 55km southeast of Manzini. The fee includes transport, meals and a guide. Guests join in on whatever activities are going on in the village – including cooking, planting and harvesting.

nated by office blocks and a couple of shopping malls running down two main streets. With the exception of the market, Manzini itself has limited appeal for the tourist.

◉ Sights

Manzini Market MARKET
(cnr Mhlakuvane & Mancishane Sts; ☺7am-5pm Mon-Sat) Manzini's main drawcard is its colourful market, whose upper section is packed with handicrafts from Swaziland and elsewhere in Africa. Thursday morning is a good time to see the rural vendors and Mozambican traders bringing in their handicrafts and textiles to sell to the retailers.

🛏 Sleeping & Eating

George Hotel BUSINESS HOTEL $$$
(☑2505 2260; www.tgh.co.sz; cnr Ngwane & Du Toit Sts; s/d incl breakfast from E1230/1750; P❄🤍🛏) Don't be discouraged by this hotel's modest exterior and unspectacular location up the main road. Manzini's fanciest hotel attempts an international atmosphere and features a respectable collection of various-size comfy rooms (tip: ask for a poolside one), two stylish restaurants, a lovely garden with a pool, a small spa (massages from E200) and conference facilities.

Baker's Delight BAKERY $
(☑2505 9181; cnr Tenbergen & Louw Sts; snacks E10-70; ☺6.30am-5pm Mon-Fri, to 2pm Sat) If you think life is unbearable without a chocolate éclair or a scone, bookmark this snazzy bakery. Also serves up snack options, including salads and burgers, at lunchtime. Good breakfasts, too.

Manzini

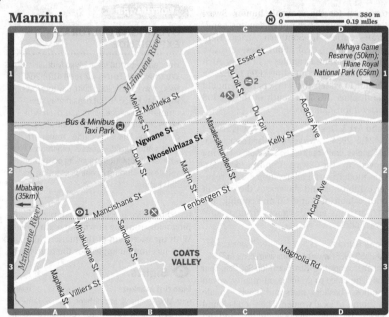

Manzini

⊙ Sights

🛏 Sleeping

🍴 Eating

Gil Vincente Restaurant   PORTUGUESE **$$**
(☎2505 3874; Ngwane St; mains R80-150;
⊙9am-10pm Tue-Sun) Despite its location in a
strip mall, gourmands saunter here for well-
prepped Portuguese-inspired dishes with a
twist, a respectable wine list, efficient ser-
vice and smart decor. Sink your teeth into a
juicy *bitoque* (beefsteak with fried egg) or a
succulent *bacalhau* (cod). Had enough pro-
tein? Pastas and salads are also available.

❶ Getting There & Away

The main bus and shared-taxi park is at the north-
ern end of Louw St, where you can also find some
nonshared taxis. A shared-taxi trip
up the Ezulwini Valley to Mbabane costs E40
(35 minutes). Shared taxis to the Maputo bus
station in Mozambique (E120) also depart
from here.

NORTHWESTERN SWAZILAND

Lush hills undulating off towards the ho-
rizon, green velvet mountains cloaked in
layers of wispy cloud, majestic plantations
and woodlands, streams and waterfalls, and
plunging ravines: these are the main fea-
tures of Swaziland's beautiful northwest. As
well as boasting the best scenery in Swazi-
land, this area offers some excellent hiking
and accommodation options.

Ngwenya
POP 1281

Tiny Ngwenya, 5km east of the border with
Mpumalanga, is the first town you'll reach if
you're arriving in Swaziland via Oshoek. If
you can't wait until you reach the Ezulwini
Valley to do your shopping, there are several
excellent craft outlets here. For history buffs,
the Ngwenya iron-ore mine is well worth a
detour.

⊙ Sights

Ngwenya Iron-Ore Mine   HISTORIC SITE
(E30; ⊙8am-4pm) Ngwenya is one of the
world's oldest known mines. The visitors cen-
tre has an interesting display of photographs

and information, including the original excavation tools. To visit the mine, even if you are travelling by vehicle, you'll need to be accompanied by a ranger, who will explain the mine's history (note: tips are appreciated).

Although the mine is part of Malolotja Nature Reserve, you can't continue in to the rest of the reserve from here.

🛏 Sleeping & Eating

Hawane Resort   RESORT $$

(📞 2444 1744; www.hawaneresort.com; Hawane; dm E120, chalet s/d incl breakfast E630/990; 🅿🛜🏊) Framed by the Malolotja peaks, these quirky chalets are a blend of traditional Swazi materials (wattle and grass) and glass, with ethnic African interiors. Backpackers are stabled in a converted barn. The resort restaurant serves African cuisine (dinner buffet E190). It's a convenient base for visiting Malolotja Nature Reserve, though some visitors say it's overpriced and service is lackadaisical.

Horse riding is available on the premises (E150 per hour), as are spa treatments (E220 to E320). Use of the wi-fi costs E20 per stay. It's about 5km up the Piggs Peak road from the junction of the MR1 and MR3, and 1.5km off the main road.

🛍 Shopping

Ngwenya Glass complex is a hub of boutiques selling all kinds of quality arts and crafts. It's well signposted off the MR3 on a road that leads to the Ngwenya iron-ore mine.

⭐ **Ngwenya Glass**   ARTS & CRAFTS

(📞 2442 4142; www.ngwenyaglass.co.sz; Ngwenya Glass Complex; 🕗8am-4.30pm Mon-Thu, to 4pm Fri-Sun) One of Swaziland's major tourist attractions, this superb glass-blowing factory and boutique showcases a fantastic selection of animal figurines, vases, decorative art glass and tableware, all made from recycled glass. On weekdays you can watch the glass-blowers at work from an overhead balcony. Magical!

The on-site cafe serves light lunches (mains E45 to E75), freshly squeezed juice and big wedges of chocolate cake.

Quazi Design Process   ARTS & CRAFTS

(📞in Mbabane 2422 0193; www.quazidesign.com; Ngwenya Glass Complex; 🕗8am-4.30pm Mon-Thu, to 4pm Fri-Sun) 🌿 Run by a group of women, this sustainable outlet sells modern accessories of cutting-edge design, made in Mbabane from recycled paper.

Tsandza Weaving   ARTS & CRAFTS

(📞7681 3595, 2518 8867; www.tsandzaweaving.com; Ngwenya Glass Complex; 🕗8am-4.30pm Mon-Thu, to 4pm Fri-Sun) 🌿 This lovely boutique was previously called Rosewood before a change of ownership, but the shop still sells top-quality handwoven shawls, cushion covers, bags, blankets and other colourful items.

🛈 Getting There & Away

Ngwenya is just 5km from the Oshoek border post and is easily accessible by car. There are shared taxis from Mbabane to the glass factory (E12.50, 25 minutes). Shared taxis from the border can also drive you to the glass factory, though it is not a normal route so be prepared to pay a bit more.

Malolotja Nature Reserve

One of Swaziland's premier natural attractions, the beautiful Malolotja Nature Reserve (📞7660 6755; www.sntc.org.sz/reserves/malolotja.asp; adult/child E40/25; 🕗6am-6pm) is a true wilderness area that's rugged and, in the most part, unspoiled. The reserve is laced by streams and cut by three rivers, including the Komati, which flows east through a gorge in a series of falls and rapids until it meets the lowveld. No prizes for guessing that this spectacular area is a fantastic playground for nature lovers and ornithologists, with more than 280 species of bird.

Fans of flora will also get their kicks here; wildflowers and rare plants are added attractions, with several (including the Woolly, Barberton and Kaapschehoop cycads) found only in this region of Africa.

🛈 MALOLOTJA NATURE RESERVE

Why Go Breathtaking mountain scenery; excellent playground for walkers and mountain bikers; abundant birdlife and diverse flora; no dangerous animals; Swaziland's sole canopy tour.

When to Go Year-round, but expect heavy mist between October and March.

Practicalities Some stretches of road that are heavily eroded require a 4WD in wet weather.

Budget Tips The reserve has camping facilities.

WORTH A TRIP

PHOPHONYANE FALLS ECOLODGE & NATURE RESERVE

This little morsel of paradise about 14km north of Piggs Peak is a dream come true for those seeking to get well and truly off the beaten track. The **lodge** (☑ 7604 2802, 2431 3429; www.phophonyane.co.sz; s/d safari tent with shared bathroom E1130/1610, s/d beehive hut E1750/2520, d cottage E2360; ℗ ⊠) lies on a river in its own nature reserve of lush indigenous forest. Accommodation is in comfortable cottages, stylish beehive huts or luxury safari tents overlooking cascades.

There's a network of walking trails around the river and waterfall. All visitors (including overnight guests) to the reserve are charged E40/30 per adult/child. Excellent meals are available in the stylish dining area. Turn at signs indicating Phophonyane Falls; then it's 4.5km on dirt road.

Don't expect to see plenty of large mammals, though. It's the scenery that's the pull here, rather than the wildlife. That said, you'll certainly come across various antelope species as well as small groups of zebras and wildebeest.

🏃 Activities

Malolotja offers some of the most inspirational **hiking** trails in Swaziland, so pack your sturdy shoes. Walking options range from short walks to multiday hikes. Well-known and much enjoyed walks include the 11.5km Malolotja Falls Trail, with superb views of the Malolotja Valley, and the 8km Komati River Trail.

Printouts of hiking trails are available for free at reception inside the reserve. Also check the SNTC website (www.sntc.org.sz/tourism/malolotjawalks.asp) for descriptions of walks and trails.

Malolotja Canopy Tour   OUTDOORS
(☑ 7660 6755; www.malolotjacanopytour.com; E650; ⊘8am-2pm) This tour is a definite must-do for those wanting to experience the Malolotja Nature Reserve from a different perspective. Here you will make your way across Malolotja's stunning, lush tree canopy on 10 slides (11 wooden platforms) and via a 50m-long suspension bridge. It's very safe and no previous experience is required.

From the restaurant inside the park you're driven to a base point, from where it's a 15-minute walk to the canopy starting point. Tours leave every 30 minutes.

🛏 Sleeping & Eating

Malolotja Cabins   CABIN $
(www.sntc.org.sz/tourism/malolotja.asp; s/d E400/660; ℗) These cosy, fully equipped, self-catering wooden cabins, each sleeping a

maximum of five, are located near Malolotja Nature Reserve reception and afford lovely mountain views. If cooking's not your thing, there's a restaurant (mains E50 to E110) also near reception.

Malolotja Camping   CAMPGROUND $
(camping E100) Camping is available at the well-equipped main site near the reserve's reception, with ablutions (hot shower) and braai (barbecue) areas.

ℹ Getting There & Away

The entrance gate for Malolotja is about 35km northwest of Mbabane, along the Piggs Peak road (MR1). It's well signposted. If taking public transport, grab a shared taxi in Mbabane heading to Piggs Peak and tell the driver you are going to Malolotja. It's a 2km walk from the road to the reception.

Komati Valley

East of Malolotja Nature Reserve, the Komati Valley is a delight, with its majestic mountainscape, rural atmosphere and impressive Maguga Dam. It's hard to believe that Mbabane is only a short drive away.

There are regular shared taxis on the MR1 road between Mbabane and Piggs Peak (E35, one hour). If you want to head to the Maguga Dam, you'll have to go up to Piggs Peak and catch another shared taxi there (E16, 25 minutes). The roads are in good shape barring a few potholes and you'll be to travel almost anywhere without a 4WD.

⊙ Sights

Maguga Dam   LANDMARK
This very scenic dam is on the Komati River, and was constructed to provide irrigation and energy to local communities. With its

glittering waters surrounded by the muscular hills of the highveld, it fits the picture-postcard ideal.

Nsangwini Rock Art Shelter   ROCK ART

(☑ 7812 1139; adult/child E50/25; ☺ 9am-4pm) Culture buffs will love this community-run archaeological site. The well-preserved paintings are under a small but impressive rock shelter, which is perched over the Komati River and affords lovely views across the mountains. The cave was believed to be that of the Nsangwini San and features the only known paintings of winged humans. Nsangwini is signed from the main Piggs Peak road and the Maguga Dam loop road. Follow a dirt road for 7.5km.

Note that conditions can get a bit rough after rain. A local guide will take you on the slightly steep and rocky walk (15 minutes down; 20 minutes up) and will give a brief explanation.

🛏 Sleeping & Eating

★ Maguga Dam Lodge   LODGE $$

(☑ 2437 3975; www.magugalodge.com; Maguga Dam; camping E160, s/d incl breakfast E760/1150; 🅿❄☀☲) Scenically positioned on the southern shore of Maguga Dam, this laid-back venture is blessed with commanding views of the dam and surrounding hills. It comprises two well-equipped camping grounds, a clutch of spacious and light-filled rondavels and an excellent restaurant (mains E65 to E85) with a deck overlooking the dam.

There is rock art near the hotel, though the art is faint in comparison to the nearby Nsangwini Rock Art. Various activities are on offer, including fishing (E120 with own fishing equipment), cultural tours (E120 per person), hiking (from E120 per person) and boat cruises (adult/child per hour E170/80). If the activities all seem a bit daunting, pay a visit to the on-site spa offering a variety of massages (E170 to E400).

Maguga Viewpoint   BURGERS $

(☑ 2437 1056, 7606 5519; mains E45-70; ☺ 8am-5pm; 🅿) While slightly dishevelled compared to the Maguga Dam Lodge, this restaurant has a nice deck overlooking the dam and it also offers several viewpoints accessible by walking trails. The menu offers a mix of burgers, steaks and sandwiches, though don't expect everything to be available.

NORTHEASTERN SWAZILAND

The remote northeastern Swaziland lowveld, nestled in the shadow of the Lebombo Mountains, is the country's top wild-life-watching region. Here you'll find a duo of excellent wildlife parks – Hlane Royal National Park and Mkhaya Game Reserve (p513) – as well as a couple of lesser-known nature reserves that also beg exploration. If it's action you're after, the superb rapids of the Great Usutu River (Lusutfu River) provide an incredible playground.

Hlane Royal National Park

Hlane Royal National Park (☑ 2383 8100, 2528 3943; www.biggameparks.org/hlane; E50; ☺ 6am-6pm) belongs in the elite of Swaziland's wildlife parks, and it's easy to see why. Here you can expect to see most safari A-listers, with the exception of buffaloes. This well-organised reserve is the country's largest protected area, and is home to elephants, lions, leopards, white rhinos and many antelope species, and offers wonderfully low-key wildlife and bird-life watching. And it's so easy to enjoy it: hippos and elephants are found around Ndlovu Camp just metres from your cottage. There's plenty to keep you occupied, including bushwalking, wildlife drives, mountain biking and cultural tours.

WORTH A TRIP

SHEWULA MOUNTAIN CAMP

This community-run camp (☑ 7605 1160, 7603 1931; www.shewulacamp.org; Shewula; camping E90, s/d E350/440) 37km northeast of Simunye in the Lebombo Mountains (21km on tarred road and 16km on dirt road; turn at signs indicating Shewula) is a marvellous 'stop the world and get off' place. Accommodation is pretty basic – you can camp or there are stone-and-thatch rondavels (no electricity) with shared ablutions (three have bathrooms).

It's wonderful to be able to enjoy the jaw-dropping views and get a taste of rural life. Activities include guided cultural walks to nearby villages. Local meals can also be arranged.

ℹ️ HLANE ROYAL NATIONAL PARK

Why Go Has four of the Big Five; the only reserve in Swaziland where you can encounter lions; dedicated rhino wildlife drive; excellent accommodation; good birdwatching; various activities on offer.

When to Go Year-round.

Practicalities You can explore most of the park with a 2WD, with the notable exception of the special lion compound, which can be visited on the wildlife drives only.

Budget Tips Ndlovu Camp has camping facilities.

🏃 Activities

All activities can be booked at Ndlovu Camp.

Mountain Biking

Mountain biking is a fun and ecofriendly way to commune with Hlane's bushveld. Guided mountain-bike outings led by expert rangers cost E280 and last two hours (minimum two people). Tours start from Ndlovu Camp at sunrise.

Bush Walks

Hlane offers guided walking trails and birding trips (per person E225, minimum two people), which afford the opportunity to see elephants and rhinos. Serious walkers or bush fanatics can book the one- or two-night fully catered Ehlatsini Bush Trails (full board from one/two days E1445/2455, April to September only and minimum two people), which take in some lesser-known areas of the park. Book ahead for the overnight trails.

Wildlife Drives

Hlane's major attraction are its large mammals and predators, and the easiest way to spot them is on a wildlife drive in an open vehicle. The 2½-hour sunrise and sunset drives (per person E370), only for those overnighting at Ndlovu Camp, are best for wildlife and photography; they include the lion enclosure, where you have good chances to see the big cats. A dedicated white-rhino drive (1½ hours, E260) will allow you to leave the vehicle and get up close to these endangered giants.

👉 Tours

Growing weary of antelope, rhinos and lions? Bookmark the Ndlovu Camp (p512)'s 'Umphakatsi Experience' cultural tour (two hours; per person E130, minimum four people), during which you'll visit a chief's village and learn about traditional Swazi culture. You'll need your own vehicle for this activity.

🛏️ Sleeping & Eating

Ndlovu Camp   CAMPGROUND, COTTAGE **$$**
(☑ 2528 3943; www.biggameparks.org/hlane; camping E125, s/d rondavels E745/1140, cottages from E775/1180; ℙ) Ndlovu Camp is a delightfully mellow spot, with spacious grounds and an atmospheric restaurant that serves outstanding food. Accommodation is in rondavels and self-catering cottages with no electricity (paraffin lanterns are provided). You can also pitch your tent on a grassy plot. Ndlovu is just inside the main gate and near a water hole that draws hippos and rhinos.

In the evening, don't miss the traditional dance performance around the campfire.

Bhubesi Camp   BUNGALOW **$$**
(☑ 2528 3943; www.biggameparks/hlane; s/d E700/1000; ℙ) Set in a pristine and secluded setting about 14km from Ndlovu Camp, Bhubesi Camp features tasteful four-person, self-catering stone bungalows that overlook a river and green lawns and are surrounded by lush growth. As there are no dangerous animals in this section of the park, you can hike freely. Electricity is available, but there's no restaurant.

ℹ️ Getting There & Away

The gate to Hlane is about 7km south of Simunye (it's signposted). If you don't have your own transport, you can book a tour through **Swazi Travel** (☑ 2416 2180; www.swazi.travel; day tour from R1850).

Mlawula Nature Reserve

The low-key Mlawula Nature Reserve (☑ 2383 8885, 2343 5108; www.sntc.org.sz/reserves/mlawula.asp; adult/child E35/16; ⏱ 6am-6pm), where the lowveld plains meet the Lebombo Mountains, boasts antelope species and a few spotted hyenas, among others, plus rewarding birdwatching. Keep your expectations in check, though; wildlife is more elusive here than anywhere else in the country and visitor infrastructure is fairly limited. The park's real highlight is its network of walking trails amid beautifully scenic landscapes. There are 10 self-guided walks ranging from a one-hour stroll to a full-day hike. Ask for the *Trails and Day Walks* brochure at the gate.

The turn-off for the entrance gates to the Mlawula Nature Reserve is about 10km north of Simunye, from where it's another 4km from the main road. You'll need your own transport to explore the reserve. If taking public transport, grab a shared taxi from Manzini to Lomahasha (E45, 1½ hours), though you'll have to walk from the main road.

🛏 Sleeping & Eating

The reserve has a campsite and a self-catering cottage, though neither are of a particularly good standard.

Magadzavane Lodge   CHALET $$
(☑2343 5108; magadzavane@sntc.org.sz; s/d incl breakfast E600/900; P🄿🛜🛏) This great option offers 20 enticing chalets in southern Mlawula, on the edge of the Lebombo escarpment, with magnificent views of the valley below. There's a restaurant and a small infinity pool. From the northern gate, it's a 17km drive on a gravel road; the last kilometres are very steep (but manageable in a standard vehicle in dry weather).

Mbuluzi Game Reserve

This small and privately owned reserve (☑2383 8861; mbuluzireception@gmail.com; E45; ☉6am-6pm) boasts a range of animals, including giraffes, zebras, warthogs, antelope species and wildebeest. Twitchers are sure to get a buzz: more than 300 bird species have been recorded here, including some rare and uncommon species. The reserve is split into two sections, divided by the public road. The southern section has a more dense wildlife population, while the northern sector offers outstanding mountain views. Most areas can be explored in a standard vehicle along well-maintained gravel roads, and no guides are necessary. There's a good network of clearly marked walking trails.

The turn-off for Mbuluzi is the same as for Mlawula; the reserve entrance is about 500m from the turn-off and on the left. If taking public transport, take a shared taxi from Manzini heading to Lomahasha (E45, 1½ hours) and then walk from the Mbuluzi turn-off.

Mbuluzi Camping   CAMPGROUND $
(☑2383 8861; mbuluzireception@gmail.com; camping E110) Campsites are available near the Mbuluzi River on the reserve's northern side. Facilities include ablution blocks with hot showers and firewood is provided.

Singwe Lodge   LODGE $$
(☑2383 8861; www.mbuluzi.com; per person E680, minimum two people; P🄿❄🛏) Located along the Mlawula River, this lodge contains four en-suite rooms with air conditioning and a lounge with DSTV. However, you'll likely spend most of your time outside, either in the pool or watching giant kingfishers from your outside deck.

Mkhaya Game Reserve

The crowning glory of Swaziland's parks, the top-notch and stunning Mkhaya Game Reserve (☑2528 3943; www.mkhaya.org) is famous for its black and white rhino populations (it boasts that you're more likely to meet rhinos here than anywhere else in Africa, and judging from our experience, this is true). Its other animals include roan and sable antelopes, giraffes, tsessebe and buffaloes, along with a rich diversity of birds. If you're lucky, you might spot the elusive narina trogon and other rare bird species.

Note that children under 10 are not allowed in the park.

> ### ⓘ MKHAYA GAME RESERVE
>
> **Why Go** Swaziland's most exclusive safari retreat; a real sense of wilderness; *really* close encounters with rhinos; atmospheric accommodation; excellent wildlife drives and sensational bush walks run by expert guides.
>
> **When to Go** Year-round.
>
> **Practicalities** You can't visit the reserve without booking in advance, and even then you can't drive in alone; you'll be met at a pick-up location just past Siphofaneni at a specified time – either 10am or 4pm – and escorted to the ranger base station, where you'll leave your vehicle.
>
> **Budget Tips** While day tours can be arranged, it's ideal (and better value) to stay for at least one night.

WHITEWATER RAFTING & CAVING

One of the highlights of Swaziland is rafting the Great Usutu River (Lusutfu River). The river varies radically from steep creeks to sluggish flats, but in the vicinity of Mkhaya Game Reserve it passes through a gorge, where a perfect mix of rapids can be encountered all year round.

Swazi Trails (p500) is the best contact to organise a rafting trip – it offers full- and half-day trips (E1300/1100 per person, including lunch and transport, minimum two people). Abseiling and cliff jumps are added for extra adrenaline in the winter months.

For an off-the-scale challenge rating, the company's adventure-caving trips offer a rare window into the elite world of cave exploration. A few kilometres from Mbabane, the vast Gobholo Cave is 98% unexplored. You can choose between the 8.30am departure (E800) and the 4.30pm dinner trip (E950; it includes a hot-spring soak, pizza and beer).

🏃 Activities

Wildlife Drives

Wildlife drives through Mkhaya in an open vehicle are included in Stone Camp's accommodation rates. For overnight guests, they take place in the early morning and late afternoon. Those on a day trip (per person E735) will have two wildlife drives, and lunch is included.

Bush Walks

Mkhaya's signature activity, guided bushwalks are an ideal way to approach wildlife, especially white rhinos. You periodically disembark from the open vehicle and track rhinos on foot, under the guidance of an experienced ranger. You'll learn plenty about rhino behaviour. Unforgettable!

Bush walks take place at 11am. Note that they're offered only to Stone Camp guests who are staying more than one night or who are picked up at 4pm for a 24-hour stay.

🛏 Sleeping & Eating

⭐ **Stone Camp**   LODGE $$$

(☏ 2528 3943; www.mkhaya.org; s/d with full board & activities from E2835/4250; P) A dream come true for nature lovers, Stone Camp consists of a series of rustic and luxurious semi-open stone-and-thatch cottages (a proper loo with a view!), located in secluded bush zones. The price includes wildlife drives, walking safaris and meals, and is excellent value compared to many of the private reserves in Southern Africa. Simply arrive, absorb and wonder. No electricity, but paraffin lanterns are provided.

ℹ Getting There & Away

The Mkhaya Game Reserve is near the hamlet of Phuzumoya, off the Manzini–Big Bend road (it's signposted off the MR8). Rangers meet you at the pick-up location to transfer you to camp. There is secure parking at the ranger base station. You can also grab a shared taxi from Manzini heading to Lomahasha (E45, 1½ hours), which can drop you off at the pick-up location.

Understand South Africa, Lesotho & Swaziland

South Africa, Lesotho & Swaziland Today

More than two decades after Nelson Mandela came to power, life in South Africa remains dominated by social inequality. Central Cape Town's mountain and beach communities contrast with the townships sprawling across the Cape Flats, lining the N2 with shacks and Portaloos. Seeing First World wealth alongside African poverty is confronting for first-time visitors. Yet every day, millions of South Africans embrace progress by trying to understand and respect the vastly different outlooks of people from other economic and racial groups.

Best in Print

Johannesburg (Fiona Melrose; 2017) Follows a diverse cast of characters on the day of Nelson Mandela's death.

Thirteen Hours (Deon Meyer; 2011) Grizzled Cape Town cop investigates a backpacker's murder. Also check out *Blood Safari* and *Fever*.

Who Killed Piet Barol? (Richard Mason; 2017) The *History of a Pleasure Seeker* sequel follows a WWI-era Dutch con artist.

Born a Crime (Trevor Noah; 2016) The comedian's autobiography.

Best on Film

Invictus (2009) Covers the historic 1995 Rugby World Cup; stars Morgan Freeman and Matt Damon. Clint Eastwood directs.

Mandela: Long Walk to Freedom (2013) Condensed but enjoyable biography, covering Madiba's journey to presidency.

District 9 (2009) Neill Blomkamp and Peter Jackson's sci-fi gem about giant alien 'prawns' overrunning Jo'burg.

Tsotsi (2005) Athol Fugard's moving Soweto tale follows a gangster and a baby.

Winnie (2017) Documentary about Nelson Mandela's second wife.

Chappie (2015) Blomkamp's equally futuristic follow-up to District 9.

Race Relations

What makes South Africa an uplifting place to visit is witnessing the dissolution of racial divisions. Projects here aim to empower inhabitants of the townships and former homelands, and to provide work in a country with over 25% unemployment. Finding common ground can be challenging in this cultural melting pot with 11 official languages, but race relations are informed by the miracle that Mandela et al performed.

However, given the decades of segregation under apartheid, South African society lacks the cohesion enjoyed by many Western countries. The ruling African National Congress (ANC) party often links current woes to apartheid, perhaps seeking to lessen its own culpability and reinforce its image as South Africa's great liberator. More extreme still are utterances by Julius Malema of the Economic Freedom Fighters (EFF), known for its Zimbabwe-style policies of land reform and nationalisation, and protesting students who accuse universities of being bastions of colonialism. Despite the courts cracking down on racist behaviour, high-profile cases still make headlines.

Xenophobia

Relations between black ethnic groups are equally as sensitive as those between different racial groups – from the Xhosa and Zulus to foreign immigrants. Economic refugees flock to the townships from neighbouring countries, intensifying pressure on infrastructure and competition for jobs. A decade after xenophobic violence swept the country, attacks on immigrants and looting of foreign-owned shops continue to be features of township life.

AIDS & Gender Issues

With the world's largest HIV-positive population (more than seven million people), South Africa saw 270,000 new infections and 110,000 deaths from AIDS-related illnesses in 2016. Educational efforts face numerous taboos, and *sangomas* (traditional healers) preach superstitious lore. South Africa's record on gender issues exemplifies the country's contradictions. Its constitution, adopted in 1996, is the world's most progressive, promoting the rights of women and LGBT people (same-sex marriage is legal). Yet the street-level reality is far harsher, with one of the world's highest rape rates, including 'corrective' rape of lesbians.

Political Scene

When Mandela died in 2013, South Africa came together in a way not seen since the 2010 World Cup. Madiba's death was, though, a reminder that the ANC is losing its apartheid-busting glow, as it presides over a country where crime, corruption and institutional incompetence are rife. As the hope surrounding 1994's election recedes, millions of South Africans still live in shacks and struggle to find work.

Cyril Ramaphosa became leader of the ANC in late 2017, but Jacob Zuma was still set to remain as president until the 2019 general elections. That was until growing controversy and pressure from within his own party came to a head in February 2018 and forced Zuma to resign. Given the gains made by the opposition Democratic Alliance (DA) and their coalitions, the ANC will have to work hard to avoid a repeat of the 2014 elections, when its majority in the National Assembly dropped to 62% from previous highs of 66% in 2009 and 70% in 2004.

Lesotho

In 2017, a general election returned Prime Minister Thomas Thabane to power, and his All Basotho Convention (ABC) party formed a coalition government. Sadly, the transfer of power was far from peaceful, and the country teetered on the edge of yet another coup.

The Basotho-dominated country did not experience apartheid and, with life revolving around subsistence farming, levels of social inequality and crime are lower than in South Africa. The mountain kingdom does face serious issues though, including unemployment, food shortages and a devastating HIV epidemic – in 2017, the new infection rate was the world's highest.

Swaziland

Democratic freedom is an issue in Swaziland, where absolute monarch King Mswati III has been accused of silencing opponents. While elections are held every five years, this is to elect just 55 of the 65 members of parliament – King Mswati III appoints the rest, as well as the entire senate and top-ranking civil servants. The king's attempt to rebrand his monarchy as a 'monarchial democracy' was met with further criticism from local and international media due to Swaziland's continual low human development index ranking.

The rural, homogeneous country has many challenges, including widespread poverty, a declining economy reliant on South Africa and the world's highest HIV prevalence at 27.2%. Life expectancy hovers around 50 years – among the lowest in the world.

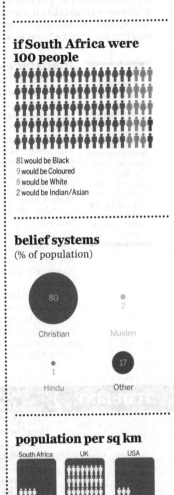

POPULATION: **SOUTH AFRICA: 55 MILLION; LESOTHO: 2.2 MILLION; SWAZILAND: 1.34 MILLION**

AREA: **SOUTH AFRICA: 1,219,090 SQ KM; LESOTHO: 30,355 SQ KM; SWAZILAND: 17,364 SQ KM**

if South Africa were 100 people

81 would be Black
9 would be Coloured
8 would be White
2 would be Indian/Asian

belief systems
(% of population)

80 Christian
2 Muslim
1 Hindu
17 Other

population per sq km

South Africa | UK | USA

= 11 people

History

Visit South Africa and you'll see reminders of its past at every turn. The country's human drama is reflected in the faces and body language of its citizens. It's on display in centuries-old rock art and modern-day urban graffiti, in isolated battlefields and sober apartheid-era memorials. It permeates every corner with its pain and injustice but also with its hope. Be prepared to immerse yourself in one of the most anguished yet most inspiring stories to be found anywhere.

Check out www.brandsouthafrica.com/people-culture/history-heritage for news and articles on South Africa's history and heritage, with everything from an infographic about the life and work of Oliver Tambo to a profile of Johannesburg's Constitutional Court.

Inauspicious Beginnings

Life at the southern tip of Africa began inauspiciously enough. A scattered collection of striking rock art provides evidence that as early as 25,000 years ago, and possibly as early as 40,000 years ago, nomadic San hunter-gatherers were living in the area that is now South Africa. Small numbers of San still live in South Africa today, making theirs one of the world's oldest continuous cultures.

Before this, the picture is murkier, but a wealth of fossil finds at Sterkfontein near Johannesburg show that the Gauteng area may have been almost as much of a population centre in prehistoric times as it is today, with human-like creatures (hominids) roaming across the highveld at least three million years ago. By about one million years ago, these creatures had come to closely resemble modern humans, and ranged well beyond Africa, including in Europe and Asia. Somewhere around 100,000 years ago, *Homo sapiens* (modern humans) came onto the scene. Although it's still a topic of debate, fossils found near the mouth of the Klasies River in the Eastern Cape indicate that our *Homo sapiens* ancestors may have been travelling around South Africa as early as 90,000 years ago.

Around 2500 years ago the shaping of modern-day South Africa took a dramatic turn, with descendants of the early San hunter-gatherer groups acquiring livestock and becoming pastoralists. This introduced concepts of personal wealth and property ownership. The pastoralist San – who became known as Khoekhoen ('men of men') – began to build more established communities and develop chieftaincies. They also began to

TIMELINE	40,000– 25,000 BC	AD 500	1200–1270
	The San – Southern Africa's first residents and one of the world's oldest traditional cultures – leave rock art documenting their nomadic lifestyle and hunter-gatherer traditions.	A centuries-long series of migrations from West Africa's Niger Delta culminates when Bantu speakers reach what is now KwaZulu-Natal. These people are the ancestors of most modern-day South Africans.	The thriving trade centre of Mapungubwe – in today's Limpopo province – rises to become centre of the largest kingdom in sub-Saharan Africa, with trade links as far afield as Egypt, India and China.

move from their traditional inland areas south towards the coast, while smaller groups of more traditionalist hunter-gatherer San continued to inhabit the interior.

New Arrivals

Around AD 500, a new group of peoples – Bantu speakers originally from the Niger Delta in West Africa – began settling in what is now South Africa. Their arrival marked the end of a long migration that had begun about 1000 BC, culminating when the first groups reached present-day KwaZulu-Natal.

The contrasts between the Bantu speakers and the early San hunter-gatherers couldn't have been greater. The Bantu speakers lived in settled villages where they tended their livestock. They were also skilled iron workers and farmers, growing maize and other crops.

Before long, the Bantu speakers, from whom most modern-day South Africans are descended, had entrenched themselves. Some groups – the ancestors of today's Nguni peoples (Zulu, Xhosa, Swazi and Ndebele) – settled near the coast. Others, now known as the Sotho-Tswana peoples (Tswana, Pedi, Basotho), settled in the highveld, while the Venda, Lemba and Shangaan-Tsonga peoples made their home in what is now northeastern South Africa.

For an overview of rock art in Southern Africa and other parts of the continent, see University of the Witwatersrand's Rock Art Research Institute page at www.wits.ac.za/rockart.

Early Kingdoms

The hills and savannahs in South Africa's northeastern corner are dotted with ruins and artefacts left by a series of highly organised and stratified Iron Age kingdoms that flourished between about AD 1200 and the mid-17th century.

The first major one, Mapungubwe, was in present-day Limpopo province at the confluence of the Limpopo and Shashe Rivers, where Botswana, Zimbabwe and South Africa meet. Although its residents – ancestors of today's Shona people – were farmers, it was trade in gold and other goods that was the source of the kingdom's power. Pottery pieces, beads, seashells and other artefacts have been found at the site, showing that Mapungubwe was one of the major inland trading hubs in the Southern Africa region from about 1220 until 1300. Its trading network extended eastwards to the coast, and from there to places as far afield as Egypt, India and China.

Mapungubwe's decline coincided with the rise nearby of a similarly structured but larger early Shona kingdom at Great Zimbabwe, over the border in present-day Zimbabwe, suggesting that the focus of trade shifted northwards.

With the abandonment of Great Zimbabwe in the mid-15th century, several of the early Shona groups made their way back to the area just south of the Limpopo River that is now part of northern Kruger National

As the pastoralist Khoekhoen mixed with the hunter-gatherer San, it soon became impossible to distinguish between the two groups – hence the oft-used term 'Khoe-San'.

1487	1497	1652	1657
Portuguese explorer Bartholomeu Dias successfully navigates the Cape of Good Hope. Although he doesn't linger, his journey marks the start of a long history of European involvement in Southern Africa.	Natal is named by Vasco da Gama, who, sighting its coast on Christmas Day 1497, names it for the natal day of Christ.	The Dutch East India Company, seeking a secure way station en route eastwards, establishes the first permanent European settlement at Table Bay, Cape Town, under Jan van Riebeeck's leadership.	The Dutch East India Company releases employees to establish their own farms and supply the settlement with produce. These farmers – known as free burghers – soon expand into the lands of the Khoekhoen.

Park. There they established numerous settlements in the Pafuri region. These included the walled kingdom of Thulamela, the last of the great Iron Age kingdoms, which flourished between the mid-16th and mid-17th centuries. Several of Thulamela's artefacts, most notably an iron gong of the type also found in Ghana, show that its trading links stretched as far as West Africa.

A Short History of Lesotho from the Late Stone Age to the 1993 Elections by Stephen J Gill is a concise and readable history of the mountain kingdom.

First Europeans

Apart from Portuguese explorer Bartholomeu Dias naming the Cabo da Boa Esperança (Cape of Good Hope) in 1487, the Portuguese showed little interest in South Africa – the Mozambican coast, further northeast, was more to their taste.

By the late 16th century, the Portuguese were being significantly challenged along their trade routes by the English and the Dutch.

In 1647 a Dutch vessel was wrecked in what is now Cape Town's Table Bay. The marooned crew built a fort and stayed for a year until they were rescued, becoming the first Europeans to attempt settlement in the area. Shortly thereafter, the Dutch East India Company (Vereenigde Oost-Indische Compagnie; VOC), one of the major European trading houses sailing the spice route to the East, decided to establish a permanent settlement. A small VOC expedition, under the command of Jan van Riebeeck, was launched, reaching Table Bay in April 1652.

No sooner were they off their boats than the Dutch found themselves in the midst of the, by then, well-established Khoekhoen peoples. Yet while the new settlers traded with the neighbouring Khoekhoen out of necessity, there were deliberate attempts on the part of the Dutch to restrict contact. To alleviate a labour shortage, the VOC released a small group of Dutch employees to establish their own farms, from which they would supply the VOC settlement. The arrangement proved highly successful.

For an overview of the famous figures who have shaped South African history, check out www.sahistory. org.za for a well-presented list of biographies. Alternatively, concentrate on the dastardly villains with Cape Town journalist Alexander Parker's fast-moving and entertaining book *50 People Who Stuffed Up South Africa* (2011).

While the majority of these free burghers (as these farmers were called) were of Dutch descent and members of the Calvinist Reformed Church of the Netherlands, there were also numerous Germans. In 1688 they were joined by French Huguenots, also Calvinists, who were fleeing religious persecution under Louis XIV.

Europeans Leave Their Mark

The VOC also began to import large numbers of slaves, primarily from Madagascar and Indonesia. With this additional labour, not only was South Africa's population mix broadened but the areas occupied by the VOC were expanded further north and east, where clashes with the Khoekhoen were inevitable. The beleaguered Khoekhoen were driven from their traditional lands, decimated by introduced diseases and destroyed by superior weapons when they fought back – which they did in

1658	1660	1786	1814
Slaves from Madagascar and Indonesia, the first to be imported into South Africa, are brought to the country by the Dutch.	Jan van Riebeeck plants a bitter-almond hedge separating the Dutch from the neighbouring Khoekhoen – in retrospect, an early step towards apartheid.	Moshoeshoe, founder of the Basotho nation, later to become Lesotho, is born; Shaka, future king of the Zulu, is born the following year.	The British, keen to outmanoeuvre the French, gain sovereignty over the Cape as Dutch mercantile power fades.

a number of major wars and with guerrilla resistance that continued into the 19th century. Most survivors were left with no option but to work for the Europeans in an arrangement that hardly differed from slavery. Over time, the Khoe-San, their European overseers and the imported slaves mixed, with the offspring of these unions forming the basis for modern South Africa's coloured population.

As the burghers continued to expand into the rugged hinterlands of the north and east, many began to take up a semi-nomadic pastoralist lifestyle, in some ways not so far removed from that of the Khoekhoen whom they were displacing. In addition to their herds, a family might have had a wagon, a tent, a Bible and a couple of guns. As they became more settled, a mud-walled cottage would be built – frequently located, by choice, days of hard travel away from the nearest European. These were the first of the Trekboers (Wandering Farmers); later shortened to Boers) – completely independent of official control, extraordinarily self-sufficient and isolated. Their harsh lifestyle produced courageous individualists, but also a people with a narrow view of the world, whose only source of written knowledge was often the Bible.

Arrival of the British

As the 18th century drew to a close, Dutch power began to fade, and the British moved in to fill the vacuum. They seized the Cape to prevent it from falling into rival French hands, then briefly relinquished it to the Dutch, before finally garnering recognition of their sovereignty of the area in 1814.

Awaiting the British at the Cape was a colony with 25,000 slaves, 20,000 white colonists, 15,000 Khoe-San and 1000 freed black slaves. Power was restricted to a white elite in Cape Town, and differentiation on the basis of race was already deeply entrenched. Outside Cape Town and the immediate hinterland, the country was populated by isolated black and white pastoralists.

One of the first tasks for the British was trying to resolve a troublesome border dispute between the Boers and the Xhosa on the colony's eastern frontier. In 1820 about 5000 middle-class British immigrants – mostly traders and business people – were persuaded to leave England and settle on tracts of land between the feuding groups with the idea, at least officially, of providing a buffer zone (they were known as the 1820 Settlers). The plan was singularly unsuccessful. By 1823 almost half of the settlers had retreated to the towns – notably Grahamstown and Port Elizabeth – to pursue the jobs they had held in Britain.

A pattern soon emerged whereby English speakers were highly urbanised and dominated politics, trade, finance, mining and manufacturing, while the largely uneducated Boers were relegated to their farms. The gap between the British settlers and the Boers further widened with

South Africa's tumultuous, still-contested history has inspired many excellent novels. Check out Barbara Mutch's *The Housemaid's Daughter* (2013), an apartheid-era drama set in the Karoo; Yvette Christiansë's *Unconfessed* (2006), about a Mozambican prisoner on Robben Island; and Brent Meersman's *Reports Before Daybreak* (2011), a moving novel set in 1980s Cape Town.

HISTORY ARRIVAL OF THE BRITISH

1816	1820	1828	1838
Shaka becomes chief of the Zulu, triggering the rise of a militaristic state and setting off the *difaqane* (forced migration), a wave of disruption and terror throughout Southern Africa.	The British try to mediate between the Boers and the Xhosa in Cape Colony by encouraging British immigration. The plan fails, but the new settlers solidify Britain's presence.	Shaka is killed by his half-brothers; as the *difaqane* continues for another decade, Dingaan seeks to establish relations with British traders.	Several thousand Zulus are killed in the Battle of Blood River. The anniversary was celebrated by white people as the Day of the Vow until 1994, when it was renamed the Day of Reconciliation.

the abolition of slavery in 1833, a move that was generally regarded by Boers as being against the God-given ordering of the races. Meanwhile, British numbers rapidly increased in Cape Town, in the area east of the Cape Colony (present-day Eastern Cape), in Natal (present-day KwaZulu-Natal) and, after the discovery of gold and diamonds, in parts of the Transvaal (mainly around present-day Gauteng).

Difaqane

The difaqane, a tumultuous period of forced migration during the 19th century, caused huge suffering and accelerated the formation of several states, notably those of the Sotho (present-day Lesotho) and Swazi (now Swaziland).

The first half of the 19th century was a time of immense upheaval and suffering among the African peoples of the region. This period is known as the *difaqane* (forced migration) in Sotho and as *mfeqane* (the crushing) in Zulu.

While the roots of the *difaqane* are disputed, certain events stand out. One of the most significant was the rise of the powerful Zulu kingdom. In the early 19th century, Nguni tribes in what is now KwaZulu-Natal began to shift from loosely organised collections of kingdoms into a centralised, militaristic state under Shaka, son of the chief of the small Zulu clan. After building large armies, Shaka sent them out on a massive program of conquest and terror. Those who stood in his way were enslaved or decimated.

Tribes in the path of Shaka's armies fled, in turn becoming aggressors against their neighbours. This wave of disruption and terror spread throughout Southern Africa and beyond, leaving death and destruction in its wake.

Great Trek & Battle of Blood River

The Boers were growing increasingly dissatisfied with British rule in the Cape Colony. The British proclamation of equality of the races was a particularly sharp thorn in their side. Beginning in 1836, several groups of Boers, together with large numbers of Khoekhoen and black servants, decided to trek off into the interior in search of greater independence. North and east of the Orange (Gariep) River (which formed the Cape Colony's frontier), these Boers, or Voortrekkers (Pioneers), found vast tracts of apparently uninhabited grazing lands. They had entered, so it seemed, their promised land, with space enough for their cattle to graze and for their culture of anti-urban independence to flourish. Little did they know that what they found – deserted pasture lands, disorganised bands of refugees and tales of brutality – were not everyday life in the hinterland, but the result of the *difaqane*.

With the exception of the relatively powerful Ndebele, the Voortrekkers encountered little resistance among the scattered peoples of the plains. Dispersed by the *difaqane* and lacking horses and firearms, the locals' weakened condition also solidified the Boers' belief that European occupation heralded the coming of civilisation to a savage land.

1843	1852	1869	1879
Boer hopes for a Natal republic are dashed when the British annex the area and set up a colony in modern-day Durban.	The Boer Republic of Transvaal is created. The first president, elected in 1857, is Marthinus Wessel Pretorius, son of Andries Pretorius, the famous Voortrekker leader.	The first diamond is found near Kimberley in the walls of a house. This spells trouble for the Boers as the British quickly move to annex the area.	The Zulus inflict one of the most humiliating defeats on the British army at the Battle of Isandlwana, but Zululand eventually comes under British control.

However, the mountains (where King Moshoeshoe I was forging the Basotho nation, later to become Lesotho) and the wooded valleys of Zululand were a more difficult proposition. Resistance here was strong, and the Boer incursions set off a series of skirmishes, squabbles and flimsy treaties that were to punctuate the next 50 years of increasing white domination.

The Great Trek's first halt was at Thaba 'Nchu, near present-day Bloemfontein, where a republic was established. Following disagreements among their leadership, the various Voortrekker groups split, with most crossing the Drakensberg into Natal to try to establish a republic there. As this was Zulu territory, Voortrekker leader Piet Retief paid a visit to King Dingaan and was promptly massacred by the suspicious Zulu. This massacre triggered others, as well as a revenge attack by the Boers. The culmination came on 16 December 1838 at the Ncome River in Natal. Several Boers were injured and several thousand Zulus were killed, reportedly causing the Ncome's waters to run red.

After this victory (the result of superior weapons) in what came to be known as the Battle of Blood River, the Boers felt that their expansion really did have that long-suspected stamp of divine approval. Yet their hopes for establishing a Natal republic were short-lived. The British annexed the area in 1843 and founded their new Natal colony at present-day Durban. Most of the Boers headed north, with yet another grievance against the British.

The British set about establishing large sugar plantations in Natal, and looked to India to resolve their labour shortage. From 1860 into the early 20th century, more than 150,000 indentured Indians arrived, as well as numerous free 'passenger Indians'.

Diamonds & Anglo-Boer Wars

The Boers meanwhile pressed on with their search for land and freedom, ultimately establishing themselves in the Transvaal (encompassing parts of present-day Gauteng, Limpopo, North West and Mpumalanga provinces) and the Orange Free State. Then the Boers' world was turned on its head in 1869 with the discovery of diamonds near Kimberley. The diamonds were found on land belonging to the Griqua – but to which both the Transvaal and Orange Free State laid claim. Among the best-known Khoekhoen groups, the Griqua had originally lived on the west coast between St Helena Bay and the Cederberg range. In the late 18th century, they managed to acquire guns and horses and began trekking northeastward. En route, they were joined by other groups of Khoe-San, coloured people and even white adventurers, and rapidly gained a reputation as a formidable military force.

Nelson Mandela's widow Graça Machel is the only woman to have been the first lady of two countries, having previously been married to the late Mozambican president Samora Machel.

1881	1886	1893	1897
First Anglo-Boer War ends with a decisive victory for the Boers at the Battle of Majuba Hill; Transvaal becomes the South African Republic.	Gold is discovered on the Witwatersrand, setting off rapid population growth and development in Johannesburg. The Witwatersrand contains the world's largest gold deposit.	Mohandas (Mahatma) Gandhi sets sail for South Africa. His early days in the country mark the beginning of his doctrine of nonviolent protest and influence his entire life's work.	Enoch Mankayi Sontonga, a choir leader from the Eastern Cape, composes 'Nkosi Sikelel' i Afrika' (God Bless Africa). It is first recorded in 1923 and made the national anthem in 1994.

Britain quickly stepped in and resolved the issue of who had rights to the diamonds by annexing the area for itself. The establishment of the Kimberley diamond mines prompted a flood of European and black labourers to the area. Towns sprang up in which the 'proper' separation of whites and blacks was ignored, and the Boers were angry that their impoverished republics were missing out on the economic benefits of the mines.

Long-standing Boer resentment became a full-blown rebellion in the Transvaal, and in 1880 the First Anglo-Boer War broke out. (Afrikaners, as the descendants of the early Boers became known, called it the War of Independence.) The war was over almost as soon as it began, with the Boers' crushing defeat of the British at the Battle of Majuba Hill in February 1881. The Transvaal Republic regained its independence as the Zuid-Afrikaansche Republiek (ZAR; South African Republic). Paul Kruger, one of the leaders of the uprising, became president in 1883.

Despite setbacks, the British forged ahead with their desire to federate the Southern African colonies and republics. In 1879 Zululand came under British control. Then in 1886 gold was discovered on the Witwatersrand (the area around Johannesburg). This accelerated the federation process and dealt the Boers yet another blow. Johannesburg's population exploded to about 100,000 by the mid-1890s, and the ZAR suddenly found itself hosting thousands of *uitlanders* (foreigners), both black and white, with the Boers squeezed to the sidelines. The influx of black labour was particularly disturbing for the Boers, many of whom were going through hard times and resented the black wage earners.

The situation peaked in 1899, when the British demanded voting rights for the 60,000 foreign whites on the Witwatersrand. (Until this point, Kruger's government had excluded all foreigners from the franchise.) Kruger refused, calling for British troops to be withdrawn from the ZAR's borders. When the British resisted, Kruger declared war. The Second Anglo-Boer War was more protracted and the British were better prepared than at Majuba Hill. By mid-1900 Pretoria, the last of the major Boer towns, had surrendered. Yet resistance by Boer *bittereinders* (bitter enders) continued for two more years with guerrilla-style battles, which in turn were met with scorched-earth tactics by the British. In May 1902 the Treaty of Vereeniging brought a superficial peace: under its terms, the Boer republics acknowledged British sovereignty.

A Fragile Peace

During the immediate postwar years, the British focused their attention on rebuilding the country, in particular the mining industry. By 1907 the mines of the Witwatersrand were producing almost one-third of the world's gold. But the peace brought by the treaty was fragile, and challenged on all sides. The Afrikaners found themselves in the position of being poor farmers in a country where big mining ventures and foreign

My Traitor's Heart is a hard-hitting memoir of apartheid by acclaimed journalist Rian Malan, who writes with a pace and vigour akin to the late Hunter S Thompson. Although the book ultimately focuses on the era's chilling violence, the beginning is a brilliant rumination on white history in South Africa.

1902	1902	1910	1912
The brutality of the Second Anglo-Boer War is shocking and causes the death of 26,000 people from disease and neglect.	The Treaty of Vereeniging ends the Anglo-Boer War, although the peace it brings is fragile and challenged by all sides.	The Union of South Africa is created. English and Dutch are made the official languages, and there are no voting rights for blacks.	Pixley ka Isaka Seme, a Columbia University–educated lawyer, calls a conference of chiefs. A union of all tribes is proposed, resulting in the formation of what will become the African National Congress (ANC).

capital rendered them irrelevant. They were particularly incensed by Britain's unsuccessful attempts to Anglicise them, and to impose English as the official language in schools and the workplace. Partly as a backlash to this, Afrikaans came to be seen as the *volkstaal* (people's language) and a symbol of Afrikaner nationhood, and several nationalistic organisations sprang up.

All the building blocks for the modern South African pariah state of the mid-20th century were now in place. Black and coloured people were completely marginalised. Harsh taxes were imposed, wages were reduced and the British caretaker administrator encouraged the immigration of thousands of Chinese to undercut any resistance. Resentment was given full vent in the Bambatha Rebellion of 1906, in which 4000 Zulus lost their lives after protesting onerous tax legislation.

The British, meanwhile, moved ahead with their plans for union. After several years of negotiation, the 1910 Act of Union was signed, bringing the republics of Cape Colony, Natal, Transvaal and Orange Free State together as the Union of South Africa. Under the provisions of the act, the Union was still a British territory, with home rule for Afrikaners. The British High Commission Territories of Basotholand (now Lesotho), Bechuanaland (now Botswana), Swaziland and Rhodesia (now Zimbabwe) continued to be ruled directly by Britain.

English and Dutch were made the official languages. Despite a major campaign by blacks and coloureds, only whites could be elected to parliament.

The first government of the new Union was headed by General Louis Botha, with General Jan Smuts as his deputy. Their South African National Party (later known as the South African Party or SAP) followed a generally pro-British, white-unity line. More radical Boers split away under the leadership of General Barry Hertzog, forming the National Party (NP) in 1914. The NP championed Afrikaner interests, advocating separate development for the two white groups and independence from Britain.

See www.anc.org.za for the official view of everything past and present related to the African National Congress (ANC), including a potted history.

Racism Entrenched & Birth of the ANC

There was no place in the new Union for black people, even though they constituted more than 75% of the population. Under the Act of Union, they were denied voting rights in the Transvaal and Orange Free State areas, and in the Cape Colony they were granted the vote only if they met a property-ownership qualification. Following British wartime propaganda promising freedom from 'Boer slavery', the failure to grant the franchise was regarded by blacks as a blatant betrayal. It wasn't long before a barrage of oppressive legislation was passed, making it illegal for black workers to strike, reserving skilled jobs for whites, barring blacks from military service and instituting pass laws. Continued under

1913	1914	1925	1927
The 1913 Immigration Law prohibits further immigration of Indians to South Africa. Any marriage not performed according to Christian rites is also illegal, invalidating Hindu and Muslim marriages.	Following demonstrations and strikes, the Indian Relief Bill is passed, restoring recognition of Hindu and Muslim marriages and convincing Gandhi of the power of nonviolent resistance.	Afrikaans is made an official language with the rise of Afrikaner nationalism. It becomes associated with apartheid, and its proposed introduction into township schools is one of the triggers of the 1976 Soweto uprising.	Kruger National Park opens to the public, although its proud history is tainted during apartheid, when the government removes people from their traditional lands to allow for the park's expansion.

apartheid, the pass laws restricted black people's movement, forcing them to carry a pass book – the forerunner of today's ID book – and only allowing them to enter certain areas for work.

In 1913 the Natives Land Act was enacted, setting aside 8% of South Africa's land for black occupancy. Whites, who made up 20% of the population, were given more than 90% of the land. Black Africans were not allowed to buy, rent or even be sharecroppers outside their designated area. Thousands of squatters were evicted from farms and forced into increasingly overcrowded and impoverished reserves or into the cities. Those who remained were reduced to the status of landless labourers.

Against this turbulent background, black and coloured opposition began to coalesce, and leading figures such as John Jabavu, Walter Rubusana and Abdullah Abdurahman laid the foundations for new nontribal black political groups. Most significantly, a Columbia University–educated attorney, Pixley ka Isaka Seme, called together representatives of the various African tribes to form a unified national organisation to represent the interests of blacks and ensure they had an effective voice in the new Union. Thus was born the South African Native National Congress, known from 1923 onwards as the African National Congress (ANC).

Almost parallel to this, Mohandas (Mahatma) Gandhi had been working with the Indian populations of Natal and the Transvaal to fight against the ever-increasing encroachments on their rights.

Nelson Mandela's autobiographical *Long Walk to Freedom* is essential reading and the ultimate recounting of the early days of resistance and the years that followed.

Rise of Afrikaner Nationalism

In 1924 the NP, under Hertzog, came to power in a coalition government, and Afrikaner nationalism gained a greater hold. Dutch was replaced by Afrikaans (previously only regarded as a low-class dialect of Dutch) as an official language of the Union, and the so-called *swart gevaar* (black threat) was made the dominant issue of the 1929 election. Any hopes of turning the tide of Afrikaner nationalism were dashed when Daniel François (DF) Malan led a radical breakaway movement, the Purified National Party, to the central position in Afrikaner political life.

Due to the booming wartime economy, black labour became increasingly important to the mining and manufacturing industries, and the black urban population nearly doubled. Enormous squatter camps grew up on the outskirts of Johannesburg and, to a lesser extent, the other major cities. Conditions in the townships were appalling, but poverty was not only suffered by blacks: wartime surveys found that 40% of white schoolchildren were malnourished.

Walls of Apartheid Go Up

In the months leading up to the 1948 elections, the NP campaigned on its policy of segregation, or 'apartheid' (an Afrikaans term for the state of being apart). The Nats, as the NP became known, defeated Smuts'

1932	1948	1955	1960
World-famous singer Miriam Makeba ('Mama Africa') is born in Johannesburg – she spends 30 years outside South Africa in exile for criticism of the apartheid government.	The darkness descends – the National Party under the leadership of DF Malan gains control of the government after campaigning on a policy of segregation, and apartheid is institutionalised.	At a congress held at Kliptown near Johannesburg, a number of organisations, including the Indian Congress and the ANC, adopt a Freedom Charter, still central to the ANC's vision of South Africa.	Sharpeville massacre; ANC and Pan African Congress (PAC) banned; Miriam Makeba is denied entry to South Africa after trying to return for her mother's funeral.

United Party, in coalition with the Afrikaner Party (AP) and under the leadership of DF Malan.

Thus it was that apartheid, long a reality of life, became institutionalised under Malan. Within short order, legislation was passed prohibiting mixed marriages, making interracial sex illegal, classifying every individual by race and establishing a classification board to rule in questionable cases. The noxious Group Areas Act of 1950 set aside desirable city properties for whites and banished nonwhites into the townships. The Separate Amenities Act created, among other things, separate beaches, buses, hospitals, schools and even park benches.

The existing pass laws were further strengthened: black and coloured people were compelled to carry identity documents at all times, and prohibited from remaining in towns, or even visiting them, without specific permission.

In 1960 tensions came to a head: on 21 March, Robert Sobukwe, who had founded ANC splinter group the Pan African Congress (PAC), protested with thousands of followers against the hated pass laws at police stations in Gauteng and the Western Cape. Police opened fire on the demonstrators surrounding a police station in Sharpeville, a township near Vereeniging, Gauteng. In what became known as the Sharpeville massacre, at least 67 people were killed and 186 wounded; most were shot in the back.

Across Boundaries: The Journey of a South African Woman Leader by Mamphela Ramphele traces the life of an extraordinary woman who was internally 'exiled' to the town of Tzaneen for seven years but later rose to become the University of Cape Town's vice-chancellor.

HISTORY WALLS OF APARTHEID GO UP

'HOME' LANDS

In 1962 the Transkei was born. It was the first of 10 so-called 'Bantustans' or 'homelands' that were intended to provide a home for all black South Africans. On these lands – so went the white South African propaganda – blacks would be self-sufficient, self-governing citizens, living together with others of their own ethnic group.

The realities were much different. The homeland areas had no infrastructure or industry, and were incapable of producing sufficient food for the growing black population. All the homelands together constituted only 14% of South Africa's land, while blacks made up close to 80% of the country's population. Tribal divisions were made arbitrarily, and once a person had been assigned to a homeland, they could not leave without a pass and permission. The resulting suffering was intense and widespread.

Following creation of the homelands, blacks flooded the cities seeking work: while life in urban squatter camps was bad, life in the homelands was worse. The government responded by banning blacks from being employed as shop assistants, receptionists, typists and clerks. The construction of housing in the black 'locations' (dormitory suburbs for black workers) was halted and enormous single-sex hostels were built instead.

Although the homelands concept came to an end with the demise of apartheid, its legacy, including completely insufficient infrastructure and distorted population concentrations in the homeland areas, continues to scar South Africa today.

1961	1961	1964	1966
Soon after the Sharpeville massacre Prime Minister Hendrik Verwoerd, the Dutch-born 'architect of apartheid', announces a referendum – in May South Africa leaves the Commonwealth and becomes a republic.	On 16 December, Umkhonto we Sizwe, the military wing of the ANC, carries out its first attacks, marking the start of the armed struggle against apartheid.	Nelson Mandela is sentenced to life imprisonment – a sentence that will span 27 years and include 18 years at the notorious Robben Island prison.	Verwoerd is stabbed to death by Dimitri Tsafendas, a parliamentary messenger, who suffers from schizophrenia and is resentful of being shunned for being dark-skinned, though he is classified as 'white'.

Soon thereafter, Prime Minister Hendrik Verwoerd, credited with the unofficial title of 'architect of apartheid', announced a referendum on whether the country should become a republic. The change was passed by a slim majority of voters. Verwoerd withdrew South Africa from the Commonwealth, and in May 1961 the Republic of South Africa came into existence.

ANC Begins the Long Walk

The further entrenchment of apartheid pushed the hitherto relatively conservative ANC into action. In 1949 it had developed an agenda that for the first time advocated open resistance in the form of strikes, acts of public disobedience and protest marches. Resistance continued throughout the 1950s and resulted in occasional violent clashes. In 1959 a group of disenchanted ANC members, seeking to sever all links with white politicians and activists, broke away to form the more militant PAC.

To many domestic and international onlookers, the struggle had crossed a crucial line at Sharpeville, and there could no longer be any lingering doubts about the nature of the white regime. In the wake of the shooting, a massive stay away from work was organised, and demonstrations continued. Prime Minister Verwoerd declared a state of emergency, giving security forces the right to detain people without trial. More than 18,000 demonstrators were arrested, including much of the ANC and PAC leadership, and both organisations were banned.

In response, the ANC and PAC began a campaign of sabotage through the armed wings of their organisations, Umkhonto we Sizwe (Spear of the Nation, MK) and Poqo ('Pure' or 'Alone'), respectively. In July 1963, 17 members of the ANC underground movement were arrested and tried for treason at the widely publicised Rivonia Trial. Among them was Nelson Mandela, an ANC leader and founder of Umkhonto we Sizwe, who had already been arrested on other charges. In June 1964 Mandela and seven others were sentenced to life imprisonment. Oliver Tambo, another member of the ANC leadership, managed to escape South Africa and lead the ANC in exile. On 20 April 1964, during the Rivonia Trial, Nelson Mandela said, 'I have fought against white domination and I have fought against black domination. I have cherished the ideal of a democratic and free society in which all persons live together in harmony and with equal opportunities. It is an ideal which I hope to live for and to achieve. But if needs be, it is an ideal for which I am prepared to die.'

Decades of Darkness

With the ANC banned, and Mandela and most of its leadership in jail or exile, South Africa moved into some of its darkest times. Apartheid legislation was enforced with increasing gusto, and the walls between

Rabble-Rouser for Peace: The Authorised Biography of Desmond Tutu by John Allen is a fascinating and inspirational look at the life of one of South Africa's most influential figures.

The Wild Almond Line by Larry Schwartz is a memoir of growing up in a segregated country and being a conscript in the apartheid-era army.

1976	1978–88	1982	1989
On 16 June the Soweto uprisings begin, setting off a chain of violence around the country and marking the first major internal challenge to the apartheid government.	During the Border War, the South African Defence Force (SADF; now the South African National Defence Force, or SANDF) launches attacks inside Angola, Mozambique, Zimbabwe, Botswana and Lesotho.	The first AIDS death is recorded in South Africa, marking the start of an ongoing scourge spreading to, and devastating, communities across the country.	Mandela pleads to President Botha from prison for negotiations to avert a civil war in South Africa. His appeal falls on deaf ears.

NELSON MANDELA

Nelson Rolihlahla Mandela, one of the last century's greatest leaders, was once vilified by South Africa's ruling whites and sentenced to life imprisonment. Almost three decades later, he emerged from incarceration calling for reconciliation and forgiveness.

Mandela, son of a Xhosa chief, was born on 18 July 1918 in the Eastern Cape village of Mveso, on the Mbashe River. After attending the University of Fort Hare, Mandela headed to Johannesburg, where he soon became immersed in politics. He finished his law degree and, together with Oliver Tambo, opened South Africa's first black law firm. Meanwhile in 1944, along with Tambo and Walter Sisulu, Mandela formed the Youth League of the African National Congress (ANC). During the 1950s, Mandela was at the forefront of the ANC's civil disobedience campaigns, for which he was arrested in 1952, and tried and acquitted. After the ANC was banned in the wake of the Sharpeville massacre, Mandela led the establishment of its underground military wing, Umkhonto we Sizwe. In 1964 Mandela was brought to trial for sabotage and fomenting revolution in the widely publicised Rivonia Trial. After brilliantly arguing his own defence, he was sentenced to life imprisonment, and spent the next 18 years in the infamous Robben Island prison before being moved to the mainland.

Throughout his incarceration, Mandela repeatedly refused to compromise his political beliefs in exchange for freedom, saying that only free men can negotiate.

In February 1990 Mandela was finally released, and in 1991 he was elected president of the ANC. In 1993 Mandela shared the Nobel Peace Prize with FW de Klerk and, in the country's first free elections the following year, was elected president of South Africa. In his much-quoted speech 'Free at Last!', made after winning the 1994 elections, he focused the nation's attention firmly on the future, declaring, 'This is the time to heal the old wounds and build a new South Africa'.

In 1997 Mandela – or Madiba, his traditional Xhosa name – stepped down as ANC president, although he continued to be revered as an elder statesman. On 5 December 2013 Nelson Mandela, aged 95 years, died from an ongoing respiratory infection. South Africans grieved openly for the man who had given so much of himself to his country. Then South African president Jacob Zuma said, 'Our nation has lost its greatest son. Nothing can diminish our sense of a profound and enduring loss'. The world also grieved for the man who had inspired so many with his moral authority. One of the largest gatherings of world leaders came together for the memorial service.

the races were built ever higher. Most odious was the creation of separate 'homelands' for blacks. Ten homelands were created within South Africa's borders – black-only 'countries' that were meant to be autonomous from South Africa, though no one outside the country recognised them. Residents were stripped of their South African citizenship and left in a puppet state with no infrastructure and plenty of corruption.

1989	1990	1993	1994
Botha suffers a stroke and FW de Klerk becomes president, lifting the ban on the ANC. He later proclaims 'we have closed the book on apartheid' after 68.7% of whites vote to end white-minority rule.	In what becomes a historic moment in South African history, Nelson Mandela is freed after 27 years in prison, preaching not hatred but forgiveness and reconciliation.	Nelson Mandela and FW de Klerk, the two men shaping the future of South Africa through tough negotiation, are awarded the Nobel Peace Prize.	In a triumph for democracy and Mandela's path of reconciliation and freedom for all, the first democratic elections are held; Nelson Mandela is elected president.

During the 1970s, resistance again gained momentum, first channelled through trade unions and strikes, and then spearheaded by the South African Students' Organisation under the leadership of the charismatic Steve Biko. Biko, a medical student, was the main force behind the growth of South Africa's Black Consciousness Movement, which stressed the need for psychological liberation, black pride and nonviolent opposition to apartheid.

Things culminated in 1976, when the Soweto Students' Representative Council organised protests against the use of Afrikaans (regarded as the language of the oppressor) in black schools. On 16 June, police opened fire on a student march led by Tsietsi Mashinini – a central figure in the book *A Burning Hunger: One Family's Struggle Against Apartheid* and now immortalised by a large monument in Soweto. This began a round of nationwide demonstrations, strikes, mass arrests, riots and violence that, over the next 12 months, took more than 1000 lives.

In September 1977, Steve Biko was killed by security police. South Africa would never be the same. A generation of young blacks committed themselves to a revolutionary struggle against apartheid ('Liberation before Education' was the catch cry) and black communities were politicised.

STEVE BIKO

Steve Biko, born in 1946 in the Eastern Cape, was one of the most prominent and influential anti-apartheid activists. His Black Consciousness Movement mobilised urban youth and was a major force behind the 1976 Soweto uprisings. As a result of his activities, Biko was high on the list of those targeted by the apartheid regime. In 1973 he was restricted to his birthplace of King William's Town and prohibited from speaking in public. Despite these restrictions, he continued his activism, as well as community work, including establishing literacy programs and a health clinic.

On 18 August 1977, Biko was detained under the Terrorism Act. Less than a month later, he was dead – from a hunger strike, according to the police. In 1997 the Truth and Reconciliation Commission reported that five former members of the South African security forces had admitted to killing Biko, although they were never prosecuted. Biko had been beaten until he fell into a coma, he went without medical treatment for three days and he finally died in Pretoria. At the subsequent inquest, the magistrate found that no one was to blame, although the South African Medical Association eventually took action against the doctors who failed to treat him.

Biko's death prompted a huge public outcry and drew international attention to the brutality of the apartheid system. Biko's funeral service, celebrated by then Bishop Desmond Tutu, was attended by thousands, including representatives from various Western countries. Thousands more were barred from attending by security forces. Biko's story was the centrepiece of the 1987 film *Cry Freedom*.

1996	1997	1999	2004
After much negotiation and debate, South Africa's parliament approves a revised version of the 1993 constitution that establishes the structure of the country's new, democratic government.	In an almost-unheard-of move by an African head of state, Nelson Mandela retires as ANC president and is succeeded by Thabo Mbeki.	The ANC wins a landslide victory in the second democratic elections held in South Africa, falling just short of the 66.7% required to change the constitution.	Mbeki guides the ANC to a decisive victory in the national elections. In accordance with his vision of an 'African renaissance', South Africa increases regional engagement.

South Africa Under Siege

As international opinion turned decisively against the white regime, the government (and most of the white population) increasingly saw the country as a bastion besieged by communism, atheism and black anarchy. Considerable effort was put into circumventing international sanctions, and the government even developed nuclear weapons (since destroyed).

Negotiating majority rule with the ANC was not considered an option (publicly, at least), which left the government reverting to the use of sheer military might. A siege mentality developed among most whites, and although many realised that a civil war against the black majority could not be won, they preferred this to 'giving in' to political reform. To them, brutal police and military actions seemed entirely justifiable.

From 1978 to 1988 the South African Defence Force (SADF; now the South African National Defence Force, or SANDF) made a number of major attacks inside Angola, Mozambique, Zimbabwe, Botswana and Lesotho. All white males were liable for national service, and thousands of them fled into exile to avoid conscription. Many more were scarred mentally and physically by the vicious struggles that ensued.

Paradoxically, the international sanctions that cut whites off from the rest of the world enabled black leaders to develop sophisticated political skills, as those in exile forged ties with regional and world leaders.

The Soft Vengeance of a Freedom Fighter by Albie Sachs is an extraordinary and moving tale of an influential ANC member who lost an arm and an eye in the struggle for freedom.

Winds of Change

In the early 1980s, a fresh wind began to blow across South Africa. Whites constituted only 16% of the total population, in comparison with 20% 50 years earlier, and the percentage was continuing to fall. Recognising the inevitability of change, President PW Botha told white South Africans to 'adapt or die'. Numerous reforms were instituted, including the repeal of the pass laws. But Botha stopped well short of full reform, and many blacks (as well as the international community) felt the changes were only cosmetic. Protests and resistance continued at full force as South Africa became increasingly polarised and fragmented, and unrest was widespread. A white backlash gave rise to a number of neo-Nazi paramilitary groups, notably the Afrikaner Weerstandsbeweging (AWB), led by Eugène Terre'Blanche. The opposition United Democratic Front (UDF) was also formed at this time. With a broad coalition of members, led by Archbishop Desmond Tutu and the Reverend Allan Boesak, it called for the government to abolish apartheid and eliminate the homelands.

International pressure also increased, as economic sanctions began to dig in harder, and the value of the rand collapsed. In 1985 the government declared a state of emergency, which was to stay in effect for five years. The media was censored and by 1988, according to ANC estimates (and backed up by those of human-rights groups), 30,000 people had been detained without trial and thousands had been tortured.

2005	2006	2007	2007
President Thabo Mbeki dismisses Jacob Zuma from his position as deputy president following corruption charges, igniting a political war between the two men that Mbeki ultimately loses.	Over five million South Africans are living with HIV/AIDS; the devastation wrought by the disease is a reflection of many years of neglect by the government.	The AIDs tragedy affects the country's most vulnerable. According to Unaids, there are approximately 280,000 South African children living with HIV and 1.4 million orphaned by AIDS.	In December Thabo Mbeki is defeated and replaced by Jacob Zuma as president of the ANC. New corruption charges – following the dropping of earlier charges in 2006 – are brought against Zuma.

Mandela is Freed

In 1986 President Botha announced to parliament that South Africa had 'outgrown' apartheid. The government started making a series of minor reforms in the direction of racial equality, while maintaining an iron grip on the media and on all anti-apartheid demonstrations.

In late 1989, a physically ailing Botha was succeeded by FW de Klerk. At his opening address to parliament in February 1990, De Klerk announced that he would repeal discriminatory laws and legalise the ANC, the PAC and the Communist Party. Media restrictions were lifted, and De Klerk released political prisoners not guilty of common-law crimes. On 11 February 1990, 27 years after he had first been incarcerated, Nelson Mandela walked out of the grounds of Paarl's Victor Verster Prison a free man.

From 1990 to 1991 the legal apparatus of apartheid was abolished. A referendum – the last whites-only vote held in South Africa – overwhelmingly gave the government authority to negotiate a new constitution with the ANC and other groups.

The Rough Road to Democracy

Despite the fact that the state of emergency had been lifted and the military presence removed, the period between apartheid and democracy was in fact one of the most violent times in South African history. There were groups on both sides who resented their leaders entering into talks with the opposition and made every effort to end the peace talks – usually by violent means. Between 1990 and 1994 there were more than 12,000 political killings.

Although Mandela and De Klerk initially enjoyed mutual respect, Mandela soon became suspicious of De Klerk's loyalty to democracy following a record number of deaths, many seemingly carried out by the police. He believed these murders and disappearances had ultimately been ordered by the government – and that meant by De Klerk. Mandela referred to the authority ordering the deaths as the Third Force. There were also many everyday South Africans opposed to the talks who likewise perpetuated violent attacks. Chaos reigned in the townships, where rival factions fought – when the police stepped in, the violence escalated further. Many ANC members had trained for guerrilla warfare and clung hopelessly to the idea that they could overthrow the government using violence and without having to accommodate white demands. In July 1991 Nelson Mandela was officially elected president of the ANC, despite an increasing distrust for a man in secret negotiations with the oppressive government.

Throughout the negotiation process huge problems were caused by the Zulu Inkatha Freedom Party (IFP), both in its own province and in townships around the country where Zulus lived and clashed with other

The Bang-Bang Club (2000) by Greg Marinovich and João Silva is a gripping account of four photographers documenting the turbulent final days of apartheid. It was dramatised as a movie starring Ryan Phillippe.

The Elders (www.theelders.org) is a group of world leaders founded by Nelson Mandela to bring voices of integrity and wisdom to resolution of global issues. Members include Archbishop Desmond Tutu and Mandela's widow, Graça Machel.

2008	**2008**	**2009**	**2010**
Long-simmering social discontent boils over and xenophobic rioting wracks townships around the country, causing more than 60 deaths and forcing many workers from neighbouring countries to return home.	The Shikota movement, headed by former Gauteng premier Mbhazima Shilowa and Mosiuoa Lekota, forms a new ANC-breakaway political party called the Congress of the People (COPE).	The ANC wins the country's fourth general election, and Jacob Zuma becomes president. Just before the election, the 'Spytape' corruption charges, which have dogged the controversial Zulu polygamist, are dropped.	The FIFA World Cup of football is held in South Africa and, despite fears that visitors would become victims of crime, it takes place without a hitch.

DESMOND TUTU

Few figures in South Africa's anti-apartheid struggle are as recognisable as Desmond Mpilo Tutu, the retired Anglican Archbishop of Cape Town. Tutu, born in 1931 in Klerksdorp, Transvaal (now in North West Province), rose from humble beginnings to become an internationally recognised activist. During the apartheid era, Tutu was a vigorous proponent of economic boycotts and international sanctions against South Africa. Following the fall of the apartheid government, he headed South Africa's Truth and Reconciliation Commission, an experience that he chronicles in his book *No Future Without Forgiveness*.

Today Tutu continues to be a tireless moral advocate. He has been a particularly outspoken critic of the ANC government, lashing out against corruption, AIDS and poverty, and taking the government to task for failing to adequately tackle poverty. Tutu has been awarded the Nobel Peace Prize, the Gandhi Peace Prize and numerous other distinctions. It is Tutu who is generally credited with coining the phrase 'rainbow nation' as a description for post-apartheid South Africa.

groups. Throughout apartheid KwaZulu had enjoyed special status, with leader Chief Mangosuthu Buthelezi sitting on a fence somewhere between African rights and white capitalism. As violence reached a new high, ANC followers demanded that the armed struggle recommence and with the country verging on anarchy, all talks collapsed. The world looked on in despair.

Slowly the government gave in to each of Mandela's demands and in doing so gradually lost control of the negotiations process. Suddenly Mandela had the upper hand. His former comrade in MK, Joe Slovo, drafted a constitution that appeased the National Party. Slovo included what he called 'sunset clauses', which allowed current public servants to continue their term, working alongside ANC members in a power-sharing plan that would ensure a smooth government changeover.

Elections & South Africa's Constitution

In 1993 an interim constitution was finalised, guaranteeing freedom of speech and religion, access to adequate housing and numerous other benefits, and explicitly prohibiting discrimination on almost any grounds. Finally, at midnight on 26/27 April 1994, the old national anthem 'Die Stem' (The Call) was sung and the old flag was lowered, followed by the raising of the new rainbow flag and the singing of the new anthem 'Nkosi Sikelel' i Afrika' (God Bless Africa). The election went off fairly peacefully, amid a palpable feeling of goodwill throughout the country. Due to their efforts in bringing reconciliation to South Africa, Mandela and De Klerk were jointly awarded the Nobel Peace Prize in

Thabo Mbeki: The Dream Deferred by Mark Gevisser is an intriguing examination of both the man who stood at the forefront of South African politics for more than a decade and of South Africa itself.

2011	2011	2012	2012
With 2 billion rand 'lost' from its national accounts, Limpopo province is declared bankrupt by the national treasury and the federal ANC government seizes direct control of the province.	South Africa becomes a member of BRICS (Brazil, Russia, India, China), an association of the most economically powerful developing nations in the world.	Wildcat strikes sweep the nation as 12,000 mine workers are fired for striking. The appalling conditions endured by many mine workers are brought to national prominence.	The ANC celebrates its 100-year anniversary with major celebrations in Bloemfontein, where it was founded; events commemorating its centennial continue throughout the year all over the country.

1993. The ANC won 62.7% of the vote, less than the 66.7% that would have enabled it to rewrite the constitution.

In 1996, after much negotiation and debate, South Africa's parliament approved a revised version of the 1993 constitution that established the structure of the country's new, democratic government. The national government consists of a 400-member National Assembly, a 90-member National Council of Provinces and a head of state (the president), who is elected by the National Assembly.

A South African president has more in common with a Westminster-style prime minister than a US president, although as head of state the South African president has some executive powers denied to most prime ministers. The constitution is most notable for its expansive Bill of Rights.

In 1999 South Africa held its second democratic elections. Two years previously Mandela had handed over ANC leadership to his deputy, Thabo Mbeki, and the ANC's share of the vote increased to put the party within one seat of the two-thirds majority that would allow it to alter the constitution.

By any account, Mbeki had huge shoes to fill as president – how close he came is the subject of sharply divided debate – and his years in office can only be characterised as a roller-coaster ride. In the early days of his presidency, Mbeki's effective denial of the HIV/AIDS crisis invited global criticism, and his conspicuous failure to condemn the forced reclamation of white-owned farms in neighbouring Zimbabwe and to speak out publicly against his long-time comrade, Zimbabwean president Robert Mugabe, unnerved both South African landowners and foreign investors.

> 'We...shall build the society in which all South Africans, both black and white, will be able to walk tall, without any fear in their hearts, assured of their inalienable right to human dignity – a rainbow nation at peace with itself and the world.' *Nelson Mandela, 1994, Inauguration Speech*

Truth & Reconciliation

Following the first elections, focus turned to the Truth and Reconciliation Commission (1995–98), which worked to expose crimes of the apartheid era. The dictum of its chairman, Archbishop Desmond Tutu, was: 'Without forgiveness there is no future, but without confession there can be no forgiveness'. Many stories of horrific brutality and injustice were heard by the commission, offering some catharsis to people and communities shattered by their past.

The commission operated by allowing victims to tell their stories and perpetrators to confess their guilt, with amnesty on offer to those who made a clean breast of it.

> Poet and journalist Antjie Krog's *Country of My Skull* (1998) is a powerful account of the Truth and Reconciliation Commission, mixing reportage with personal response.

The Zuma Era

In 2005 Mbeki dismissed his deputy president, Zulu anti-apartheid struggle veteran Jacob Zuma, in the wake of corruption charges against him, setting off a ruthless internal ANC power struggle, which Zuma won. In September 2008, in an unprecedented move by the party, Mbeki was asked to step down as president. The charges against Zuma were

2012	2013	2014	2014
Three years after charges of corruption, racketeering, tax evasion and money laundering against President Jacob Zuma are dropped, the country's supreme court rules to allow a review of the decision.	Nelson Mandela dies from respiratory failure. His death causes an outpouring of grief in South Africa and beyond. Leaders from around the world attend his memorial service.	In the episode known as Nkandlagate, President Zuma is criticised by the anti-corruption ombudsman for a 20-million-rand refurbishment of Nkandla, his private home in Zululand.	The country holds its fifth general election since the end of apartheid. The ANC wins, albeit with a reduced majority of 62.1% (compared with 65.9% in 2009), and Zuma begins his second term as president.

dropped and, as widely expected, the ANC won the 2009 election, with Zuma declared president.

In the 2014 elections, the country's media excitedly talked up the chances of the Democratic Alliance (DA), the official opposition. Disenchantment with crime and revelations of corruption, along with slow progress on providing critical services to poor communities, fed a growing desire for change. In the end, though, the ANC won comfortably, with 62.1% of the vote, and the DA won 22.2%, highlighting the mammoth task it faces in wresting government from the ANC.

The Economic Freedom Fighters, a new political party headed by the controversial firebrand Julius Malema, garnered 6.4% of votes, finishing in third place. The former ANC Youth League leader had been expelled from the ANC for corruption and bringing the party into disrepute. Once one of Zuma's greatest supporters, Malema railed against his former mentor and the corrupt practices that he accused the ANC of perpetrating. Though the Limpopo-born Malema enjoyed grassroots popularity for his Afro-socialist talk of economic equality and fighting poverty, his radical views against 'white monopoly power' and on the need for land redistribution and nationalising the mines worried many.

> More people have HIV/AIDs in South Africa than any other country – for more on the history of the epidemic in South Africa and what's being done today, see www.avert. org/aidssouth africa.htm.

New Era

The ability of opposition parties to pressure the government to tackle the country's problems continues to be an important test of South Africa's political maturity. Corruption, crime, economic inequality, quality education and HIV/AIDS all loom as major challenges. Given the country's turbulent recent history, ongoing crime problems and issues of corruption – the last two are always talking points among the populace – it's not surprising that there is a range of views among South Africans about the future of the 'rainbow nation'.

In late 2017, as Cape Town's water crisis worsened and the city experienced harsh restrictions on water usage – hoping to stave off Day Zero, when its taps would run dry – there was some good news in the shape of Cyril Ramaphosa. Mandela's old comrade replaced Zuma as leader of the ANC, and as many hoped the increasingly scandal-mired Zulu resigned as president in February 2018. Zuma's second presidential term had been dominated by allegations of the questionable influence exerted on government by three powerful Indian brothers, the Guptas. While the ANC retained its huge following of older and rural black voters, it lost the municipalities of Tshwane (Pretoria), Johannesburg and Nelson Mandela Bay (Port Elizabeth) to DA-led coalitions in the 2016 municipal elections, suggesting the ruling party had much work to do before the 2019 general elections.

> The legacy of Nelson Mandela is what he achieved with unswerving determination, generosity of spirit and lack of vengeance. And his gift to South Africans was to bring peace and reconciliation to a country torn by racial discrimination. It is a legacy that reverberates far beyond his country's borders.

2014	2015	2017	2018
The country's newest political party, the Economic Freedom Fighters, led by former disgraced ANC Youth League leader Julius Malema, captures 6.4% of the vote in the national elections.	The #RhodesMustFall movement, dedicated to 'decolonising' South African universities, succesfully pressures the University of Cape Town to remove a statue of 19th-century magnate Cecil Rhodes from campus.	Following the ANC's losses to DA-led coalitions in the 2016 municipal elections, amid allegations about corruption under President Zuma, Cyril Ramaphosa replaces Zuma as ANC president.	Water restrictions become daily realities for drought-hit South Africa, with Capetonians limited to 50L per person per day. The city's residents stockpile bottled water in fear of Day Zero, when taps will be turned off.

Environment

South Africa has incredible biological diversity, and for Africa in particular is highly urbanised. Mountainous Lesotho is far more rural while Swaziland is somewhere between the two. The wildlife in this region is Africa at its best: South Africa boasts some of the most accessible wildlife viewing on the entire continent. Probably your best chance of seeing the Big Five – rhinos, buffaloes, elephants, leopards and lions – is in the excellent parks and reserves of South Africa and Swaziland.

South Africa measures around 1,219,090 sq km, or five times the size of the UK. It's Africa's ninth-largest and fifth-most-populous country.

The Land & Sea

A windswept and beautiful coast is the face that South Africa turns to the rest of the world – tempestuous and tamed, stormy and sublime. It spans two oceans as it winds its way down the Atlantic seaboard in the west and up into the warmer Indian Ocean waters to the east. In all, the country has more than 2500km of coastline.

And this is just the start of the region's topographical wealth. Head further inland and you'll find yourself climbing from the eastern lowlands (lowveld) to the cool heights of the Drakensberg Escarpment and onto the vast plateau (highveld) that forms the heart of the country. This plateau, which averages about 1500m in height, drops off again in the northwestern part of the country to the low-lying Kalahari basin.

The Drakensberg range is at its most rugged in tiny Lesotho – a 30,355-sq-km patch of mountain peaks and highland plateau that is completely surrounded by South Africa. It has the highest lowest point of any country in the world – 1400m, in southern Lesotho's Senqu (Orange) River valley.

Swaziland is one of Africa's smallest countries at only 17,364 sq km in area, but with a remarkable diversity of landscapes, climates and ecological zones for its size. These range from low-lying savannah to the east, rolling hills towards the centre, and rainforest and perpetually fog-draped peaks in the northwest.

Wildlife
South Africa

South Africa is home to the world's three largest land mammals (the African elephant, white rhino and hippopotamus), its tallest (giraffe), fastest (cheetah) and smallest (pygmy shrew). The country's 800-plus bird species include the world's largest (ostrich), the heaviest flying bird (Kori bustard) and the smallest raptor (pygmy falcon).

Off its long coastline is a rich diversity of marine life – 11,000 species have been recorded. Eight whale species are found in South African waters, including the largest mammal in the world, the blue whale. Although it's the great white shark that snares most of the headlines, turtles, seabirds and penguins are also popular sightings.

Lesotho

Due primarily to its altitude, Lesotho is home to fewer animals than much of the rest of the region. Those you may encounter include rheboks, jackals, mongooses, meerkats, elands and rock hyraxes. However,

Lesotho's montane areas are of particular interest for their rare smaller species. Many are found only in the Drakensberg, including the highly threatened Maloti minnow, the African ice rat, several species of lizards and geckos, and the Lesotho river frog.

The country's almost 300 recorded bird species include the lammergeier (bearded vulture) and the southern bald ibis.

Among Lesotho's earliest wild inhabitants were dinosaurs: the small, fast-running Lesothosaurus was named after the country.

Swaziland

Swaziland has about 120 mammal species, representing one-third of Southern Africa's nonmarine mammal species. Many (including elephants, rhinos and lions) have been introduced, and larger animals are restricted to nature reserves and private wildlife farms. Mongooses and large-spotted genets are common, and hyenas and jackals are found in the reserves. Leopards are rarely seen.

Swaziland's varied terrain supports abundant birdlife, including the blue crane, ground woodpecker and lappet-faced vulture. More species have been spotted in Swaziland than in the larger Kruger National Park.

Watching Wildlife

The most straightforward and cheapest way to visit the parks (especially if you're in a group) is usually with a hired car. A 2WD is adequate in most parks, but during winter, when the grass is high, you'll be able to see more with a 4WD or other high-clearance vehicle. Organised safaris are readily arranged with major tour operators and with backpacker-oriented outfits.

Several major parks (including Kruger, Hluhluwe-iMfolozi and Pilanesberg) offer guided wilderness walks accompanied by armed rangers. These are highly recommended, as the subtleties of the bush can be

Endangered mammals include black rhinos (sometimes spotted in KwaZulu-Natal's uMkhuze Game Reserve and Hluhluwe-iMfolozi Park), riverine rabbits (found only near rivers in the central Karoo), wild dogs (Hluhluwe-iMfolozi Park and Kruger National Park) and roan antelope (Kruger National Park).

THE GREAT IVORY DEBATE

In 1990, following a massive campaign by various conservation organisations, the UN Convention on International Trade in Endangered Species (CITES) banned ivory trading in an effort to protect Africa's then-declining elephant populations. This promoted recovery of elephant populations in areas where they had previously been ravaged. Yet in South Africa, where elephants had long been protected, the elephant populations continued to grow, leading to widespread habitat destruction.

Solutions to the problem of elephant overpopulation have included creating transfrontier parks to allow animals to migrate over larger areas, relocating animals, small-scale elephant contraception efforts and – most controversially – culling.

In 2002, after much pressure, CITES relaxed its worldwide ivory trading ban to allow ivory from legally culled elephants to be sold. The decision has been strongly disputed by several governments on the grounds that resuming trade will increase demand for ivory and, thus, encourage poaching. The idea behind the move was that earnings would benefit elephant conservation efforts and communities living around elephant areas, and that CITES would monitor whether poaching increased after the ban was relaxed.

The most recently approved major one-off ivory sale was in mid-2008, when 108 tonnes of ivory from South Africa (51 tonnes), Namibia, Botswana and Zimbabwe was exported to China in a CITES-authorised transaction. Following such a sale, CITES mandates a nine-year resting period during which no additional ivory sales from these countries are permitted. In China – long one of the main markets for the illegal ivory trade – ivory is used for everything from jewellery and artwork to mobile-phone ornamentation. South Africa, Zimbabwe and Namibia have looked at ways to overturn the CITES restrictions to sell more of their ivory stockpiles.

much better experienced on foot than in a vehicle. Book well in advance with the relevant park authority. Shorter morning and afternoon walks are also possible at many wildlife parks, and can generally be booked the same day.

Throughout South Africa, park infrastructure is of high quality. You can often get by without a guide, although you'll almost certainly see and learn more with one. All national parks have rest camps offering good-value accommodation, ranging from campsites to self-catering cottages. Many have restaurants, shops and petrol pumps. Advance bookings for accommodation are essential during holiday periods; at other times it's available at short notice.

Sasol eBirds of Southern Africa features images, distribution maps and descriptions of birds. This great app is essentially a digital version of the Sasol field guidebook. Compare birds, store a list of sightings and verify an identity by matching it to one of 630 recorded bird calls.

Safari Safety

One of South Africa's major attractions is the chance to go on safari and get 'up close and personal' with the wildlife. Remember, however, that the animals aren't tame and their actions are often unpredictable. Some tips for staying safe:

➡ Never get between a mother and her young.

➡ Never get between a hippo and water.

➡ Watch out for black rhinos (although they are rare), which will charge just about anything.

➡ Be careful around buffalo herds – they charge without warning and the whole herd will charge together.

➡ Although elephants often appear docile, never take them for granted – be especially careful around females with young and agitated young males.

➡ Remember that a fake charge from an elephant is probably a precursor to the real thing.

When to Watch

Wildlife watching is rewarding at any time of year, although spotting tends to be easier in the cooler, dry winter months (June to September), when foliage is less dense and animals congregate at water holes. The summer (late November to March) is rainy, warmer and scenic, with greener landscapes, although animals are more widely dispersed and may be difficult to see.

Birding is good year-round, with spring (September to November) and summer generally the best times.

ENJOYING SOUTH AFRICA'S MARINE ENVIRONMENT

There are many ways to enjoy South Africa's unique and plentiful marine environment. Spending time on top of, or under, the water could prove to be a highlight of your trip. In the Western Cape, Hermanus is regarded as the best land-based whale-watching destination in the world: southern right whales cruise past from June to December.

A unique opportunity exists to come face to face with a great white shark in KwaZulu-Natal and the Western Cape. Despite its detractors, shark-cage diving remains a popular adventure sport. And scuba diving is all the rage off the coast of KwaZulu-Natal, with Aliwal Shoal considered one of the best dive sites in the world. Colourful coral, turtles, rays and many species of sharks can be seen.

The Greatest Shoal on Earth is the sardine run that occurs between May and July, when a seething mass of sardines appears off the coasts of the Eastern Cape and Kwa-Zulu-Natal, stretching for up to 15km. Predators, such as sharks, dolphins and seabirds, come from far and wide to gorge themselves, and snorkelling or diving around the shoal is an incredible experience.

THE CAPE FLORAL KINGDOM

The Cape Floral Kingdom, parts of which are now a Unesco World Heritage Site, is the smallest of the world's six floral kingdoms, but the most diverse, with 1300 species per 10,000 sq km. This is some 900 more species than are found in the South American rainforests. The main vegetation type is *fynbos* (fine bush), characterised by small, narrow leaves and stems. The *fynbos* environment hosts over 7500 plant species, most of which are unique to the area. Some members of the main *fynbos* families – ericas (heaths), proteas and restios (reeds) – have been domesticated elsewhere and are relatively widespread, but many species have a remarkably small range.

The Cape Floral Kingdom extends roughly from Cape Point east almost to Grahamstown and north to the Olifants River, and includes the Kogelberg and parts of several biosphere reserves. However, most of the remaining indigenous vegetation is found only in protected areas, such as Table Mountain and the Cape Peninsula.

Plants

South Africa's more than 20,000 plant species represent 10% of the world's total, although the country constitutes only 1% of the earth's land surface. Dozens of flowers that are domesticated elsewhere grow wild here, including gladioli, proteas, birds of paradise and African lilies. South Africa is also the only country with one of the world's six floral kingdoms entirely within its borders (in the Western Cape). In the drier northwest are succulents (dominated by euphorbias and aloes) and annuals, which flower brilliantly after the spring rains.

South Africa has few natural forests. They were never extensive, and today there are only remnants. Temperate forests occur on the southern coastal strip between George and Humansdorp, in the KwaZulu-Natal Drakensberg and in Mpumalanga. Subtropical forests are found northeast of Port Elizabeth in areas just inland from the Wild Coast, and in KwaZulu-Natal.

In the north are savannah areas, dotted with acacias and thorn trees.

National Parks & Protected Areas

South Africa

South Africa has hundreds of national parks and reserves, many featuring wildlife, while others are primarily wilderness sanctuaries or hiking areas. All national parks charge a daily conservation fee, which is discounted for South African residents and nationals of Southern African Development Community (SADC) countries.

In addition to its national parks, South Africa is party to several transfrontier conservation areas. These include Kgalagadi Transfrontier Park, combining the Northern Cape's former Kalahari Gemsbok National Park with Botswana's Gemsbok National Park; the Maloti-Drakensberg Peace Park, which links Sehlabathebe National Park and other areas of the Lesotho Drakensberg with their South African counterparts in uKhahlamba-Drakensberg; and the Great Limpopo Transfrontier Park, which spans the borders of South Africa, Mozambique and Zimbabwe. Private wildlife reserves also abound.

In total, just over 5% of South African land has national park status, with an estimated 4% to 5% more enjoying other types of protective status. The government has started teaming up with private landowners to bring private conservation land under government protection, with the goal of increasing the total amount of conservation land to more than 10%.

The Wildlife & Environmental Society of South Africa (www. wessa.org.za) is a leading environmental advocacy organisation that runs the high-profile Rhino Initiative to stop the illegal trade in rhino horn.

TOP PARKS & RESERVES

LOCATION	PARK/RESERVE	FEATURES	ACTIVITIES	BEST TIME TO VISIT
Cape Peninsula	Table Mountain National Park (p56)	rocky headlands, seascapes; African penguins, elands, water birds, bonteboks	hiking, mountain biking	year-round
Western Cape	Cederberg Wilderness Area (p173)	mountainous and rugged terrain; San rock art, sandstone formations, plant life	hiking, climbing	Mar-Oct
Mpumalanga/Limpopo	Kruger National Park (p395)	savannah, woodlands, thornveld; the 'Big Five' animals	vehicle safaris, wildlife walks	year-round
Mpumalanga	Blyde River Canyon Nature Reserve (p386)	canyon, caves, river; stunning vistas	hiking, kloofing (canyoning), scenic drives	year-round
Northern Cape	Augrabies Falls National Park (p463)	desert, river, waterfalls; klipspringers, rock dassies; striking scenery	hiking, canoeing, rafting	Apr-Sep
Northern Cape	|Ai-|Ais/Richtersveld Transfrontier Park (p467)	mountainous desert, haunting beauty; klipspringers, jackals, zebras, plants, birds	hiking, 4WD adventures	Apr-Sep
Eastern Cape	Addo Elephant National Park (p197)	dense bush, grasslands, forested kloofs; elephants, black rhinos, buffaloes	vehicle safaris, walking trails, horse riding	year-round
Eastern Cape	Garden Route National Park (Tsitsikamma section; p180)	coast, cliffs, rivers, ravines, forests; Cape clawless otters, baboons, monkeys, birdlife	hiking	year-round
KwaZulu-Natal	Hluhluwe-iMfolozi Park (p270)	lush, subtropical vegetation, savannah; rhinos, giraffes, lions, elephants, birds	wilderness walks, wildlife watching	May-Oct
KwaZulu-Natal	iSimangaliso Wetland Park (p272)	wetlands, coastal grasslands; elephants, birds, hippos, crocodiles	wilderness walks, vehicle/boat safaris	Mar-Nov
KwaZulu-Natal	uMkhuze Game Reserve (p277)	savannah, woodlands, swamp; rhinos and almost everything else; hundreds of bird species	guided walks, bird walks, vehicle safaris	year-round
KwaZulu-Natal	uKhahlamba-Drakensberg Park (p287)	awe-inspiring Drakensberg Escarpment; fantastic scenery and wilderness areas	hiking	year-round
Free State	Golden Gate Highlands National Park (p316)	spectacular sandstone cliffs and outcrops; zebras, oribis, rheboks, elands, birds	hiking	year-round

In addition to this, South Africa has over 20 Marine Protected Areas (MPAs) designed to protect and stabilise fish and other marine-life populations against overfishing, pollution, uncontrolled tourism and mining. The world's seventh-largest MPA was declared in 2013 and lies 2000km southeast of the country's coastline around Prince Edward and Marion Islands. Marine life falling under the protection of the new MPA includes albatrosses, penguins, fur seals, killer whales and Patagonian toothfish.

More information is available through online resources:

CapeNature (☎021-483 0190; www.capenature.co.za) Promotes nature conservation in the Western Cape, and is responsible for permits and bookings for Western Cape reserves.

Ezemvelo KZN Wildlife (☎033-845 1000; www.kznwildlife.com) Responsible for wildlife parks in KwaZulu-Natal.

Safcol (www.safcol.co.za) Its Komatiland Forests Eco-Tourism division oversees forest areas, promotes ecotourism and manages hiking trails around Mpumalanga and Limpopo.

South African National Parks (SANParks; ☎012-428 9111; www.sanparks.org) The best place to start your safari.

Lesotho

In part because land tenure allows communal access to natural resources, less than 1% of Lesotho is protected – the lowest protected-area coverage of any nation in Africa. Sehlabathebe National Park is the main conservation area, known for its isolated wilderness. Other protected areas include Ts'ehlanyane National Park and Bokong Nature Reserve.

Swaziland

About 4% of Swaziland's area is protected. Its conservation areas tend to be low-key, with fewer visitors than their South African counterparts, and good value for money. They include Mlilwane Wildlife Sanctuary, Mkhaya Game Reserve, Malolotja Nature Reserve, which is mainly for hiking, and Hlane Royal National Park. Mlilwane, Mkhaya and Hlane are included in South Africa's Wild Card program (www.sanparks.org/wild).

Environmental Issues
South Africa

South Africa is the world's third most biologically diverse country. It's also one of Africa's most urbanised, with over 50% of the population living in towns and cities. Major challenges for the government include managing increasing urbanisation while protecting the environment.

Land degradation is one of the country's most serious problems, with about one-quarter of South Africa's land considered to be severely degraded. In former homeland areas, years of overgrazing and overcropping have resulted in massive soil depletion. This, plus poor overall conditions, is pushing people to the cities, further increasing urban pressures. The distorted rural-urban settlement pattern is a legacy of the apartheid era, with huge population concentrations in townships that generally lack adequate utilities and infrastructure.

South Africa receives an average of only 500mm of rainfall annually, and droughts are common, with Cape Town's taps expected to run dry in 2018. To meet demand for water, all major South African rivers have been dammed or modified. While this has improved water supply to many areas, it has also disrupted local ecosystems and caused increased silting in waterways.

South Africa has long been at the forefront among African countries in conservation of its fauna. However, funding is tight and will likely remain so as long as many South Africans still lack access to basic

Rhinos aren't named for their colour, but for their lip shape: 'white' comes from *wijde* (wide), the Boers' term for the fatter-lipped white rhino.

RHINO POACHING IN SOUTH AFRICA

Rhino horn has long been a sought-after commodity in some Asian countries. It is a status symbol and is believed to be a healing agent. A single rhino horn can fetch a lot of money on the black market in countries such as Vietnam and China.

This market has provided plenty of motivation for the illegal trade in rhino horn. From the late 1970s to mid-1990s, rhino populations were periodically decimated in Africa by poaching.

In recent years rhino poaching has again escalated sharply. In 2003, 22 rhino were poached in South Africa. In 2012 this figure rose to 668, and by the end of 2014, a staggering 1020 rhino had been poached that year. Of that figure almost 700 were slaughtered in Kruger National Park, a place that is home to 60% of the world's remaining rhinos. More recent stats look equally bleak, although happily arrests of suspected poachers and traffickers are also significant – 359 in the first half of 2017.

Kruger National Park is officially part of the Great Limpopo Transfrontier Park, which combines Kruger with areas of Zimbabwe and Mozambique's Limpopo National Park. Many poachers come from Mozambique through the long, porous border between Kruger and Limpopo. The latter park's under-resourced and under-capacity anti-poaching unit does battle with poaching syndicates that have unlimited resources.

Overwhelmed by the challenge of monitoring the park's huge and largely unattended border with Mozambique, the South African government has embarked upon a massive relocation program. It is transporting rhinos to safer areas within Kruger and other parks in South Africa and neighbouring countries, while private efforts include the Rhinos Without Borders conservation project, which is translocating 100 rhinos to Botswana, funded by travel companies &Beyond and Great Plains Conservation.

In the meantime, innovative ways of tracking down poachers are being deployed. These include Shotspotter, a technology usually rolled out in crime-ridden cities in the USA. When a shot is fired, hidden microphones in the bush pick up the sound, triangulate it and feed location information to rangers and police, who can respond in real time. Poachers are turning their focus from Kruger to KwaZulu-Natal, but perhaps the most worrying recent development has been the legalisation of South Africa's domestic rhino-horn trade, despite criticisms that the move would encourage demand and poaching. An online auction went ahead in 2017, with supporters arguing that establishing a legal, regulated market could help to deter poaching, but the 264 horns attracted few bidders.

For more information on the ongoing battle to save the African rhino from extinction, check out www.savetherhino.org and www.stoprhinopoaching.com.

amenities. Rhino poaching across the country, and particularly in Kruger National Park, is exacerbated by underfunding. Potential solutions include public/private-sector conservation partnerships, and increased contributions from private donors and international conservation bodies such as the World Wide Fund for Nature (WWF).

Estimates have put South Africa's potential shale-gas deposits at 485 trillion cubic feet of gas. That's gained a lot of interest from oil companies, and according to Econometrix (in a report commissioned by Shell) the shale-gas industry could be worth R200 billion annually to GDP and lead to the creation of 700,000 jobs. Until 2012 South Africa, like many countries, had placed a moratorium on hydraulic fracturing (fracking) to extract the gas. There are serious environmental concerns about the safety of the technology used in fracking, which uses large amounts of clean water mixed with sand and a 'chemical cocktail' to crack underground rocks and release the shale gas.

Since the moratorium was lifted, the debate over fracking in South Africa's Northern Cape (in the Karoo) has continued to rage, with these environmental concerns pitted against vested economic interests – in particular large oil companies. In March 2017 the government announced that fracking would go ahead.

Going Green

More than 90% of South Africa's electricity is coal-generated – more than double the international average. Yet on a local level, there are many commendable projects showcasing the country's slow but sure progress towards going green.

Lynedoch EcoVillage (☎021-881 3196; www.sustainabilityinstitute.net) South Africa's first ecologically designed and socially mixed community is slowly taking form, with the design of energy-efficient houses and community buildings, and a focus on the establishment of a self-sufficient community.

Monwabisi Park Eco-Cottages Project (www.shaster.org.za/Past-Projects) Under the auspices of the Shaster Foundation, the Monwabisi Park squatters' settlement of Khayelitsha was transformed into an eco-village, with informal shacks replaced by community-built eco-cottages. Sandbags, earthworm waste systems and natural energy systems were employed.

The Kuyasa Project (www.kuyasacdm.co.za) More than 2000 low-income houses in Cape Town's Khayelitsha township have been retrofitted with renewable energy technologies such as solar water heaters, energy-efficient lighting and insulated ceilings. In addition to promoting energy savings (averaging about 40% per household), the project has also created jobs and offered other sustainable development benefits.

South African National Parks (SANParks; ☎012-428 9111; www.sanparks. org) Facilities at parks in the SANParks network are being upgraded with installation of solar water heaters and other energy-saving devices.

Tree planting More than 200,000 indigenous trees were planted as part of the Greening Soweto project, which sought to beautify the massive township as a legacy of the 2010 FIFA World Cup. The project incorporates ongoing environmental-awareness programs.

Wind farms One of several wind-farm projects, the Darling Wind Farm, 35km north of Cape Town, is linked to the national power grid. There are many more earmarked sites on the Eastern Cape coastline.

Lesotho

Climate change is becoming a problem for Lesotho, a country highly vulnerable to flood and drought, and now threatens the nation's food security, water supply and biodiversity. Other main issues include animal population pressure (resulting in overgrazing) and soil erosion. About 40 million tonnes of topsoil are lost annually, with a sobering prediction from the Ministry of Natural Resources that there may well be no cultivatable land left by 2040.

On a brighter note, Lesotho and South Africa are working together within the framework of the Maloti-Drakensberg Transfrontier Conservation and Development Project to protect these two alpine areas.

In addition, the once-controversial Highlands Water Project, which activists feared might disrupt traditional communities, flood agricultural lands and adversely impact the Senqu (Orange) River, is now regarded by the government as a success.

Swaziland

Three of Swaziland's major waterways (the Komati, Lomati and Usutu Rivers) arise in South Africa, and Swaziland has been closely involved in South Africa's river-control efforts. Drought is a recurring problem in eastern lowveld areas. Other concerns include lack of community participation in conservation efforts, low levels of environmental awareness and lack of government support.

Scorched: South Africa's Changing Climate by Leonie Joubert is a thought-provoking journey through South Africa. It transforms climate change and other environmental issues from dry discourse into sobering, near-at-hand realities.

Two major ocean currents shape South Africa's climate and provide for rich marine life. The chilly Benguela current surges up from Antarctica along the country's Atlantic Coast and is laden with plankton. The north-to-south Mozambique/Agulhas current gives the east coast its warmer waters.

ENVIRONMENT ENVIRONMENTAL ISSUES

Cape Town's dams are almost empty, with accusations of mismanagement flying as the drought continues. Water restrictions force residents to bathe together and hoard grey water for irrigation, as daily usage was limited to 50L per person by early 2018. Day Zero, when the taps run dry, is expected in 2018.

Responsible Travel

Tourism is big in South Africa, and making environmentally and culturally sensitive choices can have a significant impact. Following are a few guidelines for visitors:

➡ Travel involves a responsibility to local cultures and people – consider giving back to local communities through a donation of money to a reputable NGO working in the field, or through volunteering some of your time.

➡ Always ask permission before photographing people.

➡ Avoid indiscriminate gift giving. Donations to recognised projects are less destructive to local cultural values and have a better chance of reaching those who need them most.

➡ Support local enterprises, buy locally whenever possible, and buy souvenirs directly from those who make them.

➡ Seek entities that promote sustainable, community-oriented tourism. The lists on the website of Fair Trade Tourism (www.fairtrade.travel) are a good starting point.

➡ Avoid buying items made from ivory, skin, shells etc.

➡ Carry a SASSI app or pocket guide (downloadable from www.wwfsassi.co.za) if you enjoy dining at seafood restaurants.

➡ For cultural attractions, try to pay fees directly to the locals involved, rather than to tour-company guides or other middle people.

➡ Respect local culture and customs.

➡ Don't litter. On treks, in parks or when camping, carry out all your litter (most parks give you a bag for this purpose) and leave trails, parks and campsites cleaner than you found them.

➡ Maximise your 'real' time with locals, choosing itineraries that are well integrated with the communities in the areas where you will be travelling.

SIMON DANNHAUER / SHUTTERSTOCK ©

Bateleur eagle (p556)

Wildlife & Habitat

South Africa encompasses one of the most diverse landscapes on the entire continent. There are habitats ranging from verdant forests, stony deserts and soaring mountains to lush grasslands, classic African savannahs and thornbush velds. It is home to penguins and flamingos, caracals and sables, wild dogs, dwarf mongooses and hulking African elephants. The number and variation of species is astounding and a deep immersion into wildlife watching is a pure joy of travel here. Showcasing this diversity are more than 700 publicly owned reserves and about 200 private reserves.

1. Caracal 2. Lion 3. Cheetah 4. Leopard

Cats

In terms of behaviour, the cats that are found in South Africa are little more than souped-up house cats; it's just that they may weigh half as much as a horse or jet along as fast as a speeding car. With their excellent vision and keen hearing, cats are superb hunters.

Lion

Weight 120–150kg (female), 150–225kg (male); length 210–275cm (female), 240–350cm (male) Those lions sprawled out lazily in the shade are actually Africa's most feared predators. Equipped with teeth that tear effortlessly through bone and tendon, they can take down an animal as large as a bull giraffe. Females do all the hunting; swaggering males fight among themselves and eat what the females catch.

Leopard

Weight 30–60kg (female), 40–90kg (male); length 170–300cm More common than you realise, the leopard relies on expert camouflage to stay hidden. At night there is no mistaking the bone-chilling groans that sound like wood being sawn at high volume.

Caracal

Weight 8–19kg; length 80–120cm The caracal is a gorgeous tawny cat with extremely long, pointy ears. It is able to make vertical leaps of 3m and swat birds out of the air.

Wildcat

Weight 3–6.5kg; length 65–100cm If you see what looks like a tabby wandering along fields and forest edges, you may be seeing a wildcat, the direct ancestor of domesticated house cats.

Cheetah

Weight 40–60kg; length 200–220cm Less cat than greyhound, the cheetah is a world-class sprinter. Although it reaches 112km/h, the cheetah runs out of steam after 300m and must cool down for 30 minutes before hunting again.

BEN CRANKE / GETTY IMAGES ©

1. Chacma baboons **2.** Samango monkey **3.** Vervet monkey

3

Primates

East Africa is the evolutionary cradle of primate diversity, and South Africa is a relative newcomer on the scene, home to just five species of monkeys, apes and prosimians. Some of these, however, are common and widespread, meaning that you're likely to see a lot of fascinating primate behaviour.

Vervet Monkey

Weight 4–8kg; length 90–140cm If any monkey epitomises South Africa, it is the widespread and adaptable vervet monkey. If you think their appearance too drab, check out the extraordinary blue and scarlet colours of the male sexual organs when they get excited.

Greater Bushbaby

Weight up to 1.5kg; length 80cm, including 45cm tail Named for their plaintive call, bushbabies are actually primitive primates. They have small heads, large rounded ears, thick bushy tails, dark-brown fur and enormous eyes.

Chacma Baboon

Weight 12–30kg (female), 25–45kg (male); length 100–200cm Chacma baboons are worth watching for their complex social dynamics. Look for signs of friendship, deception or deal-making.

Samango Monkey

Weight 3.5–5.5kg (female), 5.5–12kg (male); length 100–160cm Samango monkeys are part of a vast group of African primates called gentle, or blue, monkeys. They are found exclusively in forests.

Greater Galago

Weight 550g–2kg; length 55–100cm A cat-sized, nocturnal creature with a doglike face, the greater galago belongs to a group of prosimians (the 'primitive' ancestors of modern primates) that have changed little in 60 million years.

Cud-Chewing Mammals

Africa is most famous for its astounding variety of ungulates – hoofed mammals that include everything from buffaloes and rhinos to giraffes and zebras. The subgroup of ungulates that ruminate (chew their cud) and have horns are bovines. Among this family, antelopes are particularly numerous, with more than 20 species in South Africa.

Wildebeest
Weight 140–290kg; length 230–340cm
Look for the black-shouldered blue wildebeest and the white-tailed black wildebeest (a South African speciality).

Impala
Weight 40–80kg; length 150–200cm
Gregarious and displaying a prodigious capacity to reproduce, impalas can reach great numbers.

Springbok
Weight 20–40kg (female), 30–60kg (male); length 135–175cm Lacking the vast grasslands of East Africa, South Africa is home to only one gazelle-like antelope – the lithe, little springbok.

Gemsbok
Weight 180–240kg; length 230cm
With straight, towering, metre-long horns and a boldly patterned face, this elegant desert antelope can survive for months on the scant water it derives from the plants it eats.

Sable
Weight 200–270kg; length 230–330cm
Looking like a colourful horse with huge soaring horns, the sable ranks as one of Africa's most visually stunning mammals.

1. Sable 2. Impalas 3. Blue wildebeests

Hoofed Mammals

A full stable of Africa's mega-charismatic animals can be found in this group of ungulates. Other than the giraffe, these ungulates are not ruminants. They have been at home in Africa for millions of years and are among the most successful mammals to have ever wandered the continent.

Mountain Zebra
Weight 230–380kg; length 260–300cm
South Africa's endemic mountain zebra differs from its savannah relative in having an unstriped belly and rusty muzzle.

Giraffe
Weight 450–1200kg (female), 1800–2000kg (male); height 3.5–5.2m
Though they stroll along casually, giraffes can outrun any predator.

African Elephant
Weight 2200–3500kg (female), 4000–6300kg (male); height 2.4–3.4m (female), 3–4m (male) Commonly referred to as 'the king of beasts', although elephant society is actually ruled by a lineage of elder females.

Hippopotamus
Weight 510–3200kg; length 320–400cm
Designed like a floating beanbag with tiny legs, the hippo spends its time in or very near water chowing down on aquatic plants.

White Rhinoceros
Weight 1400–2000kg (female), 2000–3600kg (male); length 440–520cm
Brought to the brink of extinction in the early 1990s, this majestic creature was largely saved by the efforts of South African wildlife managers. Poaching has once again become a major problem though, particularly in Kruger.

1. White rhinoceros 2. Hippopotamuses 3. Giraffes and zebras

FRANZ ABERHAM / GETTY IMAGES ©

1. Meerkats **2.** Honey badger **3.** African wild dogs

Other Carnivores

In addition to seven types of cat, South Africa is home to 25 other carnivores ranging from slinky mongooses to highly social hunting dogs. All are linked in having 'carnassial' (slicing) teeth. A highlight for visitors is witnessing the superb hunting prowess of these highly efficient hunters.

Honey Badger

Weight 7–16kg; length 75–100cm The ratel or 'honey badger' may be the fiercest of all African animals. It finds its honey by following honey guide birds to beehives.

Aardwolf

Weight 8–12kg; length 75–110cm This slender, tawny animal is actually the smallest hyena, but its fearsome carnivorous tendencies are limited to lapping up soft-bodied termites.

Spotted Hyena

Weight 40–90kg; length 125–215cm Living in packs ruled by females that grow penis-like sexual organs, these savage fighters use their bone-crushing jaws to disembowel terrified prey on the run, or to do battle with lions.

African Wild Dog

Weight 20–35kg; length 100–150cm Fabulously and uniquely patterned, hunting dogs run in packs of 20 to 60 that ruthlessly chase down antelopes and other animals. Organised in complex hierarchies maintained by rules of conduct, these highly social canids are incredibly efficient hunters.

Meerkat

Weight 0.5–1kg; length 50cm South Africa's nine species of mongoose may be best represented by the delightfully named meerkat. Energetic and highly social, meerkats spend much of their time standing up with looks of perpetual surprise.

Birds of Prey

South Africa is home to about 60 species of hawks, eagles, vultures and owls. Look for them perching on trees, soaring high overhead or gathered around a carcass. Your first clue to their presence, however, may be the scolding cries of small birds harassing one of these feared hunters.

African Fish Eagle

Length 75cm Given its name, it's not surprising that you'll see the African fish eagle hunting for fish around water. It is most familiar for the loud ringing vocalisations that have become known as 'the voice of Africa'.

Bateleur

Length 60cm The bateleur is an attractive serpent eagle. In flight, look for this eagle's white wings and odd tailless appearance; close up, look for the bold colour pattern and scarlet face.

Bearded Vulture

Length 110cm Around the soaring cliffs of the Drakensberg, you may be lucky to spot one of the world's most eagerly sought-after birds of prey – the massive bearded vulture, also known as the lammergeier.

Secretary Bird

Length 100cm In a country full of unique birds, the secretary bird literally stands head and shoulders above the masses. With the body of an eagle and the legs of a crane, this idiosyncratic, grey-bodied raptor is commonly seen striding across the savannah.

Lappet-Faced Vulture

Length 115cm Seven of South Africa's eight vulture species can be seen mingling with lions, hyenas and jackals around carcasses. Here, through sheer numbers, they often compete successfully for scraps of flesh and bone. The monstrous lappet-faced vulture, a giant among its cohorts, gets its fill before the other vultures move in.

1. African fish eagle 2. Secretary bird 3. Bearded vulture

1. Ground hornbill 2. Lesser flamingoes 3. African penguins
4. Lilac-breasted roller

JAMES HAGER / GETTY IMAGES ©

NIGEL DENNIS / GETTY IMAGES ©

Other Birds

Come to South Africa prepared to see an astounding number of birds in every shape and colour imaginable. If you're not already paying attention to every bird you see, you may find them an energising and pleasant diversion after a couple of days staring at impala and snoring lions.

Lesser Flamingo

Length 100cm Coloured deep rose-pink and gathering by the thousands on salt lakes, the lesser flamingo creates some of the most dramatic wildlife spectacles in Africa, especially when they all fly at once or perform synchronised courtship displays.

Ground Hornbill

Length 90cm Looking somewhat like a turkey, the ground hornbill spends its time on the ground stalking insects, frogs, reptiles and small mammals, which it kills with fierce stabs of its large powerful bill.

Lilac-Breasted Roller

Length 40cm Nearly everyone on safari gets to know the gorgeously coloured lilac-breasted roller. Related to kingfishers, rollers get their name from the tendency to 'roll' from side to side in flight to show off their iridescent blues, purples and greens.

Ostrich

Length 200–270cm If you think the ostrich looks prehistoric, you aren't far off. Weighing upwards of 130kg, these ancient flightless birds escape predators by running away at 70km/h or lying flat on the ground.

African Penguin

Length 60cm Yes, they are silly looking, but African penguins get their nickname, the 'jackass penguin', for their donkeylike calls, part of the ecstatic courtship displays given by the males. Found along the coast and on offshore islands, some penguin colonies are ridiculously tame.

Savannah landscape at Hluhluwe-iMfolozi Park (p270)

Habitats

Nearly all of South Africa's wildlife occupies a specific type of habitat, and you will hear rangers and fellow travellers refer to these habitats repeatedly. Your wildlife-viewing experience will be greatly enhanced if you learn how to recognise these habitats, and the animals you might expect in each one.

Savannah & Grassland

Savannah is *the* classic African landscape, with broad, rolling grasslands dotted with acacia trees, and best known in East Africa. Known as bushveld in South Africa, this open landscape is home to large herds of zebra and antelope, in addition to fast-sprinting predators such as cheetahs. Grasslands lack woody plants, and on the central plateau they are known as highveld.

Fynbos

The dense, low shrub cover that can be found around Cape Town is so utterly unique that it is considered one of the six major plant biomes in the world. Of the 7500-plus plant species found here, around 80% occur nowhere else in the world. Many of the plants are unsuitable for grazing animals, but this is a region of remarkable insect and bird diversity.

Semiarid Desert

Much of western South Africa sees so little rain that shrubs and hardy grasses are the dominant vegetation. The Karoo and Kalahari semideserts comprise a huge portion of South Africa, which merges with true desert in Namibia. Lack of water keeps larger animals such as zebras and antelopes close to water holes, but when it rains this habitat explodes with plant and animal life. During the dry season, many plants shed their leaves to conserve water.

Music

Just as music fuelled the resistance to apartheid, it continues to sing out for freedom and justice, while providing a soundtrack to everyday lives. Music is everywhere in South Africa, coming through every available medium, communicating in every imaginable style. Want a 'typical' South African sound? Forget it: South Africa has perhaps the greatest range of musical styles on the continent, and more than any country of similar size anywhere in the world.

It is a nation of record collectors, who get down to rock, jazz, classical, gospel, rap, reggae, Afro-house, *maskanda* guitar picking, *mbaqanga* township jive, *kwaito* and much more. Centuries-old traditions jostle with new genres, and Western styles are given an idiosyncratic stamp. The country's gargantuan recording industry (with its small but determined crop of independent black-owned labels) watches, ready to pounce. No one sound will ever pigeonhole South Africa, which can only be a good thing – the annual South African Music Awards (www.samusicawards.co.za) is multicategory, multitextured...and, consequently, a very long ceremony.

Two decades of freedom have proved that a recovering country can produce sophisticated talent to the highest international standards. So get humming, swing your hips and dive in.

> The first known musicians in South Africa were the San people, some 4000 years ago. They sang in a uniquely African click language, and played rattles, drums and simple flutes and even their hunting bows.

Musical History

The Zulu, Xhosa and Sotho people have been singing and dancing for thousands of years – this is the music that attracted Paul Simon and fed into his 1986 masterpiece, *Graceland* – just as the Venda have been playing their *mbiras* (thumb pianos) and reed pipes. There are eight distinct 'tribal' traditions in South Africa and the democratic era has seen a resurgence in traditional musicians making very traditional music. But from the earliest colonial times to the present day, South Africa's music has created and reinvented itself from a mixture of older local and imported styles. Most of the popular styles use either Zulu a cappella singing or harmonic *mbaqanga* as a vocal base, ensuring that whatever the instrument – and the banjo, violin, concertina and electric guitar have all had a profound influence – the sound stays proudly, resolutely African.

European Influence

Ever wondered why the chord sequences of many South African songs seem familiar? Blame the church: the Protestant missionaries of the 19th century developed a choral tradition that, in tandem with the country's first formal music education, South African composers would blend with traditional harmonic patterns. Enoch Sontonga's 1897 hymn 'Nkosi Sikelel' iAfrika' (God Bless Africa), originally written in Xhosa, is now part of the country's national anthem.

Zulu music's veteran exponents Ladysmith Black Mambazo – wrongly considered 'typical' South African music by many Westerners, thanks to their rapid-fire album releases and relentless international touring schedule – exemplify the way indigenous harmonies were neatly mixed with the sounds of European and African church choirs (a vocal style known as *mbube*). In the same way that much contemporary South African art was born from oppression, Ladysmith's 'tiptoe' *isicathamiya* music, with its high-kicking, soft-stepping dance, has its origins in all-male miners' hostels in Natal province in the 1930s, where workers were at pains not to wake their bosses. *Isicathamiya* choirs still appear in weekly competitions in Johannesburg and Durban, and such choirs, or versions thereof, often busk South African city streets.

Apartheid Sounds

Kwela music, like most modern South African styles, came out of the townships. Meaning 'get up' in Zulu, 'kwela' in township slang was both an invitation to dance and a warning that police vans (known as the *kwela-kwela*) were coming. Once-infamous areas like Soweto, Sharpeville, District Six and Sophiatown gave rise to urban, pan-tribal genres, mostly inspired by music coming in (or back) from America, such as jazz, swing, jive and soul. Black South Africans added an urban spin: *kwela,* with its penny whistles (an instrument evolved from the reed flutes of indigenous cattle herders) and one-string bass, became sax-jive, also known as *mbaqanga*. *Marabi* soul took off in the 1970s and 'bubblegum' pop dominated the 1980s.

America and Europe were the inspiration for white South African artists. Sixties phenomenon Four Jacks and a Jill were pure Western pop. British punk inspired 1970s working-class outfits such as Wild Youth, whose sound recalls the Buzzcocks and the Stooges. The 1980s saw a crossover of black and white musicians: Johnny Clegg and his former bands Juluka and Savuka used a fusion of white rock and pop with traditional Zulu music to challenge racist restrictions and set a precedent for others.

Modern Era

Kwaito, South Africa's very own hip-hop, exploded in the 1990s and remains, apart from gospel, rap and a burgeoning R&B scene, the country's most popular genre. Grunge helped shape the likes of Scooters Union, the Springbok Nude Girls and other 1990s guitar bands, while acts including Seether, Prime Circle and former Springbok frontman Arno Carstens ensure that rock continues to flourish. Afrikaans rock continues to build on the legacy of the Voëlvry movement and Fokofpolisiekar, who developed the genre and its following from the '80s onwards.

Acts such as Die Heuwels Fantasties (watch their song 'Noorderlig' on YouTube), Van Coke Cartel, Chris Chameleon and aKING entertain the alternative crowd, while singer-songwriter David Kramer's musicals have received critical acclaim. And then there's the huge cutting-edge dance scene: house, techno, acid jazz, R&B, dance hall and all grooves in between, often with live elements thrown in. South Africa's trance scene is second only to Israel's, and parties regularly happen near Cape Town. The tie-dye crowd converges on the AfrikaBurn festival (www.afrikaburn. com), held every April/May in the Tankwa Karoo.

The effects of apartheid on lives and culture are still sorely felt; musicians such as the late jazz legend Hugh Masekela have stressed the need for continued sensitivity. Award-winning protest singer Vusi 'the Voice' Mahlasela, who performed at Nelson Mandela's inauguration in 1994, has continued to spread Mandela's message by appearing at concerts to promote causes such as 46664, the former president's HIV/AIDS initiative.

The creation of a black-owned, black-run music industry and distribution network has been a long battle (resistance by moguls from

Music Websites

South African Music (www.music. org.za) Definitive reference on Southern African musicians.

Takealot (www. takealot.com) The local Amazon is a good source of South African CDs and DVDs.

MELODIC MOVIES

➡ *Searching for Sugar Man* (2012) is a brilliant documentary about Rodriguez, the Dylanesque singer-songwriter from Detroit who was bigger than Elvis in South Africa – but didn't find out until 30 years later. The Oscar-winning film shows how Rodriguez' early '70s compositions, such as 'Sugar Man', were anthems for liberal white South Africans during apartheid.

➡ Featuring music by and interviews with Abdullah Ibrahim, Hugh Masekela and Miriam Makeba among others, Lee Hirsch's *Amandla! A Revolution in Four-Part Harmony* (2003) explores the role of music in the fight against apartheid. Made over nine years, this is a deeply affecting film.

➡ Pascale Lamche's *Sophiatown* (2003) looks at Jo'burg's bustling Sophiatown, the Harlem of South Africa. Home to many artists and musicians, it was flattened for redevelopment in the 1950s. The film's archival footage and interviews make for compulsive viewing.

➡ The 2005 Oscar-winning township drama *Tsotsi* features a soundtrack composed by *kwaito* star Zola (who also plays local gang boss Fela), as well as haunting tracks by singer-songwriter Vusi Mahlasela.

➡ *Fokofpolisiekar: Forgive Them for They Know Not What They Do* (2009), a documentary about Afrikaner rockers Fokofpolisiekar (Fuckoffpolicecar), is a fascinating glimpse of contemporary Afrikanerdom. The seminal band voiced the frustrations of young Afrikaners, tired of the conservatism and Christianity of Afrikaner society, and ruffled establishment feathers.

the old-school white biz was fierce). However, South African music is becoming more Africanised, with a healthy selection of Westernised English- and Afrikaans-language indie and electronic acts in the mix. The passionate music of the anti-apartheid resistance, meanwhile, has maintained its fire by changing its focus: other scourges – such as HIV/AIDS, poverty, the abuse of women and children – are being written and sung about. Many of these issues, especially the HIV/AIDS epidemic, remain taboo despite their devastating effects on township communities, and music is a good way to get people listening and talking about these topics.

Opportunities abound in the current climate of cultural and artistic expression. Boundaries are down and styles are cross-pollinating. Many genres, especially Afro-house and R&B, are booming and venues are following suit. Democracy, so bitterly won, has never sounded so sweet.

South African Musical Styles

Marabi

In the early 20th century, travelling African American minstrel shows, vaudeville acts, ragtime piano players and gospel groups impressed local audiences in the growing cities of Cape Town and Jo'burg. Urbanisation had a domino effect on musical styles: visiting American jazz artists and records by the likes of Louis Armstrong and Duke Ellington kick-started what would later become the South African jazz scene. By the 1920s and '30s the urban ghettos were singing and swinging to *marabi,* a defining and dangerous (in Sotho it means 'gangster') small-band sound.

Played on cheap pedal organs and keyboards with accompaniment from pebble-filled cans, *marabi* flooded illegal township *shebeens* (taverns) and dance halls. Its siren call got people in and drinking, but it also offered some dignity and consolation to the oppressed working-class areas where it was played. *Marabi's* trancelike rhythms and cyclical

ESSENTIAL LISTENING

marabi – *From Marabi to Disco*, various artists

kwela – *King Kwela*, Spokes Mashiyane

mbaqanga – *Kuze Kuse*, Soul Brothers

jazz – *African Marketplace*, Abdullah Ibrahim

gospel – *Tales of Gospel SA*

neotraditional music – *Amakhansela*, Phuzekhemisi

reggae and R&B – *Respect*, Lucky Dube

soul – *Nomvula*, Freshlyground

electronic – *Perceptions of Pacha*, Goldfish

bubblegum and kwaito – *New Construction*, Bongo Maffin

zef and current trends – *Trading Change*, Jeremy Loops

harmonies had links to American Dixieland and ragtime. Subsequent decades saw the addition of penny whistle, drums, banjo, elements of big-band swing and even bebop.

Marabi made its way into the jazz-dance bands that produced the first generation of professional black musicians: the Jazz Maniacs, Merry Blackbirds and Jazz Revellers. Often referred to simply (and not always correctly) as 'African jazz' or 'jive', *marabi* went on to spawn other styles. One of these was *kwela*.

Kwela

The first popular South African style to make the world sit up and take notice was *kwela*. Initially played on acoustic guitar, banjo, one-string bass and, most importantly, the penny whistle, *kwela* was taken up by kids with no access to horns and pianos but keen to put their own spin on American swing. Groups of tin-flautists would gather to play on street corners in white areas, with the danger of arrest (for creating a 'public disturbance') upping the music's appeal and attracting rebellious white kids known as 'ducktails'. Many such groups were also lookouts for the *shebeens*.

Kwela combos gained a live following but little recording took place until 1954, when Spokes Mashinyane's 'Ace Blues' became the smash African hit of the year and sent white producers scurrying into the black market. Artists such as Sparks Nyembe and Jerry Mlotshwa became popular, while the hit 'Tom Lark' by Elias and His Zig Zag Jive Flutes even crossed over to Britain, where – probably because of its similarity to skiffle – it stayed in the charts for 14 weeks.

In the early 1960s, Mashinyane introduced the saxophone to *kwela* with his song 'Big Joe Special', ending the penny-whistle boom and creating sax-jive. Sax-jive quickly became *mbaqanga*.

Mbaqanga

The saxophone became vital to South African jazz, which, much to the dismay of white *kwela* fans, was now limited to performances in the townships. *Mbaqanga* ('daily bread' in Zulu) had its innovators: Joseph Makwela and Marks Mankwane of celebrated session players the Makhona Tshole Band added electric guitars to the cascading rhythms – notably a funky, muscular bass – while sax player and producer West Nkosi set the pace. This hugely popular electric sound backed singers whose vocal

The Voëlvry ('free as a bird') movement united Afrikaner musicians opposed to apartheid in the 1980s, culminating in a nationwide tour. For local musicians it was a watershed akin to the cultural revolution that swept the West in the '60s.

style was later christened *mqashiyo* (after a dance style), even though it was really no different from *mbaqanga*.

Mbaqanga's idiosyncratic vocals echoed 1950s groups such as the Manhattan Brothers and Miriam Makeba's Skylarks, who copied African American doo-wop outfits but used Africanised five-part harmonies instead of four. In the 1960s Aaron 'Jack' Lerole (of Elias and His Zig Zag Jive Flutes fame) added his groaning vocals to the mix, but it was the growling bass of Simon 'Mahlathini' Nkabinde and his sweet-voiced Mahotella Queens (backed by the Makhona Tshole Band) that would inspire a generation, including Izintombi Zeze Manje Manje and the Boyoyo Boys. More recently, Lerole founded the band Mango Groove and toured with the USA's Dave Matthews Band before his death in 2003. The Mahotella Queens are still going strong – sans Mahlathini – and British producer/chancer Malcolm McLaren sampled the Boyoyo Boys on his 1983 British hit, 'Double Dutch'.

Mbaqanga remains an important force in South African music, its influence apparent in everything from soul, reggae and R&B to *kwaito*, *motswako* (Tswana hip-hop) and, of course, jazz.

Jazz

Structurally, harmonically and melodically distinctive, the force that is South African jazz started as an underground movement and became a statement of protest and identity. In the hands of such talented exiled stars as singer Miriam 'Mama Africa' Makeba, pianist Abdullah Ibrahim (formerly Dollar Brand) and trumpeter Hugh Masekela, it was famously an expatriate music style that represented the suffering of a people. Legendary outfit the Blue Notes, led by Chris McGregor and featuring saxophonist Dudu Pukwana, helped change the face of European jazz after relocating to the UK. Jazzers who stayed behind kept a low profile while developing new sounds and followings with, variously, jazz-rock fusion, Latin and even Malay crossovers.

World-renowned exiles, who returned home after the end of the anti-apartheid cultural boycott, had to work hard to win back local audiences. Most now enjoy healthy followings – Makeba passed away aged 76 in 2008, making Masekela his country's most enduring musical ambassador – in what is now a mainstream scene. Frequent festivals, often featuring top overseas acts (Erykah Badu and Level 42 have appeared at the Cape Town International Jazz Festival), are providing platforms and the South African media is lending its support.

Well-known locals are moving jazz forward, working with DJs, artists, poets and dance companies. The late Coltrane-esque saxophonist Zim Ngqawana, who led a group of 100 drummers, singers and dancers at Nelson Mandela's inauguration, drew on folk and rural traditions as well as Indian, avant garde and classical music. Before his death in 2011, he founded the Zimology Institute, mentoring young jazz musicians and offering an alternative to formal music education on a farm outside Jo'burg.

Ngqawana's former sideman, pianist Andile Yenana, combines the traditional and experimental with Monk-ish flair. Renowned guitarist Jimmy Dludlu, a sort of African George Benson, takes time out to work with music-school graduates. High-profile South African chanteuses include the late Afro-jazz queen Pinise Saul, Sibongile Khumalo, Judith Sephumo and Xhosa vocalist Simphiwe Dana. The latter has been proclaimed the 'new Miriam Makeba' for her fusion of jazz, Afro-soul, rap and traditional music. Many such singers are enjoying success in another genre sharing common roots with jazz: gospel.

Late jazz icon Miriam Makeba sings her most famous song, 'Qongqothwane' (or 'The Click Song'), in the clicking Xhosa language.

Gospel

The music industry's biggest market, bolstered by the country's 80% Christian black population, South Africa's gospel is an amalgam of European choral music, American influences, Zulu a cappella singing and other African traditions incorporated within the church (Zionist, Ethiopian, Pentecostal and Apostolic). All joy, colour and exuberance, rhythm, passion and soul, gospel choirs perform throughout South Africa, lifting the roofs off big, formal venues and community halls alike. Like many big choirs, the 30-piece ensemble and overseas success story, Soweto Gospel Choir, which won Grammy awards in 2007 and 2008 for its albums *Blessed* and *African Spirit,* features a band with drummers and dancers.

This vast genre is divided into traditional gospel – personified by the International Pentecostal Church Choir (IPCC), Solly Moholo, Hlengiwe Mhlaba and Jabu Hlongwane – and contemporary gospel. Beacons of the latter include veteran superstar Rebecca 'Ribs' Malope, also a TV host; the multiplatinum-selling Zulu diva Deborah Fraser; Reverend Benjamin Dube ('the Gospel Maestro'); and the pastor and former Durban street kid Andile Ka Majola. Bethusile Mcinga, whose 'Uzundithwale' won best gospel song at the Crown Gospel Music Awards 2014, is a name to watch. Popular Swazi acts include France Dlamini, the 'father of Swazi gospel', Shongwe & Khuphuka and the Ncandweni Christ Ambassadors, fronted by former parliamentarian Timothy Myeni.

Gospel also comprises much of the oeuvre of Ladysmith Black Mambazo (whose album *Ilembe: Honoring Shaka Zulu* scooped the 2009 Grammy for Best Traditional World Music Album). Their Zulu *isicathamiya* style is a prime example of the way traditional South African music has appropriated Western sounds to produce unique musical styles. Gloria Bosman, Sibongile Khumalo, Pinise Saul and other top black South African artists are now working across a range of genres (gospel, jazz, classical, opera), having started singing in mission-school choirs or in church. Others, such as Rebecca Malope, crossed to gospel from the shiny world of pop.

Neotraditional Music

Away from the urban life of the townships and the cities' recording studios, traditional musicians from the Sotho, Zulu, Pedi and Tsonga regions have developed dynamic social music. Since the 1930s, many have mixed call-and-response singing with the dreamy 10-button concertina, an instrument that has made a comeback in Zulu pop. The Sotho took up the accordion (accordion players and groups still abound in Lesotho), the Pedi the German autoharp, and the Zulu embraced the guitar.

Maskanda (or *maskandi*) is a form of rhythmic and repetitive guitar picking born through the Zulu experience of labour migration. Many migrants made do with an *igogogo,* an instrument fashioned from an oil can – late *maskanda* stalwart Shiyani Ngcobo used the *igogogo* in his live sets. Other top-selling *maskanda* acts include virtuoso guitarist Phuzekhemisi (whose shows often include dozens of singers, dancers and instrumentalists), the popular duo Shwi No Mtkehala and the poetic Bhekumuzi Luthuli, who died in 2010.

The upbeat and vaguely Latin-sounding Tsonga music tends to feature a male leader backed by, variously, a female chorus, guitars, synths, percussion and an unabashed disco beat. Best-known acts include Doctor Sithole, George Maluleke, Conny Chauke and Fanie Rhingani.

In her traditional/urban crossovers, Xhosa artist Lungiswa is one of the few female South African musicians to play the *mbira* (thumb piano). Her songs include a Xhosa cover of Marvin Gaye's 'Inner City Blues'. The late veteran Zulu chanteuse Busi Mhlongo fused traditional Zulu sounds with hip-hop and *kwaito*.

Musical roots are being mixed with every sound imaginable, from country, blues, rap (check out Hip Hop Pantsula and Molemi) and house (see DJs Black Coffee, Mbuso and Vinny da Vinci) to rock, Afro-house, reggae and soul.

Soul, Reggae & R&B

The American-led soul music of the 1960s had a huge impact on township teenagers. The local industry tried various cheap imitations; the few South African 'soul' groups that made it did so on the back of a blend of soul and *marabi,* such as the Movers, or soul and electric-bass *mbaqanga,* such as the Soul Brothers, a band that spawned dozens of imitators. Contemporary South African soul is often filed under *mbaqanga,* the genre from which evergreen reggae star Lucky Dube – shot dead in a carjacking in Johannesburg in 2007 – grew to the status of Africa's Bob Marley. Over 25 years, he recorded two-dozen albums in Zulu, English and Afrikaans; his CDs still have pride of place in shops and market stalls throughout sub-Saharan Africa.

Dube's legacy aside, reggae in South Africa is often subsumed into other genres such as ragga and *kwaito:* Bongo Maffin throws *kwaito,* house, reggae, ragga, gospel and hip-hop into the pot. Homegrown R&B, meanwhile, has surged, with huge stars such as Loyiso Bala. The wonderful Thandiswa Mazwai (Bongo Maffin's erstwhile frontwoman) nods in the R&B direction on her second solo album, *Ibokhwe.* The soulful sounds of DJ, singer and media player Unathi Nkayi seem to be everywhere, while in Cape Town you will likely hear the upbeat local outfits Goldfish and Freshlyground – their breezy Capetonian sounds fall somewhere between soul, pop and electro.

Bubblegum & Kwaito

The disco that surfaced during the 1970s came back – slick, poppy and Africanised – in the 1980s as 'bubblegum'. Vocally led and aimed squarely at the young, this electronic dance style owed a debt to *mbaqanga* as well as America. What the Soul Brothers started, superstars such as the late Brenda Fassie, Sello 'Chicco' Twala and Yvonne 'princess of Africa' Chaka Chaka refined – Chaka Chaka's track 'Umqombothi', named after Xhosa home brew, soundtracks the opening of the film *Hotel Rwanda* (2005). Bubblegum's popularity waned in the 1990s, and in its place exploded *kwaito* (meaning 'cool' in Isicamtho, the Gauteng township slang; a bastardisation of the Afrikaans word *kwaai,* which means strict or angry).

Paul Simon's *Graceland* album has sold more than 14 million copies worldwide and, despite the controversy over breaking the global musicians' boycott of apartheid South Africa, was vital in alerting the rest of the world to South African music.

The music of young, black, urban South Africa, *kwaito* is a rowdy mix of everything from bubblegum, hip-hop, R&B and ragga to *mbaqanga,* traditional, jazz and British and American house music. It is also a fashion statement, a state of mind and a lifestyle. Chanted or sung in a mixture of English, Zulu, Sotho and Isicamtho (usually over programmed beats and backing tapes), *kwaito's* lyrics range from the anodyne to the fiercely political. A unique fusion, *kwaito* has caught the imagination of post-apartheid South Africa and is evolving even as the 'Is *kwaito* dead?' debate rages. Acts such as Zola, Boom Shaka, Mapaputsi, Spikiri and Trompies were trailblazers; the current crop includes Mandoza, Thokozani 'L'vovo Derrango' Ndlovu, Big Nuz and Howza.

Zef & Current Trends

Two acts that have created their own genres, and achieved international success in the process, are Die Antwoord and Spoek Mathambo – both have proved adept at repackaging South Africa's unique and little-known subcultures for an international audience. Die Antwoord ('the answer' in Afrikaans), featuring Ninja (Watkin Tudor Jones) and cyberpunk pixie Yolandi Visser (Anri du Toit), have created a harsh, futuristic sound and image under the banner of 'zef'. The term was long used to describe the culture of low-income white South Africans (without the negative connotations of 'bogan' in Australia or 'chav' in the UK), and Die Antwoord appropriated the word for their frenetic rap-rave and tongue-in-cheek white-trash look.

Another zef artist is rapper Jack Parow, who is like an Afrikaner version of Britain's the Streets. Describing himself as 'the pirate of the caravan park', he sings about suburban life in Cape Town. Die Antwoord, however, are currently in a league of their own in South Africa, having toured internationally with the likes of Aphex Twin and created unsettling visions in their music videos. Check out 'Enter the Ninja', 'I Fink U Freeky' and 'Ugly Boy' on YouTube.

Spoek Mathambo calls his sound, which merges electronic beats, lo-fi guitars and African influences, 'township tech'. His second album, *Father Creeper,* released in 2012 on American label Sub Pop, encapsulates the linguistic mash of the townships, switching between black African languages, English, Afrikaans, Western references and South African subjects. He has enjoyed some success abroad, gaining attention by covering British post-punk band Joy Division's 'She's Lost Control' and appearing on Damon Albarn's Africa Express tour in 2012. Other artists such as Cape Town's poppy folk muso Jeremy Loops have also made inroads internationally.

In South Africa, freedom of expression for everyone, from black youth to white middle-class rockers, is no longer the luxury it was under apartheid. The first place this freedom became visible was the music scene – a scene that is still thriving, creating and reinventing itself in ever-increasing and exciting ways.

At Kirstenbosch Summer Sunset Concerts (www.sanbi.org/gardens/kirstenbosch), local and international stars from Cat Stevens to Goldfish perform in the blissful mountainside setting of Cape Town's botanical gardens.

Lesotho & Swaziland

In Swaziland, where thousands of bare-breasted virgins dance about for polygamous absolute monarch King Mswati III in the ancient but controversial *umhlanga* (reed dance) ceremony, things aren't quite so liberal as they are in South Africa. Nonetheless, music pulses strongly here; Mswati himself has long hosted fundraising concerts that feature international stars (such as Eric Clapton) and local performers. Music, he has said, 'is a healing weapon for a depressed soul as well as an expression of joy'. Swaziland's traditional music is used as an accompaniment to harvests, weddings, births and other events. But the sounds of South Africa have an inevitable influence on its smaller neighbours, and Swaziland also has local choral music, jazz, Afropop, rock, a hip-hop scene and, above all else, gospel. Swazi acts to look out for range from African house DJ Simza and female rapper Pashu – aka Princess Sikhanyiso, King Mswati's eldest daughter – to Franco-Swazi jazzers Lilanga, sweet-voiced soul singer Bholoja and gospel act the Ncandweni Christ Ambassadors.

Up in Lesotho, the hills and valleys are alive with the sound of music. Choirs are popular, as are reggae and *famo* (singing, often with ululations, accompanied by an accordion, oil-can drum and sometimes a bass), followed by Afropop, jazz and *kwaito*. The Basotho people love their songs and instruments: children in villages harmonise their hearts out in choirs; shepherd boys play their *lekolulo* flutes and sing in pure, pitch-perfect voices; women play the stringed *thomo*; and men the *setolo-tolo,* a sort of extended Jew's harp that's played using the mouth.

Lesotho has produced jazz musician Tsepo Tshola, known for his early work with the Maseru band Sankomota and more recent solo albums such as *The Village Pope*. A group of shepherds known as Sotho Sounds play instruments made from discarded objects: one-string fiddle *(qwadinyana)*, guitars *(katara)*, drums fashioned out of disused oil cans, car tyres, twigs and a kitchen sink. A triumph at Britain's Womad Festival, they are based in Malealea, where they continue to compose and rehearse (and still perform for guests of Malealea Lodge).

Food & Drink

South Africa's culinary diversity reflects its multicultural society, ranging from African staples in the townships to seafood and steaks in globally acclaimed restaurants, and eating is an excellent way to the heart of the 'rainbow nation'. The dining scene is more limited in Lesotho and Swaziland, but you'll find good restaurants and cafes in their capital cities and rural lodges.

Need some padkos (literally 'road food') for a long journey? The classic South African choice would be a box or two of natural fruit juices along with biltong, droëwors (dried boerewors sausage), a hard-boiled egg or two and dried fruit such as guava.

The region's earliest inhabitants survived on animals hunted for meat, seafood gathered from the beaches and sea, and myriad vegetables and tubers. When it became necessary to have fresh vegetables and fruit available for passing ships, the Dutch arrived and planted their famous vegetable garden (now Cape Town's Company's Garden). Their rich cuisine was infused with nutmeg, cinnamon and cassia, as well as rice from their colonies in the East. Malay slaves from Madagascar and Indonesia added to the mix, providing spicier accompaniments to the bland fare on offer.

The Cape was the birthplace of South African cuisine, but Kwa-Zulu-Natal is important too: there were migrants from other African countries, British settlers and Mauritians who planted exotic fruits and introduced their spicy tomato sauces. And when the Indian indentured labourers arrived in the mid-19th century, they brought their spices with them. Learning the cultural influences that abound in South African cuisine leads to exciting explorations of the country's many specialities.

Cultural Staples & Specialities

Trout in Mpumalanga, mealies (or mielies; cobs of corn) in Gauteng, umngqusho (maize and bean stew) in the Eastern Cape, Free State venison and cherries, Durban curries, crayfish on the West Coast and succulent Karoo lamb – the variety of cuisine here is boundless.

The Afrikaner history of trekking led to their developing portable food, hence the traditional biltong (dried strips of salted, spiced meat), rusks (hard biscuits) for dunking, dried fruit and boerewors ('farmer's sausages' made with meat preserved with spices and vinegar; also found dried).

Cape cuisine is the product of Malay influence on Dutch staples, and you'll find dishes such as bobotie (sweet-and-spicy mince, topped with beaten egg baked to a crust, and served with rice), chicken pie and bredies (lamb and vegetable stew). Desserts can be the rich malva (sticky sponge pudding) or melktert (custard-like tart), usually brightened up with a sprinkling of cinnamon.

From Xhosa to Zulu, black African cuisine is founded on the staples of maize, sorghum and beans, enhanced with morogo (leafy greens) or imfino (maize meal and vegetables), cooked with onions, peanuts and chilli.

South African Indian cooking brings delicious curries and breyanis (similar to biryanis) and also fuses with Malay cooking, so you'll get hotter curries in Durban and milder ones in Cape Town.

FOOD MARKETS

South Africa's love affair with the artisanal is best embodied at the weekly food markets that take place across the country. You'll find organic veggies, freshly baked breads, handmade cheeses and a range of sauces, jams and pickles to take home, but the markets are as much about eating in as taking away. Vendors sell everything from chickpea pancakes and paella to delicate dim sum and hearty sandwiches filled with free-range meat. There's always lots of boutique booze available and sometimes little extras like live music, crafts for sale or a children's play area. Most markets take place on weekends and, while the bulk of them are in Cape Town and the Winelands, you'll find the odd market everywhere from small Garden Route towns to larger cities such as Bloemfontein and, of course, Johannesburg.

What brings everyone together is the cross-cultural South African institution of braaing (barbecuing). A social occasion, the braai usually features meat and vegetables – lamb chops or *sosaties* (spiced meat skewers), boerewors, corn cobs and sweet potatoes – and can be found everywhere from the *platteland* (farmland) to the townships to the cities. Braais are sometimes called *shisa nyama* in townships.

Staples

Mealie pap (maize porridge) is the most widely eaten food in South Africa. It's thinner or stiffer depending on where you eat it, and is completely bland. However, it's ideal if you want something filling and economical, and can be quite satisfying served with a good sauce or stew. *Samp* (dried and crushed maize kernels) and beans fulfil the same role, making an ideal base for vegetable or meat stews.

Rice and potatoes are widely available and you might even be served both on the same plate. From *roosterkoek* (bread traditionally cooked on the braai) to panini, bread in South Africa is good and comes in infinite varieties.

Meat

In certain areas of South Africa, meat is considered a 'staple'. Afrikaners will eat boerewors (sausages) or beef mince for breakfast, and you often hear people joking that chicken is a vegetable. Alongside the more traditional beef and lamb, you'll find game meats such as ostrich, springbok and kudu. Steaks in particular are excellent.

Seafood

Considering the fact that South Africa is lapped by two oceans, it has a remarkably modest reputation as a seafood-lover's destination. Yet Cape Town, the West Coast, the Garden Route and Durban have some delicious fish dishes. Among the highlights are lightly spiced fish stews, *snoekbraai* (grilled snoek), mussels, oysters and seawater crayfish. Pickled fish is popular in Cape cuisine, while in KwaZulu-Natal prawns are a common feature on restaurant menus, courtesy of nearby Mozambique. On the West Coast, look out for *bokkoms*, strips of salty, sun-dried mullet that can best be described as 'fish biltong'.

Drinks

Water

Tap water is generally safe in South Africa's cities. However, in rural areas (or anywhere that local conditions indicate that water sources may be contaminated, including drought-struck Cape Town), it's best to purify it or use bottled water.

The Karoo is renowned for its superlative lamb, and many meats are falsely claimed to be from the semi-desert region. A new 'meat of origin' certification has been developed to ensure that your Karoo lamb meets strict standards. See www.karoomeat oforigin.com for more information.

Homages to Food

Olive Festival, Riebeek Kasteel (May)

Oyster Festival, Knysna (July)

Meat Festival, Calvinia (August)

Cherry Festival, Ficksburg (November)

Crayfish Festival, Paternoster (December)

Beer & Cider

Beer is the national beverage. With vast breweries in all the major cities, SAB (South African Breweries) was taken over in 2016 by the world's largest brewing company, AB InBev. The country has long been a lager-drinking nation, with Castle and Black Label the bestsellers and Castle Lite a new favourite. In recent years, ales have gained popularity and a craft-beer revolution has swept across the country.

Today there are upwards of 170 breweries, scattered across every province. Larger brands such as Boston Breweries, Cape Brewing Company, Darling Brew, Jack Black and Red Rock are found throughout the country, while nano-breweries tend to only produce enough to supply their own village or town. Look out for unusual brews using local plants such as rooibos and buchu (a medicinal herb with a strong minty flavour) to add a unique South African tang.

Craft ciders, too, are in vogue, mainly produced in the Western Cape's Elgin Valley. Check out Windermere and Everson's.

Beer comes in bottles (or cans) from around R20, and bars serve draught from around R25. Craft beers are more expensive – expect to pay anything from R30 to R60 for a 500mL draught beer.

Wine

South African wine debuted in 1659. Since then it's had time to age to perfection, and is both of a high standard and reasonably priced. Wines are all certified and labels reflect their estate, vintage and origin.

Dry whites are particularly good – try sauvignon blanc, riesling, colombard and chenin blanc – while popular reds include cabernet sauvignon, pinotage (a local cross of pinot noir and cinsaut, which was known as hermitage), shiraz and pinot noir.

Although South African sparkling wine may not be called champagne, a number of producers use chardonnay and pinot noir blends and follow the *méthode champenoise* – the local name is MCC *(méthode Cap classique)*. Likewise, port-style wines cannot use 'port' in their title – look out for Cape Ruby and Cape Tawny. Calitzdorp in the Klein Karoo is well known for its fortified wines.

Wine prices average from around R50 in a bottle store, and twice that in a restaurant. Wine by the glass is often available from around R35.

Spirits

If you prefer your grapes distilled, there are some world-class brandies in the Cape Winelands – try KWV or Van Ryn's. Brandy and cola is popular in much of the country; Robertson-produced Klippies (Klipdrift) and Coke is swigged by many a braai.

> Cookbooks are big business in South Africa. Look out for those by South African celebrity chefs such as Pete Goffe-Wood, Justin Bonello, Reuben Riffel, Jenny Morris, Jan Braai and Tim Noakes.

> Published annually, *Platter's Wine Guide* is the definitive guide to South African wines. See also www.wineona platter.com, where there's an app, listings and information.

BEST CRAFT BREWERIES

Devil's Peak Brewing Company (☎021-001 4290; www.devilspeakbrewing.co.za; 166 Gunners Circle, Epping 1; ⏰8am-7pm Mon-Wed, to 2am Thu & Fri; ☎) Made in Cape Town, widely available and always a good option.

Cape Brewing Company (CBC) Another prolific Cape producer, making everything from pilsner to amber weiss in Paarl.

Mad Giant (p349) Taste the dynamic spirit of Jo'burg in these brews crafted in steam-punk-style surrounds in Newtown.

Aegir Project (p97) Sample this Noordhoek outfit's IPAs, porters and more in its brewery at Beach Road Bar.

Brauhaus am Damm (p437) Excellent *weissbier* (wheat beer) and more from the Rustenburg microbrewery.

SOUTHERN AFRICAN SUSTAINABLE SEAFOOD INITIATIVE

With more and more people turning to fish as a healthy alternative source of protein, there are fears that stocks around South Africa's coastlines (and beyond) are not sustainable. Overfishing and the use of inappropriate fishing methods are taking their toll on the populations of many fish.

With innovative foresight, South Africa's branch of the World Wide Fund for Nature (WWF) set up the Southern African Sustainable Seafood Initiative (SASSI) in 2004 to educate people about which fish are sustainable (Green List), which should be eaten with caution (Orange List) and which are so endangered that catching them is against the law (Red List).

You'll be pleased to know that most of the fish you're likely to find on a South African restaurant menu is on the Green List: snoek, yellowtail, albacore, skipjack and yellowfin tuna (depending on how they were caught), angelfish and rainbow trout. Species unlikely to be able to sustain heavy fishing, and therefore found on the Orange List, include Atlantic salmon, West Coast crayfish, haarders (mullet), prawns, red roman and swordfish. While restaurateurs are allowed to sell them, you might want to consider your actions. Bear in mind that some fish are acceptable only if caught a certain way; for example, dorado caught by traditional line-fishing are on the Green List, whereas those caught with pelagic longlines are orange and those caught with a gill net are red. Likewise, kingklip caught by longlines are green, whereas those caught by offshore trawlers are orange; check which technique has been used when ordering this South African favourite. It also varies between relatives – Namibian hake is orange, whereas Argentine and Peruvian hake are red. Absolute no-nos are galjoen, geelbek, white musselcracker, steenbras, stumpnose and blue-fin tuna.

Fortunately you don't need to remember every fish on the lists to make an informed, pro-environment choice. Simply send an SMS with the name of the fish to ☏079 499 8795 and you'll be told right away whether it's a good choice or not.

For more information, see www.wwfsassi.co.za, where you can download a pocket guide and app.

Mampoer (moonshine) and *witblits* (a grape-based spirit similar to grappa) are found throughout South Africa, but with alcohol percentages upwards of 50, these tipples can be a little rough around the edges.

Better are the hand-crafted spirits coming out of the emerging boutique-distillery scene; try Jorgensen's and Inveroche in the Western Cape – the latter uses indigenous *fynbos* plants to flavour its range of gins.

Where to Eat & Drink

If you're after fine dining in magnificent surroundings, head to the Winelands. Along the Western Cape coast, open-air beachside eateries serve multi-course fish braais, with everything cooked before your eyes. A highlight of visiting a township is experiencing some family-style cooking in a B&B or home. In addition to speciality restaurants, every larger town has several places offering homogenised Western fare at homogenised prices (from about R75). Many restaurants are licensed, but there's still a BYO wine option pretty much everywhere – corkage charges almost always apply.

All towns have cafes where you can enjoy a cappuccino and a sandwich or other light fare. In rural areas, 'cafe' *(kaffie)* usually refers to a small corner shop selling soft drinks, chips, basic groceries and braai wood. Most cafes are open from about 8am to 5pm.

Larger towns have a good selection of pubs and more upmarket cocktail lounges. Franchised bars proliferate in urban areas, and most smaller towns have at least one hotel with a bar. In townships, things

In Lesotho, look for *motoho* (a fermented sorghum porridge). Swazi variants include *sishwala* (maize and bean porridge, usually eaten with meat or vegetables) and *incwancwa* (slightly fermented maize porridge).

centre on *shebeens* (informal drinking establishments that were once illegal but are now merely unlicensed). Throughout South Africa, and in major towns in Lesotho and Swaziland, you can buy all alcoholic drinks at bottle stores and wine at supermarkets, though there are few options for take-out booze on Sunday.

Vegetarians & Vegans

South Africa is a meat-loving society, but most restaurants have at least one vegetarian option on the menu. In larger towns you might find a vegetarian restaurant. Cafes are good bets, as many will make vegetarian food to order. Indian and Italian restaurants are also useful, although many pasta sauces contain animal fat. Larger towns have health-food stores selling tofu, soy milk and other staples, and can point you towards vegetarian-friendly venues.

Eating vegan is more difficult: most nonmeat dishes contain cheese, and eggs and milk are common ingredients. Health-food shops are your best bet, though most are closed in the evening and on Sunday. Larger supermarkets also stock soy products, and nuts and fruit are widely available. Look out for farm stalls selling seasonal fruit and vegetables along the roadside throughout the country.

In Lesotho and Swaziland, you'll find plenty of bean, peanut and other legume dishes, usually offered with vegetables.

In Lesotho, watch for coloured flags hung in villages to advertise home-brewed beer or available food – white is for sorghum beer, yellow for ginger sorghum beer, green for vegetables and red to indicate that meat is for sale.

Eat Your Words

Want to know *potjie* from *umphokoqo*? Know your *skilpadjies* from your *sosaties*? Get behind the cuisine scene by getting to know the language.

Menu Decoder

It's unlikely that you'll see all of these items on the same menu, but they provide an insight into the diversity of South African cuisine.

Food

Meat Dishes

bobotie – sweet-and-spicy mince, topped with beaten egg baked to a crust, served on a bed of yellow rice with chutney

boerewors – spicy sausages, traditionally made of beef and pork plus seasonings and plenty of fat; an essential ingredient at any braai and often sold like hot dogs by street vendors

bredie – hearty Afrikaner pot stew, traditionally made with lamb and vegetables

breyani – a fusion of Hindu and Cape Malay influences, this is a spicy, layered rice-and-lentil dish with meat, similar to the Indian biryani

eisbein – pork knuckles

A LEKKER BRAAI

The national pastime and the main food-centred social event is the braai (barbecue). Even the public holiday officially named Heritage Day (24 September) is also known as National Braai Day.

If you're invited to a braai, it's customary to take a bottle of your favourite tipple and your choice of meat. Often the hosts provide salad, boerewors and other side dishes; generally guests take a side or a dessert. Dress is casual and the atmosphere relaxed. Typically, men do the cooking while women make the salads.

Jan Scannell, better known as Jan Braai, is the poster child for the national pastime and the driving force behind Braai Day. His book *Fireworks* is a good place to learn the fine art of cooking over coals. Wood is the preferred cooking material in the Cape, whereas faster-paced Gautengers cut to the chase with charcoal. Either way, don't forget the Blitz firelighters.

FOOD & DRINK EAT YOUR WORDS

COOKING COURSES

Cape Town, a gourmet's paradise, is the best place for cooking courses.

Andulela (p72) Packages include a half-day Cape Malay cookery course in the Bo-Kaap (R985) and an African cooking class (R985) in a family home in the township of Langa, where you can learn to prepare traditional Xhosa foods.

Bo-Kaap Cooking Tour (☏074 130 8124; www.bokaapcookingtour.co.za; 46 Rose St; per person R825; 🚌Church|Longmarket) After a short walking tour of the Bo-Kaap and a bit of spice shopping, join Zainie in her home for a hands-on Cape Malay cooking class.

frikkadel – fried meatball

mashonzha – name for mopane worms in Venda, where they're served with *dhofi* (peanut sauce)

mopane worms – caterpillars found on mopane trees; the legs are removed, and the caterpillar is dried and served as a crunchy snack

potjiekos – meat and vegetables layered in a three-legged pot and slowly simmered over a fire, often served with *potjiebrood* (bread cooked in another pot)

skilpadjies – (literally, 'little tortoises') lamb's liver wrapped in caul fat and braaied

smileys – slang term for boiled and roasted sheep heads; often sold in rural areas

sosatie – lamb cubes, marinated with garlic, tamarind juice and curry powder, then skewered with onions and apricots, and grilled (originally Malay); also made with chicken

venison – often springbok, but could be kudu, eland, blesbok or any other game meat

vienna – hot-dog sausage, usually pork

waterblommetjie bredie – Cape Malay stew of lamb with Cape pondweed (*Aponogeton distachyos*) flowers, lemon juice and sorrel

Curries, Condiments & Spices

atchar – Cape Malay pickle of fruit and vegetables, flavoured with garlic, onion and curry

chakalaka sauce – spicy tomato-based sauce seasoned with onions, *peri-peri*, green peppers and curry, and used to liven up pap and other dishes

curry – just as good as in India; head to Durban if you like your curry spicy, and to Cape Town (Bo-Kaap) for a milder, Malay version

peri-peri/piri piri – hot chilli

samoosa – spicy Indian pastry filled with potatoes and peas; sometimes with mince or chicken

Breads & Sweets

koeksister – plaited doughnut dripping in syrup (very gooey and figure enhancing); the Cape Malay version is fluffier, spicier and dusted with coconut

konfyt – fruit preserve

malva pudding – delicious sponge dessert; sometimes called vinegar pudding, since it's traditionally made with apricot jam and vinegar

melktert – rich, custard-like tart made with milk, eggs, flour and cinnamon

roosterkoek – bread traditionally cooked on the braai

rusk – twice-cooked and particularly hard biscuit, best dipped in tea or coffee

vetkoek – deep-fried dough ball sometimes stuffed with mince; called *amagwinya* in Xhosa

Grains, Legumes & Vegetables

amadumbe – yam-like potato; a favourite staple in KwaZulu-Natal

imbasha – Swazi fried delicacy of roasted maize and nuts

Ukutya Kwase-khaya: Tastes from Nelson Mandela's Kitchen by Xoliswa Ndoyiya includes the traditional recipes once enjoyed by Madiba. Xoliswa, who was Mandela's personal chef, includes African recipes such as *umqusho* (maize and beans) and *umsila wenkomo* (oxtail stew) alongside international dishes.

Hungry for a quick bite? Try a roasted mealie (cob of corn) or Durban's filling *bunny chow* (curry to go: half a loaf of bread, scooped out and filled with curry).

imfino – Xhosa dish of mealie meal and vegetables

mealie/mielie – cob of corn, popular when braaied

mealie meal – finely ground maize

mealie pap – maize porridge; a Southern African staple, best eaten with sauce or stew

morogo – leafy greens, usually wild spinach, boiled, seasoned and served with pap

pap and sous – maize porridge with a tomato and onion sauce or meat gravy

phutu – Zulu dish of crumbly maize porridge, often eaten with soured milk; called *umphokoqo* in Xhosa

samp – mix of maize and beans; see *umngqusho*

tincheki – boiled pumpkin cubes with sugar

ting – sorghum porridge; popular among the Tswana

umngqusho – samp (dried and crushed maize kernels) boiled then mixed with beans, salt and oil, and simmered; a Xhosa delicacy (called *nyekoe* in Sotho)

umvubo – sour milk and mealie meal

Fish

kingklip – excellent firm-fleshed fish, usually pan-fried; South Africa's favourite fish

linefish – fresh fish caught on a line

snoek – firm-fleshed migratory fish that appears off the Cape in June and July; served smoked, salted or curried, and good braaied

Drinks

mampoer – moonshine made from just about any fruit but often with peaches, citrus fruits or apricots

rooibos – (literally 'red bush' in Afrikaans) herbal tea that has therapeutic qualities; look out for the 'red cappuccino', a caffeine-free equivalent using rooibos instead of coffee

springbok – cocktail featuring crème de menthe topped with Amarula Cream liqueur

steen – chenin blanc; most common variety of white wine

sundowner – any drink, but typically alcohol, drunk at sunset

umqombothi – sorghum beer, a low-alcohol and slightly sour traditional beer that is pinkish in colour and opaque

witblits – a white spirit distilled from grapes, mostly produced in the Western Cape

Rooibos (*Aspalathus linearis*) grows only in the Cederberg region of the Western Cape and has been used as a tea since the San inhabited the area. There's a renewed pride in this South African beverage, sought after for its health benefits. Check out Clanwilliam's Rooibos Route (www.rooibos-route.co.za) and Rooibos Teahouse.

People & Culture

South Africa's multicultural society faces issues from unemployment to HIV/AIDS, with Lesotho and Swaziland grappling with many of the same problems. Especially in South Africa, the rich body of music, literature and, increasingly, film offers some understanding of the distinct characteristics and challenges of this multiracial society, where millions mix Christianity with traditional African beliefs, most people can speak a few of the 11 official languages, and the black, white, coloured and Asian communities comprise the 'rainbow nation'.

Dubbed the 'rainbow nation' by Archbishop Desmond Tutu, South Africa has become more integrated in the two decades since its first democratic elections. There's still a long way to go, perhaps a generation or two, but people tend to live and work more harmoniously these days, and the nation is divided less by colour than by class.

The numerous issues that stir racial tension and shake international confidence in South Africa include government corruption and the disparity between rich and poor, land reform and farm attacks, the controversial Black Economic Empowerment (BEE) and affirmative action, and inflammatory tirades from the likes of Economic Freedom Fighters (EFF) leader Julius Malema. All have contributed to the weakening rand: between 2011 and 2017 its value dropped from roughly seven to the US dollar to 13 to the dollar.

The country's reputation for crime continues to dent its considerable appeal as a tourism destination. It is important to keep things in perspective so as not to miss out on this inspiring and hope-filled country at the tip of Africa. Visiting South Africa provides a rare chance to experience a nation that is rebuilding itself after the profound change of replacing apartheid with democracy. A backdrop to all this change is magnificent natural scenery and the remarkably deep bond – perhaps best expressed in the country's literature – that most South Africans feel for their land.

People & Economy

South Africa

South Africa's Gauteng province, which includes Johannesburg and Pretoria, is the economic engine of the country, generating over a third of South Africa's GDP – and 10% of Africa's. It's also the most densely populated and urbanised province. At the other end of the scale is the rural and underdeveloped Eastern Cape, where around 25% of adults are illiterate.

Beyond economics, different racial groups have complicated relationships. While much of the focus in South Africa has been on black-white relations, there is also friction and distrust between black people, coloured people and South Africans of Indian descent. Yet locals are often surprisingly open when they talk about the stereotypes and prejudices that exist across racial lines. Relations within racial groups are also complex: just ask a Zulu what he or she thinks about Xhosas, or quiz English-speaking white people about their views on Afrikaners.

Below the Poverty Line

South Africa 16.6%
Lesotho 57%
Swaziland 63%

Unemployment

South Africa 27%
Lesotho 26.4%
Swaziland 28%

Lesotho

Lesotho's main link with South Africa has been the mining industry. For most of the 20th century, Lesotho's main export was labour, with about 60% of males working in South Africa, primarily in mining. In the early 1990s, at least 120,000 Basotho men were employed by South African mines and up to one-third of Lesotho's household income was from wages earned by the miners. When the mining industry was restructured, the number of Lesotho miners was halved and many have returned home to Lesotho to join the ranks of the unemployed.

Chinese-owned textile factories subsequently became the country's major employer, with 36,000 Basotho working inside them. In recent years, the US economic slowdown and increased competition from countries such as Vietnam and Bangladesh have taken their toll, while the diamond mining industry has grown, constituting as much as 8.5% of the nation's GDP.

Swaziland

Swaziland's economic scene is almost completely wrapped up in that of its larger neighbour. About two-thirds of Swazi exports go to South Africa and more than 90% of goods and services are imported. Overall, some 70% of Swazis live in rural areas and rely on subsistence farming for survival.

Swazi culture is very strong and quite distinct from that of South Africa. The monarchy influences many aspects of life, from cultural ceremonies to politics. While some Swazis are proud of the royal traditions and suspicious of those who call for greater democracy, a growing number of human-rights and opposition activists believe power should be transferred from the king to the people.

Racial Groups

Black

The vast majority of South Africans – about 80% – are black Africans. Although subdivided into dozens of smaller groups, all ultimately trace their ancestry to the Bantu speakers who migrated to Southern Africa in the early part of the 1st millennium AD. Due to the destruction and dispersal caused by the *difaqane* (forced migration) in the 19th century, and to the forced removals and separations of the apartheid era, tribal affiliation tends to be much weaker in South Africa than in other areas of the continent.

Today, discussions generally focus on ethnolinguistic groupings. With the constitution's elevation of 11 languages to the status of 'official' language, the concept of ethnicity is also gaining a second wind. The largest ethnolinguistic group is the Nguni, which includes Zulu, Swazi, Xhosa and Ndebele peoples. Other major groups are the Sotho-Tswana, the Tsonga-Shangaan and the Venda.

The Zulu maintain the highest-profile ethnic identity, and 23% of South Africans speak Zulu as a first language, including ex-president Jacob Zuma. The second-largest group is the Xhosa, who have been extremely influential in politics. Nelson Mandela was Xhosa, as were many figures in the apartheid struggle, and Xhosa have traditionally formed the heart of the black professional class. About 16% of South Africa's population uses Xhosa as a first language.

Other major groups include the Basotho (found primarily in and around Lesotho and South Africa's Free State), the Swazi (mostly in Swaziland and Mpumalanga) and the Tswana (who live primarily in the North West Province and Northern Cape, as well as neighbouring Botswana). The Ndebele and Venda peoples, found mostly in Mpumalanga and Limpopo respectively, are fewer in number, but have maintained very distinct cultures.

Economic immigrants from South Africa's neighbouring countries and beyond are widely employed in tourism and hospitality nationwide. During your stay you will likely meet waiters, hotel porters and car guards from countries including Zimbabwe, Mozambique, Malawi and the Democratic Republic of the Congo.

In South Africa's uniquely multicultural but racially conscious society, people are not shy about referring to themselves and others as black, coloured or white. This can come as a bit of a shock for visitors from countries where such referrals are considered politically incorrect.

Coloured

During apartheid, 'coloured' was generally used as a catch-all term for anyone who didn't fit into one of the other racial categories. Despite this, a distinct coloured cultural identity has developed over the years – forged, at least in part, by white people's refusal to accept coloureds as equals, and coloureds' own refusal to be grouped socially with blacks. Coloured people are renowned for their sharp sense of humour and quick-witted patter, which has helped them through hardships such as the notorious forced population removals from Cape Town's District Six (covered at the District Six Museum; p56).

Among the diverse ancestors of today's coloured population are Afrikaners and others of European descent, West African slaves, political prisoners and exiles from the Dutch East Indies and some of South Africa's original Khoe-San peoples.

One of the major subgroups of coloureds is the Cape Muslims, also know as the Cape Malays, with roots in places as widely dispersed as India, Indonesia and parts of East Africa. They have preserved their Asian-influenced culture and cuisine, which you can experience on a walking tour of Cape Town's Bo-Kaap neighbourhood.

Today most coloured people live in the Western and Northern Capes, with a significant population also in the Eastern Cape. About 20% speak English as their first language, while about 80% are Afrikaans speakers – one of the oldest Afrikaans documents is a Quran transcribed using Arabic script. South Africa's roughly 4.6 million coloured people comprise about 9% of the total population.

White

Most of South Africa's approximately 4.6 million white people (about 9% of South Africans) are either Afrikaans-speaking descendants of the early European settlers or English speakers. The Afrikaners, who constitute about 5% of the country's total population, have had a disproportionate influence on South Africa's history. Rural areas of the country, with the exception of the Eastern Cape, KwaZulu-Natal and the former homelands, continue to be dominated by Afrikaners, who are united by language and often by membership of the Dutch Reformed Church, the focal point of life in country towns.

Internet Users

....

South Africa 52%

Lesotho 20.6%

....

Swaziland 27.8%

UK 92.6%

....

USA 88.5%

For an insight into coloured society and culture, Chris van Wyk's *Shirley, Goodness & Mercy* and *Eggs to Lay, Chickens to Hatch* are entertaining memoirs about growing up in a coloured Jo'burg suburb.

SOUTH AFRICA'S MELTING POPULATION POT

There are few countries where racial and ethnic conflicts have been as turbulent and high profile as in South Africa. The country's heart pulses with the blood of diverse groups, including the ancient San, 17th-century Dutch settlers, 19th-century British traders, Bantu-speaking African peoples, Indians, Indonesians, Chinese, Jews and Portuguese. Yet it is only since 1994 that there has been any significant degree of collaboration and peace between the various groups.

During the apartheid era, the government attempted to categorise everyone into one of four major groups. The classifications – black (at various times also called African, native and Bantu), coloured, Asian or white – were often arbitrary and highly contentious. They were used to regulate where and how people could live and work, and became the basis for institutionalised inequality and intolerance. To get a feel for this, visit Jo'burg's Apartheid Museum (p335), entered through chillingly evocative racial classification gates.

Today, discrimination based on wealth is threatening to replace racial discrimination. While the apartheid-era classification terms continue to be used, they work only to a certain extent, and within each of the four major categories are dozens of subgroups that are even more subjective and less clearly defined.

While a few Afrikaners still dream of a *volkstaat* (an independent, racially pure Boer state), the urbanised middle class has become considerably more moderate. Happily, the further the distance between the apartheid era and the 'new South Africa', the more room there is for all Afrikaners to be proud of their heritage. Two reflections of this are the growing popularity of Oudtshoorn's Little Karoo National Arts Festival (p165) and the blossoming Afrikaans indie music scene.

About two-thirds of South Africa's white English speakers trace their roots to the British immigrants who began arriving in South Africa in the 1820s. Other white South Africans include about 70,000 Jews, a Greek community numbering 50,000-plus people and a similar number of Portuguese.

> The typical Afrikaner's genealogy includes about a third Dutch blood, with smaller percentages of French (mostly Huguenot), German, coloured and British blood.

Asian

The majority of South Africa's almost 1.3 million Asians are Indians. Many are descended from the indentured labourers brought to KwaZulu-Natal in the 19th century, while others trace their ancestry to the free 'passenger Indians' who came to South Africa during the same period as merchants and business people. During apartheid, Indians were both discriminated against by whites and seen as white collaborators by some blacks.

Today's South African Indian population is primarily Hindu, with about 20% Muslims and small numbers of Christians. Close to 90% live in Durban and other urban areas of KwaZulu-Natal. Most speak English as a first language; Tamil, Hindi and Afrikaans are also spoken.

There are more than 300,000 Chinese people in South Africa, concentrated primarily in Johannesburg but running shops nationwide, and small numbers of other East Asians.

> The Zulu word for grandmother is *gogo*. The *gogo* plays a vital role in many families and her monthly pension is often the only regular source of income for the extended family.

Women

Women have enjoyed a uniquely high profile during South Africa's turbulent history: they were at the centre of the anti-pass-law demonstrations and bus boycotts of the 1950s, protesting under the slogan 'You strike the woman and you strike the rock'. Women are also well represented in South Africa's current parliament, the constitution guarantees women's rights, and the ruling African National Congress (ANC) party has a 50%-women quota system.

However, the daily reality for many South African women is very different, with poverty, sexual violence and HIV infection overshadowing other gains. South Africa has one of the world's highest rape rates, with more than 50,000 offences reported to the police annually – or around 150 a day. Gang rape is common in crime-ridden areas such as the Cape Flats outside Cape Town, and, in one study, one in four men admitted to having raped a woman. The brutal gang rape and mutilation of teenager Anene Booysen in the Overberg town of Bredasdorp in 2013 was a 'Delhi moment' for South Africa, sparking protests about the horrific epidemic and echoing the previous year's outcry in India.

Women are statistically more likely than men to be infected with HIV, and many women become infected at an early age. Worsening the situation is the threat of sexual violence, which often undermines the ability of young women to ensure their partner is wearing a condom. The situation is equally dire in Swaziland and Lesotho, with some of the world's highest levels of sexual violence against women in the latter, where 19% of girls under 18 are forced into illegal marriages and one in four people have HIV – the world's highest rate of new HIV infections.

Swaziland's 2005 constitution guarantees women equal political, economic and social rights and reserves one-third of parliamentary seats for women, but this is not always instituted and discriminatory practices

> In line with its progressive constitution, South Africa's parliament is 42.3% female, placing it 8th in the world in terms of female representation. Lesotho's parliament is 22.9% female (79th in the world) and Swaziland's is 6.2% (176th).

continue. Traditional social systems discriminate against women, and one survey conducted by Unicef found that one-third of Swazi females had experienced sexual violence before they turned 18.

That said, it is estimated that over 70% of small businesses in Swaziland are operated by women, who tend to be more entrepreneurial than their countrymen. Likewise, Basotho women are often better educated than their male counterparts, and have long shouldered a big share of economic, social and family responsibilities.

Media

Having experienced decades of repression during apartheid, South Africa's media is coming into its own, despite threats to press freedom from the ANC's proposed Protection of State Information (or Secrecy) Bill. The national broadcaster, SABC, is an important source of news for South Africans, and is adjusting to its role as an independent voice. SABC currently has 20 radio stations and five TV channels; private channels are e.tv and M-Net.

South Africa's most popular English-language dailies include the *Daily Sun* (www.dailysun.co.za), *Star* (www.iol.co.za/the-star) and *Sowetan* (www.sowetanlive.co.za). All three primarily cater to English-literate black readers; the *Sowetan* began as an anti-apartheid publication and has a left-leaning editorial tone. The *Sunday Times* (www.timeslive. co.za) and *City Press* (www.citypress.co.za) are favourite Sunday papers, while the *Mail & Guardian* (www.mg.co.za) is a popular Friday paper among middle-class readers. In other languages, Afrikaans Sunday broadsheet *Rapport* and Zulu daily tabloid *Isolezwe* are the most popular reads.

South Africa's press freedom ranking, according to Reporters Without Borders, rose to 31st in the world in 2017 (the US was 43rd).

Religion

Religion plays a central role in the lives of most people in South Africa and church attendance is generally high. Christianity is dominant, with almost 80% of South Africans identifying themselves as Christians. Major South African denominations include the Dutch Reformed Church, which has more than a million members and more than 1000 churches across the country, and the considerably more flamboyant Zion Christian Church (ZCC), with up to six million followers.

About 15% of South Africans are atheist or agnostic, while Muslims, Hindus and Jews combined make up less than 5% of the population. Up to two-thirds of South Africa's Indians have retained their Hindu faith. Islam has a small but growing following, particularly in the Cape. There is a declining Jewish community of about 70,000 people, mostly in Jo'burg and the Cape.

African traditional believers make up around 1% of South Africa's population, compared with 20% in neighbouring Lesotho. However, their traditions and practices have a significant influence on the cultural fabric and life of the region. Visting the *sangoma* (traditional healer) for some *muti* (traditional medicine) is a widespread practice, even among those who practise Christianity.

Three films to look out for are *Die Wonderwerker* (2012), about the poet Eugène Marais; the surreal and tragic *Paljas* (1998), about a circus clown stranded in a tiny Karoo town; and the altogether cheesier romantic comedy *Leading Lady* (2014), which follows an aspiring British actress from London to a remote Free State farm.

Arts

Cinema

South African cinema has seen a turnaround since 1994 and the film industry is bursting with new talent. The first major feature film directed by a black South African was *Fools* (1997) by Ramadan Suleman, who later directed *Zulu Love Letter* (2004). Other directors and films to look out for include Zola Maseko *(Drum)*, Zulfah Otto-Sallies *(Raya)*, Teboho Mahlatsi, Simon Wood *(Forerunners)*, Timothy Green *(Skeem)*, Khalo

SPORT: ALMOST A RELIGION

South Africans are sports fanatics, with club sports generating passionate loyalties. Football (soccer) is the most popular spectator sport, followed by rugby and cricket. Traditionally, the majority of football fans were black, while cricket and rugby attracted predominately white crowds, but this is changing.

Hosting the 2010 World Cup was a historic event for South Africa. Rugby has also benefitted from development programs across the colour divides: the beloved national team, the Springboks (or 'Boks'), is one of the world's best, having won the 2007 and historic 1995 World Cups. South Africa's cricket team, nicknamed the Proteas, is also one of the world's best-performing, and fans enjoy a friendly rivalry with fellow members of the Commonwealth.

Matabane *(State of Violence)*, Gavin Hood *(Tsotsi)*, Oliver Hermanus *(Skoonheid)* and Sara Blecher *(Otelo Burning)*.

The most internationally acclaimed South African filmmaker is *Elysium* (2013) director Neill Blomkamp, who presents a dystopian vision of Jo'burg in *District 9* (2009) and *Chappie* (2015), both featuring the South African actor Sharlto Copley. Named one of Africa's most powerful celebrities by Forbes, Blomkamp was slated to direct Sigourney Weaver in *Alien 5* after *Chappie*.

> South Africa's national football (soccer) team is called Bafana Bafana (the Boys, in Zulu). The women's team is called Banyana Banyana (the Girls).

Literature

South Africa

South Africa has an extraordinarily rich literary history, and there's no better way to get a sense of the country than by delving into some local reads.

Many of the first black South African writers were missionary-educated, including Sol Plaatje. In 1930 his epic romance *Mhudi* became one of the first books published in English by a black South African. The first major South African novel published internationally was Olive Schreiner's *Story of an African Farm* (1883), which depicts colonial life in the Karoo.

In 1948 South Africa made an impression on the international literary scene with Alan Paton's global bestseller *Cry, the Beloved Country*. Today this beautifully crafted tale is still one of the country's most widely recognised titles.

Nadine Gordimer's acclaimed *A Guest of Honour* was published in 1970. The country's first Nobel laureate in literature (1991), her most famous novel, *July's People* (1981), depicts the collapse of white rule.

In the 1960s and '70s Afrikaner writers gained prominence as powerful voices for the opposition. Poet and novelist Breyten Breytenbach was jailed for becoming involved with the liberation movement, while André Brink's novel *Looking on Darkness* was the first Afrikaans book to be banned by the apartheid government. His autobiography, *A Fork in the Road* (2009), gives a fascinating account of anti-apartheid activities by Afrikaners.

> Although he often portrays South African society negatively, JM Coetzee's writing is exquisite and gives a sense of the violence and isolation under apartheid. Look out for *Disgrace* and *Age of Iron*.

The 1970s also gave rise to several influential black poets, including Mongane Wally Serote, a veteran of the liberation struggle. His work gives insights into the lives of black South Africans during the worst years of oppression.

JM Coetzee, now residing in Australia, gained international acclaim with his novel *Disgrace* (1999), which won him his second Booker Prize. Coetzee was awarded the Nobel Prize for Literature in 2003.

One of the most prominent contemporary authors is Zakes Mda. With the publication of *Ways of Dying* in 1995, Mda became an acclaimed novelist. His memoir, *Sometimes There is a Void* (2011), is a transfixing account of his exile in Lesotho and eventual return to South Africa.

Contemporary South African literature is a vibrant reflection of the country's multicultural society and turbulent political scene, fuelling literary events from festivals to bookshop readings and producing distinct voices such as Lauren Beukes, author of the Hillbrow-set Afrofuturist crime thriller *Zoo City* (2010).

Lesotho & Swaziland

Not much of Lesotho's literature is available in English. However, Thomas Mofolo's *Chaka* (1925), one of the greatest 20th-century African novels, and *Traveller to the East* (1907), the first Sotho novel, have been translated into English. Other authors to look out for include Mpho 'M'atsepo Nthunya, who writes about female experiences in the autobiographical *Singing Away the Hunger* (1996).

Most of the books available about Swaziland were written by Brits during the colonial era. Noted indigenous writers include James Shadrack Mkhulunyelwa Matsebula, who pioneered the use of Swati as a written language. Stanley Musa N Matsebula's novels, including *Siyisike Yinye Nje* (We Are in the Same Boat; 1989), opened up the debate about gender inequality in Swaziland. More recently, Sarah Mkhonza's novels, *Weeding the Flowers* (2008) and *Teaching English in Swaziland: Essays on the Life of Gordon James Thomas* (2011), detail her time in a boarding school in Manzini.

Architecture

Among the highlights of South African indigenous architecture are the 'beehive huts' that you'll see dotted throughout the region, including in rural parts of KwaZulu-Natal. A typical homestead, or *umuzi* as it's known in Zulu, consists of a group of these dwellings arranged in a circle around a cattle *kraal* (enclosure) and surrounded by a fence made of stones or bush. Traditionally the huts were set on an eastward-facing slope, with the chief's residence at the highest point.

In the Xhosa areas of the rural Eastern Cape, you'll see thatched, round, straight-walled huts scattered over the hillsides, often painted turquoise or pink.

Elaborately painted Ndebele houses – a relatively recent tradition – are another highlight. Their exteriors sport brightly coloured geometric motifs or more elaborate artwork, which may depict cars, street lamps, airplanes and other symbols of the modern world.

Basotho homes often feature geometric and sometimes highly symbolic mural art known as *litema*. During the anti-apartheid struggles, some Basotho women used *litema* as a political statement, painting their houses in the gold, black and green colours of the ANC. Today *litema* is used for special celebrations and holidays, such as births, weddings and religious feasts.

The colonial era left a rich architectural legacy. One of its most attractive building styles is the graceful, gabled Cape Dutch house so typical of the Western Cape. Pretoria also showpieces colonial-era architecture, with an impressive collection of conservative and stately creations, including the famous Union Buildings, designed by English architect Sir Herbert Baker.

Jo'burg grew quickly after the discovery of gold in 1886, and mining magnates were eager to display their wealth with palatial homes and grand offices. In Durban the designs show more art deco influences, giving the city its own style. Cape Town's building boom in the 1930s also

---

Afrikaner poet Ingrid Jonker is often compared to Sylvia Plath. Nelson Mandela read Jonker's poem 'The Child who was Shot Dead by Soldiers at Nyanga', inspired by protests against the pass laws, at his inauguration in 1994.

PEOPLE & CULTURE ARTS

Individual works by major 20th-century and contemporary South African artists, including Irma Stern, Pierneef, William Kentridge and Tretchikoff, have fetched over US$1 million at auction.

left a wealth of impressive art deco designs, especially around Greenmarket Sq. A highlight is the colourful houses in the Bo-Kaap area.

One of the most noteworthy examples of new South African architecture is the Constitutional Court in Jo'burg. Another is the Northern Cape Legislature Building in Kimberley, notable for its lack of columns and the minimisation of hard right angles and lines. In Pretoria, Freedom Park, an inspiring monument to people who died in the name of freedom, faces the modernist celebration of Afrikaner nationalism, the Voortrekker Monument.

Drive through Cape Town's Atlantic suburbs of Clifton and Camps Bay to see open-plan contemporary palaces worth millions of dollars, conceived by globally lauded local architecture firms such as SAOTA (www.saota.com). The city's latest architectural event is the V&A Waterfront's Zeitz MOCAA Museum, created from a monolithic 1920s grain silo by London architect Thomas Heatherwick.

Visual Arts

South African art had its beginnings with the San, who left their distinctive designs on rock faces and cave walls throughout the region. When European painters arrived, many of their early works centred on depictions of Africa for colonial enthusiasts back home, although with time a more South Africa–centred focus developed.

Black artists were sidelined for many decades. Gerard Sekoto was one of the first to break through the barriers of racism, becoming a major figure in South African modern art. Throughout the apartheid era, racism, oppression and violence were common themes. Many black artists who were unable to afford materials adopted cheaper alternatives, such as lino prints.

A recent lack of public funds for the arts sector has meant that it has become more reliant on corporate collectors and the tourism industry. Contemporary art ranges from the vibrant crafts sold in the Venda region (or on the side of the road in cities and tourist areas) to high-priced paintings hanging in galleries. Innovative township artists are using 'found' materials such as telephone wire, safety pins, beads, plastic bags and tin cans. Local sculpture is also diverse – artists working in various media include the Venda woodcarvers and bronze sculptor Dylan Lewis.

With the opening of Cape Town's Zeitz MOCAA Museum in 2017 and numerous new global art fairs covering Africa, the continent's art is increasingly attracting investors. A new generation of painters and photographers is dissecting post-apartheid South Africa, joining international luminaries such as William Kentridge and the Ndebele painter Esther Mahlangu in the canon. See www.artthrob.co.za for news, features and listings on South Africa's contemporary visual-arts scene.

The first all-race theatre venue was the Market Theatre, which opened in 1976. The run-down buildings at Jo'burg's old 'Indian' fruit market were converted and patrons and performers defied the apartheid government's notorious Group Areas Act.

Theatre & Dance

After the colonial era, homegrown playwrights, performers and directors gradually emerged. Writer and director Athol Fugard was a major influence in the 1960s in developing black talent, and more recently wrote the novel *Tsotsi*. Other big names include actor and playwright John Kani, a veteran (like Fugard) of Jo'burg's Market Theatre; try to catch a performance here or at Cape Town's Fugard Theatre, Baxter Theatre Centre or Artscape.

Jo'burg's Dance Umbrella (www.danceforumsouthafrica.co.za) festival of contemporary dance and choreography, held in March at venues including Wits University, brings together local and international artists and provides a stage for new work.

Survival
Guide

Safe Travel

CRIME

Crime is a national obsession in South Africa. Apart from car accidents, it's the major risk that you'll face here. However, try to keep things in perspective: despite the statistics and newspaper headlines, the majority of travellers visit without incident.

The risks are highest in Jo'burg, followed by some townships and other urban centres. You can minimise risks by following basic safety precautions:

➡ Store your travel documents and valuables in your room (if it's secure), in a safe or at least out of sight.

➡ If your room does not have a safe or is not secure, enquire if there is a safe at reception.

➡ Don't flash around valuables such as cameras, watches and jewellery.

➡ Don't look like you might be carrying valuables; avoid wearing expensive-looking clothes.

➡ Completely avoid external money pouches.

➡ Divide your cash into a few separate stashes, with some 'decoy' money or a 'decoy' wallet ready to hand over if you are mugged.

➡ Keep a small amount of cash handy and separate from your other money so that you don't need to pull out a large wad of bills to make a purchase.

➡ Don't keep money in your back pocket.

➡ Avoid groups of young men; older, mixed-sex groups are generally safer.

➡ Listen to local advice on unsafe areas.

➡ Avoid deserted areas day and night, including isolated beaches and parts of Cape Town's mountains.

➡ Avoid the downtown and CBD areas of larger towns and cities at night and weekends.

➡ If you're visiting a township, join a tour or hire a trusted guide.

➡ Try not to look apprehensive or lost.

➡ If you get a local phone number, bear in mind that 419-style telephone and SMS scams are rife.

In Transit

➡ On the flight over, keep your valuables in your hand luggage.

➡ If arriving or changing planes at OR Tambo International Airport (Jo'burg), vacuum-wrap your baggage. Items are sometimes pilfered from bags before they reach the carousel.

➡ To travel around towns and cities after dark, take a taxi or, if your destination is very close, drive or walk with others.

➡ As a general rule, avoid walking by yourself or driving at night.

➡ Keep your car doors locked and windows up.

TOP TIPS
....

Keep things in perspective and don't be overly paranoid, but do remember that South Africa has a high crime rate and you need to be much more cautious than in most Western countries.

➡ Look out for ATM and credit-card scams.

➡ If you're using public transport and venturing outside tourist environments, it is preferable to travel with a friend or in a group.

➡ Remember that violence against women is widespread throughout South Africa; exercise caution.

➡ Ask locals about areas to avoid and don't walk around after dark, when the risk of mugging is high.

BEATING ATM SCAMS

There are dozens of ATM scams that involve stealing your cash, your card or your personal identification number (PIN) – usually all three. Thieves are just as likely to operate in Stellenbosch as in downtown Jo'burg, and they are almost always well-dressed and well-mannered men.

In the most common scam the thief tampers with the ATM so your card becomes jammed. By the time you realise this you've entered your PIN. The thief will have seen this, and when you go inside to report that your card has been swallowed, he will take the card – along with several thousand rand. In a less common but equally surreptitious scam, a wireless device that records PINs is attached to the ATM. Bearing the following rules in mind will help you avoid mishaps.

➡ Avoid ATMs at night and in secluded places. Rows of machines in shopping malls are usually safest.

➡ Most ATMs have security guards. If there's no guard around when you're withdrawing cash, watch your back or get someone else to watch it.

➡ Watch the people using the ATM ahead of you carefully. If they look suspicious, go to another machine.

➡ Use ATMs during banking hours and, if possible, take a friend. If your card jams in a machine, one person can stay at the ATM while the other seeks assistance from the bank.

➡ Do not use an ATM if it appears to have been tampered with.

➡ When you put your card into the ATM, press cancel immediately. If the card is returned, you know there is no blockage in the machine and it should be safe to proceed.

➡ Refuse any offers of help to complete your transaction – or requests of help to complete someone else's.

➡ If someone does offer assistance, end your transaction immediately and find another machine.

➡ Carry your bank's emergency phone number, and report card loss immediately.

➡ Avoid using ATMs that inform you at the beginning of the transaction that it will not issue a receipt.

➡ If there are complications or the withdrawal fails, don't try again; retrieve your card.

➡ Put your home mobile phone on roaming, buy a local SIM card or hire a phone, especially if you'll be driving alone.

➡ Leave your car in secure parking at night and avoid parking in secluded areas during the day.

➡ Don't leave anything valuable in your car or give the impression that you are on a road trip and have bags in the boot.

➡ If you leave bags in the boot of a parked car, never open it before walking away.

➡ One of the greatest dangers during muggings or carjackings (most common

in Jo'burg) is that your assailants will assume you are armed and could kill them. Stay calm and don't resist or give them any reason to think you will fight back.

Lesotho

In Lesotho, there are some important safety tips to keep in mind.

➡ Rape is a problem; women should avoid walking alone in remote areas.

➡ Travellers should not flaunt valuables, especially in Maseru. Don't walk alone

there at night either, as muggings are common.

➡ Bag-snatching and pickpocketing are the main risks during daytime.

➡ Occasional political unrest generally affects only the capital; stay off the streets and avoid crowds at these times.

➡ There are numerous police roadblocks; halt at the first stop sign and wait to have your papers checked and be waved forward.

Hiking Tips

➡ If you're hiking without a guide, you might be hassled for money or 'gifts' by shepherds in remote areas and there's a very slight risk of robbery.

→ Hiking alone is not advised because rape is an issue.

→ Children sometimes beg and throw stones at cars, especially 4WD vehicles, on remote roads.

→ Lives are lost each year from lightning strikes; keep off high ground during electrical storms and avoid camping in the open.

→ Waterproof clothing is essential for hiking and pony trekking.

Swaziland

→ Petty crime such as pickpocketing and phone- and bag-snatching can happen in urban areas. Always take common-sense precautions and be vigilant at all times. Never walk around alone at night or flaunt valuables.

→ Schistosomiasis (bilharzia) and malaria are both present in Swaziland, although Swaziland is taking steps to be the first country in sub-Saharan Africa to move to malaria-free status.

DRUGS

→ The legal system does not distinguish between soft and hard drugs.

→ *Dagga* or *zol* (marijuana) is illegal but widely used.

→ People often use marijuana openly, as you may discover in some backpacker hostels and bars. This is not recommended; there are heavy penalties for use and possession.

→ Ecstasy is as much a part of club culture and the rave scene in South Africa as it is elsewhere.

→ South Africa is a major market for the barbiturate Mandrax (known locally as 'buttons'), which is banned here and in many other countries because of its devastating effects.

→ Drugs such as cocaine and heroin are becoming widely available and their use accounts for much crime.

→ Local drugs, including *tik* (crystal meth) in Cape Town, compound social problems in the townships. Users are irrational and aggressive.

SOLO TRAVEL

→ Solo travel is straightforward.

→ While you may be a minor curiosity in rural areas – especially so for solo women travellers – in most places it's likely that nobody will even bat an eyelid.

→ Times when you should join a tour or group include at night and on hiking trails.

→ Particularly for women, going it alone on hiking trails is not recommended. There

is normally a three-person minimum on trails for safety reasons.

→ Especially in urban areas and at night, lone women travellers should use caution and avoid isolating situations.

→ Solo female travellers may feel uncomfortable in Lesotho, where women are regularly oppressed and harassed in the patriarchal society.

GOVERNMENT TRAVEL ADVICE

For the latest information, check the following websites:

Australian Department of Foreign Affairs and Trade (www.smartraveller.gov.au)

Canadian Ministry of Foreign Affairs, Trade and Development (www.travel.gc.ca)

German Federal Foreign Office (www.auswaertiges-amt.de)

Japanese Ministry of Foreign Affairs (www.mofa.go.jp)

Netherlands Ministry of Foreign Affairs (www.minbuza.nl)

New Zealand Ministry of Foreign Affairs and Trade (www.safetravel.govt.nz)

UK Foreign and Commonwealth Office (www.gov.uk/government/organisations/foreign-common wealth-office)

US Department of State's Bureau of Consular Affairs (www.travel.state.gov)

Directory A–Z

Accommodation

The region offers excellent accommodation options for all budgets, from boutique hotels in Jo'burg and farmstays in the Western Cape to Lesotho's mountain lodges and Swaziland's backpacker hostels. You can often get away with booking a few days in advance, or not at all, but if you're travelling at Christmas or Easter, plan several months ahead. Always book park and reserve accommodation, farmstays and other rural self-catering options in advance.

Seasons Rates rise steeply during the summer school break (mid-December to early January) and the Easter break (late March to mid-April). Room prices sometimes double and minimum stays are imposed; advance bookings are essential. The other school holidays (usually late June to mid-July and late September to early October) are classified as either high or shoulder season. You can get excellent deals during the winter low season, which is also the best time for wildlife watching.

Discounts Discounted midweek and multinight rates are common, so always ask. Occasionally, in towns geared towards business travellers rather than tourists, such as mining centres, rates can be more expensive during the week.

Budget accommodation
The main budget options are campsites, backpacker hostels, self-catering cottages and community-run offerings, including homestays. Campsites are fairly ubiquitous but other budget options are often scarce outside tourist areas.

Midrange This category is particularly good value and includes guesthouses, B&Bs and many self-catering options. Accommodation in the national parks often represents fantastic value.

Top end South Africa boasts some of Africa's best wildlife lodges, as well as superb guesthouses and hotels, including historic properties and accommodation on wine estates. Prices at this level are similar to, or slightly less than, those in Europe or North America. There are also some not-so-superb hotels and guesthouses, which can be expensive disappointments, so be selective.

Townships In Soweto, Khayelitsha and several other areas you can sleep in township B&Bs, backpackers and homestays, which are excellent ways to get an insight into township life. Many owners offer township tours and unparalleled African hospitality.

Lesotho The best accommodation options, and a highlight of travelling in Lesotho, are the various tourist lodges, which offer excellent digs, good food and a range of activities. Family-run guesthouses of varying quality can be found across the country. Top-end accommodation is scarce – exceptions are a few hotels in Maseru and one superb lodge in Ts'ehlanyane National Park. Camping opportunities abound away from major towns but always ask locally for permission.

Swaziland Rates are reasonable in Swaziland and much lower than you would find in Europe or North America. There is a handful of backpacker hostels and camping is possible on the grounds of many accommodation options.

Booking Services

A few of the centralised online booking services that cover South Africa are listed here. Because most booking services charge listing fees, the cheapest places sometimes aren't included. Many regions also have B&B organisations and tourist offices or associations that

---

BOOK YOUR STAY ONLINE

For more accommodation reviews by Lonely Planet authors, check out http://lonelyplanet.com/hotels/. You'll find independent reviews, as well as recommendations on the best places to stay. Best of all, you can book online.

take bookings; they're good places to find local gems such as farmstays.

Farmstay.co.za (www.farmstay. co.za) Farmstays and rural activities.

Portfolio Collection (www. portfoliocollection.com) Upscale guesthouses, boutique hotels, lodges, self-catering and more from Cape Town and Kruger to Lesotho and Swaziland.

Safari Now (www.safarinow. com) Thousands of properties across South Africa, from tented camps to Cape Dutch villas.

SA Places (www.places.co.za) Accommodation throughout South Africa, from wildlife lodges to guesthouses.

Camp SA (http://campsa.co.za) Campsite info and bookings for South Africa, Lesotho and Swaziland.

Fair Trade Tourism (www. fairtrade.travel) Fair Trade Tourism–certified accommodation and tours, plus a magazine. Fourteen- and 21-day travel passes are available; see www. facebook.com/FairTrade TravelPass.

Rooms for Africa (www.rooms forafrica.com) Accommodation, including B&Bs and self-catering, plus travel guides.

Where To Stay (www.where tostay.co.za) Covers a range of accommodation and activities in South Africa and neighbouring countries.

Seastay (www.seastay.yolasite. com) Coastal farmstays.

Hostel World (www.hostelworld. com) Hostels, guesthouses, lodges and hotels throughout Africa.

Lonely Planet (www.lonely planet.com/south-africa/ hotels) Recommendations and bookings.

BedandBreakfast.com (www. bedandbreakfast.com/south -africa.html) B&B listings.

B&Bs & Guesthouses

B&Bs and guesthouses are two of South Africa's accommodation treats. They're found throughout the country, from cities to villages, while in rural areas you can stay on farms. Some of the cheapest places are unexciting, but in general, standards are high and rooms are good value.

Facilities Unlike B&Bs in some other countries, most South African establishments offer much more than someone's spare room. Unlike motels, the bedrooms are individual and often luxurious. Antique furniture, a private bathroom and verandah, big gardens and a pool are common. In scenic areas such as the Cape Winelands, wonderful settings are part of the deal. Breakfasts are usually large and delectable.

Rates Prices start around R400/600 per single/double, including breakfast and private bathroom. With the odd exception, starting prices tend to be higher in Cape Town, Johannesburg and the Garden Route.

Backpackers

South Africa is backpacker friendly, with a profusion of hostels in popular areas such as Cape Town and the Garden Route. Visit Travel Now Now (www.travelnownow. co.za) for more ideas.

Accommodation In addition to dorm beds (from about R160 per night), hostels often offer private rooms (en-suite singles/ doubles from about R250/500). Many will also allow you to pitch a tent on the grounds for a fee of R100 or so.

Facilities Hostels are often of a high standard, with wi-fi, self-catering facilities, a bar and a travellers' bulletin board. Some offer meals. Staff can provide information on the area and local transport, and organise pick-ups if the hostel is not on the Baz Bus route.

Hostelling International South Africa has hostels nationwide affiliated with HI (www.hihostels. com), so it's worth taking an HI card.

Camping

Camping grounds and caravan parks have long been the accommodation of choice for many South African families. Grounds in popular areas are often booked out during school holidays. Wild camping isn't recommended in South Africa, but you can often pitch your tent at backpackers for R100 or so.

Municipal Most towns have an inexpensive municipal campsite and caravan park, ranging from pleasant to unappealing. Those near larger towns are often unsafe.

Private Altogether better are privately run campsites and those in national parks. These are invariably well equipped and appealing, with ablution blocks, power points, cooking areas and water supply. Tourist areas often have fancy camping resorts, complete with swimming pool, restaurant and minimarket.

Prices Rates at private campsites are either per person (from about R130) or per site (from

---

ACCOMMODATION LINGO

If a hotel touts rooms costing, say, R300, this often means R300 *per person* in a twin or double room. Furthermore, the price is based on two people sharing, and a single supplement is normally charged – a solo traveller might pay R450 in this example, or even have to pay the same as two people.

Half-board includes breakfast and another meal (usually dinner); full board includes all meals. All-inclusive accommodation prices are also found: in game lodges they generally cover all meals, wildlife drives and sometimes also park entry fees; in coastal resorts they include all meals, access to resort facilities and some activities.

about R200). Except where noted, we have quoted camping prices per person.

Rules Some caravan parks ban nonporous groundsheets (which are sewn in to most small tents) to protect the grass. If you're only staying a night or two, you can usually convince the manager that your tent won't do any harm. Some parks may not allow tents at all, though if you explain that you're a foreigner without a caravan, it may be possible to get a site.

Hotels

These cover the full spectrum, from spartan set-ups to exclusive boutique properties.

Budget Most budget hotels are run-down and inadequate. There are a few reasonable old-style country hotels, where you can get a single/double from about R350/500, have a meal and catch up on gossip in the pub.

Midrange These options are more dependable than their budget counterparts, offering good value and atmospheric surroundings.

Top end Rates are high in local terms, and generally in line with international prices, but the appealing properties include boutique, historic and design hotels.

HOTEL CHAINS

Chain hotels are common and can be found in cities and tourist areas.

City Lodge (☏011-557 2600; www.clhg.com) Decent value, with Road Lodges (slightly superior standards to the rival SUN1 chain; about R650 for a room accommodating one to three), Town Lodges (around R1000/1200 per single/double), City Lodges (about R1300/1600 per single/double) and Courtyard Hotels (around R1700/3000 per studio/double). Lower rates are offered for online bookings.

InterContinental Hotels Group (IHG;☏086 144 4435; www.ichotelsgroup.com) Offers a range of accommodation across its Holiday Inn, Holiday Inn Express and InterContinental hotels in the major cities.

Protea (☏086 111 9000; www.proteahotels.com) A network of three- to five-star hotels across South Africa. Protea's Prokard Explorer loyalty club offers discounts of up to 10% and VIP privileges. Owned by Marriott International.

Tsogo Sun (☏011-461 9744, 086 144 7744; www.tsogosunhotels.com) Operates various chains and properties throughout South Africa, including Southern Sun Hotels, the midrange Garden Court brand and SUN1. Previously known as Formule1, SUN1 offers South Africa's cheapest chain hotels, with functional but cramped rooms accommodating one to three from about R500.

Sun International (☏011-780 7855; www.suninternational.com) Runs top-end, resort-style hotels in the former homelands, plus Swaziland, usually with casinos attached. Standards are generally high and package deals are available.

Lodges

In and around the national parks, you can relax comfortably in bush settings. Staying at a wildlife lodge is an unmissable experience. You also have to stay at one to gain access to parks such as Madikwe Game Reserve (North West Province).

Facilities Accommodation is usually in a luxurious lodge, comfortable rondavel (round hut with a conical roof) or safari tent. Expect many of the amenities you would find in a top-end hotel, including en suites with running hot and cold water, comfortable bedding, delicious cuisine and, at the top end, even a pool. However, many lodges don't have landlines, wi-fi, TVs or, in especially rustic cases, electricity. Most luxury lodges charge all-inclusive rates, which include wildlife drives and meals.

Reservations It's important to phone ahead if you plan to stay at a lodge or self-catering option in the wilderness. Not only can they be tricky to find without di-

rections, and the staff may need to pick you up if your vehicle doesn't have good clearance, but if you turn up unannounced you might find there's no one home.

Self-Catering Accommodation

This can be excellent value, from around R500 per two-person cottage – also called chalets, cabins, huts and rondavels. Options range from farm cottages and campsite accommodation to community-run camps and holiday resorts.

Facilities Apart from the occasional run-down place, most self-catering accommodation comes with bedding, towels and a fully equipped kitchen, though confirm what is included in advance. In some farm cottages you'll have to do without lights and electricity.

Locations Small-town tourist information centres and their websites are good places to find out about self-catering accommodation. Self-catering chalets, often available in campsites and caravan parks, are common in tourist areas such as the coast and around parks and reserves. Many are set in scenic but remote locations, more suited to travellers with a car, although cottages are also found in towns and villages.

Parks and reserves South African National Parks (SAN-Parks) offers well-maintained, fully equipped options, ranging from bungalows and cottages to safari tents and rondavels. You pay a premium for the privilege of staying in the park or reserve, but the units are usually appealing, with larger options for families. Some parks and reserves also have simpler huts, with shared bathrooms.

Reservations Booking ahead is essential. You normally have to pay 50% (occasionally 100%) in advance by bank deposit or transfer. In a small community, there's a chance you'll get a ride to the cottage if you don't have a car.

Customs Regulations

➡ You're permitted to bring 2L of wine, 1L of spirits and other alcoholic beverages, 200 cigarettes and up to R5000 worth of goods into South Africa without paying duties.

➡ Imported and exported protected-animal products such as ivory must be declared.

➡ For more information, visit www.brandsouthafrica.com and search for its customs guide.

➡ You may leave Lesotho with souvenirs and presents with a value of up to M500. Anything more must be declared, and any good with a serial number must also be declared.

➡ There are restrictions on bringing meat and citrus fruit into Swaziland.

Discount Cards

➡ A valid student ID will get you discounts on bus tickets, museum admissions and so on.

➡ If you're planning to spend several days in national parks, consider buying a **Wild Card** (www.sanparks. org/wild). A year pass for individual foreigners is R2430 (R3800 per

couple, R4545 per family), which gives free access to more than 80 parks and reserves run by SANParks, Ezemvelo KZN Wildlife, Cape Nature, Msinsi and Swazi organisations.

➡ Some cities also offer discount cards for a number of their attractions.

Electricity

There are frequent power cuts across the region.

Type C
220V/50Hz

Embassies & Consulates

South Africa

Most countries have their main embassy in Pretoria, with an office or consulate in Cape Town.

Most open for visa services and consular matters on weekday mornings, between about 9am and noon. For more information, see www. dirco.gov.za/foreign/forrep/ index.htm.

Australian High Commission (☎012-423 6000; www. southafrica.embassy.gov.au; 292 Orient St, Arcadia; ☺8am-4pm Mon-Fri)

Type M
230V/50Hz

Botswanan High Commission (☎012-430 9640; 24 Amos St, Colbyn; ☺9am-1pm & 2-4.30pm Mon-Fri) Also has a consulate in **Jo'burg** (☎011-403 3748; 66 Jorissen St; ☺8am-4.30pm)

Canadian High Commission (☎012-422 3000; www. canadainternational.gc.ca/ southafrica-afriquedusud; 1103 Arcadia St, Hatfield; ☺8am-noon Mon-Fri)

Dutch Embassy (☎24hr 012-425 4500; www.nether landsandyou.nl; 210 Florence Ribeiro Ave, New Muckleneuk; ☺8.30am-noon & 1-4pm Mon-Thu, 8.30am-1pm Fri) Also has a consulate in Cape Town (☎021-421 5660; http://southafrica. nlembassy.org; 100 Strand St, City Bowl; ⬚Strand).

French Embassy (☎012-425 1600; https://za.ambafrance. org; 250 Melk St, New Muckleneuk; ☺8am-noon Mon-Fri) Also has consulates in Cape Town (☎021-423 1575; https:// lecap.consulfrance.org; 78 Queen Victoria St, Gardens; ☺9am-1pm & 2-5pm Mon-Thu, 9am-1pm Fri; ⬚Upper Long|Upper Loop) and Jo'burg (☎011-778 5600; https:// johannesburg.consulfrance.org; 191 Jan Smuts Ave, Rosebank; ☺8.30am-1pm Mon-Fri).

German Embassy (☎012-427 8900; www.southafrica.diplo. de; 201 Florence Ribeiro Ave, Groenkloof; ⊗8-11.30am Mon-Fri) Also has a consulate in Cape Town (Map p82; ☎021-405 3000; e-tv Bldg, Roeland Park, 4 Stirling St, District Six; ☐Lower Long|Lower Loop).

Irish Embassy (☎012-452 1000; www.dfa.ie/irish-em bassy/south-africa; 2nd fl, Parkdev Building, Brooklyn Bridge Office Park, 570 Fehrsen St, Brooklyn; ⊗9am-noon Mon-Fri) Also has a liaison office in Cape Town (☎021-419 0636, 021-419 0637; www.embassy ofireland.org.za; 19th fl, LG Bldg, 1 Thibault Sq, Foreshore; ⊗9am-noon Mon-Fri).

Lesotho High Commission (☎012-460 7648; www.foreign. gov.ls/home; 391 Anderson St, Menlo Park; ⊗8.30am-4.30pm Mon-Fri) Also has consulates in Jo'burg (☎011-720 5644; 222 Smit St, Braamfontein; ⊗8.30am-1pm, 2-4pm Mon-Fri) and Durban (☎031-307 2168; 2nd fl, 303 Dr Pixley Kaseme St; ⊗9am-4pm Mon-Fri).

Mozambican High Commission (☎012-401 0300; www. embamoc.co.za; 529 Edmond St, Arcadia; ⊗9.30am-1pm & 2-5pm Mon-Fri) Also has consulates in Cape Town (☎021-418 2131; 3rd fl, 1 Thibault Sq, Long St, City Bowl), Nelspruit (☎013-753 2089; 32 Bell St; ⊗8am-3pm Mon-Fri), Durban (☎031-303 9204; Ste 9, Sutton Sq, 306/310 Mathews Meyiwa Rd; ⊗8am-noon Mon-Fri) and Jo'burg (☎011-327 5707; 95 Oxford Rd, Saxonwold; ⊗8am-noon, 1-4pm Mon-Fri).

Namibian High Commission (☎012-481 9100; www.namibia. org.za; 197 Blackwood St, Arcadia; ⊗8am-4.30pm Mon-Fri)

New Zealand High Commission (☎012-435 9000; www.nzem bassy.com/south-africa; 125 Middle St, New Muckleneuk; ⊗9am-noon & 1-4pm Mon-Fri) Also has an honorary consul in Cape Town (☎021-683 5762; Eastry Rd, Claremont).

Swaziland High Commission (☎012-344 1910; www.swazi

highcom.co.za; 715 Government Ave, Arcadia; ⊗8.30am-4.30pm) Also has a consulate (☎011-403 2050; Braampark Forum 7, 33 Hoofd St, Braamfontein; ⊗8.30am-4.30pm) in Jo'burg.

UK High Commission (☎012-421 7500; www.gov.uk/world/ south-africa; 255 Hill St, Arcadia; ⊗8am-5pm Mon-Thu, 8am-12.30pm Fri) Also has a consulate in Cape Town (☎021-405 2400; https:// gov.uk/world/organisations/ british-consulate-gener-al-cape-town; 15th fl, Norton Rose House, 8 Riebeeck St, Foreshore; ⊗8.30am-12.30pm Mon-Thu; ☐Adderley).

US Embassy (☎012-431 4000; http://za.usembassy.gov; 877 Pretorius St, Arcadia; ⊗8am-5pm Mon-Thu, to noon Fri) Also has consulates in Cape Town (☎021-702 7300; 2 Reddam Ave, Westlake), Durban (☎031-305 7600; 31st fl, Old Mutual Center, 303 Dr Pixley KaSeme St (West St); ⊗9am-5pm Mon-Thu, to noon Fri) and Jo'burg (☎011-290 3000; 1 Sandton Dr, Sandhurst; ⊗7.45am-5.15pm Mon-Thu, to 12.45pm Fri).

Zimbabwean Embassy (☎012-342 5125; www.zimfa.gov. zw; 798 Merton Ave, Arcadia; ⊗8am-noon & 1-5pm Mon-Fri) Also has a Jo'burg (☎011-615 5879; www.zimbabweconsulate. co.za; 13a Boeing Rd W, Bed-fordview; ⊗8.30-noon Mon, Tue, Thu & Fri) consulate.

Lesotho

Embassies and consulates are found in Maseru. Missions in South Africa gener-ally have responsibility for Lesotho. For more listings, visit www.foreign.gov.ls.

British Honorary Consul (☎223-13 929; barrett@leo. co.ls; United Nations Rd, Senti-nel Park; ⊗hours vary)

Canadian Honorary Consul (☎223-15 365; canada@leo. co.ls; 3 Orpen Rd; ⊗8.30am-1pm Tue-Thu)

French Honorary Consul (☎223-25 722; www.alliance. org.za; Alliance Française, cnr Kingsway & Pioneer Rd; ⊗9am-1pm & 2pm-7pm Mon-

Thu, 9am-1pm & 2pm-5pm Fri, 9am-1pm Sat)

Netherlands Honorary Consul (☎223-12 114; www.nether landsandyou.nl; Lancer's Inn, Pioneer Rd)

South African High Commis-sion (☎222-25 800; www. dirco.gov.za; cnr Kingsway & Old School Rd)

US Embassy (☎223-12 666; https://ls.usembassy.gov; 254 Kingsway; ⊗7.30am-5pm Mon-Thu, to 1.30pm Fri)

Swaziland

Embassies and consulates are found in Mbabane and the Ezulwini Valley. Missions in South Africa generally have responsibility for Swaziland.

German Liaison Office (☎2404 3174; www.southafrica.diplo.de; 3rd fl, Lilunga House, Samhlolo St/Gilfillan St; ⊗9am-4.30pm Mon-Thu, to 1pm Fri)

Mozambican High Commission (☎2404 1296; moz.high@ swazi.net; Princess Drive Rd, Highlands View; ⊗9am-1pm Mon-Thu, to 11am Fri)

Netherlands Honorary Consul (☎2404 3547; www.nether landsandyou.nl; 649 Ben Dunn St, Mantambe House; ⊗9-11am Mon-Fri)

South African High Commis-sion (☎2404 4651; www.dirco. gov.za; 2nd fl, the New Mall, Dr Sishayi Rd; ⊗8-10am Mon-Fri)

EATING PRICE RANGES

The following price ranges refer to a standard main course.

$ less than R75

$$ R75–R150

$$$ more than R150

In Cape Town, Johan-nesburg and the Wine-lands, prices are higher:

$ less than R100

$$ R100–R200

$$$ more than R200

US Embassy (☎2417 9000; http://swaziland.usembassy. gov; cnr MR103 & Cultural Center Dr, Lobamba; ⊙7am–5pm Mon-Thu, to noon Fri)

Insurance

➡ Travel insurance covering theft, loss and medical problems is highly recommended.

➡ Before choosing a policy, shop around; policies designed for short European package tours may not be suitable for the South African veld.

➡ Read the fine print – some policies specifically exclude 'dangerous activities', which can mean scuba diving, motorcycling, bungee jumping and more.

➡ Some policies ask you to call (reverse charges) a centre in your home country, where an immediate assessment of your problem is made.

➡ Worldwide travel insurance is available at www. lonelyplanet.com/travel-insurance. You can buy, extend and claim online any time – even if you're already on the road.

Internet Access

➡ Internet access is widely available in South Africa, though connections are often slow and temperamental outside the cities.

➡ Accommodation options usually offer wi-fi or, less commonly, a computer with internet access for guest use.

➡ Many malls, cafes, bars and restaurants (including chains) have wi-fi, often for free. Alternatively, it may be through a provider such as Skyrove (www.skyrove. com) or Red Button (www. redbutton.co.za), for which you will need to buy credit online or from the hot spot owner.

➡ Look out for the AlwaysOn (www.alwayson.co.za) network, which generally allows you 30 minutes free connection per hot spot if you sign up. It's available at airports and some cafes, malls and banks.

➡ If you are staying for some time, a USB modem or smartphone data package may be useful.

➡ Local mobile-phone companies such as MTN (www.mtn.co.za) sell USB modems and data packages.

➡ There are internet cafes in major towns and, sometimes, smaller locations. Charges are about R40 per hour.

➡ Branches of PostNet (www.postnet.co.za) often have a few computers with web access.

➡ In Lesotho, web access is available in Maseru and a few accommodation options elsewhere have wi-fi, though it is often unreliable or pay-as-you-go.

➡ Wi-fi is still rare in Swaziland, even in many accommodation establishments. Many hotels will offer paid-for wi-fi (even if staying there) and you will find a few (paid-for) wi-fi spots and internet cafes in Mbabane, Manzini and Malkerns Valley.

Language Courses

There are numerous language schools for learning Xhosa, Zulu, Afrikaans and English. You can also do Teaching English as a Foreign Language (TEFL) teacher training here.

Interlink (www.interlink.co.za) English courses in Sea Point, Cape Town.

International English School (☎021-852 8859; www.english. za.net; 142 Main Rd, Somerset West) English and TEFL courses.

Jeffrey's Bay Language School (www.jbaylanguage.co.za) One of a few English schools in surf town Jeffrey's Bay. Affiliated with Island Vibe hostel.

Language Teaching Centre (Map p58; ☎021-425 0019; www.languageteachingcentre. co.za; 705 Touchstone House, 7 Bree St, Foreshore; ⬜Lower Loop|Lower Long) Xhosa, Zulu, Afrikaans, English.

Ubuntu Bridge (www.learn xhosa.co.za; Montebello Design Centre, 31 Newlands Ave, New-lands; ⬜Newlands) Xhosa.

Wits Language School (Map p328; ☎011-717 4208; www. witslanguageschool.com; Professional Development Hub, Gate 6, 92 Empire Rd, Braam-fontein) Zulu, Sesotho, Tswana, Afrikaans, English and sign language. Part of the University of the Witwatersrand.

Legal Matters
South Africa

➡ Key areas to watch out for are traffic offences such as speeding and drink driving, and drug use and possession.

➡ Despite a relatively open drug culture, use and possession are illegal: arrests happen and penalties are stiff.

➡ South Africans may complain about police corruption and claim to have bribed police officers, but offering bribes is not recommended.

➡ If you get arrested in South Africa, you have the following rights: to remain silent; to be released on bail or warning, unless there's a good reason to keep you in jail; to a lawyer; and to food and decent conditions.

Lesotho

➡ Foreigners caught with large amounts of drugs face heavy fines, imprisonment or deportation.

➡ Theft is widely prosecuted.

➡ If you are involved in a traffic accident, you must wait (sometimes hours) for traffic police to arrive and create a report.

Swaziland

➜ All drugs, including marijuana, are illegal in Swaziland. Anyone caught in possession of marijuana faces a maximum five-year prison sentence.

➜ Tourists should carry their passport with them in case they are stopped by police, as well as their driving licence and cross-border permit if driving a rental car.

➜ Small bribery is common in Swaziland, particularly for minor traffic offences (such as a cracked windshield), for which the police will ask for a E20 fine. Rather than pay a bribe, it is best to ask for a ticket, which you can then pay at a police station.

LGBT Travellers

South Africa's constitution is one of the few in the world that explicitly prohibits discrimination on the grounds of sexual orientation. Gay sexual relationships are legal and same-sex marriages are recognised. There are active gay and lesbian communities and scenes in Cape Town and Jo'burg, and to a lesser degree in Pretoria and Durban. Cape Town is the focal point, and is the most openly gay city on the continent.

But despite the liberality of the new constitution, it will be a while before attitudes in the more conservative sections of society begin to change towards acceptance. Particularly in black communities, homosexuality remains frowned upon – homosexuals are attacked in the townships. Outside larger city centres, exercise discretion.

Lesotho's law does not protect against discrimination based on sexual orientation or gender identity. Gay sexual relationships are taboo.

Swaziland is one of the most conservative countries in Southern Africa. Male homosexual activities are illegal, and gay relationships are culturally taboo, with homosexuals subjected to discrimination and harassment.

Resources

Check chain bookstores such as CNA and gay venues for newspapers and magazines. In addition to the organisations listed here, most major cities have a gay support organisation.

Behind the Mask (@BehindThe Mask99) Jo'burg-based media and activist organisation, supplying information and a platform for dialogue about LGBTI issues in Africa.

Deo Gloria Family Church (www.deogloria.org) LGBT-affirming charismatic church in Durban, registered to conduct same-sex marriages.

Durban Lesbian & Gay Community & Health Centre (www.gaycentre.org.za) LGBTI drop-in centre.

Exit (www.exit.co.za) LGBTI monthly newspaper.

GAP Leisure (www.gapleisure.com) Gay-friendly travel agency.

Gay & Lesbian Network (www.gaylesbian.org.za) Health program in Pietermaritzburg and the KwaZulu-Natal Midlands.

Gay Pages (www.gaypagessa.co.za) Quarterly glossy magazine, available throughout South Africa.

GayCapeTown4u (www.gaycapetown4u.com) Gay guide to the Mother City.

GaySA Radio (www.gaysaradio.co.za) Download the app and podcasts or listen online.

Health4Men (www.health4men.co.za) Jo'burg-based health service.

Lunch Box Media (www.lunchboxmedia.co.za) Look out for its publications, including monthly newspaper *The Pink Tongue*.

Mamba (www.mambaonline.com) Gay news, information, listings and links.

Mamba Girl (www.mambagirl.com) Lesbian-focused site.

Pink South Africa (www.pinksa.co.za) Online gay-tourism directory.

Triangle Project (http://triangle.org.za) This Cape Town–based organisation campaigns for LGBTI rights and supports the community through various programs.

Events

Cape Town Pride (www.capetownpride.org; ⊙Feb-Mar) Parades, pageants, parties and other events, mostly in De Waterkant, from late February to early March.

Johannesburg Pride (www.johannesburgpride.co.za; ⊙Oct) Dating to 1990, Africa's first-ever gay and lesbian pride parade takes place every October.

MCQP (Mother City Queer Project; ☎021-461 4920; https://mcqp.co.za; ⊙Dec) One of Cape Town's main gay events, this fabulous fancy-dress dance party is held every December.

Miss Gay Western Cape (www.missgay.co.za; Joseph Stone Auditorium, Klipfontein Rd, Athlone; ⊙early Nov) Cape Town's long-running transgender beauty pageant, usually held in early November.

Pink Loerie Festival (www.pinkloerie.co.za; ⊙early May) Knysna's Mardi Gras in late April and early May.

Money

South Africa

CASH

➜ South Africa's currency is the rand (R), which is divided into 100 cents. The notes are R10, R20, R50, R100 and R200; the coins are R1, R2 and R5, and five, 10, 20 and 50 cents. Transactions are often rounded up or down by a few cents.

➜ The rand is weak against Western currencies, making travelling in South Africa less expensive than in Europe and North America.

➜ The best foreign currencies to bring in cash are US dollars, euros or

PRACTICALITIES

➡ All three countries use the metric system for weights and measures.

➡ *Mail & Guardian* (www.mg.co.za) is a national weekly newspaper.

➡ *The Sowetan* (www.sowetanlive.co.za) is a national daily.

➡ Other nationals include the *Sunday Independent* (www.iol.co.za/sundayindependent), the *Sunday Times* (www.timeslive.co.za) and *Business Day* (www.businessday.co.za).

➡ News24 (www.news24.com) is part of Media24's www.24.com portal, with news and features.

➡ *Getaway* (www.getaway.co.za), *Go!* (www.netwerk24.com/weg/go) and *Country Life* (www.countrylife.co.za) are South African travel magazines.

➡ SABC (www.sabc.co.za) broadcasts local TV programs from soap operas to news.

➡ M-Net (https://mnet.dstv.com) offers US films and series.

➡ e.tv (www.etv.co.za) offers local programs and international favourites.

➡ SAfm (www.sabc.co.za) broadcasts news and chat online and on 104-107FM.

➡ The *Sunday Express* (sundayexpress.co.ls) and *Lesotho Times* (www.lestimes.com) carry Lesothan news.

➡ *Times of Swaziland* (www.times.co.sz) and *Swazi Observer* (www.observer.org.sz) carry Swazi news.

British pounds, but a debit or credit card will be more useful, as most businesses only accept rand.

➡ Cash is readily exchanged at banks and foreign-exchange bureaus in the cities.

➡ Keep at least some of your exchange receipts, as you'll need them to convert leftover rand when you leave.

➡ Keep a small stash of cash hidden away if visiting rural areas, such as Kruger National Park, where ATMs are often scarce and temperamental.

CREDIT CARDS

Because South Africa has a reputation for scams, many overseas banks automatically prevent transactions in the country. If you plan to use a credit card in South Africa, contact your bank before leaving home and inform it of your travel plans to avoid having your purchases declined automatically. If you have done this and a credit- or debit-card transaction unexpectedly fails, it's safest to try another card or pay with cash, as two transac-

tions enable scammers to clone your card.

TAXES & REFUNDS

➡ South Africa has a value-added tax (VAT) of 14%, but departing foreign visitors can reclaim most of it on goods being taken out of the country.

➡ To make a claim, the goods must have been bought at a VAT-registered vendor, their total value must exceed R250 and you need a tax invoice for each item.

➡ Your receipt usually covers the requirements for a tax invoice. It must include the following: the words 'VAT invoice', the seller's name, address and 10-digit VAT registration number (starting with a 4); a description of the goods purchased; the cost of the goods in rand; the amount of VAT charged, or a statement that VAT is included in the total cost; an invoice number; the date of the transaction; the quantity or volume of the goods; and for purchases more than R3000, the buyer's name and physical address.

➡ All invoices must be originals – no photocopies.

➡ A commission of 1.3% of the reclaimed sum is charged for the service (minimum R10, maximum R250).

➡ At your point of departure, you'll need to fill in a form or two and show the goods to a customs inspector.

➡ At airports, if your purchases are too large for hand luggage, make sure you have them checked by the inspector before you check in your bags.

➡ After going through immigration, make the claim and pick up your refund, normally issued as a MasterCard or Visa electronic card, which will be loaded with your home (or another foreign) currency and can be used to make purchases or withdraw money within three days.

➡ If your claim comes to more than R3000, the refund will not be given on the spot; it will be loaded onto the card you are given up to three months later.

→ You can claim at Jo'burg, Cape Town and Durban's major international airports, and in the smaller airports at Lanseria (Jo'burg), Bloemfontein, Polokwane (Pietersburg), Nelspruit, Pilansberg, Port Elizabeth and Upington.

→ It's also possible to claim at major harbours and some train stations.

→ You can claim the refund by post within three months of leaving South Africa, but it is much easier to do it in person.

→ Visit www.taxrefunds. co.za for more information.

TRAVELLERS CHEQUES
→ Thomas Cook, Visa and American Express travellers cheques in major currencies can be cashed at banks, foreign-exchange bureaus and some hotels – with varying commissions.

→ Buying cheques in a stronger currency such as US dollars will work out better than buying them in rand.

→ If you buy rand or rand cheques, watch the market, as the currency can be pretty volatile. Failing that, buying them just before departure will minimise the effects of devaluation.

→ There are American Express (www.american expressforex.co.za) foreign-exchange offices in major cities.

Lesotho
The South African rand is universally accepted in Lesotho, but even though it's tied to its neighbour's currency, the loti is not accepted in South Africa. Most ATMs dispense maloti, so don't get caught with a pocketful. If you are spending a short time here before returning to South Africa, stocking up on rand will eliminate the worry of having to spend all your maloti before leaving Lesotho.

→ Maseru is the only place where you can reliably exchange foreign cash and travellers cheques.

→ Rand notes are usually available on request.

→ A tax of 14% is included in the stated price of hotel rooms and restaurant meals. Travellers generally cannot receive tax refunds.

Swaziland
Swaziland's currency is the lilangeni (plural emalangeni, E), divided into 100 cents. It is fixed at a value equal to the South African rand. Rand are accepted everywhere, though you will invariably be given emalangeni in change.

→ FNB and Nedbank change cash and travellers cheques – their rates are similar, but commissions vary.

→ Most banks ask to see the purchase receipt when cashing travellers cheques.

→ **Nedbank** (Corporate Place; ⊗8.30am-3.30pm Mon-Fri, to noon Sat), **FNB** (Corporate Place; ⊗8.30am-3.30pm Mon-Fri, to noon Sat) and **Standard Bank** (Corporate Place; ⊗8.30am-3.30pm Mon-Fri, to noon Sat) have branches in Mbabane, Manzini, Matsapha and around the country.

→ A 14% VAT is included in the cost of most goods and services in Swaziland. Swaziland does not have a VAT refund program.

Opening Hours

Banks 9am to 3.30pm Monday to Friday, to 11am Saturday

Post offices 8.30am to 4.30pm Monday to Friday, to noon Saturday

Government offices 8am to 3pm Monday to Friday, to noon Saturday

Cafes 8am to 5pm

Restaurants 11.30am to 3pm and 6.30pm to 10pm (last

orders); many open 3pm to 6.30pm

Bars 4pm to 2am

Businesses and shopping 8.30am to 5pm Monday to Friday, to 1pm Saturday; some supermarkets open weekday evenings, and all day Saturday and Sunday; major shopping centres until 9pm daily

Photography

→ In South Africa cameras, memory cards, film and accessories are readily available in large towns.

→ Camera and equipment choice is limited in Lesotho and Swaziland, with modest selections available in Maseru and Mbabane.

→ In all three countries, don't photograph or film soldiers, police, airports, defence installations, border posts and government buildings.

→ You should always ask permission before taking a photo of anyone, but particularly if you're in a tribal village.

→ In Cape Town a recommended camera and equipment shop is Orms (www.ormsdirect.co.za).

→ Pick up *Lonely Planet's Guide to Travel Photography* for inspiration and advice.

Post

→ Domestic and international deliveries are generally reliable but can be slow.

→ Periodic postal strikes cause further delays.

→ Delivery times are considerably quicker for items leaving South Africa than for items entering the country.

→ For mailing anything valuable or important, use a private mail service such as PostNet (www.postnet. co.za).

➡ Post Office (www. postoffice.co.za) branches are widespread.

➡ Do not have anything of value sent to you from overseas, as parcels are often impounded by customs.

Public Holidays

South Africa

New Year's Day 1 January

Human Rights Day 21 March

Good Friday March/April

Family Day March/April

Freedom Day 27 April

Workers' Day 1 May

Youth Day 16 June

National Women's Day 9 August

Heritage Day 24 September

Day of Reconciliation 16 December

Christmas Day 25 December

Day of Goodwill 26 December

Lesotho

New Year's Day 1 January

Moshoeshoe's Day 11 March

Good Friday March/April

Easter Monday March/April

Workers' Day 1 May

Africa or Heroes' Day 25 May

Ascension Day May/June

King's Birthday 17 July

Independence Day 4 October

Christmas Day 25 December

Boxing Day 26 December

Swaziland

New Year's Day 1 January

Good Friday March/April

Easter Monday March/April

King Mswati III's Birthday 19 April

National Flag Day 25 April

Workers' Day 1 May

King Sobhuza II's Birthday 22 July

Umhlanga Reed Dance Festival August/September

Somhlolo (Independence) Day 6 September

Christmas Day 25 December

Boxing Day 26 December

Incwala Ceremony December/ January

Telephone

South Africa

South Africa has good telephone facilities, operated by Telkom (www.telkom.co.za). A good way to avoid high charges when calling home, or to make reverse-charge calls, is to make a 'home direct' or 'direct dial' call through Telkom's 24-hour international call centre.

PHONECARDS

Telkom WorldCall prepaid calling cards are widely available, in denominations from R10 to R500. WorldCall charges per minute are R0.46 for domestic calls to landlines, and R1.30 for calling a mobile phone. International charges per minute from landlines include R0.93 to an Australian landline, R0.57 to Canada and R0.60 to the UK.

Rates drop between 8pm and 7am Monday to Friday, and over the weekend.

PHONE CODES

Telephone numbers in South Africa are 10 digits, including the local area code, which must always be dialled. There are several four-digit nationwide prefixes, followed by six-digit numbers. These include:

➡ ☑ 080 (usually 0800; toll free)

➡ ☑ 0860 (charged as a local call)

➡ ☑ 0861 (flat-rate calls)

MOBILE PHONES

➡ Mobile-phone networks cover most of South Africa, on GSM, 3G and 4G digital networks. GSM phones on roaming should work here, apart from older dual-band phones from North America and tri-band phones from Central and South America.

➡ South Africa's 10-digit mobile-phone numbers begin with 06, 07 or 08.

➡ The major mobile networks are Cell C (www.cellc.co.za), MTN (www.mtn.co.za), Virgin Mobile (www.virginmobile.co.za) and the Vodafone-owned Vodacom (www.vodacom.co.za).

➡ You can hire a mobile phone through your car-rental provider or a rental operation such as B4i.travel (www.b4i.travel).

➡ A cheaper alternative is to use a local prepaid SIM card in your own phone, provided it's unlocked and on roaming.

➡ SIM cards and credit are available almost everywhere in shops and malls throughout cities and larger towns.

➡ A new SIM should cost about R20; they tend to be more expensive in airport shops.

➡ You need some form of ID and proof of South African address to buy and 'RICA' (register) a SIM card. The proof of address can be a signed statement from your accommodation that you are residing with them, a receipt or a reservation with a letterhead. If you are staying at a private address, your host will need to sign an affidavit confirming that you are residing with him or her.

➡ Various prepaid plans and airtime or data bundles are available. On Vodacom's Anytime Per Second plan, for example, calls cost R1.20 per minute, local SMS texts are R0.50 and international texts R1.74.

Lesotho

➡ Lesotho's telephone system works reasonably well in the lowlands, but even landlines are temperamental in the highlands.

➡ There are no area codes.

➡ Lesotho's eight-digit landline and mobile phone (cell) numbers respectively begin with 2 and 5 or 6.

➡ International calls are expensive.

➡ For international reverse-charge calls dial 109.

➡ Booths selling phone services generally have a landline, offering calls to Lesotho and South Africa for about M8 per minute.

MOBILE PHONES

➡ Mobile phone signals are rare in the highlands and can only be picked up on a few mountain passes.

➡ The main mobile phone service providers are Vodacom Lesotho (www.vodacom.co.ls) and Econet Telecom (www.etl.co.ls).

➡ Most villages have a Vodacom or Econet booth selling credit and SIM cards (about M20; bring your passport).

➡ Mobile credit comes in R5, R10 and R20 vouchers; international bundles are available. Some South African SIMs work on roaming.

Swaziland

➡ Swaziland has a reasonably good telephone network, operated by SwaziTelecom (www.sptc.co.sz/swazitelecom).

➡ There are no area codes.

➡ Swaziland's eight-digit landline and mobile-phone numbers begin respectively with 2 and 7.

➡ MTN Swaziland (www.mtn.co.sz) provides the mobile-phone network.

MOBILE PHONES

➡ Local SIM cards can be used in most European and Australian phones. SIM cards can be bought for a nominal fee. South African SIM cards work on roaming. Other phones must be set to roaming to work, though be wary of roaming charges.

➡ International calls are most easily made using MTN phonecards.

➡ Dial 94 to make a reverse-charge call.

➡ Outside the major towns, dial 94 to book international calls.

➡ You can buy SIM cards for a nominal fee and South African SIMs work on roaming.

IMPORTANT NUMBERS

South Africa

Ambulance	☎ 10177
Emergencies (from mobiles)	☎ 112
Police	☎ 10111
Cape Town emergencies	☎ 107
Cape Town emergencies (from mobiles)	☎ 021-480 7700
Cape Town rape crisis hotline	☎ 021-447 9762
Collect/reverse-charge calls	☎ 10900
Directory services	☎ 1023
International call centre	☎ 10900, 10903
Lifeline Johannesburg (rape counselling)	☎ 011-728 1347
Mobile Yellow Pages	☎ 34310
Netcare 911 medical emergencies (private service)	☎ 082 911
Talking Yellow Pages	☎ 10118

Lesotho

Ambulance	☎ 223-13 260, 112
Fire	☎ 112
Police	☎ 588-81 010, 588-81 024, 112

Swaziland

Ambulance	☎ 977
Fire	☎ 933
Police	☎ 2404 2221, 999

Time

➡ SAST (South Africa Standard Time) is two hours ahead of GMT/UTC.

➡ There is no daylight-saving period.

➡ Lesotho and Swaziland are in the same time zone as South Africa.

➡ This is a wide region to be covered by one time zone; the sun can rise and set an hour earlier in Durban than in Cape Town.

➡ Most timetables and businesses use the 24-hour clock.

Toilets

➡ Finding a clean, sit-down toilet in South Africa is usually not a problem.

➡ There are few public toilets, but malls generally have them.

➡ Tourist offices and restaurants are normally happy to let you use their facilities.

Tourist Information

South Africa

Almost every town in the country has a tourist office. These are often private en-

tities, which will only recommend member organisations and may add commissions to bookings they make on your behalf. They are worth visiting, but you may have to push to find out about all the possible options.

In state-run offices, staff are often lacking in information and lethargic; asking for assistance at your accommodation may prove more useful.

South African Tourism (www.southafrica.net) has a helpful website, with practical information and inspirational features.

Visit www.southafrica.net for details of South African Tourism's offices and call centres in Amsterdam, Beijing, Frankfurt, London, Milan, Mumbai, New York, Paris, Tokyo and Sydney.

PROVINCIAL TOURIST BOARDS

Eastern Cape Parks & Tourism Agency (www.visiteasterncape.co.za)

Free State Tourism (www.freestatetourism.org)

Gauteng Tourism Authority (www.gauteng.net)

Limpopo Tourism Agency (www.golimpopo.com)

Mpumalanga Tourism & Parks Agency (www.mpumalanga.com)

North West Tourism (www.tourismnorthwest.co.za)

Northern Cape Tourism (www.experiencenortherncape.com)

Tourism KwaZulu-Natal (www.zulu.org.za)

Western Cape Tourism (www.goto.capetown)

Lesotho

There is a tourist office in Maseru (p479); elsewhere they are thin on the ground.

Lesotho Tourism Development Corporation (http://visitlesotho.travel)

See Lesotho (www.seelesotho.com)

Swaziland

Swaziland has tourist offices at the Oshoek border, in Mbabane and the Ezulwini and Malkerns Valleys; elsewhere they are thin on the ground.

Big Game Parks (www.biggameparks.org)

Swaziland National Trust Commission (www.sntc.org.sz)

Swaziland Tourism (www.thekingdomofswaziland.com)

Swazi.travel (www.swazi.travel)

Travellers with Disabilities

➡ South Africa is one of the best destinations on the continent for travellers with disabilities, with an ever-expanding network of facilities catering to those who are mobility impaired or blind.

➡ We've noted establishments and destinations with facilities and access for travellers with disabilities.

➡ Several gardens and nature reserves have Braille trails for the visually impaired.

➡ Boardwalks for wheelchair access are found at many parks and attractions, and some can organise activities for travellers with disabilities.

➡ Hand-controlled vehicles can be hired at major car-rental agencies.

DIFFERENCES FROM SOUTH AFRICA STANDARD TIME

COUNTRY	CAPITAL CITY	DIFFERENCE FROM SOUTH AFRICA
Australia	Canberra	+8hr
Canada	Ottawa	-7hr
France	Paris	-1hr
Germany	Berlin	-1hr
Japan	Tokyo	+7hr
Netherlands	Amsterdam	-1hr
New Zealand	Wellington	+10hr
Spain	Madrid	-1hr
UK	London	-2hr
USA	Washington, DC	-7hr

➡ Lesotho is not an accommodating place for travellers with disabilities.

➡ Swaziland can also be challenging, as it does not have any legislation mandating access to transportation and public buildings for travellers with disabilities.

➡ Many of Swaziland's larger hotels and restaurants are set up to accommodate travellers with disabilities.

➡ Download Lonely Planet's free Accessible Travel guides from http://lptravel.to/AccessibleTravel.

Resources

Brand South Africa (www.brandsouthafrica.com) Has an overview of facilities and links to tour operators and local organisations.

Cape Town Tourism (www.capetown.travel) List of wheelchair-friendly activities in the Mother City. Search for 'wheelchair' on the homepage.

Disabled Travel (www.disabledtravel.co.za) South Africa–wide recommendations of accommodation, restaurants and services from an occupational therapist.

Linx Africa (www.linx.co.za/trails/lists/disalist.html) Lists accessible nature trails.

National Council for Persons with Physical Disabilities in South Africa (☎011-452 2774; www.ncppdsa.org.za) Local information.

QuadPara Association of South Africa (www.qasa.co.za) Has wheelchairs for beach use in Durban and the KwaZulu-Natal south coast.

Safari Guide Africa (www.safariguideafrica.com) Beginner's guide to safaris for travellers with disabilities. Search for 'disabled' on the homepage and look under 'pages and posts found'.

SANParks (www.sanparks.org) Has a detailed and inspirational overview of accommodation and accessibility for blind, deaf and mobility-impaired travellers at its parks, including Kruger. Available to download as a PDF or app.

On the homepage (bottom left), look for 'People With Disabilities' under 'Special Groups'.

Sponge Project (http://thespongeproject.yolasite.com) SMS information service for people with disabilities.

Tours

Access 2 Africa Safaris (www.access2africasafaris.com) Tours including Kruger and Swaziland.

Enabled Online Travel (www.enabled-travel.com) Tours including Cape Town and the Garden Route.

Endeavour Safaris (www.endeavour-safaris.com) Southern Africa safaris.

Epic Enabled (www.epic-enabled.com) Offers accommodation and tours, including Kruger safaris.

Flamingo Tours (www.flamingotours.co.za) Tours around Cape Town, along the Garden Route and elsewhere.

RollingSA (www.rollingsa.co.za) Tours include a nine-day safari covering Kruger.

Travel with Renè (www.travelwithrene.co.za) Quadriplegic Renè Moses offers South African tours, including a whale-watching trip.

Visas

South Africa

➡ Travellers from most Commonwealth countries (excluding New Zealand), most Western European nations, Japan and the USA receive a free, 90-day visitor's permit on arrival.

➡ Your passport should be valid for at least six months from the date of your entry to South Africa.

➡ For any entry – whether you require a visa or not – you need to have at least two completely blank facing pages in your passport, excluding the last two pages.

➡ Children aged under 18 must show an unabridged birth certificate, with additional paperwork needed in some cases. Where only

one parent's particulars appear on the UBC or equivalent document, no parental consent affidavit is required when that parent travels with the child. Your airline will likely alert you to immigration regulations (p45) when you buy your flight.

➡ If you aren't entitled to a visitor's permit, you'll need to obtain a visa at a South African diplomatic mission in your home country, or one nearby. New Zealand citizens require visas.

➡ Visas are not issued at the borders.

➡ If you do need a visa, get a multiple-entry visa if you plan to visit Lesotho, Swaziland or any other neighbouring country. This avoids the hassle of applying for another South African visa.

➡ For more information, visit websites such as the Department of Home Affairs (www.dha.gov.za), Brand South Africa (www.brandsouthafrica.com) and the British Foreign and Commonwealth Office (www.gov.uk/foreign-travel-advice/south-africa/entry-requirements).

VISA EXTENSIONS

➡ It is possible to extend your visitor's permit for an additional 90 days. Apply soon after arrival through VFS Global (www.vfsglobal.com/dha/southafrica).

➡ VFS Global also processes applications for temporary residence permits, which last anything from two to five years. It has offices in 11 cities, including Cape Town, Durban, Jo'burg and Port Elizabeth.

➡ Immigration consultants include the **International English School** (☎021-852 8859; www.english.za.net; 142 Main Rd) in Somerset West, near Cape Town.

➡ Extension applications cost R1775 and take eight to 10 weeks to process. They must be submitted in person, and required documents include an onward flight ticket, three months' bank statements and medical and radiological reports.

➤ Changes made to the immigration regulations in 2014 preclude 'visa runs'. If you reenter South Africa with a still-valid visa, you will not be given a new one unless you are coming from your country of residence. If your visa has expired, you will be given a visa allowing entry for up to seven days, unless you are coming from your country of residence, in which case you will be granted your full entitlement.

Lesotho

➤ Citizens of most Western European countries, the USA and many Commonwealth countries are granted a free entry permit upon arrival for stays of up to 14 days.

➤ If you ask for a stay longer than 14 days at the border (or the ministry), it may be granted. Otherwise, you may apply at the Ministry of Home Affairs to extend your permit for another 14 days.

➤ Travellers who require a visa can get one in Pretoria, South Africa. A new electronic visa system also allows travellers to apply online at http://evisalesotho.com. The process takes 72 hours.

➤ If you arrive at the **Maseru Bridge** (Map p476; ☉24hr) border crossing without a visa, with some luck you'll be issued a temporary entry permit to allow you to get to Maseru, where you can apply for a visa. However, don't count on this method, which is unreliable.

Swaziland

➤ Visitors from most Western countries don't need a visa to enter Swaziland for up to 30 days.

➤ For stays longer than 30 days, apply at the **Ministry of Home Affairs immigration department**

(☑2404 2941; www.gov.sz; Home Affairs & Justice Bldg, Mhlambanyatsi Rd; ☉8am-4.45pm Mon-Fri).

➤ Visas cannot be obtained on arrival in Swaziland.

➤ Visa applications must be accompanied by documents including a letter of invitation. Visa applications can be submitted at your local Swaziland embassy or consulate.

Volunteering

Volunteering is a growing area, with opportunities across the region. But there are some rip-off operators, often around animal-related projects. Book through local rather than foreign organisations, get previous volunteers' opinions and check that most of your payment will go to the schemes involved rather than administration.

To work on an unpaid, voluntary basis for a short period, a visitor's permit or visa suffices. If you want to take a lengthy placement (longer than the 90 days afforded by a visitor's permit), the organisation facilitating your placement should help you apply for the correct visa.

Shorter experiences of a few hours, days or weeks are available through accommodation options and tourist businesses, which often give ongoing support to one or two local schemes. But keep in mind that while short visits are interesting for the visitor, they may be of limited use to the project, beyond any fee paid for the trip. Some prominent volunteer organisations have actually suggested that short-term volunteers may do more harm than good.

African Conservation Experience (www.conservationafrica. net) Conservation projects and courses in Southern Africa.

African Impact (www.african-impact.com) Volunteering and internship opportunities in areas such as health care and conservation.

All Out Africa (Map p501; ☑2416 2260; www.alloutafrica. com; MR103; ☉8am-5pm) Offers experiential volunteering trips, lasting from two to eight weeks and mixing travel with community volunteering.

Aviva (www.aviva-sa.com) Cape Town–based organisation offering wide-ranging volunteering opportunities, including great white shark and African penguin conservation.

Bethel Business and Community Development Centre (BBCDC; ☑590-11 384; Bethel; per person M350; 🅿️📶) 🖋 Technical school and learning centre in southern Lesotho.

GoAbroad.com (www.goabroad. com) Listings of opportunities in South Africa, Lesotho and Swaziland.

Greater Good SA (www.greater goodsa.co.za) Has details on many local charities and development projects.

Grow (www.facebook.com/ GROWMokhotlong) There are opportunities with this NGO implementing community-development programs in eastern Lesotho.

Kaya (www.kayavolunteer.com/ destinations/country/swaziland) Options in South Africa and Swaziland.

Kick4Life (www.kick4life. org) Opportunities in Lesotho, including the annual football tour, which mixes HIV education and soccer matches.

Life Skills (www.lifeskillsinsa. com) Reforestation and other green projects on the Garden Route.

One World 365 (www.one world365.org) Opportunities in areas such as human rights, conservation, English teaching and health care.

Streetfootballworld (www. streetfootballworld.org) A starting point for football-related volunteering opportunities.

Travel Now Now (www.travel nownow.co.za) Province-by-province listings of opportunities.

Uthando South Africa (www. uthandosa.org) A tour company that supports a range of charitable projects.

Wilderness Foundation (www.wildernessfoundation.org) Conservation NGO running projects throughout South Africa.

World Wide Opportunities on Organic Farms (www.wwoofsa.co.za) Opportunities to stay and work on organic farms across South Africa.

Women Travellers
Attitudes Towards Women

Old-fashioned attitudes to women are still common among South African men, regardless of colour. However, this doesn't mean sexist behaviour should be tolerated.

There's a high level of sexual assault and other violence against women in South Africa, the majority of which occurs in townships and poor rural areas. Given the HIV/AIDS epidemic, the problem is compounded by the transfer of infection. Some rape victims have escaped infection by persuading the attacker to wear a condom.

For most female visitors, patriarchal attitudes and mildly sleazy behaviour are the main issues. However, there have been incidents of travellers being raped, and women should always take precautions.

Safety Precautions

➡ Single female travellers have a curiosity value that makes them conspicuous, but it may also bring forth generous offers of assistance and hospitality. Despite the risk of assault,

many women travel alone safely in South Africa.

➡ The risk depends on where you go and what you do: riskiest (and not recommended) are hiking alone, driving after dark, hitching and picking up hitchers.

➡ Risks are reduced if two women travel together or, better, if a woman travels as part of a mixed-sex couple or group.

➡ Inland and in more traditional black communities, it's best to behave conservatively. On the coast, casual dress is the norm, but elsewhere dress modestly (full-length clothes that aren't too tight) if you do not wish to draw attention to yourself.

➡ Always keep common sense and caution at the front of your mind, particularly at night.

➡ Don't go out alone in the evenings on foot; always take a taxi, preferably with others.

➡ Even during the day, avoid isolated areas, roadsides and quiet beaches.

➡ Carry a mobile phone if you'll be driving by yourself.

➡ If you are spending a long period in a more dangerous place such as Jo'burg, consider buying a can of pepper spray or similar to keep with you.

Work
South Africa

If you would like to stay put somewhere for a month or two, the easiest option is to find informal, cash-in-hand work at a backpackers or

cafe, possibly with room and board included. Opportunities exist in the tourism and hotel industries, but your employer will have to help you procure a work permit through VFS Global (p601). Using an immigration consultant is recommended.

The same applies to other sectors such as business and aid, where there are opportunities for people with special skills. Bear in mind that jobs are poorly paid in South Africa compared with Western countries, even taking the exchange rate into account. Working remotely for foreign clients takes advantage of the weak rand.

Lesotho

Work permits for foreigners are difficult to obtain in Lesotho, and paying jobs are rare. But if you're lucky enough to find somebody willing to employ you, you can begin the process of getting a residence permit (you can apply online with a passport, a passport photograph, details of where you'll live and a letter from the employer).

It is also possible to enter Lesotho on a tourist visa and then apply for a residence permit, which is done in Maseru at the **Ministry of Home Affairs** (Map p476; ☑223-27 205; www.gov.ls; Parliament St). The residence permit can be obtained for up to two years.

Swaziland

Considering the high unemployment rate in Swaziland, it is next to impossible to be granted a work permit unless you are willing to invest and start a business in Swaziland.

Transport

GETTING THERE & AWAY

South Africa is well connected by air, with major carriers serving Johannesburg's OR Tambo International Airport, Cape Town International Airport and Durban's King Shaka International Airport. OR Tambo is a hub for the whole of Southern Africa. You can get onward flights to Lesotho's Moshoeshoe I International Airport and Swaziland's King Mswati III International Airport, but many people travel overland or pick up a domestic flight to a nearby city such as Bloemfontein or Durban. It's also worth noting that car rental is cheapest in South Africa, so the best option is to hire a car with the necessary paperwork (p608) and cross the border to Lesotho or Swaziland.

Flights, cars and tours can be booked online at lonelyplanet.com/bookings.

Entering the Region

If you have recently travelled in a yellow-fever area, or even transited for over 12 hours en route to South Africa, you need to show a vaccination certificate to enter South Africa, Lesotho and Swaziland.

South Africa

➡ South Africa is straightforward and hassle-free to enter, although airport customs officers often check bags for expensive gifts and items purchased overseas.

➡ Immigration officials rarely ask to see it, but travellers should technically be able to show an onward ticket – preferably an air ticket, although an overland ticket is also acceptable.

➡ The same applies to proof that you have sufficient funds for your stay; it pays to be neat, clean and polite.

➡ Immigration rules have been changing with regards to travelling with children (p45), which involve unabridged birth certificates etc, so check the latest details well before departure.

➡ For more information see www.brandsouthafrica.com.

Lesotho

➡ Entry permits are easy to get at Lesotho's land borders and Maseru's **Moshoeshoe I International Airport** (MSU; ☏223-50 380).

➡ If you are a citizen of a country for which a visa is required, it's best to arrange this in advance.

Swaziland

➡ Entry via Swaziland's land borders and Manzini's **King Mswati III International Airport** (SHO; ☏2518 4390; www.swacaa.co.sz) is usually hassle-free.

➡ People who need visas can get them at Swazi diplomatic

CLIMATE CHANGE & TRAVEL

Every form of transport that relies on carbon-based fuel generates CO_2, the main cause of human-induced climate change. Modern travel is dependent on aeroplanes, which might use less fuel per kilometre per person than most cars but travel much greater distances. The altitude at which aircraft emit gases (including CO_2) and particles also contributes to their climate change impact. Many websites offer 'carbon calculators' that allow people to estimate the carbon emissions generated by their journey and, for those who wish to do so, to offset the impact of the greenhouse gases emitted with contributions to portfolios of climate-friendly initiatives throughout the world. Lonely Planet offsets the carbon footprint of all staff and author travel.

missions in Johannesburg, Pretoria and elsewhere.

➡ As long as you have complied with visa and entry-permit requirements, there are no restrictions on any nationalities for entering Swaziland.

Air

Airports & Airlines

South African Airways (SAA; ☎086 160 6606; www.flysaa.com) is South Africa's national airline, with an excellent route network and safety record. In addition to its long-haul flights, it operates regional and domestic routes together with its partners **Airlink** (☎086 160 6606; www.flyairlink.com) and **SA Express** (☎086 172 9227; www.flyexpress.aero).

OR Tambo International Airport (Ortia; ☎011-921 6262; www.airports.co.za; Kempton Park), east of Jo'burg, is the major hub for Southern Africa. The other principal international airports are **Cape Town International Airport** (CPT; ☎021-937 1200; www.airports.co.za) and **King Shaka International Airport** (DUR; ☎032-436 6585; http://kingshakainternational.co.za) in Durban.

Tickets

International fares to South Africa are usually highest during December and January, and between July and September. They are lowest in April and May (except during the Easter holiday period) and November. The rest of the year falls into the shoulder-season category.

It's normally cheaper to fly via Jo'burg than directly to Cape Town. If an airline serves both, an 'open jaw' ticket may be available, allowing you to fly into one city and out of another; more commonly, you may be able to fly to Jo'burg and return from Cape Town via Jo'burg (or vice versa).

London is a hub for airlines offering discounted fares.

INTERCONTINENTAL (ROUND-THE-WORLD) TICKETS

Some standard around-the-world (RTW) itineraries include South Africa.

It's possible to include both Jo'burg and Cape Town, allowing you to fly into one city and out of the other, and make your own way between the two.

The easiest and cheapest option may be to fly in and out of Jo'burg on a RTW ticket and make separate arrangements from there for Southern African travel.

From Africa

There are good connections between Jo'burg and most major African cities.

South African Airways, Airlink, SA Express, other countries' national carriers and British Airways (www.britishairways.com) are good starting points.

Most transcontinental flights have set pricing, with little of the competition-driven discounting that you'll find in other parts of the world. To reach a far-flung part of Africa from Jo'burg, flying via Europe or the Middle East is often cheaper than travelling direct.

SOUTHERN AFRICA

Jo'burg is well connected, including to secondary Southern African airports. For example, Air Botswana (www.airbotswana.co.bw) offers direct flights from Jo'burg to Francistown and Maun as well as the Botswanan capital, Gaborone.

In addition to national carriers, budget South African airlines serve other destinations in the region:

Fastjet (☎010-500 2560; www.fastjet.com) Jo'burg to Harare and Victoria Falls (Zimbabwe), with connections from the former to Dar es Salaam (Tanzania) and Lusaka (Zambia).

Kulula (☎086 158 5852; www.kulula.com) Offers online discounts on British Airways flights from Jo'burg to Harare

(Zimbabwe), Livingstone (Zambia), Windhoek (Namibia) and Mauritius, and on Kenya Airways flights from Jo'burg to Nairobi (Kenya).

Mango (☎086 100 1234; www.flymango.com) Jo'burg to Zanzibar (Tanzania).

From Asia

Most of the major hubs have direct connections to Jo'burg.

Air Mauritius (www.airmauritius.com) Hong Kong, Shanghai, Kuala Lumpur, Singapore, Delhi, Mumbai, Bangalore and Chennai via Mauritius to Jo'burg, Cape Town and Durban.

Cathay Pacific (www.cathaypacific.com) From Hong Kong, with connections to Cape Town.

Singapore Airlines (www.singaporeair.com) From Singapore, with connections to Cape Town.

South African Airways (www.flysaa.com) From Beijing, Hong Kong and Singapore.

From Australia & New Zealand

It often works out cheaper to travel via Asia, the Middle East or London.

Air Mauritius Perth via Mauritius to Jo'burg, Cape Town and Durban, with connections to and from other major Australian cities.

Emirates (www.emirates.com) Most major cities in Australia and New Zealand via Dubai to Jo'burg, Cape Town and Durban.

Qantas (www.qantas.com.au) Sydney to Jo'burg.

Singapore Airlines Perth, Adelaide, Melbourne, Sydney, Brisbane, Darwin, Auckland and

Christchurch via Singapore to Jo'burg, with connections to Cape Town.

South African Airways Perth to Jo'burg.

From Canada & the USA

The cheapest route is often via London, continental Europe or even the Middle East. A discounted transatlantic ticket and separate onward ticket to Jo'burg or Cape Town may work out the same or cheaper than a through-fare.

Some airlines fly via West African airports such as Accra (Ghana) and Dakar (Senegal). South African Airways flies to Jo'burg from New York and Washington, DC, with a fuel stop in Dakar.

From the US west coast, you can occasionally get good deals via Asia.

From Continental Europe

You can fly to South Africa from most European capitals. Paris, Amsterdam, Frankfurt, Munich and Zurich are hubs; all are within about nine hours of Jo'burg.

Several airlines fly direct to both Jo'burg and Cape Town, including KLM (www. klm.com) from Amsterdam. South African Airways flies direct from Frankfurt, Munich and Zurich to Jo'burg.

It can work out cheaper to fly via the Middle East. Turkish Airlines (www.turkish airlines.com) often offers competitive fares to Jo'burg, Cape Town and Durban via Istanbul.

From South America

Travelling via London or continental Europe opens up more choice. South African Airways flies from São Paulo to Jo'burg.

From the Middle East

Egypt Air (www.egyptair.com) Cairo to Jo'burg, with connections to Cape Town and Durban.
Emirates Dubai to Jo'burg, Cape Town and Durban.

Qatar Airways (www.qatarairways.com) Doha to Jo'burg and Cape Town.

South African Airways Cairo to Jo'burg; Dubai to Jo'burg, Cape Town and Durban.

Turkish Airlines Istanbul to Jo'burg, Cape Town and Durban.

From the UK & Ireland

British Airways flies direct from Heathrow to Jo'burg and Cape Town, with onward connections; Virgin Atlantic (www.virginatlantic.com) and South African Airways also serve Jo'burg. You can find budget flights from Gatwick.

Cheap fares are also available via the Middle East, with airlines such as Turkish Airlines, Emirates and Qatar Airways, and continental Europe. Ethiopian Airlines (www.ethiopianairlines.com) offers competitive fares via Addis Ababa.

From Ireland, you'll need to fly via London or continental Europe.

Land

Bicycle

There are no restrictions on bringing your own bicycle into South Africa, Lesotho and Swaziland. Some sources of information:

Cycling South Africa (www.cyclingsa.com)

International Bicycle Fund (www.ibike.org)

Border Crossings
BOTSWANA

There are 15 official South Africa–Botswana border posts, open between at least 8am and 3pm.

Some of the more remote crossings are impassable to 2WD vehicles and may be closed during periods of high water. Otherwise the crossings are hassle-free.

Citizens of most Western nations do not require a visa to enter Botswana. People who do require a visa should apply in advance through

a Botswanan mission (or a British mission in countries without Botswanan representation).

Grobler's Bridge/Martin's Drift (8am to 6pm) Northwest of Polokwane (Pietersburg).

Kopfontein Gate/Tlokweng Gate (6am to midnight) Next to Madikwe Game Reserve; a main border post.

Pont Drift (8am to 4pm) Convenient for Mapungubwe National Park (Limpopo) and Tuli Block (Botswana).

Ramatlabama (6am to 10pm) North of Mahikeng; a main border post.

Skilpadshek/Pioneer Gate (6am to midnight) Northwest of Zeerust; a main border post.

Swartkopfontein Gate/Ramotswa (6am to 10pm) Northwest of Zeerust.

Twee Rivieren (7.30am to 4pm) At the South African entrance to Kgalagadi Transfrontier Park.

MOZAMBIQUE

Citizens of Western countries should apply in advance for tourist visas at a Mozambican mission. Border visas may be issued to people coming from countries where there is no Mozambican consular representation, but travellers in this situation should check with the Mozambican High Commission in Pretoria (or Mbabane, Swaziland).

Giriyondo (Map p398; ☺8am-4pm Oct-Mar, to 3pm Apr-Sep) Between Kruger National Park's Phalaborwa Gate and Massingir (Mozambique).

Kosi Bay/Ponta d'Ouro (☺8am to 4pm) On the coast, well north of Durban.

Lebombo/Ressano Garcia The main crossing, east of Nelspruit; also known as Komatipoort.

Pafuri (Sango; Map p398; ☺8am-4pm Oct-Mar, to 3pm Apr-Sep) In Kruger National Park's northeastern corner.

NAMIBIA

Citizens of most Western nations do not require a visa to enter Namibia for up to three months. People who do require a visa should apply in advance through a Namibian mission. Border posts include the following:

Alexander Bay/Oranjemund (6am to 10pm) On the Atlantic coast; access is reliant on the ferry.

Nakop/Ariamsvlei (24 hours) West of Upington.

Rietfontein/Aroab (8am to 4.30pm) Just south of Kgalagadi Transfrontier Park.

Vioolsdrif/Noordoewer (24 hours) North of Springbok, on the N7 to/from Cape Town.

SWAZILAND

There are 13 Swaziland–South Africa border posts, all of which are hassle-free. Note that small posts close at 4pm.

Bothashoop/Gege (8am to 4pm) Near Piet Retief. Unpaved roads on the South African side, followed by unkept roads on the Swaziland side.

Bulembu/Josefdal (8am to 4pm) Between Piggs Peak and Barberton (Mpumalanga); the road is in a terrible state and barely passable in a 2WD.

Houtkop/Sincunusa (8am to 6pm) Northeast of Piet Retief.

Jeppe's Reef/Matsamo (7am to 10pm) Southwest of Malelane and a possible route to Kruger National Park. Casinos nearby attract traffic, especially on weekends – good places to look for lifts into and out of the country.

Lavumisa/Golela (7am to 10pm) En route between Durban and Swaziland's Ezulwini Valley.

Lundzi/Waverly (8am to 4pm) Usually quicker to cross than Oshoek, though the road is in worse condition.

Mahamba (7am to 10pm) The best crossing to use from Piet Retief in Mpumalanga. Casinos nearby attract traffic, especially on weekends – good places to look for lifts into and out of the country.

Mananga (7am to 6pm) Southwest of Komatipoort.

Mhlumeni/Goba (24 hours) To and from Mozambique.

Namaacha/Lomahasha (7am to 10pm) The busy post in extreme northeast Swaziland is the main crossing to and from Mozambique.

Ngwenya/Oshoek (7am to midnight) The busiest crossing (and a good place to pick up lifts), about 360km southeast of Pretoria.

Salitje/Onverwacht (8am to 6pm) North of Pongola in KwaZulu-Natal.

Sandlane/Nerston (8am to 6pm) East of Amsterdam. The road is in awful condition after crossing the border.

ZIMBABWE

Citizens of most Western nations need a visa to enter Zimbabwe, and these should be purchased at the border.

Beitbridge (24 hours), on the Limpopo River, is the only border post between Zimbabwe and South Africa. The closest South African town to the border is Musina (15km south), where you can change money.

There's lots of smuggling, so searches are thorough and queues often long. Ignore touts on the Zimbabwe side trying to 'help' you through Zimbabwe immigration and customs; there's no charge for the government forms needed for immigration.

LESOTHO BORDERS

Most of the border posts with South Africa can be crossed in a 2WD. There is an M30 road toll to pay on entry to the country.

Caledonspoort (6am to 10pm) For crossing between Fouriesburg and Butha-Buthe.

Makhaleng Bridge (8am to 6pm) Near Mohale's Hoek/Zastron.

Maputsoe Bridge (24 hours) For crossing between Maputsoe and Ficksburg.

Maseru Bridge (24 hours) The busiest crossing; direct access to Maseru.

Nkonkoana Gate (8am to 4pm) Remote 4WD-only crossing near Sehlabathebe National Park.

Ongeluksnek (7am to 7pm) Remote southern post connecting Mphaki and Matatiele.

Peka Bridge (6am to 4pm) Quieter alternative to Maseru Bridge, just north of Maseru.

Qacha's Nek (8am to 10pm) Connecting Qacha's Nek and Matatiele.

Ramatseliso's Gate (8am to 6pm) Remote 4WD crossing between Tsoelike and Matatiele.

Sani Pass (8am to 4pm) Iconic border post near Himeville; 4WD required.

Sephapo's Gate (8am to 4pm) Quiet crossing near Mafeteng/Boesmanskop.

Tele Bridge (8am to 10pm) Near Quthing/Sterkspruit.

Van Rooyen's Gate (8am to 10pm) Near Mafeteng/Wepener.

Bus & Shared Taxi

Numerous bus lines cross between South Africa and its neighbours. It's the most efficient way to travel overland, unless you have your own vehicle. **Intercape** (☑021-380 4400; www.intercape.co.za) runs regular services.

Sometimes-lengthy queues are usually the only major hassle. At the border you'll have to disembark to take care of visa formalities, then reboard and carry on.

Visa prices are not included in ticket prices. You can also travel to and from South Africa's neighbours by local shared taxi. A few routes go direct, but it's normally necessary to walk across the border and pick up a new taxi on the other side. Long-distance services generally leave early in the morning.

BOTSWANA

Intercape runs daily between Gaborone (Botswana) and Jo'burg (R220 to R330, 7½ hours) via Pretoria.

Less safe and comfortable than buses, shared taxis run from Jo'burg to Gaborone (seven hours) and Lobatse (Botswana) with a change in Mahikeng (North West Province). Another route from Jo'burg is via Grobler's Bridge/Martin's Drift to Palapye (Botswana; eight hours).

LESOTHO

Shared taxis connect Jo'burg and Maseru (eight hours). It's quicker and easier to catch a bus to Bloemfontein, then continue by shared taxi to Maseru (three hours).

South African bus lines, including Intercape, also link Bloemfontein and beyond with Ladybrand (2½ hours), a few kilometres from the Maseru Bridge crossing.

Leaving Maseru, long-distance shared taxis depart from the rank at Maseru Bridge.

Other possible shared-taxi routes:

➤ Butha-Buthe to/from Fouriesburg (Free State)

➤ Leribe (Hlotse) to/from Ficksburg (Free State)

➤ Quthing to/from Sterkspruit (Eastern Cape)

➤ Qacha's Nek to/from Matatiele (Eastern Cape)

MOZAMBIQUE

Bus companies including **Greyhound** (www.grey hound.co.za), Intercape and **Translux** (www.translux.co.za) run daily 'luxury' coaches between Jo'burg/Pretoria and Maputo (Mozambique) via Nelspruit (Mbombela), Komatipoort and the Lebombo/Ressano Garcia crossing (R300, 10½ hours). Passengers must have a valid Mozambique visa before boarding the bus.

Mr Chubby (☑074 329 9114; www.mrchubbyshuttles. com) and **Cheetah Express** (☑084 244 2103, in South Africa 013-755 1988; cheetahex pressmaputo@gmail.com; cnr Avenidas Eduardo Mondlane & Julius Nyerere) run shuttles between Nelspruit (which is well served by shuttles; p391) from Jo'burg and beyond) and Maputo. Jo'burg/Pretoria–Maputo can also be tackled in shared taxis.

NAMIBIA

Intercape buses run between Windhoek (Namibia) and Cape Town (R630 to R780, 21½ hours), departing roughly every other day.

SWAZILAND

Daily shuttles run between Jo'burg and Mbabane. Shared taxi routes:

➤ Jo'burg to/from Mbabane (four hours); some continue to Manzini

➤ Durban to/from Manzini (eight hours)

➤ Manzini to/from Maputo (3¼ hours)

ZIMBABWE

Greyhound and Intercape operate daily buses between Jo'burg and Harare (Zimbabwe; R570, 17 hours), and between Jo'burg and Bulawayo (Zimbabwe; R550, 14 hours), both via Pretoria.

Shared taxis run south from Beitbridge to Musina and beyond.

Car & Motorcycle

CAR RENTAL

➤ If you rent a car in South Africa and plan to take it across an international border, you'll need a permission letter from the rental company.

➤ South African car-rental companies typically charge around R500 for cross-border travel to Lesotho and Swaziland, R1500 for Botswana, Namibia and Zimbabwe, and R2000 for Mozambique.

➤ Most companies permit entry to most neighbouring countries, though some may be reluctant regarding Mozambique and Zimbabwe.

➤ Check that the right information is on the permission letter; companies sometimes get it wrong.

➤ Taking a car across a border also raises the insurance excess.

BRINGING YOUR OWN VEHICLE

➤ You'll need the vehicle's registration papers, liability insurance and your driving licence.

➤ You'll also need a *carnet de passage en douane*, the international customs document, which allows the temporary admission of motor vehicles.

➤ Obtain a carnet through your local automobile association (from about US$300).

➤ Drivers of vehicles from outside Africa must typically pay a 50% refundable security deposit of 25% of the vehicle's value.

➡ Cars registered in South Africa, Lesotho, Swaziland, Botswana and Namibia, and driven by citizens or permanent residents of these countries, don't need a carnet to visit the other countries in this group.

BOTSWANA

The following crossings are passable in 2WD cars:

➡ Grobler's Bridge/Martin's Drift

➡ Kopfontein Gate/ Tlokweng Gate

➡ Ramatlabama

➡ Skilpadshek/Pioneer Gate

LESOTHO

Road tax of M30 (or R30) is payable on entering Lesotho. The easiest entry points for cars and motorcycles are on the northern and western sides of the country.

Most of the entry points to the south and east are unsealed, though many are passable in a 2WD, depending on weather conditions. A sealed road runs around the perimeter of the country from Qacha's Nek clockwise to Mokhotlong.

It's more economical to rent a car in South Africa than in Lesotho. You must have two red hazard triangles in your car in case of a breakdown.

MOZAMBIQUE

You must have two red hazard triangles in your car in case of a breakdown.

Giriyondo It's 95km from Kruger's Phalaborwa gate to Giriyondo, and 75km further to Massingir, the first major town on the Mozambique side. A 4WD and proof of overnight accommodation in the relevant park are required.

Kosi Bay/Ponta d'Ouro Travelling to and from Mozambique via this border post, you'll need your own 4WD vehicle. Accommodation options in Ponta d'Ouro (Mozambique) offer transfers if you need to leave your vehicle at Kosi Bay.

Lebombo/Ressano Garcia (Komatipoort) The N4 highway connects Pretoria with this post, joined by the N12 from Jo'burg. The EN4 highway runs southeast from here to Maputo. There are tolls on both sides of the border.

Namaacha/Lomahasha The roads leading to this border post with Swaziland are sealed and negotiable with 2WD.

Pafuri Just 29km from Kruger's Pafuri gate, but on the Mozambique side, there is an unbridged crossing of the Limpopo River near Mapai (makeshift ferry during rains) and a rough bush track thereafter via Mabote and Mapinhane to Vilankulo (4WD required). Allow two full days for the journey. Proof of accommodation in Kruger or Limpopo park is required.

NAMIBIA

2WD Highways lead to the Vioolsdrif/Noordoewer and Nakop/Ariamsvlei crossings.

4WD A 4WD opens up more options for crossing the border, including through the Kgalagadi and |Ai-|Ais/Richtersveld transfrontier parks.

SWAZILAND

➡ Swaziland's borders can be crossed in a 2WD.

➡ Road tax of E50 payable on entering the country.

➡ It's more economical to rent a car in South Africa than in Swaziland.

ZIMBABWE

Entering or leaving South Africa, vehicles pay a toll at the border to use the Limpopo Bridge.

Train

The Man in Seat Sixty-One (www.seat61.com) has ideas for train travel throughout Southern Africa.

MOZAMBIQUE

Caminhos de Ferro de Moçambique (www.cfm. co.mz) has a daily train between Maputo and the Lebombo/Ressano Garcia (Komatipoort) border post

(US$1, 3¾ hours), where you can cross the border on foot and continue by bus, shared taxi, shuttle or train.

NAMIBIA

TransNamib StarLine (www. transnamib.com.na) connects Walvis Bay, Swakopmund and Windhoek with Keetmanshoop and Karasburg in southern Namibia. From the latter, you can catch an **Intercape** (☎021-380 4400; www.intercape. co.za) bus across the border to Upington (Northern Cape).

Sea

South Africa is an important stop on world shipping routes. Cape Town is a major port of call for cruise ships, and many also stop at Durban. Both are good places to look for crew berths on private yachts sailing up the East African coast.

It's possible to find cruise and freighter lines linking South Africa with Mozambique, Madagascar and Mauritius. Many freighters have comfortable passenger cabins.

Even on freighter lines, the thrill of approaching the tip of the continent by sea certainly doesn't come cheap. Fares from South Africa tend to be lower than those to it.

Helpful contacts:

Cruise People (www.cruisepeople.co.uk) Based in London.

Cruiser Log (www.cruiserlog. com) Crew positions and forum.

Cunard (www.cunard.co.uk) Luxury cruises to Cape Town. Has a list of cruise travel agents around the world.

LBH Africa (www.tallships.com) Southern African freighter line.

Maris Freighter Cruises (www. freightercruises.com) Freighter cruises from North America.

Perpetual Travel (http://perpetualtravel.com/rtw/rtwfreighters. html) Suggests reference books and further links.

Royal Mail Ship St Helena (www.rms-st-helena.com) Cape Town to St Helena and Ascension Island.

Safmarine (www.safmarine. com) Cargo ships. Headquartered in Cape Town.

Tours

Dozens of tour and safari companies organise package tours to South Africa and its neighbouring countries. If you prefer a more independent approach, you can book flights and accommodation for the first few nights, then join tours locally.

Itineraries typically include Kruger National Park and Cape Town and the Cape Peninsula.

For particular interests such as birdwatching and botany, check the advertisements in specialist magazines.

Australia

Adventure World (www.adventureworld.com.au) A range of tours and safaris in South Africa and the region.

African Wildlife Safaris (www. africanwildlifesafaris.com.au) Customised tours and safaris in South Africa and neighbouring countries.

Peregrine Travel (www.peregrineadventures.com) Guided and independent tours and safaris in South Africa and beyond, including family adventures.

France

Makila Voyages (www.makila. fr) Upper-end tailored tours and safaris in South Africa and its neighbours.

UK

Dragoman (www.dragoman. co.uk) Overland tours.

Exodus Travels (www.exodus. co.uk) A variety of tours, including overland trips, walking, cycling, wildlife and cultural itineraries, covering South Africa and surrounds.

In the Saddle (www.inthesaddle. com) Strictly for horse aficionados, with various rides in South Africa (including the Wild Coast and the Cape Winelands) and its northern neighbours.

Intrepid Travel (www. intrepidtravel.com) Tours advocating the philosophy of independent travel; numerous itineraries cover South Africa, Swaziland and the region.

Naturetrek (www.naturetrek. co.uk) Specialist nature tours, visiting parts of South Africa (including the Drakensberg and Kruger National Park) as well as Botswana and Namibia.

Temple World (www.temple world.co.uk) Upper-end 'educational' tours in South Africa, Swaziland and elsewhere in the region, focusing on themes such as history, culture and wildlife.

USA & Canada

Africa Adventure Company (www.africa-adventure.com) Upper-end wildlife safaris, including the private reserves around Kruger National Park, plus itineraries in and around Cape Town.

Born Free Safaris & Tours (www.safaris2africa.com) Itineraries covering areas from the Cape to Swaziland and further north in Southern Africa.

Bushtracks Expeditions (www. bushtracks.com) Luxury safaris and private air charters.

Heritage Safari Company (www.heritagesafaris.com) Canada-based company offering wildlife-watching tours in South Africa and bordering countries.

GETTING AROUND

Air

Domestic fares are generally affordable but it depends on the route. A budget flight from Jo'burg to Cape Town, a popular route served by numerous airlines, costs around R1000, while Cape Town to East London, a less competitive route, might cost double that.

There are a number of budget airlines connecting all the major South African cities. It rarely works out cheaper to fly with the main carrier, South African Airways (SAA).

Keep costs down by booking online months before travelling, either directly or through the likes of **Computicket Travel** (☏0861 915 4000; www.computickettravel. com) or **Travelstart** (www. travelstart.co.za).

Regional Airlines

Airlink (☏086 160 6606; www. flyairlink.com) South African Airways' partner has a good network, including smaller destinations such as Upington, Mthatha and Maseru.

SA Express (☏086 172 9227; www.flyexpress.aero) This South African Airways partner has a good network, including direct flights between Cape Town and Hoedspruit (for Kruger National Park).

South African Airways (SAA; ☏086 160 6606; www.flysaa. com) The national airline, with an extensive domestic and regional network.

Budget Airlines

South Africa's budget airlines also offer hotel bookings, car rentals and holiday packages.

CemAir (☏011-390 1110; www. flycemair.co.za) A small airline connecting Port Elizabeth, Bloemfontein, George, Plettenberg Bay, Margate and other destinations.

FlySafair (☏087 135 1351; www.flysafair.co.za) Offers cheap fares between Jo'burg, Cape Town, Durban, Port Elizabeth, East London and George.

Kulula (☏086 158 5852; www. kulula.com) Budget airline connecting Jo'burg, Cape Town, Durban, George and East London. It also offers discounts on domestic flights with sister airline British Airways.

Mango (☏086 100 1234; www. flymango.com) The South African Airways subsidiary flies between Jo'burg, Cape Town, Durban, Port Elizabeth, George and Bloemfontein.

Bicycle

South Africa

As long as you're fit enough to handle the hills, South Africa offers some rewarding cycling. It has scenic and diverse terrain, abundant campsites and numerous quiet secondary roads. The major drawback is sharing the tarmac with South Africa's often erratic and aggressive drivers.

Good areas The roads around the Cape Peninsula and Winelands are popular, although busy and swept by summer wind. The Wild Coast is beautiful and challenging, and the northern lowveld offers wide plains.

Public transport Trains can carry bicycles, but most bus lines don't want bikes in their luggage holds, and shared taxis don't carry luggage on the roof.

Purchase Larger South African cities, especially Cape Town, have a good selection of mountain bikes for sale. Jo'burg and Cape Town are the best places to look for touring bikes. To resell your bicycle at the end of your trip, try hostel noticeboards, bike shops and clubs, and www.gumtree.co.za.

Rental For day rides, some hostels offers short-term mountain-bike rental. Rentals can also sometimes be arranged through bike shops in the cities; you'll usually be required to leave a credit-card deposit.

Safety Distances between major towns are often long, though, except in isolated areas such as the Karoo, you're rarely far from a village or farmhouse. Many roads don't have a hard shoulder; on those that do, motorists use the shoulder as an unofficial slow lane. It's illegal to cycle on highways, and roads near urban areas are busy and hazardous. Before heading off anywhere, contact other cyclists through local cycling clubs or bicycle shops to get recent information on the routes you're considering. Bring a good lock to counter the ever-present risk of theft, store the bike inside your accommodation (preferably inside your room) and chain it to something solid.

Spare parts Mountain bikes and parts are widely available in the cities. It's often difficult to find specialised parts for touring bikes, especially outside Cape Town and Jo'burg. Establish a relationship with a good bike shop in a city before you head off into the veld, in case you need something couriered to you.

Weather Much of the country (except for the Western Cape and west coast) gets most of its rain in summer (late November to March), often in the form of violent thunderstorms. When it isn't raining, summer days can be unpleasantly hot, especially in the steamy lowveld.

Lesotho & Swaziland

Both are excellent cycling destinations, for which you need a mountain bike. Stock up on spare parts in South Africa. Summer thunderstorms and flooding are an issue. Transporting bicycles on public transport is uncommon, but you can often arrange something with the driver.

Lesotho You'll need to bring your own bike into the country, and given the terrain you'll need legs of steel.

Swaziland Avoid the main towns and the heavily travelled Ezulwini Valley. Short pedals are available on the mountain-bike trails of **Hlane Royal National Park** (☑2383 8100, 2528 3943; www.biggameparks.org/hlane; E50; ☺6am-6pm) and **Mlilwane Wildlife Sanctuary** (Map p501; ☑2528 3943; www.biggameparks.org/mlilwane; Off MR103; E50; ☺6am-6pm), which respectively offer guided rides and bike rental.

Boat

There are few opportunities to travel by boat. The most likely possibilities are between Cape Town, Port Elizabeth and Durban. Local yacht clubs are good starting points. Cruise liners also ply the east coast between the Cape and Mozambique, with opportunities to join or leave along the way.

Bus

South Africa

A good network of buses, of varying reliability and comfort, links the major cities.

Classes There are no class tiers on the bus lines, although major companies generally offer a 'luxury' service, with features such as air-con, a toilet and films.

Discounts The major bus lines offer student, frequent-traveller and senior-citizen discounts, as well as specials – check their websites for details.

Fares Roughly calculated by distance, though short runs are disproportionately expensive. Your fare may also be based on the bus's whole journey (so travelling from Jo'burg to Bloemfontein costs the same as travelling from Pretoria). Prices rise during school holidays.

Safety Lines are generally safe. Note, however, that many long-distance services run through the night. On overnight journeys, travellers should take care of their valuables and may feel more comfortable sitting near the front of the bus.

Ticket purchase For the main lines, purchase tickets at least 24 hours in advance, and as far in advance as possible for travel during peak periods. Tickets can be bought through bus offices, **Computicket Travel** (☑0861 915 4000; www.computickettravel.com) and Shoprite/Checkers supermarkets. Computicket is particularly useful and functional, offering the major carriers in one booking engine and generally accepting foreign credit cards and mobile-phone numbers. Just note that, unless you're travelling out of a large city, you must usually pick up your physical ticket at a Shoprite or Checkers before catching your bus.

BUS LINES

City to City (☎086 158 9282; www.citytocity.co.za) In partnership with Translux, it operates the routes that once carried people between the homelands and the cities under apartheid. The no-frills service is less expensive than other lines and serves many off-the-beaten-track places, including townships and mining towns. Destinations include Mthatha (for the Wild Coast), Nelspruit (for Kruger National Park), Zeerust (for Botswana), Cape Town and Durban.

Greyhound (☎customer care 24hr 011-611 8000, reservations 087 352 0352; www.greyhound.co.za) An extensive nationwide network of comfortable buses, including Jo'burg to Durban via Richards Bay. Also operates other lines, including the cheaper Citiliner buses.

Intercape (☎021-380 4400; www.intercape.co.za) An extensive network stretching from Cape Town to Limpopo and beyond. For longer hauls (including Cape Town to Windhoek, Namibia, and Mossel Bay

to Jo'burg), it's worth paying extra for a reclining seat on an overnight Sleepliner bus.

Translux (☎086 158 9282; www.translux.co.za) The main long-distance operator, serving destinations including Cape Town, Durban, Bloemfontein, Port Elizabeth, East London, Mthatha, Nelspruit and the Garden Route.

Lesotho

Buses and shared taxis A good network of buses, minibus shared taxis (known locally as just 'taxis'), sprinters and private or shared-car taxis (known as 'four-plus-ones') covers most of the country. Minibus taxis serve the major towns and many smaller spots. Buses (cheaper and slower) and sprinters (faster and more expensive) serve the major towns. There are no classes and service is decidedly no-frills.

Departures Most departures are in the morning (generally, the longer the journey, the earlier the departure).

Northern Lesotho Heading northeast from Maseru by shared taxi, you usually have to change at Maputsoe. The transfer sometimes happens en route into Maputsoe if your vehicle meets another taxi.

Tickets On larger local buses, although you'll be quoted long-distance fares, it's best to just buy a ticket to the next major town. Most passengers will likely get off there, leaving you stuck waiting for the vehicle to fill up again while other buses and shared taxis leave. Buying tickets in stages is only slightly more expensive than buying a direct ticket. It's not necessary (or possible) to reserve a seat in advance.

Swaziland

Minibus shared taxis are the main form of public transport in Swaziland. They run almost everywhere, with frequent stops en route. They leave when full; no reservations are necessary.

Local buses connect towns and villages throughout the country. Most start and terminate at the main stop in central Mbabane; they are slightly cheaper than minibuses but are slow and often overcrowded.

BACKPACKER SHUTTLES

A convenient alternative to standard bus lines, the **Baz Bus** (☎021-422 5202, SMS bookings 076 427 3003; www.bazbus.com) caters almost exclusively to backpackers and travellers. It offers hop-on, hop-off fares and door-to-door services between Cape Town and Jo'burg via the Garden Route, Port Elizabeth, Mthatha, Durban and the Northern Drakensberg.

Baz Bus drops off and picks up at hostels, and it has transfer arrangements with those off its route in areas such as the Wild Coast. You can book directly with Baz Bus online, by email, phone or SMS, or at hostels.

Point-to-point fares are more expensive than on the major bus lines, but it can work out economically if you take advantage of the hop-on, hop-off feature. Sample one-way hop-on, hop-off fares from Cape Town are Jo'burg R5400, Durban R4470 and Port Elizabeth R2300. One-/two-/three-week travel passes cost R2600/R4100/5100.

New challenger **Mzansi Experience** (☎021-001 0651; www.mzansi.travel) offers a similar service to Baz Bus and is fast gaining popularity among travellers. Prices are lower: a hop-on, hop-off ticket from Cape Town to Jo'burg costs R4400; and three-day/one-/two-/three-week travel passes are R1500/2500/3800/5000.

Car & Motorcycle

South Africa is a spectacular country for a road trip. Away from the main bus and train routes, having your own wheels is the best way to get around, and if you're in a group, hiring a car is often the most economical option.

Road maps are a worthwhile investment and are readily available in South Africa.

Automobile Associations

Automobile Association of South Africa (AASA; ☎011-799 1000, 086 100 0234; www.aa.co.za) offers a vehicle breakdown service, which can be useful if you'll be driving in the areas it covers.

Its fleet of emergency response vehicles operates nationwide, with AA-approved operatives available elsewhere and numerous other benefits offered to members. Membership costs from R111.50 per month. Check the website for motoring news, information and tips.

Members of foreign clubs in the Fédération Internationale de l'Automobile (www.fia.com) group have access to AASA – contact your club to find out what is available to you in South Africa.

Driving Licences

➡ You can use your driving licence from your home country, provided it is in English (or you have a certified translation).

➡ For use in South Africa, your licence should also carry your photo. Otherwise you'll need an international driving permit.

➡ Police generally ask to see foreign drivers' passports, so keep a photocopy in your car.

➡ You can be fined for not being able to show your licence, passport or other ID.

Fuel & Spare Parts

➡ Unleaded petrol costs about R12 per litre.

➡ An attendant will fill your tank and clean your windows – tip R2 to R5; if they check your oil, water or tyres, tip R5 to R10.

➡ Along main roads, there are plenty of petrol stations. Many stay open 24 hours.

➡ There are petrol stations in most South African towns.

➡ In rural areas, fill up whenever you can.

LESOTHO

➡ The main petrol stations are in Maseru.

➡ Other major towns have limited facilities and unreliable fuel availability.

➡ Carry a jerry can, as fuel is not readily available in remote areas.

PARKING & CAR GUARDS

Parking is readily available at sights, eateries and accommodation throughout South Africa. Particularly in Jo'burg and other locations where crime is a problem, secure parking is often offered.

If you are parking in the street or even a car park in larger South African towns and cities, you will often be approached by a 'car guard'. They will keep an eye on your vehicle in exchange for a tip: R2 for a short period, R5 to R10 for long stays. They may also offer to wash your car for an extra R20. Do not pay them until you are leaving, or if they did not approach you when you arrived. Ensure you give the money to the right person; in Cape Town, for example, approved car guards often wear high-visibility vests.

SWAZILAND

➡ Mbabane and Manzini have the best facilities.

➡ Manzini is the best place for sourcing spare parts.

Car Hire

➡ Car rental is inexpensive in South Africa compared with Europe and North America, starting at around R200 per day for longer rentals.

➡ Many companies levy a surcharge for drivers aged under 21.

➡ Most companies ask for a credit card and will not accept a debit card. Many use a chip-and-pin machine, so you'll need to know your credit card's PIN.

➡ For low rates, book online months in advance.

➡ Many companies stipulate a daily mileage limit, with an extra fee payable for any mileage over this limit. This can be a drawback if you're planning a long road trip. Four hundred kilometres a day is generally sufficient. If you plan one- or two-day stopovers along the way, 200km a day might be sufficient.

➡ A few local companies offer unlimited mileage. If you rent through an international company and book through an overseas branch, you may get unlimited mileage for no

extra cost, except at peak times (such as December to January).

➡ Make sure that quoted prices include the 14% value-added tax (VAT).

➡ One-way rental is charged according to the distance of the relocation.

➡ There are rental operations in cities, major towns and airports, but it's generally cheapest to hire in a hub such as Jo'burg or Cape Town.

LESOTHO & SWAZILAND

It usually works out cheaper to rent a vehicle in South Africa and drive it over the border. You'll need a permission letter from the rental company to cross the border; some companies charge a fee (around R500) for this.

Lesotho has rental operations in Maseru and Moshoeshoe I International Airport.

You'll find rentals in Swaziland in Mbabane and King Mswati III International Airport.

RENTAL COMPANIES

In addition to the companies listed, check with backpacker hostels and travel agents, as many offer good deals. Local companies are usually less expensive, though they tend to come and go, and their vehicles are often older.

Argus (www.arguscarhire.com) Online consolidator, covering South Africa, Lesotho and Swaziland.

Around About Cars (www.aroundaboutcars.com) Covering South Africa and Swaziland, this recommended budget agent secures low rates with other operators, including Budget, Tempest and First. One of the few companies offering unlimited mileage.

Avis (www.avis.co.za) Covers South Africa, Lesotho and Swaziland.

Budget (www.budget.co.za) Covers South Africa and Swaziland.

Europcar (www.europcar.co.za) Covers South Africa, Lesotho and Swaziland.

First (www.firstcarrental.co.za) Covers South Africa.

Hertz (www.hertz.co.za) Covers South Africa.

Sixt (www.sixt.com) Covers South Africa.

Tempest (www.tempestcarhire.co.za) Covers South Africa.

Thrifty (www.thrifty.co.za) Covers South Africa.

CAMPERVANS, 4WD & MOTORCYCLES

➧ Some campervan and motorhome rentals include camping gear.

➧ One-way rental is not always possible.

➧ 'Bakkie' campers, sleeping two in the back of a canopied pick-up truck, are cheaper.

➧ Mopeds and scooters are available for hire in Cape Town and other tourist areas.

➧ For Lesotho and provinces such as the Northern and Eastern Capes, with many gravel roads and national parks, consider a 4WD.

➧ Besides standard rental-car companies, check Britz (www.britz.co.za) in Cape Town, Jo'burg and beyond for 4WDs; Drive South Africa (www.drivesouthafrica.co.za) in Cape Town for 4WDs and campervans, and

Maui (www.maui.co.za) in Cape Town and Jo'burg for motorhomes.

Insurance

Insurance for third-party damage and damage to or loss of your vehicle is highly recommended, though it's not legally required for private-vehicle owners. Generally it is only available on an annual basis.

If you're renting a vehicle, insurance with an excess should be included, with an excess waiver or reduction available at an extra cost.

Check that hire-car insurance or the rental agreement covers hail damage, a costly possibility during summer in the highveld and lowveld regions.

Insurance providers include the following:

Automobile Association of South Africa (AASA; www.aa.co.za)

Old Mutual iWyze (www.oldmutual.co.za)

Outsurance (www.outsurance.co.za)

Sansure (www.sansure.co.za)

Vehicle Purchase

South Africa is the best place in the region to purchase a vehicle for a Southern African, or larger sub-Saharan, journey. It's worth buying a vehicle if you plan to stay longer than about three months.

Jo'burg is the best place to buy; prices are often lower here, and cars tend to build up rust in Cape Town and coastal towns. Cape Town is the best place to resell; the market is smaller and prices tend to be higher.

In Jo'burg you'll find a good congregation of used-car dealers on Great North Rd, Benoni; in Cape Town, look on Voortrekker Rd between Maitland and Bellville metro train stations.

Buying privately, prices are considerably lower, though you won't have any dealer warranties and shop-

ping around is likely to take longer. Dealers can advise on the arduous process of registering the car, and they may have some of the forms you need. You may find one willing to agree to a buy-back deal, though the terms are likely to be unfavourable.

Prices are high. Lonely Planet readers and writers have paid R124,000, at a Benoni dealership, for a four-year-old Nissan 2.4 4WD bakkie with a canopy and 135,000km on the clock; R70,000 to a private seller in Cape Town for a seven-year-old Toyota Corolla with 95,000km on the clock; and most recently, R60,000 to a private seller in Cape Town for a 10-year-old Renault Clio with 120,000km on the clock.

PAPERWORK

Make sure the car details correspond accurately with the ownership (registration) papers, that there is a current licence disc on the windscreen and that the service-history book is up to date. Check the owner's name against their identity document, and check the car's engine and chassis numbers.

An up-to-date roadworthy certificate is required when you submit the change-of-ownership form and pay tax for a licence disc. Roadworthy test centres issue certificates for a few hundred rand and will generally overlook minor faults. In Cape Town many test centres are found on Oswald Pirow St (also known as Christiaan Barnard St), near the Civic Centre.

REGISTRATION

Registering your car is a bureaucratic headache and will likely take a couple of weeks. Officials have told travellers they cannot register a car without South African citizenship, but this is untrue.

The forms you need to complete should be available at vehicle registration offices and dealers:

➜ ANR8 (application and notice in respect of traffic register number)

➜ RLV/NCO5 (notification of change of ownership/sale of motor vehicle)

Submit your ANR8 as soon as possible, as this registers individuals to drive on South African roads. Without this piece of paperwork, you cannot register a car in your name; it takes several weeks to process. You generally need a proof of your permanent address, such as a utility bill in your name; check what is required, as this has proved to be an obstacle for foreigners.

To submit your RLV/NCO5, present yourself at a vehicle registration office along with the following items:

➜ your passport and a photocopy of it

➜ a copy of the seller's ID

➜ the registration certificate (in the seller's name)

➜ a roadworthy certificate

➜ proof of purchase

➜ proof of address (a letter from your accommodation may suffice)

➜ a valid licence

➜ your fee (in cash)

Ideally get photocopies of IDs and other documents certified at a police station before submitting them.

Charges rise annually and typically start at around R400 to register and license a car.

If the licence has expired, you will have to pay a penalty.

CONTACTS & RESOURCES

Auto Trader (www.autotrader.co.za) Car ads across South Africa.

Cape Ads (www.capeads.com) Car ads around Cape Town.

eNaTIS (www.enatis.com) Forms and information on registering vehicles.

Gumtree South Africa (www.gumtree.co.za) South African car ads.

Mahindra Benoni (www.msmdealer.co.za) Jo'burg dealer offering car and bakkie sales and trade-ins; has experience selling to foreigners and helping them register vehicles.

South African Government Services (www.gov.za) Information on applying for a traffic register number and driving licence. Click on Services, Services for Foreign Nationals and Driving.

Suedafrika-forum.net (http://suedafrika-forum.net) A forum in German.

Western Cape Government (www.westerncape.gov.za) Forms and advice on registering a vehicle in the Western Cape; click on Directories then Services and search for the Licences, Permits and Certificates link. Also details of vehicle registration offices in and around Cape Town; click on Directories then Facilities and search for the Motor Vehicle Registering Authorities link.

Road Conditions
SOUTH AFRICA

➜ A good network of highways covers the country.

➜ Major roads are generally in good condition.

➜ Outside large towns and cities you may encounter gravel (dirt) roads, most of which are graded and reasonably smooth.

➜ Check locally on tertiary and gravel roads' condition, which can deteriorate when it rains.

➜ In rural areas beware of hazards such as dangerous potholes, washed-out roads, unannounced hairpin bends, and livestock, children and dogs on the road.

➜ The N2 highway through the Wild Coast region is in poor condition.

LESOTHO

➜ Driving in Lesotho can be challenging, with steep terrain, hairpin turns and inclement weather.

➜ Roads are being built and upgraded, many financed by Chinese mining corporations and the Highlands Water Project.

➜ During roadworks, previously passable gravel and tar roads become impassable to 2WD cars.

➜ A tarred road, passable in a 2WD, runs clockwise from Qacha's Nek to Mokhotlong, with possible onward access to Sani Top.

➜ Stretches of tar and good gravel also give 2WD access to Semonkong (from both the north and south), Thaba-Tseka (from the north and west) and Ts'ehlanyane National Park.

➜ Apart from issues caused by roadworks, sealed roads in the highlands are generally good, but very steep in places.

➜ Rain will slow you down, and ice and snow in winter can make driving dangerous.

➜ If you're driving an automatic, you'll rely heavily on your brakes to negotiate steep downhill corners.

➜ Away from main roads, there are places where even a 4WD will struggle, such as the road north from Sehlabathebe National Park.

➜ Rough roads and river floodings after summer storms are the biggest problems.

➜ People and animals on the road can also be a hazard.

➜ There are sometimes police or army roadblocks.

SWAZILAND

Swaziland has a good road network and most major routes are tarred. Most unpaved roads are in reasonably good condition, except after heavy rains. The MR3, which crosses Swaziland roughly from west to east, is a major highway as far east as Manzini. Take care on Malagwane Hill, from Mbabane into the Ezulwini Valley, particularly in rainy weather or heavy traffic – it was once

CARJACKING

In Jo'burg and, to a lesser extent, in the other big cities and elsewhere in the northeastern provinces, carjacking is a danger. It's more likely if you're driving something flash, rather than a standard rental car.

➔ Stay alert, keep your taste in cars modest and avoid driving in urban areas at night; if you have to do so, keep windows wound up and doors locked.

➔ If you're waiting at a red light and notice anything suspicious, it's standard practice to check that the junction is clear and jump the light.

➔ If you do get carjacked, don't resist; just hand over the keys immediately. The carjackers are almost always armed, and people have been killed for their cars.

listed in *Guinness World Records* as the world's most dangerous road.

Away from the population centres and border-crossing areas there is little traffic, but look out for drunk drivers, wandering cattle and speeding minibuses, especially on gravel roads.

Road Hazards

➔ South Africa's roads can be treacherous, with a horrific accident rate and well over 10,000 deaths annually.

➔ Notably dangerous stretches of highway: N1 between Cape Town and Beaufort West, and between Polokwane (Pietersburg) and Louis Trichardt (Makhado); N2 between Cape Town and Caledon, along the Garden Route, between East London and Kokstad, and Durban and Tongaat; N12 between Springs and Witbank; N4 between Middelburg and Belfast.

➔ The main hazards are your fellow drivers. Motorists from all sections of society drive sloppily and often aggressively. Be particularly wary of shared-taxi drivers, who operate under pressure on little sleep in sometimes-shoddy vehicles.

➔ Overtaking blind and with insufficient passing room are common.

➔ On major roads, drivers coming up behind you will flash their lights at you and expect you to move into the hard shoulder to let them pass, even if you are approaching a corner and regardless of what is happening in the hard shoulder. Motorists often remain hard on your tail until you move over.

➔ Drivers on little-used rural roads often speed and assume there is no other traffic.

➔ Watch out for oncoming cars at blind corners on secondary roads.

➔ Despite roadblocks and alcohol breath testing in South Africa, particularly in urban areas, drink driving is widespread. Do not be seduced by the relaxed local attitude to drink driving; you can end up in a cell, so nominate a designated driver.

➔ Farm animals, wildlife (particularly baboons) and pedestrians stray onto the roads, especially in rural areas. If you hit an animal in an area where you're uncertain of your safety, continue to the nearest police station and report it there.

➔ In roads through townships (such as the N2 from Cape Town International Airport to the city), foreign objects are occasionally placed on the road and motorists robbed when they pull over after driving over the object. Continue to a garage and police station to inspect your car and report the incident.

➔ During the rainy season, thick fog can slow you to a crawl, especially in the higher areas of KwaZulu-Natal and Mpumalanga.

➔ In the highveld and lowveld, summer hail storms can damage your car.

Road Rules

➔ In South Africa, Lesotho and Swaziland, driving is on the left-hand side of the road.

➔ Seatbelts are mandatory for the driver and all passengers.

➔ The main local idiosyncrasy is the 'four-way stop' (crossroad), found even on major roads. All vehicles are required to stop, with those arriving first being the first to go (even if they're on a minor cross street).

➔ There are numerous police roadblocks in Lesotho; halt at the first stop sign and wait to be waved forward. Most police officers will quickly check your papers or just wave you on.

➔ If you're driving a car hired in South Africa and get stopped in Lesotho or Swaziland, you might have to show the letter from the rental agency giving you permission to take the car across the border.

➔ In Swaziland, if an official or royal motorcade approaches, you're required to pull over and stop.

SPEED LIMITS

Stick to speed limits, as speed traps (cameras and guns) are increasingly common in South Africa, although limits remain widely ignored by locals.

South Africa 100km/h on open roads; 120km/h on most major highways; 60km/h in built-up areas; and 40km/h in most wildlife parks and reserves.

Lesotho 80km/h on main roads; and 50km/h in villages.

Swaziland 60km/h in towns; 80km/h on open roads; and 120km/h on most major highways.

Signage

Signage is good in South Africa. Signposts are sparser on secondary and tertiary roads, sometimes only giving route numbers or directing you to nearby towns, rather than the next large town or city.

Roads are normally numbered (eg R44). When you ask directions, most people will refer to these numbers.

In Lesotho, main routes are numbered, beginning with A1 (Main North Rd). Side roads branching off from these have 'B' route numbers.

Tolls

On some South African highways a toll is payable, based on distance. You can usually pay with cash or card. Many rental cars have a transmitter attached; you will automatically be charged and the fee added to your final rental bill. If this is the case, the transmitter will beep and the toll gate will open automatically.

There's always plenty of warning that you're about to enter a toll section (marked by a black 'T' in a yellow circle), and there's normally an alternative route (marked by a black 'A' in a yellow circle).

Calculate journey tolls at Drive South Africa (www.drivesouthafrica.co.za).

Hitching

Hitch-hiking and picking up hitchers is inadvisable.

If you're strapped for cash, you can look into driveshares. Hostel noticeboards often have details of free or shared-cost lifts. Also check out FindALift (https://findalift.co.za) and Jumpin Rides (www.jumpinrides.co.za).

Local Transport
Bus

➡ Several urban areas, including Cape Town, Durban, Pretoria and Jo'burg, have city bus networks.

➡ Fares are cheap.

➡ Routes, which are often signboarded, are extensive.

➡ Services often stop running early in the evening, and there aren't many on weekends.

➡ In terms of safety and convenience, only Cape Town's MyCiTi buses and Durban People Mover are recommended.

Private Taxi
SOUTH AFRICA

➡ Larger cities have private taxi services, with taxi stands in popular areas.

➡ Phoning for a cab is often safer; you will have to wait for the taxi to arrive, but the vehicle will likely be better quality than those at the stands.

➡ Rates vary between cities; in Cape Town, rates average R10 per kilometre, often with a minimum charge of R30 or more.

➡ Uber is popular in larger cities and operates in Cape Town, Johannesburg, Pretoria, Durban and Port Elizabeth.

LESOTHO & SWAZILAND

Larger cities have private taxi services. They are more expensive than shared taxis, but the price is often negotiable. It's best to ask your accommodation to phone for a taxi rather than hailing one on the street – the vehicle will likely be better quality and you can ask your accommodation for a reputable company.

Shared Taxi

Shared minibus taxis run almost everywhere – around cities, and to the suburbs, townships and neighbouring towns. Riding them offers an insight into local life, but be aware that there are safety issues.

➡ They leave when full – though 'full' in South Africa isn't as packed as in many African countries.

➡ Most accommodate 14 to 16 people. Slightly larger 'sprinters' accommodate about 20.

➡ Away from train and bus routes, shared taxis may be the only choice of public transport.

➡ At weekends they generally have reduced services or no departures.

SHARED TAXI ETIQUETTE

➡ Passengers with luggage should sit in the first row behind the driver.

➡ Move along the seat to the window to give others easy access.

➡ Pass the money forward (your fare and those of the people around you) to the driver's assistant.

➡ If you sit on the folding seat by the sliding door, it's your job to open and close the door when passengers get out. You'll have to get out of the taxi each time.

➡ Some shared taxis, for example in Cape Town, have a conductor who calls out to potential passengers and handles the minibus door.

➡ Say: 'Thank you, driver!', when you want to get out, rather than just: 'Stop!'

→ Visit TaxiMap (http://taximap.co.za) for a useful database of minibus-taxi routes, fares and other information.

→ Car taxis are sometimes shared. In some towns, and on some longer routes, a shared car taxi may be the only transport option.

→ Shared car taxis are more expensive than minibus taxis and similar in terms of safety.

SECURITY

Money saved by taking shared taxis is generally outweighed by safety considerations.

→ Overall, taking shared taxis is not recommended.

→ Driving standards and vehicle conditions are poor.

→ There are frequent accidents.

→ There are occasional gangster-style clashes between rival companies.

→ Shared-taxi stations and their immediate surroundings are often unsafe.

→ Muggings, pickpocketing, sexual harassment and other incidents are common.

→ If you want to try riding in a shared taxi, don't travel at night, read the newspapers and seek local advice on lines and areas to avoid.

→ In a few areas shared taxis are relatively safe during daylight hours. This is notably the case in central Cape Town, where locals from all walks of life use shared taxis.

→ Do not travel with luggage, partly because most shared taxis don't carry bags on the roof, and stowing backpacks can be a hassle.

LESOTHO & SWAZILAND

Minibus shared taxis don't have stellar road-safety records but can sometimes be your only option. They are widely used for short and long routes. The downside

is that journeys can be slow, with constant stops and long waits to fill the seats.

In larger towns in Lesotho, you will find 'four-plus-ones' – normal taxis that collect passengers as they go. They are more expensive and more comfortable than minibus taxis, but are often only used for short routes.

Tours

There are dozens of tours on offer by local companies, ranging from budget overland truck journeys to exclusive luxury safaris, from 4WD adventures to weeklong horseback treks.

Backpacker hostels around the country are good sources of information on tours geared towards budget travellers. Many are affiliated with budget tour operators and have travel desks and bulletin boards.

Try to book day or overnight trips as close to the destination as possible. For example, if you're in Durban and want to visit a reserve in northern KwaZulu-Natal, it's usually cheaper to travel to a hostel near the reserve and take a day trip from there, rather than booking a longer excursion from Durban. You usually also get to spend more time at the reserve.

Acacia Africa (www.acacia-africa.com) Overland camping tours throughout Southern Africa. Also offers overland trips with accommodation and small-group safaris.

Ashworth Africa (www.ashworthafrica.com) Luxury tailored tours and safaris in South Africa and the region.

Bok Bus (www.bokbus.com) Budget-oriented tours along the Garden Route and around.

Cape Gourmet Adventure Tours (www.gourmet.cape-town.info) Mouth-watering tours of Cape Town and the Western Cape, ranging from catching your own seafood to a gourmet treasure hunt.

Drifters (www.drifters.co.za) Southern and East Africa adventures and lodges.

Go2Africa (www.go2africa.com) African safari specialist, offering experiences from beach holidays to luxury train travel.

Oasis Overland (www.oasisoverland.co.uk) UK-based overland specialist covering South Africa and the region.

Signature Tours (www.signaturetours.co.za) General-interest tours with a focus on nature and wildlife; tailored self-drive and guided packages available.

Springbok Atlas (www.springbokatlas.com) Coach tours and safaris around South Africa and the region.

Swazi Trails (www.swazitrails.co.sz) Trips on Swaziland's Great Usutu River (Lusutfu River) and around the country.

Thompsons Africa (www.thompsonsafrica.com) Midrange and top-end tours and safaris.

Wilderness Safaris (www.wilderness-safaris.com) Upscale, conservation-focused operator offering high-end safaris and special-interest trips; also operates several luxury bush camps.

Wilderness Travel (www.wildernesstravel.com) US-based company offering various small-group tours of Southern Africa, covering locations from Cape Town to the Drakensberg and focused mainly on wildlife and walking.

Wildlife Safaris (www.wildlifesaf.co.za) Midrange safaris for individuals and small groups, from Jo'burg to Kruger National Park, Madikwe Game Reserve and the Blyde River Canyon.

Train

South Africa's **Shosholoza Meyl** (☑011-774 4555, 086 000 8888; www.shosholozameyl.co.za) offers regular services connecting major cities.

For an overview of services, descriptions of trains and valuable advice, visit The Man in Seat Sixty-One (www.seat61.com/southafrica).

RIDING THE RAILS

In addition to the Shosholoza Meyl services, there are numerous special lines. Travel agents **New Fusion** (☑061 463 1089; www.newfusion.co.za) and **African Sun Travel** (☑086 584 6404; www.southafricanrailways.co.za) offer bookings on the Blue Train, Premier Classe and Rovos Rail. **JB Train Tours** (☑011-913 2442; www.jbtours.co.za) sells train holiday packages.

Blue Train

South Africa's famous **Blue Train** (☑012-334 8459; www.bluetrain.co.za) travels between Pretoria and Cape Town, stopping en route in Matjiesfontein or Kimberley. For 27 hours of luxury, one-way fares (per person sharing) are R20,280/25,615 for deluxe/luxury during high season (September to mid-November), including all meals, drinks, off-train excursions and en-suite bathroom. Fares drop by about R4000 during low season. You can book directly or through travel agents, both in South Africa and overseas. Enquire about packages including accommodation and one-way flights between Pretoria/Jo'burg and Cape Town. The train also occasionally travels between Pretoria and Hoedspruit (for Kruger National Park).

Premier Classe

Shosholoza Meyl's luxury offering, **Premier Classe** (☑086 000 8888, 011-774 4555; www.premierclasse.co.za) is an affordable alternative to the Blue Train et al. Trains run from Cape Town to Jo'burg (R3120 per person) on Tuesday, returning on Thursday; and from Jo'burg to Durban (R1230) on Thursday, returning on Sunday. The fare includes meals in the deluxe air-conditioned dining car. Single travellers occupy two-berth coupes, couples occupy four-berth compartments. There's a lounge-bar and shared bathrooms, and vehicles can be transported.

Rovos Rail

Rovos (☑012-315 8242; www.rovos.co.za) rivals the Blue Train as Africa's most luxurious and expensive service. Regular services include Pretoria–Cape Town over two nights/three days, with stops at Kimberley and Matjiesfontein; Pretoria–Durban over three days; Pretoria–Swakopmund (Namibia) over nine days, via Etosha National Park and other Namibian highlights; and Pretoria–Victoria Falls (Zimbabwe) over four days.

Shongololo Express

Rovos Rail's **Shongololo** (☑012-315 8242; www.shongololo.com) offers four train tours, including between Pretoria and Victoria Falls (12 days), and Pretoria and Cape Town via Swaziland and Durban (15 days). You travel by night and disembark during the days.

Steam Railways

Atlantic Rail (www.atlanticrail.co.za) Steam-train excursions from Cape Town to the Winelands.

Ceres Rail Company (www.ceresrail.co.za) This vintage-train company operates three steam locomotives with renovated lounge cars on a historic line reopened in 2012 from Cape Town to the mountainous, fruit-producing Ceres area. Trains normally run every other Saturday, arriving at Ceres Golf Club in time for lunch, before returning to town in the afternoon.

Umgeni Steam Railway (www.umgenisteamrailway.co.za) Steam-train day trips in KwaZulu-Natal.

Classes

Both tourist and economy class are affordable options. Unlike on long-distance buses, fares on short sectors are not inflated.

Tourist class Recommended: scenic, authentic but safe, and more comfortable than taking the bus, albeit often slower. The overnight journey from Jo'burg to Cape Town is a wonderful way to get a sense of the country's vastness, entering the Karoo as night falls and eating a celebratory lunch as the train swishes through the Winelands. There's a dining car and showers, and the fare includes accommodation in a two-berth coupe or four-berth compartment. Depending on what's available, couples are given coupes and single travellers and groups are put in compartments. If you are travelling alone and you want a coupe to yourself, you'll need to buy two tickets. There's an additional R60 charge for bedding hire. Cars can be transported on the Jo'burg–Cape Town, Jo'burg–Durban and Jo'burg–Port Elizabeth routes.

Economy class Does not have sleeping carriages and is not a comfortable or secure option for overnight travel.

Tickets & Fares

➜ At the time of writing, Jo'burg to Cape Town in tourist/economy class cost R690/440.

➜ Tickets can be purchased up to three months in advance and must be bought at least 48 hours before departure.

➜ Tourist-class sleepers can get fully booked a month or two ahead, especially on popular routes such as Jo'burg–Cape Town.

➜ The easiest way to purchase tickets is through travel agent **African Sun Travel** (086 584 6404; www.southafricanrailways.co.za). It charges a small commission (about R100 for Cape Town–Jo'burg tickets and R80 for Jo'burg–Durban tickets).

➜ Bookings can be made at train stations, by phone or through Shosholoza Meyl's website. You must then collect and pay for your tickets at a station within two days.

➜ A more complicated and lengthy option is to deposit the money in Shosholoza Meyl's bank account and send the company proof of payment; it takes four days for funds to clear in Shosholoza Meyl's account.

Routes

East London–Cape Town Via Queenstown and Beaufort West; 28 hours; tourist and economy (Tuesday and Sunday).

Jo'burg–Cape Town Via Kimberley and Beaufort West; 27 hours; tourist (Tuesday to Friday and Sunday) and economy (Wednesday, Friday and Sunday).

Jo'burg–Durban Via Ladysmith and Pietermaritzburg; 14½ hours; tourist and economy (Friday and Sunday).

Jo'burg–East London Via Bloemfontein; 20 hours; tourist and economy (Wednesday, Friday and Sunday).

Jo'burg–Komatipoort Via Nelspruit (Mbombela); 12½ hours; economy (Wednesday to Friday and Sunday).

Jo'burg–Port Elizabeth Via Bloemfontein; 20 hours; tourist and economy (Wednesday, Friday and Sunday).

Metro Trains

Cape Metro Rail (080 065 6463; http://capetowntrains.freeblog.site) Services from Cape Town south to Simon's Town are generally safe during peak daylight hours.

Gautrain (0800 428 87246; www.gautrain.co.za) The rapid-transit Gautrain is a safe and slick link between OR Tambo International Airport, Sandton, Rosebank, Park Station (downtown Jo'burg), Pretoria and Hatfield. Trains depart every 12 minutes at peak times (5.30am to 8.30am and 3pm to 6pm Monday to Friday), and every 20 to 30 minutes outside peak times. A one-way ticket between Pretoria and Park Station costs R76. If you're travelling in peak periods or staying near a station, it's a fast, state-of-the-art and cost-effective way to enter and exit Jo'burg.

Health

As long as you stay up to date with vaccinations and take basic preventative measures, you're unlikely to succumb to any hazards.

While South Africa, Lesotho and Swaziland have an impressive selection of tropical diseases, suffering from diarrhoea or a cold is more likely than contracting an exotic malady.

The main exception to this is malaria, which is a real risk in lower-lying areas of Swaziland and in northeastern South Africa.

BEFORE YOU GO

Insurance

➡ Find out in advance whether your insurer will make payments directly to providers or reimburse you later for overseas health expenditures.

➡ If your policy requires you to pay first and claim later for medical treatment, be sure to keep all documentation.

➡ Ensure that your travel insurance will cover any emergency transport required to get you to a hospital in a major city, or all the way home, by air and with a medical attendant if necessary.

➡ If you'll be in Lesotho or Swaziland, check whether the evacuation plan extends to these countries.

Medical Checklist

Get a check-up from your doctor if you have any regular medication or chronic illness. Bring medications in their original, clearly labelled containers. A signed and dated letter from your physician describing your medical conditions and medications, including generic names, is helpful. If carrying syringes or needles, ensure you have a physician's letter documenting their medical necessity. See your dentist before a long trip.

Assemble a medical and first-aid kit, especially if you will be hiking or staying in parks and reserves, and consider packing the following:

➡ antibacterial ointment (eg Bactroban) for cuts and abrasions

➡ antibiotics (if travelling off the beaten track)

➡ antidiarrhoeal drugs (eg loperamide)

➡ antihistamines (for hay fever and allergic reactions)

➡ anti-inflammatory drugs (eg ibuprofen)

➡ antimalaria pills (if you'll be in malarial areas)

➡ bandages, gauze

➡ DEET-containing insect repellent

➡ insect spray for clothing, tents and bed nets

➡ oral rehydration salts (eg Dioralyte)

➡ paracetamol or aspirin

➡ scissors, safety pins, tweezers, pocket knife

➡ sterile needles and syringes (if travelling to remote areas)

➡ sun block

➡ thermometer

➡ water-purification tablets

Websites

In addition to the information on their websites, the Centers for Disease Control and Prevention and World Health Organization publish handbooks and apps.

Centers for Disease Control and Prevention (www.cdc.gov/travel)

Health Canada (www.hc-sc.gc.ca)

Health Protection Scotland (www.fitfortravel.nhs.uk)

Immunization Action Coalition (www.immunize.org)

International Association for Medical Assistance to Travellers (www.iamat.org)

Lonely Planet (www.lonelyplanet.com)

MD Travel Health (https://redplanet.travel/mdtravelhealth)

Netdoctor (www.netdoctor.co.uk)

Smarttraveller (www.smarttraveller.gov.au)

World Health Organization (www.who.int/ith)

RECOMMENDED VACCINATIONS

Visit a doctor or travel clinic at least four weeks before departure for vaccinations; some don't ensure immunity for two weeks. America's Centers for Disease Control and Prevention (CDC; www.cdc.gov/travel) suggests immunisations, including the following, as routine for adults, in addition to routine childhood vaccines.

Ask your doctor for an International Certificate of Vaccination or Prophylaxis (ICVP or 'yellow card'), listing all the vaccinations you've received.

➡ Diphtheria

➡ Human Papillomavirus

➡ Influenza

➡ Meningococcal

➡ Pertussis (whooping cough)

➡ Pneumococcal

➡ Shingles

➡ Tetanus

The CDC also suggests the following immunisations:

➡ Hepatitis A

➡ Typhoid

The CDC suggests the following for some travellers to the region, depending on the areas to be visited:

➡ Hepatitis B

➡ Malaria

➡ Rabies

Further Reading

➡ *The Essential Guide to Travel Health* by Jane Wilson-Howarth

➡ *Travel Health Guide* by Mark Wise

➡ *Travels with Baby* by Shelly Rivoli

➡ *Traveller's Good Health Guide* by Ted Lankester

➡ *Travellers' Health* by Dr Richard Dawood

➡ *Wilderness and Travel Medicine* by Eric Weiss

Courses

If you'll be spending much time in remote rural areas, consider doing a first-aid course, for example one offered by the American Red Cross (www.redcross.org) or St John Ambulance (www.sja.org.uk).

Particularly if you're going trekking, you could take a wilderness medical training course, such as those offered in the UK by Wilderness Medical Training (http://wildernessmedical training.co.uk) and the Royal Geographical Society (www.rgs.org).

Also consider becoming a member of the International Association for Medical Assistance to Travellers (www.iamat.org), which lists trusted English-speaking doctors.

IN SOUTH AFRICA, LESOTHO & SWAZILAND

Availability & Cost of Health Care

➡ Good-quality health care is available in all of South Africa's major urban areas.

➡ Private hospitals are generally of an excellent standard.

➡ Public hospitals are often underfunded and overcrowded.

➡ In off-the-beaten-track areas, including much of Lesotho and Swaziland, reliable medical facilities are rare.

➡ Your accommodation should be able to recommend the nearest source of medical help.

➡ Western-embassy websites often list doctors and clinics, and your travel insurer might also be able to help.

➡ In an emergency, contact your embassy or consulate.

➡ Most doctors expect payment immediately after the consultation.

➡ Patients may also have to pay on admission to a hospital.

➡ Bring drugs for chronic diseases from home.

➡ Blood-transfusion services test donated blood for hepatitis B and C, syphilis and HIV, but there is nonetheless a tiny risk of contracting HIV from infected transfusions.

➡ The Blood Care Foundation (www.bloodcare.org.uk) is a useful source of safe, screened blood, which can be transported to any part of the world; join before you need its services.

➡ In Lesotho the best facility is Maseru Private Hospital, about 7km south of the city centre.

➡ Swaziland offers good health-care centres in Mbabane and Manzini, as well as in the Ezulwini Valley. Expect consultations with a GP to cost around E350 and up to E500 with a specialist.

Infectious Diseases

Cholera

Spread through Contaminated drinking water. The risk is low, and mostly confined to occasional outbreaks in rural parts of Limpopo, Mpumalanga, KwaZulu-Natal, the Eastern Cape and Swaziland.

Symptoms and effects Profuse watery diarrhoea, which causes debilitation if fluids are not replaced quickly.

Prevention and treatment In rural parts of eastern South Africa and Swaziland, pay close attention to drinking water, don't drink tap water, and avoid potentially contaminated food such as unpeeled or uncooked fruits and vegetables. Treatment is by fluid replacement (orally or via a drip); sometimes antibiotics are needed. Self-treatment is not advised.

Dengue Fever

Spread through Mosquito bites; in the north of KwaZulu-Natal's Elephant Coast and eastern Swaziland, and from there up South Africa's northeastern border to the top of Kruger National Park.

Symptoms and effects Feverish illness with headache and muscle pains, similar to those experienced during severe, prolonged influenza attacks. There might be a rash.

Prevention and treatment Avoid mosquito bites. Self-treatment: paracetamol (not asprin or non-steroidal anti-inflammatory drugs such as ibuprofen), hydration and rest. Dengue hemorrhagic fever, which mostly affects children, is more serious and requires medical attention.

Hepatitis A

Spread through Contaminated food (particularly shellfish) and water. Very occasionally, close physical contact with an infected person.

Symptoms and effects Jaundice, dark urine, a yellow colour to the whites of the eyes, fever and abdominal pain. Although rarely fatal, it can cause prolonged lethargy – recovery can be slow.

Prevention and treatment Vaccine (eg Avaxim, Vaqta, Havrix or Epaxal) is given as an injection, with a booster extending the protection offered. Can also be given as a combined single-dose vaccine with hepatitis A (Twinrix) or typhoid (Hepatyrix or Viatim). If you've had hepatitis A, you shouldn't drink alcohol for up to six months afterwards.

Hepatitis B

Spread through Infected blood, contaminated needles and sexual intercourse.

Symptoms and effects Jaundice and liver problems (occasionally failure).

Prevention and treatment Those visiting high-risk areas for long periods or those with increased social or occupational risk should be immunised. Regular travellers in sub-Saharan Africa should consider having hepatitis B as a routine vaccination. Treatments include an injection of immunoglobulin within 12 hours of exposure, rest, a nutritious diet and lots of fluids, possibly accompanied by antiviral drugs or hospital admission. Chronic cases may require ongoing antiviral medication and a liver transplant.

HIV

Spread through Infected blood and blood products; sexual intercourse with an infected partner; 'blood to blood' contacts, such as through contaminated instruments during medical, dental, acupuncture and other body-piercing procedures, or sharing intravenous needles. HIV and AIDS are widespread in South Africa, Lesotho and Swaziland.

Symptoms and effects Progressive failure of the immune system, leading to death.

Prevention and treatment Be cautious about sexual relationships with locals, regardless of their background, and don't have one-night stands. Travellers and

aid workers have been infected by locals. If you think you might have been infected, a blood test is necessary; a three-month gap after exposure is required to allow antibodies to appear in the blood. There is no cure, but medication to keep the disease under control is available.

Lymphatic Filariasis (Elephantiasis)

Spread through The bite of an infected mosquito. Larvae are deposited on the skin and migrate to the lymphatic vessels, where they turn into worms.

Symptoms and effects Localised itching and abnormal enlargement of body parts, commonly the legs and/or genitalia, causing pain and disability. In severe cases, the kidneys and lymphatic and immune systems are damaged.

Prevention and treatment Avoid mosquito bites. If infected, seek treatment, preferably by a specialist in infectious diseases or tropical medicine. Diethylcarbamazine (DEC) is commonly used to treat travellers.

Malaria

Spread through A parasite in the bloodstream, spread via the bite of the female Anopheles mosquito. Malaria is mainly confined to northeastern South Africa (parts of Kruger National Park, Limpopo, Mpumalanga and northern KwaZulu-Natal) and Swaziland (although Swaziland is taking steps to be the first country in sub-Saharan Africa to move to malaria-free status).

Symtoms and effects Falciparum malaria, the most dangerous type of malaria, is the predominant form in South Africa. The early, flu-like symptoms of malaria include headaches, fevers, aches and pains and malaise. Abdominal pain, diarrhoea and a cough can also occur. If not treated, the next stage can develop within 24 hours, particularly if falciparum malaria is the parasite: jaundice, then reduced consciousness and coma (also known as cerebral malaria), followed by death. Malaria in pregnancy frequently results in miscarriage or premature labour; the risks to both mother and foetus are considerable.

Prevention Infection rates vary with the season and climate, so check the situation before departure. During summer, prophylaxis is generally necessary. Several drugs are available and up-to-date advice from a travel clinic or similar is essential; some medication is more suitable than others (eg people with epilepsy should avoid mefloquine, and doxycycline should not be taken by pregnant women or children aged under 12). There is no conclusive evidence that antimalarial homeopathic preparations are effective, and many homeopaths do not recommend their use. It's a dangerous misconception that malaria is a mild illness and that taking antimalarial drugs causes more illness through side effects than actually getting malaria. Immunity, developed by surviving a bout of malaria, wanes after 18 months of nonexposure, so even if you have had malaria or lived in a malaria-prone area, you might no longer be immune. If you decide against taking antimalarial prophylaxis, you must understand the risks and be thorough about avoiding mosquito bites.

Treatment If you develop a fever in a malarial area, or shortly after leaving one, assume malarial infection until a blood test proves negative, even if you are or have been taking antimalarial medication. Report any fever or flu-like symptoms to a doctor as soon as possible. Treatment in hospital may be required; even in the best intensive-care facilities there is still a chance of fatality in the worst cases.

Rabies

Spread through Bites or licks on broken skin from an infected animal. Few human cases are reported in South Africa, the risks highest in rural areas.

Symptoms and effects Initial symptoms are pain or tingling at the site of the bite with fever, loss of appetite and headache. With 'furious' rabies, there is a growing sense of anxiety, jumpiness, disorientation, neck stiffness, sometimes seizures or convulsions, and hydrophobia (fear of water). 'Dumb' rabies (less common) affects the spinal cord, causing muscle paralysis, then heart and lung failure. If untreated, both forms are fatal.

Prevention and treatment People travelling to remote

areas, where a reliable source of post-bite vaccine is not available within 24 hours, should be vaccinated. Any bite, scratch or lick from a warm-blooded, furry animal should immediately be thoroughly cleaned. If you have not been vaccinated and you get bitten, you will need a course of injections starting as soon as possible after the injury. Vaccination does not provide immunity, it merely buys you more time to seek medical help.

Schistosomiasis (Bilharzia)

Spread through Flukes (minute worms) are carried by a species of freshwater snail, which sheds them into slow-moving or still water. The parasites penetrate human skin during swimming and migrate to the bladder or bowel. They are excreted via stool or urine and could contaminate fresh water, beginning the cycle again. Bilharzia is found in northeastern South Africa and Swaziland, reaching as far south as the Wild Coast and (very occasionally) as far west as the Northern Cape section of the Orange (Senqu) River.

Symptoms and effects Early symptoms may include fever, loss of appetite, weight loss, abdominal pain, weakness, headaches, joint and muscle pains, diarrhoea, nausea and cough, but most infections are asymptomatic at first. Untreated, bilharzia can cause problems such as kidney failure and permanent bowel damage.

Prevention and treatment Avoid swimming in stagnant or slow-running water, for example in a dam, lake or river. Heat baths and showers and vigorously towel yourself after swimming. A blood test can detect the parasite, and treatment is available – usually taking the drug praziquantel (Biltricide).

Tuberculosis

Spread through Close respiratory contact and, occasionally, infected unpasteurised milk or milk products. Tuberculosis is highly endemic in South Africa, Lesotho and Swaziland. People mixing closely with the local population, for example working

---

ANTIMALARIAL A TO D

A Awareness of the risk. No medication is totally effective, but protection of over 90% is achievable with most drugs, as long as other measures are taken.

B Bites, to be avoided at all costs. Sleep in a screened room, use a mosquito spray or coils, and sleep under a permethrin-impregnated net. Cover up at night with light-coloured long trousers and long sleeves – preferably permethrin-treated clothing. Apply repellent (preferably DEET-based) to all areas of exposed skin in the evenings.

C Chemical prevention (ie antimalarial drugs) is usually needed in malarial areas. Get medical advice, as resistance patterns can change, and new drugs are in development. Not all antimalarial drugs are suitable for everyone. Most antimalarial drugs need to be started at least a week beforehand and continued for four weeks after the last possible exposure to malaria.

D Diagnosis. If you have a fever or flu-like illness within a year of travel to a malarial area, malaria is a possibility, and immediate medical attention is necessary.

as a teacher or health-care worker, or planning a long stay, are most at risk.

Symptoms and effects Can be asymptomatic, although symptoms can include a cough, loss of appetite or weight, fatigue, fever or night sweats months or even years after exposure. An X-ray is the best way to confirm if you have TB.

Prevention and treatment Avoid overcrowded and unventilated environments where TB carriers might be found, such as hospitals and homeless shelters. BCG vaccine is recommended for those likely to be mixing closely with the local population; as it's a live vaccine, it should not be given to pregnant women or immunocompromised individuals. Travellers at risk should have a predeparture skin test and be re-tested after leaving the country. Treatment is a multiple-drug regimen for six to nine months.

Typhoid

Spread through Food or water that has been contaminated by infected human faeces.

Symptoms and effects Initially fever, a pink rash on the abdomen, appetite loss and listlessness. Septicaemia (blood poisoning) may also occur.

Prevention and treatment Vaccination given by injection. In some countries, an oral vaccine is available. Antibiotics are usually given as treatment.

Environmental Hazards

Heat Exhaustion

Causes Occurs following heavy sweating and excessive fluid loss with inadequate replacement of fluids and salt. This is common in hot climates when taking unaccustomed exercise before full acclimatisation.

Symptoms and effects Headache, dizziness and tiredness.

Prevention Dehydration is already happening by the time you feel thirsty – drink sufficient water such that you produce pale, diluted urine. The African sun can be fierce, so bring a hat.

Treatment Fluid replacement with water and/or fruit juice, and cooling by cold water and fans. Treat the salt loss by consuming salty fluids such as soup or broth and adding a little more table salt to foods than usual.

Heatstroke

Causes Extreme heat, high humidity, physical exertion or use of drugs or alcohol in the sun, and dehydration. Occurs when the body's heat-regulating mechanism breaks down.

Symptoms and effects An excessive rise in body temperature, accompanied by the ceasing of sweating, irrational and hyperactive behaviour and eventually loss of consciousness and death.

Treatment Rapid cooling by spraying the body with water and fanning. Emergency fluid and electrolyte replacement by intravenous drip is usually also required.

Insect Bites & Stings

Causes Mosquitoes, scorpions (found in arid areas), ticks (a risk outside urban areas), bees and wasps.

Symptoms and effects Stings can cause irritation and get infected. The scorpion's painful sting can be life-threatening. If you're stung, take a painkiller and seek medical treatment if your condition worsens. Tick-bite fever (rickettsia), a bacterial infection transmitted by ticks that can cause malaria-like symptoms, is a risk in the lowveld, including Swaziland.

Prevention and treatment Take the same precautions as for avoiding malaria, including protective clothing and repellent. If you pick up a tick, press down around its head with tweezers, grab the head and gently pull upwards. Avoid pulling the rear of the body, as this may squeeze the tick's gut contents into your mouth into your body, or leave its head inside you; both outcomes increase the risk of infection and disease. Smearing chemicals on the tick will not make it let go and is not recommended. If you suspect tick-bite fever, visit a doctor; treatment is a strong dose of antibiotics.

TAP WATER

High-quality water is widely available in South Africa and drinking from taps is fine, except in rural and drought-struck areas.

In Lesotho and Swaziland, stick to bottled water, and purify any stream or tap water before drinking it.

Snake Bites

Causes Venomous snakes found in South Africa include the black mamba, puff adder and Cape cobra. Snakes like to bask on rocks and sand, retreating during the heat of the day.

Prevention Do not walk barefoot or stick your hands into holes or cracks.

Treatment If bitten, do not panic. Half of the people bitten by venomous snakes are not actually injected with poison (envenomed). Immobilise the bitten limb with a splint (eg a stick) and apply a bandage over the site with firm pressure, similar to bandaging a sprain. Do not apply a tourniquet, or cut or suck the bite. Note the snake's appearance for identification purposes, and get medical help as soon as possible so that antivenin can be given.

Traditional Medicine

If you are ill, some locals may recommend you see a *sangoma* (traditional healer, usually a woman) or *inyanga* (traditional healer and herbalist, usually a man). These practitioners hold revered positions in many communities and are often interesting characters to meet on a tour. However, if you are ill, recourse to tried-and-tested Western medicine is a wiser option. Likewise, treat the traditional medicinal products found in local markets with circumspection.

Language

South Africa has 11 official languages – English, Afrikaans and nine indigenous languages (Ndebele, Northern Sotho, Southern Sotho, Swati, Tsonga, Tswana, Venda, Xhosa and Zulu). Forms, brochures and timetables are usually in English and Afrikaans, but road signs alternate. Most Afrikaans speakers also speak English, but this is not always the case in small rural towns and among older people. In and around Cape Town three languages are prominent: Afrikaans, English and Xhosa.

The official languages of Lesotho are Southern Sotho and English. In Swaziland, Swati and English are both official.

AFRIKAANS

Afrikaans developed from the dialect spoken by the Dutch settlers in South Africa from the 17th century. Until the late 19th century it was considered a Dutch dialect (known as 'Cape Dutch'), and in 1925 it became one of the official languages of South Africa. Today, it has about six million speakers.

If you read our coloured pronunciation guides as if they were English, you should be understood. The stressed syllables are in italics. Note that aw is pronounced as in 'law', eu as the 'u' in 'nurse', ew as the 'ee' in 'see' with rounded lips, oh as the 'o' in 'cold', uh as the 'a' in 'ago', kh as the 'ch' in the Scottish *loch*, zh as the 's' in 'pleasure', and r is trilled.

Basics

| Hello. | Hallo. | ha·loh |

WANT MORE?

For in-depth language information and handy phrases, check out Lonely Planet's *Africa Phrasebook*. You'll find it at shop.lonelyplanet.com, or you can buy Lonely Planet's iPhone phrasebooks at the Apple App Store.

Goodbye.	Totsiens.	tot·*seens*
Yes.	Ja.	yaa
No.	Nee.	ney
Please.	Asseblief.	a·si·*bleef*
Thank you.	Dankie.	*dang*·kee
Sorry.	Jammer.	*ya*·min

How are you?
Hoe gaan dit? — hu khaan dit

Fine, and you?
Goed dankie, en jy? — khut *dang*·kee en yay

What's your name?
Wat's jou naam? — vats yoh naam

My name is ...
My naam is ... — may naam is ...

Do you speak English?
Praat jy Engels? — praat yay *eng*·ils

I don't understand.
Ek verstaan nie. — ek vir·*staan* nee

Accommodation

Where's a ...?	Waar's 'n ...?	vaars i ...
campsite	kampeerplek	kam·*peyr*·plek
guesthouse	gastehuis	*khas*·ti·hays
hotel	hotel	hu·*tel*

Do you have a single/double room?
Het jy 'n enkel/dubbel kamer? — het yay i *eng*·kil/di·bil *kaa*·mir

How much is it per night/person?
Hoeveel kos dit per nag/persoon? — hu·*fil* kos dit pir nakh/pir·soon

Eating & Drinking

Can you recommend a ...?	Kan jy 'n ... aanbeveel?	kan yay i ... aan·bi·feyl
bar	kroeg	krukh
dish	gereg	khi·*rekh*

SOUTH AFRICAN ENGLISH

English has undergone some changes during its use in South Africa. Quite a few words have changed meaning, new words have been appropriated and, thanks to the influence of Afrikaans, a distinctive accent has developed. Vocabulary tends to lean more towards British rather than US English (eg 'lift', not 'elevator'; 'petrol', not 'gas'), as do grammar and spelling, and there are influences from other indigenous languages such as Zulu and Xhosa as well. Repetition for emphasis is common: something that burns you is 'hot hot', fields after the rains are 'green green', a crowded minibus with no more room is 'full full' and so on. Here's just a smattering of the local lingo you're likely to hear:

babalaas (from Zulu) – a monster hangover

bakkie – pick-up truck (US); ute/utility (Aus)

bonnet – car hood (US)

boot – car trunk (US)

cool drink – soda (US)

Howzit? – Hello/Greetings; How are you?

Izzit? – Is that so? Really?

just now – soon

lekker – nice, delicious

naartjie – tangerine

petrol – gasoline (US)

robot – traffic light

rubbish – garbage (US)

(Og) Shame! – Ohh, how cute! (in response to something like a new baby or a little puppy); Really! Oh no! (with a sympathetic tone)

soda – soda water; club soda (US)

sweeties – lollies; candy

tekkies – runners; joggers

place to eat	*eetplek*	*eyt·*plek
I'd like ..., please.	*Ek wil asseblief ... hê.*	ek vil a·si·*bleef* ... he
a table for two	*'n tafel vir twee*	i *taa·*fil fir twey
that dish	*daardie gereg*	*daar·*dee khi·*rekh*
the bill	*die rekening*	dee *rey·*ki·ning
the menu	*die spyskaart*	dee *spays·*kaart

Emergencies

Help!	*Help!*	help
Call a doctor!	*Kry 'n dokter!*	kray i *dok·*tir
Call the police!	*Kry die polisie!*	kray dee pu·*lee·*see
I'm lost. *Ek is verdwaal.*		ek is fir·*dwaal*
Where are the toilets? *Waar is die toilette?*		vaar is dee toy·*le·*ti
I need a doctor. *Ek het 'n dokter nodig.*		ek het i *dok·*tir noo·dikh

Numbers

1	*een*	eyn
2	*twee*	twey
3	*drie*	dree
4	*vier*	feer
5	*vyf*	fayf
6	*ses*	ses
7	*sewe*	*see·*vi
8	*agt*	akht
9	*nege*	*ney·*khi
10	*tien*	teen

Shopping & Services

I'm looking for ...
Ek soek na ... ek suk naa ...

How much is it?
Hoeveel kos dit? *hu·*fil kos dit

What's your lowest price?
Wat is jou laagste prys? vat is yoh *laakh·*sti prays

I want to buy a phonecard.
Ek wil asseblief   ek vil a·si·*bleef*
'n foonkaart koop.   i *foon*·kaart koop

I'd like to change money.
Ek wil asseblief geld ruil.   ek vil a·si·*bleef* khelt rayl

I want to use the internet.
Ek wil asseblief die   ek vil a·si·*bleef* dee
Internet gebruik.   in·tir·net khi·*brayk*

Transport & Directions

A ... ticket,   *Een ... kaartjie,*   eyn ... *kaar*·kee
please.   *asseblief.*   a·si·*bleef*

   one-way   *eenrigting*   eyn·*rikh*·ting
   return   *retoer*   ri·*tur*

How much is it to ...?
Hoeveel kos dit na ...?   hu·fil kos dit naa ...

Please take me to (this address).
Neem my asseblief na   neym may a·si·*bleef* naa
(hierdie adres).   (*heer*·dee a·*dres*)

Where's the (nearest) ...?
Waar's die (naaste) ...?   vaars dee (*naas*·ti) ...

Can you show me (on the map)?
Kan jy my   kan yay may
(op die kaart) wys?   (op dee kaart) vays

What's the address?
Wat is die adres?   vat is dee a·*dres*

NDEBELE

Ndebele is spoken as a first language in relatively small numbers in South Africa's northern provinces.

Hello.	*Lotsha.*
Goodbye.	*Khamaba kuhle./ Sala kuhle.*
Yes.	*I-ye.*
No.	*Awa.*
Please.	*Ngibawa.*
Thank you.	*Ngiyathokaza.*
What's your name?	*Ungubani ibizo lakho?*
My name is ...	*Ibizo lami ngu ...*
I come from ...	*Ngibuya e ...*

NORTHERN SOTO

Most mother-tongue speakers of Northern Sotho (also known as Sepedi) inhabit South Africa's northeastern provinces, with the vast majority to be found in Limpopo.

Hello.	*Thobela.*
Goodbye.	*Sala gabotse.*
Yes.	*Ee.*

No.	*Aowa.*
Please.	*Ke kgopela.*
Thank you.	*Ke ya leboga.*
What's your name?	*Ke mang lebitso la gago?*
My name is ...	*Lebitso laka ke ...*
I come from ...	*Ke bowa kwa ...*

SOUTHERN SOTO

Southern Sotho is the official language of Lesotho, alongside English. It is also spoken by the Basotho people in the Free State, North-West Province and Gauteng in South Africa. It's useful to learn some phrases if you're planning to visit Lesotho, especially if you want to trek in remote areas.

Hello.	*Dumela.*
Greetings father.	*Lumela ntate.*
Peace father.	*Khotso ntate.*
Greetings mother.	*Lumela 'me.*
Peace mother.	*Khotso 'me.*
Greetings brother.	*Lumela abuti.*
Peace brother.	*Khotso abuti.*
Greetings sister.	*Lumela ausi.*
Peace sister.	*Khotso ausi.*

There are three common ways of saying 'How are you?', each one with a standard response. Note, however, that these questions and answers are interchangeable.

How are you?	*O kae?* (sg)
	Le kae? (pl)
I'm here.	*Ke teng.*
We're here.	*Re teng.*
How do you live?	*O phela joang?* (sg)
	Le phela joang? (pl)
I live well.	*Ke phela hantle.*
We live well.	*Re phela hantle.*
How did you get up?	*O tsohile joang?* (sg)
	Le tsohile joang? (pl)
I got up well.	*Ke tsohile hantle.*
We got up well.	*Re tsohile hantle.*

When trekking, people always ask *Lea kae?* (Where are you going?) and *O tsoa kae?* or the plural *Le tsoa kae?* (Where have you come from?). When parting, use the following expressions:

Stay well.	*Sala hantle.* (sg)
	Salang hantle. (pl)
Go well.	*Tsamaea hantle.* (sg)
	Tsamaeang hantle. (pl)

'Thank you' is *kea leboha* (pronounced 'ke·ya le·bo·wa'). The herd boys may ask for *chelete* (money) or *lipompong* (sweets), pronounced 'dee·pom·pong'. If you want to reply 'I don't have any', just say *ha dio* (pronounced 'ha dee·o').

SWATI

Swati is the official language of Swaziland, along with English. It's also widely spoken as a first language in South Africa's Mpumalanga province. It's very similar to Zulu, and the two languages are mutually intelligible.

Hello. (to one person)	*Sawubona.*
Hello. (to a group)	*Sanibonani.*
How are you?	*Kunjani?*
I'm fine.	*Kulungile.*
We're very well.	*Natsi sikhona.*
Goodbye. (if leaving)	*Salakahle.*
Goodbye. (if staying)	*Hambakahle.*
Yes.	*Yebo.* (also a common all-purpose greeting)
No.	*Cha.* (pronounced as a click)
Please.	*Ngicela.*
I thank you.	*Ngiyabonga.*
We thank you.	*Siyabonga.*
Sorry.	*Lucolo.*
What's your name?	*Ngubani libito lakho?*
My name is ...	*Libitolami ngingu ...*
I'm from ...	*Ngingewekubuya e ...*
Do you have ...?	*Une yini ...?*
How much?	*Malini?*
Is there a bus to ...?	*Kukhona ibhasi yini leya ...?*
When does it leave?	*Isuka nini?*
Where is the tourist office?	*Likuphi lihovisi leti vakashi?*
morning	*ekuseni*
afternoon	*entsambaba*
evening	*kusihlwa*
night	*ebusuku*
yesterday	*itolo*
today	*lamuhla*
tomorrow	*kusasa*

TSONGA

Tsonga is spoken as a first language in South Africa's north, predominantly in the provinces of Limpopo and Gauteng, and to a lesser extent in Mpumalanga and North-West Province.

Hello. (morning)	*Avusheni.*
Hello. (afternoon)	*Inhelekani.*
Hello. (evening)	*Riperile.*
Goodbye.	*Salani kahle.*
Yes.	*Hi swona.*
No.	*A hi swona.*
Please.	*Nakombela.*
Thank you.	*I nkomu.*
What's your name?	*U mani vito ra wena?*
My name is ...	*Vito ra mina i ...*
I come from ...	*Ndzihuma e ...*

TSWANA

Tswana is spoken in South Africa as a first language mainly in Gauteng and North-West Province, with lesser numbers of first-language speakers in the eastern areas of Northern Cape and the western parts of the Free State.

Hello.	*Dumela.*
Goodbye.	*Sala sentle.*
Yes.	*Ee.*
No.	*Nnya.*
Please.	*Ke a kopa.*
Thank you.	*Ke a leboga.*
What's your name?	*Leina la gago ke mang?*
My name is ...	*Leina la me ke ...*
I come from ...	*Ke tswa ...*

VENDA

Venda is spoken mainly in the northeastern border region of South Africa's Limpopo province.

Hello. (morning)	*Ndi matseloni.*
Hello. (afternoon)	*Ndi masiari.*
Hello. (evening)	*Ndi madekwana.*
Goodbye.	*Kha vha sale zwavhudi.*
Yes.	*Ndi zwone.*
No.	*A si zwone.*
Please.	*Ndikho u humbela.*
Thank you.	*Ndo livhuwa.*
What's your name?	*Zina lavho ndi nnyi?*
My name is ...	*Zina langa ndi ...*
I come from ...	*Ndi bva ...*

XHOSA

Xhosa belongs to the Bantu language family, along with Zulu, Swati and Ndebele. It is the most widely distributed indigenous language in South Africa, and is also spoken in the Cape Town area. About six and a half million people speak Xhosa.

Numbers – Xhosa

English numbers are commonly used.

1	wani	waa·nee
2	thu	tu
3	thri	tree
4	fo	faw
5	fayifu	faa·yee·fu
6	siksi	seek'·see
7	seveni	se·ve·nee
8	eyithi	e·yee·tee
9	nayini	naa·yee·nee
10	teni	t'e·nee

In our pronunciation guides, the symbols b', ch', k', p', t' and ts' represent sounds that are 'spat out' (only in case of b' the air is sucked in), a bit like combining them with the sound in the middle of 'uh-oh'. Note also that hl is pronounced as in the Welsh *llewellyn* and dl is like hl but with the vocal cords vibrating. Xhosa has a series of 'click' sounds as well; they are not distinguished in this chapter.

Hello.	Molo.	maw·law
Goodbye.	Usale ngoxolo.	u·saa·le ngaw·kaw·law
Yes.	Ewe.	e·we
No.	Hayi.	haa·yee
Please.	Cela.	ke·laa
Thank you.	Enkosi.	e·nk'aw·see
Sorry.	Uxolo.	u·aw·law
How are you?	Kunjani?	k'u·njaa·nee

Fine, and you?
Ndiyaphila, unjani wena?
ndee·yaa·pee·laa u·njaa·nee we·naa

What's your name?
Ngubani igama lakho?
ngu·b'aa·nee ee·gaa·maa laa·kaw

My name is ...
Igama lam ngu ...
ee·gaa·maa laam ngu ...

Do you speak English?
Uyasithetha isingesi?
u·yaa·see·te·taa ee·see·nge·see

I don't understand.
Andiqondi.
aa·ndee·kaw·ndee

ZULU

Zulu is a language from the Bantu group, and it's closely related to the other Bantu languages in southern Africa, particularly Xhosa. About 10 million Africans speak Zulu as a first language, with the vast majority (more than 95 per cent) in South Africa. It is also spoken in Lesotho and Swaziland.

In our pronunciation guides, the symbols b', ch', k', p', t' and ts' represent sounds that are 'spat out' (only in case of b' the air is sucked in), a bit like combining them with the sound in the middle of 'uh-oh'. Note also that hl is pronounced as in the Welsh *llewellyn* and dl is like hl but with the vocal cords vibrating. Xhosa has a series of 'click' sounds as well; they are not distinguished in this chapter.

Hello.
Sawubona. (sg)
Sanibonani. (pl)
saa·wu·b'aw·naa
saa·nee·b'aw·naa·nee

Goodbye. (if leaving)
Sala kahle. (sg)
Salani kahle. (pl)
saa·laa gaa·hle
saa·laa·nee gaa·hle

Goodbye. (if staying)
Hamba kahle. (sg)
Hambani kahle. (pl)
haa·mbaa gaa·hle
haa·mbaa·nee gaa·hle

Yes.
Yebo.
ye·b'aw

No.
Cha.
kaa

Thank you.
Ngiyabonga.
ngee·yaa·b'aw·ngaa

Sorry.
Uxolo.
u·kaw·law

How are you?
Unjani?/Ninjani? (sg/pl)
u·njaa·nee/nee·njaa·nee

Fine. And you?
Sikhona.
Nawe?/Nani? (sg/pl)
see·kaw·naa
naa·we/naa·nee

What's your name?
Ngubani igama lakho?
ngu·b'aa·nee ee·gaa·maa laa·kaw

My name is ...
Igama lami ngu-...
ee·gaa·maa laa·mee ngu·...

Do you speak English?
Uyasikhuluma isiNgisi?
u·yaa·see·ku·lu·maa ee·see·ngee·see

I don't understand.
Angizwa.
aa·ngee·zwaa

Numbers – Zulu

English numbers are commonly used.

1	uwani	u·waa·nee
2	uthu	u·tu
3	uthri	u·three
4	ufo	u·faw
5	ufayifi	u·faa·yee·fee
6	usiksi	u·seek·see
7	usevene	u·se·ve·nee
8	u-eyithi	u·e·yeet
9	unayini	u·naa·yee·nee
10	utheni	u·the·nee

GLOSSARY

For more food and drink terms, see the Menu Decoder (p574).

Afrikaans – the language spoken by Afrikaners, derived from Cape Dutch

Afrikaner – Afrikaans-speaking white person

amahiya – traditional Swazi robe

ANC – African National Congress; national democratic organisation formed in 1912 to represent blacks

AWB – Afrikaner Weerstandsbeweging, Afrikaner Resistance Movement; an Afrikaner extremist right-wing group

bakkie – pick-up truck

balimo – ancestors (Sotho)

Bantu – literally 'people'; during the apartheid era, used derogatorily to refer to blacks; today, used only in reference to ethnolinguistics, ie Bantu languages, Bantu-speaking peoples

Bantustans – see *homelands*

BCP – Basotholand Congress Party

Big Five – lion, leopard, elephant, buffalo and black rhino

bilharzia – another name for schistosomiasis, a disease caused by blood flukes, passed on by freshwater snails

biltong – dried meat

bittereinders – 'bitter enders' in Afrikaans; Boer resisters in the 1899–1902 South African War who fought until the 'bitter end'

BNP – Basotholand National Party

bobotie – curried mince with a topping of savoury egg custard

Boers – see *Trekboers*

braai – short for *braaivleis*, a barbecue at which meat is cooked over an open fire

Broederbond – secret society open only to Protestant Afrikaner men; was highly influential under National Party rule

bubblegum – a form of township music influenced by Western pop

byala – traditional beer

coloureds – apartheid-era term used to refer to those of mixed-race descent

dagga – marijuana, also known as *zol*

Democratic Alliance – the official opposition party to the ANC

diamantveld – diamond fields

difaqane – 'forced migration' of many of Southern Africa's Nguni peoples; known as *mfeqane* in Zulu

dorp – small village or rural settlement

drostdy – residence of a *land-drost*

free-camp – camping where you want, away from a formal campsite; permission should be sought and money offered

fynbos – literally 'fine-leafed bush', primarily proteas, heaths and ericas

gogo – grandmother

highveld – high-altitude grassland region

homelands – areas established for blacks under apartheid and considered independent countries by South Africa (never accepted by the UN); reabsorbed into South Africa after 1994

IFP – Inkatha Freedom Party; black political movement, founded around 1975 and led by Chief Mangosouthu Buthelezi

igogogo – musical instrument made from an oil can

igqirha – Xhosa spiritual healer

impi – Zulu warriors; also any group of soldiers

indunas – tribal headmen

inyanga – traditional medicine man and herbalist who also studies patterns of thrown bones

isicathamiya – a soft-shoe-shuffle style of vocal music from KwaZulu-Natal

ixhwele – Xhosa herbalist

jol – party, good time

karamat – tomb of a Muslim saint

Khoekhoen – pastoralist San

Khoe-San – collective term referring to the closely related San and Khoekhoen peoples

kloof – ravine

kloofing – canyoning

knobkerry – traditional African weapon; a stick with a round knob at the end, used as a club or missile

kommando – Boer militia unit

kopje – small hill

kraal – a hut village, often with an enclosure for livestock; also a Zulu fortified village

kroeg – bar

kwaito – form of township music; a mix of *mbaqanga*, jive, hip hop, house, ragga and other dance styles

kwela – township interpretation of American swing music

landdrost – an official acting as local administrator, tax collector and magistrate

lapa – a circular building with low walls and a thatched roof, used for cooking, partying etc

LCD – Lesotho Congress for Democracy

lekgotla – place of gathering

lekker – very good, enjoyable or tasty

lekolulo – a flutelike instrument played by herd boys

lesokoana – wooden stick or spoon, traditionally used for stirring mealie pap

liqhaga – 'bottles' that are so tightly woven that they are used for carrying water

lowveld – low-altitude area, having scrub vegetation

maskanda – Zulu form of guitar playing

matjieshuis – Afrikaans term for traditional woven Nama 'mat' huts

mbaqanga – form of township music; literally 'dumpling' in Zulu, combining church choirs, doo-wop and sax-jive

mdube – vocal style mixing European and African church choirs

mfeqane – see *difaqane*

minwane – dinosaur footprints

Mkhulumnchanti – Swazi deity

mokorotlo – conical hat worn by the Basotho

molianyeoe – see *mokorotlo*

moraba-raba – popular board game played with wooden beads and four rows of hollows; known elsewhere in Africa as *mancala* and *bao*

moroka-pula – rainmaker

mqashiyo – similar vocal style to *mbaqanga*

muti – traditional medicine

Ncwala – Swazi first-fruits ceremony

ndlovukazi – she-elephant, and traditional title of the Swazi royal mother

ngaka – (also *ngaca*) learned man

ngwenyama – lion, and traditional title of the Swazi king

PAC – Pan African Congress; political organisation of blacks founded in 1959 to work for majority rule and equal rights

piri piri – hot pepper

pinotage – a type of wine, a cross between Pinot noir and Hermitage or Shiraz

pont – river ferry

Poqo – armed wing of the PAC

Rikki – an open, small van used as public transport in Cape Town

robot – traffic light

rondavel – a round hut with a conical roof

San – nomadic hunter-gatherers who were South Africa's earliest inhabitants

sandveld – dry, sandy coastal belt

sangoma – traditional healer

setolo-tolo – stringed instrument played with the mouth by men

shebeen – drinking establishment in black township; once illegal, now merely unlicensed

slaghuis – butchery

slenter – fake diamond

snoek – firm-fleshed migratory fish that appears off the Cape in June and July; served smoked, salted or curried

sourveld – a type of grassland

swart gevaar – 'black threat'; term coined by Afrikaner nationalists during the 1920s

Telkom – government telecommunications company

thkolosi – small, maliciously playful beings (Basotho)

thomo – stringed instrument played by women

thornveld – a vegetation belt dominated by acacia thorn trees and related species

tokoloshe – Xhosa malevolent spirit or short manlike animal, similar to the Sotho *thkolosi*

township – planned urban settlement of blacks and coloureds, legacy of the apartheid era

Trekboers – the first Dutch who trekked off into the interior of what is now largely Western Cape; later shortened to Boers

trokkie – truck stop

tronk – jail

tuk-tuk – motorised tricycle

uitlanders – 'foreigners'; originally the name given by Afrikaners to the immigrants who poured into the Transvaal after the discovery of gold

Umkhonto we Sizwe – the ANC's armed wing during the years of the struggle; now defunct

veld – elevated open grassland (pronounced 'felt')

velskoene – handmade leather shoes

VOC – Vereenigde Oost-Indische Compagnie (Dutch East India Company)

volk – collective Afrikaans term for Afrikaners

volkstaal – people's language

volkstaat – an independent, racially pure Boer state

Voortrekkers – original Afrikaner settlers of Orange Free State and Transvaal who migrated from the Cape Colony in the 1830s in search of greater independence

zol – marijuana, also known as *dagga*

Behind the Scenes

SEND US YOUR FEEDBACK

We love to hear from travellers – your comments keep us on our toes and help make our books better. Our well-travelled team reads every word on what you loved or loathed about this book. Although we cannot reply individually to your submissions, we always guarantee that your feedback goes straight to the appropriate authors, in time for the next edition. Each person who sends us information is thanked in the next edition – the most useful submissions are rewarded with a selection of digital PDF chapters.

Visit **lonelyplanet.com/contact** to submit your updates and suggestions or to ask for help. Our award-winning website also features inspirational travel stories, news and discussions.

Note: We may edit, reproduce and incorporate your comments in Lonely Planet products such as guidebooks, websites and digital products, so let us know if you don't want your comments reproduced or your name acknowledged. For a copy of our privacy policy visit lonelyplanet.com/privacy.

OUR READERS

Many thanks to the travellers who used the last edition and wrote to us with helpful hints, useful advice and interesting anecdotes: Adrian Solitander, Amanda Captain, Andre Sennema, Andrew Spence, Anthony Loftus, Ben Furstenau, Brian McCollom, Camilla Hughes, Christian Ungruhe, Craig Steiner, Greg Poole, Henriette Poelman, James Timmis, Jeremy Marx, Ludo van Mil, Mariska de Beer, Megan Harris, Petra O'Neill, Rafael Serrano, Thomas Dijkema, Vera de Visser

WRITER THANKS
James Bainbridge

Thanks in 11 languages to my fellow writers Simon, Lucy, Shawn and Ashley for beers and banter in the Southern Suburbs during this update; to the rest of the writer team for your contributions; to everyone who helped me on the road in Mpumalanga and Cape Town; and to Leigh-Robin, Oliver and Thomas for putting up with my long hours typing in the garden shed.

Robert Balkovich

Thank you to my mother and father. To my sister for always coming along for the ride. To everybody I met along the way, especially all of the South Africans who were eager to learn where I was coming from, and thrilled to show me their beautiful country. Especially

to Christos, Chad, Hanli and Nonhlanhla for making the planet seem less lonely.

Jean-Bernard Carillet

A huge thanks to everyone who helped out and made this trip an enlightenment, especially Doné, Renée, Esti, Leigh and all of the people I met on the road. At Lonely Planet I'm grateful to Matt for his trust, and to the hard-working editors. At home, a *gros bisou* to Eva and lots of love to Morgane, whose support was essential.

Lucy Corne

Huge thanks to the team in Kimberley – Dianna, Romano, Kim, Joy and Tebogo – and to Fayroush, Christa, Brian and Nadia at SAN Parks. *Baie dankie* to Ailsa Tudhope for making me fall in love all over again with Prince Albert, and to Johan, Debbie, Martiens and Cathy for making my life easier on the road. Big love to Shawn, who didn't help because he was busy with his own chapter, and a huge high five to Kai, who makes a pretty awesome travel buddy and helps me to see everything through the eyes of a four-year-old.

Shawn Duthie

Many thanks to Matt and the team at Lonely Planet for their great help and support, as always. In Swaziland, a massive thank you to Xolani and Nikki at Big Game Parks. Finally, thank you to Lucy and Kai, my inspirations for everything I do.

BEHIND THE SCENES

Anthony Ham

Heartfelt thanks to Matt Phillips, my Africa friend and editor of long standing for continuing to entrust me with a corner of the earth I adore. To my family, Marina, Carlota and Valentina: thank you for sharing my love of Africa and for giving me so many special memories there.

Ashley Harrell

Thanks to: editor Matt Phillips for trusting me with a piece of Africa; the Peace Corps crew (Gaby, Ryan and Hindrik) for their invaluable input; everyone at Semonkong Lodge for helping with my destroyed rental car; Madeline Moitozo and Nikki Gamer for the highly amusing company; Anne Kamau Isavwa (and Tony, Ella and Joshua) for letting me move in for a second; MAF for showing me Lesotho from the air; and Belinda Groves for renewing my faith in human goodness.

Simon Richmond

Many thanks for the help, friendship and advice from the following: fellow writers James and Lucy, Heather Mason, Bheki Dube, Gerald Garner, Mike Luptak, Sheryl Ozinsky, Nicole Biondi, Iain Harris, Lee Harris, Brent Meersman and Amber April.

ACKNOWLEDGEMENTS

Climate map data adapted from Peel MC, Finlayson BL & McMahon TA (2007) 'Updated World Map of the Köppen-Geiger Climate Classification', *Hydrology and Earth System Sciences*, 11, 1633–44.

Cover photograph: Giraffe, Hluhluwe-iMfolozi Park; Christopher Scott/Getty Images ©.

THIS BOOK

This 11th edition of Lonely Planet's *South Africa, Lesotho & Swaziland* guidebook was researched and written by James Bainbridge, Robert Balkovich, Jean-Bernard Carillet, Lucy Corne, Shawn Duthie, Anthony Ham, Ashley Harrell and Simon Richmond. This guidebook was produced by the following:

Destination Editor Matt Phillips

Senior Product Editor Elizabeth Jones

Product Editor Carolyn Boicos

Senior Cartographer Diana Von Holdt

Book Designer Lauren Egan

Assisting Editors Andrew Bain, Michelle Bennett, Peter Cruttenden, Jacqueline Danam, Andrea Dobbin, Samantha Forge, Emma Gibbs, Jennifer Hattam, Cath Lanigan, Louise McGregor, Kate Morgan, Gabrielle Stefanos, Simon Williamson

Assisting Cartographers Laura Bailey, Anita Banh

Cover Researcher Naomi Parker

Thanks to Ronan Abayawickrema, Andi Jones, Kate Kiely, Kate Mathews, Claire Naylor, Karyn Noble, Kirsten Rawlings, Alison Ridgway

Index

Map Legend

Sights

- Beach
- Bird Sanctuary
- Buddhist
- Castle/Palace
- Christian
- Confucian
- Hindu
- Islamic
- Jain
- Jewish
- Monument
- Museum/Gallery/Historic Building
- Ruin
- Shinto
- Sikh
- Taoist
- Winery/Vineyard
- Zoo/Wildlife Sanctuary
- Other Sight

Activities, Courses & Tours

- Bodysurfing
- Diving
- Canoeing/Kayaking
- Course/Tour
- Sento Hot Baths/Onsen
- Skiing
- Snorkelling
- Surfing
- Swimming/Pool
- Walking
- Windsurfing
- Other Activity

Sleeping

- Sleeping
- Camping
- Hut/Shelter

Eating

- Eating

Drinking & Nightlife

- Drinking & Nightlife
- Cafe

Entertainment

- Entertainment

Shopping

- Shopping

Information

- Bank
- Embassy/Consulate
- Hospital/Medical
- Internet
- Police
- Post Office
- Telephone
- Toilet
- Tourist Information
- Other Information

Geographic

- Beach
- Gate
- Hut/Shelter
- Lighthouse
- Lookout
- Mountain/Volcano
- Oasis
- Park
- Pass
- Picnic Area
- Waterfall

Population

- Capital (National)
- Capital (State/Province)
- City/Large Town
- Town/Village

Transport

- Airport
- Border crossing
- Bus
- Cable car/Funicular
- Cycling
- Ferry
- Metro station
- Monorail
- Parking
- Petrol station
- Subway station
- Taxi
- Train station/Railway
- Tram
- Underground station
- Other Transport

Routes

- Tollway
- Freeway
- Primary
- Secondary
- Tertiary
- Lane
- Unsealed road
- Road under construction
- Plaza/Mall
- Steps
- Tunnel
- Pedestrian overpass
- Walking Tour
- Walking Tour detour
- Path/Walking Trail

Boundaries

- International
- State/Province
- Disputed
- Regional/Suburb
- Marine Park
- Cliff
- Wall

Hydrography

- River, Creek
- Intermittent River
- Canal
- Water
- Dry/Salt/Intermittent Lake
- Reef

Areas

- Airport/Runway
- Beach/Desert
- Cemetery (Christian)
- Cemetery (Other)
- Glacier
- Mudflat
- Park/Forest
- Sight (Building)
- Sportsground
- Swamp/Mangrove

Note: Not all symbols displayed above appear on the maps in this book

Shawn Duthie

Swaziland Originally from Canada, Shawn has been travelling, studying and working around the world for the past 13 years. A love of travel merged with an interest in international politics, and led to several years of lecturing at the University of Cape Town and, now, as a freelance political risk consultant specialising in African countries. Shawn lives in South Africa and takes any excuse to travel around this amazing continent.

Anthony Ham

Kruger National Park, Limpopo, North West Province Anthony is a freelance writer and photographer who specialises in Spain, East and Southern Africa, the Arctic and the Middle East. When he's not writing for Lonely Planet, Anthony writes about and photographs Spain, Africa and the Middle East for newspapers and magazines in Australia, the UK and US.

Ashley Harrell

Free State, Lesotho After a brief stint selling day-spa coupons door-to-door in South Florida, Ashley decided that she'd rather be a writer. She went to journalism grad school, convinced a newspaper to hire her, and starting covering wildlife, crime and tourism, sometimes all in the same story. Fuelling her zest for storytelling and the unknown, she travelled widely and moved often, from a tiny NYC apartment to a vast California ranch to a jungle cabin in Costa Rica, where she started writing for Lonely Planet. From there her travels became more exotic and further flung, and she still laughs when paychecks arrive.

Simon Richmond

Cape Town, Johannesburg & Gauteng Journalist and photographer Simon has specialised as a travel writer since the early 1990s and first worked for Lonely Planet in 1999 on their *Central Asia* guide. He's long since stopped counting the number of guidebooks he's researched and written for the company, but countries covered include Australia, China, India, Iran, Japan, Korea, Malaysia, Mongolia, Myanmar (Burma), Russia, Singapore, South Africa and Turkey. For Lonely Planet's website he's penned features on topics from the world's best swimming pools to the joys of Urban Sketching – follow him on Instagram to see some of his photos and sketches.

OUR STORY

A beat-up old car, a few dollars in the pocket and a sense of adventure. In 1972 that's all Tony and Maureen Wheeler needed for the trip of a lifetime – across Europe and Asia overland to Australia. It took several months, and at the end – broke but inspired – they sat at their kitchen table writing and stapling together their first travel guide, *Across Asia on the Cheap*. Within a week they'd sold 1500 copies. Lonely Planet was born.

Today, Lonely Planet has offices in Franklin, London, Melbourne, Oakland, Dublin, Beijing and Delhi, with more than 600 staff and writers. We share Tony's belief that 'a great guidebook should do three things: inform, educate and amuse'.

OUR WRITERS

James Bainbridge

Cape Town, Mpumalanga James is a British travel writer and journalist based in Cape Town, from where he roams the globe and contributes to publications worldwide. He has been working on Lonely Planet projects for over a decade, updating dozens of guidebooks and TV hosting everywhere from the African bush to the Great Lakes. The coordinating writer of several editions of Lonely Planet's *South Africa, Lesotho & Swaziland*, *Turkey* and *Morocco* guides, his articles on travel, culture and investment appear in the likes of *BBC Travel*, the UK *Guardian* and *Independent*, *Condé Nast Traveller* and *Lonely Planet Traveller*. For this guide, James also wrote the Plan Your Trip, Understand and Survival Guide chapters.

Robert Balkovich

KwaZulu-Natal Robert was born and raised in Oregon, but has called New York City home for almost a decade. When he was a child and other families were going to theme parks and grandma's house he went to Mexico City and toured Eastern Europe by train. He's now a writer and travel enthusiast seeking experiences that are ever so slightly out of the ordinary to report back on. He's on Instagram @oh_balky.

Jean-Bernard Carillet

Eastern Cape Jean-Bernard is a Paris-based freelance writer and photographer who specialises in Africa, France, Turkey, the Indian Ocean, the Caribbean and the Pacific. He loves adventure, remote places, islands, outdoors, archaeological sites and food. His insatiable wanderlust has taken him to 114 countries across six continents, and it shows no sign of waning. It has inspired lots of articles and photos for travel magazines and some 70 Lonely Planet guidebooks, both in English and in French.

Lucy Corne

Western Cape, Northern Cape Lucy left university with a degree in journalism and a pair of perpetually itchy feet. She taught EFL for eight years in Spain, South Korea, Canada, China and India, while writing freelance features for a range of magazines, newspapers and websites. She joined the Lonely Planet team in 2008 and has since worked on a range of titles, including *Africa, Canary Islands, South Africa, Lesotho & Swaziland* and several foodie titles. Lucy lives in Cape Town with her husband and young son, where she writes on travel, food and beer. Her popular blog, www.brewmistress.co.za, documents the South African beer scene.

OVER PAGE | MORE WRITERS

Published by Lonely Planet Global Limited
CRN 554153
11th edition – November 2018
ISBN 978 1 78657 180 9
© Lonely Planet 2018   Photographs © as indicated 2018
10 9 8 7 6 5 4 3 2 1
Printed in Singapore

Although the authors and Lonely Planet have taken all reasonable care in preparing this book, we make no warranty about the accuracy or completeness of its content and, to the maximum extent permitted, disclaim all liability arising from its use.